THE ABUSED CHILD IN THE FAMILY AND IN THE COMMUNITY

VOLUME I

THE ABUSED CHILD IN THE FAMILY AND IN THE COMMUNITY

Selected papers from
The Second International Congress on Child Abuse and Neglect, London, 1978

VOLUME I

Editors

C. HENRY KEMPE
University of Colorado Medical Center, Denver

ALFRED WHITE FRANKLIN
The London Clinic, London

CHRISTINE COOPER
University Department of Child Health, Newcastle-upon-Tyne

PERGAMON PRESS
OXFORD · NEW YORK · TORONTO · SYDNEY · PARIS · FRANKFURT

U.K.	Pergamon Press Ltd., Headington Hill Hall, Oxford OX3 0BW, England
U.S.A.	Pergamon Press Inc., Maxwell House, Fairview Park, Elmsford, New York 10523, U.S.A.
CANADA	Pergamon of Canada, Suite 104, 150 Consumers Road, Willowdale, Ontario M2J 1P9, Canada
AUSTRALIA	Pergamon Press (Aust.) Pty. Ltd., P.O. Box 544, Potts Point, N.S.W. 2011, Australia
FRANCE	Pergamon Press SARL, 24 rue des Ecoles, 75240 Paris, Cedex 05, France
FEDERAL REPUBLIC OF GERMANY	Pergamon Press GmbH, 6242 Kronberg-Taunus, Pfedstrasse 1, Federal Republic of Germany

---

First edition 1980

British Library Cataloguing in Publication Data

International Congress on Child Abuse and Neglect, *2nd, London, 1978*
The abused child in the family and in the community.
1. Child abuse - Congresses
I. Title II. Kempe, Charles Henry
III. Franklin, Alfred White
IV. Cooper, Christine
362.7'1 HV707 79-42636

ISBN 0-08-023430-5

These proceedings were published originally as volume 3 of Child Abuse & Neglect, and supplied to subscribers as part of their subscription.

In order to make this volume available as economically and as rapidly as possible the authors' typescripts have been reproduced in their original forms. This method has its typographical limitations but it is hoped that they in no way distract the reader.

Printed in Great Britain by A. Wheaton & Co. Ltd., Exeter

CONTENTS

VOLUME I

CONTENTS

VOLUME II

FOREWORD

The Second International Congress on Child Abuse and Neglect was planned to promote the maximum opportunity for discussion by the delegates. Eight speakers were invited to address the plenary sessions, and a fifth plenary session was devoted to a Panel Discussion on questions from delegates. Each day had its main themes - the community, the family and lastly the child. The Scientific Programme Sub-Committee tried wherever possible to link together the latter part of the morning and the early afternoon subjects, hoping that this would encourage true discussion groups to form, although at the price of restricting the delegates' choice. Another link brought a theme, for example, the law, into focus through the whole Congress, with emphasis on its relationship with the theme of the day. Legal delegates who accepted the servitude of this link could not join in the discussions at sessions on other topics. Other continuing subjects included help from lay or non-professional groups, treatment plans and sexual abuse. These arrangements, which depended on the co-operation of the delegates as well as on the skill of the sessional chairmen, were only partially successful. Delegates to International Congresses insist on chasing favourite speakers and special subjects, despite the complications which few congresses have yet managed to overcome.

The speakers at an International Congress have four essential tasks. First they are invited to submit short abstracts of what they propose to say. For this Congress the majority of the abstracts* have been published with a supplement, 200 in all. Each writes also a version of a length suitable to the number of minutes allotted for speaking. A third task is to prepare a full-length paper for submission to the Editor who is publishing the Proceedings, in this case in the first three numbers of the Journal during 1979.

So great was the response to the "call for papers" that had all papers been accepted the Journal would be filled for seven years with a resulting great delay in publication. Selection has been inevitable. Those authors whose papers are not accepted are released from the copyright arrangement that was requested before the meeting so that they can seek publication elsewhere. The Editor is grateful to the Scientific Programme Sub-Committee for their help. As they had studied all the Abstracts carefully before planning the Scientific programme, they agreed to act as an editorial advisory board. But it is the Editor-in-Chief who takes the responsibility for the final decision.

The fourth task is for the speaker to present his material at the meeting and this causes the most difficulty. To travel halfway across the world, bursting with invaluable knowledge, and then to contain it all in a few sentences delivered within ten or fifteen minutes is more than the human spirit can bear. And yet how can all the aspirants be given their chance without such self sactifice?

The other serious problem, which we could not solve, was where to find rooms of the right size for the thirteen simultaneous sessions which occupied half of the Congress time. Inevitably delegates had to select their sessions and may then have found the selected session full. This difficulty was magnified by the unexpectedly large number of late but serious applications to attend. Because each delegate was so limited in what he could hear and do, we attach the greatest importance to putting into the hands of every delegate a copy of such parts of the proceedings as are published.

We hope that the authors whose papers are not being published in this Journal will find a suitable alternative and that they will understand the editorial problem which has resulted from the plethora of papers.

Alfred White Franklin C. Henry Kempe Christine E. Cooper

RECENT DEVELOPMENTS IN THE FIELD OF CHILD ABUSE

C. Henry Kempe, M.D., Professor of Pediatrics and Microbiology
Director, National Center for Prevention and Treatment of Child Abuse and Neglect, Department of Pediatrics, University of Colorado
4200 East Ninth Avenue, Denver, Colorado 80262

All of us concerned with the welfare of children the world over must remember that to this very day vast numbers of children, and particularly those living in portions of the third world, still face malnutrition and infectious diseases as the two major problems of survival. Nations concerned with malnutrition and the prevention of infectious diseases must first address these primary needs, but it is interesting that even in countries struggling with these basic concerns, the problem of child abuse is now being considered. In Europe and North America we see that, as birth rates drop, each child is expected to survive. Without concerns about malnutrition or infectious diseases as likely causes of death, many additional threats to the child's life and health are increasingly considered, and among them is child abuse. In a sense, therefore, the very consideration of child abuse as a problem worthy of the public's concern means that children have reached a certain plateau of basic care.

A unique event in the lives of children the world over will occur in a few weeks. 1979 will mark the International Year of the Child by order of all 149 member states of the United Nations. The International Year of the Child is a worldwide effort to better the lot of children. Broadly based national committees all over the world are planning what each country wants most urgently to do for her children. Many of the national committees are considering plans for improved childhood nutrition, immunization, and improvement in education. There seems to be a consensus among national committees working in each member country that the rights of children should be prominently considered, and child abuse has already been named as a topic by a number of them. The International Year of the Child will see broadly ordered programs throughout the world dedicated to emphasizing the unique needs of the child and for the first time, on an international basis, address the rights of all children. The United Nations is on record as saying that it is not enough for a child not to be abused, not to be neglected, not to be starved, and not to be sexually assaulted. On the contrary, the Children's Charter states that all children have the right to be in a setting that will attempt to develop each child to his or her greatest potential. To do so children need to be born well, to be valued, to enjoy optimal growth and development, to be in a nurturing family environment, to learn the skills necessary for success, to receive health assessment and health maintenance, anticipatory guidance, health education for self care, easy access to competent medical and dental treatment, and to share in the advances made possible by biomedical and biosocial research.

Your program committee asked me to provide a brief overview of developments in our field since our last meeting. I do so based on information available to me from letters and visits from many workers who contacted The International Society for the Prevention of Child Abuse and Neglect since its formation at the Geneva meetings two years ago, and based on the material submitted to the new journal, CHILD ABUSE & NEGLECT - THE INTERNATIONAL JOURNAL, which will soon be celebrating its second birthday.

In Geneva two years ago we brought together many diverse professionals who could freely exchange experiences and views. This led to collaborations and cross fertilization of ideas which have been striking.

I shall briefly deal with six selected areas where significant progress has occurred. These are:

1) Change from a closed system of child protection to a more open system involving many professions and the public at large.

Perhaps the greatest progress we have seen is in the general recognition that social workers have carried the entire burden of protective services alone for too long a time, and that they have lacked the needed support of physicians, nurses, police, the judiciary, and finally the population they serve. Wherever the system has remained too rigidly isolated so as to preclude an interdisciplinary approach, progress has been slow and pressure from the outside, primarily from enlightened and sometimes enraged citizens, has been required to bring about needed change. But in many thousands of communities throughout the world, broad interest shown by the public and all helping professionals have brought about reorientation toward joint concerns by involving the community as a whole with all its professional and lay talents, and this has greatly improved the lot of needy families as well as the lot of primary workers in the child protection field. It is now well understood, that because of the enormous emotional stress produced in coping with child abuse, the fatigue burnout of workers in the field is great. Primary care child protection workers are the only public servants willing to constantly stretch their case load to meet any demands. They do so because they are not a militant profession with defined duties. But in the process they do an injustice to their clients and to themselves. The answer lies in the increasing use of lay family aides as social work extenders.

We now understand what must be done to prevent this phenomenon by professional and community support. In a larger sense, there is the fact that the complex problems of child abuse, with the long treatment required for families, the difficult-to-treat parents and very needy children, are in themselves such a challenge to the social care system, that there is chance that, once progress has been made, it might later be lost in an exhaustion phenomenon of the system itself. It is not possible to say that it is too expensive, too time-consuming to try to treat treatable families by pronouncing them all to be untreatable. Having once committed ourselves to helping families to prevent and treat child abuse and neglect, we must not once again leave it to the constituted authorities to slide back to the isolationist days so recently overcome.

It is not surprising that every country I have analyzed goes through a specific sequence of developmental stages in addressing the problem of child abuse.

Stage One is denial that either physical or sexual abuse exists to a significant extent. Serious abuse that surfaces is ascribed to a psychotic, drunk or drugged parent or to foreign guest workers with different styles of child raising, "nothing to do with us."

Stage Two is paying attention to the more lurid abuse - the battered child, and beginning to cope in more effective ways with physical abuse including early intervention when abuse is perhaps not so severe.

Stage Three comes when physical abuse is better handled and attention is now beginning to be paid to the infant who fails to thrive, an example of passive abuse, and the general area of significant physical abuse.

Stage Four comes in recogntion of emotional abuse and neglect. Its more severe form is seen in the child who is rejected, scapegoated, unloved, and so emotionally deprived as to significantly interfere with the normal physical, intellectual, and emotional growth and development.

Stage Five is the paying attention to the serious plight of the sexually abused child, including the youngster involved in incest.

I am certain you can think of these sequences of events in your own country, and, provided you have already passed through all these phases, you might ask yourself when you might come to face Stage Six, that of guaranteeing each child that he or she is truly wanted, is provided with loving care, decent shelter and food, and first class preventive and curative health care.

If any country has solved the problem of child abuse, I have not discovered it. Some nations have moved forward in this field through all the above stages and they do possess the understanding and technical know-how to provide proper services. But even in these so-called advanced countries there are as yet only islands of excellence among a sea of ineptitude and insufficient political and financial commitment. There may yet come a time when children are seen as such a precious national resource and so possessing of total civil rights that society at large will take a benevolent interest in their welfare from the time of conception through prenatal care, birth, into infancy, early childhood, and through the school years. One of the paradoxes of our century is that society has, indeed, involved itself materially in the child's life at school age, but in many nations there remains an enormous hiatus between protection of the child affordad from conception until age six.

The question of the rights of parents to be left alone must be weighed against the rights of the child to be protected from parents unable to cope at a level assumed to be reasonable by the society in which they reside.

2) Early treatment of the abused child and his siblings.

Another relatively recent development has been the acceptance of the concept that we cannot wait to begin the emotional reconstitution of the physically or sexually abused and neglected child, regardless of age. Treatment of the child is a relatively new concept for protective service workers who have hitherto, of necessity, had to focus on the mother while the father was largely unavailable. This was known as the "trickle down" theory by which giving nurturing help to the mother was thought to improve her total life and marriage, and would then permit her to be a more competent mother and wife. It was the credo of protective service work for one hundred years, and it turns out to be woefully lacking. It should come as no surprise to anyone that it took parents twenty-five years to become what they have become, that it should be more difficult to change their child raising practices and also, even in a modest way, their character in a period of a year or two. On the other hand, it has been very encouraging to us to see how relatively quickly their children can be reconstituted emotionally, provided only that they receive appropriate emotional support of a skilled, reliable kind and at once. Individual and group treatment must be tailor-made to each child's needs. To fail to address the emotional needs of the abused child effectively and from the very first should nowadays have to be regarded as malpractice.

3) The growing recognition that sexual abuse is as numerous and, in many ways, as serious as physical abuse in considering the long term welfare of children.

More and more is being done to prevent child abuse and to intervene successfully as early as possible before it is as yet a major threat to the child's life or growth and development. This has not yet been possible in a major way in the field of sexual abuse although even there we see inroads being made by early inclusion of family life education in schools and by providing effective rescue once sexual abuse and incest come to light. Let me add here that those who believe that incest had best be left a "family affair," that it is not of serious emotional import as judged by the fact that many victims have gone on to lead apparently normal lives, fail to take into account the enormous emotional costs paid by many of these children and the scars they bear for a lifetime. Recent studies do show that a disproportionate number of prostitutes have been involved in incest in early years, and that most children involved in incest do not grow up to have happy lives. The frequency of incest is very large and the reported number is now fully equal to that of physical abuse in our Center.

Early treatment of these children, regardless of age, appears to be important in order to be successful in many cases, with some spectacular failure in others. But remember that incest is as yet hardly talked about in many countries; it is, indeed, the "last taboo." Discussing incest even at a professional level, often leads to hostile responses similar to those we heard twenty years ago when discussing the battered child.

4) The institutional abuse that occurs when society's intervention is more harmful than if intervention had not occurred.

Our concept of prevention and, when that fails, of early intervention does assume that intervention is better than doing nothing. But there are times when we clearly intervene badly and do unintended harm. An intelligent treatment plan must be made that does full justice to the rights of the child without subjecting him to the alternative, institutional abuse of unduly prolonged and frequently changing foster care or institutional placements. Many a child, having been robbed of his family for his own good, is then subsequently robbed of each new family substitute, in turn, a truly devastating blow at any attempt of bonding for the child. The incredible inertia of child protection and judicial systems the world over requires public attention and action to ameliorate this kind of institutional abuse.

Consider the plight of children who have committed no crime, but are placed in temporary shelters which are in fact juvenile correction institutions, training schools, and security detention facilities, all alternatives used by society to cope with children who simply have no place to go because they are abused at home. In many instances the money spent by the public on institutional care of such children could be better spent in treatment of the family, with the child given additional safeguards because of this increased development of helping services. But above all, the child who is in limbo is really suffering the most. Where families cannot be reconstituted, the speedy making available for adoption of a child would be certainly far superior to shuttling children from pillar to post over a period of many years.

Since our last meeting there has been lively debate about the relative importance of societal abuse of the parents by suggesting that child abuse is essentially a product of young families caught up in the stresses of poverty, racism, unemployment, poor housing and that these crises trigger the attack on the child and are the primary cause of physical abuse in children. This concept does not, of course, take care of the failure-to-thrive syndrome, or sexual abuse or incest, but it does take the therapist somewhat off the hook by blaming society's shortcomings for the parents' abusive behavior. Without underestimating the importance of external crises as a trigger phenomenon, let me just point out that we are so very struck with the high incidence and serious nature of child abuse among a group of individuals who do have a job, housing, cheap food, free comprehensive health care, are married, and live surrounded by potentially helpful people. I am talking here about a group of military families who enjoy all these societal advantages and still have a very significant problem of child abuse, with five child deaths occurring in a single military camp in my state in the past twelve months. Clearly internal and external stresses combine to trigger attacks.

5) <u>The Two legal concepts of the law guardian and of the legal requirements for involuntary termination of parental rights and the freeing of the abused child for adoption</u>.

Two legal advances which are rapidly coming to the foreground in the past two years have been the concept of a guardian <u>ad litem</u>, an adult who may not necessarily have legal training, who is assigned by the court to be the advocate of the child in all situations where the child is deemed to be in need of protection by the court. All of our states have the possibility of providing guardians <u>ad litem</u> to abused children, but an increasing number of states now mandate it.

Similarly, a number of states have now more clearly defined the situations under which involuntary termination of parental rights can be accomplished. This now usually entails either a particularly brutal or sadistic form of abuse or neglect by imprisonment or starvation or abandonment for a period of six or more months. Also considered are serious and incurable psychopathology on the part of the parent which places the child in immediate danger and is not amenable to treatment, and finally those situations where a serious effort at treatment has failed and it is felt by the court that a child cannot successfully be raised in his family. Such termination of parental rights is never undertaken lightly, but if information is well documented by a social worker, a pediatrician and a psychiatrist, we have yet to see it overturned on appeal. Early termination of parental rights to make the child available for adoption will, in years to come, be seen as a key element in the chain of progress for abused children.

6) <u>Prevention of child abuse</u>.

Since our last meeting there has also been debate around the ethics of identifying, or some people say labeling, of some families as "in need of extra services" or "at risk." Pediatricians have always preferred prevention to treatment. We felt that it was far better to develop the poliomyelitis vaccine to prevent polio than to try to improve the iron lung respirator used by the victims of the disease. There are now a number of well controlled studies that show that it is possible to identify families who might be expected to have problems in bonding and to assist many of them by an extra effort of kindness and care. It is particularly important to those of us who work in the fields of obstetrics, midwifery, pediatrics, and nursing, that every effort be made by paying careful attention to families' attitudes toward their babies before, during, and after their births, and to find those to whom we will need to reach out in order to provide extra help if parenting should fail partially or completely, and before disasters occur. There are those who believe that even looking at a mother and a child after delivery is unethical and an invasion of their privacy. Not so! We health professionals are employed by our families to help bring into the world a healthy child with the least trauma both physically and emotionally to the baby and also to the parents. As part of comprehensive health care by obstetrics and pediatrics, we must pay attention to early bonding and adjustment needs of families. Failure to provide this comprehensive health care is medical and nursing malpractice.

It should not be surprising to anyone that as we do a better job of providing early help to families in need of extra services and by educating families to seek such help when they encounter crises, we will be left with the residue of impossible-to-treat, abusive parents, who will appear to us to be more and more sick. Unless we license parenthood, this will be our lot in years to come, if we are successful in preventing the majority of instances of serious child abuse and neglect.

CONCLUSION

This Second International Congress represents a truly unique opportunity to listen and to learn: to have a totally open mind, to be humble and not dogmatic, and to assume that we all know very little.

To those who for professional satisfaction insist on a high percentage of "cures," the field of child abuse and neglect has little to offer. But to those who find an immense satisfaction in bringing happiness, even for a time, to children and to their parents, to see them all grow and develop, and to go from constant misery to at least intermittent times of joy and satisfaction, it is, indeed, a most satisfying field. It is hard to measure the ultimate effect of our care. One simply has to see hundreds and hundreds of such families to be persuaded that humane and skilled efforts in their behalf have brought about changes for the better, and this is particularly so for the children who have been neglected so long in our early rush to help their parents.

While international meetings serve a splendid purpose of acquainting us with the contributions made by many diverse groups in many countries, I should warn you that it is not always possible to transfer a program from one country to the next, even when they are neighboring countries. Differences in professional attitudes, the law, and society's readiness for change, all govern and all are important. On the other hand, it would be quite wrong to assume that just because a piece of work was done here that it cannot be useful somewhere else. Science would not have progressed if people had persisted in reinventing the wheel.

Allow me to close by quoting the preamble to the Declaration of the Rights of the Child adopted by the United Nations in 1959.

> "Mankind owes the child the best it has to give."

I wish you an exciting and memorable meeting in the cause of the abused child and his needy family.

SUMMING UP

Alfred White Franklin
Chairman, Executive Committee, The Second International Congress on Child Abuse and Neglect, London, England

As I entered the hall, I passed two delegates, one, surprised to see the other asked, "Why did you come?" "To collect experiences," was the reply. He might have answered to learn or to teach, to exchange ideas, criticizing, rejecting or accepting what seems new, to listen to lectures, to discuss papers, to talk over lunch, to get to know other delegates and to make friendships which can continue after the Congress ends. The shy worker, who came to receive may have been tempted out of his shyness to give. The teacher may have discovered how much more he needs to learn. The broad purpose of the Congress was to improve the care of children worldwide by lessening the effect of one important harmful factor - child abuse and neglect.

Behind these four simple words, "child abuse and neglect," lie crises of emotion and long drawn out, destructive agonies of body and spirit not only for the child but also for parents and care-givers. We must remember too the tensions and agonies of those caring people to whom belong the difficult prevention and ministering duties. Whatever words we use, in the end we are talking and thinking about individual people. Some of us, proud in our self-sufficiency, believe that all the answers are discoverable inside the human brain. But some of us need to commune in stillness with a power outside ourselves to find that inner peace, confidence and strength which we consume in the service of others. Mindful of this, I sought help from the Rev. Lord Soper, and he kindly composed the prayer which is printed inside the cover of the program:

> "We pray together in the belief that to care for little children is to interpret the true spirit of the world in which we live. We speak together that we may come to understand the perils that so many children have to face and the evils from which they suffer. We intend to act together that we may come to their succour and help to make a world fit to receive and to cherish all children everywhere."

The Congress was opened by the Secretary of State, Mr. David Ennals, after Henry Kempe had given us, as only he can, the overview of the present international situation. David Gil followed by presenting his theme, that personal and family violence reflect the violence of society. He demands the recreation of society. He suggests that criticism of capitalism does not mean an acceptance of communism. Both share in the misuse of the individual. That Dr. Gil, when challenged, could produce no blueprint of the good society is not surprising. What he sought was a change in the nature of the human beings who make up society, for the relationships of men, women and children to each other in the family and in society are governed less by human laws than by human nature. The members of Dr. Gil's ideal society are nowhere to be found on earth. Yet some of the damaging, stressful conditions of life could be changed. Our acquiescence and our inaction are forms of involvement, if negative ones. Our non-vote is a vote. If it be true that no act is without political significance, since it involves society, it follows that there are no innocent bystanders.

Several strands ran through the Congress, perhaps the most important being the effects of abuse and neglect on child development shown in delayed acquisition of language skills, in delayed emotional maturation, and most strikingly in deprivation dwarfism from a lack of love rather than of calories. The end result may be abuse and neglect in the next generation. We are agreed that physical abuse is always accompanied by emotional deprivation, and of the two emotional damage lasts longer, brain damage, blindness and death excepted. Sexual abuse causes additional and devastating long-term problems.

Half of our time in plenary session was devoted to the central interest of the day - the community, the family or the child. The subjects moved from David Gil's plea for the creation of a non-violent society to Murray Straus's delineation of family patterns and Christopher Ounsted's typically English account of a disturbed family, illustrated by vivid "flow-charts," to demonstrate what can happen when the affections of mother and baby fail to bond. Elizabeth Elmer illuminated the large subject of children's rights by placing this matter in historical perspective and Harold Martin described his invaluable followup studies of abused children.

A suggested working definition of child abuse and neglect, namely "any avoidable condition or act that reduces the child's ability to develop" was thought to be too wide. What the Congress delegates discussed was a situation produced by a number of complex interacting procedures, ending in either a crisis or a long drawn out and bitter conflict, punctuated perhaps by recurring crises.

Vulnerable families can certainly be identified, especially when there are multiple problems including psycho-social stresses, marital difficulties, poor housing, debts, and handicapped children, and especially when the family is isolated socially. The higher social classes can unload their children, but when there is abuse it is often subtle rather than physical. The extra stress imposed by service life adds to the risk. No definitive study exists about the direct effect of extreme poverty and misery. We know that maternal depression is commoner in families where children have behavior problems; we do not know which is cause and which effect. Post puerperal depression which may have hormonal and chemical associations, must be better diagnosed, for it always produces a crisis in infant care. Humane and considerate perinatal management, the special concern of obstetricians, midwives and medical social workers was seen as an achievable preventive measure.

Prediction or identification of vulnerable families and its concomitant prevention maintains its importance despite their voracious appetite for the time of trained staff. Some doubt was voiced that this high index of suspicion may now be so high that parents conceal legitimate injuries that require treatment. The labelling of families deemed vulnerable may even be self-fulfilling. The value and the purpose of registers raised important issues which need further study. The trend in the USA seemed to be towards aiding diagnosis through the register and in the UK towards monitoring. Better criteria are essential for inclusion and, no less, for expunging the record. The insupportable work load, resulting from mandatory reporting and penalties for failure to report, present a burden to all. Some support swapping prediction for education.

Ray Helfer demonstrated his crash course in childhood for adults. The necessity for education about family life to schoolchildren also was strongly supported. The present sophisticated methods of teaching about child abuse were demonstrated and should be employed, not only for medical students and public health nurses but also members of the legal, law enforcement professions and the general public. The use and abuse of the mass media occupied a session. Discussions about the work of parent aides and Parents Anonymous helped clarify the part which nonprofessionals should play. That these lay helpers are helpful was clear.

Many sessions were devoted to management and treatment, both of families and individuals, by group and individual therapy. Residential and day care units for families had their supporters. The interventions proposed ranged from early treatment and early removal of the child to attempts to reunite the family after ensuring a safe, nurturing environment in which their particular problems could be identified and good child-rearing techniques learned.

Intervention is not without its own dangers. Changes of caregiver are stressful, as are some aspects of the legal process. These will remain as long as child abuse is with us. Institutional care, ordered for the child's safety, produces its own hazards of emotional deprivation. Even within institutions, as in all forms of alternative care, the freedom of the child from even physical abuse can by no means be guaranteed. The plea was made to pay more attention to how the situation strikes the child. Humiliated, dignity removed, and injured, the child may still feel safer within an abusive family than when cut off at the roots. On the other hand, family life can be too dangerous, resulting in a child who develops physical illness, or even self-mutilation, preferring pain to pleasure.

A number of important questions arose during the "legal" sessions. A brilliant presentation of a Scottish children's hearing raised the whole problem of responsibility for decision-making. Difficult and harrowing as this responsibility is, many seek control. Should the social services exercise control, should it be other professionals or an independent panel of people?

The failure in English law to provide for representation of parents who are at risk of losing control of their children is seen not only as a denial of justice but as a defect which hampers the proper representation of the child. Lack of finance is blamed, but there is also a lack among lawyers' familiarity with the aims and conduct of social work and child care. Specialized courts or tribunals are strongly recommended to provide opportunities for gaining the necessary exerience in family problems. In the United States social resources are proving inadequate for handling the reports which the reporting laws produce. Especially difficult is a legal definition of abuse and neglect. What legally is emotional abuse? What would constitute acceptable evidence? How can the professionals' wish for preventive care be reconciled with parent's rights to the care of their own children?

Included in parental care is their right to raise their own children and a clearer boundary is needed between punishment and abuse. To some, the idea of corporal punishment is abhorrent and is equated with abuse. This feeling has been incorporated into Swedish law. What follows, from the application of this law, is claiming worldwide scrutiny. The question was asked, whether there are limits to physical forms of punishment universally applicable.

Another important Congress theme was sexual abuse, including incest, rape, child prostitution and "sexploitation," and the abuse of children for pornographic purposes. What can be done to help the victims, the children and also, in incest, the parents and the rest of the family? How can we minimize the added trauma inseparable from the current medical and legal management required to establish the crime?

On the subject of research, the academicians criticized many followup studies on the grounds of doubtful methodology. This criticism applied especially to the comparison of the different forms of treatment and management. In judging results the similarities between methods and successes should be looked at as well as the differences and failures. A particular difficulty stems from the observation that norms vary. Research is essential, although the researcher may be led to contaminate compassion with the "using" of families. The feeling was expressed that some issues should not be researched. Is knowledge really limited only to what has been proven by organized and controlled observation?

Case conferences were discussed, as well as more peripheral themes. These included fostering, adoption and alcohol and drug misuse. The problems as seen by "feminists" and those in the third world found their place. Society's involvement permeated the discussions, revealing itself especially in the sessions and demonstrations concerned with parent aides and other forms of lay and nonprofessional care.

To the authors and discussants to whose contributions I have not referred, I tender my apologies. May their reward be the knowledge that what they did, they did well. And so I conclude my peroration.

Let the dreamers amongst us go on dreaming their dreams and living in their worlds of fantasy. For most of us, another Monday morning will soon dawn and our tasks will be to work again within the society which exists, within the laws which govern us, administered by the judges and magistrates that we have, aided by actual police men and women. We shall be social workers, health visitors, probation officers, doctors and nurses, school teachers, parent aides. As ever numbers will be too few, time will be too short, stresses will mount.

One thing we have in common with our clients: we are all people, people with personalities that clash, people with aggression and violence inside us. Perhaps it is by helping others to develop to their maturity that we shall best develop ourselves.

The prospect is often bleak. In our work we may swing from feeling omnipotent to feeling helpless. Lack of time, pressure of work, our own exhaustion lead us on the way to "burnout." But we must leave this meeting rejoicing in hope, knowing that a spirit of compassion is abroad and that our work and our experience can contribute to a greater knowledge and understanding of life's problems, knowing what a large untapped world of helpfulness exists, and knowing that human beings are capable of good actions as well as bad. Murray Straus told us that only one third of those who are vulnerable and then severely stressed do in fact damage their children. We do not know what is the missing factor that leads them into child abuse and neglect. I will venture a guess about what stops the other two thirds. It is that they are human and that they have been able to adapt themselves to the circumstances of their lives, external as well as internal. Without adaptability and flexibility the human body would have gone from the earth and the human spirit would have been broken. Men and women are adaptable, are capable of change and change can be for the better as well as for the worse. What we learn about child abuse and neglect will surely teach us lessons which will help us to understand the needs of all children and their families. Awareness of the stresses that come from poverty of money and of power moves us deeply; we must allow also for the stresses that come from riches and status. We may even approach that utopia of David Gil's where each man and each woman relate perfectly with each other and their children, where none dominate through aggression and there are no dominated, but interaction is only through love and service to each other.

Our humanity permits us to dream of the perfect society while preventing us from its attainment. We need both our dreamers and our technical specialists, but above all we need them to work together for the common good. After the week of wide ranging discussions, we returned to our daily tasks with a little more knowledge and, I hope, refreshed by having had this opportunity of sharing with others of like mind our fears and our hopes.

In his summing up Dr Franklin quoted freely from reports on their sessions written by some of the co-chairmen to whom he expressed his grateful thanks.

Child Abuse and Neglect, Vol. 3, pp. 1 - 7.
Pergamon Press Ltd., 1979. Printed in Great Britain.

CONFRONTING SOCIETAL VIOLENCE BY RECREATING COMMUNAL INSTITUTIONS

David G. Gil

Brandeis University
Florence Heller Graduate School
Waltham, Mass. 02154

Introduction

Violence in families is, in my view, an inevitable by-product of selfish, competitive and inegalitarian values and of dehumanizing, authoritarian and exploitative social structures and dynamics which permeate many contemporary societies. Domestic violence can therefore not be overcome, as is often assumed, through administrative, legal, technical, and professional measures which leave social values, structures, and dynamics unchanged. Rather, what seems required, is political, philosophical, and consciousness-expanding, non-violent processes, aimed at changing the quality of human relations from an "I-it" to an "I-thou" mentality;[1] and aimed at transforming established values and institutions in directions conducive to the realization of everyone's intrinsic biological, social and psychological needs, and thus to the spontaneous unfolding of everyone's inherent physical, intellectual and emotional capacities.

I have discussed these propositions at a recent conference of the International Society on Family Law.[2] It will suffice, therefore, to summarize my arguments at that conference as a basis for suggesting steps people could initiate at their places of work and in their communities in order to create potentially non-violent spaces for themselves--new healthy cells of cooperation and equality within the sick and aging bodies of oppressive social orders.

To avoid misunderstandings several observations seem necessary before discussing these issues:

1. Viewing domestic violence as rooted in violent and dehumanizing values, structures and dynamics, and their complex consequences for individual behavior and human relations, enables one to transcend one-dimensional causal models according to which family violence results either from poverty or from emotional ills. One realizes instead that stresses, insecurities and frustrations, which emanate from prevailing social dynamics and relations, tend to affect everyone irrespective of position in society. There are, to be sure, important qualitative differences in the impact of these social dynamics and relations on individuals and groups in different social and economic circumstances. Family violence varies accordingly in dynamics, specifics, and incidence rates with social and economic circumstances. However, no group and no individual are presently immune from alienating experiences in everyday life and everyone's emotions are twisted by these experiences to some extent: hence we all carry seeds of violent behavior in our minds and souls, which tend to erupt when our defenses are worn down and when triggered by the social context.

2. When suggesting that political and philosophical processes aimed at transformations of social values and institutions are necessary to overcome the roots of violence in societies and families, I am not arguing against the use of administrative, legal, and professional measures to ameliorate current massive suffering. I am merely insisting that we should not confuse such amelioration with prevention and that we do not create illusions by misrepresenting ameliorative interventions as solutions to the problems of violence. I suggest, furthermore, that ameliorative services could actually be used to expand political and philosophical consciousness among service workers and service users. In this way, ameliorative practice could contribute to a revolutionary process and thus toward fundamental

solutions of structural and personal violence.[3]

3. The critique of social structures as potentially violent and thus as major sources of domestic violence is not limited to societies organized by capitalist principles and ideologies. It may apply equally to societies who claim to be organized by socialist principles and ideologies. Capitalism began as a liberation movement against feudalism and mercantilism more than 500 years ago just as socialism began as a liberation movement against the bourgeoisie in the 19th century. While both movements have contributed to the process of human liberation, neither has brought about non-violent, genuinely democratic social orders conducive to free and full development of everyone. Hence, both must be confronted critically. By the same token, it is important to maintain a critical stance toward newly emerging liberation movements in order to avoid ideological blind spots which may cover up new patterns of violence and domination.

A Radical Perspective on Violence

Human development, like other development processes in nature, tends to proceed spontaneously when individuals can realize their intrinsic biological, psychological and social needs[4] through everyday interactions with the human and material environment. In accordance with this view of human development, violence is human-originated conditions, acts or inactions, which interfere temporarily or constantly with the realization of intrinsic human needs, and which thus inhibit the unfolding of normal human development. As defined here, violence may be a result of acts of individuals--"personal violence," of societal dynamics--"structural violence," and of interactions between societal and individual dynamics.

We speak of personal violence when the agents are individuals. This is the kind of violence with which the public and professionals are usually concerned. We may speak of social-structural violence when inhibition of human development is due to institutional patterns of societies which are incompatible with the fulfillment of intrinsic human needs. We tend to view personal violence as isolated events to be understood as a function of personality, and to be dealt with through individual treatment, behavior-modification, or constraints. We tend to overlook, however, that personal violence is usually a reaction to experiences resulting from social-structural violence. For when individual development is obstructured as a result of pervasive needs-frustration in everyday life, blocked developmental energy tends to erupt as personal violence mainly in informal settings such as the home, where behavior is less inhibited than in the formal social settings in which needs-frustration originates. When personal violence is discharged in this manner in the home, it will often set in motion chain reactions of violence within and beyond families and homes.

It is a sad paradox of life in modern industrial societies, that families which are assumed to be a "haven in a heartless world"[5] have evolved also into settings for discharge of violent feelings and impulses since they now function to restore the emotional balance of individuals who encounter unsettling experiences in the course of everyday life, especially in settings of work and production. Besides, families participate in the perpetuation of violence in an even subtler manner: they serve as unwitting agents of structural violence when preparing children for adulthood in societies in which personal violence and submission to structural violence are normal aspects of life. In such societies, families tend to stress hierarchical patterns, authority, discipline, and punishment including corporal punishment. These patterns and practices transmit to children attitudes and capacities which they will require as adults in societies permeated with structural and personal violence.

To identify the prevalence of structural violence, one needs to examine the extent to which a society's major institutions are conducive to, or inhibit, the realization of people's biological, psychological, and social needs, and thus, the unfolding of their intrinsic potentials. Institutional patterns one needs to consider in this context are: (1) control of resources and means of production; (2) organization of work and production; and (3) distribution of goods and services, social prestige, civil and political rights. My knowledge of these issues is limited largely to capitalist societies and I shall therefore draw on that experience in the following brief analysis. I am, of course, aware that structural violence exists also and has existed in many non-capitalist and pre-capitalist societies.

Resources: A central feature of capitalist societies is that most life sustaining and life enhancing productive resources such as land, other natural resources, energy, human-created means of production, and human-generated knowledge, are owned and controlled by relatively small segments of the population, and are managed primarily for the material benefits of owners and their agents. The majority of the population is essentially propertyless, and is consequently dependent on the propertied minority for access to needed resources, and for opportunities to work. These circumstances result inevitably in widespread insecurity, deprivation, and frustration of basic biological, psychological, and social needs. Since those who own and control productive resources use them primarily in the pursuit of profit and further accumulation of capital, rather than to assure needs-satisfaction for everyone, the propertyless can never be sure that their intrinsic needs will be met through access to, and use of, essential resources, and that they will be able to participate productively in society. Consequently, capitalist control of productive resources and the competitive and exploitative dynamics resulting from it, are major sources of structural violence.

Work: Work and its organization in capitalist societies reflects the structurally violent manner in which productive resources are owned, controlled, and managed.[6] A reserve pool of unemployed and marginally employed workers tends to be maintained as an underclass whose circumstances are usually worse than those of the least advantaged, regular participants in the work force. They are supported and subtly stigmatized by various public income maintenance programs, and they are perceived by others and often by themselves as inferior and deserving of blame. All this provides a strong incentive for people to seek employment however exploitative and alienating the work context may be. The constant risk of unemployment keeps wages relatively low and assures discipline among workers. The artifically maintained scarcity of employment and, especially, of more desirable, more highly rewarded positions, results in fierce competition for jobs and promotions, and in antagonistic human relations among individuals and groups in the population. This structurally conditioned competition, in which there are inevitably more losers than winners, generates multi-dimensional divisions among people and ideologies which sustain these divisions. It is a major source of racism, sexism, ageism, etc.; it undermines potential solidarity among dispossessed classes by disguising the real sources of oppression, and it thus protects the established social order.

The quality of work is usually unsatisfactory and alienating. As a result of prevailing technology and sub-division of production processes, tasks of individual workers are highly routinized. Work has little intrinsic meaning and usually precludes a sense of pride and achievement and the integrated use of people's physical, intellectual, and emotional capacities. These capacities atrophy when not used, and are consequently lost to individuals and society. Furthermore, workers have usually no say in what is being produced, and how work is to be carried out; and they tend to know little about the nature of materials, products, and production processes, as this knowledge is increasingly monopolized by management.

Trade unions who have done much to improve wages and working conditions refrain from political struggles for the liberation of workers from dependence on the propertied classes. They accept implicitly the legitimacy of established property relations and focus their efforts solely on winning larger shares out of capitalist profits rather than on reversing past and ongoing processes of expropriation of the working classes.

Socialization in homes, neighborhoods, schools, and through advertising and media of communication, prepares children and adults to fit "voluntarily" into the prevailing mode of work or exclusion from work.[7] It also reinforces constantly the dominant capitalist ideology. It is an adjustment-oriented, oppressive and pacifying process which generates a widespread sense of powerlessness. It results in massive destruction of human potential, since most people's rich capacities are not needed in the established, dehumanizing mode of production in which humans are viewed and treated as factors, rather than as masters, of production.

It follows that work and socialization like capitalist control of resources from which they derive, are also structurally violent processes, since intrinsic human needs can usually not be realized at work, and the spontaneous unfolding of human potential is consequently obstructured.

Rights: The distribution of goods and services, of social prestige and of civil and political rights is in capitalist societies linked closely to ownership and control of productive resources and to people's positions in the division of labor. As noted above, most people are excluded from ownership and control of productive resources, many are also excluded from employment, and the positions of those who are employed are organized hierarchically into pyramids of status, power, prestige, and privilege. Economic, social, civil and political rights are consequently distributed unequally, with some receiving disproportionately large shares and many receiving small and utterly inadequate shares. In the United States, for instance, by the government's own count, over twenty-five million people are now living on incomes at or below the official "poverty" line, a measure derived from an "emergency food budget," and about one-third of the population live on incomes at or below a level which the government considers "low standard."

With such widespread "absolute" and "relative" poverty and deprivation many people can not satisfy basic material needs, and many more are living in constant insecurity. Under such circumstances social and psychological needs are usually frustrated. However, needs-frustration is not confined to groups who experience material deprivation. The competitive dynamics and acquisitive mentality of this societal context affect almost everyone and many individuals in all social classes suffer feelings of loneliness, alienation, powerlessness and self-doubt which often result in mental and psycho-somatic ill-health. Based on these observations, one is forced to conclude that processes of rights distribution in capitalist societies are not conducive to the realization of people's intrinsic needs. These processes must therefore be considered structurally violent.

Values: In tracing structural violence one needs to examine also the dominant philosophy and values of a society. In capitalist societies, humans are considered to be selfish, evil, unreliable, and lazy, and they are therefore, thought to require external controls and material incentives. When social institutions are designed to fit these assumptions, their structures and dynamics will inevitably bring forth the very tendencies they are expected to control, and will suppress the unfolding of alternative human tendencies. The assumptions thus become self-fulfilling prophecies, and the resulting human behavior is considered to support the validity of the assumptions.

Humans in capitalist societies view and treat others as objects rather than as equally worthy and entitled subjects. They will therefore abuse and exploit others, and expect to be abused and exploited by them. They also tend to perceive others as potential adversaries against whom they must compete for desired goods and positions. Such perceptions and interactions preclude meaningful and caring relations among people and they consequently inhibit spontaneous development of human potential.

The assumptions and values sketched above which have evolved along with the institutions of capitalism and which, in turn, sustain and reinforce these institutions are, not unexpectedly, violence-inducing assumptions and values.

Toward Non-Violent Communities

If capitalist institutions and values result inevitably in widespread frustration of intrinsic human needs and in massive destruction of human potential, which, in turn, lead to domestic violence (as well as other social problems), then capitalist institutions and values must be transformed so that domestic violence should be prevented. This proposition raises several related questions: What values and institutions should replace capitalist ones, so that everyone's intrinsic human needs may be realized and human potential may unfold freely; and how can powerful, non-violent revolutionary movements be built and what strategies should these movements pursue toward an alternative, non-violent society? There are no definitive answers to these questions. However a study of philosophy, history, anthropology, political theory, behavioral sciences, etc. suggests promising hypotheses concerning revolutionary objectives and political strategies.

It is relatively simple to sketch alternative assumptions, values, and institutions which seem logically conducive to everyone's development and thus to the emergence of non-violent communities.[8] If everyone's intrinsic needs are to be met use of productive resources must be open to all. Hence these resources must not be controlled by minorities. Rather, control should be decentralized to local communities of producers and consumers. Decentralized control requires mechanisms for horizontal, inter-community cooperation, for coordination of production, and for exchange of raw materials, knowledge, and finished products on non-exploitative, egalitarian terms of trade.

To humanize work, it would have to be redesigned structurally and qualitatively. Everyone's participation and cooperation in the design, direction, and execution of production would have to be assured. The products and the processes of work would have to be compatible with intrinsic human needs and with the integrated and creative use of human capacities. All work roles should be valued equally, and should entitle workers to equal rights concerning satisfaction of their needs. People should choose their own work from among the many tasks needed in their communities. Tasks not chosen in this voluntary fashion, as well as tasks preferred by too many people, would have to be assigned by rotation. The organization of work and the use of resources would have to conform to requirements of conservation of scarce resources in order to assure satisfaction of needs of people living elsewhere and of future generations.

Goods and services should be distributed in accordance with needs, subject to democratically developed, rational priorities. Social prestige, civil and political rights should be shared equally. Governance should be decentralized to local communities and should use processes of consensus and participatory democracy. Trans-local coordination should be worked out by delegate assemblies representing self-governing communities rather than anonymous individuals. All governance processes should be open. The task of representing one's community should be rotated and should not entitle incumbents to privileged circumstances.

The assumptions underlying these structures are that humans have the potential to cooperate, to care about self and others, and to be self-motivated, rational, creative, active and productive. The suggested institutional structures are expected to bring out and reinforce these potentials. The values implicit in these structures are that humans, though unique and different, are intrinsically equal in worth, and should be equally entitled to resources, rights, liberties and responsibilities. They should be considered subjects rather than objects and should not be exploited and dominated. Cooperation is assumed to be more compatible than competition with genuine human self-interest, survival, development, and self-actualization.

It is more difficult to generate political movements and strategies toward egalitarian, cooperative, democratic and non-violent communities than to sketch principles for their social organization. There does not seem to be a simple, correct strategy. Rather strategies need to be geared to particular social and historical contexts, and there are likely to be different complementary strategies for any particular context. The revolutionary process needs to focus simultaneously on several levels: individuals, households, workplaces, communities, societies, continents and the world. And it needs to be multidimensional, striving simultaneously to unravel prevailing oppressive ideologies by deepening comprehension of institutional realities; to change perceptions of self-interest and redefine it accordingly; to adjust assumptions and values to newly emerging perceptions of self-interest and consciousness about reality; to modify attitudes, behaviors and human relations in accordance with newly defined self-interests, values, and consciousness; and finally, to transform institutions through practices compatible with alternative perceptions, assumptions, values, and consciousness. [9]

Creating collectives among workers at places of work and in communities is one feasible component of a set of strategies aimed at transforming capitalist states into decentralized, democratic, cooperative, non-violent societies.[10] Working people in any existing enterprise could transform themselves and their households voluntarily into social, economic and political collectives. They do not require consent from the managements of their enterprises since such a step affects initially only their relations and responsibilities towards one another and does not immediately change the property and authority relations in the enterprise.

Once workers discover the potential benefits for themselves and their families in cooperation and mutual commitment, and the long-range revolutionary possibilities of this decentralized strategy, they could begin to share their wages and salaries and to make joint democratic decisions on the use of their combined economic resources in ways conducive to meeting everyone's needs in accordance with collectively developed priorities. They would learn in the process the deeper meanings, possibilities and rewards, and also the difficulties of cooperation and mutual commitments.[11] As such worker collectives spread throughout the enterprises and organizations of a capitalist state they could, in a later stage of their evolution, create federations and networks for mutual economic and social support and for joint political strategizing and action. Should such a movement gain strength and momentum, it would eventually be in a position to replace the established management of enterprises through coordinated action at a collectively chosen time. This should occur non-violently and should involve the possibility for former managers to join in the workplace collectives as equally entitled and equally responsible participants, but not as owners and managers. From that point on worker collectives would direct their respective enterprises through democratic processes and they could begin to transform the nature of products, the quality of the work process, and the direction of the economy on local and translocal levels. They could then proceed to implement the principles of equality and cooperation within and beyond their communities.

This brief sketch of the creation and expansion of workplace collectives as a feasible aspect of a revolutionary strategy has not dealt with the many internal and external difficulties one must expect in such a process. Much theoretical and practical work needs to be done for this strategy to succeed. Here I wanted merely to sketch the idea and to indicate that possibilities for non-violent revolution toward non-violent alternative modes of human existence are available, provided we commit ourselves to work toward them. The essense of this idea is that the way toward the revolution is to realize it in one's own life in the space available right now. When we begin moving in that direction our everyday experiences and human relations will change gradually, and we will be on the way to overcoming the prevailing sense of powerlessness, alienation and isolation. Thus we will no longer need to project our feelings of violence onto members of our households and domestic violence should decline as the workplace and community collectives multiply and the revolutionary movement gathers strength.

Footnotes

1. Martin Buber, Good and Evil, New York: Charles Scribner's Sons, 1952, 1953.

2. David G. Gil, "Societal Violence and Violence in Families," in J.M. Eckelaar & S.N. Katz, editors, Family Violence, Toronto: Butterworths, 1978. Presented at the Second International Conference of the International Society on Family Law, Montreal, 1977.

3. David G. Gil, "Practice in the Human Services as a Political Act," Journal of Clinical Child Psychology, Vol. 3, No. 1, Winter-Spring 1974.

   David G. Gil, "Clinical Practice and Politics of Human Liberation," Journal of Clinical Child Psychology, Vol. 5, No. 3, Winter 1976.

4. Abraham H. Maslow, Motivation and Personality, New York: Harper & Row, 1970.

5. Christopher Lasch, Haven in a Heartless World: The Family Besieged, New York: Basic Books, 1977.

6. Harry Braverman, Labor and Monopoly Capital: The Degradation of Work in the Twentieth Century, New York: Monthly Review Press, 1974.

   David G. Gil, "Social Policy and the Right to Work," Social Thought, Vol. 3, No. 1, Winter 1977.

7. Samuel Bowles and Herbert Gintis, Schooling in Capitalist America, New York: Basic Books, 1976.

8. David G. Gil, "Resolving Issues of Social Provision," in D. G. Gil, The Challenge of Social Equality, Cambridge: Schenkman Publishing Co., 1976.

9. Andre Gorz, Strategy for Labor, Boston: Beacon Press, 1967.
   Paulo Freire, Pedagogy of the Oppressed, New York: Herder and Herder, 1970.
   David G. Gil, "Thoughts on Political Practice Toward an Egalitarian, Humanistic, Democratic Social Order," in D.G. Gil, The Challenge of Social Equality, Cambridge: Schenkman Publishing Co., 1976.

10. David G. Gil, "Work Place Collectives: A Strategy Toward Decentralized Democratic Socialism," in D.G. Gil, Beyond The Jungle, Cambridge and Boston: Schenkman Publishing Co. and G. K. Hall Co., 1979.

11. Petr Kropotkin, Mutual Aid - A Factor in Evolution, Boston: Porter Sargent, 1956.

David G. Gil, "The Kibbutz - One Feasible Model for Human Survival and Liberation," Frankfurter Hefte, Vol. 32, No. 5 & No. 6, May and June 1977. (in German translation); English in D.G. Gil, Beyond The Jungle, Cambridge and Boston: Schenkman Publishing Co. and G.K. Hall Co., 1979.

Child Abuse and Neglect, Vol. 3, pp. 9 - 18.
Pergamon Press Ltd., 1979. Printed in Great Britain.

A CROSS-CULTURAL PERSPECTIVE ON THE ROLE OF THE COMMUNITY IN CHILD ABUSE AND NEGLECT*

Jill Korbin, Ph.D.

The National Center for the Prevention and Treatment of Child Abuse and Neglect
1205 Oneida Street, Denver, Colorado

In considering problems of human behavior, a distinction is often made between the so-called "folk", "primitive", "non-Western", "Third World", "simple", "less- or under-developed", "non-industrial" societies on the one hand, and the so-called "urban", "industrialized", "complex", "modernized", "Western", "developed" societies on the other. In the social sciences, this is most often referred to as the "folk-urban continuum" (Redfield 1947). It is tempting to evoke the image of the "natural state", of the "noble savage", in which all things are in harmony with nature and problem-free, including childbirth and childrearing. The nature of anthropology has been to report the norm, the ideal, for the first type of society, while researchers have often concentrated on urban ills and other such problems besetting the second type of society. This is not only a problem with respect to child abuse, but also with respect to other types of deviance -- theft, homicide, incest, substance abuse, suicide, and the like (Edgerton 1976). As well, anthropologists are not immune to a hesitancy to recognize and then report a behavior as inherently troubling as the abuse of one's offspring. A similar hesitancy has been noted as members of other disciplines entered the child abuse field.

While child abuse may occur with different frequencies, or perhaps in different forms, all communities -- rural and urban, simple and complex, Western and non-Western, contain individuals who do not measure up to their society's standards of a good parent. Our image of the "folk" end of the continuum, which I will refer to here as small-scale communities, may be somewhat distorted. Nevertheless, it does seem to be the case that the transition from small-scale, kin-based communities to large, complex societies involves changes that may well be conducive to the occurrence of child abuse and neglect. It is this loss of a sense of community that has been postulated to be at the heart of various social problems (Goodman 1956). While it is true that all societies have individuals who deviate from community norms, some communities seem to provide an environment more favorable for childrearing than do others. A cross-cultural perspective will help us to understand how the community can function either to reduce the likelihood of child abuse or to provide a milieu which seems to encourage its occurrence.

CULTURAL DEFINITIONS OF CHILD ABUSE AND NEGLECT

We must start with the basic premise that there must be a community for child abuse to be first defined, and then identified in the population. Dealing with child abuse and neglect is difficult enough within a community sharing a basic definition of abuse. The problem is exacerbated when different communities come into contact, or when sub-cultural groups, often referred to as communities in their own right, differ in their beliefs about child-rearing practices, including child abuse and neglect.

As efforts continue to deal with child abuse and neglect on an international level, cultural conflict can be expected. Western groups may consider harsh initiation rites in other parts of the world that include subincision, clitoridectomy, scarification, beatings, hazing, and

* This paper was formulated while participating in the Scholars-in-Residence Program at the National Center for the Prevention and Treatment of Child Abuse and Neglect, Denver. I would also like to thank L.L. Langness for his helpful suggestions.

the like as abusive. At the same time, many of our Western childrearing practices would be viewed as equally abusive by these same groups. Non-Western groups often conclude that anthropologists and other whites with whom they come into contact do not love their children (Benedict 1938). This belief is based on observation of our normative childrearing practices, not on instances of what we might define as abusive or neglectful. Hawaiian women, for example, were incredulous that haole (literally meaning "outsider", but used to refer to whites) mothers put their infants in a separate bed, and further in a separate room. While this might seem like a benign example, to a community that believes that such a practice is detrimental to child development, and potentially dangerous, this is a serious matter. As I have discussed elsewhere, it is not the act itself that is the major criterion in defining child abuse in a culturally appropriate fashion, but the context in which the act occurs.

Cultural conflict may also occur among sub-cultural groups encompassed by a larger community. In the United States, with its multi-cultural population, the issue of cultural conflict has arisen repeatedly concerning child abuse and neglect. For example, Asian children began to enter emergency rooms and physicisns' offices with large, circular bruises. When the first few cases of this condition arose, child abuse was suspected. The bruises were indeed inflicted, but as a part of a practice called cao gio ("coin rubbing") in which a metal coin is pressed with considerable force on the child's body. The parents, who inflicted these bruises, did so within the context of Vietnamese folk medicine. This practice is believed to reduce fever and chills (Yeatman et al. 1976). Thus, bodily injury was done to a child. But within the context of traditional Vietnamese beliefs about healing, one would be hard pressed to define the practice as child abuse. Similar issues have arisen with respect to the traditional treatment for mollera caida ("fallen fontanel") in the Mexican-American community. Listlessness, vomiting and diarrhea are treated by holding the child upside down, often with the head in water, and shaking the child (Clark 1959). This remedy, however, may result in retinal hemorrhages and other symptoms of child abuse (Guarnaschelli et al. 1972; Sandler and Haynes 1978). A seemingly harmless practice among Mainland parents in the United States, tossing small children slightly in the air to entertain them or to quiet their crying, may, according to Hawaiian folk medicine, cause injuries to a child that are equally indicative of child abuse. Hawaiians believe that this causes a condition known as opu hule ("turned stomach"), with symptoms of indigestion, fussiness, and stomach discomfort.

In acknowledging cultural variability in childrearing, and in definitions of child abuse, it is important to remember that we are not dealing with capricious and idiosyncratic harm done to a child outside of culturally accepted practices. No community sanctions the occurrence of the extreme physical evidence of the "battered child syndrome" (Kempe et al. 1962) of repeated fractures, burns, and skull injuries. The problem we must consider here, however, is just where,in a large and heterogeneous nation, is the overriding "community" that either sanctions or proscribes the treatment of children. "Community"does not refer merely to a set of local, state, or national laws, but to some sense of "belongingness" and "social solidarity", some sense of mutual obligation and responsibility. It is this type of experience that is meant by the suggestion that there has been a "loss of community" (Goodman 1956).

All communities have concepts of appropriate and inappropriate parenting behavior. Both the most indulgent of communities, in which children are rarely subjected to any sanctions, and the most punitive of communities, in which children may be severely beaten for given offenses, have definitions of abusive treatment of children. It is this violation of culturally accepted practices that is the crucial issue in defining child abuse without an ethnocentric bias. Again, the limits of acceptable behavior may vary from group to group. In one Native American/American Indian culture, the community supported a grandmother who threatened to take her grandchildren away from their mother because the mother yelled at them too often (Leighton and Kluckhohn 1947). In another group, however, severe ostracism of a child may fall within the continuum of acceptable punishments and be supported by community members. The following account by a Hopi woman of the consequences for failing to take care of her younger sister properly illustrates this:

> "My younger sister ____ was born when I was about four or five, I guess. I used to watch my father's and mother's relatives fuss over her. She didn't look like much to me. I couldn't see why people wanted to go to so much trouble over a wrinkled little thing like that baby. I guess I

didn't like babies as well as most girls did... But I had to care for her pretty soon anyway. She got fat and was hard to carry around on my back, for I was pretty little myself. First I had to watch her and joggle the cradle board when she cried. She got too big and wiggled too much and then my mother said to me, 'She is your sister -- take her out in the plaza in your shawl.'

"She made my back ache. Once I left her and ran off to play with the others for a while. I intended to go right back, but I didn't go so soon, I guess. Someone found her. I got punished for this. My mother's brother said: 'You should not have a sister to help you out when you get older. What can a woman do without her sisters? You are not one of us to leave your sister alone to die. If harm had come to her you would never have a clan, no relatives at all. No one would ever help you out or take care of you. Now you have another chance. You owe her more from now on. This is the worst thing that any of my sisters' children has ever done. You are going to eat by yourself until you are fit to be one of us.' That is what he said. That is the way he talked on and on and on. When meal time came they put a plate of food beside me and said, 'Here is your food; eat your food.' It was a long time they did this way. It seemed like a long time before they looked at me. They were all sad and quiet. They put a pan beside me at meal time and said nothing -- nothing at all, not even to scold me.

"... I would rather have been beaten or smoked. I was so ashamed all the time. Wherever I went people got sad (i.e. quiet). After a while (in about ten days as her mother remembered it) they seemed to forget it and I ate with people again...

"Sometimes now I dream I leave my children alone in the fields and I wake up in a cold sweat. Sometimes I dream I am alone in a desert place with no water and no one to help me. Then I think of this punishment when I dream this way. It was the worst thing I ever did. It was the worst thing that ever happened to me" (Eggan 1970:120).

The woman was six years old at the time. At forty, as she related the incident, she cried.

COMMUNITY FACTORS IN THE TREATMENT OF CHILDREN

Given this cultural variability among communities in terms of the definition of child abuse, some aspects of the community emerge as having an effect on the occurrence of child abuse and neglect. No practice or belief is sufficient in itself to cause or to prevent mistreatment. Rather, it is the integration of a community, a coherence of beliefs and practices, that act to prevent abusive treatment of children or to provide an environment conducive to its occurrence. Thus, extended families, neighborhood vigilance, protective services, health care, educational efforts, and so on must be viewed within the context of the community.

Beliefs about children impact upon socialization practices and in turn upon child abuse and neglect. A central issue is the value that a community places on its children. The United States and other Western nations are now facing an unprecedented situation in human history. Children are a matter of choice rather than an expected and inevitable part of the progression through the life cycle. The criteria for having children has also changed rather drastically over the generations. Children no longer have an inherent place as contributing, participating members of the household. In accentuating the value of play, and the dichotomy between childhood and adulthood in Western communities, children are often denied tasks important to the functioning of the household (Benedict 1938, Bronfenbrenner 1970). Children do not work the farm, herd the livestock, or tend to younger children. Rather than functioning as an asset, children have become a rather severe financial liability in terms of the resources that must be expended to clothe, feed, and educate them (Benning 1976). In some sections of the United States, it is becoming increasingly difficult to find housing with a child (Los Angeles Times 2/6/77). The functional importance of children in a household impacts not only on parental and community values on children, but also importantly on the value that the child places on himself/herself, on the development of self-esteem (B. Whiting 1972). Additionally, children do not necessarily support their parents in old age, either financially or emotionally.

This is a frequently-cited reason in the cross-cultural literature for having children, preferably many children. As visits to retirement homes in the United States will readily indicate, children often do not even visit their aged parents with any regularity, thus failing to provide even emotional support.

The value placed on children simply for their own sake as individual human beings and members of the community is also of concern. While the United States and other Western groups may appear to be child-oriented, largely because of the commercial orientation towards youth, children are often the lowest priority in terms of community resources expended for their welfare (Bronfenbrenner 1976). In most small-scale communities, children are valued not only for their participation in the functioning of the household, but simply for their existence. Children are considered a pleasure; interacting with and caring for infants and small children is a high prestige activity throughout the life cycle. Young children may over-report the amount of sibling caretaking they perform as an indication of the value and prestige assigned to the care of still younger children (Korbin 1978). It is not uncommon cross-culturally for very old women and men to adopt very young children. These children are often grandchildren. The primary reason expressed for this adoption is that it is a pleasure to have children in the house; that the house feels empty without a young child (Gallimore et al. 1974). Because of the nature of informal adoption and community responsibility, which will be discussed more fully below, there is no concern as to how these elderly individuals will rear the child to adulthood. Since childrearing in such societies is a community venture, there will always be someone to take over.

The effect of childbearing on the position or status of the parent in the community is also an issue. In Western communities, childbearing often removes the mother from active participation in the wider economic sphere. Women who have small children may be expected to stay at home with the primary function of taking care of the children and the house. This has arisen as a concern for women who desire a career as well as a family. Thus, the woman who has small children may be limited to an "ascribed" status on the basis of sex, rather than having access to an "achieved" status that is valued in Western communities (Greenfield 1974). In most small-scale communities, childbearing does not significantly disrupt the mother's economic contribution to the household and the community. While her central function may be overseeing the rearing of her young, this is not her only role. For instance, if women are responsible for horticultural tasks, as is common cross-culturally, children may be left with alternate caretakers such as grandmothers or siblings, or taken to work in the gardens (Minturn and Lambert 1964, Read 1968, Weisner and Gallimore 1977). The important point here is that children are not seen as an alternative to active economic participation in the community, but rather as a complement.

Another indication of the value placed on children may be the change in status that childbearing provides. In many small-scale communities, a marriage is not considered valid until the birth of the first child, sometimes even the birth of the first son. This value may persist even after conversion to Christianity with its concomitant insistence on marriage prior to sexual relations and procreation. Thus, the birth of the first child often precedes the wedding. Even if the marriage occurs first, the community may delay recognition of the couple's status until the birth of a child.

In addition to beliefs about children in general, communities have varying standards about particular categories of children. This can make a difference in the role that the community plays in insuring the welfare of different children. At a most basic level, this may involve attitudes about children of different sexes and ages. Indeed, in some groups male children may even be encouraged to physically maltreat female children (Langness 1972). Even if girl children are not more likely to be physically abused in communities with a higher value on boys, girls might well not receive the same quality of medical care as their brothers, thus decreasing their chances of survival.

A fruitful area for further investigation may be the importance ascribed to developmental stages and tasks in different communities. For example, toilet training is an especially stressful time in many households in the United States. Toilet accidents are frequently at the center of abusive incidents. Children are dunked in scalding water, given harsh enemas, and so on for soiling after their parents determine (age appropriately or not) that they are too old for such behavior. In most small-scale communities, however, toilet training is not an arena for a battle of wills between parent and child. Indeed, most of these groups would have difficulty thinking of this process as "training". It is assumed that the child will urinate and defecate in the appropriate areas -- be it a toilet or an area of the bush -- once the child has the physical maturity to control these functions as well as to follow their older siblings or parents to the proper area. Western communities tend to be on the extreme end of the cross-cultural continuum in terms of early demands and severity of toilet training (Whiting and Child 1953). Thus, individuals in Western groups may be more susceptible to mistreatment of children centered on this stage of the socialization process. If toilet training is expected at an early age to begin with, even slight deviations, in terms of age appropriate expectations, may have more disastrous effects than in communities that do not require early compliance with toilet training. Western beliefs and material culture have sometimes had an effect on the toilet training practices of other communities. For example, with increased contact with whites, the Papago Indians of North America became more punitive in their toilet training practices. This seemed to be associated with an imitation of their white neighbors,who demanded toilet training compliance earlier, and with the acceptance of wooden floors that were more difficult to clean than their previous earthen floors (Honigman 1967).

Most communities also have beliefs about child behaviors and characteristics such that some children fall outside of the range of normative parenting. While children may be highly valued in a community, this does not necessarily extend to all children. Some children may be inadequate or unacceptable. These children may then fail to receive the same standard of parenting and care accorded to children in general in the community. This may include children believed to be possessed by the devil or spirits, illegitimate children, deformed children, retarded children, or even orphans. For instance, while retarded individuals are treated with care and concern, and integrated into group life in some communities cross-culturally, some groups have been known to burn them alive (Edgerton 1976). Adopted daughters in places like Taiwan, for example, may be treated as servants. Indeed, these children may be adopted by single women with the expectation that the girl will support the woman through prostitution when old enough (Wolf 1968). Unwanted children in a Sepik River community in New Guinea were sometimes sold to a nearby tribe as homicide victims. Males of the purchasing group were required to commit homicide before being granted adult status in the community. An adult male would aid a boy in killing the infant purchased for this purpose (Gewertz 1968, Langness n.d.).

The belief that certain children need not be reared in line with community standards may be another useful place to examine the community contexts in which children are abused. We know from studies in Western nations that characteristics of the child may contribute to child abuse. These characteristics may be tangible, as in low birth weight, or perceptions on the part of the parent that the child is somehow "different(Helfer 1973; Kempe and Helfer 1972; Lynch 1976; Martin 1976; Milowe 1964).

In addition to categories of children who are not acceptable by community standards, most communities also allow considerable latitude for the psychological or personality "fit" between parent and child. Outside of Western nations, it is a rare community that believes that all children are necessarily suited to their natural parents, and vice versa. It is expected that parents will have favorite children because of their personality and other characteristics. It is also expected that some children will not be as well-liked by their parents, or that the child will prefer other adults. This is not viewed as an inadequacy or fault in either the child or the parent. Rather, individuality is expected. While community harmony is a priority, it is not expected that all individuals will get along equally well with one another. This includes parents and children. This problem is somewhat alleviated by the practice of informal adoption that is so common in non-Western groups. The birth of a child is usually accompanied by numerous requests for the child. These requests can be from grandparents, who want a child in the house, to childless relatives, to a couple that may have all boys and want a girl child. Young parents often consider themselves fortunate when social obligations and cultural/community rules allow them to keep their child to rear themselves. The practice of informal adoption is not necessarily related to a lack of fit between parent and child, or even to unwanted children. Parents sometimes relinquish children that they would very much like to keep to further community and kin-group harmony. As will be discussed below, such relinquishment does not imply a termination of the parent-child relationship. But should a lack of fit between parent and child occur, the opportunity to relinquish the child in a manner acceptable to the community at large, and thus with no stigma attached, is readily available.

Informal adoption may be initiated by the child or the parent, and may occur at different stages in the child's development. Among a group of Out-Island Bahamians, with whom I worked in 1971, an old woman was rearing a grandniece. When the child was a baby, she continually crawled away from her parents' home to the old woman's house. There were several other houses along the way such that the child's destination seemed purposeful. The parents and the old woman felt that the child was expressing a preference and decided that the child should be allowed to live with this older woman. Relations with the natural parents remained excellent, but the girl continued to live in the household of the old woman through adolescence.

In the United States and other Western communities, one is accustomed to thinking that the removal of a child from his or her parents to be brought up in another household is damaging to the child. The circumstances under which this usually occurs may mean that this is indeed the case. Western communities are again on the far end of the cross-cultural continuum concerning adoption. Only one set of parents is acknowledged, and the transaction is permanent. Adoption, which is generally formal and legal, implies a termination of the relationship with the parents of procreation in the establishment of permanent ties with the adoptive parents. In most small-scale communities, where adoption most frequently occurs among kin, ties are maintained with both the parents of procreation and the adoptive parents. This is indicative of the wider network of individuals, the community, which has a responsibility for the children. Thus, informal adoption extends the child's social ties and relationships rather than limiting them as is the case in Western adoption. Among Hawaiians, this informal adoption, called hanai (which literally means "to feed"), is considered advantageous to the child in that the child is involved in a wider network. Should something happen to one set of parents, there would be another who, through love established during the child's upbringing, and not obligation based on kinship ties alone, would take care of the child. Indeed, children who have never been hanaied, sometimes receive extra attention from their parents to compensate for this perceived disadvantage. Such informal adoption may be short or long term. It is not uncommon in such communities for children to alternate between several households -- natural parents, adoptive parents, grandparents, aunts, adult siblings, and so on.

A critical issue is whether or not children are considered a responsibility of the community as a whole, or a responsibility of the individual parents. In most small-scale communities, children are the responsibility of the entire community. They belong as much to the wider kin group, clan, lineage, and so on as they do to their individual parents. Children have certain responsibilities towards the adults of the community, and in turn, the adults have certain obligations for the welfare and education of the children. This mutual obligation structure is often reflected in the kinship terminology. For example, a child may refer to all males of his father's generation by a term that translates as "father", to all female members of his mother's generation by a term that translates as "mother", and to all cousins in his age group as "brother" or "sister". This does not imply a confusion about biological relationships. Rather, the terminology is indicative of the structure of the community and well-defined kinship obligations (Murdock 1949). Thus, for example, all members of a young man's clan may contribute pigs, cattle, cowrie shells, or whetever is necessary to aid in securing a wife for the young man. The resulting marriage will produce children that are members of the clan and that will insure its survival and prosperity. The birth of a child very often is an event celebrated by the entire community. Feasts are prepared and everyone rejoices in that the child is not only an addition to his parents' household, but also to the community at large.

If the community has an investment in the child and the child's future, childrearing becomes much more of a community issue than in Western societies where individuals so often live in isolated households, far from or not mutually involved with a wider network of kin. In small-scale communities, a child that is not thriving is of concern to the whole group. If the parent is neglectful or abusive, this has an impact on the whole community. If a mother, for example, fails to teach her daughter to weave mats, tend the garden, and so on, the daughter will be unable to find a husband and participate as an adult in the life of the community. Beyond denying the girl her own future, the mother's neglectful behavior will mean fewer resources, often in terms of a bridewealth, for the community as a whole. If a father fails to teach his son to hunt, then nobody would be expected to give a daughter in marriage to a man who cannot provide for her. The group thus loses future children. Individual failings thus have wider ramifications in small-scale communities in which the individuals have mutual obligations to one another. At the same time, in communities in which childrearing is a shared concern and responsibility, someone, usually a relative, will take over the care and education of the child as a matter of course. Situations that might turn into child abuse or neglect in a community in which individuals are isolated in the task of childrearing, may be caught before the consequences are serious for the child in terms of injury or for the parent in terms of labelling. All individuals are not expected to be equally good parents. But the maturation of the young into participating members of the community is a shared concern.

While there are ethical sanctions against behavior abusive to children, the interests of the community as a whole may reinforce these ethical positions (Nadel 1953). For example, all communities have an incest taboo. The adherence to the taboo may not be complete. Nevertheless, sexual relations between individuals are prohibited by moral or ethical sanctions. It is worthwhile to note that incest prohibitions may encompass different relationships cross-culturally. Thus, sexual relations with a member of the same clan, even if this individual is a distant cousin, may be considered incest. While these ethical sanctions are a powerful force (Langness 1973), they are buttressed by tangible community interests. For instance,males may be dependent upon the bridewealth received for females to procure their own wives. If a father, brother, or uncle has sexual relations with a culturally prohibited female, the group will be unable to secure a husband, and thus a bridewealth, for the girl. The welfare of the young men, and indeed the community as a whole, may therefore be importantly tied to compliance with incest regulations. Violations have implications not only for the child or the immediate family, but also for the wider community. The interest of the wider kin group may also be indicated by the responsibilities allocated to different adults. In matrilineal communities, in which descent is traced through the mother's blood lines, the mother's brother may fulfill many of the tasks and duties that are associated with the father in Western communities. The child thus has close ties not only with the father, but also with the mother's brother, who is often referred to by a term that translates as "male mother".

As I have discussed more fully elsewhere(Korbin 1977, 1977a), and will only touch on briefly here, structural features of the community must also be considered in the etiology of child abuse and neglect. It is of particular interest that aspects of the community that have been identified in cross-cultural studies of childrearing, have also been associated with child abuse and neglect in the United States and other Western nations. Support systems, particularly alternative sources for caretaking, are importantly related to child treatment. Individuals who are isolated in the task of child care, without others to periodically or regularly relieve or assist them, tend to be more punitive in their childrearing practices and to "blow hot and cold" towards their children (Minturn and Lambert 1964; Rohner 1975). As well, small-scale communities tend to provide a preparation for parenthood as an aspect of community responsibility and participation in child care. Sibling caretaking is common cross-culturally (Weisner and Gallimore 1977). The cross-cultural literature indicates that this is a positive experience for the young caretaker, both in terms of generating self-esteem through contributing to the welfare of another individual, and in terms of providing experience with small children prior to parenthood. In many Western communities, this lack of experience with young children is compounded by the lack of a consistent folk wisdom about childrearing,and the lack of participation by older relatives experienced in child care. Thus, Western communities may be unique in that the first time an individual has any responsibility for the care of a baby may be at the birth of his or her first child. Social isolation, low self-esteem, lack of support systems, and inadequate preparation for parenthood have been connected with the etiology of child abuse and neglect.

There are clearly differences in the childrearing environment provided by small-scale, kin-based, relatively homogeneous communities, and heterogeneous, complex, perhaps "non-communities" in which most of us now live. We do not yet have adequate information on the incidence or etiology of inadequate parenting cross-culturally. However, it does seem to be the case that the nature of the community, particularly the level of group rather than individual concern with and participation in childrearing, provides an environment that either reduces the likelihood of child abuse, or seems to encourage its occurrence. My purpose in bringing a cross-cultural perspective to child abuse and neglect work is to place Western communities, within the context of which we know the most about child abuse and neglect, into a wider picture of human behavior.

REFERENCES

Benedict, Ruth
1938 Continuities and Discontinuities in Cultural Conditioning. Psychiatry 1:161-167.

Benning, Lee E.
1976 How to Bring Up a Child Without Spending a Fortune. Garden City: Doubleday.

Bronfenbrenner, Urie
1970 Two Worlds of Childhood: U.S. and U.S.S.R. New York: Simon and Schuster.

1976 Who Cares for America's Children? In The Family -- Can it Be Saved? V. Vaughan III and T. B. Brazelton, eds. Pp. 3-32. Chicago: Year Book Medical Publishers.

Clark, Margaret
1959 Health in the Mexican-American Culture. Berkeley: University of California Press.

Edgerton, Robert B.
1976 Deviance: A Cross-Cultural Perspective. Menlo Park: Cummings.

Eggan, Dorothy
1970 Instruction and Affect in Hopi Cultural Continuity. In From Child to Adult: Studies in the Anthropology of Education. John Middleton, ed. Pp. 109-133. Garden City: Natural History Press.

Gallimore, Ronald, Joan Whitehorn Boggs, and Cathie Jordan
1974 Culture, Behavior, and Education. A Study of Hawaiian-Americans. Beverly Hills: Sage Publications.

Gewertz, Deborah
1978 Tit for Tat: Barter Markets in the Middle Sepik. Anthropological Quarterly 51(1):36-44.

Goodman, Paul
1956 Growing Up Absurd. New York: Random House.

Greenfield, Patricia Marks
1974 What We Can Learn from Cultural Variation in Child Care. Paper presented at the Meetings of the American Association for the Advancement of Science. San Francisco.

Guarnaschelli, J., J. Lee, and F.W. Pitts
1972 "Fallen Fontanelle" (Caida de Mollera): A Variant of the Battered Child Syndrome. Journal of the American Medical Association 222:1545.

Helfer, Ray E.
1973 The Etiology of Child Abuse. Pediatrics 51(4):777-779.

Honigman, John
1967 Personality in Culture. New York: Harper and Row.

Kempe, C. Henry and Ray E. Helfer
1972 Helping the Battered Child and His Family. Philadelphia: Lippincott.

Kempe, C. Henry, Frederic N. Silverman, Brandt F. Steele, William Droegmueller, and Henry K. Silver
1962 The Battered Child Syndrome. Journal of the American Medical Association 181:17-24.

Korbin, Jill
1977 Anthropological Contributions to the Study of Child Abuse. Child Abuse and Neglect: The International Journal 1(1):7-24.

1977a Changing Family Roles and Structures: Impact on Child Abuse and Neglect -- A Cross-Cultural Perspective. Proceedings of the Second National Conference on Child Abuse and Neglect.

1978 Caretaking Patterns in a Rural Hawaiian Community: Congruence of Child and Observer Reports. Ph.D. Dissertation. University of California, Los Angeles.

Langness, L.L.
1972 Violence in the New Guinea Highlands. In The Illumination of Collective Violence. James F. Short and Marvin E. Wolfgang, eds. Pp. 171-185. Chicago: Aldine.

1973 Ethics. In Anthropology in Papua New Guinea. Ian Hogbin, ed. Pp. 187-200. Melbourne: University Press.

n.d. Child Abuse and Cultural Values: The Case of New Guinea. In Child Abuse and Neglect: A Cross-Cultural Perspective. J. Korbin, ed. In preparation.

Leighton, Dorothea and Clyde Kluckhohn
1947 Children of the People. The Navaho Individual and His Development. Cambridge: Harvard University Press.

Los Angeles Times
2/6/77 Fair Housing Campaign -- For Children. V:1.

Lynch, Margaret
1976 Risk Factors in the Child: A Study of Abused Children and Their Siblings. In The Abused Child: A Multidisciplinary Approach to Developmental Issues and Treatment. Harold Martin, ed. Pp. 43-56. Cambridge: Ballinger.

Martin, Harold, ed.
1976 The Abused Child: A Multidisciplinary Approach to Developmental Issues and Treatment. Cambridge: Ballinger.

Milowe, I.D. and R.S. Lourie
1964 The Child's Role in the Battered Child Syndrome. Journal of Pediatrics 65: 1079-1081.

Minturn, Leigh and William Lambert
1964 Mothers of Six Cultures. Antecedents of Child Rearing. New York: John Wiley and Sons.

Murdock, George P.
1949 Social Structure. New York: Macmillan.

Nadel, S.F.
1953 Social Control and Self-Regulation. Social Forces 31:265-273.

Read, Margaret
1968 Children of Their Fathers: Growing Up Among the Ngoni of Malawi. New York: Holt, Rinehart and Winston.

Redfield, Robert
1947 The Folk Society. American Journal of Sociology 52:293-308.

Rohner, Ronald P.
1975 They Love Me, They Love Me Not. A Worldwide Study of the Effects of Parental Acceptance and Rejection. New Haven: HRAF Press.

Sandler, Alan P. and Vincent Haynes
1978 Nonaccidental Trauma and Medical Folk Belief: A Case of Cupping. Pediatrics 61(6):921-922.

Weisner, Thomas and Ronald Gallimore
1977 My Brother's Keeper: Child and Sibling Caretaking. Current Anthropology 18(2):169-190.

Whiting, Beatrice
1971 Folk Wisdom and Childrearing. Paper presented at the Meetings of the American Association for the Advancement of Science.

1972 Work and the Family. Cross-Cultural Perspectives. Proceedings of the conference, Women: Resource for a Changing World. Cambridge.

Whiting, John W.M. and Irvin L. Child
1953 Child Training and Personality. New Haven: Yale University Press.

Wolf, Margery
1968 The House of Lim: A Study of a Chinese Farm Family. New York: Appleton-Century, Crofts.

Yeatman, G.W., C. Shaw, M.J. Barlow, and G. Bartlett
1976 Pseudo-battering in Vietnamese Children. Pediatrics 58:616.

Child Abuse and Neglect, Vol. 3, pp. 19 - 30.
Pergamon Press Ltd., 1979. Printed in Great Britain.

THE ONTOGENY OF COMMUNICATION BEHAVIOUR AND ADRENAL PHYSIOLOGY IN THE YOUNG CHILD

Hubert MONTAGNER[+], Jean Charles HENRY[++], Michel LOMBARDOT[+], Albert RESTOIN[+], Martine BENEDINI[+], Dominique GODARD[+], Françine BOILLOT[+], Marie Thérèse PRETET[++], Danièle BOLZONI[+], Josette BURNOD[++], Rose Marie NICOLAS[++].
+ Laboratory of Psychophysiology, Faculty of Sciences, Besançon, France.
++Laboratory of Biochemistry, Faculty of Medicine, Besançon, France.

INTRODUCTION

Aggressiveness and aggression in both man and animal are among the themes which have most often been developed by behavioural biologists over the last 20 years. However, argument has often dominated critical analysis of the different factors that govern the expression of aggressive behaviour. The difficulties in mutual understanding come mainly from the differences in the methods of approach.

To better understand phylogeny certain ethologists (the Objectivists: especially K.LORENZ) have made comparative studies of the behavioural repertory of related species and in particular the expression of reproductive and aggressive behaviour. When the structure of behavioural units is invariable or varies very little from one individual to another in the same species, these units can be assimilated to organs as if they come from the genetic code of the species. The expression of these inherited behaviours depends on social releasers (see for example _On aggression_ by K.LORENZ, 1966, or _Ethology : the biology of behaviour_ by I.EIBL-EIBESFELDT, 1970).

If the inneist conceptions of the Lorenzian school are questionable, this school gives us at least two groups of conclusions that cannot be ignored in the study of aggressive behaviour : 1-aggression is part of a group of behaviours and it is artificial to try and separate them, i.e. _agonistic behaviours_ that include threat, preparation for aggression, aggression itself, submissive behaviour, fearfulness and escape. Even in a more general way aggression as such cannot be separated from other exchanges between individuals of the same species and must first be considered as an integral part of the communication systems of the species; 2-the motor manifestations of aggression are studied in free active organisms in their natural life environment in relation to the physiological events preceding or accompanying reproduction, feeding, overpopulation, etc... This way we can see the influence of different physiological states, which in turn are linked to endocrinal and metabolic variations in the structure, amplitude, frequency and duration of agonistic behaviours between individuals of the same species.

Some biologists have studied the motor expression of aggression by stimulating from a distance, using telemetry and implanted electrodes, specific nervous structures (in particular the hypothalamus and the limbic system) in different mammal species including man (see for example the work of J.M.R.DELGADO et al.). Other biologists have analysed the intra or interspecific aggressive behaviours after systematic stimulations or lesions or destructions (see for example the work of P.KARLI et al.). Many scientists have concurrently studied the enzymatic systems, cerebral amines and neuro-hormones of individuals who are "naturally" aggressive or made aggressive after surgical, electrical or chemical treatment. An interesting approach is being developed : the concurrent study of the ontogeny of nervous structures and neuro-chemical systems and the ontogeny of aggressive behaviour (see for example the work of F.ECLANCHER working in P.KARLI's laboratory).

Finally, biologists have studied the relationship between hormones and agonistic behaviours by removing endocrinal glands, injecting hormones or measuring the endocrine gland activity in individuals who are more or less aggressive in varied social contexts (confrontation during reproductive periods, despotic dominance, etc...).

Our research approach is a synthesis of that of the Objectivist ethologists (except that we do not prejudice the respective parts of the inherited and acquired behavioural expression), that of the behaviourist endocrinologists and that of T.C.SCHNEIRLA and D.S.LEHRMAN. These last two scientists have shown that to understand behavioural expression we must study concurrently and continuously the role of social factors coming from individuals of the same species and the physiological factors in this expression : for example T.C.SCHNEIRLA has studied the social and physiological factors which regulate the alternation of the sedentary and the nomadic phases in the Amazon ants of the _Eciton_ genus from Central America.

D.S.LEHRMAN has shown how social factors and hormones regulate concurrently or successively the different reproduction stages of the ring dove Streptopelia risoria .This approach appears to be absolutely necessary when individuals are studied throughout their development cycle.When an ontogenic study is made the important thing is to see at what moments during the individual development cycle (whose scenario is a translation of the genetic code) there are changes in structure,amplitude,frequency and duration of behaviour which are related to ecological and social environmental changes or physiological changes.Thus,looking for the part played by the inherited factors in behavioural expression no longer has any real meaning (see below).

OUR APPROACH AND METHODS IN THE STUDY OF CHILD RELATIONAL SYSTEMS

For 8 years we have been observing and filming the behavioural sequences in young children in a day care centre playground for children from 6 to 36 months and a kindergarten playground for children from 3 to 6 years when they turn or go towards another child.From one day to another we alternate continuous observation of children in free activities (one worker for 1 to 4 children) and the observation of the same children placed together in different competing situations (the assistant or the teacher changes only one element in the environment i.e. putting one table upon another or placing a sweet or an usually wanted object such as a coloured box,a toy car,a doll,etc... at the edge of the group of children gathered on a mat).Using a period of one month as a time unit we quantified the frequency,the duration and the linking order of the mimicries,postures,gestures and vocalisations of each child.We observed and filmed the children from October to June each year and as a matter of interest we estimate that already by 1st October 1977 we had used 80 kms of film.Some children from the day care centre are then followed up at kindergarten and then at primary school.Using questionnaires and discussions with parents we obtained information concerning events that took place in the child's family (absence or sickness of one or other of the parents,arrival or departure of familiar people,etc...).Then we were able to establish relationship between these events and possible changes in the child's behaviour and in particular on Mondays after the weekend spent with the family. At the same time, the assistant, the teacher and the parent collect the children's urine at regular intervals during the day (from waking to going to bed) and the week including the weekends. This collection is made 3 to 5 times a year. We studied the urine for derivatives of adrenal cortex hormones which play a major role in the defense and adaptation of the organism : cortisol and 17-hydroxycorticosteroids.Thus,for each child we have circadian curves for the urine elimination of corticosteroids that we study in relation to his behavioural profile (see below),experienced events and the day of the week.We also studied the urine for catecholamines, magnesium and zinc (paper in press).

CHILD COMMUNICATION SYSTEMS AND BEHAVIOURAL PROFILES

We did not try to make a list of the acts and vocalisations of children (the ethogram),but we did analyse how these acts and vocalisations link together in a communication situation. Then within these links we looked for the sequences that had the highest probability of bringing about a given response.Thus,we speak of appeasement sequences when the receiving child responds by smiling,stroking or stopping crying;soliciting sequences when the response is an offering in at least 50% of cases;threatening sequences when the receiving child responds by letting go an object,fearfulness or escape;aggressive sequences when the contact acts bring about crying; and channelling aggressive sequences when the linkings of the receiving child's acts stop,divert or subdue the beginning of aggression or threats which usually have the greatest chance of being linked with aggression.Thus,we can observe that all the children of less than 20 months present acts and vocalisations (items) which make up all these sequences and observe the sequences themselves. However only certain children express them regularly without mixing them up and appropriately to the experienced situations. The threatening sequences that are only expressed to defend an object, a situation or another child are not linked with aggressive acts ; when these acts appear they are most often only in response to aggressive behaviour by the other child.The appeasing and soliciting sequences of these children are very complex and frequent and they are rarely linked with threats or aggression.Between 24 and 36 months,some of these children participate actively in competitions and are among those who take possession of situations and objects which gave rise to competition.They are attractive and followed and are at the origin of most of the new activities and often lead games : we have called these children leaders.Figures 1 and 2 show the linking of behavioural sequences that these children are most likely to express when they see an attractive object in the hands of another child (Fig. 1) and when they have just undergone failure (Fig. 2).Other children who are also dominant or most often dominant in competitive situations can in all situations provide the linking for appeasing ,threatening and aggressive acts,but from 20 to 36 months they tend to favour more and more often aggressive sequences that are preceded or not by threats i.e. dominant-aggressive children in Fig. 1 and 2.Between 2 and 3 years and contrary to the leaders their offering behaviour and appeasement sequences are less frequent

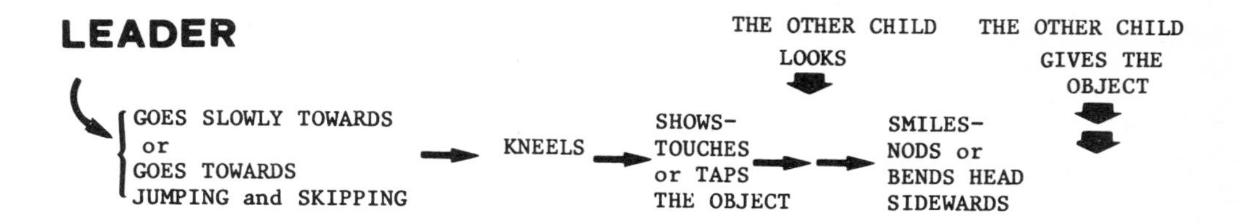

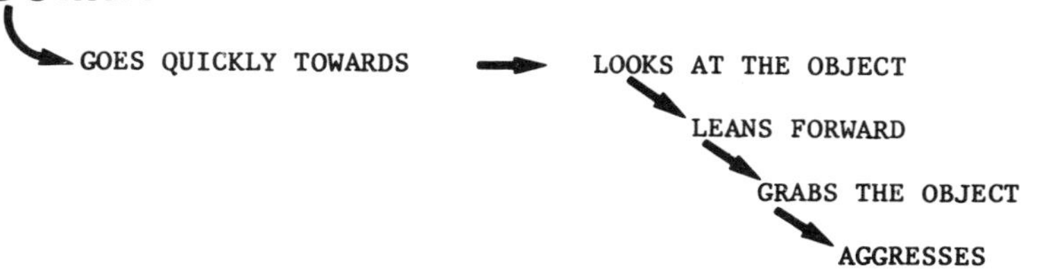

Fig. 1. Sequences of most probable behaviour items of leader and dominant-aggressive children after they have seen an attractive object in the hands of another child. If certain items (Showing, touching the object, etc...) are left out, the continuation of other items vary little in more than 60% of the cases.

LEADER

SMILES --- OFFERS (and/or STROKES) --- WAITS --- GOES AWAY.

BENDS THE HEAD ON SHOULDER or NODS --- WAITS --- GOES AWAY.

OFFERS --- BENDS THE HEAD ON SHOULDER or OTHER APPEASING ACTS --- THREATENS or BLOW IN THE AIR or BLOW SUBDUED --- GOES AWAY

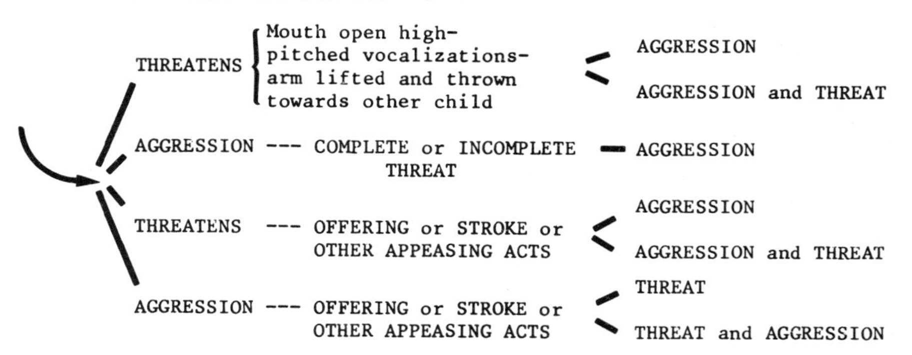

Fig. 2. Sequences of most probable behaviour of leader and dominant-aggressive children after they have failed to take an object. If certain items (offering, stroking, etc.) are left out the continuation of other items vary little in more than 60% of the cases.

than their aggression sequences (see TABLE 1).At the same time their spontaneous aggressions (without any apparent immediate cause-often described by the parents and the teachers as "gratuitous") are not ritualized or take on a symbolic form.They are not subdued or prepared for by a threatening sequence or words.They become more and more frequent,hard and repeated. These children often disorganise the activities of the other children and are much less sought after,followed and imitated than the leaders (see TABLE 1).Others avoid them or reject them that is if they themselves do not withdraw from the others.Other dominant children fluctuate between the leader profile and that of the dominant aggressive child either from one day to the next or from one week to the next.This observation added to the fact that there are differences in degree within the leader and the dominant-agressive profiles and to the fact that certain children can then change profiles (see below) shows that there is not a difference in the nature background between the leader and the dominant-aggressive children.
Among the children who do not participate in competitions or who do not manage to impose themselves we have distinguished several behavioural profiles which are still related to the linking of acts and vocalisations in communication situations : 1-those who have the same behaviour as leaders ; the dominated children with leader mechanisms.They are attractive and followed by a small number of children (1 to 4),but not by all the group;2-those who mix with their behavioural links frequent acts of fearfulness and escape ; the dominated fearful children.They approach groups,but often turn around them and often respond to an approach from others by avoidance and escape.Their periods of isolation and crying last much longer than those of the dominated children with leader mechanisms and the dominant children;3-those who alternate prolonged isolation and reinforced aggression ; dominated aggressive children. Between 3 and 5 years they also develop very pronounced fear and escape behaviour;4-those who often isolate themselves and have few gestures.They do not express structured communication behaviour in sequences even if they sometimes speak quite well.
From 3 to 6 years at the kindergarten the linking of behaviour with a communication value maintains the same structure and functions while the children become more and more fluent in their handling of language.The most appeasing children remain the most attractive,imitated and followed (see TABLE 2).We find the same behavioural profiles as we did in the day care centre even if it is a little more nuanced and even if the aggression is more ritualized and the isolations and fearfulness less pronounced than at the day care centre.The dominant-aggressive children can give the illusion of being leaders,because they can lead the others (especially the dominated children) in games with rules,but much more often than the others they go towards repeated reinforced aggression when they do not succeed in taking possession of an object or a situation which has given rise to competition.They bring about escape,fearfulness and isolation in children they have aggressed,especially the more fearful ones,and they often find themselves outside the activities of the others.The very aggressive children more often than the other children (with the exception of the dominated fearful children) find themselves in a breaking situation that they themselves have brought about.The changes in life rhythms (for example on Monday after the week end with their family) and the repression of their behaviour by the teachers reinforce the frequency of the appearance,duration and amplitude of their aggression.From 3 to 5 years,the fearful children have fearful,escape and isolation behaviour that is less frequent and less marked than between 2 and 3 years.However they still tend to respond by escape and isolation when they are aggressed or when they are rejected (when they themselves express an aggression after isolation this aggression is often reinforced and repeated).This is also what was observed when they had to change their environmental structure (change of class,school or guardian,changes in the composition of their family).These children can take 2 to 3 months to adapt to a new structure.
However some children who were isolated at 2,3 or 4 years progressively come out of their isolation at the kindergarten even if they continue to have a tendancy to remain outside the activities of the others especially when there is a conflict or just after.In particular this is the case for shortsighted and sickly children.

WHERE DO THE MAIN BEHAVIOURAL TENDENCIES OF THE YOUNG CHILD COME FROM ?

Many specialists thought and still think that the main behavioural tendencies of the young child are inherited and this is what underlies their thought when they speak of nature,character,temperament or personality.It is also known that certain specialists attribute to adult criminals atypical chromosomic formulas (this has not been proved).In actual fact the animal and man behaviourists do not have at their disposal any unquestionable method to isolate the part played by the genetic background of the species or by the genome of the individual in the expression of behaviour.This is even more true as we approach the human species.We know

TABLE 1 Quantitative study of appeasing and aggressive acts of dominant children from 27 to 36 months (between themselves and with dominated children).

		Age at 1-5-72 (Group A) and at 1-10-72 (Group B)	Period spent at the day care centre	Number of spontaneous aggressions	Number of appeasing sequences: Ritual. sollicit.	Number of appeasing sequences: Other app. acts	Ratio between N° of appeasing acts and N° of spontaneous aggressions	Number of attractions and imitations ✱	
Group A who was studied from Oct.1971 to June 1972									
OLIVIER	♂	32 months	30 months	10	11	31	4,20	82	LEADER CHILDREN
ARNAUD	♂	36 "	27 "	12	15	29	1,66	57	
STEPHANE	♂	36 "	28,5 "	18	13	22	1,94	35	
ERIC (A)	♂	36 "	14 "	22	4	16	0,99	20	DOMINANT AGGRESSIVE CHILDREN
SANDRA	♀	34,5 "	13,5 "	22	3	16	0,86	18	
CHRISTOPHE	♂	36 "	24,5 "	26	5	16	0,80	24	
ALAIN	♂	36 "	35 "	48	4	12	0,33	13	
EMMANUEL	♂	27 "	24 "	33	2	6	0,24	3	
Group B who was studied from Oct.1972 to june 1973									
LAURENT	♂	32 months	24,5 months	12	12	35	3,91	71	LEADER CHILDREN
ANNE	♀	35,5 "	33 "	14	16	28	3,14	59	
SEBASTIEN	♂	34 "	21,5 "	10	8	22	3	45	
ERIC (B)	♂	32 "	24,5 "	15	14	29	2,86	32	
EDWIGE	♀	32 "	28 "	7	3	15	2,57	42	
PHILIPPE	♂	32 "	30 "	42	0	12	0,28	11	DOM. AGG. CHILD.
FREDERIC	♂	29 "	1 "	36	1	7	0,22	7	

✱ Attractions and imitations of each child's actions.Ritual.sollicit.:Ritualized sollicitations. This table deals with observations made during the month of May 1972 (Group A) and the month of October 1973 (Group B).There were 10 observation periods for Group A :4 Monday morning,2 Monday afternoon,4 Tuesday morning;and 10 observation periods for Group B : 4 Monday morning, 3 Monday afternoon,3 Tuesday morning.Lenght of an observation period : 2hours.This table only refers to very dominant children who were present at the day care center during the 10 observation periods(such results are calculated at the end of each month).It shows that leaders are more attractive,imitated and followed than dominant aggressive children.

that certain sensory systems (it could be all of them) of the foetus are functional during the last 2 or 3 months of pregnancy and in particular audition and proprioception.This means, and as well it has been proved with several species of birds and mammals,that the embryo receives more and more varied and accurate information concerning the outside environment of the mother,her types of movements and perhaps her main behaviour and also concerning his own motor activities.This information must have an influence on the activities and motor coordination which are differenciated later on.If the new-born's behaviour is to a large extent the expression of the genetic code it also already includes a part of his own individual experiences (influences received in the foetal state) and these obviously vary from one individual to another.As the baby gets older and as the wakening periods occupy a large and larger part of the day the environmental factors direct and modulate the maturation processes which translate the genetic influences until they become indissociable one from the other. This is why we selected first to study the ecological and social environmental factors that have a profound influence on the differenciation and modifications of the behavioural profiles that we encountered.

Among the environmental factors,we gave emphasis at the outset to the behaviour of both parents in relation to the child.Three methods were used to study the relations between the parents and child of 18 to 36 months : 1-the analysis of the behavioural sequences of the

TABLE 2 Quantitative study of appeasing and aggressive acts of children from 4 to 6 years of the same kindergarten class.

	Age at 1-10-76		Weight in Kg.	Number of appeasing sequences A	Number of spontaneous aggressions B	Number of attractions and imitations C	Appeasement / Aggression Coef. D	Number of successful issues to obtain an object or a situation E
MALICA	5yrs	9mn	17	25	5	16	5	33
MOHAMED (A)	5 "	4"	19	8	13	8	0,6	14
MAGALIE	5 "	1"	17	5	6	16	0,83	40
FLORENCE	5 "		19	13	12	14	1,08	15
CLAUDE	5 "		17	4	7	3	0,57	23
DAMIEN (A)	4 "	11mn	17,5	3	7	3	0,42	6
LYDIE	4 "	10"	19	9	6	6	1,5	25
CHRISTELLE (J)	4 "	9"	17	12	5	6	2,4	25
SOPHIE (C)	4 "	9"	17,5	19	10	13	1,9	15
YANN	4 "	7"	17,5	20	21	34	0,95	38
GILDAS	4 "	5"	17	28	12	22	2,33	24
MOHAMED (B)	4 "	3"	19	3	8	5	0,37	9
CLAUDIE	4 "	2"	15	2	0	1	2	11
DAVID	4 "	2"	18	9	3	2	3	17
DAMIEN (F)	4 "	2"	20	18	14	10	1,28	44
THIBAUT	4 "		19	4	25	1	0,16	8
CHRISTELLE (G)	4 "		19	22	1	6	22	9

Correlation Coefficient between A and C : r=0,74 significant (P<0.01)
" A and E : r=0,57 significant (P<0.01)

These results were obtained during 15 observations of 1 hour on Thursdays spread out over the whole year (Wednesday is a school holiday in France).Data are also available for the other days of the week.

---

mother and father when they came to receive the child at the day care centre between 5 and 7 p.m.;2-the analysis of the behavioural sequences of both parents who came to receive the child and who prepare him to go home (without any visible observer) in the dressing room; 3-the study of thé child's behaviour on Mondays at the day care centre and the kindergarten and on Thursdays at the kindergarten in relation to the events that took place in the family during Saturday and Sunday at the day care centre and the kindergarten and on Wednesday at the kindergarten.Questionnaires that were given to the parents enabled us to obtain information on the absences and illnesses of the children and parents,on the children's and adults' visits,etc...

These three methods gave us the same response; the differentiation of the behavioural profile and the major modifications in behaviour of children from 18 to 36 months are directly related to the modifications in behaviour of the family and in particular of the mother. Thus,when the mother of a leader child and a dominated child with leader mechanisms receives her child at the day care centre,there are often the following sequences : mother's eyes look for the child - smile and stretch out 1 or 2 hands towards the child who runs towards the mother who kneels down , touches or strokes the cheek or head of the child and often speaks to him at the same time- she kisses him , takes the child in her arms. Some of these behavioural items can be left out,but when on several consecutive days the sequences of the parents' acts are reduced to a few items and include the sudden grabbing of the child,impatient speech,acts or threats we observe that in communication situations the leader child or the dominated child with leader mechanisms links appeasing,grasping,threatening and aggressive acts like the most aggressive children.At the same time,the amplitude,frequency and duration of the child's aggression increase.The behaviour changes in the mother are related to several groups of factors : physiological (illness,ovarian cycle,diet,etc...),social (work rhythms, repeated aggression in daily life,etc...) or personal (conjugal or other conflicts).The changes in the leader child's behaviour are always temporary when the above factors last for a short period of time i.e. a few days.The leader child then returns to the behavioural characteristics that he had before the changes in the mother's behaviour.However when the

TABLE 3 Comparison between the coefficient $\frac{\text{Frequency of appeasements}}{\text{Frequency of spontaneous aggressions}}$ of the child and the coefficients for the mother and father $\frac{\text{Frequency of appeasements}}{\text{Frequency of threats and aggressions}}$.

	Age of children (months) at the end of a series of observations 2 consecutive years.		Coefficient of the children : appeasements / aggressions C_1		Coefficient of the mothers : appeasements / aggressions & threats C_2	Coefficient of the fathers : appeasements / aggressions & threats C_3
O. (boy)	32 (71-72)	LEADER CHILDREN	5,20		15,30	2,03
L. (boy)	31 (72-73)	LEADER CHILDREN	4,15		8,43	3,49
A. (girl)	34,5 (72-73)	LEADER CHILDREN	3,57		4,82	1,20
S. (boy)	33 (72-73)	LEADER CHILDREN	3,24		7,38	?
E. (boy)	31 (72-73)	LEADER CHILDREN	2,90		8,43	3,49
Ed.(girl)	31 (72-73)	LEADER CHILDREN	2,85	Correlation coefficient between C_1 and C_2 : r=0.932	5,10	1,12
Ar.(boy)	36 (71-71)		2,85		8,55	1,50
St.(boy)	36 (71-72)		1,54		2,37	5,62
S. (girl)	34,5 (71-72)	DOMINANT-AGGRESSIVE CHILDREN	0,96		1,20	Mother unmarried
Er.(boy)	36 (71-72)	DOMINANT-AGGRESSIVE CHILDREN	0,82		1,39	8,31
Ch.(boy)	36 (71-72)	DOMINANT-AGGRESSIVE CHILDREN	0,74		1,10	Mother unmarried
Al.(boy)	36 (71-72)	DOMINANT-AGGRESSIVE CHILDREN	0,37		0,88	Mother unmarried
P. (boy)	31 (72-73)	DOMINANT-AGGRESSIVE CHILDREN	0,26		0,75	2,70
Em.(boy)	27 (71-72)		0,26		0,87	1,36
F. (boy)	28 (72-73)		0,22		0,48	4,25

The coefficient C_1 for each child is calculated from the appeasing sequences and spontaneous aggressions that the child expresses towards others when in free activities (10 observation sessions staggered over 1 month period).The coefficients C_2 and C_3 of the parents are calculated from the relative frequency of appeasing sequences,threats and aggressions that the parents express towards the child when bringing him to the day care centre in the morning and undressing him as well as in the evening when greeting and dressing him (20 observations of approx.15 min.each;ten were in the morning and ten in the evening).The children figuring in this table have been characterized as leaders or dominant-aggressive.

---

factors which changed the mother's behaviour continue,the child goes more and more towards the dominant-aggressive profile,without however actually reaching it if this happens after the age of 30-32 months,according to whether the mother continues to translate her difficulties into her exchanges with her child (the behaviour characteristics of the child are close to those of a dominant-aggressive child) or according to whether the mother returns to almost her prior behaviour with the child (the child only retains some of the dominant-aggressive child's mechanisms).

The receiving behaviour of the mother of a dominant-aggressive or a dominated aggressive child is shorter,more rigid and more rapid than that of the mother of a leader or a dominated child with leader mechanisms.Using a period of one month as a unit of time,we observed that the receiving behaviour of these mothers was often mixed with more or less sudden and frequent graspings,impatient acts and speech (the child shakes his limbs),threats and also aggression. It does appear that this behaviour increases in importance and frequency when the child is from 2 to 3 years : in all cases the behavioural links of the child become poorer in appeasement sequences and at the same time acts of grasping,threatening and aggression become more marked and fequent.The child disorganises even more the activities of the others.When the family environment maintains the same frequency of aggression in relation to the child, the child maintains and sometimes increases the frequency of his grasping and aggression sequences at the kindergarten.

TABLE 3 shows that when the interactions between the mother and child are quantified when the mother is alone with the child in the dressing room,there is a very high positive correlation between the $\frac{\text{frequency of appeasements}}{\text{frequency of aggressions}}$ coefficient of dominant children from 2 to 3 years who are observed among other children and the $\frac{\text{frequency of appeasements}}{\text{frequency of threats and aggressions}}$

coefficient of their mother in relation to them.We did not find any correlation between the coefficient of a child and that of his father.
The behavioural fluctuations of children who alternate from one day to the next or from one week to the next and the behavioural links of leader and dominant-aggressive children are also related to the behavioural fluctuations of the mother.
The influence of the father is translated by a reinforcement or an attenuation of the aggressive behaviour of the child,but not by the direct opposite behavioural effects to those induced by the mother's behaviour (see H.MONTAGNER,L'enfant et la communication,1978).It would seem that the paternal influence is exerted more particularly through the mother.Her aggression towards the child increases and becomes more frequent when she herself is aggressed by the father.Inversely, the frequency of maternal aggression is often attenuated when the father is rarely aggressive and provides security.
The communication behaviour of most of the dominated children also appears to be in direct relationship with the types of relationships that develop between the family and the child as from 1 to 2 months after walking (and perhaps before).The mother of dominated children with leader mechanisms has a profile that is similar to that of the mother of the leader child.But contrary to this,and despite the fact we were unable to quantify this,the mother of the dominated child with leader mechanisms appeared to be dependent on the advice of her husband.Perhaps this is one of the reasons for the low participation in competitions by dominated children with leader mechanisms and their low frequency of success in taking possession of objects and situations which have given rise to competition.Even if they are not leaders for the whole of the group,these children are often sought after and followed by some children (from 1 to 4).Leadership (leading others without there being necessarily any intention to lead) thus does not depend on the level of dominance,but on the structure of communication behaviour : children who have homogeneous linking behaviour (linking of appeasing and offering acts that are not mixed with aggressive and grasping acts;linking of threatening acts which are not mixed with aggression) and who favour appeasement rather than aggression in all cases are the most sought after,imitated and followed.They are also initiators of most of the new activities.With their families in all cases they have exchanges where appeasement dominates aggression.
The mothers of dominated fearful children appeared to be over-protective.They often restrict their child to the family circle.Four or five months after they start kindergarten (they normally start at 3 years),these children show fearful and escape behaviour that is less marked and less frequent than between 2 and 3 years except when the over-protective attitude of the mother increases.The following years at the kindergarten,then at the primary school, if the fearful and escape behaviour of the child becomes even less marked and less frequent it appears again as soon as the family goes through a difficult period (illness,unemployment, etc...) or as soon as the child has to change his environmental structure (changing school, classes,etc...).
The family of dominated aggressive children appears to be very repressive or often hurries the child up as from the beginning of the day.When such a situation continues,the child at the kindergarten alternates between very reinforced aggressive behaviour and fearful and escape behaviour that is sometimes very marked.He is often rejected by the other children and at the same time he withdraws.
Finally,we were unable to establish such a clear relationship between the very isolated but not aggressive child and the attitude of the family in relation to him.
In conclusion,the linking of behavioural sequences with a communication value and the more and more marked tendancy to favour aggression,fear and escape differentiate,as from 1 to 2 months after starting to walk,mainly under the influence of the family,but more particularly of the mother.The behavioural characteristics of the child vary like the types of relationship between the child and his parents even if the behavioural items and the sequences of items are the same in all children whatever their ethny (they have been found in the same situations in Congolese children).Thus,it can be thought that if acts and vocalisations which make up sequences with a communication value perhaps belong to the background of the human species,the tendencies to favour such or such sequences from the walking stage ,and more and more clearly from 18 months to 4 years,depend on the quality of the exchanges between the child and his family.The reinforcement of aggressive behaviour evolves just as the aggression and repression of the child by his family evolve.This also remains true for children from 5 to 6 years at the kindergarten and from 6 to 9 years at the primary school.Thus, it can be thought that the interactional climate which is established and reinforced between the young child and his family is probably responsible ,to a large extent,for the marked aggressive tendencies in older children and adolescents.The consequences of this are the rejection of these aggressive individuals by the society and the development of extremely marginal behaviour.If there are ontogenetical causes for the mother and father's behaviour, the conjunctural,physiological (illness,dissynchronisation of physiological functions related

to the relational life as sexual functions and defense functions against aggression,etc...) and ecological (especially climatical) factors play separately or jointly an essential role in the temporary reinforcement,attenuation and modifications of the availability,listening attitude and interactional way of the parents in relation to the child.To try and better understand the causes of violence in the human species (and also fearfulness and solitude), scientists must look into all these factors and not just one in isolation.

THE PHYSIOLOGY OF DEFENSE

It has been known for a long time that the defense of a mammal organism depends to a large extend on the hormones secreted by the cortex of the adrenal glands : glucocorticoids (cortisone,hydrocortisone,etc...).These hormones are anti-inflammatory and anti-allergic. When researcher workers made mammals live in aggressive situations (contention,electric shocks,aggression expressed by members of the same species,overpopulation,etc...),they also observed an increase in the secretion of catecholamines and corticosteroids.Many experiments have shown that aggressive situations are accompanied by modifications in the structure and functioning of the adrenal glands .The extension or accentuation of aggressive situations is translated by an increase in the frequency of digestive ulcers and also of the mortality rate (see for example the work of H.SELYE and S.LEVINE).
This is why we tried to see if there was a correspondance between the concentration variations in urine of corticosteroid hormones and the normal behavioural profile of the child and the special events that the child experiences.Figures 3 and 4 show the circadian cortisol and 17-hydroxycorticosteroids (or 17-OHCS) excretion curves of a 3 year old leader (Fig. 3) and of a dominant-aggressive child of 3 years (Fig. 4) belonging to the same child population over 4 consecutive days (Friday and Monday the children are at the day care centre all day, and Saturday and Sunday they are with their family).Whereas the circadian curves of the leader are rather regular from one day to the other,those of the dominant-aggressive child fluctuate much more and have higher levels of 17-OHCS at all times throughout the day except at the circadian peak.These results have continued to be confirmed over the last 8 years.Thus,Fig 5 shows that the more the child has a leader profile the less his mean circadian curve of 17-OHCS varies from one day to the other at all times throughout the day (the variability is given by the standard mean error) and the lower the mean levels of 17-OHCS are at all times throughout the day.If Magalie and Sylvie are leaders,Magalie is much more so than Sylvie : Sylvie has more frequent acts of grasping and aggression than Magalie.In the same child population the mean circadian curves of 17-OHCS of the dominant-aggressive children are much more atypical (without any circadian peak and in any case without a characteristic structure) when the frequency of aggression is higher : Damien,whose mean circadian peak is shifted to 2 p.m., is more aggressive than Isabelle who is more aggressive than Sylvie;Valerie's curve does not have a definite structure : she is even more aggressive than Damien.Thus,the more the aggression dominates the other forms of expression the more the circadian curves for the urine elimination of 17-OHCS appear to be variable (dissynchronised) from one day to the next and at the same time the 17-OHCS levels are relatively higher at all times throughout the day in relation to those of other children.Everything takes place as if in response to a very aggressive and "not available" family environment.The young child tends to differenciate both the heterogeneous and very fluctuating behavioural links where aggression dominates and a very fluctuating and increased functioning of his defense physiology.The fluctuations and the levels of 17-OHCS increase more than in other children when the dominant-aggressive child undergoes sudden and repeated changes in environmental structure and in life rhythms.The dominant-aggressive children are thus more sensitive than leader children to changes in their environment both from the behavioural and defense physiological points of view.They are also more vulnerable and are more often rejected and disorganised in their behaviour.They have the most frequent and lasting otitis and rhino-pharyngeal infections and severe sore throats. We have shown that the mean circadian 17-OHCS curves of dominated fearful and aggressive children also had atypical characteristics in relation to the curves of the leaders and the dominated children with leader mechanisms (see H.MONTAGNER "L'enfant et la communication", 1978).These children tend to favour fearful and escape behaviour (dominated fearful children) or aggressive,isolated and fearful behaviour (dominated aggressive children) and are more quickly and profoundly disorganised than leaders and dominated children with leader mechanisms in their communication behaviour and in their adrenal physiology when they are subject to aggression and when they suddenly change their environmental structure or life rhythm (we have shown that going from the kindergarten-saturday morning- to the family -saturday afternoon- and from the family to the kindergarten from sunday to monday was translated a few hours later by a shift of the circadian peak of 17-OHCS curves in some children and an increase in the levels of 17-OHCS for all the child population -see H.MONTAGNER "L'enfant et la communication", 1978).At this time of breaking of rhythm these children are more subject to otitis,rhino-pharyngeal infections and severe sore throats.

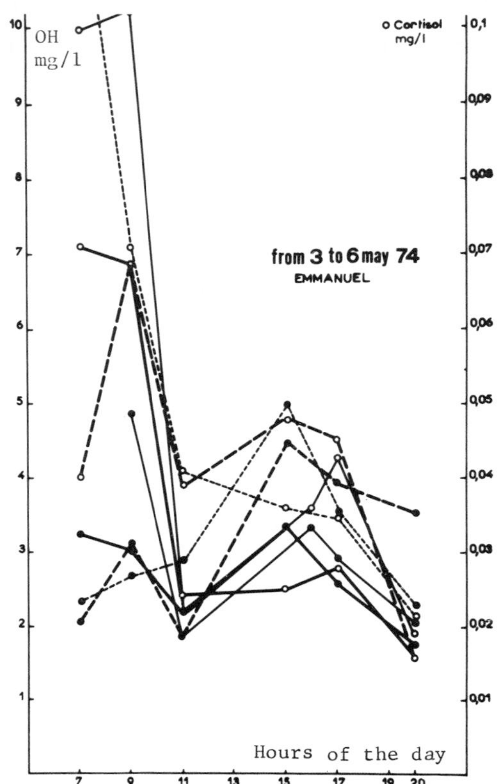

Fig. 3 Circadian cortisol and 17-OHCS excretion curves of a boy leader from Friday 3 May (fine continuous line) to Monday 6 May 1974 (thick continuous line).The curves for Saturday and Sunday are shown with short dashes (Saturday) and thick longer dashes (Monday).The boy is 3 years old.The circadian curves have a tendency to be regular,whatever the day.

The teacher's behaviour must also be added to the factors that bring about a dissynchronisation of the circadian curves of 17-OHCS and an increase in the levels of 17-OHCS at all times throughout the day (see H.MONTAGNER "L'enfant et la communication",1978).
Children who are usually the most disorganised in their behavioural structure and the most fluctuating in their adrenal physiology (the most aggressive and the most fearful) are also the most sensitive and the most vulnerable to all changes in their social environment (break in the rhythm or way of life,behaviour of their teachers outside their family environment).

CONCLUSION

The sensory and motor capacities of children have been underestimated and at the same time many scientists have had a too global approach to the child's emotional development.Language as a vector and a builder of the processes of knowledge has been given too much attention. Aggression,fearfulness and isolation as elements in their own right in communication systems have often been overlooked.The results have been that :1-rejection,marginality,violence are treated separately when they occur rather that trying to find the underlying causes; 2-discourse, as false and as impersonal as it may be, has become synonymous with communication when it is not the only way to fulfill this function;3-intelligence through discourse and abstract achievement is considered to be the noble motor of human relations.
In actual fact it is through all corporal expression including the functioning of the vocal cords(vocalisations and speech) that the young child transmits and decodes appeasement,solicitation,threat,fearfulness,aggression,isolation,etc...All profound imbalance of corporal expression in favour of aggression,fearfulness and isolation only reflects social or physiological imbalance of the family or physiological imbalance of the child himself.The imbalance persists even if it can occasionally be hidden,whatever the degree of mastery of speech and the degree of development of the mechanisms of intellectual knowledge and reflection.The mastery of reasoning and an elaborate language does not imply the possession nor the mastery of communication systems.To favour the setting up of all communication systems in the child

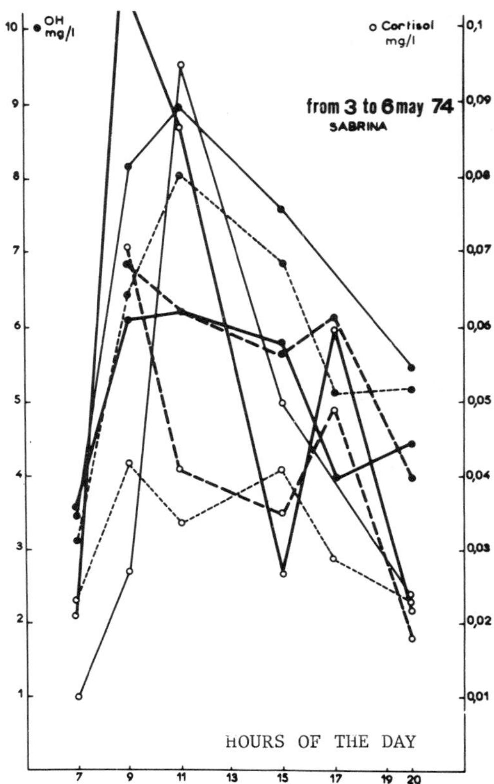

Fig. 4 Circadian cortisol and 17-OHCS excretion curves of a dominant-aggressive girl from Friday 3 May (fine continuous line) to Monday 6 May 1974 (thick continuous line). The curves for Saturday and Sunday are shown with short dashes (Saturday) and thick longer dashes (Sunday).The girl is 3 years old and belongs to the same population than the boy in Fig. 3.

---

is to avoid favouring aggression,fearfulness and isolation : it is to increase the child's capacities to respond to environmental aggression;it is to enable the child to set up and reinforce the behavioural mechanisms which help him avoid breaking with his social environment.

To do this we can no longer be satisfied with looking for an explanation of "deviant" or "asocial" behaviour in heredity,the overallness of ontogeny,the phantasms or perversions of childhood or adolescence.One of the basic priorities of our society must finally be the material and emotional support of the family : it is here that the relational behaviour of the human being is formed and reinforced.The breaking situations must be reduced by changing the social and socio-ecological factors which,when accentuating this behaviour,weigh the balance down on the side of violence and total rejection of others,in particular,work rhythms that are imposed on parents and the behaviour of adults who look after children outside the family.Only a true communication society can succeed in doing this.

<u>NOTE</u> The bibliographical references can be consulted in the book "L'enfant et la Communication",by H.MONTAGNER,Stock,Paris.

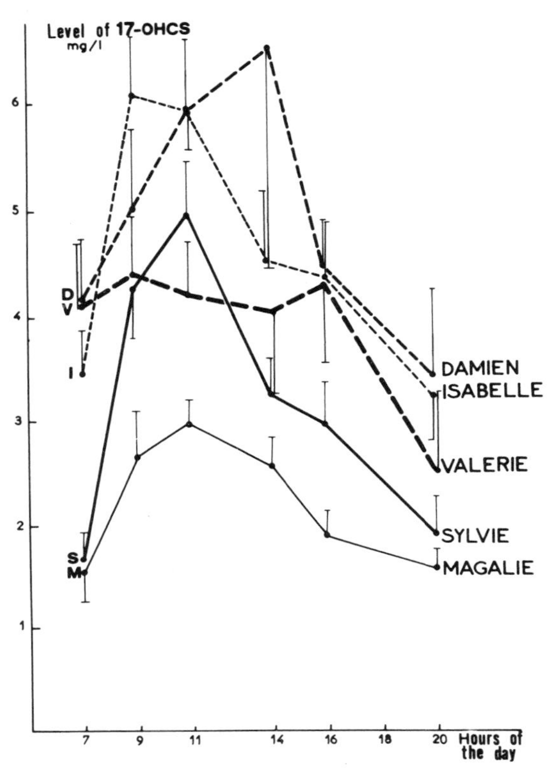

Fig. 5 Mean circadian curves of urine elimination of 17-OHCS of 2 leaders (Magalie and Sylvie : Magalie is more appeasing,attractive and less aggressive than Sylvie) and 3 dominant aggressive children (Isabelle is less aggressive than Damien who is less aggressive than Valérie).All children are 4 years old.Each point is the mean of 12 to 16 measurements which correspond to 3 or 4 series of samples from november to may over 4 consecutive days.We can see that the higher the frequency of child aggressions the more the mean circadian curve is atypical (the circadian peak shifted to 2 p.m.-Damien,or there is no peak-Valérie) and the higher the level of 17-OHCS at almost all times throughout the day.Each mean is given with its standard error : the upper (or the lower) limit gives the security coefficient at 95%.

Child Abuse and Neglect, Vol. 3, pp. 31 - 34.

0145-2134/79/0301-0031 $02.00/0.

PROPOSED LEGISLATION FOR FREEING CHILDREN FOR PERMANENT PLACEMENT

Sanford N. Katz

Professor of Law

Boston College Law School, Newton Centre, Massachusetts, U.S.A.

The basic unit in the Western world is the family. It is assigned the fundamental responsibility to care for and rear children so as to assure continuity of an ordered society made up of productive members. In the laws of the United States the family is treated not as a legally recognized unit like a business corporation or a labor unit, but as a bundle of legal relationships, one of which is that of parent and child. Although the United States Constitution does not speak directly to familial relationships, the United States Supreme Court has extracted from our Bill of Rights such phrases as "substantive due process" and "penumbra of rights" to protect these relationships from unwarranted governmental intrusion. The right to raise a child is now recognized as a fundamental personal liberty guaranteed by the United States Constitution.

But this fundamental right of a parent to the custody and care of his child - to provide for its physical, mental and moral welfare and growth - is not absolute. The State has long been recognized to have such an interest in the welfare of its children that under certain limited circumstances of health, financial support, education and morality parental rights may be overridden. Judicial termination of parental rights represents a radical intrusion into the privacy of the family unit. When it is voluntary a parent must comply with the legal requirements for relinquishment. Involuntary termination may be decreed following a statutory dependency, neglect or termination proceeding.

Severance of the parent-child relationship is so drastic, especially when involuntary, that there is a need for an entirely separate proceeding for termination, distinct from either a neglect or abuse hearing or an adoption proceeding. For this reason the United States Department of Health, Education, and Welfare appointed me to formulate a Model Act to provide guidelines to the fifty-four American jurisdictions for a judicial process to readjust parental rights and responsibilities when birth parents are no longer capable or desirous of rearing their children. Although the United States government has not yet finally approved the Model Act, it has been a catalyst for a number of state legislatures in their efforts to reform their child welfare laws.

The proposed Model Act to Free Children for Permanent Placement[1] was hammered out from six previous drafts, each of which was discussed with multi-disciplinary and ethnic groups in many meetings throughout the United States. The Act is not the work product of pure ivory tower thinking but the result of input from professional and lay persons concerned with child

[1]The Model Act to Free Children for Permanent Placement was developed under a grant to Professor Sanford N. Katz by U.S. Department of Health, Education, and Welfare (OCD-CB-473). A copy of the Act is available by writing to Professor Katz at Boston College Law School, Newton Centre, Massachusetts, U.S.A.

welfare: lawyers, judges, legislators, social workers, agency administrators, psychiatrists, foster parents and adoptive parents. The very title of the Act has significance. In the United States, proceedings designed to sever the parent-child relationship are labeled "termination proceedings." The Model Act deals with the process of adjusting the parent-child relationship. This may or may not result in termination, but it certainly results in a permanent placement for the child. The Act was planned to emphasize, not the rights or sins of the parents, but the needs of the child - especially now when over half a million American children are living outside of their birth families in legal limbo, some of them for as long as ten years. As I have said, the whole focus of the Act is on permanent placement for these children, whether that necessitates termination of parental rights, non-termination with appointment of a guardian, or other disposition. Because of the traumatic effects on children of prolonged familial disruption, the Act incorporates time frames to ensure speedy decisions.

A critical problem is to balance the needs of the child for a secure and permanent home with the State's responsibility for preserving the birth family. The Act aims to satisfy both interests by not allowing permanent placement with persons other than birth parents without giving the birth parents an opportunity for rehabilitation. This objective has been codified in a provision which mandates that the State must make a timely offer of social services to the birth parents whenever possible. To safeguard against bureaucratic inefficiencies in state welfare systems - unfortunately frequent in a large country like ours - the Act provides for the court which is making the permanent placement decision to consider the adequacy of the social services offered to the family to facilitate the reunion of the child with his birth parents. This provision is designed to ensure that the agency will be held to a high degree of accountability for making a diligent and reasonable effort to rehabilitate parents before the court has reached its decision. If social services for purposes of rehabilitation are not statutorily mandated, it is possible that the noble goals of family unity will remain simply aspirations. The provision puts legal teeth into the Act's stated purpose of attempting to preserve the birth family unit whenever possible.

The Act includes foster parents in the list of persons who can invoke the permanent planning process by a petition: a provision which aroused lengthy controversy. There was fear that this right to petition might encourage foster parents to become adversaries of the birth parents and/or the agency. There was fear that allowing foster parents procedural rights would lead to giving them some substantive advantages. Nevertheless, since foster parents may be the child's only psychological parents and the only persons with any real knowledge of or interest in the child, and since giving them the right to file a petition for an involuntary termination would flag to the court that a permanent placement had not yet been made and ensure some kind of accountability from the agency, the Model Act opted for inclusion of foster parents in its eligibility list.

The legal process by which permanent placement is accomplished is an innovative feature of the Act. I have already mentioned that foster parents may petition to invoke the process, along with other more customary petitioners such as either birth parent, a social service agency or a guardian of the child's person. The contents of the petition also strike a new note. The petitioner must indicate on his petition the legal grounds and the particular facts on which permanent placement is sought. In this way a proceeding based on vague allegations is avoided.

Following the filing of the petition a preliminary hearing is held. At this hearing, the judge determines whether all necessary parties have received proper notice and are aware of their right to counsel. In the case of an unwed or unknown father, efforts are undertaken to locate and notify him. The court appoints counsel if necessary, and also appoints an independent attorney to represent the interests of the child and to serve as the child's guardian *ad litem*. The ground rules for the decisive adjudicatory hearing are set at this preliminary hearing.

In addition, at this session the court may order a psycho-social assessment of the child. Such a mechanism will benefit the legal proceedings by the input of professionals from the behavioral sciences. A complete psycho-social assessment of the child would include consideration of his present circumstances and the results of any medical, psychiatric or psychological examinations of the child, as well as of his birth and/or de facto parents. Further, the report would analyze the strengths of the child's past and existing relationships with his birth and/or de facto parents and with his siblings and the child's own preferences for placement. With this background the report would propose plans for the child's future.

Another original feature in the Act is the characterization of the child's guardian ad litem, who is also the child's advocate and legal representative. Past experience has taught us that merely appointing an attorney for a child in juvenile proceedings does not always result in effective representation or protection. For this reason the Act spells out that the child's guardian ad litem should be an attorney experienced in the field of children's rights. His duties include a full exploration of the child's situation - his inner feelings, his attachments, his attitudes and his relationships with others. With this information in mind, the guardian ad litem's prime duty is to protect and promote the rights of the child through all stages of the proceeding.

The next stage is the hearing itself, which is conducted as a non-jury civil trial. The Model Act has adopted the clear and convincing proof standard for evidence of parental unfitness. This standard was chosen because it gives sufficient protection to the child and simultaneously is in line with the new emphasis given by the United States Supreme Court to the fundamental interest of the parent in his child. The Act rejects the milder civil standard of proof, the preponderance of the evidence, as making it too easy for the State to separate a child from its parents. It also rejects the criminal standard of beyond a reasonable doubt. Courts in the United States have attempted to refrain from criminalizing civil neglect and termination proceedings. Termination proceedings and freeing children for permanent placement proceedings are entirely different from criminal proceedings where there is a clear contest between a defendent and the State. As stated earlier, in freeing children for permanent placement, the overriding consideration is the welfare of the child rather than the culpability of the parent. The beyond a reasonable doubt standard affords the parent the most protection. In the context of the freeing children for permanent placement process, the use of the criminal standard does not sufficiently protect the child.

Once this evidentiary stage is completed, the judge must move to disposition. The Model Act's provisions on dispositions deal with the court review of the psychosocial study and the recommendation of the guardian ad litem. The Act provides three alternatives if the court believes that there are sufficient grounds for termination and so decrees. One, the court may appoint an individual as guardian of the child's person, vesting legal custody in that person. Two, the court may appoint an individual as guardian of the child's person and give legal custody. Three, it may appoint an authorized agency as guardian of the child, with legal custody of the child also in the agency. The important feature of this section is that the guardian must report back to the court within 90 days on the status of the placement plan for the child. This provision is designed to ensure accountability from the post-termination custodians and to make certain that termination has led to the most appropriate form of permanent placement. It gives the court jurisdiction to monitor the required follow-up on the disposition.

The Act also provides that, though grounds may exist, termination need not be ordered if it is not in the child's best interest: when, for instance, an older child with a sound relationship with the de facto parent still has close ties with his birth parents. In such cases the Act requires the court to stipulate what rights and responsibilities attach to the birth parent if termination is not decreed (e.g., visitation rights), and thus implements the stated policy of the Act that the birth relationship shall be recognized, strengthened and preserved. And under the same philosophy the court, when sufficient grounds for termination are not found to exist, may return the child to his parent either with or without protective supervision. Reunion with the birth family is a possibility which the court must always consider.

This description of the Model Act to Free Children for Permanent Placement exemplifies American thinking in law and the behavioral sciences on the status of children in legal limbo. A sister act, the Model State Subsidized Adoption Act,[2] was approved by the United States government in the fall of 1976. The Subsidy Act was designed to bring into permanent families of their own the 100,000 children with physical, mental or emotional handicaps, or of minority backgrounds, older children and those with siblings from whom they should not be separated. The purpose of the Subsidized Adoption Act is to provide a subsidy for a child whose prospective adoptive parents are unable to assume full financial responsibility for him during his minority. The subsidy would help with the costs of special medical care and with additional expenses incurred because of a child's continuing disabilities; would facilitate adoption by many minority group families; and would minimize the special economic drain of rearing several children from the same biological family who should remain together.

It is a national tragedy that thousands of American children are living in institutions, where their development is almost inexorably stunted, or being moved from foster home to foster home with permanent damage to their selfhood. With the Model Act to Free Children for Permanent Placement and its sister act, the Model State Subsidized Adoption Act, the basic right of every child to have a permanent and loving home may at last be achieved. At the very least, the lives of many children should be salvaged.

---

[2] The Model State Subsidized Adoption Act with Commentaries is published with a full discussion in Katz, S. N., and Gallagher, U. M., Subsidized Adoption in America, Family Law Quarterly, Vol. 10, pp. 3-54 (1976).

Child Abuse and Neglect, Vol. 3, pp. 35 - 43.

0145-2134/79/0301-0035 $02.00/0.

CHILD ABUSE IN AMERICA: A DE FACTO LEGISLATIVE SYSTEM [1]

BRIAN FRASER, J.D., EXECUTIVE DIRECTOR

THE NATIONAL COMMITTEE FOR PREVENTION OF CHILD ABUSE.

INTRODUCTION.

Probably no other country in the world has spent so much time, effort, and resources in developing a statutory framework to deal with the problems of child abuse, as America. Child Abuse legislation is regarded by many in America as a panacea to the complex problems we face. It is not.

This paper will briefly discuss the history of child abuse legislation in America, its evolution, the present relationship between such legislation and the existing state child abuse systems, and what can be reasonably expected over the next decade.

The successful resolution of a suspected case of child abuse requires the completion of three separate, yet interrelated steps. Identification. Investigation. Intervention. Child abuse legislation, especially the mandatory reporting statute, was developed in the early 1960's to address the problems of identification. Over the next two decades this legislation began to pay increasing attention to investigation and intervention.

Historically, child abuse legislation in America may be characterized as being reactive in nature. Remedial solutions are often viewed as prudent solutions. They are not. Today, this form of legislation could best be described as standing on the threshhold. It could continue to fine tune its reactive tenacles or it could begin to address the issues of planning, coordination, allocation of resources, and prevention. In a word it could begin to anticipate solutions, rather than react to problems.

FACTORS IMPACTING CHILD ABUSE LEGISLATION IN AMERICA.

A. THE EXTENT OF THE PROBLEM.

Child abuse was originally defined in 1962 as a non-accidental physical injury.[2] It was a simple and narrow definition. It reflected the extent of our knowledge at the time. In recent years, however, our knowledge of inflicted trauma has expanded substantially. As our knowledge increased, our definition of child abuse grew.

Today, child abuse is a generic term. It has four separate elements: Non-accidental physical injury. Sexual molestation. Neglect. Mental injury. Utilizing just the first three elements, it is estimated that 665,000 to 1,675,000 children are abused in America eacy year.[3] Nationally, it is estimated that 2,000 to 5,000 children die each year as a direct result of child abuse.[4]

Child abuse legislation in America has had to constantly remain cognizant of the extent of the problem. In the future it will have to pragmatically weigh the sheer number of persons affected against the limited resources available and strike a prudent balance.

B. THE STATE CHILD ABUSE SYSTEM.

Constitutionally, the problem of child abuse is the responsibility of each individual state. Each state has developed its own system to accept reports, make an investigation and provide treatment. Although definitions and receiving agencies vary from state to state, procedurally each case is handled in an identical manner. The successful resolution of a suspected case of child abuse requires three steps. One: the child must be identified as a suspected victim of child abuse and reported to the appropriate state agency. Two: An investigation must be completed by the receiving agency to determine if this is truly a case of child abuse. Three: Treatment must be made available to the child and his family.

Although one million children are abused each year in America, only one-third of that number are properly identified and reported. Although every state has identified at least one agency to receive and investigate reports of suspected child abuse, these agencies are currently functioning at or over capacity. If every child who was abused was identified and reported, the system would collapse.

When the state agency has completed its investigation, it must resolve three issues. Is this truly a case of child abuse (diagnosis)? What are the chances for successful treatment (prognosis)? What treatment is available and what treatment can be offered to the family (treatment plan)? The actual implementation of the treatment plan is referred to as intervention. The feasibility of intervention in any case of child abuse rests upon one assumption. The assumption is that treatment services are available. In most communities, however, the assumption is erroneous.

Child abuse legislation in America has had and will have to constantly grapple with the fact that only one-third of the children who are abused are reported, that the mandated agencies are already working at or over capacity, and that treatment in most communities is simply not available.

C. THE FEDERAL GOVERNMENT.

On January 31, 1978, the President of the United States signed into law the Child Abuse Prevention and Treatment Act.[5] Although this law was not binding on individual states, it did earmark a specific sum of money for state use. However, before any state was eligible to share in these funds, it was required to meet ten conditions.[6] The ten conditions are:

1. A provision for the reporting of suspected cases of child abuse.
2. A provision for a prompt investigation of each report of suspected child abuse.
3. A demonstration that the state can effectively and efficiently deal with child abuse.
4. A provision of immunity from suit for persons reporting in good faith.
5. A provision to insure the confidentiality of reports of suspected child abuse.
6. A provision for cooperation between diverse agencies dealing with the problem.
7. A provision for a guardian ad litem appointed to represent the child's interest if the case results in a judicial proceeding.
8. A demonstration that state support for child abuse does not drop below the 1973 level.
9. The public dissemination of information about the problems of child abuse, and
10. A provision to insure that parental organizations dealing with child abuse receive preferential treatment.

Today, in America 36 states meet the requirements of Public Law 93-247 and share in Federal Funds.[7]

A QUICK HISTORY OF THE MANDATORY REPORTING STATUTE.

In the early 1960's there was a feeling that professionals, especially physicians, would not voluntarily report suspected cases of child abuse. It was from this anticipated hesitation of reporting that the concept of a mandatory reporting statute was first conceived.

The first model child abuse reporting statute was proposed by the Childrens Bureau of the Department of Health, Education, and Welfare in 1963.[8] In 1965 two other model laws had been drafted and were offered to the general public.[9] By, 1964, 20 states had adopted a mandatory reporting statute [10] and by 1974 every state, Washington D.C., Puerto Rico, and the Virgin Islands had enacted into law such a statute.[11]

The first generation of reporting statutes had a rather simple focus. Their purpose was to mandate certain professionals to report suspected cases of child abuse. It was an identification function. At that time, it was believed that if a case of suspected child abuse was identified and funnelled into the existing system, appropriate relief would be provided. It was a naive assumption.

In response, a second generation of reporting statutes and model laws began to emerge.[12] The focus of these new statutes was identification and investigation. It was believed that if needs were clearly identified and if investigatory standards were clearly established existing agencies could provide adequate and appropriate relief. In a few years, that too, proved to be an erroneous assumption.

In response to this second failure, a third generation of model laws[13] and reporting statutes began to emerge. The focus of these third generation statutes was identification, investigation, and intervention. These statutes began at least tangently to address the complex issues of intervention. They began to address the needs of limited resources, limited expertise, lack of coordination, the role of the general public and a planning component. It is these issues and these needs that are now in a period of flux in America.

THE MANDATORY REPORTING STATUTE.

Today, every state in America has enacted into law a mandatory child abuse reporting statute. Unfortunately, every state has enacted its own law. As a result, there is little uniformity in the language between states. There are, however, common concepts and a common format. At an absolute minimum, every state defines child abuse, identifies a group of individuals who are mandated to report, identifies at least one state-wide agency to receive the report, and provides immunity from civil and/or criminal liability if the report is made in good faith.

A. DEFINITION

Every state defines child abuse to be a combination of one or more of the following four elements: non-accidental physical injury, neglect, sexual molestation, and mental injury. Today every state includes non-accidental physical injury in their definition. Forty-seven states include the element of neglect, forty-two states include the element of sexual molestation, and thirty-two states include the element of mental injury. While non-accidental physical injury and sexual abuse may be clearly identified and specifically defined, the elements of neglect and mental injury cannot. Neglect and mental injury are much more closely akin to acceptable standards of care and support. However, since America has never developed nor accepted such standards the actual parameters for neglect and mental injury are seriously lacking. [15]

B. WHO REPORTS.

The first generation or reporting statutes singled out the physician as the sole mandated reporter. It soon became apparent, however, that this narrow mandate was shortsignted. Experience demonstrated that the physician only had access to the child when the injuries had become severe. A more prudent approach dictated an earlier identification of the abuse. As a result, the base of mandated reporters has been substantially broadened in the last two decades. Today, the focal point is individuals who have constant access to young children and who can identify the inflicted injuries before they become severe.

C. WHEN IS A REPORT MADE?

The actual diagnosis of child abuse can be a complex and difficult task. In effect, it often requires the expertise of different professions. Since mandated reporters often lack this substantive expertise, a definitive diagnosis is not required before reporting. In every state, the obligation to report arises when the mandated individual "has reasonable cause to suspect or believe" that a child has been injured. The actual diagnosis of child abuse is made after an investigation has been completed.

D. TO WHOM AND HOW ARE REPORTS MADE.

Every state in America has identified at least one state-wide agency to receive and investigate suspected cases of child abuse. In almost every state that agency is the Department of Social Services. Almost every state requires that the mandated individual make an immediate oral report and forty-two states require that a written report be made within 48 hours of the oral report. The purpose of the oral report is to permit the receiving agency to take immediate protective action if necessary. The purpose of the written report is to provide a written record of the report and a foundation for the investigation.

E. IMMUNITY.

In an effort to encourage reporting, every state has included an immunity provision in the reporting statute. These provisions simply provide immunity from civil and criminal actions if the original report was made in good faith.

F. PENALTY PROVISION.

A majority of states now provide a specific penalty for the failure to make a required report. Penalty provisions like immunity provisions were originally drafted with the intent of encouraging reports. Immunity provisions were drafted to reassure hesitant reporters that they would not be held liable for good faith reports. Penalty provision, on the other hand, were drafted to insure hesitant reporters that they would be held liable if they failed to report. Today 36 states provide a criminal penalty for a failure to report, and five states provide a vehicle for civil suit for failure to report. [16]

BROADENING THE IMPACT AND THE SCOPE: THE INVESTIGATION.

As America's experience with reporting statutes grew, it soon became apparent that a simple identification of abused children was not sufficient. The identification mechanism increased statistics but statistics by themselves had little impact on how a state would respond.

A. INVESTIGATION.

The first generation of reporting statutes simply required that an investigation be made once a report was received. No guidelines were provided for when, what, and how. Predictably, the results were tardy and tenuous at best. As a result, almost every state has now developed specific guidelines for child abuse investigations. At a minimum, these guidelines require that the investigation be initiated immediately or promptly. They require a determination of the nature, extent, and cause of the reported injury, the name of the person responsible for such injuries, the names and conditions of all other children in the same home, the condition of the home environment, and the relationship between the child and his parents. Language such as this presumes that a thorough investigation can be mandated by statute. It cannot. The availability of trained staff, in adequate numbers with sufficient backup resources are all conditions precedent to a good investigation. In most states they are lacking.

B. PSYCHOLOGICAL/PSYCHIATRIC EVALUATIONS OF THE PARENTS.

Psychiatric/psychological evaluations of the child parents have been used rather routinely for the past ten years. These evaluations have been ordered after a finding of abuse has been made and before a final disposition is completed. Today, however, the reporting statute of seven states specifically permits a psychiatric/psychological evaluation of the parents before any finding of abuse has been made. The language of provisions such as this passively assumes that these examinations can be used to determine culpability as well as the best disposition alternative. In all likelihood such sweeping provisions will be severely challenged by those who see it as a fishing license to further intervene in the family.

C. MEDICAL EXAMINATION OF THE CHILD.

A number of states have now recognized the fact that a diagnosis of child abuse is an arduous task, requiring diverse skills. These same states have recognized that individual social workers are not resevoirs of such skills. As a result, five states now make provision in the reporting statute for a complete medical examination of the child with or without the parents permission. This medical examination, coupled with the expertise of the social worker should provide for a much more accurate diagnosis.

D. COLOR PHOTOGRAPHS AND X-RAYS.

In order to facilitate the investigation and preserve evidence, eighteen states now make provisions for the taking of color photographs and x-rays with or without the parents approval.

E. STATE-WIDE CENTRAL REGISTRY.[17]

It is well documented that child abuse is a pattern of behavior. It continues over a period of time and damage increases proportionately. It is also commonly recognized that many abusive parents doctor shop and hospital shop. They take the child to a different doctor of a different hospital with each injury. As a result the attending physician only develops a one dimensional picture of the child that he or she is examining. If, however, the physician had access to data indicating other injuries over a period of time, he might be able to see this pattern of child abuse begin to emerge. A central registry is a repository of past reports of suspected child abuse.

It is believed that a central registry which is properly conceived and properly structured can serve four functions. One, it can provide statistics. Two, it can provide raw data for research purposes. Three, it can be used as a diagnostic tool. Four, it can be used to measure the effectiveness of an agency dealing with child abuse. These beliefs have proven to be so pervasive that 40 states have now created central registries by statute and another six states have created central registries by administrative fiat.

F. TEMPORARY PROTECTIVE CUSTODY.

In cases of child abuse it is often necessary to assume temporary custody of a child believed to have been abused. The reasons are three-fold. One: there is often a need to remove the child from his home before further damage can be inflicted. Two: there is often a need to retain a child in a hospital setting because there is a strong possibility that further damage will be inflicted if the child is returned to his home. Three: the child is in need of additional medical care and there is a real possibility that the parents will not return the child.

Consequently, 28 states have enacted provisions within their reporting statute which allow professionals - doctors, hospital administrators, social workers, police officers - to assume temporary protective custody without parental permission and without the consent of the court.

G. THE CHILD PROTECTION TEAM.[18]

When the investigation has been completed, the investigatory data must be analyzed and three issues must be resolved. One: has this child been abused (diagnosis)? Two: What are the chances for successful treatment (prognosis)? Three: What treatment ought to be offered (treatment plan)?

These are complex, eclectic issues to resolve. At a minimum they require a basic understanding of medical pathology, psychiatry, social work and legalese. It is unrealistic to expect any one individual to have substantive expertise in all of these fields. In almost every state, however, it is a single social worker who must complete the investigation, analyze the data, and resolve these difficult issues. An obvious solution to the dilemma would seem to be to create a pool of necessary expertise.

These pools of expertise are called multi-disciplinary child protection teams or in short, child protection teams. Ten states in America have created these child protection teams by statute to help resolve the complex issues involved in child abuse.

TINKERING WITH THE MOST COMPLEX COMPONENT: INTERVENTION.

When the investigation has been completed, when the data has been analyzed and when the issues of diagnosis, prognosis, and treatment are resolved, it is necessary to implement the treatment plan. The actual implementation of the treatment plan is referred to as intervention. Intervention in America can take two forms. It can be a voluntary agreement between the parents and the Department of Social Services or it can be involuntary - initiated and monitored through the juvenile court. At this final stage there are two potential problems. One, if it is necessary to utilize the courts to implement the treatment plan the case often proves difficult to establish. Two, in most communities treatment programs and services simply do not exist.

The problems which surround the issues of intervention are by far the most complex to resolve. States, in their efforts to impact intervention have tentatively approached the problem from three different directions.

1. MAKING THE CASE EASIER TO PROVE.

Child abuse is a difficult case to prove. It is difficult because it takes place in the family home behind closed doors, there are no eyewitnesses willing to testify, data which is relevant is difficult to collect, and the burden of proof is high.

Five states have therefore drafted a portion of their statutes in such a way as to make a case of child abuse in the juvenile courts easier to establish. These statutes simply require that evidence of a non-accidental injury to a child be provided. They do not require a showing of who did what to whom. If a non-accidental injury is established with the requisite burden of proof, the burden of going forward then shifts to the parents. It then becomes the parent's responsibility to provide a reasonable explanation for the injuries in question. If they cannot, the evidence which has been presented is deemed sufficient for a finding of abuse.

2. PROTECTING THE CHILD'S INTEREST: THE GUARDIAN AD LITEM.[19]

No one would question the fact that a child's safety and interests not jeopardized in a case of child abuse. Until recently, however, a child suspected of being abused was not provided with any form of representation if the case proceeded into court.

Recognizing the fact that a child's interests were not adequately represented in cases of child abuse, some states in 1971 began to appoint a guardian ad litem to represent those interests. A guardian ad litem is simply a guardian appointed by the court to protect the child's short and long range interests. Although there is no requirement that the guardian ad litem be an attorney, almost every guardian ad litem who is appointed in America is an attorney.

Today, 26 states require the appointment of a guardian ad litem to represent the child's interests in a case of child abuse.

3. GETTING BETTER MILEAGE OUT OF CURRENT RESOURCES.

The single largest problem today in America in the field of child abuse is the lack of treatment services for the abused child and his family. It is a problem destined to become more severe over the next decade. Resources which are scarce now will be stretched to the breaking point. Americans are only now beginning to accept the fact that the state and federal governments can not continually increase their allocations for child abuse.

A few of the more progressive states have therefore begun to grapple with the issue of a large and increasing problem, and in some cases, shrinking resources. These states have attempted to avoid the duplication of scarce resources by making the system more efficient. These states attempt to combine the resources and expertise of different agencies. Sixteen states now require cooperation and coordination between agencies dealing with the problem of child abuse, five states require a comprehensive plan for child abuse activities within the state, and five states have created state-wide counsels to oversee child abuse activities.

Cooperation, coordination and planning, alas, are much easier to draft into legislation than they are to operationalize.

CONCLUSION.

The child abuse system in America may be characterized as a reactive system and a reactive process. The problem was formerly identified in 1962. Two years later the first mandatory reporting statute became law. Eight years later every state in America had enacted a mandatory reporting statute. The purpose of this first generation of reporting statutes was identification. The result can only be classified as being eminently successful. Unfortunately, as the number of identified and reported cases increased, the state's ability to investigate each case decreased. Consequently a second generation of reporting statute emerged which focussed on a state's responsibility to make a thorough and immediate investigation. The identification function, gasping for breath, continued to lunge forward and upward. States, now seeing the breadth of the problem and the staggering numbers involved, attempted to alter their legislation in order to absorb the tide. A third generation of reporting statutes - still reacting to the problem - was born. The birth might better be described as a stillbirth. The effort was dead before it could gasp its first breath.

The problem of child abuse in America might best be described as the following:

"Every year one and a half to two percent of our children are reported as suspected victims of child abuse. While social agencies are working to help this years two percent, they are still trying to figure out what to do with last years two percent and are pleading with legislators for more money to deal with next years two percent. The problems of abuse and neglect accumulate at the rate of one and a half to two percent more children each year."[20]

The current child abuse system in America is destined to failure. As the identification process becomes more efficient and more thorough, the system will overload and short. Treatment services which are already functioning at capacity will sink. Slowly at first then rapidly.

America if it is to be successful in dealing with the problems of child abuse must develop a new and different perspective. The perspective is prevention. To do anything less is to worship at the alter of futility.

FOOTNOTES

[1] For a much more comprehensive discussion of the aspects discussed here see:

Fraser, A Glance at the Past, A Gaze at the Present and Glimpse at the Future: A Critical Analysis of the Development of the Child Abuse Reporting Statute. Chicago Kent Law Review, Sept. 1978.

[2] Kempe et al, The Battered Child Syndrome, 181JAMA17, 1962.

[3] Light, Abused and Neglected Children in America: A Study of Alternative Policies, 43 Harvard Ed Rev. 556 at 557 , 1975.

[4] Kempe, Approach to Preventing Child Abuse, 13 Journal Dis. Child 941 at 945, 1976.

[5] Public Law 93-247 (42 U.S.C. 5101-5106, 1974.

[6] 42 U.S.C. 5103 (b) (1), 1974.

[7] Conversation with the National Center for Child Abuse and Neglect, H.E.W., Washington, D.C., 1978.

[8] U.S. Department of H.E.W., Childrens Bureau: The Abused Child; Principles and Suggested Language for the Reporting of the Physically Abused Child, 1963.

[9] American Medical Association, Physical Abuse of Children, Suggested Legislation (1965). Council of State Governments, Program for Suggested State Legislation, 1965.

[10] Shepard, The Abused Child and the Law, 22 Wash. and Lee, Law Review , 182 at 184, 1965.

[11] Fraser, A Pragmatic Alternative to Current Legislative Approaches to Child Abuse, 12 Am. Crim. Law Review 103 at 104, 1974.

[12] Fraser, Child Abuse and Neglect: Alternatives for State Legislation, Education Commission of the States, Report No. 44, 1973 (Denver, Colorado)

[13] Fraser and Besharov, Child Abuse and Neglect: Model Legislation for the States, Education Commission of the States, Report No. 71, 1975.

[14] Sussman and Cohen, Reporting Child Abuse, 1974.

[15] Wald, State Intervention on Behalf of Neglected Children, 27 Stan. Law Review 985, 1975.

[16] Comment, Civil Liability for Failing to Report Child Abuse, Detroit College of Law 135 , 1977.

[17] Fraser, Toward A Practical Central Registry, 51 Denver L. Journ. 509, 1974.

[18] Schmitt, The Child Protection Team, 1976.

[19] Fraser, Independant Representation for the Abused and Neglected Child: The Guardian Ad Litem, 13 Cal. W. L. Rev. 16, 1977.

[20] Helfer, Prevention of Serious Breakdowns in Parent Child Interaction, National Committee for Prevention of Child Abuse, 1978.

Child Abuse and Neglect, Vol. 3, pp. 45 - 49.
Pergamon Press Ltd., 1979. Printed in Great Britain.

THE ABUSED CHILD IN THE COURTS

Margaret Booth, Q.C.

1, Mitre Court Buildings, Temple, E.C.4.

Parliament has entrusted the legal protection of an abused child to the juvenile court. This court is in fact a magistrates' court and is bound by all the rules regulating the constitution, place of sitting and procedure of magistrates' courts except in so far as they are specially modified. It is composed of justices of the peace who are specially qualified to deal with juvenile cases, although there is no requirement for any formal training or qualification. Its jurisdiction extends not only to care proceedings but also to criminal charges against juveniles and to other specified matters including, at the present time, adoption.

Jurisdiction in care proceedings is principally governed by the Children and Young Persons Act 1969, under which the court may make orders committing a child to the care of a local authority (a care order) or, as an emergency measure, ordering him to be detained in a place of safety for a period of time not exceeding 28 days (a place of safety order). To make a care order the court must be satisfied first, that one or more of the conditions listed in section 1(2) (a)-(f) of the 1969 Act are satisfied and, second, that the juvenile is in need of care or control which he is unlikely to receive unless a care order is made: see section 1(2) of the 1969 Act. Broadly speaking, in the case of an abused child it must be proved to the satisfaction of the court that he has been neglected or ill-treated or that it is probable that he will be so having regard to the fact that a court has already found such a condition proved in the case of another child who is, or was, a member of the same household. Care proceedings may be instituted by a local authority, by any police constable or by the National Society for the Prevention of Cruelty to Children, who are specially authorised by the Home Secretary to do so. A parent or guardian may not bring care proceedings, although he may request the local authority to do so. He must, however, be given notice of any such proceedings and may be required to attend the hearing unless in the circumstances this is unreasonable: see section 34 of the Children and Young Persons Act 1933.

In the juvenile court the parent or guardian is not a party to care proceedings and he has no standing as such. It is the child in question who is brought before the court and who is, in effect, the defendant. The parent or guardian may, in the first instance, be regarded as representing the child for the purpose of the proceedings, but where it appears to the court that a conflict of interest exists between the child and his parent the court may direct that the parent is not to be treated as representing the child and the court may itself appoint a guardian *ad litem* for the child: see Children and Young Persons Act 1969, sections 32A, 32B, aided by the Children Act 1975, but not yet fully in force. If such an order is made the duty to safeguard the interests of the child rests with the guardian *ad litem* and the right of the parent is restricted to meeting allegations made against him and to making representations to the court: Magistrates, Courts (Children and Young Persons) Rules, 1970, r. 14B. The parent is, therefore, restricted in the scope of the evidence he may call and, not being a party to the proceedings, he has no right of appeal against any order that may be made. Indeed, the only person who has the right to appeal to the Crown Court against the making of a care order is the child itself and if he, through his guardian *ad litem*, refrains from doing so the parents themselves have no such right.

Since its jurisdiction is wholly statutory the juvenile court is strictly bound by the provisions of the relevant Acts and Rules as to the procedure it may follow and the orders it may make. But from time immemorial there has existed a much wider jurisdiction for the protection of children, that being the wardship jurisdiction of the High Court which is now exercised by the Family Division but which derives originally from the duty of the Sovereign as *parens patriae* to protect those of his subjects who are unable to protect themselves. Of this jurisdiction it was said by Lord Eldon L. C. in 1827: "It has always been the principle of this Court not to risk the incurring of damage to children which it cannot repair, but rather to prevent the damage being done". He also said that the jurisdiction "is founded on the obvious necessity that the law should place somewhere the care of individuals who cannot take care of themselves, particularly in cases where it is clear that some care should be thrown round them": see *Wellesley v. Duke of Beaufort* (1827) 2 Russ. 1. When it is invoked the wardship jurisdiction is exercised for the benefit of the child concerned and no limit has been set upon the powers of the Court, although it will take into consideration the rights and interests of third parties: but the interest of the child must be of paramount consideration.

By the simple process of issuing an originating summons in the Family Division of the High Court a child may be made a ward of Court and immediate orders may be sought for his protectio Ultimately there will follow a full hearing at which his future will be decided. If the wardship is then continued the Court retains its jurisdiction over the child until he attains his majority at the age of 18 and at any time during the continuance of the wardship the matter may be restored to the Court for further orders to be made. Such proceedings may be initiated by any person having a genuine interest in the child: see, for example, *In re D. (a minor)* [1976] Fam. 185, in which wardship proceedings were stated by an educational psychologist to protect the child against a proposed operation for sterilisation. The defendants may be the parents or guardian or any other person against whom relief is sought. Thus, such a person being a party to the proceedings is not restricted as to the nature and purport of the evidence that he calls nor is he debarred from having a right of appeal to the Court of Appeal or, with leave to the House of Lords. But unlike the procedure in the juvenile court the child himself may not be made a party except with leave of the Court and in such circumstances or otherwise where it is deemed appropriate arrangements will be made for his separate representation, usually by the Official Solicitor.

In such civil proceedings, whether in the juvenile court or in the High Court, the object to be achieved is the protection of the child. It is not then the function of the court to establish guilt and punish an offender. Nevertheless the proceedings are adversarial in form even if the purpose is to examine objectively the welfare of the child. In both courts they share certain principal characteristics. The proceedings cannot be brought by the court on its own motion: there are specified procedures as to who may be parties and witnesses give evidence on oath and in accordance with the general principles of evidence: evidence, which may be given orally and, in the case of wardship proceedings, on affidavit, may be tested by cross-examination: and it is the duty of the tribunal in either case after hearing evidence and submissions to make findings of fact, decisions as to law and orders in respect of the child.

Although the purpose of proceedings under the 1969 Act is to conduct an objective examination of the condition of the child and it is not a contest between the local authority and the parer in the majority of child abuse cases the facts are such that the local authority, its social workers, the doctors and the police are on the one side making allegations of neglect or ill-treatment against the parents or guardians on the other. If an allegation of child abuse or neglect is admitted or is established by a finding of the court it is in effect a finding of "guilt" which may lead to a criminal prosecution. So, when such an allegation is denied there immediately exists an issue as to facts, a finding of which may have serious socia consequences. The fear of such consequences may well lead parents responsible for non-accident injuries to attempt to conceal this fact and lead them in some instances falsely to protest their innocence. But over and above this, in many such cases the parents will regard this removal of the child from their care as an unjustified interference by the authorities which results for them in the "loss" of their child. Unless the parents can be satisfied that they have had a full and fair hearing before an impartial tribunal their hostility towards the social services and the all-pervading sense of injustice may prevent them from coming to terms with the situation and may prove a real obstacle in any attempt at the rehabilitation of the family. It is, therefore, of the first importance both for the child and for his parents that they should feel able to accept the decision of the Court and so accept the making of a care order.

But it cannot be denied that in disputed cases the position of the local authority and in particular of its social workers is a difficult one. The role of the social worker in court is that of a witness of fact, but however objectively his evidence may be given it is likely to be seen by the parents as damaging to their cause if not a direct personal attack upon them.

Yet outside the court the social worker must establish a working relationship of trust and understanding with the parents if the best is to be achieved for the child. Suspicion and mistrust on the part of the parents may be enhanced if they feel that inimical material is contained in the case notes of social worker which they have had no chance to see or to refute. It has been well established by the courts that since case notes should be a full and frank record public policy requires that they be privileged documents and not subject to disclosure in court proceedings. Lord Justice Harman said in *In re D. (infants)*, [1970] 1 W.L.R. 599, C.A: "These records must not be kept by people looking over their shoulders in case they should be attacked for some opinion which they feel it is their duty to express". In the House of Lords in *D. v. N.S.P.C.C.* [1978] A.C. 171 it was held that a similar immunity from disclosure of their identity in civil proceedings should be extended to those who gave information about the neglect or ill-treatment of children to a local authority or the N.S.P.C.C. to that which the law allowed to police informers, so that the identity of the informer might not be disclosed, whether by discovery, interrogatories or questions posed during the course of the hearing, the public interests being served by preserving the anonymity of both classes of informants. On the other hand, while it is clear that the demands of public interest require case records to be privileged documents, it has been said that it revolts the sense of justice that local authorities should hold all the documents while the parents are allowed access to none: see *Regina v. Greenwich Juvenile Court, ex parte Greenwich London Borough Council* (1977), The Times, 11th May. It should, perhaps, be considered in each case whether it is not desirable for the local authority to relax the rules and to make at any rate partial if not full disclosure of documents where this will ensure a greater sense of fairness and diminish the risk that the parents will feel that a full and fair hearing has not taken place.

The doctor is in court an expert witness. He may give evidence as to fact, for example as to bruises, burns, bone fractures and other injuries, and he may also express his opinion, for example as to causation. In practice his relationship with a patient and, therefore, his records relating to the patient, are subject to qualified privilege. In the High Court he may be compelled to produce his records to the Court by means of a *subpoena duces tecum* and when disclosed to the Court those records may be made available to the parties to see them. The procedure of *subpoena* and indeed the procedure of discovery as a whole is not available in the juvenile court and there is no means in that court by which such disclosure may be compelled.

The purpose of cross-examination is to test the evidence and to assit in eliciting facts in any case in which there is a dispute as to fact. The evidence of an expert witness is as open to cross-examination as that of any other witness. In a child abuse case there may exist a conflict of expert evidence of fact as occurred in *Re Cullimore (a minor)* (1976), The Times, 24th March, when the parents asserted, and the Court ultimately so found, that a child whose father had been charged with causing her grievous bodily harm, was not in fact an abused child who had been subject to non-accidental injuries but was one who suffered from osteogenesis imperfecta, or brittle bones. Disputed evidence of this nature and indeed the disputed observations and conclusions of social workers together with the evidence of other witnesses including the parents, cannot be properly evaluated until tested by cross-examination. But it is inevitable that on some occasions a strong cross-examination may be seen as a personal attack and may produce considerable resentment where its purpose has not been made clear or is not fully understood.

In determining what, if any, order to make for the protection of the child the High Court in its wardship jurisdiction may exercise its inherent as well as statutory power to do what is in the child's best interests. In the High Court in any proceedings where the custody or upbringing of a minor is in question the Court, in deciding that question, shall regard the welfare of the minor as the first and paramount consideration: section 1 of the Guardianship of Minors Act, 1971. Where satisfied that it is a proper case in which to exercise its wardship jurisdiction and where it appears that there are exceptional circumstances making it impracticable or undesirable for a ward to be, or to continue to be, under the care of either parent or of any other individual, the High Court may, if it thinks fit, make an order committing the care of the ward to a local authority: section 7(2) of the Family Law Reform Act 1969. In that case the local authority controls the day-to-day care of the child but subject to the directions of the Court: see *In re Y. (a minor) (child in care: Access)* [1979] Fam. 134, C.A. In the juvenile court a care order may only be made when the court has been satisfied as to the matters specified in section 1 of the Children and Young Persons Act 1969 and it is not open to that court to make such an order on the broad basis that it is "desirable" to do so or for some other reason outside the statutory provisions of the Act. While in addition to making a care order and a place of safety order the juvenile court may also, where appropriate, make a supervision order and have power to vary and discharge a care order, it has no inherent jurisdiction to make other orders for the general well-being and protection of the child. In this respect the powers of the High Court are considerably wider. For example, in the High Court, but not in the juvenile court, where it is necessary for the protection of the child, an injunction may be made restraining a third party, such as a parent or guardian or a stranger, from removing the child from the person having his *de facto* care; or an injunction may be made restraining a third party from molesting or handling a foster parent or some other person connected with the case as, for example, a social worker. Where necessary appropriate orders may be made in the High Court to prevent the removal of a child from the jurisdiction and where a foreign element is involved in a case reciprocity is likely to be more easily accorded to an order of the High Court by the court of a foreign country than it is to the order of a juvenile court.

Nevertheless, the High Court will not necessarily exercise its wardship jurisdiction in respect of an abused child. The possibility of conflict between the High Court on the one hand and the juvenile court or a local authority on the other has for long been recognised. It is well established that the High Court will not permit its wardship procedure to be used simply as a form of appeal from the juvenile court and where the juvenile court has already been seised of the matter the High Court will not accept jurisdiction unless there are special or good and convincing reasons for so doing. Equally, where a child is committed to the care of a local authority the exercise by the High Court of its powers in wardship proceedings have been severe restricted by decisions of the Court of Appeal: see, for example, *In re M. (an infant),* (1961) Ch. 328: *In re T. (A.J.H.) (an infant)* (1970) Ch. 688. Such restriction is based upon the principle that since Parliament has entrusted all decisions relating to the welfare of the child where that child has, in accordance with statute, been committed to the care of a local authority, the Court should only interfere if the local authority has acted improperly or unlawfully. That is the same principle which is applied by the Court in deciding whether or not it will review the exercise of ministerial or administrative discretions generally. Nevertheless, in a child case the High Court is always mindful of its considerably wider powers to act for the general welfare of the child and to what is in the best interests of the child, so that where the powers of the juvenile court are inadequate the High Court will not hesitate to intervene. Indeed, the positive advantages of the wardship jurisdiction from the point of view of local authorities has several times been emphasised: see, *In re B. (a minor) (wardship: child care)* [1975] Fam. 36 per Lane J., where wardship jurisdiction was exercised concurrently with a care order in view of the aggressive violent character of the child's step-father in respect of whom the local authority might find it necessary to seek injunctions only available from the High Court: *In re D. (a minor) (Justices' decision: Review)* [1977] Fam. 158 per Dunn J., in which wardship jurisdiction was invoked by a local authority following the discharge by a juvenile court of a care order, and where it was held appropriate that that jurisdiction shou be exercised on the basis that until it made a care order the juvenile court had no jurisdictio to consider the welfare of the child - so that where a care order was refused or discharged the High Court would exercise its jurisdiction to consider that welfare: *In re H. (a minor) (Wardshi: Jurisdiction)* [1978] 2 W.L.R. 608, C.A. per Ormrod L.J., in which, again, wardship jurisdiction was exercised to enable a child, the subject of a care order, to leave the jurisdiction with her parents, they having no right of appeal against the making of the order or against the refusal of the justices to discharge it.

In the English judicial system there is no procedure for informal arbitration in a child case, but it must be doubtful whether such a procedure is necessary or would serve any useful purpose in the context of a disputed matter. The alternatives to Court procedure would seem to be a decision made by the local authority or a decision reached by doctors, police officers or other authorised persons or a decision after some form of case conference by all persons concerned with the child. Even assuming that the parents were heard by everyone concerned before such decision was reached these procedures do not provide means by which an impartial assessment of facts can be reached nor do they provide a tribunal suitable for the determination of issues of fact or of law. Despite the obvious disadvantages of the adversarial system of court procedure, where there are disputed issues of fact in circumstances which frequently arouse strong emotions even among professional people who are experts, there is a need for a judicial process.

Undoubtedly, however, it may be thought that there are deficiencies in the present system. It is difficult to find a rational basis for the discrepancy in the positions of the parents or guardians and the child in the juvenile court and in the High Court. It is basically unsatisfactory that in the juvenile court the parents of the child cannot be fully involved in the proceedings with unrestricted rights to defend and to appeal. It is also a defect in the current legislation that no provision at present exists for appropriate cases proceeding under the 1969 Act to be transferred from the juvenile court for hearing in the High Court. The juvenile court is unlikely to be an adequate tribunal to hear and determine a case such as *Re Cullimore*. The justices though in many cases of considerable experience do not usually have the necessary qualifications or training based upon many years' practice to determine issues between expert witnesses. A case involving the future of a child and requiring considerable investigation may take many hours if not days and it is difficult for juvenile courts, most of which are under considerable pressure, to allot the necessary number of consecutive days to any one case. There do not exist in the juvenile court the interlocutory procedures for the discovery of documents nor are there the means to compel the production of documents. While the juvenile court provides a local and easily accessible tribunal which in the great majority of cases may be well adequate to protect the abused child, it is unfortunate that in those more exceptional cases when a real conflict of fact exists the use of wardship proceedings is not more generally encouraged in the absence of any statutory provision for the transfer of cases to the High Court. It is also unfortunate that there still exists a shadowy area of apparent conflict between the High Court in the exercise of its wardship jurisdiction and the juvenile court and local authorities. Again, it is for the most part an anomoly that while an appeal from the refusal of a juvenile court to rescind a resolution made by a local authority under section 2 of the Children Act 1948 now lies to the Family Division of the High Court, an appeal by a child under the 1969 Act lies not to the Family Court but still to the Crown Court.

In children's cases above all others there is a need for clarity in the legal process so that all who have recourse to it may do so in the full knowledge and understanding of what is required and what can be achieved.

Child Abuse and Neglect, Vol. 3, pp. 51 - 60.
Pergamon Press Ltd., 1979. Printed in Great Britain.

ILL-TREATMENT OF CHILDREN : THE SOCIAL AND LEGAL CONTEXT IN ENGLAND AND WALES

Jack Chapman
Court Welfare Officer

Royal Courts of Justice, London, WC2

The Varying Definitions of a 'Child'

In discussing Child Abuse in its social and legal aspects, it must first be acknowledged that there is a real problem - not just a semantic one - in arriving at an agreed definition of the term 'child'. This partly because, in England and Wales, the statutes concerned with the education and protection of children have been far from uniform in their statement of the age at which the child or 'minor' ceases to be regarded as such and becomes an adult. In 1880, when the first compulsory Education Act fixed the school leaving age at 13, this was regarded as a landmark after a long period of child exploitation during the early industrial age. Since then, the frontiers of childhood have been pushed forward steadily by legislation. One such advance was signalled by the 1933 Children and Young Persons Act, which created the English Juvenile Courts, giving them jurisdiction in respect of all young people, whether offenders or in need of care, up to their seventeenth birthday. The concept of Wardship in the High Court, and the laws regulating it, apply to 'minors' up to their eighteenth birthday, as do Care Orders made in the Juvenile Court. However, 'the age of consent' is sixteen years, this being also the threshold point for marriage: and the present legal provision for education fixes the school leaving age at the sixteenth birthday also. Finally, the age of criminal responsibility remains at ten years, though existing legislation (1) contains provisions to raise this by stages to fourteen years.

These varying concepts of what constitutes the appropriate age-span of childhood reveal not only a considerable range of officially expressed attitudes but also, of equal importance, a deep-seated sense of uncertainty in Western industrialised societies about the right methods of dealing with the transition from 'childhood' to adulthood. Contributing to this uncertainty have been a number of factors which have only emerged clearly within the past fifty years. One such development has been the well-attested earlier physical(but not emotional) maturing of older children. The dilemmas posed by this and other problems will be discussed later in relation to the increased anxieties which they bring, as the atmosphere of society becomes both more permissive and at the same time more censorious.

The Risks to Older Children

The ever-increasing output of written material concerning non-accidental injury to children has dealt predominantly with the detection, treatment and prevention of physical injury to infants and children under three years of age. There are doubtless good and compelling reasons for this: all of us, specialists and laymen alike, experience feelings of horror and revulsion on hearing of gross cruelty to helpless and innocent children of tender years. Yet the strength of our feelings, when we are confronted with such situations, tends to obscure the fact that children in all age groups are suffering abuse and that in the case of older children the infliction of physical cruelty, or even the witnessing of domestic violence, is likely to have traumatic effects. Any serious injury to a very small child, especially if it is repeated, is bound to attract the attention and concern of adults and to be referred to a doctor, whether it is accidental or not. In contrast, as a child gets older the signs of

[1]Children and Young Persons Act 1969

injury or stress become more difficult to detect and diagnose in the absence of an intimate knowledge of the interactions within the family concerned. The need to respect the privacy of the home, and the ability of parents to create elaborate systems of defence, often make prompt action difficult so that quite serious abuse of older children can continue over relatively long periods, as was seen in the case of Maria Colwell and, more recently,Stephen Menheniott, who was 18 years old when he died.

Family Fragmentation : its Extent and Effects

Much attention has been paid over a long period to the harmful effects on children of growing up in a deprived or disadvantaged family. A powerful lobby on behalf of such children has been mounted by such bodies as the Child Poverty Action Group and the National Council for One-Parent Families. By contrast, there has been far less enquiry and research into the consequences for children of family fragmentation and disruption, and the psychological effects of this on them.

The only official statistics relating to family breakdown which can be quoted with confidence are those for divorce decrees, judicial separations and matrimonial orders in magistrates' courts. While the two latter categories have remained static in recent years, the number of divorces has risen more or less steeply year by year since 1970 when new legislation came into effect. Table I shows, in addition, the percentage of divorces involving children and the numbers of such children.

TABLE 1

Children involved in Divorces during the period 1970 - 1975

	No. of Divorce Petitions	No. of Divorce Decrees involving children	Total No. of children concerned
1970	71,700	35,900	71,300
1971	110,900	42,000	82,300
1972	110,700	66,800	130,900
1973	115,491	73,800	126,900
1974	131,700	68,600	135,300
1975	140,100	73,900	145,100
(1976)	146,400	N/A	N/A
(1977)	167,000	N/A	N/A

Source : Office of Population Censuses and Surveys 1978 Series FM2. No. 2. All figures to the nearest hundred.

However, the marriage figures during the same period show that the number of remarriages after divorce have also increased sharply and it is estimated that approximately 60% of divorcees are now remarrying, many within a short time. Thus there has been a cumulative increase in the number of children growing up in either one-parent families, or in family groups where there is a step-parent because of a previous separation. Estimates of the present number of such children must necessarily be tentative, but it is thought to be in the region of 950,000 if one includes those whose parents have parted without legal process. In all such cases there has been a break in the continuity of loving care by united parents, which so many writers regard as a fundamental postulate of healthy child development. It is worth noting the finding of one study quoted by Rutter(1975), that children suffer less disturbance through the loss of a parent by death than from prolonged disharmony in the home, whether or not this ends in the separation of their parents. To most children, especially younger ones, such experiences are traumatic because they are incomprehensible, and all that the children are aware of is the impending break-up of their familiar world, bringing an end to the routine which spells security for them.

The main reason for the lack of firm evidence about the extent of family breakdown, both statistically and in qualitative terms, is that so much of what goes on within the four walls of a home is regarded as private and is therefore not easily susceptible to scientific analysis. Only when there is an attempt to portray in documentary form the day-to-day life of an ordinary, randomly-selected, household, as in the B.B.C. television series "The Walkers" shown in 1975, do we obtain a glimpse of the real nature of contemporary family life, and the stresses that lurk beneath the surface facade which most families strive to present to their neighbours. Relatively few people with the necessary skills of observation and analysis are able to penetrate this veil of secrecy and possess the authority to enter homes either on official duties or to facilitate research into the texture of family relationships. The Newsons, in their long-term studies of 700 Nottingham homes, are among the few social scientists who have attempted the task and they are conscious of the serious gaps in their painstaking task, notably the reluctance of fathers to be drawn in and interviewed. The N.S.P.C.C. encountered the same difficulty in obtaining information from or about fathers when carrying out the research on which their study, "At Risk"(1976), is based.

In considering the total number (admittedly imprecise) of children who have experienced the separation of their parents or have been affected by long-standing disharmony between them, it would be easy to give way to pessimism and to exaggerate the results of this. Not all such children are affected in equal measure and, fortunately, many are resilient enough or adaptable enough to emerge from such situations with few outward signs of disturbance in spite of the inner anxieties which must have been engendered in the great majority of them. Nevertheless, doctors, health visitors, social workers and others who see such children in their homes are well aware that a substantial proportion do exhibit the classic symptoms of vulnerability and stress to a minor degree, and a smaller but significant number are deeply and lastingly affected.

The symptoms which most often occur in both groups are enuresis, sometimes accompanied by soiling, nightmares, speech impediments, facial 'tics' or other involuntary movements, skin complaints, and asthma or bronchitis. Whilst it is plain that some of these ailments can arise from an innate constitutional tendency and may occur among children in 'normal' and supportive families, it is often evident that there is a strong psychosomatic element involved, particularly when the onset of an attack coincides regularly with a recurrent stressful sequence of events, e.g. access by a separated parent towards whom the child has ambivalent feelings.

In many cases there are also behavioural problems of greater or lesser severity. One of the most common and widespread of these is under-achievement at school and a failure by the child to realise the potential of which it is capable. Associated with this may be school phobia (as distinct from truanting) caused by the child's instinctive need to cling to a parent for security. Children under stress may react by becoming on the one hand unnaturally withdrawn and timid, or on the other, hyperactive or aggressive. Stealing within the home is a frequent danger signal. Finally, when one or more of these symptoms have become persistent, there follows a referral to a child guidance clinic with the further possibility of a place having to be found at a special school for maladjusted children.

Social Isolation : its Origins and Effects

The risk factors associated with Child Abuse have now been so clearly defined and described that it is unnecessary to refer to them in detail in this paper. However, there is one such factor, namely social isolation, which has such a strong bearing on the stress experienced by older children and their subsequent behaviour as parents that its causation and effects repay a fuller analysis.

The usual approach to the phenomenon of social isolation is to see it largely in terms of the feelings of shame and embarrassment arising from the current behaviour of parents towards the children in their home. The remedy usually prescribed is that parents who have abused their children, or appear to be in danger of doing so, should be encouraged to join mutually supportive groups where they can meet and talk about their difficulties openly.

The need for such groups is undoubted: but unfortunately this simple solution to the problem of social isolation is likely to fail if it ignores the existence of a rooted predisposition arising from an upbringing in an unhappy or disrupted family. Too often, conflict between parents, from whatever cause, starts a process of retreat from everyday social contacts which inevitably has repercussions on the children involved. In this situation a child can suffer quite as much from seeing his parents hitting one another or a brother or sister as if he himself were assaulted. Continuous verbal warfare in the home, particularly if accompanied by obscenities, can have the same effect.

No longer can such a child chatter spontaneously to his friends at school about all that is happening at home. For him, as for his parents, a shutter has come down cutting him off from the natural enjoyment of sharing and comparing his experiences with others. He can take no pride in his family and therefore feels devalued. The title chosen by Erin Pizzey for her book, "Scream quietly lest the neighbours should hear", epitomises the dilemmas faced by adults and children alike in such situations.

The important point to be grasped is that in contemporary conditions this is by no means an uncommon experience. School teachers, especially those who act as counsellors, are acutely aware of the rising proportion of their pupils whose home circumstances must be referred to circumspectly. Where there has been actual family breakdown and separation, teachers and social workers frequently become involved in webs of suspicion and secretiveness, with addresses withheld by one parent from the other, telephone numbers ex-directory, risks of embarrassment, or worse, when both parents attend prize giving, and other by-products of parental conflict.

A further problem which often arises and causes distress in varying degrees to the children concerned is over their surnames, when these differ from that of the parent with whom they are living. At school a child has to try to explain to his peers why his name is not the same as his mother's, if she has remarried. This has both social and legal aspects: it causes a sense of confused identity, particularly if there is a half-brother or half-sister with the mother's surname; yet for the past five years it has been forbidden in divorce and wardship cases to change a child's surname without the express permission of the Court(2). When mothers contract successive marriages or have more than one 'liaison', the anxiety and confusion arising from changes of family surname can in itself be extremely damaging to a child's developing self-image.

While many children manage to emerge relatively unscathed from these internal and often unsuspected ordeals, it is not surprising that a small proportion become permanently scarred and find it difficult, if not impossible, to form normal confident relationships in adult life. These are often the ones who marry early, find adjustment to parenthood too difficult, and become depressed and isolated giving rise to the classic conditions within which child abuse is likely to occur. But the seeds of their social isolation were often sown at an earlier stage of their life.

The Link between Criminality and Child Abuse

During the past ten years the steeply rising divorce rate has been paralleled by a sharp increase in crime of all types, but particularly in offences of violence. It is not suggested that there is necessarily a close correlation between these trends which are probably separate symptoms of a common underlying social malaise. Nevertheless, if one puts the following facts together, it becomes possible to discern a direct link between criminal behaviour and gross ill-treatment of children.

First, there has been a dramatic and disproportionate increase in offending in the 14 - 21 age group, which is now responsible for one third of the whole total of indictable offences in England and Wales.

Secondly, it is by now well established that a high proportion of the parents who injure their children deliberately were married between the ages of 16 and 20, and when the wife was already pregnant.

Thirdly, both the Home Office and the N.S.P.C.C., in separate researches, have found a high incidence of previous criminal behaviour by such parents or their partners.

Is it not likely that deviant behaviour and precipitate marriage are symptomatic of the

[2] Matrimonial Causes Rules 1973

feelings of alienation experienced by adolescents in bitterly disrupted homes ? And if they have either experienced or witnessed violence in their original home, is this not probably another link in the chain of causation leading ultimately to child abuse in its grosser forms ? This whole area needs to be illuminated by research, taking as its starting point the widespread incidence of law-breaking in the community at large and the inevitable bearing of this on ordinary family relationships and the kind of behaviour which children come to regard as 'normal' within their home circle.

A Strategy for Restoring Family Stability

In the light of what has so far been said, is it possible to chart some lines of approach to the education of parents and parents-to-be concerning the elements of family stability and the essentials of child rearing ? In spite of the publication of a host of books on the subject, there appears to be no settled opinion on these matters which commands universal respect; and experts have too often appeared to be at variance in their views. Yet there is now a wide consensus over the basic needs of children to ensure their full mental and emotional development. A distillation of knowledge about this is, for example, provided by Kellmer Pringle in "The Needs of Children"(1975) in which she quotes ten basic precepts for the upbringing of children.

What may be required is reading matter which attempts to apply such precepts, based on the insights of paediatricians and psychiatrists, to the kind of situations in which typical contemporary families find themselves. The House of Commons Select Committee on Violence in the Family evidently believes this to be so: in their First Report(1977) they noted the need for a widely-available handbook on Bringing Up Children and recommended that such a publication should be produced.

Closely related to this and no doubt using suitable reading material as a basis for discussion there should be a determined attempt to produce an agreed syllabus for adolescent groups on Preparation for Marriage and Parenthood. Such groups, with appropriately trained leaders, should be part of the teaching programme of every secondary school and could be widely introduced in youth clubs, and in church groups for young people where the stress would naturally be placed on the imperatives of Christian morality.

In planning future educational programmes in this field, whether they are intended for young adults or adolescents still at school, there should be a much firmer emphasis on the vital need for continuity in the nurturing of children within a domestic situation, be it a married relationship or one of cohabitation only. It should be pointed out that since children are the natural outcome of setting up a home, their deepest and most fundamental needs must be foreseen and provided for with reasonable certainty when the time comes. The demands of parents for release from marital or domestic stress must at least be measured against the indispensable requirements of children - unspoken and inarticulate as these may be - but none the less real and urgent both for them and for the society of which they are a part. Even though many people would regard this as primarily a moral question, the arguments can be put in purely practical terms, and it is likely that only on this plane will an impact be made on the minds of the majority, in an age dominated by material considerations.

Argument has raged, and will continue to do so, over mothers of young children going out to work. In relation to the unmet need for nursery schools, it has recently been estimated that 4 out of 10 such mothers in London now have a job outside the home. It is said, (a) that families need the extra income and, (b) that mothers benefit from the release which this brings them from domestic routine. Yet most social workers would confirm the prevalence of homes where standards are high and there may be a plethora of toys, but where living contact with the children by either parent is at an unacceptably low level. As an example, in a home recently visited by the writer, with the father in a well-paid full-time occupation, the mother was found to be working five evenings a week, going out as soon as the father returned from work. When questioned the mother stated quite frankly that her only motive for working was to provide her with a diversion from her home duties.

The Present Legal Framework of Child Protection in England and Wales

When Parliament passed the first legislation for the specific protection of children in the latter half of the 19th Century, the aim was solely to prevent the exploitation of children who were being put to work in industry and the mines. Although this constituted an interference with the established rights of heads of families - and was resented for this reason - it would have seemed unthinkable at that stage to question and to regulate in any way what went on behind the closed doors of the home.

It has only been in the 20th century that the focus has shifted from the abuses of child labour to a concern for the more general welfare of children in the home, the school and the community. This concern has been expressed in three separate ways : first, by a strengthening and extension of the adult criminal law in relation to children; secondly, by the introduction and development of the principle of 'care' of children who are at risk; and thirdly by legislation designed to safeguard the rights of children caught up in the divorce or separation of their parents.

It is clearly beyond the scope of this paper to list and describe in detail the bewildering and complex array of statutes which now exist to protect the interests of children(3). All that will be attempted is a mention of some legal landmarks over the past 75 years, and an estimate of the effectiveness of the law in preventing child abuse and neglect or moderating its incidence.

The Criminal Law and Children

Offences committed against children may be divided into two categories: those which are applicable to adults and children alike, and those which relate specifically to children. In the former category are the major offences against the person - murder, manslaughter, rape, kidnapping and serious assaults. In the latter category are infanticide(rarely invoked now), incest, homosexual practices with minors, intercourse with a girl under the age of consent, and neglect causing avoidable suffering. There is still legislation restricting the employment of children. An adult offence which is now virtually obsolete, though still on the statute book, is being drunk in charge of a child.

One of the commonest offences against children, which is applicable to adults also, is indecency. The problems involved in bringing the law to bear on deviant behaviour towards children is clearly illustrated by the offence of indecent assault. This may occur within the home and be committed by a parent or relative; or it may take place outside the home and be by a stranger, or perhaps by someone in charge of children. Whatever the circumstances, the offender is often in the grip of an obsessive urge and may be as much in need of treatment as of punishment. In appropriate cases this is recognised by the Judge or Magistrate when passing sentence and is dealt with leniently. But the general public, unaware of the full background of individual cases, may feel a sense of outrage at what appears to be a condonation of child abuse. The same individual may exhibit the greatest laxity in his own morals and behaviour and yet be among the most censorious where offences against children are concerned. A well-known example of this tendency is the need to segregate such offenders who are imprisoned from other prisoners for their own protection.

The Caring Principle : Wardship, Guardianship and the Juvenile Courts

It is in the application of the principle of caring for children and safeguarding their interests that there has been the most continuous, and sometimes confusing, growth of legislation. This has occurred mainly during the 20th century; but historically the oldest jurisdiction which has included children within its scope has been that of Wardship, now exercised by the Family Division of the High Court. Originally invoked comparatively rarely, and then chiefly to prevent minors from exploitation over money matters, Wardship is now undergoing an upsurge of popularity as a speedy method of shielding children who appear to be gravely at risk by bringing them under the umbrella of the Court's protection. The immediate effect of a Wardship application is that the Court assumes the custody of the child and can either impose a stand-still on events (as when it seems likely that a child may be removed from the jurisdiction of the Court) or may make a temporary Order ensuring the child's safety until a satisfactory long-term plan can be devised and sanctioned by the Court. In almost all such cases a Court Welfare Officer's report is called for, but in some the Official Solicitor is invited to act as Guardian-ad-Litem in order that the child may be legally represented in

[3] The standard work is Clark Hall and Morrison on Children: 9th Edition,1976

Court, independently of the parents. An advantage of Wardship is that anyone closely connected with the child, but not necessarily a relative, can initiate proceedings. Many Local Authorities are now taking this course.

Guardianship of Minors (formerly called Guardianship of Infants) is within the jurisdiction of the Magistrates' Courts primarily, but also of the High Court. It provides for relatives of children whose parents may be dead, missing or incapable of providing proper care, to apply to the Court for an Order giving the relative formal and legal responsibility for the child. It also provides for a parent to seek custody of, or access to, a child, including an illegitimate child, where no other proceedings(e.g. divorce) are appropriate. Sometimes such proceedings later become combined with custody suits in the Divorce Court. However,the caring principle has been given its fullest and most developed expression in the Juvenile Courts, created as a separate section of the Magistrates' Courts in 1933. In this paper only the most salient features of the Juvenile Courts can be mentioned. From the beginning they have been concerned both with the criminal law relating to offences by children and young persons and with the civil law concerning their care and protection. From 1933 till 1969 the procedure for dealing with these two categories remained distinct, though children from both 'streams' could be committed to Care and then received identical treatment. There was thus an acknowledgement that children, even if over the age of criminal responsibility, could not be held fully to account for their delinquency and were deserving of care as much as those who needed protection because of their family circumstances. Since 1969 this principle has been made more explicit: in order to make a Care Order after a child has been charged with an offence which has been found proved, the Court must also be satisfied that the child is in need of care and control which he is unlikely to receive unless the Court makes an Order.

Two of the most important developments in Juvenile Court law relating to Child Abuse or Neglect have been the provision for the making of a Place of Safety Order, embodied in the original 1933 Act and the Assumption of Parental Rights by Local Authorities under Section 2 of the 1948 Children Act. Unfortunately, some recent legal decisions have appeared to place serious obstacles in the way of Local Authorities taking speedy and decisive action when this seems necessary - hence their increasing use of the Wardship jurisdiction, as noted earlier.

Some of the latest legislation concerned with the protection of children was embodied in the 1975 Children Act, the 1976 Domestic Violence and Matrimonial Proceedings Act and, most recently, in the Domestic Proceedings and Magistrates' Courts Act which received the Royal Assent on 30th June 1978, though there must be some delay in its implementation. As a direct result of the deficiencies in Juvenile Court procedure which came to light following the death of Maria Colwell in 1974, there was provision in the 1975 Act for separate representation of children and the appointment of a guardian-ad-litem in unopposed applications for the revocation of Care Orders. The 1976 Act was an attempt to deal with the problem of violence within the home by giving County Courts powers to issue injunctions restraining spouses of cohabitees from assaulting their partners or their children, and to make an Order excluding the offending partner from the home. If the Judge is satisfied that the offending person has caused actual bodily harm to the applicant or a child concerned, and that he is likely to do so again, he can attach a power of arrest to the Order. A constable may then arrest the person if he suspects a breach of the Order; but he must bring the person arrested before a Judge within 24 hours.

Some Appeal Court Judges had doubts about the over-riding of property rights; but following a House of Lords ruling a compromise appears to have been reached and 'exclusion' injunctions are now usually made for a period of one to three months to give time for the problems to be resolved, or action taken. Whether this will provide a sufficient safeguard is open to some doubt.

Now the 1978 Act, which will radically alter the nature of proceedings in the matrimonial jurisdiction of magistrates, will give them carefully defined powers, where there has been violence, to make personal protection Orders and exclusion Orders and to back them with a power of arrest. When these provisions of the 1978 Act come into operation, it is hoped that this armoury will provide an effective means of dealing with the scourge of domestic violence and afford protection to children and mothers - and sometimes to fathers also.

The latest Act to arrive on the statute book is the Child Protection Act which originated in a private member's Bill and is designed to prevent the exploitation of children for pornographic purposes.

Children caught up in Divorces and Separations

Divorce is dealt with by the High Court and County Courts: matrimonial Orders following separations and, as in divorce, often involving disputes over the custody of children, are made in Magistrates Courts or the Domestic Courts. In all such cases a Court Welfare Officer's Report (in the Magistrates' Court) can be called for. A divorce decree cannot be made absolute unless the Judge declares that the arrangements proposed for the future of the children are satisfactory or are the best that can be devised in the circumstances. These arrangements normally include provision for access and reports are sometimes required concerning this. Supervision Orders on children can be made in all courts.

Thus, every effort has been made in the legislation relating to divorce and matrimonial disputes to provide built-in safeguards against disregard of the children's long-term interests. To some extent this is successful in mitigating the worst effects of the anxiety and bitterness generated by family disruption. But inevitably there will in many cases be damaging consequences which the best-intentioned legislation cannot prevent. Because of lack of manpower and resources in the Probation Service, which provides Court Welfare Officers, there is in many areas of the country, including the High Court, a strict limitation on the number of reports for the Court that can be ordered. This means that only in the most obviously difficult cases is there any in-depth examination of the situation as it affects the children. It is probable that some divorces go through without adequate assurance that the children's interests have been fully considered.

The Prospects for Constructive Legal Reform

It is evident that in many respects the present body of English law relating to children is not wholly effective and has become unnecessarily complex and confusing to lawyers and laymen alike. One of the main reasons for this is the variety of jurisdictions and the consequent overlapping of functions exercised by Courts at different levels. In order to eliminate much of this, and at least to simplify the area of civil law, proposals have been put forward for the establishment in England and Wales of Family Courts on a similar basis to those operating successfully in other countries, notably Australia. Such Courts, if introduced, would have the following advantages :-

1. They would enable family disputes to be adjudicated, and the welfare of children to be considered, in a non-criminal setting.

2. They would have an experienced welfare staff, the members of which could be available to give general help and advice to those facing the possibility of family disruption, or coping with the results of it.

It is now abundantly clear that although legal process will always be necessary for the settling of stubborn family divisions and for the protection of children who suffer as the result or because of, criminal offences, the law is often a blunt instrument in dealing with sensitive areas of human conduct where emotions run high and reason is at a premium.

Contradictions in Public and Private Attitudes

The growth during the past 45 years of such a veritable forest of legislative provision is the firmest evidence that there has been a high level of public anxiety over the welfare of children in England and Wales. Yet in recent years, the conventional attitude towards children, especially young children, has been to idealise them almost to the point of sentimentality. As most social workers would confirm, children are nowadays far more often over-indulged than ill-treated in a direct way. Why, then, has it been necessary to create such a complex framework of protection for them during a period when living standards have improved throughout the population ?

The explanation of this seeming paradox may lie in a conscious awareness (or more often a dim discernment) of the profound social malaise which has overtaken the family and rendered all its component members, including children, vulnerable in new ways. Some of the possible causes of this vulnerability have been sketched in this paper. But it should be noted that an important factor has been a growing divergence between what people say about children and what they do. The same individual who would publicly express horror over any instance of cruelty to children and would wax indignant at the thought of his or her child receiving corporal punishment at school, will often think nothing of going out for the evening leaving his own very young children alone in the home or with another child a year or two older in charge of them. There seems to be little adult understanding of the effect on children of all ages of disruption within the home or frequent breaks in the continuity of their care. Unfortunately, the predominance in this era of the nuclear family and the consequent retreat into a jealously guarded domestic privacy make it extremely difficult, if not impossible, to detect with accuracy the current patterns of family behaviour. Any would-be researchers are, in effect, faced with a massive 'cover-up' by parents intent on projecting the best possible image of themselves. Only through, for example, television viewing figures can it be inferred how much or how little time parents spend in vital and active contact with their children. Only by weaving together many strands of such indirect evidence can a picture be built up of the extent to which children's basic needs are being left unmet; often in homes where material affluence is considerable.

As many social workers and police will testify, parents of truants often show indifference or, worse, involve their children in tasks which keep them from school. There is frequently a similar reaction to offences committed by their children, for example burglary, vandalism, taking motor vehicles and robbery with violence. A strong case can therefore be made for a more general enforcement of legal penalties in the shape of fines or compensation against the parents of truants and delinquents. So long as society, in England and Wales, maintains that the young cannot be held fully responsible for deviant behaviour because this is essentially linked to lack of parental control, it must logically follow that adults should not only share the blame but be penalised for the consequences of their children's behaviour(4). There would doubtless be situations where no shadow of blame could be attributed to the parents; but discretion could be exercised in these cases, which would not alter the principle that parents should be held accountable to some degree for the anti-social manifestations of their methods of dealing with their children.

Conclusion

At a time when politicians of all parties are vieing with one another in stressing the role of the family as the keystone of society, the view seems to be taken that its well-being and stability can be assured through tax changes and other measures of financial support. This paper argues that a broader vision is necessary to ensure the conditions in which children can receive not only adequate material care and nourishment but the kind of supportive nurture which will promote their fullest intellectual and emotional development. While avoidable poverty is in itself an evil and can cause severe tensions contributing to child abuse, there is a less easily definable poverty in the quality of many family relationships which can cause psychological deprivation and suffering, whether or not this is linked with the infliction of physical cruelty.

During 1979, the International Year of the Child, attention will be focused in many less fortunate countries on securing for children the means of bare survival. In Western industrialised societies, on the other hand, the aim should be to throw more light on the disintegrating forces which cause widespread unhappiness among children and in some cases result in their death or permanent injury. Much has been said and written about the Cycle of Deprivation, and how to break it in order to help the many families which become enmeshed in it. Urgent study needs now to be given to what may be described as the Cycle of Family Disruption, and our efforts should be directed to restoring the continuity and wholeness of family relationships which are equally indispensable to the health and safety of children in our society.

---

[4] Under the Criminal Law Act 1977, parents can now be held responsible for paying fines imposed on their children.

REFERENCES

CENTRAL COUNCIL FOR EDUCATION AND TRAINING IN SOCIAL WORK: Study No. 1. 1978. Good Enough Parenting.

EEKELAAR J. 1978 : Family Law and Social Policy.

GOLDSTEIN J., FREUD A., SOLNIT, A.J. 1973 : Beyond the Best Interests of the Child.

KELLMER PRINGLE M. 1975 : The Needs of Children.

OFFICE OF POPULATION CENSUSES AND SURVEY 1978 : Series FM2., No. 2. Marriage and Divorce Statistics.

RUTTER M. 1975 : Helping Troubled Children.

SELECT COMMITTEE ON VIOLENCE IN THE FAMILY : Session 1976 - 77. First Report : Violence to Children.

Child Abuse and Neglect, Vol. 3, pp. 61 - 66.

0145-2134/79/0301-0061 $02.00/0.

SEXUAL AND COMMERCIAL EXPLOITATION OF CHILDREN: LEGISLATIVE RESPONSES AND TREATMENT CHALLENGES

Judianne Densen-Gerber, J.D., M.D., F.C.L.M.
President and Founder of Odyssey Institute, Inc.
Stephen F. Hutchinson, Esq.
Vice President and General Counsel of Odyssey Institute, Inc.

A popular lay description of child abuse and neglect typically includes the battering or starving of a child by a parent who hates the child or is mentally deranged. Many child abuse and neglect cases fall under such descriptions, but there are significant numbers of cases in which the parent or adult perpetrator is motivated by sexual and/or commercial influences. The use of the child as an adjunct or tool in fulfilling the parent's aberrant personal desires or needs is a form of child abuse distinguishable from the traditional formulation, yet often more devastating to the child.

Within the context of this paper, sexploitation is a term coined from sexual exploitation and abuse of children and will be defined as physical or emotional harm to a child arising from 1) use of the child by the parent or someone in loco parentis for his or her own sexual needs, and 2) the use of the child in explicit sexual performances, whether for the purposes of prostitution, sexual exhibition or the production of pornographic materials.

Let us consider the second category first because it raises the least controversy for the public at large; the majority of whom are definite in their lack of understanding or compassion for persons who sell their children sexually or for others who commercially sexually exploit children for economic gain but are confused and sympathetic in the area of incest. The sexual use of children, ranging in age from three to sixteen, has become a multimillion dollar industry within the United States and has spread around the world. Many of the same materials I found in New York were also being sold in Europe, Southeast Asia, Australia and Japan. Child prostitutes mark the streets of every major city I have visited in these countries. This is truly an international issue.

Turning first to the commercial use of children in sexually explicit magazines, films and other items of child pornography, it must be noted that child pornography includes both heterosexual and homosexual acts. By recent count, there are at least 264 different magazines being produced and sold each month in adult bookstores across the country dealing with sexual acts between children or between children and adults. These magazines -- slickly produced -- sell for prices averaging over $7.00 each. This number of 264 does not include the vast number of films or other media. Until recently, it was incorrectly assumed that child pornography was produced mostly in Europe, but investigations have now revealed that much of it is produced in the United States -- even some materials which are packaged in such a manner as to represent foreign origin.

Film makers and magazine photographers have little difficulty recruiting youngsters for these performances. Some simply use their own children, or buy the children of others; some rely on runaways. Recent findings of a U.S. Senate subcommittee on juvenile delinquency indicate that more than one million American children run away from home each year, often for good cause, having been victims of intolerable conditions, with physical and sexual abuse present.[1] From this vast army of dispossessed children, exploiters select literally thousands of participants for their production needs and prostitution rings. Los Angeles police estimate that adults in that city alone sexually exploited over 30,000 children under seventeen in 1976, and photographed many of them in the act. Five thousand of these children were under twelve. In 1975, Houston police arrested a man after finding a warehouse full of pornography including 15,000 color slides of boys in homosexual acts, over 1,000 magazines and paperback books plus a thousand reels of film.[2]

In New York City, Father Bruce Ritter of Covenant House, a group of shelters for runaway children, has reported that the first ten children who entered Covenant House had all been given money to appear in pornographic films. These children, in their early teens, could not return to their homes because of extreme conditions of abuse and neglect, and could not find jobs or take care of themselves other than in illegal ways. There is no other way for a child of twelve to support him or herself,and sadly, too few sheltering alternative environments are provided by our communities.

Despite the highly secretive nature of the recruitment and sexploitation process, a growing body of information about the children involved confirms that psychological scarring and emotional distress which occur in the vast majority of these cases lead to significant other problems, many of which include the illicit use of drugs to deaden memories and desensitize present experiences.[3]

Pre-pubescent sexual activity, especially under conditions of exploitation and coercion, is highly destructive to the child's psychological development and social maturation. Psychiatrists report that such inappropriate sexuality is highly destructive to children. It predisposes them to join society's deviant populations; drug addicts, prostitutes, criminals, the promiscuous and pre-adult precocious parents.

Over 17,000 babies were born to mothers under fourteen years of age in 1976. Venereal diseases in children have now reached epidemic figures. Although there may not be a proven link between adult pornography and sexual abuse, there is no doubt that this sexploitation of our young in order to produce child pornography often scars the children so used for life. This opinion is not based purely on intelligent conjecture, for a number of children and young adults who had been involved in posing and/or performing for sexually explicit films and magazines have surfaced. These children are now or have been in treatment programs for substance abuse, delinquency or other aberrant behavior. Some of these children have voluntarily recounted their experiences to law enforcement, mental health workers, and news media people who are attempting to learn more about the recruitment process, the type of activities involved, the treatment needs, and the long-term effects upon the victims.

Psychiatry has not yet developed a treatment design for these youngsters, however, we have proposed to establish small treatment centers in New York City which will adapt many components of the highly successful modality created by Dr. Henry Giarretto and Anna Giarretto (discussed, supra). The target patient group is distinct in several characteristics from the other groups of child abuse victims. They show a more marked inability than other patients to trust any adult or establish the therapeutic rapport which is so necessary for rehabilitation. Other children who are abuse victims hunger for affection and caring, and are immediately or shortly thereafter responsive to any adult who shares affection and warmth. This is far from the case with children who have been sexually used. They, better than almost anybody else, know when such exploitation and abuse masquerades as "love." It is "love" and its closeness as defined previously in their lives that they most fear.

Many previously were victimized in a most brutal fashion. Experienced law enforcement investigators reject the commonly stated belief that nude posing is harmless to the children. They have found that the child pornographer is also often a child molester. Photography is often only a sideline to prostitution, sexual abuse and drugs. It is important to note that the victimization in the child pornography process goes beyond the child actor. For example, authorities in Rockingham, New Hampshire, reported recently that, in 1977, every one of the 27 cases of incest reported in their jurisdiction included child pornography preceding and accompanying the assaults on the children.

The men who support this billion-dollar industry do so because they are seeking justification and rationalization for their deviant behavior. Indeed, one magazine in the Odyssey Institute files, Lust For Children, is a primer for the sex molester, teaching him how to go to the park and pick up two little girls, what games to play to induce them to cooperate and what acts to perform which will leave the least evidence for the police, should the children report him. Another, entitled Schoolgirls, instructs a father in text and photographs as to those positions for intercourse best used with pre-pubescent girls (in this instance a girl of 9) and still another shows in serial photographs how to affix a lock to one's daughter's labia so that no other man may "get to her." Such sadomasochistic and snuff activities are an integral part of the "kiddie porn" market.

Furthermore, not only are these activities harmful emotionally, developmentally and psychologically to the child actors and children subsequently sexually abused, but physically, as many suffer lacerations of the vagina and rectum. Additionally, the research of Dr. Malcolm Coppleson, one of the leading gynecologists in Sydney, Australia, has shown the vaginal pH of the pre-pubescent is not sufficient to neutralize infections that come with intercourse, so that she is subject not only to vaginitis, but early onset of cervical cancer often necessitating hysterectomies prior to attaining thirty years of age.[4] It is obvious that children were not meant to satisfy the sexual needs of adults, and such use of them is like rape, a crime of power and abuse.

Child prostitution is defined as: the use of or participation by children under the age of majority (or sometimes defined as under sixteen years of age) in sexual acts with adults or other minors where no force is present. Prostitution differs from statutory rape and incest in that there is an element of payment, usually in money, but often in drugs, gifts, clothing, food or other items.

How many children are involved? Experts in the field of juvenile delinquency have shown that in the United States, there is a minimum of 300,000 active boy prostitutes under the age of sixteen.[5] Approximately 30,000 of these are located in New York City, with at least 2,000 concentrated in the Times Square area. The Los Angeles Police Department has identified 30,000 boys working as prostitutes within that city of whom 5,000 are under fourteen years of age, and several hundred are as young as eight. No one has counted the number of girls involved in sex-for-sale, but most authorities agree that there are probably as many girls involved as boys. In other words, there are more than one-half million children in the United States who are actively engaged in prostitution. Some experts estimate the number of children involved is easily twice that number -- 1.2 million, and this includes only children under the age of sixteen. The number nearly doubles again if sixteen and seventeen year olds are added.[6]

American children engaged in prostitution often are recruited from rural areas or midwestern cities. There are more than one million runaway children each year, many of whom turn to prostitution for survival; others as rebellion. Many leave homes of violence and sexual abuse, others are lonely because of distant neglectful personally preoccupied families, and still others are overwhelmingly bored and unchallenged -- a few are severely mentally ill but untreated. The longing for adventure and to be rid of parental abuses, leads hundreds of thousands into the streets, brothels and bus terminals. Their common fervent needs are affection and attention. These needs make them vulnerable to smooth-talking pimps who woo them with protestations of love and promises of fun and big money. For some, drugs and alcohol are part of the enticement; for others, these habits follow. Most are involved in substance abuse sooner or later. The drug habit only insures their captivity in the lifestyle of domination by the pimps.

Child prostitutes are rotated around the country like country circuit riders because the men who desire children also desire variety. These men need the illusion of innocence and virginity. One child I have treated literally claimed to have sold her maidenhood forty-four times. In other cases, the wandering is to avoid arrest or territorial disputes with local established prostitutes. Still others follow conventions of professional and business groups.

What happens to these children? The life of a child prostitute is generally far different from what may have been promised to or anticipated by the child victim. Besides the drug and alcohol abuse, there are frequent beatings by pimps, violence from customers, and conditions of slavery. If the girl has a child, her pimp often takes her baby from her; he sends the infant out of state to be cared for by one of his relatives whose name or whereabouts she does not know; thereby if the prostitute tries to leave his stable (the name for a pimp's group of girls) he threatens her with the reality that she may never see the child again.

These forms of sexploitation challenge the community's limit setting and service delivery mandates. The legislative response has been strong and swift after an awareness of the problem of child pornography was created last year. The helping professions must act quickly to fill the need for support and therapeutic services to the victims and families afflicted.

The menace of sexploitation will not be removed by simple changes in law or harsh penalties, although these are essential components of the complete strategy. There must be a public awareness in each community that sexploitation exists, both as a big business, (in large part run by organized crime) and within individual families, that it victimizes children in every community, that it can be stopped and that it will only be stopped by a commitment to the children of the community manifested in explicit actions:

1. Amendment of child abuse and neglect statutes to include sexual exploitation, and to prescribe harsh criminal penalties for offenders.

2. Amend the Civil Code to provide for licensing of all children used in commercial modeling or performing, with carefully worded proscriptions and substantial sanctions against the use of such children in sexually explicit activities.

3. Extend criminal liability to promoters and distributors of child pornography, without whose promotion and marketing of the finished product there would be no financial motive for the sexploitation of children in the first place.

4. Strengthen sexual assault and incest statutes, and modify the judicial process with respect to the evidentiary process vis-a-vis young children.[7]

5. Develop intervention and treatment models for children victimized by this process, to mend their emotional and psychological injuries to and return them to the mainstream of society.

With respect to sexploitation, the helping professions must assume a leadership and advocacy role. Let us, for once, get off our sterile, clinical or academic towers and reverse this very critical disease process.

What can be done? First, we must recognize that a sexually permissive society without humanistic caring contributes to the defective values presently being developed in children. Children need structure; they need to learn that sex is more than just doing what mechanically feels good or earns them money. Sex is part of a relationship -- a special kind of friendship which is not exploitive. Second, children must be given attention and affection in the home. This includes loving, cuddling, warmth and concern -- basic psychological needs devoid of genital sexual overtones. If these warm touching experiences are missing in the home, the child may seek them elsewhere becoming vulnerable to sexual exploitation by others with their own agendas.

Third, we must develop and provide all children with thorough sex education, but not simply information on techniques and mechanics, but what to do with their feelings and honest information about human sexuality, including the preciousness of human relatedness, caring, and commitment. Anatomy and warnings about masturbation are not a substitute for dealing with the very real concerns and frustrations of adolescence, but all information shared with our young must be appropriate for them, not for sophisticated adults.

Fourth, when a child gets involved in prostitution, authorities should recognize the behavior as a symptom of more serious problems. The juvenile justice system or other strictly legalistic approaches can not alone prevent or stop the problem. We must take a comprehensive look at the child in trouble, including psychological, medical, educational, legal and intra-family issues.

Fifth, communities must recognize that child prostitution and pedophilia are very serious threats to all children in the community and to the community itself. Delivery of community resources must be organized to maximize the impact of appropriate skills and resources to return the victimized child to a happy, healthy, and appropriate lifestyle. At the present writing, there are no treatment centers specially designed to treat child sex abuse victims.[8]

Much remains to be done but at least we have begun by identifying that these problems exist; now we must create a society where children can enjoy love and affection without being subject to sexual abuse. All children should have an inalienable right to love and affection.

When Odyssey began its campaign against child pornography in January, 1977, there was very little legislation on the federal or state level dealing with the use of children in sexually explicit materials or performances. On the federal level, five laws prohibit the distribution of "obscene" materials. Laws pertaining to the dissemination of obscene material to minors have been enacted in 47 states and the District of Columbia, however only six states specifically prohibited the participation of minors in an obscene performance that could be harmful to them.[9] Enforcement of the then-existing statutes did not seem likely to significantly curtail the activity.

Statutes dealing with sex crimes often are not helpful. The physical activity involved in sexploitation of minors in pornography may not meet the criteria of the statute, e.g., rape, sodomy, sexual abuse. Or the statutes may be so broadly worded as to discourage courts from applying them in terms of significant sanctions. Many states have child welfare provisions within their education laws that regulate the employment of children in commercial activities. Unfortunately, these same laws either abdicate control when the child is working for a parent[10] or the sanctions are so limited as to pose no deterrant.[11]

Given the paucity of legislation specifically relating to this activity, there can be little wonder at the relatively scarce previous attempts at law enforcement. The problems of case-finding and evidence are compounded by a confusion between sexploitation as a form of child abuse and adult obscenity matters. These problems and the attitudes of many judges discourage and actually thwart the few criminal investigations attempted.

Today, one year later, in early 1978, Congress has passed and the President signed a significant federal statute, and more than 30 state legislatures have introduced or passed child porn legislation. Such legislation can achieve maximum success by prohibiting specific sexual acts when performed by minors for the purpose of producing a film or magazine. The production, distribution and sale is forbidden as crime of sexual exploitation of children as opposed to obscenity which focuses on the reader or viewer. Thus, the preferred view is to legislate against the exploitation as a form of child abuse, and the material as a contraband product of the exploitation. There is ample historical precedent for this in the child labor law area.

These statutes criminalize the activities but do not themselves respond to the evidentiary problems. In this area, the New York appproach wherein the standard rules of criminal evidence are inapplicable to child protective proceedings is recommended.[12] This should be extended, though perhaps with minor modifications, to criminal proceedings in sexploitation cases.

Under traditional evidentiary statutes, such as in Massachusetts, severe evidentiary limitations handicap resolution of cases. These limitations are threefold. First,that in many jurisdictions a child under the age of seven is *non sui juris*. A recent study conducted at the Odyssey House facilities resulted in a finding that eighteen percent (18%) of the incest victim population had had their initial cross-generational incest experience under the age of seven. Incest is a crime that generally occurs in the home environment, with no witnesses present other than the participants in the act. The *non sui juris* rule automatically eliminates much of the ability to aid that portion of the population which is most in need of protection by the social institutions. Second, in all jurisdictions studied children between the ages of seven and twelve routinely may give unsworn testimony. Such unsworn testimony is insufficient grounds upon which to base a conviction in a sexual abuse case. Again, given the nature of the act, it is improbable that such corroboration is available. Finally, in all states studied, with the exception of New York, the evidentiary rules requiring corroboration of charges of sexual misconduct again serve to severly restrict the probability of success of prosecution for sexual abuse. A survey of the case law reveals only one case discussing sexual abuse of the child, *In Re Hawkins*.[13] In that case a finding of abuse by the Family Court was made possible only because the act was corroborated by the victim's thirteen-year-old brother. The victim's unsworn statement that the act occurred would have been insufficient, standing alone, to support a finding of abuse and thereby protect her.

Professors Holmstrom and Burgess have written extensively on the preparation of a child for court, and have identified significant factors decreasing or increasing stress, which underscore the need for a new approach to the fact-finding process:

Guidelines for Preparing the Child or Adolescent for Court [14]

Factors Decreasing Stress	*Factors Increasing Stress*
Talking about the court process: who does what in court.	Public setting of the courtroom
Visiting and walking around an empty court room.	Being unfamiliar with court room and court personnel
Using a private, quiet room for interviewing about the assault	Speaking into a court microphone
Availability of crayons and paper and age-related toys for young witnesses during interview	Being sequestered and no familiar faces in court
Presence of a parent or familiar person in court	Different DAs at district court and superior court
Explanation of purpose of interview and testimony	Legal and/or technical jargon
Use of clear, simple language, as well as carefully chosen questions	Seeing the defendant
Practicing the style of the DA and/or defense counselor through role-play of testifying	Linguistic strategies of the defense
Flexibility of the interviewer	Rigid, indifferent style of some DAs
Including the family and/or familiar persons in the preparation process	Judgmental attitude of the situation
Keep a written account of the testimony for victims to refresh their memory	Long delays and postponements
Instructions about where to go in the courthouse	Memory loss
Instructions on how to respond to the DA and on cross-examination	

The legal process, in other words, must be handled delicately with regard to child victims. Otherwise, the court room can be as traumatic as many forms of sexploitation, if not more so.

There must be created within the helping professions a greatly increased recognition of the need for effective treatment and counselling services. The California project has demonstrated an effective model with a remarkable record of intervention. They work predominantly with incest victims and their families, however, the approach may well be adaptable for use in working with child prostitutes, victims of sexual assault and child pornography victims.

> The child victim needs to be convinced that he or she is not to blame for the incestuous behavior or for the family disruption that ensued when the incest secret was disclosed. Regardless of how seductive or provocative the child's behavior, all family members must acknowledge that the total responsibility for incest rests with the adults involved. The child victim must hear from the mother, "You are not to blame. Daddy and I did not have a good marriage. That is why Daddy turned to you." Likewise, the child victim must receive an acknowledgement of complete responsibility for the incest behavior from the father and an apology from the father.
>
> A girl who has been a victim of incest needs to receive the message that sexual feelings are good and normal, despite the guilt and confusion attending the sexual relationship with her father. Great care must be taken to prevent girls from coping with the enormity of what has happened to them by "turning off" sexually. Contrary to popular opinion, most victims do not enjoy the incest relationship, especially on a long-term basis. It is an oppressive relationship for the child victim and an exploitation of parental authority. Daughters often describe a feeling of "a heavy weight pressing on me." This feeling is lessened and frequently will disappear after counseling, if the daughter has been successfully relieved of her guilt and helped to become comfortable with her sexual feelings.[15]

SUMMARY

In the brief space allowed for this paper, we have attempted to describe a very serious and complex problem which threatens our children and challenges our professional and governmental resources. The legal and medical professions must develop new tools and systems to significantly impact the plight of sexploited children. Detection, protective intervention, placement and treatment should each involve a coordinated multi-disciplinary system.

We are not going to produce mentally healthy and happy children by issuing an executive order that all children must be loved. But we can enact and enforce legislation to protect them and give them a fighting chance in this world. As Eric Ericson wrote:

> Someday, maybe, there will exist a well-informed, well considered, and yet fervent public conviction that the most deadly of all possible sins is the mutilation of a child's spirit; for such mutilation undercuts the life principle of trust, without which every human act, may it feel ever so good, and seem ever so right, is prone to perversion by destructive forms of consciousness.

FOOTNOTES

1. House of Representatives, Committee on Judiciary, Subcommittee on Crime. Hearing: March 8, 1977.

2. Lloyd Martin, Sgt., Los Angeles Police Department, personal communication with the author, and Congressional Record, May, 1977, Committee on Judiciary, Subcommittee on Crime.

3. Robin Lloyd, Obscene But Not Forgotten, Howard McCann, 1979.

4. Malcolm Coppleson, M.D., personal communication with author.

5. Robin Lloyd, Boy Prostitution in America -- For Money or Love, Vanguard, 1976.

6. Id.

7. Judianne Densen-Gerber, J.D., M.D., F.C.L.M., "Child Prostitution and Child Pornography: Medical, Legal, and Societal Aspects of the Commercial Exploitation of Children," Sexual Abuse of Children: Selected Readings edited by MacFarlane, Jones and Jenstrom, National Center of Child Abuse & Neglect, Fall, 1978.

8. Id.

9. Judianne Densen-Gerber, J.D., M.D., F.C.L.M. and Stephen F. Hutchinson, J.D., "Developing Federal and State Legislation to Combat The Exploitation of Children In the Production of Pornography," The Journal of Legal Medicine, September, 1977.

10. Mich. Act 157, Public Acts of 1947 (as amended) Section 409.14.

11. N.Y. Educ. Law Section 3231(a),(c).

12. New York Family Court Act Section 1046.

13. 351 N.Y.S. 2d 574 (New York County Family Court, 1974).

14. Ann Wolbert Burgess and Lynda Lytle Holmstrom, "The Child and Family During the Court Process," Sexual Assault of Children and Adolescents, Lexington, Mass., D.C. Heath and Co., 1978, p. 229.

15. Henry Giarretto, Anna Giarretto and Suzanne M. Sgroi, "Coordinated Community Treatment of Incest," Sexual Assault of Children and Adolescents, Lexington, Mass., D.C. Heath and Co., 1978, p. 236.

Child Abuse and Neglect, Vol. 3, pp. 67 - 72.
Pergamon Press Ltd., 1979. Printed in Great Britain.

THE REPETITION OF CHILD ABUSE: HOW FREQUENTLY DOES IT OCCUR?*

Roy C. Herrenkohl, Ellen C. Herrenkohl, Brenda Egolf, Monica Seech

Center for Social Research, Lehigh University, Bethlehem, Pa. USA

INTRODUCTION

Results from previously reported studies indicate varying percentages of recurrence of child abuse. The range is large. Some studies report 20% or lower recurrence; others report as high as 60% of families in which abuse or neglect recurs. In one study of 25 abused and neglected children (Morse, Sahler, and Friedman, 1970; Friedman, 1972), it was found that one-third of the children were abused or neglected again. Johnson and Morse (1968) reported that 20% of the survivors of abuse were found to have been re-abused or grossly neglected when studied 42 months later. Skinner and Castle (1969) reported the highest percentage, 60%, as having been re-battered. It is notable that some reports combine abuse and neglect, while others report only abuse.

The overall objective of this paper is to present data on recurrence and recidivism and to clarify conceptual and methodological difficulties involved in the assessment of repetition of abuse.

In this paper, four types of child abuse are described. Physical abuse is serious non-accidental, physical harm to a child. Emotional abuse is serious emotional harm to a child. Sexual abuse is sexual activity with a child. Gross neglect is nutritional or medical neglect which is immediately dangerous to the health of the child, and includes the "failure-to-thrive" syndrome.

METHODS

Overview

The present report is based on a follow-up study of 328 families who were provided services for child abuse in two counties of eastern Pennsylvania (USA) during the ten-year period, 1967 to 1976. All cases had been closed or had received at least one year of service. The study included three parts: (1) an analysis of the case records of all 328 families; (2) interviews with one or both (original) heads of household who could be located and would agree to the interview; (3) an analysis of the birth records of children in the families where the parents would give permission to read the records. The present report is based on data drawn almost exclusively from the analysis of the case records.

Measures

Two approaches were used to measure repetition of abuse. One was defined as "recurrence," that is, the occurrence of one or more abuse incidents after an initial incident.

---

*The study reported here was funded by the National Center on Child Abuse and Neglect, Children's Bureau/Administration for Children, Youth and Families, U. S. Department of Health, Education, and Welfare, Contract No. 90-C-428.

Two measures were used to reflect recurrence. One was a frequency count of legal charges of abuse (citations). A second measure was a frequency count of verified abuse incidents noted in the case records. In reading the case records it was found that there were more verified incidents of abuse than there were corresponding legal charges of abuse. For both citations and incidents, perpetrators and targets of abuse were identified, and the four types of abuse - physical, emotional, sexual, and gross neglect - were distinguished.

A second approach to the repetition of abuse was defined as "recidivism," that is, a further occurrence of abuse after termination of service to a family following the first citation for abuse. There were also two measures of recidivism. One was a frequency count of legal charges (citations) which occurred after the termination of service which was provided in response to a family's first charge of abuse. The second measure was a frequency count of verified incidents of abuse which occurred during that same period. It is important to note that the identification of incidents after case closing was possible only after the case had been re-opened.

RESULTS

Characteristics of the Families

Among the female heads of household agreeing to be interviewed (N = 151), 83.5% were white, 11.9% were Spanish-surnamed, and 4.6% were black. Almost two-thirds (62.3%) were Protestant, almost one-quarter (23.8%) were Roman Catholic, less than one percent was Jewish, and the remainder (13.2%) had no religious preference. Among the female heads of household, approximately two-thirds (65.5%) had less than 12 years of education. A lower percentage (50.0%) of male heads of household had less than 12 years of education. Most of the 328 families (86.0%) had both a male and a female head of household during the period when abuse occurred. Where comparisons between characteristics of the interview sample and the total abuse population were possible, the figures given here were found to be reasonable approximations of the population characteristics.

Indications of Repetition in Families

Among the 328 families served for abuse during the study period, 260 had at least one valid charge. However, case records of 286 families revealed verified incidents of abuse. In the case records of the 26 families for which there was not a validated charge, there was evidence that abuse had occurred; however, for various reasons, including self-referral of the family, there was not a validated charge.

Recurrence. There was a total of 349 citations in the 260 families with at least one valid citation. As can be determined from Table 1, 66 (25.4%) of the 260 families had repeated citations; 50 (19.2%) had 2 citations, 10 (3.9%) had 3 citations, and 5 (1.9%) had 4 citations.

TABLE 1 Recurrence: Citations and Incidents for Families

	Citations				Incidents			
Number of Occurrences	All Families		Families with Valid Citations		All Families		Families with Verified Incidents	
	No.	Percent	No.	Percent	No.	Percent	No.	Percent
0	10	3.1	-	-	39	11.9	-	-
1	245	74.7	194	74.6	97	29.6	95	33.2
2	57	17.3	50	19.2	82	25.0	81	28.3
3	10	3.1	10	3.9	28	8.5	28	9.8
4	5	1.5	5	1.9	29	8.9	29	10.1
5	1	0.3	1	0.4	14	4.3	14	4.9
6-10	0	0.0	0	0.0	24	7.3	24	8.3
11-15	0	0.0	0	0.0	11	3.3	11	4.0
Over 15	0	0.0	0	0.0	4	1.2	4	1.4
Total	328	100.0	260	100.0	328	100.0	286	100.0

There were 903 incidents of abuse in the 286 families with verified incidents. As can be seen in Table 1, among the 286 families, 191 (66.8%) had at least a second recorded incident; 53.1% had from 2 to 5 incidents, 8.3% had from 6 to 10 incidents, and 5.4% had over 10 incidents.

Recidivism. Table 2 indicates the numbers of citations and incidents which occurred after the termination of service following the first citation. There were 192 cases which closed among the 260 validly cited families, 73 of which re-opened. Twenty-one (28.8%) of the families with re-opened cases were re-cited for abuse (8.0% of the 260 families or 10.9% of those families whose cases had been closed).

Among the 286 families with a verified incident there were 206 cases which closed, 84 of which were re-opened. Among those families with re-opened cases, 38 (45.2%) were found to have further incidents of abuse. This number represents 13.2% of all 286 families or 18.5% of those families whose cases had been closed.

TABLE 2 Recidivism: Citations and Incidents for Families after Case Closing

	Citations			Incidents		
Case Status	Number	All Cases Percent	Closed Cases Percent	Number	All Cases Percent	Closed Cases Percent
Not closed	68	26.2	-	80	28.0	-
Closed, not re-opened	119	45.8	62.0	122	42.7	59.2
Closed, re-opened	73	28.0	38.0	84	29.3	40.8
Total	260	100.0	100.0	286	100.0	100.0
Number of Occurrences in Re-opened Cases						
None	52	20.0	27.1	46	16.1	22.3
1	17	6.5	8.8	24	8.4	11.7
2-3	4	1.5	2.1	7	2.4	3.4
4-5	-	-	-	5	1.7	2.4
More than 5	-	-	-	2	0.7	1.0
Total	73	28.0	38.0	84	29.3	40.8

Indications of Recurrence by Parties to the Abuse

Perpetrators of abuse. Indices of recurrence can also be calculated for perpetrators and targets of abuse. Table 3 indicates recurrence rates for perpetrators of abuse. Among the 362 perpetrators in the families with a valid citation, 58 (16.1%) were formally charged with abuse more than once. Among the 404 perpetrators in families where there was at least one verified incident of abuse, 197 (48.8%) were involved in more than one incident.

TABLE 3 Recurrence: Citations and Incidents for Perpetrators

	Citations		Incidents	
Number	Number of Perpetrators	Percent	Number of Perpetrators	Percent
0	79	21.8	-	-
1	225	62.1	207	51.2
2	44	12.2	89	22.0
3	12	3.3	44	10.9
4	-	-	28	7.0
5	2	0.6	11	2.7
6-10	-	-	19	4.7
11-15	-	-	6	1.5
Total	362 (260 families)	100.0	404 (286 families)	100.0

Targets of abuse. Turning to the targets of abuse, Table 4 indicates that 37 (8.0%) of the 460 children who were targets of abuse in validly cited families were listed as targets in repeated citations. Table 4 also indicates that 253 (49.5%) of the 511 children in families with abuse incidents were targets of repeated incidents.

TABLE 4 Recurrence: Citations and Incidents for Targets

Number	Citations: Number of Targets	Citations: Percent	Incidents: Number of Targets	Incidents: Percent
0	154	33.5	-	-
1	269	58.5	258	50.5
2	31	6.7	133	26.0
3	5	1.1	64	12.5
4	1	0.2	24	4.7
5	-	-	11	2.2
6-10	-	-	19	3.7
Over 10	-	-	2	0.4
Total	460	100.0	511	100.0
	(260 families)		(286 families)	

The lower recurrence rates for perpetrators and for targets as compared to the family rates for recurrence reflect the fact that in any one family more than one adult may assume the role of perpetrator and more than one child may assume the role of target, often at different points in time. In fact, 44.2% of the 260 families had more than one perpetrator and 45.3% had more than one target.

Indications of Recurrence by Type of Abuse

Another way to examine the recurrence of abuse is to consider different types of abuse, that is, physical, emotional, and sexual abuse, and gross (life-threatening) neglect.

Table 5 indicates that among 286 families with at least one verified incident, 90.5% were involved in physical abuse, 14.7% were involved in emotional abuse, 9.4% were involved in sexual abuse, and 28.3% in gross (life-threatening) neglect. As can also be determined from Table 5, among families in which physical abuse occurs, 54.1% have repeated incidents; among families in which emotional abuse occurs, 21.4% have repeated incidents; among families in which sexual abuse occurs, 29.6% have repeated incidents, and in families exhibiting gross neglect, 44.4% have repeated incidents.

TABLE 5 Number of Incidents by Type of Abuse

Number of Incidents	Physical No.	Physical Percent	Emotional No.	Emotional Percent	Sexual No.	Sexual Percent	Neglect No.	Neglect Percent
0	27	9.5	244	85.3	259	90.6	205	71.7
1	119	41.6	33	11.6	19	6.7	45	15.7
2	65	22.7	6	2.1	1	0.3	18	6.2
3	26	9.1	1	0.3	5	1.8	8	2.8
4	14	4.9	2	0.7	-	-	3	1.1
5	13	4.5	-	-	1	0.3	2	0.7
6-10	15	5.3	-	-	1	0.3	5	1.8
11 & over	7	2.4	-	-	-	-	-	-
Total	286	100.0	286	100.0	286	100.0	286	100.0

Indications of Recurrence by Combination of Abuse Types

Still another way to consider recurrence is to examine the different combinations of abuse types with which these families were associated. Approximately two-thirds (64.7%) of the 286 families were involved in one type of abuse. Twenty-eight percent were involved in two types of abuse, 7.0% in three types, and less than one percent (0.3%) in four types. When calculating percentages of recurrence, a conservative approach is to allow each family the same number of occurrences as they have types of abuse before considering recurrence to exist. Using this approach, recurrence percentages for combinations are 51.9% for single types, 66.3% for double types, and 85.0% for triple types. There was no fifth incident in the one family with four types of abuse.

Does Recurrent Abuse Occur in Families with Younger or Older Children?

In view of the amount of recurrent abuse identified in the present study, a further question that can be considered is whether the families in which the abuse recurs have younger or older children. The importance of this question derives from the greater developmental vulnerability of younger children.

Obtaining an answer to this question is complicated by the fact that children in a family cover a range of ages. As a preliminary step, however, families were categorized in terms of the age(s) of their younger child(ren) who were or became targets of abuse. If a family had at least one target child in the 0-5 year age group at the time of the family's first abuse incident, the family was placed in the 0-5 year category. If the family had at least one target child who was 6-11 years of age and none in the 0-5 year group when the family's first abuse incident occurred, the family was placed in the 6-11 year group. Families with all target children over 11 years of age at the time of the family's first incident were placed in the over 11 year group.

Table 6 gives the results when the age categories are cross-tabulated with the presence or absence of recurrence. There is a significant association ($X^2 = 23.37$, $p < .01$, df = 2) between recurrence and the age categorization. Greater than expected frequencies occur in the 0-5 year, recurrent group and the over 11 year, non-recurrent group. Among families where there are target children under six, which constitute over two-thirds of the families, 74.2% (144) are in the recurrence group. This has serious implications for children who are in families where abuse occurs when they are at a vulnerable and impressionable age. It should be noted that younger children have more opportunity to experience recurrent abuse than older children.

TABLE 6 Recurrence Status by Age of Target Children

Recurrence Status	Age of Youngest Target Child at Time of Family's First Incident: 0-5 years		6-11 years		Over 11 years			
	Number	Percent	Number	Percent	Number	Percent	Total	Percent
No recurrence	50	17.8	23	8.2	22	7.8	95	33.8
Recurrence	144	51.3	31	11.0	11	3.9	186	66.2
Total	194	69.1	54	19.2	33	11.7	281*	100.0

$X^2 = 23.37$, $p < .01$, df = 2

*The age of target children at the time of the first incident was unknown for five families.

DISCUSSION

What Can Be Concluded from the Present Results?

Official reports of abuse underestimate repetition. An important finding is the degree to which official reports of abuse underestimate the degree of recurrent abuse. For families with identified abuse, the low recurrence percentage for official reports (25.4%) as compared to the much higher percentage for verified incidents (66.8%) means that the magnitude of the problem is underestimated if recurrence is assessed by means of charges. A practical consequence of this underestimation may be that the potential for recurrent abuse may not be given the attention it deserves.

Abuse frequently recurs. The generally held view that abuse frequently recurs is supported by the present study. This, however, is only part of the picture. More than one perpetrator was identified in 44.2% of the validly cited families, and in 45.3% of these families more than one child was abused. Furthermore, where there is only one type of abuse the percentage of recurrence is 51.9%, while in families where there are two and three types, the percentages are 66.3% and 85.0%, respectively. Thus, among the families studied, recurrence of abuse may involve more than one perpetrator of abuse, more than one target of abuse, and more than one type of abuse.

Abuse occurs after the termination of services. The term "recidivism" has been reserved for abuse that occurs after service is terminated. The percentage of families that had incidents which occurred after the case closing is 13.2% of the 286 families with verified incidents or 18.5% of the 206 families whose cases had closed. While there are no uniform criteria by which to judge the seriousness of this level of recidivism, this percentage is high when it is considered that many of the more disturbed or disorganized family situations are provided many months of service before case closing. Twenty-five percent of the families with verified incidents had received over 36 months of service. Furthermore, some of the more serious cases were still open at the time the present study was done.

In conclusion, "recurrence" appears to be a more appropriate focus for assessing the risk of repeated abuse to the child than "recidivism". The latter term implies termination of service followed by further abuse and, in the case of service to abusive families, case closings are greatly affected by agency policy with regard to families who are chronically disorganized or resistant to service. From the perspective of "recurrence," repetition of abuse may be a more serious problem than has been generally recognized, highlighting the need to identify those factors which are predictive of repeated abuse. Currently, analyses of data from the study reported here are under way in order to identify such predictors. One report (Herrenkohl and Herrenkohl, 1978) which focuses on factors associated with the births of targets of abuse has been completed. Other reports assessing additional predictive factors are in preparation.

REFERENCES

Friedman, S.B. The need for intensive follow-up of abused children. In C.H. Kempe and R.E. Helfer (Eds.) (1972), Helping the Battered Child and His Family, Philadelphia: Lippincott.

Herrenkohl, E., and Herrenkohl, R. A comparison of abused children and their non-abused siblings. Submitted for publication (1978).

Johnson, B., and Morse, H. The Battered Child: A Study of Children with Inflicted Injuries. Denver Department of Welfare (1968).

Jones, C.O. The fate of abused children. In A.W. Franklin (Ed.) (1977), The Challenge of Child Abuse, New York: Grune and Stratton.

Morse, C.W., Sahler, O.J.Z., and Friedman, S.B., A three-year follow-up study of abused and neglected children. American Journal of Diseases of Children, (1970), 120, 439-446. cited in Jones, op. cit.

Skinner, A.E., and Castle, R.L. 78 Battered Children: A Retrospective Study. National Society for the Prevention of Cruelty to Children, London (1969).

Child Abuse and Neglect, Vol. 3, pp. 73 - 80.

0145-2134/79/0301-0073 $02.00/0.

"GOOD ENOUGH CARE"? [1] A STUDY OF CHILDREN WHO WENT HOME "ON TRIAL".

June Thoburn

Visiting Lecturer in Social Policy,
University of East Anglia, Norwich, England.

ABSTRACT

This paper is based on a descriptive study of thirty-four children in statutory care, who had returned home at least two years previously. Parents and social workers were interviewed about their perceptions of the problems which led to court action, the help given, the placement in care, the reasons for the children going home, and their assessments of the well-being of parents and children. The author stresses the importance of the appropriate placement, and of skilled and imaginative work in improving the material and emotional environment. She explores the delicate relationship between parents, children, and social workers when care and control must be combined; and also considers the degree of risk to the children, whilst suggesting ways of minimising this risk.

INTRODUCTION

The study on which this paper is based (Thoburn, 1977) was carried out in 1976 and 1977 and aimed at examining the debate about "the least detrimental alternative" (Goldstein, Freud, and Solnit, 1973) for children at risk, from the point of view of social workers and parents. The majority of earlier studies on the management of child abuse cases have concentrated on the decision about whether the child should be placed away from home, but more recent studies have suggested that "hospitalization, separation from parents, frequent home changes, and poor quality foster homes or institutional placements may be more damaging to the child in the long term than the physical trauma itself." (Jones, 1978). This study starts with the problem facing the social worker when a care order is made. Does he work towards returning the child home, or providing long term substitute care? How does he decide whether parents who have been unable to meet their child's needs in the past may be able to do so in the future, and if there is a reasonable possibility of them being able to provide good enough care, where should he place the child? Other studies, (George, 1970; Jenkins, 1972; Kadushin, 1970; Rowe, 1973; Tizard, 1977) have looked at children mostly placed voluntarily in foster, residential, or adoptive care, but there is a lack of information about children who have been found by a court or committee to be in need of care and who subsequently return home. Yet in England and Wales at any one time approximately 30% of all children in care on care orders are living at home "on trial". It should also be noted that this study is not confined to abused children, but is based on a general population of children coming into statutory care under the age of fourteen. The author believes with Jones (1978) that physical abuse is only one manifestation of "those malevolent aspects of home life which result in emotional disorder, inhibited intellectual capacity and a propensity to resort to violence in adult life." Elmer (1977) using matched comparison groups of abused and accident prone children and non-abused children found substantial psychological handicap at the age of eight in all three groups.

[1] This term is used in the sense explored extensively by Winnicott (1960) and implies that perfect care does not exist and that for each child what is "good enough" will vary with individual circumstances. Goldstein's (1973) "least detrimental alternative" implies a similar way of looking at services for children already deprived of a normal family life.

THE STUDY

The methodological problems of follow-up studies are well documented (Jones, 1978), the main problems being to assess "success", and to identify a representative sample and a control group. Where figures are used in this paper, these difficulties should be borne in mind, especially as no control group was used. For this reason, and because it is felt that the "in depth" study of a small group of families can play a part in suggesting hypotheses and revealing important differences which may be lost in large scale quantitative surveys, this study is essentially descriptive. It was carried out in a county authority in the South of England, and was representative of the county in terms of urban, rural, and new town populations. Fifty six children were identified, being, as far as could be ascertained, [2] the total number of those from the area from which the sample was taken who had gone home "on trial" between 1969 and 1975. The final sample was made up of twenty-two of these families plus two whose circumstances were very similar but where a supervision order was made and not a care order. Twenty of the twenty-five families agreed to be interviewed, but another five were included where the social worker was reluctant for the family to be contacted but which exemplified important issues which would otherwise have been inadequately covered. The families were chosen to include roughly equal proportions of children placed initially in residential care, in foster care, and directly home, and also in three roughly equal groups according to the reasons for care. Group A consisted of ten children from nine families who were either actual or suspected abuse cases; group B consisted of fourteen children under ten, (from seven families) covered losely by the heading "unsatisfactory home conditions", but including some children who had been physically abused, and in group C were ten children from nine families aged between ten and fourteen when they came into care for delinquency or behaviour or school problems. Thus the sample was deliberately selected to cover a range of placements and problems, rather than being a random sample. The main systematic bias is that a higher proportion of the children were younger on reception into care than was the case in the county as a whole, they were more likely to be placed initially in foster care, and there were fewer offenders.

The twenty families were interviewed by appointment in their own homes, and the interviews were recorded. Six of the interviews were with the mother and father, two with single fathers, two with step mothers, and ten with the mother. A guided interview schedule was used, covering the parents' perceptions of their own and their children's problems since before care proceedings to the time of the interview, their views of the help offered, and their assessments of the present situation for themselves and their children. The social worker at the time of the study was interviewed, and information was supplemented from the file. A questionnaire was used but interviews were also recorded in order to gain information about attitudes as well as factual information. Five children from two families in group B were interviewed, and I chatted briefly with others. The material was also discussed with residential workers, foster parents and social services managers, but in assessing the conclusions it should be borne in mind that only the views of social workers and parents were systematically included.

THE PARENTS AND CHILDREN

Information was gathered about the material circumstances, and emotional and physical health of members of the family before care and when the children went home. The findings are similar to those of other studies of children in care. (George, 1970; Holman, 1973; Thorpe, 1974; Aldgate, 1977). There were two middle class families, but even here incomes were low. About half of the families had housing problems before the children came into care, but almost all spoke of serious housing difficulties in the early stages of marriage and bringing up children. None of the parents, nor the social workers thought inadequate income or housing were major reasons for statutory action. However, there were indications that material deprivation, particularly when the children were very young, could in several cases have led to inappropriate child care practices or to marital problems which subsequently led to the need for court action.

[2] Because of methods of recording changes of placements it was difficult to be sure that all children who had been home and returned to care were included.

A high proportion of the families before care, and almost half at the time of interview, were single parent families, and several of the children came into care in traumatic circumstances at the time of the break-up of the marriage. One parent in almost half of the families was known to have a physical illness or handicap of a debilitating nature, and almost half the adults involved, from all except one of the families, had some form of psychiatric or serious emotional problem. At least eleven of the parents had experienced serious discontinuity of parental care during their childhood and another had been adopted as an infant. The main underlying reasons for the parents being unable to meet their children's needs were their own emotional or marital problems, sometimes aggravated by practical problems. Social workers tended to refer to them as "immature", "disorganised", or "trying but just unable to cope", and none of them were thought to be deliberately cruel, despite the fact that several of the children were physically injured. The majority of the children, then, came into care because of their parents' rather than their own problems, but in nineteen of the twenty-five families at least one child did have health or behaviour problems which made the parents' task more difficult. These included educational or physical handicap in seven cases, disturbances probably due to late adoptive placement in two cases, and five cases of delinquency associated with school problems. The rest involved behaviour problems clearly resulting from inappropriate child care practices, or, with infants, from undernourishment or untreated injuries received earlier.

THE SOCIAL WORKERS

It is generally agreed that the decision about whether children can remain at or return home must be to some extent dependant on the resources available to support the parents and protect the child, and that this must include the availability of skilled social work help. Baher and her colleagues (1976) comment that they were working in "near ideal conditions" and that "there remains a large gap between the provision of an ideal service, such as we have attempted, and the normal facilities available to the battering family without access to a special treatment centre." Others made the same point in a series of papers edited by Carter (1974). This study was not about the services which _ought_ to be offered, but what is in fact offered by a Social Services Department whose standards and resources are about average for an English county. It confirms other findings that unqualified and inexperienced social workers are undertaking work which it is generally agreed should be allocated to only qualified workers with special skills in this area of work. In all, fifty different local authority social workers had been involved with these families, six families having been visited by only one, but ten having had three or more workers. The parents were painfully conscious of the differences between workers, and some unqualified or inexperienced workers also regretted their lack of expertise.

Mother. "I think they should be trained before they are let on cases. He was practising on us. He didn't know his job. He once said, "I don't care how you feel. I've taken her away, and thats that." We were just a case to him. All he could say if we asked him anything was "I'll have to ask my superiors.""

Social Worker. "You want to give them the best service you can offer. I can't offer them the best service because I don't know what there is to offer."

On the other hand, at the time of interview, 76% of the families had a qualified worker. Since the proportion of qualified social workers for the county as a whole was 40% this does indicate that attempts were made to allocate these cases to qualified workers. Similarly, although one family had had six different workers, eleven families had had the same social worker for more than two years. Most of the social workers _did_ have good relationships with their clients, (this being confirmed by the parents themselves), and said that these families mattered to them more than most of their other clients. It was particularly important to the parents that the social worker should care about them as people; that he should be honest with them about plans for the children, consulting them as much as possible, and that he should be dependable and not make empty promises.

Mother. "They've got to get involved to understand the situation. Once we thought Bill had run away. The social worker got onto them the same night and came round that night and said "Don't worry, he is still there." He seemed more like one of the family. Although he was so busy, he always seemed to have time."

Mother. She _did_ care, because if she said something she would do it. It was not a false promise. She always seemed to know when I was unhappy.

THE HELP OFFERED

Prevention

The focus of this paper being on services offered after care proceedings, the issue of prevention will be touched on only briefly. Six of the families were offered a planned social work service prior to statutory action, but it must be a matter of regret that a further five families, who should clearly have been identified as at risk, (because the parents themselves had a history of emotional problems whilst in care, or because children had been placed for adoption or been in temporary care) were offered only a crisis service by a succession of social workers. The other fourteen families were not known to the Social Services Department prior to the events which led to court action. Although, given the severity of the problems, practical help alone would not have been sufficient, it was estimated by the researcher that a combination of skilled social work help, together with day care, help in the home, or a battered wives' hostel could have prevented the need for statutory action for about a third of the children. This was particularly the case when problems resulting from the breakdown of a marriage led to care. Since some of the children concerned stayed in care for several years, and were most likely to be caught up in "tug-of-love" situations, the necessary investment in time and resources at an earlier stage would have saved a great deal of unhappiness, for children, foster parents, and parents. The availability of such resources would have allowed some children to go home more quickly, and more safely.

Mother. "If that hostel for battered wives had been there it would have been allright. Because he couldn't have got there to get me back. I went to a place where I could only keep the baby, and the others were taken into care. So I went back to him. Then he started interfering with them, and they had to go to court."

It was noted that at the point of marriage breakdown the potential of the fathers to care for the children was not adequately considered in some cases. This led to the inappropriate placement of children in long term care.

Placement

For most children, the major form of help was placement away from home, either as a means of offering protection, or in order to achieve a change in behaviour. All except two of the children originally placed at home spent some time away from home, usually for less than three months, and two children on supervision orders were either in hospital or foster care on interim orders. The length of time away from home varied from three months to six years with half of the children spending over a year away before returning home. However, for forty out of a total 100 years which these thirty-four children had spent technically "in care" they had lived at home "on trial". Eight of the children, mostly the older ones, had only one placement in care, but fourteen had three or more placements, and one child had six. Eleven of the children were placed initially at home, six in residential care, and seventeen in foster care. One child returned home on a supervision order directly from hospital.

No objective measure of the well-being of the children whilst away from home is available, and this in any case changed over time, but social workers were asked to make a rough assessment. Eleven were thought to have been happy or fairly happy, six to be fairly happy but also anxious, and twelve to be anxious, apathetic, confused or unhappy. One aspect of these cases which should be noted is that eighteen of the children were visited at least once a week by at least one parent, and only one child was not visited at least once monthly. This finding supports the conclusion of Jenkins (1972) that return home from care is related to frequency of parental visiting. Although some of the social workers encouraged visits by taking parents, paying fares, and talking about the feelings aroused, this was done in a minority of cases. In most cases the quality of social work at the time of placement of the children was of the generally low standard documented in larger studies. (George, 1970; Holman, 1973; Rowe, 1973). Very few children, and even fewer parents made a pre-placement visit; if a child changed placement, the parents were usually told after the event; and only six parents actually went with the social worker when the child was taken to his placement. Thus, it must be concluded that the regularity with which these parents visited had more to do with their own determination to keep in contact than with the efforts of the social workers.

In common with other researchers I found that almost all the parents, with the exception of a few visiting older children in residential care, found visiting their children a painful experience.

Mother." It was about three weeks before I visited. I had to make the first move, but I think the social worker did want me to visit in a way. The foster mother thought I was a nuisance. I couldn't make conversation. You feel as though you are interfering. You sit there and you think: "Does she want to keep him?". I used to swear under my breath and think: "you've got my baby and I can't have him. You think they look on you as somebody who can't look after children, as though you will drop him. In a way I enjoyed seeing him. But you get all confused, and the distance from here to there, and not having anywhere to go if you take him out, and you just don't seem to bother any more. I thought, what's the point of going to see him if I can't have him back."

Mother. "I hated it. I used to think she was watching me, and I couldn't express how I felt, because I didn't feel anything. I went twice a week, but out of duty. I thought I ought to, seeing as he was coming home."

Although most of the parents who had visited children in both said that they found it easier to go to see them in residential than foster care, most of those interviewed said they preferred foster placements because they thought this was better for their children. They did however make the proviso that they should be able to play as full a part as possible in their children's lives, and were clearly thinking in terms of "professional" foster parents. (Holman, 1975; Rowe, 1976). Most of the parents and social workers were satisfied with the physical care given, but only in a third of cases was this the placement the social worker would have chosen if a more suitable alternative had been available. More "professional" foster parents were needed for children of all ages, and also residential assessment facilities for a small number of younger children. Social workers gave examples of children remaining at home, or returning home too soon, because the right placement in care was not available, but also of other, usually younger, children who for the same reason stayed in care permanently, or longer than was necessary and at greater cost to their emotional health. Two children were exposed to the extreme stress of conflicting loyalties because they were placed with foster parents who really wanted to adopt a child, although it should have been obvious at the time of placement that parental contact would be maintained.

Mother. "Foster homes are fine for long term children, where the children are not wanted, but to me, Pat has always been wanted. What she had was a substitute home, and what she needed was a foster home where we could still be involved."

Thus the decision about where to place the child can be as crucial to his future development as the original decision about whether to do so. It can diminish or increase the stresses to which he is exposed, and have an important influence on the likelihood of his maintaining bonds with his parents and therefore of successful return home. At best, a good placement in care can improve the relationship between parents and children and some of the residential workers and foster parents in the study did manage to perform this very difficult and demanding task.

Return Home

One of the most important questions which this study sought to answer was why these particular children went home. It has been noted that the parents had many problems, and although no control group was used, comparison with Thorpe's (1974) study of parents of children in long term care suggests that these parents were no more stable emotionally than others whose children do not go home. On the other hand, none were considered to be deliberately cruel, over a period of time and this was the one group where social workers said they would not consider rehabilitation. Three major influences on the decision to let the children go home were noted: the attitudes of parents and children, and their reactions to placement; the attitudes of the social workers; and the nature of the practical and emotional support offered and of the placement. Of these three the author concluded that the most important factor was the determination of the parents, and where old enough the children, to stay together as a family. Several of the parents reported numbness and depression after their parting with their children similar to what Jenkins (1972) describes as "filial deprivation". However, these parents were more likely than those in other studies to feel anger, and to worry about their children. The extent to which parental determination resulted from anger, from fear of losing control, from feelings about "possession" or the "blood tie", or from the existence of strong bonds with the children, was not clear. Probably all four played a part. Whatever the reason it led them to overcome the pain of visiting, and in some cases fight long legal battles or make strenuous efforts to improve their circumstances or behaviour to get the children back home.

Social workers by no means agreed about the weight to be placed on "birth identity", and for nineteen of the thirty four children the original plan was for them to stay in long term care. All those interviewed said that the most important factor was the ability of the parents to provide good enough care. However, the attitude of the social workers towards parental rights and the importance of birth identity indirectly influenced the likelihood of a child returning home, in that it influenced the decision about the level of care which would be considered "good enough". Social workers who considered birth identity to be important were more likely to help parents to overcome their sense of numbness and the pain of visiting, and more likely to offer emotional and practical support to enable the parents to improve the care they could offer to the children. The skill of the social workers in mobilising resources and in relating to parents was also important, but perhaps less so than the availability of the right placement in care.

Social worker "The attitude of the foster parents influences our decisions, because it influences the child's development. If the foster parents want to hang onto the child, and convey it to the child, inevitably if it goes on long enough you are influenced by the wishes of the child, and you stop thinking of him going home."

The brother of two of the children in the study who had gone home quite successfully remained in long term care with no contact with his natural family for this reason.

Social Work and Protection

Although there were criticisms to be made of the level of service offered before statutory action, and at the time of placement, once a decision had been made to work towards rehabilitation the parents were likely to be offered a skilled and dependable service. An analysis of the work of the social workers showed that a wide range of practical help, emotional support and, to a lesser extent, therapy was offered. The most difficult problem for the workers was to combine their protective role towards the children with their helping, caring, and sometimes parental role with the parents. Most managed to do so, but some clearly did not. Even those who had a good relationship with the parents tended to underestimate the importance given to their supervisory role, and the anger and resentment felt, even years after the event, about the statutory action which they or their colleagues took. Several writers (Baher, 1976; Kempe, 1972; Lynch, 1978) have discussed the extreme difficulty of relating to some abusing parents whose behaviour is characterised by a lack of trust, and the consequent need to be in control, and at the same time by infantile dependancy. Several of the most disturbed parents had left the home when the children returned, but in about half of the cases the parents needed, and the social workers tried to offer, the sort of nurturing relationship described by Baher (1976). The lack of suitable working conditions and back-up resources in a busy local authority department placed considerable stress on the workers, and increased the risk to the children.

Mother. "She is more or less like a mother to me, not a social worker. I can't talk to my mother like I talk to her. I can always look on her as someone to go to if I'm ever in trouble. Sometimes I go and she says she is too busy and I feel she is brushing me off. But she does care, I know that.

Social worker "Jim is at risk because of my lack of time. His mother knows I will try to be there if she really needs me. But sometimes she comes so often I have to tell her to go away. I'm afraid one day I will misjudge it."

The impact of the authority role of the social worker on those clients who needed to be in control led to "testing out" behaviour, such as threatening to remove a child from care, which needed particularly skilled handling. The timing of the return home of the children also placed stress on the social workers' relationships with such parents. Because of their strong identification with the parents, and the pressures placed upon them for the children to come home, most stressed the importance of good consultation from an experienced child care worker who was familiar with the case. In some cases the involvement of senior management or a case conference in the decision about return home reduced the stress on the social worker. In others delays caused by the attempt to eliminate all risk weakened the relationship between social worker and client at a time when it was most important, and arguably placed the child at even greater risk. Having decided that return home had a reasonable chance of providing the least detrimental alternative, social workers or case conferences sometimes demanded a pattern of behaviour and level of frustration tolerance which many more stable families would have found difficult. Clients were also well aware of recording, and the hierarchical nature of decision making, and this undermined in some cases their trust in the social worker. The right balance between the helpful sharing of responsibility and encouraging the professional autonomy essential for building up a trusting relationship is perhaps more difficult to achieve than has been recognised.

Mother. "It doesn't make sense. They are trying to help you. You tell them what is wrong. They go to somebody higher up that doesn't even know you and they start making orders above your head."

It is perhaps not surprising, that a substantial number of the parents, including some who spoke very highly of the social workers, were not prepared to be completely honest with them. This was especially so at the crucial stages just before and just after the children went home.

Stepmother. "She did play me up at first quite a lot. But I didn't feel able to be honest in case he would take her away."

In view of this it is disturbing that parents and social workers agreed that the service offered to the children was less than adequate in most, though not all cases. It seemed that the children were even less able than their parents to understand that the person who had taken them away was trying to help them.

Social worker. "After nearly a year at home, he barely manages to speak to me."

This lends support to the suggestion that for every child an adult should be identified who knows him well enough to detect signs of distress. This could be the family social worker, but if he is unable to play this role, a teacher, or health visitor, the residential worker or foster mother, or in some cases a friend or relative could do so, as they in fact did for some of the children in this study.

"THE LEAST DETRIMENTAL ALTERNATIVE"?

Although this was essentially a descriptive study some attempt was made to assess whether return home had offered the "least detrimental alternative". The crudest measure of success was whether the children were still at home at the time of interview. Children from eighteen of the families were at home, (though some had had brief spells, usually planned, back in care), those from four families were likely to stay in long term care, and those from three families would be returning home shortly. As these children were not selected on a random basis, the outcome of the placements of the fifty-nine children from whom they were selected was also examined, and 71% of those children were at home at the time of the study. Breakdown rates, however, are an unsatisfactory measure of "success", and an attempt was also made to assess the well-being of parents and children, and to compare the position with what it had been before court action. In assessing this the views of parents and social workers were sought, and for twelve children in the appropriate age range Rutter's scale A2 (Rutter, 1968) was used. Twelve of the children were thought to be slightly disturbed, and one seriously so. The majority of the parents, including some whose children were back in care, were thought to be emotionally and materially better off, and several commented that this was due to the help they had been given. Several of the children went through periods of severe "testing out" behaviour, but in no case was this the main reason for return to care. Only one ten year old child returned to care because he was again abused. Where children were thought to be worse off than before care, this was associated with the weakening of bonds for infants, especially with their fathers, and problems in care usually associated with having to cope with divided loyalties. The researcher estimated that there seemed a reasonable chance that twenty of the thirty-four children would grow up without further serious problems. Because of the stresses to which they had all been exposed it was unlikely that these children would be living completely trouble-free lives. In no case, however, was it clear that a child had been further damaged by the decision to allow him to go home. Even for those back in care long term plans had been made once the role which the parents could be expected to play had been clarified. All except one had the sense of identity which comes from being in regular contact with at least one parent, and only one was still in the sort of "limbo" described by Rowe (1973). It must, however, be said that on the evidence of parents themselves some of the children had been at risk in the early days of their return home. The study suggests ways in which the risk can be minimised, and especially points to the need to ensure that each child has a trusted adult to whom he can turn, and that the availability and working environment of social workers facilitates the provision of a dependable and skilled service to parents. Supportive resources must be more readily available, but perhaps most important of all is the need for a range of placements in care which will decrease rather than increase the stresses on the child.

CONCLUSION

Some children have returned home to their parents with tragic consequences. These thirty-four children went home and survived. How well they fared will not be known until they become parents themselves, but in the meantime more children will go home, and efforts must be made to improve the services available to them. It is hoped that this study will provide clues as to how this may be done.

REFERENCES

Aldgate, J. (1976) The Child in Care and His Parents. Adoption and Fostering, 2, 29-40

Baher, E., C. Hyman, C. Jones, R. Jones, A. Kerr, and R. Mitchell (1976) At Risk. Routledge & Kegan Paul, London.

Carter, J. (Ed.) (1974). The Maltreated Child. Priory Press, London.

Elmer, E. (1977). Follow-up study of Traumatised Children. The International Journal of Child Abuse & Neglect, Vol. 1, 105-109

George, V. (1970) Foster Care. Routledge & Kegan Paul, London.

Goldstein, J., A. Freud, and A.J. Solnit, (1973) Beyond the Best Interests of the Child, Collier-Macmillan, London.

Holman, R. (1973) Trading in Children. Routledge and Kegan Paul, London.

Holman, R. (1975 The Place of Fostering in Social Work. Brit. Journal of Social Work, Vol. 5 No. 1.

Jenkins, S. and E. Norman (1972). Filial Deprivation and Foster Care. Columbia University Press, New York.

Jones, C. O. (1978). The Predicament of Abused Children. In C.M. Lee (Ed.) Child Abuse. The Open University Press, Milton Keynes.

Kadushin, A. (1970) Adopting Older Children. Columbia University Press.

Kempe, C. H., and R. E. Helfer, (1972) Helping the Battered Child and his Family. Lippincott, Philadelphia.

Lynch, M. and J. Roberts (1978) Predisposing Factors within the Family. In V. Carver (Ed.) Child Abuse. Open University Press, Milton Keynes.

Rowe, J., and L. Lambert. (1973). Children Who Wait. Association of British Adoption Agencies London.

Rowe, J. (1977) Fostering in the Seventies. Adoption and Fostering Vol. 90 15-20.

Rutter, M. and P. Graham. (1968) The Reliability and Validity of the Psychiatric Assessment of the Child. British Journal of Psychiatry Vol. 114.

Thoburn, J. (1977) Who Goes Home? Unpublished Research Report for the Central Council for Education and Training in Social Work, London.

Thorpe, R. (1974). Mum and Mrs. So and So. Social Work Today, Vol. 4, No. 22.

Tizard, B. (1977). Adoption: A Second Chance. Open Books, London.

Winnicott, D. W. (1960) The Theory of the Parent Infant Relationship. In The Maturational Process and the Facilitating Environment. Hogarth Press. London.

Child Abuse and Neglect, Vol. 3, pp. 81 - 87.
Pergamon Press Ltd., 1979. Printed in Great Britain.

VIOLENCE IN COMMUNITY HOME SCHOOLS

Kenneth Hosie

Dartington Social Research Unit,
The Courtyard,
Dartington Hall,
Totnes,
Devon.

The investigation of violence in community home schools for boys undertaken by the Dartington Social Research Unit in 1974 had several aims. As so little was known about the extent and nature of aggressive behaviour among deprived and difficult children in residential institutions, we wished to establish some facts about violence in these schools. Concern was being expressed about the so-called 'rising tide of violence' which, it seemed, had attained a cyclical peak and pressure for an expansion of secure facilities for problem children was growing. Our interest in the subject was not new for as early as 1968, when we began our research into the old approved school system, the Heads' Association had just written to the Home Secretary urging decisive action to save their schools from disruption by violent inmates. More recently, we have completed a study of secure treatment settings in the child care system and the discussions of the presenting characteristics of candidates for closed units incorporate some of our researches into violence in residential institutions.

The main focus of interest in this investigation of violence in community home schools (now called CHE's) was the aggressive boy who, in a residential context, is generally viewed as the abuser rather than the abused. This is a somewhat different perspective from that of this conference but, during the course of our studies, we gained considerable insight into the nature and extent of violence offered by, as well as to, children and I hope you will find these thoughts relevant to your present discussions.

Problems of Evidence and Definition. An initial problem in our study of violence stems from the difficulties in using documentary evidence from residential schools but this is not because material is supressed or unavailable. On the contrary, violent incidents, when they occur,are reported at length to case conferences or in boys' records. However, such accounts are not written with research in mind, thus the actual details of any violent incident become difficult to unravel. This is important because when we set out to measure violence, we largely find the situations we look for. It is interesting that staff anxiety over violent adolescents which we shall shortly illustrate, bears little relation to the actual levels of violence in the institution. There were several CHE's in our research where staff frequently hit children and where the formal punishment records underestimated the number of violent situations that occurred but which, nevertheless, were quite happy with their levels of violence. No one seemed particularly anxious in this rumbustious environment, except possibly a visitor, and in such establishments violence was not defined as a problem.

In contrast, in several cosy family group CHE's for younger children, where staff were particularly sensitive to boys' needs, violent behaviour was often viewed as a major concern. Staff complained that children swore, that they hit each other, that they damaged property or were noisy and defiant. In contrast, staff perspectives in more permissive regimes are quite different. In such contexts, violence is frequently defined as acting-out behaviour and perceived in a way that is very different from that found in more rigid regimes such as those for boys of senior age. Thus,with all these real problems in the way of any investigation into violence among adolescents in residential schools, it is not surprising that so little empirical research has been undertaken.

Despite these research problems. we had gathered considerable material during our previous researches into seventeen boys' approved schools. We had complete case histories of the 1,120 boys in them and more recently we had been closely studying four community homes with education as they made major changes in their regimes. So, notwithstanding all these deficiencies in approaching the number and nature of violent incidents in residential schools for young offenders, we made the following explorations.

We chose to define violence as "the use of force in a social situation in a way that those in power define as illegitimate". In a school situation, it is usually the headmaster and staff, the power holders, that define the sorts of force that are forbidden. In most schools physical attack of boy on boy, of boy on staff or of staff on boy are all areas that are defined as being unacceptable. But, as we come to examine these situations, there are many problems.

This institutional perspective fails to distinguish affective, that is where aggression takes place between parties with reciprocating emotional ties, and non-affective violence, a difference which is often clearly made by participants. It is also very difficult to get a reliable set of figures for attacks of boy on boy in schools. Serious attacks which precipitate other crises, such as absconding or which demand medical attention, are entered up with more reliability than others where there are no such effects. The actual dynamics of the boy-boy incident are difficult to follow, however, and all that is clear is that some violence occurred. Much more reliable are the figures and descriptions of boys' attacks on staff in residential institutions. Any striking of staff by a boy, even if a relatively minor incident, is carefully recorded. In therapeutic communities too,you find this pattern is adhered to, even though the interpretation that is given to the aggression is rather different. Careful reporting probably springs from the fact that such behaviour is viewed as having serious prognosis implications for the offender.

However, in one area, where violence is offered by staff to children, we suspect that the reporting is deficient. This is not only because it rests with staff themselves to make uncomplimentary reports on their own actions, but also because much of the violence that we as adults offer to children - the vigorous shove, the shaking of a little boy, the grabbing by the scruff of the neck and frequently the clout - are not perceived by us as violence. This supported by the fact that every report we found in the CHE's of assaults of staff on boys seemed to have come to light as the result of some subsequent action on the part of the child. For example, he has absconded, he has refused to go into the class or workshop or, of course, he has retaliated. In the school's subsequent investigation of these incidents, the initial involvement of the member of staff comes to light.

Differences in the levels of violence. The first thing that became apparent when we looked at the seventeen boys' approved schools was that levels of violence differed considerably between each of the age groups and between individual schools. Also, the number of recorded incidents did not correspond in any direct way to concern expressed by staff over boys' violence or to boys' aggressive histories. It was clear that the schools themselves greatly influenced the amount of violence they experienced. Using material gathered during our general survey, we compared three contrasting aspects of violent behaviour in these residential communities:the concern about troublesome behaviour expressed by 187 staff during interviews, the proportion of boys defined as violent or aggressive during assessment and, thirdly, the number of violent incidents of all kinds recorded in school records.

The greatest discrepancies between the three aspects we have described were found among the schools for junior boys aged 10-13. Although we found that juniors were twice as likely as others to be labelled violent or aggressive, both staff concern about young boys' behaviour and the recorded levels of violence in junior schools were low. But, as the boys grew older, the correlations between staff concern, the number of incidents and the proportion of boys with aggressive histories increased. Staff attached little significance to violent behaviour among younger children and many outbursts probably passed unrecorded but, as the boys grew older, adult concern increased. An initial assessment or reputation for aggression led staff to be more cautious and, consequently, more conscientious in recording violent outbursts. Hence, the schools for older boys appeared to be more violent, particularly in incidents involving staff.

This evidence provides an example of the ways in which ideas on violence reflect people's underlying fear and insecurities rather than reality. Adult anxiety seemed quite unrelated either to the actual number of incidents or to children's potential for aggression. Powerful stereotypes appear to be operating in these situations and, as we shall see, these perspectives are fashioned by institutional regimes and social climates. Parallels can be drawn in the context of the family where rearing practices are passed on from parent to offspring and where perceptions of paternal and maternal roles are transferred from one generation to another.

Institutional regimes also seem to have an influence on violence. In the schools we looked at, the more relaxed the regime, the greater the incidence of aggressive behaviour of all sorts. But, the number of serious incidents is so small as to make such comparisons unreliable and it certainly does not follow that violent environments are necessarily anarchic or threatening to staff.

These changing patterns of violence can be more clearly seen if we look more closely at four CHE's which we have studied during the past three years. These establishments have all moved towards more open flexible structures, offering care in small groups and have abandoned all the training structure of the orthodox approved school which they had operated previously. All of these establishments display some increase in the levels of violence during the changes but the rates for recorded incidents per boy are still very small and vary widely, so that one CHE still has a rate four times greater than the others.

If we look more closely at a typical community home sheltering boys in their mid-teens, we note that, despite the increase mentioned, serious incidents of violence are few and far between and that almost three-quarters of the incidents recorded are boy-boy assaults. In a three year period between 1972 and 1974, boys hit staff on only eleven occasions. In those three years, nearly 120 boys will have been in the school, so the frequency of assaults on staff works out at one incident in every 3 months. This pattern is repeated in the other schools and hardly corroborates popular ideas of a surging tide of violence in residential establishments. Even in secure child care establishments where regular outbursts of aggression might be expected, violence was rare. For example, there were in the first 3 years at one unit, only 79 violent incidents in a period equivalent to 714 boy months. What is more, only 21 of these assaults involved staff and all this during an unsettled period when routines were being established. These findings are important because assaults on staff are the most likely of all violent acts to be systematically recorded and attacks of this sort question the way in which the aggressor should be approached in the future. Such infrequent incidents are hardly what the heads of the old approved schools had in mind when they wrote to the Home Office in 1968 expressing concern about violence. More perturbing than all this and most certainly what staff did not suspect are the greater number of incidents of staff hitting boys which appears from our evidence, especially as the notification of such incidents is very likely to be an underestimate of the truth.

Our findings about staff violence to children, it must be stressed, only apply to long term treatment establishments and not to short term assessment or remand institutions where the situation is rather different. The brief stay of the children, rather than the nature of the regime seems to account for the very high levels of non-affective violence observed in these places. Among the CHE's, we had found a clear relationships between rates of premature transfer and levels of recorded violence and this would suggest that the roots of this aggression, as with many cases of non-accidental injury within the family, lie mostly in the tenuousness of the relationships between the parties involved. Residential assessment and remand facilities are, by their nature, characterised by a shifting population whose stay is very short and who have little opportunity to develop relationships. This hypothesis is also supported by Prison Department statistics which reveal that the most violent penal establishments are not those providing long stay maximum security for serious offenders but are the remand and detention facilities, especially junior detention centres where the length of stay is shortest.

Violent behaviour in residential establishments also appears to be cyclical. Because there are so very few serious incidents it is difficult to talk of cycles, but offences do seem to cluster, mainly between home leaves. It is also noteworthy that the boy-boy incidents seem to cluster in senior establishments with changes in the leading group. There is also some evidence from our study of our 4 CHE's over time that violence is increasing. The number of incidents seems to have doubled over a couple of years and, although earlier figures are less reliable, 1974 rates seem to be about three times those of 1969, even when we take into account fluctuations in school populations. It is probably this rate of increase in violence that has alarmed the headmasters and staff of residential establishments rather than the actual levels but, again, it must be emphasised that very few of these incidents are serious and almost all the increase has been in violence between the boys. In any case, we should be mindful of the fact that increasingly difficult behaviour does not correspond with a greater high risk clientele.

Characteristics of violent boys. One of the tasks we faced with the 1,120 boys in our earlier studies of the approved schools was to decide which types of boy were being admitted to each of the schools. Those schools that took second-time-round offenders or the more disturbed children could hardly be expected to be as successful as those that were taking tranquil boys who were new to the residential experience. For each boy in our study, 41 characteristics were relentlessly plotted, ranging from early separation from parents to aspects of personality, intelligence and educational attainments. This is a common technique when approaching such a research problem and by a process of multi-correlation, we are able to see which types of boy have a history of being actively involved in at least one violent act during their stay.

From these correlations, we learn that boys who are violent in their community homes are more likely to be less intelligent than others, to have spent long periods in residential care and to come from families which have other violent members, particularly the father. Paternal absence seems to affect boys more than girls, making the boys less aggressive when young but more violent during adolescence. It has also been demonstrated that those parents who condone violence, who are violent themselves or who reward aggression, are more likely to have aggressive children. Parental discipline will have been fitful. The boy's father in particular will have been ambivalent in his attitude towards his sons, a point corroborated by the fact that aggressive examples are very likely to be copied by boys if violence is seen to be rewarded or goes unpunished. There is also a suggestion that institutionalised boys and those with low self-esteem are particularly prone to this sort of modelling. There were, however, no significant differences between the backgrounds of the boys and girls who were the aggressors and those who were the victims.

Correlations are also clear between violence in adolescence and boys displaying difficult behaviour from an early age, many of whom have been noted as being highly aggressive during their primary education. While such lads are clearly subject to the influence of 'labelling' it does seem that boys who have been violent before are expected by staff to be violent again and so frequently are. Almost half the boys concerned in violent incidents in one of the CHE's we studied had been previously involved more than once, suggesting that expectations can render conflict more likely and more fierce.

Unfortunately, it is not possible to trace the parallel violent histories of adults in the institutions, although there is considerable evidence that certain staff are more likely to be involved in violent acts than others. Here again, there are parallels with N-A.I.C. in the community where research has indicated that the abused and abuser often have similar distinguishing personal and social characteristics that interact to produce violence. High risk individuals and families tend to bear high risk progeny.

I would suggest that in a similar way we can identify high risk institutions which, as they fail to act as therapeutic environments, pass on their difficult inmates to a set of equally ineffective establishments which can be observed as being bedevilled by problems. In our investigations of absconding from CHE's, for example, we found a similar pattern. Boys with histories of absconding were usually transferred to institutions with even higher rates of running away. But, while we were able to conclude that high absconding was always an indication of an ineffective regime, in the case of violence, the situation is rather more complex. We found that aggressive boys, like the absconders, were transferred to institutions with even higher levels of staff-boy and boy-boy violence but that this transfer only aggravated aggressive behaviour where the increased violence did not stem from greater emphasis on relationships and small group work and when the violence itself was of a non-affective kind. When this was the case, high levels of recorded violence were found to be associated with high rates for transfer and staff turnover and with low staff morale and these CHE's also had few trained staff and displayed high levels of absconding.

Group Violence.

Occasionally in residential institutions, violent outbursts involve large numbers of people. We can add little to what has already been written on group violence because, thankfully, no riots marred our many visits to these institutions. However, it is worth considering Clarke and Sinclair's valuable review of the available literature on violence as so much that they suggest is supported by our own work on school regimes (1). They comment that "the likelihood of a riot is increased by such factors as the admission of new disruptive residents or the discharging of old stabilising ones, the formation of cliques of difficult residents and the existence of grievances among them. Such patterns are accompanied by a lack of communication between residents and staff which makes it difficult for grievances to be dealt with and which grow worse as the trouble begins. The two groups, staff and inmates, grow apart in mutual hostility. The riots frequently take place during a change from a strict to a more permissive regime and may be triggered off by the staff disunity which often accompanies these changes". They comment that the reports of disturbances at Carlton and Standon Farm schools revealed similar tensions, "the existence of boredom, a wide-spread sense of grievance, the presence of a number of difficult boys, poor communications between boys and staff and among the staff themselves, the undermining of staff authority and the absence of key staff at crisis moments". Here again, we see from another course the role of the institution being stressed and that the context has to be right for confrontation.

Wider Perspectives on Adolescent Violence. A good deal more can be learned about adolescent violence than that simply afforded by the statistics we have accumulated. These can be studied in greater detail elsewhere (2). First of all, it is clear from a careful examination of staff-boy conflicts that almost all are entirely avoidable. Unfortunately, it seems that few staff have had even the simplest instructions on how take preventive action. Frequently, they hasten into confrontation situations in which neither staff nor boy feels he can back down without significant loss of face. Such confrontation often takes place in group situations where the esteem of others will be lost by backing down and, inevitably, the chances of an aggressive response are heightened.

Stress on the need for such awareness on the part of staff is reinforced by the fact that in those incidents where staff hit boys, over half the boys involved had violent histories. The staff had quite clearly set up the situation in two-thirds of the incidents and were the ones who hit first. Yet, people can be trained to avoid these situations, either by side-stepping the confrontation or by meeting it in much the same way as violent patients are contained in mental hospitals. It is an unfortunate fact that few of these strategies ever form part of the courses offered to students for posts in schools or residential homes.

Particularly interesting also is the whole area of the relationship between the hitter and the hit. It is not necessarily one of constant and mutual hostility. Most aggression in CHE's is affective, part of an on-going friendship and only in rare cases is it the result of carefully nurtured hostility or indifference. We undertook a number of sociometric studies during our studies of community homes to contrast the friendship patterns between block institutions and those which emphasised small group settings in house units. Not only did highly aggressive boys have a wider friendship network but they were more likely to be involved in conflict with their reciprocating friends. It seems that signals between boys in paired or triangular relationships are often misinterpreted and a fight ensues but this violence is not damaging to the institution and probably reflects the stress put on fostering warm relationships.

It can be hypothesised that, in the light of these relationships, there may be links between sexual and violent behaviour among adolescent boys. We have noted that violent boys have not only suffered from the absence of father but also spent a long time in institutional care. This poses them with considerable identity problems, particularly those of sexual identity. We also know that single sex communities tend to engender anxiety over masculinity. This problem is aggravated for the young offenders by the fact that they are bound by strong and pervasive norms on what constitutes masculine behaviour. This does not imply that these boys hasten into earrings and keep their high-heeled shoes under the bed - indeed, the situation might be less fraught if they did - but it does mean that in residential settings, boys' masculine self-image is constantly being threatened by what they feel about other people and what other people feel about them. They and their schools have developed none of the mechanisms which abound in more esteemed residential settings and which release or displace such anxieties. Consequently, young offenders will be more difficult and allay their tensions by overtly masculine display of which aggressive, violent behaviour is the most immediate, as well as being an unmistakeable badge of courage.

In a modified way some of these identity problems must affect male staff and would explain why women, on those rare occasions they are allowed to intervene, seem so much more successful in handling boys' aggressive outbursts than are men. In co-educational settings it is noticeable that whatever problems may abound, the aggressive behaviour of boys and the belligerent stance of male staff is much reduced.

Cultural Perspectives on Violence. The interpretation which we put on aggressive behaviour differs not only with age but with social class. Generally, juvenile aggression is concerned with establishing position and forming relationships. Fights between juveniles are highly ritualised and do very little damage. They are an exciting, enjoyable experience which gains attention, informal status and, frequently, the bonus of adult disapproval. This is particularly true of working class adolescents whose vehicles for aggression are more limited than their contemporaries in a higher social class. In the outside world, the football excursion and the motor bike offer some chances for aggressive working class youths to explode but, for children in residential care, opportunities are much more restricted. It is interesting to contrast the CHE's with independent boarding schools. Not only are the latter highly aggressive places but their release mechanisms are also intrinsic to their functions. The relentless competition, the myriad of status positions, fierce and particular loyalties and monastic isolation all create antagonism and conflict. Of course, such aggression is highly creative. Sporting, cultural, social, academic and even spiritual arenas abound where the drive, iconoclasm, hostility and brimming resentment of adolescents can find expression.

However, the problem of adolescent aggression is not simply one of cultural relativism and some comment is necessary on the rate of increase of reported violent incidents in residential settings. Actual violence levels are not yet large but, if present trends continue, they could become worrying as they will increase demands for secure accommodation.

Future Trends in Violence. Our own studies and much other research would suggest that violence increases in the institution when the stability of the inmate and staff informal world is either threatened or absent. When radical changes in roles, perceptions and relationships are demanded, considerable disruptions result. This is why moves towards a more benevolent regime, such as the introduction of pastoral staff, changes in control or the release of informal leaders, all of which may be ameliorative, can initiate unrest.

In times of change the many components of an institution do not necessarily change at the same rate and this can lead to a state of confusion among staff and children. For example, the norms of one sub-unit such as the residential house may conflict with the expectations of educational facilities. The frustrations arising from this state of anomie, when the normative demands of particular sub-systems are dissonant from those of the wider institution, can provoke aggressive outbursts. This means that all changes in institutions, however immediately benevolent they may be, need very careful engineering, especially as disruptive behaviour by adolescents following liberal innovations not only strengthens the hand of those who dismiss change as permissive but also saps the confidence of radical staff. Critics perhaps fail to realise that it is just as likely that change in a more custodial direction would have produced similar tremors of boy dissatisfaction. Whatever the views of staff, it is clear that recent changes in the aims, administration, staffing patterns, accommodation and clientele that have faced CHE's must be partly responsible for the increasing conflict that is reported.

While disturbances are usually short-lived, there is evidence which would suggest that moves towards more benign regimes in a wide variety of residential schools, not only the community homes, have been accompanied by an increase in reported physical violence and disruptive behaviour. However, as we have seen, most of the increase is in affective violence which does not challenge institutional aims. A number of explanations for this offer themselves. In settings where close relationships are encouraged between children and staff and where affective displays and involvement are mutually cherished, those sharing a relationship will have a strong interest in knowing all the activities of each other. With such boys as those sheltered by the community homes, whose vulnerability, emotional deprivation and difficulties in relationships have been relentlessly chronicled elsewhere, the competition and jealousy over the attention of caring adults must add yet another dimension to unrest.

Residential institutions differ from schools in the outside world in that such boy-boy and boy-staff relationships are public and their development scrutinised by all. Boys become jealous of their friends' involvements with others and also of the affections of staff. The widespread and successful efforts to bring about closer relationships between boys and between staff and children in community homes through small group living and working situations, must be related to the increase on conflict. It accounts for the frequency of violence which we have already noted as being between reciprocating friends. It would seem reasonable to suggest that in those situations where adolescents are kept longer under scrutiny than ever before, such as in day schools, youth clubs and residential schools, where adolescents are maturing earlier and where children are encouraged to be open and communicative about their feelings, aggressive behaviour of an affective kind must increase.

All this would imply that while violence to us may appear wanton, motiveless and spasmodic, it is none of these things. For the participants conflict is logical, frequently moral and often fulfilling. In fact, it is the essential logic of much adolescent violence that should give us the greatest encouragement. If it is a response to demanding social situations rather than an uncontrolled drive, then youthful aggressions can be checked and confrontation can be manipulated by adults.

Although the main focus of this paper has been the aggressive adolescent in CHE's, there are one or two conclusions that have a bearing on our general understanding of violence in institutions. Firstly, serious incidents are not common,attacks on staff or by staff are rare and staff are as likely to initiate aggressive confrontations as are boys. As with N-A.I.C., there is often a complex interaction between aggressor and victim. In institutions with continually shifting populations or where staff are inexperienced and untrained, non-affective conflicts are more likely to occur. Changes towards a more benign, psychotherapeutic regime in CHE's are also likely to raise levels of aggression but this must not be interpreted as a threat to institutional stability or as an index of ineffectiveness. We would suggest that only repeated and extreme violence of a non-affective type and where physical harm is inflicted need raise doubts about the viability of an institution and create the issue of transferring inmates to more custodial settings.

Finally, there may well be a case for an 'at risk' register for institutions where, as with families or children, certain characteristics are used to predict possible problems. Factors such as high turnover of staff and children, high absconding rates, high levels of transfer, high failure rates, low staff morale, low proportions of trained or experienced staff and high levels of non-affective violence could be used to identify a residential institution in distress and indicate where child abuse is likely to occur. There are, of course, dangers in this suggestion for, as with violent families, one can end up finding what one looks for or merely chart situations that are the most apparent. The fact that social classes IV and V of the population are over-represented in most analyses of child abuse does not mean that we should restrict our concerns to these groups. Similarly, in institutional contexts, we must be aware of the dangers of studying what is most apparent or obvious. It is all too easy to ignore the more subtle and less visible forms of violence that occur in unexpected contexts. Far from being the genesis of a problem, violence is nearly always a symptom of other factors and we have suggested that these must not always be viewed as undesirable. When looking at violence in institutions, it is important not to concentrate on the violence alone for an institution that abuses its children, like a parent, is in clear need of help in a much wider range of areas.

References.

1. R.V.G.Clarke and I. A.C.Sinclair, Literature Survey on Aggression. Unpublished survey, Home Office Research Unit, 1970.

2. The full report of the research on which this paper is based can be found in S.Millham, R.Bullock and K. Hosie, 'On Violence in Community Homes', in N. Tutt (ed.), Violence, London, H.M.S.O. 1976, pp.126 - 65.

Child Abuse and Neglect, Vol. 3, pp. 89 - 92.
Pergamon Press Ltd., 1979. Printed in Great Britain.

THE NEGLECT OF CHILDREN IN LONG-STAY HOSPITALS

Maureen Oswin

U.K.

More than 6000 handicapped children in England and Wales are living permanently in National Health Service hospitals. Just under 5000 are in mental handicap hospitals and about 1500 are in other types of hospitals.

The children are handicapped by a variety of mental and/or physical disabilities caused by such conditions as cerebral palsy, muscular dystrophy and spinal diseases; some have irreversible brain damage caused by illnesses, accidents or physical abuse. The majority of these children are living in institutions because the community is unable, or unwilling, to provide them and their parents with the support that they need; for example, some handicapped children may actually spend a childhood in a mental handicap hospital simply because their families have housing needs which are not being met by the local authority. Some children live in long-stay hospitals because their parents are ill, or dead, and the local Children's Home will not accept handicapped children.

Society accepts the institutionalisation of more than 6000 handicapped children because, in the United Kingdom, there has long been a tradition that dependent people such as the elderly, the mentally ill, the mentally handicapped and the physically disabled should live apart from the rest of society. It is difficult to break down this tradition of putting people into institutions, and, although there has been some progress made in the development of community care in the last twenty years, all sorts of excuses are still being found to delay the widespread development of community care.

One excuse is built around the idea that severely handicapped children need some sort of medical and nursing care that they will only get if they live in a hospital. But how true is this?

My own studies (1, 2) show that if multiple-handicapped children live permanently in hospital they are likely to suffer from physical and emotional neglect that may be so serious that their handicaps will be *increased* rather than *alleviated*. In view of this I would go so far as to describe the child in a long-stay hospital as a child who is *abused by society*. He is abused by society because society too easily accepts the institutionalisation of handicapped children.

His social abuse has three major facets:

First: he is deprived of ordinary childhood experiences when he lives in a long-stay hospital;

Second: he is likely to suffer physical neglect in a long-stay hospital;

Third: he is likely to be emotionally deprived when he lives in a long-stay hospital.

Let us look more closely at these three facets of childhood institutionalisation:

First: his deprivation of ordinary childhood experiences. It does not require much stretch of the imagination to realise that if a handicapped child lives in a hospital he cannot enjoy ordinary neighbourhood or family-type experiences, such as going to the local supermarket, having a bus or train ride, playing in a small garden whilst his parents plant seeds or dig, or watching his parents wash clothes, iron, sew, do the housework.

Hospitalised children never experience that most normal of childhood experiences — hearing their mum talk to another mum over the garden fence. They do not have any opportunities to make a relationship with a grandparent or a baby brother or sister, or an uncle or auntie.

They may never enter a kitchen and see a meal being cooked, because their food in the hospital is always pre-cooked in a central kitchen and then delivered to the ward in a trolley. So, the children never see potatoes peeled or cakes made or a joint of meat carved or pastry being rolled. They will only experience these things if an enterprising member of the teaching or nursing staff makes a special arrangement for these simple home-making tasks to take place in the ward, as a special treat.

When I was working as a teacher in a long-stay hospital during the years 1959-1974 I tried to create the sort of homely situation that the children needed by taking them down to the local shops outside the hospital gates to buy a few potatoes to take back to the ward to peel and cook on a little cooker which I had fixed in the classroom. We would also buy buns and toast them, and grill sausages. And we mixed pastry and boiled eggs.

The children were always very interested and excited about doing these things, because it was a novelty to them and they enjoyed the experience. But my attempt to make a home life in the ward classroom was really a very poor substitute for the real thing.

Official visitors would sometimes come around the hospital and say how marvellous it was of the staff to do all these things. But, to be honest, I felt that what we were doing was not marvellous at all, but only a rather pathetic attempt to compensate the children for their loss of normal childhood experiences. No matter what we did, we would never have been able to make up for their loss of ordinary family life, which they were denied through having to live in hospital.

My second point was: he is likely to suffer physical neglect in a long-stay hospital. This may seem a strange statement, for one assumes that a child in hospital will at least get his physical needs met, even if he is deprived of ordinary childhood experiences. However, this may not be so; it is common knowledge that long-stay hospitals in the United Kingdom are very short of specialist staff such as physiotherapists, speech therapists and paediatric occupational therapists. The result of these shortages means that children who have physical disabilities caused by cerebral palsy and allied conditions are at risk to increased disability and even serious deformities.

The research that I did from 1975 to 1977 (2) which looked at the care of 223 multiple-handicapped children living in mental handicap hospitals, showed that only 75 of the 223 children were receiving physiotherapy, and none had speech therapy and none had the advice of paediatric occupational therapists.

As a result of that neglect there were some horrifying incidences of deformities. For example, I visited one ward where there were 26 children, 21 of whom had been admitted before the age of four years old. Nineteen of the 26 children had already been in the hospital for more than ten years. The children of that ward had never received regular physiotherapy, and, indeed, there was no therapist employed in the hospital at the time I visited and there had not been one for more than a year.

My personal (unpublished) notes for that particular ward are as follows:

> "1975. X Ward: Y Hospital: The children are so physically deformed that they are difficult to dress and feed. Some of them, especially Ivor, Margaret and Bill, are grossly twisted to one side, and their legs and arms are contracted up, their wrists and hands bent in the opposite direction, and their legs scissored. After years of lying on one side they must now *always* be on that side as their limbs are bent that way like the roots of a tree that deform themselves against a wall. Even their faces are squashed, on the side they have always lain on. It is a terrible indictment of medical neglect: Ivor has lived in the hospital for 11 years, Margaret for 13 years, and Bill for 12 years; they are still under 16 years of age.
>
> I cannot see that these children have ever received any physiotherapy or orthopaedic care ... When these deformed children are undressed it is difficult to see where their ribs end and their hips begin. Putting a pair of pants on them is a major task ... so severe is their scoliosis that it is difficult to put their dresses and shirts on. Poor Margaret,

now bent for ever into this screwed-up, lying-sideways position, she can only look up at us with her left eye... She is a beautiful child ... and aware of what is going on, although so handicapped..."

When that sort of physical neglect occurs in National Health Service Hospitals I think that it can justifiably be called *public abuse*, for it is, indeed, a social disgrace that the public show such little concern for these children who start life at a disadvantage because they are handicapped and are then caused further handicaps because society chooses to "put them away" in hospitals that lack specialist staff to help their conditions.

My third point was that a child in a long-stay hospital is likely to be emotionally deprived. What does this rather vague statement mean? It simply means that children in long-stay wards are deprived of mothering attention from their staff, such as cuddles, play, talking to. They are deprived of mothering care because their hospitals are understaffed and there are many changes of staff, and this makes it very difficult for ward staff to develop good close loving relationships with the children.

In the recent research that I referred to earlier I often went into wards where there were 30 children and only three staff, or 20 children and only two staff. Sometimes I would find one nurse working for 12 hours a day looking after 15 very helpless spastic children with the help of perhaps only one unqualified student aged about 18. In some hospitals there were so many changes of staff that the nurse on duty did not know the names of the children she would be putting to bed.

Under these conditions it was impossible for the staff to give the children all the love and mothering that they needed. The ward staff were aware that they could not meet the children's needs for mothering, and many of them felt very depressed about the situation. And the children were likely to suffer great personal loneliness, although they were living in what looked like busy wards.

After many months observing the amount of attention received by the children I found that a multiple-handicapped child who lives in a long-stay ward can expect to receive an average of only five minutes, mothering attention in every 10 hours of the day.

The children in my research study often sat for seven, eight, nine hours a day, totally ignored except when they needed to be washed and fed and changed.

Some of these very lonely children just sat playing with their hands. Others sat motionless. Some developed bizarre habits of self-stimulation to compensate for their boredom, such as dribbling on their hands and clapping them together.

Fourteen year old Sally, who had been in hospital for 11 years, would spend most of the day chewing the straps of her wheel-chair. One afternoon she spent six hours and fifty minutes sucking these straps, and nobody spoke to her or touched her during that time.

We have now looked briefly at the three damaging aspects of childhood institutionalisation that I listed at the beginning of this paper, which were:

1. Children living in long-stay hospitals are deprived of ordinary childhood experiences.

2. They are likely to suffer physical neglect.

3. They are likely to be emotionally deprived.

This now brings me to a final question: how can any responsible modern society that professes to care about its children continue to let handicapped children live in long-stay hospitals when it is *known* that they are likely to be neglected in such places? We have 6000 children in this situation in England and Wales; what happens in other countries? Are there thousands of handicapped children suffering similar childhood deprivations in institutions in France, U.S.A., Germany, Russia, Japan, Holland?

I would like to close with a reference to one particular child; perhaps her story may illustrate my point that society has a responsibility to see that handicapped children do not live for ever in institutions.

Thirteen-year-old Dorothy was only 18 months old when her father abused her, causing her to suffer multiple injuries. Dorothy was admitted to the General Hospital in need of urgent treatment. She remained in the children's ward for many months and received expert care for her injuries, and eventually it became obvious that she would survive the assault. She would, however, be permanently brain-damaged and physically and mentally handicapped for the rest of her life.

When Dorothy was two years old she no longer needed treatment in the General Hospital. She now needed a family, a caring home, and regular physiotherapy for her physical disabilities. The local Children's Home, however, would not accept handicapped children, so Dorothy was transferred to the mental handicap hospital for long-term care and put into a ward for spastic children. She has now been there for more than 11 years.

In her ward there are 20 other multiple-handicapped children, some of whom were brain-damaged at birth; others were handicapped through rubella, and some were handicapped by road accidents or childhood illnesses such as measles. All the children are there for long-term care, because their families cannot manage without some support and help and because there are no places for them in Children's Homes in the community.

Dorothy's parents were prosecuted for abusing her, and her father then served a term of imprisonment. After the trial, with its public chastisement of the mother and the subsequent imprisonment of the father for this act of violence to Dorothy, the case appeared to have been neatly tied up. Justice was seen to be done — Dorothy was now being safely cared for in the mental handicap hospital and all self-righteous members of society felt that they could heave a sigh of relief.

But I would ask you, who is the most guilty of abuse and neglect: the father who batters his child in a fit of anger caused perhaps by mental illness, marital stress, drink or intolerable poverty, or the society which then sits complacently by and lets that disabled child go and live for the rest of her life in an understaffed and underfinanced institution?

When Dorothy entered the mental handicap hospital for permanent care all those years ago she was ensured of a roof over her head, she would be dressed, fed, and kept warm. Nobody in the hospital would be cruel to her. But, she *would* suffer from the abuses which are inseparable from institutionalisation — those abuses which I have described in this paper as "social abuses": a lack of ordinary childhood experiences, a lack of therapy for her disabilities and a lack of mothering.

Dorothy is only one amongst the 6000 handicapped children now living in long-stay hospitals in this country. Unless there are some radical reforms to prevent the future institutionalisation of handicapped children, then I am afraid that Dorothy and her 6000 contemporaries will continue to suffer the abuse of an uncaring society which condones the "putting away" of handicapped children.

REFERENCES

1. *The Empty Hours*, Maureen Oswin (1971), Allen Lane.

2. *Children Living in Long-stay Hospitals*, Maureen Oswin (1978), Heinemann Medical Books.

Child Abuse and Neglect, Vol. 3, pp. 93 - 97.
Pergamon Press Ltd., 1979. Printed in Great Britain.

CHILDREN'S RIGHTS AND PARENTS' RIGHTS IN CHILD ABUSE: NEW DIAGNOSTIC PROBLEMS

Irwin E. Redlener, M.D.
Department of Pediatrics*
University of Miami School of Medicine
Miami, Florida 33152, U.S.A.

Parenting embraces a variety of styles almost as wide as the range of human behavior itself. A person ultimately parents according to the dictates and limits of his or her personality, intellect, family traditions and cultural background. But any number of individual variations of parenting approaches may yield well-adjusted children who grow up to be happy and productive adults. On the other hand, over the past twenty years we have become increasingly aware of certain disorders of the parenting process which have lead to considerable societal concern. These disorders have been variously termed the battered child syndrome, the maltreated child, non-accidental injury, trauma-x, child abuse and neglect and so forth. Lately, those terms which have a mostly physical connotation (e.g. the battered child) are seen as inadequate to describe the entire problem. It is clear that physical abuse is only one manifestation of a vast complex of parenting disorders that also include emotional and verbal abuse, neglect of various sorts and sexual abuse.

Observing the behavior of parents toward their children can be an enlightening process. A parent can be minimally verbal yet notably affectionate and supportive of his or her child. Another parent can verbalize affection but demonstrate hostility and anger. One parent can utilize a judicious slap on the backside to emphasize a point about not walking into the street while another parent's lack of self-control turns a mild spanking into a violent outburst of rage.

Identifying child abuse can be seen as a process functioning simultaneously on several different levels. Ultimately, we want to determine if a particular caretaker has behaved in a way that would be considered outside the acceptable range of parenting for a given society. In addition, however, we are looking to see if the child has suffered as a result of the inadequate parenting. For example, in the case of physical abuse we see a child with some set of injuries and attempt to determine if these were accidental or not. If not accidental, we attempt to link these injuries with potentially negative aspects of the parenting process. If this relationship can be established we presume that the child has been abused or neglected by the parent. The presumption is therefore based upon the parent's behavior as well as the effect of this behavior upon the child.

The process for determining the presence of maltreatment cannot function unless one accepts two principles. First, any child has the inherent right to live in safety and without threat of intentional injury or significant deprivation. Second, the right of an adult to express and exhibit individual modalities of parenting does not supersede the basic rights of the child as stated in the first principle. Unfortunately, there are few universally accepted limits of parenting and little agreement about what inherent rights, if any, children possess.

On the other hand, there are certain parental behaviors which are considered by most standards to be clearly unacceptable. Gross, uninhibited violence toward children as well as sexual molestation or starvation is often dealt with most harshly by society. However, the problems

---

*Current Affiliation: Department of Pediatrics, Albert Einstein College of Medicine, Bronx, New York 10461, U.S.A.

of identifying aberrant parenting behavior relate to a vast grey zone which hovers between the clearly acceptable and the clearly unacceptable. It is the interface between physical discipline and abuse, between affection and fondling and between verbal reprimand and emotional deprecation which is so very difficult to delineate. This grey zone has great importance. The better we are able to differentiate between reasonable and unreasonable parenting, the greater will be the likelihood of making early determinations of intra-familial dysfunction. The earlier this determination can be made, the better we can prevent serious abuse and neglect and the more enhanced will be our potential for preserving the integrity of the families involved.

ESTABLISHING GUIDELINES

The guidelines for making the determination of either the child abuse/neglect syndrome or a family in need of intervention usually requires an appraisal from two perspectives: parent and child. Sometimes a unidirectional approach will suffice to make a determination. For example, a mother hostily rejecting a newborn infant is clearly in need of major intervention. A toddler with multiple serious injuries, skeletal fractures of varying age and a withdrawn personality can be diagnosed prior to an interview with his parents.

Most cases are much less obvious than these examples. It then becomes critical for the examiner to evaluate the parenting techniques and attitudes as well as the manifestations in the child. Data from a variety of resources will be collected and integrated during the diagnostic process.

The characteristics of the abusing parent have been well described by Kempe, Helfer, Steele and others (Ref. 7, 9, 17). In addition, much information is available with reference to physical manifestations of abuse in the child (Ref. 7, 9, 12, 15, 17). However, we have been impressed with the lack of emphasis upon behavioral features which may facilitate the diagnosis of child abuse or neglect during the early phases of the clinical evaluation. Not only are there very frequent associations of behavioral abnormalities with physical abuse, but sometimes the behavioral findings can precede the discovery or appearance of traumatic injury. The delineation of specific personality or behavioral observations in the child may enable the evaluator to differentiate between a situation of a simple variance of parenting style from actual or potential abuse.

BEHAVIORAL ALERTING SIGNALS

Compliance

In 1974 E. Lenoski described a phenomenon of catatonoid-like posturing in children who had been physically abused (Ref. 11). We routinely test all abused and suspect abuse cases for this phenonenon. Termed postural compliance it may be elicited by approaching the child's bedside or crib and with as few words as possible, the examiner takes one or more extremity and raises them into some elevated and awkward position. In a test considered positive, the child will retain the position for at least fifteen seconds. The test should be performed on children between approximately ten months and five years of age. Normally, a child of this age range will be most resistant to attempts by a stranger to elevate one of the extremities. Non-cooperation with such bizarre and uncomfortable requests is the overwhelming norm for children in the late infancy, toddler and pre-school stages. Abused children in the same age groups differ dramatically in their response to this test. While these children may appear very apprehensive when approached (called "frozen watchfullness" by Ounsted) (Ref. 13), they are so fearful of violent consequences for disobeying an adult that they will make every effort to comply with the demands of the stranger. Thus, this impressive phenomenon, called postural compliance, is seen with significant frequency in the chronically abused child. It is also notable that after a period of time in a protected and more predictable environment like the hospital, postural compliance disappears.

In our own experience, 85-90% of abused children will show compliance at the time of initial observation. It is considered to be important adjunctive data which supports the suspected diagnosis of non-accidental trauma and is also reflective of the profound psychological consequences arising from chronic maltreatment by the caretaker. The phenomenon of postural compliance does not appear to be simply a function of acute anxiety related to the hospital experience for a young child, since less than 5% of children in the same age range admitted for accidental trauma or other illness will be compliant for more than fifteen seconds.

Compliance as a personality feature along with general passivity is noted by Gray and R. Kempe to occur in some 75% of abused children in Denver. (Ref. 6). The remaining 25%, like some 10 to 15% of our cases tend to exhibit markedly different personalities including hyperactivity and aggressive tendencies.

Inappropriate Interactions

Inappropriate interpersonal interactions are another kind of behavioral observation which may be very helpful in assessing whether or not a child has been subjected to chronic maltreatment. For example, we would expect normal one to three year old children to be fearful of the emergency room and seek comfort from a parent. Failure to exhibit this behavior, or excessive and inappropriate affection exhibited to strangers may be signs of parent-child interactional dysfunction. Again, observations of this type would lend support to suspicions of abuse.

Of the maltreated children admitted to our hospital, approximately 50% will have inappropriate responses to strangers or to their parents or both. On a number of occasions we have been struck with the sight of a toddler clinging to a police officer as the family is brought into the emergency room for evaluation of possible battering. Sometimes the child may go to the parent because he senses the parent wants him and is fearful to disobey. This is explainable by the child's compliance as described earlier although it is also related to ambivalence of feelings the youngster has toward even the abusing parent. In any case, the fact that a child is seen sitting on the parent's lap should not rule out the possibility of an abusive relationship. Clinging to strangers is more important diagnostic data than is rejection or acceptance of the parent.

Actually, the behavioral observations made during the clinical evaluation can be most helpful in evaluating historical information as well as physical findings. As an analogy of sorts we can discuss the evaluation of feeding techniques in infancy. There are many ways of accomplishing the task of nourishing an infant with respectable proponents in every major school of thought. There are also many parental variations of approach to the feeding process. If we are seeing a family and want to determine whether a particular method is acceptable or not, the first thing we do is evaluate the child's health and growth pattern. By and large, if the health is good and the weight gain adequate it is difficult to incriminate feeding technique. On the other hand, if a parent describes a well-accepted feeding plan in a baby who is not thriving, but without underlying organic disease, we would be correctly concerned that the feeding was not being administered as described. In other words, the growth pattern and general health become indices or guidelines for evaluating the quality of the nutritional regimen. Likewise, the behavioral manifestations in a child may serve as markers for the quality of the on-going parenting process.

USE AND ABUSE OF PHYSICAL PUNISHMENT

Many parents have rather definitive ideas concerning the appropriateness of physical punishment in children. Attitudes on this subject can be extreme: "I never spank my children" to "children must be disciplined lest they grow up spoiled". Some parents who use physical discipline have well-established patterns such as using a hairbrush, switch, belt or other object. Sometimes disciplining actions are assigned to one parent only. Parents may habitually use severe violence in punishing children during moments of rage. One parent may plan disciplinary actions with military-like deliberateness and never feel guilt or regret, while another may hurt a child and be overcome with remorse.

Cultural and familial preferences for the use or avoidance of physical discipline also plays a role in the individual parenting and punishment pattern (Ref. 10). In addition, individual variations in impulse control and momentary alterations in level of external stress have an impact on when and how children are punished.

How is the practitioner to evaluate a specific family's disciplinary approach? Many episodes of physical abuse have been inappropriately rationalized as "excessive discipline" or a parent "carried away" and "too angry" while punishing the child.

At times the situation is clear. A six-month old struck on the head because "he wouldn't stop crying" or a five-year old covered with belt bruises and lash marks have not merely been punished within the acceptable range of parental prerogative.

Fine-tuning the interface between discipline and abuse - especially when the visible injuries are not prominent - can be an exceptionally difficult task. Nonetheless, this distinction can make the critical difference between risking serious abuse later on by missing a warning sign versus offering early intervention and preventing a future calamity.

Published child guidance books available to the public usually include some discussion of discipline and punishment. We reviewed eight of these volumes and found that five of these discouraged any physical punishment whatsoever (Ref. 1, 3, 5, 8, 18) while three allowed for occasional spanking (open hand on backside) for emphasizing certain points under selected circumstances (Ref. 2, 14, 16). The overall tendency was against corporal punishment. Nonetheless, public opinion, as might be gauged by the actual proportion of parents who utilize physical discipline, probably opposes the theoretical objections espoused by many experts in the field. Do we have misguided arm-chair advisors or, a great portion of our population who must resort to physical punishment as a substitute for better parenting techniques? The question remains, for the most part, unresolved.

In any case, parent attitudes and techniques of punishment must be considered as another set of important data in the overall evaluation of possible abuse. Maybe the best we can do at this point is to agree on certain kinds of punishment which are universally appreciated as behavior which demonstrates abuse potential in a parent and which violates the right of the child to live without unnecessary fear or personal violence.

CONCLUSION: ALERTING SIGNALS

Diagnosing child abuse involves gathering and integrating a great deal of medical and non-medical data. The practitioner is faced with greater complexity and confusion in making the appropriate decision as the definition of abuse and neglect becomes increasingly wider. What are the real limits of a parent's prerogative? When is corporal punishment acceptable or appropriate? Is the concept of "children's rights" valid? Which families need and deserve minimal intervention and what is the mechanism for assuring that these services are delivered?

It is true that we are just beginning to face some of these questions and that answers are not likely to come easily. Particularly in the cases of such highly charged issues as parent's rights and family intervention do we face fierce conflicts in moral and political arenas. Nonetheless, as child advocates we must develop the appropriate forums for the issues to be heard and ultimately resolved.

The following represents a list of alerting signals which, in our experience, provide special guidelines for assisting in the determination of inappropriate parenting. They are not necessarily all-inclusive but may serve as important baseline data in the determination of when help is needed:

1. Non-accidental injuries
2. Any physical punishment of an infant less than 18 months of age
3. Striking a child with any object or fist or other than upon the hand or buttock
4. Striking a child during periods of extreme parental anger
5. Inappropriate for age postural or behavioral compliance in a child
6. Inappropriate interpersonal interactions
7. Non-organic delays in physical or developmental growth
8. Obvious deficiencies of general care provision

The presence of any of these findings should be cause for concern about the family. This is not to say that if alerting signals are discovered the children will necessarily need immediate removal. Some cases will require little more than an offer of additional services like parenting classes or minimal supportive counselling. It is hoped that by establishing specific guidelines upon which early intervention decisions can be made, clinicians will be able to increase the confidence in and efficiency of their dispositional decisions. Ultimately, if alerting signals are heeded, the practitioner can become an advocate for the child and his family - not a referee over the conflicting rights of parents and their children.

REFERENCES

1. Becker, W. (1971) Parents Are Teachers, Research Press, Illinois.

2. Dodson, F. (1970) How To Parent, Signet, New York.

3. Fraiberg, S. (1959) The Magic Years, Scribner's Sons, New York.

4. Franklin, A. W. (Ed.) (1975) Concerning Child Abuse, Churchill Livingstone, London.

5. Ginott, H. (1965) Between Parent and Child, Avon, New York.

6. Gray, J. and R. Kempe, The Abused Child at Time of Injury, in H. Martin (Ed.), The Abused Child, Cambridge: Ballinger, 1976.

7. Helfer, R. E. and C. H. Kempe (1968) The Battered Child, University of Chicago Press, Chicago.

8. Ilg,F.and L. Ames (1955) Child Behavior, Harper and Row, New York.

9. Kempe, C. H. and R. E. Helfer (1972) Helping the Battered Child and His Family, Lippincott, Philadelphia.

10. Korbin, J. , Anthropological Contributions to the Study of Child Abuse, Child Abuse and Neglect, The International Journal, Vol 1, 1977.

11. Lenoski, E. F. , Paper presented at Seminar on Child Abuse, Denver, September 1974.

12. McNeese, M. and J. Hebeler, The Abused Child, Clinical Symposia, Vol. 29, 1977.

13. Ounsted, C. (1972) Proceedings of the 8th International Study Group on Child Neurology and Development (unpublished).

14. Salk, L. (1972) What Every Child Would Like His Parents to Know, Warner, New York.

15. Schmitt, B. and C. H. Kempe, The Pediatrician's Role in Child Abuse and Neglect, Current Problems in Pediatrics, Vol. V, March 1975.

16. Spock, B. (1971) Baby and Child Care, Pocket Books, New York.

17. Steele, B. and C. A. Pollack, A Psychiatric Study of Parents Who Abuse Infants and Small Children, in R. Helfer and C. H. Kempe (Eds.) The Battered Child, University of Chicago Press, Chicago, 1968.

18. United States Government Report (1970) Your Child from 1 to 12, Signet, New York.

Child Abuse and Neglect, Vol. 3, pp. 99 - 105.

0145-2134/79/0301-0099 $02.00/0.

THE POLITICS OF CHILD ABUSE AND NEGLECT: NEW GOVERNMENTAL RECOGNITION FOR AN OLD PROBLEM

Barbara J. Nelson

Woodrow Wilson School of Public and International Affairs
Princeton University, Princeton, New Jersey, U.S.A.

ABSTRACT

In the 1870s child abuse and neglect was transformed from a "non-issue" to the responsibility of the civic-sector charity groups and, more recently, to a charge of the public sector. The objective of this article is to examine the cause of these shifts of responsibility by covering three topics: (1) a discussion of spheres of responsibility for social problems, (2) a definition and discussion of what constitutes a shift of risk from one sphere to another, and (3) an analysis of the shift of responsibility for child abuse and neglect from individuals to the civic sector and then to the public sector. In both instances the shift of risk was caused by slack resources, willing leadership, and the absence of any organized opposition to the changing locus of responsibility.

INTRODUCTION

Records from the English colonies in America depict all manner of child abuse and neglect. In 1655, Robert Latham of the Plymouth Colony beat, starved, overworked, and eventually caused the death of his apprentice, John Walker.[1] In Maryland in 1660, Arthur Turner so neglected the indentured orphan, John Ward, that "the voice of the people crieth shame..."[2] In both instances the authorities responded with relative severity against the abusers. For the death of his apprentice, Robert Latham was "'burned in the hand' and 'all his goods confiscated,'"[3] and the court ordered John Ward freed from his master. In neither case, however, did the authorities urge a more general investigation of the extensiveness of abuse and neglect among apprentices or indentured servants. Child abuse and neglect were viewed as the isolated, extreme acts of atypical individuals. Because of this view, there was no emphasis on preventing abuse or neglect, and "collective" response was limited to the punishment of offenders.

Punishment of those found guilty of excessive violence or gross inattention remained the major "collective" response to child abuse and neglect until the Guilded Era (1870s), to be supplanted by the work of voluntary protective societies. The protective societies, some of which emphasized rescuing "the child from the dens and slums of the City"[4] and others of which worked for social reform as the method of improving the care of children, signaled a move toward viewing child abuse and neglect as a social problem with societal causes, as well as an individual problem with psychopathic roots. The protective societies sought out dignified press coverage of their activities and encouraged the general public to recognize child abuse and neglect as an important social issue, although they retained a definite bias toward labeling violence against well-to-do children as eccentricity and violence against poor

---

[1]Robert H. Bremner, ed., Children and Youth in America: A Documentary History, Vol. I: 1600-1865 (Cambridge, Mass.: Harvard University Press, 1970) pp. 123-124.

[2]Ibid., p. 125

[3]Ibid., p. 123

[4]Robert H. Bremner, ed., Children and Youth in America: A Documentary History, Vol. II: 1866-1932, Parts One through Six (Cambridge, Mass:: Harvard University Press, 1971) p. 190.

children as abuse. The number of protective societies grew rapidly from 1874 when the New York Society for the Prevention of Cruelty to Children (NYSPCC) was founded, until the turn of the century. After that, the societies declined in number and stature because they divorced themselves from long-term support services after "rescuing" the child. The case-finding function devolved on other groups, most notably public benefit agencies and private child residences. Without a specific label and a vocal constituency, child abuse and neglect melted into a more general concern with child welfare and then largely disappeared from the scrutiny of child welfare workers and the general public.

In 1957, child abuse and neglect reemerged as a social problem, this time as an issue for which government had some direct responsibility. That year, the Children's Bureau (CB) published its "Proposals for Drafting Principles and Suggested Language for Legislation on Public Child Welfare and Youth Services,"[5] which contained a short section urging each state's Child Welfare Department[6] to investigate neglect, abuse, and abandonment; offer social services or bring the situation to the attention of a law-enforcement agency. The Children's Bureau insured government's continuing interest in the issue by supporting research, most notably C. Henry Kempe's[7] study of the etiology of physical abuse of children and David Gil's[8] nationwide survey of attitudes toward child abuse. As a result of this research, and increased media attention, all states passed child abuse (and sometimes neglect) reporting laws between 1963 and 1967, and the federal government supported research and services through the Child Abuse Prevention and Treatment Act of 1974 (now the Child Abuse Prevention and Adoption Reform Act).

This brief history of response to child abuse and neglect demonstrates that the locus of responsibility for the problem shifted twice, once from being a "non-issue" to a civic-sector (private, voluntary) concern and then to a public (governmental) social welfare issue. The objective of this article is to examine the cause of these shifts. We will cover three topics: (1) a discussion of spheres of responsibility for social problems, (2) a definition and discussion of what constitutes a shift of risk from one sphere to another, and (3) an analysis of the causes of the shift of responsibility for child abuse and neglect from individuals to the civic sector and then to the public sector. The data for this study derive from two sources: the written record as found in historical documents, books, journals, memos, correspondence, and unpublished reports; and confidential interviews with 32 public- and civic-sector leaders who participated in the agenda-setting process. The interviews, which took place in the spring and summer of 1977, lasted thirty minutes to three hours. and were conducted with past and present high-ranking officials in the executive branch, members of Congress, and with several of their past and present personal and committee staff, noted researchers, professors, legal and medical practitioners in the child abuse field, and national leaders in relevant private charity groups.

SPHERES OF RESPONSIBILITY FOR SOCIAL PROBLEMS

Not all social and economic conditions which might be considered deleterious are designated by individuals or societies as problems. When there is no designation of conditions as problems, there is also no socially designated sphere of responsibility for them (though in practice the consequences of "non-problems" are usually borne by individuals or families). However, when conditions are collectively deemed unacceptable, there exist four possible spheres of responsibility: (1) individuals or families, (2) the civic (voluntary, non-profit) sector, (3) the private (profit-making) sector, or (4) the public sector. The assignment of a problem to one or another sphere may be a formal act by a powerful person

---

[5]United States Children's Bureau, "Proposals for Drafting Principles and Suggested Language for Legislation on Public Child Welfare and Youth Services," (Washington, D.C.: United States Department of Health, Education and Welfare, Social Security Administration, Children's Bureau, 1957).

[6]The term "Child Welfare Department" is employed to cover any state administrative unit dealing with child welfare services and benefits, regardless of name.

[7]C. Henry Kempe, et al., "The Battered-Child Syndrome," Journal of the American Medical Association, Vol. 181 (July 7, 1962), pp. 17-24, 42.

[8]David G. Gil, Violence Against Children: Physical Child Abuse Against Children (Cambridge, Mass.: Harvard University Press, 1970).

or group, but frequently it is not. Tradition may account for responsibility for a problem being located in a particular sphere, or strong groups may choose to accept certain risks which are economically profitable or socially and personally rewarding.

Social issues include the individual and collective problems arising from the social and economic dependency--youth, old age, illness and disability, and the imperfect match between skills and employment. In the past two hundred years responsibility for social problems has frequently (but not universally) progressed from families to voluntary groups to profit-making firms to government. However, responsibility for a problem does not move wholesale from one sphere to another, rather new spheres of responsibility are layered on older ones. The movement of a problem from total individual-familial responsibility to more group responsibility is usually accompanied by an infusion of resources for people facing the problem. However, the extra resources are by no means universally available. Even government's adoption of responsibility does not insure increased resources for those facing a social problem. The federal system and the power of interest-group politics has created a patchwork of public social policy varying from place to place and group to group.

Responsibility for income maintenance among the work disabled is a good example both of the "progression" and imperfect overlap of spheres of responsibility. In agricultural societies, the burden of work disability falls on the disabled worker or his or her family. With industrialization, benevolent societies began to assist members in meeting this problem. These volunteer self-help and "do-good" groups were characterized by their ability to exclude those not wanted, a trait solidified by increasingly specific tax exemptions for charities, exemptions which remain today. Somewhat later, entrepreneurs discovered that the disability benefits available to members of friendly societies might be successfully commercialized as disability insurance (though not as successfully commercialized as life insurance). Only the well-to-do could afford such coverage, however, and a variety of public programs (e.g. Workers Compensation, Social Security) were instituted to respond both to residual need and high risk. Nonetheless, with all these resources, work disability socially and economically disrupts those who lose some or all ability to be gainfully employed.[9]

DEFINING AND DISCUSSING SHIFT OF RESPONSIBILITY

Responsibility for the vicissitudes of life and economic cycles may formally be assigned to individuals or families or may be woven imperceptibly into unquestioned social norms. The great psychological leap is to a commonly held belief that certain problems are a collective responsibility, or at least have a collective element. The first component of collective responsibility entails amassing resources, either human resources for providing services, or goods or money. Second, collective responsibility requires devising an organizational mechanism for distributing resources. Third and last, collective responsibility necessitates mobilizing moral energy (leadership and commitment) for promoting interest in the problem and the proposed response.

All these do not, however, guarantee a general perception of the legitimacy or collective response to a problem. Realistically, it is not merely the fact that a few people believe that a problem is a collective responsibility, but that a "critical mass" of people share that belief. Of course, the actual number or percentage of people holding that view, or their social position, is not easily defined. It is particularly difficult to determine this "critical mass" when collective responsibility is more limited than the scope of the problem, as was the case with the creation of the child-saving movement in the 1870s and the 1880s. Indeed, the severely limited responsibility assumed by many protective societies is one reason civic-sector (that is, early collective) interest in child abuse eventually declined.

What transforms the unacceptable conditions of individuals into the group problems of societies? Certainly such a transformation requires cultural and institutional readiness, or what Smelser[10] calls the structural conduciveness for change. Beyond this, a notable event frequently focuses attention on a topic. But even such an occurrence does not insure the emergence of a general interest or collective response. The direction of leadership (that

---

[9] Monroe Berkowitz and William G. Johnson, "Towards an Economics of Disability: The Magnitude and Structure of Transfer and Medical Costs," The Journal of Human Resources, Vol. 5 (Summer, 1970) pp. 271-297.

[10] Neil Smelser, Theory of Collective Behavior (New York: Free Press, 1962).

is, the willingness of individuals to provide the organizational framework or program for activity) is the final requirement for transforming numberless individual experiences into a class of experiences. Sometimes such leadership has been provided by those newly converted to a particular cause. But for child abuse, as for many other social issues, leadership for the transformation of private experience to collective responsibility came from issue partisans, people with established interests in similar issues. For these people, the decision to create organizations or policies in which others might share was not difficult.

SHIFTS OF RESPONSIBILITY FOR CHILD ABUSE AND NEGLECT

As noted, child abuse and neglect underwent two major shifts of responsibility, from individuals and families to the civic sector and then to the public sector. The popular version of the first transformation finds Henry Bergh, the founder of the American Society for Prevention of Cruelty to Animals, successfully arguing in court that the foster child, Mary Ellen, ought to be removed from her cruel guardians because she, as a member of the animal kingdom, deserved the same protection as abused animals. In actuality, the case was argued by Bergh's friend and counsel, Elbridge T. Gerry who had Mary Ellen removed from her unwholesome surroundings by a petition for a writ de homine replegando , an old English writ to remove the custody of one person from another.[11] It was Gerry, not Bergh, who suggested forming the New York Society for the Prevention of Cruelty to Children. However, Gerry did have a formal connection with animal protection, being the Counsel to the Society for Prevention of Cruelty to Animals.

Gerry and his associate, John D. Wright, undertook the legwork to create the NYSPCC. They provided what is technically called a "public or collective good," that is, a good which once provided by someone cannot by its nature be (easily) denied to anyone.[12] We can imagine that he thought his motives were purely generous, but the rhetoric of the Society has a strong class bias, as well as implicit nativist and anti-Catholic sentiment. Even the Massachusetts SPCC, which took a more social reform view of ameliorating child abuse and neglect, evinced this class bias. The class-specific emphasis of these societies in this early period is typified by this case summary from the Massachusetts SPCC, First Annual Report:

> (Case No.:)1375. Four children, five months to nine years. Father intemperate, sickly. Mother negligent and dissolute, absenting herself for weeks at a time, abandoning her nursing infant. Under 'neglect law' children sent to Marcella Street Home and City Nursery.[13]

Although led in the early period by men, prevention societies were primarily staffed by women. These women were for the most part wealthy, or at least middle-class, and had the leisure time (or more technically, the slack resources) to invest as they felt profitable. A social-darwinistic view of Christian charity is ascribed to them; the hierarchical nature of peoples was self-evident; some people were evidently more "fit" than others, but vigilant attention to the lower order could aid, if not redeem, them.[14] It was a gospel of social control with the tiny safety-valve of upward mobility for those who conformed to the norms of higher strata.

In addition to merging social control with social concern, the female (and sometimes male) members of prevention societies can be described as domestic or social feminists.[15] Domestic feminists felt that a home and family were the proper ambitions of a young girl, and by teaching or assuring that young lower-class girls learned homemaking skills, domestic feminists both supported their own conservative, middle-class values while expanding their own

---

[11] Mason P. Thomas, Jr., "Child Abuse and Neglect, Part 1: Historical Overview, Legal Matrix and Social Perspectives," North Carolina Law Review, Vol. 50 (February, 1972) pp. 293-349.

[12] Mancur Olson, Jr., The Logic of Collective Action: Public Goods and the Theory of Groups (New York: Schocken Books, 1971).

[13] Bremner, op. cit., 1971, p. 204.

[14] Anthony M. Platt, The Child Savers: The Invention of Delinquency (Chicago: The University of Chicago Press, 1977, second, enlarged edition) pp. 28-36.

[15] William O'Neill, Everyone Was Brave (Chicago: Quadrangle Books, 1969).

experience and influence. The early days of the NYSPCC was characterized by an ambiance of domestic feminism. Social feminists, on the other hand, supported a second fairly conservative belief, the purity of women. When women addressed such problems as child abuse, child labor, ramshackle housing, or piece labor (all issues which directly touched traditional family concerns) they brought the purity and selflessness to the effort. Many such women belonged to the Massachusetts SPCC, a society which emphasized social reform over social control. The early child abuse movement (as well as the more recent movement) did not have many, if any, ideological feminists, people who examined the power relationship betwen women and men, and whose social activism was based on attempts to alter that power relationship. Indeed, a fascinating question comes to mind: did any of the women (or men) involved in the early child-saving movement draw the legal, if not sociological, analogy between the relationship of child and father, and wife and husband?

Whatever the views of the prevention society members, state legislatures increasingly recognized and in some cases regulated charity activity. Prior to the rise of prevention societies the Massachusetts legislature created the Board of State Charities (later called the State Board of Charities) which coordinated the four public and four quasi-public charitable and correctional institutions in the state. In regard to child protection, the New York Assembly passed legislation making it a misdemeanor to interfere with a prevention society worker.[16] In this last act, the legislature was enfranchising, as it were, private groups to perform a social control function.

"Enfranchising legislation" did not, however, indicate a shift to, or sharing of, responsibility for prevention and treatment of child abuse to the public sector. Rather it acknowledged and strengthened the existing role of private prevention societies, aiding them with recognition and in some cases quasi-judicial powers. The prevention societies and enfranchising legislation were more prevalent in older Eastern and Midwestern states where the formal charity tradition was stronger than in the West and Southwest. Thus, there was no geographically uniform governmental recognition for the need to protect children. But more importantly, the kind of recognition afforded by state legislatures ("enfranchising" laws) said in essence, "If private charitable groups want to provide this service they may do so with our blessing. However, if charities do not wish to engage in this activity the state acknowledges no responsibility for providing similar services." Such a stance on the part of state officials was consistent with the era of "dual federalism,"[17] an era when Supreme Court opinions on issues such as child labor stated that the federal government had no right to intervene in a person's opportunity to sell his or her labor, and the state,which had the right, had no binding responsibility.

Prevention societies began to decline in the 1900s and were with rare exceptions defunct or decimated by the end of the Depression, victims of their own unwillingness to provide services to "rescued" children, as well as the demise of private giving. What, then, caused the Children's Bureau (and later all 50 state legislatures and Congress) to recognize and respond to the problem of child abuse, an issue with a decreasing constituency?[18] As was the case in civic sector recognition, the necessary conditions for recognition were leadership and slack resources, in this case slack organizational rather than personal resources. In addition, the shift from tenuous civic responsibility to public responsibility was aided by the care issue partisans used in describing child abuse as an issue of child protection and welfare and not as a situation of excessive discipline. Attacks on a parent's right to discipline a child always eroded the consensual quality of the issue, a quality necessary to encourage political leaders to invest their time on the issue.

The Children's Bureau did not independently revive an interest in child abuse; rather it sponded to the research findings of the American Humane Association (AHA), a private charity specializing in research (not service) on child and animal protection. From 1955 through 1959, the AHA coordinated a semi-annual meeting of child welfare experts. At a meeting in 1956, the AHA presented findings of research on the status of state child abuse and neglect

---

[16]Thomas, op. cit., p. 311.

[17]Edwin S. Corwin, The Constitution and What It Means Today (Princeton, New Jersey: Princeton University Press, 13th Edition, 1973, revised by Harold W. Chase and Craig R. Ducat) p. 228.

[18]For a more detailed discussion of how the issue of child abuse and neglect achieved the public agenda, see Barbara J. Nelson with the assistance of Thomas Lindenfeld, "Setting the Public Agenda: The Case of Child Abuse," in Judith May and Aaron Wildavsky, eds., The Policy Cycle (Beverly Hills, California: Sage Publications, forthcoming 1978).

laws and services.[19] Annie Lee Sandusky was the CB representative at that meeting. She was the bridge between the AHA's research and the CB adoption of the issue.

Steiner[20] suggests that the Children's Bureau was a bureaucratically intractable organization, which because of its insistence on providing services to middle-class rather than impoverished children, was not particularly overworked. In that respect it had the slack resources to accept new issues, if the issues were perceived to be within its legitimate authority. Because the Children's Bureau had many staff members whose previous experience included civic-sector child welfare work, it was easy to include child abuse on the Bureau's agenda. For administrators child abuse was not so much a new issue, but a new emphasis, a nuance easily incorporated in the 1957 "Proposals...for Legislation on Public Child Welfare." More importantly, the growing significance and centrality of the issue of child abuse to the CB was marked by the funding of several research projects. In that research, the CB avoided the major pitfall in the child abuse issue (an attack on parental rights) by focusing on extreme physical abuse. Indeed, it was the results of the CB's conference on the physical abuse of children which helped to solidify governmental responsibility for treatment of child abuse and neglect.

The conference suggested that states pass child abuse reporting statutes. In its 1963 pamphlet, "The Abused Child: Principles and Suggested Language for Legislation on Reporting of the Physically Abused Child,"[21] the CB suggested that reports of child abuse be made to police officers. Between 1963 and 1967 the American Humane Association, the Council of State Governments, the American Medical Association and the American Academy of Pediatrics all published guidelines for legislation or model statutes. State legislatures were virtually bombarded with requests for child abuse legislation, and during the same years (1963-1967) every state passed child abuse (and sometimes neglect) reporting laws. However, only the Illinois law carried an appropriation.

The incentives for state legislators to provide leadership for, or merely support, child abuse reporting laws are obvious. Legislators could demonstrate their rectitude by supporting legislation protecting children from brutality (the early laws emphasized the physical aspects of abuse) while not spending the taxpayers money. Such a political situation (no-cost rectitude) is admittedly rare. Because of the virtual absence of political or monetary costs, support for child abuse legislation was similar to organizational expansion to take up slack resources (the case in the Children's Bureau). State legislators were able to increase government responsiveness with almost no expenditure of political or actual capital. However, such responsiveness had unanticipated (though predictable) consequences. By requiring reporting, state legislators created a wildly-growing demand for service which became increasingly difficult to meet.

The 1960s saw an enormous upsurge in expenditures on public social services, with demand outstripping supply no matter how fast service expenditures grew. Derthick[22] has chronicled this growth through a history of Title XX of the Social Security Act (Services for Individuals and Families). Many child welfare leaders, especially in private charity, channeled their national lobbying efforts related to child abuse and neglect into regularizing the very confused arrangements for financing services. Indeed it was not private groups, so active in encouraging the Children's Bureau and state legislatures to take responsibility, who urged Congressional response to child abuse as a separate issue. Rather, initial recognition came from Congressman Mario Biaggi (D., N.Y.) who introduced the first of several Congressional child abuse bills in 1968. It required, however, the leadership of then Senator Walter F. Mondale (D., Minn.) to catapult the issue to prominence in Congress. In 1973, Mondale

[19] Vincent DeFrancis, Child Protective Services in the United States (Denver, Colorado: Children's Division, the American Humane Association, 1956).

[20] Gilbert Y. Steiner, The Children's Cause (Washington, D.C.: The Brookings Institution, 1976) pp. 36-89.

[21] United States Children's Bureau, "The Abused Child: Principles and Suggested Language for Legislation on Reporting of the Physically Abused Child," (Washington, D.C.: Department of Health, Education and Welfare Administration, Children's Bureau, 1963).

[22] Martha Derthick, Uncontrollable Spending for Social Services Grants (Washington, D.C.: The Brookings Institution, 1975).

chaired the Subcommittee on Children and Youth (now the Subcommittee on Child and Human Development), a new subcommittee with able, eager staff. Because the Subcommittee was only two years old it did not have a recurring fixed agenda of legislation which must be renewed.[23] At that time Mondale was considering running for President. The combination of a fairly unencumbered subcommittee (once again slack organizational resources), political motivation and a previously demonstrated concern for children which made the political motivation both genuine and palatable, encouraged Mondale to press for specific national legislation identifying child abuse as a significant child welfare issue. Supported in the House by the rather unlikely triumverate of novice Congresswoman Patricia Schroeder (D., Colo.), Subcommittee on Select Education Chairman John Brademus (D., Ind.), and Congressman Biaggi, the Child Abuse Prevention and Treatment Act (CAPTA became law on January 31, 1974. CAPTA (now, as noted, the Child Abuse Prevention and Treatment and Adoption Reform Act) supported research on child abuse and neglect and supported a relatively low level (as compared with Title XX) of service provision. With the passage of CAPTA, the United States had a visible national commitment to recognizing child abuse.

The shift from minimal civic-sector responsibility to a public and civic partnership in response to child abuse took almost twenty years. Although the adoption of the issue of child abuse by the Children's Bureau, state legislatures, and Congress rested each time on slack organizational resources, the consensual nature (or packaging) of the issue and critical infusions of leadership; the process was more generally facilitated by the active encouragement of many private charity groups. Individual charitable groups had varying preferences for the content of governmental responsibility. For example, the American Humane Association preferred greater state responsibility and authority for child abuse policy, a preference which caused the AHA to be a peripheral actor in passing the national legislation. However, the civic sector encouraged (or at least did not hamper) governmental recognition and responsibility for child abuse for two reasons. First, government attention was a method for rejuvenating and legitimizing the issue. Second, and more importantly, civic sector groups believed (quite rightly) that government attention would yield government money. The increasing use of services purchased from private providers rather than the creation of new public agencies encouraged (again, quite rightly) the leaders of private child protection groups to believe that the government's adoption of "their" issue would not threaten the organizational integrity of the groups. Thus, in sum, government's present day responsibility for child abuse is a matter of the pull of governmental leadership and slack resources, and the push of private agencies for increased funds and social legitimacy. It is a pattern which repeats itself for many other issues of social policy in the last two decades.

[23]Jack L. Walker, "Setting the Agenda in the U.S. Senate: A Theory of Problem Selection," British Journal of Political Science, Vol. 7 (October, 1977) pp. 423-445.

Child Abuse and Neglect, Vol. 3, pp. 107 - 114.
Pergamon Press Ltd., 1979. Printed in Great Britain.

STRATEGIES FOR CHANGE: AN EXPLORATION OF GUIDE LINES

Maxwell H. Paterson,

57 Oxgangs Farm Grove,
EDINBURGH, EH13 9PP.

At a stage in human history when the discovery, preservation and allocation of natural resources pre-occupy the minds of governments, we continue to neglect the immeasurable resource available to us through an understanding of the human psyche.

The primary task which faces civilisation is the conversion of growing knowledge into managed and egalitarian systems of use. Whatever our ideological divisions, skills have grown in the management of these systems by which we distribute our natural resources, but the dissemination of knowledge as a resource, and especially knowledge of the psyche, finds no such skill. While the knowledge available to us of childhood if given systematic application would transform our culture, we continue to meet in unresolved confrontation.

Explanation for this selective failure to use the study of the psyche lies in our fear of those aspects of the psyche which we subsume under the term 'unconscious'. This fear is expressed in the dismissive view of psychology as 'common sense', and are we not all rich in our possession of that commodity? If we are to hold to a distinction between disciplined knowledge of the psyche and 'common sense', as a distillation from a culture of its beliefs and traditions, then it is the latter which informs and determines the practice of child care in our society. We deny to children, that is, our knowledge of childhood and human growth, and of the intra-psychic forces which sustain behaviour. If it were not so, then those to whom we, as a society, delegate responsibility for our children, for their education and their care, would be the carriers of all the information and the insights available about childhood growth. Our failure to ensure this apparently simple basic measure on behalf of childhood, is the index of our resistance to change. This is not to suggest that society remains fixed in its cultural modes. Change has been effected in many facets of the care and education of children. But within these as evolving systems of provision the residual content from our primitive origins remains to confound our best intentions. The essential centre to this content may be uncovered if we pursue the thread of evolution of the psyche.

The genius of our century lies embodied in the monumental studies of the psyche by Freud and Jung and the schools which derive from their originality of thought. But we retreat from Oedipus and our Archetypal nature as if threatened by the onset of cataclysm. Resistance to the application of knowledge, Freud (1) viewed as inevitable, and from his gloom he predicted the failure of the League of Nations, and, more generally, the incapacity of mankind so to manage its affairs as to bring freedom from war, persecution and bigotry; sickness and misery would persist in the midst of growing knowledge and growing wealth of resources. This pessimism followed from the role which Freud attributed in the development of civilisation to the guilt which arises as aggressive instinctive forces within the psyche are held in balance by the opposing forces of love. The outcome is remorse and guilt. The arena for the expression of this psychic struggle, in its primal form, is identified in the feelings experienced by children toward their parents and in the responses of parents to their children.

The application of psychoanalytic theory to our field of interest, child abuse, has been described and discussed by Lloyd de Mause (2) in his "History of Childhood", an invaluable source for further reference. It is the basis to the development of this theory that adults do respond to children 'projectively', supposing the child to be the bearer of those adult feelings most forbidden and so disavowed. Such feelings assume destructive forms when they represent the psychic 'debris' consequent upon the failure of the parents to resolve those problems which had arisen for them in primary relationships, experienced as destructive, with their own parents. There is considerable evidence to support the view that parents responsible for the gross abuse of their children have themselves experienced gross abuse in childhood. The evidence is presented and discussed in a recent paper by Margaret Lynch (3). It is important to note the evidence presented to show that children who have survived the most gross abuse are likely to become socially isolated and be identified as 'hostile' by their teachers. The prognosis as we study the subsequent development of abused children must appal us and return us to pessimism and gloom. Dr. Lynch concludes her comment "If the prognosis of child abuse is to improve, those working with these families must be prepared to look behind and beyond the overt abuse and be prepared to commit themselves to more than crisis intervention". (4) There is a clear indication that we should not abandon the abused child once infancy has passed and our meeting then is with the 'hostile' child in confrontation with authority. Yet the further evidence must lead us to conclude that as a society we all too quickly hold children to be self-responsible and bring to bear upon them punitive controls which can serve only to re-inforce the damage already done to them.

While the scene of institutional care in the United Kingdom has no such chronicler as Kenneth Wooden, (5) his documentation of the incarceration of children in the United States has chords of meaning for all contemporary society. In his comment on Wooden's work, Karl Menninger wrote "Wooden is uncovering the terrible things that are done to our children with our money, but are unknown to most of us." The risk in this response is that we then identify others as the culprits to become in turn the victims of our anger as we survey a scene so wretched. The disavowal of responsibility requires a victim as scapegoat. We may neglect the evidence that we as a society select those who will represent us in the care of children. In our conduct, as we manage our social relations, we sanction the violence exercised by those whom we appoint in the punitive control of those children whom we abandon to institutional life. Knowledge of the institutional scene has always been available to us. If we do not know, then we do not wish to know. This, in turn, is the expression of a guilt to which we do not wish to give substance. To meet through the stress of our knowledge with the psychic forces within ourselves, to encounter the 'debris' from our own primary relationships, is to enter the territory of our own distress. The Nurenberg defence, that we do not know, we may reject, but the alternative is the acknowledgement of a responsibility as a society; and this acknowledgement must be supported by the release of greater resources on behalf of children. But money is not enough. The primacy of need on behalf of children is for the release of knowledge about childhood and the management of its application. The history of the development of provision for children, in education and in child care, is a history of the rejection of knowledge and ideas and their subsequent partial acceptance in a form diluted by the ambivalent feelings of those entrusted with their application (6).

Lloyd de Mause opens his account of the evolution of childhood with the comment, "The history of childhood is a nightmare from which we have only recently begun to awaken". This awakening is represented by an increasing volume of study and writing about childhood, as it is by the apparent intent of agencies of government to improve the experience of childhood and the training of those employed to work with children. The nightmare, as Wooden illustrates, is yet with us. The extent of violence in our culture and especially its diffusion within practices of parenting and child-care is described in a set of papers edited by Norman Tutt (7) under the title 'Violence'. The evidence is before us that within our culture the basis to the control and management of children lies in the violence of adults, whether parents or teachers or child-care workers, to the children in their charge. The evidence is equally before us that the incarceration of adults, in prisons and in some institutions for the care of the mentally handicapped and elderly. occurs in conditions which encourage the application or interchange of violence.

The evidence is available to us that within the United Kingdom the greater the extremity of the distress of children the more likely are they to be retained in conditions of incarceration, whether in prisons or in children's institutions constructed to provide care under conditions of 'maximum security'. The recent construction of such institutions in England may not be within popular 'knowledge', yet the current development of the model represents official policy, openly implemented, toward such massively distressed children. The solution to the incarceration of children in a prison system devised for adults, (8) is to devise a system of imprisonment for children within the child-care services. We should not misunderstand the pressures within child-care services to make the decisions which give rise to these institutions. It is child-care workers, and their advisers, who carry on behalf of the wider society a responsibility to meet the problems presented by distressed children in confrontation with the world which has already damaged them. The perspective within which decisions are made contains unremitting pressure to achieve a solution to problems often experienced as insoluble. To remove such problems from the vision of society, while it brings comfort with the illusion of responsible action, is in itself an evasion of the essential problem, to find means whereby damaged children may encounter their hurt and surmount, in their further growth, its consequence for the distortion of their minds. The dilemma has an awesome reality. Personal commitment to the relief of stress in others brings exposure to areas of stress within ourselves; such a commitment to severely stressed children reveals to us the unresolved psychic debris from our early relationships with parents. Unless we are trained in the understanding of childhood and supported in meeting and resolving personal stress we must come to treat children with indifference or hostility. It is a consequence that those who work with children, unless so trained and supported, come to be the least capable of achieving the aims of a child-care service. The defensive responses of adults who work in institutions coalesce to form systems of management and control whose overt aim, to achieve efficiency of care, covers the reality of the covert aim, to protect adults from the immediacy of experienced stress. The seminal study of this phenomenon as a flight into organisational systems, is to be found in Isobel Menzie's (9) paper on her observation of nursing practice in a general hospital. It is a message which we have not yet received into the practice of care, nurture and education; nor yet has it informed practice in adult institutions. So disturbing is this message that it is given no more than token response, if at all, in the formulation of programmes for the training of the basic practitioners in these fields.

Training in the institutional care of children is formally and officially determined as a training of inferior status to that of field social workers. (10) In consequence the practice of residential child-care is largely determined by those beliefs and traditions of child-care carried from their culture by inadequately prepared and supported staff (11). Traditions in the training of teachers have not yet been so breached as to ensure their knowledge of childhood and understanding of the nature of growth. That teachers must in their everyday practice encounter distress, both chronic and acute, in children, is not acknowledged in the core of their training and, once again, it is the consequence that teachers bring to their responses to the stresses of childhood whatever assumptions and beliefs they carry from their culture. Indeed a pursuit of this question of the training of professional practitioners, across the total range of provision for children, leads to the strange conclusion that no single profession trains its practitioners to understand childhood and growth in terms which recognise the nature of the human psyche. Before we begin we are in headlong flight. Yet from those whom we deny the acquisition of such knowledge and from whose support in practice we withdraw, we demand those levels of achievement required for our comfort.

There is a sequence of response which we may identify. Illustrated in teaching practice, this sequence is initiated by the appointment of a teacher to bring children, in a conformity with social norms, to an agreed standard of academic attainment; it is continued in the challenge offered by children to social norms as these are represented by the authority of the adult world; it is taken yet one further stage in the exasperated failure of the teacher to bring all children to conformity with the norms; it is concluded in the attack by teachers upon parents for their failure to act in responsible authority over the children. Illustrated is the unacknowledged stress contained within the professional role. This is a sequence which may be recognised wherever adults are identified as bearing authority in the lives of children. The anxieties which determine its course lead us back to the Freudian hypothesis embodied in the myth of Oedipus. The guilt which we carry and which determines the evolution of cultures, derives from the aggressive instinct by which sons hold their fathers as objects which bar their development to adult status. This aggression is energised by those further forces within the psyche whose objective is the survival of the 'self'. The father, in this analysis, represents a threat to survival and to growth. While the final hostile act, the killing of the father, is rejected, the energies evoked by the rejected wish must be given outlet. To pursue this hypothesis into contempory society, we may conjecture that as authority passes from the father into those social institutions which have proliferated in the modern state, child hostility must come to be directed upon those social institutions which most powerfully assume that authority. Erosion of the authority of the father and the primacy of the family, as the context for child growth, encourages the expression of hostility by children toward those institutions responsible for that erosion. In the context of family life, it is the child's love for the father which so balances hostile impulses as to constrain their direct expression in aggressive action. As love constrains aggression, the response in experienced guilt releases energy for alternative 'conforming' interests. Attack on the institutions of society has no such balancing power as love of institutional authority, nor does its expression find a consequence in guilt. Schools above all other social institutions find themselves the objects of child hostility. Response which seeks to 'stamp out' the expression of this hostility serves to substantiate the basic assumption in which it finds its origin, that authority intends to suppress growth and punish its challenge. If however we are to look at the erosion of parental authority and the diminishing role of family in the developmental phase of growth through childhood then we may discover alternative and less destructive strategies. The conclusion from this premise in the Freudian hypothesis is that the primary aim of the professions is not the education or care of children, but the control of their conduct and the containment of their hostilities. It is the observed role of the adult in authority to control. Thus, it is argued in institutional practice "You cannot help the body if you don't have it with you". This is a view which gives priority to the containment of children within institutions; it ignores the evident response of children when under compulsion to resist that compulsion, if not by absconding when the consequence is too greatly feared, then by rejecting as valid the attempts by adults to influence their growth.

The power to influence the growth of children derives from the capacity to form empathetic bonds with them. Empathy is the avenue by which we escape from our projective identification with children and so from the conversion of our guilt into punitive action. It is the failure to empathise which sets the scene for child abuse; it is the critical upsurge of those feelings which impute to the child our own denied aggressive impulses which seem to justify the act of abuse. Consequently we cannot be surprised to find that the primary condition for child abuse derives from the failure of 'bonding' between mother and child in the beginnings of child life. Bowlby's (12) seminal writing has led to important further studies of the bonding process. These are discussed elsewhere by Klaus and Kennell (13).

Beyond this as a source for psychic change, we must be aware of the changing roles of men and women in contempory western society and give our attention to the consequent exploration of the roles developed and relationships formed by parents as they conceive and prepare for the birth of their children. Once viewed as the exclusive domain for women, childbirth is increasingly accepted by parents as a shared experience. This reflects the development of roles within heterosexual relationships and within the act of conception itself. Modifications in sexual role arose as women came to explore their capacity to share with men the experience of the sexual act as non-reproductive, pleasurable, self-fulfilling, and as an aspect of the bond within relationship. The discovery of the 'pill' encouraged further developments of role and relationship for it brought the decision to procreate within the authority of women. As women have been increasingly released from 'chattel' roles, their relationship with men has been opened to negotiation, and from this men have been compelled to face new stresses and acknowledge new facets of role and relationship, new systems of authority within families.

As procreation follows increasingly from negotiated agreements between partners, the size of families has reduced and the significance of each child in the psychic life of the parents may be expected to assume an enhanced value. Reduction in family size may also be seen to follow from reduction in infant mortality rates and from the major social changes effecting economic life and opportunity. Each such factor must introduce further matter for negotiation and consequently the sharing of that authority from which decisions arise. Traditional distinctions in family and social roles of men and women thus questioned, the expectations which parents adopt toward their children must also modify. The concept of unisexual work-tasks brings the girl to share with her brother his traditional role as the child through whom the father may derive surrogate achievement of unrealised ambitions.

We begin, at this point, to engage in the exploration of new dimensions for change, for our engagement concerns the psychic life of individuals, the spring from which cultural evolution is energised and determined.

Less gloomy than Freud in his study of contemporary society, Jung (14) emphasises the neutrality of the unconscious, "... it contains all aspects of human nature - light and dark, beautiful and ugly, good and evil, profound and silly." There are answers to the wretched human equations, the 'animalism' which we impute to terrorists, to political monsters and to those who murder their fellows; and to those who abuse children. But if there are answers, or routes to their discovery, these must reflect, not the decisions of governments, but radical change in the psychic lives of individuals. It is the role of government to pursue strategies to create the conditions for psychic health and psychic evolution. Clearly the condition which should be given such strategic priority is the condition into which babies are born and empathetic bonds experienced.

A massive responsibility may be seen to attach to those responsible, on behalf of our society, for the decisions which effect the conditions for birth. This responsibility carries two major lines for thought and decisions. The first concerns authority. Whatever erodes the authority of parents as the decisive figures in the psychic experience of their children, whatever erodes the validity of family life as the context for their early development denies to children the opportunity to experience parental authority, identify with authority responsibility held, and so to incorporate this experience as a personal dimension of the psyche. The balance which should be sought lies between the authority appropriate to parents and that appropriate to the maternity services. The Court Report (15) on the child health services recommends that professional workers "... should see their task not as usurping the responsibility of the family, but as encouraging it, so that families are better able to exercise responsibility for their children." This definition of the role of the professional moves toward the view contained in play-group literature (16) that professional people should adopt roles and acquire skills to support parents in their authority. The recommendation of the Court Committee seems strangely at odds with the content of its Report when practice of child-birth is under survey, for Court encourages the continuation of the practice whereby 90% of births in England and Wales in 1975 took place in hospital. The right to decide upon home or hospital as the venue for confinement has been substantially removed from parents and the authority of the parents effectively diminished at source. From this we may draw one conclusion, that the priority professionally determined in the experience of birth is attached to the physical health of the mother and child and to the survival of the child, whatever recognition may be given to the consequence of the birth experience for the psychic bonding of mother and her baby. In further illustration of the problems in effecting change when opposed to traditional practices, we may refer to the White Paper on "Violence in the Family"(17) and to its response to the recommendation of the Parliamentary Select Committee (18) that "serious attention should be given to making more generally available the option of having a home confinement for all those mothers who wish it." The Government acknowledging the conflict of views between "chiefly non-medical groups" on grounds of "child care" and the health care professions on the grounds of "safety", "supported the professions' view that women should be encouraged to have their babies in hospital". It must be hoped that the Select Committee in its further work will question this response because of the challenge it represents to the authority of the individual in self-determination.

As we move to our second major line for governmental thought and action, we may note the reality acknowledged in the Court Report of those institutional practices by which babies are taken from their mothers, nursed in 80% of cases in routine nurseries, and in all but a quarter of instances, denied the breast on the first day of life.

As we study these documents we may wonder at the paucity of interest shown toward birth as an experience for the baby critically influential in establishing a base for psychic growth. While this knowledge has informed psycho-analytic practice in the treatment of individual stress, advocacy of its application to obstetric practice is associated with the work of Leboyer (19) whose concern it is to prepare for the new-born child an experience devoid of pain and fear. In contrast, scientific obstetric practice is concerned to reduce the experience of pain and fear by the mother and to prepare for any dangerous complication. This scientific approach also serves the interest of the organisation to maximise the economic use of professional time and resources. Association of childbirth with pain and danger has its origin in unconscious psychic life. Not only is it present in the individual but by derivation from the unconscious of all individuals in our society, it is present as an unconscious determinant of our culture. Accordingly, in our stage of social evolution, we have required obstetricians to deal with birth as a process within which pain and danger have a natural presence. This reflects from the further association of birth with sexual experience not yet freed from its place in the psyche as the forbidden experience, the very essence of sin. Pain and danger belong to birth, as punishment belongs to sin. The child as the product of the sinful act is 'full of the stains and pollutions of sin'(20). While we have no conscious impulse to effect the suffering of the baby, we obscure our perception of its suffering because to do so would bring us to awareness of repressed aspects of ourselves. It is as if we retain our stance as 'good', free from moral pollution, through the psychic mechanism which allows others to bear our guilt and so, vicariously, our punishment.

This is to suggest that, as with institutions for child-care and education, important aspects of obstetric practice are culturally determined however far its conduct appears to be governed by careful professional and governmental consideration.

The experience of birth, in Leboyer's terms, is an experience of abuse and violence. (21) It is an occasion for the incorporation into the infantile psyche of an experience which establishes the condition for the abuse of others.

Reason will seak to reject this hypothesis. Yet we cannot suppose that an event of such psychic value as birth may escape the weight of unconscious intervention. Its retuals colour the pages of anthropological study. Nor can our culture evade its evolutionary role. We, as primitives to the future, evolve as we glimpse the realities of our nature through the windows of self-perception. Jung writes (22) "Our present lives are dominated by the Goddess Reason, who is our greatest and most tragic illusion. By the aid of reason, so we assure ourselves we have 'conquered nature'."

The dubious role for reason in the management of our affairs further emphasises the complex nature of the task which separates the identification of a problem from its resolution; indeed we must wonder how capricious is the definition of the problem. Public anxiety, concentrated upon the plight of infants who are victims of massive injury, has obscured the wider reality that abuse of children and insensitivity to childhood may be demonstrated in diverse ways, many of which have been incorporated into traditions of childbirth, parenting, education and care of children. In support of this view we may take cognizance of relevant contributions by The National Children's Bureau (23), The Dartington Hall Social Research Unit (24, 25), and John and Elizabeth Newson (26, 27, 28). We must be aware that abuse of children, however diluted it may be in our judgement, provides social sanction for those acts which result in massive injury. This is to say that abuse is indivisible, however diverse its consequence. So too for concern. If we are to effect radical change in the patterns of child abuse our concern must be with violence of person to person wherever we find this in our society. We cannot thrash or belt or cane, whatever our indignation or displeasure, but we sanction violence. The ultimate illusion is that by violent means we can stamp out violence.

Violence in our institutions we may equate with stress upon staff. The revolution in our prison system will follow from a revolution in the experience of working in prisons. We must come to accept that any post which carries responsibility for the total care of others must be of the highest professional status. The application of this argument to the nurture of children, the handicapped and the elderly confronts us with the enormity of past neglect.

As a society we need to give urgent attention to the formulation of policies which will support families as the units of society and especially we must help to provide for parents those supports which will help them to achieve confidence as parents and clarity of parental role. The current defence of those in statutory authority, as children test and challenge that authority, is to place responsibility for child behaviour upon its parents. Without consistent policies in support of parents this will remain an evasion of evident realities.

The professions must come to a redefinition of professional role. It is the professional tradition to hold specialised knowledge, dispute its possession by others and so to maintain discrete preserves of competence. The concept of the expert as a consultant to others supporting their growth to an authoritative use of knowledge requires new perspectives in professional practice, new forms of training and experience. Whatever the professional task, the siting of basic training in understanding of growth and stress would provide that common ground essential for the interlocking of professional services and for effective corporate action with other specialists and with non-specialists who share that understanding.

Professional practice must be located within the communities served. The role of supportive consultant to parents will at best develop when consultancy is located within a physical setting which belongs to the community and is managed by its representatives. Current interest in the concept of 'family centres' within 'pram distance' may bring us to achievements in environmental planning and community responsibility. The essential is that absolute responsibility be held by the community. Consultancy with professionals and the use of statutory services should reflect insight into their nature and full acknowledgement of their value. Consequently a range of services should evolve through negotiation between specialist and community. The experience acquired by voluntary groups in the care of alcoholism and handicap provides a rich resource for our further learning of how responsibility may be held and negotiation effected by those most compassionately concerned with others. There can be no central blueprint for such community controlled centres; each must be an expression of its locality. An immediate consequence of a shared experience of interest in environment and the wellbeing of others, as the atmospheric component of a meeting place, is the reduction of isolation and the opening to others of experience of stress. Within this setting we may offer an alternative to the despairing self-inadequacy which is the emotional context of child abuse. We may bring this stress within the wider perspective of concern for all children within a community and supportive understanding of parental stress.

The objective must be to restore to parents their authority, to challenge all statutory action which threatens that authority, to make available the information which will permit decision and choice to be informed, to enter into a creative partnership based in parity but determined by acknowledgement of the primacy of their role.

Whatever the great debates which divide our society, whatever the confrontations and the discussions, the accusations and the justifications of self or group, there is a harmony of otherwise discordant voices when parents are held responsible for the waywardness of children. The debate will be resumed as we study the means by which parents may be helped or hindered in their responsibilities. But this is the essential ground for study and debate. We may as a nation find confrontation upon us as we present views and feelings upon law and order, education, immigration, wage levels and social status. The nuclear centre from which all such confrontations emerge is 'authority'. It will be in the management of problems of authority that each confrontation will be brought to resolution; it will be from the support of parents in their proper authority roles that resolution will be brought to these difficulties carried through the lives of children as they grow. Parents are the primary source for the healthy growth of our children and as children carry our culture into their future they will reflect our insights, our empathy and our competence. (29)

REFERENCES

(1) Freud, S. Civilisation and its Discontents, Hogarth Press, London. The theme which is carried throughout Freud's writing is discussed in his philosophical enquiry into Freud by Marcuse, H. (1956) Eros and Civilisation, Routledge and Kegan Paul, London.

(2) Lloyd de Mause (1974) The History of Childhood, Souvenir Press, London.

(3) M.A. Lynch, The Prognosis of Child Abuse, J. Child Psychol. Psychiat. 19, 175 - 180 (1978)

(4) Many documents and papers equate prevention with early recognition. Prognosis will be improved if we understand prevention in those wider terms which seek so to change the source of abuse in psychic conflict as to inhibit the origin of the abusive process. Early recognition has its own importance.

(5) Wooden, K. (1976) Weeping in the Playtime of Others, McGraw - Hill, New York.

(6) The history of Homer Lane's 'Little Commonwealth' exemplifies this phenomenon, while the life of A.S. Neil presents the case in classical form. For a survey of innovation in education and a source of further material, reference may be made to: Skidelsky, R. (1969) English Progressive Schools, Penguin, London.

(7) Tutt, N. (Ed) (1976) Violence, H.M.S.O. London.

(8) Recent data suggests that in England and Wales, in any one day, upwards of 4,000 young people, defined as those who have not yet reached the age of seventeen, are retained within the authority of Her Majesty's Prisons. While the preportionate number in Scotland is smaller, a higher proportion of children are retained in juvenile institutions.

(9) Menzies, I.E.P. (1970) The functioning of Social Systems as a Defence Against Anxiety, The Tavistock Institute, London.

(10) Central Council for Education and Training in Social Work (CCETSW) Various Papers. C.C.E.T.S.W., London.

(11) Illustration is to be found in the forms of practice applied to tantrum behaviour. The common response remains the shock tactic of slapping or applying cold water, or enclosing in a confined space. This response is often professionally sanctioned or advised. Non-violent holding and comforting of the child in tantrum, based in an understanding of its anxiety, does not satisfy a cultural response to tantrum behaviour as an act of disobedience and so of violence to the adult ego. The cultural aim is to regain control rather than to respond to the anxiety which determines this behaviour in children.

(12) Bowlby, J. Nature of a Child's tie to his Mother, Int. J. Psychoanal, 39, 350 - 373 (1958). Bowlby, J. (1969) Attachment and Loss, Basic Books, New York.

(13) Klaus, H and Kennell, J.H. (1976) Maternal - Infant Bonding, C.V. Mosby, Saint Louis.

(14) Jung, K. (Ed) (1964) Man and His Symbols, Pan Books, London.

(15) The Report of the Committee on Child Health Services (1976) Chairman, Court, S.D.M. Fit for the Future, H.M.S.O. London.

(16) England and Wales, Scotland, Northern Ireland have their own Playgroup Associations. The Philosophy and practice of playgroups in England has been best described by Brenda Crowe. The magazines 'Contact' and 'Under 5' are published by P.P.A. London. Parental authority and its support have been discussed by Max Paterson in a series of papers. All playgroup literature is available from The Pre-School Playgroups Association, Alford House, Aveline Street, London.

(17) D.H.S.S. and other Departments (1978) Violence to Children: A response to the First Report from the Select Committee, H.M.S.O. London.

(18) First Report from the Select Committee on Violence in The Family (1977) Violence to Children, H.M.S.O. London.

(19) Leboyer, F. (1977) Birth Without Violence Fontana/Collins, Glasgow.

(20) De Mause offers this quotation from Richard Allestree (1676). The pollution comes from our "first parents through our loins". This reference to the Garden of Eden and to the descent from Grace to Sin consequent upon the discovery of sexual desire is echoed in the concepts of a childhood Age of Innocence also terminated by the awakening of sexual feelings. The apparent contradiction between the sinfullness of the infant and its innocence reflects those polarities within the human psyche. We are good and we are evil; we love as we are gratified and hate as we are denied. It lies within the authority of the 'ego' to preserve a balance. When crisis - as the infant beyond control or satisfying - threatens the authority of the ego it may fail to preserve the balance and hitherto repressed forces given outlet. The baby may then be experienced as the more powerful because it has overwhelmed an inadequate ego, and as evil in its intent, because the loss of ego control induces a state of fear and impending disaster. In this event the extremity of violence follows as if the infant were indeed a powerful, threatening adult. In its extremity the baby is experienced as threatening death to the adult, for such are the fears and phantasies of the unconscious; child abuse, in this extremity, is conducted as an act of personal survival.

(21) Leboyer says of newly born babies that they look like tortured prisoners. It is of interest to compare his account of birth with Marcel Foucault's account of legal execution. There is fascination too in comparison of execution rituals, with the condemned as the object, and birth rituals, with the mother as the object. What is denied in both is the authority to control what is happening to the body.

Foucault, M. (1977) Discipline and Punish, The Birth of the Prison, Penguin Books, London. "The body is caught up in a system of constraints and privations, obligations and prohibitions". Present is "an army of technicians" with the doctor ".. the agent of welfare .. the alleviator of pain." "When the moment of execution approaches, the patients (sic) are injected with tranquillizers. A utopia of judicial reverence; take away life, but prevent the patient from feeling it.

(22) Jung, K. Man and His Symbols, Op. Cit.

(23) Pringle, M.K. et al Concern (1977-78) National Children's Bureau, London.

(24) Millham, S. Bullock, R., Cherrett, P. (1975) After Grace - Teeth, Human Context Books, London.

(25) Millham, S., Bullock, R., Cherrett, P. (1975) On Violence in Community Homes, Violence, op. cit.

(26) Newson J. and Newson, E. (1963) Infant Care in an Urban Community, Allen & Unwin, London.

(27) Newson J. and Newson, E. (1968) Four Years Old in an Urban Community, Allen & Unwin, London.

(28) Newson J. and Newson, E. (1976) Seven Years Old in the Home Environment, Allen & Unwin, London.

(29) For an introduction to Psychogenic Theory: A Paradigm for History, see Lloyd de Mause, The History of Childhood p. 54 Op. Cit.

Child Abuse and Neglect, Vol. 3, pp. 115 - 121.

0145-2134/79/0301-0115 $02.00/0.

THE MULTI-DISCIPLINARY TEAM IN AN URBAN SETTING: THE SPECIAL UNIT CONCEPT.

John Pickett and Andy Maton.

N.S.P.C.C. Special Unit, Manchester, England.

When a parent physically or emotionally damages a child we are witness to a fundamental break down in the most vital of all interpersonal relationships. This breakdown is symptomatic of a complex interaction of social, biological and intra-psychic stresses. There is no simple solution. Child abuse is not only a crisis for the child and its family but also for the community and its helping professions. All are debilitated in their different ways. The outcome may be a progressive return to a relative state of equilibrium or a rapid or insidious regression into a chronic state of disequilibrium. All depends on the family's, the community's and the profession's response to that crisis.

The psychological defence mechanisms which are part and parcel of the individual person's response to threat can and do find expression in the wider context of groups and the community. There is much to suggest that these psychological defences operate with considerable force as a reaction to the inescapable fact of our personal aggressive drives being mirrored in their most pathological form - destructive, interpersonal violence. Denial seems to be the most persistent form of defence against the threatening phenomenon of child abuse. This is either acted out by pretending the problem doesn't exist, or by partialising the problem in the hope of reducing its size and complexity to manageable proportions. Thus, the problem (and solutions) can become either medical, social, legal, or cultural but never all and each at the same time. It is only when pioneers like Caffey and Kempe force us to look again that we are able to see beyond our own professional and personal boundaries, exploring new territory, in search of real solutions. The real solutions we seek demand a comprehensive perspective which soon makes it apparent that none of the professions or agencies can provide all the services alone. And so we have to find our place within the multi-disciplinary team.

In the field of child abuse teamwork is of critical importance. Early epidemiological studies in the U.K. showed serious failure in diagnosis and early case finding and an alarming incidence of re-injury even amongst diagnosed cases. Skinner and Castle (1969) demonstrated these two crucial points at which failure occurred and recommended that the early identification of child abuse would be assisted by the wider distribution of existing knowledge; it was suggested that mandatory reporting laws should be considered; they pointed out the need for education of the medical, nursing, legal and social work professions in techniques of treatment to deal with the problems of stress and crisis encountering by parents suffering from character disorders.

Considerable debate followed the publication of this important report and one study (Hall, 1972) suggested that as many as 757 children a year died as the result of child abuse. Subsequent research by the NSPCC (Rose and others 1975, Creighton and Owtram, 1977) drastically revised these estimates but not before they had gained considerable currency and had contributed to a generally alarmist atmosphere. Some of these cases led to official enquiries into the reasons for the child's death. The first such enquiry being into the death of Maria Colwell (DHSS, 1974). Other enquiries have followed with the unfortunate consequence of arousing considerable professional anxiety. Much of this anxiety has become projected into a consistently popular scapegoat 'lack of communication' between the professions concerned. Here we see the pressure to reduce complex issues to manageable proportions in the search for a single cause and a single solution. The fact of the matter is that although good inter-disciplinary communication is important, so too is an adequate level of knowledge, professional expertise, good clinical judgement and available treatment resources. These elements have tended to be subordinated to the need for good communication.

In 1974 the Department of Health and Social Security (DHSS, 1974 R) reinforced earlier advice by recommending the creation of Area Review Committees (ARD's) multi-disciplinary committees responsible for co-ordinating the management of cases of child abuse. They also recommended the setting up of central registers to aid identification and follow up. It should be noted that this circular made no attempt to define child abuse and gave little advice about the complex problems raised in the social management of these cases, nor did it comment on the need for adequate treatment facilities being available once the cases had been identified and assigned to the child protection services.

Without exception, all local authorities have responded to the circular and systems of co-ordination have developed largely based on the use of procedural guidelines, registers and case conferencing services. A recent study has shown that many of the registers are not effectively managed and the absence of expertise and resources are major contributory causes in their failure (BASW, 1978). The study noted that where teams of child abuse specialists operated the registers and related services much higher standards could be achieved. The report recommends that Child Abuse Consultants should be appointed in each local authority "empowered by the Area Review Committee to act on its behalf in all aspects of child abuse management......". It was clear to the authors of this report that there is little hope of achieving an efficient level of co-ordination in the absence of adequate levels of expertise. It was noted that in many areas of the country these complex cases are carried by untrained, unqualified social workers.

It is interesting to contrast the statutory services' response to the problem of child abuse with that of the NSPCC whose particular response to the management, study and treatment of child abuse has been considerable. Through research studies, articles in professional journals, conferences and use of the media it has played a large part in alerting the community to the nature and extent of child abuse. The Society has attempted to retain a comprehensive view of the problem, providing specialist services which include a significant level of direct service to the abused child and its parents. Since 1973 it has created seven Special Units which are designed to meet both the individual needs of parent and child and the needs of the professions concerned. The first of these Units was established in Manchester and the others are all run on similar lines.

The City of Manchester has a population of 490,000 of whom 106,000 are children under 15 years. It is typical of many large, urban communities with a declining population, inner-city decay and a high index of social problems creating heavy demands on the over-stretched community services. The need for planned teamwork and effective means of communication becomes very obvious in a city where the law enforcement, social, medical, nursing and educational services have between them approximately 9,600 personnel who may during the course of their daily work come into contact with an abused child.

A system of notification, intervention, co-ordination and review has been developed in Manchester which may provide a useful model for others to adopt (Pickett, 1976). The system is based on the assumption that effective communication and co-ordination can only occur where responsibility for its existence and maintenance is clearly defined and vested in practitioners who have the kind of specialised knowledge which enables them to work across professional boundaries and who also have a clear sense of commitment to their task and authority to carry it out. These attributes can only exist within a multi-disciplinary team.

The Manchester scheme began to evolve in 1970 when a multi-disciplinary committee was established under the chairmanship of John Davis, Professor of Child Health, Manchester University. In its early days the committee's work was confined to cases of non-accidental injury occurring to children under four years of age. Since January, 1975, its work has extended to include all non-accidentally injured children under sixteen years. The committee is known as the Manchester Child Abuse Policy Committee and functions as an Area Review Committee.

In 1971-72 the committee considered how it might increase effectiveness in the management of cases, and recognised the need for a specialist team to supplement and strengthen existing services. Following detailed discussions the Social Services Department and the N.S.P.C.C. jointly funded and set up a Special Unit with the Child Abuse Policy Committee acting as an advisory body. The Unit became operational in January, 1973, and its main functions are:-

1) To provide social work services for families referred where non-accidental injury is known or thought to have occurred.

2) To provide opportunities for consultation and discussion of such cases held by other social workers, health and medical personnel, with the aim of promoting good practice.

3) To maintain a central case register of all suspected cases of non-accidental injury to children under 16 years of age.

4) To co-ordinate services within the City of Manchester, ensuring that case conferences are held, where appropriate; all notified cases are periodically reviewed, and good communication maintained between the professions involved.

5) To undertake research into the problem.

6) To provide information to the professions and general public about the nature and extent of the problem.

The Unit is staffed by a team of six qualified social workers who provide casework services to referred families and consultative services to the professions; a Health Visitor on full-time secondment from the Area Health Authority who provides intensive health visiting to the Unit's caseload and acts as a consultant within the team; a Unit Co-ordinator who is responsible for the maintenance of the central case register, maintaining the co-ordination and review procedures associated with the registered cases and reporting to the Area Review Committees who contribute to the register. The Unit includes a Family Centre staffed by five qualified Nursery Nurses. There is also a team of consultants in Paediatrics, Psychiatry, Psychology, Gynaecology and Obstetrics and the Law, each playing an important part in the work of the Unit. A team of volunteers is also used to provide direct service to families both within the Family Centre and within the parents' homes. There are also supporting clerical staff who play a significant role not only within the office but in their contact with staff and clients.

High priority is given to creating a caring millieu and staff support, supervision and training represent a major proportion of the Team Leader's work.

THE CASEWORK SERVICE:

One of the prime functions of the Special Unit has been the provision of a casework service to families where non-accidental injury has occurred. Our casework experience is in many ways the bedrock of our value as credibility as consultants in child abuse. We believe that our validity as consultants depends on our practice experience with such family situations. What we have to advise as consultants is therefore rooted in ongoing practice experience which necessarily has regard both to the paradoxes and uncertainties of human behaviour and to the constraints of social reality.

The Unit does not provide an investigatory service, its casework service begins at the point where a clear diagnosis of non-accidental injury has been made, which is usually in the context of a case conference. In a few cases we have become involved nearer to the initial crisis where a medical consultant has been able to give a fairly unequivocal diagnosis and where there is no other social work involvement at the time. We accept cases on the understanding that our intervention will involve relatively intensive medium to long-term therapy. In a few cases we have accepted cases for a shorter diagnostic period in the first instance, usually these cases pose particularly difficult prognostic issues.

Caseloads have been limited to 10 - 12 per caseworker, recognising the demanding nature of work with many of the families and in order to maintain the other functions of the Unit.

During the first five years of the Unit's work 81 families have been taken on the caseload, this represents approximately 25% of Manchester's registered injured children. During the first two of those five years intake was below present levels but increased in 1975 when the size of the team was increased from 3 to 6 workers. The team has tended to concentrate its efforts on those families where the diagnosis and prognosis seem set at the more serious end of the spectrum of child abuse. All the team members are 'authorised persons' empowered to remove children and institute care proceedings. The team are on 24 hour call for all its services and radio paging equipment is used to achieve total availability.

The primary focus of social work treatment is the preservation of the life and health of the child, preferably within its natural home surroundings. In an attempt to meet the unmet dependency needs which seem to characterise many abusing parents, a supportive 'on-demand' service is offered with frequent contact and home visiting as part of the reaching out process. Detailed discussion of the casework process is reported elsewhere. (Pickett and Maton, 1977).

The therapeutic potential of the Unit services was considerably enhanced by the addition of a health visitor during 1976. She has been seconded by the Manchester Area Health Authority initially for an experimental period of two years (now extended a further two years), to explore the potential of intensive health visiting and parent education programmes. A preliminary discussion of her work can be found elsewhere. (Clarke, 1978).

THE FAMILY CENTRE:

In late 1976 the Family Centre was added to the range of services offered by the Unit. The Centre provides a treatment service for children and their parents and consists of a twenty place day nursery for children under five and facilities for their parents. Children who attend the Centre do so for a specified number of days ranging from one - five days per week, depending on their individual needs. All children attending the Centre are psychologically tested on admission and periodically reviewed by an Educational Psychologist attending on a sessional basis and provided by the School Psychological Services. The psychological assessment includes recommendations for a remedial programme for each child which is provided by the Centre staff under the supervision of the Family Centre Matron who is provided with consultation and support by the psychologist. Psychological assessment of the parents is also provided where this is required for therapeutic reasons. The children's Child Health records are transferred to the Centre for the duration of their attendance and a clinical medical officer (from the Child Health Services) is attached to the Centre and carries out developmental checks on a routine, regular basis. This service includes the full range of prophylactic procedures normally carried out in community clinics. Where necessary, arrangements are made for specialist remedial treatment by, for example, audiologists, ophthalmologists, etc. either by attendance at specialist clinics or by visiting specialists attending the Centre. The Centre offers the major advantage of bringing together all the community services within the context of a multi-disciplinary team in close communication. Regular multi-disciplinary reviews are carried out on each child and family.

Parents enter into a contract of attendance at the time that the family are admitted to the Centre, and usually attend for a minimum of one day per week but usually two days. Parents take part in various group work activities designed to improve their social functioning; their understanding of child/parent interaction; their awareness of their child's needs and a fuller understanding of child development. During the first full year there were 2625 child attendances and 1,054 parent attendances. It will be some time before it is possible to evaluate the value of this service but one interesting by-product has been a considerable advance in the observational skills of social workers brought into daily contact with abused children and this has obvious value for their consultative work.

CO-ORDINATION IN MANCHESTER:

The case register maintained by the Special Unit is in essence a depository of information from all sources, to which all designated personnel can relate as a first step in diagnosis and treatment. This aspect of the Unit's work is fully discussed elsewhere. (Maton and Pickett, 1978).

The Manchester Child Abuse Policy Committee (ARC) has delegated responsibility to the Special Unit to initiate appropriate action to protect the child and bring help to the family once a case has been notified to them.

Members of the Child Abuse Policy Committee have collaborated to produce procedural guidelines in the form of a 19 page booklet giving detailed advice on the steps to be taken once non-accidental injury is suspected. 10,000 copies of these guidelines have been distributed in conjunction with a pamphlet on non-accidental injury, which is designed as an aid to the identification of suspected cases.

The procedural guidelines are specifically designed to take account of the inter-related functions of the personnel involved, and to guide personnel into channels of communication both inter-departmentally and inter-professionally. Special emphasis has been given to delineating the role of senior designated staff members in advising and supporting field staff. Provision is also made for specialist social work and paediatric consultation to be available

The procedures cover cases coming to the notice of clinical medical officers, day nursery staff, education welfare officers, general practitioners, health visitors, hospitals, police, schools, school medical services and social workers (authorised and unauthorised).

For example:

Procedures for cases coming to the notice of Social Workers authorised under the C. & Y.P. Act, 1969.

1. Immediately consult with a senior designated staff member, who will be responsible for:-

   (a) Supporting and advising the social worker about the management of the case throughout these procedures and subsequently.

   (b) Checking the Special Unit register, and notifying the case to the register after investigation, if appropriate.

   (c) Having liaison with the Special Unit which will arrange a case conference, unless it is mutually agreed that one is unnecessary.

2. Consult with all other agencies who may have information about the child or family, including the child's general practitioner, clinical medical officer, health visitor and appropriate staff of school attended.

3. Interview the parents (or other persons having custody, charge or care of the child).

4. See the child, carefully note and record the child's condition and any observed injuries.

5. Ensure that the child receives medical diagnosis and treatment, either through the general practitioner or the casualty department.

6. Obtain a Place of Safety Order where it is necessary to afford immediate protection to the child.

7. If during step 2 it is ascertained that an authorised social worker in another agency is servicing the family, mutually agree and confirm with that worker who will carry out these procedures. If it is agreed that the other worker accepts responsibility for action as above, the social worker to whom the case was referred must satisfy himself that the other worker follows these procedures and ensure that he receives a report of any decisions made about the case. Both social workers should attend the case conference, if one is held.

Once a case is notified to the Special Unit, steps are immediately taken to check that communication is occurring between those involved. A decision is reached as to whether a case conference is necessary. In most cases it is. Unit staff are responsible for ensuring that the case conference is held, and that all appropriate personnel are invited. A Unit staff member attends, acting as a chairman and consultant to the conference, and representing the Child Abuse Policy Committee. In addition the three major children's hospitals have co-ordinating paediatricians who are available to attend case conferences or provide a further opinion or advice to other medical consultants. These Paediatricians also act as consultants to the Special Unit Staff. The Unit's Consultants in Psychiatry, Gynaecology and Obstetrics are also available for consultation and referral. A situation has now been achieved where every case conference in Manchester has available to is a specialist team experienced in dealing with large numbers of child abuse cases in the medical, nursing, social work and legal professions.

THE CONSULTATION SERVICE.

In our consultation service our management responsibilities and casework experience meet, although we regard consultation, functionally, as part of our management task. It has been one of our main functions from the planning stage of 1972, and has been available to all agencies and professions in the whole region since then. In the first five years we have undertaken 1,138 consultations. It was envisaged at the beginning that a specialist team of social workers and consultants from the discipline involved would be able to offer a high level of advice on diagnosis, case management planning and therapeutic aspects of non-accidental injury. It was also expected that the case conference would be an important context for our consultation service. This kind of management procedure was felt to facilitate, more than any other, the inter-professional liaison and communication that were seen as crucial to effective management of non-accidental injury at all levels.

We are aware that the case conference is sometimes subject to criticism, particularly on account of the professional time they absorb. The role of chairman of the case conference is crucial to the efficiency and economy with which it sets about its task. This is often complex, as are the family problems under review there. The chairman's task is to enable the group to share information, diagnostic thinking, case management planning and therapeutic insights. As chairman of the Manchester case conferences we seek to promote efficient and economical meetings without cutting them short of their task.

The tasks of the case conference combine to produce a set of recommendations to the various agencies concerned, for ongoing action. Interagency co-operation is essential to the overall diagnosis of the families' situations, and to a rounded view of therapeutic possibilities. We also feel it is increasingly important that recommendations about resource availability, the question of care proceedings and so on, should come from as wide a community base as possible, rather than any one professional group or agency, the case conference setting facilitates this.

It is always hard for one professional to appreciate another's view of a social problem, and to make the necessary accommodation. Occasionally during or after a case conference inter-professional difficulties may arise. It is good when they come to the surface during the meeting, as that is often the context where they can most appropriately be resolved. We see our task in the Special Unit as facilitating mutual understanding, and the fact that we represent an independent and voluntary agency, often helps.

We know from experience that liaison and co-operation between agencies often do not happen spontaneously and informally as they should, without a face-to-face meeting of the interested parties. There is also something about the dynamics of a case discussion that enables fresh insights and emphasis to emerge, that were previously not appreciated. Sometimes at a case conference it is appropriate to clarify the procedures, roles or responsibilities of different agencies and it is then particularly important for the chairman to be relatively neutral. Undoubtedly part of our effectiveness derives from the impartial and neutral stance that we are able to take. The same could certainly be said for the monitoring procedure that we operate. It is a credit to the Manchester scene that by and large co-operation and good will exist at the case conference and worker level. There seems little doubt that the tone for this is set by policy and decision making levels of the agencies involved.

For co-ordination to work effectively at the case conference level, there must be an underlying commitment to co-operation, in an atmosphere of good will, at the topmost level of each agency and profession. The setting for this to be worked out and maintained is the Area Review Committee, on which those agencies and professionals are represented. The Special Unit is a member of each of the ten Area Review Committees in Greater Manchester and serves the Manchester Area Review Committee (Child Abuse Policy Committee) in a secretarial and executive capacity. If the Special Unit exists in large part to facilitate co-operation and co-ordination between agencies, and if these qualities are essential to effective intervention in non-accidental injury, then any success in Manchester is a tribute ultimately to the agencies concerned and the Child Abuse Policy Committee in particular. We believe, in fact, that a measure of success can be demonstrated in Manchester from the trends that the register research has shown (Maton and Pickett, 1978). Nevertheless, this does not give grounds for complacency. The data also shows that non-accidental injury is still with us.

CONCLUSION.

The primary and explicit aim of the Manchester Special Unit is to provide a specialist service for helping the community services deal adequately with families who severely maltreat their children.

We seek to do this through, the formal procedures we operate, specialist advice we are able to offer, and the practical experience of casework, derived from direct work with abused children and their parents. The effectiveness of each of these relies on teamwork and co-operation between agencies and professions, and within individual departments. Trends have been identified which indicate a measure of success in effectively responding to the problem of child abuse in Manchester. Because success is an index of teamwork, any measure of success in Manchester is a reflection of everybody's corporate effort.

The Manchester agencies and professions share with us the aim of effectively responding to child abuse. We all, therefore, need to retain a high level of awareness of the problem, skill of identifying it and evaluation of the relevant procedures for managing it. Effort always needs to be made to retain a given level of practice and until the incidence of child abuse becomes markedly reduced none of us has any justification for complacency. Our ultimate goals must remain first the reduction in its incidence, especially of serious injury, and to young children; second, effective response when it occurs, and third, sufficient community-based resource and skill to reduce to a minimum the need for alternative care for the children.

We in the Unit are well aware that non-accidental injury is but one form of serious child abuse. We suspect that other forms of abuse are in fact more prevalent and as serious, e.g. failure to thrive, sexual and emotional abuse. As we fully realise that they may be harder to effectively manage than physical abuse. We hope that, as the problem of non-accidental injury becomes effectively and stably contained, we will be able to widen our scope in order to give attention to some of the wider problems of child abuse that are equally deserving.

ACKNOWLEDGEMENTS:

The Special Unit staff are indebted to all their professional colleagues for their help and support and to the Area Health Authority and Education Department for providing specialist consultants. All the professions involved are especially indebted to the Manchester Social Services. It is their support allied to that of the N.S.P.C.C. which has made our work possible.

REFERENCES:

British Association of Social Workers, (1978). The Central Child Abuse Register: A BASW Working Party Report.

Clarke, A. (1978). Ante-Natal Problems and Health Care in Abusing Families. In a paper presented to the Second International Congress of Child Abuse and Neglect. London, 1978.

Creighton, S. Owtram, P. (1977). Child Victims of Physical Abuse: A report on the Findings of N.S.P.C.C. Special Units' Registers. N.S.P.C.C. London.

D.H.S.S. (1974a) Report of the Committee of Enquiry into the Care and Supervision Provided in Relation to Maria Colwell. H.M.S.O. London.

D.H.S.S. (1974b.). Non-Accidental Injury to Children. LASSL (74) 13.

Hall, M.H. (1972). Non-Accidental Injuries in Children: In Royal Society of Health, 79th Annual Congress. April, 1972.

Maton, A. Pickett, J. (1978). Central Registration of Child Abuse in Manchester: An Evaluation. In a paper presented to the Second International Congress of Child Abuse and Neglect. London. 1978.

Pickett, J. (1976). The Management of Non-Accidental Injury to Children in the City of Manchester, in Borland, M. (Ed), Violence in the Family, Manchester University Press pp.61-87.

Pickett, J. Maton, A. (1977). Protective Casework and Child Abuse in A. W. Franklin (Ed). The Challenge of Child Abuse. Priory Press. London.

Rose, R. Owtram, P. Pickett, J. Masson, B. Maton, A. (1976). Registers of Suspected Non-Accidental Injury. A report on registers maintained in Leeds and Manchester by N.S.P.C.C. Special Units, N.S.P.C.C. London.

Skinner, A. E., Castle, R.L., (1969). Seventy Eight Battered Children: A Retrospective Study. N.S.P.C.C. London.

Child Abuse and Neglect, Vol. 3, pp. 123 - 130.
Pergamon Press Ltd., 1979. Printed in Great Britain.

TRAINING PROGRAM IN CHILD ABUSE FOR COMMUNITY HEALTH WORKERS

Stuart Copans, M.D.*, Helen Krell, M.D.*, John Gundy, M.D.*, Frances Field, M.N.*, Janet Rogan, ACSW**

*Dartmouth Medical School, Hanover, New Hampshire 03755
**Mary Hitchcock Memorial Hospital, Hanover, New Hampshire 03755

ABSTRACT

A wide range of health workers in the community provide care for families that abuse or have a potential for abusing their children. Frequently these workers are unable to work effectively because of difficulty dealing with feelings aroused by contact with such families.

An experimental child abuse training program for community health workers was designed by a pediatrician, a social worker, a public health nurse and two child psychiatrists. This program included a six-month study group which met weekly to focus on feelings and conflcts aroused during the course of work with abusing or potentially abusing families.

Through analysis of the group experience, the leaders identified eleven sets of feelings or conflicts which seemed to interfere consistently with effective delivery of care: 1)anxieties about a) being physically harmed by angry parents and b) about the effects of a decision; 2) denial and inhibition of anger; 3) need for emotional gratification from clients; 4) lack of professional support; 5) feelings of incompetence; 6) denial and projection of responsbility; 7) feeling total responsibility for assigned families; 8) difficulty separating personal from professional responsibility; 9) feelings of being a victim; 10) ambivalent feelings a) toward clients and b) about one's professional role; 11) need to be in control.

This type of group experience seems to be an effective method for exploration and resolution of feelings and conflicts.

group community workers feelings conflicts child abuse

INTRODUCTION

Child maltreatment is a serious and widespread problem. It is estimated that in the United States alone more than one million children are victims of physical abuse or neglect each year and at least 2,000 children die annually from circumstances associated with abuse or neglect.[1] There has been a tremendous increase in the number of reported cases in the nation over the past several years.

With increased public and professional awareness of this problem, increased attention has been focused on the care given to families with actual or potential child abuse and neglect. A wide range of community workers and agencies have traditionally provided basic human services to these high risk families: private physicians, public health nurses, visiting nurses, school health personnel, child health clinics, neighborhood health centers, physician's assistants, hospital emergency room personnel, welfare departments, and mental health centers.

As increased knowledge of the etiology and treatment of child abuse is gained, these community personnel are asked to provide specific psychological treatments along with the medical follow-up and social support traditionally given.

Work with these high-risk families is difficult, and often does not help the family's problem. In some cases this is because resources are too limited or intervention began too late, but in many cases, the lack of adequate training and support for workers impairs delivery of care.

Work with high-risk families is particularly difficult because of the highly charged feelings aroused in such work. These feelings often prevent the making of proper decisions and good management of cases even when cases are adequately understood. A crucial part of training involves learning to recognize, examine, and work with these feelings. This process does not stop with training, however, and on-going support for such self-examination should be part of any job involving work with high-risk families.

This paper has two purposes:

1. To describe a training group developed for a wide range of community workers involved in the care of high-risk families.

2. To examine the factors that frequently interfere with the delivery of effective care to high-risk families.

ORIGINS AND DESCRIPTION OF THE TRAINING GROUP

The training group grew out of a monthly pediatric conference initiated at a rural medical center in 1975 by an interdisciplinary regional child abuse program, the Children-At-Risk Program. The task of this monthly pediatric conference is to coordinate the care given to high-risk families seen in the hospital or its out-patient clinics with the care given in neighboring community human service agencies. During these conferences it became apparent that the many professionals and paraprofessionals available to work with these families were familiar with the literature related to child abuse, but often felt that they lacked sufficient emotional support for their efforts and lacked training in dealing with their own feelings aroused during their work. As a result, they were uncomfortable about working with these families and often made inappropriate decisions about how to manage cases.

For example, after one conference, a physician who was an authority on child abuse casually mentioned a case that had recently come through the emergency room of his hospital. The emergency room nurse and pediatric social worker had consulted him about a child seen in the emergency room with a laceration, which the mother stated she had inflicted; the physician was ambivalent about making a child abuse report--even though he knew the significant risk to the child of future serious injury and recognized the parents' need for child behavior counseling--because he was a friend of the family and he saw reporting as a punitive act.

A second case, presented at one of the conferences, involved a child who had been brought into the emergency room eight times because of injuries, including one instance in which it was reported by the parents that the child had fallen on an ice pick. The father's cardiologist and the father's psychotherapist, who had been asked to attend the high-risk conference, both stated that they would not permit the pediatrician involved to report this case to Protective Services because it would be harmful to the father. Another worker present at the conference stated that the mother worked in the hospital as another reason for not reporting to Protective Services.

In a third case, a diagnosis of child abuse had been made and Protective Services notified. Since the protective Services worker had too large a caseload to see the family as often as necessary, the reporting physician arranged to have a public health nurse also work closely with the family. The public health nurse was moralistic and judgmental. The Protective Services worker could see that the nurse's approach to the family was inappropriate and ineffective but was unable to discuss this fact with the nurse or the reporting physician.

A fourth case involved an adolescent girl brought to the mental health center by her mother, who was angry because the girl had complained of neglect by her mother. During the evaluation, the psychiatrist learned that the mother's boyfriend was currently living with the family and had engaged in serious sexual play with the girl, once directly in front of the mother, who claimed she was "too tired to protest". A Protective Services worker made one visit to the family, at which time the incident was admitted to but minimized, and decided no additional involvement was necessary. The psychiatrist felt this decision was inappropriate, but did not directly follow up on the case himself.

In these case examples it was not lack of knowledge that interfered with providing adequate care for high-risk families, but rather an inability to translate knowledge into action because the professionals involved lacked training and support in dealing with feelings.

For these reasons, group training was planned for community workers. The group consisted of two co-leaders and eleven participants, including four social workers, two case-aide workers, five registered nurses and one outreach worker. The agencies represented included three home health agencies from two states, a day care center, a community mental health center, a medical school outreach project, and a federaly funded Children and Youth Project.

The group began with a one-day seminar to present basic knowledge about child abuse and continued as a group meeting for one and one-half hours, once a week, for six months. The task of the group was to examine the feelings aroused in the workers by their work, and to discuss how these feelings aided or interefered with effective delivery of care to high-risk families.

FACTORS THAT INTERFERE WITH DELIVERY OF CARE

It is clear that knowledge about child abuse does not always lead to effective management of cases. What makes it so difficult for workers with adequate knowledge to function as competent professionals when dealing with high-risk families?

Discussions in the group led to identification of eleven major sets of feelings and processes that frequently interfered with the effective delivery of care to high-risk families:

1. Anxieties
   a) about being physically harmed by angry parents
   b) about the effects of a decision
2. Denial and inhibition of anger
3. Need for emotional gratification from clients
4. Lack of professional support
5. Feelings of incompetence
6. Denial and projection of responsibility
7. Feeling totally responsible for assigned families
8. Difficulty separating personal from professional responsibility
9. Feelings of being a victim
10. Ambivalent feelings
    a) toward clients
    b) about one's professional role
11. Need to be in control

Each of these warrants more detailed discussion.

1a) Anxiety About Physical Harm

Anxieties about physical harm are common in work with high-risk families. In many cases there is a history of violence and it is appropriate and realistic to be frightened and ask for assistance. However, very often the anxiety is irrational and unconsciously determined.

One worker visited a mother in a family with a history of abuse. She told the mother about the need to involve Protective Services and said she would return the next day to discuss this with the father and mother together. The mother predicted that the father, who had beaten her in the past, would surely "beat up" the worker when she returned. Initially the worker became quite fearful, and panicky, and felt totally unable to return to the home. After discussion with her supervisor, she arranged to have another worker accompany her on her visit with the father. In the group she was able to describe her initial anxiety and inability to proceed with the case as mostly irrational and related to her own childhood experiences. As a result of this group discussion, she was able to return to this family without fear. In fact, once she had stopped reacting to the father as if he were her own father, she found him to be in great distress and willing to have her help.

1b) Anxiety About the Effects of Making a Decision

An example of this was given by one of the nurses who had been working with an alcoholic mother for over a year. The children were clearly being mistreated; yet the mother kept promising to do better, threatening to kill herself if the children were taken away. The nurse was reluctant to report the case to Protective Services because of the mother's threat. After much discussion in the group, the worker filed a report, the children were removed from the home, and the mother actively sought help from a local Alcoholics Anonymous group for the first time. The nurse was able to see that her fear that she would be responsible for the mother's suicide had led her to act inappropriately and to allow unnecessary risk for the children.

2) <u>Denial and Inhibition of Anger</u>

One worker described a case inwhich she waited outside in the rain for hours knowing that the mother was inside. When asked how she felt, the worker said, "Oh no, I wasn't angry" but after further discussion in the group discovered she did have angry feelings toward the family. Other members of the group stated that they usually avoided this type of case and became aware that their avoidance was a way of expressing anger which was not consciously recognized. As one worker put it "the nice thing about a large case load is that when a case gets too difficult or frustrating, you can ignore it for a while because you always have too much to do".

3) <u>Need for Emotional Gratification from Clients</u>

Most workers badly wanted to be liked by their clients and to feel professionally competent. High-risk families typically do not gratify these needs, causing much frustration for the worker. One worker from an outreach project recognized her need for gratification from the discussion of the following case. She was seeing a family at home several times weekly. Each time she visited they asked her to do a favor for them. It soon took the whole visit, and more, for her to do these favors, which included driving the mother to an art show and borrowing money from a local priest for them. The worker began feeling "used" but hated herself for having that feeling. The family liked her, but she was getting angry at them and furthermore the family was making no progress at all. As she discussed this case in the group it became obvious to her that she did these favors for the family because she needed them to like her and to be grateful to her. By satisfying her own need to be liked, the worker was fostering excessive dependency. Once the group had helped her identify her need to be gratified by her clients, she was able to set limits on their demands of her, and they began to solve their own problems more effectively. This same worker also began questioning her motives about other behaviors on this case. Through individual introspection in the group as well as insights obtained from other members, she realized that she had been avoiding the mother's boyfriend and his continued bruising of the child because she was afraid of him. As a result of working through her feelings in the group, she was able to approach the boyfriend therapeutically, found him to be sad, lonely, jealous of the attention the mother had gotten from her and very responsive to help. Subsequently the complaints from the neighbors about the boyfriend beating and holding the child out the window stopped. Other group members also discovered they acted inappropriately at times out of fear or to make their clients like them. Almost every member also stated that one of the most difficult things about their work was their client's lack of appreciation of them.

4) <u>Lack of Professional Support</u>

Lack of support from their "professional family" of co-workers seemed a universal phenomenon. This lack of ability to support each other was closely linked to the need for support mentioned earlier. As one worker put it, "I've got so much crap to deal with, I don't feel like having anybody else unload theirs on me".

One worker gave an example of this within her own agency. A new worker in the agency was having severe emotional difficulties. The other workers in the agency refused to recognize the man's symptoms and continued to allow him to work. The group member who was attempting to deal with with the situation alone became so angry and agitated that she was unable to do her work effectively. She did finally come to the group in tears asking for support, yet held back for fear of "breaking down" in front of the group. Apparent in this case was a reluctance to admit "weakness" in self or others. Such reluctance is common and leads to difficulty in asking for, or giving, professional support.

After discussion in the group of this difficult problem, the worker returned to her agency and by dealing directly with the head of the program was able to obtain professional help for the disturbed worker as well as to have him temporarily relieved of clinical responsibilities.

Workers frequently came to the group with difficult cases they have not been able to discuss with their fellow workers or supervisors. Prior to the group, they had rarely discussed uncomfortable feelings aroused in their work. As the group progressed, they were able to bring feelings and conflicts to discussion and resolution in their own agencies.

5) Feelings of Incompetence

Feelings of incompetence seemed universal in the members of our group. These feelings are hardly surprising given the difficulties inherent in their work, and their inability to support each other.

One very competent worker said she felt professionally inadequate most of the time. Since she rarely received comments on her work, she assumed it was not good. It was a great relief to her to discover that others in the group shared these feelings of failure. As a result of recognizing this problem in the group, many workers returned to their agencies and asked for critical feedback on their work. Most of them also felt much less incompetent, as they could see from case discussions in the group that there is generally no "best way" or "right answer" in their work.

6) Denial and Projection of Responsibility

An outreach worker had been working with a family for several months and suspected abuse of one of the children. She made a report and discussed the case briefly with the Protective Services worker who agreed to see the family very soon. The outreach worker ceased to work with the family, assuming the Protective Services worker had taken over. Two months later she checked on the family, discovering that they had never been seen by the Protective Services worker. The outreach worker was furious. After "stewing" about it for several days, she called the Protective Services worker and "gave him hell" for not seeing the family. He became defensive and angry. He stated that since he had such an overwhelming case load, he first attended to cases in which no other agency was involved, and that she should have been following the family. Each denied his own responsibility and assigned it to the other. Meanwhile the family had been attended by no one. However, in the group, these two people were able to resolve their differences and devise a treatment plan by which the family obtained the necessary services.

7) Feeling Totally Responsible for Assigned Families

Workers frequently described feeling that they were totally responsible for assigned families. This was generally much more of a problem than their refusing to assume responsibility.

One Protective Services worker Mr. R. was following an infant being cared for by his 86 year old grandfather and mentally retarded mother. The worker knew removal of the child would be very painful for the grandfather who was quite attached to the child and felt that if he removed the child, he would be personally responsible for the grandfather's suffering. After much discussion in the group, Mr. R. was able to see that he had taken too much responsibility in this case. Once he realized this and some of the reasons for such behavior were worked through, he was able to see his responsibility much more realistically. As a result, he went to court and asked for removal of the child who a year later was dramatically improved in his foster home.

8) Difficulty Separating Personal Responsibility from Professional Responsibility

One worker had been a public health nurse in her small town for several years. She had been hard-working, diligent, and competent, and had worked with many high-risk families. One family began calling her at any hour of the night for minor complaints and she responded by going out to the home each time. The nurse became exhausted and unable to carry out her normal work and care for herself and her family because of the drain and strain of these middle-of-the-night visits. The nurse thought it wrong to refuse to come whenever someone called; she felt it was her personal, professional responsibility to meet the needs of the townspeople whenever they asked. After much discussion in the group, she was able to take a day off, missing an important meeting, to celebrate her daughter's birthday--something she would never have done before. She was also able to limit the excessive demands of the townspeople.

A second manifestation of separating personal from professional responsibilities is demonstrated by emotional involvement. One of the group members was asked to testify as an expert witness in a case of child abuse in which the state petitioned the court for termination of parental rights. The worker, after a thorough investigation of the children and mother, thought it best to terminate parental rights and so testified in court. The mother was in the courtroom at the time. During the hearing the worker began to feel guilty about her testimony, avoided looking at the mother's pleading eyes, and had to keep telling herself "remember you were asked to make a recommendation regarding the children, not the mother". The worker felt remorseful afterwards: she thought herself a failure as a professional and a bad person for having recommended that the mother be "deprived of her children". It was only after discussing her feelings and frustrations in detail that she was able to see that she had acted properly.

Another example, but in reverse, was given by one of the workers. After a fight with her boyfriend, she described feelings that she was a failure as a person, and went to work that day feeling depressed that she was also a failure in her job. Most group members could identify with this phenomenon and decided they could most effectively deal with it either by discussing the feelings with a co-worker or by taking off part of the day until they felt better.

9) Feelings of Being a Victim

Repeatedly the workers in the group blamed case failures and frustrations on the families who "just weren't motivated", on "other agencies who weren't cooperating", or on the state government which was "full of bureaucrats who wanted to glorify themselves". This enabled the workers to avoid facing their limitations, their failures, and the disturbing fact that for certain families there is nothing one can do. Often a hopeless attitude towards the system kept them from advocating change in the system. Workers from one Protective Services office said, "We'll never get any more workers in our office, why try?" Shortly after they had discussed this in the group, a new director was able to hire two more workers for that same office.

Other group members observed that members from that particular office were overly and unrealistically pessimistic. This engendered group discussion about how expecting too much from families can leave workers feeling depressed and demoralized. Case discussions among group members enabled each of them to be more realistic about their families and as a result, members felt less "burnt out".

10a) Ambilvalent Feelings Toward Clients

Ambivalent feelings frequently interfered with effective client care. One worker had been visiting a home for months. Each time she came, the mother's boyfriend disappeared into the bedroom, but then asked for a ride as she was getting ready to leave. He "looked like a hippie" and had a history of "serving time for assault". She wanted to help the family but hated making home visits because of the boyfriend. Through individual introspection in the group as well as insights obtained from other members, she realized that she had been avoiding the mother's boyfriend and his continued brusing of the child because she was afraid of him. As a result of working through her feelings in the group, she was able to approach the boyfriend therapeutically, found him to be sad, lonely, jealous of the attention the mother had gotten from her and very responsive to help. Subsequently the complaints from the neighbors about the boyfriend beating and holding the child out the window stopped. Other group members also discovered they acted inappropriately because of ambivalent feelings toward their clients.

10b) Ambivalent Feelings About One's Professional Role

One worker talked about quitting his job. He often worked twelve-hour days, seven days a week, but then complained bitterly about the long hours. He was unable to reach a balance between feeling responsible and liking his job and feeling overworked and hating it. At times when a case truly demanded after-hour care, he would be resentful of that particular family. Many other group members also admitted feeling the same way. The worker in the above example, partly as a result of the group experience, left his job as a Protective Services worker and made furniture for over a year. Subsequently, he sought work again in the area of child abuse and in his current role he has set limits on what he can do and feels much more satisfied and less ambivalent about his professional responsibilities.

11) Need to be in Control

Most workers at some time mentioned a need to control their situation with clients, or to control the clients themselves. Some insisted on a certain degree of motivation in the family before they would work with a family, in spite of having knowledge from conferences and literature that aubsing parents are difficult to work with because of their poor motivation, and that reaching out to them is nonetheless crucial to establishing a working relationship.

A nurse was working with an older woman whose husband was dying in the local hospital. The wife did not visit him. The nurse did not understand this, condemned the wife for not visiting, and finally insisted on taking her to the hospital. The woman refused to go, saying she was not feeling well, and the nurse, believing she was making excuses, was angry and wanted to stop trying to help the wife. Group members confronted her with her insensitivity to the mother's feelings out of her own need to control and impose her own feelings upon her. Initially the nurse was defensive but gradually as a result of group feedback, she came to her own conclusion that she was not in touch with her own feelings, and that this in turn led her to be insensitive to others. As she discussed her own feelings more, she was able to be less rigid with her clients.

DISCUSSION

Many persons who work with high-risk families experience their own feelings, actions and doubts as evidence of their personal and professional unfitness. The members of our group felt this way even though they were in fact highly competent workers. Careful selection of people hired to work with abusing families will not eliminate these problems.

It has long been known that patients re-establish with their therapists the relationships they had with the significant people in their lives. It has also been reported that therapists receiving supervision of their work with such patients try to establish this same relationship with their supervisors. In the same way, problems that characterize high-risk families seemed to be recapitulated in the relationship of the workers to the group leaders. There was a remarkable similarity between the problems and issues raised by the workers in our group and the problems and questions noted in high-risk families.[2]

One method of dealing with the difficulties encountered in this work is to develop a continuing support group of individuals who work together. In rural areas where the families are far apart and workers often work alone, this is not feasible. In such areas, it is necessary to develop methods of training and sources of support for the workers. The group described in this paper seemed to provide an effective method for exploration and resolution of feelings and conflicts.

SUMMARY

Training methods in psychiatry, pediatrics, nursing or social work do not prepare workers for the feelings and reactions stimulated by work with families at risk for child abuse. These feelings, if not recognized and examined, often interfere with providing good care. These feelings and reactions include: anxieties about physical harm and about the effects of a decision; the denial and inhibition of anger; the need for emotional gratification from clients; lack of professional support; feelings of incompetence; denial and projection of responsibility; feelings of total responsibility; difficulty distinguishing personal from professional responsibility; feelings of being a victim; ambivalent feelings toward clients and about one's professional role; and need to be in control.

Workers assigned to high-risk families must be given the training and support necessary to recognize and deal with these feelings and processes in ways helpful to the care of clients.[3]

REFERENCES

1. From statistics gathered for the United States Department of Health, Education and Welfare in the Newsletter of the American Orthopsychiatric Association, Inc. Summer 1976, page 8.

2. Galdston, Richard, M.D. 1976, "Child Abuse and the Epidemiology of Violence", in Proceedings, Second Annual Children's Advocacy Conference, Durham, New Hampshire, April 23 and 24.

3. Sanders, Wyman R. 1972, "Resistance to Dealing with Parents of Battered Children", Pediatrics 50(6):835-857

Child Abuse and Neglect, Vol. 3, pp. 131 - 135.

0145-2134/79/0301-0131 $02.00/0.

A STATE-WIDE CHILD ABUSE TRAINING PROGRAM FOR PUBLIC HEALTH NURSES

Elizabeth Elmer, Harriet G. Bennett, Carol G. Sankey

Parental Stress Center, 918 South Negley Avenue,
Pittsburgh, Pennsylvania 15232, U.S.A.

BACKGROUND

Today, child abuse is one of the most difficult problems facing professionals who work with families. There are no simple solutions; one cannot simply prescribe a pill to make it go away. Indeed, many people have a difficult time even looking at child abuse. This, coupled with the difficulty of defining abuse and neglect, makes the problem even more complex. Legal definitions are often ambiguous, the causes and forms of abuse vary, and controversy often surrounds the issues.

In view of these complexities, the Public Health Nurse's (PHN's) role in relation to child abuse and neglect can be difficult, particularly when one considers her role in the community. While conducting clinics and doing home visits, the PHN is in an excellent position to identify possible cases of abuse. However, because of the non-threatening image of the PHN and because she may frequently be one of the few resources available in small communities, she is an appropriate person to do intervention work with these troubled families. This dual responsibility is not easily resolved.

The passage of the new Pennsylvania child abuse law in 1975 compounded the problem by naming the public health nurse as a mandated reporter and as an additional assessment resource for child welfare services. While the PHN possessed a basic body of knowledge related to child development, her knowledge of child abuse, particularly its identification and management, was still minimal. In addition, the PHN had to learn to understand and deal with her feelings toward people who abuse in order that her emotions should not interfere with her legal obligation to report abusive situations, nor her ability to continue working with a family. Training the nurse to assume her expanded role became vital.

OVERALL DESIGN AND PROGRAM GOALS

In response to this need, the Pennsylvania Department of Health contracted with the Parental Stress Center of Pittsburgh to develop a training program for the 300 state PHNs, which would enhance the PHN's knowledge of child abuse and neglect and enable her to deal more effectively with such cases. The contract called for the Parental Stress Center project staff to develop the training program and the necessary tools for its implementation: a detailed curriculum including a trainer's manual, a selected readings manual to augment the program, and a film specifically designed to portray the role of a public health nurse. The project staff would then demonstrate the training program and train eight public health nurses to act as nurse-trainers,conducting workshops throughout the state. Finally, to assess the total impact of the program, evaluation procedures would be designed.

Following initial consultation to establish the grantor's priorities for the training, the project staff defined the following goals for the workshops: (1) to increase the competence of the PHNs in identifying suspected cases of child abuse and neglect; (2) to acquaint the PHNs with relevant child abuse laws and the reporting process; (3) to clarify the role of the PHNs in prevention, intervention, and ongoing case management of suspected and reported cases; and (4) to enhance collaboration between the PHNs and child welfare services workers.

CURRICULUM DEVELOPMENT

As an early step in planning we needed information regarding some of the characteristics of the nurses to whom the workshops would be directed. A questionnaire was developed by our evaluation consultant and sent to a 20% sample of the nurses. The results acquainted the project staff with the nurses' background and experience in abuse and showed that one of the greatest gaps in the knowledge of nurses was in relation to the law and law-related personnel. The validity of one of the chief objectives of the program was confirmed - that of augmenting the nurses' knowledge of Pennsylvania child abuse laws and the use of the legal process and reporting.

Though the project staff had the necessary content knowledge for the projected training, they recognized the need for a consultant skilled in curriculum development. The task of that individual was to provide input regarding the optimum structure for content presentation, to help determine appropriate teaching techniques, and to help set the time frame for the workshop presentation. In addition, consultation was obtained from other sources such as health department administrative personnel, child welfare services staff, lawyers, and physicians.

This input, combined with our formal statement of the program goals, led to the following as principal items for curriculum content: feelings and attitudes towards abuse; etiology; identification of abuse and high risk families; laws relating to abuse and the legal process; an overview of child welfare services and their methods of case management; prevention; intervention; and the PHN's role. We found it necessary to define certain boundaries for the program. The focus would be primarily on the pre-school child (birth - 5 years) and the content would deal in depth with physical abuse and neglect rather than sexual and emotional abuse. The program would concentrate on abused and neglected children whom the PHN would most likely see during routine clinic and home visits. We assumed that severely abused children (i.e., those with fractures and lacerations) would be seen more often in hospital emergency rooms.

As curriculum content emerged, we considered possible teaching techniques to effectively present the material. We learned that the nurses chosen by the Health Department to be trainers had no particular background in abuse or teaching methods. Therefore, the objectives, content, and techniques had to be developed in the most minute detail. We would have to provide the nurse-trainers with a wide but simple variety of options and techniques for their presentations such as the use of small groups, role play, and group-centered discussion; there would be little emphasis on and use of the lecture method. Always present was the idea that the nurse-trainers would need sufficient confidence in their skills and presentations so that they would be accepted as teachers by their peers.

A focal point of the curriculum was a 25-minute movie, Ordinary People: A Film on Child Abuse. The film was designed to heighten the awareness of the dynamics of abusive families and increase the feeling of empathy for abusive adults. It was a tool to stimulate discussion of the etiology, identification, and prevention of abuse by presenting a series of incidents in the life of an abusive family where a public health nurse was involved. Ordinary People won first prize in the Training and Education category of the National Industrial Film Festival (United States) in September, 1977 and is now being distributed nationally.

The Selected Readings Manual Related to Child Abuse was compiled for the trainees as a supplement to the curriculum. Given to each participant, this printed manual provided them with additional viewpoints for discussion. The first two sections of the manual dealt with general aspects of child abuse; the remaining sections followed the subject order of the curriculum. A list of selected references appeared at the end of the manual.

The Trainer's Manual was designed to assist the nurse-trainers in conducting workshops for their co-workers. Though each trainer would attend a demonstration of the curriculum and an intensive, week-long program on conducting workshops, the manual became a vital supplement and reference for each nurse-trainer. It explained the rationale and goals of the program, the necessary planning phases of the workshop, explanations of recommended teaching methods and techniques and finally a day-by-day account of the curriculum and its presentation. We suggested that the trainer might want to adapt techniques and expand the basic content to suit her own particular style of teaching as well as the needs of each group of trainees. Though flexibility and personalization were encouraged, the project staff cautioned the trainers to respect the recommended content in order to preserve the integrity of the evaluation.

PREPARATION OF NURSE-TRAINERS

The culmination of all our planning and preparation was two demonstrations of the curriculum by the project staff. Our staff presented the entire program, as the nurse-trainers would, alternating the sessions they led to avoid excessive fatigue. Workshops lasted a total of four days, with two consecutive days at the beginning of one week and two days of the following week. This maximized the participant's ability to absorb the material.

Four prospective nurse-trainers attended each demonstration as participants to gain information, see the design in action, and observe the project staff as role models. Following each of the two demonstrations, the nurse-trainers met with the project staff to discuss their new roles, thus giving them an opportunity to air concerns and questions in this first stage of their training and formalize their commitment to the program.

The second phase in the preparation of the nurse-trainers was a week of intensive training in Pittsburgh where they acquired more in-depth knowledge of the curriculum as well as methods for effective presentation. Local experts on child abuse gave didactic presentations covering those areas of the curriculum in which trainers seemed most lacking. This, coupled with the opportunity for the nurse-trainers to interact with these resource people, served to reinforce curriculum content. We focused on providing the trainers with an enlarged pool of knowledge from which to draw should questions beyond the immediate course content arise in their own workshops.

Our curriculum consultant conducted two full days of the training week. During this time she discussed methods and techniques of teaching in addition to providing experiential sessions to facilitate the nurse-trainers' learning. The value and use of the group process was particularly emphasized. The project staff also focused on enhancing group interaction and cohesiveness among the nurse-trainers which ultimately established an informal network of peer support.

IMPLEMENTATION

After the intensive training week, the nurse-trainers began to plan the workshops for the other state PHNs. To concentrate on their new role, the neophyte trainers were freed of their nursing responsibilities by temporary replacements.

Each pair of trainers arranged the workshops in their own communities with the assistance of their local nurse administrator and, when needed, the project staff. Health Department social workers, familiar with the project, provided additional support.

As the final stage in the training process, the maiden workshop of each pair of trainers was monitored by a project staff member. This monitoring provided support to the nurse-trainers, clarified the trainer's role and helped in the assessment of the nurse-trainer's effectiveness. Following the initial monitoring, the project staff and the nurse-trainers kept in touch through written reports and regular phone calls. We found that the nurse-trainers also formed an internal peer support system by frequently sharing experiences by the phone. In all there were 20 workshops across the state, including the two initial demonstrations. A total of more than 300 state nurses were trained over a 17-week period.

FORMAL EVALUATION

In addition to the initial questionnaire assessing the nurses' needs prior to curriculum development, a second questionnaire was developed to assess the effects of the total training program. By using ongoing evaluation procedures, we were able to follow group progress to assure the effective presentation of the curriculum.

The questionnaire consisted of two parts. First a 94-item true-false test covering the curriculum topics was administered at the beginning and close of each four-day workshop. Second, five-point scales were used for the nurses to rate their perception of the amount of information gained on various workshop topics and the usefulness of specific exercises and activities. Altogether, forty-two topics and workshop activities were rated. To assure anonymity of the trainees' responses, all questionnaires were identified by code number which enabled the evaluation team to determine the workshop each nurse attended and her job level.

An independent analysis of all the questionnaires was conducted by a University of Pittsburgh psychologist specializing in evaluation. A statistically significant increase occurred in the nurses' scores between the pre- and post-workshop administrations of the true-false test ($t = 23.4$, $p < .001$). Analysis according to job level also showed an increase of knowledge, thus proving the value of the program to all nursing personnel, both line workers and supervisors.

According to the rating scales, the topic areas on which the nurses felt they received most new information were the laws related to child abuse, the role of the courts, reporting procedures, and the identification of child abuse. These results were consistent with the goals of the program. In addition, the ratings for reporting procedures and laws related to child abuse were significantly correlated with the gains in test scores from the beginning to the end of the workshops. Nurses who felt they had obtained the most new information of these topics tended to make the greatest improvement on the true-false test.

Finally, in regard to specific activities of the workshop, the most valued activities were the presence of an attorney, the opportunity to share experiences with other PHNs, the lecture on legal issues related to abuse, the discussion of the nurse's role in the court process, and the presence of a representative from Child Welfare Services. Again the results were consistent with the goals of the program and also showed the value of sharing experiences with colleagues.

The results of the questionnaires indicate that not only did the workshops contribute significantly to increasing the PHN's knowledge of child abuse, but the nurses perceived the workshops as worthwhile. The findings also support the conclusion that, given a well developed workshop format and appropriate curriculum materials, public health nurses can be taught to successfully implement a program for their colleagues. Further, the evaluation yielded pertinent information which can be useful in refining the curriculum for other professionals.

ASSESSMENT

In looking back on the experience, we feel that the nurse-trainers were asked to take on an enormous job. Initially, they had to learn a broad new concept area characterized by few facts, many opinions and prejudices, and by shifts in general knowledge from year to year. Next, the nurse-trainers needed to learn completely new techniques of teaching beyond the lecture method that was most familiar to them. Third, the nurse-trainers' colleagues had to accept them as having some expertise in presenting a workshop on child abuse. Trainee groups proved to be somewhat resistant to methods utilizing participation and discussion. This may have been due to the emotionally charged nature of the subject matter.

Though we emphasized that the nurse-trainers were facilitators of learning rather than teachers, we found them to be much more confident about their nursing role than their teaching role. It also became apparent that nurses, on the whole, had low self-esteem in relation to child welfare personnel. Though we felt that they had much expertise in handling complex family and community problems in the course of their professional duties, they felt it necessary to bow to the judgment of other professionals. The PHNs implied that child welfare staff were better trained and more skilled regarding children's needs. This feeling was often illustrated by the reluctance of the PHN to insist upon getting a report from child welfare about a child known to both agencies. Sometimes a PHN was left out of case planning even though she had made the initial referral and her continued input could be helpful. Her acceptance of this rejection indicated her lack of confidence. We questioned whether this also affected her dealings with other professionals and clients.

As the workshops progressed and the PHNs could see and talk to representatives of child welfare and other professions, they began to evidence a gain in stature. They could see that their professional training was fully as adequate as the training of child welfare staff; in fact, their knowledge of child development frequently surpassed that of others. In addition, the child welfare representatives treated the nurses with respect. By meeting face to face in the workshops, both PHNs and child welfare representatives discovered how much they could help each other in working with troubled families.

In summary, our project staff derived much professional satisfaction from developing this training program for the Pennsylvania State Public Health Nurses. We were continually impressed with the quality of both nurses and nurse-trainers, who proved willing, dedicated, and knowledgeable.

To our knowledge no other state in our country has developed and implemented a training program for any one profession which has covered the entire state group. In presenting this paper we hope that other states or countries, as well as other professional groups, may become interested enough to develop similar programs.

Child Abuse and Neglect, Vol. 3, pp. 137 - 143.
Pergamon Press Ltd., 1979. Printed in Great Britain.

INTERDISCIPLINARY EDUCATION OF LAWYERS AND SOCIAL WORKERS AS ADVOCATES FOR ABUSED CHILDREN AND THEIR FAMILIES

Donald N. Duquette, Law School
Carolyn Okell Jones, School of Social Work

University of Michigan

INTERDISCIPLINARY CHILD ADVOCACY PROJECT AT THE UNIVERSITY OF MICHIGAN

Working effectively with families who have abused or neglected their children demands enormous commitment and cooperation from a variety of disciplines and agencies. In recognition of this fact the Towsley Foundation funded in 1976 a three year project called the Interdisciplinary Project on Child Abuse and Neglect involving the Schools of Law, Medicine and Social Work at the University of Michigan. The Project's main goals are to develop models of interdisciplinary collaboration and training in child advocacy in the context of child abuse and neglect and to produce teaching materials that can be used by a variety of professionals in this field. In addition to a full-time administrative coordinator, the Project is staffed by professionals representing law, social work, pediatrics, child psychiatry and pediatric psychology. Three members (1 lawyer and 2 social workers) are employed by the Project full-time; the majority are engaged on a part-time basis to undertake clinical, academic and executive responsibilities.

Medical School

Part of the Project is located in Mott Children's Hospital at the University Medical Center. The Project staff participate in several facets of the medical education curriculum. Drawing on their clinical experience in the hospital, they teach students in the Law and Social Work Schools and train social workers in community agencies concerned with the protection of children.

Primarily, the staff serve as working members of the University Hospital Child Abuse or Neglect (SCAN) team providing consultation, assisting in the diagnosis and management of cases and cooperating with community agencies in developing a treatment plan for the abused or neglected child and his family.

School of Social Work

In the School of Social Work two faculty positions are funded by the Project. These faculty persons perform traditional clinical, in-service and teaching functions including offering graduate students two specialized courses in child abuse and neglect. Each semester several social work students have field placements with the SCAN team and work closely with law students from the Child Advocacy Law Clinic on cases of child abuse and neglect.

Law School

The other major component of the Project is the Child Advocacy Law Clinic whose activities will be cited in detail as an example of the way in which the goals of interdisciplinary education are pursued. In addition to the Child Advocacy Law Clinic, teaching is provided by the Project staff in the non-clinical law school curriculum focusing on legal, medical, psychiatric and social aspects of child abuse and neglect.

CHILD ADVOCACY LAW CLINIC

The Child Advocacy Law Clinic is a speciality clinical law experience offered by the University of Michigan Law School as part of the Interdisciplinary Project. An objective of the Child Advocacy Clinic is to provide eight law students per semester with a clinical

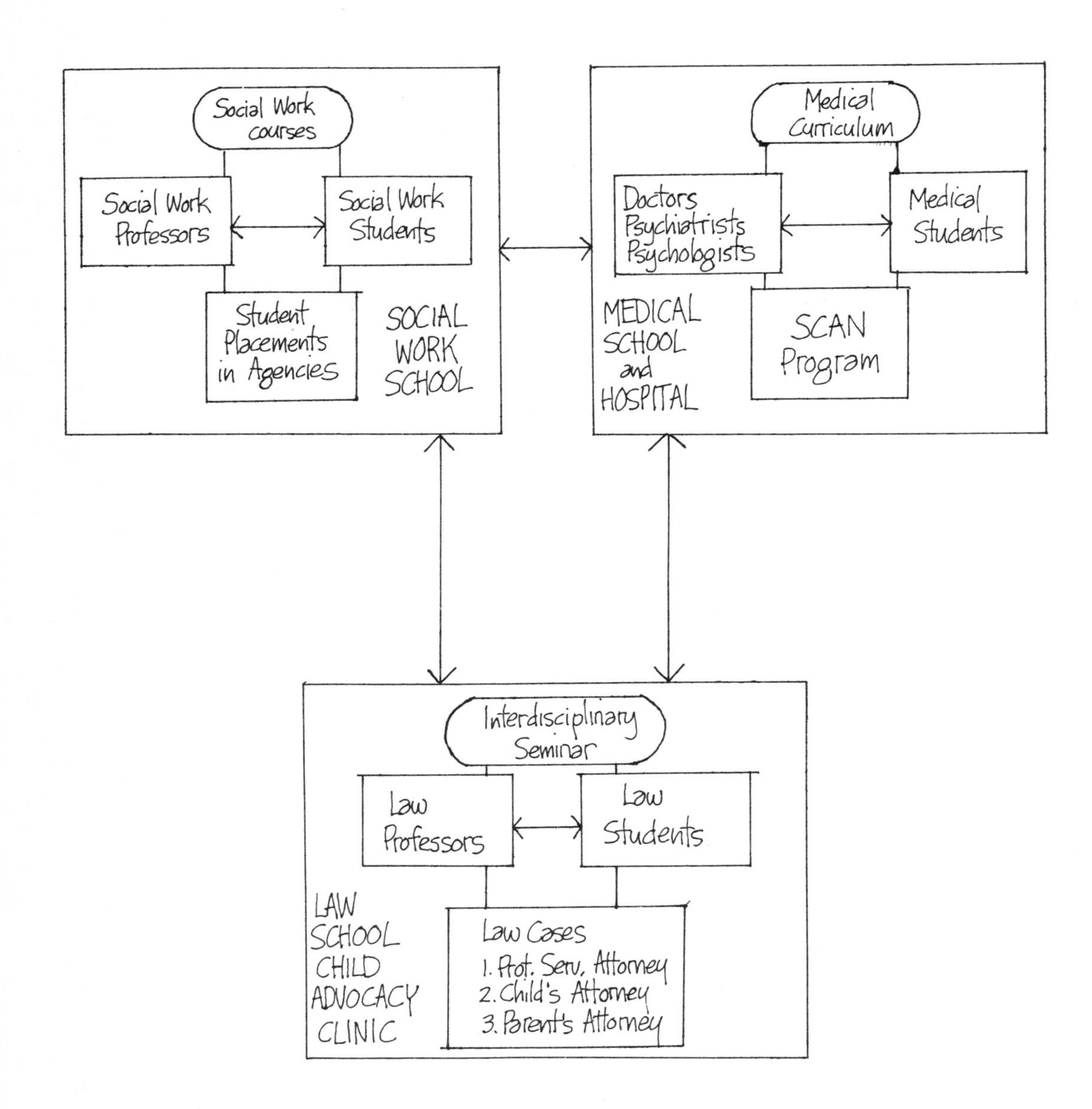

INTERDISCIPLINARY PROJECT ON CHILD ABUSE AND NEGLECT
UNIVERSITY OF MICHIGAN

Figure 1

experience handling actual child abuse and neglect cases in a setting of close collaboration with several different professions.

Actual case handling, under the supervision of a law faculty member and in consultation with social work, psychiatry, psychology and pediatric faculty, is the core of the Child Advocacy experience for law students. Recognizing that the lawyer responsibility in child protection cases in the American legal system cannot be examined or learned from a single perspective, and that child advocacy by necessity requires family advocacy, law students handle cases in three distinct legal roles in separate Michigan counties. In Washtenaw County (Ann Arbor and vicinity) the Clinic acts as attorney for the Child Protection Agency who is the petitioner (moving party) in child protection legal actions. In Wayne County (Detroit) the Clinic represents the child in abuse or neglect cases. In Jackson County, a mostly rural county to the west of Ann Arbor, the Clinic represents parents accused of child abuse or neglect.

Several advantages result from the different legal roles and geographical diversity of cases handled. First, both students and faculty experience the role demands and personal and interprofessional conflicts evoked by representation of the various parties. Second, the court and social service delivery systems in each county vary significantly in the amount of resources available and in their efficiency and effectiveness. Third, the community standards of child care vary appreciably among the counties. For example, a case that would not even be brought to the attention of the Court in one county may result in a child being removed from his home in another. A case that would prompt marshalling of extensive assessments and treatment resources in one county may receive only monitoring by a single caseworker in another county.

The Child Advocacy Clinic is offered cases by Court authorities in each county. Cases are screened by the supervising attorney for educational value and opportunity for interdisciplinary collaboration. Students' time commitments and existing caseload are also a consideration in the choice of cases.

The Clinic's interdisciplinary staff offer the law students traditional legal skills training as well as seminars in medical aspects of child abuse and neglect, child development, interpersonal and family dynamics, functioning of human service agencies, intervention strategies, interviewing and counseling. Each student is provided with a Child Advocacy Manual compiled by the interdisciplinary staff on the legal, medical and social-psychological aspects of child abuse and neglect. Through interacting with the interdisciplinary faculty and social work students in seminars and through consultation on cases, students gain an appreciation of the roles and functions of the other disciplines and begin to understand the legal role in relation to the other professions.

Attorney for Child Protection Agency

To prepare the law student for the role of Protective Services attorney, the Clinic simulates the development of a case early in each semester. Mock interviews between social work students and law students are conducted, sample petitions are drafted and courtroom advocacy is simulated. Student performances are video-taped for private review and for review with the faculty. Prior to actually handling a case, students see video-tapes of other students and of lawyers in courtroom settings. They also observe the supervising attorneys in court on cases with which they are already familiar.

In all the attorney roles, the Child Advocacy law students are encouraged to define their responsibilities more broadly than merely in-court advocacy. Client counseling, negotiation, case preparation, and social advocacy are just as important for the lawyer as is traditional trial advocacy. As attorney for the child protection agency, however, traditional trial advocacy skills are especially important. Child protection cases are often difficult to prove. The incidents often occur without witnesses. If a parent denies allegations of child abuse or neglect the agency attorney must marshall whatever evidence is available and organize and present it in a persuasive fashion to the Court. Proofs in such cases often require testimony from physicians, psychiatrists and psychologists. The social workers nearly always testify and are essential colleagues in developing the legal case.

The interface between the social agency and the Court must be explored and understood by both lawyers and social workers. In the Clinic the role of the Court in child protection is placed in context for both social workers and lawyers.

Delivery of services to the dysfunctional family remains the duty of the social agency whether or not court action is taken. It is the social workers who have the mandate, the expertise and the resources to actually provide assistance to the children and their families. Legal action becomes necessary only when the intervention strategy of the agency infringes important personal liberties of the parents or the children. Essentially, the agency asks the Court to suspend parental rights and authorize coercive intervention in a particular family on behalf of the children. The Court's authorization may facilitate the agency intervention. The Court itself, however, has no treatment expertise nor should it be relied upon to develop a treatment plan.

The law student, when representing Protective Services should understand and appreciate the responsibilities, skills, available resources and even the limitations of the social workers with whom he is working. The lawyer for Protective Services should not view the social worker's goals only in terms of legal objectives, but should identify the social objectives of the agency as separate and distinct from immediate legal objectives. With the help of the social workers, the lawyer should identify the social goals of the agency with as much specificity as possible, and appraise what realistically can be expected to be achieved with a family and in what time span. Thereafter the lawyer or law student, by creative use of the court process, may be able to accomplish the social goals whether or not the most obvious legal goals are attainable. Knowing the social work plan and its bases the lawyer is better able to support it in court through expert and material witnesses.

The further challenge for the lawyer is to achieve the social results in an efficient, effective and direct way which avoids or minimizes the negative effects of the adversary process. The legal process itself may contribute to the family dysfunction and tension to which the social worker is trying to respond. A process of mediation or negotiation may provide an alternative to the adversary system in which family members must testify against family members; and helpers, such as social workers and physicians, must testify against the parents they are trying to assist. Skills and tactics in negotiation, mediation and pacing the litigation are stressed within the Child Advocacy Clinic in addition to traditional trial advocacy.

Through the clinic experience law and social work students come to recognize the mutual benefits that accrue through early consultation and collaboration on a case. Social workers discern with lawyers whether there are grounds and sufficient evidence to take a case before the Juvenile Court. The social workers obtain an informed opinion on the likely outcome if the decision is made to proceed to Court. Legal assistance is provided in petition drafting. Lawyers utilize the assistance of social workers in preparing a strong case by advising them on the exact nature of documentation and other evidence required, including focusing on hard facts and actual observations of behavior rather than relying on vague opinion.

In the Clinic, students are encouraged to reflect on the impact of legal and social work intervention on the families with which they deal. Potential role conflicts within and between the legal and social work professions are also explored. Lawyers learn to appreciate the difficulties that social workers encounter when trying to deal with and determine what is best for the whole family in contrast to the lawyer's role of representing one party as client. Social workers learn to understand the lawyer's role in protecting the due process rights of their particular client in the complex arena of child protection.

The Child's Attorney

The lawyer as child's attorney in Michigan, as in many other of the United States, is charged with representing the "best interests" of the child. The lawyer, then, must form an independent judgement and be an independent and objective advocate for the child. In preparation for and in support of the child's attorney role, law students in the Child Advocacy Law Clinic are introduced to the basics of child development, as well as to the family dynamics associated with abuse and neglect and the expectations and responsibilities of the various social and medical agencies involved. A child's need for secure attachment and the potential short and long term consequences of separation, foster placement and adoption subsequent to termination of parental rights are among the subjects examined.

Throughout their Clinic experience and in particular when preparing individual cases in consultation with the interdisciplinary faculty, law and social work students are encouraged to reflect on what good professional practice in child abuse and neglect cases ought to be. Provided a model of good practice, the law and social work students are able to evaluate shortfalls when they occur; and conversely, appreciate good professional practice when they witness it.

The child's attorney role is introduced as a vigorous and active one. On some cases social work students work with law students. Students, with the advice and supervision of faculty, act as advocates within the social service delivery system as well as legal advocates. The child's attorney presses and persuades the responsible social agencies for services and attention which the client needs. Preferably such nudging is done in a collegial and non-accusatory manner and is often quite effective. If, however, a social worker or his agency is not fulfilling their responsibility to a particular child or parent, the Child Advocacy Law Clinic insists on a higher standard of service either by a direct request to the agency or by formally raising the issue before the Court.

Must the child's representative in child protection cases be a lawyer? This question is continually under consideration in the Clinic even though current Michigan law may limit what experimentation can be done. Many of the functions performed by the child's attorney could be done as well or better by social workers or other behavioral scientists; however, some responsibilities do require legal skills. Is the solution to have social workers represent children in child protection cases with lawyers' support as needed? Or is the solution representation by a team of social worker and lawyer?

Parents' Attorney

Representation of parents in cases of alleged child abuse and neglect requires certain skills and resources in addition to the ones discussed above. Lawyers and law students must first deal with their negative feelings toward the client parent accused of child abuse or neglect. The feelings toward a client parent, unless dealt with properly, can sabotage a lawyer's advocacy either consciously or unconsciously. These feelings are dealt with from the beginning of the Child Advocacy experience. At first through films and video-tapes of abusive parents, then through discussions of actual cases, the personal reactions of students surface and are dealt with. An intellectual understanding of the dynamics of abuse and neglect gained through seminar and case experiences also tends to soften the negative personal reaction to client parents.

Considerable attention is paid to family and personal dynamics associated with child abuse and neglect. Among the dynamics identified is that of parental ambivalence toward both their children and the helping personnel. Law students are warned about parental ambivalence so that they can identify and understand it and perhaps avoid parents' changing their positions at the last minute or sabotaging gains for which the lawyer has worked very hard.

Lawyers are counselors at law as well as advocates. In the agency attorney role the lawyer may advise a client social worker to pursue non-legal avenues in a case before taking legal action or to consult other professionals about treatment strategy before initiating court action.

The lawyer as counselor to parents must feel comfortable engaging the parent as a person. He must evaluate the parents' difficulties and their legal and social situation, and then provide legal counsel as to how to accomplish their goals. The lawyer may well explore with parents whether or not personal and family problems exist with which the social agencies may assist. He may counsel parents to accept certain services, seeking postponement of the Court process in the interim. As a result the parents may be willing to accept some limited assistance from an agency voluntarily. The parents may even be well-advised to forego immediate legal advantage in order to benefit from a social intervention that is calculated to prevent recurrence of abuse or neglect.

Where the client parents are willing to accept some services under the shadow of court action, the parents' lawyer should obtain from the social worker a detailed treatment plan for the family. The social worker should also make a contract with the parents defining in concrete terms the problems that are to be worked on, the obligations of the parents and of the agency, and what is expected to be achieved by the parents prior to return of the child or termination of intervention by the agency.

The counselor role is quite consistent with traditional lawyer functioning. It is based on trust and dealing with the client parents as important individuals. However, these non-adversarial tasks of the lawyer may be even more important in child protection than in other areas of the law. In exercising his counselor function the lawyer must be careful to establish whatever trust he can with the clients. When recommendations of cooperation with social agencies are made they should be made carefully so that the clients understand that if the suggestions of the lawyer are not accepted, the lawyer will stand by them as advocate of their position in subsequent proceedings.

After exercising his counselor function the lawyer may decide that vigorous advocacy to accomplish his clients' goals is necessary. This decision may be based on an appraisal that the case against the parents is weak or unfounded, or the agency response may seem unduly harsh or drastic in light of the problems identified by the agency or the parent. The decision may also be based on the clients' firm denial of the allegations in the petition and their instructions to contest the case. After fulfilling the counselor function, the lawyer must zealously advocate his client's position. It is recognized that others may believe that a child may be at grave risk, but it is the lawyer's duty to advocate for his client no matter the opinion of others and no matter his personal beliefs in the matter.

Other professionals often find the lawyer's role as zealous advocate for the parent in serious child abuse cases disquieting and difficult to understand. This issue is one raised regularly in the Child Advocacy Law Clinic.

The lawyer's advocacy should start in the agency itself. Some discussion and negotiation may lead to a resolution of the conflict between parents and agency. Law students are tutored in the important but little taught art of persuading a large bureaucracy, convinced of the inherent rightness of its position, to modify it. In spite of the desirability of non-judicial resolutions of disputes between the parent and the social agency it is often necessary to proceed to trial. The Child Advocacy students are first trained in traditional skills of trial advocacy and are ready to go to trial when necessary.

IMPLICATIONS FOR THE COMMUNITY

Participation in an interdisciplinary process involves continuous appraisal of the scope and limits of each profession's expertise and simultaneously promotes understanding of the interdependent roles. It becomes apparent that the quality of each profession's functioning is contingent on the performance of other members of the team. The realization that one's own professional performance depends on others creates a system of checks and balances.

Inevitably, at the interface between the different professions in an interdisciplinary team there is an overlap of skills. Team members have to establish mutual trust before they are in a position to negotiate how tasks should be allocated to avoid unnecessary duplication. However, the balance is delicate and care must be taken to avoid blurring of roles. For example, social workers trying to adopt a lawyer's role and vice versa.

A major pre-requisite for functioning well in an interdisciplinary team is that each member hold a strong sense of his/her own professional identity while being able to appreciate the views and practices of professionals coming from different conceptual orientations. Failure to recognize the part played by traditional professional systems and theoretical orientations of different professional groups in the diagnosis and treatment of child abuse and neglect is at the bottom of many professional disputes and misunderstandings.

By providing an interdisciplinary teaching and clinical experience for students before their professional stance becomes set and their belief systems entrenched, some of the problems in interdisciplinary collaboration can be ameliorated or at the very least aired and better understood. Interdisciplinary education also ensures that students from different disciplines gain a clearcut understanding of what the responsibilities of each discipline are in the management and treatment of child abuse and neglect. Expectations are thus created about standards of practice. Professionals are encouraged to hold each other and their different agencies accountable for their performance.

It is recognized that students who go through the clinic may not ultimately specialize in this field, but, as a result of the experiences to which they have been exposed, it is hoped that they will not lose their humanist "child advocacy" orientation. Having worked cooperatively and fruitfully with other disciplines, the law students are more likely to seek out an interdisciplinary network of supportive expertise in whatever field of law they enter. Throughout their careers they are likely to use their influence to bring legal and political pressure to bear on other child and family issues.

Child abuse and neglect is an important field for the well-trained lawyer to enter. It is a field, along with much of family law, not traditionally considered important or prestigious within the Bar. The Child Advocacy Law Clinic, as a family law speciality clinic in a major law school, may help enhance the image and importance of child and family law.

It is hoped that well-trained social workers will be stimulated by the interdisciplinary educational experience in child abuse and neglect to become more involved in Child Protective Services and reaching out to unmotivated clients. Also as a result of their Child Advocacy experience they will be able to cooperate better with lawyers on all cases involving families.

In Social Work education generally there has been a marked reluctance to discard sentimental notions of the family and to consider the role which force and violence play in family life and the extent to which it may be a potentially endemic property of the family as a system. However, manifestations of family violence such as spouse assault and child abuse are commonplace in social work practice today and are cause for much anxiety within the profession. Hence, it is important that social work curricula include specialized courses on family violence and that the phenomenon be recognized as a complex legal - medical - social problem demanding serious scientific investigation, skilled intervention and the flexible provision of resources and interdisciplinary effort.

Acknowledgment

The authors wish to thank Sally Russo and Daniel Madaj for preparing the diagram and Betty Scheffler for typing this manuscript.

Child Abuse and Neglect, Vol. 3, pp. 145 - 149.

0145-2134/79/0301-0145 $02.00/0.

HOW TO AVOID BURNOUT: A STUDY OF THE RELATIONSHIP BETWEEN BURNOUT AND WORKER, ORGANIZATIONAL AND MANAGEMENT CHARACTERISTICS IN ELEVEN CHILD ABUSE AND NEGLECT PROJECTS

Dr. Katherine L. Armstrong

Childrens Rights Group, 693 Mission, 5th floor, San Francisco, CA 94105

INTRODUCTION

Traveling across the United States, Studs Terkel ascertained from his interviews that people are looking for meaning and fulfillment in their jobs. When work is not purposeful, anger, frustration, and apathy often follow. The problem portrayed in Terkel's book, Working,[1] is not uniquely a blue collar crisis, but commonly exists in human service industries, among which are universities, protective service agencies, mental health clinics, and small demonstration child abuse projects. Professionals, like secretaries and janitors, share the quest for meaning and purpose in their jobs. If, as Terkel's interviews suggest, when a person's needs are not met by his/her job, dissatisfaction is express through hostility, resentment and physical ill health, we must be concerned, for in addition to being a serious mental health problem for workers, clients are victimized and depersonalized by worker estrangement.

Evidence of social workers' dissatisfaction with their work in social and health agencies can be found in the high turnover rate and absenteeism experienced by most agencies. The average social worker changes jobs every two years. Many agencies have a yearly turnover rate of 25% or more, almost twice that experienced among professionals in private industry. (Katzell, Korman & Levine, 1971) In addition to job turnover, there exists among workers in the helping fields a phenomenon that characterizes worker estrangement from his/her job, popularily referred to as burnout. Burnout is the process whereby workers become detached or alienated from the meaning and purpose of their work and are estranged from clients and their suffering. It has occurred when a worker reflects a cynism regarding the meaning and purpose of his/her work with clients and is no longer sure that the time and energy needed to solve human problems is worth the effort. The symptoms of burnout include:[2]

- high resistance to going to work every day (dragging your feet);
- somatic symptoms; a nagging cold, frequent bouts with a virus or flu;
- feeling tired and exhausted all day, frequent clockwatching to see how late it is, usually accompanied by tiredness after work;
- postponing client contacts, resisting client phone calls and office visits;
- stereotyping clients -- "Here goes the same old story";
- an inability to concentrate or listen to what the client is saying;
- feeling intolerant of client's anger, an inability to understand and interpret client anger;

[1] Terkel, S.: Working, New York: Avon Books, 1972.

[2] This list is derived from personal interviews with workers at the demonstration projects in this study.

- driving the long way to a client's home, driving around the block before entering the client's home;
- feeling immobilized -- "There is nothing I can do to help these people";
- excessive anxiety about investigating a new client referral or making a home visit;
- walking through department stores, frequently in the afternoon between home visits;
- problems sleeping at night, tossing and turning, feeling restless;
- cynicism regarding clients, an emerging blaming attitude -- "These clients create their own problems"; and
- increasing reliance on rules to deal with client demands.

Similar feelings and behaviors have been experienced by all of us, but those workers who experience a constellation of these symptoms frequently are feeling "burned out".

There is evidence that burnout effects the quality of service delivery, workers' mental health and the agency performance. Clients of burned out workers are likely to receive fewer services and to be depersonalized in the process. (Maslach, 1976; Armstrong, 1978) Burned out workers suffer physical and emotional ills, such as flu, viruses, depression, apathy, and cynicism. Because workers who have burned out often terminate their jobs, agencies must spend scarse resources and time recruiting and selecting new staff, and imposing upon other workers extra caseload responsibilities that, in turn, interfere with their work duties. As new workers are hired and trained, client services are interrupted and continuity of service is disrupted. Further, if burned out workers who do not leave the job have trouble delivering services, agency performance is effected.

Why does burnout occur? What causes the transformation of a worker from a humanitarian into a cynic, indifferent to individuals and their needs for assistance? Under what circumstances does this metamorphosis occur? What can be done to prevent it?

In an effort to answer these questions and to determine how this problem can be avoided, an investigation of burnout and its contributing factors was undertaken under the auspicies of Berkeley Planning Associates (BPA) in conjunction with a three year evaluation of the Joint Office of Child Development (OCD/SRS) National Demonstration Program in Child Abuse and Neglect.[3] In this demonstration effort, eleven communities across the United States received three year grants to test alternative strategies for treating child abuse and neglect. The BPA evaluation was concerned with the issues of cost effectiveness, quality of case management, goal accomplishment, adult client impact and community systems impact. In the second year, the study of worker burnout was added.

METHODOLOGY

Data were collected during site visits to the eleven projects using questionnaires, interviews and record reviews. All workers presently employed in the project completed a five page questionnaire that included questions on demographics, burnout, job satisfaction, work environment and views on project mangement. Individuals who had terminated with the agency received the same questionnaire with an addendum surveying the reasons for termination of employment. There was a 97% response rate. The survey sample consisted of 162 workers,

---

[3] This evaluation was sponsored by the Health Resources Administration (HRA) National Center for Health Services Research, Division of Health Services Evaluation, under contract numbers HRA 106-74-120 and HRA 230-75-0076.

representative of all levels of jobs in the eleven child abuse projects located throughout the United States. Of the 162 workers, 113, both terminated and non-terminated, were interviewed. The interviews ranged from 30 to 60 minutes in length and took place in a secure room where the employee could talk without inhibition. A standard instrument was used with all interviewees, but the interview style was informal and designed to explore the participant's personal feelings and reflections about his/her job and the project management.

Interviews were also conducted with each project director and a representative from the host agency to obtain descriptions of the project operation and functioning. Project records were used to collect information on absenteeism, turnover and other relevant data. Data collected on a prior site visit by BPA staff on the project's organizational characteristics, size, complexity, span of control, formalization and centralization completed the data set.

FINDINGS

Burnout is commonly addressed by inservice training or staff retreats that focus on the individual, suggesting ways of coping with work responsibilities and for effectively dealing with the stress created by the helping role. In this study, the basic assumption that burnout is primarily due to the individual worker's characteristics or that of the clients and can, therefore, be prevented or corrected by intervening with individuals is challenged. Rather, it is hypothesized that burnout is more likely caused by the way programs are organized and managed; and to avoid burnout we must better understand what management and organizational practices contribute to burnout. In this study a multi-dimensional design was used to clarify the most significant factors associated with burnout. Worker demographics, organizational structure and management processes as well as the interrelationships among these subsystems were examined.

Reservation about these findngs and their interpretation must be expressed. The survey data regarding management, burnout, and some of the organizational measures --formulization and centralizational--relied on respondents'; perceptions of their environment and their status. No objective measures of these factors were used. Because of weaknesses related to a field study methodology, response bias is difficult to know and control. Unfortunately, data analysis techniques do not specify the direction of causality. Furthermore, this sample is of 11 demonstration projects and it is difficult to know to what extent they are representative of typical child abuse programs. Given these methodological problems in studying burnout, this study does suggest a number of interesting findings for your consideration.

A number of factors among worker, organizational and management characteristics were highly associated with burnout. Employees most likely to burnout are young, inexperienced workers; those supervised by others; clerical, management and professional staff; and perhaps male employees. The interview findings suggest that many burned out workers have interests in specialty areas other than abuse and neglect; feel stagnated by limited opportunities for personal growth; have strong interest in treatment versus case management duties; and have skills and abilities incompatible with the job.

Large caseloads, highly formalized rules and regulations as well as centralization of decision making are organizational characteristics that tend to be significantly associated with burnout. Workers in interviews reported that they experience a great deal of stress trying to cope with large caseloads. Large caseloads result in infrequent client visits and inadequate case supervision; workers feel behind, overworked and unable to do a good job. In addition to feeling overwhelmed by caseload duties, workers have little time to do a variety of other job activities (e.g. community education, training of paraprofessionals and innovative program development) that could revitalize them. Other conditions associated with burnout --formalized rule observation and centralized decision making--confirm previous research findings. Professionals want to have clear job responsibilities, but resent excessive supervision of their behavior in observing rules. Many professionals resent centralized decision-making that excludes their input and imposes arbitrary decisions unrelated to "real work conditions".

TABLE 1 The Relationship Between Poor Scores on Key Management Variables and Burnout among Workers in Eleven Child Abuse and Neglect Projects* (N=162)

Characteristics of Management	% Burned Out	% Moderately Burned Out	% Not Burned Out
Inadequate Leadership: The extent to which leaders are able to provide structure and support to workers	85	15	0
Inadequate Communication: The extent to which information is timely, appropriate, and adequate	86	14	0
Inadequate Clarity: The extent to which workers know what to expect in their daily routines and how explicitly rules and policies are communicated	57	26	17
Inadequate Job Autonomy: The extent to which workers are encouraged to make their own decisions	81	19	0
Inadequate Innovation: The extent to which variety, change and new approaches are emphasized in the work environment	69	19	11
Inadequte Supervision: The extent to which management is supportive of workers and encourages workers to be supportive of each other	80	15	5
High Work Pressure: The extent to which the press of work dominates the job milieu	68	23	10

*Significant $P < .01$

Management processes are those integrative activities that form the interface between the organizational structure and personnel characteristics. This study shows highly significant relationships exist between burnout and project leadership, communication, supervision, job clarity, job autonomy, task innovation and work pressure. (Table 1) An ability to provide support and structure is, of all the variables, most likely to explain the variation in burnout among workers and is the chief discriminating factor in separating burned out and non burned out workers. Of those who reported an inability by their project leadership to provide support and structure, 85% were scored as burned out. (Table 1) The tendency is maintained when examining the relationship between communication and job clarity and burnout. When workers report that the communication in their agencies is not timely, appropriate or relevant, 86% of them also are burned out. Or, when agencies' rules and regulations are not clearly communicated, the workers are more likely to be burned out (57%). Similarily, when workers perceive the work environment as having little worker autonomy, not valuing innovation, and having inadequate staff support or supervision, the majority of workers are likely to be burned out.

During the interviews, workers reported consistent problem areas, in project management that interfered with their work and led to burnout. These internal management difficulties, more often than client problems, were reported to cause job exhaustion and after work stress. Problems in the agency occurred because project leadership could not cope with staff anger, did not handle his/her authority well, was unable to trust the staff, and/or unable to give support and positive feedback.

Inadequate communication was another key complaint. Duplication of work often occurred because pertinent changes in rules and regulations were not conveyed to the workers by administration. Poor communication was said to exacerbate poor working relationships among staff. Workers also complained of the poor quality of supervision received. Many were never told what was expected of them on the job and did not receive feedback on their performance. Many felt isolated from both staff and supervisor and complained of having to make difficult case decisions without consultation and support.
Another chief complaint was related to the lack of diversion on their jobs, or opportunities to use a variety of their skills and abilities. Finally, the crisis atmosphere which pervaded most of the projects was a significant contributing factor in burnout. Because of high work pressure, workers always feel behind and unproductive; therefore, tend to question the meaningfulness of their work. Interestingly, these management problems were consistently discussed by workers, supervisors, and administrators in relationship to their own level in the hierarchy of the organization.

Further analysis of the data suggest a possible hierarchy among worker, management and organizational factors and their relationship to burnout. Demographic characteristics only slightly influenced the relationship between management and burnout (i.e., the relationship between management factors and burnout remained strong even when controlling for personnel characteristics). The relationships between management and organizational factors were highly significant, suggesting a strong interaction between management and organizational factors. But the significant relationships between structural variables and burnout were substantially decreased when controlling for the influence of management variables, suggesting management has a mediating influence on the relationship between organizational structure and worker burnout. These findings suggest a comprehensive strategy is needed to prevent burnout. Any effort to avoid burnout must examine the unique interrelationships in the agency between worker management and organizational characteristics. The popular approach to dealing with burnout by intervening with individuals or the common attempts to improve the agency's effectiveness by a major reorganization are contra-indicated by this study, unless such efforts first consider how changes affect the quality of management and the work environment and complements the preferences and needs of the workers and the demands of service delivery.

SUMMARY

In conclusion this study affirms the hypothesis that burnout occurs when a constellation of factors--relating to worker, organizational and management--interact to create an alienating work environment. It suggests that solutions to the problem of worker burnout and performance require a systematic assessment of each of these areas to determine how and in what ways they contribute to burnout in any one particular agency. Further study and investigation that focuses on the interaction among worker, organizational and management characteristics is needed to affirm what common practices in social agencies lead to burnout and interfere with performance. Thereby, developing a relevant theory of management for social agencies that deals effectively with a high degree of uncertainty in the work task, that meets the needs and expectations of a professional manpower, and that can respond to changing and often hostile environmental conditions.

Child Abuse and Neglect, Vol. 3, pp. 151 - 156.
Pergamon Press Ltd., 1979. Printed in Great Britain.

USING CENTRAL REGISTERS TO MONITOR AND GUIDE CHILD ABUSE TREATMENT ACTIVITIES

Jay Olson, MSW, Special Assistant to the Director
Douglas J. Besharov, J.D., LlM, Director
National Center on Child Abuse and Neglect
Administration for Children, Youth and Families/Children's Bureau
P.O. Box 1182, Washington, D.C. 20013

This paper concerns one management weakness under which many child protective agencies suffer, namely: the failure to take advantage of the scientific and technological revolution which has changed so radically much of American society during the past two decades. Technologically, most social service agencies, including child protective agencies, are 50 years or more out of date. To paraphrase the words of The President's Commission on Crime: Even small businesses employ modern technological devices and systems, but the Nation's child protective network is closer to the era of the quill pen than it is to the age of electronic data processing.

One way that states have sought to use modern technology to improve their child protective systems has been through the installation of a "Central Register of Child Protection Cases."

The rapid proliferation of central registers has been extraordinary. The first registers were established in 1964 and 1965 by five cities. In 1965 and 1966 four States established registers by legislation: California, Illinois, Virginia and Maryland. An additional four states did so by administrative decision: Colorado, Florida, North Dakota and Utah. By late 1970, 19 States had legislatively established central registers while 26 States had administratively established registers. Two years later 33 States had legislation creating central registers while another 13 States had administratively established child abuse registers. Since 1974, 46 States, the District of Columbia, Puerto Rico, American Samoa and Guam have had some kind of central register of child protection cases. Of these, 39 States now have legislation establishing a central register. In virtually all States it is maintained by the State social service agency.

Registers vary in scope and purpose from those that merely collect monthly statistical reports to those that are used for case monitoring and management planning. In one state, the central register is a handful of 3 x 5 index cards in a shoe-box file; in another, it is a sophisticated "on-line," electronic data processing system with remote terminals for input and access through cathode ray tubes (T.V. screens) and computer printouts. In some states, reports are made to local agencies which forward copies to the statewide central register; in others, reports are made directly to the register. Thus, to say that a state has a central register does not say very much about what kind of facility it has.

It is the principal purpose of this paper to discuss the use of modern information management technology to strengthen child protective systems. Child protective information systems are usually called "Central Registers" because they are usually an upgraded (second generation) version of the central registers and the first are often confused with each other. This paper uses the term in both senses, but conceptualizes a second generation central register as a multi-purpose information system with, at its center, a county-wide or state-wide facility which receives, stores, monitors, and analyzes reports of known and suspected child abuse and neglect.

Central registers have been criticized because they raise genuine concerns over unwarranted record keeping and potential "Big Brotherism" and, because, in the past, many have not proven useful. But those who say there should be no central register--either because registers are dangerous or because they do not work--misunderstand a register's nature and functions. For, a central register fundamentally is nothing more than an index of cases handled by an agency or a number of agencies. Those who advocate the abolition of central registers do not realize that all agencies--as bureaucratic institutions--must have an index of cases if they are to function coherently. Without an index, or register, there would be no way of knowing whether a case was currently being handled by an agency without polling every member of the agency's staff each time a letter or referral arrived at the agency. Every worker then would have to consult his own individual index of cases or rely on his memory. Such chaotic arrangement would cause far greater harm to children and families needing help than would a centralized index.

So, there can be no question about the need for some type of register; no service agency could function without a master index. But there is reasonable dispute about how a register should be organized and operated, who should have access to it, which functions it should perform, and especially over whether it should be state-wide in scope. Central registers take on their character--either good or bad--either successful or unsuccessful--according to the data they contain, how the data is maintained, who has access to the data, and how those who have access to the data use it. Just as there is no "best" way to offer child protective services, neither is there one "true" way to operate a central register. Each state must re-think the concept of the central register in light of its own circumstances and then design its register system to fit them.

Most state laws, until now, have not been specific about the operations of their registers. Generally, they only provide that a specified state agency "maintain a central register of reports" and, perhaps, go on to recite its diagnostic and/or statistical purpose, sometimes also describing what information is to be kept in the register. The register's actual organization and mode of operation is left to administrative decision.

If a central register is upgraded to become a comprehensive management information system and if it is coupled with a statewide hotline for reporting cases, it can serve four vital functions: 1. Facilitate management planning by providing statistical data on the characteristics of reported cases and their handling; 2. Assist assessments of danger to children by providing information on prior reports and prior treatment efforts; 3. Encourage reporting of known and suspected child abuse and neglect by providing a convenient hotline for reporting, by providing a focus for public and professional education campaigns and by providing convenient consultation to caseworkers and potential reporters; and 4. Sharpen child protective accountability by monitoring follow-up reports.

However, many existing registers perform none or only some of the above functions, because of financial limitations, the absence of support from agency decision-makers, and civil liberties concerns, or because other information systems perform them. Taking these issues into account, the next sections of this paper discuss these possible functions of an upgraded register.

1. Facilitate Management Planning By Providing Statistical Data on The Characteristics of Reported Cases and Their Handling

There are many needs in child protective services, but the greatest need is the need to know. No activity, process, program, or administrative procedure in the child protective system is operating so smoothly that it could not benefit from systematic evaluation and improvement. But agency managers and policy-makers largely lack meaningful information about the child protective system--the characteristics and needs of clients, the services they receive, and how well they are served. Such information is fundamental to intelligent planning and program development. Virtually all efforts to plan and develop child protective services are hampered by a pervasive lack of adequate, objective, and quantifiable information. Presently, planning is based upon rules of thumb that have evolved out of experience and are justified through the use of anecdotal vignettes. Sometimes, these assumptions are based upon one dimensional statistical tabulations, lacking detailed data or a control group. As a result, planning for children and families cannot be conducted in a predictable or reasoned pattern. Agency planners cannot give the comprehensive direction that child protective services need. They cannot maximize the effectiveness of existing resources; they cannot assign thoughtful priorities in the development of additional resources; and they cannot point to a concrete record of accomplishment--or of need--in their periodic bouts with legislative and budgetary officials.

The desirability of having statistical data to gauge the effects of different services and treatment approaches cannot be over estimated. For example, if a register collects data on the outcomes of investigations, it provides hard and fast proof when we fail to improve the lives of children and families. Subsequent reports on the same child or family (if valid) are concrete evidence of the failure of the child protective services to treat or ameliorate the abuse or neglect.

The records in most existing registers are grievously incomplete because of fragmented and complicated reporting procedures. Many reports received by local agencies are never forwarded to the central register. Some states place a further obstacle to reporting by not providing printed forms for making reports to the register. In one state, ordinary local police arrest reports, sometimes called "injured child reports," which differ from community to community, are used to make reports to the central register.

The narrow, incomplete, and one dimensional statistical reports generated by most existing registers present a superficial and distorted picture of the problems facing child protective agencies. Little real program planning can be done with such elementary data, especially since electronic data processing and immediate retrieval capability is rare.

Though greatly needed, statistical information must be pursued and used with great caution. The idea of uni-dimensional cause and effect relationships in the real world of child abuse and child neglect can be misleadingly superficial. True relationships are complex and inextricably interwoven with many different, and sometimes hidden, factors. Even now, the most basic relationships are poorly understood. Moreover, it is often impossible to attempt to apply scientific measures of cost effectiveness to child protective procedures. Even financial costs include indirect as well as direct burdens that cannot always be discovered. Hence, although techniques of numerical analysis should be used, human values must also be weighed. Numerical measures tend to oversimplify and distort issues, since considerations such as justice, individual liberty, privacy rights, and humaneness cannot be quantified. The cost effectiveness approach can not decide questions involving unmeasurable human values. It must be recognized as a limited focus on the critical issues that face planners, legislators, and administrators.

The danger is not only that too much information may be stored in central registers, but that too little thought may be given to the usefulness of what comes out. If unchecked, the passion for collecting statistics can be the undoing of registers. Modern information systems can generate great quantities of data without meeting management's information needs. The statistics, charts, and reports which a central register can churn out have the potential to overwhelm managers with enormous quantities of data, much more than they can possibly ever read, let alone use. Unless the proper thought and planning are given to the register's output it is possible that a monster may have been created--a monster that could destroy the register and its usefulness to the child protective service system.

2. Assist Assessments of Danger to Children By Providing Information On Prior Reports and Prior Treatment Efforts

Determining the existence of child abuse or neglect is almost always difficult; often it is impossible. Most child abuse and neglect occurs in the privacy of the home. Even the most thorough investigation may not reveal clear evidence of what happened; a medical report describing severe physical injuries that suggest child abuse may not establish a connection between the parents and the condition of the child. Most maltreated children are too young or too frightened to seek help on their own or are reluctant to criticize their parents. Unless a family member is willing and able to tell what happened, there are usually no witnesses to step forward.

Hence, the identification of child abuse or neglect usually means that a professional has formed an opinion, based upon certain signs or indicators, that the child is most likely abused or neglected.

The most crucial factor in the diagnosis and evaluation of child abuse and neglect, especially for physicans, is often circumstantial evidence showing a pattern of previous suspicious injuries. Since child abuse and neglect are usually part of a repetitive or continuing pattern information concerning the existence of prior injuries or other manifestations of maltreatment can assist in determining whether an incident is an isolated occurrence or one of a series of injuries or reports suggesting abuse or neglect. Knowledge of a previous incident, similar in kind, can turn uncertain doubt into relative certainty. For example, a physican who examines a child with numerous bruises on his leg will be much less apt to accept the parents' explanation of the injury as accidental if he is aware of a series of previous suspicious or unexplained injuries.

Unfortunately, because the provision of health and social services is fragmented in most communities and because abusing parents often take their children to different doctors or hospitals for treatment each time they are injured, a cumulative record on prior suspicious injuries and social service treatment efforts is not ordinarily available. By maintaining a community-wide or statewide record of prior reports and treatment efforts--and their outcomes--central register are said to be able to provide assistance to professionals who need such information to determine whether a child is being abused or neglected.

Since most central registers are statewide in scope, they could be an important tool for locating the records of families that have moved from county to county. While school, welfare, employment, and driving records are often helpful in tracing a family, sometimes they are unavailable or incomplete. In some cases, the existence of a statewide index is the only thing that could enable the physican or protective worker to discover past history. And in almost all cases, it could be faster.

Reflecting one of the original purposes of central registers, the rhetoric of diagnosis still permeates the public discussion of the register's purpose. As of 1974, twenty-seven of the then thirty-three state laws creating central registers made specific reference to the diagnostic function of the register.

Nevertheless, no state can point to more than a handful of instances in which a professional requested that register's assistance to diagnose suspicious circumstances; most states cannot point to any instances. And it is a good thing that professionals do not request diagnostic assistance, for the central registers in almost all states could not provide the needed information.

Since information on prior suspicious occurrences and treatment efforts can assist any person who must decide whether a child is abused or neglected, one might assume that all "mandated" reporters should have access to the register for diagnostic and evaluative assistance. However, although a few states allow all mandated reporters to have direct access to the register, the great majority severely limit access to the register.

The reason for limiting access is a twofold concern over the misuse of the information in the register. First, authorizing access to all mandated reporters creates immense practical problems in guarding against unauthorized disclosure of information. For example, there are over 27,000 school teachers in Chicago, and over 4,000 social workers in Los Angeles. It would be impractical to issue to every possible mandated professional an identifying code number, much like a credit card number, which must be recited together with a password in order to gain information.

Secondly, there is a real danger that potential reporters might allow the presence or absence of a prior record to influence their actions inordinately. The presence or absence of such information may be used as a crutch by those who do not take the time or trouble to evaluate a family situation carefully. As a consequence, many children may not be reported who should be and many children will be reported who should not be. Therefore, access should be limited to child protective personnel, police, physicans treatment agencies, courts, and grand juries.

Direct access to the register for all reporting professionals coming in contact with abused and neglected children is not necessary. Protective workers can share information with other appropriate agencies and professionals as a cooperative treatment plan is developed. Professionals who know and trust each other should be able to discuss a case in their professional capacities without concern that information shared may be misused.

3. Encourage Reporting of Known and Suspected Child Abuse and Neglect

a. By Providing a Convenient Hotline for Reporting

A confused and confusing reporting process often discourages professionals and private citizens from reporting. Ignorance of the local agency's telephone number and the frequent absence of a specialized phone line at the agency can be major obstacles to more complete reporting. Consequently, in the early 1970's, a number of states established centralized, statewide reporting hotlines, at least ten through legislation. If a reporting hotline is established in association with the central register as the 24 hour recipient of all reports, the resultant uniform and easy to use procedure of calling a statewide hotline encourages more complete reporting.

b. By Providing a Focus for Public and Professional Education

The sensational death of a young child is too great a price to pay for increased reporting. A more humane way to encourage better recognition and reporting is to sensitize and educate the general public and professional personnel. However, most local and state authorities have been unable to mount sustained educational and training programs. Medical and child caring professionals--including physicans, nurses, social workers, teachers and day care personnel--and the general public must be made aware of the prevalence of child maltreatment and must know how to identify and report it. An educational program that meets these objectives while emphasizing that child protective procedures are not punitive but are designed, instead, to protect the child and rehabilitate the family can result in vastly increased reporting. "The Central Register (sic) assists in alerting the public to the nature and extent of the problem of child abuse in the State," by facilitating the collection, analysis, and distribution of statistics and other information about the incidence and severity of child abuse and neglect.

c. By Providing Immediate Consultation To Child Protective Personnel, Potential Reporters, And Parents Seeking Assistance

If there is a hotline established together with a central register and if the persons assigned to the hotline are trained in protective services--and preferably have field experience as well as training--then the register can provide helpful consultation to those seeking to protect children. Professionals (including child protective workers) and private citizens may not know what to make of a case before them or how to handle it. They often need someone to call who can help them understand the situation, their legal rights and responsibilities, and the appropriate steps to take; they need someone with whom to consult, to plan, and to begin with cooperative dialogue that determines the handling of a case. Hotline staff can refer inappropriate reports and self reports (from parents seeking help), can advise potential reports about the law and child protective procedures, can assist in diagnosis and evaluation, and can consult about the necessity of photographs, x-rays, and protective custody. Diagnostic accuracy and the handling of later stages of cases would improve almost immediately. Thus, whether a state of local system is used, staff answering the telephone should have social work or comparable qualifications, enabling them to offer effective and sensitive assistance to parents and others calling for help.

4. Sharpen Child Protective Accountability By Monitoring Follow-up Reports

Once a report is accepted by a child protective agency, it is assigned to one of the agency's protective workers, who is responsible for the field investigation and for the provision of protective and treatment services. Individual workers have the greatest influence on investigations and the ultimate handling of cases. Many of their decisions can mean life or death for the children under their care. Theoretically, they are supervised by an administrative bureaucracy and are accountable to it, but they have enormous discretion in their determinations, and their decisions usually become the agency's.

Based upon the "investigations," the protective worker decides if the report of suspected abuse or neglect seems true and, if so, what further action is required. If the worker decides that the child's or family's situation requires services, the decision must be made whether to work with the family members, refer them to another social agency, or initiate court action. In some cases, the worker may decide that the child is in such imminent danger that treatment services will not suffice and that the child's removal from the home is necessary. Even in such situations, the worker seeks to avoid court action by persuading the parents to agree to place their child in foster care.

The protective worker's decisions divide into two interrelated and simultaneously explored issues:

(1) Verification of the report: Do the allegations seem to be true? Has the child been abused or neglected? Who is responsible?

(2) Determination of the needs of the child and family: Is the child and family in need of protective services? Is there a need for immediate action? Should the child be placed in protective custody? What kinds of ameliorative or treatment services are necessary? Are they available? Must the child be removed from his home permanently or for a long period of time? Is court action necessary?

The need to make these hard child protective decisions--to investigate and verify third-person reports offer treatment services and determine the need for court action sets child protective casework apart from most other types of social casework and in many ways makes it more difficult, more trying, but also less rewarding.

Viewed realistically, child protective intervention is, in part, an investigative and decisional process--a process in which the protective worker must intrude into the family, often against the parent's will, in order to gain sufficient information about the family to decide whether a child is in jeopardy and whether ameliorative or rehabilitative services are needed. However, simultaneously, the protective worker is expected to begin treating the parents, either directly or by preparing them for referral to a treatment program or facility.

A system that monitors case handling from intake through disposition by means of progress reports to the register encourages workers to make early and precise decisions on the protective objectives and services needs of individual clients. Requiring structured follow-up reports to a register can help guide the worker's decision making process by specifying decision points and by verbalizing service goals. With this information a register can produce individual reports designed to monitor each child's and each family's progress in achieving the goal initially set. It also can generate case management information which can identify, among other things, time spent at each state of the protective decision-making process, services provided compared to services needed or requested, and total caseworker time spent with each case, classified by type of case and type of activity.

A register system with follow-up capability sharpens agency and worker accountability. It can be an unparalleled tool for managing and monitoring the handling of cases in this age of geographically disbursed and bureaucratically structured child protective agencies. Although many workers bridle at the notion of being monitored by a machine, conscientious and competent workers should not be troubled by such accountability, which is only another form of supervision. Indeed, they often welcome such a "fail-safe" system to help them keep track of the many tasks that must be performed to protect children and serve families.

Finally, there is nothing so striking as the failure of almost all central register systems to fulfill their stated statistical, diagnostic and case monitoring functions. The failure of the central register to realize its potential is not necessarily because the theory is wrong, for it has never been adequately tested. Controversy will continue over the feasibility of establishing and operating central registers however there can be no doubt that an effective register could help protective agencies save the lives of some children and stop the suffering of many by aiding case assessment and agency planning and monitoring.

Child Abuse and Neglect, Vol. 3, pp. 157 - 166.

0145-2134/79/0301-0157 $02.00/0.

CENTRAL CHILD ABUSE REGISTERS: THE BRITISH EXPERIENCE

DAVID N. JONES
B.A. (Oxon), M.A., C.Q.S.W.
Unit Member, Nottinghamshire and NSPCC Special Unit
Chairman, British Assoc. of Social Workers Working Party on Child Abuse Registers.

K. PATRICIA HILL
A.A.P.S.W.
Unit Leader, Nottinghamshire and NSPCC Special Unit
CCETSW Fellow (researching child abuse management).

ROSAMUND THORPE
B.Soc.Sc., Ph.D., Dip. Grad. Studies (Social Work)
Currently Lecturer in Social Work, Sydney Univ., Australia
Formerly Lecturer in Social Work, Nottingham Univ., Member BASW Working Party on Child Abuse Registers, Hon. Consultant in Groupwork to Notts. and NSPCC Special Unit.

Multi-disciplinary co-operation, including use of central registers, is now regarded as essential to the management of child abuse, both in the UK and USA. There are significant differences in register operation in the UK and USA, however. This paper describes two research studies of registers in the UK, discusses various issues of register operation and contrasts the UK and USA experience as reflected in research and literature.

HISTORICAL DEVELOPMENT OF REGISTERS

The compilation of specific lists of abused children, separate from other agency records, originated in the USA in the mid 60's as part of mandatory reporting laws, (16,40a) - a response to the emotional public reaction to the "discovery of the battered baby syndrome" and the finding that professionals of all disciplines had frequently ignored or failed to diagnose child abuse. Reporting laws were intended to protect children by obliging professionals to identify, report and investigate suspected child abuse. It was assumed "treatment" would follow where appropriate, although lack of trained personnel and resources has inhibited development of adequate follow-up services (6,40a). Registers were expected to serve three main purposes: i) record previous abuse/suspicion as a diagnostic aid, ii) eliminate dangers of "hospital shopping", iii) statistics and research. It seems reasonable to assume that, in the absence of statutory registers, agencies would have maintained records of children reported to them under Reporting Laws; it is a moot point when such records become "a register". "Those who advocate the abolition of central registers fail to realise that all agencies - as bureaucratic institutions - must have an index of cases if they are to function" (3).

There are no statutory reporting laws in the UK, the balance of public and professional opinion seems opposed. Management of child abuse is thus based on voluntary co-operation at local level within a structure "strongly recommended" by Central Government (13,14, see also 27,33). Responsibility for policy co-ordination is vested in the Area Review Committee (ARC), a non-statutory, advisory body including senior members of all professions and agencies involved with children in the area (boundaries usually co-terminous with Area Health Authorities and local authority Social Services Departments. The duty to report and investigate is now generally accepted however, and professional employees of most health and social service agencies have written instructions embodied in multi-disciplinary procedures co-ordinated and approved by the ARC (e.g. 10,29).

There was no national consideration of child abuse registers in the UK prior to 1970. However the NSPCC published research on child abuse in 1969 and 1972 (9,38), including recommendations on registers. Professionals were also aware of developments in the USA (39). Some areas soon established registers, and some adapted existing "at risk registers" previously concerned with medical aspects of mental and physical handicap, resulting in serious confusion especially among medical and community nursing staffs. In the 1950's and '60's some areas had operated inter-agency, "problem family co-ordinating committees", frequently with housing problems as the main focus; a list of families considered by such committees would be available (a register?). It could be argued that the Government circulars in 1974 and 1976 formalised a "quasi-statutory", uniform system of co-operation in all areas. Some have suggested that these circulars have had greater influence on social policy and resulted in a greater commitment of resources than many acts of Parliament concerning social service provision (e.g. 1 and reply 14).

The first Government comment on registers, stated "there is value in the setting up of a registry" (12) in the 1970 circular. In 1974 Government advised ARCs to consider establishing a register "within existing resources": "a central record of information in each area is essential to good communications between the many disciplines involved in the management of these cases" (13). In 1976 the advice was strengthened: "all areas which have not yet established a central register should now do so" (14). Research by the British Association of Social Workers (BASW) (6) suggests the advice has been followed, but it would appear that many registers were established in haste, with insufficient attention to the implications of the structure and systems adopted and to the purposes they were to serve.

PURPOSE AND FUNCTIONS OF REGISTERS

The purpose of registers is to facilitate and improve the protection of and services to children at risk of abuse: "if this is not achieved they should be abandoned" (6). As yet there is no "hard" evidence that registers fulfil this purpose, although there is some evidence that a closely co-ordinated, multi-disciplinary approach, including a register, can reduce the incidence of death and serious injury by abuse (11,36). Various authors have suggested that registers will fulfil this overall purpose in a number of ways. These are listed below, although space does not allow full discussion of each. (For extended discussion of relevant issues see 6,40).

a. DIAGNOSIS - detection of a sequence of injuries could prove child abuse although each alone would be less suspicious (6,16,40c,41,44,45);
b. DETECTION - tracking of mobile families/"hospital shopping"/"roving cohabitees" (6,11,40c,44,45);
c. CO-ORDINATION - identification of agencies/workers already involved with a family should a subsequent incident be reported to another agency, thus preventing duplication (40c);
d. CONSULTATION - providing a readily identifiable, easily accessible resource point for fieldworkers encountering child abuse in the community (providing the register is professionally administered) (3);
e. ACTIVATION - presence of the register compels consideration of essential questions for relevant case management (e.g. degree of risk, need for case conference) (3,23);
f. CO-OPERATION - providing a unifying administrative focus for all agencies concerned with child abuse (23);
g. SUPERVISION - ensuring monitoring of the child's future safety by formalised review of multi-disciplinary work with the family (3,6,36,45);
h. ADMINISTRATION - storage and easy retrieval of records of cases investigated under the area multi-disciplinary system and considered by case conference (primarily UK) (3,23,40);
i. RESOURCE ALLOCATION - identification of clients with priority need (e.g. for social work time, daycare, housing) (6);
j. JUDICIAL - providing evidence for court proceedings (not in the UK) (40c);
k. PREDICTION - identification of a group of "potential deviants" who require "treatment" (i.e. children whose childhood experience may predispose future anti-social behaviour) (17,19);
l. EVALUATION - facilitates review of service delivery system and procedures (3);
m. INFORMATION - provides statistics on incidence for planning future services (6,40c);
n. RESEARCH - facilitates identification of a target group for research (6,40c,45).

REGISTER SYSTEMS IN THE UK AND USA COMPARED

A comparison of register systems is, in effect, a comparison of different approaches to the management of child abuse. The register is a useful focus, highlighting the similarities and differences. This section is largely based on research in the USA by SUSSMAN and COHEN (40) and in the UK by one of the authors, on behalf of the British Association of Social Workers (6).

A major difference between the two countries is the legal position. In the USA registers are established by law in most states (16) and certain professionals are mandated to report suspicion of abuse (i.e. register the child). Those reporting usually have immunity from criminal and civil action arising out of registration, some states have enlarged the common law of negligence to include failure to report suspected child abuse (16), and some states have legislated that a child's future safety and welfare must come before traditional concepts of confidentiality. In contrast, the UK system is built on voluntary co-operation between agencies and practitioners, with no specific legislation on child abuse management. Social Services

Departments (Social Work Departments in Scotland) do have a legal duty to investigate all reports of child ill-treatment (Children and Young Persons Act, S.2(1).) The S.S.D., and Police and NSPCC can all seek a Place of Safety Order (temporary removal) and initiate care proceedings in the Juvenile Court. There are no penalties for failure to report and no legal cases involving child abuse registers have been reported. There are no laws waiving professional/client confidentiality, although it is inconceivable that a court would sustain legal action against a professional for taking action in good faith on suspicion of child abuse. The DHSS (14), BASW (5), and Medical Defence Union have indicated that confidentiality should not be a bar to ensuring the safety of a child (e.g. by sharing in a case conference).

In both the UK and USA there are wide variations between areas in the detailed operation of registers, although in both the register is usually administered by a social work agency. UK registers are never held by a court or police, unlike some states in the USA. Perhaps the single most significant overall difference between the UK and USA systems is the process of registration. In the USA a child's name is usually registered by an individual professional who suspects child abuse (i.e. prior to checking previous suspicion and before investigation), only some states expunging names if suspicion is not found proven. Registration usually implies a referral for investigation to a child protective agency. In the UK a register enquiry is usually for information only and a separate referral must be made for investigation. Registration itself usually only follows a multi-disciplinary case conference (i.e. after at least preliminary investigation) (6,14). Some UK areas do record details of register enquiries (see below) (22) and it has been argued that this is itself a register. Nevertheless there remains a significant difference in conception and use of the register, the US being, in effect, a register of professional concern, the UK being a list of children identified by a multi-disciplinary group in contact with the family as having suffered from or being at risk of abuse (proved or highly suspected), the implication being that all on the register should have received/be receiving intervention/treatment.

The criteria for registration vary widely in both countries (6,16), some including injured children only, some including children at risk of injury and some including some or all of failure to thrive, general neglect, sexual abuse, emotional risk, "general concern". Some USA registers also specifically include child abuse in state institutions (schools, residential establishments,) whilst UK registers have focused purely on child abuse in private homes, although it has been suggested in one area that children sustaining injuries whilst being caned in a residential establishment should be registered (39). There are also variations in the age range, most registers in both countries extending to between the 16th/18th birthday.

The differences in register conception influence the issue of access to the information. In many USA states this was restricted to medical personnel because a medical opinion was considered essential to child abuse diagnosis (32), but there is now a trend to enlarging the scope of those mandated to report (16). The BASW survey revealed that access in the UK was usually allowed to most medical, social (including the police) and educational agencies, usually at "middle management level", a case conference being required before the child was formally registered. It would appear that the issue of removal from the register (when risk has declined, and/or following a given period and/or when suspicion has not been proved) has still to be resolved in both countries.

CRITICISMS OF CHILD ABUSE REGISTERS

Any evaluation must consider some fundamental criticisms of registers. Broadly these embrace: a) civil liberty issues, b) professional autonomy and c) managerial effects.

a) There is international concern about the potential infringement of civil liberties by databanks and records of personal details, particularly when computerised (20,41). Concern focuses on the effect of being listed, who decides who is listed and why, any right of appeal, who has access to the data recorded, how and when. Such questions apply equally to all health and social records: "we are aware that standards of confidentiality in all agencies should be improved and do not consider that registers should require tighter security than all other personal records" (6). Nevertheless registers have attracted specific criticism, perhaps reflecting public and professional ambivalence about the authority/therapeutic dimensions of child abuse management.

The Younger Report on privacy in Britain (42) recognised an individual's right to decide what information about him should be passed to others, subject only to a clearly established, over-riding community interest (para. 57). Child abuse could be such an interest, however the principle implies that there should be a system of inclusion and exclusion which is standardised and guards against "the haphazard exercise of professional discretion" (7) (i.e. all should be treated alike). The report recognised a second principle, namely individual freedom from being placed in a false light (para. 69). If registers include suspected or "at risk" cases, they would appear to infringe this principle (3). US concerns appear to be influenced more by constitutional concern for the right to "due process of law" and court rulings that it is unconstitutional publicly to stigmatise a person without right of appeal (40c), but the basic issues are common to both countries, namely how to balance the need of child protection agencies to consider and record suspicion against the right of individuals to be treated equitably respecting their rights (45, para.48).

It is suggested that procedures should be uniformly applied, but the issue of data disclosure is possibly even more important in the civil liberty context. Some argue that there should be penalties for wrongful disclosure (37) and circumstances when an enquiry is appropriate should be clearly identified. The problem of secondary disclosure has also been considered (i.e. information given to a person without direct access by one who has) (40c). There is concern that register data could be used in ways other than originally intended, for example by exchange between computers (20). However stringent the safeguards, mistakes can also happen once a register is computerised (3,41), although others suggest that computers can offer safeguards impossible in manual systems (40c).

The impact of registration on clients cannot be ignored. The Younger Report referred to "tension induced mental illness" following "black listing" (42, para.111). Given that stress is a factor in child abuse, others have argued that registration may increase risk, the reverse effect to that intended (28), although the investigation process would seem more likely to be stressful than registration per se. Labelling theory (2) suggests that once registered, subsequent actions may be misinterpreted as confirmation of the original label; the register can distort decisions and encourage mistaken diagnosis (19). Definite registration (implied in some registers) can also inhibit rehabilitation: "the positive results of intervention can be undermined by the pernicious effects of labelling and it also implies a lack of trust in social work intervention" (6). "The belief that things can get better is possibly the single most important motivating force behind professionals and clients alike and should not be discouraged by administrative systems" (6). Others have argued that registration of suspected or "at risk" cases could lead to the unwanted and unnecessary imposition of "treatment" or surveillance (40c).

b) "Human problems require human responses: machines can provide data for decision taking but can do no more" (41). Child abuse diagnosis ultimately depends on the knowledge and skills of practitioners, but the existence of a register could foster undue reliance on records, undermining individual competence and confidence (40c). It has been suggested that the inherent caution of bureaucracies probably tends to increase the risk of wrongful inclusion and also diverts attention from developing treatment services to improving administration as an end in itself (7). Caution probably leads to lengthy or even indefinite registration, possibly resulting in commitment of staff to unnecessary involvement, despite evidence suggesting that the highest risk period for rebattering, for example, is the first three months (36) and also of the potential of skilled, short term crisis intervention and behaviour modification (e.g. 35). The register should be responsive to developments in treatment theory and practice.

c) Inescapable consequences follow establishment of a register, some specific others reflecting well documented tensions in all bureaucracies offering a personal service. "Unless these are anticipated, we think the entire system will become untrustworthy, fall into disrepute and thus become redundant; a major commitment of professional time and public money will be to no avail" (6) (see also 3,40). The potential conflict between service development and administrative improvement is discussed above. Inherent in this are financial considerations. Maintaining an accurate index is time consuming and costly, employing professional and administrative staff in sifting, following up, reviewing and updating reports, costs increasing with scope, size and availability (e.g. 24 hour access). "The greater the safeguards the greater the cost" (6).

There is also a danger that the register will skew resource allocation decisions (e.g. daycare, professional time) to the detriment of "unregisterable" but equally needy groups (6). Public and professional knowledge of the register (and associated procedures) does seem to encourage detection and reporting, at least initially, necessitating a management evaluation of whether adeqaute staff exist to investigate and follow up cases: "reporting without follow up is meaningless and even harmful" (40). Finally, the presence of a register can be used to give the impression of urgent activity in response to the problem of child abuse, although without adequate service delivery capability, the register means nothing (4,15,18,40).

There are clearly serious, inter-related problems arising from the use of registers; unless their effectiveness can be shown, they should be abandoned in their present form. If retained they should offer a system which a) facilitates effective professional intervention and b) affords protection for the child and parent, not only against child abuse but also against unnecessary and unjustified erosion of civil liberties.

A CASE STUDY IN REGISTER OPERATION - NOTTINGHAMSHIRE

Having considered the rationale for and criticisms of child abuse registers, and before discussing general research and opinion on how registers have in fact operated and how they could be improved, we consider some evidence from a UK register which is fully integrated with the child abuse management procedures in its locality (Nottinghamshire) and well used by professionals. This is a summary of a more detailed analysis available elsewhere (21). The authors have been associated with this register in differing capacities.

The register was established when the Notts. and NSPCC Special Unit became operational in May 1976. The Unit includes a specialist group of social workers and administrative staff with advisory, co-ordinating and educational functions and the register must be seen in that context. It provides an administrative link between the various services offered by the Unit and other health and social agencies. (The establishment and operation of the Notts. child abuse system is described and discussed elsewhere - 24). This discussion will have little relevance to registers operated purely by clerks/administrators (6). The purpose and functions of a register can only be fulfilled if the register has day to day professional oversight.

365 enquiries were made to the Notts. register in the first 12 months, possibly the highest level of enquiries in the UK (6). This probably reflects the emphasis of the procedures and the time spent by Unit members in educational and publicity work with all agencies, both prior to the Unit opening and subsequently. A register enquiry is frequently the first contact which the Unit has with a case of suspected child abuse; the ARC procedures advise/instruct that a register enquiry be made whenever any professional finds a case of suspected abuse (29).

It must be stressed that an enquiry does not lead to automatic registration but is simply an initial search for information at an early stage in the investigation. However Unit members are sometimes asked to comment on the case in question and advise on procedures and management; this is one aspect of the Unit's consultation work. Even mandatory reporting laws in the USA do not necessarily generate use of the register (3,40b,40c). It would appear that the register will not be used unless the individual professional considers that it will benefit his own practice. The continuing high rate of enquiries (increasing in subsequent years) seems to reflect not only the agreed procedures but also the value placed on Unit services linked to the register, by staff of other agencies.

SOURCE AND OUTCOME OF ENQUIRIES TO THE NOTTS. REGISTER 1976/77

Enquiring Agency	I Number	(%)	II Known Already	(%)	III Case Conference	(%)	IV Registered Subsequently	(%)
All Agencies	365	(100)	36	(10)	128	(35)	101	(28)
S.S.D.	141	(38.6)	16	(11)	52	(37)	44	(31)
Schools	53	(14.5)	4	(7.5)	4	(7.5)	2	(4)
* Hospitals	52	(14.2)	3	(6)	25	(48)	19	(36.5)
Police	36	(9.9)	3	(8)	19	(52)	18	(50)
Probation	26	(7.1)	5	(19)	6	(23)	5	(19)
Community Nurses	24	(6.6)	3	(12.5)	12	(50)	5	(21)
NSPCC Inspectors	14	(3.8)	1	(7)	6	(42)	6	(42)
School Welfare	13	(3.6)	-	-	-	-	-	-
** Doctors	2	(0.5)	-	-	-	-	-	-
Others	4	(1.1)	-	-	-	-	-	-

Notes: a) Percentages in Column I represent the proportion of total enquiries by agency. Percentages in Columns II, III, IV represent the proportion of all enquiries by that agency included under that heading.

* Includes all hospital staff, social workers usually enquiring on behalf of medical and nursing staff.

** Includes family and school medical service doctors.

The high number of enquiries from the Social Services Department (SSD) probably reflects the procedures which channel most suspected cases to that agency at an early stage for preliminary investigation. This is recommended because of the statutory powers of the SSD (see above), but more important is the need to centralise investigation in one agency so as to co-ordinate activity and avoid purposeless, multiple visiting of the family, which can increase stress and therefore risk to the children. The SSD is also known to the public as concerned about child ill-treatment. Schools show the second highest enquiry rate and this is particularly significan given the main focus of much child abuse literature on under school age children. The 5 - 16 years group provided 30% of actual registrations in the latest NSPCC register research (11).

In contrast family doctors, who might be expected to encounter a high proportion of cases, made very few enquiries. Only two community based doctors made a register enquiry, in contrast with hospital based colleagues, particularly paediatric specialists, who are deeply involved in child abuse management and the inter-agency procedures. This finding is typical of other studie which have shown either the apparent reluctance of family doctors to become involved in multi-disciplinary co-operation in this field or their peripheral contact with the problem (see below) (3,14,25,40a,40b).

Two very different patterns of enquiry can be identified. Those made by the police (10%), NSPCC Inspectors (4%), SSD (39%) and hospital (14%) resulted in a high proportion of subsequent registrations (i.e. abuse was confirmed or highly suspected) (50%, 42%,31%,36.5% respectively). At the other extreme, only 7.5% of the enquiries made by schools were found on initial investigation, to require a case conference, which is mandatory in every case of suspected and confirmed abuse (24,29) and only 4% of these enquiries resulted in registration. Perhaps ironically, neither of the enquiries by community based doctors led to a case conference or registration. This pattern can perhaps be explained by the comparative seriousness of cases which reach the police, hospital, NSPCC and SSD. There is also a high level of interest, anxiety about the problem and willingness to communicate in many Headteachers, coupled with a lack of detailed knowledge of the medical and social symptoms of child abuse, resulting in a high proportion of "inappropriate" enquiries, although we consider that this is proper use of the register. A further explanation for this dichotomy may be differing abilities of agencies to command adequate investigation of suspected cases.

A limited follow up of initial enquiries (by phone) showed that in a small number of cases there had been failures of communication between agencies, even within the short period of initial intervention, which could have led to inadequate investigation. It is clearly important to monitor the quality of the service and communications, especially where knowledge is restricted, to ensure suspicion is adequately assessed and followed up (e.g. schools). Even this small proportion of inadequate investigations emphasises the danger of allowing the existence of agreed procedures and the register to foster complacency. There must be a commitment to in-service training, and the existence of a specialist team to support community staff is also helpful, if not essential (6,24).

10% of enquiries were in respect of children already known to the register. 128 enquiries (35%) led to a case conference because of suspicion/proof of child abuse and 28% (101 families) resulted in registration of one or more children. An analysis of the forms of abuse and circumstances of these families, including similar statistics from the other six NSPCC Special Units, will be available in due course, following those for earlier years already published by the NSPCC (11,36).

The Notts. register, unlike many others (6,40) is available 24 hours a day. 35 enquiries (9.6%) were made out of office hours and the proportion is increasing. Many of the functions of registers depend upon 24 hour access.

RESEARCH INTO THE OPERATION OF REGISTERS

It is perhaps surprising that, despite extensive professional and political commitment to the concept of registers, there has been so little research into their operation. This section draws on some USA studies, comparing these with the BASW survey (which included returns from areas including 61.4% of the child under 15 population in England, Scotland and Wales). The analysis is divided into categories suggested by Besharov (3) as the fundamental factors determining a register's character.

DATA SUPPLIED: There is no doubt that the result of the "battered baby" publicity has been a dramatic rise in detection rates in the UK and many areas of the USA. However the increased concern has not resulted in significant use of registers. The BASW survey revealed wide variation in enquiry rates, a few areas reporting no enquiries made in the 12 month period, over 50% under 100 and 8% over 200, the range not being significantly related to population. Suggested reasons for this include (a) variations in area procedures, not all mandating enquiries, (b) improved skill in detection/diagnosis making need to gain supporting historical evidence less acute, (c) feeling that there is unlikely to be positive identification by the register, (d) improved follow up making repeated abuse less likely, (e) improved inter-agency co-operation meaning awareness of involvement of others is more likely. All the US studies comment on a similar pattern of under reporting (3,40b,40c). Suggested reasons include a) ignorance of reporting laws, (b) a belief that a report should only be made when diagnosis was certain, (c) intra-agency confusions over forms and accountability, (d) fear of entanglement in court proceedings, (e) reluctance to appear punitive, (f) confusion over access and operation. In both the USA and UK there is a professional fear that reporting child abuse will alienate the client/patient and damage the possibility of future work (6,40c). This applies particularly to family doctors in both countries (14,25,40a,40b): "everyone knows how serious a case must be before a private physician reports" (3). It begins to seem that the organisation of family doctors positively inhibits their involvement in child abuse management. This certainly appears to be the one major group in the UK which remains distrustful of the multi-disciplinary system now accepted by virtually all groups, including other branches of the medical profession.

The low levels of reporting in some US states renders entire registers unreliable. The UK pattern is potentially different, many registrations not being preceded by a register enquiry. It would seem probable that the UK system of considering registration at the case conference should enhance the reliability of the register, compared with the USA. The BASW research also revealed that around half the areas had a named senior official empowered to veto or insist on registrations when case conferences ignored or misinterpreted the criteria. There is thus a double check which should eliminate individual idiosyncracies, and act as a check against wrongful registration, thereby protecting the clients' rights to some extent. However many areas in both countries do not delete registrations, even when injuries have been found to be accidental (14,40c but see 37). There are also wide variations in the amount of data recorded (3,6,19).

HOW DATA IS MAINTAINED: The BASW survey showed that in most UK areas the register was physically separate from all other filing/index systems. It is generally agreed in the UK that the onus should be on the professional to suspect abuse and make an enquiry. We have found no comment on US practice. Most areas in the UK also have a system of register review for professional and administrative purposes, usually at least half yearly, which should update data. In contrast many US registers seem not to have this facility, New York being an exception (40b). It seems only realistic to assume that, to ensure accuracy, the register administrator must initiate a regular, routine review by contacting those with the information (6). The question of de-registration has been identified above as one many registers have still to resolve.

ACCESS TO THE DATA: There seems to be an area of confusion in many areas of the USA and possibly the UK also. The widening of those allowed access is noted above. This renders confidentiality procedures very important. In the UK this is controlled by use of the "ring back" system and restriction of access to middle management staff in many areas (6,14). Some writers have recommended civil and/or criminal sanctions against wrongful disclosure of register data (3,19) and this has been enacted in Iowa (37), including penalties of up to 2 years prison or fine plus civil liability. There is no such specific provision in the UK and no case law.

HOW DATA IS USED: "Almost all existing register systems fail to fulfil their stated diagnostic and statistical functions" (3,44). It is already clear that the data is not used as originally intended, largely because of under reporting and reasons suggested above for the reluctance to make reports/enquiries. There is also evidence that "hospital shopping" is not as prevalent as once anticipated (21,40c) and re-injury rates (following initial intervention) have fallen (11,40b - New York recidivism around 2%). However some UK registers have been valuable in tracking "roving cohabitees" (young, violent men who injure children in a sequence of short stay homes) (11). The evidence therefore suggests that, of the functions listed above, (a and b) are rarely used, although in a few cases these could still prove crucial. UK register systems probably relate more significantly to the inter-agency co-ordination functions (c,d,e, f) and co-ordinated follow-up (g,h) (6), although consultation (d) is irrelevant if the register is not in fact used by professionals; this seems far more developed in the UK than the USA (3,40b). The UK concentration on improving procedures and awareness in the routine community services (14), in contrast to some US schemes involving small, specialised teams is possibly one explanation for the decrease in serious abuse and re-injury (11,24,34).

The dangers of using registers as indicators of priority need (resource allocation) have been mentioned above, but registers appear to fulfil this function in the UK (6). This would seem less likely in the USA. Conversely the judicial use of registers seems prevalent in the USA but has not featured in UK discussions, the view being that courts should be informed of substantive fact about incidents. Lack of register accuracy and incomplete reporting suggest that registers would be misleading judicial instruments. The suggestion that registers should be used to predict future anti-social/deviant behaviour by abused children (k) seems fraught with danger and has never been identified in the UK, except in sofar as such children are usually considered to require services at the time of abuse and subsequently. Any suggestion that registers should be used to enable indefinite follow-up of potential deviants seems abhorent in Western society. Even the use of registers for follow-up studies has attracted ethical criticism, although there is little doubt that the generational pattern of violent family relationships will re-emerge (31). Inaccurate data is a poor basis for service evaluation planning and research (l,m,n), although some UK areas have attempted research, (e.g. Hampshire and Lewisham), the most significant ongoing study being undertaken by NSPCC Special Units (11,36).

RECOMMENDATIONS FOR PRACTICE

It seems clear from this analysis that there must be a re-evaluation of the contribution of registers to child abuse management. As indicated above, it is unrealistic to talk of abandoning registers, because some form of index will still be required. It is sensible, therefore, to develop a viable, manageable system with realistic objectives, respecting civil liberties, which is both useful and effective.

The British Association of Social Workers has published a thorough review of register operation in the UK, on which much of this paper is based (6). The working party made 38 specific recommendations for practice, drawing on discussions with representatives of the British Paediatric Association, all but two or three of which have now been adopted as BASW policy. The policy views the register in an operational perspective - "a working repository of information about reported cases" (22) which is in constant use. The recommendations are based on the following principles: a) effective child abuse detection, treatment and prevention must involve basic community health and social services; b) child abuse management requires multi-disciplinary co-operation; c) such inter-agency co-operation requires active co-ordination by a professional individual/team; d) individuals will tend to work in isolation unless procedures clearly facilitate/instruct co-ordination and this is frequently reinforced by training; e) the register and related procedures must have professional oversight; f) the system must be open and honest with clients, staff and public, respecting civil rights of parents and children although aware these may conflict. Working with all agencies in their areas, NSPCC Special Units have been operating a system similar in many respects to that proposed by BASW (24,33). It is workable and does seem effective. National implementation of the BASW proposals would probably require some additional expenditure, but this would seem likely to be cost effective and therefore necessary as a component in the system of prevention and treatment of child abuse.

REFERENCES

1. Association of Directors of Social Services, First Report from The House of Commons Select Committee on Violence in the Family, Vol. 2, Minutes of Evidence (29.6.76), HMSO, London, (1977).

2. Becker H., Outsiders, Free Press, New York, (1963).

3. Besharov D.J., An appraisal of current use and abuse of central registries, American Humane Society, 5th National Symposium on Child Abuse, Denver, Col., (1976).

4. British Association of Social Workers, First Report from the House of Commons Select Committee on Violence in the Family, Vol. 2, Minutes of Evidence (29.6.76) HMSO, London, (1977) (reprinted in 6 below).

5. British Association of Social Workers, Confidentiality in Social Work, Report of a working party (Chairman P. Oakley), (1977).

6. British Association of Social Workers, The Central Child Abuse Register, Report of a working party (Chairman D.N. Jones), (1978).

7. Carter J., Co-ordination and child abuse, Social Work Service, 9, 22-28, (1976).

8. Carver V., Child Abuse: A Study Text, Open University Press, Milton Keynes, (1978).

9. Castle R.L., A Study of Suspected Child Abuse, NSPCC, London, (1972).

10. Coventry Area Review Committee, A Professional Guide on Detection and Treatment of Child Abuse, City of Coventry, (1976) (reprinted in part in Lee C.M. op. cit.).

11. Creighton S.J. & Owtram P.J., Child Victims of Physical Abuse, NSPCC, London, (1977).

12. Department of Health and Social Security, The Battered Baby, HMSO, (1970).

13. Department of Health and Social Security, Memorandum on Non-Accidental Injury to Children, Lassl (74) 13, CMO (74) 8, (1974) (reprinted in part in Lee C.M. op. cit.)

14. Department of Health and Social Security, Non-Accidental Injury to Children: Reports from Area Review Committees, Lassl (76)2, CMO (76)2, CNO (76)3, (1976) (reprinted in part in Lee C.M. op.cit.)

15. Desborough C., Government Guidelines on Child Abuse, ch 15 in Carver V. (op. cit.) (1978).

16. Education Commission of the States, Trends in Child Abuse and Neglect Reporting Statutes, Report 95, Denver, Col., (1977).

17. Fontana V.J., Somewhere a Child is Crying, Macmillan, New York, (1973).

18. Fry A., NAI: Danger of Over-Reaction, Community Care, 14.7.1976.

19. Garinger G. & Hyde J.N., Child Abuse and the Central Registry, ch 25 in Ebeling N.B. & Hill D.A., Child Abuse: Intervention and Treatment, Public Sciences Group Inc., Acton, Mass., (1975).

20. Hewitt P., Privacy: The Information Gatherers, National Council for Civil Liberties, London, (1977).

21. Hill K.P., Evaluating inquiries to Notts' NAI register, Social Work Today, 9,29, 19-20 (1978).

22. Ireland W.H., Mission and functions of central registers, American Humane Society, 5th National Symposium on Child Abuse, Denver, Col., (1976).

23. Jones D.N., Hill K.P. & Thorpe R. original idea, (1978).

24. Jones D.N., McClean R., Vobe R.J.S., Case conference on child abuse: the Nottinghamshire approach, paper to be presented to the 2nd International Congress on Child Abuse and Neglect, (1978).

25. Lancet, The, The battered......, The Lancet, 1228-9, 31.5.1975.

26. Lee C.M., Child abuse: a source book, Open University Press, Milton Keynes, (1978).

27. Lupton G.C.M., Prevention, recognition, management and treatment of cases of non-accidental injury to children: arrangements in the United Kingdom, International Journal of Child Abuse and Neglect, 1,1, 203-209, (1977).

28. Martel S., Non-accidental injury, (including Survey of the operation of at risk registers), Family Service Units, London, (1977).

29. Nottinghamshire Area Review Committee, Non-accidental injury to children: guidance notes and procedures, Notts. County Council, Nottingham, (1976).

30. Nottinghamshire Branch, British Association of Social Workers, Corporal punishment - professional advice to members, reported in Social Work Today, 9,24,2 (1978).

31. Oliver J.E., Cox J., Taylor A., & Baldwin J., Severely ill-treated children in north-east Wiltshire, Oxford Regional Health Authority, (1974).

32. Paulsen M.G., The legal framework for child protection, Columbia Law Review, 66, 679, 710-717, (1966).

33. Pickett J., The management of non-accidental injury to children in the City of Manchester, in Borland M., Violence in the family, Manchester University Press, (1976).

34. Pickett J. & Maton A., The multi-disciplinary team in an urban setting: The Special Unit concept, paper to be presented to the 2nd International Congress on Child Abuse and Neglect, (1978).

35. Reavley W. & Gilbert M.T., The behavioural treatment approach to potential child abuse cases: two illustrative case reports, Social Work Today, 7,6,166-8, (1976).

36 Rose R., Owtram P., Pickett J., Marran B. & Mann A., Registers of suspected non-accidental injury: a report on registers maintained in Leeds and Manchester by NSPCC Special Units, NSPCC, London, (1976).

37. Sheeley J.A., Use and control of abuse of a central child abuse registry, American Humane Society, 5th National Symposium on Child Abuse, Denver, Col., (1976).

38. Skinner A.E. & Castle R.L., 78 battered children: a retrospective study, NSPCC London, (1969).

39. Stark J., The battered child - does Britain need a reporting law?, Public Law, Spring, 48-63, (1969).

40. Sussman A. & Cohen S.J., Reporting child abuse and neglect: guidelines for legislation, Ballinger, Camb., Mass., (1975) (especially ch 3 A review of the literture - 40a, ch 6 Child abuse reporting in four states - 40b, ch 7 Central registers and the problem of databanks: an introduction - 40c, also 27 page bibliography).

41. Whiting L., The central registry for child abuse cases, rethinking basic assumptions, Child Welfare, 56,1,761-767, (1977).

42. Report of the committee on privacy (Chairman K. Younger), Privacy, Cmnd 5012, HMSO, London, (1972).

43. Report of the committee on child health services (Chairman S.D.M. Court) Fit for the future, (especially Appendix F "At risk registers", 413-5) Cmnd 6654, HMSO, London, (1976).

44. First report from the House of Commons Select Committee on Violence in the Family, Violence to children, 329-i, HMSO, London, (1977).

45. UK Government (DHSS, DES, DOE, Home Office, etc.), Violence to children: a response to the first report from the Select Committee on violence in the family, Cmnd 7123, HMSO, London, (1978).

46. 1969 Children and Young Persons Act, HMSO, London, (1969).

NB For extended bibliographies refer to (6) and (40).

ACKNOWLEDGEMENTS

We ackowledge help and co-operation from Unit colleagues (Celia Doyle, John Hawke, Alma Crabtree, Anne Dowling and Vicky Stevenson), other members of the BASW Working Party (Sally Beer, Phil Cooke, Ann Gegg, John Pickett), and from Dr. P. Bean, Dr. C. Cooper and Dr. R. H. Jackson.

Child Abuse and Neglect, Vol. 3, pp. 167 - 174.

0145-2134/79/0301-0167 $02.00/0.

CENTRAL REGISTRATION OF CHILD ABUSE IN MANCHESTER: AN EVALUATION.

Andy Maton and John Pickett.

N.S.P.C.C. Special Unit, Manchester, England.

INTRODUCTION.

Central registration of cases of child abuse has become prevalent in the U.K. as one of the professional responses to growing concern about child abuse. Professional awareness of the phenomenon in the U.K. developed in the 1960's (Baher and others, 1976; Lupton 1977), following the pioneering work that had been done in the U.S.A., where, for example, all 52 states had by 1968 passed mandatory reporting laws. In many of the state schemes some form of central registration was included (Stark, 1969; Court, 1969; Sussman and Cohen, 1975). Experience derived from the state of Illinois scheme suggested that registers had four main values (Ireland, 1966), as follows:-

1. Identification of multiple abuse in the same family;
2. Development of an intervention and treatment programme;
3. Provision of a basis for the further definition of the phenomenon;
4. Education of the public about the nature and extent of the problem.

Professional concern in the U.K., reinforced by the case of Maria Colwell (Lupton, 1977; DHSS, A, 1974), led to the Department of Health and Social Security (D.H.S.S.) recommending in 1974 (DHSS,B, 1974) that Area Review Committees be set up, to devise standard procedures for the management of child abuse, including a central record of information, in order to facilitate inter-disciplinary communication. Such communication has rightly been identified as essential to effective intervention in cases of child abuse (DHSS,A, 1974; Carter, 1974; Tomlinson, 1976).

In 1976 more specific recommendations were made by the D.H.S.S. in a circular letter (DHSS, 1976) which recognised the wider variation in practice among those local authorities which were by then operating central registers. The British Association of Social Workers also addressed itself to the problems and criticisms attached to central registration, and the variations in practice. The report of a working party was published in 1978 (BASW, 1978).

DEVELOPMENT OF THE REGISTER IN MANCHESTER.

A central register of child abuse commenced operation in the City of Manchester at the beginning of 1973, in anticipation of the D.H.S.S. recommendation made the following year. Since then it has been operated and managed by a Special Unit of the National Society for the Prevention of Cruelty to Children on behalf of the Child Abuse Policy Committee of the City of Manchester. This is a multi-disciplinary body that formed itself in 1970; also in anticipation of the D.H.S.S. recommendation that local authorities establish Area Review Committees (Pickett, 1976).

During 1973-1974 the Manchester register was concerned with children under the age of 4 years, who had suffered from certain or suspected non-accidental injury at the hands of a parent or other care-taker. It was intended that the relevant social agencies and professionals would notify such cases to the register, and consult with the register regarding other cases which gave cause for concern. Any previous knowledge the register contained regarding a previous history of suspected non-accidental injury in that case, would then be available to the workers involved in order to assist their overall understanding and judgements about the case. The functions of the register were precisely those that Ireland had suggested from his study of the Illinois scheme (Ireland, 1966).

In 1975 the Social Services Department of Manchester Corporation published the "City of Manchester Guidelines" (Manchester SSD, 1975) on behalf of the Child Abuse Policy Committee, which set out the standard procedures to be followed by the various disciplines involved, when cases of suspected non-accidental injury came to light. The procedures included register inquiries and register notifications, and expanded the criteria to, "All physically injured children under the age of 16 years where the nature of the injury is not consistent with the account of how it occurred, or where other factors indicate that there is reasonable suspicion that the injury was inflicted, or not prevented by any person having custody, charge or care of the child".

The N.S.P.C.C. Special Unit which has operated the Manchester register, has had additonal functions (Owtram, 1975), some of which have operated since 1973, others of which, developing during 1973-74, were also formalised in the City of Manchester Guidelines in 1975. The former group of functions comprised the following:-

1. Monitoring the progress of registered children and their siblings through the social worker and health visitor involved with the family. The monitoring process occurs at 3-monthly intervals, until neither worker feels there is a risk of further abuse.

2. Offering a consultative service on child abuse to other professions and agencies.

3. Offering a therapeutic social casework service to families where suspected non-accidental injury has been inflicted on a child (Pickett and Maton, 1977).

4. Organising and participating in educative events regarding child abuse.

The latter group of functions comprised the following:-

5. Convening case conferences on children felt to be at risk of abuse.

6. Providing a social work consultant in child abuse to chair and minute the case conferences.

7. Maintaining a duplicate of the registers operated by the 9 metropolitan boroughs which together with the City of Manchester, comprise the Greater Manchester County.

The Manchester register therefore has not operated in isolation from other procedures and services for the abused child and his family. The purpose of the remainder of this paper is to evaluate its operation within its wider context during the five-year period 1973-1977. Significant criticisms of central registration as a technique, make such an evaluation an important exercise in order to justify its further use and/or to underline its limitations.

THE OBJECTIONS TO, AND PROBELMS OF, REGISTERS.

The concept of central registration raises problems and objections by its essential nature. Unlike most lists of individuals maintained by social and medical agencies the central register of child abuse is a pool of information that is shared by and equally accessable to a number of agencies and professions. This raises problems of confidentiality, professional autonomy and civil liberty (Sussman and Cohen, 1975). While it is to be expected that the same problems are to be encountered regarding lists of individuals confined to a single agency, especially where that is a large organisation, the inter-disciplinary and inter-agency sharing of information and judgements in cases of child abuse, heighten the problems regarding central registration of these cases.

The following paragraphs outline the ways in which the Manchester register has attempted to meet the problems and criticisms:-

1. Confidentiality

It is undoubtedly true that central registration stretches the concept of professional confidentiality to a considerable degree. Professional workers can easily see this to be a serious ethical problem. Indeed, the fact that doctors in the U.S.A. also saw it as a potentially serious legal problem for them, was in part, accountable for the passing of mandatory reporting laws there (Stark, 1969). The legal situation in the U.K. is not the same (Medical Defence Union., 1974) but the ethical problem has led to reticence among some professional in participating in a central register scheme.

It is also undoubtedly true that no register can operate without a climate of mutual trust between the agencies and professions and where this is validated by a mutual respect for each other's confidences (Pickett, 1976). To this end, for example, in Manchester, each copy of any child abuse case conference minute is prefaced by a statement that information contained therein should not be divulged to any third party without the prior consent of the originator of that information.

Similarly, various ways have been employed to preserve the confidentiality of the information recorded on the register. The information is kept under conditions of strict security within the Special Unit office, and only one identifiable copy of the register entry is made. Regarding register inquiries, generally made by telephone, a ring-back procedure is used, by which the inquirer is telephoned back with the answer as to whether or not a given child is already known to the register. This enables the authenticity of the inquirer to be checked. Also the information given to the inquirer is kept to a minimum; wherever possible, if a child's name has already been registered, the inquirer would then be directed to contact the previously identified key worker for that child.

Access to the register is limited to doctors and senior designated professional personnel in the social and medical agencies involved, rather than to all personnel in what are often large and complex organisations. When information is extracted from the register for research purposes, all personal identifying details are omitted so that the researchers deal only with anonymous data.

In Manchester, resistances to the register on the ground of its conflict with professional confidentiality has withered away to a large extent; as far as it is possible to identify this. This is a reflection on the inter-disciplinary trust which appears to exists, the credibility of the register and other management procedures, and on a recognition that rigid adherence to a strict professional confidentiality, does not necessarily serve the interests of the abused child and his family, better than a commitment to inter-professional co-operation.

2. Professional Autonomy.

It is undoubtedly true that central registration and the procedures linked to it, restrict individual professional autonomy, by placing constraints on the professional worker's adherence to procedures, his time, energy, skill in judgement and practice, and his general accountability. His professional practice is open to scrutiny in an inter-disciplinary context, and this can be quite threatening to him. Alternatively the professional worker may honestly believe his own resources are sufficient to effectively deal with the problems he encounters, in his own way.

The desire to maximise professional autonomy has been manifested as a resistance to the idea of central registration, and to complying with the whole of the procedures, in the same way as the desire to maintain strict professional confidentiality. These two aspects of professionalism can easily be seen in association with each other, but while the medical profession in general has been particularly concerned with confidentiality, the professions of teaching, social work and psychiatry appear to have been rather more sensitive regarding their individual professional autonomy.

A reconciliation between central registration and the problem it poses to professional autonomy, has not been effected in Manchester, as satisfactorily as in preserving confidentiality. A small number of abused children were registered as late as 1977, where a professional worker had deliberately decided not to notify that child to the register, or otherwise invoke the procedures, only months earlier. The reasons for this type of decision or the tendency towards it are various. In some cases the professional worker has wished to avoid the personal exposure of judgements, attitudes and practice to the corporate nature of the multi-disciplinary procedures. In others the resistant professional worker has felt reluctant to share his professional status or role with another of different perceived rank (H.M.S.O., 1977). A third reason has been the professional worker's fear that by registering a child, or otherwise invoking the procedures, the child and his family would subsequently be deluged by professional intervention operating independently of the original worker, and jeopardising his own standing with the family.

The main reason why the problem of professional autonomy has been less effectively met in Manchester, is that this particular phenomenon has been expressed much less overtly than for example the problems of confidentiality and civil liberty. The factors underlying professional autonomy are rather more subjective and less respectable. Few could deny rationally and intellectually, for example the relevance of inter-disciplinary communication, co-operation and teamwork in the identification, diagnosis, management or treatment of child abuse (DHSS.A, 1974; DHSS,B, 1974; Carter, 1974). More subjectively therefore is the problem of professional autonomy felt and expressed. It is consequently more difficult to effectively meet the problem.

Nevertheless despite the inevitable blurring of professional roles in a multi-disciplinary setting, which Bentovim (H.M.S.O., 1977) feels is a very positive development with wider applicability than merely to child abuse, each profession needs to preserve role identity and clarity, and a degree of autonomy is inevitable where the professional role is defined by legal statute. In Manchester registration and the procedures have been designed to encourage inter-professional communication and co-operation, respective role clarification and teamwork. Wherever possible a case conference is used to make the judgement as to registration, generally on a basis of concensus. Once made that judgement would not necessarily be beyond review, and an automatic and irrevocable sequence of interventions would not follow either the registration of a child or a prior register inquiry.

3. Non-professional Response.

Central registration has been criticised as being a beaureaucratic reaction to a human situation, and which undermines professional judgement by imposing an automatic response or intervention to the problem of child abuse (Carter, 1974; Whiting, 1977). The criticism is pertinent, particularly where the register is operated by non-professionals or by managers whose principal concern is administration (BASW, 1978).

The Manchester register has sought to avoid this danger by using a team of social workers, to operate the register, who are also consultants, practitioners and teachers in child abuse. In accepting registrations, as in the conduct of case conferences, professional judgement is thereby underlined, rather than beaureaucratic response.

4. Civil Liberty.

A very significant objection to central registration has to do with the effect that registering an abused child has on the child and the family members, implicated. Labelling theory, for example implies that a parent identified as an actual or potential abuser will tend to be seen in that light thereafter: his actions will be taken to confirm the original label whatever they are. Also there is a feeling that a register operates as a blacklist and that a stigma is attached to the parent against which there is no appeal (H.M.S.O., 1972; Martel, 1976).

Now, given that the register information is secure, the stigmatising effect of registers is probably more a reflection on the attitude and conduct of the professional workers concerned, than on the system itself. But, it remains true that the registration system makes the 'label' potentially more widely known among the professions, and may confer an added authenticity to the 'label'.

The Manchester register has sought to meet this objection by using strict criteria for registration. Degrees of suspicion that the injuries to the child were non-accidental have been employed, each determined by a more or less forensic type of factor, for example by a definable discrepancy between the injuries and the account of how they occured. This has meant that for each registration, objective factors could be given to the family by the social worker or doctor for example, as to why the registration was made, and what were the areas of concern shared by the agencies and professions involved. The Manchester register therefore contrasts with 'At-risk' registers maintained by some other local authorities where the criteria are more subjective and variable.

The British Association of Social Workers (1978) has recommended that de-registration should follow a 12-month period in which regular monitoring of the child's progress indicated that there was no further risk of abuse. One year after de-registration, provided that there was no further concern, the register record would be destroyed.

In Manchester the ongoing monitor records of registered children are carefully reviewed every three months. The monitoring procedure ceases after there has been a 12-month period free from risk of further abuse. The register record then becomes less accessible. Until recently Manchester had no process of de-registration but the N.S.P.C.C. Special Unit supports the recommendations made by B.A.S.W. and a policy for de-registration is being formulated along these lines.

THE PERFORMANCE OF THE MANCHESTER REGISTER.

The objections to and criticisms of the central registration of child abuse, place on the operation of the register a serious responsibility as to its mode of operation and the quality of judgement on which it is based. They also seek that the register should demonstrate its effectiveness. The following paragraphs will outlines to what extent the Manchester register has fulfilled the functions with which it began in 1973.

1. The identification of multiple abuse in the same family.

One of the principal functions of central registration was originally seen as diagnostic. This followed from experience with abusing families where for example a repeatedly injured child might be taken to different medical facilities for treatment on subsequent occasions. It was hoped that a central register of all such individually suspicious instances of abuse would reveal patterns of abuse within a family, that might otherwise remain unidentified, and thereby contribute an important diagnostic factor (Castle and Kerr, 1972; DHSS, 1987): Hence the important place given to the initial register inquiry by the Manchester procedural guidelines.

Currently around 500 inquiries each year are being made of the Manchester register, of which around one third apply to the City of Manchester. No more than 4% of the inquiries have referred to children already registered. Among these 20 or so cases per annum, the register has proved diagnostically very helpful in some individual cases, revealing a history of past abuse, or identifying a highly mobile family or adult who moves from family to family, precipitating abuse in each one in turn.

However the scale of diagnostic usefulness of the Manchester register has been lower than was originally envisaged. It compares for example with the Nottinghamshire register where 10% of all inquiries were in respect of children already registered (Hill, 1978).

There are two aspects to this. On the one hand, the forensic nature of the Manchester register's criteria means that registration is unlikely to occur unless there is a reasonably high degree of suspicion. Injuries to children which do no more than cause vague concern are not likely to be followed by registration. In other words the constraint placed on the register by the consideration of civil liberty, tends to mitigate against its usefulness as a diagnostic tool. It follows that the value of registration in identifying abuse would be reduced, since cases would already be identified when they were registered.

On the other hand it is also to be expected that effective registration and procedures will tend to make the register's diagnostic role redundant. Where a case of child abuse is identified and subsequently offered appropriate medical, psychiatric and social work help, then either subsequent abuse is likely to be less frequent (Creighton and Owtram, 1977) or when it does occur, it is more likely to be known about by the local professional nexus. Although registration has been criticised because of the implication' it carries for resource allocation (BASW, 1978), one of its effects has been to lessen the probability that cases of child abuse will be ignored by the agencies and professions concerned.

Both factors outlined above have operated in the case of the Manchester register. The question that remains, is whether, in the absence of the encouragement to intervention that the register implies, there would be a reversion to the sort of situation Skinner and Castle (1969) describe, where in the absence of effective intervention, there was a reinjury rate of 60%.

2. Development of an Intervention and Treatment Programme.

In Manchester the central register is an operationally integrated part of the whole set of management procedures. This totality is described elsewhere (Pickett and Maton, 1978). The initial register inquiry initiates a flow of action, not necessarily automatic, and which is designed not only to facilitate inter-agency and professional communication' and co-operation but which also incorporates a consultative element designed to promote a high level of professional judgement and confidence in handling child abuse cases. Professional advice and support, the convening, chairing and minuting of a case conference, registration and subsequent monitoring are all available from the same office, and arise as appropriate from the initial inquiry. In all of this the attempt is made to formulate treatment goals, and specify resources and techniques that may help the particular family in question (Pickett and Maton, 1977).

The Manchester procedures therefore contrast with arrangements elsewhere (both in the U.K. and U.S.A.) which, firstly isolate registration from the other procedures such as case conferences, so that the register is little more than a passive list of known cases, and those which secondly separate procedures from the ready availability and scrutiny of professional advice and skill. In the U.S.A. Sussman and Cohen (1975) have recognised the need for registers to be an integral part of a comprehensive and integrated inter-disciplinary response and this is reflected in their recommended model child abuse reporting laws for the U.S.A. In the U.K. there is also need for revision of notification systems which fail to integrate the total processes of inter-disciplinary co-ordination in the way we have described.

Whatever credibility the Manchester register has attracted locally, this has undoubtedly derived in large part from the integration of the procedural elements incorporating professional judgement.

3. Provision of a basis for further definition and public education about the problem.

Data has been extracted from the Manchester register for epidemiological research, which has shown certain trends which point to a degree of effectiveness for the Manchester procedures. Two reports have been published by the N.S.P.C.C. The first (Rose and others, 1976) covers the registers in Manchester during 1973-1974 and in Leeds in 1974. The second covers seven N.S.P.C.C. Special Unit registers, which were operating in 1975, including Manchester (Creighton and Owtram 1977), and which together covered 10% of the population of England and Wales.

These register studies have highlighted several features of child abuse, on a basis of careful statistical calculation; for example the particular vulnerability to abuse of the low birth-weight baby, the marginal vulnerability of children in large families, the relative youthfulness of parents, the relative fluidity of their marital and domestic arrangements.

The studies have also revealed trends which point to the effectiveness of the registers. First there has been a decline in the number of children registered with a previous or subsequent injury. In 1973 60% of injured registered children (aged 0 - 4 years) in Manchester had suffered suspected non-accidental injury prior to the injury at registration. In 1974 and 1975 this had fallen to 34%. Also, in 1973 and 1974, 20% of registered injured children (aged 0 - 4 years) suffered reinjury after registration. In 1975 this had fallen to 9%.

Secondly there has been a decline in the number of children registered with fatal or serious injury (fractures, internal injuries, serious burns and scalds). In 1973 and 1974 about 45% of registered injured children (aged 0 - 4 years) had sustained fatal or serious suspected non-accidental injury. In 1975, 1976 and 1977 this has fallen to around 22%.

The rate of registration has been fairly constant, at around 1.2 children per 1000 (aged

0 - 4 years) during the period 1973-1977, and at around 0.5 per 1000 (aged 4 - 16 years) during the period 1975-1977. Proportional decreases in reinjured and seriously injured children have therefore also been decreasing in the actual number of children in those categories. This was true even of 1975 which saw a rather larger number of registrations of the younger age group (67 injured children aged 0 - 4 years, compared with 35 in 1973, 38 in 1974, 37 in 1976 and 49 in 1977).

The reduction in the number and proportion of seriously injured and repeatedly injured children in Manchester are trends which imply that Manchester's procedural model, together with a concomitant development of professional awareness of the problem, has achieved a modest but measurable effect on the scale of child abuse in the city. In particular the trends imply that the social and medical services have been enabled to intervene more effectively and earlier in the escalating pattern of intra-familial violence to children, than had previously been the case. The register must take an important part of the credit for this, since it remains the operational foundation and initiation-point for the rest of the procedures.

CONCLUSION.

The Manchester register of child abuse has two features which distinguish it from many registers operating in the U.K. Firstly it is not operated independently of the rest of the procedures. Secondly it is not operated independently of professional scrutiny, judgement and advice. The register is the foundation of a procedural package that incorporates professional skill and expertise at every step. Its effects can be demonstrated from statistical trends and its mode of operation shows that conflict with issues of professional and social ethics can be reduced. The conflict that then remains must needs be balanced with the commitment profession share to effectively break into the cycle of family violence.

REFERENCES:

Baher, E. et al (1976). 'At Risk: an account of the work of the Battered Child Research Dept. of the N.S.P.C.C.'. RKP. London.
BASW (1978). 'The Central Child Abuse Register'. British Association of Social Workers, Birmingham, 1978.
Carter, J. (1974). 'Coordination and planning of Services' in 'The Maltreated Child'. Priory Press, London.
Castle, R.L., and Kerr, A.D. (1972). 'A Study of Suspected Child Abuse'. N.S.P.C.C. London.
Court, J. (1969). 'An historical review of the American child abuse laws'. Child Care News, 92.
Creighton, S.J. and Owtram, P.J. (1977). 'Child Victims of Physical Abuse: a report on the findings of N.S.P.C.C. Special Units' registers'. N.S.P.C.C. London.
D.H.S.S. (1970). 'The Battered Baby'. Standing Medical Advisory Committee.
D.H.S.S. A (1974). 'Report of the Committee of Inquiry into the care and supervision provided in relation to Maria Colwell'.
D.H.S.S. B (1974) 'Non-accidental injury to children'. (LASSL (74) 13, CMO (74) 8).
D.H.S.S. (1976). 'Non-accidental injury to children : Area Review Committees'. (LASSL (76) 2; CMO (76) 2). 1976.
Hill, P. (1978). 'Evaluating inquiries to the Nottinghamshire Non-accidental injury register'. Social Work Today, Vol.9, No.29, 21.3.78.
H.M.S.O. (1972). 'Report of the Committee on Privacy (Younger Report).
H.M.S.O. (1977). Evidence of Dr. A. Bentovim to the Select Parliamentary Committee on 'Violence in the Family'. Vol. 3.
Ireland, W.H. (1966). 'A registry of Child Abuse'. in Children, Vol.13, May-June 1966.
Lupton, G.C.M. (1977). 'Prevention, Recognition, Management and Treatment of cases of non-accidental injury to children: Arrangements in the U.K.'. Child Abuse and Neglect. Vol.1, No.1, Pergamon Press.
Martel, S. (1976) 'Non-Accidental Injury' in F.S.U. Quarterly (28th Annual Report) Family Service Units, London.
City of Manchester Social Services Dept. (1975). 'Non-Accidental injury to children: City of Manchester Guidelines'.
Medical Defence Union (1974). Annual Report.
Owtram, P.J. (1975) 'N.S.P.C.C. Special Units' in Social Service, D.H.S.S.
Pickett, John (1976). 'The Management of Non-Accidental injury to children in the City of Manchester' in 'Violence in the Family' (ed by M. Borland Manchester University Press.

Pickett, John and Maton Andy (1977). 'Protective Casework: Practice and Problems' in 'The Challenge of Child Abuse' (ed. A. White Franklin), Academic Press, London.
Pickett, John and Maton, Andy (1978). in a paper presented to the Second International Congress of Child Abuse and Neglect. London.
Rose, Owtram, Pickett, Marran and Maton, (1976). 'Registers of Suspected Non-Accidental Injury'. N.S.P.C.C. London.
Skinner, A.E. and Castle, R.L. (1969). '78 Battered children: A retrospective study'. N.S.P.C.C. London.
Stark, J. (1969). 'The battered child - Does Britain need a reporting law ?' in Public Law, Spring, 1969.
Sussman, A. and Cohen, S.J. (1975). 'Reporting Child Abuse and Neglect: Guidelines for Legislation' Ballinger, Cambridge, Mass.
Tomlinson, T. (1976). 'Inter-agency collaboration: issues and problems' in 'Violence in the Family' (ed. M. Borland) Manchester University Press.
Whiting, L. (1977). 'The central registry for child abuse cases: rethinking basic assumptions'. Child Welfare, Vol.56, No.1, pp 761-767.

Child Abuse and Neglect, Vol. 3, pp. 175 - 177.

0145-2134/79/0301-0175 $02.00/0.

STUDY OF CENTRAL CHILD ABUSE REGISTERS IN ENGLAND AND WALES 1977

Mrs. Jane Jenkins

South Glamorgan Social Services Department
Cardiff.

1978

INTRODUCTION

A Department of Health and Social Security memorandum[1] circulated to all Local Authorities in 1974 recommended the setting up of registers of all known cases of Child Abuse :-

> " A central record of information in each area is essential to good communication between the many disciplines involved in the management of these cases".

Child Abuse Registers were intended to be one element of a comprehensive system of a multi-disciplinary approach to the effective management of cases of Child Abuse. As little detailed guidance was available to those responsible for setting up these registers, it became clear that there was not standardization of approach throughout the country and concern was expressed as to their general effectiveness both locally and nationally.

The object of this study is to examine the extent of these variations in register management throughout England and Wales and to a assess the efectiveness of registers for the purpose for which they were originally intended.

METHOD

115 comprehensive questionnaires were sent to Local Authorities in England and Wales in January 1977. Topics covered included the size of registers; criteria for inclusion; the times at which the registers were made available and to whom; confidentiality and general safety precautions; reviewing and de-registration procedures; the range of information contained on a register and the extent to which the register was used.

102 completed questionnaires were returned and 100 were selected as being suitable for analysis.

FINDINGS

Analysis revealed a considerable variation in the way in which registers were designed and subsequently maintained.

The number of cases on any one register varied from 5 to over 1000 cases. Whilst this is partially related to the population of each area which the register covers, it is also influenced, more significantly, to the stricking variation in the criteria for inclusion. (See Table 1)

TABLE I

Criteria	Number of Registers
N.A.I. Overt and Suspected	13
N.A.I. Overt and Suspected; Potential N.A.I.	39
N.A.I. Overt and Suspected;Clearcut Neglect	11
N.A.I. Overt and Suspected; Potential N.A.I.; Clearcut Neglect	3
N.A.I. Overt and Suspected; Potential N.A.I.; Clearcut Neglect and Potential Neglect	28
No response to this question	6
TOTAL	100

Only 13% Authorities restricted inclusion to only clearcut cases.

42% Authorities indicated that they also included cases of neglect on their register. A few also included "emotional" battering, moral danger and ingestion of toxic material.

69% Authorities stated that they included potential or 'at risk' cases but it was also very clear that this category is defined in a variety of ways. For example, where a register is administered by the N.S.P.C.C. special units, very few potential cases are included, whereas in my own Authority of South Glamorgan two-thirds of registered cases are classified as potential.

In 44% Authorities the register was only made available for checking information during office hours.

Just over half the Authorities indicated that they only had one copy of the register. 44% had at least one duplicate copy; this was often necessary in order to provide twenty-four hour cover, in that the duplicate copy would be lodged in a place where there was full time cover already, such as a hospital casualty department or a residential children's home. The administrative task of maintaining up-to-date information on the register increases with each duplicate copy.

Another very stricking variation of approach is related to access to the registers. To sum this up, 42% Authorities allowed only very limited access and 49% indicated that they adopted a definite policy of allowing access to all agencies who might find the information useful. In this latter group however the wider access was frequently only via senior members of staff. The remaining 9% had no clear access policy.

Information contained on the registers varied from a few identifying items only to a very comprehensive and detailed list of all aspects of the childs socialand medical background; more than 50 different items of information were recorded. This finding, I suggest, indicates the varying attitudes as to the purpose of the register and also poses important questions about confidentiality and therefore access policy.

95% Authorities stated that the "phone back" system was employed for checking the authenticity of telephone enquiries. This seemed to be the most popular means of safeguarding the register, but several Authorities also said that the register was kept locked and specifically stated that only limited information was recorded in order to cut down the possibility of breaches of confidentiality. This policy may conflict with the usefulness of a register in that the availability of very limited details of the case only, may not provide the enquirer with sufficient information on which to base a decision about appropriate action.

5% of Authorities stated that they did not undertake any reviewing of registered cases. The remaining 95% employed a great variety of methods which ranged from reconvening the original case conference to an informal discussion between key workers.

Reviewing procedures can broadly be divided into two types :- firstly, Active Reviewing - i.e. reviewing initiated centrally by the register administrator, usually by means of a simple questionnaire tobe completed by the key workers of the various agencies involved, and independently assessed. Secondly, Passive Reviewing, which is left to the discretion of the area or district offices. The findings of this study indicate that 38% Authorities employ some form of 'active' reviewing or monitoring procedure, and 52% had adopted the 'passive' approach which I suggest is probably less efficient and comprehensive. The remaining 5% did not give enough information about reviewing procedures.

Table II shows graphically the great variation in the frequency with which reviews are carried out.

TABLE II

Frequency of Reviewing of Cases on a Register - Maximum time interval

Frequency	Number of Registers
According to Need	13
Monthly	9
3 Monthly	35
6 Monthly	34
Annually	3
Less Frequently	1
Inadequate information or no reviewing	5
TOTAL	100

12% Authorities had no procedure for removing a name from the register. Procedures for 'off-listing' once again varied a great deal although in nearly all Authorities the decision was a multi-disciplinary one. At least 12% Authorities maintain off-listed cases in a dormant or inactive list and do not destroy records.

One of the most stricking findings of this study was the discovery that 65% Authorities claimed that their register was rarely used, especially by agencies outside Social Services. Only 23% Authorities said that their register was regularly used - this included most of the registers administered by the N.S.P.C.C. special units where a tradition of register use seems to exist. The remaining 12% claimed moderate usage. Many Authorities clearly implied a degree of disappointment at how little their register was being used.

DISCUSSION

Examination of the findings in closer detail did not reveal any clear solution to the problem of limited usage except that, as might be expected, those registers which were available on a 24 hour basis, were used significantly more. Broad access policy did not appear to lead to greater usage neither did the existance of duplicate copies. The larger registers, which favoured a broader definition of Child Abuse and Potential Child Abuse, were not used to any greater extent than those which included only clearcut cases.

These findings, I suggest, may lead one to question the validity of the very existance of the Child Abuse Register. Do they serve any really useful purpose? Are checks for identification purposes really necessary? Are registers ethically acceptable? Do they undermine professionaly autonomy, discretion and judgement? It is not in the scope of this study to look at these questions in detail but I do believe that the principal of the Child Abuse Register is valid if it serves to prevent even a few tragedies. I believe this study shows, however, that the lack of standardization in approach to their administration makes it a less useful tool than it could be. They should provide a central focus for thorough inter-disciplinary monitoring and ongoing assessment of identified cases of child abuse and, I believe, potential cases of child abuse. In order to do this there must be nationally understood criteria for inclusion and reviewing and de-registration procedures. They must be efficiently administered by specifically nominated personnel. Once a universal approach is adopted, not only could they become vital in ensuring more efficient management of Child Abuse cases at a local level but also provide a very valuable source of reliable statistical data on a national level in order that our understanding of the full extent of the problem will increase and a more accurate idea of resource allocation can be achieved.

Reference (1) D.H.S.S. Memorandum April 1974 (LASSL(74)13/CMO(74)8).

Child Abuse and Neglect, Vol. 3, pp. 179 - 184.

0145-2134/79/0301-0179 $02.00/0.

AMERICAN EDUCATIONAL SYSTEMS AND CHILD ABUSE AND NEGLECT

C.D. Jones, Jr., Ph.D and Phil Fox, M.S.
Education Commission of the States, 1860 Lincoln Street, Suite 300
Denver, Colorado 80295

INTRODUCTION AND BACKGROUND

Because the school system is the most comprehensive social system for the total growth of a child, educators are a major resource for assisting abused and neglected children and their families. Recent legal mandates at the state level both require educators to report incidents of child abuse and neglect and provide protection for such reporting.

In 1975 the Education Commission of the States (ECS) received a grant from the National Center on Child Abuse and Neglect, Administration for Children, Youth and Families (ACYF), Department of Health, Education and Welfare (DHEW) to explore the role of American education in the identification, treatment and prevention of child abuse and neglect. More specifically, ECS was charged with exploring ways for educators to become more actively involved in identification, treatment and prevention programs.

As a means of gathering baseline data to assist in carrying out this charge, the project staff conducted a nationwide assessment of current education policies and practices regarding child abuse and neglect (in December 1975). Representatives of 390 selected education associations and school districts were interviewed to collect information on 1) existing policies, procedures and regulations for identifying and reporting suspected cases of child abuse and neglect; 2) the nature and extent of training activities for school personnel; and 3) the types of sponsored programs and activities regarding child abuse and neglect. The findings of the assessment are documented in ECS Report No. 85, Education Policies and Practices Regarding Child Abuse and Neglect and Recommendations for Policy Development.

In 1978 ECS conducted a follow-up assessment identical to the 1975 study. The purpose of that study was to determine and document whether there has been a noticeable increase or change in the development of policies, precedures, regulations, training activities and programs in education institutions regarding the identification and reporting of child abuse. The findings of this assessment are documented in ECS Report No. 109, Education Policies and Practices Regarding Child Abuse and Neglect: 1978. Phone calls were made from the ECS offices during November and December 1977 to a total population of 393 respondents representing the following institutions:

- State boards of education (35)
- State departments of education (50), plus the District of Columbia
- The largest district of each state, selection based on enrollment size (50)
- A small district of each state, selection based on student enrollment at the 33 rd percentile level (50), plus the District of Columbia
- The largest private school by enrollment in every state (50), and the District of Columbia

POLICY DEVELOPMENT

Every education institution engages in some measure of policy making, depending on state statutes and the governance structure of the individual state. While it is clear that American education has not reached the ideal in the area of child abuse and neglect, it is equally clear that there have been significant increases in policy development at all levels, as indicated in Table 1.

TABLE 1 SCHOOL DISTRICTS, PRIVATE SCHOOLS AND STATE LEVEL EDUCATION AGENCIES THAT HAD A POLICY ON CHILD ABUSE AND NEGLECT IN 1975 AND 1978

	Large Districts		Small Districts		Private Schools		State Boards of Education		State Departments of Education	
	Number	Percent	Number	Percent	Number	Percent	Number	Percent	Number	Percent
1975	22	44	14	28	5	10	6	17	8	16
1978	40	80	32	64	8	16	9	26	21	42
Percentage Increase Since 1975										
	82		129		60		50		163	

In reviewing the data, the following changes can be noted. Among large school districts, 80 percent report having policy commitments in 1978. This is a dramatic increase from 1975 when only 44 percent had such policies. While a smaller number of small school districts have child abuse and neglect policies (64 percent in 1978), the increase during the two years is significant.

While public education has made dramatic progress in adopting policies on child abuse and neglect, the private education sector lags behind. Only eight of the largest private schools had child abuse and neglect policies in 1978, as compared to five in 1975. These data are puzzling because most of the largest private schools are in urban or suburban areas. However, some private school administrators indicated a reluctance to report suspected cases of child abuse and neglect for fear that it would result in a loss of tuition fees. Furthermore, since a majority of the private schools interviewed were parochial, there were expressions of conviction by some that child abuse and neglect does not occur in religiously oriented families.

Both state boards of education and state departments of education reported increases in child abuse and neglect policy development. Of those agencies that have not developed any policy before or after 1975, the most frequently reported reason was that such an effort would interfere with local autonomy.

PROGRAMS AND SERVICES

Training Programs

Training can entail 1) developing an awareness of the problem in order to be responsive, 2) developing an in-depth information base or 3) pinpointing specific information and skills to develop or expand one's competency.

Within the last three years there has been an increase in the number of schools and state departments of education providing training programs for school personnel, as shown in Table 2.

TABLE 2 SCHOOL DISTRICTS, PRIVATE SCHOOLS AND STATE DEPARTMENTS OF EDUCATION THAT HAD SPONSORED TRAINING PROGRAMS IN 1975 and 1978

	Large School Districts		Small School Districts		Private Schools		State Departments of Education	
	Number	Percent	Number	Percent	Number	Percent	Number	Percent
1975	30	60	8	16	5	10	15	30
1978	36	72	21	42	10	20	31	62
Percentage Increase Since 1975								
	20		163		100		106	

State departments have shown an increasing commitment to sponsoring training. In 1975, only 15 departments reported sponsoring training, compared with 31 (over 60%) in 1978. Of the different types of schools, large districts reflect widespread commitment to training. Thirty large districts sponsored training in 1975 and 36 (over 70%) in 1978. However, small districts have made notable strides in this with only 8 small districts sponsoring training in 1975, and 21 (over 40%) in 1978. However, this represents a 163 percent increase since 1975.

Awareness Programs

Instrumental in the development of policies relating to child abuse and neglect are the public and professional awareness campaigns sponsored by the school districts, private schools and state departments of education. An increase in activity in this area has occurred since 1975, as indicated in Table 3.

TABLE 3 PUBLIC AND PROFESSIONAL AWARENESS CAMPAIGNS CONDUCTED BY STATE AND LOCAL EDUCATION AGENCIES IN 1975 AND 1978

	Large School Districts		Small School Districts		Private Schools		State Departments of Education	
	Number	Percent	Number	Percent	Number	Percent	Number	Percent
1975	18	36	1	2	2	4	12	24
1978	29	58	9	18	4	8	22	44
Percentage Increase Since 1975								
	61		800		100		83	

Only among large school districts have a majority of those polled in 1978 conducted public and professional awareness campaigns. This is an increase of 61 percent over those conducting such campaigns in 1975. Very few small districts and private schools have begun such activities, although the increase in numbers from 1975 to 1978 for small districts (1 to 9) is significant. State departments also reflect an increased commitment in this program area from 1975 to 1978, with 12 departments active in 1975 and 22 in 1978.

Services

There has been an increase in services provided by school districts to children identified as abused and neglected. Ninety-six percent of the large school districts sampled reported that they provided referrals and counselling services in 1978, while 76 percent and 82 percent of the small districts and private schools respectively provided such services. However, there was a sharp decrease in the number of state departments of education sampled in providing services.

TABLE 4 SERVICES PROVIDED BY SCHOOL DISTRICTS TO CHILDREN IDENTIFIED AS ABUSED AND NEGLECTED IN 1975 AND 1978

	Large School Districts		Small School Districts		Private Schools		State Departments of Education	
	Number	Percent	Number	Percent	Number	Percent	Number	Percent
1975	42	84	36	72	33	66	13	27
1978	48	96	38	76	42	84	6	12
Percentage Increase Since 1975								
	14		6		27		-(54)	

Interdisciplinary Involvement

As of 1978, seven of 51 states have mandated the creation of multidisciplinary child protection teams. Because of the interdisciplinary nature of the problem of child abuse and neglect, this concept provides for a broader range of input from a variety of disciplines to determine whether or not the child has been abused or neglected.

School systems are increasingly becoming involved with other service providers through representation on child protection teams. Fifty-two percent of the large districts responded that they were represented on a child protection team; 10 percent of the small districts were represented. However, 96 percent of the private schools responded that they were not represented and 4 percent "did not know".

Problems

Types of problems encountered by school personnel in dealing with suspected cases of child abuse and neglect are outlined below. Table 5 includes data on the number of large and small school districts and private schools that encounter problems.

TABLE 5 DISTRICTS AND PRIVATE SCHOOLS THAT ENCOUNTERED PROBLEMS IN CHILD ABUSE AND NEGLECT IN 1975 AND 1978

	Large School Districts		Small School Districts		Private Schools	
	Number	Percent	Number	Percent	Number	Percent
1975	41	82	26	52	16	31
1978	31	62	10	22	11	22
Decrease Since 1975						
	24		62		31	

TYPES OF PROBLEMS ENCOUNTERED IN 1978 ONLY (Rank Order)

Large School Districts - N=50

1) Lack of community resources
2) Lack of cooperation after referral
3) Lack of knowledge of characteristics of child abuse and neglect
4) Reluctance by school personnel to become involved

Small School Districts - N=50

1) Reluctance by school personnel to become involved
2) Lack of cooperation from community after referral
3) Other - parents

Private Schools - N=51

1) Lack of cooperation from community after referral
2) Other - parents, children protective of parents
3) Lack of knowledge of characteristics
4) Limited community resources

Perception of Incidence Among School Personnel

In the 1978 survey, an assessment was done of the perception of the incidence of child abuse and neglect. Table 6 indicates the responses from the school districts and private schools regarding whether the number of reported cases of child abuse and neglect was rising, falling or constant.

TABLE 6 PERCEPTION OF INCIDENCE OF CHILD ABUSE AND NEGLECT BY EDUCATION PERSONNEL IN 1978 ONLY

Incidence	Large School Districts	Small School Districts	Private Schools
Rising	31	8	6
Falling	1	1	0
Constant	10	32	34
Don't Know	8	5	4
No Cases	0	4	7
	N=50	N=50	N=51

The contrast in perception of the rate of incidence between large school districts and small districts and private schools is puzzling. A majority of the large schools indicated that the incidence of reported cases is increasing, while small districts and private schools indicated the incidence of cases is about the same. In analyzing this data, one should ask the following questions: Is there a widespread perception that child abuse is only an urban problem? Are larger communities identifying cases more effectively than the smaller communities are? Have public and professional awareness campaigns had more impact on urban areas? Equally puzzling is that although 8 percent of the small school districts and 14 percent of the private schools perceived cases of child abuse and neglect as nonexistent, research and professional opinion strongly indicate the contrary.

SUMMARY AND RECOMMENDATIONS

Traditionally, American education is more reactive to social change than proactive. While the above figures are at first glance, not encouraging, the rate of increase is quite dramatic and promising.

American educational systems and personnel can no longer avoid involvement in the recognized problem of child abuse and neglect. The history of American education records that when society becomes sufficiently aroused of a major social concern, it invariably turns to the schools for solutions because, schools, if not universally respected, are at least accepted as a prime influence, perhaps next only to the family, in the child's life.

The areas of education's greatest potential to help deal with the problem of child abuse are identification, precrisis intervention and primary prevention. Specifically, education groups and institutions could:

- Cultivate an awareness of child abuse among both lay citizens and the professional community.
- Promote needed legislation on the local, state and national levels.
- Provide preservice and inservice training for professionals, including social workers, mental health workers, police officers and all school personnel.
- Help coordinate health, welfare and other services throughout the community.
- Provide special, in-class attention to the educational, emotional and developmental needs of the abused child and counselling services for children and parents.
- Provide child-care services such as crisis nursery facilities, pre-school day care and emergency baby sitting.
- Offer courses for both secondary students and adults on appropriate parenting behaviors.
- Include information in the primary, intermediate and secondary curricula on child development, family life, discipline and agression, and other topics potentially useful to future parents.

Child Abuse and Neglect, Vol. 3, pp. 185 - 190.
Pergamon Press Ltd., 1979. Printed in Great Britain.

CHILD ABUSE : THE GREEK SCENE

Helen Maroulis
Institute of Child Health - Athens - Greece

Child abuse was totally unexplored in Greece until recently when we began our own pilot study. Therefore, in this paper, I will first describe some features of Greek society which may predispose families to abuse or neglect their children and secondly, to touch upon some of the methodological and practical problems encountered in our attempt to study these families.

I. A DESCRIPTION OF GREEK SOCIETY

A basic feature of Greek society today is its rapid transition from an agricultural economy to an industrial one. This has influenced radically most aspects of living, especially family life and values. The changes have affected the population's demographic characteristics, the role of women, marriage, the family, migration and the law, and these will be briefly considered.

A. Demographic characteristics

Greece has a population of 8.7m.[1] of which more than half live in urban areas. For the last 45 years the population's growth rate has been steadily declining. From 30 births per 1000 in 1928 to 16 births per 1000 in 1976.[2] This decline has been attributed to[3]

1. Increased participation of women in the labor force.
2. Decline in infant mortality rates (since survival ratio is greater, parents plan pregnancies).
3. Abortion (used as the main method of birth control).
4. Parents' increasing educational level.
5. High urbanization rate.
6. High emigration rate in young people.

The difficult living conditions in Greece are reflected in the official statistics[4] : 18% of homes in the cities described as " normal dwellings " and 40% in rural areas have no running water in the house, 12% have no electricity (27% in rural areas); 47% have a toilet with no plumbing (72% in rural areas).

However, there have been rapid changes particularly in rural areas where electricity and running water have been widely provided during the last ten years.

B. Education

Statistics on the extent of illiteracy in Greece show that there has been a significant drop but there is a marked difference between the sexes[4] .

Table I

Percentage distribution of Greek Population over 10 years into literate and illiterate

	Literate			Illiterate		
Census Year	Total	Male	Female	Total	Male	Female
1907	39	60	20	61	40	80
1920	48	66	30	52	34	70
1928	58	76	41	42	24	59
1951	76	89	65	24	11	35
1961*	82	92	73	18	8	27
1971	86	94	78	14	6	22

* Including those not stating if they know reading or writing

In spite of this improvement one should note that :

1. In 1971 more than 1m. people were illiterate out of which 79% were women.
2. The gap between the sexes is still great although tending to be reduced.
3. Today, 84% of women over 10 years have had six years of schooling or less. Nowadays, however, the law on education requires obligatory schooling for nine years.

C. Woman's role

Because the fate and well-being of children all over the world is closely related to the role of women, especially mothers, some interesting developments which took place between 1961 and 1971 deserve to be mentioned.[4]

1. An increase in the number of graduate and self-employed women.
2. An increase in the proportion and total number of women who participate in office-work, or in the salesmarket.
3. A stability in the proportion and total of skilled women workers.
4. A decrease in the proportion and total of women in agricultural work.

In 1971, 54% of the Greek female labor force were married (and of these 71% were in agriculture); 12% were divorced or widowed, and one third were unmarried.

On the whole, Greek women, even if they work full-time outside the home, also have the responsibility for running their home, bringing up their childre and maintaining the family's well-being.

D. Marriage and the family

A characteristic of the Greek society which still survives is arranged marriages. This used to be the only way by which two young people met and married. Parents and relatives or the village's "special woman" acted as match-makers. This method ensured family approval, dowries eased the financial situation of the young couple but burdened the bride's parents, while marriage guaranteed social acceptance and provided a stable environment for rearing children. Divorce was virtually non-existent. This custom is now less prominent particularly in the cities. The present divorce rate is comparatively low but with a tendency to rise (e.g. in 1971, 1.5 per 100 married)[4]. The proportion of divorced women is higher compared to men, which reflects the difficulty of remarrying among women.

The low divorce rate may be seen as an indicator of marriage stability; but it is more likely the result of social taboos about separation or divorce, sexual inhibitions, inequality between the sexes, economic problems, the lack of welfare systems to help working mothers and their children and, consequently, the women's reluctance to face life alone.

The steady decline in the number of household members is a crucial characteristic of the modern Greek family. On average, the present household has 3.3 members (1971 Census). This is attributable to the decreasing fertility and to a move towards the nuclear family.

The nuclear family lacks the support of the extended one but one notices that in the present transitional state relatives help most readily when a crisis occurs.

A further significant feature of families in Greece today is their attitude to contraception. Abortions-officially illegal and prohibited also by religion are still the most popular means of birth control. In every 100 women 40 resort to or consider abortion as the best method of birth control[5]. In Athens only, official estimates of abortions are up to 100.000 per year but unofficial sources double this number, while 130.000 children are born every year. The extremely high rate of abortion is correlated with low level of education and lack of information about birth control. In general the parents' wish for fewer children has been attributed to :[6]

1. The changing role of women-not only as wives and mothers, but also as participants in a career or in social life.
2. The desire for social and economic upward mobility - fewer responsibilities and economic dependence of children.
3. The lessening of religious beliefs that encouraged large families and prohibited birth control.

E. Migration

The Greek population through the ages has had migration, both internal and external.

Internal migration mainly takes the form of moving from rural to urban or semi-urban areas; 61% of internal migrants are young women aged 20 - 24 years and more women migrating to urban settings belong to the economically active population.[4] The children of these migrants leave behind village life - an extended family,space, no pollution, to live in the city's cement flats with much less clean air to breathe, little space to play and mothers who now face new problems of adjustment and social isolation.

Migrant families (e.g. to Western Germany) have their problems, too, while following various patterns related to care of their children. In some, the father migrates alone, while others take the children with them; others still take only one, usually the eldest. Some migrants leave the children behind in the care of relatives or send them back and forth for periods ranging from days to months or years. Whatever the pattern, those children are seen as obstacles in the family's struggle to survive and are treated as such.

Migration has been a blow to the traditional family structure which barely survives the adverse cultural, economic and phychological circumstances. One wonders what kind of adults the children of migrants will be, growing up as family burdens and leading a life of emotional deprivation - especially during the formative years - language problems, lack of both adequate basic education and educational opportunities to mention only a few. To these thousands of children we can add others belonging to the 100.000 seamen absent from home for long.

F. The Law

According to the Constitution of 1952 Greek women attained equal voting rights with men, the lack of equality between the sexes is obvious both culturally and legally. Some major legal obstacles to equality are paternal custody over children, dowry system, unequal pay, lack of or inadequate protection of motherhood.

The present law not only fails to help women and children but reinforces the current state. Mothers have no rights over their children while they usually bear the responsibility for their upbringing. The father has the supreme custody over his children until the age of 21, including the right to bring up the child, to supervise, to educate, to take the " appropriate " disciplinary measures and to determine the place of domicile.

From the foregoing, one would conclude that in the Greek family too much is happening too soon. Meanwhile, lack of adequate services and the inability of the existing ones to meet current needs have contributed towards a general feeling of insecurity, isolation and doubt, especially among the most deprived members of the population.

II. THE CHILD ABUSE SCENE

From this description one would anticipate that the stress experienced by many Greek families will place them particularly at risk for child abuse and neglect. And it was this consideration that prompted us to embark upon the pilot investigation of abused children and their families.

Predictably, our first obstacle was the lack of awareness of the problem among doctors and hospital personel which made our task of case identification rather difficult.

Initially, there was a tendency for doctors to disregard the extent of the problem. This attitude was probably shaped on the traditional view of the Greek extended family as a caring and protecting unit which is generally thought to make many sacrifices for the benefit of children.

Some evidence of child abuse and neglect has already been presented.[8,9] Our aim in those studies had been to explore the characteristics of abused and neglected children in Greece, and our findings were in line with those reported in the literature. An interesting feature, however, was the large number of children abused by parental substitutes.

It has been frequently said that interest in a particular problem tends to generate the material for its study. As our pilot study went on we found a greater willingness on the part of doctors to refer cases not only of blatant but of suspected abuse. Such cases may have not been focused upon previously, mainly because of the inadequacy of supporting services and the doctors' traditional reluctance to intrude in family problems.

Corporal punishment in our culture seems to involve no guilt and is viewed as an acceptable way of shaping a child's behaviour. One of the aims of our study, therefore, is to investigate the area of discipline among abusing families and controls. It is important to focus on the area of discipline. Children are spanked, beaten, deprived of love, all within the process of socialization. In our sample, parents showed little guilt for bruises and marks on their children's bodies. A mother of a 3 - year olf boy who was severely abused said: " It's natural for me to slap him on the face, to make his nose bleed, to break a tooth or two, I'm his mother after all". That child had sustained a fractured skull, broken limbs and nose, and multiple bruises and burns.

We have seen so far extreme cases of abuse and neglect mostly in multi-problem families where child abuse is only one of the signs of social maladjustment. Most parents were found to have abnormal personalities or mental illness. Their lives revealed a long history of deprivation, violence, poverty or broken homes. Most were of low education and currently unemployed. To these people, our interest in their problems was a new and somewhat threatening experience and it was only after repeated home visits and continuous care that they realized that somebody genuinely cared for them and wanted nothing in return. Appart from the recurrent nature of their problem another reason for such feelings and reactions may have been due to the inadequacy of the existing services.

Another area worthy of investigation is the distribution of authority in the Greek family. While existing laws support paternal authority, mothers usually have responsibility over their home and children. Furthermore, grandparents, though not always living with the young couples, still exert influence and encourage the young parents' dependency which often leads to conflicting values. From observations in 600 homes with young children in a Greek rural region,[10] it was revealed that paternal grandparents play a decisive role in the family, acting not only as authority figures for the young but also for the daughters in law.

In conclusion, I could state that the area of child abuse in Greece should be investigated within a cultural perspective that would include:

1. The study of child rearing practices with special reference to discipline.
2. The study of authority figures in the Greek family and their role in the socialization of children.
3. Assessment of the existing social services with special reference to child protection.
4. The study of the existing family law and areas for change.

Our aim , therefore, is not only to study child abuse and neglect in Greece from a clinical and social point of view but to examine the nature of the problem from a cultural perspective which, hopefully, may lead to the development of appropriate services and ultimately lead towards prevention.

BIBLIOGRAPHY

1. Résultats due Recensement de la Population et des Habitations, effectué le 14 Mars 1971, Office National de Statistique en Grèce, Athènes, 1975.

2. N.S.S.G., Statistical Yearbook of Greece 1977, Athens, 1977.

3. Symeonidou-Alatopoulou, H., An Account of Factors Affecting Fertility in Greece. Paper presented at the International Symposium " The Child in the World of Tomorrow ", Athens, July 1978.

4. Mousourou, L., I. The contemporary Greek Woman (Basic Data). (In Greek). Gutenberg, Athens, 1976.

5. Valaoras, Vas., Subfertility in Greeks and previous abortions. (In Greek). Athens, 1969.

6. Polyzos, N., Birth Control, First Yearly Report of the Center of Social Studies, Higher School of Industrial Studies, Athens 1957-58.

7. Manganara, J., Selective Problems of Intraeuropean Migrant Children in Sending and Receiving Societies. Paper presented at the International Symposium on the " Child in the World of Tomorrow ", Athens, July 1978.

8. Marouli, H., A Retrospective Study on the Child Abuse Syndrome. The Greek Review of Social Research, 30-31, 1977.

9. Nakou, S., Marouli, H., Doxiadis, S., The Syndrome of Child Abuse in Greece. (In Greek). Paper presented at the 4th Panhellenic Medical Congress, Athens,April 1978.

10. Tsitoura, S., Personal Communication.

Child Abuse and Neglect, Vol. 3, pp. 191 - 197.
Pergamon Press Ltd., 1979. Printed in Great Britain.

L'ECOLE MATERNELLE ET LES ENFANTS MALTRAITES
(INFANT SCHOOLS AND ABUSED CHILDREN)

P. STRAUS

Institut de Pédiatrie Sociale
Hôpital des Enfants Malades
149, rue de Sèvres 75015 PARIS

ENGLISH ABSTRACT

To-day in France more than 20 % of 2 to 3 year olds, 60 % of 3 to 4 year olds, 80 % of 4 to 6 year olds attend french infant schools. The author presents the results of a survey on abused children carried out in 1974 on a population of infant school headmistresses of a Paris suburb district under the form of a series of free or semi-directive interviews tape-recorded, then described and analysed.

Results

During the interviews, the headmistresses mentioned the cases of 52 children between 2 and 6 which they considered more or less in danger.

Concern arousing signs are triggered off mainly by the child's state of health and behaviour.

a) Marks of body injuries are only found on 25 % of the children mentioned, even though 50% of them are suspected of being battered by their parents. This assumption is based on the children's tales, neighbours reports, or even on parents remarks.

b) Overall bad state of health, physical deficiency, filth are sometimes stated.

c) But mainly the child's behaviour disorders and adjustment problems to school arouse attention : instability and agitation, sometimes hidden under aggressiveness, introversion, anxiety ; excessive emotional quest, overall backwardness in learning with lack of participation to class activities.

Attention is also drawn to demonstrations of verbal aggressiveness and emotional rejection as shown by the parents on bringing their child to or fetching it from school. Elective rejection of one child among siblings is also often noted without the reasons for this elective rejection being clearly perceived.

Teachers do not know the families well, do not see them at home. It is therefore difficult for them to assess living conditions and parents personality.

In the case of a child thought to be battered or rejected, the headmistresses call the parents in, give advice, suggest they consult a child doctor or a child guidance clinic.

Only 25 % of these children are reported by the headmistresses to child protection agencies. Reports to juvenile courts are exceptional. In most cases action is confined to body care given to the child in school, or psycho-emotional support when severe emotional deficiency is detected.

To conclude, the majority of children in France between 2 and 6 years old attend infant school. They generally receive careful attention from the teaching staff.

Due to their essentially psycho-educational aim infant schools are cut off form other child care agencies. Coordination with the latter is quite inadequate and therefore restricts the privileged part infant schools could play in protecting the children's rights and safety.

INTRODUCTION

L'école maternelle française est une structure d'enseignement préscolaire qui dépend du Ministère de l'Education Nationale.

Elle accueille aujourd'hui plus de 20 % des enfants de 2 à 3 ans, 60 % des enfants de 3 à 4 ans et 80 % des enfants entre 4 et 6 ans.

La plupart de ces enfants fréquentent l'école trois heures le matin et trois heures l'après-midi, mais beaucoup d'entre eux dont les mères travaillent mangent également à la cantine scolaire et sont gardés par des femmes de service le soir jusqu'à 18 h ou 19 h.

L'auteur expose ici les résultats d'une enquête sur les enfants maltraités, effectuée dans deux communes de la région parisienne comportant plus de 150.000 habitants, auprès de 18 Directrices d'Ecole Maternelle.

METHODOLOGIE

L'enquête s'est déroulée sous la forme d'une série d'interviews libres ou semi-directives, enregistrées au magnétophone puis secondairement décriptées et analysées.

La technique par interview a été préférée au questionnaire en raison du malaise exprimé par le personnel enseignant devant le problème des sévices physiques exercés par des parents sur leurs enfants. Ce malaise était tel qu'il aurait certainement entrainé un blocage des réponses par la méthode du questionnaire alors qu'au cours d'une interview la personne interrogée peut s'exprimer plus librement et citer des cas "limites" ou "douteux" sans se sentir culpabilisée pour ne pas avoir signalé l'enfant aux structures administratives ou judiciaires de la protection de l'enfance.

Le point de départ des entretiens était la question suivante : "Connaissez-vous des enfants dans votre école dont vous pensez qu'ils sont victimes de mauvais traitements ou risquent de l'être ? La notion de mauvais traitements pouvant inclure des cas de négligence ou des sévices moraux ayant des conséquences physiques."

En règle générale les interviews sont surtout riches en ce qui concerne l'état physique de l'enfant et son comportement en classe. Elles abordent de façon plus ou moins "impressionniste" le problème des relations parents-enfants telles qu'on peut les observer au moment de la rentrée ou de la sortie de l'école mais comportent très peu de précisions sur l'état civil , les conditions de vie, la structure familiale et les antécédents de l'enfant. Enfin, le caractère assez libre des entretiens et leur mode d'enregistrement donnent aux propos des directrices d'école beaucoup de richesse mais ne permettent pas une véritable analyse statistique.

RESULTATS

Une petite minorité des directrices d'école se sont refusées à admettre la réalité du problème ou à citer des exemples concrets, faute de preuves suffisantes. Elles se sont bornées à traiter des problèmes généraux concernant les parents et les enfants, s'étendant sur les caractères généraux de la population scolaire et sur les difficultés de coordinations avec les services sociaux.

Beaucoup plus fréquentes et significatives furent les réflexions concernant la spécificité et les limites de la définition proposée :

Les propos suivants extraits des interviews en sont une bonne illustration:

"Je ne comprends pas votre enquête : Qu'est ce qui est physique et qu'est-ce qui est psychique quand on est un enfant. C'est un domaine où tout est entremelé."

"Le manque d'affection c'est la même chose que les coups, avec les coups en moins".

Pour la plupart des directrices d'école la distinction entre sévice physique et rejet affectif de l'enfant parait artificielle.

Au total les Directrices d'école ont évoqué dans leurs interviews les cas de 52 enfants agés de 2 à 6 ans, considérés par elles comme plus ou moins en danger.

1°) Les signes d'alarme concernent avant tout l'état physique et le comportement de l'enfant.

a) Des traces physiques de sévices corporels (ecchymoses, hématomes, plaies ou brûlures) n'ont été retrouvées que sur 10 enfants, mais la moitié des cas rapportés (25 enfants) sont cependant considérés par les enseignants comme battus par leurs parents. Cette notion découlant des dires des enfants, de la dénonciation du voisinage ou même des propos tenus par les parents à la directrice.

Ex :
- "L'enfant est arrivée avec des marques sur le visage, elle disait que c'était son papa qui l'avait battue."
- "Plusieurs fois il est arrivé avec des ecchymoses sur le visage et même une brûlure, le père a dû le pousser contre le poêle."
- "Il portait des marques très fortes de griffures, des traces de doigts et lorsqu'on l'a dit à la mère, elle a reconnu qu'elle ne pouvait en venir à bout."
- "La mère n'avait jamais un geste tendre vis à vis de son fils, toujours des gestes brusques : un jour une institutrice l'a surprise dans la rue rouant l'enfant de coups de pieds parce qu'il avait oublié son cartable."
- "L'enfant avait 2 ans, elle a fait pipi dans sa culotte. Comme je disais à la mère que ce n'était pas grave, elle me rétorqua : "Comment, mais vous laissez passer cela, mais c'est affreux, vous ne vous rendez pas compte, il faut lui donner la fessée, il faut lui mettre le nez dedans", et sans que j'ai pu l'en empêcher, devant moi elle a mis une fessée à l'enfant."
- "Les voisins sont venus me trouver disant qu'il fallait faire quelque chose, que c'était toute la journée des hurlements, que les enfants étaient battus et particulièrement celle que j'avais à l'école."

b) Le mauvais état général, la déficience physique, la saleté sont fréquemment évoqués comme témoins de négligences graves ou d'abandonnisme.

c) Mais ce sont surtout les troubles du comportement de l'enfant et son inadaptation au milieu scolaire qui attirent l'attention.

- Certains enfants frappent par leur :
  . Instabilité et leur agitation qui prend parfois le masque de l'agressivité.

Ex :
- "C'était comme un petit animal paniqué qui mordait et griffait dès qu'on s'approchait d'elle."
- "Le matin, quand il y a eu un drame familial, elle est énervée et agressive, s'acharne sur les autres enfants."
- "Elle s'ennuie profondément en classe. Toujours le pouce dans la bouche ou bien s'agite et tourbillonne."
- "Elle est agitée, instable, perturbe toute la classe, dérange ses voisins.

- D'autres, au contraire inquiètent par leur apathie, leur repliement sur eux-mêmes et l'on retrouve dans les interviews toute une série d'expressions imagées : peu épanoui, bloqué, éteint, muet, recroquevillé, paralysé, replié, morne, figé, air fatigué.

- Parfois l'anxiété parait prédominer, d'où les termes de : triste, craintif, terrorisé, air malheureux, esquisse des gestes de défense.

Ex : - "Elle était d'un mutisme absolu comme une petite bête qui se renferme sur elle-même, toujours prête à servir de souffre douleur à la classe."

- Les perturbations psychologiques de l'enfant se manifestent fréquemment sous la forme d'une quête affective dont l'intensité trouble et inquiète la maitresse.

Ex : - "Il a vraiment besoin d'un contact physique, il lui faut toucher la peau, toucher les mains de la maitresse, les embrasser."

- "Il était constamment en quête d'affection, on voyait toujours une main qui se tendait ou un visage à la recherche d'un baiser. C'était poignant".

- "Elle a besoin que je m'occupe d'elle tout le temps : "Moi maitresse, moi maitresse."

- L'inadaptation scolaire est presque toujours sous-entendue dans le discours des enseignants. Elle est souvent décrite sous forme de retard des acquisitions et de non participation à la classe.

Ex : - "Elle semble assez maladroite, craintive et peu épanouie, elle a peur des autres, elle a un vocabulaire des plus pauvres et on ne comprend pas bien ce qu'elle dit."

d) Enfin dans certains cas le dépot d'un jeune enfant tôt le matin et sa reprise tard le soir inquiète comme un témoignage d'abandon ou de rejet de la part des parents.

Ex : - "La mère travaille sur place, elle n'a pas de longs transports donc pourquoi met-elle sa fille si tôt le matin et la reprend-elle si tard le soir ? Elle avoue d'ailleurs que son enfant est impossible et qu'elle veut la laisser à l'école le plus tard possible. C'est presque aussi important que les coups que laisser ainsi un enfant."

Les relations Parents-Enfants

Plus que les brutalités corporelles, ce qui attire l'attention des directrices ce sont les manifestations d'agressivité verbale et de rejet affectif des parents à l'égard de l'enfant telles qu'on peut les observer au moment de l'entrée ou de la sortie de l'école; Brusquerie des gestes, refus d'embrasser un enfant ou même de le toucher, langage agressif tenus à son égard ou devant lui. "C'est un voyou." "Il est infernal." "Je le tuerai." "Je ne peux pas le supporter, il me rend malade." etc...

Le rejet électif d'un enfant parmi ses frères et soeurs est également fréquemment observé sans que les raisons de ce rejet soient toujours bien perçues.

Ex : - "La mère laissait à la cantine sa fillette de 3 ans et reprenait le garçon. Comme je lui en faisais la remarque elle me dit : "Je me suis mise d'accord avec elle, elle sait que je ne peux la supporter, elle me rend malade. Quand je sais qu'il faut que j'aille la chercher, j'en ai l'estomac qui se serre."

- "La mère disait qu'elle ne pouvait le supporter, qu'elle continuerait à le battre, qu'il fallait qu'on le lui place... Quand elle venait le chercher à l'école avec sa petite soeur, elle embrassait la petite fille mais pas lui, elle donnait la main à sa fille et lui suivait, elle ne le touchait pas."

Il s'agit d'ailleurs souvent d'un enfant qui manifeste à l'école une instabilité ou une agressivité particulière sans que l'on saisisse bien quel est l'élèment premier : est-ce le comportement de l'enfant qui conduit la mère à ne plus pouvoir le supporter, ou bien ce comportement est-il réactionnel à l'agressivité maternelle.

Dans 1/3 des cas cependant le vrai sujet d'inquiètude réside dans l'état de négligence grave, voire d'abandonnisme dans lequel se trouve l'enfant :

Enfant mal nourri ou dénutri, que ses parents ne viennent pas chercher, qui traine dans la rue, qui n'est jamais lavé, qui porte des vêtements d'été en hiver, etc... Il s'agit d'ailleurs souvent dans ces cas de familles nombreuses ou tous les enfants sont également l'objet de la préoccupation des directrices.

L'Ecole et les Familles

Les enseignants connaissent mal les familles. En l'absence d'assistante scolaire, les visites à domicile sont rares. Il leur est donc souvent difficile de faire une évaluation des conditions de vie des parents.

Pour la moitié des enfants (26) signalés par les écoles, les familles sont considérées comme des "cas sociaux" en raison de difficulté socio-économique particulière, de mauvaises conditions de logement, d'instabilité conjugale, de problème d'éthylisme ou de maladie mentale, par suite de placements ou de retraits antérieurs d'enfants ou parce qu'il s'agit de mères célibataires ou de travailleurs immigrés.

Ex : - "Il y a 6 enfants, la mère a eu son 4e enfant à l'âge de 20 ans, elle n'est pas mariée, elle en a placé deux avec l'aide des Services Sociaux."

- "Il y a 6 enfants, le père est algérien, la mère française, il n'y a jamais d'argent. L'enfant était tellement maigre qu'on a réussi à faire peur au père pour qu'il le laisse manger à la cantine."

- "La mère est cuisinière dans un hôpital. Elle est plus ou moins débile, elle a eu 4 enfants de trois pères différents. Celui qui vit avec elle actuellement est ivrogne et ne travaille pas. Chez elle, c'est affreux.

Dans 11 cas la structure familiale leur apparait normale, la situation économique "moyenne" ou "bonne".

Enfin, dans 15 observations les renseignements concernant l'environnement de l'enfant sont absolument insuffisants voire inexistants ce qui rend impossible une évaluation quelconque des conditions de vie de la famille.

Lorsqu'un enfant dans l'école leur parait en danger, qu'il soit l'objet de brutalités physiques, d'un rejet affectif ou de négligences graves, les directrices s'efforcent d'établir un contact avec les parents dans le but de mieux comprendre la situation et d'agir autant que possible sur les relations parents-enfants.

Ce contact se heurte a plusieurs difficultés :

Dans certaines familles nombreuses, les jeunes enfants sont amenés à l'école par leurs ainés. Lorsque la mère travaille, elle confie parfois l'enfant à l'école tôt le matin et le reprend tard le soir à des heures ou la directrice est absente.

Mais ce qui ressort surtout des interviews, c'est la difficulté d'évaluer la personnalité des parents.

Ex : - "Le père m'a fait bonne impression, si je ne savais pas ce qu'il faisait à son enfant, jamais je ne l'aurais soupçonné. Il est bien de sa personne, il a l'air sympathique, je ne l'aurais pas cru capable de taper comme cela sur son enfant".

- "La maman est charmante et il s'agit d'un milieu "bien". Quand on discute avec elle on a l'impression d'une mère aux petits soins avec ses enfants et finalement on s'est rendu compte qu'elle est brutale avec son fils pour des petits riens, qu'elle n'a jamais de geste affectif, qu'elle le secoue violemment; elle est maniaque, veut que tout soit parfait et réagit par des coups."

Cette difficulté d'évaluation constitue un des principaux obstacles qui freine le signalement des enfants en danger aux services de la Protection Maternelle et Infantile ou aux Structures Judiciaires.

Le rôle de l'Ecole Maternelle

Devant un enfant qui préoccupe la structure scolaire en raison de son état physique, de son comportement ou de son inadaptation, l'école maternelle se sent une responsabilité spécifique en liaison avec sa double finalité: sociale et psychopédagogique et du fait que l'enfant passe à l'école une importante partie de son temps.

Le Maternage consiste à assurer à l'enfant des soins qui ne peuvent lui être fournis par une mère absente ou parfois une mère déficiente.

Il peut s'agir de soins corporels : laver l'enfant, lui fournir des vêtements, lui assurer une alimentation rationnelle à la cantine scolaire, organiser son placement pour les vacances, mais les directrices d'école insistent surtout sur le rôle de soutien psycho-affectif joué par les institutrices en face d'enfants pour lesquels elles croient deviner une importante carence affective.

Ce rôle nécessite d'ailleurs une disponibilité qui n'est pas toujours facile en raison du trop grand nombre d'enfants par classe (les normes actuelles de l'Education Nationale fixent ce nombre à 35).

Par ailleurs si l'attention particulière dont il est l'objet rend l'enfant plus heureux et plus épanoui en classe, il ne tient plus à rentrer à la maison ce qui avive les conflits entre les parents et les enseignants et peut exacerber les manifestations d'agressivité dont il est l'objet chez lui.

L'Ecole maternelle et le Service de Santé Scolaire

En principe le service de Santé Scolaire (médecin de santé scolaire, assistante sociale scolaire, groupe d'action psychologique) ne s'occupe que des enfants fréquentant l'enseignement primaire et secondaire.

La santé et la protection des enfants de moins de 6 ans reste du ressort des services départementaux de la Protection Maternelle et Infantile et ce sont les assistantes polyvalentes de secteur qui ont en charge les jeunes enfants fréquentant l'école maternelle.

Cette situation est mal acceptée par les Directrices d'école qui préféreraient travailler avec une assistante sociale intégrée dans le groupe scolaire, connaissant bien les enfants et en contact permanent avec le personnel enseignant. C'est pourquoi dans quelques cas les directrices utilisent les services de santé scolaire de l'école primaire pour contacter une famille ou rédiger un certificat médical.

L'Ecole maternelle et les Services Sociaux

Les relations entre les directrices d'école et les assistantes sociales de secteur ne sont pas faciles. Elles les connaissent mal, ne leur font pas toujours confiance, et quand un secteur est "vacant", elles ne savent pas à qui s'adresser.

Ces difficultés de coordination entre services sociaux et écoles maternelles et les difficultés d'évaluer la gravité d'un cas expliquent que 13 enfants seulement ont fait l'objet d'un signalement aux services sociaux de secteur. Ces signalements concernent le plus souvent des familles défavorisées ou marginales déjà connues par les services sociaux ou des enfants victimes de sévices graves. Les signalements effectués directement par l'école à la police ou aux autorités judiciaires sont beaucoup plus rares (3 cas).

Lorsque le milieu familial leur parait "normal" ou plus simplement leur est mal connu, les directrices hésitent à faire un signalement et se contentent de convoquer les parents, de discuter avec eux, de leur donner des conseils et de les orienter vers un pédiatre, une consultation de P.M.I. ou une structure d'hygiène mentale infantile.

Rapports avec l'Hygiène Mentale Infantile

Dans 7 cas, l'école maternelle a recours au C.M.P.P. (Centre Médico-Psycho-Pédagogique) pour tenter d'améliorer les troubles du comportement présentés par un enfant ou pour essayer d'agir sur les relations parents-enfants.

Ce recours à l'Hygiène Mentale Infantile parait plus facile à l'école et répond mieux à son problème qui est avant tout celui de l'inadaptation scolaire de l'enfant.

L'Hygiène Mentale Infantile bénéficie d'un prestige certain mais l'attente de l'école est loin d'être toujours satisfaite et les interviews révelent parfois une certaine desillusion.

Ex : - "C'est une enfant mal-aimée, elle n'a pas de père, elle a été en nourrice depuis sa naissance et sa mère ne peut pas l'accepter. Nous avons conseillé à la maman d'aller consulter au C.M.P.P. mais sans résultat. On peut bien obliger les gens à y aller une ou deux fois, mais après, s'ils ne veulent pas y retourner on ne peut rien faire."

Enfin, le manque de liaisons entre l'Hygiène Mentale Infantile et l'école est souligné dans plusieurs observations :

Ex : - "Le C.M.P.P. nous a demandé des renseignements au début, mais depuis nous n'avons plus aucun contact, et pourtant à cette époque nous ne savions pas que la mère la battait".

CONCLUSION

La majorité des enfants français entre 2 et 6 ans fréquentent l'école maternelle. Ils y sont en général l'objet de beaucoup d'attention de la part du personnel enseignant et les perturbations secondaires à l'agressivité ou à la négligence de leurs parents y sont souvent finement analysées.

Mais la finalité essentiellement psychopédagogique de l'école maternelle l'isole des autres structures de la Protection Médico Sociale de l'enfance. Les coordinations avec ces dernières sont actuellement tout à fait insuffisantes et ceci limite le rôle privilégié que l'Ecole maternelle peut jouer pour la sauvegarde des intérêts et de la sécurité des jeunes enfants.

REFERENCES

P. STRAUS et M. MANCIAUX, Les Jeunes Enfants Victimes de Mauvais Traitements, Edition C.T.N.R.E.H.I. - 1978, 27, quai de la Tournelle 75005 PARIS.

Child Abuse and Neglect, Vol. 3, pp. 199 - 204.

0145-2134/79/0301-0199 $02.00/0.

LOW BUDGET PLAY THERAPY FOR VERY YOUNG CHILDREN

Elizabeth Davoren

5080 Paradise Drive, Tiburon, California 94920 USA

There is growing agreement in the field that children who have been abused and neglected need direct therapy; but only a small portion of those who need the treatment get it. Lack of money, lack of therapists, and parental resistance are among the deterrents to the needed therapy[1]. I inadvertantly discovered one way around these three obstacles when working as a consultant forthe Extended Family Center in San Francisco[2]. The Extended Family Center provided day care for infants, toddlers, and preschool children who had been severely abused or neglected, and treatment for their parents.

Excessive Violence -- the Presenting Problem

One day during consultation the day care staff were discussing problems caused by the excessive violence of the three to five year old preschoolers. Physical attacks directed toward the staff could be handled. However, the attacks the children directed toward each other could not always be anticipated and prevented. They hurt each other, which was bad enough in and of itself, but in addition the resulting bruises, bite marks and scratches enraged the parents of the injured. "How come," their parents wanted to know, "we have to answer for anything that you don't like about the way the kids look when we bring them in, but when we pick them up, they have marks on them that would put us in jail?" Although such statements were not accurate, there was an uncomfortable element of truth in them. It was embarrassing to try to answer parents under the circumstances.

Doll House Play -- a Trial Solution

We considered what could be done to diminish the children's hitting each other that had not already been tried. It was the staff assumption, based on considerable experience, that the children were bringing to day care an overflow of anxiety and rage from home. I suggested that doll house play might be used to alleviate the tension that resulted in aggressive interaction while allowing a child to share home bound worries in a non-threatening way. Since the staff did not know how to encourage or handle doll house play, we arranged to use some of my consultation time for a demonstration of play techniques.

The first demonstration took place in a corner of the preschool play room. The doll house, typical of those used in play therapy, consisted of heavy rectilinear boards with appropriately placed holes to represent windows and doors. The boards could be fitted together in a number of ways, thus allowing for variable room sizes. The house was roofless and all play took place looking down on the rooms. Indestructible wooden furniture was arranged in the rooms. Flexible plastic dolls with felt clothes were placed at random throughout the house. The dolls represented mothers, fathers, sisters and brothers. The popular baby dolls had to be replaced frequently because some of the youngsters swallowed them. There were black dolls and white dolls, but none to represent the appearance of latinos and orientals who were an important part of the play school population.

[1]For details of obstacles experienced at the National Center for Prevention and Treatment of Child Abuse and Neglect in Denver, see Chapter 21, pp. 265-273 in Martin, Harold, The Abused Child, Ballinger Publishing, Cambridge, 1976.

[2]For a fuller description, see: Ten Broeck, Elsa, The Extended Family Center, Children Today, Vol. 3, No. 2, 2 (1974).

We could have guessed that doll house play in an open setting would soon become the free-for-all it did. The amount of staff attention focused on the activity caused the children to contest for attention rather than play in the house. The winner of the contest sat himself down on the house, covering the rooms and their contents, thereby ending the play and enraging the other children. After this brief introduction, which at least allowed all of the children to have a look at the doll house and dolls, we moved into a separate structure only a few steps away. The tiny cottage normally used for staff meetings contained little that could damage or be damaged. There were no windows. The skylight was too high to be reached by objects hurled in its direction, and what furniture there was could be jumped on and otherwise abused without causing concern. On the minus side, the room was exceptionally unattractive and there was no heat. Since broken toys and other objects were stored in the room, it was important to remember to remove them before play sessions began.

From Play Demonstrations to Play Therapy

After a few weeks I felt that being in the role of demonstrator affected my relationship with the children, making the sessions less productive than they should be. Also the staff who wer used to being spontaneous with the children tended to interrupt the flow of their play by asking questions and making suggestions. I asked to see the children for a while without staff to give me a chance to refine techniques. The time spent with the children was so intriguing that what started out as brief demonstrations of doll house play for the staff evolved into 18 months of play therapy sessions for the children.

I had only two hours each week to be divided among the 10 to 15 children in the preschool group. There were always more requests for play sessions than could be met. Frustrated by having to tell children too young to understand that I would see them next week, I tried in one session "encouraging" each one to leave after about 10 minutes. The week following I had the play room and the time to myself. The children had felt pushed out and unwanted, and did not want to return. With the free time I went shopping at a nearby sweet shop for candy bribes. An assortment of small candies was selected, from which the children could choose an three that appealed to them at the completion of their play. The bribes were intentionally small. That way no child would find it too much of a drawing card if he/she didn't want to come for a play period nor would any child find it too much of a disappointment if time, ther fore the candy treat, were not available.

Agatha

At first the candies were given only to those who came for a play session, but an experience with four year old Agatha soon changed that. Agatha walked on tip toe all the time. She was one of the most disturbed and frightened children at the Center. Her mother had smothered on baby before Agatha was born, and, although Agatha had never been physically harmed or neglected, she had been locked in a closet for as much as five hours at a time. Unlike the others, she took weeks to get used to me. I chatted with her every week, or tried to. Slowly she responded, and after six weeks she even managed to tiptoe into the play room and ask if she could have some candies. I invited her in to play. She refused. I explained that candies came at the end of a play session. Agatha looked indignant and betrayed. She had worked up courage to come into a strange room for nothing. The next week I took her aside and told her the rule on candy was changed, so any time she wanted to come in and just ask for candies, th would be all right. She didn't come right away, but when she did she decided she would stay and play.

Developing the Play Sessions

The time spent in the play room by each child varied from a few minutes to thirty minutes. learned to gauge how much time each child needed by taking into account: 1) the general appe ance and affect of the child, 2) the importance of the subject matter tackled and the intens of the play.

In the beginning I very gently tried to focus the children's attention on the house and doll play. It became apparent that it was better to let each child choose what to do. The limit toy supply did some of the focusing for us. Any control which was tried experimentally in order to streamline the use of the limited time available was soon relinquished. As it deve oped our brief play period became a time in which the children had almost complete control o their activities, as well as undivided, non-critical adult attention. The sort of non-direc play therapy[3] that was being used was a unique experience for these children who were accustomed to exceptional demands, control, and criticism from their parents. Even the day care staff, who were pro-child, warm, and supportive, had to set limits continuously to avoid chaos.

The children showed strength and insight in their play one would never believe possible. However, their play was so different from the non-Center children I had known in several states and settings that I asked staff who had preschool children if they would bring them in for a brief play session. The staff were of the same ethnic mix and lived in the same neighborhoods as the Center families. Their children's play did prove to be different from that of the Center children, and comparable to the other non-Center children I had known.

Characteristics of Play

As others have found with abused and neglected children, the language skills of the Center's children were notably deficient[4]. They used less fantasy in their play[5]. There was an abundance of anticipated violence. Some of it was played out with the dolls. The parent dolls continuously threatened the child dolls, and beat them to reinforce threats. Mass violence -- all the dolls beating and killing each other -- was common. Interestingly enough, with the exception of one 4-year old boy, no one used any television themes even though all of them had seen a great deal of television. The play house furniture was thrown around and stomped on many times. It was rarely placed in anything near an orderly fashion. If a child found the furniture arranged he/she would ask who put it that way, and, without waiting for an answer, would mess it up and stack it. Dolls, too, were often piled on top of one another. As most children do, they took off the dolls' clothes to look for genitals. However, their knowledge of sexual behavior exhibited in doll play was far more extensive than that of most children of comparable ages.

Most non-violent play started with the dolls being put down to sleep. For many of the children putting the dolls to sleep was their major activity. An unusual amount of attention was paid to the refrigerator, but it was more likely to be used as a place to sleep than a source of food. I was surprised that food or eating was not more of a theme because of the enormous amount of time each child at the Center normally devoted to eating. The TV was probably the most commented on and used piece of furniture in the play house. The dolls were put about a room to watch TV -- that's all. The toilet was also used fairly frequently. Going "pee" or "ca-ca" seemed to be regarded with much more embarrassment or sense of doing the forbidden than any of the sexual activity that was played out with the dolls. The bathtub was used for sleeping, as was every other piece of furniture in the house. Beds were used occasionally for sex, as well as sleeping.

Agatha -- Reprise

Although there were many similarities in their play, each child had his or her own agenda -- played out from week to week, until reaching what appeared to be a resolution. For instance, Agatha, the child who had been so reluctant to try the play room, stayed for only brief periods at first. She was somewhat threatened by the locked door, which was necessary to keep the other children out. Her first day was spent picking up dolls and pieces of furniture naming each in a tentative sort of way, then quickly putting them down. "I want my candy now", she said. She snatched three pieces of candy and left as quickly as her tiptoeing would allow. Over a period of four months she progressed through four stages: 1) picking up, identifying by name and quickly putting down each piece of furniture and each doll (almost as if they were hot coals), 2) holding on to each object longer and naming each with increasing assurance, 3) piling dolls and furniture randomly about the rooms of the house, 4) making specific placement of the furniture and the dolls. Stage 3, the piling, went on the longest time, and stage 4, the specific placement, was epitomized in her last play session when she organized the furniture and sat the dolls, each in a place of its own. "There!" she said, looking quite satisfied. She had already increased her time of deliberation over the candy selection, but this time she was the most careful she had ever been. In her play room behavior, Agatha seemed to be taking

[3] The form of therapy used with the children did not differ markedly from that described by Virginia Axline in Play Therapy, Ballantine Books, New York, 1969 and Dibs in Search of Self, Ballantine Books, New York, 1964.

[4] As noted p. 85 of: Martin, Harold, The Abused Child, Ballinger Publishing, Cambridge, 1976.

[5] Compared, for instance, to the play of a normal four year old child as cited in Erikson, Erik, Toys and Reasons, Norton Publishers, New York, 1977.

increasing charge of the turmoil that she felt inside of herself, becoming less afraid and more sure of her surroundings. She also could begin to make decisions about what she wanted for herself.

April

Unlike the reluctant Agatha, April was an enthusiastic and aggressive participant. She almost always managed to be the first play room participant of the day, no matter how severe the competition. April was 3½ years old at the time she started play therapy. She had been "in charge" of a household and two younger brothers since whe was 3. Her mother was partially paralyzed and on occasion overtly psychotic. She stayed in bed a lot. Whatever was done while the father was at work had to be done by this child. April's main theme in play therapy was house cleaning. "Clean the house or go to jail" a policeman would roar to the assembled doll family. Everyone would refuse to clean the house and its piled up furniture. So they would be taken to jail. Elaborate, usually successful, plots to escape from jail took place, sometimes ending with the policeman locked in his own jail. This sort of play went on for about a year -- not every week, but with a high degree of frequency. The concluding episode of the slowly evolving drama had the house being cleaned by all of its inhabitants, followed by the policeman's moving in as a family member. April seemed to be both the policeman and the householder -- at the same time she was the powerful person who would see to it that the house was in order and she was also one of those who would attempt to escape the responsibility. Her resolution of the dilemma was to spread the responsibility around, and change the role of the policeman from overseer to equal. Toward the end of her play room visits she stopped fighting ferociously to be first. At the time I thought she was less invested in play sessions, which may have been so, but it also seems likely that it was not as necessary for her to run things anymore. She could be one of the group -- which for her was an achievement.

Mark

April had run everybody else's life, but Mark was only responsible for his own. Mark was known in the neighborhood bars where he spent most of his time as the child who could take care of himself. By age three he was already a rough, tough street kid who had fallen out of a second story window onto the street below and survived with a scraped face and a broken arm. His mother had no investment in him and his stepfather was so passive he seemed not to exist. At the Center, Mark spent most of his time testing limits and his teacher's endurance. His interest in play sessions developed slowly. He came first for the candy and ended up staying to play. As might be expected, his play was full of violence -- kicking off " the cop's weewee", and killing all the dolls over and over again -- but eventually rescuing one doll that seemed clearly to be himself. There were many violent themes and much sex play. However, the most relevant happening was not around the doll house play.

At first the testing of limits which I had expected from Mark did not materialize. There are so few limits to test, I thought, he can't be bothered, or possibly he is content here because there are so few limits -- he doesn't need to test. I was wrong. As soon as Mark's intense interest in play diminished, he found the limit to test -- the three candy limit. One day after picking three candies he announced he wanted more. The rule was simply explained, but he could not accept it. Reflective techniques[6] were used successfully for a couple of weeks with such comments as: "you wish you had more candy", "you're mad because I don't let you have it". By the third week he was ready with a new tactic. As soon as the candies were presented he dived for them -- prepared to take a fistful. I saw what was coming and closed the container. "I promise I will just take three" he aaid and he did when the candy was again offered. But he quickly threw these candies away and showed his empty hands. "I don't have any candies now. Can I have my three candies?" he asked. "You can pick up those you threw if you like", I said. Instead of candy, he picked up tricycle handlebars that had not been removed from the room as they should have been. "Give me candy or I'll hit you", he said. "You want to control the number of candies you pick. You have a hard time deciding to follow the rule", I countered I prepared mentally to protect myself, but did not move. He was poised to strike for a few momemts. It was with relief that I watched him lower the handle bars to the floor.

These vigorous attempts to get his way were tried with variation over a two-week period, and then on the third week after a short play period, he aaid "I'm ready for my candy." He looked

[6] As discussed p. 73 Axline, Virginia, Play Therapy, idem, and p. 16 Moustakas, Clark, Children in Play Therapy, Ballantine Books, New York, 1953.

over the offered mix for a long, long time, then slowly and deliberately picked out three, scrutinizing my face after each candy selection and building up considerable suspense. This behavior was repeated for several weeks. It seemed as if this were the first time Mark knowingly internalized someone else's rule and made it his own. "I will have three candies," he said on his last visit -- "not one, or two, or four, just three."

Allen

I was surprised when one of the staff members told me that Allen couldn't talk. I had passed him on the way through the Center to the play therapy room and he was saying a very understandable "fuck you" into a toy phone. We did not know it, at first, but Allen's use of language reflected his whole state of being. In the play room after weeks of playing out hitting and killing scenarios and abundant sex themes, (using a few words, when necessary), he turned his attention to the cassette recorder which was recording the sessions. Unlike the other children, who liked to speak briefly into it, rewind the tape and listen to themselves, Allen wanted only to talk.

On guessing he wished to use the recorder, since he wasn't explicit about it, I put him on my lap and we put the recorder with its conddnser microphone in his lap. What followed was a bit of a shock. He made noises as if talking, but there were no understandable words said. He "talked" for half an hour without pause, saying nothing. When the tape clicked off, he left. Thirty minutes was a long time to spend with one child, but it was strange to spend it with a child making wordless noises into a tape recorder. I played the tape at home one evening, and was shocked again. After having been lulled almost to inattention I was startled to hear the word "hospital" said quite clearly. There was one more discernable word several minutes later, "hurt". Allen spoke more often and more clearly during play sessions after that. As you have probably guessed he was physically abused and was in a hospital at one time. We had very little information about the hospitalization. Perhaps what Allen wanted to say had no words, or could not be said, except in the special way he used. I played the tape for the staff in a training meeting several months after Allen made it. They found the sounds that Allen uttered too painful to listen to, although they couldn't say why.

Melissa

I rarely talked with the staff about the content of sessions with the children. The exception was one session with Melissa. Melissa came from a very chaotic family. Melissa's mother had been severely abused as a child, physically by her mother and sexually by her father. Hot grease had been poured on her as a child -- and she poured hot grease on one of her children, causing him severe burns. Although Melissa had not been hurt, she was considered at risk and placed in the Center when she was five years old along with her younger siblings. I looked forward to her visits to the play room because, unlike the other children, her speech was easily understood and she played out stories of family life. One day she played out a story of murder. The girl doll (herself) and the mother doll were hiding from the father doll who was chasing them with a gun, having already killed the rest of the family. I had interviewed Melissa's parents sometime before this play episode and knew them to have murderous impulses as well as the guns to implement them. I was, therefore, very concerned that Melissa's play might be closer to reality than fantasy. The staff was alerted and devised a plan for closer support and supervision of the family. We had no way of knowing what would have happened without intervention. With intervention the family relationships improved and no one was hurt. Melissa, however, did not play out family themes again. It was unlikely that the staff made any overt reference to the play that stimulated the intervention, but the subsequent change in Melissa's behavior made me think she sensed that I had talked about her with others.

Advantages and Disadvantages of Time Constraints

One of the advantages of low budget therapy turned out to be that there was relatively little time to share information about the content of play sessions with the staff. This meant that the confidences of my young patients were not violated, except for the described episode with Melissa. Equally important, the staff did not fell deliberately left out of what went on between the children and me.

In addition to the minimal cost of providing 40 children with a play therapy experience there were other benefits. There were no subtle pressures on the children to attend or not attend play sessions as there can be when parents or others are involved in transporting a child at a set time to a waiting therapist. Since the decision was completely theirs to make on the spur of the moment, they controlled the first step of treatment; would they or would they not attend.

As for the parents, they considered the time their children spent with me another preschool activity and no threat to their self-image. They did not feel that the need for play therapy implied they were inadequate or at fault in their childrearing practices. The brief time I had with each child did not allow for much of a bond between us, so that parents did not perceive my time with their children a challenge to their relationship[7]. The time factor also seemed to encourage autonomy, which supported the children in working out ways that they could deal with their lives. The surprise was that they were able to accomplish as much as they did. They had been so traumatized and they were so young. Their youth, however, was an advantage. They had not built up many defenses, nor had they become as fixed in their ways as they would in a few years. The limited amount of play materials provided them with less to pick from to express themselves, but fewer toys meant there was also less to distract children who were highly distractable.

Time limitations have disadvantages, too, of course. To name a few, there is less planning time, less recording time, and a good deal more wear and tear on the therapist.

All told, however, most disadvantages changed into advantages as play therapy developed and moved beyond its original purpose of reducing physical conflict among the preschool children at the Extended Family Center through doll house play. Low budget play therapy became a useful tool for dealing with the overwhelming aggression and other problems as well of very young children who had been severely abused and neglected and were continuing to stay in their own homes while in day care.

[7]For a significant elaboration of the psychology of the parent-child relationship see: Goldstein, Joseph; Freud, Anna; Solnit, Albert J., Beyond the Best Interests of the Child, Free Pr New York, 1973.

Child Abuse and Neglect, Vol. 3, pp. 205 - 211.
© Pergamon Press Ltd., 1979. Printed in Great Britain.

0145-2134/79/0301-0205 $02.00/0.

OCCURRENCE OF ABUSE AND NEGLECT OF CHILDREN BORN TO AMPHETAMINE ADDICTED MOTHERS

Lars Billing, Margareta Eriksson, Gunilla Larsson and Rolf Zetterström

Department of Pediatrics, Karolinska Institute, St. Göran's Children's Hospital, Stockholm, Sweden

Parental addiction must be considered to constitute an undesirable and insecure environment for children both physically and emotionally. The drug addicted woman usually demonstrates very special characteristics as unstable background, inconsistent mothering, low frustration tolerance adding to the severe direct consequences of the drug dependency (Ref. 1). Drug addiction during pregnancy may also make the child hard to care for due to prolonged withdrawal symptoms. The feeling of guilt following the drug induced fetal damage may make the child less acceptable to the parents (Ref. 7). Further, the mother-child relationship may be jeopardized if the newborn infant requires hospitalization due to withdrawal symptoms or other perinatal complications. Thus, there are several interacting adverse factors which place a child born to an addicted woman at a very high risk for abuse and neglect.

Withdrawal symptoms in the newborn infant is a well-known consequence of heroin abuse during pregnancy (Ref. 9, 15). As has been found in a retrospective study and has been documented in a few case reports, amphetamine addiction may also be associated with complications although less severe (Ref. 3, 11). Follow-up studies of children to addicted mothers are scarce (Ref. 10, 13). In one retrospective study concerning treated opiate addicted families, 12% of the addicts admitted that they had subjected their child to physical abuse (Ref. 7).

In Sweden, amphetamine addiction is the major drug problem. The estimated number of female amphetamine addicts is 4000. Almost all of them are in fertile ages and many of them have children. To elucidate the relation between maternal amphetamine addiction and the occurrence of child abuse and neglect, a prospective study has been undertaken.

MATERIAL

In the study we have tried to include all children born to amphetamine addicted mothers in the Stockholm area (population ca: 1.5 millions). The deliveries took place in different maternity hospitals during a period of 14 months (1.6.1976 - 30.7.1977).

Concerning the intensity of maternal amphetamine intake, our estimations are based on the mother's own statements in interviews the week after delivery. The information is limited to the number of months during pregnancy that the drug abuse has been going on and whether it has been regular throughout pregnancy i.e. more than 100 injections during pregnancy.

Out of a total number of 51 children that have come to our knowledge, two were stillborn and another two died during the first seven days of life. All of these four infants had a gestational age of less than 37 weeks. Perinatal morbidity rate was thus 8% compared to 1.3% in the general Swedish population.

The 47 surviving infants have been referred to three different groups according to the extent of maternal abuse and whether the infant left the maternity ward in their mother's custody or was placed in a foster home.

The classification of children is:

Group A consists of 13 infants born to mothers who claimed that they had discontinued their amphetamine abuse after becoming aware of pregnancy which means that they had not taken any drugs during the second and third trimester. All these babies remained in their mother's custody.

Group B includes 25 infants. The maternal abuse continued regularly throughout pregnancy. The infants left the maternity hospitals in their mother's custody.

Group C consists of 9 infants born to mothers with a continuous amphetamine intake during pregnancy. Mother and child were separated after birth and the child discharged from the maternity clinic to an institution or foster home.

The majority of the women in all three groups have been addicted to amphetamine for more than five years. Most mothers confirm that they have been using the drug regularly before they realized being pregnant. Approximately 20% of the women have an excessive use of alcohol as well, but the drug dependency is the predominant social and medical problem. There does not seem to be any difference among the groups as to drug experiences before pregnancy.

METHODS OF FOLLOW-UP STUDY

At an age of 12 months, medical, psychological and social information has been collected about the child from personal interviews with the mother or the caretaker. This information has been supplemented by interviews with the nurse at the well-baby clinic as well as the social worker. For evaluating the psychological development of the children the same psychologist (L.B.) has seen the children in their own environment. Gesell's method has been used. Further, medical, well-baby clinic and social welfare records have been studied.

ANALYSIS OF POSSIBLE ADVERSE FACTORS

The General Psycho-Social Situation of the Mother

The age distribution of the mothers at delivery ranged from 20-29 years (median 22) in Group A, 16-38 years (median 22) in Group B and 20-33 years (median 26) in Group C. In Group B, 40% of the mothers were younger than 20 years. The proportion of teen-age deliveries is significantly higher in this group than in Groups A and C and the figure for all teen-age deliveries in Sweden is 5.4%.

Many of the mothers have been raised under poor social conditions. Thus, 42% in Group A, 72% in Group B and 78% in Group C have been periodically in foster homes because of unstable home conditions often associated with parental alcoholism or the child's social disintegration. As a consequence, the educational level was very poor. In Group A 34%, in Group B 57% and in Group C 80% of the women had left school before having completed the minimal school education which is 9 years' attendance. Only a few of them have been employed for a significant period of time.

During the first year of follow-up after delivery, two mothers in Group A, who each lived together with a drug addicted man, had relapsed into drug abuse. All but two of the mothers in Group B have been taking amphetamine more or less regularly. No such information is available for Group C, as the mothers do not have the custody of their children.

Prenatal Care

Information on the prenatal care is given in Table 1.

TABLE 1 Prenatal Care

	Group A (n = 13)	Group B (n = 25)	Group C (n = 9)
First week of pregnancy (median and range)	12 (9-13)	22 (7-38)	22 (8-38)
Number of visits (median and range)	13 (1-21)	6 (2-21)	3 (0-8)

The women in Group A have made their first visit to the maternal health clinic significantly earlier as well as paid significantly more visits than the women in the Groups B and C. The corresponding figures for registered pregnancies in Sweden are that 75% make their first visit to prenatal clinics before 13 weeks of pregnancy and the average number of visits is 12.6. One-third of the women in the Groups B and C have come too late to the prenatal clinic to even discuss interruption of pregnancy. The number of visits varies widely and it seems that the women with a continuing addiction are less prepared for delivery as well as motherhood.

Prenatal Situation

During the neonatal period as is shown in Table 2, 25% of the infants were separated from the mother directly after birth and transferred to a pediatric ward because of low gestational age, respiratory distress and feeding difficulties.

TABLE 2 Hospital Care and Separation Mother-Child during the Neonatal Period

	Group A (n = 13)	Group B (n = 25)	Group C (n = 9)
Hospital care	1	5	7
Separation mother-child >48 hours	1	4	7

The Family Situation after the Birth of the Child

The number of mothers living alone or together with an addicted man is shown in Table 3. In Group A, 25% of the mothers and their children live together with men who have a habitual drug abuse. Two mothers are single. Here there is a difference compared to the family structure in Group B where 80% of the children's environment include an addicted father. During the last year, two of the men in either group have been or are still in jail charged with crimes associated with drugs.

TABLE 3 Family Structure in Groups A and B

Mothers' living situation	Group A (n = 13)	Group B (n = 25)
Single	2	1
With a drug-free man	6	-
With an addicted man	3	22
With an addict temporarily in jail	2	2

The interviews have given the following results regarding the social network of the families. In Group A, 9 of 13 mothers have very few contacts outside the family and none associated with the drug subculture. Thirty percent of the mothers consider that they have support in the child rearing from their mothers. Forty-five percent of the women have no contact at all with their parents. The corresponding figure for Group B is that 12% regard the relation with their mothers as relatively good and 45% lack contact. As all but two mothers are living as drug addicts they are socially isolated and rejected by others.

The children belonging to Group C live in foster families who are socially well-established and consisting of parents with no known abuse. Fifty percent of them are undeliberately childless and have a desire to adopt their foster children.

RESULTS OF FOLLOW-UP STUDY

Custody of the Children

The children belonging to Groups A and C have remained in the same environment during their first year of life (Table 4). In contrast, the children in Group B have had very unstable conditions. Nine of the 24 children were taken from their mother's custody after having been subjected to neglect.

Seven of the surviving 24 children in Group B have been separated from their mothers between four to six times due to acute crises in the family resulting in neglect of the infant. The parental addiction has in these cases been continous and the child has been temporary placed in an institution or foster home.

TABLE 4 Custody of the 12-Month-Old Children

	Biological mother	Foster parents
Group A (n = 13)	13	-
Group B (n = 24)*	15	9
Group C (n = 9)	-	9

* One case of sudden unexpected death

General Health Situation of the Children

As is shown in Table 5, two infants in Group A and one child in Group C have been admitted to pediatric wards due to acute infections. In Group B, 41% of the children have been hospitalized once or several times with the following diagnosis; failure to thrive (n = 2), accidental burn (n = 1) and infections (n = 6). There is one case of sudden unexpected death in infancy in Group B. The child was 6 weeks old and died at home. There seems here to be significant differences between the groups in as well the need of hospital care as the diagnosis. For comparison, the corresponding figure for hospitalization during the first year of life is 22% in the general population of Sweden.

The two children with failure to thrive were brought to hospital by the nurse at the child health center due to an poor weight gain. After hospital care,the children were placed in foster homes where they have gained weight normally.

All children but two in Group B have been followed regularly at the child health centers. The high attendance of the children especially in Group B is a result of insistent work by the nurse. All except four children in Group B have had a normal growth pattern during the first year of life.

TABLE 5 Separation Mother-Child during the Infant's First Year of Life

	Group A (n = 13)	Group B (n = 24)*	Group C (n = 9)
Hospital care	2	9	1
Temporary placement in foster home or institution	-	7	-

* One case of sudden unexpected death

Psychological Development of the Children

When evaluating the results of the examination of the psychological development it has to be considered that the psycho-social as well as the medical situation differs markedly between the three groups. In Group A, there has only been fetal exposure to the drug during early pregnancy. In Group B, the fetus has been continuously exposed to the drug, prenatal care has been poor and the infant has been subjected to psycho-social deprivation. In Group C, the fetus has been continuously exposed to the drug, prenatal care has been poor but after birth the psycho-social conditions have been quite acceptable.

In addition, on our visits we found that the children in Group B were living under very different social conditions and they have been divided into three groups. Subgroup III includes children who have been in foster homes for more than 3 months.

Table 6 presents the results from the evaluation of the psychological examination.

TABLE 6 Psychological Development

	Fine motor and gross motor development	Emotional and social development	
	Retarded	Signs of deprivation	Hyper-sensitivity
Group A (n = 13)	1	2	
Group B (n = 24)			
I 7 infants in dysfunctional homes	2	5	
II 8 infants in their mothers' custody	2	2	
III 9 infants in foster homes	1	1	
Group C (n = 9)	1*		1

* This child has a moderate cerebral palsy.

The definition of being late in fine or gross motor is a 2 month delay in development. In Group A, one child was found to be retarded in the fine and gross motor skills. Corresponding figures for Group B was five and for Group C one child who has a moderate cerebral palsy (spastic diplegia) resulting in a reduced seizing function.

Characteristics such as empty eyes in a face without expression, difficulties in getting response to various stimuli, as a total lack of distance to strangers have been defined as symptoms of deprivation. Two children in Group A have shown moderate symptoms of deprivation. Those are the two infants who are living with a drug addicted father and periodically also an addicted mother. In Group B, one-third of the children have shown symptoms of emotional deprivation. Most of them living in dysfunctional families. The difference is significant concerning the emotional and social adaptation of the infants between on one hand Groups A and C and on the other Group B.

In six cases, foster parents have found the child to be extremely slow in development and showing a high degree of lassitude. These circumstances have in three cases led to suspicion of impaired hearing both by the foster parents and the well baby clinic. Audiological examinations have, however, shown a normal hearing function. When the children have reached an age of 6 - 8 months they have rapidly caught up on their development and have been evaluated as having a normal psychomotor development at an age of 12 months.

Measures Undertaken by the Social Welfare Department

Table 7 presents the varying support to the families with a 12-month-old infant in their custody. In Group A, 75% of the families and in Group B, 93% have been continuously on welfare. The most common support is financial help. Besides the fact that all children in Group A have remained in their mothers' custody also few interventions have been undertaken in comparison with Group B. Several measures have been undertaken in Group B and in some cases more than one.

TABLE 7 Social Welfare Support and Measures Given to the Families during the First Year after Birth

	Group A (n = 13)	Group B (n = 15)
Social welfare	9	14
Day nursery	3	7
Family therapy	-	3
Probation	-	7

DISCUSSION

This population of children may be characterized as a minority in the Swedish society but a very high risk for abuse and neglect. They have been exposed to amphetamine *in utero* through maternal abuse and a total of 80% have remained in their mothers' custody on discharge from the maternity clinics. Some of the infants have also been subjected to the exposure of alcohol during fetal life.

The amphetamine exposure *in utero* does not seem to result in the same serious consequences of mental retardation as alcohol is reported to give (Ref. 2). Behavioral disturbances as hyperactivity and altered sleep patterns which are noted in children to heroin addicted mothers have not been identified in the present study (Ref. 14). On the contrary, some of the children born to mothers with an extensive amphetamine intake during pregnancy have shown apathy. This fact has been noted by foster parents and could be a long lasting withdrawal effect. In the above mentioned studies, however, it is impossible to separate the sequel of intrauterine exposure from the effect of living in unstable environment.

The local social authorities have in different ways evaluated the impact of adverse factors. The situation for the infants in Group A has in general been judged more favorable as the mother has been motivated for psycho-social rehabilitation and the child has not manifested any withdrawal symptoms. The infants born to mothers with a continuous amphetamine abuse during pregnancy have in addition to a longer drug exposure also several other known risk factors, such as less prenatal care and more perinatal complications to be taken into consideration (Ref. 6). In consequence, the society has undertaken more interventions. However, unfortunately most of the children in the Groups B and C have met very heterogeneous environments, which in these children have led to manifestations of neglect, emotional deprivation as well as more physical symptoms. According to our knowledge there has not been any case of more severe physical abuse in the present material up to an age of one year. In infants, included into this study but not yet 12 months old we are aware of physical abuse leading to hospitalization.

There is no definition of what is a minimum standard of an environment and where the lower limits are of an acceptable home for a growing child. Our conclusion is, however, that the majority of the children in Group B have been living in an undesirable environment with several stress factors interacting. Thus, approximately one-third of the children have shown severe symptoms of neglect; all of these infants have been moved to foster homes.

The need of a psychological parent and continuity in infancy and early childhood have been documented and stressed (Ref. 4). There are seven children in Group B who have been separated from their mothers several times and can be classified as "migrant children". The separation of mother and newborn are known to be unfortunate for the bonding process and places the child at a greater risk of abuse (Ref. 5, 6). Disturbances in the emotional and social adaptation have occurred in several cases in this sample, when the infant has been subjected to perpetual separations. These children definitely have been exposed to social abuse.

A large number of the infants in families with ongoing amphetamine addiction has shown symptoms of emotional deprivation interpreted as a reaction to the undesirable home conditions. Other children demonstrate more physical symptoms as failure to thrive. There are conflicting opinions as to the significance of hospital admissions as indicators of children at risk (Ref. 6, 12). We found that 41% of the children in our high risk group have been admitted to hospitals. There is one case of sudden unexpected death in infancy. This cause of death which has also been reported to occur in a high incidence in opiate and methadone addicted families (Ref. 8).

CONCLUSION

As there have been several adverse factors in common concerning both mothers and infants, it is obvious that the predominant characteristic for neglect and emotional deprivation of the children is the parental drug addiction *per se*. This opinion is based on the fact that the children who have shown symptoms are those in either Group A or B who live in an amphetamine addicted environment. The rights of mothers to treatment as well as the rights of the children to an optimal social, psychological and somatic development must be met. The delicate balance between the integrity of the parents and the rights of the child must not result in social abuse. To a large extent the development of these infants depends on the society's responsiveness to their needs.

REFERENCES

1. Carr, J.N., Psychological aspects of pregnancy, childbirth and parenting in drug dependent women in J.L. Rementeria (ed.) Drug Abuse in Pregnancy and Neonatal Effects. C.V. Mosby, Saint Louis, 1977.

2. Clarren, S.K. and Smith, D.W.,The fetal alcohol syndrome. N. Engl. J. Med. 298, 1063 (1978).

3. Eriksson, M., et al.,The influence of amphetamine addiction on pregnancy and the newborn infant. Acta Paediat.Scand. 67, 95 (1978).

4. Goldstein, J. and Freud, A. (1973) Beyond the Best Interests of the Child. Free Press.

5. Holman, R.R. and Kanwar, S., Early life of the battered child. Arch. Dis. Childh. 50, 78 (1975).

6. Lynch, M.A., Ill-health and child abuse. Lancet II, 317 (1975).

7. Mayer, J. and Black, R., Child abuse and neglect in families with an alcohol or opiate addicted parent. Child Abuse & Neglect 1, 85 (1977).

8. Pierson, P.S. et al., Sudden deaths in infants born to methadone-maintained addicts. JAMA 220, 1733 (1972).

9. Rothstein, P. and Gould, J.B., Born with a habit. Infants of drug-addicted mothers. Pediat. Clin. N. Amer. 21, 307 (1974).

10. Sardeman, H. et al., Follow-up of children of drug-addicted mothers. Arch. Dis. Childh. 51, 131 (1976).

11. Sussman, S., Narcotic and methaamphetamine use during pregnancy. Am. J. Dis. Child. 106, 325 (1963).

12. Wadsworth, M.E.J. and Morris, S., Assessing chances of hospital admission in preschool children. Arch. Dis. Childh. 53, 159 (1978).

13. Wilson, G.S. et al., Early development of infants of heroin-addicted mothers. Am. J. Dis. Child. 126, 457 (1973).

14. Wilson, G.S., Somatic growth effects of perinatal addiction. Add. Dis. 2, 333 (1975).

15. Zelson, C., Infant of the addicted mother. N. Engl. J. Med. 288, 1393 (1973).

Child Abuse and Neglect, Vol. 3, pp. 213 - 225.
Pergamon Press Ltd., 1979. Printed in Great Britain.

FAMILY PATTERNS AND CHILD ABUSE IN A NATIONALLY REPRESENTATIVE AMERICAN SAMPLE*

Murray A. Straus
University of New Hampshire, Durham, N.H. 03824, USA

ABSTRACT

Data on 1,146 families with a child age 3 through 17 at home are presented. Child abuse information was obtained for a randomly selected child in each family. Child abuse was defined as an attack by a parent involving punching, kicking, biting, hitting with an object, "beating up," or using a knife or gun. Over 14 out of every 100 American children 3-17 are subjected to abusive violence each year. These figures are at least 26 times greater than those of the National Center For Child Abuse and Neglect. Even so, for reasons outlined in the paper, they are underestimates. Families in which child abuse occurred are compared with other families. The results suggest that child abuse is brought about by the very nature of the society and its family system. This has profound implications for the prevention and treatment of child abuse. Although psychotherapy may be appropriate in some cases, a more fundamental approach lies in such things as a more equal sharing of the burdens of child care, replacement of physical punishment with non-violent methods of child care and training, eliminating the stresses and insecurity which now characterize our economic system, and strengthening the ties of individual families to the extended family and the community.

THE SOCIAL CAUSES OF CHILD ABUSE

What can cause a parent to punch, kick, bite, burn, or stab a child? The causes are complex in at least two ways.

First, there seem to be a multitude of factors, each of which increases the probability of a violent physical attack on a child. At the same time no one of these factors accounts for a very large proportion of the cases of child abuse. For example, this paper will show that men who hit their wives are much more likely to abuse a child than are other men. Still, most men who hit their wives do _not_ attack a child violently enough for it to be considered child abuse by contemporary standards.

---

*This paper is part of the Family Violence Research Program at the University of New Hampshire. The Program is supported by NIMH grants T32 MH15161 and MH27557, and by the University of New Hampshire. A list of Program publications is available on request.

I am grateful to Sieglinde Fizz for the care and skill with which she arranged the computer typesetting of this article, to Shari Hagar for the same qualities in her work on the innumberable computer runs for the statistical analysis, and to Arnold Linsky for insightful comments and suggestions on an earlier draft.

A second complication making it difficult to pinpoint the causes of child abuse is that these factors do not operate in isolation from each other. Rather, it is likely that certain combinations of factors are much more potent than either of the factors by themselves; and also much more potent than one might imagine by just adding together the effects of each of the two factors. For example, unemployment is associated with child abuse, as is a history of hitting one's wife. Let us say that each of these factors increases the chances of a child being abused by 75%. But the combination of unemployment and a prior history of having hit one's wife may increase the probability of child abuse by 300 or 400% rather than 150%. In short, there are likely to be "explosive combinations." Combinations like that are what statisticians call "interaction effects."

Both of these complicating factors must be kept in mind when evaluating what has been written about the causes of child abuse because neither is usually considered. Instead, there is a tendency to focus on one or two factors as though they offered the key to explaining this baffling phenomenon. Even when several factors are considered, the effects of the "interactive combinations" of these factors is not. These criticism also apply to this paper. I am stating them at the beginning to alert readers to the limitations of what is to be presented.

To be more specific, the data to be presented relate 25 different factors to child abuse. One might therefore think that the first criticism--ignoring the multiplicity of causal factors--has been met. But that is not the case because all of the factors to be discussed are, broadly speaking, social variables. That is, they describe the social characteristics and social interactions of parents and children. Not considered are the psychological characteristics of the parents, for example, their mental health, aggressiveness, anxiety, rigidity, etc. Such psychological characteristics may well be part of the explanation for child abuse. The research to be described, however, ignores psychological variables, not because they are unimportant, but because this research was designed to find out about the social causes of child abuse.

The second criticism of child abuse research--that it has by and large ignored the consequences of different combinations of factors--also applies to this paper. However, this is a limitation which will be corrected in the next stage of the research. What is presented here are the results of the work we have so far been able to do.

SAMPLE AND METHOD

The data come from interviews with a nationally representative sample of 1,146 American families who have a child age 3 through 17 at home. A limitation of the sample is that one and two year olds--a high risk age--are omitted. This was because of other purposes of the study required older children. Further details on the sampling method and on the reasons for limiting the study to children between 3 and 17 are given elsewhere (Straus, Gelles, and Steinmetz, 1979). In any case, the absence of children under age three is one of several factors which suggest that the child abuse incidence rates to be reported are underestimates.

Interviews were conducted with the father in a random half of the families, and with the mother in the other half of the families. In each family, the data on physical violence was obtained for only one child, and only for the parent who was interviewed. When there was more than one child, the "referent child" for the study was selected by a random number table.

The interview covered a great many aspects of family patterns and life circumstances. It included the Conflict Tactics Scales (Straus, 1979). The items in those scales which pertain to severe violence by the parent toward the referent child were combined to form a Child Abuse Index. These are all the items which refer to violence more severe than pushing, shoving, slapping, and throwing things. Specifically, the list consists of whether, during the 12 months up to the interview, the parent had ever kicked, bit, punched, hit with an object, beaten up the child, or used a knife or gun (in the sense of having actually tried to stab or shoot the child). A parent who did any of these things was counted as having abused the child.

INCIDENCE OF CHILD ABUSE

The rates of child abuse revealed by this method are truly astounding. Each year, over 14 out of every 100 American parents of a child 3 through 17 is violent enough to a child to be included in our Child Abuse Index. This means that of the 46 million children of this age group in the United States, approximately six and a half million are abused each year.

It might be objected that this index uses too lax a definition of child abuse because one of the items is "hitting with an object." For some parents that could be the traditional strap or paddle rather than an out of control assault. So we recomputed the index leaving out the data on hitting with objects. The rates drop sharply to "only" three or four out of every hundred parents, and to an estimate of 1.7 million children per year.

The data just presented might overstate the amount of child abuse because a family is included if even one isolated incident of abusive violence occurred during the year. On the other hand, these rates may understate the extent to which children are severely assaulted by their parents because the figures do not take into account how often such assaults occurred. The answer to this question is that if one assault occurred, several were likely. In fact, a single incident occurred in only six percent of the child abuse cases. Mean number of assaults per year was 10.5 and the median 4.5.

It is obvious that the incidence of child abuse obtained by this method is many times that estimated by the U.S. National Center on Child Abuse and Neglect (NCCAN). They have published figures indicating approximately a million children per year are abused. However, that includes neglect, sexual abuse, and psychological abuse. The physical abuse figure they report is apporoximately 250,000. What accounts for the difference between that quarter of a million and our figure of almost two million? There are two main reasons:

(1) THE NCCAN figures are based on incidents which come to official attention. This leaves out the vast number of cases in which physical abuse is suspected and not reported, as well as the equally vast number of cases in which a child is injured but there is no suspicion of abuse.

(2) Probably the most important reason why our rates are so much higher is that our data is based on violent acts carried out, rather than on injuries produced. Fortunately, children are resilient. Many is the child who has been thrown against a wall and who simply bounces off with at most a bruise. Only the relatively rare instances in which a concussion occurs stand even a chance of being suspected of parental abuse.

In describing the sample, I said that the omission of children in the high abuse risk age of birth to age three is one of several factors which make even our very high rates of child abuse an underestimate. There are several other factors which push in the same direction. The second such factor is that these are self-reports by parents to a stranger doing a survey. Not every parent who had punched or kicked a child is going to admit that in such an interview. Third, the Conflict Tactics Scales include only a limited list of all the possible abusive acts. For example, we omitted burning a child, wiping out the child's mouth with soap or more noxious substances, and sexual abuse. Fourth, we interviewed either the father or the mother and have data only on that person's abuse of the child. But most children have two parents and therefore twice the risk--or at least a higher risk--of being abused than our figures show. A fifth factor making these underestimates is that our data are based on children living with two parents. The two parents need not be the child's natural parents. However, the omission of children living in one-parent households may lead to underestimating because there are reasons to think that child abuse is greater under the strain of trying to raise children without the aid of a partner.

MEN, WOMEN, AND JOBS

I will start this examination of the social causes of child abuse with two of the most elementary but also two of the most important characteristics which are associated with child abuse: sex and socioeconomic status.

It is widely known that women are less violent than men. The assault and murder rates of women are a fraction of the rates for men. But in the family it is different. Using our index of child abuse, the rate for men is 10.1 per hundred childred whereas the rate for women is 75% greater: 17.7 per hundred children.

I have started with the simple fact of the sex of the parent to emphasize the importance of social factors as compared to psychological factors in understanding child abuse. These, after all, are the same women who, outside the family, are much less violent than men. So the reasons underlying their much greater violence toward their own children is unlikely to be anything in the personality or other mental characteristics of women as compared to men. Rather, the reasons start with the simple fact that husbands and wives do not have equal responsibility for care of children. The way our type of society is organized, child care is the responsibility of women. So women are simply exposed more to both the joys and the trials and tribulations of caring for children--they experience more time "at risk." Moreover, since our sample of children did not include any infants, it is even more clear that this is a matter of culturally determined rules and arrangements. Fathers are just as capable--biologically, even if not by training--of caring for children of this age.

"Time at risk," however is not the whole story. The factors underlying the much greater frequency of child abuse by mothers go well beyond that. At least two other factors need to be considered. First, it is that mothers who tend to be blamed if the child misbehaves or does not achieve what is expected of children at a given age. Since all children misbehave, and since standards of achievement are ambiguous, almost all mothers tend to feel anxiety, frustration, and guilt about their children and their adequacy as mothers. This is not because women are any more anxiety prone than men, but because society sets up a situation in which a high level of anxiety and frustration is just about inevitable.

A third factor which might account for the higher child abuse rate of women is that the unequal division of labor and the responsibility for the child's conduct is not a voluntary choice. These are roles assigned to women by long historical tradition, and on which most husbands insist. It is no problem for those women who wish to focus their lives on the role of mother and housewife. But in a society where other opportunities beckon, millions of women feel blocked and frustrated by the fact that they--not their husbands--will have the overwhelming responsibility for the children.

Housewives

Most of us are so imbued with the cultural ideology of women as mothers and housewives that it may be difficult to see the argument just presented. There is neither the space nor the evidence to prove the point. But there is a way of getting at this issue indirectly. We can compare mothers who are full time housewives with mothers who are also employed outside the home.

From one point of view, the highest rate of child abuse should be among women who have paid employment in addition to their work as mothers and housekeepers. This is because the research shows that such women continue to have the major burden of housekeeping and child care. They therefore carry a double burden. The opposite point of view is also plausible. Women who have jobs outside the home may have a lower rate of child abuse because the hours the child spends at a nursery or with a baby-sitter reduces their time at risk, because they can escape the stress and frustration of being employed full time in a role which is not of their own choosing, and because being employed for wages gives women more power in the family and control over their own lives.

The results of this study clearly support the second line of reasoning. The child abuse rate for women who are full time housewives is half again higher than the rate for women who, in addition to their responsibilities as housekeeper and mother, also have a job outside the home (15.7 versus 10.3). One can also see that the child abuse rate for women with paid employment is almost identical to the rate for men (10.1).*1

Socioeconomic Status

One should not be misled by the above into thinking of the workplace as heaven. Millions of men and women work at boring, demeaning, and underpaid work. But for women, even these jobs may be a lesser evil than the confines of the type of family typical of industrial societies. Even inadequate wages can help alleviate the economic stress faced by working class families. For men, however, we will see that the situation is quite different.

Child abuse is found at all social levels, from paupers to royalty. But that is not the same as saying that the rates are equal at all social levels. Officially reported cases of child abuse are much higher among the poor. Perhaps this is because the poor must use public rather than private medical facilities and because the police and other officials are quicker to make charges against the poor?

Our data do not depend on official reports. Yet they reveal a child abuse rate in families where the husband is a manual worker which is 41% higher than for families in which the husband is a white-collar worker (16.4 versus 11.6). Although this is a substantial difference, it is a much smaller difference than is typical when officially reported child abuse rates are used to compare social classes. Thus, part of the social class difference in officially reported child abuse does seem to be the result of biases in the system of reporting. At the same time, the data also suggest that there is a considerably higher rate of actual child abuse in families in which the husband is a manual worker.

There are many factors which could produce the higher rate of child abuse found in manual worker families. One such factor is the stress of maintaining a family on a low or sometimes entirely inadequate income. That this is one of the underlying factors is indicated by the child abuse rate for families with incomes under $6,000 a year. It is 62% greater than for other families (21.1 versus 13.4). The same pattern of higher rates low income families applies to abuse by the father (15.6 versus 9.6) and abuse by mothers (24.4 versus 16.7).

Of course, it is not just the absolute level of poverty which matters, important as that is. Also entering the situation is the meaning of income as a symbol of personal worth. Anyone with a family income of under $6,000 in the USA in 1976, in effect received with each paycheck a reminder that he or she is not worth very much. The child abuse rate for husbands who were dissatisfied with their standard of living was 61% greater than the rate for other husbands (14.4 versus 8.9); and for wives who were not satisfied with their standard of living the rate was 77% greater than for other wives (22.3

---

1. This could be a spurious relationship, reflecting the confounding of employment with such things as better education. That possibility will be checked in a future analysis.

versus 12.6).

Then there is the frustration imposed by an unstable economic system. Families in which the husband was unemployed at the time of the survey have a child abuse rate that is 62% greater than other families (22.5 versus 13.9). A similar high rate of child abuse is associated with part-time employment of the husband (27.3 versus 14.1).

Finally, there are a number of factors on which we do not have data but are likely to enter the picture. Working class parents are known to be more authoritarian with their children, to have greater faith in physical punishment as a means of child rearing, and a lesser understanding of child psychology. In addition, low income areas of American cities have much higher rates of violence outside the family. Each of these in their own way are conditions making for parental violence.

FAMILY STRUCTURE AND CHILD ABUSE

Some analysts of child abuse, for example David Gil (1975) write as though the direct and indirect effects of an unjust and unstable economic system, and its associated oppression of women and minorities, fully explain the paradox of child abuse. Unfortunately, the etiology of child abuse is far more complicated. One can see this from a comparison of child abuse in Black and in white families. Blacks are one of the most economically and socially oppressed groups in American society. Yet both this study and some studies of officially reported child abuse (Billingsley, 1969; Young, 1963) show that Blacks do _not_ have a significantly higher rate of child abuse than whites. Blacks in this sample have a rate of 15.7, which is only 11% greater than the white rate of 14.1. One reason why Blacks have a rate of child abuse that is much lower than expected on the basis of their low income, high unemployment, and rejection by the rest of the society, seems to be the aid and support, especially in the care of children, provided by Black extended families (Cazenave and Straus, 1978).

Cazenave and Straus's findings about Black extended families points to the structure of the family as another important set of factors leading to or insulating parents from child abuse: the patterns of interaction within the family.

Years Married

An indirect indicator of the effect of family patterns is the duration of the marriage. The early years of a marriage carry the highest risk of child abuse: those married less than 10 years have a rate of 20.3 compared to 11.5 for other couples. A number of factors could account for this. (1) It could be the greater experience with children which comes over time. (2) It could be just the greater tendency toward violence of the young since the difference between the child abuse rate of those age 30 or under versus older parents (21.2 versus 12.1) is similar to the difference between those married less than ten years and other couples. (3) The lower child abuse rate for marriages of 10 or more years could simply reflect a greater tendency for the most violent marriages to be terminated by divorce or separation. (4) Finally, the higher rate could reflect the fact that very young children are more frequent victims of abuse.*2 Each of these possibilities will be checked in the next phase of the research.

---

2. However, in this sample, we found a bimodal distribution, with high incidence of child abuse in both our youngest group (age 3-4) and among the 15 to 17 year olds. Moreover, another indication that age of the child is not the only factor is that wife-beating and husband-beating is also most frequent among those married less than 10 years.

Husband-Wife Conflict

A more direct indicator of the patterns of interaction in the family is the amount of conflict between husband and wife. To measure the extent of such conflict we obtained information on how often the couple disagreed on five issues: money, sex, social activities, housekeeping and maintenance, and children. Couples with more than the average amount of conflict have a higher incidence of child abuse. The effect is moderate for wives: a 28% greater rate (20.0 versus 15.6 for those low in conflict). For husbands, a high level of conflict with a wife is associated with a 79% greater rate of child abuse (12.7 versus 7.1).

Verbal Abuse and Physical Abuse

Even more important are the tactics used when a couple has a conflict. Some family therapists argue that the best tactic is to let go and not repress one's anger. "Don't be afraid to be a real shrew, a real bitch. Tell them where your really at. Let it be total, vicious, exaggerated, hyperbole..." as one advocate of this approach put it (Howard, 1970:54). Venting one's anger in this way is claimed to provide a release from the tension of a dispute, and therefore helps avoid physical aggression. On the contrary, the research evidence shows that the more husbands and wives are verbally aggressive to each other the <u>higher</u> the rate of violence (Straus, 1974). The main reason for this is that verbal aggression, no matter how emotionally satisfying it may be, does not come to grips with the substance of the dispute. Rather, it creates additional animosity which makes it even more difficult to deal with the original source of the conflict.

Exactly the same results were found in this study for the relation between verbal aggression and child abuse. Parents who were verbally aggressive to the referent child*3 have a child abuse rate which is six times that of other parents (21.0 versus 3.6).

It could be argued that the verbal aggression is a consequence rather than a cause of this high rate of violence. A child has been slapped, and then either slaps back or kicks, or insults the parent. The parent then verbally assaults the child. No doubt that does happen. But such a sequence does not explain another finding: that the rate of child abuse is also higher for parents who are verbally agressive to each other. Husbands who were verbally aggressive to their wives have a child abuse rate of 17.3 compared to 6.3 for other husbands: and wives who were verbally aggressive to their husband have a child abuse rate of 17.9 compared to 4.5 for other wives. All of this suggests that verbal aggression is a relatively stable pattern in such families and, as just suggested, it is a mode of relating which interferes with dealing with the actual issues, creates additional problems, and often sets in motion an escalating cycle of events which ends in physical violence.

Number of Children

We expected the rate of child abuse to increase with each additional child. It turns out that there is a 42% greater incidence of child abuse among couples with two or more children at home as compared to those with only one child at home (15.1 versus 10.6). However, the rate for those with three or more children is not greater than the rate for those with two children. Just why a second child seems to be a critical threshold after which further children make little difference is an issue which will be studied in the next phase of the research.

---

3. As measured by the Verbal Aggression scale of the Conflict Tactics Scales (Straus, 1979). This includes such things as insults, sulking, venting anger by smashing things and slamming doors, and cutting remarks.

VIOLENCE AS A MODE OF RELATING

One of the clearest findings to emerge from the Family Violence Research Program, as well as from the findings of the study reported in this paper, is that violence in one sphere of life is related to violence in other spheres of life (Straus, 1977). Early in life, most of us receive a kind of basic training in violence in the form of physical punishment. Mommy slaps an infant's hand to teach the child not to put dirty things in his or her mouth. But this also teaches the child that love and violence go together. Moreover, it does more than establish the empirical fact that those who love you are those who hit you. Ironically, it also teaches that the use of violence within the family is morally right.

In some families slapping a child is replaced by non-violent forms of punishment, and by the use of reasoning and negotiation. If this happens, what is learned in infancy and early childhood can be replaced by non-violent modes of dealing with others--though the earlier patterns may still emerge in extreme conditions. But when the use of physical punishment continues into the early teen ages, and when children observe their parents being violent to each other (as is the experience of millions of American children), the chances are great that the use of physical force will become a regular part of the way such people interact with others (Gelles and Straus, 1975, 1978; Owens and Straus, 1975).

Physical Punishment as Training for Child Abuse

The ideas expressed in the previous two paragraphs are based on plausible reasoning, and on the results of our pilot studies. To what extent are they supported by the data for this nationally representative sample of parents? To find out we asked the parents how much their own parents had used physical punishment when they were 13 or older. Those who said their mother had used physical punishment twice or more a year had a child abuse rate of 18.5, which is 57% greater than the rate for parents who experienced less physical punishment (11.8). Physical punishment by the _fathers_ of the parents in this sample made less difference: the child abuse rate for those whose fathers punished them two or more times was 16.7, compared to 13.2 for other parents.

An interesting additional finding is that the effects of physical punishment are greater when the sex of the parents we interviewed is considered. There seems to be a greater effect if the physical punishment was done by the parent of the opposite sex. Men who were punished by their mothers have a child abuse rate that is double that of other men (14.2 versus 7.4), whereas for women, physical punishment by their mother is associated with a child abuse rate that is "only" 52% greater (23.0 versus 15.1). The reverse is the case for men who had been punished by their fathers. They have a child abuse rate which is "only" 31% greater than other men (11.8 versus 9.0); whereas women who had been physically punished by their fathers have a rate which is 53% greater than other women (24.2 versus 15.1).

Observing Parents Fight As Training For Child Abuse

The data just presented suggest that children learn to be violent to others by being the victims of violence by their parents. Ironically, the learning effect is probably enhanced because, by and large, parental violence is done out of concern for the child and for other morally desirable ends. Parents also teach violence to their children in number of other ways, for example, by teaching boys to "stand up and fight like a man" (Stark and McEvoy, 1970), and by example through violence towards each other.

More than one out of ten of the parents in this sample (11.5%) could remember at least one instance when they saw their own parents hitting each other.

The effects of observing one's father hit one's mother are greater than effects of observing one's mother hit one's father. Being the child of a father who hit his wife is associated with a 39% greater rate of child abuse compared to men whose fathers did not hit their wives (13.3 versus 9.7). However, being the daughter of a father who hit his wife is associated with only a slightly greater rate of child abuse (19.7 versus 17.4). On the other hand, being the daughter of a mother who hit her husband is associated with a substantially higher incidence of child abuse as compared to the abuse rates of other women (24.4 versus 17.2). The greater effect of father's violence to his wife on sons, and of mother's violence to her husband on daughters, suggests that violence by a parent of the same sex as the child provides the strongest role-model.*4

Husband-Wife Violence and Child Abuse

Now let us turn to another way in which the principle that child abuse tends to be associated with violence in other spheres of family life. In this case, the question is whether couples who hit each other, also tend to abuse their children. The answer is an emphatic "yes."

In families where the husband had hit his wife during the year of the survey, even if the violence was restricted to slaps, pushes, and throwing things, the incidence of child abuse was 129% greater than in other families (28.0 versus 12.2). If the violence was more severe, the difference was even greater: Almost a third of the couples (31.9%) in which there was an incident of wife-beating also abused a child that year. If it is the wife who hits the husband, this is associated with a 120% greater incidence of child abuse (27.7 versus 12.6). But surprisingly, if the wife was very violent, this did not produce the same further increase in child abuse as occurred when the husband went beyond "ordinary" pushing, slapping, and throwing things.

ISOLATION FROM KIN AND COMMUNITY

Earlier in this paper I referred to the important role played by the extended family among American Blacks. The same process seems to be a work for the entire sample, but the differences in child abuse rates between couples with weak ties to the community and other couples is not as large as for Black families, and fewer whites than Blacks have such ties. Taking the sample as a whole, parents who lived in the neighborhood for a relatively short period (0 to 3 years) have a 54% higher rate of child abuse (18.5 versus 12.03).

An even larger difference in child abuse was found using an index of participation in organizations such as clubs, lodges, unions, church groups, etc. One point was given for each such group belonged to, and one point for each meeting of such a group attended in a month. Those who neither belonged to or attended such meetings have a child abuse rate which is 72% greater than for parents with a score of one or more (19.9 versus 11.6).

Since long residence and involvement in organizations tends to be assoicated with being more settled in life, the same comparison was computed for those married less than ten years and for those married ten or more years. For the younger group, their generally high rate of child abuse reduced the effect of residental stability and organizational involvement. Among couples married 10 or more years, the differences between those with and without the social ties which come from being a long term resident, or from being involved in organizations, is similar to but larger than the differences for the sample

4. However, as indicated in an earlier section, the opposite seems to be the case in respect to which parent's physical punishment is most associated with child abuse.

as a whole. Both these data and the results of other studies (see the review in Maden and Wrench, 1977; Smith, 1975) all point to a strong association between child abuse and social isolation.

A CHILD ABUSE CHECK LIST

Up to this point, each of the factors associated with child abuse has been considered separately from the others. This is clearly inadequate. These factors do not exist in isolation. Some overlap with the others, and the existence of certain combinations may be particularly important. As a first approach to at least partly overcoming these limitations, a child abuse checklist score was computed.

TABLE 1 Characteristics Included in Child Abuse Checklist

Characteristic Associated With Child Abuse
A. Important for Child Abuse by Either Parent
Was verbally aggressive to the child (insulted, smashed things etc.)
B. Important for Child Abuse by Fathers
Married less than ten years
Wife is a full-time housewife
Husband was physically punished at age 13+ by mother
Lived in neighborhood less than two years
Above average conflict between husband and wife
No participation in organized groups
Grew up in family where mother hit father
Two or more children at home
C. Important for Child Abuse by Mothers
Husband was physically violent to wife
Husband dissatisfied with standard of living
Husband a manual worker
Husband was verbally aggressive to wife
Wife was physically punished at age 13+ by father
Wife age 30 or under
Wife a manual worker

The procedure started with a "discriminant analysis" using the SPSS program DISCRIMINANT (Nie *et al*, 1975). This identified 16 of the variables described in this paper as the most useful in distinguishing between abusing parents and other parents, and which do not significantly overlap with each oTher. These 16 variables are listed in Table 1.

Each couple was then given a score by assigning a point for any of the 16 variables on which their characteristics matched that of the abusing parents. A couple could therefore have a score ranging from 0 (none of the factors is present) to 16 (all of the factors present).

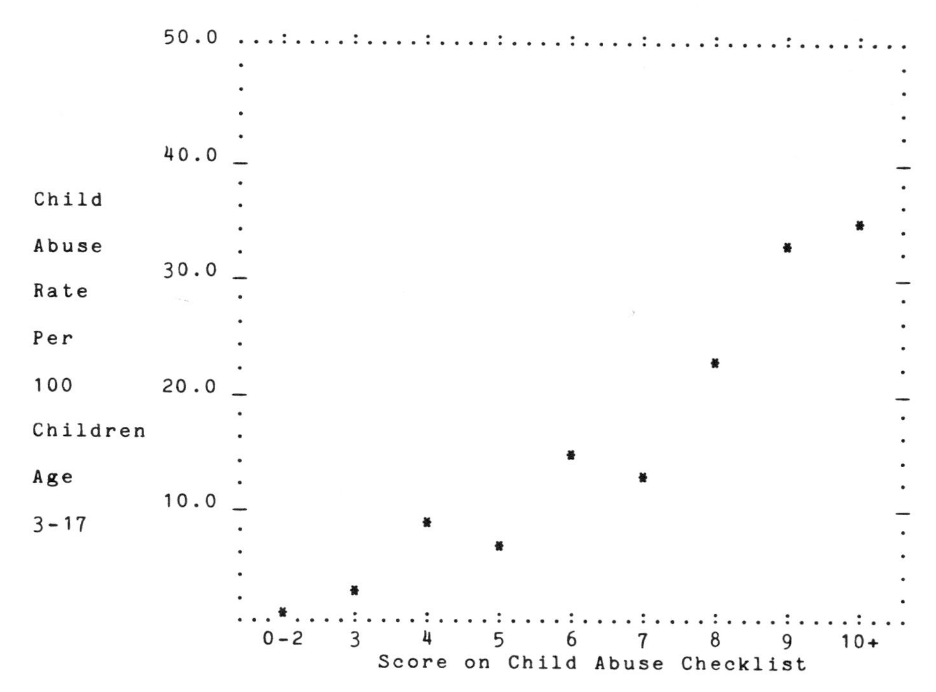

Fig.1. Incidence of child abuse by score on child abuse checklist

Figure 1 clearly shows the powerful relationship between the combination of these factors and the incidence of child abuse. Couples with scores of 0 to 2 were entirely free of child abuse. The incidence of child abuse climbs steadily from there on, reaching a rate of 33 per hundred children in families characterized by 10 or more of these factors.

The social factors identified in this research obviously are strongly associated with child abuse. The incidence of abuse for those unfortunate enough to be characterized by all the elements of the syndrome is staggering. But even among this group of parents, two thirds did <u>not</u> abuse a child. This fact should serve as a caution against attempting to use the Child Abuse Checklist as a means of locating high risk parents in order to provide services which might prevent child abuse.

Tempting as is that possibility, any potential gains in preventing child abuse have to be weighed against the costs and potential dangers. One large cost is the creation of an intrusive system of family surveillance. A potential danger lies in the consequence of falsely labeling millions of partners as "potential abusers" or "high risk parents."

The fact that the child abuse rate for parents with scores of ten or more is "only" 33 per hundred children also indicates that we still have a long way to go in pinpointing the causes of child abuse. As suggested in the introduction, there is an obvious need to include data on the psychological characteristics of the parents <u>and</u> the characteristics of the child. If such characteristics were included, and if we were to use more adequate methods of taking account of the unique combinations of factors, it might be possible to account for even more of the cases of child abuse. But even limiting the study to purely social factors, and using the simple methodology which there has so far been time to apply, it is clear that we have been able to isolate many of the factors associated with child abuse.

SUMMARY AND CONCLUSIONS

This paper reports the incidence of physical abuse for a nationally representative sample of American families with a child age 3 through 17 at home. The rate of 14 per 100 children is vastly higher than previous estimates. This difference reflects the fact that the present study was not dependent on officially reported instances of abuse, and the fact that "abuse" was defined by the nature of the violent acts carried out, rather than by the nature of the injury produced.

The main part of the paper examined social factors which might account for the extremely high incidence of child abuse. The findings suggest that the causes of child abuse can be found in (but are not limited to) the following factors: (1) The structure of the contemporary American family, for example, the practice of placing almost the whole burden on child care on mothers. This is a main reason why women have a much higher rate of child abuse than men, despite lower rates of violence outside the family. (2) The economic and psychological stress created by poverty and an unstable economic system. Illustrative of this is the finding of a higher incidence of child abuse among manual workers and among the unemployed. (3) Isolation from the help and social control which occurs when a family is embedded in a network of kin and community. This is illustrated by the finding that short term residents of a neighborhood have a higher incidence of child abuse when compared to longer established residents. (4) Unintended but powerful training in the use of violence as a means of teaching and resolving conflicts. Parents who had been physically punished abuse their children much more often, as do parents who engage in physical fights with each other. Parents who saw their parents hit each other have a much higher rate of child abuse than other parents.

Overall, the results of this study suggest that child abuse is brought about by the very nature of the society and its family system. This has profound implications for the prevention and treatment of child abuse. Although psychotherapy may be appropriate in some cases, a more fundamental approach lies in such things as a more equal sharing of the burdens of child care, replacement of physical punishment with non-violent methods of child care and training, eliminating the stresses and insecurity which now characterize our economic system, and strengthening the ties of individual families to the extended family and the community.

Considerable caution is needed in respect to these suggestions concerning prevention and treatment. First, there is an ideological bias on my part, for example, in suggesting greater sharing of child care and equality between husband and wife. I do not think it affected the data analysis, but that possibility is present. Second, the findings reflect the situation in the USA at a particular point in history. The findings could be quite different in another society or at a previous point in American society. An example is the higher rate of child abuse by mothers who are full time housewives. This could reflect such things as feelings of inadequacy generated by the growing expectation that everyone--wives as well as husbands--should be in the paid labor force. A generation or two ago the situation was reversed. Then the adequacy and psycholgocial normality of the "career woman" who did not stay home with her children was questioned and gave rise to feelings of doubt and insecurity on the part of women with full time jobs.

Although this research revealed an extremely high rate of child abuse in a cross section of American families, the findings also offer hope for the future. This is because the changes which are needed to reduce the level of abuse of children coincide with changes already in progress, or with changes in the family and society advocated on other grounds.

REFERENCES

Billingsley, Andrew, Family functioning in the low-income black community, Casework 50, 563-572 (1969).

Cazenave, Noel A. and Murray A. Straus, The effect of social network embeddedness on Black marital violence attitudes and behavior: a search for potent support systems. Paper presented at the American Sociological Association, San Francisco, (September 7, 1978).

Gelles, Richard J. and Murray A. Straus, Family experience and public support of the death penalty, American Journal of Orthopsychiatry 45, 596-613 (1975).

Gelles, Richard J. and Murray A. Straus, Determinants of violence in the family: towards a theoretical integration, In Wesley R. Burr, Rueben Hill, F. Ivan Nye, and Ira L. Reiss (eds.), Contemporary Theories About the Family, Free Press, New York (1978).

Gil, David G., Unraveling child abuse, American Journal of Orthopsychiatry 45, 346-356 (1975).

Howard, Jane, (1970) Please Touch, Delta, New York.

Maden, Marc F. and David F. Wrench, Significant Findings in Child Abuse Research, Victimology 2, 196-224 (1977).

Nie, Norman, H., C. Hadlai Hull, Jean G. Jenkins, Karin Steinbrenner, and Dale H. Brent, (1975) Statistical Package for the Social Sciences, Second Edition, McGraw-Hill, New York.

Owens, David M. and Murray A. Straus, The social structure of violence in childhood and approval of violence as an adult, Aggressive Behavior 1, 193-211, (1975).

Smith, S. M., (1975) The Battered Child Syndrome. Butterworths, London.

Stark, Rodney and James McEvoy III, Middle class violence, Psychology Today 4, 52-65, (1970).

Straus, Murray A., Societal morphogenesis and intrafamily violence in cross-cultural perspective, In Leonore Loeb Adler (ed.), Issues in Cross-Cultural Research, Annals of the New York Academy of Sciences 285, 717-730, New York(1977)

Straus, Murray A., Measuring intrafamily conflict and violence: the Conflict Tactics (CT) scales, Journal of Marriage and the Family 41 (1979).

Straus, Murray A., Richard J. Gelles, and Suzanne K. Steinmetz, (1979) Violence in the American Family, Doubleday/Anchor, New York, in press.

Young, Leontine R., The behavior syndromes of parents who neglect and abuse their children, Doctoral Dissertation, Columbia University School of Social Work (1963).

Child Abuse and Neglect, Vol. 3, pp. 227 - 233.

0145-2134/79/0301-0227 $02.00/0.

A COURSE IN INTERVENTION STRATEGIES IN CHILD ABUSE AND NEGLECT

Kathleen Coulborn Faller, M.S.W. and M. Leora Bowden, A.C.S.W.
University of Michigan, School of Social Work, Ann Arbor, Michigan

GENERAL INTRODUCTION

During recent years in the United States, and also in Western European countries, considerable emphasis has been placed upon the identification and reporting of families where child abuse or neglect is suspected. As a consequence, we have had, in the United States, an astronomical increase in the number of substantiated cases of child maltreatment. Unfortunately, we have not seen a comparable increase in treatment services and personnel. By and large practitioners in Child Protective Services have all they can do, and sometimes more, to investigate reports and provide emergency intervention to protect the child. Practitioners in treatment agencies, outside the Child Protection System, who could and should be providing ongoing treatment to families where abuse and neglect have been identified, have been slow to respond to the problem. Further they feel their skills are inadequate to meet the needs of these families.

As a response to this dilemma, we have developed a course called Intervention Strategies in Child Abuse and Neglect designed to be useful both for Protective Services workers and for other mental health practitioners. We have taught it to second year masters level students in social work and have opened it up free of charge to practitioners already in the field of child abuse and neglect. Most of the students were concurrently doing field placements with families and/or children, but not necessarily with maltreating families. Therefore, we felt that our bringing in practitioners would enhance our capacity to relate directly to the problems of child abuse and neglect. In addition, of course, it provided an opportunity to impart new skills to practitioners. To further anchor the course in the real world of treatment, we had as guest lecturers four persons involved in practice with abusive and neglectful families.

An essential characteristic of the course was that it was experiential. Because it was a "how to" course, it required that the participants try out what they were learning. Thus class sessions included role play of the strategies being taught, and course assignments were to employ the methods with clients and bring in tapes or written material demonstrating these efforts.

We chose to expose our students to five different approaches. The first uses linguistics as a therapy base and demonstrates how language can be a tool for therapy. The Structure of Magic, Vol. 1 and 2, 1975 by Richard Bandler and John Grinder served as the text. Our goal was to have their approach form an overarching framework because it can be utilized regardless of the therapist's theoretical proclivity.

As for the remaining four approaches, we took what we regarded as some major hypotheses about the kinds of family malfunction which lead to child abuse and neglect, and addressed these with currently practiced therapies. An important criterion for the therapies chosen was that they be useful in short-term intervention. In the United States, delivery of services to families suspected of abuse and neglect generally mandates time-limited involvement, ranging from three months in some states to a maximum of about two years in others. While in actual practice, cases are often open longer than the Child Protection Program specifies, clearly we are in a situation where there is no support for such long-term methods as psychotherapy. Moreover, the bulk of population presently being identified in our country does not have the verbal skills nor the motivation to commit themselves to long-term psychotherapy.

A second criterion for the therapies that we taught was that they have an interpersonal, rather than an intrapersonal, orientation, and that they be methods which are especially useful within a family context. The rationale for such a choice is that if one is to have an impact within a brief period, one must include as many of the relevant actors as possible.

The first hypothesis we considered is that child abuse and neglect is a consequence of maladaptive family interaction and chose family systems therapy as a strategy to address the diagnosis. Second, we looked beyond the family *per se* to the hypothesis that a major factor in child abuse and neglect is the social isolation of the family and dealt with this issue by teaching network therapy. Third, we took Ray Helfer's (1975) formulation of the War Cycle (the world of abnormal child rearing) and taught our students how to use Transactional Analysis to break the cycle. Finally, taking as a hypothesis that parents who abuse and neglect their children have had a poor learning history for parenthood and thus do not know how to nurture, we used some methods based upon behavior modification.

Perhaps, before moving to more detailed descriptions of the intervention strategies, it should be noted that while these hypotheses are overlapping, they do represent different points of view about what leads to child abuse and neglect. However, rather than seeing the teaching of such diverse analyses as inconsistent, we viewed it as reflective of the fact that the crucial dynamics of causation vary considerably from case to case. Thus the clinician must do a careful assessment during the initial stages of involvement and choose a therapy which speaks to the critical problems of the family. We also counselled flexibility of mind on the part of our students, encouraging them to have ready more than one approach for dealing with a particular problem. But we cautioned them that when they switched strategies, they should be clear that they were switching models of therapy as well.

LINGUISTIC ANALYSIS

The major concept that we attempted to convey in presenting a linguistic approach is based on the idea that human beings do not operate directly on the world. Instead, they build a map or model which they use as a basis for their behavior. In addition, individuals' models of the world determine how they experience the world and what choices in life they perceive as being available. People have difficulty when they have models of the world that are too limited to deal with reality. By listening to a person's language, an assessment can be made of a person's model of the world and its limitations. Then appropriate interventions can be selected.

Three major mechanisms that people use to limit their models of the world were covered in the course. These were generalizations, deletions, and distortions. Generalizations refer to the process by which single elements or parts of a person's experience come to represent an entire category of experiences; e.g. a hot stove which causes a burned hand leads to a generalization that all stoves are hot and all kitchens dangerous. Deletion refers to the process of selectively paying attention to certain sensory experiences and excluding others; e.g. noticing the child has a sore leg, but not being aware the child has two broken bones in the leg. Distortion is the process which happens when a person reinterprets sensory data to correspond with his model of the world; e.g. a person may maintain low self-esteem by stating to self the positive comments about behavior were "just made to make me feel better."

Students were taught to recognize and confront these mechanisms in interview situations with the use of role playing exercises. We have found that these exercises improve the interviewing skills of students and enhance their assessment ability and the clarity of their communications with clients.

FAMILY SYSTEMS INTERVENTION

Readers who have a working knowledge of family therapies which regard the family as a system know that, in fact, we are talking about several different schools of family therapy. To have tried to teach students all of these approaches would have confused them and inhibited them from trying anything, particularly in a course where they were learning other therapies as well. Thus, we were selective in what we chose.

First we presented material to help students understand what is meant by viewing the family as a system of interacting parts. Students learned how to redefine the presenting symptom, for themselves and the family, as a family problem. In abuse and neglect the difficulty is usually viewed by the family as a parental deficit or child misbehavior. We focused on strategies which elucidate the contributions of other family members to the symptomatic behavior.

We also spent a fair amount of time on how to assess and intervene in the power configuration in the family system. Power is a very salient issue in maltreating families. In abusive families we see fixation on the need to control. Neglectful families often present with signs that family functioning is out of control or that parents are failing to exercise power. We defined power in two ways: the ability to influence the behavior of another individual and control over family decisions. Within the context of power we deal with scapegoating.

Recognizing the difficulty of diagnosing power, we offer students several different strategies to be used concurrently: 1) Evaluating sources of power; 2) Using an assessment instrument which examines family's decision-making processes and division of labor; 3) Observing the process of family interaction.

With reference to the first strategy, we noted that every family member has some power, but that parents usually have the preponderance. We took as a starting point French and Raven's (1968) five bases of social power: reward power, coercive power, legitimate power, referrent power, and expert power. We concentrated on elaborating sources which are coercive, as these are the most heavily relied upon in maltreating families. Their willingness to use physical force is one obvious basis of power, but there are others as well. In fact we regard this source as part of a larger class we have called the willingness to engage in deviant behavior.

Research on normal families (e.g. Blood and Wolfe, 1960; Safilios and Rothchild, 1971) cites bringing money into the household, the ability to provide services, and the ability to find an alternate living arrangement as important sources of power. In maltreating families these are relied upon in a coercive manner; in the first two instances family members overtly or covertly threaten to withhold these things in order to control others' behavior. With the third instance they threaten to leave the home or become uninvolved in order to control.

The assessment instrument we used is one based on protocols employed in studies of many different types of families in the United States and abroad (e.g. Blood and Wolfe, 1960; Centers, Raven and Rodriguez, 1971; Heer, 1962; Herbst, 1952; Olson and Cromwell, 1975; Safilios-Rothchild, 1971). It examines how family members say decisions are made and labor is distributed in the family, and how they would <u>like</u> these things to be done. Four areas of family functioning are covered: economic, child-related, homemaking, and recreational.

For our approach to family process we drew upon a substantial body of research on power in small groups (e.g. Cartwright and Zander, 1968; Parsons and Bales, 1954) as well as upon family therapists and researchers who have examined family interaction in normal and abnormal families on a number of dimensions, including power, (e.g. Winter and Ferreira, 1969; Jay Haley, 1969; Strodbeck, 1969; Riskin and Faunce, 1972; Winter, Ferreira and Bowers, 1973).

Some aspects of the process which we deemed important are who talks the most, who interrupts, who disagrees, who speaks for whom, and who has the final say about matters.

We urged students to use all three of these strategies in a given case because power can be complex. For example, family members may have control in some areas but not others and the power configuration can change. Further, persons may exercise power in an indirect rather than direct manner.

We focus on two general strategies related to the power structure and treatment: 1) How to manipulate the family's current power configuration so that it supports appropriate change; 2) How to alter the power structure, by a variety of means, so that it enhances adequate family functioning.

In our material on scapegoating, we use a broad definition, identifying it as any circumstance where the parent attacks, belittles, or otherwise maltreats the child when her/his real target is someone or something against which s/he feels a sense of impotence. Thus the target of frustration may be a more powerful spouse, but may also be a boss, a job, or a society which fails to provide a job, subsistence, or adequate housing. Based on diagnosis, the therapist might choose from a range of intervention strategies. Some are focused on changes within the family system, such as working on the marital problem or setting up positive interchanges between the scapegoater and the scapegoat. Others are targeted outside the system; for example, teaching the scapegoater how to be assertive with the boss, or assisting the family in getting better housing, or financial assistance.

A systems approach is one very compatible with the current Child Protection service delivery system and is already being used by some practitioners in the field.

NETWORK THERAPY

When we taught network therapy, we attempted to do two things: to teach how to accurately assess the network and then how to do therapy employing social network members as change agents. The reason for attention to the former is that as we refine our research on social isolation in abusive and neglectful families, we are discovering that to state these families are isolated is an over-simplification. A majority of them have extensive contact with formal network resources, helping professionals and human service agencies. However, often these relationships are uncoordinated, unproductive, and sometimes counterproductive. On the other hand, their contacts with friends, neighbors, and particularly relatives are truncated. In assessing the network, some of the factors which are examined are the number of persons in the family network, network density (i.e., whether members know and have contact with one another independent of the target family), network embeddedness (i.e., whether members are neighbors, friends, relatives, professionals), frequency of contact, geographic proximity, degree of reciprocity between the family and network member, degree of comfort, and degree of obligation the family feels in maintaining the contact.

The network therapy model we teach is one modified from that of Ross Speck and Carolyn Attneave (1972). Its structure is as follows: Persons who participate from the network should be chosen and invited by the family in consultation with the therapists. The therapists want to assure that all family members have allies in the therapy group and that some persons who are peripheral to the family's network are invited (to renew the network). Most should be from the family's informal network but some professionals should also be involved. We recommend 10 to 20 people be invited and that two to three therapists participate. The therapy is short-term, comprised of two to six meetings, but these are spaced about three weeks apart. Between sessions network subgroups are active and there is considerable telephone contact with the therapists. Often the network continues to meet after therapist contact ceases.

The process of therapy is one in which therapists take a very active role in mobilizing the network to help the family with its problems. They deal with conflicting definitions of the problem and with varieties of resistance by members of the group to being involved in the solution. They enrich or create new bonds between network members and loosen others. What the network members do in their efforts is highly variable. This is as it should be because we know that abuse and neglect are symptoms of family malfunction--which can entail a range of problems. Thus the network may take turns visiting a desperate and lonely mother, may provide a drop-in babysitting service, might help a father or mother find employment, may help with transportation, or might provide a home for a rebellious adolescent.

A major asset of this type of intervention is the fact that it creates an ongoing system to augment family functioning, which will persist after professional involvement has ended. Its drawback is that it is a step beyond what traditional agencies see as appropriate modes of intervention. Thus practitioners may encounter agency resistance to its utilization.

TRANSACTIONAL ANALYSIS

Justice and Justice utilized their knowledge of Transactional Analysis to understand and work with parents who had abused and neglected their children. (Described in their book The Abusing Family, 1976.) One of their major hypotheses is that a pattern of unresolved symbiosis is a contributor to abuse in families. Transactional Analysis, trisects individual functioning into parent, adult, and child states. Symbiosis occurs when two individuals transact in such a way that one person functions in the adult and parent state and the other in the child. This pattern, learned in the family of origin and perpetuated in the existing family, is one in which either the spouses are tightly bound together, one parent is fused with the child, or the husband or wife is still intensely bound up with the family of origin. Generally the person fused with is seen as the major source of gratification. In these families there is considerable competition over who will be nurtured. The winner gets taken care of and the others have to resort to extreme behavior to obtain nurturance. The family's symbiotic pattern can be identified by analysing transactional patterns and/or obtaining information from observation and interviews on how care and attention are obtained and provided for by members of the family.

We presented basic information about theoretical concepts from Transactional Analysis in order to teach three strategies for intervening in a symbiotic family:

1) A symbiosis exists when persons are not using all their ego states. Identifying ego states being excluded is the first step. The second step is to encourage the use of the excluded ego states.
2) In symbiotic relationships one may need to recognize and confront forms of passivity. People may engage in passivity to avoid autonomous response to stimuli, options or problems. In so doing they meet their needs or reach their goals within the structure of unhealthy relationships. (Schiff and Schiff, 1971.)
3) Discounting may be present and need to be addressed by the therapist. There are four levels of discounting people use to minimize or ignore some aspects of themselves, others, or the reality of the situation. (Schiff, 1975.)

Transactional Analysis may offer a useful interpretation of relationships and behavior in both abusive and neglectful families, particularly those preoccupied with their families of origin.

BEHAVIOR MODIFICATION

Experts in the field of abuse and neglect will know that behavior modification, particularly in the form of child management, is currently being utilized as an intervention strategy with abusive and neglectful parents (e.g. Epstein and Shainline, 1975). In this case the hypothesis is that these parents' upbringings did not afford them an adequate child rearing experience. It is assumed that one learns to parent primarily from one's own parents, and thus maltreating parents have deficient skills and few options in methods of controlling their children because of their own rearing. Strategies we used included teaching parents to use positive reinforcement with children and each other. We taught several behavioral strategies. First students learned how to get parents to use positive reinforcement with children. For example parents learn to employ concrete rewards (such as toys, money, or food) and privileges contingent upon good behavior, in order to increase the likelihood of the behavior happening in the future. Similarly parents are taught to praise and hug their children when children are good. Parents also learn about less punitive methods, such as "time out" (short-term isolation) to control or diminish unacceptable behavior.

In addition, because marital difficulty is a common presenting problem in child maltreatment, we taught behavioral marital contracting, utilizing the structure developed by the Oregon Research Institute (Patterson *et al.*, 1970). In this model parallel independent contracts are developed for each spouse.

When we teach students how to utilize behavioral strategies, we emphasize that didactic explanations are insufficient, even when accompanied by a written plan and arrangements for monitoring. For such intervention to be effective, the therapist must model the expected behavior and relevant family members must practice perhaps several times in the therapist's presence. Great care needs to be taken to specify when, where, and how the methods should be used, and initially the therapist will have to call daily to see how the intervention is progressing.

Although students were instructed in behavioral contracting and how to use monitoring forms with families and couples, emphasis was placed upon simplicity. We advocated the use of the least complicated and most compatible intervention feasible. Such an approach greatly improves the likelihood of its permanent impact on family functioning.

CONCLUSION

All courses taught at the University of Michigan School of Social Work are evaluated by students taking them, and this course got excellent ratings. Nevertheless we would like to note some of the ways we will teach the course differently next year. First, we have attempted to cover too much material to treat in-depth in four months. Therefore we will not teach so many different models of therapy, probably eliminating Transactional Analysis and Behavior Modification. Second, although a substantial proportion of class time was spent practicing techniques, more time should be so allocated. We will endeavor to offer a lab for additional credit which will be devoted to practice and stimulation.

In conclusion, we hope that this description of our work will stimulate and inspire others in the field to attend to the treatment of families suspected of abuse and neglect in innovative yet feasible ways.

REFERENCES

1. Bandler, Richard and Grinder, John, The Structure of Magic, Vols. 1 and 2, Palo Alto, California, Science and Behavior Books, 1975.

2. Blood, Robert and Wolfe, D., Husbands and Wives, Glencoe, Illinois, Free Press, 1960.

3. Cartwright, Dorwin and Zander, Alvin, eds., Group Dynamics, New York, Harper and Row Publishers, 1968.

4. Centers, R., Raven, B., and Rodriguez, A., "Conjugal Power Structure: A Reexamination", American Sociological Review, Vol. 36, (April) 1971, 264-278.

5. Epstein, N. and Shainline, A., "Paraprofessional Parent Aides and Disadvantaged Families", Social Casework, Vol. 55.4, 1974, 230-236.

6. French, C. and Raven, B., "Bases of Social Power", in Cartwright, D. and Zander, A., eds., Group Dynamics, New York, Harper and Row Publishers, 1968.

7. Haley, Jay, "Research in Family Patterns: An Instrument of Measurement", in Winter, D. and Ferriera, A., Research in Family Interaction: Readings and Commentary, Palo Alto, California, Science and Behavior Books, 1969.

8. Heer, David, "Husband and Wife Perceptions of Family Power Structure", Marriage and Family Living, (February) 1962, 62-65.

9. Helfer, Ray, The Diagnostic Process and Treatment Programs, Washington, D. C., DHEW Publication (OHD), 75-69.

10. Herbst, P. G., "The Measurement of Family Relationships", Human Relations, Vol. 5, 1952, 3-35.

11. Justice, Blair and Justice, Rita, The Abusing Family, New York, Human Sciences Press, 1976.

12. Parsons, Talcott, and Bales, Robert, Family Socialization and Interaction Process, Glencoe, Illinois, The Free Press, 1954.

13. Patterson, Gerald, et al., A Social Learning Approach to Family Intervention, Eugene, Oregon, Castillia Publishing Company, 1975.

14. Olson, David and Cromwell, R., Power in Families, New York, 1975.

15. Riskin, Jules and Faunce, E., "An Evaluative Review of Family Interaction Research", Family Process, (December) 1972

16. Safilios-Rothchild, Constantina, "The Study of Family Power Structure: A Review, 1960-1969", in Broderick, Carlfred, ed., A Decade of Family Research and Action, Minneapolis, Minnesota, National Council on Family Relations, 1971.

17. Schiff, A. W. and Schiff, J., "Passivity", Transactional Analysis, Vol. 1.1, (January) 1971, 71-78.

18. Schiff, Jacque, "Discounting", Transactional Analysis, Vol. 4.1, 1975.

19. Speck, Ross and Attneave, Carolyn, "Network Therapy", in Sager, C. and Kaplan, H. S., Progress in Group and Family Therapy, New York, Brunner-Mazel, 1972.

20. Strodbeck, F. L., "The Family As A Three Person Group", in Winter, D. and Ferreira, A., eds., Research in Family Interaction, Palo Alto, California, Science and Behavior Books, 1969.

21. Winter, D. and Ferreira, A., Research in Family Interaction: Readings and Commentary, Palo Alto, California, Science and Behavior Books, 1969.

22. Winter, W. D., Ferreira, A. and Bowers, D., "Decision-Making in Married and Unrelated Couples", Family Process, (March) 1973.

Child Abuse and Neglect, Vol. 3, pp. 235 - 239.
Pergamon Press Ltd., 1979. Printed in Great Britain.

THE PARENTS ANONYMOUS SERVICE PROVIDER/SERVICE RECIPIENT EXPERIMENTAL TRAINING PROJECT

Margot E. Fritz and Jean M. Baker
Parents Anonymous, 2810 Artesia Blvd., Suite F, Redondo Beach, CA 90278
Behavior Associates, 330 E. 13th Street, Tucson, Arizona, 85701

BACKGROUND AND RATIONALE

The National Office of the Parents Anonymous Self-Help for Child Abusing Parents program has received a grant from the National Institute of Mental Health (DHEW) for the purpose of conducting an innovative training program. The unique aspect of the Parents Anonymous training approach is that it brings together the service provider, that is, the professional working in the field of child abuse, and the service recipient, the parent with abuse problems. The training approach is based on the concept that knowing through experiencing must precede intellectual comprehension. The approach also assumes that in the field of human services people learn best in interaction and relationship with each other, and that the best learning takes place when the learner is an active participant in the learning process. By utilizing an experiential approach, working in small groups, and focusing on individual experiences, participants are given the opportunity to relate in feeling, as opposed to intellectual, terms. We are supported in these ideas by Dr. Carl Rogers (1) who states in a chapter written by him in the Humanistic Education Sourcebook, "Teaching is, for me, a relatively unimportant and vastly overvalued activity. We are faced with an entirely new situation in education where the goal is the facilitation of change and learning. When I have been able to transform a group - and here I mean all the members of a group, myself included - into a community of learners, then the excitement has been almost beyond belief."

How does one go about facilitating learning in the group setting? Certain factors which facilitate learning in the group setting are a sense on the part of each individual that he is valued as a participant in the group; a sense of shared commonality of experience which helps to overcome the barrier of the 'not I'; and adherence to a basic principle for all Parents Anonymous Chapters - something called Lieber's Law: Trust the Group. This principle will be discussed in more detail later in the paper.

In order to facilitate group learning it is also necessary to take into account the factors which are inhibiting to change. Among the most important of these are fear, defensiveness and competitiveness, the latter often resulting in aggressive postures. In a deeper psychological sense the fear of difference in another, the perception of the other as 'not me' is an important issue and must be dealt with if good communication is to occur. In the introduction to both the workshop and the lab, I, as the leader, point out that the extent to which I am out of touch with some part of myself is precisely the extent to which I will be unable to respond or relate to that part of another person. To be in touch with my own sexuality, violence, or need for intimacy means that part of me can be responsive to those feeling states in the other. Overcoming the sense of difference is a basic task of the training.

In the field of child abuse, more than in most areas of human services, fear is an important factor to be reckoned with. It is a potent force and one which greatly impedes communication and the ability of one human being to help, or to accept help, from another. This fear may arise from the stereotypes we carry around with us of persons in roles, and is based on the mechanism of splitting in which we split off bad, unwanted and feared parts of ourselves and project them onto others. This process may occur for the professional in relation to the fear of violence. The parent with abuse problems may become a projection of the professional's fears of violence within himself and the parent is then perceived as possessing those qualities which the professional cannot countenance within himself. A stereotype is developed which serves as a defense and an impediment to the professional's perceiving the parent as in any way like himself. The parent, in other words, becomes for the professional the 'not I.' I have many times had this clearly revealed to me when, in the course of a conversation or an interview, I have revealed that I am a parent with abuse problems and the person to whom I am speaking reacts with shock to discover that this person whom they have identified as being in many ways like themselves turns out to be someone who possesses qualities which they definitely cannot accept in themselves. Some of you may be experiencing that same sense of disbelief and shock at this moment.

The splitting process occurs for the child abusing parent as well. In Kleinian terms what happens for so many of them is that they have failed to integrate the good parent with the bad, they are stuck in a developmental phase in which they can only allow themselves to perceive the bad parent. This reaction is often most marked toward anyone in the role of an authority figure, as professionals so often are. One of the tasks which the training attempts to accomplish is an opening into this closed perception of the other as the 'not I.'

DESCRIPTION OF THE TRAINING APPROACH

Since I felt that it was important that both parents and professionals be able to make their initial contact with one another other freed from role identification, I use first names only on name tags for all participants, thus assuring them anonymity as well as freedom from their usual roles. This generates some anxiety, but it also puts people vividly in touch with their need for identifying labels.

The first exercise acts as a social leveler because no one is sure how to do it 'right'. It is very simple. Participants are asked to form a circle and move around the circle greeting each other non-verbally, they may touch, but are asked not to speak. Everyone experiences some anxiety doing this exercise and, because speech cannot be used participants are more aware of what they are experiencing at a feeling level. The exercise acts as a social leveler because all the usual verbal means we use to present ourselves as acceptable, O.K. people are eliminated. Participants experience the feeling of being very vulnerable, and fears of rejection come to the fore. When the exercise has ended, the participants form groups, determined on a random basis by numbering off, and discuss the exercise. In the discussion that ensues, people begin the process of identifying with one another,the stereotypes begin to crumble and the group usually starts to feel a sense of shared commonality of experience.

The next exercises are designed to further facilitate cohesiveness in the group as well as provide learning opportunities. A simple sentence such as, "When I was 16 I..." elicits much painful material for most participants, but it can also result in insights, as long repressed feelings are brought to consciousness. Professionals often get in touch with the ways in which they may have experienced abuse as children, and parents are faced with the recognition that they are not alone in having been abused as children. Parents also have an opportunity to experience professionals as people who can feel anger, hurt, bitterness, envy, insecurity and this can be a real eye-opener for parents who have never had a personal relationship with a professional. As parents reveal their histories, professionals are afforded a first-hand opportunity to learn about the historical and present day factors which contribute to abuse problem. Almost always there are surprises. Someone whom the group has identified as a parent turns out to be a professional, and the reverse occurs as well. This, more than anything tends to destroy the stereotypes. By the end of the morning session it no longer matters very much to most participants who are the parents and who the professionals They have connected with each other along dimensions of identification and commonality of shared experience, the person has become paramount in importance and the role has receded. Each participant feels important to the group and this lessens competetiveness. A climate of safety has usually developed which make it possible for group members to take risks. When this climate develops it serves to build trust in the group and lessens the need for defensiveness.

Following the lunch break I give a lecture which focuses on the morning's exercises. I ask for audience responses to the non-verbal mill, and, using the words which clearly denote an uncomfortable feeling state, I point out that if you magnified those feelings by a power of 10 you will have some idea of how parents feel walking through the door of their first P.A. chapter meeting. Because participants still have the feeling memory with them, my words have much greater impact. I continue the lecture by discussing the variables which are facilitative to developing group cohesiveness as opposed to those which are not. I end the lecture with Lieber's Law. This simple concept is a key factor in the success and growth of P.A. Chapters. It is "Trust the Group". Leonard Lieber, who founded P.A., has used that as a guiding principle, both for individual chapters and for the organization as a whole. It permits a maximum degree of autonomy to the chapters and places the power and responsibility for the chapter with the parents. For people who have felt powerless and helpless most of their lives this sense of chapter as 'theirs' is a key factor in their growth.

During the afternoon session participants are asked to state the specific needs, personal or professional, which brought them to the workshop. Very often parents will say that they wanted to come because they felt that since it was something P.A. was offering it would be a good experience for them no matter what went on. Professionals often have questions about P.A. -- how it functions or what it achieves for those who experience it. Usually I am able to take a back seat in these sessions. If there is a good representation of chapter people their dialogue with each other will give professionals much information about how chapters function, what kinds of problems they encounter, the differences between chapters, and, most importantly, what parents get from the chapter experience. Hearing this last from parents themselves carries far more weight than if I were to enumerate the benefits.

For parents the gain from the afternoon session may often be the feeling that they have been able to give professionals something for a change, instead of vice versa. Professionals will often get into discussions with each other about the problems they encounter within their agencies and this helps both to clarify the professional's role and to give parents more realistic expectations about what professionals can do for them.

For me a workshop or lab has been successful if participants take away with them some "knowing" upon which they can build intellectually as well as some recognition of the fact that we are all rather more alike in our humanness than not.

EVALUATION OF THE PROGRAM

An outside evaluation firm, Behavior Associates of Tucson, Arizona, was asked to assess the effectiveness of this training program and to measure participant satisfaction with the training. Questionnaires designed by the evaluators were administered on a pre, post, and follow-up (3 to 4 months) basis to all of the training program participants. Preliminary results are as follows:

Changes in Opinions About Child Abuse

In general,the training appears to result in a greater willingness to work with child abusing persons, increased feelings of competence and comfortableness in working with such persons and more positive feelings toward persons with child abuse problems. The individual questions relative to these areas and the results for those trainees participanting in the three day training program are presented in the following graphs:

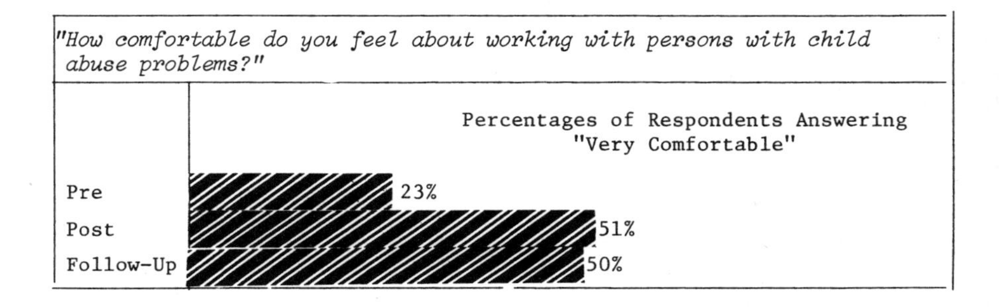

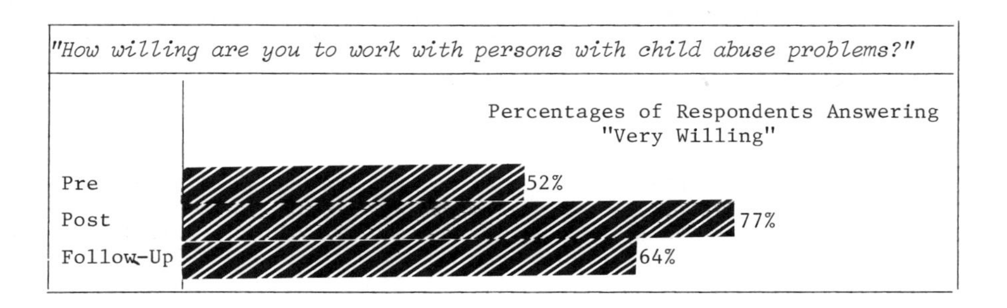

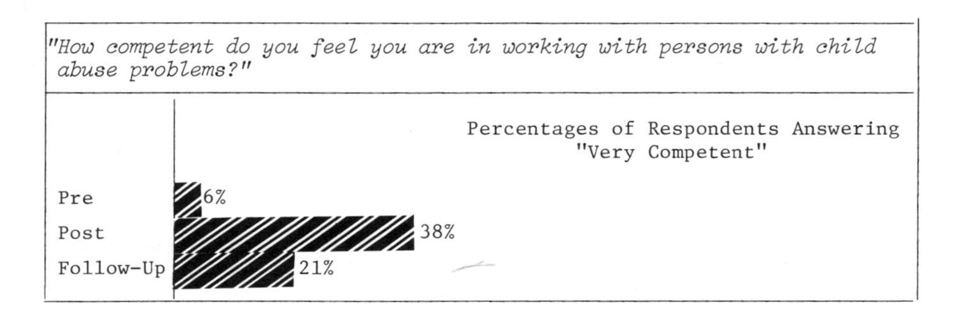

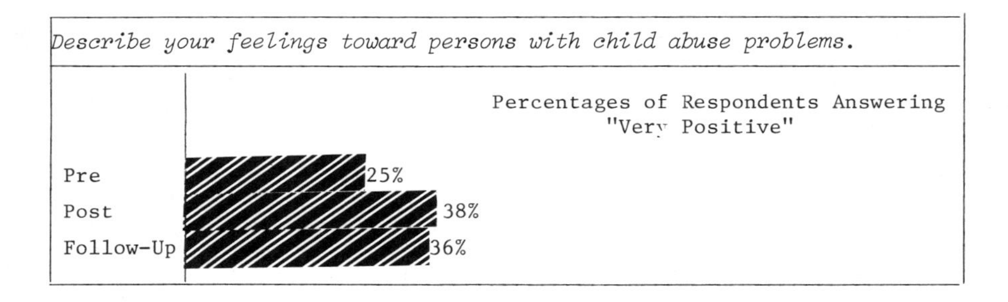

It can be noted that for each of the items there was a consistent positive change from pre to post measures and only a slight drop from post to follow-up.

An increase in awareness of the seriousness of the effects of child abuse on the children involved, was another apparent effect of the training. For example:

...48% of the participants rated physical abuse as an"Extremely Serious"problem on the pre-test, while 53% on the post test and 61% on the follow-up rated it as an "Extremely Serious" problem.

...The results were similar for the various forms of abuse (verbal, emotional, sexual) and for neglect (physical, emotional). That is there was an increasing awareness of the seriousness of the problems from pre training to post training to follow-up.

Changes in Knowledge of and Attitudes Toward the Parents Anonymous Program

Pre and most measures demonstrated that the attitudes of the non-P.A. affiliated trainees toward the Parents Anonymous program became much more positive after the training. The findings of the pre, post and follow-up questionnaires demonstrated that:

...Opinions of the non-P.A. professional toward the Parents Anonymous program became significantly more positive from the pre to post measure and from the pre to follow-up measure.

...The number of referrals which these professionals made to Parents Anonymous increased from an average of 1.9 per two month period to 2.8 per two month period.

...The professionals (non P.A. persons) became more emphathic with the feelings of child abusing persons as evidenced by their answers to questions which asked them to judge how they felt child abusers would feel toward their children. They answered these questions at the follow-up almost identically to the way the child abusing people answered them (Average score for 4 questions was 11.03 for the professionals and 11.33 for the P.A. people, whereas the scores at pre-test were 10.00 for professionals and 12.8 for P.A. people).

Changes in Feelings of Parents Anonymous Members, Chairpersons and Sponsors Toward Professionals and Community Services

Pre, post and follow-up measures demonstrated that Parents Anonymous people became more positive about professionals and community resources after their training. The results showed that:

...P.A. people made almost twice as many referrals to mental health services and other community services three to four months after their training than they did prior to their training.

Impact of the Training on Agencies and Communities

Three to four months after training the participants who were professionals in the child abuse field were asked about ways in which they may have influenced their agencies or communities as a result of their training. The results indicated that:

...58% of the three day training program participants had helped their agencies become involved in inter-agency collaboration for child abuse treatment or prevention.

...42% had conducted staff training programs to disseminate information or skills learned during the training.

...39% had been instrumental in developing new child abuse programs in their agencies.

...39% had developed new programs for community education on child abuse issues.

...31% had been instrumental in establishing closer liaison between their agency and Parents Anonymous Chapters in their communities.

Participants' Evaluation of the Training

The results of the participant evaluation of the training were very positive.

...70% of the three day training program participants rated the training as "Outstanding" and 30% rated it as "Good".

...At a three to four month follow-up these participants rated the effectiveness of the training in a number of areas. Eighty-four percent rated it as "Very Effective" in increasing their understanding of persons with child abuse problems; 71% rated it as "Extremely Effective" in increasing their understanding of Parents Anonymous; 69% rated it as "Extremely Effective" in increasing their understanding of professionals working in the field of child abuse; and 63% rated it as "Extremely Effective" in increasing their skills in working with persons who have child abuse problems.

Summary of Evaluation

These preliminary evaluation results suggest that the training approach is positively perceived by participants and that it has positive effects in changing their attitudes and behavior.

Rogers, Carl R. (1975) The interpersonal relationship in the facilitation of learning. In Donald C. Read and Sidney B. Simon (Eds.) The Humanistic Education Sourcebook. Prentice-Hall, Inglewood Cliffs, New Jersey.

Child Abuse and Neglect, Vol. 3, pp. 241 - 246.
© Pergamon Press Ltd., 1979. Printed in Great Britain.

0145-2134/79/0301-0241 $02.00/0.

AN OBSERVATIONAL STUDY OF MOTHER-INFANT INTERACTION IN ABUSING FAMILIES

Clare A. Hyman, Robert Parr & Kevin Browne

University of Surrey

The present controlled study represents an attempt to study mother-child interaction directly. Our previous research with abusive families at the NSPCC's National Advisory Centre and in the Surrey Health Authority's Area (Hyman & Mitchell, 1975; Hyman, 1977, 1978a, 1978b) has given strong support to the idea that psychological factors, probably operating from a very early stage in an infant's experience with his mother, serve to distort and damage the relationship between them in a cumulative way.

Immaturity, in terms both of maternal age (even when social class is controlled (Boyd 1978)) and in terms of ego-control and integration as revealed in responses to the Sixteen P.F. Personality Questionnaire (Hyman 1977; NSPCC Battered Child Research Team 1976), seems to be a prime handicap in abusive mothers. It might be thought that this in itself, implying, as it does, a greater degree of egocentricity in the Piagetian sense, may largely explain the unreal expectations and perceptions of her infant reported commonly in studies of abusing mothers (Steele & Pollock 1968).

We have also suggested that the distortion is shared by the children. Reporting the responses of abused children to the Bene-Anthony Test of Family Relations (Bene & Anthony 1957) we noted that as early as three and four years such children reveal disturbances in their interactions with their mothers (Hyman & Mitchell 1975).

Having, as it were, approached the problem obliquely through the analysis of the responses to psychometric tests and interview schedules we decided to confront the question of distorted interaction directly and set about making video recordings of mothers and infants attending the National Advisory Centre.

SAMPLE

At the time of writing some twenty abusing dyads and an approximately equal number of matched control dyads have been filmed. To date twelve experimental and twelve control video tapes have been analysed in terms to be described, and it is this sample which forms the basis of this report.

The experimental and control families have been matched for sex, infant's age, ordinal position, parental age, ethnic group and home accommodation. All the infants ranged in age from six to twenty four months with a mean age of 13.8 months for the abused infants and 13.6 months for the control infants - an insignificant difference. There were equal numbers of boys and girls in each group.

Bayley developmental quotients shewed developmental lag in the abused infants, with a mean motor quotient of 95 and a mean mental scale quotient of 89 for the abused infants. Such differences have been shewn by us (NSPCC Battered Child Research Team 1976) as well as by Martin (1976) to arise through inhibiting influences in the abusive environment and to ameliorate when there is effective therapeutic intervention, as for example at the special therapeutic nursery which many of the children at the NSPCC's National Advisory Centre attended.

METHOD

For this first step in the observation of abusive mother-infant dyads it was decided that a short standard sequence should be used which would include the separation and reunion of mother and infant. Because of the use of a fixed angle video camera the child was placed in a high-chair for the duration of the observation session.

The video recordings of the referred cases were made at roughly one month after referral and were carried out at the National Advisory Centre on the Battered Child. The occasion of the recording was the first visit that each mother and infant had made to the centre. The cases were asked to participate in the research by their social workers. It was explained to each mother that this would involve a visit to the NAC during which testing would be carried out and a short film made of her child. Thus, the actual recording was a small part of the whole visit and no stress was placed upon the filming. In later discussion few mothers indicated any awareness of being filmed. Control cases were obtained from Health Visitor files of the same London Borough from which the majority of the referred cases came.

On being escorted to the centre all cases were shewn into the observation room by a social worker. The observation room was furnished as an office but with two arm-chairs and the child's high-chair placed in a shallow arc perpendicular to the line of the camera, which was mounted on the wall in one corner. The infant was placed in the high-chair and the mother shewn to a chair beside the infant. The mother was told that someone would be in to see her shortly and recording began as the social worker left the room.

This first episode, the mother and infant alone in the strange room, lasted three minutes and was ended by the entry of a stranger. The stranger introduced herself and took a seat next to the child. After thirty seconds another stranger entered and asked the mother to accompany her in order to answer a number of questions. Episode C began as the mother left the room. This episode lasted three minutes during which time the mother was asked questions relating to the pregnancy and birth of her child. The stranger carried a stop-watch during this episode and with thirty seconds of the episode left to run, withdrew from interaction with the infant.

After the return of the mother to the observation room a further two minutes of recording was completed. The mother was then told that she had been filmed, was shewn the recording and told that the tape would be wiped clean if she wished.

The first stage in the analysis of the recorded behaviour of mother and infant was the compilation of a behaviour catalogue which in its final form consisted of over one hundred items, defined where possible in anatomical terms. This catalogue was devised in such a way as to allow for as detailed a description of behaviour as possible without destroying the integrity of behaviour. Thus, an action such as 'offers-toy-to-another' was coded as such and no attempt was made to reduce such a behaviour to individual arm and body movements. On the other hand neither was it, as is the case in the majority of observational studies of mother-infant interaction, merely included in the broader category of 'plays-with'. This tendency to use broad categories of behaviour was the principle reason why an existing catalogue of behaviour items could not be used for this study.

The transcripts of behaviour produced by the application of the behaviour catalogue in accordance with a set of scoring rules, were analysed in two ways by the Primate Computer package (Humphreys 1973). Amounts of individual behaviours were obtained by a behaviour frequency analysis which merely counted the number of times specified behaviour items appeared in a transcript. In order that these analyses should accurately reflect amounts of behaviours a three second time grid was imposed upon the behavioural sequences. Amounts of behaviour were also analysed using groups of items. The main items contributing to the grouping of manipulative behaviours for example, were - general handling of a toy; inspection of a toy; banging of toys; dropping a toy and picking up a toy.

The analysis of interactions carried out by Primate was accomplished by the coding of interactive initiatives in the transcripts of behaviour, for which Primate supplies a special symbol. An interactive initiative may be considered broadly as a behaviour directed at another individual. The interaction results to be reported later are concerned with the responses to interactive initiatives on the part of those to whom they are directed.

For example, when a mother leans toward, smiles at and talks to her infant, what is the infant's response? In order to simplify the analysis we may classify the responses as reciprocal or non-reciprocal. A reciprocal response would be one which involved a behaviour being directed back at the initiator of the interaction. A non-reciprocal response clearly, would be any other non-directed behaviour.

Instances in which an interactive initiative on the part of one individual is responded to by reciprocal directed behaviour are labelled as mutual interactions in the results to follow, and those which meet with no response, as failed interactive initiatives.

Provisional inter-observer reliabilities were calculated during the course of the pilot study in order to indicate particular weaknesses in the behaviour catalogue and coding procedure. Correlations of between .82 and .99 were obtained for distributions of behaviour items and percentage agreement of 67% for the coding of the interaction symbol by which interactive initiatives were identified.

RESULTS OF FREQUENCY ANALYSIS OF INFANTS' BEHAVIOUR

Significant differences were found in the separation (C) and reunion (D) episodes:-

Episode C

In the separation episode (C) several differences in the infants' behaviour arose. These are shewn in Fig. 1.

Looking at the first column - There was less looking at the stranger by all the abused children than was true of the control children.

Looking at the second column - It seems that the battered children were engaged in searching for the mother rather than in looking at the stranger, turning or gazing toward the door from which she left.

Looking at the third column - We find a sex linked reaction in that the male abused infants shewed more signs of physical discomfort, such as struggling and kicking than was found in the control male children.

Finally the last two columns - Shew lower levels of toy interest by the male abused infants. They neither looked at the toys nor manipulated the toys as much as was true for the control male infants.

We interpret these results to mean that the abused children, especially, but not uniquely the males, were more emotionally upset by the mother's departure than was true of their control counterparts and that this shewed itself directly in the type of reactions noted, including less participation with the stranger, and indirectly in depressing the play levels as shewn in the toy directed measures.

Episode D

These signs of emotional distress in the abused children as a group were sustained into the reunion episode, as shewn in Fig. 2.

Looking at the first column - We can see greater signs of distress in the abused children. In this catagory is included fretting, sobbing, puckering the face.

Looking at column two - There was less vocalisation by all the battered infants. This includes babbling and cooing as well as talking.

Looking at columns three and four - Again, as in the preceding episode, there was less interest in the toys on the part of the abused males with lower outputs of looking at, and manipulation of the toys.

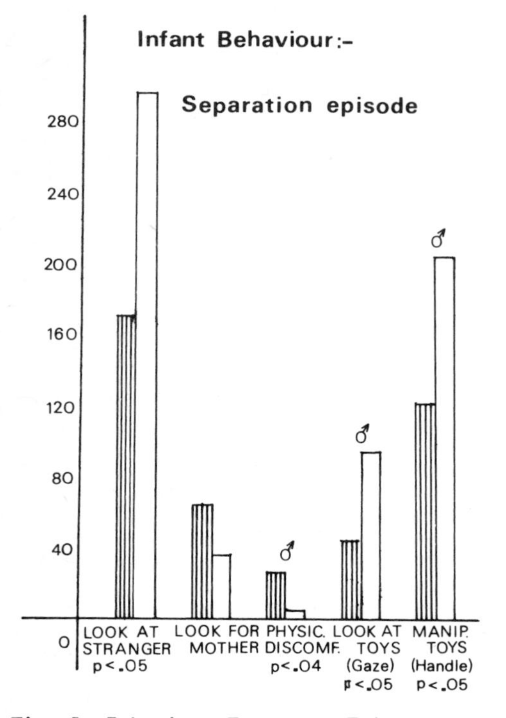

Fig. 1. Behaviour Frequency Episode C.

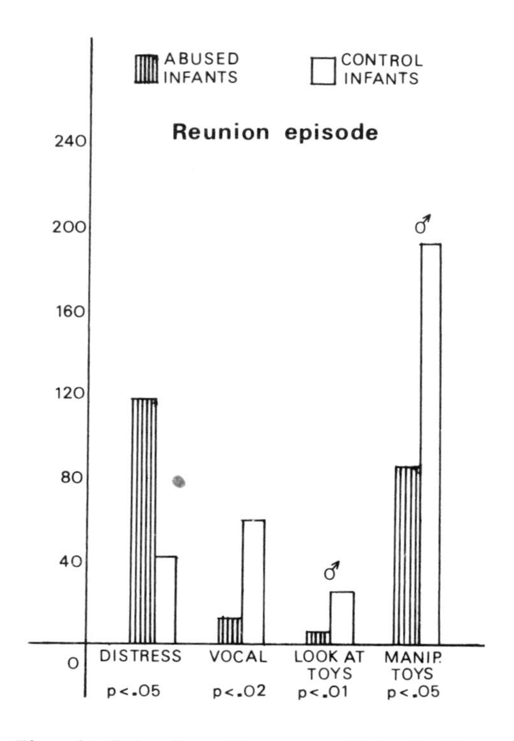

Fig. 2. Behaviour Frequency Episode D.

The distress aroused in the abused children by the mother's departure was therefore not allayed by her return, especially in the case of the male infants. Thus although in the low stress situation in which mother and child are alone together the abused and control infants shewed similar patterns of behaviour, the introduction of the stranger and the departure of the mother potentiated different types of response in the two groups of children.

RESULTS OF FREQUENCY ANALYSIS OF MOTHERS' BEHAVIOURS

Turning to an examination of the mothers' behaviours, few differences were found in episodes C and D. However, in episode A an interesting contrast was found between control and and abusive mothers.

While the abusive mothers shewed disproportionately more visual behaviours directed toward their infants, the control mothers visually explored the room and manipulated the toys more as is shewn in Fig. 3. This was especially pronounced for the mothers of female infants.

We conclude from these results that the control mothers were less anxiously preoccupied with their infants than the experimental mothers.

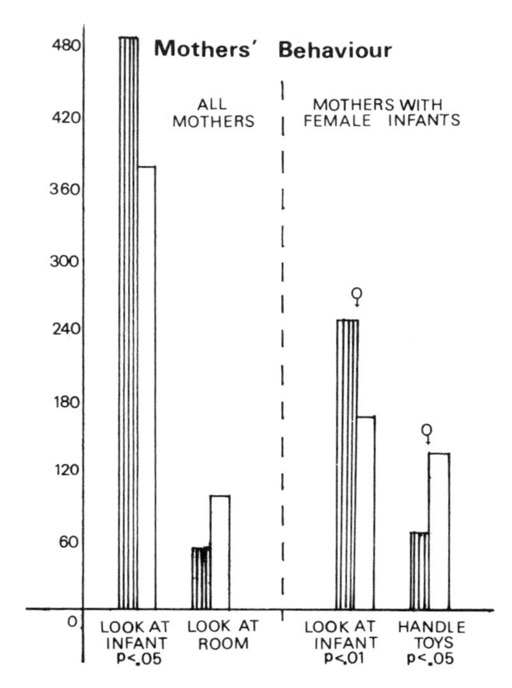

Fig. 3. Behaviour Frequency Episode A.

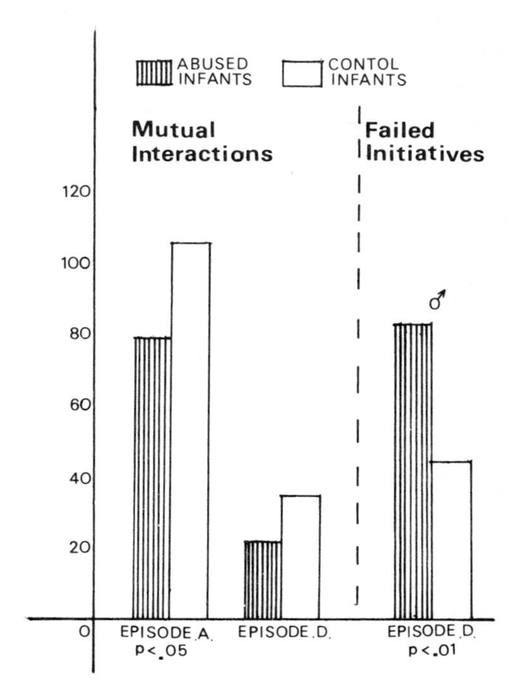

Fig. 4. Mother-Infant Interactions.

RESULTS OF INTERACTION ANALYSES

None of the infants' response patterns to the mothers' initiatives shewed any differences between the abused and normal children. Differences in the mothers' interactive behaviours are of two types:-

1. Mothers' responses to infants' initiatives (mutual interactions)
2. Mothers' failed interactive initiatives in which behaviours are directed at the infant but a response is not forthcoming.

Fig. 4 shews that the abusive mothers shewed fewer of the first mutual type of interaction with their infants both in the initial episode A in which mother and infant are alone in the strange room together and in the final reunion episode D. They also shewed more failed interactive initiatives in the reunion episode than the control mothers. This is however, primarily due to the mothers of male infants for whom in fact this difference is the significant one.

Thus these interaction analyses suggest that the disturbances in infant behaviour shewn in the separation and reunion episodes form part of a broader pattern of disturbance which involves the style of interaction between battering mother and infant, observable from the outset of the strange situation experiment. This we think, involves a more intrusive manner of relating to their infants by the abusive mothers of male infants, who appear to send out too much behavioural initiative for their infants effectively to respond to. In addition, the different style of the abusing mothers involves a generally less reciprocal manner of interaction throughout the experimental period by the abusive mothers as a whole. These important differences were not the result of the infants' being more disturbed. The correlation between distress behaviours in the infants and failed initiatives in the mothers in episode D was not significant for abused dyads, ($r = 0.35$ $p > .05$).

DISCUSSION

The results so far obtained in this ongoing observational study suggest that in the period of infancy and early childhood it is possible to detect differences in child, in maternal and in dyadic behaviour which differentiate abused from normal pairs.

Comparing our results with those of Ainsworth who originated the strange situation procedure, we are struck by the similarity between our abused infants and a small group of insecurely attached children on whom she reported and who she described as having been mothered in an inconsistent and insensitive fashion (Ainsworth, Bell & Stayton 1971).

The intrusiveness of our mothers' interactions is also very similar to the coerciveness reported by Burgess and Conger with an observational study of older abused children and their families (Burgess & Conger 1977). They too reported a lack of reciprocity in adult-child interactions.

We are now in the process of extending this work which is supported by a grant from the Department of Health & Social Services. The next step is to analyse an enlarged sample of video tapes and then to carry our observation into the home employing a graduate Health Visitor who will be specially trained for this work and will also be readily acceptable to workers in the field. Our aim is essentially a prophylactic one; that is, to refine a set of diagnostic behavioural signs which will alert workers to the risk of abuse before violence has arisen.

REFERENCES

Ainsworth, M., Bell, S. & Stayton, D. (1971). In Schaffer, R. (Ed.), Origin of Human Social Relations. Academic Press, London. 3-52.

Bene, E. & Anthony, J. (1957). The Family Relations Test. N.F.E.R.

Boyd, K. (1978). A Comparative Study of N.A.I. to Infants and Young Children in Surrey. Unpublished Dissertation, University of Surrey.

Burgess, R.L. & Conger, R.D. (1977). Family Interaction Patterns Related to Child Abuse & Neglect. Child Abuse & Neglect, 1, 2-4, 269.

Humphreys, P. (1973). Primate. Brunel University.

Hyman, C. & Mitchell, R. (1975). A Psychological Study of Child Battering. Health Visitor, 48, 8, 294-296.

Hyman, C. (1977). A Report on the Psychological Test Results of Battering Parents. Br. J. Soc. & Clin. Psychol., 16, (3).

Hyman, C. (1978a). Some Characteristics of Abusing Families Referred to the NSPCC. Br. J. Social Work, 8.2, 31-36.

Hyman, C. (1978b). Non-Accidental Injury. Health Visitor, 51.5, 168.

Lynch, M. & Roberts, J. (1977). Predicting Child Abuse. Child Abuse & Neglect, 1, 2-4, 491-2.

Martin, H. (1976). The Abused Child. Ballinger.

NSPCC Battered Child Research Team. (1976). At Risk. Routledge & Kegan Paul.

Steele, B.F. & Pollock, C.B. (1968). In Helfer, R.E. & Kempe, C.H. (Eds.), The Battered Child. University of Chicago Press.

Child Abuse and Neglect, Vol. 3, pp. 247 - 251.
Pergamon Press Ltd., 1979. Printed in Great Britain.

SOME FURTHER FINDINGS ON THE TREATMENT OF THE MOTHER-CHILD DYAD IN CHILD ABUSE

Esther Robison, Ph.D. and Frances Solomon*

INTRODUCTION

A follow up study of the first 60 patients to complete treatment in a residential treatment facility for child abusers and their children, which provides psychiatric services, social supports and client advocacy revealed an encouraging success rate (Fontana and Robison, *Pediatrics*, 1976). There was a diminution of abuse in about 60% of the cases; however, these results were interpreted with caution. Ancillary factors such as continued contact with the program and maturation of the participating children beyond age of highest risk may have been contributing to the positive outcome. Of greatest concern were observations of the interaction process between mother and child. Although patients had met criteria for discharge including the major criterion of no overt violent incidents, when they returned for aftercare visits patterns in the interaction process which augured poorly for non violent interchange were observed to persist.

Despite methods of re-education using paraprofessional role models, psychiatric intervention and didactic materials on parenting, "graduating" mothers were still typically exhibiting an insensitivity to the moods and signals of their children. This was often accompanied by high intensity demands for compliance with directives.

Recent research (Schaffer, 1977), has shown that *successful* cueing in is a crucial ingredient in the positive development of the mother child dyad, yet its absence appeared pervasive even in the "cured" abusers we observed. Closer scrutiny of the interaction process in the mother child dyad seemed warranted.

Systematic observational techniques to incoming patients were applied after 1976. From this vantage point, we were able to see even more dramatic examples of this lack of mutuality. For example, many incidents of unprovoked, highly insensitive handling of children were observed; these appeared almost at random: an obviously sleepy 9 month old would be tossed in the air playfully and break into shrieking howls; a toddler would be abruptly aroused from a nap and forced to stand up while being dressed for lunch; a mother wants a child to relinquish a toy, twists her arm to release it; a three year old must sit perfectly still while his mother braids his hair. Here it was noted that the child's cries of discomfort do not have the expected inhibiting effect on the mother's pursuit of her own goals. There is growing awareness of how early a mutually modulating feed back system of signals of mother-to-child and back develops (Stern, 1974; Brazelton, 1974). This synchronous pattern is deemed important for both cognitive and social development. But, beyond development of good rapport, findings suggest that there are surplus benefits in attunement to children's signals, specifically in the area of control. Bell and Ainsworth (1972) found that consistency and promptness of maternal response to infant

---

* Esther Robison is Program Consultant at the New York Foundling Hospital and a Research Fellow at Albert Einstein College of Medicine, New York. Frances Solomon is an Early Childhood Supervisor at the New York Foundling Hospital. The project discussed in this paper is part of the Temporary Shelter/I Care Programs of the Parent Child Development Center, New York Foundling Hospital, New York. The entire program is under the direction of Dr. Vincent J. Fontana.

crying was highly associated with a decline in frequency and duration of crying by the end of the baby's first year.

Stayton, Hogan and Ainsworth (1976) found that a one year old child whose mother had been accepting, cooperative and *sensitive* to *signals* in his infancy later obeyed her verbal commands and prohibitions more consistently than one whose mother had been rejecting, interfering and insensitive. This has particular relevance to abusers. In our observations of abusing mothers it appeared that so many of their strategies in handling (or mishandling) their children stemmed from fear of loss of control: confinement of the child, restraint of his/her movements, restriction of his space, physically forcing responses and rarely questioning the child's desires. It appeared as if acknowledging the reality of the child's existence as a *person* threatens their own existence--hence they must ignore him, overwhelm him or destroy him.

In 1977 an article appeared in *Social Work* (Jayaranthe) arguing against the proliferation of parent-training programs for abusing parents. The argument was based principally on the point that studies of child abuse fail to delineate how parenting styles of abusing parent differ from non-abusing parents and lead to abusive behavior.

Much of the criticism in the paper rested on the inconsistency in reports on *traits* of child abusers. Granted, it has been fairly well established, that no specific, personality trait useful for the screening and detection of potential child abusers exists (Gelles, 1973). Furthermore other investigators have shown that abusing parents do not expound parenting practices that are significantly different from those of non-abusing parents (Wolock and Horowitz, 1978). All evidence in these reports and findings is based on *clinical interviews* and responses to questionnaires. There has, however, not been any direct observational research on *styles of parenting among abusing parents.* Clinical intervention in parenting often fails not because of lack of "empirical data" since there appears to be no lack of that in the literature: what does appear to be missing is direct observational data of parent and child interaction. Only a detailed exploration of the actual patterns of interaction between mother and child will more clearly delineate a specific abuseogenic style. Observation of the interaction itself can yield information on the *conditions* which elicit abusive behavior and/or the factors which maintain abusive patterns. We therefore felt that an approach to treating mother-child interaction which addressed the specific patterns and deficits peculiar to abusers was essential. It was deemed particularly important for mothers of toddlers. The toddler stage is a period when the child's thrust for autonomy and his well-documented negativism are particularly difficult for these mothers to negotiate. The following outlines the program that grew from the above observation.

Triadic Approach: Model and Rationale

A mother and child are seen first in an initial session which is videotaped. To provide a frame work, three types of activities are made available, typically, a small motor task with a self contained goal such as stacking toys, nesting cups or puzzles; a large motor activity such as balls, darts, a slide, and objects for imaginative play such as dolls, wagon, etc. Other toys and books are also available from which the mother and child are free to select: These permit us to examine several dimensions of interaction. We see how well the mother deals with unstructured play, how she handles the child's movements toward physical independence, and what types of activities she is most comfortable with. The interaction is assessed from the following stand points: child's developmental level, mother's use of language, use of materials, the mother's availability to the child, repertoire of means of controlling the child, affect, eye contact, engagement with the child, and the age appropriateness of her demands. From these observations a prescription is developed for the mother-child interaction sessions which follow. A hierarchy of goals is developed and the means for approaching each of them through the techniques developed (to be described below).

Three months later the mother and child are taped again and any changes noted.

In attempting to develop reliable behavioral measures of change, it became clear that a two-fold measurement issue existed. Earlier, aspects of behavior were selected for scrutiny which we speculated were abuse connected. First, was the problem of specifying this behavior in a way that could be measured reliably. Secondly, even if we could specify, measure and alter behaviors in the direction desired we had to establish a connection between the original behavior and abuse.

A pilot study was designed to address the above issues.*

A comparison group of non-abusers from the sams SES background was videotaped. This group consisted of mothers and children who are part of another residential treatment program; these mothers are slightly younger in age; they average 18 years and are in treatment for reasons other than child abuse. The mothers in the comparison group were matched for race and age of child. They share with abusers in our sample a low socio-economic status, disorganized backgrounds involving foster care and institutional placement. They also report being maltreated by their parents but have not abused their children.

A third comparison group consisted of upper middle class non-abusing mothers serving as a contrast group.

This study is still in progress and results will be reported elsewhere; however, some preliminary analyses are of interest since the results point in the direction justifying our parent training effort. The primary finding was that there are real differences in some *routine patterns* of mother-child interactions indeed among abusing mothers, relative to non-abusing mothers, regardless of background and socioeconomic factors. While some deficits are class related (use of language), other correlate only with abuse. For example an abusing mother "looks at" (maintains her child in her perceptual sphere) on the average 30% of the time compared to 55% for comparison group mothers (77% for middle class mothers). Even when looking at her children abusers spend a lower proportion of that time actually attending to (focused attention) (25%) compared to 50% for the other two groups. If one is to accurately read signals it is apparent that one must look at the sender.

Secondly, the abusers also initiate actions at about twice the frequency of non-abusers. Abusers, however, respond only 1/10 as frequently as they initiate and about 1/3 as frequently as the other two groups. Thirdly, the content of their *verbal behavior* consists largely of orders and directions, which interestingly their children respond to with slightly lower frequencies than children in the other two groups, i.e., they don't "obey" orders and directions as much as non-abused children of either class.

One can speculate as to why this occurs, however, the major picture that emerges is of a dyad "out of sync." Non-obeying children vis a vis abusing mothers often spell trouble. Several questions arise: do demands escalate? Are only very high intensity commands or physical force effective in getting compliance? Is an abused child conditioned to react only to the most extreme constraints? Irrespective of the answers, an attempt to attune the mother to her child's behavior and make the mother feel in command by giving her a repertoire of interactive skills (other than violence) appears warranted.

Program Structure and Content

A mother, child, and teacher (the triad) meet for twenty minute sessions twice a week. The goal of the session is to "help" the mother better handle her child, and to promote his development.

Four areas are always kept in mind: the mother's:

1. feelings of inadequacy re: control of child
2. fear of loss of self-esteem in eyes of teacher and of child
3. competition with child for supplies, (teacher & materials)
4. lack of *resources* and *skills* in teaching the child constructively.

The teacher avoids the following:

1. vagueness: instructions and directions to the mother are simple in language and unelaborated
2. enthusiasm over "cuteness" or accomplishments of child
3. Passivity: letting mother take back seat; she must be actively engaged and she must be drawn into plans during transitions between activities. Also the rationale for change must be given for any activity.

Materials utilized are ordinary household materials (pots and pans) or commonly used toys (ball, blocks, dolls).

Work is done with duplicate materials so that mother and child each has access to the same item.

Initially, the emphasis is placed on getting the mother to *look at her* child and to accurately label what the child is signalling (these mothers often cannot tell that a smile means pleasure); it is crucial for her to have a capacity to recognize and label feelings. We have observed that very little physical movement occurs with the mother; many of them maintain a hovering stance over their young children as if in readiness to react instantly to any movement. Paradoxically, this hovering is usually coupled with a lack of eye contact and a lack of responsiveness to the child's gestures for involvement.

Next, (simultaneously to some extent) we expand her repertoire of responses through coaching and modeling.

To avoid rote imitation of the teachers actions (which are modeled) any technique is taught with an alternative i.e.--in handing a block to a child we can label for color or form; in bathing the baby we can label body parts or talk about what we will do next. This also encourages the mother to look to her child to signal a change in mood or interest and it automatically doubles the mother's repertoire of responses.

As mother and child share nursery school equipment the opportunity for the mother to experience these materials is offered. This is an advantage she has missed in her childhood; however, the mother's "executive" role is always acknowledged--encouraged vis a vis the child. The teacher plays the role of a knowledgeable facilitor. She helps the mother become a more effective teacher to her child while the focus of the task is the child.

We concentrate on the mother's use of *proximity* or *distance*. Our observations lead us to believe that proper postural distancing will often enhance proper psychological distancing from the child. Clumsiness and retarded motor development have been noted in these children. Thses symptons can derive as much from the mothers peculiar "pseudo-protective" stance (hovering over child, keeping him constrained on her lap, pinning his arms to his body while holding him) as from injuries incurred, or from congenital abnormalities. A child unacquainted with exploring his environment often can't differentiate between the potentially dangerous and non-dangerous. When this child is permitted freedom of mobility the mother has to be cued into potential safety hazards, since they often fail to be attentive to these.

We have isolated 24 basic interventive interactions; among them are modeling, coaching, confirming, encouraging, explaining, didactic information, corrective feedback, sharing enjoyment. Each occurs in specific contexts.

The pivotal approaches utilized are *coaching* and *modeling;* the mother and child start an activity while the teacher acts as an interpreter, rewarder and ally for the mother. The mother's receptivity is monitored and demands are escalated or de-escalated accordingly.

Didactic information or direct instruction (e.g. equivalent activities to be done at home) is conveyed when the child is absorbed in an activity. This can be done in a collegial manner. It also "trains" the mother to disengage from her child at the appropriate time (when he is involved in constructive play). Vigilance for the safety of the child is maintained during these exchanges.

Explanations take the form of simple interpretations of how a child learns, and how he makes demands at his presenting development stage. Explanations are usually offered only when the mother finds the child's behavior unacceptable.

Questions usually take the form of asking the mother "what does he seem to want," to reinforce her role as primary authority over her child and reinforce the importance of attending to the child's signals.

Discussion of general characteristics of the child are avoided. Discussion should relate only to behavior which is immediately observable and interpretable. If a mother wants to discuss an incident which occurred at another time, naturally it is not dismissed. But the central "work" of these sessions revolves around the present.

Sessions are ended with a strong assertion of the mother's authority. Her control over her child is reestablished with a new skill such as terminating his activity through distraction. She leaves feeling in charge and competent.

(Presentation of samples of Videotape sessions of pre, post and actual interventions)

Conclusion

No simple model or set of factors has yet been established which can fully account for the occurrence of child abuse. The perspective and approach offered here appears to be one which holds forth some promise of contributing to a diminution of violence perpetrated against children by their primary caretakers.

The intervention addresses the evidenced lack of reciprocity, and incapacity to "tune in" to a child's cues of abusing mothers. This pattern creates a highly volatile situation, exacerbated by the mother's inability to terminate undesirable behavior by the child other than by extreme means.

An absence of expected restraints in face of the child's cries of distress has led to the conclusion that these inhibitors may be developed by humanizing the child for the mother and enhancing her competence to achieve her desired effectiveness without injury to the child.

Questions relating to selection and training of teachers to provide this intervention in a home setting are currently being considered.

Bibliography

Ainsworth, M. D. S. and S. M. Bell, Infant Crying and Maternal Responsiveness, *Child Development;* 1972, Vol. 43, 1171-1190.

Brazelton, T. B., B. Koslowski and M. Main, "The Origins of Reciprocity: The Early Mother-Infant Interaction" In Lewis and Rosenblum, *The Effect of the Infant on the Caregiver,* New York: Wiley, 1974.

Gelles, R. Child Abuse as Psychopathology: A Sociological Critique and reformulation, *American Journal of Orthopsychiatry,* 43, 611 (1973).

Jayaranthe, S. "Child Abusers as Parents and Children: A Review", *Social Work,* Jan., Vol 22, 1: 5-9, 1977.

Schaffer, R. *Mothering.* series: The Developing Child, Jerome Bruner, e.d., Harvard University Press, 1977.

Stayton, D., R. Hogan and M. Ainsworth, "Infant Obedience and Maternal Behavior: The Origins of Socialization Reconsidered," *Child Development,* 1971, Vol.42, 1057-1069.

Stern, D. N. "Mother and Infant at Play: The Dyadic Interaction Involving facial, vocal and gaze behaviors." In M. Lewis and L. A. Rosenblum, eds, *The Effects of the Infant on It's Caregiver,* New York: Wiley, 1974.

Wolock, Isabel and Bernard Horowitz, presenters on panel: The Demography of Child Abuse: Implications for Policy and Program, 1978 National Conference on Child Abuse and Neglect, New York City,.

---

*The authors wish to thank Gene Mundee, R. N., for assistance in data gathering.

Child Abuse and Neglect, Vol. 3, pp. 253 - 257.
Pergamon Press Ltd., 1979. Printed in Great Britain.

LE PLACEMENT FAMILIAL, MODE DE PROTECTION DE NOURRISSONS DE MERE PSYCHOTIQUE

Docteur Myriam David
Centre Familial d'Action Thérapeutique, Soisy-sur-Seine, France

La relation précoce entre une mère activement psychotique et son nourrisson peut mettre l'enfant en danger. Notre propos est de rappeler la nature des risques encourus par l'enfant et de discuter de l'intérêt du placement familial précoce et des conditions nécessaires pour en faire une mesure de protection et de traitement.

I - Le placement familial d'un nourrisson de mère psychotique se présente toujours comme une urgence lorsque plus ou moins inopinément sa mère le met en danger au cours d'une bouffée délirante, ou encore, lorsque l'équipe soignante qui soigne la mère et le nourrisson découvre qu'elle malmène l'enfant, refuse de le soigner sans supporter de voir une autre personne s'en occuper.

L'intolérance de la mère à l'égard de l'enfant se manifeste le plus souvent au cours des premières semaines de vie de l'enfant, ou encore à divers moments qui correspondent à la progression de l'enfant dans le processus d'individuation autour de 8 mois à 1 an, de 18 mois à 2 ans, ou encore à la fin du congé maternité.

Il faut noter qu'il s'agit toujours de mère isolée, célibataire ou divorcée. La conception de l'enfant s'est faite dans des situations aléatoires pour donner satisfaction au désir caché ou manifeste de maternité de la jeune femme, parfois à la suite du retrait et placement d'un autre enfant. Dans la plupart des cas une interruption de grossesse a été discutée et refusée par la mère. Souvent aussi l'abandon a été envisagé à la naissance par la mère, ou/et par l'équipe soignante, puis repoussée.

On comprend mieux aujourd'hui la nature de l'impasse dans laquelle se trouvent ces malades qui, comme le montre bien Odette Masson (1) cherchent confusément et inconsciemment à travers leur grossesse à échapper à leur relation symbiotique à leur propre mère, et, qui vont osciller en elle-même entre le désir de se faire remplacer par l'enfant pour échapper à son emprise, et la compulsion de renouer avec lui le même lien fusionnel. Le contact avec le nourrisson, à certains moments critiques de son développement, peut alors susciter chez la mère un assaut pulsionnel se traduisant par des mouvements simultanés, aussi violents l'un que l'autre, de captation et de rejet si bien que l'on voit la mère dans un acting de rapprochement serrer à l'étouffer son nourrisson ; ou encore, en faire un objet délirant de persécution, la mettant elle en danger et qu'elle tient à distance sans soins ni alimentation, ou en qui elle voit son "mauvais moi" qu'il faut punir, voire détruire et qu'elle secoue dangereusement.

Cette maternité tant désirée a pris une forme et force intolérable, exposant la mère délirante et son enfant aux angoisses archaïques de dévoration, morcellement, anéantissement mutuels.

La mère peut alors mettre la vie de l'enfant en danger. Mais il faut remarquer aussi que ces mères s'arrangent inconsciemment pour ameuter l'entourage et que la démonstration de leurs violences est probablement une forme de demande de retrait de l'enfant, vis-à-vis duquel d'ailleurs, elles offrent peu de résistance.

Madame X. pousse des cris en tenant son enfant dans le vide par la fenêtre ; Madame Y. enfermée à clé, laisse le sien dans un cabinet noir sans le nourrir et fait elle-même la morte sur son lit jusqu'à ce que sa voisine inquiète appelle au secours.

Une fois la séparation consommée, la mère reste parfois longtemps sans parler de son bébé. Lorsqu'elle est rétablie elle nie ou ne garde pas de souvenirs de sa violence, fait plutôt état d'une entente idéale entre elle et l'enfant. C'est alors que va se manifester son désir de revoir l'enfant et de le reprendre.

II - Il est possible maintenant d'examiner les dangers de diverses natures qui guettent l'enfant : les uns sont en rapport direct avec la maladie de sa mère, il s'y ajoute ceux propres à tout placement lorsque celui-ci devient nécessaire, ces risques étant encore accrus ici par la fragilité éventuelle de ces enfants conçus de façon hasardeuse, exposés pendant la vie intra-utérine aux médications et troubles de leur mère, puis à une relation maternelle pathogène après leur naissance.

1°) Risques en rapport avec la pathologie de la mère

Si comme on l'a vu, l'alerte donnée par la mère évite habituellement le danger de mort pour l'enfant, il n'en reste pas moins vrai qu'il est redoutable pour le nourrisson d'avoir été exposé à cette violence, à ces mouvements de captation et de rejet, tout comme il est dangereux pour l'intégrité de sa santé mentale d'être traité par elle en objet, exclusivement en fonction de ses projections à elle, de ne pas être vu par elle en tant que sujet et de ne pas recevoir d'elle de réponse adéquate à ses manifestations et initiatives propres et à l'ensemble de ses besoins.

Il existe une abondante littérature sur les mères schizophrènes et psychotiques, des travaux moins nombreux sur l'avenir de leurs enfants, (Réf. 1-2-3), mais rien à notre connaissance concernant le développement premier de ces nourrissons et leurs réactions propres envers leur mère malade. Dans le cadre de l'Unité de Soins Spécialisés à domicile et à l'occasion de rencontres entre le nourrisson et sa mère en placement familial, nous sommes témoins des réactions et troubles de ces enfants dont nous donnerons quelques exemples.

Parmi les enfants qui tant bien que mal se sont maintenus dans leur famille beaucoup d'entre eux montrent des signes de fragilité physique, une riche symptomatologie psychosomatique (troubles digestifs, infections répétées des voies respiratoires supérieures). Celles-ci sont d'autant plus florissantes, lorsqu'en l'absence d'aide, les soins maternels peuvent prendre un caractère aberrant retentissant aussi sur le développement général. Les poussées fébriles peuvent alors provoquer des hospitalisations courtes mais à caractère répétitif. Les enfants sont rapidement améliorés par les soins hospitaliers et vivement repris par les parents qui ne supportent pas l'hospitalisation, mais ils sont aussi vite réhospitalisés par eux comme si c'était là un moyen de répondre à leurs mouvements internes de captation et de rejet. L'enfant vit alors dans un état de discontinuité telle qu'il ne peut élaborer ni investir aucune relation. C'est dans ce genre de contexte que l'on observe des arrêts de développement dûs aux soins inadéquats compliqués par les effets de ces hospitalisations répétées. "Claude avant son placement à l'âge de 15 mois avait déjà été hospitalisé 12 fois pour des périodes de 8 à 15 jours et jamais dans le même service. Il se présentait comme un enfant vide, inaffectif, inexpressif et silencieux, gravement anorexique, son développement somatique et psychomoteur étant à peine de 5 à 6 mois. Il bénéficia alors, mais bien tard, d'un traitement en Placement Familial Spécialisé.

L'observation directe des interactions entre certaines mères et leur enfant psychotique nous ont permis aussi de constater comment certains d'entre eux évitent le contact, font le vide en eux, fuient dans le sommeil ou à l'inverse exercent une vigilance excessive au point de s'endormir difficilement.

"Julie dans les bras de sa mère se tortille, s'écarte quand elle veut l'embrasser, fuit le regard de sa mère qui la cherche, mais la regarde et se manifeste à elle quand celle-ci l'ignore".

"Cécile, placée depuis quelques mois ne supporte pas les visites. Lorsque au cours de ces rencontres, sa mère prend possession d'elle sans ménagement, la manipule sans tenir compte de sa peur manifeste ou de son état de sommeil, Cécile, 3-4 mois, devient livide, son regard se vide de toute vie, elle se fait molle comme une poupée de chiffon, est prostrée et perd la possibilité de se maintenir. Dès la visite terminée elle tombe dans un sommeil profond dont elle sort dès qu'elle se retrouve dans les bras de sa nourrice. Un strabisme apparaît".

Notons aussi que tous ces enfants présentent des difficultés persistantes à se séparer de leur mère ou de leur nourrice et une angoisse très aigue à l'égard des étrangers.

C'est peut-être le lieu ici d'attirer l'attention sur le fait que les troubles de ces enfants sont rarement reconnus et signalés alors que des observations systématiques de nourrissons de mère malade mentale permettraient de déceler des manifestations de souffrance du nourrisson sans attendre que ne se constituent ces situations d'urgence nécessitant une mesure rapide de séparation et avant que ne se constituent des troubles structurés de la personnalité. Il serait possible alors d'intervenir précocément par une aide à domicile qui pourrait éviter parfois l'aggravation de l'état de la mère et le placement ou qui, en tout état de cause, permettrait de préparer celui-ci en évitant qu'il se fasse en urgence si le maintien à domicile s'avèrait impossible.

2°) Risques en rapport avec le Placement

Nous voulons rappeler ici que le placement d'un nourrisson comporte toujours de grands risques, mais pour le nourrisson de mère psychotique, en raison même de sa vulnérabilité liée à ce passé court mais hautement pathogène, le placement peut être plus redoutable encore pour l'avenir de son développement que les avatars de sa relation avec sa mère psychotique, à moins que ce placement ne lui apporte les garanties de stabilité et de sécurité.

Nous ne rappellerons pas ici les risques des placements mais insisterons seulement sur deux points : les carences affectives liées à l'instabilité des placements, le danger de la coupure du lien avec sa mère à moins qu'il ne soit adoptable et adopté rapidement.

a - La stabilité du placement est une nécessité absolue et il est ridicule de séparer un bébé de sa mère si le service auquel il est confié, par son organisation, sa surcharge et son manque de personnel, n'assure pas d'emblée cette stabilité et fait vivre à ce nourrisson une série de changements qui le font passer de foyer d'accueil en hôpital et en pouponnière avant d'aller de nourrice en nourrice. Or sauf exception, tel est le sort commun de ces enfants. Dans ces conditions le nourrisson fragile est assuré d'aller rejoindre la cohorte lamentable et nombreuse des enfants victimes de carences affectives précoces. Tout à la fois débile, psychotique et psychopathe il reproduira pour ses enfants, s'il parvient à l'âge adulte, les situations de traumatismes et de carences dont il ou elle a été victime.

b - L'adoption serait une solution idéale pour un nourrisson lorsque sa mère accepte de l'abandonner, ce qui est impossible pour une mère psychotique ou si l'on estime que la gravité et la chronicité de son état ne lui laisse aucune chance d'être la mère effective de son bébé. Bien des facteurs s'opposent à l'adoption : la peur de l'hérédité, le souci de préserver les droits de la mère, ne dut-elle jamais être capable d'en faire usage, celui de garantir aussi le droit des parents adoptifs à avoir un enfant "sans risques", l'emportent pour le moment sur la nécessité de donner priorité au seul intérêt de l'enfant.

Si bien qu'en France il n'est guère possible à un nourrisson de mère malade mentale d'être adopté. C'est là un grave préjudice sur lequel Anna Freud, Goldstein et Solnit (4) ont à juste titre beaucoup insisté.

Dans ces conditions, il est indispensable de maintenir le nourrisson en contact avec sa mère et que des liens étroits existent entre le service qui soigne la mère et celui qui surveille son enfant. En l'absence de telle mesure, l'enfant risque d'être confronté soudainement avec une mère inconnue qui vient tout naturellement le récupérer après une absence de plusieurs mois ou années, lorsque son état s'est amélioré et qu'elle tente de recréer un foyer. La rupture avec une famille où à grand peine il s'est créé une sécurité, la rencontre avec une mère inconnue ne peuvent être qu'un drame pour l'enfant qui peut réagir par la terreur, l'opposition et un état dépressif anxieux, un drame pour la mère dont toute l'angoisse sera réveillée par celle de l'enfant qui risque alors d'être maltraité puis,replacé sans qu'il ait grande chance de retrouver sa nourrice parce que d'une part sa mère l'aura prise en grippe et que de toute façon un autre enfant lui aura été confié.

III - Il est possible maintenant de préciser quelles sont les indications du placement et comment apporter à l'enfant les garanties de sécurité, de stabilité, de soins affectueux nécessaires et indispensables à son développement normal et au traitement des troubles qu'il a déjà contractés éventuellement.

Le placement familial de l'enfant doit être réservé aux enfants envers lesquels il n'a pas été possible par des soins adéquats de protéger mère et enfant de cette dangerosité de la pathologie maternelle.

Il est presque inévitable, lorsque comme c'est souvent le cas, la mère est isolée ; ou encore si l'enfant est amené à vivre avec elle chez ses propres parents, l'enfant risquant de devenir l'objet de l'enjeu de la relation symbiotique qui préexiste et demeure entre sa mère et sa grand-mère maternelle.

Il est indiqué également lorsque le père, du fait de sa pathologie et de celle du couple ne peut jouer le rôle de médiation et que l'anarchie des soins alliée aux mouvements alternés de captation et de rejet entraînent des hospitalisations répétées ou une errance de l'enfant.

Le but du placement familial est de protéger l'enfant de la dangerosité de sa mère, tout en tentant de réaménager cette relation "impossible" pour en faire à long terme une relation "possible". Nous espérons de cette façon trouver un moyen terme entre l'intérêt de l'enfant et celui de sa mère à qui le retrait de l'enfant est nuisible alors que son maintien dans certains cas peut contribuer à sa guérison (réf. 5).

Au début de ce périple, le retrait total de l'enfant, comme mesure provisoire, doit être compris comme une mise à distance maxima nécessaire dans ces états extrêmes de dangérosité où mère et enfant ne peuvent que se renvoyer en miroir leurs angoisses mutuelles.

Les visites organisées selon un plan, accordé à l'évolution de la mère et de l'enfant, leur offrent des possibilités progressives de rapprochement et sont la clef de voûte du traitement. Elles ont intérêt à être pratiquées par deux co-équipiers, d'accord entre eux pour que l'un assiste plutôt l'enfant, l'autre plutôt la mère, en se proposant comme but commun d'abord de permettre à mère et enfant de simplement co-exister, puis de rendre possible et faciliter la communication entre eux, chacun restant très proche des mouvements que celui-ci suit chez l'enfant, celui-là chez la mère.

Ces visites sont si pénibles au début qu'on y sursoirait volontiers si on ne s'y trouvait engagé par l'équipe soignante de la mère. Cette difficulté explique en partie au moins la fréquente impossibilité de communication entre les équipes "adulte" et "enfant". C'est là un premier obstacle à surmonter.

Au début, et cela dure parfois bien longtemps, la mère ne peut être que rigide et glacée devant cet enfant qui toujours la repousse, la fuit et réagit par des cris à ses tentatives de le prendre, tentatives qui ont un caractère impulsif, maladroit et inquiétant. Les témoins que nous sommes sont envahis par l'angoisse qui sue de toute part. Aussi la visite se termine vite, mais chacun découvre ensuite qu'on y a survécu. C'est sans doute ainsi qu'au fil des semaines et des mois, voire des années, les choses changent insensiblement, les fantasmes angoissants cédant le pas au testing de la réalité. L'enfant feint moins d'ignorer la présence de sa mère, il s'y intéresse de loin du regard, refusant encore tout rapprochement. La mère se défend un peu de le prendre, à la place tente de lui donner un jouet, une friandise, il les refuse puis les prend et se sauve jusqu'au jour où comme Viviane, âgée de 2 ans ½ et séparée à l'âge de 6 semaines, il peut s'instaurer un jeu entre eux. "C'est au cours d'un jeu de dinette où sa mère lui donne des pastilles de chocolat que Viviane ravie découvre la similitude de couleur entre sa main, celle de sa mère et le chocolat ; Viviane dévisage sa mère et semble découvrir ce jour là qu'elle est sa mère. La fois suivante elle reproduit ce jeu, mais est toute animée, saute de joie, fait le pitre pour faire rire sa mère et se retrouve dans ses bras où elle se laisse aller tendrement. Madame pleure en la câlinant doucement".

Que les visites aient lieu au Centre, à l'hôpital ou au domicile de la nourrice , avec ou sans elle , à un rythme rapproché ou distant , que l'enfant soit laissé seul ou non avec sa mère , qu'il sorte ou non avec elle , qu'il y passe un week-end comme vient de le faire Patrick (âgé de 7 ans, séparé à 18 mois) pour la première fois avec un vif plaisir partagé par sa mère, telles sont les questions auxquelles il n'est possible de répondre qu'au jour le jour en fonction de l'état de la mère et des réactions de l'enfant.

On pouvait croire Viviane et sa mère prêtes à se rencontrer sans nous, or peu après cette visite qui a dû à nouveau ébranler la mère, celle-ci rechute et est hospitalisée six mois pendant lesquels elle préfère ne pas voir sa fille. Elle est maintenant sortie, a repris son travail et a revu sa fille. L'enfant a été plus vite que la mère, et c'est là un risque fréquent.

Tout ce travail n'est possible du point de vue de l'enfant que parce qu'il est soutenu tout au long par la stabilité de sa relation affectueuse avec sa famille d'accueil. Il faut bien réaliser que la bonne qualité et évolution de cette relation "ne va pas de soi" mais est soumise à de rudes épreuves que la famille d'accueil et l'enfant vont avoir à résoudre. Il n'est pas possible d'en faire ici l'exposé. Nous mentionnerons seulement deux points.

Le mouvement d'ensemble de ce travail est de permettre à l'enfant de vivre une relation engagée de type parentale en veillant tout particulièrement au processus "d'individuation" et de "sevrage progressif" en veillant à éviter que ne se reproduise entre la nourrice et l'enfant la relation symbiotique que celui-ci a eu avec sa mère. Or c'est notre expérience, que la fragilité de l'enfant, son état de nourrisson, son "malheur", sont des points d'appel apparemment très tenaillant. Une nourrice bonne, aimante et intuitive se laisse facilement aller à cet appel, plus facilement qu'avec ses propres enfants, comme si elle se permettait avec ce nourrisson qui n'est pas le sien de s'engager davantage que son mari et elle-même ne se le sont permis avec leurs propres enfants. C'est la responsabilité de l'équipe de l'aider à vivre cette relation sans s'y engouffrer avec l'enfant, et de remplir cette fonction de médiation de type "paternel".

Dans tous les cas de notre connaissance, la problématique des 8 à 15 mois est particulièrement difficile à vivre pour l'enfant et sa nourrice et se dénoue avec plus de difficultés et dans un temps plus long que la moyenne, sans aucun doute du fait de l'expérience antérieure de l'enfant, de son "vécu" de la situation présente et de ce que tout cela peut susciter en la nourrice.

C'est dans le cadre de cette relation, au fur et à mesure de son évolution et de la maturation de l'enfant, que se précise pour lui l'image de ses deux mères qu'il a à situer l'une par rapport à l'autre. Nous espérons pouvoir un jour en décrire les mouvements et étapes successifs ainsi que le travail à faire pour que cette épreuve puisse être plutôt maturante qu'invalidante pour l'enfant.

La relation de soutien et d'accompagnement offerte à l'enfant et à la famille d'accueil par le "responsable" chargé de suivre l'enfant dans son placement, les consultations thérapeutiques régulières, les groupes de familles d'accueil, les baby-club, sont autant de moyens intéressants à utiliser.

Il est trop tôt pour conclure : à ce jour les enfants se portent bien. Ils sont physiquement bien développés, leur développement psychomoteur et intellectuel est satisfaisant, ils apprennent tôt à utiliser le langage comme mode d'expression. A certains moments ces jeunes enfants nous paraissent pleinement épanouis, à d'autres moments les difficultés surgissent et posent des interrogations quant au mode de structuration de leur personnalité. Seule la poursuite de cette expérience, de leur vie et de notre aide nous dira s'il a été possible de trouver un compromis acceptable entre les besoins du nourrisson et ceux de sa mère et de déterminer la valeur de cette tentative de prévention et de traitement précoce.

(1) MASSON O. Casuistique d'enfants de mères schizophrènes. Evolution Psychiatrique N° 5 Tome XL fasc. 2 (1975).

Réflexions sur les possibilités d'approches thérapeutiques et préventives chez les enfants de mères schizophrènes. Revue de neuropsychiatrie infantile 24, 5 à 16 (1976).

(2) ANTHONY E.J. , A clinical evaluation of children with psychotic parents American J. Psychiatry 126, : 177--184 (1969).

The contagious subculture of psychoses. In Sagir, H.S. Kaplan Progress in group and family therapy. W Y Brunner et Mard pp 636-658 (1972).

(3) LANDAU R., HART H.P., OTHNAY N., SCHARFHERTZ C. The influence of the psychotic parents on their children's development American J. Psychiatry 129, 38-43 (1972).

(4) GOLDSTEIN J., FREUD A., SOLNIT A.J. Beyond the Best Interest of the child Free Press-London. Traduit en français E.S.F.

(5) RACAMIER P.C., SENS C. et CARRETIER. La mère et l'enfant dans les psychoses du post partum Evolution Psychiatrique 26 : 525-570 (1961).

Child Abuse and Neglect, Vol. 3, pp. 259 - 267.
Pergamon Press Ltd., 1979. Printed in Great Britain.

PREDICTIVE STUDY OF EARLY MOTHER-CHILD RELATIONSHIPS*

Jeanette Funke-Furber, M.Sc., Nurse, Researcher,
Royal Inland Hospital, Kamloops, B.C., Canada

ABSTRACT

In this project, reliable and valid instruments which indicate maternal adaptive behavior during pregnancy and early childrearing were created, tested and revised. A longitudinal examination of a variety of maternal infant variables was made through periodic measures from the 12th week of gestation to six months postpartum. The sample size consisted of 76 mother-child pairs. A reliable, valid and practical questionnaire was devised, which when used at 34-36 weeks gestation is predictive of maternal postnatal behavior.

KEY WORDS

Mothering, Maternal behavior, Psychosomatic Obstetrics, Pregnancy, Mother-Child Interaction, Infant behavior.

INTRODUCTION

The chief purpose of this research project was to create and test the reliability and validity of instruments which indicate maternal adaptive behavior during pregnancy and the early childrearing phase. These instruments could become vital assessment tools for those primary health workers whose goals are directed toward meeting the health needs of families. A secondary purpose of the study was to determine the inter-relationships between antenatal behaviors, postnatal behaviors and infant development. The results of the study indicate that certain aspects of the mothers prenatal behavior are significantly related to her postnatal behavior and her infants development.

A longitudinal examination of a variety of maternal and infant variables was made through periodic measurements (Table I). The complete experiment took place over a period of 18 months, with any one expectant mother and mother-child pair continuing as a sample subject for a period of 10-12 months. The study population (N=76) was obtained from one obstetricians' private clients. While this may have been a limitation of the study, it was noted that the sample was of varied socio-economic status and appeared to be similar to the generalized population of expectant couples in a large urban area. As stated, this study was designed to test the reliability and validity of indicators of maternal adaptive behavior. In an effort to minimize invalidity, a quasi-experimental design was instituted. (Campbell and Stanley, 1963.) A summary of measures taken in the study to establish the reliability and validity of indicators of maternal adaptive behavior is described in Appendix I.

*This project was supported by the Toronto Sick Children's Hospital Foundation and carried out at the Faculty of Nursing, University of Alberta, Edmonton, Canada.

TABLE I

Data Collection Schedule

		When Rated	Raters
Pregnancy			
$FMAP_I$	life history, adaptation to pregnancy	12-16 weeks	investigator nurse researcher
MAS Pitts	anxiety scale depression scale	12-16 weeks	self-administered
$FMAP_2$	adaptation to pregnancy	24-26 weeks	investigator nurse researcher
$FMAP_3$	adaptation to pregnancy	36-38 weeks	investigator
MAS Pitts	anxiety scale depression scale	36-38 weeks	self-administered
Labor/Delivery			
Hospital Experience Record	observation of labor, delivery	at delivery	various delivery room nurses
Postpartum			
Hospital Experience Record	observation of postpartum	during the 4 days p.p.	various staff nurses
$FMII_I$	observation of mother-infant interaction	4th day p.p.	investigator & other nurse observer
$FMII_2$ $FMII_3$ $FMII_4$	observation of mother-infant interaction	1 mon., 3 mon., 6 mon.	investigator & other nurse observer
Infant Evaluation			
Brazelton	Neonatal Behavior	72 hours	family physician
Griffiths, D.D.S.T.	Infant development	6 months	investigator & nurse observer

Organic and enviornmental variables which were held constant are: each subject had an established residence and reported to live with the father of the infant, not be under severe financial distress (as specified later) and live within the city's telephone exchange system. Variables which were not controlled but were recorded for retrospective analysis on each subject were: age, parity, ethnicity, socio-economic class, attendance at prenatal classes, husband's presence at labor and/or delivery, length and type of labor, analgesic medications and anesthetics during labor and delivery, sex of infant, Apgar of neonate at one minute and five minutes after delivery, type of feeding - bottle or breast, birth weight of infant, rooming-in experience, number of days in hospital, mother's return to employment, pregnancy, labor, and/or delivery complications, infant developmental deviations and Neonatal Assessment Score. (Brazelton, 1973.) Most of these variables relate to events that occurred between the periodic data collection from early pregnancy to six months post delivery. These events were systematically documented and became a fundamental part of the data collection procedure and analysis. Those subjects with complicated pregnancies, labors, deliveries and/or whose infants had developmental deviations, were removed from the primary analysis and a separate descriptive analysis was carried out.

ANALYSIS

Classification of Mothers

Having tested the reliability and validity of the revised instruments, the investigator proceeded on to answer those questions which were the guiding hypotheses in this study of maternal adaptive behavior. This process involved the examination of the interrelationships amongst the antenatal behavior, the postnatal behavior and infant behavior. The most important feature of this process was to assess the ability of the prenatal indicators in predicting the postnatal maladaptive and adaptive mothers. In order to assess the predictive value of the prenatal variables, it was first necessary to identify those postnatal mothers who were adaptive and those who were maladaptive. The procedure used was Wards (1963) method of clustering cases to determine optimum groupings among cases. In applying Wards (1963) method of grouping, the series of prenatal score profiles and postnatal score profiles for each N were used for the reduction process independently until eventually the entire population was reduced to four (4) and then two (2) distinct groups. The classification was done on the basis of each of the prenatal score profiles and postnatal score profiles. To investigate the characteristics of the postnatal group further discriminant analysis was carried out. Initially all sets of postnatal score profiles were analyzed. Through this proceedure twenty-one (21) of the thirty-six (36) indicators were identified that best discriminated between Group I (adaptive mothers) and Group 2 (maladaptive mothers).

Once having identified those indicators which provided satisfactory discrimination, prediction was calculated on the two Postnatal Groups, using all the Postnatal score profiles. The ability to accurately predict the maladaptive mothers was 100% while the ability to predict the adaptive mothers was 98.2%.

TABLE II

Variables Correlated with Postnatal Groups

	Group I Adaptive	Group II Maladaptive
1. Sedation During Labor		
No sedation	69.3%	29.7%
Heavy sedation	50.0%	50.0%
II. Rooming-In		
Yes	73.6%	26.4%
No	47.2%	52.8%
III. Breastfeeding		
Yes	72.6%	27.4%
No	40.7%	59.3%

A number of variables that were not controlled in the data collection were correlated with the two Postnatal Groups. This was done in an effort to understand the relationships between these extraneous variables and Postnatal maternal behavior. Firstly, wifes' age was correlated with the Postnatal Groups. It is interesting to observe that there were thirteen mothers under the age of twenty, and twelve of these mothers were in the maladaptive group, which indicates a significant relationship. Secondly, parity was correlated with the Postnatal Groups, while there were thirty-five (35) mothers who were Para 0, nineteen (19) were adaptive and fourteen (14) were maladaptive, thus indicating that parity did not appear to have an influence on the postnatal variables. In examining the amount of sedation received by the mothers during labor and delivery, there appears to be a definite difference between the two groups, in that of those mothers who had no sedation, 69.3% of them were adaptive mothers. In addition to this, amongst those mothers who received heavy sedation, there is no difference between the two groups. (See Table II). Amongst those mothers who had their baby Rooming-in with them during the four days postpartum, 73.6% were in the adaptive group and 26.4% were in the maladaptive group. Similar differences were apparent with those mothers who were breastfeeding.

In order to assess the effect of the infant's behavior on the mother, Brazelton (1973) scores were correlated with the two Postnatal Groups. There was no significant difference between the infant's state and interactive processes, and the adaptive/maladaptive groups.

In examining the indicators that best discriminate between the Postnatal Groups at 4 days postpartum, 1 month, 3 months and 6 months postpartum, some indicators show evidence of stability through these three time periods, while others are time dependent. The quality and amount of verbal stimulation, expression of affection and speed of response continued to be significant discriminators through to 6 months postpartum. It is believed that as the mothers progressed through the phases of early childrearing, the adaptive mothers became more sensitive and responded more quickly and appropriately to their infants, as illustrated in Table III.

TABLE III

Time Dependent Postnatal Indicators

Mother-Infant Interaction	4 Days P.P.	1 Month	3 Months	6 Months
Eye to Eye Contact			X	
Acceptance Rejection	X			X
Physical Closeness		X		
Speed of Response	X		X	X
Sensitivity		X	X	
Expression of Affection		X		X
Verbal Stimulation Amount	X	X	X	
Verbal Stimulation Type, Quality		X	X	X

The postnatal infant development indicators (Griffith, 1956), (Frankenburg and Dodds, 1971.) that best discriminated the adaptive mothers from the maladaptive mothers were the following infants' competence levels at six months of age: (i) personal-social, (ii) hearing and speech, and (iii) eye to hand coordination. It was anticipated that the mothers' quality of interaction and stimulation efforts would influence their infant's development, specifically in the three competencies which have been defined as the best indicators. Previous studies by Klaus et al (1975) have suggested similar findings, where mothers who were given extended early contact with their infants, subsequent testing of these infants at one year displayed advanced language scores.

Prediction from Prenatal to Postnatal

The next step was to analyze the relationships among the postnatal groups and the prenatal variables. To do this, the three trimester sets of prenatal score profiles were discriminantly analyzed. Thirteen (13) of the thirty-two (32) prenatal indicators were identified that could best discriminate between Postnatal Group I (adaptive mothers) and Postnatal Group 2 (maladaptive mothers).

In order to calculate the predictive value of these thirteen prenatal indicators, the discriminant function derived from these prenatal indicators was fitted to the Postnatal Groups and used to classify all subjects. The level of sensitivity and specificity derived from this analysis resulted in a 96% accurate prediction of the maladaptive mothers and a 89.1% accurate prediction of the adaptive mothers. These predictive values provided for a sound premise upon which one can infer that these thirteen (13) prenatal indicators are reliable in predicting postnatal maternal behavior.

Revised Predictive Questionnaire

The thirteen indicators deduced from the discriminant analyses cover the mothers problem with (i) her own relationship with parents and her parents childrearing practices, (ii) expectations related to adjusting to a new role, (iii) physical preparations for her infant and expressed need for help with her infant, (iv) high expectations for her infant, (v) denial of pregnancy and (vi) her inability to find pleasure with quickening and subsequent movements of the developing fetus. These six problem areas, as identified from the thirteen indicators have shown large differences between low and high risk mothers in the direction predicted in recent studies of early recognition of "at risk" mothers (Helfer et al 1976.). The single best item for predicting individual mothers to the adaptive or maladaptive postnatal group is an item from the third trimester questionnaire. This item measures the mothers' expectations of their infants appearance and behavior at 5-7 days of age. It was anticipated by the investigator that the maladaptive group would tend to express unrealistic expectations, in that they would have high expectations for their infant, with a felt need to regulate and control their infants actions and reactions. The data analyses does lend support to this inference, since 75% of the adaptive mothers and 18.8% of the maladaptive mothers had realistic expectations of their infants. Also important to note is that 62.5% of the maladaptive mothers and 19.6% of the adaptive mothers were vague in their expectations related to their infants behavior.

As an approach to designing an edited, reliable and valid yet practical and simplified Prenatal Questionnaire, which would be predictive of maternal behavior from prenatal to postnatal, a variety of alternative mothering ability equations were computed. The equations were computed by utilizing a multiple number of combinations of the thirteen prenatal indicators. Consideration was given to the number of data collections that would be necessary, since several of the prenatal indicators were time dependent, that is, maternal behaviors were anticipated to occur at a specific time in the pregnancy as a result of progress through developmental stages. The following formula was identified as having the best reliable and valid predictive value in the assessment of maternal behavior during pregnancy:

Predictive Maternal Ability (Pred. M.A.) = 3(Q5) + 2(Q4) + (Q3) +1(Q1) + 1(Q2)

Q1, Q2, Q3, etc; correspond to question 1, 2, 3, 4, and 5 in the Revised Questionnaire (Appendix (II)

The manner in which this formula (Pred. M.A.) measures the maternal behavior during pregnancy is illustrated in Table IV. A score of 8-20 indicates a highly maladaptive mother, in need of immediate intervention, a score of 35-40 indicates a highly adaptive mother, and scores of 21-30 indicate questionable "at risk" mothers, and further evaluation and assessment of this group would be necessary in an effort to intervene appropriately.

TABLE XVI

Pred. M.A. Scores Related to Prenatal Groups

	8-20	21-30	31-34	35-40
Adaptive	0	4	22	21
N = 47	0%	8.6%	46.8%	44.6%
Maladaptive	3	30	4	0
N = 37	8.1%	81%	10.9%	

The Pred M.A. has been developed into a practical assessment tool, and its usage requires an initial data collection visit at 34 to 36 weeks gestation. This assessment would then form the basis for further intervention and follow-up.

The Revised Questionnaire covers the following areas: 1) mothers expectations for her baby, 2) mothers perceived need for help upon discharge from hospital, 3) adjusting life style with the new role of parenting, 4) mothers own background and 5) denial of the pregnancy.

CONCLUSIONS

While there may be limitations to this study, emphasis must be given to the fact that the Revised Maternal Adaptation to Pregnancy Questionnaire appears to be capable of separating groups of mothers who are adaptive and maladaptive in terms of maternal behavior. The data strongly supports the authors conviction that clearly substantiate the need for systematic assessment during the prenatal period. The Revised Questionnaire when used as a screening device, will assist in the identification of those families who are in need of further evaluation, follow-up and intervention during pregnancy, parturition and postpartum.

REFERENCES

Brazelton, T.B. (1973). Neonatal Behavioral Assessment Scale. J.B. Lippincott, Philadelphia.

Campbell, D., J. Stanley (1963). Experimental and Quasi-experimental Designs for Research. Rand McNally College Publishing Co., Chicago.

Frankenburg and Dodds. (1972). Denver Developmental Screening Test Manual. W.K. Frankenburg, Denver, Colorado.

Griffith, R. (1956). Ability of Babies. Butterworths, London.

Helfer, Schneider, and Hoffmeister. (1976). "A predictive screening questionnaire for potential problems in mother-child interaction." In H. Kempe and R. Helfer (Eds.) Child Abuse and Neglect: The Family and the Community. Ballenger Publishing Co., Cambridge, Mass.

Klaus, M. et al. (1975). Mother to child speech at two years: effects of early postnatal contacts. Journal of Pediatrics, 86, 141-144.

Pitt, Brice. (1968). Atypical Depression following Childbirth. British Journal of Psychiatry, 114, 1325-1335.

Taylor, Janet. (1953). A personality scale of manifest anxiety. Journal of Abnormal and Social Psychology, 8, 285-290.

Wards, Joe. (1963). Hierarchial grouping to optimize an objective function. Journal of American Statistics Association, 58, 236-244.

APPENDIX I

Reliability and Validity Measures

Instrument	Reliability	Validity
FMAP Funke Maternal Adaptation During Pregnancy Questionnaire	-Pretest to correlate scores of 2 interviewers, if reliability level is less than .80 revision of instrument will be done. -Minimum test-retest reliability at .80 level.	-Content validation of items and categories by Panel of Reviewers (standard for agreement was at 75% level). -Instrument validity through the consistent use of structured open-ended questionnaire. -Internal validity obtained through correlation of levels from early experimental measures with later measures. -MAS Scores correlated with FMAP -Predictive validity, data from FMAP used as a prediction of future behavior (postnatal maternal behavior and infant development).
FMII Funke Mother-Infant Interaction assessment	-Pretest to correlate scores of 2 observers where reliability level is less than .80, revision of instrument was done. -Dual observer, minimum reliability at .80 level. -Correlated scores from Neonatal Assessment Scale with FMII.	-Content validation of items and weightings by Panel of Reviewers. -Instrument validity through the consistent use of a structured category rating scale. -Correlated scores from early experimental measures with later measures to check for constancy of scores. -Predictive validity data from FMII used as a prediction of infant development (Neonatal Behavioral Assessment, DDST, Griffiths Scales).
Neonatal Behavior Assessment Scale	-Trained tester's test-retest at a minimum reliability level of .80. -Published reports indicate reliabilities of independent testers at the same time as .85 to 1. (Brazelton, 1973). -Test-retest stability data indicate an item reliability of .783. (Brazelton, 1973).	
Griffiths Mental and Motor Performance Scale	-Published reports indicate reliabilities of independent testers at same time to be at .87 (Griffiths, 1956). Test was standardized on a total of 604 testings of 552 children.	

APPENDIX II

Revised Maternal Adaptation to Pregnancy Questionnaire

(To be used at 34 to 36 weeks gestation)

1. When did you first see a doctor about your pregnancy? Can you tell me why you chose to go at this particular time?

Score

______ 1. Saw doctor after third missed menstruation didn't realize was pregnant, thought the lack of menstruation maybe due to something else. Went to see the doctor to have this investigated.

______ 2. Saw doctor after 2nd or 3rd missed menstruation, went to see doctor because husband observed wife's irritablilty and/or went to have the I.U.D. checked.

______ 3. Vague about when visit to doctor was made, thinks she missed 2 menstruations, unplanned pregnancy, wanted to validate.

______ 4. Saw doctor about 1 week after 2nd missed menstruation, knew she was already pregnant, planned, wanted to validate.

______ 5. Saw a doctor about 1 week after first missed menstruation, wanted to have planned pregnancy validated.

2. As a child, was there someone in your immediate family that you see as a loving kind of person? Who was the most loving person in your family? Your mother, your father? What were your parents like?

Score

______ 1. Does not have anyone in family that she sees as a loving person; expresses dislike and negative feelings about early childhood, may have been in numerous foster homes. Parents very strict or very lenient.

______ 2. Defines problems in childhood; had separations from parents, definite problems, i.e. alcoholism. Parents inconsistent.

______ 3. Vague about family, unable to give definite ideas re "a loving person", ambivalent feelings expressed, unable to define characteristics.

______ 4. Describes relationship with a parent as being satisfactory, with warmth but wants the relationship with own child to be stronger.

______ 5. Mother or father seen as very positive, very warm person, expresses positive feelings.

3. What thoughts and ideas have you and your partner had on the changing of life styles, working hours, or other adjustments pertaining to this pregnancy and new baby?

Score

______ 1. Has thought about it, but feels no changes or adjustments are necessary, states that they feel this is important, not to change things for a baby.

______ 2. Hasn't thought about the adjustments and changes, wonders if there will be a need to change, questioning the possibility.

______ 3. Has had some thoughts about the changes, feels they want to wait to see what it will be like once the baby arrives, thinks that it's easier to do after the baby comes.

______ 4. Has already made a few changes, thinks that there will be a need for further changes, have spent time talking about it, have tentative plans.

______ 5. Have made changes to suit wife's needs for increased rest, have spent time thinking about the changes, have plans for help, baby sitter, relatives visiting, etc.

4. Do you think you will need help when you get home from the hospital? Have you made any plans for help, if so what are they?

Score

______ 2. No, do not want anyone interfering.

______ 4. No, feels can manage well by self.

______ 6. Ambivalent, don't know.

________ 8. No help available, has made definite plans on how to try to manage, or plan involves calling someone in case of emergency.

______ 10. Yes, has specific plans for husband or other person to be there for help.

5. Have you had any thoughts, ideas, hunches about your baby's appearance and behavior after you bring him/her home from the hospital?

Score

______ 2. Describes very unrealistic behavior such as regular sleeping, sleeping through the night or describes 3 or 4 negative aspects.

______ 4. Describes 1 - 2 negative aspects along with 2 - 3 fears re not knowing what to do or has no idea, gives it no thought.

______ 6. Unable to describe, only in vague terms, describes fears relating to baby's crying.

______ 8. Can describe a few aspects (1 - 2) of baby's behavior.

______ 10. Describes realistically baby's sleeping, feeding, crying behavior, has a few questions to have clarified.

Scoring:

Add scores from each question: 1.______

2.______

3.______

4.______

5.______

Total =______

Scores of 8-20 = very high risk, needing intervention

21-30 = questionable "at risk" needing further follow-up

31-33 = low risk

34-40 = no risk

Child Abuse and Neglect, Vol. 3, pp. 269 - 278.

0145-2134/79/0301-0269 $02.00/0.

PRELIMINARY RESULTS OF A PROSPECTIVE STUDY OF THE ANTECEDENTS OF CHILD ABUSE [1]

Byron Egeland

University of Minnesota, n548 Elliott Hall, Minneapolis, Minnesota 55455

An analysis of the existing child abuse literature suggests the presence of three broad quasi-independent factors: characteristics of the parents, environmental and sociological stress, and characteristics of the child. The majority of the investigations have focused on the contributory role of the parent. Results of this research have portrayed the abusive parent as a member of a multi-problem family whose deficits and liabilities encompass the entire spectrum of personal and social pathology (Parke and Collmer, 1976; Sameroff and Chandler, 1975). Specifically, research has attempted to show that abusive parents possess a unique constellation of personality traits or characteristics which presumably increase the likelihood that they will engage in abusive behavior. However, studies aiming to delineate personality characteristics of abusive parents have yielded no consistent findings, but instead have implicated a wide array of disparate, sometimes contradictory, traits (Gelles, 1973; Parke and Collmer, 1976; Spinetta and Rigler, 1972). Many authors also assert that abusing parents share some common misunderstanding with regard to the nature of child rearing and tend to look to the child for satisfaction of their own parental emotional needs. The personal histories of these parents include evidence that they were themselves abused, neglected, or emotionally deprived as children and consequently lack parenting skills and adequate understanding of appropriate child rearing practices (Smith and Hansen, 1975). In addition, it is argued that abusing parents lack knowledge of child rearing and have unrealistic expectations of normal child development (Smith and Hansen, 1975).

A number of investigators have also suggested that environmental and sociological stress factors impinging on the family are prepotent elicitors of child abuse (Justice and Justice, 1976). A basic tenet of this prospective is that hardship and stress create frustration which leads to aggression, often exhibited towards children, primarily because they do not pose a threat of retaliation. It follows from this assumption that populations exposed to the greatest amount of environmental stress would exhibit the greatest incidence of child abuse. This is particularly applicable to low socioeconomic status populations where people are faced with the problems of simply providing the basic necessities of life for their families. Families in general, and low socioeconomic families in particular, are subject to a variety of stresses that threaten the integrity of the individual members and the family functioning and interaction as a whole. Poverty, unemployment, poor and crowded living conditions, illness, death, desertion, social isolation, and marital conflict all serve to heighten frustration, increasing the possibility of aggressive outbursts (Egeland, Cicchetti, and Taraldson, 1976).

While research has suggested that in a large majority of the reported cases of child abuse the perpetrator was of low socioeconomic status, nonetheless there are studies which maintain that child abusers are made up of a cross-section of individuals of different socioeconomic status and education (Blumberg, 1976) and that social, economic, and demographic factors are irrelavant to the act of child beating (Steele and Pollack, 1968). Even though it may be true that child abusing families are experiencing a great deal of stress, it is clear that every family undergoing an equal amount of stress does not abuse their children. Since the majority of parents from lower socioeconomic backgrounds do not abuse their children, it is obvious that

1) This research was funded by a grant from the Administration for Children, Youth and Families, National Center for Child Abuse and Neglect, U.S. Dept. of Health, Education and Welfare

environmental stress alone is not a sufficient explanation for the occurrence of abuse.

Only recently has any consideration been given to the behavior of the child and how these behaviors may tend to elicit abuse or neglect from the parents. It is possible that the reason some parents abuse their children, while others displaying the same personality characteristics and inundated by the same stress do not, is that certain characteristics of the child may lead to some parents taking out their frustrations by abusing and neglecting the child. The child may be the major source of the parents' hostility and aggressiveness, not just the outlet for those already existing characteristics. Gelles (1973) and Parke and Collmer (1976) have suggested that certain traits, characteristics, or behaviors may render a child particularly unrewarding and difficult to care for or tolerate and therefore increase the probability of abuse. Terr (1970) found that many children in his sample were mentally retarded or hyperactive. Kemp (1971) found the adopted child, premature baby, and the precocious child to be high risk for abuse. Infant characteristics alone do not offer a viable etiology for child abuse since the majority of premature babies and children showing other problems are not abused. However, it would appear that the deviancies and caretaking behavior which characterize the parents of abused children can only be understood if the nature of the child's contribution to the disordered relationship is also taken into consideration. There is evidence in the child development literature which suggests that the child does affect the caretaker (cf. Lewis and Rosenblum, 1974).

From the diversity of findings of previous research in the area of child abuse, it is inevitable that any search for a single simple etiological factor is doomed to failure. Thus, it is imperative that we examine the interactions of the parents, environmental and sociological stress, and the child. All three factors occur within the context of the family in conjunction with each other, so that the effects and significance of any one must be explored with respect to its relationship with the other factors. One factor by itself may mean nothing, but in combination with specific others may create a particular malignant situation.

It should also be noted that the approach used in the vast majority of child abuse research is retrospective. Retrospective research attempts to identify factors that differentiate abusing from nonabusing parents after the abuse has occurred. As pointed out earlier, the conclusions drawn from such retrospective research are that environmental stress, poverty, and certain parental personality characteristics are among the causes of child abuse. A most important question remains unanswered: Why do some parents abuse or neglect their children while others, displaying the same personality characteristics or under the same stress, do not? We need to identify the precipitating factors that differentiate the family that abuses a child from the similar family that does not; an at-risk model of research is the best design for this task.

This investigation studies the interaction of a wide but carefully chosen set of variables in the lives of a group of high-risk mothers who are being followed throughout their children's first year of life. In the research reported here, characteristics of the mothers, infant temperament and the organization of neonatal behavior, environmental stress factors , and the interaction of the caretaker and infant are examined in an attempt to identify differences between mothers who mistreat their children and those who do not. It is hoped that by studying the relationship between mother and infant during the first year of life we can gain a better understanding of the causes of child abuse, neglect, and more mild forms of mistreatment for a high-risk sample. The following specific factors are looked at in terms of how well they differentiate a group of mothers who eventually mistreated their children from a group who provided adequate care: during the last trimester and three months after the baby is born, parental personality characteristics, anxiety, locus of control, and feelings, perceptions and expectations regarding pregnancy, delivery, and the baby are assessed; infant temperament is assessed at birth and 3 months; and mother-infant interaction are observed at three and six months of age. The results reported in this paper are preliminary in that only the data collected prenatally, at birth, and at three and six months are used in the analyses.

METHOD

Selection of the Sample

A sample of 275 primiparous women receiving prenatal care at the Maternal and Infant Care Clinics, Minneapolis Health Department, were enrolled in the investigation during the last trimester of pregnancy. The families are from lower socioeconomic backgrounds (the majority were on welfare), which for this investigation defines the at-risk nature of the sample. The base rate for abuse and neglect in the Public Health Clinic population is approximately 1 to 2%, which is considerably higher than for the state in general. Even though every attempt has been made to enroll fathers, only 29% agreed to participate. Sixty percent of the mothers were unwed at the time of delivery.

During the past 20 months, 26 infants have been identified as not receiving proper care in that the caretaker is to some extent irresponsible in managing the day-to-day childcare activities. While the problems are not as severe as those found in children referred to Child Protection (six from the total of 26 are or have been active Child Protection cases), there is reason to expect some adverse psychological impact on the child. According to the results obtained from the Child Care Rating Scale, the care these children receive is similar to the care received by the children from our sample who have been referred to Child Protection. At each visit to the mother's home, the Child Care Rating Scale, which involves ratings of any evidence of violence in the household, particularly toward the child, poor physical care, bad living conditions, neglect, and failure to thrive, is completed. Actual physical abuse was noted in five cases; failure to thrive in four (medically diagnosed), neglect and abuse in three cases, and severe neglect in 14 cases. The Child Care Rating Scale was filled out by the tester after each scheduled visit to the home. The items on the scale represent specific incidents of abuse or obvious examples of neglect and mistreatment which in no way overlapped with mother-infant interaction observed during feeding.

A group of 25 good mothers offering high-quality care to their children was identified, based on observations and results from the Child Care Rating Scales. These mothers all cared for their children well in terms of feeding, providing health care, protecting the child from possible dangerous situations in the home, not leaving the baby alone or with unknown babysitters, and in general caring for the child adequately. Comparisons were made on a number of variables between the group offering high-quality mothering and the group offering low-quality mothering.

Data Gathering Procedures

At approximately 36 weeks of pregnancy, a battery of tests was given to assess personality characteristics -- aggression, defendence, impulsivity, and succorance (Jackson, 1967), dependency and depression (Schaefer and Manheimer, 1960), anxiety (Cattell and Scheier, 1963), locus of control (Egeland, Hunt, and Hardt, 1970; Rotter, 1966), and parents' feelings and perceptions of pregnancy, delivery, and their expected child (Cohler, Weiss, and Grunebaum, 1970; Schaefer and Manheimer, 1960). Specifically, these latter tests measure such characteristics as fear for self and baby, lack of desire for pregnancy, appropriate vs. inappropriate control of child's aggression, encouragement of reciprocity, feelings of competence in meeting baby's needs, etc. The battery of tests given to the parents prenatally was administered again when the infant was three months old.

At birth and at three months an attempt was made to characterize the temperament of the infant using three different approaches: direct assessment of the neonate using the Brazelton Neonatal Assessment Scale (1973); naturalistic observation, for which nurses in the newborn nursery rated the child on such factors as irritability, activity level, soothability, etc., and maternal assessment of the infant at three months using the Carey Infant Temperament Questionnaire (1970). A detailed analysis of the three infant measures of temperament (Taraldson, Brunnquell, Deinard, and Egeland, 1977) showed that interrater reliability on the Nurse's Rating Scale and the Brazelton was very good. However, the stability of the baby's behavior across the four days in the newborn nursery was moderate, and the correlations of Brazelton scores from day seven to day ten were quite low. In order to improve reliability, the Brazelton scores used in the analyses consisted of a combination of scores obtained when the baby was in an optimal state.

At three and six months mother-infant interaction is observed in a feeding situation in the home, and at six months mother and infant are observed in play. Some of the behaviors observed include quality of verbalization, expressiveness, quality of physical contact, facility in caretaking, sensitivity, cooperation, responsiveness to baby's initiation of interactions, and positive and negative regard. Twenty-four different variables are rated, and the observations are recorded using a nine-point rating scale based on Ainsworth, Staton, and Bell's work (1969) and extensive pilot work (cf. Egeland, Taraldson, and Brunnquell, 1977). Interrater reliabilities for the 24 feeding variables were quite good, with high ratings on such items as quality of physical contact (.78); facility in caretaking (.84); and general sensitivity (.82). The range for 24 items was .43 to .86 and the Lawlis-Lu measure of interrater agreement for all items was highly significant.

RESULTS

One problem with using the at-risk approach in the area of child abuse is that the number of actual cases will not be large enough to study in any systematic fashion. The incidence figure typically quoted is approximately .09% (Nagi, 1976) and the figure reported for the Minneapolis Public Health population is 1-2%. This means that the projected occurrence of abuse in our sample of 275 would be five cases. Our findings of 26 abused, neglected, and mistreated children suggests that the incidence is considerably higher than the figures typically reported. It appears that by going into the home and getting to know the families, considerably more abuse and neglect is discovered than typically comes to the attention of local hospitals and other social agencies.

All of the 26 mothers in the inadequate group are receiving some sort of social service by way of a public health nurse, social worker, and six families are under child protection. Our first analysis was an attempt to determine if the severity of maltreatment differed between the six inadequate mothers under child protection compared to the 20 who were not. According to the results, there were no differences between the two groups on the number of items checked on The Child Care Rating Scale, nor were there any differences on the type of item checked (e.g. physical violence vs. inadequate living conditions). As the 20 children not under child protection get older, there is little doubt that an increasing number of them will be placed under child protection. The results reported in the remainder of the paper involve comparisons between the 25 good mothers and the total group of 26 inadequate mothers.

Demographic and Medical Characteristics

Data regarding demographic characteristics and social and medical histories of the good and inadequate mothers were obtained from the prenatal clinic and the hospital delivery files. To summarize the results which were reported in an earlier paper (Egeland and Brunnquell, in press), there were basically no differences between the two groups regarding the sex of the baby, prematurity (approximately 10% of the babies in each group were premature), infant abnormalities, Apgar scores at one and five minutes, gestational age, and type of delivery. However, pregnancy complications were reported for 45% of the good mothers and 58% of the inadequate mothers, and delivery complications for 45% and 68% of the good and inadequate mothers, respectively. (These differences only approached significance, $p < .10$).

Perhaps the most significant factor distinguishing the two groups is the mother's age. The mean ages at delivery were 24.5 years for the good mothers and 19.3 years for the inadequate mothers. The difference is certainly related to mothers' differing abilities in preparing for and meeting the demands of pregnancy, delivery, and childrearing. The factors which do seem to distinguish between the two groups of mothers fall into two general categories: first, environmental support for the mother, and second, general education and specific preparation for the baby by the mother. General support is seen in the striking difference in marital status between the two groups. Only 32% of the good mothers were single at the time of delivery, while 74% of the inadequate mothers were single ($x^2 = 15.10$, $p < .009$). Supportiveness of the alleged father and the mother's family was reported to be 75% and 100%, respectively, for the good mothers and only 37% and 45% for the inadequate group. Interestingly the reported supportiveness of the mother's friends was approximately the same for the two groups, which suggests that friends, in many instances, do not provide significant and adequate support to the mother, particularly in the absence of more stable support from a partner or family member.

There are striking differences in education and preparation for caring for the baby. One-hundred percent of the good mothers have completed at least 12 years in school, compared to only 30% of the irresponsible mothers. Given this finding, it is not surprising that large differences in specific preparation for the baby exist. For example, 100% of the good mothers attended child birth classes whereas 30% of the inadequate mothers attended.

Discriminant Analyses

Given the large amount of data collected on the mother-infant pairs, the most appropriate way to contrast the two groups is through the technique of discriminant function analysis. The actual program used was the Discriminant from the Statistical Package for the Social Scientist (Tatsuoka, 1971). This technique, similar to regression, obtains the optimal prediction of predetermined group membership (criterion groups) using a given set of variables. In this case, the good and inadequate groups were criterion groups, and the various sets of test scores and observations data were used to estimate how well that set of variables differentiates the two preselected groups. The results are reported in terms of percentage correct classification. Since the sample size for the two groups of mothers was relatively small, it was not possible to use the separate test scores or observation ratings in the discriminant function analysis. Instead, factor scores derived from each of the factors reported in Table 1 were used. These factor scores are based on separate factor analyses of the 17 pre- and postnatal parent measures, the 27 Brazelton items, 17 nurses' ratings; and the 24 feeding ratings for the entire sample of 275 mothers and infants. The factors resulting from the principle axes factors analysis (varimax rotations) are presented in Table 1.

The results from the first set of discriminant function analyses were used to determine to what extent certain infant characteristics influence the quality of care he or she receives. Using the ratings done by nurses during the child's stay in the nursery after delivery, an overall correct classification rate of 60.8% was found ($p < .13$). Using the Brazelton Neonatal Inventory, the correct classification rose to 70.5% ($p < .007$), with most errors resulting from predicting that babies would fall into the good mother group when actually they were in the inadequate group. Factor I, Orientation, and Factor II, Irritability, contributed most to the prediction. These findings suggest that the infant plays only a moderate role in causing his or her own mistreatment.

Regarding the question of the relationship between the pattern of mother-infant interaction and later quality of care, the results clearly indicate that deviant patterns of interaction observed in a feeding situation at three and six months and in a play situation at six months were highly predictive of maltreatment and neglect later on. The prediction based on the three-month feeding observation achieved an overall correct classification rate of 81.8% ($p < .0001$). Factors I (mother's caretaking skill), II (mother's affect towards baby), and III (baby's social behavior) all contribute to the predictions, with Factor I by far the most important. The discriminant analysis using six-month feeding and play observation resulted in a higher correct classification rate and when the three-month mother personality and child care scores were added to six-month mother-infant observations, the percent of mothers correctly classified rose to 95.8%. Only one mother in each group was incorrectly classified.

Based on the personality testing of the mothers in their 36th week of pregnancy, the correct classification rate was 84.0% ($p < .0001$) with Mother Factor III, which measures the mother's ability to deal with the psychological complexity of childrearing, contributing by far the largest portion of the prediction. The good mothers had a better understanding of the psychological complexity of childrearing, that is, they seemed to be more aware of the difficulties and demands involved in being a parent and to be able to accept in an appropriate manner the ambivalent feelings which accompany healthy mothering. Factors I and IV, which focus primarily on aspects of mother's personality such as aggression and impulsivity, contribute little to predicting group membership.

The same tests repeated at three months after delivery yielded a 79.5% correct classification ($p < .0001$). While the factor structure of this set of tests differs slightly from that of the prenatal testing, the psychological complexity factor again clearly emerges as the largest contributor to the prediction and the second most important predictor was Factor V, Low Desire for Motherhood.

In an attempt to maximize correct prediction of group membership, nine variables were selected from the data presented above. Due to sample size limitation, nine was the maximum number of variables which could be included in the analysis. These variables were selected on the basis of: a) the amount of variance accounted for by each factor in its own data set, or b) rational expectation of relation to prediction of group membership. The variables selected were Brazelton I, II, and V, Mother's Prenatal I, II, and III, and three-month feeding with a direct discriminant function analysis. A set-wise solution using Wilks Lambda as criterion entered the variables in the following order: three-month feeding I and II; Brazelton I;

Feeding III; Mother Prenatal III; Brazelton II; Mother Prenatal I and II; Brazelton V. This solution also achieved an 85% final correct classification rate.

Cluster Analysis

This analysis seeks to statistically define groups or clusters within the 51 mother-child pairs used for the discriminant function analysis. In other words, are there subgroups of mothers which display different personality characteristics or interaction patterns? If so, are the subgroups related to the severity or type of maltreatment and do they represent different etiological patterns? The cluster analysis, which has as its goal identifying groups of subjects more similar to each other than to other subjects within the same general group, was performed using the same measures as described above and the 51 mothers in the good and inadequate groups. The statistical process (Dixon, 1975) begins by "clustering" the two cases with the shortest distance between them; these cases are then amalgamated and treated as one case, then joined with the other clusters (which may be individual cases or actual clusters of two or more cases); this continues until all cases are joined into one cluster. The distance calculation is done by a sum of squares procedure using the square root of sums of squares as a distance measure; the amalgamation is a weighted average of values where the weight is the number of cases in a cluster (Dixon, 1975).

To carry out this procedure the set of 51 mothers was reduced to 29 on whom a complete set of prenatal, neonatal, and postnatal measurements had been made. These included 14 good mothers and 15 inadequate mothers. In order to have a sufficient, though minimal, number of subjects per variable for this analysis, the set of variables was reduced to six. All of these had been used in the discriminant analysis, and were chosen on a rational basis as most likely to provide an adequate clustering. The variables are factor scores as in the discriminant analyses and consist of: three month Feeding Factors I, II, and III, Brazelton Factor I, Nurses Factor II, and Mother's Prenatal Factor III.

From the results of the cluster analysis four subgroups emerge. Most striking is the first large subgroup, A ,which includes thirteen of the 29 cases in the analysis. This sub-cluster includes all of the good mothers except one and none of the inadequate mothers. Among the remaining 15 cases, three groups clearly emerge, all of which contain mothers from the inadequate group (Subgroup B, N = 6; Subgroup C, N = 5; Subgroup D, N = 4). The results are extremely interesting in that the subgroups formed by the clustering procedure clearly break down into a subgroup comprising the good mothers and three subgroups comprising the inadequate mothers. The fact that the groups clustered in this way indicates that the psychological and observational factors used here are a major contributor to group differentiation. The measures used account for the formation of meaningful groups rather than random effects or observer-related error variance. The fact that three subgroups of mothers from the inadequate group clustered indicates that there are three distinct patterns of mother-infant characteristics which certainly supports the notion of multiple etiologies.

A most interesting examination of this clustered data involves looking at the subgroups within the inadequate mothers group to discover characteristics which may indicate differences between groups and similarity within groups. This was done in two ways, first by comparing the clusters to a rational grouping according to reported severity of the problem. This comparison for the 15 inadequate mothers used in the cluster analysis indicates that there is little relation between the clusters here and the severity of the abuse and neglect known to our investigators. Secondly, a look at the case histories of the mothers in the different subgroups of inadequate mothers, does yield interesting differences.

The information about each of the sub-clusters is taken from the observers' notes on conditions and events in the homes on the various visits made to each mother-child pair. There seemed to be an equal frequency of comments regarding the unsanitary conditions in all three subgroups. The sub-clusters also seemed similar in regard to generally rough handling or generally ignoring the child. One notable difference was the frequency of other people caring for the child much of the time in sub-clusters C and D but not for those in sub-cluster B. This seems to be related to a larger number of mothers in sub-clusters C and D who are teenagers and who are described as lacking skill in caring for their child and managing their own lives. On the other hand, reports of physical violence by boyfriend or husband to the mother occurred in 5 of 6 cases in sub-cluster B but not at all in sub-clusters C and D. This was accompanied by frequent change of residence in 4 of 6 cases in sub-cluster B but again not at all in sub-clusters C and D.

The results based on the cluster analyses are tentative and difficult to interpret at the present time. However, by running additional cluster analyses with different combinations of life stress, interactional, parental, and child variables and by using more of a descriptive case study approach in attempting to characterize the mother-infant pairs in each cluster; there is no doubt that we will be better able to understand the complex phenomena of child abuse and neglect. The results presented here suggest that the prospective, multivariate approach offers appropriate methodology and statistical techniques for the study of child abuse and neglect.

DISCUSSION

This investigation represents a first attempt at differentiating good from inadequate mothers based on data collected before any specific abuse or neglect has occurred. Before discussing the results and their implications, it should be pointed out that the findings reported in this paper are preliminary. By including data collected at nine and 12 months and beyond, the relative importance of certain prenatal, birth, and three-month variables for predicting group membership may change significantly. It is also the case that the good and inadequate mothers groups are changing. As more information becomes available additional mothers will be added to the two groups and in some cases mothers already in the groups will be removed.

Separate discriminant function analyses were performed using the mother, infant, and mother-infant interaction variables in an attempt to differentiate between the good and inadequate mother groups. The two measures based primarily on assessment of the infants were least effective in differentiation when used alone. It seems that the condition of the baby cannot in itself predict abuse or neglect within a mother-child pair, although the trends indicate that baby variables are involved. The importance of baby's behavior in determining the quality of care he/she receives is noted in the results of the discriminant analysis involving the combination of mother, infant and interaction variables when it was found that Brazelton Factor I, baby's orientation is the third best predictor of group membership.

There are three additional aspects of the results that will be discussed in some detail: the failure to find personality differences between the two groups of mothers; the importance of the interactional data; and the significance of the mother's understanding of the psychological complexity of the infant and her relationship with the infant.

Basically, the two groups of mothers did not differ on the personality measures. The Impulsive/Anxious and the Hostile/Suspicious factors did not differentiate the two groups which suggests that anxiety and the traits of aggression, impulsivity, and suspiciousness are not predictive of the quality of care the mother provides. These results support the notion that there is no particular abusing personality. The implications for treatment suggest that a psychiatric approach which has as its goal the modification of basic personality traits is not the most effective intervention strategy. Helping a hostile, anxious, or suspicious mother gain insight and understanding of these behaviors will probably have little effect on how she relates to her child. The generalizability of the conclusion that personality variables are relatively unimportant as an etiology of child abuse may only apply to a young, relatively uneducated, lower socioeconomic sample similar to the mothers in this investigation. It is quite possible that the psychiatric model is appropriate for abusers with different educational and socioeconomic backgrounds.

One characteristic the inadequate mothers have in common is that they misunderstand their child and the nature of child rearing. The inadequate mothers obtained lower scores on the psychological complexity factor which is based on three scales from Cohler, Weiss, and Grunebaum's (1970) Maternal Attitude Scale. The three scales measure: the appropriateness of the mother's attitude toward the child's aggression; the appropriateness of her attitude toward encouraging reciprocity, and her appropriate acceptance of the ambivalent feelings that of necessity accompany pregnancy and mothering. On the prenatal testing these three elements are accompanied by a higher than average score (for our sample) on a vocabulary test, indicating that intellectual ability is related to these three scales. This seems to be a factor related more to interpersonal understanding and empathy than to a broad personality style. Mothers scoring high on this test are more aware of the difficulties and demands involved in being a parent and are able to accept in an appropriate manner the ambivalent feelings which accompany healthy mothering. They are able to see themselves as autonomous and separate from their infants, but, on the other hand, they recognize the need to provide an environment that supports the development of a strong attachment between mother and infant. Some of the inadequate mothers seem to have difficulty maintaining their own identity or autonomy within this close mother-infant relationship while others were frightened of or did not see the need for promoting this close emotional tie. These findings suggest that intervention must focus on the mother child relationship, particularly the mother's feelings about various aspects of this relationship and her understanding of the need to promote a secure attachment. She must also recognize that as the child gets older she must encourage separation and individuation. This can only be done in an atmosphere where the mother feels a close emotional tie to the child but yet can function as a separate, autonomous person.

The importance of an adequate reciprocal relationship between mother and infant is most clearly seen in the results of the feeding and play observations. In the step-wise discriminant function analysis using the nine selected variables, the feeding observation factors, mother's caretaking skills and mother's affective behavior were the first two variables entered, that is, those which contributed most to the prediction of group membership.

In the feeding and play situations, the inadequate mothers were less sensitive to the child's cues and signals. They were more apt to interfere with baby's activities and were less likely to "cooperate" with the baby during feeding. These mothers paid little attention to baby's needs and activities, and during feeding they would often interrupt the baby's ongoing activity rather than gearing feeding in both timing and quality to the baby's state, mood, and interests. For many of the inadequate mothers, feeding was something they did to their infants, and it was done in a highly mechanical way, which precluded any reciprocal interaction. The babies would attempt to engage the mothers in social interaction, but generally the inadequate mothers were either insensitive to the baby's social cues or chose not to respond to them.

It should be pointed out that these analyses and the conclusions are an initial attempt at relating certain factors to good and poor outcomes with a high-risk sample. The results are preliminary and there is a need for further analyses and replication. Applied to another sample the results may be quite different. However, the degree of significance in differentiating the good and inadequte mother groups based on the interaction and psychological variables indicates that a powerful effect is being tapped.

REFERENCES

Ainsworth, M., Staton, M., and Bell, S. Some contemporary patterns of mother-infant interaction in the feeding situation. In J.A. Ambrose, Ed., Stimulation in Early Infancy, Academic Press, London (1969).

Blumberg, M.L. Psychopathology of the abusing parent, Amer. J. of Psychotherapy 28, 21-29 (1974).

Brazelton, T.B. (1973) Neonatal Behavioral Assessment Scale, J.B. Lippincott, Philadelphia.

Carey, W. A simplified method for measuring temperament, J. of Pediatrics 70, 188-194 (1970)

Cattell, R.B. and Scheier, I.H. (1963) Handbook for the IPAT Anxiety Scale, Second Edition, Inst. of Personality and Ability Testing, Champaign, Illinois.

Cohler, B., Weiss, J., and Grunebaum, H. Childcare attitudes and emotional disturbance among mothers of young children, Genetic Psychological Monograph 82, 3-47 (1970).

Dixon, W.J. (1975) BMDP: Biomedical Computer Programs, U. of California Press, Berkeley.

Egeland, B. and Brunnquell, D. An at-risk approach to the study of child abuse: some preliminary findings, J. American Academy of Child Psychiatry, in press.

Egeland, B., Cicchetti, D., and Taraldson, B. Child abuse: a family affair, Proceedings of the N.P. Masse Research Seminar on Child Abuse, 28-52 (1976) Paper presented April 26, 1976, Paris, France.

Egeland, B., Hunt, D., and Hardt, D. College enrollment of upward-bound students as a function of attitudes and motivation, J. of Ed. Psychology 61, 375-379 (1970).

Egeland, B., Taraldson, B., and Brunnquell, D. Observation of Waiting Room and Feeding Situation: Technical Report, U. of Minnesota, Minneapolis (1977).

Gelles, R.J. Child abuse as psychopathology: a sociological critique and reformulation, American J. of Orthopsychiatry 43, 611-621 (1973).

Jackson, D.N. (1967) Personality Research Form Manual, Research Psychologists Press, N.Y.

Justice, B. and Justice, R. (1976) The Abusing Family, Human Sciences Press, N.Y.

Kempe, C.H. Pediatric implications of the battered baby syndrome, Archives of Disease in Childhood 46, 28-37 (1971).

Lewis, M. and Rosenblum, L.A. (1974) The Effect of the Infant on its Caregiver, Wiley, N.Y.

Nagi, S.Z. Child abuse and neglect programs: a national overview, Children Today 4, 13-17 (1975).

Parke, R.D. and Collmer, C.W. Child abuse: an interdisciplinary analysis, In. E.M. Hetherington, Ed., Review of Child Development Research 5, 509-590, University of Chicago Press, Chicago (1976).

Rotter, J.B. Generalized expectancies for internal versus external control of reinforcement, Psychological Monographs ,80 (1966).

Sameroff, A.J. and Chandler, M.J. Reproductive risk and the continuum of caretaking casualty, In F.D. Horowitz, E.M. Hetherington, S. Scarr-Salapatek, and G.M. Siegel, Eds., Review of Child Development Research 4, 187-244, U. of Chicago Press, Chicago (1975).

Schaefer, M.S. and Manheimer, H. Dimensions of perinatal adjustment. Paper presented to Eastern Psychological Assocation, New York (1960).

Smith, S.M. and Hansen, R. Interpersonal relationships and child-rearing practices in 214 parents of battered children, Brit. J. of Psychiatry 127, 513-525 (1975).

Spinetta, J.J. and Rigler, D. The child-abusing parent: a psychological review, Psychological Bulletin 77, 296-304 (1972).

Steele, B.F. and Pollock, C.B. A psychiatric study of parents who abuse infants and small children, In R.B. Helfer and C.H. Kempe, Eds., The Battered Child, 103-147, U. of Chicago Press, Chicago (1968).

Taraldson, B., Brunnquell, D., Deinard, A., and Egeland, B. Psychometric and theoretical credibility of three measures of infant temperament, Society for Research in Child Development, New Orleans, Louisiana (1977).

Tatsuoka, M. (1971) Multivariate Analyses, Wiley, N.Y.

Terr, L. A family study of child abuse, American J. of Psychiatry 127, 665-671 (1970).

TABLE 1 Factors Resulting from Factor Analyses of Mother, Infant, and Mother-Infant Interaction Variables

Mother's Prenatal Testing

Factors	
I	Impulsive/Anxious
II	Negative Reactions to Pregnancy
III	Psychological Complexity
IV	Hostile/Suspicious

Brazelton

Factors	
I	Orientation
II	Irritability
III	Motor Maturity
IV	Physical Ability/Body Tonus
V	Consolability

Three-Month Feeding Interaction

Factors	
I	Mother's Caretaking Skills
II	Mother's Affective Behavior
III	Baby's Social Behavior
IV	Muscle Tone/Cuddling

Six-Month Play Interaction

Factors	
I	Mother's Support and Cooperation
II	Baby's Activity and Coordination
III	Amount of Reciprocal Play
IV	Baby's Satisfaction

Nurses' Ratings

Factors	
I	Baby's Alertness/Activity
II	Mother's Interest
III	Baby's Contentment
IV	Ease of Care for Baby

Mother's Three-Month Testing

Factors	
I	Hostile/Suspicious
II	Negative Reactions to Pregnancy
III	Psychological Complexity
IV	Impulsive/Anxious
V	Low Desire for Motherhood
VI	Dependence

Six-Month Feeding Interaction

Factors	
I	Mother's Caretaking Skills
II	Mother's Affective Behavior
III	Baby's Social Behavior

Child Abuse and Neglect, Vol. 3, pp. 279 - 283.
Pergamon Press Ltd., 1979. Printed in Great Britain.

PARENT-INFANT RELATIONSHIP AFTER IMMEDIATE POST-PARTUM CONTACT

Peter de Chateau

Departments of Pediatrics and Child Psychiatry, University Hospital,

S-901 85 Umeå, Sweden

During the last decades maternal and infant morbidity and mortality have been reduced to a very low level. Hospital personal has been focused upon providing a high quality of physical care, both for the mother and her infant, but little active interest has been directed towards the importance of the neonatal period for the development of the unique mother-father-infant relationship. Many routines in our neonatal and maternity wards, such as separation, restricted visiting hours for fathers and siblings etc., were introduced to prevent infections and to improve treatment of the newborn, and while the adverse influences on parent-infant relationship were recognized, many parents today are still not allowed to touch, hold and care for their newborn premature or sick infants. If the period immediately following delivery is a particularly sensitive or critical one many changes in our day-to-day care and hospital practices have to be made to ensure that mother and infant remain together during that period. To counteract the possible negative influences of hospital routines on the developing family relation we designed a study of enrichement of the immediate post-partum period.

MATERIAL

The basic condition for participation in the study was that mothers and infants should be healthy and live in the Umeå area, and that pregnancy and delivery should have been normal. Other criteria that all mother-infant pairs had to meet were: first pregnancy, no history of previous abortions or miscarriages, no use of drugs except iron-medication and vitamins during pregnancy, normal weight gain, normal blood-pressure and Hb-percentage and no protein-uria. The mother had to have come into labour spontaneously at full-term. All infants had to have been born in vertex presentation and to have had no signs of intra- or extra-uterine asphyxia. There had to have been no signs or symptoms of congenital malformation or disease at physical examination 1 day and 6 days post partum. The midwives made a preliminary selection of the mothers to study when they arrived at the hospital for delivery. At this point mothers and midwives were not familiar with each other. This preliminary selection was thus solely based on existing data concerning previous obstetric history, present pregnancy and residence within the Umeå area. By this procedure 50 mother-infant dyads were selected for the study. Eight mother-infant pairs who did not fulfil the established criteria concerning residence, delivery, infant and neonatal period were excluded. The final study group thus comprised 42 mother-infant pairs. After delivery the mothers were randomly assigned to one of two groups:

1. P + group (N=22): Primiparous women, given extra contact with their newborn infants.
2. P group (N=20): Primiparous women, given routine care with their newborn infants.

In routine care the infant is after delivery shown to the mother for a brief glance and thereafter taken away to another part of the delivery room for weighing, bathing, physical examination, Credé prophylaxis and dressing. Approximately 30 minutes later the infant is, fully dressed, put in a crib beside the mother's bed. Two hours after the actual time of birth the mother and infant are transferred to the maternity ward.

In extra contact the infant is put onto the mother's abdomen a few minutes after birth. A little wile later the midwife moves the baby upwards onto the mother's abdomen and helps him to suckle from the breast. This extra skin-to-skin and suckling contact lasts for about 15 minutes during the first hour following delivery. After this period the normal routine procedure as described above is continued. During the rest of the stay at the maternity ward both groups are cared for in the same way (1,2).

METHODS

A. At 36 hours after delivery a direct observation of maternal and infant behaviour during breastfeeding was made by means of a time-sampling technique (1,2).

B. Three months after delivery, during a home-visit, direct observation of mother-infant free-play and a personal interview with the mothers was carried out (1,3).

C. At one year post-partum a new follow study was made, including: observation of mother and infant behaviour during a physical examination of the infant, an interview with the mother, the Gesell Development Test, the C.M.P.S. and the Vineland Scale. Mothers also kept a diary of the childrens sleep and food habits and the duration of breastfeeding was checked.

RESULTS

A. The results of the observation at 36 hours have been published in detail elsewhere (1,2). Fig. 1 summarizes the most important differences between the two groups: significantly more holding, encompassing and looking en face in the P + group.

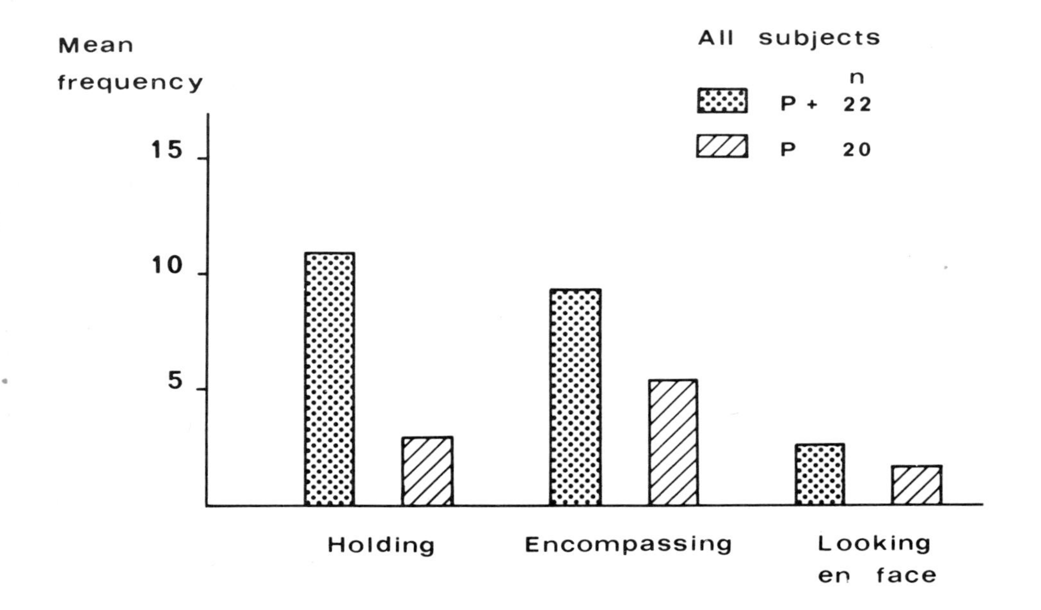

Fig. 1. Maternal behaviour 36 hours after delivery. P+ = extra contact; P = routine care

B. At three months significant differences in maternal and infant behaviour were found : mothers in the extra contact group spent more time kissing and looking en face at their infants; these infants smiled more often and cried less frequently (Fig. 2). A greater proportion of the mothers with extra contact was fully breastfeeding (3).

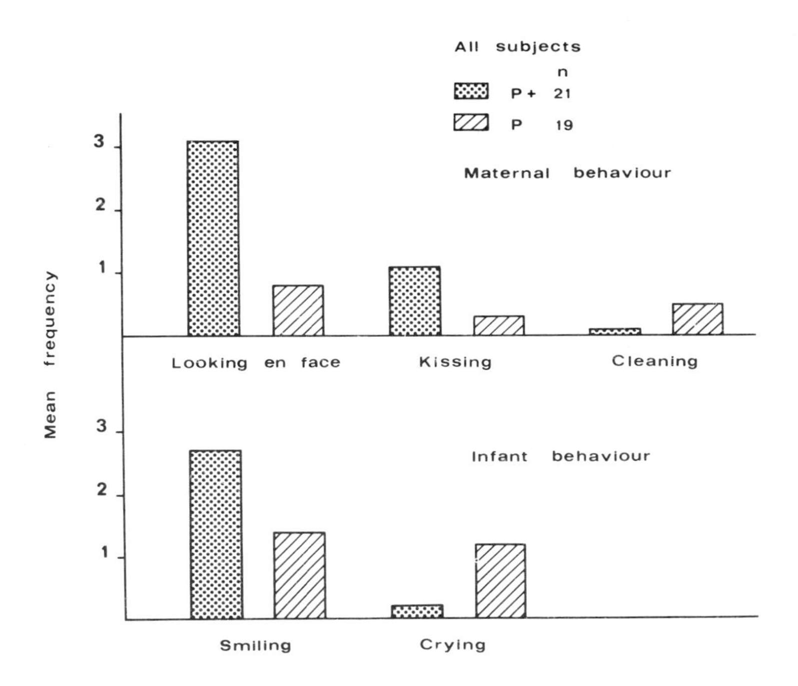

Fig. 2. Maternal and infant behaviour at 3 months. P+ = extra contact; P = routine care.

C. Mothers with extra contact were holding their infants, during observation at one year, with close body contact for a longer proportion of the total observation time. They also used a more positive and comforting language and caressed and touched, not related to caregiving, their children more frequently (Table 1).

TABLE 1 Maternal behaviour at one year

MATERNAL BEHAVIOUR	MEAN FREQUENCIES	
	P +	P
BODY-CONTACT	6.8	4.6
TALKS POSITIVELY	3.0	1.8
TOUCHING	2.1	0.8

The personal interview revealed a number of significant differences between the two groups. Mothers with extra contact had returned to their professional employement to a lesser extent, their consorts were less engaged in the daily care of the infants. More infants in the P+ group slept in a room of their own, fewer P+ mothers had started bladder training of these infants. (Table 2).

TABLE 2 Some results of the interview at one year

MOTHER AT HOME:	P + > P
SLEEPS IN OWN ROOM:	P + > P
BLADDER TRAINING:	P + < P
FATHER ENGAGED:	P + < P

In all five parts of the Gesell Developmental Test infants with extra contact after delivery (P+) were ahead of those in the control group (P). The main differences were found in gross motor and liguistic development. (Table 3).

TABLE 3 Results of the Gesell Developmental Test at one year

	P +	P
	WEEKS	WEEKS
GROSS MOTOR	+ 5.6	+ 2.4
FINE MOTOR	+ 2.4	+ 1.3
ADAPTIVE	+ 0.3	+ 0.2
LINGUISTIC	+ 0.2	- 2.4
SOCIAL	- 1.1	- 2.5
TOTAL	+ 7.4	- 1.1

weeks +(-) = mean number of weeks ahead (behind) in development in relation to biological age.

The C.M.P.S., the Vinland Scale and mother's diaries did not show any major differences between the two groups. Details of these parts of the study will be published elsewhere (4). Mothers with extra contact did breastfeed their infants for 175 days, as opposed to the mean duration for control mothers of 108 days. At all three occasions (A,B and C) boy-mother pairs seemed to be more influenced by the extra contact than girl-mother pairs.

DISCUSSION

The interpretation of studies on extra contact, early stimulation and so forth, is still very hazardous and must be made with great caution. It is, however, notable how results of different studies, both in humans and in animals, tend to fit into a similar pattern. In our study maternal and infant behaviour, child development, duration of breastfeeding and certain opinions on child-rearing practices seem to undergo changes correlated to the presence of extra contact. Early extra contact after delivery between mother and infant seems to facilitate a more synchronous development of the mother-infant relationship. Not all families however can benefit of such an extra contact, for example may mothers with an unwanted pregnancy in fact refuse the extra contact offered to them. One has therefore to be very cautious in offering all mothers this opportunity immediately after delivery. The offer should be made in an open-minded way, permitting the mother to make her own choice and decision, prefarable together with her consort.

REFERENCES

1. de Chateau, P.: Neonatal Care Routines. Dissertation, Umeå University, N.S. 20, 1976.

2. de Chateau, P. and Wiberg, B.: Long-term effect on mother-infant behaviour of extra contact during the first post-partum hour. I. First observations at 36 hours. Acta Paediatr. Scand. 66, 137 (1977).

3. de Chateau, P. and Wiberg, B.: Long-term effect on mother-infant behaviour of extra contact during the first post-partum hour. II. Follow-up at three months. Acta Paediatr. Scand 66, 141 (1977).

4. de Chateau, P. and Wiberg, B.: Long-term effect on mother-infant behaviour of extra contact during the first post-partum hour. III. One year follow-up. Dev. Med. Child Neurol.: in press.

Child Abuse and Neglect, Vol. 3, pp. 285 - 290.

0145-2134/79/0301-0285 $02.00/0.

TREATING SEXUALLY ABUSED CHILDREN

Paula Slager Jorné, Ph.D.

The Children's Center
101 Alexandrine E.
Detroit, Michigan 48201
U.S.A.

There is an enormous incidence of sexual abuse of children, many times greater than reported, and perhaps many times greater than the occurrence of physical abuse. The occurrence of child sexual abuse in the U.S. population is estimated at from 5% to 15% (Boekelheide 1978). The offender is most likely to be male and is known approximately 80% of the time. Almost 30% are members of the child victim's household, and almost 25% are parents or parent substitutes. Almost one-half of the incidents of sexual abuse of children that take place have been repeated over a period of time. Sixty percent of the offenders are male relatives or boyfriends of the mother. Sixty percent of the offenders use force or threat. In 50% of the incidents the child reports at once, and this usually occurs when the offender is a stranger or used force. Family support for the victim is much more likely when the offender is a stranger, and psychological problems are most likely when the offender is known to the child. In the case of known offenders, family loyalties may be split and the interests of the child lost. The parent response is two-thirds offender oriented, i.e., thought of punishment, wishes to protect or fears of family disruption (Brant & Tisza 1977; DeFrancis 1969; Guthiel & Avery 1977; Lustig 1966; Peters 1976).

Most reported cases come from low income families, but the occurrence of sexual abuse toward children, as with physical abuse, cuts across all economic and social lines. The family situation in homes where sexual abuse tends to occur is usually already severely troubled by other problems, such as an alcoholic father or mother, marital dysfunction, financial stress and delinquent acts already taking place. The reported sexual offense is often not the first one to have taken place in the family, and in fact one is likely to find a history of sexual abuse in the parent's childhood. More girls than boys appear to be victims, with a reported 10 cases of father-daughter incest to every one reported mother-son case (Boekelheide 1978). Boys who are sexually abused tend to be approached in a homosexual manner, though the offender may not actually be a homosexual. Some researchers assert that mother-son sexual abuse is potentially more destructive than father-daughter sexual abuse, with psychosis, alcoholism or other substance abuse involved.

Two-thirds of the children who are sexually abused appear to suffer emotional difficulties. The child's immediate response may be guilt, anxiety, fear and/or anger. Guilt may result from a variety of causes, such as having derived gratification from the event, feeling like the seducer, or feeling that something bad will happen to the offender, especially if the offender is a loved or respected adult. Quite often the child's interests are overlooked after the exposure. Parents should be encouraged to allow the child to ventilate feelings, if possible, especially with a one-time offense by a stranger, instead of attempting to suppress the event(s) as quickly as possible. Parents should also be encouraged to respond to the event as they would to a non-sexual crime, i.e., with calm, support for and acceptance of the child, and an honest attempt to assess the situation objectively. A family's response to sexual abuse is highly influential on the child's later emotional development.

The conclusion one must draw from the literature as to how sexual abuse of children occurs, is that most incidents are due to consequence of parent derelection of duty or covert conspiracy to provide the opportunity, and prevent disclosure. When treating a family where sexual abuse has occurred, one must help the family explore the underlying stresses that caused them to act out their fears, anxieties and frustrations in such a manner.

Sexual Abuse Defined

Sexual abuse, or "sexual misuse", as it is sometimes called, is defined as "exposure of a child to sexual stimulation inappropriate for the child's age, level of psychosocial development, and role in the family" (Brant & Tisza 1977, p. 80). The sexual event or events can be of any type, including overstimulation, indecent exposure, fondling, intercourse and rape. Sexual abuse generally does not reach the stage of intercourse, which is the most obvious event, but rather may take many other forms over a long period of time. Sexual abuse in the family is seen as the problem of the entire family. Incest is viewed as the expression of "the collective pathology of all the family members as well as their common adaptational capacities ...a collusive act, with the child active and even seductive and the parents driven to repeat certain childhood experiences or conflicts with a new generation" (Guthiel & Avery 1977, p.105). Sexual abuse is usually a manifestation of family pathology, and all family members are active in perpetuating the abuse.

There appears to be a distinction between sexual abuse that is brutal and sexual abuse that is not. The non-violent incident is more likely with children, while brutality is more likely with adolescents and especially adults. Violence is usually not a part of child sexual abuse, and in a family, physical abuse is not likely to occur with sexual abuse, though neglect often accompanies both.

It is important to note that the sexual abuse is not for sexual pleasure per se, but for the gratification of underlying emotional needs. Thus a man can be involved in homosexual acts with a male child in his household, but not actually be seeking sex with a male partner. Or, the father may begin first with the oldest child in the family and proceed to sexually abuse one child after the other, sequentially, regardless of the child's sex.

The following are examples of sexual abuse, ranging from less severe to quite severe:

--Boyfriend of mother putting little girl on his lap and rubbing her pelvic area against his genitals.
--Parents having sex with their bedroom door and child's bedroom door open; parents making much noise, overstimulating and frightening child.
--Mother taking a bath with older children present, especially boys.
--Mother letting seven year old child fondle her breasts.
--Parent sexually fondling child, i.e., fondling genitalia or breasts, mutually fondling each other, oral sex.
--Father having intercourse with each child successively, regardless of child's sex.
--Exposing children to pornographic literature and then further engaging in sexual relations under the guise of sex education.

Symptoms And Consequences Of Sexual Abuse

Much of the information we obtain about a child's sexual abuse comes to us by way of the psychosocial history. We may, under certain circumstances, ask about sexual abuse by posing the question to the mother, "Do you know of any sexual abuse your child may have experienced?" It is interesting to note that most of the cases we see that involve sexual abuse come to us for other problems, such as sexual acting out of a daughter, overt sexual behavior toward women in a small boy, and so on. What we see most often are the symptoms of earlier and sometimes on-going sexual abuse, which is itself symptomatic of other problems. We are most likely to see a child immediately after an incident if the offender is unknown or if the act is brutal. With fathers and daughters, we are likely to see the family when the daughter reaches adolescence and wishes to establish relationships with boys, or when an older child is attempting to separate from a highly dependent relationship. These cases may come to us with entering problems that are symptomatic of the family disturbance, such as the daughter suddenly doing very poorly in school and becoming rebellious or unmanageable. We sometimes only suspect that sexual abuse has occurred, and may never know the true history of the problems. Our approach is that the sexual abuse is not necessarily the cause of symptomatic behavior in a child but is itself symptomatic of family stress.

The following are examples of cases and entering problems seen over the past year at our child serving mental health facility:

- Ten year old boy who experienced several sexual episodes at age four with his mother's girlfriend.

Presenting problem: Aggressive behavior with younger children.
- Thirteen year old girl experienced sexual intercourse at an early age with both her natural father and her step-father. Presenting problem: evoking seductive responses from strange men.
- Thirteen year old girl raped at age eight by her church minister and later by her brother. Presenting problem: preoccupation with sex, talking about it constantly.
- Four year old boy sexually abused by his 14 year old sister. Presenting problem: very aggressive sexually with women and exposing himself.
- Fifteen year old girl had incestuous relations with her father for several years. The father had sexual relations with all his sons and daughters. Presenting problem: fainting spells, hysteria.

We once uncovered the startling information, in a group of six mothers who were being seen for physically abusing their own children, that five of the six women clients had experienced incestuous relations with their fathers.

One can see in the cases described that the sexual abuse may be of any type,and that the symptoms often have to do with sexually aggressive behavior. We also see in these and other cases that in families where sexual abuse occurs, if the father is replaced by the mother's boyfriend, the situation may well repeat itself. There are numerous examples, as well, of a child removed from home because of sexual abuse, only to have the abuse recur in the foster home. We see these last examples as cases of repetitive family psychodynamics in operation.

The symptoms we are most aware of in cases of sexual abuse is the disinhibition of the sexual impulses of the child. The child often begins to seek love through sexual contact. There appears to be little or poor control of sexual impulses. The reverse may also be seen, with an individual who has become greatly inhibited sexually as a result of earlier sexual abuse. Thus we may see a woman who was sexually abused as a child become fearful of sex and non-orgasmic, or to the contrary, be unhibited and seek out sexually aggressive, brutal partners, or be promiscuous without orgasm. Symptoms appear to be related to the developmental age of the child when the sexual abuse took place (Lewis & Sarrel 1969).

A great deal of anxiety is generated in the child when sexual abuse occurs, which may be seen in sudden nightmares or other sleep disturbances, eating difficulties, tics, sudden excessive fears, eneuresis, and so on. Psychological confusion results when the offender is known, particularly when the offender is an authority figure or trusted adult. The sexually abusive act cannot be easily assimilated, and conflict between guilt and wish fulfillment may take place.

Physical brutality such as with rape, often causes the child to associate sex with aggression. This view then interferes with normal sexual development. Great fears may be created about sex, or the individual may choose brutal partners. Fathers who are sexually brutal are often alcoholics (DeFrancis 1969).

In many cases of incest, the residual effects may not be so damaging if the incest has not gone on for very long, if there is no brutality, if the offending parent is ambivalent about his or her role, and if the family receives treatment. If the child has enough ego strength, the event can be put into perspective. The child may be able to understand the sexual abuse in terms of the problem. This is particularly true if there are positive aspects to the relationships between the parent and child. On the other hand, the child may blame him or herself. If the parent is incarcerated or sent away, the child may feel very guilty, and aside from the guilt there is the very real fact that a parent will be lost. Thus in some cases incarceration of the offending parent may have disastrous effects upon the family, unless the child cannot be protected from continuing sexual abuse, particularly brutal abuse. Many times a father who has been sent away is quickly replaced by the mother with a similar type of man, another indication that the sexual abuse is a family problem. The child , too, without treatment, tends to recreate the family situation in a foster home.

The mother of a family where sexual abuse is occurring seems to play a pivotal role in establishing the father-daughter incestuous tie (Guthiel & Avery 1977). The typical mother in such a family is depressed, isolated , withdrawn, and feeling inadequate as a mother and wife. She may feel overburdened by her sexual role, and consciously or unconsciously, provides the opportunity for sexual abuse to occur (Guthiel & Avery 1977). In this case the child involved becomes the "household and sexual surrogate" for the mother (Boekelheide 1978, p. 88). When evidence is presented to the mother that sexual abuse is occurring in her family, she either "grossly denies evidence of the incest or takes no consequent action if she does acknowledge it" (Guthiel & Avery 1977, p. 113). Some mothers refuse to believe the child, and may go so far as to punish the child severely. Girls often feel rage at their mothers for being left unprotected in such situations.

When infants are overstimulated, such as with the manipulation of the baby's genitalia, they may exhibit eating and sleeping disturbances, along with changed levels of activity. Toddlers and school age children may not be able to verbalize their fears. One may see regressive behavior, and the withdrawal into a fantasy world, simulating retardation. Young children who have been sexually abused may find it difficult or uncomfortable to sit in a chair or participate in sports. Other possible affects may be physical complaints, increased fearfulness, eating and sleeping disturbances, inappropriate play, learning problems, compulsive masturbation, poor peer relations, and sexual play.

Pre-adolescents and adolescents may act out their fears and concerns through sexually aggressive behavior, the wearing of seductive clothing, delinquency, hostility towards others, sexual promiscuity, prostitution, truancy from home, substance abuse, and increased fearfulness. Adolescent girls may confide in others directly or indirectly, such as expressing fear about going home.

There are certain situations at home that may create the opportunity for sexual abuse to occur. There may be gross overcrowding, with inadequate sleeping arrangements. Or one parent may be absent for some time, due to death, divorce or separation. The family may be socially isolated, a parent may be extremely overly protective, or supervision of children may be inadequate. Other factors that may contribute are alcoholism and substance abuse in both men and women, financial stress, change in economic status, or recent job loss.

Many aspects of family life are already disrupted by the time sexual abuse occurs. Marital conflict is quite likely. Parent-child boundaries may be ill defined, causing family members to take on inappropriate roles. Parents may have experienced sexual abuse in their own childhoods, and repeat the learned behavior with the next generation.

A typical family in which sexual abuse has occurred is usually undergoing a particularly stressful period, and is also socially isolated. The mother may be emotionally cold, depressed and withdrawn, and cannot or does not wish to provide nurturance to the father. The father is immature and cannot relate to females adequately; thus he turns to his daughter or more than one of his children, male or female, in an attempt to satisfy his emotional needs. Often incest in such a family is a final attempt to remain together and restore some order.

Treatment Approaches

The therapist working with sexually abused children and their families must always strive to convey support, understanding and compassion for all who are involved, including the offender as well as the victim. This is very important if we are to facilitate the growth of self-esteem in individuals who have already shown themselves to feel inadequate in coping with problems in appropriate ways. Thus both child and offender need to be reassured that they are not "bad people." We further need to engender a feeling of acceptance and trust, so that family members can talk more freely with the therapist and each other.

During treatment, one does not need to focus on the sexual abuse simply because it has occurred. There must, however, be recognition on the part of family members that the sexual abuse is a contributing factor to feelings of shame, guilt, and loss of sexual impulse control. If the problem in a family where sexual abuse has occurred is seen as family stress, the therapist may begin on the level the family is capable of functioning, and treat the symptoms as one would for any other family stress problem.

If a child does not bring up the sexual abuse in treatment, then the therapist generally should not, because the child's silence may indicate an inability to deal with the feelings aroused. The therapist should continue to treat the child's symptoms, which can be done in any number of ways, including behavior modification techniques to eliminate undesirable behaviors and teach acceptable ones. Children whose major problems relate to sexual abuse are not seen as appropriate candidates for group therapy, although their parents are good group candidates, since they are usually isolated and fearful of sharing feelings. If many family members have been involved in the sexual abuse, they may all be counseled individually and together. Parents may also be counseled together, without other family members. Individual treatment is recommended over group if the family has more or less erected a wall against any outsiders, such as the therapist; in these cases a family member may talk more freely when alone with the therapist. Group may be tried after more trust is established.

When sexual acting out is involved, the underlying issues should be explored, such as the seeking of assurances of being worhtwhile and loveable by using sex. It should be explained that the acting out produces the opposite effect of feeling loved, i.e., one usually feels worthless, used and guilty. In all instances the therapist must convey an understanding of the motivation and the results. The child's anxiety about being unloved must be dealt with.

A child may not be able to talk about the sexual abuse, but the problem may be demonstrated through play, such as the child sucking the genitals of an anatomically correct doll. The therapist's role in play therapy is to help the child work problems out through the play. The child can also be instructed that no one should ever touch him or her in an uncomfortable place, except a doctor. The therapist must let the child know that the responsibility for what happened is not his or hers, and that the consequences will not be so terrible. The child may be able to understand that the offender is troubled and could not help committing the offense.

Parents must come to see the similarities in their own histories to their present behavior, and recognize that patterns are being repeated. Sexual abuse in the family is essentially behavior that was learned by the parents when they were children, and is perpetuated with their own children in times of stress or crisis. These parents also did not learn appropriate parenting roles, and one finds that role boundaries in the family are very unclear. The counselor must help the parents learn what appropriate parenting is, and how relationships ought to work in a family.

The entire family should be looked at in terms of roles, i.e., who does what, when, and to whom. The family needs to examine what happens under stress, and how problems get resolved. The problems of the family need to be understood, and how the family functions in day-to-day living is important; e.g., what happens if a family member is ill. If one adult in the home is not safe for the child, the other adult must examine what his or her responsibilities are toward the child and toward the offender.

Both victim and offender need to be counseled, and treated with compassion and understanding. The offender is the family scapegoat, the member who acts out the problems of the entire family. Every family member must examine his or her responsibility and motivations regarding family functioning. Thus one must consider the problem of sexual abuse a family problem, treat the abuse as if it were another symtom of family stress handled in a maladaptive way, and begin working on family roles and relationships.

REFERENCES

Boekelheide, P.D.
Incest and the Family Physician
The Journal of Family Practice, 6(1), 1978, pp 87-90

Brant, R.S.T. & Tisza, V.B.
The Sexually Misused Child
American J. of Orthopsychiatry, January, 1977, 47(1), pp 80-90

DeFrancis, V.
Protecting the Child Victim of Sex Crimes Committed by Adults
The American Humane Society, Denver, 1969

Guthiel, T. G. & Avery, N.C.
Multiple Overt Incest as Family Defense Against Loss
Family Process, March 1977, 16(1), pp 105-116

Lewis, M.L. & Sarrel, P.M.
Some Psychological Aspects of Seduction, Incest and Rape in Childhood
J. of Amer. Academy of Child Psychiatry, 8:606, 1969.

Lustig, N.
Incest: A Family Group Survival Pattern
Arch. General Psychiatry, 1966, 14, pp 31-40

Peters, J.J.
Children Who Are Victims of Sexual Assault and the Psychology of Offenders
American J. of Psychotherapy, July, 1976, 30(3), pp 398-421

Child Abuse and Neglect, Vol. 3, pp. 291 - 296.
0145-2134/79/0301-0291 $02.00/0.

OPTIONS IN "BIG BROTHER'S" INVOLVEMENT WITH INCEST

Anne B. Topper
Social Services Administrator
El Paso County, Colorado Springs, Colorado
Adjunct Professor, Univ. of Denver

Only in recent years have the therapeutic and legal communities become somewhat self-consciously aware of the prevalence and incidence of sexual molestation of incest practiced within nuclear families. The growing awareness of incest is relatively new; the practice of incest is not. Methods of treatment of victims and punishment of offenders are developing in a rather scattershot manner, both being conditioned in part by the laws of the locale and even more, by the attitudes of the community. The State of Colorado requires that "any case in which a child is subjected to sexual assault or molestation" be considered as child abuse and as such must be reported to the County Department of Social Services or local law enforcement agency. Though the law is intended to be enforced uniformly across the state, the variations in application and interpretation are many and result in accompanying variations in punishment and treatment. Since I have served as a consultant on incest on a state-wide basis, I have learned that in some areas law enforcement prefers not to be involved at all unless the evidence is irrefutable. Since irrefutable evidence is virtually never available, neither help nor hindrance is meted out and we can assume that the situation may become even less tolerable for the victim and the family. If the alleged perpetrator is a man of position and influence in the community, and well he may be, there is a distinct tendency to "hush the whole thing up," to assume the report is a fabrication, especially if made by the victim, because as one physician stated, "I know this guy. We play tennis together. He would never do such a thing." Such discomfort with and denial of the very existence of incest has interfered with development of an encompassing model of effective intervention. Even when the procedures followed are within the letter of the law, the fall-out on the family is more often destructive than rehabilitative. I concede that a degree of disruption to the family is not only inevitable, but is necessary if the family is to reconstruct itself into more beneficial patterns---however, immediate and forceful therapeutic intervention <u>must</u> accompany such disruption if the concepts of safety for the children and unity for the family are ever to be achieved.

In my own county, adherence to the law and to a philosophy of harass and then help has been fairly widespread among the agencies and individuals working with incestuous families. When a case is reported, intervention by law enforcement, and by social services is speedy and fairly efficient. Fathers are hustled off to jail, daughters are bundled off to foster care and mothers deny all knowledge of events. Social workers counsel, lawyers defend, psychologists test, physicians examine, custody hearings are held, criminal prosecutions grind on, and eventually a sentence is handed down. The fragmented family, under great stress and embroiled in a mass of confusing procedures and pulled in several directions by various systems, cannot (until most of this is resolved) dedicate itself to becoming whole and healthy.

Because of certain provisions of the Criminal Justice Records Act (Colo. Rev. Stat. 1973, as amended, 24-72-303 (1) & 24-72-304 & the (USA) Federal Criminal History Information Act (Fed. Reg. 20-3) time limitations are placed upon the use of information contained in criminal records, the District Attorney's Office in El Paso County, Colorado, may utilize a deferred sentence rather than deferred prosecution in those cases in which it is determined that the perpetrator may be rehabilitated.

The perpetrator must admit to the charges, must enter a plea, must agree to evaluation and treatment for a period of time not to exceed the length of sentence he could receive and then he may be granted a deferred sentence. Or, he could go to trial, receive a sentence and be placed on probation, again under condition of receiving treatment. In both instances, failure to comply with the conditions set forth by the Court would result in incarceration.

Some of the advantages that accrue in using these procedures are these; the perpetrator is "motivated" to stay in treatment, he may be able to hold his job and maintain the family's economic security, the family may be re-united more quickly and begin its work, and social support systems, formal and informal, such as neighborhood, friends, schools, church, in addition to the prescribed therapeutic agents, can be integrated into the family's lifestyle. In the meanwhile, the criminal justice system will not be as limited by constraints of time as it would be if deferred prosecution and diversion were used. Among the disadvantages are the punitive aspects, the time lag involved in getting the mechanisms moving, the notoriety that inevitably occurs - the latter especially is a source of great distress to the family. And if a conviction is obtained, it of course becomes a matter of record, at least for a time. As a result, treatment (or the "help" aspect) of families caught up in the tangled relationships bred by incest may thus be delayed beyond the time when it might be most effective. Treatment is too often seen as not helpful by the families, at least at first, and is particularly so regarded by the young victims who often feel they are only further victimized. Relevancy of the course of treatment is not clearly understood by some and certain areas needing particular attention appear to be overlooked.

The purpose of this paper, then, is to present some alternatives to the current "state of the art" of society's intervention with incestuous families. The following is based primarily upon a professional study which I conducted comparing the perceptions of a group of adult women who had been incestuously molested with the perceptions of a number of teenagers who also have been victims of incest. It is limited to cases of incest between fathers or father-surrogates and daughters.

Information was gathered from the two subject populations by means of interviews, treatment groups, questionnaires and of greatest interest, a specifically formed group of adult victims who met to consider current methods of treatment and the generally accepted reporting procedure in their location (Colorado Springs, Colorado, USA). Information from approximately 85 individuals including therapists was gathered. A number of agencies participated, including the local Department of Social Services, the Mental Health Center, the Victim Service Bureau, the District Attorney's Office, as well as physicians, and therapists in private practice. All of the participants and all of the agencies involved were aware of the research project.

All subjects are now or have been in therapy of some form. This was considered to be important because it was felt that the subjects would probably require some therapeutic follow-up during and after the questioning/interviewing process. Demographic characteristics of the subjects are not detailed in this study because such information has been dealt with in some of the literature referred to in the references. Furthermore, the demographics appeared to be significant only because they were so variable, particularly in the cases of the teenagers. There were some socio-economic commonalities among the women's group---they were in substantial financial circumstances, were all married, were all parents.

A questionnaire drawn up by the author was reviewed and revised after consultation with co-workers, therapists, the women's group and various teenagers. It consisted of 34 open-ended questions dealing with the following general areas: demographic data, the incestuous activity, relationships within the family, a self-assessment (present and projected) and an evaluation of the reporting process and of the treatment received.

A total of 53 questionnaires was completed by girls ranging in age from 13 to 19. One questionnaire had to be disqualified because the girl who completed it had been raped by a non-related male,** leaving 52 questionnaires to be considered. Interviews with an additional 12 girls were conducted to determine if data collected in this manner were similar to the written data.

In the women's group, a total of 11 women participated in meetings for 25 weeks. The concerns expressed by these subjects as individuals led first to the formation of the group then to the search for more information and alternate reporting and treatment procedures. While, as mentioned previously, all the subjects are or had been in therapy of some form, the stated reasons for entering treatment differed sharply between the two populations. The girls without exception had all been referred to treatment because of the sexual assault by a father or father-surrogate. The women had initially sought treatment for a variety of problems, but none identified incest as the reason for entering therapy; rather, the focus on incest occurred either on the initiative of the therapist or after a casual "by the way... my father molested me" comment from the patient.

Some areas of agreement between the groups are these: all subjects deplored the current criminal investigatory approach---a few said they would not have reported or would have lied when questioned had they known what would follow---such as possible imprisonment of father, possible placement out of the home, going to court, having a gynecological examination, "having the (news)papers get ahold of it," undergoing a polygraph examination, having a "counselor", dealing with police, social services, doctors, "breaking up the whole family", the lsst being particularly terrifying. On the other hand, all recognized the need for some authoritative "handle" to reinforce the need for family treatment--though some youngsters felt that only treatment of the father was necessary. All felt the sexual relationship with the father would have continued had there been no intervention unless they, the victims, left home or another sister became a serial rather than concurrent sex partner for the father. All worried about "what people thought" and the women were particularly sensitive to the possibility of social stigma even now attaching to themselves or their families. All repeatedly and strongly referred to feeling "ashamed" during much of the experience, both before and after intervention. Most were aware of their feelings of guilt which confused, bewildered, and angered them--i.e., "He's the one that did it! Why do I feel like it's my fault?" The teenagers were very much concerned about the here and now --- how long would they have to stay in foster care or continue to come to group or have a social worker? What was going to happen to them, the fathers, the families? Most seemed anxious to move on, to forget, to pretend nothing "like that" had ever happened. Few were concerned about long-range effects of their experiences. Some felt they'd be fine if everyone would just leave them alone and concentrate on the fathers. The girls were concerned about what "the boys" might think, or how they'd react if they knew about the incest. Only two averred no interest at all in boys. Most of them planned to marry and to have children. They split their preferences as to wanting sons or daughters. Each had advantages and disadvantages. About one-fifth thought children would be too much of a chore. Most of the casual responses to questions about dating, sexual experiences with boys, plans to marry, etc., generally approximate the responses given by other teenagers who have not had incestuous experiences. However, the girls' concerns about being different, their feelings of being "dirty," and their memories of being unable to enforce limitations on the physical uses and responses of their own bodies were troublesome and pervasive. Factual information about sex, physiology, etc. was scant. With several there was a "Lady MacBeth" fear of never feeling or being clean again. The girls generally expressed a great deal of anger, sometimes "disgust" with their fathers. Surprisingly, few (six) said that they continued to be afraid of their fathers though an additional number said they could not or would not stay or go home if the fathers were also in the home. Only two had been subjected to other physical abuse such as severe beatings. Some were threatened, spanked, pinched. A number felt their fathers were "not like fathers anymore."

**This was discovered primarily because the responses varied remarkedly from the others.

An overwhelming and most startling finding was that the majority of girls did not want to know that their mothers knew of the incidents. This very large majority could not acknowledge that their mothers were aware of the molestation, even though the girls, in some instances, had told their mothers.** Had the mothers known, the girls felt, they would have made the fathers stop! In general, the girls had fewer complaints about their mothers than the fathers, but did indicate that the mothers were somewhat ineffective. For example, "My mother didn't know about me and my dad, but she couldn't (or wouldn't) have done nothing anyhow." Occasionally a response indicated that the mother was "lazy" -- "she doesn't do anything around the house," etc. The girls' great need to believe that they could depend on at least one parent seems clearly apparent.

The women's group was concerned about how to parent their own children, especially their daughters. They felt they had not had good relationships with their own mothers and that they knew little about being a mother to a daughter. They felt much more comfortable with sons. All of the women indicated that the inadequate or inappropriate relationships between themselves and their respective mothers were perhaps the most long-lasting and destructive elements in the incestuous system and they, in direct contrast to the views of the teenagers, expressed still unresolved and probably growing anger at their mothers who had failed them and had perhaps failed the fathers as well. This adult anger has, in the author's experience, proved to be least responsive to treatment of all manifested symptoms.

Attitudes toward fathers had become much less hostile and the women tend to see them, from a vantage point many years after the sexual activity, as rather weak human beings, sometimes almost as fellow victims of a cold uncaring ineffective mother/wife. The women recollect having had feelings of deep anger toward the fathers but without exception in this group, these feelings had mellowed. All of the women maintain contact of some sort with the still-living parents.

The women felt their experiences with their fathers had affected their choice of husbands, their attitudes toward sex and sexual experience, their feelings about themselves and their bodies. Learning to relate to males in other than sexual ways had been and for some still is, difficult. While they all said they "knew" their mates would not indulge in incest, they worried about it and had discussed it within the family (after being in treatment). They feel as wives and mothers that they can prevent the incestuous system from developing---again after being in treatment.

CONCLUSIONS AND RECOMMENDATIONS

1. The need for legal/judicial intervention is affirmed, for maintaining families in treatment on a voluntary basis has not been successful. Furthermore, the seriousness of incest as a social offense is underscored by such attention. However, such intervention in most cases should be speedy and decisive, directed toward the family as a unit with therapeutic involvement as a prerequisite for non-punitive disposition.

2. Identification of the perpetrator in the news media, notice of his incarceration, printing his home address and other such news stories cause much distress to the affected family. Further, such publicity may destroy or weaken the support now especially needed by the family from non-agency and agency social systems. Incestuous fathers virtually always limit their sexual activities to their own families or within their own homes so that the public does not require such notice for its own safety. Cooperation from the media is needed and should be addressed via education, petitions, etc.

3. Education of young incest partners about sex and their own sexuality is indicated to alleviate some of the guilt aroused by physiological responses and to deal with "dirty" feelings. Victims, teenaged or adult, have little knowledge of

---

**In four cases, the mothers had reported the sexual activity.

what constitutes a mature and gratifying sexual experience. Contrary to a belief held by much of society, the teenaged incest partner generally has knowledge only of rather immature or exploitative sexual practice and though she may be provocative, she is and may remain through adulthood somewhat juvenile and emotionally inhibited in sexual relations. The implications of such sexual attitudes added to other feelings are many and could include unsatisfying marriages, incestuous husbands, promiscuity, variant sexual practices --- all of which have been noted in social histories of many incest victims.

4. Strong modeling of parental roles and especially maternal roles for the victim is essential in the various therapy situations--individual, couple, family, group. Such modeling may be critical in preventing a recurrence of incest in the next generation for incest, like other forms of abuse is generational and the victim of incest may well become the mother of an incest victim.

5. While the perspectives of victims appear to change over the years, the damage done by the incestuous experience does not "go away" so that effective intervention is necessary and as indicated above, must consist of more than removing the father and/or the daughter from the household either temporarily or permanently. Resistance may be high so the therapy, as ordered by the court, must be intensive and confrontive and the therapists must be nurturing and understanding.

6. Since incest is a multi-layered, multi-person problem it requires a multi-therapist multi-method approach. Such cases confound the usual workload standards imposed on most agencies particularly when coupled with increasing numbers of incest reports.** The need for adequate numbers of well-trained staff of various disciplines must be emphasized.

7. Finally, it is unrealistic to expect a youngster to withstand the sexual advances of a parent who represents authority and security. However as professionals we should champion the concepts that a child belongs to himself to be guided and nurtured by his parents and that his rights as an individual should not be subjugated without question to destructive parental perogatives.

REFERENCES

Beezley, Patricia "Sexual Mistreatment of Children: An Intervention Model", National Center for Prevention and Treatment of Child Abuse and Neglect (1977).

Behavior Today "Sex: A New Frontier for Children's Rights" (8-29-77).

Brownmiller, Susan Against Our Will: Men, Women and Rape Simon & Schuster, New York (1975).

Colorado Revised Statutes, 1973 As Amended "Title 19, Children's Code", L.G. Printing Co., Denver, CO., September (1977).

Giarretto, Henry "Humanistic Treatment of Father-Daughter Incest", Child Abuse and Neglect, The International Journal, 1, 2-4 (1977). pp 411-426

Helfer, Ray E. & Kempe, C. Henry, Eds. Child Abuse & Neglect, Ballinger, Cambridge, Mass (1976).

Henderson, P. James "Incest, A Synthesis of Data" Canadian Psychiatric Assoc. Journal 17 (1972).

Lustig, Noel, Dresser, John et.al. "Incest, A Family Group Survival Pattern" Archives of General Psychiatry 14, January (1966). pp 31-39

**Of the cases open in child protective service units in our agency, the number of incest cases increased from 12% to 17% from 1976 to 1977.

Machotka, Paul, Pittman, Frank, et.al. "Incest as a Family Affair" Family Process (1967). pp 98-116

Satchell, Michael, "The Unspeakable Subject" Criminal Justice Digest, May (1975).

Schechter, Marshall and Roberge "Sexual Exploitation" Child Abuse & Neglect Helfer & Kempe, Eds. Ballinger, Cambridge, Mass. (1976).

Stein, Robert Incest & Human Love, Penguin, Baltimore, (1973).

Summit, Roland & Kryso, Joann "Sexual Abuse of Children: A Clinical Spectrum" American Journal of Ortho-psychiatry 48, #2, April (1978). pp 237

(Appreciation is expressed to John P. Kelley who edited and critiqued, to J. Worth Linn who also critiqued and to Darlene Collins who typed and re-typed.)

Child Abuse and Neglect, Vol. 3, pp. 297 - 302. 0145-2134/79/0301-0297 $02.00/0.

FAMILY THERAPY IMPACT ON INTRAFAMILIAL CHILD SEXUAL ABUSE

Jerome A. Kroth

University of Santa Clara, Santa Clara, California

ABSTRACT

A family therapy treatment program is evaluated using a cross-sectional longitudinal design. Three groups of intrafamilial sexual abuse clients at different stages of therapy are measured on 44 indices of behavioral and attitudinal change. Results are discussed in terms of the generally positive outcomes observed for this therapeutic modality in the treatment of incest.

INTRODUCTION

The Child Sexual Abuse Treatment Program (CSATP) in San Jose, California is one of the largest incest treatment facilities in the United States. In the first half of 1978 an external evaluation of the CSATP program was funded by the Office of Child Abuse Prevention and the local county to assess the efficacy of the family therapy model. The CSATP approach is clinically organized around traditional individual and family counseling and the use of the Parents United/Daughters United programs. The aim of this model is to reconstitute and resocialize the incestuous family through therapy whenever possible, returning the perpetrator and/or victim to the home when such reunification seems clinically warranted (about 3 in 4 cases).

Literature in the area of treatment outcome in child sexual abuse is almost wholly based on authority and opinion. Little if any literature exists which describes reasonably sized samples of clients measured before and after treatment on any even remotely objective indices of change. One has little difficulty, for example, finding essays on incest as a desire to possess the father's penis (1) or as an unconscious revenge against the pre-Oedipal mother (2), but any activity in contrasting behavioral, psychoanalytic, counseling or penal approaches to the treatment of offenders and their families is minimal. The list of scientific issues which remain neglected in this era of the micro-chip computer processor has been delineated by Schuchter (3) and is likely to prove an embarrassment to any professional involved in the treatment of these client populations.

To some degree the inaccessibility of incest samples has handicapped outcome research, but, perhaps equally accountable is the self-indulgent psychiatric and psychoanalytic tradition which has actively been treating child sexual abuse cases for decades without providing the professional community even one reasonably experimental,longitudinal investigation of treatment efficacy.

There is, as a result, considerable equivocation in incest research. One study suggests the victims of incest were active and initiating in the episode (4) while another holds that victims who may be described as "participants" were in the minority (5). One investigation suggests victims suffer long term psychological damage from the experience (6) while another reveals a majority were unaffected by the molest(7); still another holds that in some cases the incest experience is emotionally beneficial to psychological development(8).

The same equivocation is found in studies on the offender. One study describes the offender as a criminal personality(9); another reports incest offenders have little other criminal involvements (10). One investigation contends the offender can be reunited with his family with minimal recidivism (11)followed, almost at the same time, by a study which claims reuniting the offender with his family is like considering "the fox for a position as guard of the henhouse (12, p.33).

The need, therefore, to develop a more definite data base is important, not only in demographic samplings of incest cases, but most immediately in the study of treatment effectiveness. It is probable that the research in support of Laetrile as an effective cancercure is more sophisticated and prolific than any research which claims a certain therapeutic approach is effective in the treatment of the family experiencing incest.

METHOD AND RESULTS

The CSATP evaluation project constructed three comparison groups representing an intake sample of clients (perpetrators and spouses), a midterm sample and a near termination group. This cross-sectional, longitudinal design necessitated that the groups be matched rigorously to permit comparison such that an assessment of the efficacy and changes induced by family therapy might be measured. The groups were matched on 10 criteria: age of perpetrators, age of non-offending spouses, age of victims, total number of victims, percent of victims under 13 at molest, percent homosexual offender-victim relationships, duration of molest, education of the perpetrator, education of the non-offending spouse, and relation of perpetrator to victim. The three samples were composed of 9 perpetrators and 8 unrelated non-offending spouses constituting a sample size of 17 for each stage of therapy. The intake sample had been at the facility for about 2-3 weeks, the midterm sample approximately 5.1 months and the near termination sample 14 months. The total of all three samples shows 51 respondents who provide descriptions on a total of 70 victims. Some 44 separate measures were used and given to these clients under confidential and anonymous conditions. Twenty of these comparisons resulted in statistically significant effects which in each case favored the positive evaluation of CSATP family therapy. No statistically significant effects were noted which would point to psycho-social or familial deterioration as a consequence (or despite) treatment. Some statistically non-significant effects were noted in which case the investigator attempted to classify trends that were noted as either positively favoring the treatment model, negative findings or neutral and/or ambiguous data.

Composite Portrait of Changes from Intake to Termination

The intrafamilial sexual abuse case, typically comprised of a father-perpetrator, a non-offending spouse and one or more victims, provides the following general picture at intake. The victims on the average were 12-13 years of age with a range from 6 to 21 in all three samples. Over half of the victims had been molested from at least 6 months to three or more years duration. Some 29% of the victims had been molested within the two months prior to intake. Nearly half of all the victims at intake display nervous or psychosomatic symptoms. The parents of these children report at intake that they are in some way close to a "nervous breakdown" (67%), and 88% express the feeling that they are "emotionally devastated". Most of the marital partners are unsure they will continue to live together or are actively contemplating separation or divorce. A substantial number of perpetrators and spouses (38%) describe themselves as arguing "quite a lot" in the two months prior to intake, and 80% report either non-existent or declining sexual contacts with eachother. There are, therefore, some very prevalent symptoms of family disorganization at intake, but the degree of pathology in general does not appear as pronounced as described elsewhere in the literature.

As we move toward the termination sample, quite a different picture emerges. The majority of victims who, at intake, evidenced some form of nervous or psychosomatic symptomatology may be described as "symtom free" (94%) ($p < .05$).* The social skills of the victims are improving with 46% reported to show improving relationships with friends and peers versus only 4% in the intake sample ($p < .01$). Further, they seem to be improving their relationships with their fathers ($p < .05$) as well as with the mother (N.S., trend only). Extremely low levels of aberrant behavior seem to be maintained throughout the 14 month period of therapy and are indicative of a general failure to deteriorate when most of the literature, almost none of which is longitudinal, offers primarily dire prognostications. No significant changes are noted in this area, primarily because the victim samples are showing low levels of aberrant characteristics and continue to maintain this absence of delinquency-symptomatic behavior. The rates observed in these samples are as follows: substance abuse 3%, promiscuity 3%, involvement with authorities 6%, runaway 1%.

At termination only 6% of the parents report deteriorating relationships in the prior two months versus 47% at intake ($p < .05$), and none are still undecided or actively contemplating a divorce or separation that has not already happened while over 57% fell in this category at intake ($p < .05$). It is estimated that about 76% of the couples remain together and are reconciled as a consequence of therapy. A majority report overall improving relationships with their spouses ($p < .05$), and none describe themselves as arguing "quite a lot" in the prior two months versus 38% at intake ($p < .05$). Their conjugal life has markedly improved with 41% reporting increased sexual activity in the prior two months versus 0% at intake ($p < .01$). Some 63% report quite a few to many sexual contacts between perpetrator and spouse in the prior two months versus 0% falling in this category at intake ($p < .02$). Further, the non-offending spouses are apparently enjoying these sexual contacts more in that 50% report they have experienced orgasm "quite a bit" or "a great deal" in the prior two months in the termination sample versus 0% in the intake sample ($p < .05$).

There is a general clarification of feelings occurring with regard to guilt and responsibility for the molest. At intake the clients appear overwhelmed with intense feelings of guilt(65%) while at termination the group as a whole moves into a more moderate level ($p < .05$). Perpetrators tend to maintain a fairly high level of personal responsibility for the molest with 78% admitting they were very much to completely responsible for the molest at intake versus 89% at termination (N.S.). Curiously, the non-offending spouses profess they were "only in part responsible" for the molest's occurrence at intake (87%), but seem to clarify their own roles and understandings with respect to it by termination such that this group splits, and 50% increase their sense of responsibility and culpability by indicating they feel "very much responsible" for the molest while another group appears to increasingly exonerate itself indicating at termination they were "not responsible at all"(37%). This clarification phenomena was considered a positive therapeutic outcome and was significant from intake to termination ($p < .05$).

The perpetrator and spouse have mixed feelings about counseling and CSATP at intake. Only 1 in 4 feels with any confidence that the offending father can be helped by therapy while over 3 in 4 feel he can by termination ($p < .05$). Further, 41% of the clients do not yet express a sense that CSATP has helped them or that they necessarily believe it can at intake while none express such a feeling in the termination sample ($p < .01$).

---

*All statistical comparisons were Chi Square analyses. Data presented here is a summary of material contained in the "CSATP Interim Evaluation", Office of Child Abuse Prevention, Department of Health, Sacramento, California. The author wishes to express his gratitude to this agency as well as to the County of Santa Clara, California for funding this research. An expanded version of this evaluation will also be published by Charles C. Thomas Publishers, Springfied, Illinois in 1978-79.

Twice as many perpetrators and spouses feel "more open, honest and in contro of themselves at termination as they did at intake ($p < .01$), and 100% feel "things are a lot better than they used to be" versus 29% at intake ($p < .01$)

The perpetrator shows a consistently low level of substance abuse with 67% entirely free of any form of intoxication in the prior two months in the intake sample and 89% at termination (N.S.). Further, the perpetrator's attendance at work tends to slightly improve with therapy with a majority at intake absent from work 3 or more days in the prior two months as contras with a majority in the termination sample not missing any days of work at al (N.S.). None of the perpetrators, moreover, report any contact with the law or authorities other than for the molest situation in any of the 3 samples. Finally there appears to be a resurgence of self-esteem in the perpetrators over time, particularly in their assessment of whether they see themselves as having a "sexual problem". A large majority at intake feel that they do, while the reverse self-assessment occurs at termination ($p < .05$).

Recidivism in this sample of clients was non-existent with 29% reporting sex contacts with the victim in the two months prior to coming to CSATP and none reporting any sexual contacts in either the midterm or near termination samples ($p < .02$). (Note that this data is gathered from both perpetrators and spouses). At intake, in this regard, 76% were quite sure the molest could not happen again while at termination 94% felt this high degree of confidenc (N.S.). Additionally 35% of the parents felt the victim might keep a future molest a secret at intake, but in the near termination sample only 4% felt she might not report it ($p < .05$).

Only three measures were considered to reflect in some negative way on the otherwise positive effects noted for a family therapy/Parents United model employed by CSATP. All these negative signs were statistically non-signific but, in the investigators view, they represented some marginal degree of failure and are deserving of mention. The first was a slight increase in th reluctance of the perpetrators and spouses to report a future molest if it happened with 18% who "might keep it a secret" at intake increasing to 41% who might hold it back at termination (N.S.). While there is much internal as well as external evidence to suggest a low recidivism rate for intrafamil sexual abuse, such data tends to increase one's suspicion, although their increasing reluctance may be a reflection of the client's unhappiness with the criminal justice system more so than with CSATP.

The second negative finding is that non-molested siblings continue to show some nervous signs across samples (12% at termination versus 18% at intake--N.S.); CSATP's remarkable success with symptom elimination in victims is not paralleled with non-molested siblings (who probably are not receiving counseling when they should be); this phenomena, however marginal or small in size, represents in the investigator's opinion a clinical oversight and needs to be rectified in the treatment design.

A final non-significant but negative finding was that although much data indicates drastically improved personal and sexual relations between the perpetrators and spouses, some 24% of these clients still evidence signs of recent and long-lasting sexual dysfunction at termination; since improved relationships of perpetrator and spouse represents a major cornerstone in th family reconstitution hypothesis, and since sexuality apparently plays a large role in this reconciliation, some therapeutic effort needs to be made in reaching this sexually dysfunctional minority which successfully resists therapeutic impact. A more specific sex therapy program has, as a consequen been recommended.

Some mention should be made regarding the methodological flaws that may be involved in this investigation. First, although matching was used, there may be some illusive selective attrition between comparison groups which has gone unnoticed. Secondly, the respondents in this study were adults who provided data on child-victims; other literature has suggested that their accuracy in describing their children is often questionable. Finally it sho be noted that this study focussed on the largest group of CSATP clients, intrafamilial sexual abuse cases, and that other kinds of sexual abuse treatment e.g. adults molested as children, victims of extrafamilial sexual abuse, minor offenders, were not examined.

Of the 44 measures used in the present investigation, 20 were statistically significant, all in a positive direction with respect to the efficacy of CSATP family therapy. An additional 17 statistically non-significant effects were interpreted as potentially positive signs. No statistically significant negative indications appeared, but 3 non-significant differences were interpreted as negative evidence. Four measures were interepreted as neutral and/or ambiguous data. From this summary, 82% of the measures used favored family therapy while 6% did not. It was the investigator's conclusion from this first preliminary study that the family therapy/Parents United model employed by the Child Sexual Abuse Treatment Program was a workable therapeutic paradigm whose effects were unmistakable.

DISCUSSION

There is still very little that is known about how to clinically treat offenders, victims and the family structure. This investigation has no outside normative data with which it can compare itself. Only rough estimates were made to draw contrasts with other populations, and these were highly speculative. Of course, no one's review of the literature is ever complete, but the current investigator's deliberate attempt to find a single pre-post treatment effectiveness study in incest research proved fruitless. On the one hand, the result is a sense of having crossed a frontier in breaking through the psychiatric-psychoanalytic tradition of speculative, arm-chair ruminations on the intrapsychic vicissitudes of father-daughter incest; hopefully this metapsychological polemic will soon be circumscribed to a place in the background with respect to how these clients ought to be addressed in the therapeutic milieu. On the other hand, in the absence of other external and empirical data, one must necessarily draw conclusions with hesitation. Only when professionals have a sampling of comparable longitudinal studies which show reunification rates, recidivism rates, delinquency rates, sexual dysfunction rates, and other kinds of variables by treatment modality e.g. behavioral, psychoanalytic, systems approaches, penal and judicial approaches, will judgements be possible with respect to how best to treat this unique population.

In the meantime the professional community, itself influenced by the pervasive incest taboo, must try to discriminate between the potpourri of mythologies heretofore given to it as explanation of the problem and advice on how to treat it. The male chauvanist Freudian, armed with the concept of penis envy, tends to suggest the victims sought out and initiated the episode. Weighted on the other side of this polarity is the caricature of the rabid feminist who sees incest as a continued extension of male dominance and sexism right into the daughter's bedroom; this bias tends to minimize the degree of the daughter's collusion and participation as well as to exaggerate the long term debilitation the incestuous experience establishes in her psychological development. It may be that one of these points of view is more accurate than the other, but until an empirical outlook is developed in this area and a scientific "bias" established, this flag-waving and professional sabre-rattling serves no other purpose than to perpetuate various therapeutic myths which are then concientiously applied to child-clients whose victimization and/or exploitation is perhaps only beginning!

REFERENCES

1. J. Tomkins, Penis envy and incest, Psychoanalytic Review. 27, 319-325, 1940.

2. L. Gordon, Incest as revenge against the pre-Oedipal mother, Psychoanalytic Review. 42, 284-292, 1955.

3. A. Schuchter, Prescriptive package: child abuse intervention, U.S. Government Printing Office.(Stock No. 027-000-00387-7), 1976.

4. L. Bender, & A. Blau, The reaction of children to sexual relationships with adults, American Journal of Orthopsychiatry. 22, 825-837, 1952.

5. V. De Francis. (1969) Protecting the Child Victim of Sex Crimes Committed by Adults. American Humane Association, Denver, Colorado.

6. E. Vestergaard, Father-daughter incest. (German): Fader-dotter incest. Nord. T. for Kriminal. 3, 188-193, 1960.

7. J. Landis, Experiences of 500 children with adult sexual deviation, Psychiatric Quarterly Supplement. 30, 91-109, 1956.

8. A. Rascovsky, & M. Rascovsky, On consummated incest, International Journal of Psychoanalysis. 31, 42, 1950.

9. A. Ebner, Incest. (German): Die Blutschande. Krim. Abh, 11, 68-70,1937.

10. H. Maisch. (1972) Incest. Stein and Day, New York.

11. H. Giaretto, Humanistic treatment of father-daughter incest, In. R. Helfer & C. Kempe. (1976) Child Abuse and Neglect: The Family in the Community Ballinger Publishing Co., Cambridge, Mass.

12. V. De Francis. (1969) Child Victims of Incest. American Humane Association Denver, Colorado.

Child Abuse and Neglect, Vol. 3, pp. 303 - 314.
Pergamon Press Ltd., 1979. Printed in Great Britain.

SOCIAL AND LEGAL PERCEPTIONS OF CHILD NEGLECT: SOME PRELIMINARY CONSIDERATIONS

Robert Dingwall
SSRC Centre for Socio-Legal Studies, Oxford
John Eekelaar
Fellow of Pembroke College and
SSRC Centre for Socio-Legal Studies, Oxford

Over the last ten to fifteen years, child abuse and neglect have been widely canvassed as social problems, most notably in the USA but to some degree in all societies whose health and welfare services are influenced by American experience. As is characteristic of such campaigns, the evils alleged are held to be self-evident. Most research has taken the nature of the problem for granted and confined itself to questions of incidence, prevalence, aetiology and therapy. Our investigation, however, takes the formulation of child abuse as a social problem for its central topic. This paper constitutes a preliminary report on our activities.

In Britain, as in most Western societies, an allegation that a child has been abused or neglected can, in the last analysis, only be established at a legal or quasi-legal hearing. The right to bring a child before such a hearing is limited to the police, the National Society for the Prevention of Cruelty to Children (NSPCC) and the social services departments of local authorities. Wherever the complaint originates it must, in practice, pass through one of these three channels. Unless the NSPCC happens to have an active unit in the area, local authorities handle virtually all cases concerned with child protection, acts against children, rather than delinquency, acts by children. In sustaining an allegation of abuse or neglect the social services must usually introduce medical evidence. The third important agency, then, is the health service, both as a source of interpretations for physical signs and symptoms and in case-finding, through presentations at GPs' surgeries or hospital casualty departments or through routine population screening by health visitors.

Our research is studying the interaction between these three key agencies in determining that a child has been abused or neglected and how the relevant disposal decisions are reached. For the last eighteen months we have been conducting fieldwork in an English County. Although we make no particular claims to its representativeness, we would regard it as fairly typical of England outside the conurbations, containing both urban and rural communities of varying sizes and social composition. The main data used in this paper are derived from participant observation and taped interviews with key personnel on 13 cases where legal intervention was considered in a period of 9 months. This included all cases which came to court in that period but it does not claim to include all cases where legal intervention was considered. Partial data have also been collected on a further 7 cases which raised issues of analytic interest over the subsequent 9 months. Typically our case data include field notes on case conferences and court hearings, interviews with solicitors representing various parties, social workers and health visitors and dictated summaries of the records kept by social workers, health visitors and local authority solicitors. The next phase of our fieldwork will attempt to develop our understanding of the pre-legal screening through participant observation in social work and health visiting services and to extend our understanding of the whole by interviews with additional parties including paediatricians, magistrates and court clerks.

This paper falls into three sections. We begin by describing some of the values which are invoked to identify child abuse as a social problem and delineating some of the constraints which are derived from other social values. We shall then, in turn, show how particular orientations to these values shape the activities of health, welfare and legal personnel and the consequences for the recognition, formulation and description of child abuse.

CHILD PROTECTION AS A SOCIAL PROBLEM

The identification of some situations as a social problem turns on implicit or explicit notions of some set of ideas about what that situation ought to be like. Such a set of ideas, which we may term a society member's commonsense knowledge of social structure, provides for the recognition of ordinary states of affairs such that the observer can affirm his membership competence through his ability to identify and bear witness to the world in the same way as any other competent member of that society. By corollary these ideas also provide that a failure to interpret the world correctly or a failure on the part of the world to render itself available for correct interpretation may be an accountable matter.

In the present context, the character of the problem of child protection depends on some set of ideas about what childhood ought to be like. This scheme can be used by observers to recognise events as relevant-to-childhood, to define their nature and to warrant subsequent courses of action. Among other features of this characterisation is a claim that children merit special attention from legal and paralegal agencies over and above that which is available to other society members. This claim involves two assertions: that children are precious and must, therefore, be protected from harm and, secondly, that children are incapable of protecting themselves, either by physical self-defence or by invoking the conventional remedies available to adult victims through citizenship claims.

By 'citizenship claim' we mean those duties which members of a society are thought to owe each other by virtue of their common membership. We draw it very broadly to cover topics ranging over protection from arbitrary violence against person or property to the provision of at least a minimally adequate standard of living sufficient to sustain life, health or whatever. These claims may be enforced in a variety of ways, - for example by informal sanctions, through the legal process or through political action. Since children are denied direct access to such claim enforcement institutions, despite being valued to the degree that they are thought to have a claim to a decent existence, others must speak for them. In child protection there is a widely-shared expectation that parents will play a special role in speaking to society on behalf of their children. If a child is injured, it is its parents who will bring an action for compensation. If a child is hungry it is its parents who will take political or industrial action to raise the household income so that it can be fed. At an everyday level, it is expected that when a child is sick or injured, the parents will activate the medical services on the child's behalf and when it is hungry the parents will bring in the necessary income to feed it. A parent who does not fill this role adequately by the standards of some observer may be exposed to some form of moral or other sanction. A substantial proportion of family law is devoted to defining and elucidating the rights of children and duties of parents in this respect. Where the parent is unable to meet these responsibilities, in the case, for instance, of orphans, family law provides for the identification and licensing of some other proxy.

Child protection proceedings are a special case. Here parental conduct is being evaluated by some agency charged with the regulation of family life. Where that conduct is deemed unsatisfactory, either by virtue of the parents' neglect of their 'proper duties' or by improper behaviour towards their children, this welfare agency may seek to displace the parents, or whoever else is standing proxy for the child.

Like most movements promoting some set of events as a social problem, the child protection lobby conflates both humanitarian and organisational motives.(1) The humanitarian motives are fairly self-evident. There are those who find child abuse and neglect morally objectionable in the same way that any unregulated exercise of naked power by a dominant class is offensive. Children have the same right to protection from physical violence as any other group of people, however stigmatised those people may be - terrorists, mental patients, criminals or whatever. The same argument may even be extended to animal rights.

It is possible, though, to identify at least two organisational motives. The revival of concern for child welfare in the USA during the 1960's presents interesting parallels with the surge of child protection activity in the UK in the two decades before the First World War as a liberal response to perceived problems of social disorganisation, symptomatised by military setbacks, economic crises and civil unrest.(2) Great emphasis was placed on the failure of, particularly working-class, parents to prepare their children adequately for their proper station in life; to be law-abiding, conservative and fit workers and soldiers. It was argued that this failure could only be remedied by purposeful State intervention to regulate the physical and moral environment in which children were raised. A less turbulent society would result, at peace with itself and better equipped to match its international rivals. One can push the analogy too far but similar themes are evident in at least some of the contemporary American literature, suggesting that, whatever their authors' motives, this is expected to elicit a favourable response from government and policy-makers.

These broader concerns can be linked with more specific developments within medicine. Pfohl has analysed the part played by paediatric radiologists in promoting concern about child abuse as a way of advancing the general status of their speciality.(3) It gave a dimension of clinical relevance to a marginal, research-oriented sub-field. These radiologists formed a coalition with paediatricians. Pfohl is less explicit about the paediatricians' motives which rendered them receptive to this newly identified task. As Strong notes, with the exception of a few entrepreneurs, doctors are less ready to take on new areas of work than most proponents of the medicalisation thesis would admit.(4) Pfohl does, however, suggest that the success of preventative medicine in eradicating the infectious diseases of childhood had largely eliminated the prestigious acute elements of paediatric practice and that it was sliding back towards professional marginality.(5)

This argument carries some weight. Becker et al. and Freidson have noted that prestige in medical practice varies with the degree of risk run by the speciality's patients.(6,7) Child abuse and neglect brought life and death elements back into paediatrics. On the other hand it does not seem a sufficient explanation. Children's health remains threatened by a variety of obscure but largely fatal conditions. The singling out of child abuse has to be related both to the overall defensive strategy of paediatrics and to specific economic pressures.

Paediatrics as a speciality becomes possible only at the point where children acquire significant individual value, as birthrates fall and life-expectancy improves. Where high infant mortality is normal there is little reason to invest in medical treatment, since children are replaceable. As the birthrate declines further, each child represents a large investment to be protected. On the other hand, the risk of infectious disease also declines so that there is less need for medical treatment. In the American market situation for health care, paediatricians' incomes are threatened. There is a shrinking client population which is at decreasing risk of disease. In comparison with, say, obstetrics, the price-elasticity of demand for paediatric care may be thought to be relatively high. Obstetricians could raise their fees; paediatricians must find new areas of work and sources of income. The economic incentives in the UK are less direct but even here paediatrics has recently been identified as a relatively low priority.(7a)

The paediatricians have responded by redefining the scope of their speciality in an holistic fashion, claiming a concern for the whole of childhood life.(8,9) It is argued that we are moving towards a position where children's normality depends on continuing <u>professional</u> validation rather than being a matter of commonsense judgement. In this process, neglect and abuse are identified. This mandate, assumed by the speciality, is linked to the broader State concerns discussed earlier.

One must also note the role of budgetary defence and 'slack resources' in this process. Nelson's analysis of the Federal sponsorship of child abuse as a social problem in the U.S. draws attention to the important part played by the Children's Bureau of HEW.(10) Despite its title, the CB had few duties and a low political profile. Child abuse was a problem whose management could be made consistent with the CB's casework ideology and which gave it a more substantial and secure place in the public bureaucracy. Nelson herself discounts the financial aspects of slack resources, noting that the problem was promoted during an economic recession. However, one could argue for this as a <u>defensive</u> response by a part of the Federal government which might be peculiarly vulnerable to public spending cuts, representing, as it did, a weak client group and an unregarded agency. At a more local level Gelles remarks on the influence of the general economic recession on agency willingness to encompass child protection work in order to maintain programmes and staff employment.(11) Other services might be cut but the appeal to a nation's future remained strong for legislators.

The UK position is less well understood at present. It may well be that an additional element relates to the internal politics of the generic social services departments created by the Seebohm reorganisation and the struggles for hegemony between social workers with different specialist backgrounds. An account of the importation of this social problem is still needed.

THE STATUTORY FRAMEWORK

Reflecting these disparate but global concerns, child protection statutes tend to be relatively loosely drafted in terms of what constitutes grounds to challenge an existing proxy's actions in relation to a child. In England, the particular statute, the 1969 Children and Young Persons' Act, is exceptionally widely drawn. It attempts to protect persons and property from children, (the delinquency ground) to enforce school attendance (truancy), to require due obedience to licenced proxies ('beyond control') to regulate sexual conduct ('moral danger') and to defend children against abuse and neglect. The form of words specified under this latter ground is typical of many jurisdictions. Intervention respecting the exercise of a proxy's rights in a child is permitted if:

> his proper development is being avoidably prevented or neglected or his health is being avoidably impaired or neglected or he is being ill-treated.

On the one hand this appears to give a great deal of scope to welfare agencies and the law in determining whether the customary rights of proxy actors, generally parents, should be restricted or removed. On the other, its very indeterminacy creates a host of practical problems for agency staff. Medical and social workers are enjoined to regard certain acts as incompatible with legislators' expectations of appropriate standards of child-rearing in their community. At the same time, the statute gives little guidance in determining what in fact will count as an illegitimate act. Legal personnel are left similarly in the dark about what standards they should apply in interpreting the statute and ruling on the legitimacy of its application in particular instances. The traditional legal remedy for vague statutes, the development of case law is, in England, unavailable due to the appellate structure in this area which makes High Court rulings with national application very uncommon.

There is, then, a high degree of indeterminacy. Medical and social workers do not know what the law will recognise as meriting intervention. Lawyers and magistrates do not know how to evaluate the cases presented to them. In consequence, those involved resort either to specialised occupational theories or commonsense judgements as they attempt to fill in the language of the act and determine the future of particular cases. Whichever is followed, there is no guarantee of any degree of consistency and this is, indeed, militated against by the prevalent social philosophy of "commonsense individualism".

COMMONSENSE INDIVIDUALISM

Against the pressures for intervention, deriving from the child protection movement, described above, we must set the constraints of the individualistic philosophy which prevails in most Western societies. In its classic form this philosophy encapsulates a view of society as constituted from a series of free contracts between individuals in a universal market. Individuals are wholly responsible for their own actions and ultimately free to exercise whatever choices they like in disposing of their own lives, provided that they accept the personal consequences. The role of the State is limited to providing the conditions in which this market can flourish and acting as a residual arbiter between the exercise of conflicting liberties. Although there are few places where this doctrine survives in a pure form today, it has deep historical roots and suffuses all classes in Western societies. What an individual does, especially in the legally protected sanctity of his own home is his own business.(12) He is entitled to conduct it without outside intervention or interference.

Given the presumed social incompetence of children, they are excluded from these individual rights. As J.S. Mill observes in On Liberty, (12a), individualism only applies to 'human beings in the maturity of their faculties', which excludes children and barbarians. Mill, himself, concedes a place for State intervention to enforce parental duties or, as we might put it, to assert citizenship claims on behalf of children. They have a right to support, maintenance, education and the like which should be assumed by the State where parents are neglectful. However, Mill remarked that this doctrine found little general acceptance and parental powers over children were jealously guarded. As a television interviewer remarked in discussing a recent case we were following, '...something we all take for granted - the parents' natural right to their children, often seems to carry very little weight in the eyes of the Law'.

Agency personnel, then, are torn between two conflicting injunctions; that their duty is to intervene to protect children and that their duty is to avoid restricting the liberties of adults. This last is, of course, particularly difficult because the whole raison d'etre of the Welfare State is that the unbridled exercise of individual liberties has undesirable consequences and that a degree of uniformity must be imposed in social life. While medicine, social work and family law entail, in practice, the definition of standards of family life and the restriction of deviations, they are expected to work in a society which is profoundly sceptical about the desirability of such an enterprise.

SOCIAL SERVICES AND 'NEGLECT'

The tensions between intervention and individualism are felt in all areas of child protection, but most particularly in cases of alleged neglect. The identification of a child as neglected depends on an implicit theory about the proper development of children which is used to evaluate the data on any particular child. This evaluation matches the child against the ideals of the theorist. Whether or not these ideals are couched as statistical norms, they have an unavoidably moral character. We can, for example, take the argument that any child below the third centile in weight is neglected. As far as we know, however, weight is normally distributed so that low weight in any particular case is, in itself, as likely to be a matter of constitutional chance as of any other cause. In practice, then, workers must investigate the social meaning of low weight which, in itself, is merely a _prima facie_ charge. This involves them in an assessment of the child's overall situation and in judgements of his associated cognitive and/or affectual development. Can the charge of low weight be defeated, in other words, by pointing to a good standard of family life and otherwise normal development such that no-one is to blame? Such judgements involve reference to conceptions of 'normal lives'; that parents normally behave in certain ways towards their children, that children normally develop in a more or less continuous trajectory from some less to some more desirable cognitive or affectual condition. The particular version involved here is grounded in the experience of its principal proponents, the body of professionals licenced to assess children, more particularly the intellectuals among them whose role is to develop and propagate theories to be used in a cookbook fashion by front-line workers. It is a version which exalts formal intellectual skills and balanced emotional expression in a relatively informal and democratically organised family. (An example of this version is described by Dingwall in his discussion of health visiting (13)). The identification of a child as 'neglected' turns on the failure of a family to defeat a _prima facie_ charge based on the child's physical state, by pointing to its correspondence with other features of some 'normal life'.

There is, of course, no guarantee of the appropriateness of applying this theory. A child may well have been raised in surroundings where aberrant behaviour, in the eyes of child protection agencies, is a normal way of life. Observers of that child sharing the child's own cultural background may judge him or her to be a competent user of that native culture and to meet its cognitive and affectual standards. This judgement can, however, always be undercut by the importation of other criteria used by socially licensed specialists with their intrinsically coercive mandate of promoting a particular sectional view of family life.

This 'cultural relativism' argument is a familiar one and has had a substantial influence on the everyday practice of agencies, asserting as it does the integrity of clients' own experiences. Agency staff have been discouraged from adopting explicitly judgemental attitudes and behaviour. As a working approach it has much to commend it. At the same time it tends to obscure the control elements of the agencies' mandates. While they are enjoined to promote certain standards of family life, they are, equally, presented with a correctional task in reconciling deviants with the promulgated ideals. A non-judgemental, relativist approach is, however, one way of reconciling the strain created by the disjuncture between a control mandate and the prevailing ideology of individualism. While intervention may always be justified by invoking a control mandate, it can always be criticised on individualist libertarian grounds.

These libertarian arguments converge with other organisational pressures to bias the system against intervention. Not intervening always costs less both economically and socially in the short run.

It is often argued that agency resources are invariably perceived as scarce. Our data do not show this as a constraint once an intervention decision has been taken, but it seems reasonable to suppose that this may influence thinking at an earlier stage. We intend to investigate this more closely in our next phase of fieldwork. Intervention poses a threat to the relationship between the worker and his most potentially troublesome clients, the child's parents. The charge of neglect impugns their essential moral character by attacking their competence as socially recognised proxies enjoying 'natural rights'. It is a characteristic of 'natural' phenomena that they are seen as independent of human agency, so that such a charge is peculiarly threatening almost to the extent of questioning the capacity of the parents as moral agents possessing 'normal human parental instincts'.(14) Whatever the formal requirements of the law, the parents recognise the nature of this charge and their defence against inhumanity is to call evidence of their ordinariness, which is strictly irrelevant to the court hearing. The gravity of the charge is, equally, such that agents are reluctant to make it, especially given the indeterminacy of the legal provisions and their application discussed earlier. Finally, it must be noted that a charge of abuse or neglect can be tantamount to an admission of therapeutic failure on the part of the agency. It may be the point at which the control element of the agency mandate becomes transparent. Given the role of the therapeutic ideology in mystifying this regulatory aspect of the agency's work, its recognition may be profoundly unsettling for, particularly, basic-grade workers, constituting a crisis between the ideals of their teachers and the realities of everyday practice.

This has its own consequences. Cases are rarely brought to the law so that few people in the legal system gain any real experience in handling them. The law, consequently, is inconsistently applied and this in turn deters workers from bringing cases. Once a case is launched, a worker rapidly becomes bogged down in a morass of confusion and uncertainty which make heavy demands on his or her time and sets up strong personal pressures, especially in the face of parental hostility and the threat of public exposure. These factors also act as a deterrent against taking legal proceedings, so that few people ever handle enough cases to be able to dispose of them in a routine fashion. In consequence, legal cases are seen as threatening and are considered only as a final resort.

In the specific instance of neglect, the cultural relativism influence leads to a desire to avoid appearing to proceed for the removal of children merely because they come from working class homes. This theme features in headquarters advice to local teams of social workers, in case conferences and in court hearings. While the absolutist mandate does sustain the view that all working class children are deprived, some exceptional degree of deprivation must be established for a case to be considered a candidate for legal intervention. This would seem to create a more stringent ground than the statute itself. It is, however, still only a necessary rather than a sufficient condition. At least two other conditions seem to be required to justify a decision to invoke legal proceedings: the parents must seem incorrigible and there must be a threat of the problem being uncontainable within a small group of people.

By 'parental incorrigibility', we mean to imply, again, a more stringent test than the statute's 'in need of care and control which he is unlikely to receive'. What must be established is not so much a failure of voluntary intervention as a parental repudiation of the services' right to intervene. In this situation, of course, the parent/worker relationship has already broken down and there is less to lose by going to court. Characteristically, such parents appeal to the rhetoric of individualism to assert their right to evaluate their own children and to choose their own mode of 'normal life'. Parental opposition becomes an issue in showing that the services had no choice but to appeal to legal coercive intervention, thereby potentially defeating libertarian criticism.

The failure of containment is similarly linked to the risk of criticism for non-intervention. We have not yet delineated the boundaries of this containment, but our provisional view is that it is the primary care team of general practitioner, health visitor and social worker and the immediate bureaucratic superiors of the latter two workers. Where a case becomes sufficiently serious to justify hospital involvement or there is some chance of it becoming known to the police, school or other outside agency, the workers involved may initiate proceedings to defeat potential criticism of the ineffectiveness of their joint voluntary programme, whether or not the parents are seen as incorrigible. This is, in part, also associated with the media interest in child protection and the coverage of a number of inquiries in recent years. The value placed on children gives this coverage a dramatic and emotive quality which many workers feel threatened by. Given that most coverage has been directed at the consequences of non-intervention, workers may choose to cover themselves by invoking the legal process.

THE LEGAL PROCESS

One of the criticisms which Bourne and Newberger make of the Standards Relating to Abuse and Neglect promulgated by the Juvenile Standards Project of the Institute of Judicial Administration and the American Bar Association is the failure of the Standards to distinguish between removal of a child from home and court-ordered provision of services.(15) They argue that threshold requirements should differ according to the degree of interference in family autonomy contemplated. It is arguable that many of the confusions, ambivalences and perhaps failures of the English system owe their origin, in large part, in a similar failure.

In England it is necessary, before the court decided on what dispositional order to make, or even, strictly, before it knows what degree of intervention the social services contemplate respecting the family in question, for the court to be satisfied that one of the fact-situations triggering this jurisdiction set out in section 1 of the 1969 Act has been established. While the court should theoretically be able to separate in its mind the two questions of making a finding of neglect or abuse and the actions contemplated thereon, this is in practice difficult to do. But still more significant is the extreme narrowness of the types of dispositional orders available to a court should it make a finding. Normally the local authority will ask that the child be committed into its care (a 'care order'), whereby the authority acquires parental rights over the child. It is not, however, a final termination as a parent may at any time apply for the revocation of the order. A 'care order' is necessary if the child is physically to be removed from the parents but, as we discovered, it is by no means always the intention of the authority to make such a removal. The only other order available to the court is a 'supervision order'. This entitles the social services department to supervise the child (not the parent or any other adult) and a condition may be attached requiring the child to be medically examined. These orders were widely regarded by almost all parties in our study to be of little use, and, indeed, often to be dangerous. As one informant put it, they achieved maximum provocation with minimum effectiveness.

Our data suggests that consideration should be given to making available a far wider and more flexible range of measures as a response to abuse and neglect short of a care order. Four considerations support this point. The first arises from our earlier observation that one of the major factors precipitating a decision to initiate the legal process is the perceived 'incorrigibility' of the parents. Time and again the agency personnel relate attempts to advise, persuade or cajole the aberrant parent(s) into accepting home helps, attending clinics with their children, taking the children to playgroups or nursery schools (either for developmental reasons or to keep them out of the way when a suspect spouse or cohabitee might visit the home) or undergoing parental training. One cannot be sure, but it is at least possible that some of these cases might not have deteriorated to the condition we found them if some more formal kind of 'pressure' could have been exerted at an earlier stage.

The second reason for raising the possibility of intervention by direction rather than committal to care is that quite often this seemed in any case to be the major purpose of bringing the proceedings. A care order might, therefore, be sought despite the fact that the children were at home and were expected to remain there in order to give the authority a bargaining position in its insistence that a husband should not spend such long periods away from his neurotic wife; conversely, the authority might be prepared to leave the children at home provided that a third party, an undesirable influence in their eyes, kept away from them. Of course, 'playing' a care order in this way may have many advantages for a local authority. Unless the court discharges the order, it has an almost untrammelled discretion in deciding where the child should be and what conditions to impose. But there are also objections. It may be counter-productive to subject the parents to the trauma of full 'care proceedings', and agency personnel may themselves be inhibited from initiating this process. Having children at home with them while under a care order may subject the parents to an unnerving degree of helplessness. As one of them said: "little things make it slightly infuriating to tell people what you are doing all the time; not being treated as a responsible adult; being treated as though you were a child yourself. Like today, we wouldn't have brought the children to court, but the County Council insisted. They are with us but they are not our children."

The third consideration is that in some cases the courts seek to achieve a form of coercive intervention short of committal to care by exacting undertakings from parties. The undertaking might be to co-operate more fully with social services or the provision of home help; or to spend more time at home. In one case where a cohabitee, who was not even party to the proceedings, made an undertaking to the court, the local authority solicitor said that, as he was not a party, the magistrates would have abdicated their responsibility if they took any notice of it. But technically the parents are not parties to care proceedings either, and undertakings are sometimes sought from them. Finally, the use of "intermediate" measures would mitigate the conflict between the control element in the agencies' mandate and the individualist ideology.

ROLE OF LAWYERS AND CONCEPTS OF EVIDENCE

The strain between intervention and individualism is apparent once cases come to court. In England and Wales, matters arising under the 1969 Children and Young Persons Act are heard, in the first instance by lay juvenile magistrates. Whichever grounds the case is brought under it is, technically, treated as an action by the State, through the local authority or police, against the child. The parents are not parties and have no right to Legal Aid. The model here is, essentially, one derived from criminal prosecutions, although proceedings under the 1969 Act are, in fact, civil matters. As such it fits the delinquency grounds reasonably well. When dealing with child protection matters, however, it gives rise to a number of serious anomalies.

We have already shown that the charge of abuse and neglect is, in commonsense terms, a severe indictment of the moral standing of the existing recognised proxy for the child, usually its parents. If the matter gets to court, though, the parent is, strictly, shut out. In practice, of course, a considerable degree of discretion is often exercised by the courts in accordance with their sense of natural justice. In our experience, parents will invariably be heard by a court and, if they are not represented, court clerks often partially adopt an advocate's role in examining witnesses. But this discretion means that parental interests are represented in an ad hoc and inconsistent fashion. Much depends on whether they have the private means to engage a lawyer.

This places the child's lawyer in a difficult position. Although representing the child's interests, most of the children in such cases are too young, by any standard, to give meaningful instructions, even if their advocates were willing to take seriously what the children had to say. The obvious source of information is the recognised proxies, the parents. Children's lawyers depended on parental co-operation, shared a sense of the natural injustice of excluding parents and, typically, lacked experience in these matters. While a private practice solicitor accepting advocacy work will have a fair experience of delinquency cases under this Act, child protection cases, as we have shown, are rare events. The solicitors lack a readily available stock of knowledge and recipes for action. In consequence, their actions run on a commonsense foundation and lean heavily on the delinquency model.

Thus, while these solicitors recognised the potential conflict of interest between parents and children, and stated that they would advise parents to seek separate representation in such circumstances, they were reluctant to discover such conflicts in the particular cases they were dealing with. Their commonsense assumptions about family life made it unlikely that they would 'see' the case for abrogating proxy rights, especially where they were dealing with vague allegations of neglect or emotional damage. The criminal model of proceedings made available a rhetoric of 'testing' the local authority's case to justify vigorous cross-examination, especially when combined with the lawyer's traditional individualism which held that any State intervention required the strongest possible warrant. Examinations and closing addresses were, then, often based on an implicit espousal of the strict criminal burden of proof rather than the lighter civil burden which is technically applicable. Such considerations, then, could generate closing remarks like these from a solicitor representing a child in a case of alleged physical damage (denied by the parents).

> 'In the end it comes down to whether you feel that these two people before you are of the nature that they could lose control of themselves and deliberately inflict injuries of this nature. Unless you are satisfied of that you ought not to make the order...If you have reservations in your mind about their child care that is not relevant...I invite you to say that the Council has not made out its case.'

Yet that solicitor was still able to say to us, after the hearing, that, when he had heard all the evidence, he personally thought the care order should be made.

The influence of individualist thought ensures that the local authority cannot be seen as representing the child, as giving him independent access to society to enforce a citizenship claim. It is, rather, depicted as a faintly sinister interventionist bureaucracy. Nevertheless the local authority has such a duty laid upon it by statute and is exposed to public censure if it fails in that duty to the extent that death or serious injury results. If they are reluctant to bring cases initially, once a case is brought there are pressures to succeed. A failure may lead to the local authority being shut out and leave the child unprotected. These pressures must, however, be set against the therapeutic ideology of the social services departments. For them a court hearing is, ideally, only one phase of a continuing relationship with both children and parents. There is, then, a frequent ambivalence among social workers over their desire to win the case without compromising their therapeutic goals.

The lawyers from the solicitors' department of the local authority, who represent the social services department in these proceedings, recognise this ambivalence at a formal level. When they are asked for a statement of their role, they assert that their duty is to present all the evidence, as they see it, about the child's interests and leave it to the court to make a decision. These solicitors, however, face the occupational contingencies of any professional group in a bureaucratic setting.(16,17) The defence of their claim to professional status involves certain assertions and orientations more characteristic of a profession rooted in private practice. We intend to pursue this issue in a separate paper elsewhere. For the moment, it is sufficient to note their tendency in other contexts to slide into a more traditional lawyer/client model, where their task is to win the case for their client by putting their clients' arguments in the most favourable light.
(Interview)

JE: Did the magistrates get a full and proper picture (of the evidence)...?

LA lawyer: I certainly put our side of it. If they were clouded in one way that's up to (the opposing solicitor) to do something about it.

(Case Conference)

LA lawyer (to social worker): We've got to get this over. We've got to take a slant on this and present our evidence in such a way. Your report says that as time has gone on, family relationships have improved. I'm not going to ask you that.

The interaction of these adversarial models can lead to apparently unfortunate consequences. For fear of his adopting an adversarial role, the child's solicitor may be denied access to the information which the local authority has used to reach its decision. The solicitor is, then, obliged to rely on parents' accounts and eased into an adversarial role.

The local authority's defensiveness may be compounded by anxieties over the strength of its case. The solicitors' department usually come in at a late stage when the social workers have already decided that proceedings should be taken. To a legal eye, however, the case may look much thinner when assessed by a court's standards of evidence.

We have seen how the identification of a child as neglected turns on an implicit evaluation of the data on that child in the light of a general theory about 'normal development'. Social workers' judgements are formed on the basis of a subtle amalgam of factual observation and critical evaluation, interpreting those facts in the light of the shared knowledge of their occupational community. A social worker described one typical situation:

> '...I'm sure that anybody going into the Clarke household especially, you know, at a time after Mrs. Clarke had taken an overdose or there's something happened, I mean one can't sort of fail to feel for these children and think, you know, what effect it is having on them. But that's different to actually measuring it and being able to say in court that these children are sort of emotionally disturbed.'

While such evaluations form an integral part of social workers' 'professional judgement', their legal status is uncertain.

This uncertainty derives from the wider social uncertainty about the professional claims of social work and the degree to which they can be regarded as expert in comparison with, say, doctors:

(Hearing)

GP: ...there's no admission or criminal records of her being a psychopath; but I could easily give my opinion.

(Case Conference)

SSW: What if they say to me, 'What about if the child goes home; do you think she will be abandoned again?'

LA lawyer: You'll have to say you don't know. Nobody could answer that. Anybody from the street could have an opinion on that. You could ask an expert psychiatrist if she was the sort of person who was likely to do this. Only an expert psychiatrist can answer that, not you or I.

SW (aside): Not a mere social worker.

English law bases its suspicion of opinion evidence on the general principle that 'litigants are entitled to have their disputes settled by a judge with or without a jury and not by the statement of witnesses'.(18) This principle holds in care proceedings on the assumption that it is for the court to make the crucial, final, evaluation. It is, however, modified in two circumstances. One is where it is thought that the subject matter requires a sufficient degree of specialised knowledge to make 'expert' opinion valuable and the witness is adjudged an 'expert'. The other is where it is impossible to separate facts from the inferences based on those facts. Decisions on both these issues are taken pragmatically by the courts. Doctors, as we have seen, assume and are accorded expert status regardless of whether or not they have specialised knowledge of children or, in the above quotation, psychiatry. Social work evidence on matters relating to child-rearing and parental competence does not have such clear recognition. Sometimes it is held that these are matters in which anyone is an expert; sometimes lawyers and magistrates will ask for expert opinion from social workers.

INTERVENTION, INDIVIDUALISM AND CHILD PROTECTION

It seems that this ambiguity in relation to social worker evidence reflects a general ambiguity in society's mandate to social workers. While the medical profession has an accepted mandate to pass judgement upon practices relating to physical health, it is not clear whether the social work profession is perceived as an agency licensed by the community to regulate, in accordance with professionally accepted criteria, standards of child care. The sense of assuredness of the medical and para-medical occupations in their role may be one reason for what appears to be a greater readiness on their part to seek intervention in child abuse and neglect cases than is evident in the social services. Newberger and Bourne have noted that there is need for physicians "to be more aware of the complexity of human life, especially in its social and psychological dimensions" and thus to broaden the conceptual basis of medical practice.(19) Our own observations would confirm a tendency in that profession to make judgements based on limited evidence (perhaps only observation of parents in a hospital setting).

Newberger and Bourne consider that "the workers who seem best to be able to conceptualise the familial and social context of problems of violence are social workers and nurses" and add that their own interdisciplinary child abuse consultation programme is organised under the aegis of the administration rather than the medical clinical department. These observations would seem to apply _a fortiori_ to child neglect. In our own research the primacy of social service involvement seems to have been recognised by those doctors who have accepted social service chairmanship of case conferences even when held on hospital premises. Such an ordering of the inter-agency decision-making structure should have implications for the status of social worker evidence in care proceedings.

We are it seems left with a situation where the best may be the enemy of the good. In a thoroughgoing individualist society, we would have no State intervention and an acceptance of the liberty of any proxy acting for the child to dispose of that child as he will. This would include the right to deprive that child of its life. Indeed dead children might even serve as moral exemplars for the living as they did in Victorian days. This doctrine has the virtue of consistency, but we have as a society rejected it. At the same time, we have not, as a society, been prepared to countenance State intervention to promote some optimal standards of family life, whether by material redistribution, education or statutory regulation. Although workers in the field may be instructed in the professionally optimal standards and encouraged to use these in evaluating actual situations, they are painfully aware that the consequent implications for action are such as to command little general support. They console themselves with a therapeutic rhetoric based on persuasion as a means of effecting personal change rather than a reformative rhetoric based on direction.

In a democratic society, it may be that one can go no further, in which case we must concede the amount of avoidable damage to children which ensues. If, however, we were more explicit about the role of health and welfare agencies in enforcing social control, then we could at least have an open debate about what it was that was being enforced. This might then lead towards a more consistent policy of public information through education, mass media, etc. which would have the important libertarian benefit of allowing potential offenders to know when they were committing an offence. The libertarian losses from a degree of enlightened despotism may be offset against the gains from a greater determinacy of offence. At the same time, health and welfare workers would be relieved of the occasionally traumatic burden of combining both therapeutic and reformative roles.

METHODOLOGICAL NOTE

This paper offers a preliminary and interim account of our research which is continuing for another eighteen months or two years. Accordingly, much of it is based on our perceptions and interpretations of the data we have been collecting rather than a systematic and rigorous inspection of them. Where we have included quotations from our interviews or field notes, these should be regarded as illustrative rather than evidential.

ACKNOWLEDGEMENTS

The research described in this paper is supported by the Social Science Research Council and the Department of Health and Social Security. We are grateful to the necessarily anonymous authorities for their generous co-operation in this study. Earlier versions of this paper were read at the London Medical Sociology Group and the Ninth World Congress of Sociology. We are particularly grateful to Margot Jefferys, Bob Harrison, Phil Strong, Janet Askham and Topsy Murray for their comments but responsibility for this version is, of course, ours alone.

BIBLIOGRAPHY

1. MACINTYRE, S.J., Old Age as a Social Problem. In R. Dingwall et al., eds., Health Care and Health Knowledge, Croom Helm, London (1977).

2. DINGWALL, R.W.J., Collectivism, Regionalism and Feminism: Health Visiting and British Social Policy 1850-1975, Journal of Social Policy 6, 291-315 (1977).

3. PFOHL, S.J., The 'Discovery' of Child Abuse, Social Problems 24, 310-23 (1977).

4. STRONG, P.M., Sociological Imperialism and the Profession of Medicine: A Critical Examination of the Thesis of Medical Imperialism, Social Science and Medicine (in press).

5. BUCHER, R. and STRAUSS, A.L., Professions in Process, American Journal of Sociology 66, 325-34 (1961).

6. BECKER, H.S. et al., (1961) Boys in White, University of Chicago Press, Chicago.

7. FREIDSON, E. (1971) Profession of Medicine, Dodd, Mead, New York.

7a. D.H.S.S., Priorities for Health and Personal Social Services in England; A Consultative Document, H.M.S.O., London (1976).

8. ARMSTRONG, D., Child Development and Medical Ontology, Social Science and Medicine (in press).

9. DINGWALL, R.W.J., Problems of Teamwork in Primary Care. Paper presented at PSSC seminar, London, to be published by PSSC (1978).

10. NELSON, B.J. with LINDENFELD, T., Setting the Public Agenda: The Case of Child Abuse. In J. May and A. Wildavsky, eds., The Policy Cycle, Sage, Beverly Hills (1978).

11. GELLES, R.J., Community Agencies and Child Abuse: Labelling and Gatekeeping (1975).

12. STINCHCOMBE, A.L., Institutions of Privacy in the Determination of Police Administrative Practice, American Journal of Sociology, 69, 150-60 (1963).

12a. MILL, J.S., (1962) Utilitarianism, ed. Warnock M., Fontana, London.

13. DINGWALL, R.W.J., (1977) The Social Organisation of Health Visitor Training, Croom Helm, London.

14. GOFFMAN, E., (1975) Frame Analysis, Penguin, Harmondsworth.

15. BOURNE, R. and NEWBERGER, E.H., 'Family Autonomy' or 'Coercive Intervention'? Ambiguity and Conflict in the Proposed Standards for Child Abuse and Neglect, Boston University Law Review, 57, 670 (1977).

16. HALL, R.H., Professionalisation and Bureaucratisation, American Sociological Review, 33, 92-104 (1968).

17. BUCHER, R. and STELLING, J., Characteristics of Professional Organisations, Social Problems, 10, 3-15 (1969).

18. CROSS, R., (1974) Evidence, 4th Edition, Butterworths, London.

19. NEWBERGER, E.H. and BOURNE, R., The Medicalisation and Legalisation of Child Abuse. In J.M. Eekelaar and S.N. Katz, eds., Family Violence, Butterworths, Toronto (1978).

Child Abuse and Neglect, Vol. 3, pp. 315 - 321.
Pergamon Press Ltd., 1979. Printed in Great Britain.

ENGLISH CHILD PROTECTION LEGISLATION AND PROCEDURE
- An aid or a hindrance to the abused child and the family?

Michael Wilford, Pat McBain, Naomi Angell, Suzanne Tarlin and Others

6, Bowden Street, London, S.E.11.

Introduction

This paper is based on our experience as members of a firm of London Solicitors (only relatively recently set up) dealing exclusively with cases relating to children. The problems discussed are those which we encounter in practice and we are conscious that our viewpoint as Lawyers may seem to be a narrow one. We, therefore, hope that in the discussion the viewpoints of other professions will be expressed. We also look forward to contributions from Lawyers from other countries because we realise that, in many respects, including particularly the representation of children and parents in abuse and neglect cases, Lawyers in this country have much to learn.

Our concern is that the existing law and procedure in this country often inhibits the solution of problems instead of helping towards their resolution. We do not intend to discuss the criminal law and the prosecution of parents or guardians who ill-treat or neglect their children. The place of criminal prosecution in abuse cases is a subject in itself and, in any event, the representation of parents in such proceedings is largely outside the scope of our practice. In this context, we are concerned mainly with "Care proceedings" or "Wardship proceedings" in which the result or potential result is the transfer of responsibility for the child, including parental rights, from the child's parents to a Local Authority, to the Court or to some other person, and with that, the right to remove the child from his or her parents or guardians on a temporary or permanent basis. In Care proceedings, this is effected by making a Care Order in favour of the Local Authority. In Wardship proceedings, the child is made a ward of Court.

In cases of abuse and neglect, Care proceedings may be brought under Section 1(2) of the Children & Young Persons Act, 1969 (as amended by the Children Act, 1975), by a Local Authority, the Police or the National Society for Prevention of Cruelty to Children, where:-

(a) (the child's) proper development is being avoidably prevented or neglected, or his health is being avoidably impaired or neglected, or he is being ill-treated;

(b) it is probable that condition (a) will be satisfied, having regard to the fact that the Court or another Court has found that it is or was satisfied in the case of a child or young person who is or was a member of the household to which (the child) belongs;

(bb) it is probable that condition (a) will be satisfied, having regard to the fact that a person who has been convicted of certain specified offences against children is, or may become, a member of the same household as the child.

In Wardship proceedings, the High Court has jurisdiction to assume the guardianship of children in any case in which it seems necessary in the child's interest, and may then exercise parental rights. The Court has the legal custody of the child, but assigns his or her actual care to whoever seems most suitable. Any person with a legitimate interest in the child may apply to make the child a ward of Court. In cases of abuse or neglect, the Court will, in general, exercise its jurisdiction unless Care proceedings have already been initiated by a Local Authority, in which case it will normally be reluctant to do so. However, it is not uncommon for a Local Authority itself to apply to make a child ward of Court rather than initiate Care proceedings in the Juvenile Court. In abuse and neglect cases, such applications are usually made immediately following the child's removal from home under a Place of Safety Order.

Removal from home

No-one would, we think, dispute the necessity of a simple and rapid procedure for removing children who are at risk of injury from those with whom they are presently living, whether they be parents, guardians of the child, or others. Where there is reasonable suspicion of a danger of serious injury, immediate removal is obviously of paramount importance; or an Order may be required to prevent the child being taken away from hospital. Such a procedure is provided by Section 28 of the Children & Young Persons Act, 1969, and also by Section 40 of the Children & Young Persons Act, 1933. Under the former provision, "any person" may apply for such an Order to a single Magistrate and an Order may be made authorising the child to be removed to a place of safety (normally a children's home) for a period not exceeding twenty-eight days. An Order may be made under Section 28 if the Magistrate is satisfied that the person making the application has reasonable cause to believe that any of the grounds for care proceedings are satisfied in respect of the particular child. The applicant merely has to satisfy a Magistrate that he or she has a reasonable suspicion: no facts have to be proved, no expert evidence has to be adduced. The application under Section 40 of the 1933 Act relates specifically to cases of abuse or neglect; the application may be made by any person acting in the interests of the child and the Magistrate may issue a Warrant authorising the Police to search for and remove the child to a place of safety. Again, the Magistrate has only to be satisfied that the person applying has a reasonable suspicion that the child is being abused or neglected and the Order may be made for a period up to twenty-eight days.

In practice, we have found that these procedures have been used in almost all cases where Care proceedings are subsequently brought on the grounds of alleged abuse or neglect. It is in the less serious cases and the cases where it is very doubtful whether injuries are non-accidental that there is, to our minds, grave cause for concern about these procedures. The parents do not have to be notified of the applicant's intention, they are not represented before the Magistrate and the only obligation upon the applicant is, after the Order has been executed, to "take such steps as are practicable for informing (the child's) parent or guardian of (the child's) detention and of the reason for it". (Section 28(3) of the 1969 Act) Nothing has to be put in writing, nor do the parents have to be told of the child's whereabouts. The parents have no right of appeal against the Order. They may seek to make the child a ward of Court, but generally only if the Local Authority has not previously initiated Care proceedings, and even Wardship proceedings may be ineffective in such circumstances.

In the result, the parents and child may be separated for up to twenty-eight days without contact, the parents may have no clear idea of the reasons for the removal of the child and there may be no opportunity for independent investigation during this period of the necessity for the Order.

In one case, we were concerned for children aged 5 and 7 who were removed by Police under a Place of Safety Order. They had been with their father with whom they had been living without previous separation. When the Police came to take the children away, the father was told only that there were serious allegations against him, but nothing specific was said. The father was married, but the children were from a previous relationship. The wife had recently left the family home. For a week, the father did not know the whereabouts of the children. As a result of a case conference which was then held, the father was allowed to visit the children, but the children were put on the "at risk" register. After ten days, the Local Authority said they did not intend to institute Care proceedings. Three weeks after their removal, the children were returned home by the Police who stated that no criminal proceedings would be instituted. There was no evidence of any injuries to the children. Three months after the Place of Safety Order was taken, the children were removed from the "at risk" register.

In another case, an unmarried mother bringing up her baby alone consulted her G.P. because of the baby's incessant crying and failure to thrive. The G.P. noticed a bruise on the baby's head and referred the case to hospital. An initial X-ray suggested a fracture and the mother was told of this. A second X-ray shortly thereafter established, however, that there was no fracture, but the mother was not told of the second X-ray. A Place of Safety Order was then applied for and Care proceedings were instituted. The mother only learned that there was, in fact, no fracture of the baby's skull shortly before the matter came before the Juvenile Court a month later when the Court refused to grant an Interim Care Order. There was no Social Work support for the mother either from the hospital or the local Authority at any stage.

We cannot believe that separation is axiomatic in every abuse or neglect case. Even in those cases where separation is thought to be necessary, there will presumably be two ends to the scale: at the one end, cases in which permanent separation is thought to be necessary, and at the other, cases in which a short period of separation is considered to be desirable. But action initiated by an application for a Place of Safety Order may, in fact, result, and often will result, in a long period of separation because, as matters stand at the moment in London Juvenile Courts, it may be many months before Care proceedings are determined if the Care Order wanted by the Local Authority is opposed. What may be seen as a measure to effect a temporary separation may actually have effects upon bonding and other developmental aspects which were by no means intended. This is quite apart from considerations of justice and the right of child or parent, both of whom may be traumatically affected by such an Order, to challenge the necessity for it. We suggest, therefore, that while it should be possible for an Order for removal of the child to be obtained rapidly in an emergency on an ex parte application to the Court, the same requirements should be imposed as are imposed on an application for an Injunction in the High Court - namely, to produce evidence either oral or on Affidavit in support of the application giving grounds for the applicant's reasonable belief that the child is at risk. A copy of an Affidavit setting out such evidence should be served on the parents at the time the child is removed and it should then be open to representatives of the child or the parents to challenge the order at any time thereafter, the child being independently represented at the hearing.

The extensive use of the Place of Safety procedure is, no doubt, the result of the increasing social pressure on relevant Agencies to take effective action in cases of abuse or neglect. Apart from any harmful effects on the child resulting from sudden removal and lengthy separation, we have been forcefully struck in all the cases with which we have been concerned by the attitude of the parents following their child's removal, particularly when the removal has been effected by the Police. Invariably, the feeling of resentment on the part of the parents is profound; they feel betrayed by their Social Worker and antagonistic to any further contact with that Worker - and this at a time when it would seem most important to intensify social work with the family, particularly if a return of the child to the family is contemplated in the shorter or even in the longer term. A tightening up of the Place of Safety procedure would not, it is suggested, detract from the necessity for simple and rapid action in the serious cases, but would make it necessary to justify separation and a denial of access in the marginal cases. As it is the degree of contact between child and parents often seems to depend on the individual approach of the Social Worker.

We recently had a case concerning a young couple with a history of abuse by the father. The family's Social Worker indicated an intention to take a Place of Safety Order on the third baby as soon as it was born, but then gave us the opportunity to make the child a ward of Court immediately thereafter with the consequence that an Order could be obtained under which the mother and child could remain in hospital and enquiries could be put in hand to see if there was a family unit which could take the parents and child on a longterm basis. The expert advice received was that had the child been taken away immediately with a denial of access - an approach which has been adopted in other similar cases - the parent/child relationship would have been affected, the couple would have been left with a lasting sense of grievance and the likelihood was that the pattern would repeat itself with further pregnancies.

Care Orders to Local Authorities

There is legitimate concern that in abuse cases it is often very difficult to prove that injuries to a child were caused non-accidentally. The criticism of the present adversary system - and Care proceedings in the Juvenile Court in England are adversary proceedings, despite a statement to the contrary by the Lord Chief Justice in Humberside C.C. v. D.P.R. /1977/ 2 All England Law Reports 964) - is that if those applying for the child to be taken into care do not present their evidence convincingly, or if the advocate of the parent is particularly persuasive, the case will fail and the child will be exposed to dangers which ought to have been prevented. We would certainly endorse the view that it is of prime importance that in those cases where a child is at risk of injury, whether physical or psychological, the Court should be able to identify the danger and make appropriate Orders. Care proceedings in this country are, in our opinion, open to considerable criticism. In the first place, they are distorted by the fact that the Respondent to the proceedings is the child, whereas, upto recently, it was tacitly accepted that the parents (who are not parties to the proceedings) conducted the case on the child's behalf (see the report of the Maria Colwell case, Humberside C.C. v. D.P.R. and R. v. Worthing Justices ex parte Stevenson (1976) 2 All England Reports 194). The Maria Colwell case influenced that part of the Children Act, 1975, which gives the Court discretion to prevent the parents or guardian conducting the case on behalf of the child. But even if the 1975 Act were fully implemented, the procedure in Care cases would not, in our view, be satisfactory.

We believe that (i) Care proceedings must be adversarial and that it is essential that the parents be parties to them; (ii) that both the child and the parents be represented; (iii) that the Lawyer representing the child must either take instructions from the child if of an age to express his or her wishes, or, if not, must ensure that the Court has all the relevant evidence before it, including the evidence of independent experts in any relevant field on what is in the child's best interests; (iv) that the Court should have an investigative power to require witnesses of fact to be called who appear to have relevant evidence to give and also, if necessary, to require expert evidence on any particular topic which seems to the Court not to be adequately covered by expert evidence produced by the parties; (v) that counter-balanced against the importance of the Court being able to identify cases in which there is risk to the child is the importance of not transferring responsibility for the child from the parents to the Local Authority unless a strong case for the necessity of such transfer is made out; (vi) that Care proceedings should be conducted before a highly qualified Family Court. A Care Order to a Local Authority may not only determine the child's way of life or abode until he or she is eighteen, but may affect the child's whole future. In terms of decision-making, it might reasonably be said that there are few more important decisions in any context, whether criminal or civil, yet the responsibility for this decision is put upon the most junior level of Court - the Magistrates Court - in the judicial hierarchy.

The gravity, from both the child's point of view as well as the parents', of transferring the rights and obligations of parents to Local Authorities or to the Court, is, we believe, under-emphasised.

We have the subjective impression that Care Orders are sometimes wanted by Local Authorities for reasons which are not directly relevant to a consideration of the best interests of the child. They sometimes seem to be wanted mainly for ease of control or to obtain priority in the allocation of resources. Yet, on the other hand, in the allocation of financial resources to children under Care Orders, there often seems to be an unnecessary inflexibility. So, in a neglect case in which five children of a family were placed in three different residential homes at a cost to the Local Authority at that time well in excess of £300 per week, the alternative of intensive social work help for the family at home on a daily basis was ruled out not on social work grounds, but because administratively, there appeared to be no way in which the Department could employ a worker on that basis, despite the fact that the cost to the Authority would obviously have been considerably less.

We also have the impression that once the decision has been made by a Local Authority to apply for a Care Order, there is often a tendency to withdraw support from the family, rather than to intensify the support which might be thought to be the preferable course at a time when, in abuse or neglect cases, the child will almost always have been removed from the home. Local Authorities are in a dilemma. On the one hand, they are fearful of doing anything that would jeopardise the success of their case and any improvement in the home conditions or in the relationship between the child and the parents might be thought by the Court to run counter to the Local Authority's application. On the other hand, they are, by virtue of Section 1 of the Children & Young Persons Act, 1963, under a statutory duty to try to prevent children coming into Care.

It might help to solve this dilemma and ease the strain put upon the relationship between the family and the Social Worker by removal of the child from home, if the decision to initiate Care proceedings were removed from Social Services Departments and put in the hands of some independent initiating authority to whom Social Services Departments would be able to refer. If this is not practicable, consideration could be given to finding a way of absolving the family Social Worker of the necessity of playing the role of prosecutor as well as counsellor and confidant. In any event, we believe that more emphasis should be placed on the duty on the Local Authority under Section 1 of the 1963 Act to prevent children being taken into care. Although we understand the social pressures on Local Authorities to take legal action in this type of case, we consider that more emphasis in the marginal cases should be placed upon working out agreed courses of action with the family and less emphasis on Court proceedings.

Reviews

It is no secret that children in the care of Local Authorities sometimes get "lost" in the system and that decisions regarding their welfare and upbringing are taken on grounds of administrative expediency rather than the child's best interests. A review of each child's case is required by Section 27 of the 1969 Act, to be carried out at 6-monthly intervals, but in many cases this is a perfunctory procedure. In many cases also, because of staffing difficulties, children in care are not allocated a Social Worker and there is consequently no proper monitoring of the child's progress and development. It may well happen in such circumstances that the child is psychologically or even physically damaged because of the unsuitable environment, and that matters are as bad, if not worse, than had the child not been made the subject of a Care Order in the first place. Although, under the Children Act, 1975, the Secretary of State has power to make regulations regarding reviews which could effect a reform in this area, the present indications are that the regulations when made will affect matters very little. We agree that what is required is a Children's Ombudsman service set up to investigate complaints regarding the treatment of children in care and, coupled with that, a National Review body to whom representation could be made regarding the administration of Care Orders (see Justice 1975 and Law Centres' Working Group Recommendations on 11th Report of House of Commons Expenditure Committee on the working of the 1969 Act).

Procedural and evidential problems

As is already evident from what we have said, under the present system in England, abuse and neglect cases are not the exclusive province of any one Court. Any particular case of child abuse or neglect may be the subject of proceedings before as many as four different Courts - the Magistrates Court and/or the Crown Court in connection with the criminal aspects: the Juvenile Court and/or the High Court in connection with the civil aspects (Care proceedings and Wardship). This may involve numerous different investigations being conducted at the same time. There may be investigations by the Police, investigations by the relevant Social Services Department, investigations by a hospital, by the Official Solicitor (in Wardship cases) and by professional advisers appointed by representatives of the child and representatives of the parents. This in itself is confusing enough, but where there is a criminal prosecution, then it is almost invariably the practice of the Juvenile Court to postpone any decision on the case, other than to make Interim Orders allowing the child (who will have been removed to a children's home or to temporary foster parents under a Place of Safety Order) to be retained in care pending the final hearing. It is not uncommon, in our experience, for the child to be kept in this limbo for periods of up to six months, meanwhile being subjected to the various investigations and enquiries to which we have already referred. Save in the most serious criminal cases, there seem to be no arguments against these matters being dealt with by a single Court equipped with suitably qualified Judges.

Neither the present Juvenile Court system nor the Wardship jurisdiction of the High Court seem to us to provide the pattern for such a single Court. The procedure of the Juvenile Court reflects the fact that it is, in essence, a Court of summary jurisdiction in criminal matters. It has neither the resources nor the procedural facilities to examine in depth the issues that arise in Care proceedings nor the flexibility to make the varying orders which, in different circumstances, may be necessary. Thus, for example, in the Juvenile Court, the nature of the applicant's case does not have to be disclosed before the hearing; the parents and those representing the child only have to be informed on what ground, under the Children & Young Persons Act, 1969, the proceedings are brought. This would not, in itself, be so grave a disadvantage if those independently representing the child had access to information about the child and the family which the Local Authority had on their files. In practice, however - and it has to be said that there is no consistency here - it is very often the case that a Local Authority will refuse access to any information and will not permit the Social Worker concerned to discuss the matter with the Lawyer representing the child. This attitude is comprehensible in the light of the fact that Lawyers ostensibly representing the child have, in the past and, no doubt, still do in some cases, taken their instructions exclusively from the parents of the child. But restrictions on full investigation, coupled with the inadequate procedures of the Court, militate against any really thorough enquiry into this type of case by a Juvenile Court.

From many points of view, Wardship proceedings have greater advantages. Any person with a legitimate interest in the child is entitled to appear and be heard. Whereas, for instance, grandparents or the mother's co-habitee would have no standing in a Juvenile Court in Care proceedings, they are entitled to take part in and be represented in Wardship proceedings. Evidence, in the early stages of Wardship, is all generally given by way of Affidavit and, in our experience, this has a less destructive effect on relationships than does the giving of oral evidence - particularly when hearings follow relatively soon after the children have been removed from their parents. The High Court, in Wardship proceedings, is more flexible in the Interim Orders it can make. It may make Orders in regard to access and deal with day-to-day problems that crop up in a way which is wholly beyond the power of the Juvenile Court, which effectively can either make a Care Order in favour of the Local Authority (or a Supervision Order) or, alternatively, make no Order at all. There is also a wide flexibility in the final Orders that the High Court can make in Wardship. While retaining the legal custody of the child, the Court can grant the care and control to any person, including the Local Authority, whom it thinks most suitable and can make further Orders from time to time as and when it may become necessary to alter the existing state of things.

There is, however, in Wardship proceedings, no provision for independent representation of the child other than by the Official Solicitor, and the Official Solicitor's office, which is a civil service department, is over-burdened. Wardship is expensive and the delays are certainly no less than they are in the Juvenile Court and very often much longer. So while Interim Orders may make the period of limbo more tolerable, a final decision is often longer postponed, to the possible detriment of the child as well as the parents.

Training of Judges and Lawyers

Cases of abuse or neglect of children obviously involve medical, psychological and social factors. They also involve complex legal issues, not only because the law relating to children is becoming increasingly complex, but because of the difficulty of sifting and evaluating the factual and expert evidence in cases of this kind. Juvenile Court magistrates may have relevant qualifications but that is not by any means always the case and they are seldom legally trained. Professional Judges are well used to evaluating evidence of a technical nature, but seldom have any particular training in the other fields. Since we believe that thorough investigation and evaluation of the facts and of the opinions of experts is a matter of prime importance in this type of case, we consider that the Court which deals with them should include legally qualified Judges. We also believe, however, that good decisions are only likely to be made by those who are also sensitive to the medical, psychological and social aspects of the case. We are, therefore, of the view that if a Family Court were set up, the Judges of that Court and the advocates who practise before it should be required to have training in the other relevant fields.

Representation

One consequence of Care proceedings in this country being conducted in the lowest level of the Court hierarchy is that those who represent children and parents in those proceedings have tended to be in the past - and still tend to be in certain areas - the most junior and inexperienced advocates. If this type of case were accorded a Court which reflected the importance of the sort of decisions it had to take, one would hope that the quality and experience of the advocates who practised before it would improve. There would also be a strong case in any future system for bringing together those Lawyers and practitioners who are specially interested in the representation of children into a Child Advocacy Agency in which there would be provision for initial and continuing training in all related fields.

That perhaps is looking too far into the future. There are immediate measures which should be taken to correct distortions in the present system. As matters stand at the moment, parents are not parties to Care proceedings in the Juvenile Court and their rights to independent representation are restricted. Furthermore, save in one particular type of case (when the Local Authority agrees to the revocation of a Care Order), the parents are not, at present, entitled to legal aid. This means that, in many cases before the Juvenile Court, the parents go unrepresented unless a Law Centre can be found able and willing to represent them free of charge. Secondly, it seems to us urgent that some form of independent representation be accorded to every child when parental rights are vested in a Local Authority. Whether that independent representation should be representation by a Lawyer or by a "guardian" with some other professional status is a matter which requires careful consideration.

Conclusions

(a) Child protection legislation and the Courts at present applying it should be consolidated. A Family Court should be instituted dealing with all legal problems relating to the child and the family.

(b) The Judges of such a Family Court and the Lawyers practising before it should have medical and social work training. The Court should have its own investigatory powers and greater flexibility in the Orders it could make in Care cases than has the present Juvenile Court in England.

(c) Social Services Departments of Local Authorities should seek alternatives to legal action in less serious cases and should place more emphasis upon working out agreed courses of action with the family.

(d) Local Authorities should be accountable for children in their care to a much greater extent than at present. There should be an independent Review system and independent representation of children throughout the period they are in Care.

Child Abuse and Neglect, Vol. 3, pp. 323 - 326.
Pergamon Press Ltd., 1979. Printed in Great Britain.

THE CHILDREN'S HEARING SYSTEM IN SCOTLAND IN RELATION TO CASES OF CHILD ABUSE AND CHILD NEGLECT

Malcolm Schaffer

Assistant Reporter to the Children's Panel, Tayside.

The Children's Hearing system was set up by the Social Work (Scotland) Act 1968 to provide a new legal structure for dealing with children at risk. The main focus of subsequent publicity has been directed at cases of juvenile offenders, not surprisingly since they provide the bulk of work for Children's Hearings accounting for about 90% of referrals. However, much of the most significant and emotive work of Children's Hearings concerns their handling of cases of abused and neglected children. This paper sets out the main features of the Children's Hearing system which render it appropriate to deal with such cases and, exemplifies its working with reference to practice in one Scottish region, Tayside, during 1976 and 1977.

The grounds under which a child may be referred to a Children's Hearing initially are contained in Section 32(2) of the Social Work (Scotland) Act 1968. Three grounds in particular are relevant to cases of child abuse and neglect. These are Sections 32(2)(c), (d), and (dd) which read respectively:

> "lack of parental care is likely to cause him" (the child) "unnecessary suffering or impair his health and development";
>
> "an offence mentioned in Schedule 1 to the Criminal Procedure (Scotland) Act 1975 has been committed in respect of the child or in respect of a child who is a member of the same household"; and
>
> "the child is a member of the same household as a person who has committed an offence mentioned in Schedule 1 to the Criminal Procedure (Scotland) Act 1975".

The offences covered by Schedule 1 to the Criminal Procedure (Scotland) Act 1975 refer to sexual offences including incest, abandonment and assault.

Anyone who considers a child to be in need of compulsory measures of care may refer the case to the Reporter to the Children's Panel (Ref. 1). In Tayside, the vast majority of referrals came from the Social Work Department though other cases originated from R.S.S.P.C.C. and the Police and, in one case, from a parent worried about the standard of care provided by the other parent from whom she was now separated.

The Reporter has several important functions of which the most important is to decide whether to refer a child on to a Children's Hearing. He also is responsible for the administration of Children's Hearing system, acts as clerk and adviser on points of law and procedure within a Children's Hearing, and deals with court work arising out of the decisions of Children's Hearings. No precise qualifications have been laid down yet for Reporters (Ref. 2) although the job requires a knowledge of law and an understanding of Social Work. On receiving a referral he will investigate the case (Ref. 3) by calling for reports from any agency involved in the child's welfare, e.g. health visitor, school, hospital, and he will then make a double assessment of the case: first, as to whether there is enough evidence to support a referral in terms of Section 32(2) ; secondly, as to whether the child is in need of compulsory measures of care.

The Reporter is not obliged to refer a case to a Children's Hearing. If there is not sufficient evidence, then he will be obliged to take no further action (Ref. 4). Even if there is sufficient evidence, the Reporter may decide that a Children's Hearing is inappropriate either because the child is now receiving adequate parental care and further abuse or neglect is considered unlikely, or because the case can be disposed of by voluntary measures of care (Ref. 5). The family may be willing to accept the supervision of a social worker on a voluntary basis or may even have requested the child's removal into care which can be done on a voluntary basis. In these circumstances, formal measures of care may not be necessary. However, it is of interest that in Tayside about 52% of referrals under all grounds were not referred to Hearings in 1976 but, only 20% of child abuse and neglect cases did not reach Children's Hearings.

Within the Hearing system, processes of legal adjudication and social assessment are kept separate. Thus, if a child is referred to a Hearing and, either he or his parents fail to understand or deny the grounds of referral, the case is normally sent for proof to the Sheriff (Ref. 6). Because of the youthful age of most of the children alleged to have been neglected or abused, (average age in Tayside is five years) virtually all such cases have to be sent for proof because the child is too young to understand. The application for proof is normally heard by the Sheriff in Chambers rather than in open court and the family are entitled, at this part of the proceedings, to be legally represented. If the grounds are established, the case will be remitted to a Children's Hearing for disposal, if otherwise, the case will be discharged. In only two cases, in 1976 and 1977, were grounds not established in Tayside.

The Hearing itself (Ref. 7) is held in an ordinary room without any of the trappings of a Court. Three people sit on each Hearing, drawn from a panel of lay people who have been selected from all sections of the local community and given some training before sitting as a member of a Hearing. At least one member of each sex must sit at each Hearing.

The Hearing members will receive, in advance, copies of all relevant reports on a child's background and at the Hearing will discuss these fully with child, parents, social worker and any other relevant person. The aim is to keep proceedings fairly informal and relaxed within the loose structure provided by the Social Work (Scotland) Act 1968 and its accompanying statutory instruments, and removing the legal dispute into the domain of the Sheriff Court obviously helps achieve this ideal. Hearings last as long as they merit, on average about forty-five minutes and parents have a right to be present at all stages of the proceedings. At the end, each member of the Hearing will give his decision and the reasons for it.

The range of decisions available to a Hearing vary from complete discharge, (Ref. 8) where further action is considered unnecessary, through supervision of a social worker, (Ref. 9) to removal from home (Ref. 10). A supervision order requiring a child to live at home may also include such conditions as the Hearing consider necessary. For instance, the child may be required to attend day nursery regularly, or be subject to regular medical examination. Where a child is removed from home the resource most frequently used by Hearings in Tayside are foster homes, with Children's Homes a close second. The serious nature of the cases referred to Hearings is shown by the fact that in 1976 and 1977 about 50% of children referred on grounds of child abuse or neglect in Tayside were removed from home while only one case in 1976 and four in 1977 were discharged.

The length of time that the process will take from initial referral to final disposal will vary from case to case but may take several months. However, measures may be required for the child's immediate protection (Ref. 11). A social worker or other authorised person may obtain a place of safety order from a Justice of the Peace to permit the child's immediate removal from home. Hearings have the power to issue warrants to ensure that a child is in a place of safety while the case is in process. There are limits to the length of time that warrants can be issued, ninety-one days being the maximum period covered. In Tayside, place of safety orders were taken out in twenty-six out of one hundred and twenty-six cases in 1976, and in twenty-seven out of ninety-one cases in 1977.

One of the most important features of the Children's Hearing system is the review procedure for supervision requirements (Ref. 12). A social worker may call a review at any time if he feels the current requirement needs to be altered: the parents or child also have the right to call a review Hearing after a period of three or six months. If neither of these occurs, then a Hearing will automatically be arranged to review the child's case when a requirement has run for a year. When a review Hearing is called, supplementary reports will be asked for and the Hearing itself will contain another full discussion with all relevant parties. Once placed on supervision, a child may remain on supervision under the Children's Hearing system until he is eighteen years of age but his case must be reviewed at least once every year by a Children's Hearing. It is important to note too that every decision made by a Children's Hearing may be appealed against (Ref. 13). Appeals are heard by the sheriff.

Such is the framework within which Children's Hearings operate. In Tayside, out of a child population of approximately 103,000, around one hundred and thirty cases are referred to the Reporter each year alleging child abuse or child neglect. In 1976, the most frequent concern of the person making the referral has been the effect on the care of the child caused by the parents' life style. This may take the form of addiction to drugs or alcohol; frequent changes of address made without regard to the unsettling influence on the child or the suitability of the place that they may be moving to: or a mental disturbance in one or both of the parents. This sort of information came up in around seventy cases out of the one hundred and twenty-four cases referred in 1976.

The bad home conditions in which a child resides was a cause for referral in fifty-three cases during 1976. Concern arises where conditions are such that a child's health or safety is seriously at risk, e.g. unprotected fire-places, dirt or excrement caked on walls or floor, urine soaked bed sheets, overcrowded home conditions, no means of light or heating other than an open fire. In forty-four of these cases, the child was also being physically neglected by being left alone in the house while parents went out in the evening, or by being left in the care of an unsuitable person, or by being abandoned without arrangements being made for the child's care.

Emotional deprivation is a common feature of children in need of care but problems of proof arise. A large proportion of the cases which a Reporter does not refer to a Hearing because of lack of evidence are where emotional deprivation is feared but there is no valid factual backing to support this. In several cases, the child at risk was also failing to thrive; he appears pale and listless and fails to put on weight or even loses weight while in the care of his parents. If regular weight checks have been made at the child's nursery, proof is simplified.

Surprisingly, cases involving physical abuse of children take up a relatively small proportion of referrals. Only fifteen cases were referred to the Reporter in Tayside during 1976. Five of these were 'no actioned' or sent for voluntary measures by the Reporter due to lack of evidence and in a further two cases the grounds were not established before the Sheriff. Thus, only eight cases of direct physical abuse of a child were established in 1976.

It is important to examine the general background of such cases in order to build a proper back-cloth. In twenty-one cases in 1976, one parent or the other had attempted suicide on at least one occasion and was consequently receiving psychiatric treatment. In forty-three cases, the child was living in households where violence, e.g. wife assault or fights between parent and co-habitee, was a serious enough feature to be subject to regular police intervention. In forty-six cases, serious abuse of alcohol by the parents was also a strong feature.

All these factors indicate the absence of a stable family unit for many of the children. Thus, in sixty-one cases the natural parents of the child had split up by the time of the referral while in twenty-one cases, the child was illegitimate. Overall, in forty-eight cases, the child was, at the time of the referral, being brought up by one adult only.

Many of the problems in the household arose from inadequate income or inadequate budgeting or a combination of these two factors, and the single parent appears particularly vulnerable. As a result, in forty-one cases there were substantial rent arrears and unpaid electricity bills, often leading to threatened eviction and disconnection of electricity in the household with the resultant dangers to the child's safety and health.

This depressing picture is completed by one further statistic. In one hundred and six out of the one hundred and twenty-four cases, both parents (or in the case of single parent households, the only parent) were unemployed. This figure includes not only parents but also any co-habitee in the household, helping to maintain the family.

This indicates the very difficult family situations that Children's Hearings have to come to terms with in assessing cases. To assess their overall success is difficult because of these prevailing factors but there is much to commend in the Children's Hearing system as a model system of care which protects a child from risk of further abuse or neglect and from overzealous intervention by concerned welfare agencies.

NOTES FOR REFERENCE

1. Section 37(1), Social Work (Scotland) Act 1968.
   Section 83, Children Act 1975.

2. Section 36, Social Work (Scotland) Act 1968.
   Section 82, Children Act 1975.
   Reporters (Conduct of Proceedings Before the Sheriff) (Scotland) Regulations 1975.

3. Section 38, Social Work (Scotland) Act 1968.

4. Section 39(1), Social Work (Scotland) Act 1968.

5. Section 39(2), Social Work (Scotland) Act 1968.

6. Section 42, Social Work (Scotland) Act 1968.

7. Children's Hearings (Scotland) Rules 1971.

8. Section 43(2), Social Work (Scotland) Act 1968.

9. Section 44(1)(a), Social Work (Scotland) Act 1968.

10. Section 44(1)(b), Social Work (Scotland) Act 1968.

11. Section 37, Social Work (Scotland) Act 1968.
    Section 40(4), (7), and (8) Social Work (Scotland) Act 1968.
    Section 323 Criminal Procedure (Scotland) Act 1975.
    Section 83 and 84 Children Act 1975.

12. Sections 47 and 48 Social Work (Scotland) Act 1968.

13. Section 49 Social Work (Scotland) Act 1968.

BIBLIOGRAPHY

"Children and Young Persons, Scotland" - Report by the Kilbrandon Committee 1964

"Children's Hearings" - Social Work Services Group H.M.S.O. publication 1976

"Model Procedure for a Children's Hearing" - John Grant Scots Law Times (News) 1974 Page 229

"Face to Face with Families" - Nigel Bruce and John Spencer

"Children's Hearings" - F. Martin and K. Murray

Child Abuse and Neglect, Vol. 3, pp. 327 - 330.
0145-2134/79/0301-0327 $02.00/0.

TWO HIDDEN PREDISPOSING FACTORS IN CHILD ABUSE

Emanuel Lewis
Department of Child and Family Psychiatry,
Charing Cross Hospital, Fulham Palace Road, London W6
and
Adult Department, Tavistock Clinic, 120 Belsize Lane, London NW3 5BA

ABSTRACT

It is in the nature of stillbirth that it is very difficult to mourn. The psychological characteristics of stillbirth that give rise to the difficulty with mourning also tend to lead to its mismanagement. This exacerbates the problem so that stillbirths are often very inadequately mourned. Furthermore, the quick replacement pregnancy which frequently follows a stillbirth, and is unfortunately so often encouraged by others, impedes the mourning of the stillbirth. In the puerperium the mother, though preoccupied with her live baby, is haunted by the unmourned stillbirth. This can result in profound difficulty with the mothering of a baby born subsequent to a stillbirth. Often the baby screams. In addition, as a stillbirth can lead to marital difficulty, the mother often feels undermined by her husband. If there is a family difficulty with containing violence, the child may be battered.

Pregnancy tends to inhibit the normal processes of mourning. It is particularly difficult to mourn a dead baby during pregnancy. However, with <u>all</u> bereavements which occur during, or shortly before or after pregnancy, mourning tends to be inhibited. Once delayed by pregnancy and the maternal preoccupation with the new baby, the work of mourning may never get properly under way again. A case will be described of a woman who murdered her eldest child eight months after the birth of a baby, her husband having died suddenly during the pregnancy.

It is important to be aware of the difficulty of mourning during and around pregnancy in the understanding and prevention of child abuse. Methods to facilitate the mourning of a stillbirth and other bereavements during pregnancy and in the perinatal period will be described .

INTRODUCTION

A bereavement that occurs during or shortly after pregnancy is often inadequately mourned. This is because pregnancy tends to inhibit the normal process of mourning (Ref. 1). The resulting inadequate or failed mourning undermines a woman's mothering ability and can therefore be a predisposing factor in child abuse.

In comparing mourning with melancholia Freud (2) wrote, "Profound mourning, the reaction to the loss of someone who is loved, contains the same painful frame of mind, the same loss of interest in the outside world - in so far as it does not recall him - the same loss of capacity to adopt any new object of love (which would mean replacing him) and the same turning-away from any activity that is not connected with thoughts of him. It is easy to see that this inhibition and circumscription of the ego is the expression of an exclusive devotion to mourning which leaves nothing over for other purposes or interests. It is really only because we know so well how to explain it that the attitude does not seem to us pathological."

Freud's description of the personality in mourning has similarities with Winnicott's (3) description of the personality of the devoted mother in the state of primary maternal preoccupation which "could be compared with a withdrawn state, or a dissociated state, or a fugue, or even with a disturbance at a deeper level such as a schizoid episode ....". Strikingly similar to what Freud said of mourning is Winnicott's description of primary maternal preoccupation as a state "that would be an illness were it not for the fact of the pregnancy". A pregnant mother is so occupied with thoughts and feelings about the new life growing within her that she has little emotional space left for anyone else. A bereavement which occurs during the period of primary maternal preoccupation confronts a woman with the impossible need to make "an exclusive devotion" to two separate relationships. The bereave mother opts for her live baby and mourning tends to be postponed. Once the mourning proces has been delayed by pregnancy, many women are unable to get their mourning adequately going again.

Stillbirth is a particularly poignant perinatal bereavement. Bourne (4) has described how the abhorrence of stillbirth has led to the neglect of the study of its psychology. A moth in the state of primary maternal preoccupation makes herself psychologically vulnerable by trusting her baby to survive. If a stillbirth occurs it devastates the very foundation of her basic trust in life. The bereaved mother, primed to be devoted to her baby, has to cop with a void - there is no baby to take care of. But there is a double loss, for the live foetus is gone as well. There is a terrible emptiness where there was so obviously a fullness.

Case 1

A woman, the daughter of a depressed mother, became quickly pregnant after an inadequately mourned stillbirth. During the replacement pregnancy she refused help from a social worker except just before the birth of her daughter. After delivery she was euphoric but she beca increasingly depressed. Her husband was happy to take over much of the care of the baby. When the baby was three months old she threatened to batter her baby or commit suicide unle they were parted. The baby was admitted to hospital. She hated her daughter who she felt deliberately refused her feeds, or vomited to spite her, and then seemed to mock her with a smile. The husband and wife were helped to mourn their stillbirth by the technique of "bringing the baby back to death" (Ref. 5) and the mother was then able to care for her daughter.

With other bereavements there is much to remember. Memory facilitates the normal processes essential for psychological recovery from loss. But a stillbirth is a non-person, an intangible non-event, that is difficult to think and talk about. A stillbirth is unknown and unknowable. There is little to remember. A stillbirth is a void and it cannot fill a potential space in our minds. A stillbirth is an empty drama that takes place at the interface between life and death: there is no catharsis. Sexual creativity is mocked by th corpse - and there is a sense of murder. The mother is great with child and then we are confronted with a seemingly motiveless murder (Ref. 6). However, mourning may be facilitat by managing a stillbirth so as to make the most of what is available and can be remembered (Ref. 7).

Apart from the obvious and natural desire to have a baby, a reason for the quick replacemer which frequently follows a stillbirth is the need to fill the painful void left by the dead baby. Doctors and other professionals frequently recommend this quick pregnancy, and this part is to fill the painful emptiness they also experience. Case 1 illustrates how failure to mourn a stillbirth can impair a mother's relationship with her live baby. Only speedy intervention prevented catastrophe.

I have described how in order to escape from the predicament of needing to make an "exclusi devotion" to two separate relationships a bereaved woman in primary maternal preoccupation avoids mourning. In addition there is another impediment to mourning. It is difficult for pregnant woman to keep separate her ideas and feelings about her stillborn and her live foetus. A bereaved mother has little or no experience of her stillborn except as a foetus. Like identical twins, until you know them, there is little to help distinguish between one foetus and the next. And since the next pregnancy often follows quickly after a stillbirth this adds to the difficulty of keeping feelings about the two foetus' separate. As a resul of the confusion of feelings about the dead and the live baby, the intensely ambivalent feelings for a stillborn that are associated with mourning are easily confused with the milder mixed feelings that a pregnant woman normally has for a live foetus. This causes an intolerable fear that the anger originally directed at the stillbirth during the process of mourning may in the confusion be deflected and harm the live foetus, and so to protect her foetus the mother tends to avoid mourning.

It is after the birth of a subsequent live baby that these women are depressed and can have profound difficulty with mothering. They are haunted by their lost hopes for the dead child. Because there are no memories to test reality, the dead child tends to become an idealized ghost. The idealization of the ghost-like dead baby tends to highlight the imagined "faults" of the live baby. In Case 1, when the baby vomited the mother contrasted this behaviour with her fantasy that her dead son would have been easy to feed. This made her angry with the "bad" baby who replaced her "good" baby.

The mother is resentful of the baby whom she finds difficult to nurse. She feels guilty because of her resentment. This increases her anxiety so that mothering is further undermined. For a vulnerable mother, who may as a child have received a poor model of babycare from her own mother, this undermining of her fragile confidence can result in a disastrous failure in her mothering.

BEREAVEMENT DURING PREGNANCY

I believe that when any bereavement occurs during pregnancy then there can be difficulty with mourning. It is difficult for a woman to grieve for an adult who dies during her pregnancy, and it is probably even more difficult to cope with the loss of a child. The discomfort of pregnancy, the anxiety about the health of the baby, the responsibilities of parenthood, and concern about how the baby will alter the mother's life all give rise to apprehension and misgivings about any pregnancy. The worries are a reason for the most wanted baby to at times be disliked or hated by a pregnant woman. These ambivalent feelings that a mother has for her foetus may be conscious, though the more violently hateful thoughts and feelings are usually unconscious. There are similar ambivalent feelings about a dead loved adult or child. It is part of the work of mourning to understand and accept these ambivalent feelings. During the process of mourning the dead person is unconsciously imagined as being taken inside our minds and our bodies. The dead can be felt as dead inside us. The dead person and the live foetus both inhabit the mother's body and mind. The live foetus inside the mother has a nebulous personality so that feelings about the foetus tend, I believe, to be confused with feelings about the dead person (Ref. 1). Because of the difficulties of clearly separating a nebulous foetus from an incorporated dead person, the bereaved pregnant woman unconsciously fears that the anger and hate felt for the dead as part of her grieving can, in the confusion of unconscious thoughts, be added to any feelings of resentment she may have about her foetus. To protect her foetus from imagined harm she inhibits the process of mourning. Once mourning has been interrupted it may be difficult to get it going again. Moreover, the mother's preoccupation with life while she nurtures her baby is not condusive to hard thinking and feeling about the dead.

Case 2

A woman in her first pregnancy produced a baby which died shortly after birth. The mother's father had died in her early adolescence. During the third trimester of her fourth pregnancy her husband was killed. The three-year-old eldest child kept asking his mother for his father. The mother felt helpless about how to cope with the questions. This child was playing by a staircase equipped with a gate and his mother told him to keep away as it was dangerous, but the boy continued to play there. The mother did not close the gate and the child fell downstairs and broke his leg. When the G.P. came and wanted to examine the tender leg the mother threatened to hit him. Since the father's death the mother's relationship with her son has been painfully constrained. The mother has been surprised and frightened by the violence with which she has hit him on subsequent occasions.

This mother had to cope with a bereaved child who asked painful and awkward questions. These would be especially difficult to answer at a time when the mother, preoccupied with caring for her foetus, was avoiding thinking and feeling about her dead husband. The child angered his mother by threatening to undermine her attempt to delay mourning. The child may have sensed that his mother's preoccupation with her foetus made her less available to him in his bereavement. This would inflame the usual jealousy of a new baby. He was consequently more demanding. Thus playing in a dangerous spot was a bid for attention and a worry that Mother, preoccupied with her foetus, would want to be rid of him. He may have feared that his mother had dismissed his father from her life now that she was expecting. The mother felt guilty about not being able to pay more attention to her bereaved son, and this increased her anger with the demanding child. She continued to have a poor relationship with her son, her eldest surviving child, who carried the brunt of her painful, unworked through ambivalence for her dead first born and her husband. The mother may also have had the unconscious fear that her son's inflamed jealousy might magically harm the foetus.

An extreme example of the psychological crisis that may be precipitated by a bereavement in pregnancy is provided by the following case.

Case 3

A mother's husband died suddenly during her third pregnancy. When the child of this pregnancy was eight months old the depressed mother strangled her eldest daughter and then tried to hang herself. She said that she thought that her two younger sons would not miss her, but that her daughter would. She was sent to Broadmoor for three years. She came for help at the age of 69 after the death of her second husband. She felt she had never really mourned her first husband, whose death had not seemed real to her. She had a distant relationship with her second husband, but now recognized her need for help with her mourning.

The death of her husband seemed unreal to this mother as she was unable to get her mourning going again after its inhibition during pregnancy. The murdered child missed her father. She angered her mother by reminding her of the loss of her husband whom she was unable to mourn. It may also be that the mother projected her unmanageable grief into her sad daughter and then unconsciously tried to eliminate her grief by murdering it in her daughter.

It needs to be recognized that it is extremely difficult for some women to mourn during pregnancy and the puerperium, and that mourning failure puts them at psychological risk. The relationship with their children can be profoundly affected and may result in child abuse.

THE MANAGEMENT OF PERINATAL BEREAVEMENT

In all perinatal bereavement it is necessary to help the mother differentiate between the foetus and the dead. She should be encouraged to do those things which help this differentiation which cannot be repeated such as looking at and touching the corpse and attending the funeral. During pregnancy a holding relationship may be best. After delivery and when the baby is a going concern then memories of the dead are shared and the death made real. This is an artifice to revive the normal mourning process inhibited by pregnancy so as to avoid a pathological mourning reaction such as child abuse.

If psychotherapy is attempted during pregnancy it ought to be undertaken only by a skilled person who should focus on helping the mother to achieve a clear psychic separation between her baby and the dead. This is particularly difficult if the dead person is a child.

REFERENCES

(1) E. Lewis, Inhibition of Mourning by Pregnancy, Bulletin of Brit. Psycho-Analytical Soc. 10, Nov., (1977).

(2) S. Freud. (1957) Mourning and melancholia, in Complete psychological works, Standard ed., 14, Hogarth Press and Institute of Psychoanalysis, London.

(3) D.W. Winnicott. (1958) Primary Maternal Preoccupation, in Collected Papers, Tavistock, London.

(4) S. Bourne, The Psychological Effects of Stillbirths on Women and their Doctors, J. Royal College of General Practitioners. 16, 103 (1968).

(5) E. Lewis, A. Page, Failure to Mourn a Stillbirth: An Overlooked Catastrophe, Brit. J. Medical Psychology. Oct (1978).

(6) E. Lewis, Psychological dilemmas confronting the physician and the parents of a malformed abortus, stillborn, and deceased newborn, Proceedings of National Birth Defects Conference 1978, March of Dimes: National Foundation, in press.

(7) E. Lewis, The Management of Stillbirth: Coping with an Unreality, The Lancet, 619, Sep., (1977).

Child Abuse and Neglect, Vol. 3, pp. 331 - 333.
Pergamon Press Ltd., 1979. Printed in Great Britain.

PARENTAL ANGER: A GENERAL POPULATION SURVEY

Neil Frude and Alison Goss

University College, Cardiff, Wales

There are two sharply differing public reactions to child abuse. According to one school of thought, any parent who injures his or her child is vicious, inhuman and probably has a gross psychiatric problem. According to another common position, however, abuse is an understandable reaction by some parents pushed to the end of their tether by extreme difficulties with the child. This position is often based on empathy originating in the individual's own experiences as a parent and it regards abusive behaviour as differing only in its intensity and in its injurious consequences from other, more common, expressions of parental anger and desperation.

Undoubtedly, both of these extreme positions, as well as many of those in between, do have a certain validity. Cases differ profoundly and abuse is not a phenomenon with a uniform pattern of causal antecedents. If, however, we take the second school of thought to have _some_ validity then this does suggest that we might obtain a good deal of information relevant to an understanding of abuse and of its treatment and prevention from an examination of "normal" parenting difficulties and reactions.

At the end of 1977 a postal questionnaire was sent to a local general population sample in Cardiff, Wales, of mothers with a child between one-and-a-half and four years old. It enquired about their experiences with the child, and more specifically about their difficulties, their reactions to the child's naughtiness and the ways in which they dealt with feelings of anger. Names and addresses were taken from hospital birth records and the return of 111 suitably completed questionnaires was calculated to be a little over 45% of those which had reached the selected respondent.

This was not intended as a survey which would allow definitive estimation of the general population parameters of the variables examined, and any conclusions based on the analysis must take into account the relatively small sample size. Nevertheless, some indication was gained of at least the relative and minimal frequencies of certain values, difficulties and reactions of the mothers in the sample, it was possible to examine relationships between variables within the questionnaire and also between questionnaire items and information from hospital records, and responses to open-ended questions were content analysed.

Responses To Particular Questions

One fifth (20%) of the mothers in the sample return claimed that the child had been more difficult to care for than they had anticipated, and the same proportion (22%) reported that at times they had had problems with the child which made them feel that they couldn't cope with him any longer. As well as some persistent toilet-training and eating difficulties, these included many problems associated with bedtime and sleeping, especially difficulties in getting the child to go to bed, bedwetting, and persistent crying or screaming. One mother of a two-and-a-half year old boy claimed that she had rarely had a decent night's sleep since the birth.

Almost all of the respondents (96%) reported that there had been days on which "everything got on top of them", making them less patient with the child. Factors which seemed to contribute to this feeling were housework, marital disharmony, isolation in the house and worries about the children and about money. However, the variables most strongly reported in this context were tiredness and paramenstrual symptoms. Two-thirds of the women recognised that the monthly cycle affected their tolerance towards the child.

A large proportion of the mothers expressed some anxiety over the adequacy of their control over the child and it was clear that the maintenance of discipline was highly valued in this population. Only 10% disagreed with the statement that "too many children are allowed to do just as they like, and .... some strong discipline would do them good". Physical methods of punishment were much used; only 4% said that they "never" smacked the child, and 50% did this either "very often" or "fairly often". Over half (57%) admitted that on at least one occasion they had "lost their temper completely and hit the child really hard" and about half of these (20% of the total sample) were able to recall some details of a particular incident of this type.

Considering the apparent frequency with which parents seem to become angry with the child, the reported number of such incidents could even be seen as low, and it does suggest that in many cases mothers are fairly well able to control their angry reaction. Nearly all of the respondents, in fact, (84%) reported that they were sometimes able to stop themselves losing their temper but in many cases this control appeared to be somewhat precarious, and 40% of the mothers had entertained a fear that one day they might lose their temper completely and "really hurt" the child.

Relationships Between Variables

Analysis was made of associations between selected demographic, perinatal and questionnaire variables. Values were cross-tabulated and relationships examined using appropriate statistical tests, most commonly Kendall's "tau" or "chi-square". Some indication of the findings which emerged will be given by looking at the associations which were shown between a single central item - the response to the question "Are you ever afraid that one day you may lose your temper completely and really hurt your child?" - and other variables.

Mothers who fear that they could one day hurt the child (and 40% of the sample admitted that they had had such a feeling) tend to be those who use physical punishment relatively frequently. They worry about loss of control over the child, they feel that they are somewhat erratic in their disciplining and they admit that they sometimes find themselves using punishment methods that they believe to be wrong. Each of these relationships is associated with a probability level of less than 1/1000. This subgroup also tends to report more loneliness and isolation, they are more influenced by the effects of marital rows and lack of sleep and they experience greater irritation in response to the child's crying. There is also an association with social class, with lower class mothers more frequently reporting a fear of harming the child.

Anger Control

84% of the sample said that there had been times when they had stopped themselves losing their temper. Many of the classic anger control methods like counting to ten, deep breathing, leaving the scene and stamping the foot were represented among the techniques reported, but some of the strategies were more elaborate and many of them are similar to self-instructional and cognitive management techniques which have recently entered the therapeutic repertoire of cognitive-behaviour modification.

Some strategies were used to affect principally the appraisal of the child's annoying behaviour, either by setting a frame of mind to view the child sympathetically or by distraction. Examples of setting a positive appraisal style include the mother who used the strategy of reminding herself that children know no better and another who concentrated on how small and dependent the child was. A strategy which seems to combine this with distraction is illustrated in the case of the mother who would call to mind scriptural references on how to bring up children and build a happy family life. One mother distracted herself from the annoyance by systematically recalling moments from a very happy holiday and two mothers reported that when the older child provoked them they would turn their attention to the baby, who evoked a quite different emotional reaction. One said "I take a deep breath and look at my baby. He is so cute I cannot help laughing at him" and the other talked to the baby which, she remarked, "obviously requires a different attitude and tone of voice".

Some other strategies seemed to be principally aimed at "calming" the individual by directly affecting the anger arousal. Deep breathing and "counting to ten" might fit best in this context and stamping the foot, screaming or "screaming inside" which were all reported are classic examples of physical acts which may lead to aggression catharsis. Cigarettes were also used for their calming effect, one mother reported that she had used a tranquilliser in such a situation and others had put on a favourite record or splashed the face with cold water. One woman used "level B of the relaxation I learnt for the birth of my babies".

Finally there are those techniques which serve to substitute for or to directly inhibit aggressive behaviour. Actions which are incompatible with physical abuse of the child are often deliberately initiated; examples include knitting, "getting on with the housework", and making a cup of tea. Inhibition-maximising strategies included concentrating on the damage that could result from hitting the child and anticipating later feelings of guilt and remorse.

Accounts Of Particular Incidents

Twenty-two respondents were able to give an account of a particular incident in which they had really lost their temper and hit the child. In all but one of these cases the child was reported as doing something to trigger the outburst, and in the exceptional case the mother had been suffering from severe pre-menstrual symptoms. Several elements recurred in these accounts of the child's behaviour at the time of the incident: irritating "nuisance" behaviour was predominant in $\frac{1}{3}$ of the cases and included constant interference or clinging and persistent screaming in the night; "defiance" was the apparent key feature in another $\frac{1}{3}$ of cases and included food throwing and "deliberate" dirtying (what is important here, of course, is the mother's interpretation of the child's action rather than its real nature). In a few other cases there was real "cost" of effort or money involved - a glass wedding present was smashed, scouring powder was tipped over a floor, a dressing table had been painted with nail-varnish; and finally, in some cases the child's action had placed him in real danger, for example setting fire to paper and running across a busy road.

In most cases, however, the mother recognised that her reaction reflected her own mood as well as the child's action. Asked if other things had happened to affect their mood on the day of the incident, half of these mothers did recall such things as a frustrating shopping trip or a substantial loss of sleep. A mood check list was also provided and mothers were able to indicate how they had been feeling immediately prior to the incident. Only five respondents checked "normal", and these included the three in which the child's behaviour had been self-endangering. "Tired", "depressed" and "irritated" were the most commonly indicated moods, and "anxiety" and "tension" also featured in a number of cases.

The incident accounts suggest, then, that in many (though not all) cases, the angry outburst arose from an interaction between the mother's current mood and some perceived action of the child. Other data from the study show that incident reporting parents also more generally use physical punishment frequently, they report more unjustifiable punishment and they are more likely to see themselves in danger of one day losing control and hurting the child. Thus both immediate and also more distant, long-term, variables are related to the incident, and a complex multifactorial antecedent pattern is indicated.

Conclusion

The findings from this small study suggest that a relatively large proportion of mothers have difficulties with their young children and often experience anger towards them. Many are very good at dealing with and controlling such feelings, but angry hitting of the child is not rare and a substantial number of parents are not confident that they themselves could never constitute a positive danger to their child. Some of the incident accounts are not dissimilar to case reports from the clinical literature and it is suggested that the findings as a whole support the view that some cases of clinical abuse may best be regarded as extreme forms of reactions which are relatively common in the general parent population.

Child Abuse and Neglect, Vol. 3, pp. 335 - 340.
Pergamon Press Ltd., 1979. Printed in Great Britain.

"I KNEW IF I HIT HIM I'D GO TOO FAR"

Brenda Crowe NFU, National Adviser to PPA, 1967-1977

18 Rainsford Avenue, Chelmsford, Essex CM1 2PJ

An unexpected spin-off from the playgroup movement has been that those involved with it over a significant period of time during its seventeen years of existence have had a unique opportunity to build up a considerable body of knowledge about ordinary normal parents, particularly mothers, coping with the joys, sorrows, anxieties and stresses of daily life lived in close proximity with their pre-school children.

Doctors, nurses, health visitors, social workers, psychologists, psychiatrists, police, the legal profession, and others are trained to cope with specific types of deviation from physical, mental and social health: in the course of their work with individuals and families they all acquire deep insights into family life, but the fact remains that they are not usually called in until something has gone significantly wrong.

All these professionals do preventive work, but again the fact remains that the pressure of case loads is such that in practice most of their time and skill is devoted to those individuals and families who have reached crisis point.

The playgroup movement is about ordinary normal families who come together in their own local communities to provide safe and satisfying play for their children, and it is from this happy, positive, responsible background that their hidden anxieties, strains and stresses have spontaneously emerged, been shared, and the burden lessened.

It is the outwardly happy and well-adjusted families who have added to our knowledge of child abuse and neglect that we once associated more easily with those who came to playgroups as referrals from social workers, doctors, health visitors and others.

Before offering some of the insights gained it is necessary to explain the ethos of the playgroup movement, and to make clear the short-comings, as well as the strengths, of our young democratic voluntary association.

Any individual or playgroup can join the Pre-School Playgroup Association (PPA), including those who are 'doing it wrong', for we believe that exposure to other ideas and methods in a caring group is one of the best ways for people to learn and grow in understanding and insight.

Since we believe this it follows that there are many playgroups within PPA that are not (but hopefully may be in time) ascribing to our ideas and ideals. We hope that the wider community will come to understand that although we work steadfastly towards our stated aims we have to accept the fact that the very nature of learning through personal experience is such that playgroups will always be in a state of 'becoming', and therefore at no time can we forsee a point when every playgroup will simultaneously have 'arrived'. As one generation of parents moves on to school so new parents will come in to take their place, and the learning re-commences.

The essential ethos is that parents should be encouraged to understand and provide together for the needs of their own and each other's young children.

In the early years these self-help groups of parents called upon the 'experts' for help, and I was one of many nursery school teachers who, feeling grave concern for the children in playgroups, started to run courses 'telling them how it should be done'.

The so-called experts soon learned from this mistake: without realizing it we were trying to turn a wide cross-section of mothers into uniform imitations of nursery school teachers.

The result was that although the majority responded and contributed beyond all our expectations the minority gave rise to concern.

Some became over-confident and applied knowledge without sensitivity, and it was clear that the issuing of any certificate (other than mere attendance) could exacerbate this problem: since then it has been explained to all those attending playgroup fieldwork or 'doorstep' courses that there is nothing at the end of them that 'qualifies' anyone to do anything - the courses are for the interest, comfort, and stimulation of those who attend, and everyone is free to take from them what she or he wants and needs at that stage, and to interpret it in the best interests of their own playgroup children and parents and their own families. The enduring friendships, the exchange of visits to each other's playgroups, and involvement in the local playgroup community is often where the learning comes to fruition later (much later quite often).

Some of those on courses became strained and burdened with guilt, for they took to heart everything that was said about children's development and play needs, and felt that they had failed as parents - this defeated the aim of wanting them to feel increasingly happy, confident and aware, for if confidence and self-esteem is lost the spur to learn is blunted.

Another pitfall was the realization that when some parents began to learn about the needs of children they found themselves in the stressful position of wanting to change some of their attitudes and practices, which meant being disloyal to their own upbringing, parents, and in some cases to their husbands and parents-in-law as well.

Repeated experiences of parents' reactions on courses and in playgroups led to the understanding that although the courses were originally geared to the children, play activities and adult/child relationships in the playgroup, the first repercussion was in the homes of those on the courses.

The responsibility following this unexpected discovery led to radical rethinking.

The aim of the playgroup movement now is to create community situations in which the parents learn predominantly from each other, and any 'experts' responsible for the input of knowledge have to ask themselves "How much of all that I know on my particular subject is relevant to these particular parents, in this particular neighbourhood, at this particular time in their family and playgroup experience?"

Great sensitivity is required if the needs of children are to be upheld whilst trying to bridge the gap between ideal childhood and the many and varied childhood experiences (which are usually being re-lived with their own children) of those on the courses.

Cultural and family roots mustn't be severed, neither must inappropriate new growth be grafted on to long-established rootstock - each family must be allowed to grow in its own way, and all that 'experts' can do is to enrich the ground, find new ways to let in the light, and build in such supports as are necessary to uphold the natural growth.

You may have gathered by now that the playgroup movement is significantly more than the sum total of its playgroups: it is those who enthuse groups of parents to start their own playgroup, those who support and encourage the parents through their stages of preparation, those who organise courses, those who sustain the playgroup with visits, those who organise the local Branches of PPA to bring people together for continued learning and a happy social life, those who organise bulk buying, those who produce newsletters, publications and visual aids, and the local community which contributes in so many ways.

The courses are for playgroup leaders and parent helpers, for local groups of mothers who are interested in learning more about children; for the teenage boys and girls who help in playgroups (but who also need to regress to catch up on their own missed play experiences); for those who want to be playgroup visitors, or area organisers, or course tutors, and for any group that has a special interest that they want to pursue (such as music, first aid, story telling, leading discussion groups).

Once a group of parents makes the vital decision to do something for their own children, and to use all the available resources in order to do it to the best of their ability, then they experience a great surge of new growth.

Love of their children is the spur that drives them on, and because the movement holds parents to be as important as children their own needs and abilities are considered just as fully as those of their children.

In the accepting climate of both the courses and the playgroups parents are free to be themselves, and as trust and friendship develop the barriers come down and they dare to talk about the way it is at home rather than the way they like to pretend it is for the sake of appearances, or sometimes out of a need to protect their own illusions.

This is how we have come to know what lies behind the smiling public faces of so many outwardly happy, confident, capable and well-adjusted parents - and what we have learned confirms our belief that the mother or mother substitute at home with her young children all day needs companionship for herself as well as her child, and access to knowledge that will enhance what she already knows rather than detract from her status as the most important person her child will ever know.

Before giving examples of the types of abuse and neglect that are present in <u>any</u> community I must stress our belief that the positive aspects of mothering and fathering far outweigh the negative aspects in any community - even when parents are thought to be doing 'the wrong thing', or failing to do 'the right thing', the child is very often receiving the most vital communication of all which is that, come hell or high water, his parents love him and are doing their best according to their knowledge and ability.

The collected experience of course-tutors, playgroup leaders, discussion leaders and playgroup movement workers is that the fear of violence, and their ignorance of what constitutes abuse and neglect are expressed by parents in every type of community, and they may be loosely categorised as follows:

The Single Act of Violence

The degree of violence varies but what is constant when someone is unable to forget or forgive themselves is that at the time of the act they were 'out-of-control' and had no power to stop themselves.

Others have been driven to unaccustomed excess but felt that they had had the choice of stopping or continuing at the time, but 'allowed' themselves to continue.

Many parents have thrown their child violently on the bed, but they knew in that vital split second that they had chosen the bed rather than the floor.

Many parents who don't believe in smacking have reached a point of desperation when they resort to it, and once they start they can't stop until their own hands are so hot and sore that they cease for their own sake - but again they are aware that they have chosen to smack a leg or a bottom in preference to the head or body (the contents and workings of which are a mystery to many of them but they fear they might do real harm to a vital organ).

The release of guilt that follows these admissions is very real, and so is the relief of finding that there is always someone else in the group who has done the same thing.

One social worker kept quiet in a discussion but came up afterwards to say that at last she could forgive herself, for someone she greatly admired in the group had confessed to a once-only excess. She spoke for others when she said "I didn't know how I was going to tell my husband, for I felt that he couldn't go on loving me when he knew what sort of a woman I was".

<u>Violence that is Deflected from the Child</u>

A local authority playgroup Adviser recalled a time when she felt her control slipping, and she had four hours to wait before her husband would be home to come to the rescue. She said "I remember shutting myself in the bathroom, but then I remember nothing until I was aware that I had gripped the towelrail so tightly that I had broken it with my bare hands - I was terrified to think what might have happened if that same grip had been applied to Nick's neck." The act calmed her but the scar of the fear remained.

Another mother of a toddler and younger twins (a Chartered Accountant and later Marriage Guidance Counsellor) said that she remembered throwing the twins in the cot "to keep them safe", and putting the toddler in a safe place, before her control snapped: when she came to she was bashing her head against the kitchen wall and said "It was such a relief only having a hurt head instead of screaming nerve-endings."

<u>A Long History of Violence</u>

One mother's account is typical of many others, particularly in areas of deep deprivation and innocent ignorance.

She was unable to cope with her five children before the twins arrived, and they were the breaking point - she alternately battered them or locked them in their bedroom to keep them safe.

The health visitor suggested that she should take them to the local playgroup, but the idea was rejected out of hand with the words "No. Playgroups are only for bad mothers. I won't be a bad mother."

The health visitor asked why she thought they were for bad mothers, and the answer was "Because that's what I think when I see mothers taking them along to dump them - I'm not going to dump mine." It was explained that there were good mothers who were taking it in turns to help the local playgroup leader and her helper to provide three hours of happy play for the local children.

Assured that it was 'good', the mother took her twins along and the playgroup leader said later, "they duly behaved like incoherent little wild animals for days on end - but nobody complained, and the mother was treated as a friend and neighbour."

In her own words the mother told me how she got to the point where, on bad days, she could say to the playleader "For God's sake let me stay with you this morning or I shall murder the buggers", and how she would then have a rug put on the floor by the radiator, and how the other mothers would fetch a cushion to put at her back "just thick enough so the warmth came through but the ridges didn't stick in my back", and how they would bring her tea and biscuits.

These so-called ignorant mothers acted from their shared experience and compassion, even to knowing that sitting on the floor is more restful than sitting on a chair, and that warmth on the back is comforting.

The mother looked happy and well, and the twins were relaxed, articulate and well adjusted by the time she told me all this, but her next words shocked me, "...I could never have gone into a nursery school like I used to go into the playgroup": I wanted to tell her that I used to be a nursery school teacher and that plenty of mothers and fathers came in to say just those sort of things, and to drink tea and be comforted. But that would have been pointless for people have to be taken seriously when they say "<u>I</u> couldn't go into a nursery school like that ...": what they mean is that their particular memories of schools and authority figures is such that <u>they</u> genuinely couldn't go into a 'proper' school easily, naturally and as of right.

The playgroups, led by local mothers, have a place to play for such parents that nothing else can quite replace.

Another illustration of this is that parents will hand over their children saying "You'll have to wallop him, he won't take a bit of notice if you don't - hit him all you like, we shall understand." They are not afraid to admit this to another local mother, in fact it is almost an invitation to her to hit the child for then the parents can feel justified in their own hitting.

The sensitive playgroup leader explains, without expressing condemnation, that children are not hit in the playgroup for the strain of looking after other people's children is much less than in looking after one's own.

One such mother came to enjoy her days helping in the playgroup and said that she goes home and tries out playgroup ways when her child is playing her up - and that they work.

Another said in amazement "'E minds 'er, an' she don't 'it 'im or shout!"

The Perpetual Borderline of Violence

Many mothers or mother substitutes, shut up alone with one or more under-fives, live perpetually on the borderline of violence: this is aggravated when the accommodation is limited or shared, when the health and morale of the mother is low, when there is ignorance of children's needs, and when the child is particularly demanding.

One such family speaks for itself in the ten minute film "I Knew If I Hit Him I'd Go Too Far". The father has been out of work for two years, they have two children under five, and the young mother is again pregnant. They live in a first floor flat in a depressing housing estate. The back yards and the grass in front of the flats are fouled with dog muck and broken glass, and dogs shut out all day by their working owners roam the area in packs.

The parents talk about the strain of bringing children up under these conditions and the mother describes what she does to keep the four year old safe when she knows she could batter him.

"I go into my room, kneel on the bed, punch the eiderdown and scream at the top of my voice ... it's the only thing I can do ... it's the only outlet ... many a time I've pulled my hair out. Then other times I shut Gerald in his room and bang the door, and open it and bang it about ten times until the door frame begins to come away from the wall.

"Then there's another thing I do, I have a bath and wash my hair and put on all clean clothes, and then I go and stand on the balcony, and I'll feel better that way."

Both parents said the playgroup was the turning point for them all because of the interest it gave to the whole family.

Yet experienced social workers have seen this film, and heard the mother say how near she comes to hurting the children, only to say at the end "Why did you choose to film a family who were managing all right? Why didn't you show some of the desperate families who need playgroups?"

They were only managing all right because of the playgroup: and the playgroup was only managing all right because not too many of the families were really desperate referrals from other agencies.

The essence of a valuable community playgroup is that the predominant feeling is one of optimism, happiness, difficulties overcome and responsibilities shared, with enough people going on courses to feed insights back into the playgroup for the benefit of both children and parents, and enough people going on to do fieldwork among the new playgroups and Branches that gather playgroups and families together into a big happy family.

Only in this positive and happy atmosphere can parents begin to learn about children from other parents and other children, and only as the local level of understanding increases are parents prepared to rethink their own attitudes as they meet differing ones in people that they like and trust.

Parents compare notes about naughtiness, and punishment, and discipline, all issues of crucial importance to families and society - they come to see that play is learning for living, not just playing-about or a short-term policy of 'getting ready for school' - they come to see children as persons, not live dolls, or pets, or small-sized adults, or as a means of re-living their own lives - they begin to think about words like good, bad, dirty, messy, clever, right, wrong, responsibility, involvement, contribution, freedom, control and self-control, fair and equal.

All these words are interpreted differently in each family, and some of the misinterpretations can give rise to a real abuse of children, their play, their childhood, and ultimately their lives.

Nothing happens quickly, for real learning is slow and painful in those areas of our lives where we most need to learn.

Perhaps the key to the success of playgroup learning lies in the fact that playgroups and their courses have obliterated the barriers of education, politics, income, culture, colour, class and creed because the point of unity is at the greatest depth of human experience - we have all been children, most of us can remember being mothered and fathered, most of us can remember how we played, and most of us are parents ourselves (but are very careful not to exclude those who may not be for one of many reasons).

The learning is based on our shared experience of living, which is difficult, and trying to bring up our children, which is more difficult still.

The playgroup movement brought parents together for their children's sake and for mutual support and learning; the learning couldn't begin until people felt free to be honest; when they were honest they admitted their repressed violent feelings and areas of ignorance; then they developed an insatiable appetite for learning on courses, and by putting it into practice in a master/apprentice relationship in their playgroups. A very old wheel has turned full circle.

Child Abuse and Neglect, Vol. 3, pp. 341 - 350.
0145-2134/79/0301-0341 $02.00/0.

TOWARD THE DEFINITION OF "ABUSE PROVOKING CHILD"

Vladimir de Lissovoy, Ph.D.

College of Human Development
The Pennsylvania State University

Studies are legion that document violence by parents or other caretakers which result in physical insults of various degrees and, in some cases, the death of a child (Martin, 1977; Helfer and Kempe, 1974; Fontana, 1973; Gil, 1970; Elmer, 1967). Excellent review articles have served to give order to a vast amount of material enabling the researcher and the practitioner to grasp the significance of past labors. Spinetta and Rigler (1972), Parke and Collmer (1975), Burgess, (1978) have contributed comprehensive analyses and critical evaluations of theoretical and research efforts. The three major theoretical approaches that subsume present research efforts include: 1. The Psychiatric Model, (defined by Gelles (1973) as the Psychopathological Model, 2. The Sociological Model, and 3. The Social-situational Model (Parke and Collmer, 1975), which Burgess (1978) calls the Social Interactional Model. All of the above have demonstrated clearly that child abuse is a multicausal phenomenon and that research must be oriented in theory, in sampling procedures, and in methodological sophistication to deal with complex interactions. What is evident is that child abuse is a transactional phenomenon within the family and socio-cultural systems. Any single variable or even combinations of variables that may look promising in a retrospective analysis would not, necessarily, have predictive value. Thus Gil's (1971) wide ranging proposals of, ". . . unconditional elimination of poverty ..." while commendable as a national priority would not eliminate child abuse in the affluent population.

The practitioner (usually a social worker) at the local community level is faced with the task of ameliorating the problem. By legal dictum a reported case must be investigated and a disposition made. When compared to the support systems of teaching hospitals, the local social worker has few resources and limited authority. The awesome responsibility to arrive at a judgment and a decision that may well affect the life of the child and label a parent cannot be taken lightly. Of the myriads of findings in research to date what useful knowledge, what data and what skills can be provided? The reality is crisis intervention in one case of the routine forty to sixty others that await. There is no luxury of the therapeutic hour, the deliberations of a trauma team or even further consultations. Except in gravest situations the child remains within the family with the hope that somehow, through fear, coercion, perhaps support (if the client views it as such) abuse will cease.

This is not a critique of past research; indeed it is out of painstaking investigations that one aspect of child abuse has been receiving more attention in the last few years and it is this area that is emphasized here not as an answer to the solution of child abuse but as an area that can be translated into an applied format useful to the average practitioner. As long as the child is viewed solely in the role of victim it will be difficult to change parental abusive behavior. This limitation of perspective is dysfunctional not only in the practical aspect of assisting parents to cope with their children but also in the broader theoretical approach to the understanding of abusive acts. As an active member of the family transactional system the child's behavior, innocent in terms of motivation and, in some cases, instigative, may serve as an abuse provoking stimulus.

In a review article dealing with the role of the child Friedrich and Boriskin (1976) suggest that the "depraved-parent" model of abuse may discourage parents from seeking assistance. These authors urge a broader dissemination of the fact that some children induce stress and that parental perception that the child is "different" can be enough to be a factor in abuse.

Bidirectionality of Parent-child Relationships

Unidirectional parent effect was a convenient research model but inadequate in presenting the parent-child transactional system. Bronfenbrenner (1973) defines parent-child interaction as a reciprocal system in which the behavior of each participant is reciprocal; each participant affects the behavior of the other. The child is viewed "not merely as a reactive agent but as an instigator of behavior in others" (Bronfenbrenner, 1973, p. 3). The child as a stimulus becomes an important factor in any situation involving close proximity over time. In the family context not only does a parent produce changes in the child but vice versa. In this regard Brim (1968) noted,

> It is a commonly, if informally, reported experience by most not overly defensive parents that one or more of their children influenced them in profound ways and at deep levels on occasion and that they are different persons because of their continued intense interaction with children. It is erroneous to think of the socialization process in the parent-child relationship as a one way process. (pp. 213-214).

The role of the child as a stimulus and instigator of response has been stressed by Bell (1968, 1971). Burgess (1978) proposes a Social Interactional Model acknowledging that "abused children may contribute to the abusive behavior they receive." (p. 17). Bidirectionality is an established principle in developmental psychology; its import lies in the potential of an expanded model for understanding parent-child interaction. It is the reciprocal participation of both parent and child that shape relations but as Bell (1978) notes, the identification of child effects does not explain parental behavior, "... demonstration of a child affect indicates only that it plays some role in parent behavior." (p. 81).

In much of the early research children were identified as passive victims. Careful attention was given to the descriptive diagnoses of inflicted damage but little or no consideration was given to their roles in the abusive act (Galdston, 1971). Primary attention was given to the parents with a view of prevention and remediation (Sameroff and Chandler, 1975). Currently much more attention is being paid to the role of the child in the abusive situation.

The Abuse Provoking Child

Negatively stimulating behavior in the child may be motivationally innocent (such as appearance or activity rate) or it may have some motivational component, that is, the child may have learned behaviors that are abuse provoking. Excellent reviews now available of the child's potential role in abuse cover a wide spectrum of evidence (Parke and Collmer, 1975; Friedrick and Boriskin, 1976; Belsky, 1977; Martin, 1977). The studies cited are illustrative of main areas of evidence suggesting the role of the child in abuse.

In a study of adolescent parents de Lissovoy (1973) noted a predisposition for physical punishment by parents who were socially isolated, with little knowledge of development which resulted in unrealistic expectations of behavior. Their children were restless, colicky and irritable. Fontana (1973) in discussing parental reasons given for hurting a child notes the repeated answer that the child would not stop crying. An earlier report by Milowe and Lourie (1964) suggested potentially "abuse inviting" characteristics of the child such as difficult to manage, unappealing and excessive crying. In a descriptive study oriented to psychotherapeutic treatment of abusing families Ounsted et al. (1974) reported maternal descriptions of their children as being clingy, aggressive, timid and disobedient. Developmental histories included colic, vomiting, sleeping difficulties, excessive crying, and irritability.

Gil (1971) analyzed responses of 1,380 cases of a sample cohort that attempted to define types of child abuse. The typology presented is defined by the author as "admittedly crude" represented "most of the circumstances of abuse observed by social workers who completed the checklists." (p. 643) A factor analysis derived from the checklists identified a factor defined by Gil as "Child Originated Abuse." The behavioral descriptions that served to identify this factor included the item "persistent behavioral atypicality of child, e.g., hyperactivity, high annoyance potential, etc. Cases checked positively on this item may be considered as child-initiated or child-provoked abuse. This item was checked in 24.5 percent of the cases." (p. 643) A factor analysis of circumstances of child abuse resulted in a high loading of "misconduct of the child" in relation to "repeated abuse of the same child."

Johnson and Morse (1968) investigated child abuse utilizing caseworkers reports. Over 70% of the subjects had some physical or developmental deviation prior to the report of injury. The reports indicated that the children were hard to care for and were unresponsive. Case workers described the younger children as fussy, whiny, listless, demanding, stubborn, unresponsive and fearful. The data led these investigators to conclude that children who were most likely to be abused were overactive and difficult to supervise.

Terr (1970) reported that the abusing parents she studied manifested "fears" of the child. These included punishment from the child, fear of the infant's helplessness, fear of the child's seductiveness and disappointment in the child's inability to meet preconceived hope.

Temperamental variations in children are well documented. Many years ago Levy (1944) noted that hyperactive children showed other associated behavior disturbances such as emotional lability, feeding problems and a predisposition to personality disorders. Likewise Fries (1944) demonstrated a persistent pattern of acute response to stimuli which she defined "congenital activity." She advocated differential care according to the needs of the child. Fries and Woolf (1953) documented congenital differences in the excitability of the neuromuscular system that stemmed from inheritance, intra-uterine factors and birth trauma. Kostenburg, cited in this study observed that the hyperactive child is more likely to express aggression overtly while the hypoactive child will revert to more inward expression. Thomas et al. (1968) identified nine categories of basic tendencies present at birth which each infant possesses and which are measurable on a high-low continuum. From a sample of children that defined the study population a clinical cohort with behavioral disorders was obtained. The children were compared for each of the temperamental characteristics with the non clinical group. By this means it was possible to identify "easy" and "difficult" children. The "easy child" was one whose temperamental constellation comprises regularity, positive approach responses to new stimuli, high adaptability to changes and a preponderance of positive mood of mild or moderate intensity. In behavioral terms, this child develops regular sleep and feeding habits easily, takes to most new foods at once, smiles at strangers, adapts quickly to a new school, accepts most frustrations with a minimum fuss and learns rules easily. The "difficult child" is one who is irregular in biological functions, predominantly displays withdrawal responses to new stimuli, nonadaptability or slow adaptability to change, negative mood and predominantly intense reactions. This child manifests irregular sleeping and feeding habits, is slow to accept new foods, has prolonged adjustment periods to new stimuli and routine, and has frequent and loud periods of crying. This study indicated that it was the "difficult child" who ran the risk of being most susceptible to develop behavioral disorders at a later time.

In commenting about interaction of temperament and environment the authors note:

> ...Environment and temperament not only interact, but they also can modify each other. A parents' attitudes toward and practices with a specific child may reflect preexisting, long standing aspects of the parent's personality structure. But these attitudes and practices may also be reactive and reflect a response to the temperamental characteristics of the given child. The ease or difficulty of caring for the child, the degree of congeniality of the child's temperament for the parent, the congruence of parental expectations with the behavior of the child, all may influence not only the parent's behavior with the child, but also the form of expression of parental attitude...Environmental influences may profoundly modify the expression of temperament...A very adaptable child who is repeatedly faced with impossible demands and expectations may, after a time, become increasingly less adaptable in his behavior (p. 74-75).

In assessing this study Sameroff and Chandler (1975) caution that prediction of later emotional difficulties without additional longitudinal studies would not prove accurate. They note,

> What made the difference in outcome for these children appeared to be the behavior of their parents. If the parents were able to adjust to the child's difficult temperament, a good behavioral outcome was likely. If not, the difficulties were exacerbated and behavioral disturbance often resulted.
>
> The transaction was not simply the unidirectional influence of parents on the child, but also the reciprocal influence of the child on his parents. The impact of these

difficult children was such as to disrupt the normal caretaking abilities of their parents. (p. 229)

Extremes in temperamental reactivity could effect what Bell (1968) defined as upper-limit-control behavior, those parental responses which regulate and reduce the child's behavior which exceeds parental tolerance or expectations. Thus excessive crying, irritability, hyperactivity would be subject to upper-limit-control behavior. On the other hand a low level of reactivity such as developmental lag, lethargy, apathy, would elicit lower-limit-control behavior. Parental stability and consistency in discipline appear to be critical in controlling aversive behavior before it leads to potentially abusive responses (Elmer, 1967; Deur and Parke, 1970).

Yarrow, Waxler and Scott (1971), Osofsky and O'Connell (1972) and Dion (1974) are among a growing number of investigators to suggest that child characteristics may have a strong effect in the elicitation of adult behaviors. The latter study utilized children's physical attractiveness and sex as variables in testing adults' predisposition to invoke penalties for task errors. While the results were not clear cut there was evidence that "... women's behavior toward children was influenced primarily by the children's sex and physical attractiveness unmediated by differential attributions of ability or motivation." (p. 776)

An impressive body of literature has demonstrated a relationship between low birth weight and the likelihood of abuse. There are many variables that suggest such a relationship. Low birth infants require considerably more care and may tax the ability of some mothers (Elmer & Greg, 1967; Klaus & Kenell, 1970; Klein & Stern, 1971; Klaus and Fanaroff, 1973). Premature infants tend to cry more and be more irritable. Indications that low birth infants have a slower developmental progess have led Steele and Pollock (1968) to suggest that discrepancy in parental expectations may lead to abusive acts.

Another line of reasoning suggests that low birth weight results in separation of the mother and child. This early and often prolonged separation may interfere in the formation of attachment and the development of sensitivity to the infants needs. This view suggests that mothers who do not have the opportunity for immediate care of the newborn or who are not intimately involved with the care of the premature infant are hindered in the subsequent tasks of care taking. They lack confidence, sensitivity and skills (Leifer, Leiderman, & Barnett, 1970; Fanaroff, Kennell & Klaus, 1972; Seashore, Leifer, Barnett & Leidermann, 1973).

In sum it is clear that the child as an abuse provoking stimulus is a viable factor in the family transactional system. Parental variables in the abusing situations have been the focus of much research and only a very brief summary is presented.

The Abusive Parents

In a survey of a large number of studies assessing personality characteristics of abusing parents Spinetta and Rigler (1972) concluded that, at best, the only common denominator was "a general defect in character...allowing aggressive impulses to be expressed too freely." (p. 301). From case reports Steele (1975) suggests that abusive parents are characterized by immaturity, low self-esteem, low sense of competence, social isolation with a lack of environmental supports, misconception of the infant, punishment orientation, and a lack of ability to perceive the needs of infants in order to respond to their needs. A number of investigators have reported that abusing parents were abused as children (Curtis, 1963; Kempe et al., 1962; Fontana, 1973; Steele & Pollack, 1968). A behavioral analysis of the cycle of the abused parent abusing the child is given by Burgess (1978); he suggests that abusive behavior may be reinforced by siblings or parents that or the child may acquire aggressive behavior through observational learning. It is interesting that the notion of the cycle of abuse has not been questioned; this issue will be raised in a later section of this paper.

Preliminary Report of a Prospective Study

The emphasis of this paper has been upon the delineation of the abuse provoking variables of the child. This is not an attempt to suggest a main effect, it is this writer's contention that this is the variable that needs more attention in intervention. Gelles (1973), presents a comprehensive social-psychological model demonstrating the complexity of the transactional systems within which abuse takes place, this model takes into account child effect. Three conditions for abuse to occur are defined by Helfer (1973), the potential for abuse, a precipitating or crisis situation, and a very special kind of a child. A four factor equation of causes of abuse is suggested by Green, (cited by Friedrich & Boriskin, 1976): Special child + special parent + crisis + cultural tolerance = abuse. The authors suggest an expansion of this paradigm to two other equations which, "have all too often been ignored" (p. 588): (a) special child + normal parents + crisis + cultural tolerance = abuse; (b) special child + normal parents + cultural tolerance = abuse.

The importance of the child having abuse provoking potential is to be noted in reports of the same children being abused in different foster homes (Milowe & Lourie, 1964). In the same vein Ebbin (cited by Friedrick & Boriskin, 1976) and others have shown that in families with several children only one child was abused (Wooley & Evans, 1955; Nurse, 1964; Gil, 1970). Exceptions to this are also to be noted (Skinner & Castle, 1969).

In an ongoing prospective study de Lissovoy (1978) obtained answers to questions especially designed for incorporation into an intake interview of mothers who were identified as primary participants in abusive acts. In each case the child required medical treatment but none of the cases were severe enough to assume that the child's life was "at risk." Seven social workers dispersed geographically and unknown to one another contributed 34 answers to the following questions:

1. Will you please describe (name of the child)? (Probe)

2. How would you compare (him/her) to your other children?
(If this is the only child or if age differences are wide substitute, How would you compare (him/her) to your other children when they were the same age?)

3. Now, when you think of other children you have seen who are about the same age, how are they similar to (name of the child)?
How are they different?

In addition the mothers were read a list of adjectives and asked to answer <u>yes</u> or <u>no</u> as this applied to their child. This question was as follows:

4. Here are some words that describe many children. Which words do you feel apply to (child's name)?
affectionate, alert, aggressive, bossy, calm, careless, cheerful, curious, demanding, excitable, friendly, high strung, helpful, impulsive, jolly, nervous, patient, quiet, restless, show-off, rude.

This study is not yet finished and only the data for the "adjudicated group" are available. The control group data are now in the process of collection and because of the necessary demographic matching restrictions this is a tedious task. The preliminary analysis of the answers of the "adjudicated group" have interesting implications.

The answers to the question asking for a description of the child support Friedrick and Boriskin's (1976) notion that abusive parents perceive their child as "different." Modal descriptions included: "never slept," "cries alot," "always sick," "does not stay still," "follows me around," "gets into everything."

Comparisons to one's own children resulted in three modal answers: "sick more than others," "cries alot more," "takes more time," ("just different").

Comparison to children of others suggested few modalities in answers and a considerable number of answers that seemed defensive. Similarity to others apparently had a suggestive effect since the modal answers were, "about like other kids," or "about average." When asked about differences between own child and others again the answers seemed defensive: "he is larger," "I don't know," or "maybe noisier." The answers to the adjectives are tabulated in Table 1. They represent "forced choices" of mothers of 20 boys and 14 girls, ranging in age 2-8 to 7-2; the data are presented in raw scores.

TABLE I

Maternal Answers to Adjectives

	BOYS (N=20)		GIRLS (N=14)		TOTAL (N=34)	
	Yes	No	Yes	No	Yes	No
Affectionate	14	6	7	7	21	13
Alert	16	4	9	5	25	9
Aggressive	17	3	10	4	27	7
Bossy	15	5	8	6	23	11
Calm	2	18	4	10	6	28
Careless	12	8	7	7	19	15
Cheerful	9	11	7	7	16	18
Curious	13	7	6	8	19	15
Demanding	18	2	10	4	28	6
Excitable	17	3	11	3	28	6
Friendly	10	10	6	8	16	18
High Strung	18	2	10	4	28	6
Helpful	8	12	6	8	14	20
Impulsive	18	2	12	2	30	4
Jolly	6	14	3	11	9	25
Nervous	17	3	13	1	30	4
Patient	2	18	3	11	5	29
Quiet	3	17	4	10	7	27
Restless	19	1	4	10	23	11
Show Off	9	11	7	7	16	18
Rude	9	11	4	10	13	21

The data of maternal perception suggest that the following attributes predominate in this sample of abused boys: affectionate, alert, aggressive, bossy (assertive), not calm, curious, demanding, excitable, noisy (or active), and restless.

The girls are described as alert, aggressive, not calm, demanding, excitable, high strung, impulsive, unhappy, nervous, impatient, noisy (or active) and restless.

The semantic redundancy of the adjectives i.e., high strung, nervous, impulsive, restless apears to give an overloaded negative affect, nevertheless, the general picture is one reported in much research. With the exception of affectionate, defined yes by 61% of the mothers (interestingly more boys than girls were so defined) the affect oriented adjectives show that 47% of the children were defined as cheerful, 47% friendly, 41% helpful and 26% as jolly. A more thorough analysis will be presented along with the results of the control group in a subsequent publication.

Implications for the Practitioner

The question is raised once again, "Of the known research findings what help can be given to the practitioner (social worker) who may be the primary (and only) functionary in the intervention process?" Before attempting suggestions it is imperative to reiterate the complexity of the abusive act.

The Social Psychological model of the causes of child abuse (Gelles, 1973) illustrates the multicausal aspects of this phenomenon. At the risk of oversimplifying this excellent paradigm only the main variables will be noted in discussing implications for intervention. These are A. The Socialization Experience of the Parents, B. Possible Psychopathic States, C. Situational Stress, comprised of the variables; (1) Relations between parents, (2) Structural stress (excess children, unemployment, isolation) threats to parental authority, (3) Child produced stress, D. The Social position of Parent, E. Class and Community (values regarding violence), F. Immediate Precipitating Situations.

The practitioner can do nothing that would produce tangible long lasting results in most of the areas outlined. Short of dramatic social reorganization which would restrict personal freedom by imposing controls on family structure and function, awareness of the child abuse phenomenon and education at all levels utilizing total media seems to be the logical approach at the public level. Programs of intervention now operate in many areas of the United States.

The reports of success vary and it is not always clear whether the positive results are due to parental selection in the training procedures, to the techniques of training or to other intangibles (Parke and Collmer, 1975). Parental training programs are functional in populated areas, with fiscal integrity, professional staff and wide community support systems (cf. Patterson, 1974). They are difficult to attempt in rural and semi-rural areas.

The social worker who, in the United States, is often employed at the county government level is usually the person who investigates "at risk" or "reported abuse cases." Often it is the social worker who is the key person in the verification of abuse and who is responsible for whatever action is to follow. One of the key results in research since Dr. Kempe's pioneering paper is that child abuse is the product of a family transactional system. This view should broaden the practitioner's frame of reference to look beyond the child as the victim and the "depraved parent" orientation. Recognition of the potential of the child's role in abuse can assist in the development of supportive intervention. Since it is the social worker who by law in most states in America must follow up cases of suspected or adjudicated abuse, appreciation of mutuality of effect can assist the instigation of basic information such as realistic expectations in child development and explanation of possible alternatives to physical punishment.

This review of the delineation of abuse provoking variables is not meant as a defense of abusing parents. It is recognized that the great majority of parents are faced with many of the noted problems without resorting to abuse. If the abusing parent is to be "rehabilitated" it is imperative to be aware of the situational milieu and the critical incident that led to the violence. While it is not always possible to change parents' personal characteristics or the social milieu, one can explain normative development of children, suggest more realistic expectations, assess individual differences and assist the parent to cope with behaviors that are especially annoying (Spinetta & Rigler, 1972).

Social caseworker can be considered therapeutic insofar as the client-caseworker relationship is carried out in a milieu of affective neutrality and excludes attitudes suggesting guilt or innocence. Unfortunately the caseworker investigating alleged abuse is placed in a double bind of contradictory roles. As the investigator the social worker must arrive at a conclusion whether abuse has, in effect, taken place. In the role of "follow up" intervention a different approach is required in order to assist the client in attitudinal and behavioral change. Much of the literature oriented to SCAN programs and comprehensive hospital oriented research and training endeavors are "ideal types." The reality of what can be done in most communities falls short of such ideals.

It was noted earlier that a great many studies have found that abusive parents were themselves abused. This is apparently accepted as a fact and to the best knowledge of this writer no question of these findings has been raised. Such conclusions are so logical and fit the prevalent theories so well that it seems irrelevant to question such assumptions. Sears et al. (1957) give an interesting caveat in this regard noting that when good theory is supported by good data there is a tendency to close the doors to further research. At the risk of introducing the proverbial mouse to confront the elephant our data does not follow the previous findings.

Eleven abusive parents were interviewed and it was established in the investigation of their histories that all were abused as children. Some months later this investigator interviewed the parents about their childhood experiences. The questions used dealt with the community, school, siblings, family rituals, and significant people in their childhood. Within this framework of questions the subjects were asked the following:

"Children get into all kinds of trouble and sometimes parents must discipline them. Do you recall of any such experiences?" Another question asked directly "How often were you spanked as a child?"

Ten of the eleven parents described spanking, deprivation of privileges and "being yelled at." None suggested that they were physically hurt to an extreme point and not one had been hospitalized. Six volunteered that sometimes they "had it coming to them." One of the ten did describe acts by parents that were indeed abusive and required medical attention.

The introduction of these data on the basis of such a dimunitive sample may merit an apology. Nevertheless it raises an issue that has not yet been confronted. When an abusive parent is faced with the magnitude of the deed against a helpless child is it possible that the most natural defense in ego preservation is projection. In fact the parent is saying "I can't help it, it was done to me" not in the sense of fact but defensively. Another possibility is one of semantics; what punishment was really abuse? It would be useful to focus retrospectively on cases with medical records showing that abusive parents were in fact abused.

The vast amount of research under way is encouraging. Thus far predictive studies have not been successful, Monahan, cited by Parke and Collmer (1975), reviewed violence prediction research and concluded that there was overprediction (false positives) of between 65 and 99 per cent. Undoubtedly the years to come will witness refinements in the understanding of abusive acts. The seminal work of Patterson and Reid (1970) in explanation of coercive involvements, improved application of behavior theory with carefully controlled interaction studies such as those of Burgess and Conger (1977, 1978), the continuing efforts by Helfer and his colleagues, and the tireless efforts of Gil (1970) in fostering social progress as well as the theoretical work of Straus (1973) and Steinmetz (1974) will shed further light on violence.

Meanwhile the practitioner must do all possible to ameliorate existing abuse, to educate the parent and to prevent repeated acts of violence. As Fontana (1973) so graphically said, "Somewhere a child is crying"; there must be a response now.

References

Bell, R. Q. A reinterpretation of the direction of effects in studies of socialization. Psychological Review, 75, 81-95, (1968).

Bell, R. Q. Stimulus control of parent or caretaker behavior by offspring. Developmental Psychology, 4, 63-72 (1971).

Belsky, J. Child abuse: From research to remediation. Paper presented at the Groves Conference on Marriage and the Family. Liberty, New York, May, 1977.

Brim, O. Adult socialization. In J. A. Clausen (Ed.) (1968), Socialization and Society, Little, Brown, Boston.

Bronfenbrenner, U. An emerging theoretical perspective for research in human development. Unpublished manuscript, 1973.

Burgess, R. L. Child abuse: A behavioral analysis. In B. B. Lahey and A. E. Kazdin (Eds.), (1978), Advances in Child Clinical Psychology. Plenum, New York (in press).

Burgess, R. L. & Conger, R. D. Family interaction patterns related to child abuse and neglect: some preliminary findings. Child Abuse and Neglect: The International Journal, 1, 269-277 (1977).

Curtis, G. Violence breeds violence. American Journal of Psychiatry, 120, 386-387 (1963).

de Lissovoy, V. Child care by adolescent parents. Children Today, 14, 22 (1973)

de Lissovoy, V. Maternal descriptions of abused children. Unpublished study. (1978)

Deur, J. L. & Parke, R. D. The effects of inconsistent punishment on aggression in children. Developmental Psychology, 2, 403-411 (1970).

Dion, K. K. Children's physical attractiveness and sex as determinants of adult punitiveness. Developmental Psychology, 10, 772-778 (1974).

Elmer, E. (1967), Children in Jeopardy: A Study of Abused Minors and Their Families, University of Pittsburgh Press, Pittsburgh.

Elmer, E. & Gregg, G. S. Developmental characteristics of abused children. Pediatrics, 40, 596-602 (1967).

Fanaroff, A. A., Kennell, J. H., & Klaus, M. H. Follow-up of low birth weight infants--the predictise value of maternal visiting patterns. Pediatrics, 49, 287-290 (1972).

Fontana, V. J. (1973), Somewhere a Child is Crying, Macmillan, New York.

Friedrick, W. N. & Boriskin, J. A. The role of the child is abuse: A review of the literature, American Journal of Orthopsychiatry, 46, 580-590 (1976).

Fries, M. Psychosomatic relationships between mother and infant. Psychosomatic Medicine, 6, 159-162 (1944).

Fries, M. & Woolf, P. J. Some hypotheses of the role of the congenital activity type in personality development. Psychoanalytic Study of the Child, (1953), Volume VIII. International Universities Press, New York.

Galdston, R. Violence begins at home: The parents center project for the study and prevention of child abuse. Journal of the American Academy of Child Psychiatry, 10, 336-350 (1971).

Gelles, R. J. Child abuse as psychopathology: A sociological critique and reformulation. American Journal of Orthopsychiatry, 43, 611-621 (1973).

Gil, D. G. Violence against children, Journal of Marriage and the Family, 33, 637-648 (1971).

Gil, D. G. (1970) Violence Against Children: Physical Abuse in the United States, Harvard University Press, Cambridge.

Helfer, R. The etiology of child abuse. Pediatrics, 51, 777-779 (1973).

Helfer, R. E. & Kempe, C. H. (Eds.) (1974), The Battered Child (2nd ed.), The University of Chicago Press, Chicago.

Johnson, B. & Morse, H. A. Injured children and their parents. Children, 15, 147-152 (1968).

Kempe, C. H., Silverman, F. N., Steele, B. B., Droegemuller, W., Silver, H. K. The battered child syndrome. Journal of the American Medical Association, 181, 17-24 (1962).

Klaus, M. H., & Fanaroff, A. A. (1973), Care of the High Risk Neonate. Saunders, Philadelphia.

Klaus, M. H. & Kennell, J. H. Mothers separated from their newborn infants. Pediatric Clinics of North America, 17, 1015-1037 (1970).

Klein, M. & Stern, L. Low birth weight and the battered child syndrome. American Journal of Diseases of Children, 122, 15-18 (1971).

Leifer, A. D. Leiderman, P. H., Barnett, C. R., & Williams, J. A. Effects of mother-infant separation on maternal attachment behavior. Child Development, 43, 1203-1218 (1972).

Levy, D. On the problem of movement restraint; tics, stereotyped movements, hyperactivity. American Journal of Orthopsychiatry, 14, 664-671 (1944).

Martin, H. (Ed.) (1977) The Abused Child: A Multidisciplinary Approach to Developmental Issues and Treatment, Ballinger Press, Cambridge, Massachusetts.

Milowe, J. D., & Lourie, R. S. The child's role in the battered child syndrome. Journal of Pediatrics, 65, 1079-1081 (1964).

Nurse, S. M. Familial patterns of parents who abuse their children. Smith College Studies in Social Work, 35, 11-25 (1964).

Osofsky, J. D. & O'Connell, E. J. Daughters' effects upon mothers' and fathers' behaviors. Developmental Psychology, 7, 157-168 (1972).

Ounsted, C., Oppenheimer, R., & Lindsay, J. Aspects of bonding failure: The psychopathology and psychotherapeutic treatment of families of battered children. Developmental Medicine and Child Neurology, 16, 447-452 (1974).

Parke, R. & Collmer, C. Child abuse: An interdisciplinary analysis. In M. Hetherington (Ed.) (1975), Review of Child Development Research (Vol. 5). The University of Chicago Press, Chicago.

Patterson, G. R. Interventions for boys with conduct problems: multiple settings, treatments and criteria. Journal of Consulting and Clinical Psychology, 42, 471-481 (1974).

Patterson, G. R., & Reid, J. B. Reciprocity and coercion: Two facets of social systems. In C. Newunger and J. Michael (Eds.) (1970), Behavior Modification in Clinical Psychology. Appleton-Century-Crofts, New York.

Sameroff, A. J. & Chandler, M. J. Reproductive risk and the continuum of caretaking casualty. In F. D. Horowitz (Ed.) (1975), Review of Child Development Research, Vol. 4, The University of Chicago Press, Chicago.

Sears, R. R., Maccoby, E. E., & Levin, M. (1957), Patterns of Child Rearing. Row, Peterson, Evanston.

Seashore, M. J., Leifer, A. D., Bernett, C. R., & Leiderman, P. H. The effects of denial of early mother-infant interaction on maternal self confidence. Journal of Personality and Social Psychology, 26, 369-378 (1973).

Skinner, A. E. & Castle, R. L. (1969), 78 Battered Children: A Retrospective Study. National Society for the Prevention of Cruelty to Children. London

Spinetta, J. J. & Rigler, D. The child abusing parent: A psychological review, Psychological Bulletin, 77, 296-304 (1972).

Steele, B. F. Working with abusive parents from a psychiatric point of view. U.S. Department of Health, Education and Welfare. DHEW Publication No. (OHD) 75-70 (1975).

Steele, B. F. & Pollack, D. A psychiatric study of parents who abuse infants and young children. In R. E. Helfer and C. H. Kempe (Eds.) (1968), The Battered Child. University of Chicago Press, Chicago.

Steinmetz, S. K. & Straus, M. A. (1974) Violence in the Family. Dodd and Mead, New York.

Straus, M. A. A general systems theory approach to a theory of violence between family members. Social Science Information, 12 (1973).

Terr, L. C. A family study of child abuse. American Journal of Psychiatry, 127, 665-671, (1970).

Thomas, A., Chess, S., & Birch, H. (1968), Temperament and Behavior Disorders in Children. New York University Press, New York.

Woolley, P. V., & Evans, W. A. Significance of skeletal lesions in infants resembling those of traumatic origin. Journal of the American Medical Association, 158, 539-543, (1955).

Yarrow, M. R., Waxler, C. Z., & Scott, P. M. Child effects on adult behavior. Developmental Psychology, 5, 300-311 (1971).

Child Abuse and Neglect, Vol. 3, pp. 351 - 355.

SCOPE - FOR PARENTS AND CHILDREN

Geoff Poulton*, MA. and Lin Poulton

*Department of Sociology and Social Administration,
University of Southampton

SCOPE is a very young organisation. It formally came into existence a little over two years ago but it has its roots in work which started experimentally in Yorkshire eight years previously. One of the key ideas to emerge from the West Riding Educational Priority Area Project's pre-school programme * was that parents play a vital part in their children's education and that their teaching capacity needs to be recognised. Reinforcing the potential of parents to educate their own children became an important feature of the pre-school work in Yorkshire and various ways were tried out in working with families, both in their homes and in pre-school groups. Unemployment was high in the town at this time (1970) and a number of families had to live on very low incomes. It quickly became apparent that a number of families were living through frequent periods of high stress caused by financial pressures or relationship difficulties with other members of the family or neighbourhood, etc. Educational programmes were not likely to have much impact under such circumstances and it was therefore necessary to link the idea of 'care' and 'support' to education very firmly. So the work with young children developed to some extent into a family support service for those involved to use as required.

In Southampton many young families face similar difficulties to those in Yorkshire, but one of the strengths of a mining town comes from a sense of belonging which people have to a community where a large proportion of them share the same risks and dangers in their work. Families intermarried and remained in the area, so that it was rare to find people who felt lonely and without support in their street or neighbourhood. The town was well established having gone through its initial stages of development in the 1890's. In contrast, most of SCOPE's work is carried out on post-war housing estates, some built during the past ten years. Many young families are concentrated on the newer estates around Southampton. A number of these families have difficulties which often wear down the parents, particularly the mothers. Since they do not often have close neighbourhood links or relatives living nearby, problems become magnified and sometimes appear insurmountable. The result is a sense of powerlessness over the life of the family, including the way the children are growing up. Southampton is not unique in this experience, of course, it is a common feature of many urban areas.

SCOPE's main concern is to create a neighbourhood support system for families in order to reduce feelings of loneliness and powerlessness experienced by some people during various times in their lives. The neighbourhood groups which are formed as a result, concentrate on helping people to face periods of extreme stress before going on to reinforce the potential of parents to educate their own children. In the process, social elements of caring become blurred with educational elements of learning. The 'curriculum' of the groups is determined by the points reached in the members' lives, together with the developmental requirements of their children.

* Detailed information will be found in Educational Priority Vol. 4, HMSO (1975) and in Poulton, G. & James, T. Pre-school learning in the community R. & K.P. (1975)

The autonomy of groups is important. The members, many of whom may need to develop a greater sense of autonomy and worth, must be able to determine the group's path of development. So there is no central plan of activities or topics imposed on the groups. They plan and carry out their own activities. SCOPE is a support structure for a number of groups (at present, thirteen) who, through representation on the management committee, can determine the organisation's running and policy.

We arrived at the present structure in May 1976 by building a plan together with representatives from health, education and social service departments. A management committee was established in order to keep an overview of developments within SCOPE and to maintain links with other organisations such as Local Authority Departments, Government Departments, voluntary bodies and Trusts. The committee's responsibility was to control the finances, to maintain records of decisions made, and to reflect on the functioning of SCOPE so that changes could be made if and when necessary.

Since some changes have had to be made fairly quickly and the management committee meets eight times per year, the weekly training sessions for convenors have included a period of time to examine working problems and to find solutions. For instance, like many network organisations we have had to overcome problems of communication between groups, the management and social committees and the coordinator. We rely to a large extent on personal contact and telephone messages, but we also now produce a bi-monthly leaflet which carries information on meetings and events within SCOPE as well as individual items of news.

Support is a key feature of the organisation and is the primary reason for its existence. The groups offer support for individual families in their own neighbourhoods. The network of groups offers a supportive structure for individual groups and their convenors. The convenors meet regularly for training sessions, led by the coordinator and also may take part in support meetings conducted by a senior social worker and a psychiatrist. The coordinator herself is supervised by a social worker and also receives guidance from the Management Committee. Since the Management Committee consists mainly of group representatives, the support system of SCOPE tends to be circular rather than hierarchical, Fig. 1.

So much for organisational description. On what assumptions do we base our work with families and their young children? Our assumptions are not radical or very surprising. Stated briefly they are:

1. The early years of a child's life are very important to later development, but not irreversible. Birth to the age of thirty months is a particularly vital stage in development.

2. Close, consistent, loving, rational adult contact is necessary for a child during this period if stable emotional, intellectual and moral development is to occur. Diet, hygiene, clothing, housing are important but follow a loving relationship in order of priority.

3. Where consistent adult stimulus exists for a child then it is likely that development will be near to his potential development. The natural parents are usually in the most advantageous position to provide such stimulus in the majority of cases.

4. When social stress factors reduce an adult's capacity to maintain consistent stimulus for the child, behavioural difficulties frequently arise.

5. The effect of (4) is to lower the parent's self-concept which, in turn, can contribute to low achievement in children.

6. A neighbourhood group can help to reduce isolation, and improve a member's self-concept and sense of autonomy. In the process the child's development may be enhanced.

So far, we have presented an organisational model which, combined with the above assumptions, appears orderly and tidy. The ends have all been tied neatly around a family service package. But before opening the package in the presence of people who are likely to become involved with its contents, a further assumption has to be made. Family life is untidy and complex. Parents and their children are likely to behave irrationally rather than rationally - according to my values and standards and the outcomes of involvement with them will remain unpredictable. So a flexible, reflective operational method has to be used by everyone taking part in the action of SCOPE.

In practice the majority of families are referred to us by social agencies. As coordinator, I receive requests from health visitors, social workers, psychiatrists, general practitioners, teachers etc. to consider introducing individual families to SCOPE. Detailed information is not required, I prefer to visit a family on as equal a footing as possible. They will only have agreed with the social worker to meet and discuss with me the possibility of joining SCOPE. I have also agreed to the same contract. It is only necessary to know the names of children and their ages. My first visit to the family becomes an important introductory meeting during which we can assess each other and possibly arrive at a decision for future action. Not every visit results in the mother and child joining a group, of course. During the four months period ending in July 1978, of sixty four families referred, thirty one joined groups, twenty were visited on further occasions, five expressed interest but did not come to a group, five were encouraged to join other organisations and three families were not interested in taking part.

Sometimes a mother will feel very unsure about meeting a group of strangers. Her current difficulties may be over-powering and she may well feel that her experiences are the manifestation of her inadequacy. So further visits may be necessary before she summons the confidence to meet others. We may well take her and her child to the first meeting when she is ready to attend. The point I am making is that we start with the mother's feelings, senses and perceptions as they are presented during the first meeting and build on them together. Once in the group, the process is continued with the convenor and the other members helping the mother to develop a sense of identity in a new situation. Fathers are not excluded from SCOPE groups, of course, but referrals invariably relate to mothers and their children. During initial and subsequent visits I frequently find it necessary to involve fathers in the discussions, if they are present. Roughly sixty per cent of SCOPE members are lone parents however.

The people who come to us have a variety of backgrounds. They all have in common, at least one child under the age of five years and this provides the basis for the activities of groups. Each group has a creche, so that the children can play together, under supervision, during discussion sessions. Although the groups meet only once per week throughout the year, other social events are often arranged which provide further opportunities to reduce loneliness. In addition the group convenors, most of whom have been group members in the past, maintain contact with families between meetings, if necessary. In this way a locally based support system is available for families undergoing periods of high stress.

Further to the group system of offering support, we also hold short residential sessions for families who are needing a period of peace. These sessions offer a brief respite for families under pressure and they also provide a way of helping parents to clarify their positions in a setting which is neutral and, hopefully, un-threatening. The majority of families using this service contain only one adult, but those with physically or mentally handicapped children have also been included. While the parents rest or visit shops, cinemas etc., their children are cared for. Meals and accommodation are provided in a city-centre house owned by Winchester Diocese. SCOPE covers all costs and staffing requirements for the sessions, with the help of the Social Services Department.

To return to the subject of membership in the groups. Apart from the criterion of families with children under five years, distance to be travelled to the nearest group is also important. We usually recommend people to groups within pram-pushing distance of their homes. Initially we experienced difficulties in accepting referrals from social agencies of people who clearly could not relate to a neighbourhood group. There have been alcohol and drug abusers referred to us in the past but they have tended to place heavy demands on groups of people who themselves are fairly tender beings. So who are the SCOPE members? I include three descriptions with the agreement of the members concerned.

Penny is twenty seven, she has two girls, one aged two years and the other eight months. Her husband is a school teacher and they live on a new estate of owner-occupied houses, which is adjacent to a large local authority estate. Penny found a SCOPE group by herself. Her health visitor had told her that a group for young mothers was meeting in the area. The group consisted of mothers who recently had had their babies. The health visitor sees this group as a place where young mothers can share experiences in child-rearing and avoid becoming anxious and obsessive about particular aspects of raising children. Penny found that a number of the people in the group were her neighbours. She became friendly with them and in time arranged for them to meet in her home for coffee before the group meetings. Penny eventually took over the convening role in the group and has encouraged new members to join. She attends the training sessions with other SCOPE convenors. She feels however that her group differs from others in SCOPE because neither she nor the members have insurmountable difficulties. She can however contribute strongly in discussions on child management and development, and she provides good support for other group convenors.

Joan is twenty four with a three year old boy and four year old girl. She was referred by a social services department family aide and by a health visitor as a lonely, isolated mother who found going out of the house difficult. At the first visit by the coordinator, Joan seemed pleased to see a visitor and soon relaxed and began to talk about her difficulties. Her husband's work took him away from home and he only returned at weekends. She found the children difficult to handle especially when they reluctantly went to bed at night and took advantage of her tiredness. The coordinator gave Joan information about SCOPE and arranged another visit. Five subsequent visits by the coordinator, a group convenor and a group member, were necessary before Joan had gained enough confidence to venture out of the house. She was given a lift to the meeting and was assured that she could be taken home whenever she wished during the afternoon. After the meeting Joan walked home with another group member who lived nearby. This member was to be an important source of help to Joan, subsequently. Joan was asked if she would bring her kettle to the group the following week as the one used to make tea had broken. She turned up with her kettle at the next meeting and has not stopped coming since.

Joan says that by bringing her kettle she had an opportunity to give something after experiencing a long period at home during which she became increasingly depressed and feeling more and more useless. She had a new incentive to wash herself and put on make-up which was a very positive step towards recovering her sense of self-esteem. As Joan gained in confidence and trust, she gradually shared her worries and anxieties with the group members who often identified with Joan. Sharing experiences helped her to realise that she was not alone in trying to find solutions to difficulties. She received help and encouragement in dealing with her children who benefited by Joan being more relaxed in her relationship with them.

Marcia, aged twenty six, has three girls, four years, eighteen months and three months old. She lives on a large new local authority estate. At the time of referral she was overwhelmed with the strain of coping with a premature baby and two sickly children. She had little support or help from her husband. She was welcoming and friendly during the coordinator's first visit. She said that she was tired and spent much of the time trying to encourage her tiny baby to feed. Marcia suffers from a chest complaint and has spent long periods of her life in hospital. The coordinator played with the children and eventually examined with Marcia her present difficulties. Marcia said she failed at everything but wanted to be a good mother.

During a second visit SCOPE was mentioned and Marcia agreed to the local group convenor visiting her. She later joined the group and enjoyed having a chance to relax while her children were taken to play in the creche where they made new friends. Marcia was able to contribute to discussions on child development. Marcia has now separated from her husband who found the strain of bringing up three children under five years too great. She continues to be supported by group members and has taken part in residential weekend breaks.

During the past two years, roughly six hundred families have been in contact with SCOPE for the varying periods of time. Fortunately we have very few instances of parents abusing their children to cause permanent emotional and physical harm. There have been instances when children have been decidedly at risk and we have had to take preventative action. Our primary aim is to offer a de-fusing process to take the heat out of crises and whenever possible, we work to reduce the possibility of such crises in relationships.

Two groups have included secondary school students in their discussions and creche activities. These sessions have proved to be powerful sources of learning for the youngsters involved and good experiences for the adults, who are only a few years older. In the long run, however, the most realistic preventative service we can offer lies in a readily accessible system of support for the families with whom SCOPE has contact.

Such a system has to cut across the boundaries of disciplines established by formal agencies and it suggests that a more unified approach to family services is required in this country. It is interesting to observe the reactions of various departmental representatives to SCOPE's work. Educationists identify the possibilities of working with the under fives and adults and we certainly take a broad view of the educational opportunities presented in the organisation. Organising and running a group is an educational experience. The learning which takes place may be related to health or be based on the social, emotional or political needs of people living on housing estates. And there is no limit to the groups' potential for discussing and developing a wide range of interests.

Social workers find that the groups offer potential for establishing relationships between people who feel isolated or overcome by the pressures of raising a family. They have also commented on the efficacy of the residential weekends which provide some relief from such pressures. Health visitors and general practitioners recognise that the groups offer families chances to obtain support during periods of stress. The groups also are able to consider aspects of health education and preventive medicine in an atmosphere of normality - amongst friends and neighbours. Interestingly the groups have also contributed to the training of social workers and health visitors. Recordings made during a series of SCOPE radio discussions last year have been heavily used on local professional training courses.

Clearly our work in SCOPE cannot be biased towards either health, or education, or welfare of families because all three are inter-related at the point of contact with individuals. We are sure that the families involved in the work form the primary source of strength, dynamism and support available. Additional forms of help and service may be negotiated from statutory organisations. Services which are maintained and controlled entirely by professionals may have a negative effect on the very people who need most to develop confidence, poise and the ability to join others in local movements of education and care. We cannot, and do not provide a panacea to meet all problems and to deal with all forms of family crisis. By offering locally based points to which people can come easily and without fuss, it is possible that some family difficulties are prevented from escalating into states of extreme crisis. Our start point lies in helping people to value themselves, to feel valued and then to enable them to create the same feelings in others. Reinforcement of the parents' roles as primary care-givers and educators of their children then follows naturally.

Child Abuse and Neglect, Vol. 3, pp. 357 - 362.

0145-2134/79/0301-0357 $02.00/0.

THE PARENT SUPPORT SERVICE (AUSTRALIAN CAPITAL TERRITORY)

Elizabeth Smart
74 MacKenzie Street
HACKETT. A.C.T. 2602
AUSTRALIA

Barbara Hicks
Mental Health Branch
Capital Territory Health Commission
A.C.T. AUSTRALIA

INTRODUCTION

"Speak roughly to your little boy
And beat him when he sneezes,
He only does it to annoy
Because he knows it teases".

The words of the Duchess in Lewis Caroll's "Alice in Wonderland" suggest a fairly massive projection of adult feelings onto a child in care. The hypothesis that was fundamental to the establishment of the Capital Territory Parent Support Service was that this phenomenon of projection regularly occurs when parents are under stress.

It seems probable that, in Australia, holier-than-thou attitudes to those known to have abused a child, mask a generalised anxiety about personal parenting skills in today's complex society. The P.S.S. was therefore designed primarily as a preventive measure, to provide supportive counselling for parents experiencing stress, and publicity for the service has aimed at creating a climate in which ANY parent can admit feelings of aggression, frustration and inadequacy.

As the universality and normality of parents' "bad" feelings about themselves and their children is recognised and accepted it should become easier for those with deep-rooted problems to seek help before a crisis occurs.

THE COMMUNITY BEING SERVED

The site for the capital of the newly created country of Australia was chosen in 1909, but Canberra only developed slowly until well after World War II. At that time the government became increasingly centralised and there was such an influx of public servants, academics, and employees of service industries that the population increased from 39,000 to over 200,000 in 20 years.

Land in the Capital Territory is vested in the Commonwealth Government, so each suburb is carefully planned. In theory neighbourhood groups are established. In practise there are problems comparable to those met in other rapidly developing suburban areas, but accentuated because the city is far from the centres of population where many residents still have their roots. Low density housing, and poor public transport mean reliance on the motor-car, and it is easy to feel isolated, especially if tied to the house with young children.

The residents of Canberra are younger and more affluent than the national average, and generally expect a high standard of living. Since 1977, however, the rate of unemployment has increased more rapidly than anywhere else in Australia. There is also a high divorce rate, which can partly be accounted for by the age structure of the population. Together, all this suggests that many families are probably under considerable stress. None the less the reported incidence of child abuse and neglect has been comparatively low up to date.

BACKGROUND TO THE SERVICE

"A City Without Soul" is a term used by many non-residents to describe Canberra, but in reply to these critics it could be argued that it has a "heart" manifested by a wealth of individuals and groups concerned about community welfare.

In 1975 the 1st Australian National Conference on "The Battered Child" was held in Perth (W.A.), and for a time Child Abuse was "news". Jan Carter addressed a meeting of workers in the Welfare Industry; housewives discussed the issues at local "friendship meetings"; the two statutory Health and Welfare Agencies struggled to come to grips with problems of inter-agency policy; and 18 different groups were found to be looking at ways to prevent child maltreatment.

Eventually a voluntary service organiser and a senior social worker with the Statutory Mental Health Service took the initiative in bringing together those who were interested in co-ordinating their thinking, and rationalising their planning.

Many meetings later a Committee of Management was set up to establish the PARENT SUPPORT SERVICE, as an autonomous telephone counselling service for parents, staffed by trained volunteers working under the supervision of professional consultants. The aims of the service were:-

- To help clients to clarify their problems
- To provide information about community resources and to enable clients to use these effectively
- To provide clients with a reliable and supportive listener whom they could trust in times of crisis.

The decision to act was essentially made by individuals, supported in principle by the Mental Health Service and by a few community organisations. Three groups agreed to have official representation on the Committee, and of these "LIFE LINE" - (an organisation similar to the Samaritans) - was the most significant. Life Line's willingness to provide the initial contact with clients, and their expertise in the training of volunteers, made the P.S.S. a viable proposition.

Immediately there was opposition from those who saw that problems would arise if the service infringed on the statutory duties already being carried out by government agencies. Time was taken to gain the co-operation of these antagonists, and in order to attain credibility and recognition, a detailed policy document was drawn up. This document sets out the philosophy of the service, together with procedural guidelines for dealing with all situations that could conceivably involve legal liability.

THE SERVICE

As the P.S.S. was established without any financial backing it has no office facilities of its own. Those wanting to use the service have to ring the "Lifeline" number for their initial contact and within 24 hours the case is allocated to a volunteer who phones the client back (or makes a home visit if there is no phone). From then on the frequency of contact and the way in which the relationship develops, depend on the needs of the client.

A client who described her counsellor as "somewhere between my mother and a social worker" was probably typical of those who have benefitted most from the service. In other words, the counsellor is someone who cares, but who is without the emotional involvement of a member of the family: someone who accepts feelings of anger, resentment and inadequacy without condemnation, but who also gives positive encouragement and reassurance; someone who has skills, but with whom there are not the barriers that some clients feel separate them from professional workers.

It is made clear to the client that the service is confidential, but that each volunteer is responsible to a consultant. Permission to consult with other agencies or workers, is always obtained from the client, except when emergency action has to be taken on behalf of a child, and against the client's wishes. So far no such crisis has occurred, but if it does, responsibility for action will rest with the consultant and not with the volunteer.

The disadvantage of using "Life Line" for clients' first contact is that, after ventilating their feelings, some subsequently deny that they have a problem. Under these circumstances it is hard for the P.S.S. volunteer to establish a relationship, and all that can be done is to leave the way open for the client to call back if another crisis occurs.

THE VOLUNTEER COUNSELLORS AND CONSULTANTS

The present group of 14 counsellors are all mothers. They differ widely in age and in cultural background, but they all possess the ability to listen to other people, and to care about their clients. They also share a readiness to risk having to make radical changes in their own attitudes.

Men are not excluded, but so far none have volunteered.

The selection of volunteers is crucial to the service. Not only are they expected to undertake rigorous training, to use the consultants regularly, and to accept considerable responsibilities, but their families must be ready for the service to intrude, at times, into the privacy of their home life. Personal interviews, before and after training, have proved effective in selecting out, by mutual agreement, those not ready to undertake the work.

The three consultants are professional social workers practising in local counselling agencies. Each is responsible for a group of volunteers and is available to them for consultation about their own or their client's problems.

THE TRAINING

All volunteers undertake a basic training course of at least 3 months. At first it was thought necessary to provide them with a fairly comprehensive knowledge of the medico-legal aspects of child maltreatment, so that they would be fully conversant with pitfalls that they should avoid. As it turned out the first group of trainees were well armed for problems they seldom met.

After six months work with clients, it became increasingly clear that the role of the volunteer is to stand alongside the client as a supportive friend, avoiding as far as possible action that would link them in the client's mind with the statutory, legal, or medical authorities. The focus of the second training course was therefore radically altered. The didactic presentation of factual information was cut to an essential minimum, and trainees were taught to develop intra-personal awareness and inter-personal skills through such means as role plays and group discussion. In this way they were better prepared for the central core of the work that they were actually to undertake.

Inservice training takes the form of regular monthly meetings, supplemented by more intensive learning experiences as they are found necessary. An example of this is a recent 6 week-course on child development, and age-related problems that parents can expect to encounter.

FINANCE AND PUBLICITY

The decision to risk starting the service without independant funds was justified at the end of 1977, when the Parent Support Service won the Canberra Community Service Award for the year. This award is given annually and is sponsored by a major Canberra Building Society and by Radio 2CA.

With the $1000 cash and $1000 worth of radio publicity a public relations campaign was set in motion. Letters were sent to all medical practitioners in Canberra describing the service, and offering to co-operate with them by giving support to parents who seem anxious about their children's physical or emotional development. Liaison was established with other community health and welfare workers, and requests for speakers about the service were welcomed. Cards were produced for widespread letter-box distribution and for display at primary information centres.

Radio and television stations arranged interviews with members of the service, and local newspapers printed news items and articles about the needs of parents and ways in which the P.S.S. could help. An effective form of publicity was the frequent repetition of 10 second RADIO "blurbs" such as "If you are feeling uptight, or anxious about your child, phone 82.2222 and ask for the Parent Support Service".

Until the service becomes a bye-word in the community the work of the Public Relations Sub Committee will have to continue. Only then will parents automatically think about phoning the service rather than abusing their child.

THE FIRST 12 MONTHS OF OPERATION

During the period under review 55 women and 2 men consulted the service, and their families included 125 children of school age or below. The number is not large, but with growing public awareness of what is available, the numbers are steadily increasing.

The degree of actual abuse a client has meted out to a child is hard to assess on a telephone contact, but 49% of clients stated that they had reacted more violently than they had intended towards at least one of their children, and expressed fear of what they might do if they did not have help. 77% of clients presented a child of 5 years or under as their main problem. More often than not a mother who had coped reasonably well with one young child, was finding the strain of having two children more than she could handle.

As clients came to trust their counsellors it became increasingly clear that all were under stress for a multiplicity of reasons. Of the 44 clients living with their husbands 60% admitted that problems in their marriage were critical in their feelings towards their children. Many accused their partners of failing to give them the support they felt they needed in bringing up the children.

Low self esteem was common amongst clients, and seven were conscious of reenacting their own childhood experiences of poor parenting. Loneliness, isolation, and the feeling of being tied to the house and children, were major factors in the problems of more than half the clients. In 10 cases counsellors worked closely with professionals in other agencies. These clients all had long histories of failure and inadequacy. In this situation the role of the volunteer is that of a nurturing parent helping the client to use community resources more effectively.

The Length of time spent with clients naturally varied considerably - from the 7 who rejected the service on the first contact, to the 20 who have been working with a counsellor for between 2 and 10 months. It was encouraging that 4 clients re-contacted their counsellor when a new crisis arose, after termination had been mutually agreed on some time before. "Thank you for caring" was perhaps, the highest tribute paid to a volunteer.

The value of the service to the client did not appear to depend on the length of contact. Effective intervention at the time of crisis enabled some to mobilise their own strengths after 2 or 3 contacts, and altogether the volunteers assessed that on termination 28 clients were coping satisfactorily either on their own or in conjunction with other community resources. 12 ceased contact with results unknown, and 10 were continuing with the service on 31.5.78.

THE FUTURE

The committee has applied for financial support from the Government, and so plans for expansion of the service depend to some extent on the outcome of this application. They include the provision of a "befriending" service to clients in their own homes, and the establishment of a centre where parenting skills can be taught and where parents can come together to share their problems.

The results of an independant evaluation of the service are not known as this paper goes to press, but they too will influence future decisions.

DISCUSSION

This paper describes the experiences of a group of people working with a small number of parents and children in a particular community. As the emphasis of the work being done was on prevention and not on research, no significant conclusions can be reached, but the observations of the team are comparable to those reported in the literature on Child Abuse and Neglect.

Guthrie (1) makes the supposition that a child entering the Health System from the suburbs is diagnosed as "Failure to Thrive" whereas the diagnosis would be "Question of Neglect" if the same child came from an urban area. Kempe (2) believes that "the poor are far more likely to be reported, accused, and convicted". Thus it may be presumed that there are "at risk" families in affluent suburban Canberra, despite the low incidence of reported abuse and neglect. The admission of 49% of clients that they feared for their children's safety suggests that the service is in fact reaching some of these families.

Smith (3) claims that it is unrealistic to expect battering parents to take the initiative, and to use a 24 hour telephone counselling service. This seems a valid criticism of some such services, but it ignores the on-going nature of the relationship of trust between the volunteer and client, which, if built up steadily, should make it easier for the parent to seek help in a crisis. As Lipner (4) points out "The consistent and supportive involvement of a good friend is often the key to a change in the parent-child relationship", and this is how most clients see their volunteer counsellor.

The high incidence of marital disharmony disclosed by clients as being a factor in their "bad" feelings about their children, bears out not only the observations of Walker (5), who has found that couples project their hostile feelings about each other onto their children, but also that of Smith (6) whose research showed that "abusing mothers had problems with their partners ... more frequently than did the controls". These problems involved a lack of support in child-rearing, which has also been a consistent complaint amongst the Canberra mothers.

Avery (7), discusses the way in which clients must "have their own needs met, so that they are able to respond more appropriately to their children". This describes almost exactly the observation of the volunteers, and applies particularly to the clients for whom they acted as 'nurturing parent', while complementing the work of the professionals involved with a family.

Smith (8) records that loneliness and social isolation were reported by both control and abusing mothers, but that the former were better able to compensate. This is relevant to the Canberra setting where so many of the clients feel isolated and it suggests that those who use the service briefly (mainly as an information-giving resource) are acting constructively and are less likely to be "at risk".

The insistence on adequate training and support services for the volunteers themselves is confirmed by Lipner (9) who says "all who offer to help families in crisis need supervision and a forum to air feelings connected with this work".

Using one of Kempe's (10) criteria for assessing achievement in intervention, the Parent Support Service claims to be a success in that it has been instrumental in ensuring that a few "parents who were joyless, now seem to have some fun".

REFERENCES

1. Guthrie A.D. "Child Abuse on Main Street" In Belling N. and Hill D. (1975) (Eds.) "Child Abuse Intervention and Treatment" p.24 Publishing Sciences Group Acton Mass

2. Kempe C.H. "Paediatric Implications of the Battered Baby Syndrome" Archives of Disease in Childhood 1971.46.28

3. Smith S.M. (1975) "The Battered Child Syndrome" Butterworth's London p210

4. Lipner J.D. "The Use of Community Resources in Work with Abusive Families" in Belling N. and Hill D. (Eds.) Op. cit. p131

5. Walker A. "Social Assessment" in Carter J. (Ed.) 1974 "The Maltreated Child" Priory Press London p70

6. Smith S.M. Op Cit p213

7. Avery N.C. "Viewing Child Abuse and Neglect as Symptoms of Family Dysfunctioning" in Belling N. and Hill D. (Eds.) Op. cit. p89

8. Smith S.M. Op. cit. p209

9. Lipner J.D. Op. cit. p132

10. Kemp C.H. (1975) "The Battered Child" Proceedings of the 1st Australian National Conference on the Battered Child. Department of Comm. Welfare. W.A. 1975

Child Abuse and Neglect, Vol. 3, pp. 363 - 365.
Pergamon Press Ltd., 1979. Printed in Great Britain.

ADELAIDE'S CRISIS CARE UNIT

B.J. Fotheringham
Modbury Hospital, South Australia

At the first International Congress on Child Abuse held in Geneva two years ago it was reported that the South Australian Government was giving consideration to changes in the law regarding child abuse. These changes have now taken place and doctors, dentists, nurses, teachers, employees of agencies established to promote child welfare or community welfare and even the Police are all required to notify cases of child abuse to the Department for Community Welfare. Such notifications are then forwarded to one of five Regional Panels whose responsibility it is to decide appropriate action and to keep notified families under review. The Panels consist of five persons, viz.

1. A member of the Department for Community Welfare
2. A mothercraft (M.B.H.A.) nurse
3. A psychiatrist experienced in child psychiatry
4. A policeman
5. A doctor

These Panels work well in rationalising the treatment programmes extended to abusing families but, working as they do as committees, they could become ponderous and of little use in crisis situations.

To deal with the acute aspects of child abuse a 24 hour Crisis Care Unit has been developed in Adelaide, the capital city. This Unit is a co-operative venture between the Department for Community Welfare and the Police. It is therefore unusual, for in many other cities the two departments scarcely may talk to one another, let alone combine in a successful joint venture.

The Unit began operating on 16th February 1976 and has continued to operate 24 hours a day, 7 days a week since that time.

The Crisis Care Unit consists of 14 Crisis Care workers and one supervisor. They are rostered on day, night and evening shifts to cover the 24 hours. The workers, who are academically qualified in the areas of social work and psychology, are assisted by trained volunteers who help maintain the Unit's base operation during evenings and at weekends. This allows more time for the paid staff to undertake field duties.

The Unit's central office has a direct telephone link with the Police Department and four lines are available for the general public. There is a modern communication system between the base and mobile cars equipped with two-way radios and radio telephones.

The work of the Unit is based on the theory that the best time to intervene in personal crisis situations is at the time they are happening. Crisis Care workers are trained to enter situations where there is considerable stress and tension and to work with the people involved. The mobility of the Unit enables workers to attend people in crisis in their own environment. The problems are discussed, any immediate steps necessary are taken and appropriate referrals are made for follow-up consultations. The Crisis Care Unit itself does not get involved with long term follow-up work but ensures that other agencies do.

Common problems that are dealt with include:-

Domestic disputes with or without violence
Alcoholics in need of treatment
Parent/child disputes
Bereavement situations
Vehicular accident problems, e.g. helping the bereaved
Attempted suicide
Overdose and other drug reactions
Migrants in unfamiliar surroundings
Runaway children
Violent assaults on children
Emergency financial problems
Counselling of rape victims.

Since the Unit started two and a half years ago nearly 60,000 telephone calls for help have been received and more than 4,000 immediate visits have been made to crisis situations. 2,687 of these visits were made in the 18 months from June 1976 to December 1977 and the following is an analysis of some of these visits.

In only 34 cases (1.3%) was child abuse given as the main reasons for contacting Crisis Care. However in another 100 cases (3.7%) child abuse either was proved subsequently or was rated as being highly suspected.

This paper focuses on those 100 cases where child abuse was not given as a problem at the time of the call for help but where it was found by the Unit's worker upon arrival at the scene. These cases are important as they represent one facet of the preventive work done by the Unit.

Details of those 100 calls are as follows:-

<u>Time of Call</u>

The most popular time of call was between 5.00 pm and 6.00 pm (10% of the suspected or positive child abuse cases). In general the Unit's busiest time was later in the evening, between 8.00 and 10.00 pm.

<u>Source of Call</u>

Police	46%
Client	33%
Neighbour	8%
D.C.W.	4%

Please note that this is basically a social work service, but one accepted and used by the Police. Policemen are also accepted and valuable team members of the Regional Panels mentioned earlier.

<u>Age of Guardian</u>

Less than 21 years	34%
21 to 30 years	23%
31 to 40 years	28%
41 to 50 years	10%

Note that one third were less than 21 years of age.

Guardian's Sex

Female	76%
Male	23%
Unknown	1%

Three-quarters of those using the Crisis Care service in relation to child abuse problems were women.

Guardian's Ethnicity

Australian	69%
U.K.	10%
Italian	4%
Greek	4%
Aboriginal	1%

These percentages reflect the composition of Adelaide's community generally.

An assessment was made by the Crisis Care workers of the main underlying factors in these cases of child abuse. The results are as follows:-

Prime Contributing Factor

Personal inadequacy	35%
Communication problem	23%
Alcohol	13%
Mental illness	12%
Finance	5%
Other drugs	3%

Note that drugs other than alcohol do not rate highly, at least for the time being.

An attempt was made to rate the Guardian's attitude to the Crisis Care workers at the beginning and again at the end of the contact period. There was increasing acceptance of the workers during the contact.

Guardian's attitude

	At start	At finish
Welcoming	71%	79%
Neutral	20%	12%
Rejecting	8%	8%

Crisis Care does not aim to provide a long term follow-up service. It was therefore of interest to note that 71% had not used the service at all in the preceding 12 months.

Crisis Care work is time-consuming with most visits lasting between one and four hours. However time well spent in this crisis phase may well mean a subsequent saving in time and resources if complicating issues can be foreseen and avoided.

Conclusions

It is true that only 5% of the problems encountered by Adelaide's Crisis Care Unit are directly related to child abuse. It is nevertheless contended that despite this low percentage the service is a most worthwhile one, partly and importantly because it detects children at risk who are not recognised as such by their guardians. A multi-faceted Crisis Care service is seen as a reasonable and economical means of providing emergency care. It is particularly applicable in cities such as Adelaide where the population (900,000) does not warrant separate services to deal with each of the various social problems which feature in Western urban society.

Child Abuse and Neglect, Vol. 3, pp. 367 - 371.

0145-2134/79/0301-0367 $02.00/0.

BRUTALITY AND FAMILY LIFE: A STRATEGY OF CHANGE IN COMMUNITY MENTAL HEALTH CONSULTATION

Harvey A. Barocas, Ph.D.
Psychology Department
Baruch College
City University of New York

Carol B. Barocas, M.S.W.
Adelphi University
School of Social Work
New York

This paper examines the relationship between family violence and the preventive community mental health possibilities inherent in training police in family crisis intervention. Traditionally, police have been associated with law enforcement; however, they also provide a vital community therapeutic service to people from all socioeconomic strata. Today, they represent a primary domestic violence service delivery system. Although prevention in police work has been considered for many years, it is only recently that police organizations have emphasized this service. The utilization of police as a mental health resource for troubled families is an innovative approach that may help to identify high risk parents before they commit abuses against their children. We must recognize that the prevention of family violence is a community mental health problem akin to suicide prevention to which similar techniques and principles can be applied.

Most psychotherapists frequently accept only highly selected patients and view serious emergencies and life-stress situations as contra-indications for traditional treatment. Psychotherapists involved in clinics or office practice frequently observe only the ritualized and socially acceptable expressions of intrafamilial violence and aggression. Acknowledging that the family has become a cradle of violence (Steinmetz & Straus 1, Martin 2), urban police more frequently have the opportunity to observe and intervene in cases of direct aggression involving family members. In short, the more serious social and family pathology, ignored by psychotherapists is ministered to by the urban policeman, who is assigned the responsibility for monitoring the dimensions of interpersonal conflict and intervention in a family crisis situation.

Any policeman knows that one of the most dangerous calls he must answer is the family quarrel, where bitter hot emotion erupts into violence, where injury is as close as a knife blade, and when the despair of misery focuses suddenly on a blue uniform. Family disturbance calls currently represent the single most frequent source of injury and death to police officers. Policemen, intervening in family disturbance calls become easy targets of displaced aggression, particularly in cases of wife-beating, infidelity, child abuse and incest. We cannot assume that police are aseptic instruments, since their own life experience and family values may be imposed on others, with disastrous consequences.

That murders and serious physical injuries occur more frequently between people who are related supports the notion, "the family that slays together stays together" often in a sadomasochistic bind. Within this family circle, if police are left to draw upon their own biased notions of family psychodynamics, they may actually behave in ways to induce a tragic outcome (e.g. by forming protective, seductive alliances with helpless women against brutal husbands, contributing to the emasculation of male disputants, unconsciously inviting retaliation by intimidating family members, and inadvertently setting themselves up as potential homicide victims). This situation is further complicated since many father-absent families and families with common-law husbands in low-income ghetto areas may rely on policemen as family bouncers or substitute authority figures to compensate for the lack of a male role model.

In helping to promote the development of preventive psychiatry in the community, the police officer is in a unique position as a case finder in situations of child abuse. He not only performs a service for the child by protecting it from further abuse, but also assists the parents to learn better ways of handling their emotions by making appropriate referrals to agencies who specialize in working with child abusers. What the policeman can provide in a family crisis situation is the crucial service of early recognition and initial intervention which may ultimately determine the difference between successful prevention and destructive violence. Intervention in disturbed families is desirable at the earliest point possible in order to prevent a fixed pattern of family interaction which may be impossible to reverse.

The success of police crisis intervention designed to prevent violent action depends upon the policeman's readiness to perceive the behavioural and verbal cues that point to a potential for violent activity, and upon his ability to recognize the special nature of measures he can apply. Resort to violence bespeaks the despair which comes from failure to have or to perceive any alternatives. The fundamental task therefore during a preventive intervention is to help the individual search effectively for alternatives. By questioning the individual about the immediate threat of violence, about alternatives to it, about the consequences of various possible actions, about his unrealized aims, hopes and needs, the policeman simultaneously fosters the search for violence-avoiding alternatives, and teaches a method of problem solving the individual can learn to use. However, since the police approach is a temporary intervention at a time of crisis, it is imperative that the police engage other resources in whatever supportive or deterrent measures may be required. The ability of police to work preventively at times of crisis is greatly enhanced by the development of close effective working relationships with a variety of mental health services in the community. Police must become familiar with the psychiatric and social service resources in their community including specific contacts at the various agencies.

During a crisis period, the potential for change is greatly increased (Caplan 3, Bellak & Small 4), and police assistance provided at this point, with appropriate community follow-ups, can be very effective and assist in stabilizing family relationships. A family oriented intervention in a behavioral disturbance can produce significant and durable results in a short time. As Bard & Berkowitz (5) demonstrated in their family crisis intervention project in New York, the family's emotional resources could be mobilized into giving each other sufficient support to work through the crisis area. Basically, the crisis intervenor wants to halt further family deterioration, help restore the impaired ego coping functions, and promote the family's functioning as a stress mediating system again. He must provide a means of coping with the immediate family crisis, while serving as a liason to help establish support facilities for the family to reduce the potential of further abuse and injury.

The diversity and complexity of family quarrels where excessive violent potential is present, make police crisis intervention extremely volatile and hazardous. It is impossible to do away with intrafamilial aggression completely, but police can play a crucial role in reducing the potential for violence and helping to regulate it within the family system. However, to serve this cause, we need greater restraints on the use of official violence, impartial law enforcement, meaningful alternatives to arrest, and a more viable mediation system for families in conflict so that we do not continue to innundate our family courts with referrals.

Psychotherapists have much to offer police and society in the control and prevention of human violence. Brief emergency crisis intervention police training may work better than the traditional police approaches for defusing potentially explosive family situations. Family crisis intervention provides an opportunity to offer brief emergency psychiatric services, identify unmet needs, and act as a referral source to community agencies. Therefore, policemen must be given the psychological skills that are realistically consistent with their daily functioning or run the risk of exacerbating family conflict (Barocas 6). Psychological training in crisis intervention, by increasing the response repertoire of patrolmen, should have a positive influence on general police functioning and assist police in the prevention of violence.

A MODEL PROGRAM IN POLICE-FAMILY CRISIS INTERVENTION

Recently, the National Association of Social Workers urged Congress to establish a national program for the study, prevention and treatment of domestic violence. Emphasis was placed on setting up a nationwide network of domestic violence services. Throughout the country, police, law enforcement officials, mental health professionals, and social scientists are now placing a high priority on developing and improving the domestic violence service delivery system. Many experimental and innovative methods have emerged in the development of an integrated support system for families in crisis. New community and therapeutic approaches to the amelioration of family conflict are rapidly appearing in the psychological literature (Spector & Claiborn 7, McGee 8, and Schonborn 9).

During the past five years, the authors have been actively involved as consultants in designing and implementing police training programs in family crisis intervention. We have interviewed and talked with dozens of police officers and family members in an attempt to generate a clearer understanding of the dynamics of family violence, enhance police crisis intervention skills and outline preventive measures.

The project involved the selection and training of 20 police officers recruited from disadvantaged communities wherein a high incidence of family violence and child abuse had been identified. The officers were provided with a two-week training program emphasizing crisis intervention skills, family psychodynamics and counseling-mediation techniques. Based on experience with several metropolitan police departments, it became evident that training police in family crisis intervention could not be delivered through conventional teaching methods which were too intellectualized and devoid of significant relevance for patrolmen. Therefore, a small group interaction model which provided an opportunity for exchanging attitudes and discussing family violence was utilized throughout.

Unfortunately, many police academy training programs generally address themselves to the technical knowledge necessary for police work and tend to disregard the emotionally-affected uncertainties inherent in family crisis intervention and their ensuing anxieties. Consequently, in addition to traditional mental health lectures, the two-week training program was spent in a group workshop, using an experiential-educational model, highlighted by a conflict intervention training laboratory, which provided a unique opportunity to "learn by doing."

Laboratory demonstrations consisted of re-enacted, dramatized police-family crisis calls drawn from police records. Professional actors and actresses enacted family fights developed from actual police-family distrubance calls. Police officers paired off in teams to run through a crisis intervention case during the simulation. The plays were written without conclusions. The outcomes were improvised by the actors in response to the behavior of the policemen. Simulated conflicts involved a wide range of family life issues, including: child abuse, incest, alcoholism, infidelity, unemployment, money and wife-beating.

All simulated interventions were videotaped and focused videotape feedback was subsequently utilized in small group workshops. Conflict situations were role-played twice to permit different police teams to intervene in the same crisis call and demonstrate differential approaches and intervention styles, as well as the possibility of different outcomes. All the simulated interventions were also subjected to extensive critique and review by police participants in small group discussions. Several issues were explored in group discussions, expecially disputants response to the intervention, new problems that emerged as a result of the intervention (iatrogenic reactions) and the officers understanding and reactions to the family conflict.

Focused video-tape feedback, served as an additional vehicle for confronting patrolmen with an immediate, objective audio-visual transcript of their approaches to a family crisis call. Such feedback and group discussions helped alert many patrolmen to blind spots and patterns of maladaptive behavior by giving them information about themselves as they interacted with disputants during an intervention. The feedback process was doubly enhanced by the actors who entered the group discussions and expressed their reactions to the different police interventions.

A standard family crisis intervention technique that was emphasized involved having two policemen separate the disputants, each officer taking a disputant into a separate room to alleviate the immediate tension. They would then encourage the individual to explain his side of the conflict, trying to be empathic and supportive. Next, the officers would switch disputants to verify stories and make a more realistic assessment of the total situation. They would also attempt to get a previous history of family quarrels, and finally bring the couple together to recount their stories to each other, but permitting only one to talk at a time. This approach permits officers to point out discrepancies, contradictions, or common feelings, and get a reaction from family members.

Policemen found that certain disarming gestures of goodwill were particularly effective in facilitating communication and assisting in conflict resolution without resorting to arrest (e.g., police taking their hats off, introducing themselves, separating disputants, sitting down with disputants, talking about their own families, and offering information about community resources). Other officers found they had more of an impact on disputants when they refused to take sides. They found men were not as hostile toward them when they did not side with women automatically during a domestic quarrel.

Handling family disputes was viewed in three stages: the first stage being the initial intervention, the second consisted of assessment and diagnosis of the family problem, and the third stage involved resolution and/or referral. In assessing the seriousness and chronicity of the family dispute, police would ask non-threatening questions about the frequency of family fights, how long it existed, what precipitated it, and what were the underlying unconscious motives for the family dispute as well as the more obvious ones. They also had to ascertain whether the family disturbances required professional help. Furthermore, throughout the training program, the identification, reporting and referral of child abuse and neglect was repeatedly emphasized.

Attempts were actively made to alert policemen to potential counter-transference reactions, sensitize them to principles of individual and family psychodynamics, point out particular areas of difficulty, the role that policemen saw themselves playing in particular conflict situations. Unless a policeman was continuously alert to his own gut reactions, he was apt to find himself responding negatively and irrationally in many crisis situations, especially against the marital partner who was more obviously abusive and cruel, because of his own identification with the more mistreated spouse and not fully recognizing the latter's less obvious provocative behavior in sado-masochistic interactions. Moreover, violence against children and wife-beating frequently provoked self-righteous outrage and sadistic retaliatory urges in policemen.

During some simulated interventions, two policewomen or a policeman and policewoman would intervene in the family crisis. Although there was considerable resistance to the idea that women could perform patrol duties as effectively as men, particularly in incidents involving family violence, the results were quite surprising. When given the same responsibilities as policemen, women proved to be highly effective in neutralizing family friction and violence and greatly reduced the potential for iatrogenic violence within the family, particularly in instances of child abuse and wife beating. There was less danger of paranoid and homosexual panic reactions in male disputants when confronted by policewomen. Policemen kicking in doors and accepting the challenge of a provocative suspect very often led to physical violence.

In time, police began to examine the damaging stereotypes they held toward members of the minority communities and the extent to which these stereotypes affected their behavior during a crisis intervention. In addition, since police were frequently witness to pathological family interactions, they became more alerted to the influences of their own family psychodynamics during an intervention. Many patrolmen saw their own parents as irresponsible and recalled being viciously beaten by alcoholic fathers. This created complications when they were called upon to subdue alcoholic husbands during marital quarrels. Feeling that their competence was being personally threatened, they would sometimes become belligerent and minimize mediation techniques. Such regressions in the service and intense anxiety were not uncommon.

In order to deal with intense personal reactions, the basic training also included human relations workshops and optional brief counseling sessions which helped sensitize policemen to their own values and attitudes about disrupted family life. To further reinforce the initial training, weekly small group discussions were held over a six month period. Regularly scheduled de-briefings and continuous sensitivity training permitted an on-going review of the methods and biases which affect the crisis interventions.

Overall, the project findings were very impressive. Despite the high hazards involved in family crisis intervention, injuries to family members as well as police officers were reduced substantially. In general, the project has had a positive influence on methods of police training, helped to identify and reduce child abuse and family violence, and has significant implications for a new strategy of change in community mental health, while simultaneously alleviating the critical manpower shortage in the mental health field. The methods and approaches described here may also help prevent or mitigate the sufferings of family victims. Eventually, this approach may provide further insight into the complex social and family conditions that precipitate violence and brutality.

REFERENCES

(1) Steinmetz, S. K. & Straus, M. A. (Eds.) (1975) Violence in the Family, Dodd-Mead, New York.
(2) Martin, J. P. (Ed.),(1975) Violence and the Family, Wiley, New York.
(3) Caplan, G. (1964) Principles of Preventive Psychiatry, Tavistock, London.
(4) Bellak, L. & Small, L. (1965) Emergency Psychotherapy and Brief Psychotherapy, Grune & Stratton, New York.
(5) Bard, M. & Berkowitz, B. Training police as specialists in family crisis intervention, Community Mental Health Journal. 315, (1971).
(6) Barocas, H. A. Urban Policemen: Crisis Mediators or Crisis Creators? Am. J. Orthopsychiatry. 43, 632 (1973).
(7) Specter, G. A. & Claiborn, W. L. (1973) Crisis Intervention, Behavioral Publications, New York.
(8) McGee, R. K. (1974) Crisis Intervention in the Community, University Park Press, Baltimore.
(9) Schonborn, K. (1975) Dealing With Violence, Thomas, Springfield, Ill.

Child Abuse and Neglect, Vol. 3, pp. 373 - 379.
0145-2134/79/0301-0373 $02.00/0.

MMPI PROFILES OF HIGH-RISK AND OUTPATIENT MOTHERS

LAILLE GABINET, PH. D.

CLEVELAND METROPOLITAN GENERAL HOSPITAL
DEPARTMENT OF PSYCHIATRY
3395 SCRANTON ROAD
CLEVELAND, OHIO 44109 USA

Despite the burgeoning literature on every aspect of child abuse and neglect, there is a dearth of material pertaining to identification and treatment of the potential abuser of children. Information in this area is badly needed so that abuse and neglect may be prevented.

Spinetta and Rigler (1) in 1972 surveyed the extensive literature on the personalities of parents who abuse children. They found a general consensus about the abusing parents' own emotionally deprived upbringing, their misinformed ideas of childrearing methods, and their deficient capacity to control impulses. Helfer and Kempe (2) find the parents to be "immature, yearning people," very few of whom "seriously mentally ill." But there are many 'immature,' 'yearning,' and 'deprived' parents who do not actually become seriously abusive to their children. Others do. In order to select families for preventive treatment, some method must be found for determining who is at high risk.

The reasoning behind this conclusion is that abuse of children which is severe enough to come to the attention of Protective Service workers is only a very small tip of the iceberg of a much larger social problem. People neglect and abuse their children in many destructive ways which never are reported. If treatment is limited to those who have perpetrated a severe injury, the problem of abuse and neglect will not be effectively addressed. For this reason, absolutely accurate prediction of "reportable" abuse is not the point. If there is a typical "abusive" personality, it should include many more than those actually convicted of child abuse. Help should be offered to as many of those parents who abuse or neglect their children as possible, regardless of whether or not they are the ones who have the specific potential to injure a child so severely that protective agencies are called in.

Approaches to identification of potentially abusive parents have taken two major forms:: Clinical assessments and objective tests. In trying to effectively deal with the problem of child abuse, we would like to have a screening test that can be used routinely to identify the potential child abuser so that he or she may be treated before abuse occurs. Without entering into a discussion of practicality of testing all prospective parents or issues of civil liberties, efforts are being made to determine whether, in fact, such a test exists, or can be devised. Ray Helfer (3) is working on a new test. Paulson et al (4) found differences in the Minnesota Multiphasic Personality Inventory (MMPI) profiles of abusers and controls.

In a study conducted at UCLA School of Medicine (4), it was found that male and female child abusers had significantly higher T-scores than non-abusers on Scales 4 (psychopathic deviate) and 9 (mania) of the MMPI. In this lower middle class population, all MMPI scales were at or below T-score 70, i.e., within two standard deviations from the mean. Validity scales of abusive and control groups were below T-score 60.

The profile with Pd and Ma scales as peaks were found to differentiate between groups of abusive and non-abusive parents.

Clearly, this approach to identification of abusive parents is only in the developmental stages, and cannot yet be used for selecting families for preventive intervention. But if the findings are corroborated, they may increase our understanding of the child abuse syndrome.

Workers in obstetrics and pediatrics settings feel that they cannot and need not wait for objective screening measures. They frequently see families which they feel are at risk of abusing children. In fact, professionals in pediatric, obstetric, and psychiatric services do identify individuals about whose parenting capacities they are concerned. Because they are not making an accusation, but hoping to offer additional services, these workers use their clinical judgment in selecting "high-risk" patients. Criteria of risk (5) include such things as "poor capacity for parenting," abuse of a child in the past, ambivalence about pregnancy or the child, inability to respond to infant, mother's chaotic living situation, a mother who is unprepared for or cannot seem to plan for the child's care. These are all subjective judgments on the part of the professionals who work with pregnant women and mothers. They refer other cases because a child has been injured or had too many accidents, or one or more suspected abuses.

In Cleveland, a number of high risk families so identified are referred to the Parenting Program of the Department of Psychiatry at Cleveland Metropolitan General Hospital for therapy aimed at the prevention of child abuse.

The purpose of the present study was to identify the personality profiles of high risk mothers selected by the clinical assessment summarized above, and to compare them with the profiles of a group of mothers who have actually abused a child, and with a matched group of psychiatric outpatients _not_ selected as potential abusers. If 4-9 and 9-4 profiles proved to differentiate between abusers and non-abusers, Paulson's study would be replicated. In addition, if clinical assessment of high-risk patients produced a group with high 4-9 profiles, there would be agreement between the subjective and objective methods of assessment of "abusive" parents.

Method

All subjects were patients at Cleveland Metropolitan General Hospital. The nature of this population is described elsewhere (5). Comparison was made between Minnesota Multiphasic Personality Inventory (MMPI) profiles of 90 patients referred to the Parenting Program and 90 mothers of the same ages (18-35) who were patients of the Department of Psychiatry Outpatient Clinic. Since all referrals to the Parenting Program have been women with children, only females were used for comparison. These groups are not perfectly matched, since MMPI's are given routinely to Parenting Program patients and not to Clinic patients. In the Clinic, an MMPI is given when there is an unanswered diagnostic or treatment question. Because these Clinic patients represented the group best-matched with the Parenting Program patients whose MMPI's were available, it was decided to use them for comparison. Actual abusers were mothers who were known to have abused a child or children. This group includes all the known abusers who were referred to the Parenting Program from whom we were able to obtain MMPI's.

Three measurements were used: (1) average elevation of all scales, (2) most frequent peak scales, and (3) the most frequent 2-point profiles.

Results

Mean profiles of all groups are presented in Fig. 1. The most salient feature of these profiles is their similarity. The tendency is for all groups to have profiles with the same general configurations: Scores on F and K, the validity scales, are in the same range for all groups. Since F represents a complaining set, and K, a defensive set, the fact that F-K scores do not exceed 3 is evidence of the validity of the profiles. Once profile validity is established, the most important result is that all groups show peaks on Scales 2 (depression), 4 (psychopathic deviate), 6 (paranoia), and 8 (schizophrenia). Only in the outpatient group does the score on Scale 7, sometimes referred to as the "anxiety scale," exceed the score on Scale 6.

This whole population exhibited more pathology than Paulson's subjects since scores on all four of the peak scales (2, 4, 6, and 8) were over T-score 70 (except mean score of 68 on Scale 6 for the outpatient group). Mean elevation of all scales was the same for all groups. Table 1 lists the average scores for the groups on each scale. It is clear from inspection

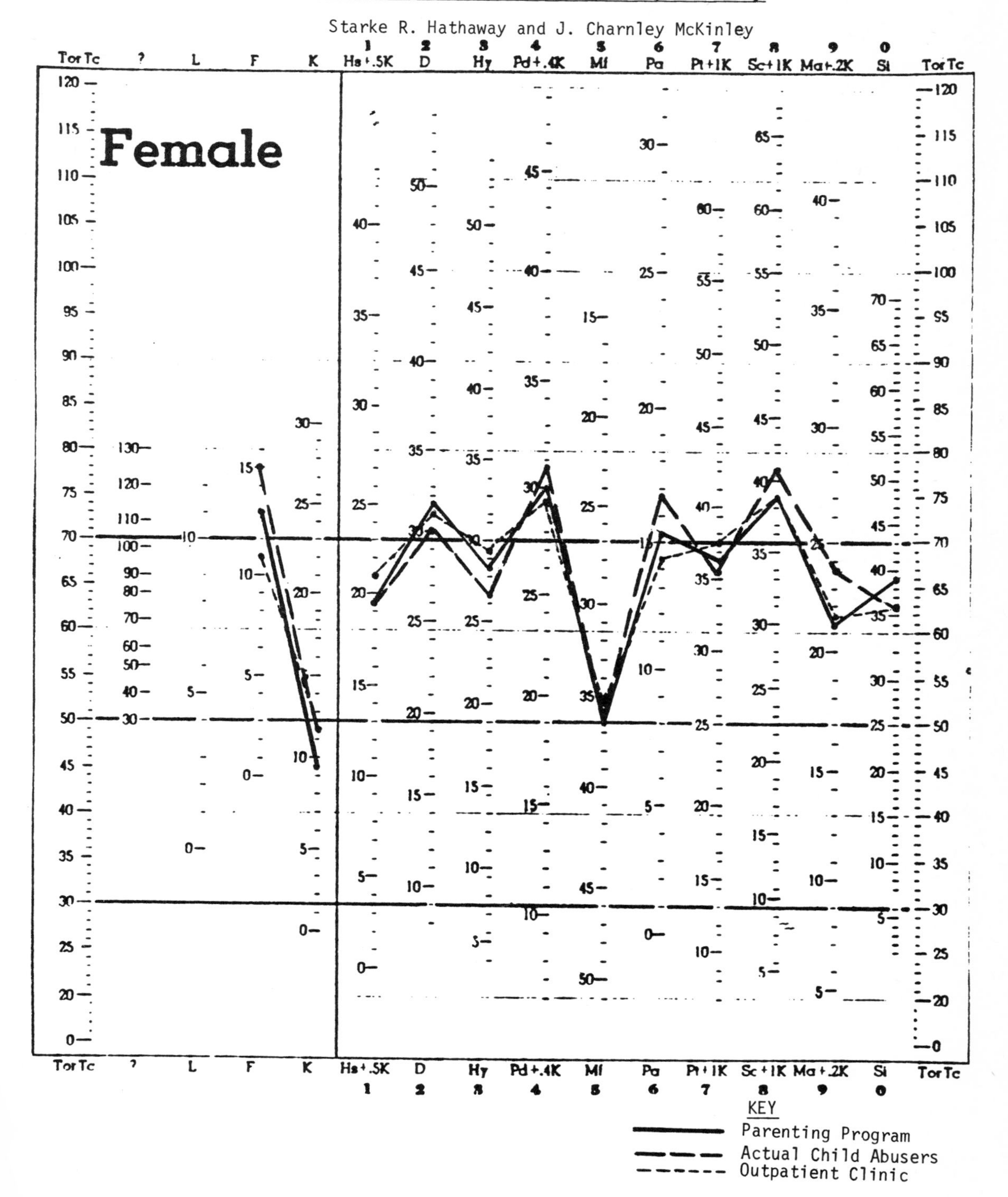
The Minnesota Multiphasic Personality Inventory
Starke R. Hathaway and J. Charnley McKinley
Female
TorTc ? L F K Hs+.5K D Hy Pd+.4K Mf Pa Pt+1K Sc+1K Ma+.2K Si TorTc
1 2 3 4 5 6 7 8 9 0
KEY
Parenting Program
Actual Child Abusers
Outpatient Clinic

Fig. 1

that none of the experimental scales: acceptance of passivity, overcontrolled hostility (7), or the McAndrews alcoholism scale, distinguished between any of the groups. This confirms Paulson's findings on overcontrolled hostility.

TABLE 1 Average Elevation on MMPI Scales

	T-Scores		
	Actual Abusers	High-risk	Outpatient
F	78	73	68
K	49	45	49
1	63	63	66
2	71	74	73
3	64	67	69
4	78	76	75
5	51	50	52
6	75	71	68
7	67	68	70
8	78	75	75
9	67	61	62
0	63	66	63
Mean	67.7	67.1	67.3
Ap	42	45	48
Oh	52	50	52
McAl *	23/24	23/24	22/24

* Not T-scores. A score of 24 is considered the point of risk for alcohol abuse.

There were 2 MMPI scales which distinguished actual abusers from the other groups. The scale on which actual abusers scored higher than both high-risk and outpatient groups was Scale 9 (mania) ($p < .05$). This scale measures such characteristics as hyperactivity, restlessness, pressure of thought, and distractibility, often summarized as hyperactivity (8). Although actual abusers scored higher than both high-risk and outpatient groups on Scale 6, this difference was significant only between actual abusers and the outpatient group. Scale 6 measures qualities of suspiciousness, interpersonal sensitivity, rigidity in adherence to ideas, and feelings of persecution (8). One may conclude that actual abusers tend to be more suspicious and have more persecutory ideas than the outpatient group, as well as being more agitated than both of the other groups. But one must not interpret the personalities of these patients as if they had 6-9 profiles. The elevated Scales 6 and 9 occurred in profiles in which neither 6 nor 9 was a peak score. The highest scales for all groups were Scales 4 and 8, with Scale 2 the next highest for both high-risk and outpatient groups and Scale 6 next for the actual abuser group.

Because some of the most common profiles in the high-risk group (6-8 and 2-4) and the clinic group (2-4 and 4-8) had so nearly the same number of patients, and because numbers in the "Abuse" group are so small, it seems less than useful to look at the differences between most frequent and second most frequent 2-point profiles. The pervasiveness of scales 2, 4, 6, and 8 is dominant, with non-significant variations in frequency of various 2-point combinations in different groups. The trend toward alienation, rebelliousness, and impulsivity, (Scale 4), pervades all the groups. Likewise, disturbance in thought processes, with some difficulties in cognitive control (Scale 8), and chronic feelings of depression (Scale 2), are common to all the groups. Projection of blame, self-righteousness, and paranoid ideas (Scale 6), are also prominent in all the groups. The higher score of the identified abusers on Scale 6 may possibly be attributable to the fact that they have been accused of wrongdoing by County authorities and have reason to feel that someone is "against" them.

Once it is recognized that the similarities among the groups are more prominent than the differences, it is possible to examine the most common 2-point profiles in all the groups combined. The most frequent profiles were: 2-8, 4-8, and 2-4 (Table 2).

Patients with the 2-8 or 8-2 profile are commonly depressed, anxious, and agitated. They feel tense and jumpy, and often fear losing control over their impulses. They often tend to have difficulty with close relationships (8). The 8-4, 4-8 code was the second most common in this population. This profile, frequent among adolescents, is associated with a high rate of delinquency. People with this profile have often learned from early life to see the world as hostile, rejecting, and dangerous (8). They do not see other people as sources of help. They feel confused about their own identity, often confused also about sexuality, have family problems and difficulty with authority, and peculiar ideation. They cope either by angry, rebellious, impulsive behavior or by social withdrawal. They are often called schizoid personalities.

This third frequent profile across all the groups was 4-2, 2-4, described as agitated depression, often combined with self-punitive rather than outwardly directed behavior. This profile was most frequent in the outpatient group, but it did appear in all of the groups. (It is not listed in the frequency list for the Actual Abuse group because it occurred only once in that group.)

Discussion

These results seem to indicate many common features of the Abusive, High-risk Program, and Outpatient groups. All groups tend to exhibit depression, rebelliousness and impulsitivity, and cognitive pathologies. Hysteria, with its common defense of denial, does not seem to be a major coping mechanism, with the possible exception of the outpatient group. Although many of these patients have numerous somatic complaints, somatic concerns are not a major feature of the profiles. Despite the finding that some outpatients had the 2-7 profile, anxiety and obsessiveness (Scale 7) are not commonly experienced in pure form. Not surprisingly, most of the patients in this inner city population can be considered to have characterological problems. There were no overtly psychotic patients in the high risk or abuse groups. We do not have clinical data on psychosis in the outpatient group.

Any efforts to understand the differences between the two groups must be based on understanding of the mechanisms of referral to the Psychiatry Outpatient Clinic and the Parenting Program.

Both programs depend primarily, though not exclusively, on referrals from within the hospital and its various satellite clinics. Often the patient does not adequately understand the reason for referral. The Outpatient Clinic receives most of its referrals from the Primary Health Care Clinic and other medical and surgical clinics. Most of these referrals are made because the physician feels that the patient's somatic complaints or "nervousness" are psychogenic. The Parenting Program's major source of referrals is social workers and physicians in Obstetrics, and Pediatrics. The Department of Psychiatry Outpatient Clinic itself refers a number of cases, as does the Protective Services Division of the County Welfare Department.

Thus, patients who come to the Psychiatry Outpatient Clinic typically are complaining about themselves; those who are referred to the Parenting Program, whether actual abusers or high-risk, are being complained *about*. Yet, the groups are more alike than they are different. Are clinic patients less likely to abuse their children than Parenting Program patients? There is nothing in the MMPI profiles to indicate that this is so. It is possible that the only reason for different referrals is that the psychiatric problems of the clinic group are identified in the context of their own medical problems, usually in the absence of their children, while the high risk group is identified when seeking obstetric or pediatric care. In the latter case, children are present, or, in obstetrics clinics, workers are concerned with the capacity to care for the unborn infant.

Our finding of similarity between the high risk and clinic groups suggests two possibilities. The first is that MMPI profiles are not an effective instrument for identification of potentially abusive individuals. Coupled with earlier research (4,9), they show that there is no one abusive personality. Out of control violence toward children cuts across personality configurations and psychiatric diagnoses as well as across socioeconomic classes. It is predictable more from history and other samples of behavior rather than by personality testing.

The other possible interpretation of our findings is based on the fact that identification of risk may be to some extent a function of point-of-entry into the health care system, i.e., children-related vs. not child-related. This raises the question of whether high risk to children is more pervasive than we suspect. This would mean that examination of the parent-child relationships in, e.g., a medical clinic population, would reveal a number of high-risk families which have not come to attention because they have not been seen or noticed in child related settings.

There is evidence to support this suggestion in casual observations of adults' behavior with children in stores, restaurants, and in our city streets. Violence toward children is an accepted pattern (10, 11) in our society. Perhaps "actual abusers" are only the ones who went too far or got caught. Many people, in this population at least, abuse their children physically and emotionally. Only a few of these come to the attention of the County's Protective Services Division and even fewer commit abuses that can be proved so clearly that the courts adjudge removal of the child to be warranted.

The fact that actual abusers had significantly higher scores than others in the same population on Scale 9 of the MMPI may indicate that, all other factors being equal, inner agitation, restlessness, or hyperactivity may be a significant factor in causing the individual to lose impulse control. This finding contributes to our understanding, but it must be viewed with caution as a predictor. It raises the whole issue of clinical vs. statistical prediction(12). We find that in this population, as in Paulson's (4), abusers tend to have higher scores on Scale 9. But the average includes a wide range of scores and even a cutting score would not safely identify the abusive individual. Similarly, although it is interesting to see that actual abusers have higher scores than clinic patients on Scale 6, the fact that they have been accused of child abuse suggests that ideas of persecution may have some basis in reality, and the finding requires further study.

It may be that high risk of abuse is more predictable by means of clinical assessment, which takes into consideration the patient's history and other samples of behavior (5), than by personality profiles. This project clearly suggests that MMPI profiles using standard scales are not a predictive measure, but may add to our understanding of the child abuse syndrome. It also provides a reminder that abuse potential is independent of personality type, that various settings serve populations which may have definite group characteristics as well as extreme variability with the group.

It is possible that in settings different from ours, individuals who abuse their children may have personalities atypical for the setting. The implication of this study, on the other hand, is that this is not the case, but that the personalities of high risk and known abusive parents are similar to those of the rest of the patients of the setting.

TABLE 2 MOST FREQUENT MMPI 2-POINT PROFILES

Actual abusers	High-risk	Outpatient
n=22	n=90	n=90
4-8 (4)	2-8 (13.5)	2-4 (10.5)
3-4 (3)	6-8 (8.5)	4-8 (10)
2-8 (2)	2-4 (8)	1-3 (7)
3-8 (2)	4-8 (6.5)	2-3 (6.5)
4-6 (2)	4-6 (5.5)	2-7 (6)
6-8 (2)	4-0 (5.5)	2-8 (6)
8-9 (2)	8-9 (4)	4-6 (6)
		8-9 (6)

* Numbers in parenthesis indicate number of subjects with that particular profile.

** If the same number of patients had two different profiles, 0.5 was assigned to each appropriate profile. So the difference between profiles 6-8 and 2-4 in the high-risk group and 2-4 and 4-8 in the outpatient group represent only one person.

BIBLIOGRAPHY

1. Spinetta, J. and Rigler, D. "the child-abusing parent: A psychological review." Psychological Bulletin, 77 (4): 296-304 (1959).

2. Helfer, R. E. and Kempe, H. C. (1972) Helping the Battered Child and His Family, Lippincott, Philadelphia.

3. Schneider, G., Helfer, R. E., and Pollock, C. The predictive questionnaire: A preliminary report. in Helfer, R. E. and Kempe, H. C. (1972) Helping the Battered Child and His Family, Lippincott, Philadelphia.

4. Paulson, M. J., Afifi, A. A., Thomason, M. L., and Chaleff, A. The MMPI: A descriptive measure of psychopathology in abusive parents. J. Clin. Psychol. 30, 387-390 (1974).

5. Gabinet, L. Prevention of child abuse and neglect in an inner city population: I. Criteria for selection and description of families. Proceeding of The Second International Congress on Child Abuse and Neglect, London, 1978.

6. Paulson, M. J., Schweimer, G. T., and Bendel, R. B. Clinical application of the Pd, Ma, and (OH) experimental MMPI scales to further understanding of abusive parents. J. J. Clin. Psychol. 32 (3): 558-564 (1976).

7. Megargee, E. Undercontrolled and overcontrolled personality types in extreme antisocial aggression. Psychol. Monogr., 80: 1-29 (1966).

8. Marks, P. A., and Seeman, W. (1963) Actuarial Description of Abnormal Personality, Williams and Wilkins, Baltimore.

9. Jameson, P. A. and Schellenbach, C. J. Sociological and psychological factors in the backgrounds of male and female perpetrators of child abuse. Child Abuse and Neglect: The Internat. J. 1 (1): 77-83 (1977).

10. Gil, D. Unraveling child abuse. Am. J. of Orthopsychiatry, 45 (3): 346-356 (1975).

11. Lystad, M. H. Violence at home: A review of the literature. Am. J. of Orthopsychiatry, 45 (3): 328-345 (1975).

12. Meehl, P. E. (1954) Clinical versus statistical prediction, U. of Minn. Press, Minneapolis.

This program has been supported in part by The Grant Foundation, The Maternity and Infant Care Project of the Dept. of Health, Education and Welfare, and The Cleveland Foundation.

Child Abuse and Neglect, Vol. 3, pp. 381 - 390.

0145-2134/79/0301-0381 $02.00/0.

A RESEARCH PROJECT ON ABUSING PARENTS AND THEIR SPOUSES

R.S. Jacobson and G. Straker

University of the Witwatersrand, Johannesburg, S. Africa.

ACKNOWLEDGEMENTS

We are grateful to Mrs E. Woodrow, who evaluated the Rorschach protocols, to the staff of the Child, Adolescent and Family Unit of the Hospital who helped with provision of subjects and Dr G. Kass and Mr G. Gott who provided ready help with the statistical analysis. The study was supported by a grant from the Medical Research Council, the George Elkin Bequest and the University Senior Bursary Fund.

INTRODUCTION

Despite a recent spate of literature, controversy surrounds the problem of the abused child (Smith, Hanson and Noble, 1975; Schneider, Helfer and Pollock, 1972). On the one hand, some see the problem as a response to stressful social circumstances and society's permissive attitude to violence (Gil, 1970). On the other hand, others consider abuse primarily as a manifestation of parental maladjustment (Steele and Pollock, 1968). Even within these two basic orientations there are differing opinions. For example, Galdston (1965) and Schloesser (1964) report a high incidence of low income occupations amongst the abusing parents, while Allen, Ten Bensel and Raile (1968) state that these parents may come from any income group and any educational level.

In commenting on the relationship of social class to abuse, Smith, Hanson and Noble (1974) stated that while material status may be significantly related to abuse it is not a primary causative factor, while personality pathology might be. They came to this conclusion because in studies where the material position of abusing parents had been improved there was not a reduction in the incidence of abuse (Gil, 1970). Thus these authors proposed that personality factors are most important in the battered baby syndrome.

In light of this, many workers have proposed psychodynamic formulations of the battered child syndrome (Green, 1973; Steele and Pollock, 1968). These formulations mainly involve the idea that abuse is related to an ego deficit in the perpetrator (Anthony and Benedek, 1970; Currie, 1970). The abusers have an ego deficit, concurs with reports of their extremely poor childhood experiences (Bleiberg, 1965; Fairburn and Hunt, 1964; Kempe, Silverman, Steele, Droegmueller and Silver, 1962; Paulson and Blake, 1969). Quality of childhood experiences is believed to be the single most important factor in the development of ego functions by most ego analyst and object relations theorists (Erikson, 1950; Hartman, 1939; Winnicott, 1965).

The subjective descriptions of abusers as impulsive (Elmer, 1967), immature (Cohen, Raphling and Green, 1966), lacking in self control (Wasserman, 1967), and unable to empathise with their children (Melnick and Hurley, 1969) further supports the notion that they have an ego deficit, since impulse control and empathy are considered to be prime ego functions (Beres, 1956; Arlow and Brenner, 1964).

Despite the theoretical soundness of proposing an ego deficit in batterers on the basis of their poor childhood experiences and the subjective descriptions of abusers found in the literature, it is necessary to empirically evaluate this notion. The first aim of the present study therefore was to examine ego functions in a group of abusers and a matched control group of non-abusers to assess whether abusers show evidence of an ego deficit.

A second aim was to specify the nature of this deficit more accurately. A third aim of the study was to try and examine ego functions in the context of the abusing parents' early family relationships as measured empirically on the Bene Anthony test rather than subjectively through clinical material.

In addition to the above, other factors were considered by the present authors as essential for a more complete investigation of abuse. More specifically, many workers reported that abusing parents have unrealistic expectations of their infant's attainment in relation to its age and stage of development. (Bain, 1963; Helfer and Pollock 1968) A distorted perception of the infant's needs and the parents own limited abilities and helplessness is coupled with a desire to get the child to behave at all costs. This emotional as opposed to intellectual block understanding children's normal developmental behaviour and needs is reported to be an important aspect of the parent's pathology. (Kempe, 1971; Schneider Helfer and Pollock, 1972). Thus a fourth aim of the study was to examine the child rearing attitudes of a group of abusers as compared to matched control groups.

Finally the present authors were struck by the lack of emphasis in the literature on the role of the non-abusing spouse in regard to the genesis of abuse. This was all the more surprising in view of Gil's 1970 findings that in 30% of 1380 reported cases of child abuse, the other parent or parent substitute was present during the abusive incident. Clinicians have reported that the spouses of abusers are similar to the abusers themselves in regard to their childhood experiences (Steele and Pollock, 1968). Furthermore the feelings of inferiority and the belief that children should satisfy parental needs, common to abusers, has also been reported in the non-abusing spouse (Green, 1973; Steele and Pollock, (1968). Thus the authors of the present study felt it would be worthwhile to research more fully the non abusing spouse in terms of his/her similarity to the abuser in regard to ego functions, childhood experiences and child rearing attitudes to test the idea that enmeshing of personality dynamics is one of the factors of abuse. Hence the fifth and final aim of the study was to determine whether there were significant differences between the actual abuser and his/her non-abusing spouse in terms of childhood experiences, ego functions and child rearing attitudes (as compared to a matched control group).

Subjects

All abusers on file during 1974 and 1975 at the largest children's hospital in the Transvaal, who consented to the investigation and where an unequivocal diagnosis of battering had been made were included in the study. The diagnosis of abuse was made either by the ward consultant and a psychiatrist or by the fact that the parents had confessed to battering. Fourteen subjects were recruited in this way, the small sample size being a function of the stringent criteria applied to establish an unequivocal diagnosis of battering.

The control subjects were parents of children under three years of age who were on file for minor ailments, such as colds, flat fleet and eye inflammations, at the same hospital. The parents of the children in the control group were matched on a one to one basis with the abusers in terms of age, sex, marital status at the time of the birth of the child, home language, financial, occupational and educational status. The children in the control group were also carefully screened by the ward consultant to eliminate any possibility of abuse having occurred.

In addition the spouses of both the index and the control group were tested.

Apparatus

(a) Childhood family relationships were measured on the Adult Version of the Bene-Anthony Family Relations Test (FRT) and two specific dimensions were examined:

(i) negative feelings towards both parents

(ii) sibling rivalry.

(b) Ego functions were measured by the Rorschach Test administered and scored using the Klopfer (1954) method with the following scoring dimensions as the focus:

(i) M, which is said to relate to the ability to delay responses, capacity for empathy, emotional adjustment and flexibility (Levitt and Truumau, 1972)

(ii) MQ, which represents a more refined way of scoring M and which specifically adjusts for the quality of the form produced by the subject (Rappaport, Gil and Schafer, 1968)

(iii) Fc which indicates degree of awareness and acceptance of recipient affectional needs, a prerequisite for the formation of mature object relations (Klopfer, 1954)

(iv) FC: CF + C, which is said to reflect the degree of control the individual has over his impulses.

(c) Michigan Screening Profile of Parenting (MSPP) was used to assess child rearing attitudes. All Questionnaires were returned to Michigan State University, USA, where they were classified "at risk" or "not at risk" and returned to the present authors.

Procedure

All subjects were approached telephonically and told that they had been randomly selected from the hospital files to participate in a study aimed at providing a better understanding of what modern parents felt about children. If the subject agreed to the investigation, an appointment was made to test them in their own homes. The order of administration of the tests remained constant and was :

1. The Family Relations Test.

2. The Rorschach Test.

3. The fact sheet giving information as to educational, economic and family backgrounds.

4. The Michigan Screening Profile of Parenting.

These tests were administered first to the mothers and then immediately to the fathers so that all possible discussion of the tests were precluded. Once the index cases had all been tested, the control cases were carefully selected and matched on a one to one basis and the same procedure as for the index cases was carried out.

RESULTS

All Rorschach protocols were scored independently by the senior author and a blind rater. The correlations obtained, using the Pearson Product Moment Correlation were never less than .80 on any of the four variables.

The results will be discussed in two parts, firstly those pertaining to the first four aims of the study which compare the actual abuser with a matched control. The findings pertaining to the fifth aim of the study viz those involving the non-abusing spouse are discussed later.

(a) Comparison of actual Abuser with matched control.

A matched pairs t-test was used to assess the direction or significance of differences in sibling rivalry, negative attitudes towards both parents, M, MQ, Fc and FC: CF + C scores produced by the abusing and control parents. A Fischer exact probability test (Siegel, 1956) was used to assess the group differences on child rearing attitudes between actual abusers and matched controls. As shown in Table I*and II*only one measure reliably differentiated between index and control group. Batterers revealed a significantly lower Fc score than the matched control group ($p < ,02$). In other words the abusing group had significantly poorer awareness and acceptance of their own affectional needs than did a matched control group.

*see appendix

(b) Results examining the Non-abusing Spouse.

In order to fully examine the hypothesis that abusing spouses had had similar childhood experiences, personality dynamics and child rearing attitudes to their abusing partners, the following statistical procedure was carried out.

Firstly the scores of the abusers on the variables sibling rivalry, negative attitudes towards parents, M, MQ, Fc, FC: FC + C were subtracted from those of their spouses and a similar procedure was followed for the control group. A t-test was carried out on these absolute differences to ascertain the significance in scores obtained by each matched couple on these variables. As shown in Table III*, none of these measures differentiated between the couples of the index and control groups.

The spouse differences on the MSPP were calculated by the use of Fischer exact probability test.

A significant difference was found between index and control groups ($p < 0,05$) in a direction indicating that in the index group significantly more couples had had both partners "at risk" than in the matched control couple (See Table IV*).

Discussion

The findings of the present study that the childhood experiences of the abusers as measured on the FRT were not significantly different from a matched control group was unexpected. Thus these findings did not confirm the bulk of clinical evidence with regard to the childhood experiences of abusers.

It could be postulated that the data derived from the clinical evidence concerning the abusing parents' poor childhood experiences was derived from their own retrospective histories which may have been subject to their own distortions during history taking, and that they were in fact not abused or emotionally deprived as children. However, this argument is not convincing when cognisance is taken of the objective confirmation of these histories provided by Steele (1966). It therefore seems that there is indisputable evidence that abusing parents were themselves subjected to punitive and rejecting experiences during childhood.

An alternative explanation for the negative findings of the present study with regard to the childhood experiences of the abusing parents is found on closer inspection of the Family Relations Test itself. On inspection of the Family Relations Test, it appears that this test taps something other than just the actual factual experiences as elicited by the case history; rather it taps feelings and attitudes about significant persons during childhood, specifically those feelings of a positive and negative affectional nature. It is therefore the contention of the authors that abusing parents are able to give descriptive, factual information concerning their traumatic childhood experiences but they have divorced or "split off" the affect associated with such memories and hence cannot report it.

Support for this contention is found in the work of Smith, Hanson and Noble (1975), who stressed that battering parents reported their childhoods as having been severely traumatic but they did not report any lack of affection to any greater extent than others of the same social class, which seems incongruous in view of their actual experiences.

The ideas that individuals who have had physically and/or emotionally traumatic childhoods have "split off" the affect associated with their traumatic experiences is one which would have been predicted by psychoanalytic theorists, viz. Freud (1936), Sterba (1934), Klein (1932) and Fairburn (1952).

Thus it seems that abusers have separated the intellectual awareness of their traumatic childhood experiences from the experiential aspects and this can be linked with the findings of the present study on the Rorschach test.

The single significant findings with regard to ego functions on the Rorschach test was that the abusers gave significantly fewer Fc responses than did the non-abusing control group.

* see appendix

Before dealing with the importance of this finding and the explanation thereof, consideration must be given to its statistical significance. One could dismiss the finding as a chance phenomenon, which does not need explanation. It is of course up to the individual to decide how much data he will require before he will abandon the null hypothesis. It is also true that it can be hazardous to rely on directional data and marginal p values. Nevertheless, the fact that the authors predicted results in line with the clinical descriptions of the battering individual would dictate against retaining the null hypothesis. In light of this, the authors of the present study felt justified in accepting this finding as significant and therefore requiring explanation.

Although abusers fall along a wide spectrum as to personality type, (Smith, Hanson & Noble, 1974) the findings of the present study with regard to the paucity of Fc responses in the abusing sample as compared to the non-abusing control group would indicate that there is one "basic fault" common to the abusers as a group, regardless of personality type, control mechanisms, intelligence, and tie with reality, etc., viz. that the abusing group demonstrate a lack of awareness of their own affectional needs (Klopfer, 1954) and a cautiousness in reaching outward for emotionally rewarding relationships (Hertz, 1960). This finding was not unexpected in view of the extensive clinical evidence.

Abusing parents have been found to be socially isolated, reluctant to avail themselves of social support (Davoren, 1968; Nurse, 1966; Young, 1964); to have difficulty in "mothering" (Steele, 1966). More specifically in relation to parental role, Steele (1966) stated:

> "that a significant breakdown occurs in the maternal affectional system of the area of sensitive emotional interaction with the warm empathic awareness of the infant's needs and feeling which we call mothering".

Thus, the one common factor in the abusing sample, as indicated in the present study, is the breakdown in the affectional system which evidences as a lack of awareness of affectional needs, and a cautiousness in making meaningful contact with others.

Having dealt with the single siginificant finding of the present study on the Rorschach it remains to deal with the insignificant findings with regard to ego function.

Firstly, insignificant difference between abusers and non-abusers was found on MQ and M denoting that they do not differ in terms of intelligence, empathy, flexibility of perceptual processes, imagination, ability to delay response, and tie with reality.

There are two possible explanations for this. First, that M and MQ do not measure empathy and the ability to delay response. This explanation is not likely because the consensus of experts on the Rorschach is that M is a measure of all those ego functions listed above but is most particularly a measure of intelligence and empathy (Levitt and Truumaa, 1972). A second explanation is that the similarities between abusers and non-abusers on ego functons other than empathy and ability to delay response which are also measured by M and MQ, such as intelligence, tie with reality and flexibility of perceptual processes, are more important than their differences in terms of empathy and delay of response. In other words, M and MQ do not measure a single function and the differences between the abusers and non-abusers could be masked by the similarities, for example their difference in empathy could be masked by their similarity on intelligence which was one of the factors controlled for in the present study, in that the subjects were matched on a one-to-one basis for educationallevel and occupational category. Therefore the result that abusers and non-abusers did not differ in terms of empathy as measured by M on the Rorschach test therefore remains unexplained except for the possibility of a compounding of ego functions in the measurement of M and MQ.

Having dealt with M and MQ, it is now possible to turn to the control of the primitive impulses as measured by the ratio FC: CF + C. No significant difference was found in the degree of impulse control between the abusers and non-abusers. This result is at variance with those authors who have associated battering with deficient impulse control (Kempe et al., 1962; Wasserman, 1967; Steele and Pollack, 1968).

Some explanation for this may be found in linking the work of researchers into abuse who show that as far as personality type is concerned abusers range from the undercontrolled psychopath (Smith, Hanson and Noble, 1974) to the overcontrolled obsessive compulsive (Bryant, 1963) with the work of Blackburn (1971), who showed that differing control mechanisms were associated with differing personality types in overtly aggressive individuals.

The point being made is that the lack of control exhibited by some members of the abusing sample may have been cancelled out by the over-control of other members, as a variety of personality types probably constituted the abusing sample in the present study and different control mechanisms are associated with different personality types.

Having dealt with the findings on the FRT and the Rorschach test, it is now possible to turn to the MSPP. The findings were that the child rearing attitudes of the abusers did not differ significantly from the non-abusing controls. This finding is at variance with those of many researchers in the field, inter alia Bain (1963), and Gregg (1968).

Turning to an explanation for the negative findings of the present study on this questionnaire, emphasis must be given to the fact that the compilers themselves (Helfer and Schneider, 1972) stressed that the questionnaire only appears to be capable of separating groups of women who are classed as "high risk" in terms of their lack of ability in rearing their children adequately from those at "low risk". From this statement two important points emerge:-

Firstly, that this questionnaire has not been fully validated nor has its reliability been fully assessed on the American population. It is noteworthy that Gil (1971) has suggested that attitudes towards child rearing are a function of cultural background. The point that clearly emerges is that the South African population may indeed have different cultural norms with regard to child rearing and this questionnaire may therefore have limited reliability and validity for the South African population.

Secondly, this questionnaire is not specific to abuse as it aims at the identification of individuals who have unusual child rearing tendencies. Although this questionnaire identifies "high risk" individuals, it does not discriminate between those parents who are physical abusers and those who are emotional abusers . Thus, when the authors examined the results of the present study more closely the 41% of the non-abusing group who were identified as "at risk" may not be at risk of physical abusing per se but of emotionally abusing their children. This then would account for the lack of difference between the index and control groups.

Turning now to the role of the non-abusing spouse.

The final hypothesis of the present study was that there is a greater similarity between the spouses of the battering parents than non-abusing parents, in terms of childhood experiences, ego strength and child rearing attitudes. As can be seen in Table III and IV, only one variable, child rearing attitudes, reflected a greater similarity between the spouses in the abusing group as compared to the spouses in the non-abusing group. More specifically this greater similarity amongst the abusing couples was in the predicted direction in that there was a significantly greater number of couples in the abusing group where both partners were classified as at risk when compared to the couples of the control group.

However, before dealing with the implications of the significant results of the present study, careful consideration must be given to the reason for the numerous insignificant findings of the present study. One such explanation could be in a possible methodological fault in the research design. However, the writers of the present study felt that, at face value at least, adequate controls were built into the study and that the only possible glaring fault could be the small subject sample. However, in defence of the small subject sample, the authors wish to point out that the number of abusers available for research is limited and that the authors further limited the possible number of batterers available by applying strict criteria for inclusion, especially along the dimension of diagnosis, where only unequivocal cases of abuse were selected.

Another explanation of the insignificant results could be that physical force is culturally sanctioned in child rearing (Gil, 1970) and that physical abuse may be sparked off by chance events which were not measured in the present stury. In other words, physical abuse of a child may result from the interaction effects of societal and individual forces, rather than from one or other of these sets of forces acting alone. In addition no cognisance was taken of the life stresses the abusers had experienced 1 year prior to the abusive incident. These societal forces and life stresses were not accounted for in the present study where the dominant theme was an individual one and this might be the key factor in the insignificant results found.

To summarise, the only significant findings of the present study were, firstly, a relationship between abuse and the specific ego deficit of lack of awareness of affectional needs and secondly, a similarity in terms of aberrant child rearing attitudes between both spouses of an abused child.

Despite the limitations of the present study (small sample size and test selection) the implications of the findings may be quite far reaching.

The first major implication of the present study is that it pinpoints as the common denominator of the abusers as a group, the following factors:

(i) affective impoverishment (Exner, 1974);

(ii) a lack of awareness of their own and hence inability to deal with affectional needs (Klopfer, 1954);

(iii) an excessive use of repressive mechanisms (Klopfer, 1954);

(iv) extreme cautiousness in reaching out to others for emotionally rewarding relationships.

This finding concurs with the view of Steele (1966), that there is a "breakdown in the affectional system" of the abusing parent, but it goes further in delineating the specific ego deficit involved, viz a lack of awareness of affectional needs and the use of extensive repressor mechanisms. This has important implications for prognosis.

As regards prognosis, if abusing is indeed associated with a specific ego deficit, viz. lack of awareness of affectional needs, this augurs poorly. A lack of awareness of affectional needs seriously impairs the individual's ability to reach out for emotionally rewarding relationships (Hertz, 1970). For personality change to occur a relationship of mutual warmth and trust must be established between patient and therapist, as a trusting relationship is the basic building block of all therapy, regardless of specific treatment strategy (Rogers and Dymond, 1954). Thus the fact that abusers are greatly impaired in their ability to reach out and form relationships is a serious impediment to the therapeutic process.

In terms of this, any treatment offered to abusers cannot be expected to be effective over the short term and this implies that serious thought should be given to actively protecting the child, despite the fact that its parents are involved in a therapeutic programme.

A final implication of the present study seems to lie in highlighting the role of the non-abusing spouse. Indeed, the present study points to an overt or active role on the part of the non-abusing spouse in that he does not intervene to protect the child not because of his unconscious needs, but rather because he believes the abuser is merely carrying out an act of discipline. This might be of significance when assessing the possibility of treatment for an abusing family and may have important prognostic implications, i.e. if both parents have similar aberrant child rearing attitudes the prognosis may indeed be a guarded one.

In conclusion, it is suggested that the results of the present study are indeed indicative of a specific ego deficit in abusers and that this augurs poorly for prognosis. It is further suggested that it is the presence of this ego deficit which is partly to blame for the poor success obtained in the treatment of abusers as reported in the literature (Polansky, 1968; Smith _et al_., 1975). Finally, it is suggested that in light of this, and where both spouses in an abusing couple share similar aberrant child rearing attitudes the child is at risk and the sagacity of leaving the child in the home, even though the parents are in therapy, should once again be seriously re-examined.

Appendix

TABLE I

Comparison of Childhood Experiences and Ego Functions of Abusers and Non-Abusers

Variable	t-value	df	Probability
Sibling rivalry	-0.70	13	0.247
Negative feelings towards parents	-0.29	13	0.387
M	0.20	13	0.422
MQ	0.89	13	0.195
Fc	2.15	13	0.0026*
FC: CF + C	0.0	13	0.5

* $p < 0.02$ one-tailed

TABLE II

Contingency Table of data on the MSPP

	At Risk	Not at Risk	TOTAL
Index group	10	4	14
Control group	6	8	14
Total	16	12	28

TABLE III

Differences between Spouses of Index Group Compared to Control Group

Variable	t-value	df	1 tail prob.
Sibling rivalry	0.80	13	.05
Negative feelings towards parents	0.50	13	.05
M	-0.89	13	.05
MQ	-1.64	13	.05
Fc	-0.50	13	.05
FC: (CF + C)	0.25	13	.05

TABLE IV

Contingency table : Spouse Differences on Attitudes towards Bringing up Children

	Both at Risk	One at Risk	TOTAL
Index couples	7	6	13*
Control couples	1	10	11
Total	8	16	24

* $p < 0.05$

Allen, H.D., Ten Bensel, R.W., and Raile, R.B. The battered child syndrome - II. Social and psychiatric aspects. Minn. Med., 1968, 52: 155-156.

Anthony, E.J., and Benedek, T. (eds.), Parenthood. Boston: Little Brown and Co., 1970.

Arlow, J., and Brenner, C. Psychoanalytic Concepts and the Structural Theory. New York: International Universities, 1964.

Bain, K. The physically abused child. Paediatrics, 1963, 31: 895-897.

Beres, D. Ego deviation and the concept of schizophrenia. In: R. Eissler et al. (eds.), The Psychoanalytic Study of the Child, Vol. XI. New York: International Universities, 1956.

Blackburn, R. Personality types among abnormal homicides. Brit. J. Criminology, 1971, 11: 14.31

Bleiberg, N. The neglected child and the child health conference. N.Y. St. J. Med., 1965 65: 1880-1885.

Blue, M.J. The battered child syndrome from a social worker's viewpoint. Can. J. publ. Health, 1965, 56: 197-198.

Cohen, M.I., Raphling, D.L., and Green, P.E. Psychological aspects of the maltreatment syndrome of childhood. Pediatrics, 1966, 69: 279-284.

Currie, J.R.B., A psychiatric assessment of the battered child syndrome. S.A. Medical Journal, May 1970, 635-639.

Davoren, E. The role of the social worker. In: R.E. Delfer and C.H. Kempe (eds.), The Battered Child. Chicago: Chicago University Press, 1968. Pp. 153-68.

Elmer, E. Children in Jeopardy: A Study of Abused Minors and their Families. Pittsburgh: Pittsburgh University Press, 1967.

Erikson, E.H. Childhood and Society. Penguin Books Ltd., 1950.

Exner, J.E. The Rorschach: a Comprehensive System. New York: John Wiley and Sons, 1974.

Fairbairn, R. An Object-Relations Theory of the Personality. New York: Basic Books, 1952.

Fairburn, A.C., and Hunt, A.C. Caffey's "third syndrome": a critical evaluation ("The battered baby"). Med. Sc. and Law, 1964, 4: 123-126.

Freud, A. The Ego and the Mechanisms of Defence. New York: International Universities, 1936.

Galdston, R. Observations on children who have been physically abused and their parents. American Journal of Psychiatry, 1965, 122: 440-443.

Gil, D.G. Violence against children. Journal of Marriage and the Family, 1971, Vol. 33.

Green, A.H. The Psychological Effects of Child Abuse and Neglect. Presented at Brotherhood in Action, February 7, 1973.

Hartman, H. Ego Psychology and the Problem of Adaptation. New York: International Universities, 1939.

Helfer, R.E., and Pollock, C.H. The battered child syndrome.Adv. Paediat., 1968, 15: 9.27.

Helfer, R.E., and Schneider, C. Summary of current status of screening questionnaire for unusual child rearing practises. Personal communication, 1972.

Hertz, M.R. Frequency Tables for Screening Rorschach responses. Fifth Edition. Cleveland: Press of Case Western Reserve University, 1970.

Kempe, C.H. Paediatric implications of the battered baby syndrome. Arch. Dis. Childh., 1971, 46: 28-37.

Kempe, C.H., Silverman, F.N., Steele, B.F., Droegmueller, W., and Silver, H.K. J. American Medical Association, 1962, 181(1): 17-24.

Klopfer, B., Ainsworth, M.D., Klopfer, W.G., and Holt, R.R. Development in the Rorschach Technique, Volume 1: Technique and theory. New York: Harcourt, Brace and World, 1954.

Levitt, E.E., and Truumaa, A. The Rorschach Technique with Children and Adolescents: Application and Norms. New York: Grune and Stratton, 1972.

Melnick, B., and Hurley, J.R. Distinctive personality attributes of child-abusing mothers. J. Consult. Clin. Psych., 1969, 33(6): 746-749.

Nurse, S.M. Familial patterns of parents who abuse their children. Smith College Studies in Social Work, 1966, 35: 11-25.

Paulson, M.J., and Blake, P.R. The physically abused child: a focus on prevention. Child Welfare, 1969, 48: 86-95.

Polansky, N. The current status of child abuse and child neglect in this country. Report to the Joint Commission on Mental Health for Children. In: D.G. Gil, Violence Against Children: Physical Abuse in the United States. Cambridge, Massachusetts: Harvard University Press, 1970.

Rapaport, D., Gill, M.M., and Schafer, R. Diagnostic Psychological Testing. New York: International Universities Press, 1968.

Schloesser, P.T. The abused child. Bulletin of the Menniger Clinic, 1964, 28: 260-68.

Schneider, C., Helfer, R.C., and Pollock, C. The predictive questionnaire, a preliminary report. In: C.H. Kempe and R.E. Helfer (eds.) Helping the Battered Child and his Family. Philadelphia and Toronto: J.B. Lippincott, 1972.

Smith, S.M., Hanson, R., and Noble, S. Social aspects of the battered baby syndrome. Brit. J. Psychiatry, 1974, 125: 568-582.

Smith, S.M., Hanson, R., and Noble, S. Interpersonal relationships and child-rearing practices in 214 parents of battered children. Brit. J. Psychiat., 1975, 127, 513-25.

Steele, B.F., and Pollock, C.B. A psychiatric study of parents who abuse infants and small children. In: RE. Helfer and C.H. Kempe (eds.), The Battered Child. Chicago: Chicago University Press, 1968. Pp. 103-147.

Wasserman, S. The abused parent of the abused child. Children, 1967, 14: 175-179.

Winnicott, D. Primary maternal pre-occupation. In: Collected Papers. New York: Basic Books, 1965.

Young, L. Wednesday's Children: A study of Child Neglect and Abuse. New York, McGraw-Hill, 1964.

Child Abuse and Neglect, Vol. 3, pp. 391 - 400.

0145-2134/79/0301-0391 $02.00/0.

FAMILY INTERACTION ASSOCIATED WITH ABUSE OF CHILDREN OVER 5 YEARS OF AGE

Jean G. Moore & Beryl M. Day

NSPCC School of Social Work, London

I THE STUDY

Over the past decade a considerable volume of literature has emerged which throws light on the reasons why some parents physically injure their very young children. The literature concentrates mainly on the 0 - 4 age group and has enabled guidelines to be produced for all the disciplines involved concerning procedures to be adopted to ensure as far as possible the protection of the children involved.

The staff of the NSPCC School of Social Work, concerned at lack of material relating to school age children and, therefore, the lack of knowledge as to whether the constellation of factors operating in a family when an older child is injured is similar to that observed when the victim is a young baby, decided to study a number of cases in depth to discover similarities and differences. It was hoped that such a study would also highlight the areas in which research would be profitable.

As an integral part of the NSPCC, the School has access to records of cases throughout England, Wales and Northern Ireland. The sample consisted of the first three cases arising within a specified period in every third work group from the Society's alphabetical list. The geographical distribution of the 32 cases (involving 35 injured children of 5 years or over) studied is shown in Table 1.

II THE FAMILIES IN THE SAMPLE

It is necessary here to define the use of the word 'family' in the study. Because of the number of second marriages or cohabitations and the presence of children of different parentage, 'family' is used to describe the group of adults and children living together as a family at the time of referral.

(1) Age and Occupation of Parents

The ages of the parents range from 24 to 51 years and are shown in Table 2. The fathers were employed in a wide range of occupations. See Table 3. In 17 cases the mother was gainfully employed outside the home and it is interesting to note that 8 of the mothers were working with people in some way - nursing, school meals, barmaid, etc.

(2) In view of the importance of marital problems which were highlighted as a causative factor in the study, it is useful to look at evidence of marital status from the sample. See Table 4.

In only half the cases (16) was the couple married without any previous marriage or cohabiting. In these cases the children in the family would be the children of the couple concerned, although in some cases the oldest child may have been conceived or born before the date of the marriage.

In 5 other cases the couple were legally married to each other but one or both had been married or cohabited before with someone else. In one instance the woman concerned had been married 3 times.

In six of the families there was a fairly consistant cohabitation with one or both of the parties married to someone else, while in four families there were frequent changes of cohabitee.

Only one case can accurately be described as a one parent family. This was where a father whose wife had left him had given up his job to enable him to take his children out of the care of the local authority.

(3) Size of Family

The number of children living in each family ranged from 1 to 9, the average being 3.56. In some cases there were also adult children living in the family home. In half the families in the study (see under Marital Status above) the children living in the family home at the time of referral did not all belong to the couple currently acting as parents.

III THE INJURIES

One of the elements in diagnosing to what degree a child is at risk and in what way he is currently suffering is the nature and extent of his injuries. These injuries were studied from the following angles:-

(1) Location of Injury

The location of the injuries is shown in Table 5. Injuries to the face and head were mainly inflicted by hand and included a number of black eyes. The injuries to the arms and shoulders were caused in a variety of ways and sometimes were quite serious. A girl of just under 6 was bruised and beaten on her arm by her mother for biting her older sister (aged 8½). She was also found to have the letters I.L.M. tattooed with a pin on her wrist and inked in with biro. These were said by the mother to mean "I love M......" This child was also found to have previously been locked in a cupboard and very actively rejected by her mother. The mother was kinder to her other children, who were all handicapped in various ways, and on one occasion she said M...... (who was physically whole) "she is the only one I can bash."

The injuries to the trunk were the cases where the force of the parent's hand was backed up by an instrument of some kind. The instruments used were belts (sometimes the buckle end), a pan scraper, a wooden sandal, a curtain rail and a fishing rod. One child was injured on the legs with a wooden spoon. This was a 7-year-old girl in a middle-class family who had lied about stealing biscuits at home.

(2) By Whom Inflicted

Nothing emerged from the study to suggest that a step-parent is particularly likely to injure a child of school age. See Table 6. From reading the cases there was a strong impression that the mother or step-mother played a significant part in the events leading up to the injury when the father or step-father actually committed the assault. In looking further at the 20 cases where the father or step-father had hit the child, the following pattern emerged.

In 7 of these cases the mother's behaviour acted as a trigger for the assault. Either she had provoked her husband in some way and then made sure - perhaps by going out - that the child got the full weight of the anger produced, or she had complained to her husband about the child's behaviour (sometimes, perhaps, to take the spotlight off herself in an explosive situation). For instance, in one family the 6-year-old daughter was very close to her father. Her mother resented this and used an opportunity when her husband was in an aggressive mood to complain about the daughter's behaviour. The father responded to this by bruising the daughter's eye, neck and arm.

In 5 other cases where the father was the injurer the mother used the incident when the child was hit for her own ends, as a means of getting help for herself or as a stated reason for deciding finally to leave home.

IV THE PARENTS

The comments in this section refer to all the parents and step-parents and not simply to those who actually committed the injuries and it is suggested that the personalities of such parents would prove a useful subject for research to establish possible causal relationships.

(1) The Mothers

Some of the mothers appeared to be projecting their own negative attributes on to the child.[1] One mother, for instance, could not tolerate her own messiness and so had to ensure that her child was punished when he left his wet, soiled clothes in the parents' bedroom. Other mothers had very low self-esteem relating to their own feelings of being rejected as children. One mother, whose step-father beat her when she was a child, in turn beat her 6¾-year-old son when she thought he was showing signs of delinquency.

There were indications that some of the mothers had been considerably at risk themselves as children - either physically or emotionally - and it could be a valuable line of further study to pursue details of these mothers' relationships with their own fathers.

(2) The Fathers

The fathers in the study were frequently seen as contributing to the violence by their inadequate passivity in some other areas of their lives and particularly in their marital relationships. The men seem to have married or are cohabiting with women who have little or no respect for them. The complaints from the women are largely about what their husbands leave undone rather than about what they actually do. In one case a worker describes the father as playing ".... a 'soft' role in the family, being very much manipulated by his wife." In another case the father, although in the room, quietly opted out of the discussion with the worker about the child's injury. The mother was "highly strung" and complained that her husband "would not let me hit them." (the children). She also complained that a neighbour spied on her if she hit them. The father's response to this seems to have been to leave the disciplining of the children to the mother, only responding (rather ineffectively) when the situation had got out of hand and one of the children had been injured.

The fathers' responses to the situation were varied. One took up judo, while another tried to be very strict with the children and a few committted minor offences outside the home (only one of which involved violence). One even resorted to black magic. This same man brought another woman into the house on one occasion because his wife "had called him a homosexual and he was out to prove he was not." The most common response was to play a very passive role in the family - virtually to opt out - apart from situations in which they became very angry because they were aware they had lost control. These situations usually involved the behaviour of one of the children. It was when the child answered back or refused to do as he was told that a number of the assaults occurred.

(3) The Marital Relationship (includes cohabitation)

In 20 cases there was mention of current and often severe marital problems. In a further 9 cases there was evidence of previous marital problems - usually with a former partner. Thus in 29 of the 32 cases (90.6%) one or more of the children had been in a family where there was at some time serious disruption in the relationship between the adults in the parenting roles.

The implications of this part of the study, which was retrospective, cannot be presented in statistical form, but there were quite strong indications that the marital problems in the different families had the following common features.

(i) Violence between husband and wife was not a feature. The children probably would have been safer if some of the aggressive feelings between their parents had been acted out more openly.

(ii) Decisions were not jointly arrived at and feelings were not acknowledged, but simmered until they reached boiling point and were often acted out around whatever was happening in the family at the time. In one case the 12-year-old daughter was hit with a belt and bruised by her father because she had shown her mother some confidential papers of his. Here, in a somewhat negative way, the child had been attempting to make her parents interact and she was punished for it.

(iii) The description which most aptly fits these marriages is "non-absorbant". In any relationship there are many things which arise that are absorbed either jointly or by one of the partners in the relationship. Sometimes this process enhances the relationship. Sometimes it is uneven as when one partner simply absorbs criticism from the other and does not retaliate.

However, in many of the cases under consideration each partner was too weak or too defended to absorb either his own or the other's aggression. Because of the problems between them there was no possibility of joint absorption, e.g. to make a concerted attack on someone or something else outside the family. However, although this means that effectively there was a great gulf between the parents, there was a link between them - the children. For various reasons, which will be discussed in the following section, some of the children were able to act out the few positive elements in the link between the parents and so were to a large extent immune. This usually left one child to carry the aggression - and also the guilt that accompanied it. Thus the child was either emotionally or physically kicked around the marital or family arena like a football - a football in a game in which all the participants were losers.

V THE CHILDREN

The 32 cases in the sample were studied to discover the characteristics of the 35 children singled out to play the "football" role. The following important clues emerged for the earlier identification of school age children at risk in this way.

(1) Age and Sex of Injured Child

The average age of the children injured (Table 7) was 9.49. The children at the older end of the age span represent a group which warrants a special study to establish possible links with socially deviant behaviour. In the sample, 22 of the children were male and 13 female.

(2) The Oldest Child

In 21 cases (60%) the oldest child in the family at the time of referral was injured. Sometimes the child was conceived before marriage or before cohabitation had been fully established and these children were often blamed for the marital problems. Their main crime was in being born. Other oldest children belonged to an earlier marriage or liaison of one of the parents and were thus a reminder for one parent of an unhappy or guilt-provoking episode and for the other parent an object which stirred jealousy.

However, it was found that there was an often stronger reason for the assault on the oldest child. This child had to operate in many situations as the parent substitute and in most of the parents in the sample, the adult role models were inadequate. The children were often given responsibilities beyond their capacity or were placed in situations where they could be wrong whatever they did. If they performed the parenting role adequately they were liable to make their parents feel guilty or envious. If something went wrong while they were held responsible then they could expect harsh punishment. An illustration of this from the sample was when a boy of 11 was told by his mother to stay off school to wait for a man to come to empty the gas meter. After his mother had gone to work, the boy told his 8-year-old sister that he was going to school and she must stay at home. The girl stayed, but when her task was completed she wanted to light the gas on the cooker. She lit this by using a long piece of paper and getting a light from the gas fire. In doing so she dropped the lighted paper and burned a hole in the carpet which had only been laid 3 weeks previously. When the father came home he caused sufficient injury to the boy to necessitate the G.P. referring him to hospital. He also caught hold of the girl by the throat and left marks on her neck.

(3) The Different Child

In some cases the child injured was "different in some way - having one different parent, being overactive or alternatively withdrawn, or having a physical condition, a characteristic which singled him out. In one case it was the only physically whole child, the other children of the family being handicapped. The mother held back from hitting the handicapped children, leaving only one child on which to vent her frustration and anger.

Some children had projected on to them the inadequacies or guilt of the parent. The child chosen is likely to be the one who most nearly fits the projection.

(4) The Contribution or Collusion of the Child

Some children more readily adopted the role of victim and drew punishment to themselves. A 6-year-old boy, hearing his mother crying after she had vainly tried to seek help with her marriage problem, and seeking to reach out to his mother, pathetically asked for a drink. His mother prepared warm milk, but he fidgeted with it and it was spilt. This caused his mother, her attention finally drawn to him in great anger, to hit him, shake him and throw him to the floor, fracturing his collar bone.

Some older children fanned the flames of parental problems, perhaps in a desperate attempt to work out a relationship with both parents, e.g. the 12-year-old girl who showed father's confidential correspondence to the mother.

VI EMOTIONAL ABUSE

The effect of the actual injury on the child was difficult to assess because of the many other complicating factors. Small injuries, unless discovered quickly at school, tended to have been left to heal themselves. Many children played down the physical effects and at least on the surface accepted their parents' view of the incident. They also accepted blame and would, therefore, not attempt to use the injuries for sympathy.

It is also interesting that even the children who went to hospital did not excite much sympathy. For instance, the boy who did not stay off school when told to, and his sister burned the carpet, was in hospital for two days. The ward sister told the worker, "He is a menace and no wonder his father hit him." It is conjectured that this boy was playing the same role in hospital that he had learned to play at home; an indication of the nature of the emotional abuse that was found.

Indications were found in many of the cases that the children had been manoeuvred into what might be termed a Laingian "Knots" situation:

> My mother does not love me.
> I feel bad.
> I feel bad because she does not love me.
> I am bad because I feel bad.[2]

A boy of 6 whose intelligence and physical development was said by the doctor who examined him at school to be far advanced for his age, was beaten by his mother. The boy said it was because he had not looked after his young brother properly and let him fall. His mother said it was for stealing 50p out of her boyfriend's pocket. This mother had a very deprived background and was also ill-treated as a child. She ran away from home and was eventually sent to an approved school. The bad behaviour she attributes to her son is reminiscent of her own behaviour as a child. By the time of referral it was difficult to know how many of the complaints about the boy were projections and which were real. This boy had not only become scapegoat for his mother's sins and for her feelings about her own childhood; he had also begun to repeat them himself.

A similar pattern is implicit in many of the cases and the abused child felt doubly punished in some instances when he was able to point to another child in the family who was 'getting away with it'. Being placed in this kind of role in a family has very serious implications for the child's development and amounts to emotional abuse in that it is actually causing the child to suffer, (as distinct from emotional deprivation which is failure to respond to a child at a basic level). Another disturbing element in many cases was the fact that in the families studied there was no evidence of any "kiss and make up" process after the so-called punishment of the child.

A child in this kind of role in his family is likely to seek a similar role elsewhere out of sheer familiarity and unless someone can help him find a more satisfying role with an individual and in a group, his development is likely to be seriously impaired.

VII THE ROLE OF THE SCHOOL

The involvement of the school was found to be of crucial importance in a number of cases. 10 of the 32 cases were actually referred from the school setting. In 6 cases teachers or education welfare officers were actively involved in the monitoring process when there were fears about possible further injury or about emotional abuse. Also in 6 cases (only 2 of them the same as for the monitoring), the school was involved in the treatment process. This included referral for child guidance and various kinds of medical treatment. In a number of other cases the school was able to supply useful information from records or in discussion.

VIII IMPLICATIONS ARISING FROM THE STUDY

When a baby or toddler is non-accidentally injured the immediate focus of attention must be upon the detection and assessment of the severity of the physical injury. When older children are non-accidentally injured it is likely that there is less risk to life, but what is critical is the early detection and identification of the nature of the inter-relationship between physical injury and emotional damage, and ensuring that due weight is given to the severity of the emotional damage.

The study raises the following issues:-

(1) Referral

(i) The school is an important referral centre, as physical injuries can be detected when children undress for sporting activities, etc.

(ii) Teachers and all those in contact with the schoolchild need training to detect the relationship between the repeating pattern of physical injuries and the pattern of the child's disturbed behaviour at school, which often reflects the emotional damage to the child at home.

(iii) In England non-accidental injury referral procedures within the school form a long chain which militates against the sense of urgency and information can lose its significance. This is particularly so as accidental bruises and other minor injuries are not an unusual feature of childhood. The minor injuries themselves do not cause alarm, therefore the emotional damage to the child is overlooked.

(2) Assessment

(i) When investigating a case where an older child has been abused it is essential to assess the way the child is caught up in and is part of the parents' disfunctional marital interaction.

(ii) As the older abused child often sees himself as deserving the physical abuse and believes the parents' projections, the social worker needs to see the child in his own right and to have special training to develop the appropriate skills for interviewing and later working directly with the child. This particularly entails distinguishing fact from fantasy with a child who has so long been the receptacle of someone else's negative projections.

(iii) The risks to the siblings of the injured child need careful assessment. Not only are they being brought up in an abusing atmosphere, but they are also subject to the risk of having a scapegoat readily available and thus not learning to internalise their own negative feelings.

(iv) Social workers must be aware that the very process of investigation can tend to fixate the child as the problem. Skill is needed to ensure that a holistic approach is used. Where appropriate, consideration should be given as to whether adult court proceedings could be used therapeutically so as to facilitate the parents perceiving and taking responsibility for their underlying attitudes and behaviour.

(v) In the initial assessment the degree of intractability of the marital patterns and their projection on the child are important predictive factors as to whether substitute care should be considered. They are also indicators of the way the child is likely to be handled within his own home in the future.

(3) Treatment

(i) Workers in these cases have to take account of the differing time scales for treatment. Work with the parents' marital problems is often necessarily of a long term nature, but to ensure the good enough emotional development of the child, some continuing satisfactions must be found immediately.

(ii) Due to their family background these children tend to bring aggression on to themselves in many settings. It is, therefore, important to ensure that the treatment process is threefold:

(a) Face-to-face therapeutic work with the child;

(b) Work with significant people in all the systems in which the child currently functions;

(c) The provision of constructive experiences for the child through the creation of new systems.

(4) Inter-disciplinary Treatment Programmes

(i) In the treatment programmes for the older abused child often a wider range of professions are involved than are traditionally used when the concern is for a younger abused child. This has several implications with regard to confidentiality, communication across the disciplines and a multiplicity of frames of reference. In contrast to the younger child, the older abused child, because of his mobility, may choose to have contacts with a very wide range of people. The implication of this is that, due to the choice of the child, the most appropriate key worker may in fact not be a professional. Due to the range of workers likely to be involved, it is essential that a team is built up and that the leadership and focus of the team is geared to meet the particular needs of the older child. The administrative and casework management processes which have been worked out to meet the needs of the very young child may be totally inappropriate for the very different needs of the older abused child.

(ii) In the handling of the younger abused child the paediatrician is of considerable importance, with the social worker often placed in the key role. In the handling of the older abused child the teacher, being in daily contact, may play the key role. The school health services, particularly the educational psychologist and the education welfare officer, also become of considerable significance.

(5) At Risk Procedures

(i) In England the 'at risk' procedures have been framed mainly with the younger abused child in mind, e.g. "When there is reasonable suspicion of non-accidental injury the child should at once be admitted to hospital for diagnosis and for his own safety."[3] The physical injury to the older child does not often require in-patient treatment and the hospital ward is not an appropriate assessment centre for him.

(ii) At risk procedures should, therefore, give more appropriate weight to indications of emotional abuse and how these can be more accurately observed by all the professionals involved. Bearing in mind the older abused child, this study gives support to present discussions that the criteria for placing the child's name on an 'at risk' register should be considerably widened and clarified, with particular reference to emotional as well as physical abuse.[4]

(6) Wider Implications

Among the wider implications of the study are:

(i) Further indication of the need for preparation for parenthood,[5] which gives emphasis to experiential teaching about relationships - probably starting much earlier than at adolescence;

(ii) The need for skilful intervention at the time of a marriage break-up, to include insight into the selection of the next partner. This is emphasized in the study by the number of children belonging to previous unions;

(iii) Consideration needs to be given to an on-going dialogue in the community with regard to the disciplining of children and to acceptable manifestations of aggression in the family and in community life generally.

TABLE 1 Sources of Cases

Bedford	3
Beds & Northants	3
Durham	3
East Anglia	3
Hants & Wilts	3
Lake District	1
Liverpool South	3
North Central London	3
Notts & Derby	3
South West Yorkshire	3
Sussex	3
Ulster	1
Total	32

TABLE 2 Age of Parents

	Age Span	Average age
Mother	24 - 47 years	32 years
Father	25 - 51 years	36 years

TABLE 3 Father's Occupation at Time of Referral

Skilled or semi-skilled	8
Professional	1
Mines	1
Clerical or distribution	2
Armed Services	1
Labourers and Factory Workers	8
Self-Employed	1
Unemployed	4
Exact nature not established at referral stage	6
Total	32

TABLE 4 Marital Status at Time of Referral

Married	16
Married but with previous marriage or cohabitation	5
Continuing cohabitation	6
Different cohabitees	4
Single Parent	1
Total	32

TABLE 5 Location of Injury

Face and Head	12 cases
Arms and Shoulders	6 cases
Trunk	13 cases
Legs	1 case
Total	32

TABLE 6 By Whom Inflicted

Inflicted by	Number
Mother	10
Father	14
Cohabitee/Step-Father	6
Child's own father and mother both inflicted injury	2
Total	32

TABLE 7 Age of Child at Time of Referral

(Note 35 children involved)

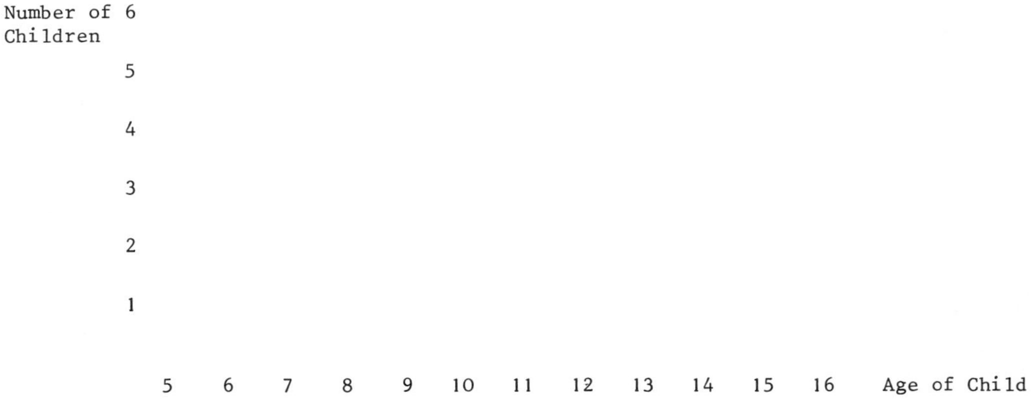

Number of Children

6

5

4

3

2

1

5 6 7 8 9 10 11 12 13 14 15 16 Age of Child

REFERENCES

1. See also Green, Gaines & Sandgrund (August, 1974) Child Abuse: Pathological Syndrome of Family Interaction, American Journal of Psychiatry.

2. R.D. Laing (1972) Knots, Penguin.

3. DHSS Circular, CMO(74)8, (22nd April, 1974), Non-Accidental Injury to Children.

4. BASW (1977), National Survey of Child Abuse Registers.

5. First Report from Select Committee on Violence in the Family (1977) - Violence to Children, Vol. 1, para. 60, HMSO.

Child Abuse and Neglect, Vol. 3, pp. 401 - 405.

0145-2134/79/0301-0401 $02.00/0.

THE PSYCHIATRIST IN CHILD ABUSE - ETHICAL AND ROLE CONFLICTS

Professor Sydney Brandon

Department of Psychiatry, Clinical Sciences Building,
Leicester Royal Infirmary, P.O. Box 65, Leicester, LE2 7LX

INTRODUCTION

Ethical and role conflicts are liable to develop for any physician concerned in the assessment and management of families or of their individual members who may be involved in violence towards children. These problems are particularly evident in the case of the psychiatrist for the exercise of his skills demands the exploration of feelings, motivation and behaviour in the context of a detailed historical review which often extends far beyond that which may have been exposed to the other professionals involved. Psychiatrists are physicians whose training is based largely upon the concept of the personal physician whose medical skills are employed within an individual doctor-patient relationship. Many are by inclination or training concerned with psychodynamic, social or behavioural models of behaviour which often lead them to involvement with groups rather than with individuals. Even when a single 'patient' is referred the sickness or disease is often found to have its roots within the family or other social group and the psychiatrist turns his major treatment endeavour towards others than the labelled patient. Nonetheless the patterns of medical practice and referral in this country ensure that most psychiatrists receive individuals as patients and become to them his or her doctor.

Psychiatric consultation is still resisted by a significant proportion of those for which it is regarded as appropriate and of the smaller group who are actually referred. One in three new psychiatric outpatients fail to keep their appointments (Whyte, 1975) in sharp contrast to almost every other medical specialty and it seems likely that stigma is now a less important deterrent than fear - fear of ridicule, of exposure, or of loss of control. Once embarked upon treatment the drop out rate is high and it is not surprising that psychiatrists are reluctant to take any action which could be interpreted as a betrayal of confidence or other breach of faith with the patient.

Although coercion in the form of compulsory treatment does form a very small and strictly limited part of psychiatric practice few, if any such cases are found in the management of child abuse. Psychiatric assessment or treatment is a joint venture and without the confidence and cooperation of the patient very little can be achieved.

Five major issues are identified for discussion in this paper; these are

1. multiple roles,

2. confidentiality,

3. conflict between treatment and management needs,

4. the right to intervene, and

5. treatment rejection.

These problems are by no means confined to but will be discussed from the viewpoint of the practising psychiatrist. The views discussed are not necessarily those of the author but all are legitimate areas of concern which need to be recognised and discussed. We will never deal with such conflicts by law or regulation but must depend upon informed and insightful professional attitudes developed in a climate of open discussion and respect of one professional for another.

MULTIPLE ROLES

First to consider the problems of multiple and changing roles, the psychiatrist may be consulted by or on behalf of an individual, a family, an agency or the courts and each implies a different contractual relationship which may be threatened when multiple consultation roles are required in an individual case.

The relationship with an individual patient may be placed in jeopardy if the psychiatrist wishes to extend his therapeutic involvement beyond the presenting patient. A marital or mothering problem might be identified by interviews with the parent alone but is less likely to be satisfactorily resolved if permission to engage the involved others is refused. The primary patient may fear exposure, resent sharing a concerned therapist or have more complex motivation for refusing, but once the wider involvement is accepted shifts in the balance of concern are to some degree inevitable. A pathologically jealous male patient may reluctantly accept his wifes involvement and find that as a consequence she decides to leave him. A depressed or severely anxious mother may find that accepting the help of the psychiatric team involves the social work member supported by the psychiatrist applying for a care order for the children.

The dilemma may be even worse when during or after individual therapy the psychiatrist is approached by the NSPCC or a local authority social service department who are seeking either information arising out of the treatment relationship or are asking for a specific consultation to advise the agency on the prognosis or management of the individual because of involvement in a case of suspected non-accidental injury. The social agency is primarily concerned with the risk to the child and may be unwilling to consider the needs of the parent patient, the psychiatrist may be apprehensive about the effects of disclosure or removal of the child upon his patient, fearing perhaps suicide or serious decompensation and the patient may be bewildered if 'his' doctor reveals to a health visitor or social worker events from the past unknown to anyone else or 'takes sides against him' in court. In these circumstances the engagement with the psychiatrist had been a voluntary one initiated by the patient whereas the agency involvement was unsought and a consequence of its social controlling practice.

The reverse situation may occur when the agency initiates the first contact as an agency consultation. Here the individual parent or parents is seen by the psychiatrist in order to advise the agency and often does so under some degree of coercion. A skilled psychiatrist may be able to coax a reluctant patient to provide sufficient information for diagnosis and assessment, indeed an extremely hostile patient may produce telling information which enables an accurate prognosis and diagnosis but it is important that in these cases the nature of the consultation and the limits of confidentiality are clearly explained to the client at the onset. Having established rapport with the reluctant informant the psychiatrist may identify problems which he believes will benefit from psychiatric treatment and offers to provide this so that the reluctant client-informant becomes patient.

In this country the legal advocacy system is such that the solicitor or barrister seeks to 'win' the case on behalf of his client. In the past the lawyer would often seek out 'favourable' medical witnesses and seek to discount medical evidence produced by the 'other side'. Most medical witnesses strive to be objective, providing for the court the relevant evidence and stating an opinion based upon that evidence; they would argue that they are unbiased and scientific. In fact it is clear that the majority of reports are 'strategic' in the sense that the information presented is necessarily selective and often incorporates a bias towards a particular outcome (Brandon, 1977). The pressures, overt and covert, upon the psychiatrist depend upon his involvement with the client, the agency, the lawyers and his colleagues and this is an area in which many role conflicts develop.

CONFIDENTIALITY

Personal responsibility towards the individual patient is the essence of medical ethics. The doctor in accepting responsibility for an individual patient undertakes to exercise proper clinical care and concern, a responsibility which he can share but cannot delegate for he remains responsible for the actions of others to whom he refers or with whom he shares the care of his patient. Included in the concern he shows must be the preservation of the confidentiality of any information about his patient which is acquired during the professional relationship. Certain statutory exceptions exist e.g. the notification of infectious disease, and the courts may direct a physician to produce records or information which he will not voluntarily disclose. The confidential relationship as between doctor and patient is not, in law, an absolute one and the doctor is entitled to break it if he has a compelling social obligation to do so. His responsibility to maintain concern continues after the patient has been discharged or otherwise withdrawn from his clinical care.

Every individual has a fundamental right to privacy and the fact of having consulted or been under the care of a psychiatrist is in itself a confidential matter not to be lightly disclosed. Most discussions on the ethics of disclosure in the child abuse situation have assumed that 'the child is the patient and all other considerations must be subservient to this paramount requirement that the child must be protected', and that 'there must be no concealment, no unilateral action on the part of any section and communications throughout must be full and comprehensive' (Hall, 1975). The problems of confidentiality are less easy to resolve when the primary commitment and clinical responsibility of the psychiatrist are in relation to one or other parent. We are concerned here not merely with information which may be of relevance in determining whether or not the child has been injured and by whom, but with a wide range of highly personal data often of a compromising or embarassing nature. The total disclosure of all available information is neither desirable nor feasible, say in the situation of an N.A.I. Case Conference,[4] and yet anything less requires what may be a fine judgement of relevance or 'need to know' by a practitioner who may be skilled in other fields but inexperienced in the child abuse situation. The presence of the police poses a particularly acute dilemma when actual evidence or patient self accusation relating to possible offences is relevant to diagnosis but might well result in action against the patient.

The police cannot give an undertaking not to take action and will sometimes remind us that it may be an offence to conceal evidence related to the commission of an offence. In law this is true but in practice a physician, especially a psychiatrist, who voluntarily discloses confidential communications which indicate that an offence has been committed will rapidly lose the confidence of his patients and be rendered impotent as a therapist. It is accepted that a compelling social obligation may exist but this is a matter for individual conscience and is not susceptible to legislative control. How is risk to be assessed, where does justifiable or excusable violence become a criminal offence, how is the greater good of society to be evaluated? Murder would appear to be a straightforward case which always calls for consultation with the police but what of the woman caring effectively for her large family who confesses that some years earlier in the desperation of a puerperal depression she smothered her first child or the man who admits that he gave his dying wife a lethal overdose. Incest, bigamy, social security frauds, shoplifting are not uncommon offences which come to light during psychiatric assessment or treatment, the psychiatrist cannot condone them but must he report them? Each situation is unique but the assessment of risk to others is usually the major determinant in deciding on disclosure. Where such a risk is great the patient should be persuaded to inform the police himself and only if he refuses to do so should he be informed that the physician proposes to take the initiative in contacting the police.

The problem of sharing is not however confined to the police for the presence of other members of the case conference may cause as much anxiety. A psychiatrist may be invited to a case conference or his report introduced by a general practitioner, paediatrician or social worker in circumstances in which the psychiatrist does not know from personal experience the qualities or the qualifications of those attending the conference. Can he exercise any control over the further disclosure of sensitive information which he provides and how can he be sure that all participants fully comprehend the significance of data or judgements contained in his report? What is his position if as personal doctor to the mother (or father) he believes that disclosure of information regarded as necessary by the case conference would be detrimental to the mental health of his patient?

CONFLICT BETWEEN TREATMENT AND MANAGEMENT NEEDS

The conflict between treatment and management needs is one of the commonest tensions experienced by the psychiatrist in cases of non-accidental injury for the parents are often vulnerable, immature individuals seriously in need of professional help. Treatment of such individuals always carries a risk of impulsive behaviour such as self injury, suicide, or violence towards the infant. There is often a point in successful treatments when current and future stability would be threatened by removal of the child. The risk to the child associated with intermittent or long term care as well as the physical risk have to be carefully considered in arriving at a decision. When the psychiatrist responsible for treatment and the social worker responsible for taking out the care order have not previously worked together a sharp polarisation of attitudes may occur. Here there is a case for the more frequent use of a second psychiatrist as agency consultant to make an independant assessment and act as mediator. In other circumstances the return or the removal of a child may conflict with a treatment plan particularly when there are some tensions between different teams involved in management. For example a patient admitted to hospital for a puerperal psychosis may be the concern of a multidisciplinary therapeutic team whose philosophy, techniques and objectives may come into conflict with a social worker in the community whose focus is the welfare of the children and team links are with a paediatric or primary care team.

THE RIGHT TO INTERVENE

The right to intervene in the interests of the child is accepted so far as community workers are concerned. Any information, from any source which raises a serious doubt regarding the welfare of a child must be responded to for we now accept that the rights of the child to protection may override the rights of the parents to privacy and independance. Whilst it is possible to take physical action to protect the child it does not follow that psychiatric intervention should or could follow. Many psychiatrists argue that the limits of intervention must be set by the patient, particularly the right not to be a patient. Certainly within the context of child abuse there is no scope for passive treatment; without the active cooperation of the patient no therapy is possible and a patient may be unwilling to accept more than a limited involvement in his life.

During the course of psychiatric treatment there may emerge problems or information relating to relationships with the child or other family members which are relevant to the occurrence or risk of abuse. The conflict regarding disclosure has already been discussed but there is the further problem of intervention. A patient may be willingly undergoing treatment for a depressive or phobic state but be unwilling to permit the psychiatrist to extend his therapeutic involvement into the treatment of the mother-child or parental relationship.

THERAPEUTIC REJECTION

Finally we come to what is here described as therapeutic rejection. We are making slow progress towards the identification of relationships at risk (Brandon, 1971; Frommer and O'Shea, 1973; Lynch and Roberts, 1977) but are less secure in identifying individuals whose personality is so disordered that they appear to be unable to show permanent benefit from any treatment or intervention and who appear to be permanently unfitted for parenthood. Most professionals are reluctant to make such judgements and some reject completely any attempt to do so. Yet all of us are familiar with individuals or families who repeatedly abuse one or more children despite the provision of the best care, support and supervision which is currently available.

Such individuals commonly consume a disproportionate share of scarce resources for the sense of hopelessness which is engendered in the worker by the failure to achieve change despite massive investment may result in a variety of inappropriate coping strategies. Collusion in denial is perhaps the most hazardous, where the worker relates to the positive aspects of the parent, establishes considerable empathy and, like other relatives or the parent him or herself, cannot believe that re-injury has occurred and accepts facile explanations. Commonly the worker feels that the lack of progress is due to some failure in him or his knowledge and experience leading to the conviction that if only more time, a more experienced or more sensitive worker, a psychiatrist, a behaviour therapist, - some other professional - were available then he would see what was wrong and be able to put it right. The consequence, apart from demoralisation of the worker, is a tendency to seek new therapists or treatment regimes and often the new worker embarks in the confidence that previous workers had not understood the client and that their newly established understanding will provide an effective base for treatment.

A consequence may be a child locked in a repetitive cycle of abuse, entry into care and return home. With each entry into care placement becomes more difficult and short of death or severe brain damage, a badly damaged older child enters a long term childrens home or foster care.

If such situations are to be prevented we must clarify the criteria by which such severe personality disordered parents can be recognised and psychiatrists must play an important part in this task. When a diagnosis of severe personality disorder with high risk of repeated violence is made this should be the occasion for a careful and detailed assessment by all the professionals involved. A comprehensive medical, including psychiatric, and social diagnosis should be made and a treatment plan agreed and given a high priority in terms of staff and other resources. The treatment plan should include limited objectives, a periodic review of progress, the provision of adequate supervision and a firm time limit. If at the periodic reviews and within the time limits set the individual shows no capacity to benefit from treatment a clear decision should be made to terminate treatment directed towards restoration of the parental role. The best possible arrangements should be made for the long term care of the child to provide an optimal opportunity for normal development and for the parent adequate and continuing provision should be made for supportive care and supervision.

Such disordered parents faced with permanent separation from their child not uncommonly embark upon another pregnancy or go to other, sometimes extraordinary lengths, to assume the care of a dependant child. Society cannot for much longer delay a decision to make possible the permanent deprivation of the right to parenthood of a small number of individuals who are a danger to children in their care.

REFERENCES

L. J. H. Arthur, M. W. Moncrieff, W. Milburn, P. S. Bayliss and J. Heath, Non-accidental injury in children: what we do in Derby, British Medical Journal 1, 1363-66 (1976).

S. Brandon, The mother-infant relationship, 3rd International Congress on Psychosomatic Medicine in Obstetrics and Gynaecology 311-313 (1971) London.

Brandon, S. (1977) The psychiatric report in cases of non-accidental injury, In The Challenge of Child Abuse, Franklin, Academic Press, London.

E. A. Frommer, and G. O'Shea, Antenatal identification of women likely to have problems in managing their infants, British Journal of Psychiatry 123, 149-156 (1973).

Hall, M. (1975) A view from the emergency and accident department, In Concerning Child Abuse, Franklin, Churchill Livingstone, Edinburgh.

M. Lynch and J. Roberts, Predicting child abuse: signs of bonding failure in the maternity hospital, British Medical Journal 1, 624-26 (1977).

R. Whyte, Psychiatric new patient clinic non-attenders, British Journal of Psychiatry 127, 160-62 (1975).

Child Abuse and Neglect, Vol. 3, pp. 407 - 413.

0145-2134/79/0301-0407 $02.00/0.

A QUANTIFICATION SYSTEM AS AN AID TO THE ASSESSMENT OF PROGNOSIS AND THE PLANNING OF TREATMENT FOR CHILD ABUSERS

G. Straker and R. Jacobson

University of the Witwatersrand, Johannesburg, S. Africa.

The statement that child abuse is multi-determined would probably elicit little disagreement from workers in the field. Neither would the notion that treatment of abusers should be multi-faceted. However, in practice, with one or two notable exceptions, treatment of abusers has often focussed on only one or two of the factors recognised in the literature as being important in abuse. The reasons for this narrow treatment focus have often been valid ones pertaining to limited time and resources.

However, while acknowledging that at times a fairly narrow treatment focus is unavoidable, the problem, as the present authors see it, is the way the factors selected for treatment are chosen by the case workers. Often it appears that the factors chosen as the treatment focus are dictated more by the workers personal theoretical orientation than by the variables in the abusers own situation.

Treatment preferences have ranged from a conventional psychoanalytic approach to therapy based on more direct mothering of the mother including actually teaching her problem solving, social and mothering skills to family therapy both on an in patient and an out patient basis.

Given the variety of treatment approaches available and the number of factors implicated in the etiology and maintainance of abuse, the present authors perceived a need for the development of a system which would help professionals to focus more sharply on the major factors contributing to abuse in a particular instance of its occurrence and thus provide guide lines for the assessment of prognosis and the type of therapy likely to be most effective.

The intention was not to develop a new method of assessment but rather to present a format for summarising and systematising the type of data which is usually elicited by workers in the area of child abuse in the normal course of an assessment, provided this includes such procedures as a clinical interview, a psychiatric history, a family interview, a home visit and a psychometric assessment. The only suggested addition to these fairly standard procedures is the administration of the Holmes and Rahe Social Readjustment Scale (1967) which is a short questionnaire aimed at assessing the life stresses which have occurred in the individual's life in the 12 months preceding the completion of the questionnaire.

Returning then to the quantification system; following a review of the literature the authors concluded that most of the elements thought to be related to child abuse could be subsumed under one of the eight following headings:- Level of Psychiatric Psychopathology, Personality Dynamic Factors, Educational Factors, Family Relationship Factors, Immediate Stimulus Factors, Social Factors, Economic Factors, Life Stresses.

These eight factors differ however in terms of the causal significance for abuse ascribed to them in the literature. Economic factors for example, while they have been shown by a number of researchers to be associated with abuse, have also been shown not to be of primary causal significance (Gil 1970, Smith, Harrison & Noble 1974). On the other hand level of Psychiatric Psychopathology and Personality Dynamic Factors have been pinpointed as having primary causal significance (Gelles 1975, Scott 1973).

Despite this issue of differential causal importance, it is the contention of the authors that all the eight factors mentioned, contribute something to the potential for abuse, thus all eight factors will be included in the proposed quantification system. However in the suggested guide lines to assessing prognosis and the intensity of treatment required, some attempt will be made to reflect the differential contributions of these eight factors to the causation and maintainance of child abuse. This attempt will of necessity be subjective as will be the attempt to weight the elements which make up the eight factors proposed by the authors. Thus the whole system is subject to the same criticism regarding lack of empirical validation, which was leveled against the earlier systems aimed at categorisation of abusers by researchers such as Merril (1962); Delsorda (1963) and Zalba (1967). The present system though; unlike the earlier ones is thought to be more comprehensive in the number of elements and factors it utilises in arriving at its guide-lines for treatment and the assessment of prognosis.

The proposed system is presented below. The numbers in brackets represent the relative importance on a scale of 0 - 7 each of the elements are thought to have in contributing to a particular factor. Excepting one factor - i.e. Level of Psychopathology, the total possible score for each factor is 7; if the individual scores the maximum possible on each element in the factor. On Factor I the total score possible for an individual is 46 because of the importance and number of elements contributing to this Factor. In establishing a score for Level of Psychiatric Psychopathology, Personality Dynamic Factors, Educational Factors and Life Stresses, these Factors should be scored separately for both the abuser and their spouses or spouse surrogates if these persons are available. The separate scores should then be summed and divided by 2. If the abuser's spouse is not available the scores on these Factors is merely calculated for the abuser and left undivided.

After the presentation of the quantification system, a prognostic chart based on the system is presented. A chart, showing guide lines for which treatment strategies should be given priority, if an individual has a high score on a particular factor is also presented. Again however it must be stressed that the quantification system presented below is merely a suggested way to summarise and systematise data and neither the system itself, nor the prognostic indications and suggested treatment strategies have been empirically validated.

Factor I
Level of Psychiatric Psychopathology
Assessment Procedure : Psychiatric Interview, Psychometric Assessment of each parent or parent surrogate.

<u>Elements</u>

(a) Psychopathy (7)
(b) Psychosis (7)
(c) General abusiveness (i.e. violent in all relationships) (7)
(d) Level of Immaturity and Inadequacy (7)
(e) Alcoholism (7)
(f) Drug Dependence (7)
(g) Criminal Recidivism (7)
(h) Depression (4)
(i) Obsessive-Compulsiveness (4)

Treatment Procedure: If a high score were obtained on this factor, the removal of the child from the family would seem indicated. If the score obtained was somewhat lower so as not to necessitate the actual removal of the child the general treatment indications would still involve residential care treatment or treatment involving day care for the child, as protection of the child would seem to be of paramount importance if a relatively high score on this Factor were obtained.

Factor II
Level of Personality Disturbance
Assessment Procedure :- Psychiatric Interview, Psychometric Assessment of both parents or parent surrogates.

<u>Elements</u>

(a) Denial of guilt (2)

(b) Unmotivated for treatment (2)
(c) Poor impulse control (1)
(d) Poor self concept (1)
(e) Disturbed identity (1)

Treatment Procedures:- If the abusive unit had a very high score on this factor, prognosis would again be questionable as personality factors are highly indicated etiological factors in abuse. Once more treatment strategies which provided for the protection of the child would have to have a high priority. Long term intensive treatment for each of the individuals of the abusing unit would also seem to be indicated.

Factor III
Educational Factors
Assessment Procedures: Clinical Interview, Psychometric Assessment, Home Visit aimed at assessing social contacts and the individual's skill in dealing with day to day living.

Elements

(a) Unrealistic Expectations of the Child (2)
(b) Inadequate Social Skills (Social Isolation) (2)
(c) Inadequate Problem Solving Skills (Housekeeping-mothering etc.) (2)
(d) Low I.Q. (1)

Treatment Procedures:- Reeducative type therapy aimed at helping the parents develop coping skills for living would seem to be indicated. Mothering the mother would seem important as would group therapy to try and facilitate and foster social skills.

Factor IV
Family Relationship Factor
Assessment Procedure:- Clinical Interview, Family Diagnostic Interview.

Elements

(a) Marital Dysharmony 2
(b) A no-adult family 2
(c) Poor Childhood Experiences 2
(d) Provocative Siblings 1

Treatment:- Family therapy would be the therapy of choice possibly combined with more intensive help for any member who seemed to warrant it.

Factor V
Immediate Stimulus Factors
Assessment Procedures:- Clinical Interview, Examination of the Infant, Home Visit to assess stimulus factors in the house.

Elements

(a) Colicky ill baby (1)
(b) Premature baby (1)
(c) Rebellious child (1)
(d) Provocative difficult baby (1)
(e) Unresponsive baby (1)
(f) Continually crying baby (2)

Treatment Procedures:- Assisting the mother in developing better mothering skills would seem important. The provision of practical services like a relief baby sitter or partial day care for the infant might be important. In the older child some sort of play therapy or a big brother system might be useful.

Factor VI
Social Factors
Assessment Procedure :- Clinical Interview

Elements

(a) Illigitimacy (1)
(b) Premarital Conception (1)
(c) Unwanted Pregnancy (1)
(d) Current Youthful age of mother i.e. under 23 (1)
(e) Absence of biological father (1)
(f) Unstable liasons (2)

Treatment Procedures:- The above factors are thought to be associated with unstable personality structures. Thus intensive psychotherapy seems indicated, perhaps with a special emphasis on helping the mother accept her unwanted baby and with an emphasis on helping her with relationship skills.

Factor VII
Economic Factors
Assessment Procedures:- Clinical Interview
Elements

(a)	Frequently Unemployed	2
(b)	Currently Unemployed	2
(c)	Low, misspent income	2
(d)	Poor accommodation	1

Treatment Procedure:- Like social factors, this factor is also often associated with an unstable personality structure. Thus intensive therapy would seem indicated rather than the provision only of financial help. Training in some practical trade might also however have some value.

Factor VIII
Life Stresses
Assessment Procedure:- Holmes & Rahe Social Readjustment Rating Questionnaire.
This factor is based on scores obtained on the above scale which reflect whether on the basis of his life's experiences over the past twelve months the individual is currently in nil, mild, moderate or severe life crisis. In terms of this, the elements for abusers could be weighed on this factor as follows :

Individual in severe life crisis and the precipitating events are recent i.e. his coping resources are not consolidated	(7)
Individual not in crisis at all i.e. the abuse seems motivated by more intrinsic factors than external stress	(7)
Individual in moderate life crisis and the precipitating events are recent	(5)
Individual in mild crisis at the time of abuse	(5)
Individual in moderate or severe stress at the time of abuse but precipitating events are now receding	(3)

Treatment. If stress seemed a precipitating factor some family therapy to help consolidate resources would be indicated. Strategies such as residential care would probably be counter-indicated as this would represent another major change for the family. If however the abuse was not associated with stress at all, then longer term intervention would be indicated as abuse would seem to be internally rather than externally motivated.

Having presented the quantification system a system for differentiating controllable from uncontrollable abuse is suggested in the prognostic chart below. Following this, a chart suggesting which treatment strategies should take priority, when an individual has a relatively high score on a specific factor is outlined. Again in conclusion the authors point out that the aim of the paper is to facilitate case workers in focussing more systematically on the factors which seem important in a specific instance of abuse rather than to provide hard and fast rules. It is hoped that the paper succeeds in this endeavour and that workers will use the system and eventually provide information as to its validity.

A small pilot study by the present authors which involved coding 20 case studies of abusers where treatment was known to be successful vs unsuccessful showed that the system differentiated successfully between the controllable and uncontrollable abusers in all the cases studied. However this is flimsy evidence and the importance of the system is still felt to be primarily in the provision of a way of forcing objectivity in the highly emotionally charged area of child abuse.

Prognostic Chart
Abuse Probably Uncontrollable
Score of 6 - 7 on any one element in Factor I
Total score of 15 or more on Factor I
Score of 6 or above on Factor 2
Score of 5 or above on any 3 Factors
Score of 4 or above on any 4 Factors

References

Birrell, R.G. and Birrell, J.H. Maltreatment syndrome in children. The Medical Journal of Australia, 1968, 2, 23: 1023-1029

Delsordo, J. (1963). 'Protective casework for abused children.' Children 10, 213-218

Gelles, R.J. Child abuse as psychopathology: a sociological critique and reformulation. American J. of Orthopsychiatry, 1973, 43(4): 611-621.

Gil, D.G. Violence against Children: Physical child abuse in the United States. Cambridge, Massachusetts, Harvard University Press, 1970.

Gil, D.G. Violence against children. Journal of Marriage and the Family, 1971, Vol. 33.

Holmes, T.H., and Rahe, R.H.: The social readjustment rating scale. J. Psychosom Res 11: 213-218 (1967).

Kempe, C.H. Position paper for hearing of the subcommittee on children and youth of the committee on labour and public welfare, United States Senate, March 31, 1973, Denver, Colorado, unpublished. In: S.M. Smith, The Battered Child Syndrome. London: Butterworths, 1975.

Kempe, C.H., and Helfer, R.E. In: C.H. Kempe and R.E. Helfer (eds.). Helping the Battered Child and his Family. Oxford: Lippincott, 1972.

Kempe, C.H., Silverman, F.N., Steels, B.F., Droegmueller, W., and Silver, H.K. J. American Medical Association, 1962, 181(1): 17-24.

Melnick, B., and Hurley, J.R. Distinctive personality attributes of child-abusing mothers. J. Consult. Clin. Psych., 1969, 33(6): 746-749.

Merrill, E.J., (1962). 'Physical abuse of children: An agency study.' In Protecting the Battered Child, Ed. by V. de Francis, Denver, Colorado: Children's Division, American Humane Association.

Polansky, N. The current status of child abuse and child neglect in this country. Report to the Joint Commission on Mental Health for Children. In: D.G. Gil, Violence Against Children: Physical Abuse in the United States. Cambridge, Massachusetts: Harvard University Press, 1970.

Smith, S.S. The Battered Child Syndrome. London: Butterworth, 1975.

Smith, S.M., Hanson, R., and Noble, S. Parents of battered babies: a controlled study. British Medical Journal, 1973, iv, 388-391.

Smith, S.M., Hanson, R., and Noble, S. Social aspects of the battered baby syndrome. Brit. J. Psychiatry, 1974, 125: 568-582.

Steele, B.F., and Pollock, C.B. A psychiatric study of parents who abuse infants and small children. In: R.E. Helfer and C.H. Kempe (eds.), The Battered Child. Chicago: Chicago University Press, 1968. Pp. 103-147.

Zalba, S.R. The abused child: I. A survey of the problem. Social Work, 1966, 11: 3-16.

Zalba, S.R. (1967) 'The abused child - II. A typology for classification and treatment,' Social Work 12, 70-79.

TREATMENT PRIORITIES

TYPE OF INTERVENTION

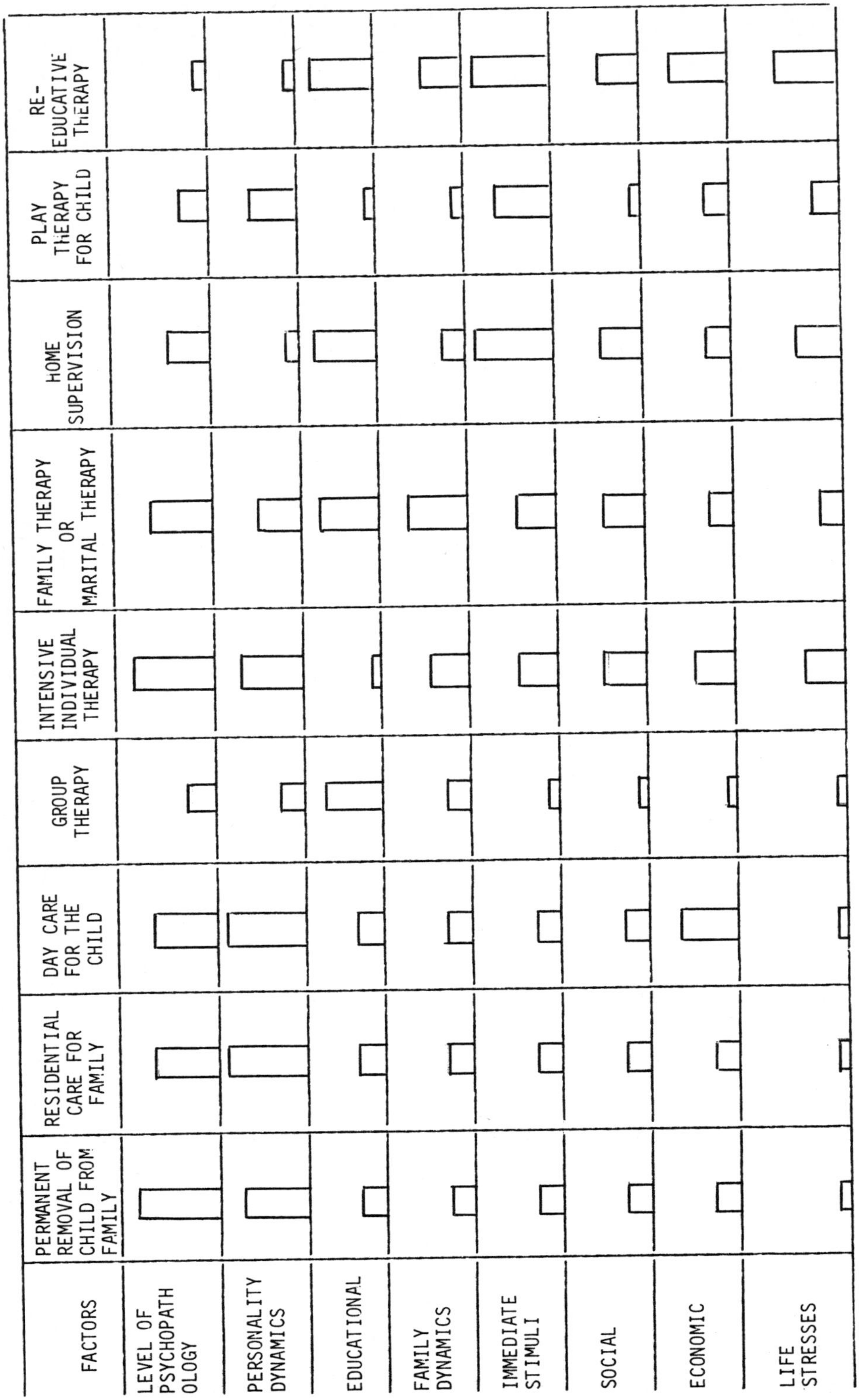

FACTORS	PERMANENT REMOVAL OF CHILD FROM FAMILY	RESIDENTIAL CARE FOR FAMILY	DAY CARE FOR THE CHILD	GROUP THERAPY	INTENSIVE INDIVIDUAL THERAPY	FAMILY THERAPY OR MARITAL THERAPY	HOME SUPERVISION	PLAY THERAPY FOR CHILD	RE-EDUCATIVE THERAPY
LEVEL OF PSYCHOPATHOLOGY									
PERSONALITY DYNAMICS									
EDUCATIONAL									
FAMILY DYNAMICS									
IMMEDIATE STIMULI									
SOCIAL									
ECONOMIC									
LIFE STRESSES									

Key: Treatment Priorities

1st 2nd 3rd 4th 5th

Child Abuse and Neglect, Vol. 3, pp. 415 - 421.
Pergamon Press Ltd., 1979. Printed in Great Britain.

CHILD ABUSE AND CHILD DEVELOPMENT

Harold P. Martin, M.D.

University of Colorado Medical Center, Denver, Colorado

I have been asked to give a presentation this morning to set the tone for today's papers. The theme of today's presentations is the child. And so I have chosen to piece together some rather disparate thoughts and observations concerning mistreated children in an attempt to meet the expectations and requirements of those who asked me to speak.

It is easy to lose sight of the primary reason for our interest and concern in child abuse and neglect. Different professionals and scientists may get so involved and intrigued with various facets of this phenomenon that we require a reminder that the ultimate and overriding concern is the child who has been abused or neglected. It is the child's welfare which is the ultimate reason to research this phenomenon; it is the child's welfare which justified the monies and energies that are spent on a Congress such as this. At bedrock is the conviction that indifference and physical violence are stressful and harmful to children. We know that children can be killed or permanently maimed by such mistreatment. We also hold the conviction that abuse and neglect of children shape children's growth and development in very harmful and malevolent ways.

Mistreatment of children is wrong. It is unjust and sullies the dignity of the child and the society which allows it to occur. But, we cannot stop at the point of condemnation of mistreatment of children. Statements such as the United Nations' Bill of Rights for Children are lofty and morally persuasive. But moral persuasion alone is not enough to influence societies to prevent such abuse or to implement mechanisms of helping such children. It is up to us to explore and investigate the effects of abuse and neglect on children. It is a challenge to us to find ways to help bind up the physical, neurological, and psychological wounds of the mistreated child. We must explore ways to put aright the derailed development of the mistreated child.

We are not starting at point zero. We do have some information about the consequences of abuse and neglect. Kempe, Helfer, (1, 2, 3, 4) and others have documented the alarming risk of death over the past 15 years. Other investigators, led by the pioneering work of Elmer (5, 6), have shown the even greater risk of serious deviations in growth and development in the survivors. In addition to the ultimate deviation in growth and development - complete cessation; i.e., death, we know that mistreatment leads to mental retardation, brain damage, neuromotor disabilities, sensory deficit, language delay, and learning disorders, in addition to a host of psychological scars and wounds which may last a lifetime (7, 8, 9).

The question is no longer "Does child abuse and neglect alter development?", but the question is now, "How does child abuse and neglect alter development?" And what can be done to set growth and development back on a normal course.

Child abuse and neglect are not typical biological diseases like measles or polio. They must be viewed in other conceptual frameworks to understand their genesis and consequences. They may be viewed as a syndrome. In such a framework, it is recognized that the acts of physical abuse or neglect per se are not the disease but part of a mosaic pattern. If abuse and neglect of a child are present in a family, then it must be assumed that there are other pathological characteristics in that family and in the parent-child relationship. Abuse and neglect can be viewed as signals; as signs that there is family disorganization and failure in parenting. The individual acts of abuse and neglect, indeed, may not be as harmful to the child as the whole pattern of aberrant parenting and family function. We have learned time and time again that children are returned to their biologic parents and through the efforts of professionals, there are no more overt acts of physical abuse or neglect. And yet, when the family structure and function have not been appreciably changed, we see the child continue to be unloved, rejected, ignored, and scapegoated. It is rare to see a child who has been physically abused come from a home which is otherwise quite healthy and normal. Instead, we see that the abused child is also exposed to and shaped by a number of malevolent environmental factors; e.g., poverty, social stress, sexual exploitation, maternal deprivation, malnutrition, rejection, psychopathological parents, inadequate cognitive and social stimulation, and inadequate emotional support. It is the abusive environment which derails the child's development. Abuse or neglect are to be considered signs of such pathology much as a high fever alerts the clinician to a biological disease state. The abuse and neglect, themselves, may be harmful, just as an inordinately high fever may cause damage, but more often, it is the underlying pathology or disease state which causes harm and which must be treated. We must not narrowly focus on the acts of abuse and neglect, just as we would not narrowly focus on the fever and headache of a child with meningitis.

There are different views at this Congress as to what the most basic underlying pathology is in this syndrome. Some of you feel that the underlying pathology is embedded in societal values and societal systems. And so there will be suggestions for prevention and treatment which stress the need to change societies. There are others of you who feel that the underlying pathology is to be seen in the personalities and life experiences of the abusing adults. And flowing from this conceptual framework are suggestions to alter and try to heal the psychological bruises and abrasions of the adult.

However, for today's focus, let us look at the child. It is my contention, supported by the work of many, that the basis for 50% to 75% of mistreated children having very serious and significant deviations in development lies in family environment or more specifically, in the parent-child relationship, which is obviously shaped by a host of factors within that specific family.

The first point I should like to make this morning is a plea for more discerning and microscopic investigations of the effects of abuse and neglect on children and their development. As stated earlier, a number of investigators have documented deviations in language, perceptual, cognitive, and learning abilities in most abused children. But to this point, we have highlighted the most gross and obvious consequences of mistreatment. When we go to document neurological damage, we have pulled out the most global measures of neurological function, such as the standard I.Q. test, the standard neurologic examination, an EEG, or measurements of language skills, etc. When we have wanted to document the psychological damage to such children, we have looked to see if they are psychotic, serious behavior problems, antisocial, or learning disabled. And, indeed, that is where we needed to start. But we are no longer at the starting gate; we have now progressed to a point where we must change our strategies and our goals. It is now time to exchange our spectacles and our telescopes for the fine scrutiny of the microscope of behavior.

Let me digress for a moment and discuss what has historically happened in researching some related areas of inadequate parenting. Indeed, I think this shall not be a digression, but perhaps a journey through recent history from which we may be well counselled.

I should like to take the study of childhood malnutrition as an example (10, 11, 12, 13, 14). The earliest studies of childhood undernutrition focused on biochemical and structural damage to the brain. This work had to be done primarily on animals; and when done on children, necessarily required study of a very biased sample of malnourished children. Then a second wave of interest focused on neurologic function in the malnourished child. And so investigators took out their I.Q. tests, performed their standard neurologic examinations, completed their EEGs, and observed school learning performance. These measurements are too global and nondiscriminating. Only the most deviant of children will be identified by such measures. Indeed, using such gross measurements, investigators often found no statistically significant differences between severely malnourished and well nourished children, even though the clinician knows that they are different. One of the offshoots of such approaches was to raise question as to whether inadequate nutrition in infancy had <u>any</u> longlasting effect on the growing child. Finally, a few investigators went further. Birch and Cravioto and colleagues (15, 16), for example, measured transmodal perceptual abilities of Mexican children who had been malnourished in infancy. Another exception was Hoorweg (17), who recently published a 15-year follow-up of Ugandan children who had suffered malnutrition in early childhood. He looked at nine different measures of cognition, tests of motor skills, and personality traits in the survivors. By these more discriminating measures, these investigators not only could document the significant effects of malnutrition, but gave us clues as to how to treat or intervene with children who had suffered the insult of calorie and protein malnutrition.

It seems to this clinician that we have followed a similar pattern in the past with regard to the psychological effects of sexual exploitation of children. Through the exclusive use of only very broad measures for psychopathology, many experts, and, unfortunately, many lay persons, have been led to believe that sexual abuse of children does not lead to any serious psychological trauma. What happened? Investigators have interviewed adults who had been sexually molested in childhood. They looked to see if these adults were psychotic, sociopaths, or severely neurotic. If such adults were married, held jobs, had stayed out of jail, and had raised children, they were considered "normal" and healthy, as if those were valid discriminating measures of normalcy. What the investigator did <u>not</u> do was to look to see if the person was happy or content. What the investigator did <u>not</u> persue were the state of object relations, capacity for sexual pleasure, self-esteem, vulnerability to stress, etc. Parenthetically, this same inappropriate global approach is too often used in measuring the effects of divorce or parent loss on children.

And now to return to abused and neglected children. What should be looked for in trying to assess the effects on growth and development? While I am not a soothsayer, surely our clinical observations suggest that neurologic integrity might be assessed by investigating such behaviors as attention span, visual-motor perception, short-term versus long-term memory, somatosensory perception, spatial organization, processing of speech, etc.

And what of the psychological wounds of such children? Again, I am not sure I know where to start, but I <u>do</u> know from examining and interviewing hundreds of mistreated children that there are a number of clues as to where to explore. If one accepts the concept that many mistreated children will grow up to be like their parents then one might well look for the early analage of personality characteristics one finds in the abusive adult, such as those enumerated by Steele (18). Taking this approach, the investigator would be interested in the child's conscience or superego development, aggression, impulse control, self-concept, state of interpersonal relations, etc.

I should like to briefly mention some issues that my colleagues at the JFK Child Development Center in Denver and I are just beginning to explore. And while our studies are not at a point of having results to share, some beginning trends are being noted.

Very recently Dr. Robert Barahal and Dr. Jill Waterman, two clinical child psychologists, and I have started to explore some rather specific issues in a population of 6-8 year-old abused children and a control group of non-abused children from similar socioeconomic background. We started from the point of thinking that if, indeed, the mistreated child is at risk of becoming an abusive adult then we should be able to see the early beginning deviations in personality that one so often sees in the adult perpetrator. And so we are trying to look at early development of conscience or superego in these early latency-aged children. One measure we are using attempts to measure whether the child's perceived locus of control is internal or external to himself. Role-taking and ability to empathize seemed pertinent areas to explore. And finally, we are trying to see how capable the abused 6-8 year-old is in his ability to recognize and identify emotions, both negative emotions of anger and hurt and disappointment, as well as positive feelings of happiness, gratitude, and well-being. While we do not have sufficient control data to present any firm conclusions, we are noting some trends which we think will show up as significant differences. One would certainly hypothesize that abused children might well label behaviors as good or bad more on the basis of the consequences of those behaviors (i.e., did one get caught and was an adult angry at the behavior) rather than on the basis of the intent or motivation of the child. We are seeing that these children have great difficulty in developing a sense of self and in empathetically taking the role of others. The results of our studies are not really the purpose of this presentation. Rather, the point is that one might hope that such studies would give rationale to specific treatment approaches for such children. The hope is that one might find ways to intervene in the cycle of "abuse begatting abuse" by identifying and isolating psychological trauma of the abuse syndrome in such a way as to lead to rational treatment approaches for the child.

Let me continue this digression abit longer by sharing with you another area of interest in the development of abused children. Again, the specific areas of development to be studied are not so important as the idea of the need to scrutinize more carefully developmental issues of childhood in mistreated children. A number of child clinicians have repeatedly been impressed by the seeming incompetence of abused children which does not appear to be based on neurologic dysfunction. Why should so many mistreated children fare so poorly on the various measures of cognition, language, or learning? This question may take us many directions in seeking for an answer. One area it has recently taken me is to an intense interest in the developmental line of mastery and competence. Observers of children have noted for centuries that there seems to be an unrelenting drive of infants and babies toward ever increasing and sophisticated knowledge and skill acquisition. It is as if children take some inherent joy in causing things to happen. As one looks at young animals, including the human, one gets a feeling that curiosity is part of the organisms birthright. Hendrick (19) suggested in the 1940's that babies have an inborn drive to do, and to learn how to do. White (20) suggests that the human baby is born with an innate instinct or drive for mastery of the environment; a drive which is aimed at learning, understanding, affecting, and conquering the environment; e.g., problems, toys, riddles, relationships, etc. He defines competence as an organisms's capacity to interact effectively with its environment. He maintains that effectance motivation is persistant in that it regularly occupies the spare waking time of children when they are not involved in episodes of homeostatic crisis, such as hunger, pain, anxiety, etc. From such a theoretical paradigm, then, one might well consider what it could be in the abusive environment which diverts and subverts this innate drive for mastery and competence.

The child will often receive verbal or physical abuse when he is striving for mastery of his environment. Mastery requires the child to be curious, to get into things, to ask questions, and to develop his own autonomy. It is just such behaviors which are apt to be met with abuse. Abusive parents are typically impatient with the child's attempts at mastery. For any child to learn some new ability or a new concept, he must practice; he must make approximations; he must be able to fail or only partially succeed in the task. For the child to successfully negotiate mastery, he needs the support of parents in those first failures or approximations or half-successful attempts. If the process of becoming successful are not supported, indeed, if those attempts at new successes are met with impatience and punishment, the drive towards effectiveness will be derailed. Even when the child has developed abilities and skills, the abusive parent may not tolerate his growing autonomy and independence, so that some abused children will hide or disguise their real abilities and potentials.

Let us assume for the moment that the abused and neglected child is discouraged from developing competence, that his drive or instinct for mastery or effectiveness is derailed. If, indeed, this is the case, then treatment approaches might be quite radically different than for a child whose incompetencies are based in neurologic deficit, lack of stimulation, or some other psychodynamic basis. If, for instance, the abused child's paucity of speech and language is really a manifestation of impairment in mastery or competence, then the speech therapist or preschool teacher might well find a traditional approach to therapy quite unsuccessful. Rather, the approach should be one of trying to help the child learn to take the risk of developing competency in language, and learning to appreciate the joy and gratification from such mastery. Drill in sound production, vocabulary, listening, auditory association, or processing may only be successful if the basic deficit in developing a sense of pleasure in effectance or mastery is dealt with. Similarly, this concept might be appropriate to children with motor delays or learning disabilities. The issue may not so much be one of teaching motor abilities or teaching reading skills, but the issue may be one of fostering the child's sense of worth and competence, of working on the developmental line of mastery and competence rather than the developmental line of motor acquisition or of processing of visual stimulae.

I am trying to emphasize the need for careful clinical study of developmental issues in mistreated children. There is a need to more carefully document just what the consequences of mistreatment are to a child's development. Many important developmental consequences may be so subtle that they will be completely disguised or obscured by the gross measures of intelligence tests or other standard measures of ego functions. I am also suggesting that such careful documentation of developmental sequellae of mistreatment can offer us logical courses to take in trying to treat the developmental lags of these children.

One other example for fruitful investigation involves those mistreated children who have seemingly escaped some of the usual consequences of their malevolent environment. Unfortunately, it is all too seldom that research is directed to explain the lack of pathology from biologic or social insult. Why, indeed, do a small percentage of abused children escape the developmental delays or the impaired intellectual functioning that is more commonly seen?

I recently reviewed the records of 11 abused children Ms. Beezley and I studied who had I.Q.'s above 115. Some interesting leads resulted. For one, four of these children had been abused and then rather quickly relinquished and adopted during their first year of life. Three other children had been abused in adoptive homes, a striking fact since these were the only three of the 58 children studied who had been abused by adoptive parents. Of the four remaining children, each had other factors which might have spared them intellectual deficit. Two of the four had had adequate parenting for the first three to four years of their life. In one instance, the mother had a rather acute psychiatric disturbance when the child was four years old. A second child had been raised by his grand parents for the first three to four years while mother had repeated psychiatric hospitalizations. A third child had a physician father and a college professor mother who encouraged intellectual persuits. Indeed, this child was clearly escaping from a world of feelings, emotions, and interpersonal relationships to find solace and some measure of peace and well-being in the mastery of the world of books, ideas, and scientific truths. I have a feeling that when a child is in an abusive home where academic competence is not punished and ridiculed, that sublimation and escape from the "real world" to the world of academics and scholarliness is not uncommon.

It seems clear that investigations of the supposedly "invulnerable" children should provide us with information which might be most helpful in planning treatment strategies for less fortunate, more "vulnerable" mistreated children.

We, of course, must be careful to not justify or rationalize narrow, irrelevant research to which there are no pragmatic clinical implications. I do not wish to open up here the whole debate over the value of basic research. But I do wish to emphasize that we have a very pressing and urgent need to find out more about mistreated children. And, further, that there are critically important reasons for needing this information. We need to know much more about how to help and treat the abused and neglected child. Protection from re-injury is not an adequate repertoire of treatment for abused children. The tremendous developmental morbidity of this syndrome needs our attention. We need information and evidence of the consequences of mistreatment of children so as to be able to influence social policy and disbursement of funds for the treatment of the victims. We need, therefore, data and conclusions which have practical implications for evaluation and treatment of mistreated children.

We are on very weak ground if we condemn the mistreatment of children solely on the basis that it is cruel, unjust. We will not be taken seriously if we base our requests for help for these families solely on the basis of moral persuasion. Our wish to prevent, to identify, and to offer treatment for abuse and neglect is not embedded in a reactionary punitive superego which wants to stamp out evil. Rather, as any group of clinicians, scientists, and social activitists, we have started out from an awareness that abuse and neglect not only threaten a child's life, but in the larger population of survivors, leaves children with deep, neurological and developmental wounds. If those developmental wounds are not identified and treated, or if they are not prevented, the child suffers; and the society in which he will grow up suffers. The early pioneers in abuse and neglect were men and women whose interests and energies were fired by a concern about children and their development.

I look forward to the presentations of today. Most of the papers being presented will shed considerable light on such important developmental issues of childhood. I look forward to future Congresses where, it is my hope, the focus will increasingly be attuned to finding ways to help mistreated children have a chance to grow and develop into healthy and happy adults.

REFERENCES

1. C.H. Kempe, et al, The battered child syndrome, Journal of American Medical Association, 181, 17-24 (July, 1962).

2. Kempe, C.H., and Helfer, R.E. (Eds) (1972): Helping the Battered Child and His Family, Philadelphia, Lippincott.

3. Helfer, R.E., and Kempe, C.H. (Eds) (1974): The Battered Child, Chicago, Univ. Chicago Press.

4. Helfer, R.E., and Kempe, C.H. (Eds) (1976): Child Abuse and Neglect: The Family and the Community, Cambridge, Mass, Ballinger.

5. Elmer, E. (1967): Children in Jeopardy, Pittsburgh,Pa, Univ. Pittsburgh Press.

6. E. Elmer and G.S. Gregg, Developmental characteristics of abused children, Journal of Pediatrics, 40, 596-602 (1967).

7. H.P. Martin, et al, The development of abused children-Part I: A review of the literature, Part II: Physical, neurologic and intellectual outcome, Advances in Pediatrics, 21, 25-73 (1974).

8. H.P. Martin and M. Rodeheffer, Psychologic impact of child abuse, Journal of Pediatric Psychology, 1, 12-16 (Spring, 1976).

9. Martin, H.P. (Ed) (1976): The Abused Child: A Multidisciplinary Approach to Developmental Issues and Treatment, Cambridge, Mass, Ballinger.

10. Canosa, C. (Ed) (1975): Nutrition, Growth and Development: Modern Problems in Pediatrics, Basel, Switzerland, Karger.

11. Chavez, A. (Ed) (1975): Prognosis for the Undernourished Surviving Child, Basel, Switzerland, Karger.

12. Prescott, J.W.,et al (Eds) (1975): Brain Function and Malnutrition: Neuropsychological Methods of Assessment, New York, Wiley.

13. Lloyd-Still, J.(Ed)(1976): Malnutrition and Intellectual Development, Littleton, Mass, Publishing Sciences Group.

14. Winick, M, (Ed) (1976): Malnutrition and Brain Development, New York, Oxford Univ. Press.

15. H. Birch and A. Leffard, Intersensory development in children, Monograph Society Research in Child Development, 28, 1-48 (1963).

16. J. Cravioto, et al, Nutrition, growth, and neurointegrative development: An experimental and ecologic study, Journal of Pediatrics, 38, 319-372 (1966).

17. Hoorweg, J.D. (Ed) (1976): Protein-Energy Malnutrition and Intellectual Abilities, The Hague, Netherlands, Mouton.

18. B. Steele, Working with abusive parents: From a psychiatric point of view, U.S. Dept. of HEW - Office of Child Development, #OHO75-70 (1975).

19. I. Hendrick, Instinct and the ego during infancy, Psychoanalytic Quarterly, 11, 33-58 (1942).

20. R.W. White, Ego and reality in psychoanalytic theory, Psychological Issues, 3, 1-196 (1963).

Child Abuse and Neglect, Vol. 3, pp. 423 - 428.
© Pergamon Press Ltd., 1979. Printed in Great Britain.

0145-2134/79/0601-0423 $02.00/0.

RECOGNITION OF SIGNS OF EMOTIONAL DEPRIVATION: A FORM OF CHILD ABUSE.

DR. DERMOD MACCARTHY.

THE INSTITUTE OF CHILD PSYCHOLOGY. 6 PEMBRIDGE VILLAS, LONDON W11 2SU.

The reason for presenting the subject of emotional privation or maternal rejection in the context of a symposium on child abuse is that it affords another example, with a different presentation, of a child evoking hostility in a parent. The maladjustment is however more continuous and less impulsive so that the child escapes the severer forms of abuse resulting in injuries that require treatment, but suffers instead from a gradual impairment of health, growth and personality development. A syndrome of dwarfism with other physical signs and characteristic behaviour is produced, which when discovered in early childhood is a certain sign of long standing severe emotional privation. The consequences of this to mental health in childhood and after are serious. Although well known to some the picture in all its physical and behavioural manifestations is perhaps not sufficiently widely recognised, especially as fringe forms exist for which, if taken in time, intervention might be more effective.

Description of the syndrome. The clinical picture has been described by a number of authors working on particular aspects of the problem, viz. : Maternal Deprivation Syndrome,[1] Deprivation Dwarfism, Maternal Rejection and Stunting of Growth,[2] Psycho-social Dwarfism, the Maltreatment Syndrome[3] and Non-organic failure to thrive.[4]
Imagine a child between 2½ to 4 years of age.

(i) Stature:

The body proportions are infantile for their age, i.e. though the head is normal size for the age, the trunk is rather short and the legs distinctly short. The state of nutrition may be poor but is not one of emaciation as a rule and they would appear to have enough flesh on their bones for them to be making some growth. Yet growth is at a standstill. (Hence the search for an endocrine cause by several teams of research workers).

(ii) An expression of dejection, apathy, indifference, submission.

(iii) Circulatory changes in the limbs. The hands and feet are cold and pink, or in winter cyanosed. Even in summer when not looking pink they feel cold. Small ulcers, ruptured chilblains or abraisons that do not heal are commonly present on both hands and feet. The condition is probably mainly due to inactivity, for these children spend much time standing around doing nothing or sitting on cold floors. It reminds one of "pink disease" (acrodynia) now a forgotten children's disease due to ingestion of mercury. It was associated with great apathy and mental misery. Cold extremities are found in anorexia nervosa, mental subnormality and in some children at boarding schools or normal children with so-called poor circulation, so this is not a specific diagnostic sign of emotional deprivation. However, all the above conditions, excepting normal children, have in common some degree of mental depression causing inertia. The degree of circulatory stasis in the limbs therefore becomes significant. An extreme form was described in the 19th century as "oedème blue" (Charcot's blue oedema) in which an arm might become so swollen blue and ulcerated as to invite a decision to amputate; the condition responding however to psychotherapy! Healthy babies quite commonly have rather pink hands and feet, but a marked degree of coldness, pinkness or blueness must arouse suspicion, for babies also are capable of feeling lonely, deprived, rejected.

(iv) The Hair:

Hair which is coarse, lacking in lustre and becoming thin is, when associated with dwarfism, suggestive of hypothyroidism. Thyroid hormone deficiency has not however been found present in these children. True alopecia areata is sometimes present and this by reputation is strongly associated with nervous stress.

(v) "Catatonia" (flexibilitas cerea). To anyone accustomed to the clinical examination of children the compliance and passivity of these, with the deprivation syndrome, is quite striking. Furthermore when put in some staturesque position they will retain it for several minutes while the observer is busy with something else or even leaves the room; whereas normal children will not hold the pose for more than a few seconds or half a minute. What does it signify? Zchizophrenia? No. Excessive obedience? Possibly. A passive attitude? Certainly. These children are unable to produce any counter aggression and are easily bullied by others.

(vi) Eating and digestion: Highly characteristic feeding behaviour is described by the mother or observed when the child is admitted to hospital: sometimes a reluctance to swallow and the holding of food for a long time in the mouth without swallowing, or the converse gulping it down like a dog; eating of scraps out of dustbins or picked up out of doors; scavenging, or eating the leavings on other children's plates or pets' food. Some mothers say the child eats "nothing", others that he "eats a lot"; more than the other children. Stealing of food is common and when left alone with food the child may gorge himself to the point of vomiting. When in hospital these children eat prodigiously and seem to have no sense of satiety. While under the depriving conditions they commonly have a gassy abdomen and loose stools resembling coeliac disease. No malabsorption state has been demonstrated on investigation, however.

(vii) State of nutrition: Although generally below the expected weight for height (dwarfed) and sometimes much under weight they do not present a "famine" picture. There are some rare exceptions however (see below). Where conditions have permitted gorging, or during a period of plentiful meals, as in hospital before a growth spurt can begin, they will become well nourished or even obese. There is also the hypothesis that the so-called well-nourished dwarf having become accustomed to a meagre food supply is able to maintain health, and energy from the limited calories available, by preserving his essential proteins and diminishing nitrogen excretion almost to zero.[5,6] But without additional protein he cannot grow.

Good evidence is available that the stunting of growth begins in the first year of life. At this period growth is faster than at any subsequent time in childhood[7] and the moderate or severe failure to thrive that goes with emotional deprivation or maternal rejection profoundly reduces it, and when continuing for several years the ultimate potential height is impaired. Babies are occasionally taken into hospital, supposedly for gastro enteritis or malabsorption states, who are simply being starved. There could hardly be a greater expression of maternal rejection than this. Nor could we have greater doubts about the wisdom of returning a child to his mother for future up-bringing than in such a case.

(viii) Language development is retarded.

(ix) Overall development and maturation impaired.

Intelligence tends to be poor. If undernutrition is the true cause of the dwarfism and has been present from the early months, then brain growth may have been influenced; but under-stimulation and lack of exploratory drive must contribute very much to the impoverishment of mental performance in these early years.[8]

(x) Characteristic behaviour: (a) at home; inability to play, alone or with others; solitariness, lack of normal aggression, but provoking aggression in other children and parents. Encopresis and enuresis common, but these are non specific symptoms of distress. Lack of attachment and affectionate bonding with the mother is shown by their indifference to being separated and absence of anyfretting behaviour when taken into hospital.

(b) in hospital or with foster parents; they become cheerful and active in a few days and seem to thrive in any atmosphere of normal care and kindness. After a while they resort to attention seeking (i.e. attention needing) from adults and become indiscriminately and shallowly affectionate towards them. Unpleasant traits such as spitefulness, cheekiness and selfishness begin to appear and petty stealing is common. Bad temper tantrums occur easily when frustrated and in younger children this may go with aggressive soiling, bed stripping and faecal smearing. All this is well known 'deprived child behaviour'. Unfortunately it persists long after removal from the depriving conditions of home and language development is very slow to improve.[9]

(xi) The diagnosis of rejection and emotional deprivation.

Although this may confidently be inferred from the presence of the above physical signs and behaviour traits, there should be positive confirmation of the psychological diagnosis. Sometimes it is openly admitted by the mother. Sometimes it is conscious but denied. She points to her other children who are thriving, as proof that she is a good mother. Sometimes it is unconscious and therefore denied. Sometimes it is an intermittent state. In any case evidence of a rejecting attitude is afforded by lack of concern over illness, nutrition, the state of the skin and by the disparaging, hostile or embittered tone with which the mother speaks about her child. It is common to find a depriving childhood in the personal history of the mother. The assessment of 15 mothers of 16 children (two of them were siblings) seen consecutively was as follows:-

Incompatibility	1	(baby fostered with a view to adoption, but failed to thrive).
Inadequate	2	(poor intelligence, lack of imagination, lack of normal concern).
Depressed	3	(This was a reactive depression. One mother was pregnant).
Rejecting	10	(conscious hostility, or ambivalence or unconscious rejection).

(xii) Explanation of the syndrome. An explanation of the dwarfism and failure to thrive (which involves failure of linear growth as well as ponderal growth) in terms of nutrition is supported by strong evidence. Children with a long history of feeding difficulties, fads, and food battles grow up with a significantly shorter stature, though within the normal range, than others without these problems.[10] Studies of infants aged 6 months to 2 years in hospital and in their homes, with severe failure to thrive and signs of deprivation[11] have shown (a) that when an adequate calorie intake is assured the children will put on weight dramatically, (b) that mother's statements as to her (rejected) child's food consumption are unreliable and (c) that rejecting mothers are indifferent as to how little or how seldom her child eats. There is also the world wide and timeless observation that severe food shortage stunts growth. Inventories made of the diets of children living at home with non-organic failure to thrive have revealed that the calorie value of the food they eat is little more than half the accepted amount for normal children.[12] Impairment of digestion by emotional upset is well supported by observations and by a certain amount of experimental work.[13]

We have to assume then that the infant or young child who is rejected or emotionally deprived is under-eating (a) because he is given too little and in spite of hunger is too depressed, too passive to protest or take what he wants or (b) because his depression or emotional apathy makes him anorexic.

(xiii) Is Deprivation Dwarfism an Indocrine Disorder?

It has been suggested [1] that the mental state of being constantly rejected and emotionally deprived reverberates upon the hypothalamus (rhinencephalon or "visceral" brain) to cause a disturbance of growth hormone release. Investigations carried out at home before the effects of a better ambiance have begun to work, have indeed shown abnormally low levels of G.H. and depressed responses to growth hormone stimulation tests in a few cases.[14] Other investigations have however been unable to confirm these findings.[12] In many conditions involving malnutrition or starvation fasting growth hormone levels are in fact raised. The hypothesis of functional pituatary deficiency with growth hormone insufficiency requires proof only for the sake of its interest, for we know that as soon as the child is released from the depriving conditons and the under-eating that goes with them, catch-up growth begins and continues till his stature is within the normal range and no persistent endocrine insufficiency will ever be found.

(xiv) Role of fathers. Fathers often show concern for these children but seem to be unable to prevent the damage that is going on; perhaps because of insufficient contact or because of their own too great dependency on this mother. At all events their contributions as husbands or as fathers to the family life, when studied, have been found to be minimal.[4]

(xv) Similarities with the "battered child syndrome".

Signs of maltreatment are a common additional clinical finding, but more serious forms of abuse involving fractures, in the author's experience, are exceptional. Certain features in the mother's story are however common to both syndromes and their pathways of determination.

(a) a childhood of privation of maternal love and concern
(b) a concept of self as "no good"
(c) paternity of child in doubt
(d) child not of the marriage, or of the cohabitation
(e) child not the wanted sex
(f) parents socially isolated
(g) child is identified with something or someone who is hated

When this syndrome of physical appearances with dwarfism is encountered in a child it is, alas, a certainty that great harm to her or his emotional development has occurred and will continue if no work on behalf of the child and family is undertaken. It is therefore important that the features should be as widely known as possible. Minor degress of the syndrome, especially in the youngest range and babies, may then be recognised and treated, with better chances of success.

References:

1 Patton, R.G. and Gardner, L.I. (1962), "Influence of Family Environment on Growth: the Syndrome of 'Maternal Deprivation'." Pediatrics,30,957-962.

2 MacCarthy D. and Booth, E.M. (1970). "Parental Rejection and Stunting of Growth," J.Psychosomatic Res.,14,259-265.

3 Fontana, U.J. et al.(1963), "The 'Maltreatment Syndrome' in Children," New England J. Med.,269, 1389-1394.

4 Togut M.R. et al. (1969), 'A Psychological Exploration of the Nonorganic Failure to Thrive Syndrome," Dev.Med.Ch.Neurol.,11,601-607.

5 Talbot N.B. et al. "Dwarfism in Healthy Children: Its Possible Relation to Emotional, Nutritional and Endocrine Disturbances," New Engl.J.Med., 263, 783-793. (1947)

6 Waterlow J.C. (1968), "Observations on the Mechanism of Adaptation to Low Protein Intake," Charles West Lecture delivered in London, October 3rd, Lancet,ii,1091-1097.

7 Hubble D.V.(1957), "Hormonal Influence on Growth," Brit.med.J.,i, 601-607.

8 Cravioto,J. and Delicardie, E.R. (1966),"Nutrition, Growth and Neurointegrative Development," Supplement to Pediatrics,38,319-372.

9 Cooper C.E. Personal communication.

10 Brandon,S.(1970),"Epidemiological Study of Eating Disturbances," J.Psychosomatic Res., 14, 253-257.

11 Whitton C.F. et al. (1969), "Evidence that Growth Failure from Maternal Deprivation is Secondary to Undereating," J.Amer.med.Ass., 209, 1675-1682.

12 Apley, J. et al. (1971), "Dwarfism Without Apparent Cause." Proc.roy.Soc.Med. 64, 135-138.

13 Widdowson, E.M. (1951), "Mental Contentment and Physical Growth", Lancet,i, 1316-1318.

14 Powell, G.F. et al. (1967), "Emotional Deprivation and Growth Retardation Simulating Idiopathic Hypopituitarism," New.Engl.J.Med., 276, 1271-1283.

LIST OF SLIDES ILLUSTRATING THE PAPER

Growth

1. Dwarfed girl with control, 9 months older.
2. List of physical features of the syndrome.
3. Boy with characteristic aspect.
4. Infantile body proportions.
5. A "well nourished dwarf".
6. Cystic fibrosis. Good leg length because of late onset of failure to thrive.
7. Giardiasis. Similar picture; girl aged 6.

Circulatory changes in the limbs.

8. Baby with acrocyanosis.
9. Same baby naked.
10. Pseudo - acrodynia.
11. Marasmus precipitated by acute infection.
12. Gross neglect and lack of concern.
13. Incipient gangrene of toe
14. Same; detail
15. The child as a whole.
16. Same child , periods of complete growth arrest.
17. Four years later, after catch-up growth
18. Amenorrhoea and slowing of growth on returning home after residential school.

The hair

19. Thinning on crown of head.
20. Unexplained cuts in scalp.

Characteristic behaviour of child

21. List of behaviour traits.

Character disorder in the mother

22. the cycle of deprivation.
23. the pathway to rejection.

Examples of simple starvation

24. Boy. (by permission of Dr Buchanan)
25. Boy. " " " " "
26. Baby girl, and later appearance.
27. Same child thriving in hospital.
28.) 29.) 30.) Onset of deprivation syndrome after change from hospital to foster-mother(1) then to foster-mother (2).
31. Catatonia.

Catch - up growth.

32. Example in boy 3 to 4 years
33. Example in boy aged 4 to 8 years.

Hormonal theories

34. Growth hormone assays on one patient.

Nutritional theories.

35. Effect of protein deficiency and of severe calorie deficiency(piglets)
36. Rate of growth in early childhood. Critic-al years for calorie deprivation.

Child Abuse and Neglect, Vol. 3, pp. 429 - 438.

0145-2134/79/0601-0429 $02.00/0.

EARLY SIGNS AND SYMPTOMS IN NEGLECTED CHILDREN

Elisabeth Jakobsson, Dagmar Lagerberg and Monica Ohlsson/PRU team

Department of Child Psychiatry, Academic Hospital, S-750 14 Uppsala, Sweden
Department of Paediatrics, Academic Hospital, S-750 14 Uppsala, Sweden

Since the beginning of 1976, a multi-disciplinary study of children at risk of physical and emotional damage in their homes has been in progress in Uppsala, Sweden. In this paper an account is given of disturbances and symptoms shown by the children.* The term "neglect" is used as a common designation for abuse, neglect and unfavourable home conditions.

MATERIAL AND METHODS

The following criteria were applied for inclusion in the material:

1. The first criterion was provided by the formulations of the Swedish Child Welfare Act, § 25 a:

   The social service agency is directed to take measures...
   if anyone below the age of 18 years is being abused in his/her home or is otherwise treated there in a manner that endangers his physical or mental health, or if his development is being jeopardized by incompetence of his parents or other fosterer as a fosterer or their incapability to foster him.

2. The families were to be selected by the social workers. It was expected that the workers should feel concerned about the well-being of the children. This concern thus functioned as a second criterion. The cases could be old or new.

3. The third requirement was that the children be of preschool age, 0 to 7 years. Of course, there could be older siblings in the family.

4. The selection of cases was restricted to one of Uppsala's four social service districts.

By this procedure 26 families with a total of 50 children were selected by the local social workers. As far as we know, physical abuse or beating was occurring or suspected in 10 children. Nineteen children were neglected in the strict sense of the word. Although abuse or neglect, according to these estimates, was occurring in 13 of the families, it was the general climate of instability and emotional deprivation that seemed the most alarming to the social workers. An obvious feature of the families was their multi-problem characteristic. There was a concentration of interwoven and mostly inveterated social, economic, psychological and medical problems, which exposed the children to varying kinds of risks.

Cases were discussed in weekly team conferences. The role of the team was advisory, and not

---

* Other papers emanating from the study are:
"A Multi-disciplinary Approach to the Child Abuse and Neglect Problem" (Gustafsson, Lagerberg and Larsson) and "Life Style Patterns in Families with Neglected Children" (Lagerberg, Nilsson and Sundelin).

responsibility-sharing. After an interval of at least one year, the case was followed up. On both occasions a record was written. The record was unstructured and based on the verbal report of the social worker. Variables in the statistical sense were not used in this context.

The process applied engenders some problems. Data gathering may be unsystematic and yield information which is vague. Sometimes important facts may be forgotten, which results in under-reporting. Furthermore, the team's knowledge of the families remains second-hand, since it is based on hearsay, except when some team member is already involved in a case and able to recognise it. The families' identities were not revealed to the team. The method of gathering information was chosen, despite its deficiencies, because it was expected to facilitate collaboration with the social workers, who were already overwhelmed by duties and would probably appreciate informal discussions where they would not have to reveal the identity of their clients.

Some children were already in foster care or in a children's home, which may have been inconsistent with our first criterion (see above). In these cases the discussion mainly concerned the future placement of the child.

The major part of the information was thus derived from the accounts of the social workers. However, data about the children were also gathered from the outpatient child health centres.*

A questionnaire was prepared and sent to the nurses responsible for the child health centres to which our children belonged. In order to provide control groups, it was required that the same questionnaire be filled in on behalf of two additional children. The control children were selected as follows:

Control 1: First child encountered after the proband child in the register, living with both parents.

Control 2: Same procedure as for control 1, except that this child was required to live with only one parent.

Control 1, consequently, represented a "normal" group and control 2 a group traditionally considered as a risk category.

Some methodological problems have to be mentioned. The probands and controls were not matched according to sex - a major defect since the proband boys outweigh the proband girls (Table 1) - nor according to family type. The latter was due to the fact that the probands could live in single-parent as well as complete families. To divide the probands according to family type would be difficult, since the patterns were transitory in this group.

The selection procedure implies a reasonably, though not entirely, safe age matching. The control children will be slightly younger than the probands, since the nurses were instructed to go forwards in the register (which is arranged according to time of birth). In one case, where there were difficulties in finding a control 2, the nurse was told to go backwards instead. The main difference between probands and controls was that the probands were, by definition, known to the social agencies as difficult cases, whereas for the controls this risk was the same as for the population at large.

A few probands had just started school or were on the point of doing so. If their records had been sent on to the school, data were provided by the school health nurses instead of nurses at the child health centres.

---

*In Sweden child health care is the responsibility of the county councils. The system is uniformly organized over the country and embraces all children from birth to the start of school, when the child health care records are sent on to the school health authorities. Registration of all preschool age children with the centres is compulsory, while actual participation takes place on a voluntary basis. The services are used for about 99 per cent of infants below one year. Participation is also high in older age groups. The centres provide regular examinations, screening of vision and hearing, rickets prophylaxis and inoculations. When the child is four years old, the "four-year control" is offered to the family. This is a thorough examination of the child's physical, emotional, language and motor development, vision and hearing etc.

The number of probands for whom child health care data were collected differs from the total given in Table 1. The reason is that answers for some probands still remain to be gathered (moved out of town, school closed, child born at a late stage of the study, indecisiveness about whether an older half-sibling should be included or not). In some cases no control 2 could be found or the nurse felt uncertain about the selection procedure. The probands are therefore more numerous than the controls. The n value of control group 1 also exceeds that of group 2.

The distribution of the probands by age (year of birth) and sex is shown in Table 1.

TABLE 1 Distribution of Probands by Year of Birth and Sex

Year of birth	Boys	Girls	Both sexes
1969	2	1	3
1970	3	1	4
1971	5	5	10
1972	1	4	5
1973	4	4	8
1974	3	3	6
1975	8	-	8
1976	2	2	4
1977	2	-	2
Total	30	20	50

Our findings will be presented in two parts in the following. The controlled study is reported on in the next section. The following part concerns the probands alone and describes some mental, behavioral, somatic and psycho-somatic aspects.

COMPARISON OF PROBANDS AND CONTROLS

In the controlled study, based on reports from the child health centres, eleven variables were used. The answer categories were: "yes", "no", and "information lacking". The variables were:

1) complicated pregnancy, 2) complicated delivery, 3) separation from mother during first year of life, 4) inpatient hospital care, 5) visit to the outpatient (hospital) paediatric clinic (data about items 4 and 5 are routinely supplied to the child health centres), 6) disturbances in weight development (defined in terms of slowness and unevenness), 7) disturbances in height development, 8) disturbances in psychomotor development, 9) disturbances in language development, 10) significant findings at the four-year control, 11) special problems (e.g. feeding, sleeping).

The first four items were inspired by the findings of Lynch (1975), who revealed significant correlations between abnormalities of pregnancy and of delivery, early separations and early illnesses in the child, on the one hand, and subsequent abuse, on the other.

The last item (item 11) has been excluded here since it appeared to overlap too much with the others and the information given was highly variable.

Table 2 shows the percentages of positive answers to the ten remaining items. The statistical calculations relate to proband-control comparisons. Percentages are given instead of absolute numbers because of the differences in n values.

It is seen in the table that the probands and controls differed in several respects. Pregnancy and delivery complications, however, did not differ significantly between the groups. Separations were recorded more often for probands than for either control group. The nature of these separations varied; hospitalization was most frequent. There were also placements in foster homes, children's homes and with relatives.

TABLE 2 Positive Answers (per cent) from the Child Health Centres

Item	Proband group n=44	Control 2 (single parent) n=38	Control 1 (both parents) n=41
1. Complicated pregnancy	16	13	12
2. Complicated delivery	11	11	27
3. Separation from mother during first year of life	41	13**	20*
4. Inpatient hospital care	64	26***	39*
5. Visit to the outpatient paediatric clinic	75	76	54
6. Disturbances in weight development	30	8*	2***
7. Disturbances in height development	14	0*	2
8. Disturbances in psychomotor development	25	0***	2**
9. Disturbances in language development	36	8***	5***
10. Significant findings at the four-year control	34	18*	15**
Mean number of positive items (out of 10 possible)	3.9	1.7	1.8
Range	0-9	0-5	0-6

*$p < 0.05$
**$p < 0.01$
***$p < 0.001$

The separation variable reflects the high frequency of hospitalization in the probands. Therefore, items 3 and 4 partly overlap each other. By way of distinction, however, the hospital care item covers the child's whole life, not only the first year. Both separation and hospital care show statistically significant differences between probands and controls.

Visits to the outpatient paediatric clinic were recorded more often, though not significantly so, for probands than for controls living with both parents. For controls with single parents the rate was about the same as for the probands. We assume that this fact reflects the vulnerability of many single parents whose anxiety is easily aroused by symptoms in the children.

Disturbances in weight development were significantly more frequent in the proband group. This also held true for height development when probands and single-parent controls were compared. Disturbances in psychomotor development were recorded for 25 per cent of the probands but very rarely for the controls (in fact, for none of controls 2). Language disturbances were found in 36 per cent of the probands, versus 8 and 5 per cent in controls 2 and 1, respectively. The differences in both these items were highly statistically significant. The four-year control revealed disturbances more often in the probands (also a statistically significant finding).

It would perhaps have been appropriate to exclude the very young children from items 9 and 10 (language development and four-year control), which are irrelevant in infants and toddlers. This has not been done, however, since the probands and controls appeared to be sufficiently well age matched.

The mean number of positive items was more than twice as high for probands as for controls (Table 2). None of the controls reached more than six positive items, whereas this was true for 16 per cent of the probands.

Table 3 shows the distribution of "developmental indices" in the three groups. An index was calculated on items 6-9, i.e. weight, height, psychomotor and language disturbances. Those with no disturbances recorded in these respects were scored 0, those with a positive answer to one item were scored 1, and so forth. A clear difference could be seen between the probands, on the one hand, and the two control groups, on the other. Just as before, the probands were more afflicted.

Parenthetically, it may be mentioned that controls 1 and 2 did not generally differ much from each other. This suggests that single parenthood is perhaps not a very great hazard in Sweden today, when the community provides health care for all children and financial support and day care facilities for single parents.

TABLE 3 Percentage Distributions of "Developmental Indices" for Probands and Controls

Developmental index	Proband group n=44	Control 2 (single parent) n=38	Control 1 (both parents) n=41
0	46	84	88
1	20	16	12
2	20	-	-
3	11	-	-
4	2	-	-
Total	100 (99)	100	100

The interpretation of the findings presented in this section involves some complications which should be considered. The separation and hospital care variables are theoretically somewhat unsatisfactory, since they may be interpreted both as dependent and independent in relation to developmental items. A child may become retarded or disturbed following separation or hospital care. But the reverse may also be true, with separation or hospitalization as a consequence of developmental disturbances. We are not, however, in a position to discuss this problem exhaustively in the present context.

It may be argued further that the figures just reflect our own selection procedures. If we define the probands as children with symptoms, it is only natural that higher frequencies of symptoms will be found among them than among controls. Our argument becomes a circle. However, this objection does not invalidate our results. The children came from families already known to the social agencies for various reasons, e.g. scarcity of financial resources or alcohol abuse.

Another complication is that in those cases where the child health nurse knew the family well, she may have been more prone to notice symptoms and disturbances, or to interpret normal behaviour as disturbed. The mere fact that she was asked by social agency personnel to fill in the questionnaire on behalf of a certain child may also have influenced her recording. In principle, the fact that the hospitalizations of the probands were so numerous may have had the same effect. Symptoms and disturbances in the controls were then perhaps overlooked. We do not, however, consider this objection significant. The communication between hospitals, social service agencies and child health centres is often superficial and does not generally make the nurses intimately acquainted with the children involved. Furthermore, the questionnaires were filled in from the routine records, which include such "hard" material as weight and height curves.

We thus consider that the findings may well be viewed in terms of unfavourable environmental conditions (cf. below).

THE PROBANDS

In this section an account will be given of some aspects of the mental and physical health of the probands. No control groups were used in this part of the study.

The social workers' descriptions confirm the child health centre data about the children's developmental disturbances. In addition, they give information concerning mental and behavioral items that are not always recorded by the child health centres.

Mental and Behavioral Disturbances

In several respects, common traits are displayed by the home conditions of the probands. They are typically characterized by a lack of security and continuity, by separations, by mental disturbances and/or drug or alcohol abuse in the parents, by variability and inconsistency in standards and rearing. It is to be expected that children living under conditions like these may react with mental and behavioral disturbances. High frequencies of disturbances were in fact found (Table 4). This was true in spite of the fact that six children were very young (born in 1976–77).

TABLE 4 Mental and Behavioral Disturbances in the Probands

Disturbance	Number of children n=50
Anxiety	14
Excessive adaptation	13
Aggressiveness/destructiveness	12
Contact disturbances/peer problems	10
Behaviour characterized by lack of distance	10
Hyperactive behaviour	8
Depressiveness	6

3–5 of the above: 15 children
2 " " " 8 "
1 " " " 7 "
0 " " " 20 " (including lack of information)

Sources: Reports by social workers and child health centre nurses.

As can be seen from the table, anxiety is the symptom most often recorded, followed by excessive adaptation. The "excessively adapted" children may be obedient, passive and unreacting. They may also assume a much greater responsibility for themselves, their sibs and sometimes also for their parents than is appropriate for their age. In eight cases, anxiety and adaptation are recorded for the same child. Aggressiveness/destructiveness and hyperactive behaviour coincide in seven children. The contact disturbances and peer problems described vary in character, e.g. difficulties in interacting in groups, and may sometimes relate to occasional events, in other cases to more significantly disturbed reactions. Distance-lacking behaviour, i.e. unselective contact-seeking with unknown adults, superficially and without shyness, is considered by us to be a serious mental symptom expressing a long-lasting lack of secure and continuous interaction with the parents. Six children display a depressive pattern which must also be regarded as a serious symptom.*

It follows from Table 4 (bottom) that several children in the study suffer from more than one symptom. Fifteen exhibit three to five of the symptoms listed in the table. Only twenty (less than half) have no records of mental or behavioral disturbances.

As few as thirteen children, i.e. about one-fourth, have seen a child psychologist or a child psychiatrist, which is remarkable. For three additional children arrangements have been made to see a psychiatrist or a psychologist, but the appointments have not been kept by the parents. Thirty-eight children, i.e. about four-fifths, have had access to day care centres, but their behaviour in this context has not been investigated by us.

*The data did not permit calculations of sleeping problems, encopresis, enuresis or other symptoms of regression.

Somatic and Psycho-somatic Symptoms

We have seen that the probands are characterized by high hospitalization rates. Both the social workers and the child health centre nurses have reported health problems.

Thirty-nine of the 50 children show physical symptoms and diseases or psycho-somatic symptoms which we consider significant. When calculating this, previous hospitalizations for unknown causes were included as signs of disease. Six children (12 per cent) suffer from serious, chronic or congenital somatic illnesses. These are:

Heart disease, skin defects of one arm, hand and chest with loss of sensation, severe impairment of vision, minimal brain dysfunction with developmental delays and motor disturbances, cystic fibrosis, and diabetes mellitus.

In a normal population of a Swedish county, the frequency of serious chronical illnesses in children aged 0-15 years has been calculated at 1.24 per cent (Herlitz and Redin 1956).

Nine children have vision problems and five hearing problems. In a normal population of four-year-olds, the rate of vision problems has been found to be 6.7 per cent and the rate of hearing impairments 1.6 per cent (Sundelin and Vuille 1975).

Sixteen children (32 per cent) have records of feeding disturbances or intestinal symptoms. For comparison it may be mentioned that in a study by Ohlsson and Östberg (1974) 20 per cent of parents of normal 5½-year-olds complained of previous food or feeding problems of a certain duration. We believe that many of the intestinal disturbances found in the neglected children may be psycho-somatic in nature.

The children in the study are affected in several ways. Seventeen suffer from disturbances in three respects: developmental (weight, height, psychomotor, language), mental/behavioral, and somatic/psycho-somatic. Sixteen are afflicted in two respects and ten in one. Only seven children are entirely free from recorded disturbances or illnesses.

In point of fact, it might not be surprising that children with somatic ailments occur frequently in the material. The figures may be due to the fact that handicapped children are more likely to get into contact with the social authorities. The seeming over-representation of somatic illnesses may, at least partly, be explained in this way.

SUMMARY AND CONCLUDING REMARKS

Summary

The findings in this study show that the probands, compared with control groups of children from single-parent and complete families, exhibit higher rates of disturbances of weight, height, psychomotor and language development. All these differences are statistically significant, except for the height variable when probands are compared with controls living with both parents. Furthermore, the probands have been separated from their mothers in their first year of life and also hospitalized to a significantly greater extent than the controls.

The neglected children display high rates of mental health and behavioral disturbances, in many cases of a serious nature. Their somatic health is generally impaired. They give evidence of a heavy pattern of physical illnesses and psycho-somatic symptoms, e.g. intestinal ailments.

When considering the symptoms of the children, it is important to observe the total picture. Many probands are disturbed in more than one respect, and only a few are "blank" in development as well as mental and somatic health.

The results of this study support the conclusion drawn in numerous other investigations of a high correlation between developmental disturbances and child abuse or neglect (e.g. Baher et al. 1976, Eppler and Brown 1976, Smith and Hanson 1974). Ohlsson (1976) has emphasized the relationship between emotional deprivation and weight disturbances. Martin (1976) has pointed out the challenging fact that abused children appear to show particularly severe disturbances in speech and gross motor development, more than in fine motor development, for example. Speech development has been considered especially sensitive to emotional stress and lack of stimulation (Klackenberg 1971, 1974), findings confirmed by the present data.

Interpretation of Results

The high rates of serious physical illnesses, psycho-somatic symptoms, developmental delays and mental disturbances in the neglected children studied may be interpreted in different ways. We believe, for instance, that both genetic/constitutional and environmental factors, e.g. insecurity and lack of stimulation, have occasioned developmental delays and disturbances. In several cases, concurring factors seem to be present. However, the data do not permit the exact proportions of external and internal aetiologies to be calculated.

It may, further, be hypothesized that in some cases illnesses and impairments have been the very determining factor engendering a family breakdown. Our families live burdensome lives. If, on top of that, they have a child with a physical or mental handicap, this may result in total incapability of mastering the situation (cf. Mattsson 1972).

To us, however, it seems important to consider signs and symptoms like those presented here mainly as consequences of environmental deficits. This kind of approach fosters prevention-prone attitudes and enhances societal efforts to help children at risk. Even where the picture is dominated by genetic factors, it may in fact be especially important to compensate for these factors by environmental improvements.

Nylander (1960) has extensively investigated children of alcoholic fathers. Social, mental, developmental, psychological and clinical characteristics were studied. The author draws the conclusion that when physical assessments fail to disclose the causes behind psycho-somatic symptoms of a certain duration, intensity and resistance to treatment, deficiencies in the home situation ought to be suspected.

When the children are trying to tell us - by displaying symptoms - that they are suffering, their unspecific messages must be understood and taken seriously. At the same time, it must be kept in mind that some children suffer without showing any symptoms at all.

Learning Problems

Many probands live chaotic lives. Their basis for a sane development is defective and they are probably impaired in intellectual and social respects. We believe that the children's emotional problems prevent them from learning effectively. Therefore, it seems to us of primary importance that their emotional needs be met for learning to take place. This view has significant implications for treatment planning. Steps taken to create security, continuity and emotional gratification must go abreast with teaching measures in these cases (cf. Martin and Miller 1976). Some special form of day care may be needed, different from the normal pre-school activity.

Professional Tasks

Attention should be paid to the probands' extensive records of medical contacts. They have visited the paediatric clinic, both as inpatients and outpatients. They have been examined at the child health centres. In some instances, their home conditions have been revealed by the personnel, but very often they have not, which may be due to professional inclinations or to a scarcity of time or resources for considering psycho-social aspects. This is unfortunate since rather few of our children have seen a child psychologist or a child psychiatrist (cf. above).

Investigations have shown that a large proportion of paediatric visits are caused by psycho-somatic ailments and that the doctor is often ignorant about the total family situation (Jonsell 1974, Norstedt 1971). Our study confirms the opinion that health and medical personnel may overlook psycho-social realities and focus entirely on somatic symptoms. It is a matter of importance that child health centre and hospital personnel consider the total family situation in emotional and sociological terms when they see children with developmental disturbances or somatic/psycho-somatic symptoms.

In this context we want to emphasize the value of deeper collaboration between social workers, child health centre nurses, child psychologists and child psychiatrists. Families with neglected children very often express negative attitudes towards social service agencies. It is possible that inter-disciplinary work involving several professions may promote more positive and supportive contacts.

The present investigation should primarily be viewed as a pilot study. Some of the data are unsystematic and vague, which makes them unsuitable for quantitative descriptions. Underreporting of symptoms may have occurred. The numbers are small. Nevertheless, our findings provide a fruitful basis for continued research. We believe they indicate basic characteristics of neglected children. All professionals working with children at risk must inquire about developmental delays, mental and psycho-somatic symptoms and other signs. They must know their significance and consider them seriously. Perhaps some procedure of this kind should be included in the routine examination schedules of social, health and medical agencies.

REFERENCES

Baher, E., Hyman, C., Jones, C., Jones, R., Kerr, A. and Mitchell, R. (1976) At risk: An account of the work of the battered child research department, NSPCC. Routledge & Kegan Paul, London and Boston.

Eppler, M. and Brown, G. (1976) Child Abuse and Neglect: Preventable causes of Mental Retardation. World Health Organization: International Congress on Child Abuse and Neglect, p. 123. Geneva, Switzerland.

Herlitz, G. and Redin, B.: Children chronically diseased. Acta paediat. 45, 85 (1956).

Jonsell, R. (1974) Patienter som söker barnmedicinsk öppen vård (Patients seeking outpatient paediatric medical care). Umeå.

Klackenberg, G.: A prospective longitudinal study of children. Data on psychic health and development up to 8 years of age. Dissertation. Acta paediat., Suppl. 224 (1971).

Klackenberg, G.: Förskoleåldrarnas föränderliga symptombild. Något om förutsägbarhetens begränsningar. (The changing pattern of symptoms in preschool age children. A few notes about the limits of predictability.) Socialmed. tidskr. 51, 88 (1974).

Lynch, M.A.: Ill-health and Child Abuse. The Lancet, August 16, 317 (1975).

Martin, H.P. (1976) Neurologic Status of Abused Children. Chapter 6 in: Martin, H.P. (ed.): The Abused Child. A Multidisciplinary Approach to Developmental Issues and Treatment. Cambridge, Massachusetts.

Martin, H.P. and Miller, T. (1976) Treatment of Specific Delays and Deficits. Chapter 14 in: Martin, H.P. (ed.): The Abused Child. A Multidisciplinary Approach to Developmental Issues and Treatment. Cambridge, Massachusetts.

Mattsson, Å.: Long-term physical illness in childhood: A challenge to psychosocial adaptation. Pediatrics 50, 801 (1972).

Norstedt, S.: Psykisk och psykosomatisk sjukdom hos barn i allmänpraktik (Psychological and psycho-somatic diseases in children in general practice). Läkartidn. 68, 105 (1971).

Nylander, I.: Children of Alcoholic Fathers. Dissertation. Acta paediat., Suppl. 121 (1960).

Ohlsson, A.: Störningar i föräldra-barn-relationen under späd- och småbarnsåldern (Disturbances in the parent-child relationship in infancy and early childhood). Paediatricus 6, 28 (1976).

Ohlsson, M. and Östberg, M. (1974) En undersökning rörande behovet av psykologisk rådgivning på barnavårdscentraler inom Uppsala kommun (An investigation on the need for psychological counselling at child health centres in the municipality of Uppsala).

Dissertation. Pedagogiska institutionen, Uppsala universitet.

Smith, S.M. and Hanson, R.: 134 Battered Children: A Medical and Psychological Study. British Medical Journal, September 14, 666 (1974).

Sundelin, C. and Vuille, J.-C.: Health Screening of Four-year-olds in a Swedish County. II. Effectiveness in Detecting Health Problems. Acta paediat. 64, 801 (1975).

Child Abuse and Neglect, Vol. 3, pp. 439 - 447.

0145-2134/79/0601-0439 $02.00/0.

PSYCHOSOCIAL DWARFISM: DETECTION, EVALUATION AND MANAGEMENT

Nancy J. Hopwood, M.D. and Dorothy J. Becker, M.B., B.Ch., F.C.P. (Paed)
University of Michigan Medical Center, Ann Arbor, Michigan and Children's Hospital of Pittsburgh, Pittsburgh, Pennsylvania, USA

ABSTRACT

Our experience with 35 children with psychosocial dwarfism (PSD) over five years is reviewed. Diagnosis and management are difficult. A multidisciplinary approach to the evaluation allows for maximal observation of family psychodynamics and intervention. Foster placement remains the intervention of choice in children over four years of age.

INTRODUCTION

Environmentally-induced growth retardation associated with psychosocial deprivation, emotional stress and/or neglect is probably the most common single cause of deviant growth in infants and children in the United States today. All too often, however, the child's small stature is ascribed to other etiologies because environmental factors are unappreciated. In 1967, Powell and associates described 13 young children with severe growth retardation, developmental delay, and bizarre behavior who had histories suggestive of emotional deprivation (1). These children were found to have hypopituitarism which resulved with change in their environment (2). Catch-up in physical and emotional growth was often dramatic. This syndrome of deprivation or psychosocial dwarfism has subsequently become more widely recognized by pediatric endocrinologists but it still remains often undiagnosed by many health professionals. It is important that there be awareness of this condition because earlier detection may help to prevent physical and developmental lags which often appear to be irreversible when intervention is delayed.

We have had wide experience with children with psychosocial dwarfism (PSD) over the age of two years who have had extensive initial medical evaluations and long term follow-up. Family assessment and intervention has often been difficult and frustrating. Our present approach to the evaluation and management of these children is based on this experience and is outlined in this report.

METHODS

The 35 children reported here represent approximately 70 percent of children over the age of two years that the authors have personally seen in whom the diagnosis of PSD was suspected or made between 1973 and 1978. Only the children for whom thorough initial evaluation and/or follow-up information is available have been included. The diagnosis of PSD was made in all instances by demonstration of behavioral, physical and/or hormonal changes during a diagnostic hospitalization and/or during subsequent foster placement. All children were referred to general pediatric or pediatric endocrine clinics or services of the University of Michigan Medical Center, Ann Arbor, Michigan or Children's Hospital, Pittsburgh, Pennsylvania for evaluation of small size. All children were seen and evaluated by one or both authors. Rarely was the family the initiator in seeking medical evaluation. Referral resulted from physicians and community clinics by concerned schools, Protective Service workers, public health nurses, neighbors or relatives. At least 17 children had been known to Children's Protective Services in the past. Three had previously been in foster homes and returned home after 6-18 months when they were less than two years of age.

TABLE 1 Early Developmental History

	Number of Children
Difficult Pregnancy	11
Difficult Birth	10
Neonatal Illness	13
Prematurity	4
Twin	2
Early Feeding Difficulty	7
Slow Developmental Milestones	
Speech	16
Motor	16
Hospitalizations for Failure to Thrive	6
Caretaker First 3 mo. Not Mother	6
Physical Abuse	13
Prior Protective Service Referral	17
Prior Foster Placement < 2 Years of Age	3

Patients

The patient population consisted of 35 children, 21 boys and 14 girls. Mean age was 5.7 years (range 2.0-14.0 years). All had growth retardation (4 to 10 standard deviations below the mean height for chronologic age). There were three sibling pairs. No child had prior evidence of organic illness which might have been a contributing factor to his or her growth retardation. Growth velocities of 14 children were unknown. The remaining 21 children were all growing less than 4.0 cm./year; half of these had essentially no linear gain for 6 to 12 months prior to admission.

Diagnostic Procedures

Thirty-two of the children were hospitalized for periods of two to four weeks for initial diagnostic evaluation; four of these children remained hospitalized for several additional weeks while management plans were being developed. Three children were seen in consultation after hospitalization elsewhere or after placement in foster homes and the evaluation was done in the outpatient clinic. A multidisciplinary team approach was used to evaluate most children and to provide serial observations of the child's behavior, eating pattern, child-parent interaction as well as interpersonal relationships with hospital staff and peer groups. The majority of children were seen by several pediatricians, nursing staff, a social worker, a child psychologist and/or a child psychiatrist. The presence or absence of poor sleeping, hoarding of food, self-destructive behavior, temper tantrums, enuresis, vomiting and abnormal stools were recorded. Diets were unlimited and daily caloric intake was recorded. Periodic team meetings were useful for sharing information, interpretation of the changes in the child, and assessment of the families' ability to change, a factor which determined the basis for subsequent intervention and management.

A general medical diagnostic evaluation was completed for each child to exclude organic illness. In 30 children, investigation of the hypothalamic-pituitary-axis was performed by means of one or more of the following diagnostic tests: arginine-insulin infusion, oral glucose tolerance and/or metapyrone. Whenever possible, these tests were performed on the first or second hospital day and repeated after 10 to 20 days of observation.

RESULTS

Child's History

Early developmental histories were often difficult to obtain due to poor recall by the parent, absence of parent or reluctance to share information. Table 1 lists some of the identified problem areas, all of which are expected to be an underestimate of the true incidence. Developmental milestones, especially expressive language and gross motor skills, were delayed in 16 of the 28 children in whom some history was available. Most often problems were dated retrospectively to age 2-3 years, the time where growth deviation occurred or became more prominent.

TABLE 2 Symptoms and Behavior

	#/35	%
Polyphagia	30	86
Bizzare oral intake	19	54
Abdominal distension	17	49
Stealing or hoarding food	15	48*
Obsession with food	15	43
Vomiting	15	43
Increased number of stools	11	31
Encopresis	10	32*
Decreased food intake	7	20
Malodorous stools	7	20
Constipation	5	14
Enuresis	16	52*
Polydipsia	9	26
Polyuria	6	17
Drinking from toilet bowl	5	14
Temper tantrums	17	49
Withdrawn behavior	17	49
Poor peer or sibling interaction	17	49
Poor sleeping	15	43
Decreased physical activity	14	40
Increased physical activity	13	37
Destructive behavior	10	29
Pain Agnosia	10	29
Self injury	3	9

* Percentage of children over 4 years of age.

Symptoms and behaviors reported by the parents are listed in Table 2. An altered relationship with food was by far the most common symptom. Most children were reported to have a large appetite. Frequently it was voracious. Reports of ingestion of unusual or excessive quantities of food (a jar of mayonnaise, a loaf of bread, two whole pies, etc.) or non-food items (dirt, paper, crayons, hair, garbage, dog food) were common. Abdominal distension, vomiting, diarrhea and/or abnormal stools often followed such ingestions. This eating behavior was frequently accompanied by parental attempts to control types or quantity of food intake and would usually be followed by the child making night raids on the cupboards or refrigerator, hoarding, begging or stealing food from other people. Many of the children preferred to play in the kitchen, talked mostly about food and evidenced considerable animation and excitement in relating to food.

Regressive behaviors such as enuresis and temper tantrums were present in half the children at the time they were seen and had been present in the majority sometime in the past. Many parents reported their children as being withdrawn and seldom playing with siblings or peers. Behavior which alternated between periods of marked passitivity (e.g. sitting in one spot and staring at the floor) and hyperactivity (often leading to destructive behavior and temper tantrums) was common. Several parents complained about poor sleeping as their primary concern. Sometimes poor sleeping was accompanied by night eating, drinking or self-injury such as hair pulling (trichotillomania). Unusual thirst was also present in nine children; five were said to drink from the toilet bowl, one drank out of the fish bowl and another drank his urine.

Even though the histories were probably unreliable for some children, every child had at least one symptom listed in Table 2. The mean number of these behaviors for each child range was 8.7 (range 1-16). The behavioral history elicited often differed with each interviewer. A detailed retrospective review at each time period in the child's development was often necessary because many of the families did not view these behaviors as abnormal or disturbing.

Physical Appearance

All children were below the third percentile on the growth grid for both height and weight. Twenty-seven children were mildly underweight for height when weight age was compared with height age from the growth charts but their appearance suggested undernutrition in less than 10 percent. Head circumference was less than 2 S.D. for age in 12 children. Head circumference age (mean for normal children) was less than height age in 11 children. Immature body proportions, facies and dress were present in almost all children. Many had abdominal distension. While liver enlargement was occasionally noted on initial evaluation, it often became palpable during rapid weight gain. Many children had multiple bruises but only one child had overt evidence of other physical injury (burns) when initially seen.

Laboratory Studies

Common biochemical abnormalities included mild elevations of blood eosinophils, sedimentation rate, blood urea nitrogen, and SGOT. Three of 11 children had mild elevations of sweat sodium or chloride; one child had elevation to 73 mEq/L which gradually declined into the normal range during catch-up growth. Only one child had an initially low serum albumin. Stools were negative for ova and parasites in all but one child tested.

Endocrine testing revealed normal serum thyroxine in all except two children who had slightly low levels before but normal levels during catch-up growth. Twenty-four hour urinary 17-hydroxysteroids were less than 1.0 mg/day in 11/16 children, but responses to oral or intravenous metapyrone were usually normal (9/11). Some children had glucose intolerance and a paradoxical rise of serum growth hormone to oral glucose. Half the children tested (14/28) had blunted growth hormone release to provocative stimuli.

Bone maturation was delayed in all but one child and was compatible with height age. Skull roentgenograms were normal; approximately half the children who had repeat roentgenograms during catch-up growth had splitting of cranial sutures (3). Several children were noted to have gastric dilatation (4) and many had evidence of growth lines in the metaphyses of long bones (5).

Twelve children were studied serially for changes in fasting blood lipids after it was noted that marked abnormalities were often present. Turbidity of fasting serum and a distinctive pattern of changing lipids were observed during the first week. A dramatic rise in serum triglyceride (36-594%) occurred during the first four days in 10 children and returned to normal by day 6-8. Cholesterol rose more slowly, then also returned to normal. Lipoprotein electrophoreses were initially normal except for presence of chylomicrons in 6/12; during the first week of hospitalization of pre-beta band frequently appeared. During this time the serum turbidity cleared. Turbidity reoccurred after 13/18 parent visits and cleared again after parent-child separation. This observation was a useful diagnostic aid in assessing the stress of the parent-child interaction and in supporting the diagnosis of PSD.

Family History and Psychodynamics

Family history was often very difficult to obtain. Most families were guarded and were reluctant to share information. Many never admitted there were problems at all. Some parents agreed that discipline of the child was difficult, but in intact families it was unusual for them to admit that marital or other conflicts existed. Initially many of these families presented a facade of stability and appeared nurturing, a factor which had often delayed the correct diagnosis previously.

The natural parents were no longer living together in 14 cases; many of these parents had remarried prior to the onset of symptoms (as stated by the parent) in the child. Birth order in natural families was: first (5), second (19), third (6), fourth (1), fifth (2), sixth (1). Thirteen of the children were the youngest children in the family at the time of evaluation. Two children had been adopted in the first post-natal month. Three were only children.

Important diagnostic clues in the family included maternal depression, marital conflict, an angry-hostile parent, an emotionally absent father, physical abuse between parents or between parent and child, and history of deprivation in parental background. Multiple family stresses which included unemployment, financial difficulties, illness, drug abuse or alcoholism were common. Poor communication between parents was present in all families interviewed. Power struggles between parent and child usually focused around food. In almost all instances, one or both parents demonstrated denial about the child's small size. Failure-to-thrive was often present in other siblings (12/35) or in the extended family. Scapegoating of the child by the parents and/or siblings was documented in at least ten children. Symbiotic relationships between child and parent were common in the most severely delayed children.

Hospital Observations

All of the children were observed during their hospital stay at least part of the time without parental presence. The comparison of behaviors between child-parent and child-staff was extremely important both for diagnosis as well as for weight gain. Initially, most of the younger children showed decreased stranger anxiety and were indiscriminate in their affections with ward personnel. All children craved attention and preferred adult to peer interaction. Labile age appropriateness was often striking. In parental presence, speech was often immature and indistinct and behavior was frequently regressive. Careful documentation of the variability of behavior was very useful in the total assessment of the family psychopathology. Many children also showed pain agnosia initially to painful diagnostic procedures; usually this disappeared after the first week. Although hoarding of food was not uncommon, the absence of other bizarre behaviors frequently contrasted with parental histories. Weight gain was often dramatic (1-3 kg/week) and caloric intakes high. Some children who had a weight age appropriate for height age did not gain excessively; rather linear growth was detectable during the next four weeks. Psychologic and/or psychiatric evaluation revealed that most children were functioning in the mildly impaired intellectual range. Only three children had an IQ greater than 90 on initial testing. Many children were preoccupied with loss and rejection, appeared frightened, had poor self-esteem and evidence of limited emotional attachments

Management and Follow-up

Initial assessment showed that most families had minimal insight into family psychopathology and very little motivation to change. Seventeen children were discharged from the hospital into foster placements under court order. Three children were removed from the hospital against medical advice before intervention strategy could be completed. In these instances foster placement was delayed several weeks until court hearings could be held. Two children were voluntarily placed in foster care one and three months after discharge because of the striking regression and weight loss they demonstrated at home. Community intervention was attempted in the remaining 15 children. Day care programs, home visits by public health nurses and parental or family counseling were intervention strategies attempted in some instances. Eight of these children were subsequently placed in foster homes because they did not show normal or catch-up growth even when the family appeared to be cooperative. Most often, however, appointments to counseling or medical evaluations were not kept and minimal excuses were given by the parents.

Thirty-one children had evidence of rapid weight gain and/or linear growth during hospitalization. In two children weight gain was not significant but on the first follow-up clinic visit one to two months later, growth acceleration was noted, reflective of changes initiated during the observation period. Three of the older children (age 8, 9, 9 years), had some weight gain and hormonal changes during their hospitalization compatible with reversible hypopituitarism, but failed to have catch-up growth during six to 18 months of foster placement. Permanent hypopituitarism is now suspected.

Seven children remained in their natural homes. Of these, two families moved out of state immediately after hospitalization, and another was lost to follow-up after the family refused to keep appointments at a mental health clinic. One child was made a court ward in her own home, grew poorly, and later moved without trace. The youngest child, age two years, was said to begin to grow after public health nursing visits but has not been seen by us again. A severely delayed four year old boy who had a strong symbiotic relationship with his mother had begun to show catch-up growth when he entered day school prior to hospitalization. The family refused counseling, had marital conflicts and continuing stresses. Two subsequent reports to Protective Services were made by the school because of the presence of bruises. Catch-up growth and developmental progress has continued in the natural home, although at a slower rate than we would have anticipated in foster care. The final child, a five year old girl, remained in her natural home after her parents refused foster placement. Three months later after marital counseling, the parents separated. The child said shortly thereafter, "my mommy and daddy are no longer mad at me; they are now mad at each other". Only then did she begin to have continued catch-up growth and behavioral changes.

Follow-up of six months to five years ($\bar{x}$ 2.6 yrs) is available for 30 of the children. Parental rights have been terminated for nine children. Six of these children have been subsequently adopted; three of them into their original foster home. With regard to behavior, the children who have been adopted appear to have made the best adjustments. Eight children have had multiple placements due to continued behavior problems. Of these children, three were placed in residential centers at some time in their management. Frequent continued visitation with natural families often precipitated behavioral regression sometimes associated with deceleration in growth velocity. When this association was evident, usually further visitation with family members was limited. Figure 1 shows a development growth curve for the height of a 9 year old boy with PSD who had good initial catch-up in height when placed in a foster home at age 3 years as the only child. When his younger brother, also with PSD, joined him six months later, both boys had marked regressive and destructive behavior and cessation of emotional and physical growth. We saw him initially at age 5.5 years and recommended placement in new and separate environments where good catch-up growth initially occurred in both boys until one brother developed a symbiotic relationship with a member of the residential center staff. Linear growth thereafter was minimal for two years. Repeat hospitalization at age 9 years documented hypopituitarism which did not completely reverse in four weeks observation. An adoptive home subsequently rejected him because of unmanageable behavior after which he remained in a shelter until he entered a second adoptive home. While linear growth seems to be approximating normal, to date no catch-up growth has been demonstrated. It remains to be seen if this child has the potential for rebound growth after so long a period of growth suppression.

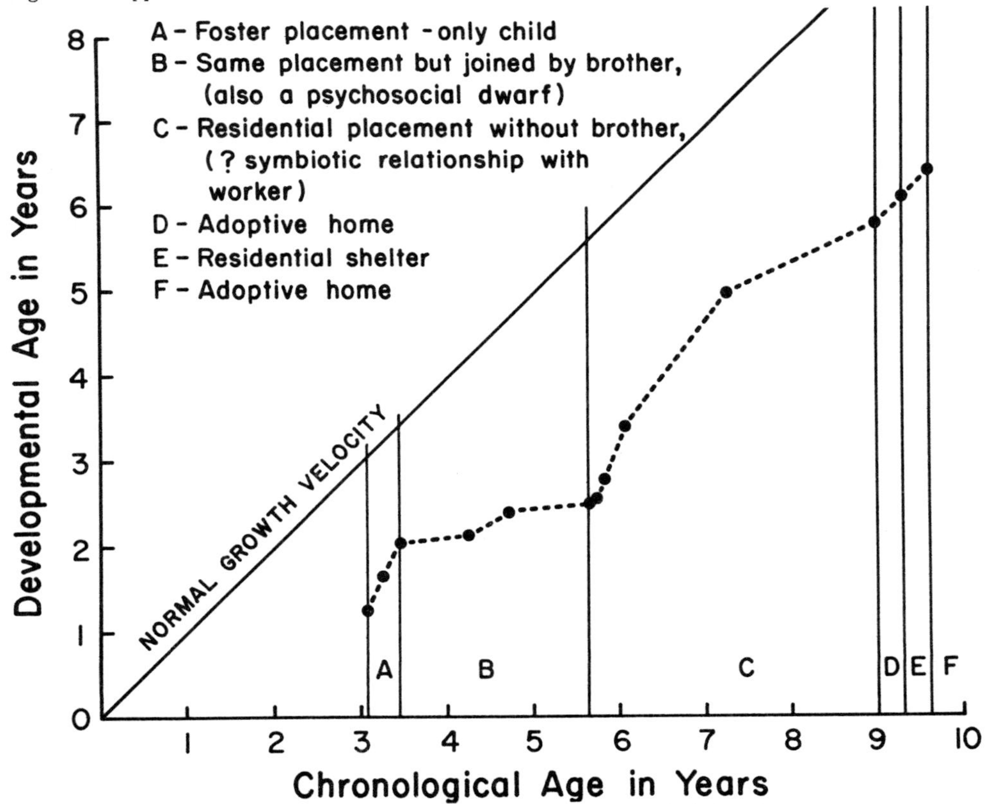

Fig. 1. Course for one of two brothers who had multiple placements (• = height)

Five boys who spent one to two years in foster placement have been returned to their natural homes. Two of these boys have been lost to follow-up. A third boy is said to be having severe behavior problems and remains very small but has not been seen by us. During the two years the fourth boy spent in foster care, his parents separated and divorced. During the first six months back in his mother's home, he continued to have a normal growth velocity but catch-up growth ceased. The family has subsequently failed to keep medical appointments over a nine month period. The fifth boy was returned home by the court after one year in foster placement where catch-up growth was noted. There was no growth or weight gain at all during the next six months in his natural home, necessitating placement into a second foster home where catch-up growth was again noted. The course of a sixth boy who will soon return home is shown in Fig. 2. Reversible hypopituitarism was documented on two occasions at age 4 and 5.5 years. Intervention over two years in the natural home was unsuccessful in reversing deviant velocity and severe developmental lags. After placement in a foster home at 6.5 years, he grew 30 cm. in the next 27 months. Placement of two infants into his foster home led to marked regression of behavior necessitating placement in a second foster home. He is now at the third percentile on the growth chart. Plans are being made for return to his natural home after a period of more frequent home visitations. The last family has been involved in psychotherapy for the past three years whereas in the first four cases, the families refused psychological help or were unmotivated to change.

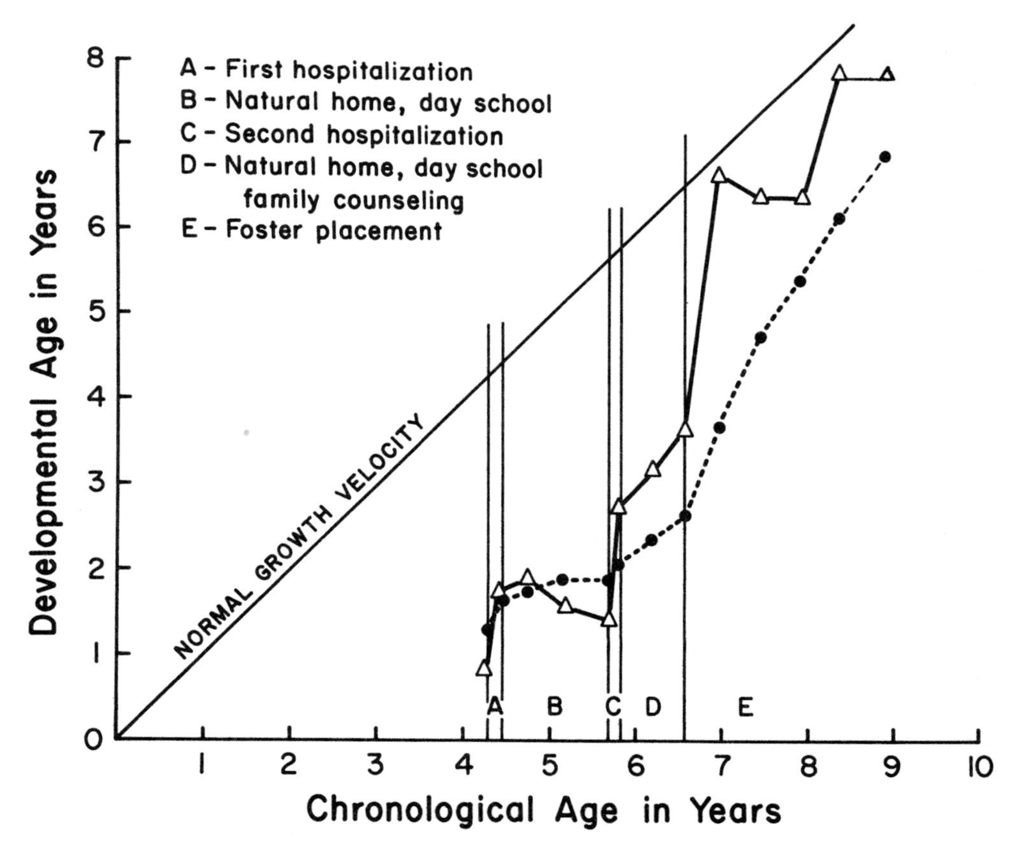

Fig. 2. Follow-up course for a four year old boy who had unsuccessful intervention in the natural home (• = height, Δ = weight)

During foster placements 13 children have now reached the third percentile on the growth chart for height and when last seen 11 were still showing catch-up acceleration. Thirteen are still below the third percentile for height; four of these are no longer showing catch-up growth but are maintaining normal growth velocity. Recent height and weight are unknown for the four other children not lost to follow-up. To our surpirse, catch-up in IQ has been minimal in 9 children serially tested; only one child had gains of greater than 10 IQ points. This may reflect decreased potential for intellectual gains at older ages ($\bar{x}$ 6.5 yrs, range 4-10 yrs). Psychological reevaluation of the children remaining in foster care is incomplete. Most children are adapting well to their homes. Almost all have needed special help at school. Immature behavior continues to be a problem in the oldest boy, now age 16, who has reached the 50th percentile in growth. He has had minimal catch-up in emotional or intellectual development during four foster placements over five years.

DISCUSSION AND RECOMMENDATIONS

Psychosocial dwarfism is a perplexing and frustrating disorder for the health professional. The relationship which results in emotional and physical growth arrest is most difficult to detect or if detected to substantiate in an empirical manner. A high degree of significance must be attached to historical and behavioral details. It requires the expertise of a variety of disciplines both from within the hospital and the community to diagnose and develope an intervention program that will reverse the process. Therefore, immediate involvement of a multidisciplinary team who can explore both organic and nonorganic etiologies for the growth retardation simultaneously should be provided during the hospital evaluation. Delay until after exclusion of organic disease leads to loss of valuable observations as well as opportunity to engage with the family. It should be explained that organic and emotional causes of growth retardation are being sought at the onset of the evaluation. Our experience is that families are more willing to consider an emotional etiology if that has been presented in a "matter of fact" manner from the beginning.

Once the diagnosis has been made a plan for intervention must be developed. All too often simplistic solutions are offered to the community and family for these extremely complex cases. Because a major symptomatology of these children is centered around their bizarre relationship to food many people erroneously believe that a failure to feed the children or failure to feed appropriately is the cause and therefore the solution becomes one of feeding the child. The marked rebound in linear growth that many of these children demonstrate on removal from their home environment is not usually due to nutritional improvement in the hospital or in foster care. The rebound seems to be due to relief from stress present in the home environment which interferes with the child's ability to grow through some as yet unexplained process.

Only one out of 35 children in our group had initiation of catch-up growth while in the natural home. In addition, catch-up growth after discharge continued in only one child over four years of age when the child returned to the same home environment. Therefore, we feel that initial separation of the child from his or her family through a diagnostic evaluation is essential. Unless given strong evidence of parental motivation and ability to change (and we are increasingly pessimistic about this possibility) our recommendation is that the children be placed in a foster placement at a minimum until they reach the third percentile in height. Usually this is accomplished in 1-1/2 to 2 years. Affected siblings should receive separate placements at least initially for maximal success. Three of our cases provide clear evidence for deceleration of growth or cessation of catch-up growth once natural siblings were reunited. After placement in separate homes two brothers (Fig. 1) met accidentally at a clinic visit. Foster parents reported enuresis and temper tantrums thereafter for almost a month. Because of our observation that the presence of younger foster siblings can also precipitate regressive behavior, we encourage a placement into a home with limited children, preferably none younger than the affected child.

Our initial recommendations are usually for a maximum visitation with natural parents of once a month for several hours. Even then, many children become anxious in anticipation of these visits. Foster parents often report behavior and school problems surrounding these visits. Likewise, contact initiated by the natural parents through phone calls, letters and/or presents is discouraged. As this type of recommendation is opposite to how physicians, psychologists and social workers have been trained, we have to repeatedly remind ourselves that the parent is stressful to the child.

Criteria for success is difficult to establish because long term evaluations have been infrequent in this condition. We have been impressed that emotional growth does not proceed without physical growth. We therefore recommend frequent monitoring (every 3 months) of weight gain and linear growth. Most children show dramatic emotional gains which parallel this rebound physical growth. Unfortunately in those children who have had unstable or poor parenting in foster homes due to poor placements, frequent moves or due to the child's lack of attachment to natural or foster parents, emotional development usually lags appreciably behind physical growth. Repeat psychological evaluations at yearly intervals can be helpful in assessing the child's emotional needs.

Continued reassessment of the natural family while the child is in foster care is important to determine if it will ever be possible to reunite the child and family. In order for this to be determined it is essential that full community intervention and psychological help for the family be offered when the child is first placed in foster care and not after one or two years when return home is being considered. The family will need more time for change than the child and this time must not be wasted. It is also crucial that the family's therapist be familiar with the syndrome affecting the child.

With the few exceptions mentioned in the paper, it is our experience that therapy has not been successful in bringing about enough of a change in these families that the child is able to grow. Factors affecting this failure must be further evaluated but it seems that some families are resistent to change and refuse help of any type. Others are isolated and referral agencies unavailable. Another reason is the lack of trained mental health professionals who can deal with these very difficult families. We could cite several instances wherein the therapist clearly became caught up in the family system and denied what was happening to the child while defending the parents. The mother of the child in Fig. 2 was extremely depressed. The father and the helpers in the community feared total mental collapse if the mother-child symbiosis was interrupted. During the second hospitalization, the mother was 8 months pregnant and she stated "if you take -- away, the next one will be the same". It was only after outside placement of the child took place that the mother began to deal with her depression and her isolation noticably decreased. What will happen to this child, soon to be returned again on a trial basis after 2 1/2 years remains to be seen.

The concept of time is important to consider when planning for the child (6). A delay of six months or a year before the child has an opportunity to grow may well represent a fourth or fifth of the child's lifetime. In addition, it may be that the child has a finite capacity to reverse this process over time and each delay or the longer the delay adds to the ultimate damage done. In our group of children, the older the child was at the time of placement, the less the significant change noted. The child cannot wait for this family to change. When family change is limited, a decision to seek permanent custody should be made and made as quickly as possible. This would free the child for adoption at a young enough age to permit stability and improved prognosis for emotional adjustment.

REFERENCES

1. G. F. Powell, J. A. Brasel and R. M. Blizzard, Emotional deprivation and growth retardation simulating idiopathic hypopituitarism I. Clinical evaluation of the syndrome, New Eng. J. Med. 276, 1271 (1967).

2. G. F. Powell, J. A. Brasel, S. Raiti and R. M. Blizzard, Emotional deprivation and growth retardation simulating idiopathic hypopituitarism II. Endocrinologic evaluation of the syndrome, New Eng. J. Med. 276, 1279 (1967).

3. M. A. Capitanio, and J. A. Kirkpatrick, Widening of the cranial sutures. A roentgen observation during periods of accelerated growth in patients treated for deprivation dwarfism. Radiology 92, 53 (1969).

4. E. A. Franken, Jr., M. Fox, J. A. Smith and W. L. Smith, Acute gastric dilatation in neglected children, Am. J. Roent. 130, 297 (1978).

5. R. J. Hernandez, A. K. Poznanski, N. J. Hopwood and R. P. Kelch, Incidence of growth lines in psychosocial dwarfs and idiopathic hypopituitarism, Am. J. Roen. (in press)

6. J. Goldstein, A. Freud and A. J. Soluit (1973) Beyond the Best Interests of the Child, The Free Press Macmillan Publ. Co. Inc.

Child Abuse and Neglect, Vol. 3, pp. 449 - 459.

0145-2134/79/0601-0449 $02.00/0.

NON-ORGANIC FAILURE TO THRIVE

Arne Ohlsson, M.D.

Barnmedicinska kliniken Regionsjukhuset
701 85 Orebro Sweden
King Faisal Specialist Hospital and Research Centre
P.O. Box 3354, Riyadh, Saudi Arabia

ABSTRACT

The purpose of this study is to identify aetiological stress factors in cases on non-organic failure to thrive admitted to a paediatric clinic in Sweden. The growth charts and the case histories of 11 children less than three years old and fulfilling the following diagnostic criteria are presented: (1) Weight 3SD below mean or a deviation of 3SD from an earlier growth pattern, (2) no organic disease to explain the underweight, (3) signs of retarded development or deprivation, and (4) weight gain, improved development and disappearance of symptoms on adequate caloric intake and psychosocial intervention in the families. Most children were referred from a Well Baby Clinic (WBC) because of deviation in the growth pattern attributed to organic disease. A combined paediatric and child psychiatric approach excluded organic disease but revealed different psychosocial stress factors such as insecure parental childhood, immigrant parents, father absent or inadequate, alcoholism, psychiatric, or marital problems in the parents, and somatic or child psychiatric disease among siblings. Except for poor weight gain the children presented with feeding difficulties, vomiting, diarroea, apathy, sterotypies, and varying degrees of retardation. A deviation in the growth pattern should always stimulate the health worker to initiate psychosocial investigations to prevent unnecessary somatic investigations and severe neglect or abuse.

KEYWORDS

Failure to thrive, child abuse, growth charts, psychosocial stress factors.

INTRODUCTION

Retardation of growth and psychomotor development in combination with a variety of somatic and psychiatric symptoms has been described in infants living in institutions and receiving inadequate emotional, physicial, intellectual, and social stimulation. The syndrome has been named hospitalism (Spitz, 1945), emotional deprivation (Bakwin, 1949), affect deprivation (Lowrey, 1940), and maternal deprivation (Bowlby, 1952). The same clinical picture may also develop in children living at home and has been presented as environmental retardation (Gesell and Amatruda, 1954; Coleman and Provence, 1957), failure to thrive (Elmer, 1960), and deprivation dwarfism (Silver and Finkelstein, 1967). The features of the non-organic failure to thrive syndrome are growth and developmental failure accompanied by psychosocial disruption followed by improvement on placement in a nurturing environment (Barbero and Shaheen, 1967; Shaheen and colleagues, 1968).

It is commonly agreed that the retarded psychomotor development is caused by inadequate or distorted interaction between the child and the mother or her substitute (Bowlby, 1952). The aetiology of the growth retardation is more controversial. Patton and Gardner (1962) presented six cases of dwarfism as a psychosomatic disorder resulting in functional hypopituitarism. Powell and colleagues (1967) found low growth hormone levels in similar cases. The levels returned to normal when the emotional climate was improved. MacCarthy and Booth (1970) consider the growth retardation to be part of a psychosomatic disease. Whitten and colleagues (1969) showed that the caloric intake in cases of failure to thrive was insufficient either because the child was not offered enough food or did not accept it. They did not believe in any psychologically induced defect in absorption or metabolism. Krieger (1974) described ten cases of psychosocial dwarfism where she found direct or indirect proof that the child was not given adequate food. Homicide by starvation was described by Adelson (1963) in three children. Koel (1969) reported children admitted for non-organic failure to thrive who were later severely abused. Fischoff and colleagues (1971) found a high incidence of character disorders among the mothers of children with failure to thrive. Leonard and colleagues (1966) pointed out psychosocial stress factors such as financial problems, bad housing, unemployment, marital conflicts, children born in close succession, depressed or socially isolated mothers. They described the parents as having failed to thrive in their roles as mother and father. The father was as a rule very little involved in family life and did not support the mother or was physically absent. Several other studies (Elmer and colleagues, 1969; Evans and colleagues, 1972; Oates and Yu, 1971; Powell and colleagues, 1967; Shaheen and colleagues, 1968) confirmed the importance of adverse psychosocial factors. Leonard and colleagues (1969) and Shaheen and colleagues (1968) did not find an increased incidence of failure to thrive among siblings but Elmer and colleagues (1969) found evidence of growth failure in more than one child in the same family. The infant himself might be the stress factor that exhausts the resources of the guardian. Oates and Yu (1971) found that behaviour problems were common among siblings although their health was good. Elmer (1969) found, however, an increased incidence of somatic disease and retardation in siblings as did Shaheen and colleagues (1968). Mental retardation, behaviour and emotional problems, and continued growth deficit have been found in follow-up studies of children with failure to thrive (Elmer and colleagues, 1969; Glaser and colleagues, 1968; Oates and Yu, 1971; Pollit and Eichler, 1976).

Pollit and colleagues (1975) did not find any clear evidence of psychopathology in the mothers but their interaction with the child deviated from the normal. The mothers related less often to their children, were less affectionate, and were more likely to use physical punishment. The psychopathology was seen only in the interaction between the parents and the child. The person might function either marginally or adequately if not challenged by the role of being parent (Koel, 1969). This would explain the discrepancy often experienced in the evaluation of parents by a psychiatrist and by a paediatrician.

At the time of this study there were only case reports of non-organic failure to thrive from Sweden (Hook, 1974; Ohlsson, 1976). Nylander and Zetterstrom (1977) in a study of 22 infants admitted to a pediatric clinic in Stockholm for feeding problems classified seven as having failure to thrive but did not present their diagnostic criteria. They showed that the mothers of infants with feeding problems had a higher "life stress score" (composed of 29 different psychosocial stress factors) compared with a control group of mothers of babies attending Well Baby Clinics. The purpose of this study is to describe the clinical picture and living conditions of children with non-organic failure to thrive admitted to a paediatric clinic in Sweden and to identify possible psychosocial stress factors in aetiology. With increased understanding of these children and their families it should be possible to prevent the condition or at least recognize the condition early to prevent severe neglect or abuse.

MATERIAL AND METHODS

In the county of Orebro, Sweden, there is only one paediatric unit located at the Regional Hospital, Orebro, to which all children with significant disease are admitted. Its catchment area is, therefore, well defined. All patients less than three years old admitted to the unit during the period July 1975 to December 1976 and fulfilling the following criteria were included in the study: (1) Weight 3SD below mean or a deviation of 3SD from an earlier growth pattern, (2) no organic disease to explain the underweight, (3) signs of retarded development or deprivation, and (4) weight gain, improved development and disappearance of symptoms on adequate caloric intake and psychosocial intervention in the family. During the study period there were 11,000 children less than three years old in the catchment area and during this period, 1850 of these children were admitted to the paediatric ward from their homes. Eleven cases of non-organic failure to thrive were diagnosed. Ten of these belonged to the catchment area, i.e., 0.5% of the admissions in that age group. Nine children were referred from a WBC mainly because of poor weight gain and two infants were admitted as emergencies because of diarrhoea. One of these two had earlier been referred from a WBC to another paediatric clinic in Sweden because of poor weight gain. One Norwegian child was admitted while on a holiday with her parents. A combined paediatric and child psychiatric case history was taken by the investigator. In all cases except one where the father was in prison, both parents were interviewed by the investigator and a social worker, who also spoke Finnish. Additional information was obtained from the records on previous hospital admissions. All children except one had visited a WBC and thanks to the WBC records, it was possible to plot the growth pattern of the children on the standard anthropometric charts used in Sweden (Fig. 1-11). In seven cases a home visit was undertaken by a staff member. Information was also obtained from social welfare agencies. At least one of the parents was encouraged to spend most of the day with the patient on the ward. One child was never visited by the parents and one only occasionally by the mother, in spite of intensive encouragement. The parent-child interaction was observed by the ward staff. All patients underwent thorough physical examination and appropriate investigation to rule out organic disorders. Human growth hormone studies and bone age determinations were undertaken and found normal in the patients who also were short for age. The psychomotor development was assessed by the investigator in the children less than one year old and by a child psychologist in the older children.

CASE REPORTS

Case 1 (Fig. 1). Nine month old girl, younger of two half-sisters; birth weight +1SD; referred from a WBC because of poor weight gain, feeding problems, and sleep disturbance. Clinical features: Weight -3SD, length normal; inactive with delayed social development and poor interaction with parents. Father had one daughter, now a teen-ager, born in his first marriage. She was brought up from the age of two by him and the step-mother. She had just left home. Mother well-educated but had remained a housewife with domestic help. Fourteen years of unintentional infertility preceded this pregnancy. Mother had had depression periods for six years requiring psychiatric treatment. On tricyclic antidepressants in early pregnancy and afraid these could cause malformation of the child. Because of her age, 36 years, and the long period of infertility, she was delivered by Caesarean section which was preceded and followed by extreme anxiety. The newborn girl had slight instability of her hips which were splinted for 6 weeks with consequent maternal anxiety. Father, age 42, a successful businessman; was very little involved with the care of the baby. As a result of feeding problems from birth, mother had intensive contact with the WBC and the baby required two hospital admissions. When the mother visited the child on the ward she preferred to watch the child being fed by a nurse rather than feed her herself. She was, however, convinced she would be capable of handling the child from the age of two years, from which time she had cared for her step-daughter. The feeding problems became worse at the time of holidays which the parents would earlier have spent abroad. Mother was referred to a psychiatrist, a social worker was placed in the home, and the father was encouraged to take a more active part in the care of the child who thereafter improved.

Case 2 (Fig. 2). Fifteen month old boy; only child. Normal weight at birth and +2SD at two months. Referred from a WBC because of poor weight gain and diarrhoea. Clinical features: Weight -2.5SD, length -1SD; four months regarded, verbally more than in motor functions, with sterotypic, apathetic behaviour. Maternal grandfather had committee suicide and maternal grandmother had died in an accident after chronic illness when mother was a teenager. Mother placed in foster home. Young parents (Mother 18, Father 20). Father, an unskilled, unemployed worker with psychosomatic problems, had had poor contact with his own parents, who were strictly religious. The family were receiving social welfare aid. The parents often left the boy alone at home in his bed with a cat while they went for long rides in their big, old, American car. He had no toys at home but for long periods of time would sit and rock back and forth in his bed. The parents were taught the basic needs of a child and a social worker was placed with them for a long period. The parents started training for employment and at that time the child was placed with a family during part of the day. He recovered completely after a few months.

Case 3 (Fig. 3). Five month old boy; youngest of three. Normal birth weight. Admitted as an emergency because of diarrhoea but had earlier been referred to another hospital from a WBC because of poor weight gain. Clinical features: Weight -3SD, length -2SD; delayed development and poor emotional contact with parents who were non-Swedish speaking gypsies, immigrants from Finland. Mother housewife and father unskilled worker (in prison). They were receiving social welfare aid. Mother abandoned child in hospital and visited him only once in spite of intensive encouragement and home visits by the staff. He had to be placed in a foster home, where he rapidly improved.

Case 4 (Fig. 4). Eleven month old girl; younger of two. Weight at birth normal and +2SD at five months. Referred from a WBC because of poor weight gain and delayed development. Clinical

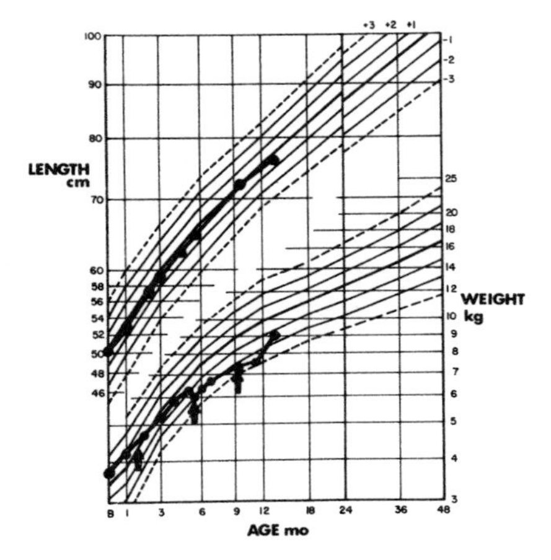

Fig. 1. Case 1.

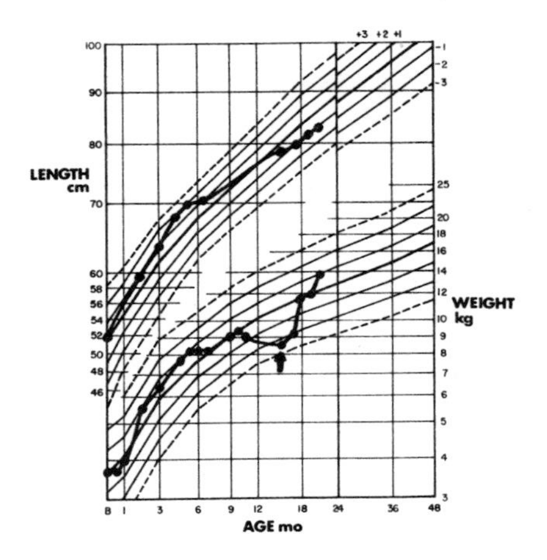

Fig. 2. Case 2.

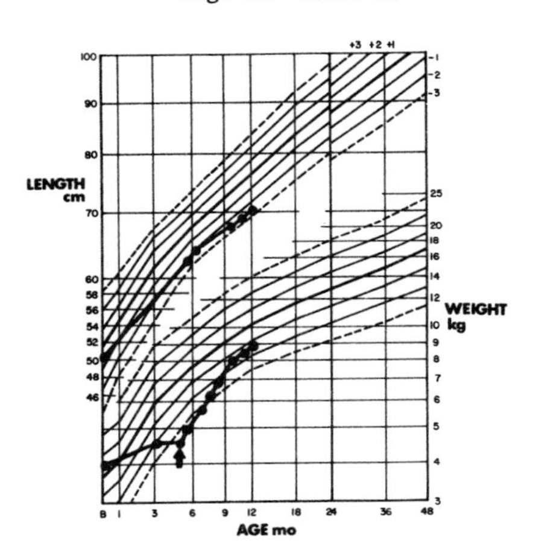

Fig. 3. Case 3.

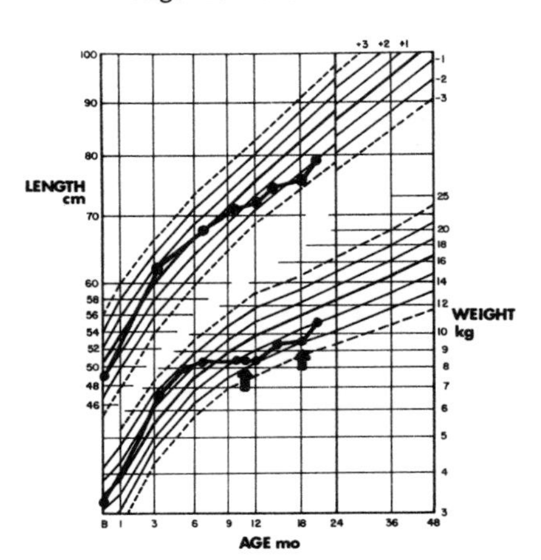

Fig. 4. Case 4.

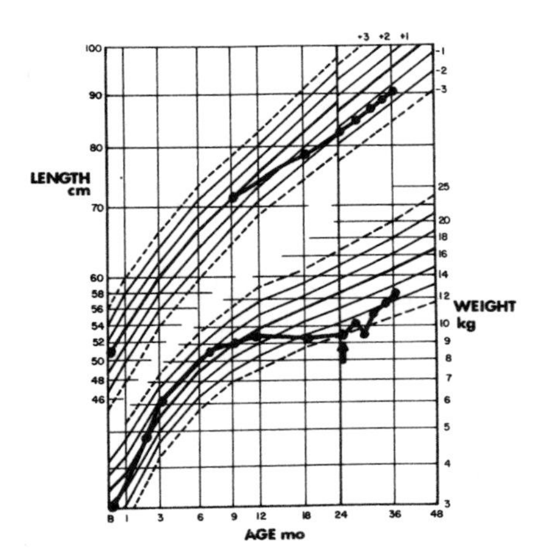

Fig. 5. Case 5.

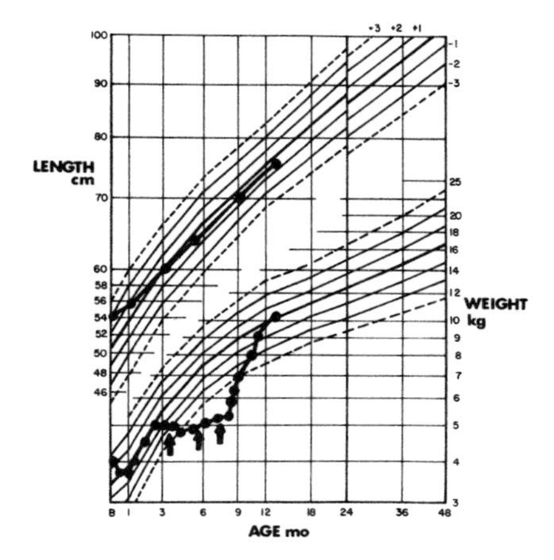

Fig. 6. Case 6.

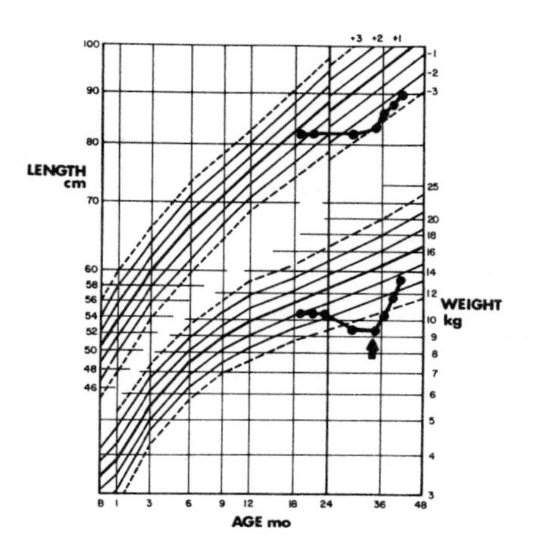

Fig. 7. Case 7.

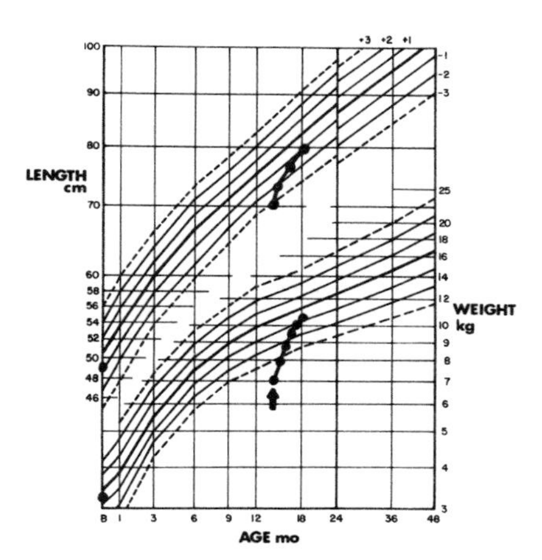

Fig. 8. Case 8.

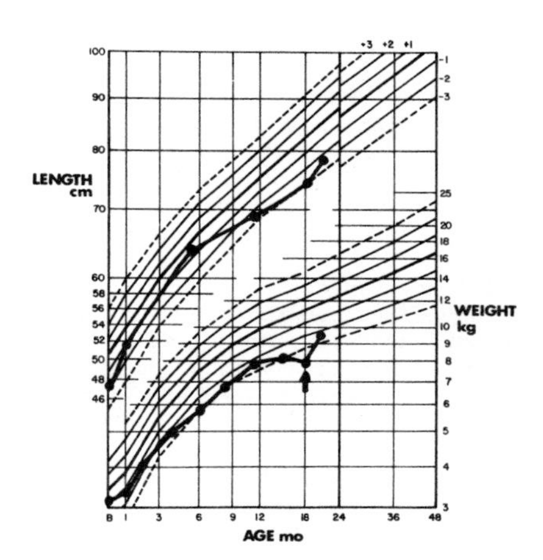

Fig. 9. Case 9.

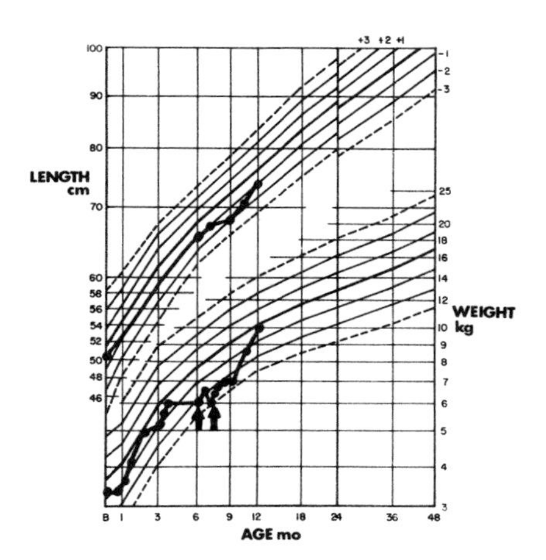

Fig. 10. Case 10.

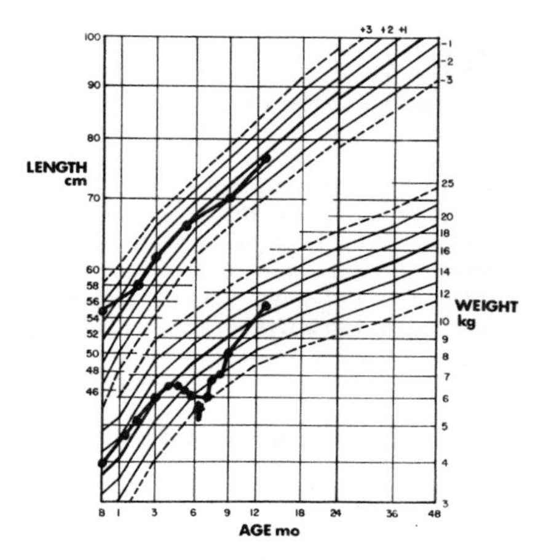

Fig. 11. Case 11.

features: Weight -2SD, length -1SD; three months retarded, more in verbal than in motor functions; manneristic behaviour and poor emotional contact. Mother, a dentist, resumed work when the baby was six months old and the father, a journalist, stayed at home with the child. From this time, the child stopped gaining weight. The father, emotionally cold, stimulated the child very little. In hospital, with stimulation and handling, the child improved physically and mentally but after discharge, again stopped gaining weight. On admission to a child psychiatric ward she was later diagnosed as a case of anaclitic depression and once more gained weight and improved mentally.

Case 5 (Fig. 5). Twenty-four month old girl; only child. Normal birthweight. Referred from a WBC because of poor weight gain and feeding problems. Clinical features: Weight -3SD, length -2SD; inactive with delay in social and language development. Both parents had been adopted as children and had poor relations with their parents. Mother, pregnant, was extremely anxious and tense and had marital problems. On home visits the child was found left on her own in bed and poor interaction with the mother was observed. With supportive therapy through the family doctor, social worker, and child psychologist, the child improved. The father, who related better with the girl, was encouraged to spend more time with her.

Case 6 (Fig. 6). Seven month old girl; youngest of four. Birth weight +1SD. Referred from a WBC initially at one month of age because of feeding problems. Underwent extensive investigation several times on account of failure to thrive. Failed to gain weight despite high caloric intake (at least 170 kcal/kg). Also investigated at a university clinic where pancreatic and small intestine studies were normal. Clinical features: Marasmic on admission at seven months of age with weight well below -3SD, length normal; inactive, poverty of vocalization, strange hand and finger movements and poor interaction with the mother. Two siblings with severe allergic problems and one with psychiatric problems. Both parents intelligent. Father, an accountant, was in military service for one month just before admission of the child. Mother, a successful mature student planning to become a journalist, came from a broken home. Parents emotionally cold, especially the mother, who in hospital stayed with the child from early morning till late evening and gave all the feeds. After five days, however, it was discovered she did not actually feed the baby but put the food alongside the mouth of the baby in a paper napkin and discarded it. When feeding was taken over by the staff the girl rapidly gained weight and recovered completely in a foster home, where she was placed temporarily, while investigations and psychiatric treatment of the parents were undertaken.

Case 7 (Fig. 7). Thirty-two month old girl; younger of two siblings. Adopted from Southeast Asia with unknown birth weight but known to have had normal length and weight on arrival in Sweden at sixteen months of age. On arrival in Sweden, she had tuberculosis that was successfully treated. She was referred from a WBC because of poor weight gain, feeding problems, enuresis, and encopresis. Clinical features: Weight below -3SD; length -3SD; severely disturbed, enuretic, encopretic with self-destructive and sterotypic behaviour and promiscuous in her contacts. Mother emotionally disturbed and intellectually dull. Father rigid and emotionally cold. The parents had one boy of their own who was doing well. The parents stated the girl did not fulfill their expectations. She was referred for psychiatric treatment and improved rapidly in weight and more slowly mentally.

Case 8 (Fig. 8). Fourteen month old girl; youngest of three. Normal birth weight. Admitted as an emergency because of diarrhoea and poor weight gain. Clinical features: Weight below -3SD, length -3SD; delayed especially in linguistic and emotional development; apathetic with poor emotional contact. The parents, gypsies from Norway, abandoned the child while on holiday in Sweden. Two days after admission the parents called from a place 1000 kilometers away, in the north of Sweden and after than, all contact with them was lost. After temporary placement in an orphanage, she later did well in a foster home.

Case 9 (Fig. 9). Eighteen month old girl; only child. Normal birth weight. Referred from a WBC because of poor weight gain. Clinical features: Weight below -3SD, length -3SD; apathetic and rejecting emotional and physical contact with everyone including her parents; delayed motor and linguistic development. At birth the child was found to have bilateral dislocation of the hips that needed treatment with plaster of Paris for 18 months. She had 12 hospital admissions, mainly to an orthopedic clinic 300 kilometers away, during which the mother, who was working, could not stay with the child. The parents were both non-Swedish speaking immigrants from Finland and no one spoke Finnish to the girl while in hospital. The parents noted the child would cry when left in hospital until latterly when she showed no reaction to being left alone. She also regressed in linguistic development. When the mother was encouraged to stay with the child in hospital (the hospital admission was necessary for treatment of the hips) the girl improved emotionally and gained 800 grams in two weeks.

Case 10 (Fig. 10). Seven month old boy; youngest of two. Normal birth weight. Referred from a WBC because of poor weight gain. Clinical features: Weight-3SD, length-1SD; apathetic. Father, an unskilled, unemployed worker, had been an alcoholic for eight years since his mother's death. Mother was working part time delivering newspapers early in the morning. A deaf, 80-year old grandmother and the father took care of the baby. Family received social welfare aid. One five-year old brother had psychiatric problems. Father referred for psychiatric treatment. The child was placed with another family for part of the day and family therapy was initiated. The boy improved.

Case 11 (Fig. 11). Six month old boy; only child. Normal birth weight. Referred from a WBC because of weight loss and vomiting. Clinical features: Weight -3SD, length normal; delayed social development and poor interaction with the mother, ruminating. Father who worked 200 kilometers from home, was absent during the week. Mother came from the north of Sweden and father from the south; as a compromise they had settled in the middle where neither had relatives and they had few social contacts. Mother, an occupational therapist, interacted very little with the boy and did not stimulate him. The father, who related much better, was encouraged to stay and feed the boy. The boy stopped ruminating on simple stimulation and improved interaction with the parents. At twelve months he was completely normal.

RESULTS AND DISCUSSION

Children

Non-organic failure to thrive constituted 0.5% of hospital admissions of children under three years of age during the study period. Elmer and colleagues (1969) reported that 5% of infant admissions in 1966 to Children's Hospital, Pittsburgh, were for non-organic growth failure. Nylander and Zetterstrom (1976) found that 3.5% of hospital admissions under one year old were for non-organic feeding difficulties and classified one-third as non-organic failure to thrive (1.2%). Six of the cases reported in this study were below 12 months of age, three were between 12 and 24 months, and two were between 24 and 36 months; their mean age at the time of diagnosis was 13 months. It is recognized that younger children are more vulnerable to all forms of child abuse and neglect (Schmitt and Kempe, 1975). Every child was the youngest in the sibship, and was born term with normal birth weight. One girl was adopted from Southeast Asia with unknown birth weight but had normal length and weight on arrival in Sweden. One child had bilateral dislocation of the hips and another a slight instability of the hips at birth. One child was separated from her parents for long periods of time because of hospitalization. Two children were often left alone at home. Given adequate food, stimulation, and psychosocial intervention in the families, all children improved. Their clinical features are summarized in Table 1.

TABLE 1. Clinical Features in 11 Children with Non-Organic Failure to Thrive

Clinical Feature:	Number of Cases:
Weight 3SD below mean, or a deviation of 3SD from an earlier weight pattern	11
Length 3SD below mean, or a deviation of 3SD from an earlier growth pattern	6
Distorted interaction between child and father or mother	11
Delayed development	9
Feeding difficulties	8
Apathy	6
Diarrhoea and/or vomiting	6
Sterotypic behaviour	3

Parents

Psycho-social stress factors frequently encountered among parents in this study are presented in Table 2. Similar factors have been found in earlier studies (Elmer and colleagues, 1969; Evans and colleagues, 1972; Leonard and colleagues, 1966; Oates and Yu, 1971; Powell and colleagues, 1967, and Shaheen and colleagues, 1968).

Mothers. The mean age of the mothers at birth of the babies was 25.3 years, two years less than the mean age for mothers who gave birth to babies in Stockholm in 1975 (27.3 years) (Nylander and Zetterstrom, 1977). The youngest mother was 17 and the oldest 36 when they delivered. Six were primigravidae, of whom one was delivered by Caesarean section. Seven mothers had low educational attainment, three were well-educated, and one had higher education. Three were working and one was a mature student. All mothers were physically healthy but eight had psychiatric disease, emotional disturbance, or inadequate personalities. Three were non-Swedish speaking immigrants. One mother interacted normally with her child but she was working and the child was cared for by the father. In all other cases the interaction between mother and child was disturbed. The mothers interacted verbally and physically very little with their children, did not cuddle them, and did not respond appropriately to their needs. One mother was found deliberately to deprive her child of food as described earlier by Krieger (1974). Another mother did not want to feed her baby herself.

Fathers. The mean age of the fathers at birth of the baby was 27.2 years. The youngest was 19 and the oldest 41 years. Of the 11 fathers, six were unskilled and two skilled workers. The others comprised an accountant, a director of private business, and a journalist with higher education. Three of the fathers were unemployed (one in prison, one alcoholic). Some fathers spent very little time at home for reasons of excessive work, work away from home, and military service. The fathers who were at home unfortunately related poorly to their children because of their own problems of alcoholism, emotional and psychosomatic problems, and personality traits. Three of the fathers had a better relation to the child than the mother, but because of their work, this relation was limited in time. Three fathers were non-Swedish speaking immigrants.

Siblings

There were 12 siblings, but no accurate information was available on five of them. Two had psychiatric problems and two had severe allergies. None had failed to thrive.

Social group

On a three-graded scale, two families belonged to social group 1, three to social group 2, and six to social group 3. Three families were receiving social welfare aid.

CONCLUSIONS

A distorted parent-child relation was found in all cases of non-organic failure to thrive. In three cases this was seen mainly in relation to the father. The parent, who was the main guardian, did not stimulate the child verbally and physically. This was usually due to stress factors which impaired the ability of the father or the mother to interact normally with the child. In one case parents and child had been separated for long periods by the child's hospitalization. The psycho-social stress factors found included: insecure parental childhood, young or old parents, immigrant parents, absent or inadequate father, working mother, alcoholism, psychiatric or marital problems in the parents, somatic or psychiatric disease among siblings, and separation between parents and child. In the study, five families belonged to social groups 1 and 2, and six to social group 3. The problem can occur in all social groups.

The results of this study, in particular the psycho-social stress factors, should make it possible to detect families at risk during antenatal period and stimulate appropriate intervention. Deviation in the growth pattern of a child should always suggest the possible need for psycho-social investigation to prevent unnecessary physical investigation on the one hand and severe neglect or abuse on the other.

TABLE 2. Stress Factors in Cases of Non-Organic Failure to Thrive

Case	Mother	Father	Social Group. Family-Child
1	Age 36; well-educated housewife on psychiatric treatment for depression for six years and on tri-cyclic antidepressants during early pregnancy. She was afraid this could cause malformations. Caesarean section. Tense, anxious.	Age 42; Director of private business. Second marriage. Little involved in care of the child.	Social Group 1. Fourteen years of unintentional infertility prior to this pregnancy. The child had instability of the hips at birth and was splinted for six weeks.
2	Age 18; housewife. As a teenager, her father committed suicide and her mother died. She was placed in a foster home. Passive. Immature.	Age 20; unemployed, unskilled worker. Poor relations with his parents. Psychosomatic problems. Aggressive. Tense. Immature.	Social Group 3. Received social welfare aid. The parents often left the child alone at home for several hours.
3	Age 27; housewife. Non-Swedish speaking immigrant from Finland. Gypsy. Inadequate.	Age 23; unskilled worker. Non-Swedish speaking immigrant from Finland. Gypsy. In prison.	Social Group 3. Received social welfare aid. Child abandoned on hospital admission.
4	Age 31; dentist who resumed work when the child was 6 months old.	Age 34; journalist. Emotionally cold. He took care of the child from 6 months of age.	Social Group 1.
5	Age 27; housewife. Adopted Psychiatric problems; extremely anxious and tense. Poor relations with her parents. Pregnant.	Age 25; unskilled worker. Adopted. Poor relations with his parents.	Social Group 3. Marital conflict. Child was often left alone in her bed at home.
6	Age 28; mature student. Parents divorced; insecure childhood. Emotionally cold. Deprived the child of food.	Age 30; accountant. In military service for one month. Denied the severity of the child's condition.	Social Group 2. Severe allergy in two siblings; one sibling with child psychiatric problems Suspected allergy in the child.
7	Age 28; housewife. Emotionally disturbed.	Age 32; skilled worker. Rigid. Emotionally cold.	Social Group 2. Child adopted; did not fulfill expectations of parents.
8	Age 27; Gypsy from Norway.	Age unknown; unskilled worker from Norway.	Social Group 3. Child abandoned when parents on holiday in Sweden.

TABLE 2. Stress Factors in Cases of Non-Organic Failure to Thrive

(Continued)

Case	Mother	Father	Social Group. Family-Chil
9	Age 22; unskilled worker. Non-Swedish speaking immigrant from Finland.	Age 24; unskilled worker. Non-Swedish speaking immigrant from Finland.	Social Group 3. The child ha congenital luxation of the hi treated with Plaster of Paris for 18 months; 12 hospital admissions during this period.
10	Age 26; unskilled shift-worker. Resumed work when the boy was 4½ months old. Anxious. Tense.	Age 29; unemployed and unskilled worker with severe alcohol problems for 8 years since the death of his mother. Psychosomatic problems.	Social Group 3. One sibling with child psychiatric problem Cared for by deaf, 80-year old grandmother. Received social welfare aid.
11	Age 23; occupational therapist. Emotionally cold. Passive in relation to the child.	Age 26 years; skilled worker; working 200 km away from home, and absent from home during the week.	Social Group 2. The family ha recently moved into the area a was socially isolated.

REFERENCES

Adelson, L. (1963). Homicide by starvation. The nutritional variant of the "battered child. JAMA, 186, 458-460.

Bakwin, H. (1949). Psychologic aspects of pediatrics. Emotional deprivation in infants. J. Pediatr., 35, 512-521.

Barbero, G.J., and E. Shaheen (1967). Environmental failure to thrive: A clinical view. J. Pediatr., 71, 639-644.

Bowlby, J. (1952). Maternal Care and Mental Health. WHO monograph series, No. 2, 2nd ed. WHO, Geneva.

Coleman, R.W., and S. Provance (1957). Environmental retardation (hospitalism) in infants living in families. Pediatrics, 19, 285-292.

Elmer, E. (1960). Failure to thrive. Role of the mother. Pediatrics, 25, 717-725.

Elmer, E., G.S. Gregg, and P. Ellison (1969). Late results of the "Failure to Thrive" syndrome. Clin. Pediatr., 8, 584-589.

Evans, S.L., J.B. Reinhart, and R.A. Succop (1972). Failure to thrive. A study of 45 children and their families. J. Am. Acad. Child Psychiatry, 11, 440-457.

Fischoff, J., C.F. Whitten, and M.G. Pettit (1971). A psychiatric study of mothers of infants with growth failure secondary to maternal deprivation. J. Pediatr., 79, 209-215.

Gesell, A., and C.S. Amatruda (1954). Developmental Diagnosis, 2nd ed. Hoeber, New York.

Glaser, H.H., M.C. Heagarty, D.M. Bullard, and E.C. Pivchik (1968). Physical and psychologic development of children with early failure to thrive. J. Pediatr., 73, 690-698.

Hook, K. (1974). Barnpsykiatriska synpunkter pa behandling av misshandlade barn. Socialmedicinsk tidskrift (Stockholm), 51, 543-547.

Koel, B.S. (1969). Failure to thrive and fatal injury as a continuum. Am. J. Dis. Child., 118, 565-567.

Krieger, I. (1974). Food restriction as a form of child abuse in ten cases of psychosocial deprivation dwarfism. Clin Pediatr., 13, No. 2, 127-133.

Leonard, M.F., J.P. Rhymes, and A.J. Solnit (1966). Failure to thrive in infants. Am. J. Dis. Child., 111, 600-612.

Lowrey, L.G. (1940). Personality distortion and early institutional care. Am. J. Orthopsychiatry, 10, 576-585.

MacCarthy, D., and E.M. Booth (1970). Parental rejection and stunting of growth. J. Psychosom. Res., 14, 259-265.
Nylander, I. and R. Zetterstrom (1977). Feeding difficulties in infants--a psychosocial problem. Lakartidningen, 74, 4199-4202.
Oates, R.K., and J.S. Yu (1971). Children with non-organic failure to thrive. A community problem. Med. J. Aust., 2, 199-203.
Ohlsson, A. (1976). Storningar i foraldra-barn relationen under spad-och smabarns aldern. Pediatricus (Stockholm), 6, No. 2, 28-37.
Patton, R.G., and L.I. Gardner (1962). Influence of family environment and growth: the syndrome of "maternal deprivation." Pediatrics, 30, 957-962.
Pollitt, E., A.W. Eichler, and C.K. Chan (1973). Psychosocial development and behavior of mothers of failure to thrive children. Am. J. Orthopsychiatry, 45, 525-537.
Pollitt, E., and A. Eichler (1976). Behavioral disturbances among failure to thrive children. Am. J. Dis. Child., 130, 24-29.
Powell, G.F., J.A. Brasel, and R.M. Blizzard (1967). Emotional deprivation and growth retardation simulating idiopathic hypopituitarism: I. clinical evaluation of the syndrome. New Engl. J. Med., 276, 1271-1283.
Schmitt, B.D., and C.H. Kempe (1975). Neglect and abuse of children. In V.C. Vaughan, R.J. McKay, and W.E. Nelson (Eds.), Nelson Textbook of Pediatrics, 10th ed. W.B. Saunders, Philadelphia, London, Toronto. pp. 107-111.
Shaheen, E., D. Alexander, M. Truskowsky, and G.J. Barbero (1968). Failure to thrive--A retrospective profile. Clin. Pediatr., 7, 255-261.
Silver, H.K., and M. Finkelstein (1967). Deprivation dwarfism. J. Pediatr., 70, 317-324.
Spitz, R.A. (1945). Hospitalism. An inquiry into the genesis of psychiatric conditions in early childhood. In O. Fenichel (Ed.), Psychoanal. Study Child., Vol. 1, International Universities Press, New York. pp. 53-74.
Whitten, C.F., M.G. Pettit, and J. Fischhoff (1969). Evidence that growth failure from maternal deprivation is secondary to undereating. JAMA, 209, 1675-1682.

Child Abuse and Neglect, Vol. 3, pp. 461 - 466.
Pergamon Press Ltd., 1979. Printed in Great Britain.

PROBLEMS IN THE IDENTIFICATION OF CHILD DEPRIVATION

H. McC. Giles

Selly Oak Hospital, Birmingham, England

The last decade has seen a remarkable advance in the breadth and depth of understanding of non-accidental injury, and the gradual, painful and not always edifying development of community codes within which to resolve the ethical dilemmas of diagnosis and management. However, in relation to the wider field of child deprivation and neglect this process has barely begun, though the *Children and Young Persons Act* in 1969 accepted "avoidable prevention or neglect of the child's proper development, or impairment or neglect of his health" as valid alternatives to ill-treatment on which to base court proceedings. Obvious problems arising in this area include the practical difficulties of quantifying a child's emotional or intellectual development and of judging whether it be impaired, and if so, how far such impairment can be regarded as attributable to action or inaction by the parents and whether such parental contribution was "avoidable" and hence culpable. In the case of physical development, measurement at least is reasonably simple, though the interpretative difficulties remain. Height and weight can define a child's physical status in relation to a comparable population of normals; but two major difficulties arise. Firstly, it may be necessary to obtain serial measurements in order to define the dynamics of the situation; and secondly, complete elucidation may require a study of the child's progress in a controlled environment, that is, other than his own home. Clearly, it is precisely those parents who are most conscious that their care of their child has been inadequate, or suspicious that it may be judged so by others, who are least likely to co-operate with procedures which may result in establishing culpability. It is with the problem of these recalcitrant families, a special section of a broader group, that I am presently concerned. Their numbers are by no means negligible; during a two-year period they have constituted about one fifth of all the families (and a higher proportion of the children, since the pattern tends to be repeated consistently throughout a sibship) presenting to my paediatric service with problems of child abuse.

Case Reports

Louise E. Louise was born on July 5th, 1970. On two occasions within the first five months she was brought to hospital and was found to be febrile and hyperelectrolytaemic. On the first occasion, at the age of 3½ months, she had burns on her feet which were attributed by mother to "dangling her feet over the edge of a windowsill onto a radiator". These events naturally aroused great anxiety as to the quality of Louise's care; but strenuous and unremitting efforts achieved only a single hospital outpatient attendance between five months and five years of age. This exception occurred through the efforts of the then children's officer and because the parents thought their application for rehousing might be expedited. Louise was then a pale, wan 2-year old, below the 3rd centile for both height and weight. Throughout this period a succession of attempts were made by homehelps, housemothers, health visitors, play group leaders, social workers and others to establish a rapport with mother and thus to facilitate regular monitoring of Louise's progress. Even after the birth of a sister on whom every attention was lavished, Louise was always kept in the background and as far as possible out of the sight of any worker who managed to gain access to the home, and was never brought to the clinic with the baby. In 1976, after Louise had completed a year in school, her head teacher became so concerned about her behaviour, her ravenous appetite and her mother's rejecting attitude towards her that she consulted the school medical officer who recommended residential open-air school. Her parents rejected this proposal but eventually yielded to firm pressure from the educational welfare officer. In her first full term at residential school Louise gained 2 kg in weight and in 6 months she grew 7.5 cm. During the next year careful and frequently weighing showed a remarkable pattern of weight gain in term time and weight loss in holiday, but with an overall advance in weight from the 3rd to the 50th centile and in height from the 3rd almost to the 25th centile. In the autumn of 1977, Louise returned from her half-term holiday with a severe napkin dermatitis. On questioning she stated that she had spent the weekend tied to her bed by her wrists and ankles. A place of safety order was obtained and a care order sought in the juvenile court. The parents failed to brief their solicitor or attend court for the hearing. On the evidence of the height and weight charts the magistrates granted a care order until the age of 18. Louise's physical growth deficits have already largely been repaired; it is doubtful whether the damage to her emotional health and intellectual development can ever be.

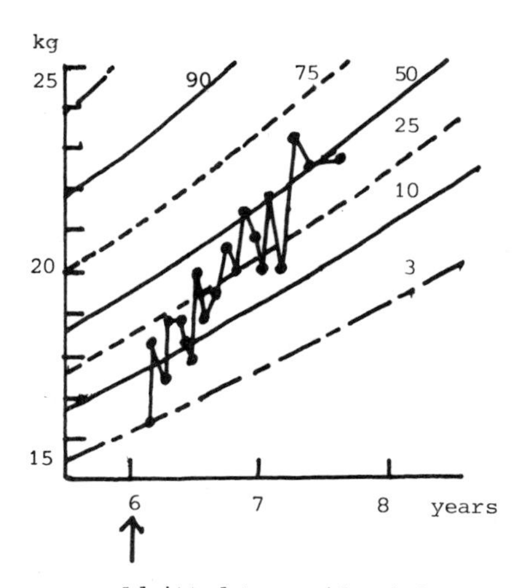

Fig. 1. Weight record of Louise E. following admission to residential school.

Anne and Marie W. Mrs. W. was 21 years old and had three children ranging up to 5 years old when the twins were born one month prematurely on 28th July 1973. Mother approached the NSPCC for help but concern about poor growth and weight gain and about the twins' behaviour, and mother's response to it, led in 1975 to admission, at the NSPCC's behest, to another hospital. Here the twins were noted to be below the 3rd centile for height and weight but as mother herself was very short it was judged that this was likely to be constitutional. After another year the NSPCC inspector again became concerned, to the extent of using his influence with mother to persuade her to have the twins admitted to our hospital. Measurements showed that over the year the twins' weight had remained constant or dropped, and their heights had increased by no more than 3 cms. Within a week of admission to hospital each twin had gained well over a kilogram in weight. As soon as she realised the implications of what was happening mother became hysterical and demanded to take the children home. A place of safety order was obtained, the children were discharged to a community home and on the strength of the height and weight measurements and with the concurrence of every professional concerned in the case, the juvenile court was approached for a care order. The parents opposed the petition and another child psychiatrist was briefed, as a result of whose sanguine forcasts the magistrates decided to impose only a supervision order. A multiplicity of stratagems were adopted including regular domiciliary psychiatric counselling and admission of the children to nursery school to try to ensure adequate surveillance, but sooner or later every agency concluded that it was impossible to develop a constructive relationship with mother. Eventually the entire family were brought under a place of safety order and a case conference decided to approach the juvenile court again for a care order, laying the major emphasis on the height and weight charts. The hearing is awaited; meanwhile the father has announced his intention of suing the local authority because the nursery school (at my behest) had submitted the twins to the procedures of weighing and measuring without obtaining his permission.

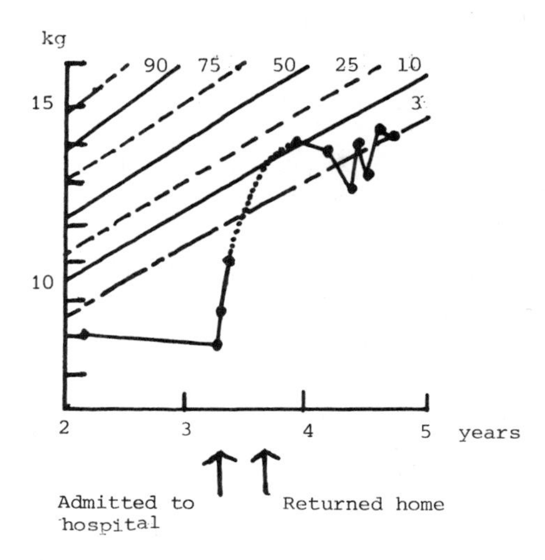

Fig. 2. Weight record of Marie W. following admission to hospital.

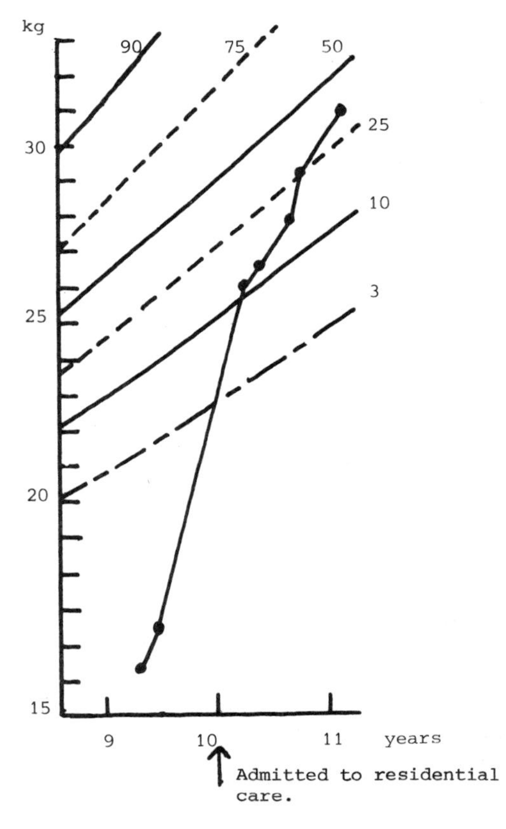

Fig. 3. Weight record of Julie G. following reception into care.

Julie G. This girl, born of a schizophrenic mother on July 29th, 1966, had a chequered early career. In July, 1968, aged 2 years, she was admitted to hospital with bilateral subdural haematomas attributed to a fall from her foster mother's arms. She was thin to the point of emaciation, her length being near the 3rd centile but her weight well below it. However, her weight quickly recovered to the 10th centile. Because of inadvertent failure to check on a missed outpatient appointment, hospital contact was lost with Julie until December, 1976. During this period Julie's longterm foster parents, who had adopted three children and short-term fostered 32 others, moved house and later became estranged. Marginal doubts about Julie's care accumulated, especially after the foster-father left home, until in 1976 she was admitted to a reception centre for assessment and was referred back to me as a candidate for growth hormone treatment, her height being 9 cm and her weight 6 kg below the respective 3rd centiles. However, at or around the time of her reception into care Julie began to grow and gain weight in the most spectacular fashion, being now on the 25th centile for height and the 50th centile for weight. She has grown 27 cms in 2½ years. None of the many observers who had contact with Julie over her later years in foster-care, though alert to the possibility, could define any specific evidence of emotional deprivation. But the physical measurements leave no retrospective doubt about the severity of her total deprivation, and more critical assessment of these measurements might have led to prompter intervention. Like Louise E., Julie's physical deficits have proved easily rectifiable, but the scars on her emotional and intellectual development are likely to be irreparable.

In a field where every case history is both complex and unique one cannot sensibly speak of "representative" examples. What these children have in common is severe growth failure resulting from deprivation. But my immediate concern (though this did not apply in the case of Julie G.) goes further, if more narrowly, and relates specifically to families where parental attitudes obstruct the assembly of essential observations. Various facets of this problem are illustrated in the reported histories. Difficulties arise essentially because we are working in an area where there is no absolute distinction between normal and abnormal, or rather between acceptable and unacceptable. A broken bone is unambiguously different from a whole bone; but we are all inadequate and neglectful parents, albeit in varying degrees. Furthermore, we are grappling with complicated interrelationships involving physical disorder, demographic differences, the interplay of physical emotional and intellectual deprivation, parental motivation and guilt, cultural variation and the independent and sometimes conflicting "rights" with which parents and children are respectively endowed through their membership of a community. Appendix III of the report on the first Tunbridge Wells conference (Ref.1) drew cogent attention to much of this, but the absence of any discussion at the time was commented upon, and not much has been contributed since.

Unravelling the possible reasons for a child's real or apparent failure to thrive is, as paediatricians know only too well, at best a difficult and time-consuming task, even with the help of serial observations and parental co-operation. Without these it can be well-nigh impossible. Disease, genetic factors and the cultural and child-rearing norms of the community have all to be taken into account and may wholly account for slow physical progress, even in families where other considerations might suggest the possibility of deprivation. The role of inadequate nutrition (in the physical sense) in the stunting of growth has long been common knowledge. The ability of emotional deprivation to inhibit weight gain was demonstrated in the classical studies of Widdowson (2) as long ago as 1951, and our understanding of the physiological mechanisms involved was well reviewed by MacCarthy in 1975 (Ref.3). But even this plethora of causes does not explain every case of growth impairment. Russell Davies (4), for example, has recently reported a series of children whose heights were below the 3rd centile as the result of prolonged deficiency in caloric intake, for which a small or capricious appetite was thought to be responsible.

The paediatrician, confronted with an undersized child whose parents are caring, responsible and concerned may have difficult decisions to make about investigation and is often likely to seek a prolonged period of observation with serial measurements of height and weight as a minimum requirement. Increasingly, however, the motive for the child's appearance is not parental concern but the anxiety of the health visitor, social worker or other professionals, whose casual and unsolicited observations have led to the devising of a rendezvous with the paediatrician - and who to achieve this end has often had to resort to something not far removed from subterfuge. Attempts to arrange hospital surveillance of these children are doomed to frustration and failure, be explanations to the parents never so tactful and sympathetic. The relationship is false from the start; such parents do not perceive their children as requiring hospital care, particularly when no "treatment" is forthcoming; their natural suspicion of and hostility towards the establishment is rapidly reinforced and such tenous links as they may have with health clinics, play groups, health visitors and the like are jeopardised and finally ruptured.

Can such an impasse be avoided? The answer must be determined to some extent by the characteristics of the families concerned. Few generalisations are possible. We are not dealing with battering families. Of 10 children in 5 families, none were known to have been physically injured except Louise E., whose physical insults were sustained on two widely separated and probably isolated occasions. In all five families the marital relationship, though hardly tranquil, had been notably stable over a number of years, in constrast to the casual comings and goings so often found in battering families. In general the mothers gave the impression that they believed themselves to be providing acceptable care for their children and to be in no need of help, thereby adding to the poignancy of their situation. And while it comes as no surprise to find that these mothers had all experienced some degree of deprivation during their own childhood, it is of interest that they are also all of markedly short stature and poor physique. If this physical characteristic is even in part constitutional, it would be expected to exaggerate the small size of their offspring and thus presumably make the latter more likely to attract adverse comment than the perhaps equally deprived children of taller mothers. And by way of explaining the persistent hostility of our mothers towards proffered help, might it be that they are asserting their own normality by insisting on the normality of the children they are moulding into their own image?

The quest for ideal long-term solutions usually comes back to prevention, which in the present content means, as so often, improving the social milieu that generates such problems and, more specifically, strengthening the health visitor, social and other services; and these aims must be energetically pursued. But the more sceptical, especially those among us who work in districts which combine the highest rates for non-accidental injury with the lowest ratios of health visitors and social workers to child population, will be excused for also seeking more immediate remedies.

Nevertheless, we must not deny our over-riding obligation to inform and educate. The Court Committee's report (Ref. 5) identified the primary professional responsibility of workers in the child health preventive services as "the oversight of health and *physical growth of all children*" (my italics) and went on to state unambiguously that "...evaluation of a child's state of health and pattern of growth requires ...... serial measurements of weight, height and head circumference suitably recorded on standardised charts giving centile norms .....". The Select Committee on Violence in the Family (Ref. 6) made the same point in recommending that "All children under school age should have the right to regular medical examinations" and its chairman subsequently expressed her perplexity at the Government's reluctance to accept this proposal (Ref. 7). The enactment of such proposals must be energetically urged upon the authorities, with the aim of re-establishing a climate of opinion in which the recording of heights and weights at regular and frequent intervals throughout the growth period again becomes a routine whose determined implementation would no longer carry threatening or pejorative overtones. And while we can indeed understand and sympathise with the misgivings of those who see such procedures as yet another erosion by the professionals of the responsibilites and prerogatives of parents, the stakes are high - no less than the long-term wellbeing, and perhaps even the lives, of some of our children. Our social worker colleagues, too, have not always been adequately briefed in the reasoning that leads paediatricians to agitate for the collection of firm physical data,even when this may threaten the developing rapport on which successful case work must depend.

Much harm has been done by those who have urged the abandonment of routine measurements and even the removal of weighing machines from health clinics. They would have been more usefully employed in pressing for the additional provision of reliable apparatus for measuring length and height and for the wider availability of both kinds of equipment in nurseries, nursery schools, play groups, perhaps even with child minders, and elsewhere. Such establishments might well be more successful than hospitals in obtaining the kind of serial records we are seeking. As things are, their staffs too often find that even when they have been concerned about the quality of home care provided for some of their charges the absence of the necessary appliances makes it impossible for them to make the simple measurements that might validate their concern.

But even when the community has been indoctrinated, the policies enunciated, the equipment installed, and every last ounce of sympathetic persuasiveness exerted by the most dedicated health visitor, there will still be a residual hard core of non-compliant families. What then?

Financial sanctions and legal compulsion remain. In the contemporary climate of opinion in the United Kingdom neither of these are greatly favoured. There are indeed certain practical and administrative difficulties in the way of tying child benefit directly to the acceptance of a programme of health surveillance; but these constitute no argument for consigning to oblivion the admirable principle that in general rewards should so far as possible be linked with the discharge of attendant responsibilities. Consideration of the legal side reveals a crucial deficit; the absence of any mechanism for enforcing so much as the weighing and measuring of a child, much less his medical appraisal, other than by obtaining a court order. Whether this order be for place of safety, supervision, or care, the necessary procedure is either unduly cumbersome or likely to be inappropriate in some other respect. One small advance in recent years, perhaps not yet sufficiently well known, is that in 1976 the Magistrates' Courts Rules were amended to enable a court to add to a supervision order the requirement that "he/she [the supervised person] shall be medically examined in accordance with the arrangements made by the supervisor". This at least does something to ease one of the social worker's difficulties in that when pressing reluctant parents to bring the child for measurement or examination she can refer to the authority of the court rather than having herself to appear as the enforcing agency. In reality, however, if the parents persist in their recalcitrance, she has no resort other than to go back to the courts for a care order (or, in emergency, to obtain a place of safety order), with no prior assurance that her application would be successful. The necessity remains for the more fundamental reform advocated by the Court Committee (Ref. 8): "..... the powers of a Local Authority ..... should be extended to enable a legally enforceable medical examination to be sought separately from a removal order." That Committee also identified three specific situations in which it judged the introduction of a legal sanction to be justifiable and expedient; the supporting arguments are set out in the Committee's report and need not be recapitulated. The relevant recommendations are (i) that the school entry medical examination should again become statutory; (ii) that where there is suspicion of serious ill-health for which medical help is not being sought, the health visitor should first seek access by persuasion, but in the event of failure should have the right to apply for a legally enforceable medical examination; and (iii) that head teachers should have the right, on reasonable grounds for concern, to request the examination of a child under their charge, if necessary without the consent of the parents (Ref. 9). These proposals require serious debate and evaluation; the problems they reflect are not going to go away until the millennium.

Conclusion

There are children who are stunted in growth and development and whose disability may be a consequence of inadequate nurture; and there are families who for reasons which may be deepseated, complex and ineradicable, cannot be persuaded voluntarily to accept the services of which their children are in such dire need. When these conditions coincide, problems of exceptional complexity are created for the caring professions in regard to diagnosis, management, the decision to intervene and the exercise of authority. Examples have been given of the important contribution that may be made to the management of such problems by simple measurement of height and weight and a plea is made for the general re-establishment of these procedures. Yet the protection of the child will still require on occasion a resort to legal sanction. In an area where no *a priori* boundaries can exist between the acceptable and the unacceptable, it is essential for the community, by informed discussion and debate, now to seek a consensus which when necessary can be expressed through the decisions of the courts.

References

(1) Franklin, A.W. (Ed.) (1975) Concerning Child Abuse, Churchill Livingstone, Edinburgh.
(2) Widdowson, E.M., Mental contentment and physical growth, Lancet, i, 1316 (1951).
(3) MacCarthy, D.de la C. in Davis, J.A. and Dobbing, J. (Eds) (1974) Scientific Foundations of Paediatrics, p 56, William Heinemann, London.
(4) Davis, D. Russell, Apley, J., Fill, G., and Grimaldi, C., Diet and retarded growth, Brit. Med. J. i, 539 (1978).
(5) Fit for the Future, para. 9.7. (1976) H.M. Stationery Office, London.
(6) Violence to Children, Recommendation 42, (1978) H.M. Stationery Office, London.
(7) The Times, Parliamentary Report (June 17, 1978) Times Newspapers Ltd., London.
(8),(9) Fit for the Future, paras 16.6, 16.7, 16.8 (1976) H.M. Stationery Office, London.

Child Abuse and Neglect, Vol. 3, pp. 467 - 475. 0145-2134/79/0601-0467 $02.00/0.

ABUSE AND NEGLECT AS A CAUSE OF MENTAL RETARDATION
A Study of 140 Children Admitted to Subnormality Hospitals in Wiltshire

by Ann Buchanan and J.E. Oliver
Burderop Hospital, Swindon, Wilts. Pewsey Hospital, Wilts

INTRODUCTION

A survey of severely ill-treated young children in North-East Wiltshire (Oliver et al 1974) found that, out of 30 severely ill-treated children, eight had been rendered intellectually impaired. At least three of these eight suffered severe or profound mental handicap due to massive, obvious brain damage associated with abuse. Their cases were described in a further paper 'Microcephaly following baby battering and shaking' (Oliver 1975a).

Recently several authors have drawn attention to the consequences of child abuse in relation to brain damage and mental function (Guthkelch 1971, Martin 1972, Martin et al 1974, Caffey 1974, Sarsfield 1974, Smith and Hanson 1974, MacKeith 1975, Jones 1976). At the first International Congress on Child Abuse and Neglect, Eppler and Brown showed 5.5 per cent of persons diagnosed mentally retarded had strongly suggestive evidence that abuse and/or neglect was the cause of their mental retardation (Eppler and Brown 1976). The British Paediatric Association Survey reported to the Parliamentary Select Committee on Violence in the Family that 92 out of 869 'Non-Accidental Injury' cases reported by paediatricians in the United Kingdom were left with brain damage and 48 with visual defects (BPA 1976). The Royal College of Psychiatrists, reporting to the same Committee, estimated that '..if 75 young children per million of total population are severely attacked each year, then 18-19 million could suffer intellectual impairment each year, often of a profound degree' (RCPsych 1976). Baldwin, projecting from the N.E. Wilts data, gives a crude minimum estimate of 240 new cases of severe subnormality (IQ below 50) in England and Wales per year resulting directly from parental assaults on babies and toddlers (Baldwin 1976).

Closely related to the effects of abuse on mental function are the effects of neglect and deprivation on intellectual development. Psycho-social deprivation as a cause of mental handicap is of course recognised by all the international classification systems (for instance General Register Office 1968, Grossman 1973). Different aspects of this important field of research, in particular the effects of underfeeding and under-stimulation on the brains of young children are considered by the following: Stott 1962, Bullard 1968, Birch and Gussow 1970, Hertzig et al 1972, Pilling 1973, Chase et al 1974, Dobbing 1974, Lewin 1974, Blackie et al 1975, Forrest 1975, Watts 1976.

However, we are not aware of any systematic survey planned to assess the number of children in subnormality hospitals in Britain whose handicap might be related to abuse or neglect. We therefore set out to discover, in children in NHS subnormality hospitals in Wilts:

1. What proportion had been victims of neglect and abuse.
2. What proportion had been definitely rendered mentally handicapped as a direct result of assaults.
3. What proportion with previously healthy brains had possibly been rendered mentally handicapped as a result of abuse.
4. What part neglect and deprivation had played in reducing intellectual potential, with resultant admission to hospital.

THE CHILDREN

The 140 children admitted or resident in the two Wiltshire subnormality hospitals during 1972 and 1973, under 16 years old in the year of their admission, constituted the basis for the study.

These 140 children came from 137 families. Three families had two children each in hospital. Seventy-seven of the cases in the survey were short-term or programmed admissions only; the remainder were long-term or had become so by 1975. Twenty children, of the 140, were admitted only to the unit in one of the hospitals which specialises in emotionally disturbed and/or psychotic children. Table 1 gives the diagnostic groupings. For most children there were ostensible medical, psychiatric or education-training reasons for admission but for three-quarters of the survey social pressures were often the most forceful arguments used to get the child into hospital. Pressure to admit children of parents in the armed services (from families transiently in the locality) on a permanent basis has always been resisted - not always successfully. Neither hospital was viewed as a special refuge for maltreated children. Despite these factors, we felt that the children admitted to the two hospitals were fairly typical of children admitted to other subnormality hospitals in Britain.

Most children in the survey had had fairly extensive investigations for their mental handicap before admission to our hospitals. Seventy-two children (51 per cent) had been investigated or treated at specialist centres outside our districts (at neurological units, paediatric hospitals, paediatric departments of Teaching Hospitals). Of these 72, 18 had been seen at Great Ormond Street. Ninety-two children (66 per cent) had been investigated at the paediatric departments of local District General Hospitals (some had also been investigated at specialist units elsewhere). Only 19 children (14 per cent) had had no detailed investigations outside our two hospitals. Of these, 10 children had been given a clear-cut diagnosis at, or very soon after, birth (9 children of Down's syndrome); five were mentally handicapped but came to hospital through the Child Guidance Departments comparatively late in development; and the remaining four were not mentally handicapped.

METHODS OF STUDY

Efforts were made to obtain all medical and social records of the 140 children, to link these with family records, and to relate them to current clinical findings. This entailed searches of records from at least 25 different types of medical or social agencies concerned with child welfare. Starting with our own hospital file on each patient, possible sources of records were followed-up. Scanning checks were made in all areas of the child's and sibs' residence, with vigilance over the frequent occurrence of alternative names and addresses. Our work did not just depend on retrospective collated data. All the children and many of the families were known to one of us (Oliver) during or before their admission to hospital. Ongoing information was obtained from Oliver's clinical work in the field of mental handicap, child guidance and child abuse; and also from the three paediatric and two other psychiatric consultants who had clinical responsibilities within the hospital. Some of the children and some of the relatives had been studied in the previous survey, 'Severely Ill-treated Young Children in N.E. Wilts' (Oliver et al 1974). In most cases it was possible to obtain original data relating to the child's birth and to plot the child's development through paediatric and health visitor notes and specialist investigations. These findings could then be linked to corresponding events in the social history of the family and related to current clinical findings. The huge amount of previously uncollated material collected is indicative of the help and co-operation from the medical and social agencies approached.

Definitions

VIH (Violence-induced handicap): Mental handicap following brain damage caused by assault(s). Assaults included fierce or repetitive shaking and/or throwing of a baby or young toddler - more dangerous practices than simple fist blows. It should be noted that VIH is not so difficult to confirm where a child has previously been entirely normal and healthy. Nevertheless, abnormal children may be most at risk. This definition, therefore, includes doubtfully healthy or abnormal children, whose intellect was unequivocally further impaired following assaults affecting the brain. In this latter instance, the VIH must usually have been severe.
Abuse: Independent professional evidence that before admission to hospital, the child had been a victim of physical assault(s) inappropriate to his age or development, and to an extent which warranted concern and/or intervention on the child's behalf.
Neglect: Independent professional evidence that the child was suffering as a result of inadequate parental care, which warranted concern and/or intervention on the child's behalf.

(See Table 4 for instances).

Diagnoses

Diagnoses and codings under the International Classification of Diseases (General Register Office 1968) were made by three consultants, in the combined sub-specialities of Child Psychiatry and Mental Handicap, and three paediatricians, as part of their routine clinical commitment. These diagnoses were based predominately on the investigations and opinions of paediatricians. Where our research elicited new medical information which might be relevant to diagnosis, aspects of this information were discussed with the appropriate specialist. In many cases, specialists in other areas discussed their findings with us.

TABLE 1 Medical Diagnoses under the ICD System

ICD code, together with the appropriate (broad) category description	No. of children
Causation of Mental Handicap	
.0 Mental handicap following infections and intoxications	16
.1 Mental handicap following trauma or physical agents (including birth anoxia,etc)	24
.2 Mental handicap associated with disorders of metabolism, growth or nutrition	1
.3 Mental handicap associated with gross brain disease	6
.4 Mental handicap associated with diseases and conditions due to (unknown) pre-natal influence	28
.5 Mental handicap with chromosal abnormalities	9
.6 Mental handicap associated with prematurity	2
.7 Mental handicap following major psychiatric disorder	13
.8 Mental handicap associated with psycho-social (environmental) deprivation	12
.9 Mental handicap - other and unspecified	25
Children admitted to hospital who were not mentally handicapped	4
Total children	140
Degree of mental handicap	
313-314 Severe and profound mental retardation (IQ under 35)	77
312 Moderate mental retardation (IQ 36-51)	36
311-310 Mild and borderline mental retardation (IQ 52-85)..	23
Not mentally handicapped	4
Total children	140

Ascertainment of Violence-induced Handicap(VIH cases)

Minimum figure: in this survey, to ascertain definite VIH cases, the following four methods of substantiation were used. In the cases reported under Results, we were in fact able to substantiate each case under three or four of the headings. In other localities, only strong suspicions may be possible.

1. Paediatric evidence at the time of the assault(s) or soon afterwards. Microcephaly following assaults can also be confirmed by serial head measurements (Oliver 1975a)
2. Statements by parent(s) or persons responsible
3. Direct observations by relatives and others.
4. Consensus on diagnosis amongst all professionals concerned with the family.

Maximum figure: because it was felt that the minimum figure for VIH cases gave no indication of the likely size of the problem, a further screening procedure was undertaken to produce a possible maximum VIH figure. The aim was to find out how many additional children with seemingly healthy brains in early infancy might have been damaged as a result of concealed abuse, for instance secret shaking of crying or troublesome babies. It was recognised that this screening procedure might miss some children who, because they had pre-existing abnormalities, might be particularly at risk of abuse (Lynch 1975). Furthermore, it might include other children who had pre-existing 'biological' abnormalities which had not been recognized by doctors. The following screening procedure was undertaken:

1. Inclusion only of children who had been passed as normal neonatally and up to three months old (sometimes for much longer)

2. Inclusion only of children whose families showed factors and behaviour generally associated with child abuse at the critical period when the child ceased to develop normally. (Assaults on sibs, violence between marital partners, mental or physical illness in parent, multi-agency involvement, severe social/domestic stress especially 'diffuse' social problems (Lynch 1976a) and situations leading to bonding failure (Lynch 1975,1976b)

3. Inclusion only of children for whom there had been professional concern that the child in question had been at risk of abuse and/or evidence that the child had actually been the victim of assaults in his first three years, during the period of maximum (postnatal) brain growth spurt.

4. Inclusion only of children for whom there were no indications that birth trauma or factors in pregnancy had caused mental handicap.

5. Exclusion of children with clear-cut diagnoses under the ICD system, related to biological causes - for instance, all children with Down's syndrome (000.5)

6. Exclusion of children from families where there were indications that mental handicap or still-births, involving parents and/or sibs, were part of a family inheritance; and exclusion of children with congenital stigmata associated with mental handicap.

Ascertainment of neglect and deprivation as a contributory factor in reducing intellectual potential

It was recognised that there would be no easy means of incriminating neglect as a sole cause of mental handicap (BMJ 1976a,b). The medical diagnosis under the ICD 000.8 (mental retardation associated with psycho-social/environmental deprivation) does not allow for the interactions of other factors in the causation of mental handicap. Nevertheless, it was felt important to ascertain those children for whom neglect had been a contributory factor in reducing intellectual potential.

All children, therefore, for whom there was evidence of neglect, in particular at the critical period of post-natal brain growth spurt (Dobbing 1974), were reassessed in detail. Diagnoses, early paediatric evidence (especially episodes of 'failure to thrive' for non-medical reasons), and social evidence (NSPCC records of neglect) were considered, and the children were assigned to the following categories:

1. Neglect - a predominating cause of mental handicap in the absence of other important identifiable features which could contribute to the reduced intelligence.

2. Neglect - a major contributory factor, with no other clear-cut causes of mental handicap.

3. Neglect - an important contributory factor but in the presence of other identifiable causes of mental handicap. All the children in this group appeared to have multiple causes for their mental handicap rather than one clear-cut cause - thus no children with Down's syndrome appear here.

RESULTS

Abused children

There was independent professional evidence that 31 children had been victims of physical assaults inappropriate to their age or development, before admission to hospital, which had warranted concern and/or intervention on the child's behalf. This was 22 per cent of the total survey cases. For three-quarters of the assaulted children, the physical abuse was not an isolated incident, but a habitual rearing pattern.

Table 2 gives details of injuries and the age at which these were sustained. There were a number of fractures occurring in children under the age of 2, some of which might have been overlooked or unsuspected if the X-ray investigations had not been carried out at critical times in relation to the assaults and the child's development.

In addition to the abused children, there was evidence of recorded professional concern that the child was at risk of assault in a further 10 per cent of the cases. Furthermore, 13 children had been threatened with injury or death by their parents.

TABLE 2 Abused children - type of, and age at, abuse among 140 children

Type of abuse	Under 2 years	2-5	6+	Total
Abused children with head injuries	6	5	1	12
Fractures associated with physical abuse:				
1. Number of children with skull fractures	2	1	-	3
(number of skull fractures)	(4)	(1)	-	(5)
2. Number of children with rib fractures	3	1	-	4
(number of rib fractures) *	(4-7)	(1)	-	(5-8)
3. Number of children with other fractures	3	2	-	5
(number of other fractures)	(4)	(2)	-	(6)
4. Total number of children with fractures associated with physical abuse	6	3	-	9
(total number of fractures) *	(12-15)	(4)	-	(16-19)
Children receiving beatings, or bruisings and other surface injuries associated with abuse	14	11	2	27
Child victims of killing attempts	2	-	-	2
Total numbers of children with evidence of abuse	15	14	2	31

* Sometimes old fractures were uncertain on X-ray. Where there are two figures in brackets, these represent the maximum and minimum numbers of fractures.

Violence-induced Handicap (VIH): Minimum confirmed figure

At least four children (3 per cent) had definitely suffered assaults as babies which caused brain damage, rendering them severely or profoundly mentally handicapped. These children were ascertained by the methods already described.

Three of the children had been mentally and biologically normal before suffering the assaults which caused very severe and obvious brain damage. These three children were twelve months old or under at the time of the assault. They all had evidence of retinal haemorrhages and intracranial bleeding; but only two of them had skull fractures. Today they are all severely mentally handicapped, spastic, with small heads (Oliver 1975). A fourth child had suffered assaults at a year old. He had suffered severe bruising to the head and face. When found, he was partially asphyxiated; his throat had been forcibly obstructed by materials. Fits, cyanosis and coma ensued, with subsequent slow and partial recovery. This child had evidence of neurofibromatosis, but was reported by his father, the family doctor and hospital doctors to have been developing normally before the catastrophe. The assault episode and/or its complications were seen to have been the main cause of the severe mental handicap. Fits and neurological features were conspicuous in the period following the assaults. At 4 years he still had not reached again some of his achievements at the age of one. The fits diminished as he grew older, but he now has an IQ of less than 30.

Violence-induced Handicap (VIH): Maximum (possible) figure

A maximum of 16 children (11 per cent of the total survey) could have been rendered mentally handicapped as a result of abuse. This figure includes the four children definitely rendered mentally handicapped as a result of abuse.

Eleven children were ascertained by the screening procedure for the Maximum VIH figure previously described. A further child is included in the maximum VIH figure because, although he was not ascertained by the screening procedure, it is highly probable that repeated trauma to the head, which was well documented, was responsible for brain damage and a subsequent impairment of intellectual ability. This child, from a mobile chaotic family, had more than ten episodes of (mostly severe) head injury from assaults, before the age of 5, the main episodes being at 4 months, 2½ years and 3 years. He had been described as a 'bright' baby and toddler but subsequently became a severely mentally and emotionally disturbed boy who required admission to the special unit within the subnormality hospital. He is now, after much special care in the range of borderline subnormal intelligence, with a clearly abnormal EEG and clinical features suggesting brain damage. It seems probable, but not certain, that repeated trauma to the head was responsible for brain damage and subsequent impairment of intellectual ability.

This case illustrates the weaknesses of our screening procedure, and is typical of three or four others in the survey. These extra 3-4 cases are not included in the Maximum (possible) VIH figure because the assault episodes are less well documented.

Table 3 details the clinical features seen in the 16 children included in the Maximum VIH figure. None of these features were part of the original screening procedure. No child had less than two of the features. Four of the children were profoundly mentally retarded, 7 were severely mentally retarded, 1 was moderately retarded and 4 had mild or borderline mental retardation, but with severe behaviour disorders.

TABLE 3 Incidence of certain clinical features seen in the 16 children who comprised the maximum (possible) figures for violence-induced handicap

Clinical feature present	Number of children out of possible 16 children with feature
1. Gross and persistent CNS damage associated with spasticity, sensory defects and severe or profound mental retardation	5
2. Spasticity reported (usually by paediatrician) at some stage in the life of child	8
3. As for 2 above, but also including children with a variety of 'softer CNS signs', often with mention of organic psychosis or organic brain damage	14
4. Epileptic fits	10
5. Rages or frenzies a prominent feature of the child's behaviour - excluding 1 above	10 *
6. Abnormal EEG, often with indications of 'multiple patchy areas of damage' or 'multi-focal cerebral damage' etc - excluding 1 above	10 *

* Out of 11

Special mention must be made of one of the eleven children derived by the screening process. There was well-documented evidence that the child had suffered suffocatory episodes by being held under water at the age of 2. Although the child was already mentally handicapped at the time of the documented incidents, there were strong indications that he suffered frequent or severe suffocatory episodes at a much earlier age. A recent Australian paper suggests that this in itself can be a cause of mental handicap (Nixon & Pearn 1977).

VIH Children in the Wessex Region

Seven part-time or full-time consultants in mental subnormality, the entire membership of the Wessex Regional Consultants in Subnormality Group, gave individual independent estimates of the numbers of children in institutions for which they had responsibility, who might have been brain damaged as a consequence of battering. The mean estimate was 2.5 per cent. This broad, partly guessed, clinical estimate compares well with the actual Minimum VIH figure given in this survey of 2.8 per cent. Two of the consultants stressed that severe shaking causes greater damage to the brains of babies than fist blows or other 'batterings'.

Neglected children

For 67 out of the 140 children (48 per cent of the total) there was recorded evidence in the notes by independent professionals that the child was suffering as a result of inadequate parental care. For 57 of these children (41 per cent) this represented a habitual pattern of rearing. In most cases, the first evidence of inadequate parental care was initially recorded for children under the age of 2 (Table 4).

TABLE 4 - Neglected children - type of neglect amont 140 children

Type of neglect	Total children
1. General low standards of care or neglect specified	33
2. General low standards of care or neglect specified, with consequential multi-agency involvement	28
3. Inadequate feeding specified	16
4. Experiential (psycho-social) deprivation	33
5. Failure to seek essential medical care, or co-operate in treatment of child	13
6. Child exposed to unnecessary hazards	5
7. Child exposed to cold with inadequate clothing	5
8. Sexual abuse	2
9. Professional intervention necessary as child was unattended for long periods	6
10. Other forms of neglect or unspecified	12
Habitual pattern of rearing	57
Isolated incident	10
Total children suffering as a result of inadequate parental care	67

Neglect as a contributory factor in reducing intellectual potential

In 34 children (24 per cent. of the survey) neglect was felt to be a contributory factor in reducing intellectual potential. In two of these, with mild or borderline mental handicap, neglect appeared to be the predominating cause of mental handicap in the absence of other important identifiable features which could contribute to the reduced intelligence. In another 15, neglect was a major contributory factor, with no other clear-cut causes of mental handicap. In the remaining 17 children, neglect and deprivation were considered to be important contributory factors, but in the presence of other identifiable causes of mental handicap. In all 17 children there were multiple adverse factors in the history of the child's birth and development.

Out of the total 34 children, 20 had been known to the NSPCC, primarily for neglect. For 9 children there were detailed records of 'failure to thrive' for non-medical reasons. Twelve of these 34 children had been diagnosed as mental retardation associated with pyscho-social (environmental) deprivation.

Children who suffered abuse and neglect

In the case of 29 children (21 per cent. of the survey) there was evidence of both abuse and neglect. There was no clear-cut cause for the handicap in 22 out of the 29, so it appears possible that the combination of abuse and neglect could have contributed in an important way to impairment of the intellects of these 22 children.

DISCUSSION

VIH should be recognised as a major cause of mental handicap

Children rendered mentally handicapped as a result of abuse may account for many more cases than phenylketonuria. The consequences are frequently more severe than those of Down's syndrome.

Difficulty of recognition of VIH

In this survey we were fortunate in having the time and facilities for investigation which would not normally be available to other specialists. An awareness of the following difficulties which we experienced in our investigations may help the recognition of VIH:

1. Evidence for VIH, if not realised, investigated and documented soon after an assault, may not be available at a later date. In brain damage resulting from shaking, the retinal haemorrhages (which may also signify punctuate haemorrhages within the brain substance) may be unnoticed or may have resolved by the time a child is admitted to a subnormality hospital. Similar considerations may apply to rib, skull or other fractures.

2. Before 1973, standard medical files seldom included details of, or even any reference to, the NSPCC the Social Services, the Probation Department or other agencies concerned with the welfare of the child in question, or with his sibs. These agencies, in turn, may have been unaware of the crucially important medical considerations of leaving children under two at risk. This may still be the case in many localities, even now.

3. Identification of abused children is at all times difficult. It is especially so in the case of mentally handicapped children. The caring professions are usually sympathetic to the difficulties of a family with a mentally handicapped child, and tend not to record evidence derogatory to the parents.

4. It is much easier to incriminate tangible factors in the causation of mental handicap - toxaemia of pregnancy, damaged placenta, difficult birth - than emotionally charged medico-social factors - cruelty or neglect in rearing. Parents assist in the distortion of emphasis by concealing more than they reveal to the trusting doctor or social worker.

5. The method of diagnostic coding used by the main subnormality hospitals in Wiltshire follows the International Classification of Diseases system (General Register Office 1968). The insistence on a primary (single) diagnosis can rule out the probability of interactions. In particular, it is unsatisfactory to code neglect/deprivation (000.8) as an all-or nothing effect in isolation from other possible aetiological factors (including abuse).

Combinations of neglect and abuse

These may be a handicapping factor for much larger numbers of children than is generally recognized, especially for those children with already 'vulnerable' brains. Some of the neglected children had adverse genetic inheritance, or had suffered damage in the pre-natal or peri-natal period. Such children seemed particularly vulnerable to aspects of inadequate care which might not have so adversely affected the brains of children from healthier backgrounds. One case of a child with potentially preventable brain damage was not recognized until too late because the mother refused to see health visitors or take her child to the clinic. This clear-cut case was nevertheless the exception. The effects of underfeeding, maternal rejection and psycho-social deprivation most often seemed to exaggerate the impaired development of a child already in precarious health. This was so in 32 out of these 34 neglected children whose intellectual potential appeared to have suffered as a consequence of inadequate rearing.

Need for recognition of the extent of VIH and the role of neglect

There is not a sufficient awareness among the general public of the vulnerability of young brains and their susceptibility to stress, especially during the period of maximum brain growth spurt (up to 2 years). In particular, the dangers of shaking a young child could be emphasized. A suffocatory act (for instance, holding a young child under water) may also induce mental handicap (Nixon and Pearn 1977) and this is more widespread than is generally recognised (Oliver et al 1974).

The high incidence of maltreatment in children admitted to Subnormality Hospitals

The rate for children who suffered abuse and/or neglect in our survey is approximately 12 times greater than that found in a comparable survey of children in the general population in N.E. Wilts (Oliver 1975b). This survey used identical definitions and covered a similar area.

Inadequate families

A proportion of children admitted to subnormality hospitals must inevitably come from families who have been unable to care for their mentally handicapped offspring adequately. Nevertheless, we would like to stress that, for nearly half the children in the survey, there was evidence of at least adequate, and in some instances, exceptionally devoted parental care before the child's admission to hospital.

ACKNOWLEDGEMENTS

The authors would like to express their appreciation to their colleagues and to the many other professionals who co-operated in this survey, and to Dr. J.A. Baldwin who helped in the design of the study.

REFERENCES

Baldwin, J.A. (1976) Personal communication
Birch, H.G. & Gussow,J.D. (1970) Disadvantaged Children Grune & Stratton, New York
Blackie,J.Forrest,A. & Witcher,G.(1975) Subcultural mental handicap Brit.J.Psychiat.127,535-9
British Paediatric Association (1976) Evidence presented to the Select Committee on Violence in the Family, 8 June 1976.
Bullard, D.M.,Glaser,H.H.,Heagarty,M.C. & Pivchik,E.C.(1968) Failure to Thrive in the 'Neglected' Child. Annual Progress in Child Psychiatry and Child Development,Chapter 32 540-54 Brunner-Mazel, New York
Caffey, J. (1974) The Whiplash shaken infant syndrome. Paediatrics 54 no. 4 396-403
Chase,H.P.,Canosa,C.A.,Dabiere,C.S.,Welch,N.N.,& O'Brien,D.(1974) Postnatal undernutrition and human brain development. Journal of Mental Deficiency Research 18,355-66
Dobbing,J. (1974) The later development of the brain and its vulnerability.Chapter 32 in Scientific Foundations of Paediatrics, Heinemann, London
Editorial (1976a) The ultimate cost of malnutrition. B.M.J.ii, 1158-9
Editorial (1976b) Kolchova's twins. B.M.J. ii,897-8
Eppler, M & Brown,G. (1976) "Child Abuse and Neglect: Preventable causes of Mental Retardation" from the First International Congress on Child Abuse and Neglect, Geneva.
Forrest, A.D. (1975) Mental handicap and syndromes of brain damage in children,B.M.J.ii 71-3
General Register Office. Studies on Medical and Population Subjects (1968 amended 1973) A Glossary of Mental Disorders, No.22.HMSO
Grossman,, H.J.(1973) Manual on Terminology and Classification in Mental Retardation. American Association on Mental Deficiency, Special Publication No. 2, Washington.
Guthkelch, A.N.(1971) Infantile subdural haematoma and its relationship to whiplash injuries. B. M.J. ii, 430-1.
Hertzig,M.E.,Birch,H.G.,Richardson,S.H & Tizard,J. (1972) Intellectual levels of school-children severely malnourished during the first two years of life.Paediatrics 49(6)814-24
Jones, C.(1976) The fate of abused children. Presented at the Symposium on Child Abuse, held at the Royal Society of Medicine 2-4 June 1976,London.
Lewin, J. (1974) Malnutrition and the human brain. World Medicine, 10(5),19-21
Lynch,M.A. (1975) Ill-health and child abuse. Lancet ii, 317-19
--------Roberts, J. & Gordon, M. (1976a) Early warning of child abuse in the maternity hospital. Developmental Medicine and Child Neurology, 18, 759-66
--------(1976b) Child abuse - the critical path. Journal of Maternal & Child Health,July 25-9
Martin,H.P. (1972) The Child and his development.Chapter 7 in Helping the Battered Child and his family (eds.C.H. Kempe and R.E.Helfer).Lippincott,Philadelphia and Toronto.
--------et al (1974) The Development of abused children.Advances in Paediatrics 21,25-73 Year book Medical Publishers, Chicago.
MacKeith, R.(1975) Speculation on some possible long-term effects of child abuse.Chapter 8 in Concerning Child Abuse (ed.A.W.Franklin). Churchill Livingstone.
Nixon,J., & Pearn,J.(1977) Non-accidental immersion in bath water: another aspect of child abuse. B.M.J. i, 271-2.
Oliver, J.E.,Cox,J.,Taylor A. & Baldwin,J.A.(1974) Severely Ill-treated Young Children in North-East Wiltshire. Oxford University Unit of Clinical Epidemiology, Oxford Record Linkage Study, Research Report No.4
-------(1975a) Microcephaly following baby battering and shaking. B.M.J. 262-4
-------(1975b) Child Abuse. Chapter in Social Crises in Service Communities. Proceedings of Triservice Multi-disciplinary Conference pp 73-136.(taken from Symposium held at Amport House, Hants. 30 September, 1975
Pilling,D.(1973) The Handicapped Child: Research Review Vol.III.From Studies in Child Development,Longman Press (in association with the National Children's Bureau)
Royal College of Psychiatrists (1976) Evidence presented to the Select Committee on Violence in the Family, 8 June 1976.
Sarsfield,J.K.(1974) The neurological sequelae of non accidental injury.Developmental Medicine and Child Neurology 16, 826-7
Smith, S.M. & Hanson,R.(1974) 134 Battered Children: a medical and Psychological study B.M.J.,iii 660-70
Stott, D.H.(1962) Abnormal mothering as a cause of mental subnormality. Journal of Child Psychology and Psychiatry, 3 79-91 and 133-48
Watts,G. (1976) Malnutrition in context. World Medicine, 11,(10),57-60.

Ann Buchanan, Dip.Soc.Studies, Research Social Worker
J.E. Oliver, M.B., B.S.,M.R.C.Psych, Consultant in Child Psychiatry and Mental Handicap.
(Reprint requests from J.E. Oliver)

Child Abuse and Neglect, Vol. 3, pp. 477 - 482.
0145-2134/79/0601-0477 $02.00/0.

BURNS AS A MANIFESTATION OF CHILD ABUSE

Catherine Ayoub and Donald R. Pfeifer

Hillcrest Medical Center, Tulsa, Oklahoma, U.S.A.

INTRODUCTION

Few articles in the literature specifically deal with non-accidental burns. Keen[1] described fractures and burns as concomitant injuries suggesting skeletal roentgenograms in instances of non-accidental burns. Stone[2] specifically addressed child abuse by burning, and listed twelve criteria used to suspect a burn as a non-accidental injury.

METHODS

From January 1, 1974, to December 31, 1976, Stone's criteria were used by a multidisciplinary child abuse team to investigate children with burns admitted to Hillcrest Medical Center, the burn center for Northeast Oklahoma. Each child received a physical examination in which both old and new physical injuries were described in detail. Skeletal roentgenograms were performed for fractures. In cases where bruising was apparent, blood clotting studies were obtained. A detailed psychosocial history was obtained from each mother. Fathers or other adults living in the home were asked to be interviewed. In no case was such an interview denied, although the fathers repeatedly failed the appointments.

SUBJECTS

Twenty-six children with burns received child abuse team consultations. Fourteen were classified as accidental, seven were accidental with extreme neglect, and five children appeared to have inflicted burns. A combination of physical findings and psychosocial assessment provided predictive criteria which aided the multidisciplinary child abuse team in the assessment and followup expectations.

FINDINGS

Accidental Burns

The fourteen children with accidental burns consisted of nine scald burns, two hot grease burns, and three flame burns from clothes catching on fire. In all instances the home environment of the accidentally burned child was found to be stable with few chronic social or emotional problems. Children demonstrated no developmental delays, nor did they display significant characteristics of withdrawal. In every case of accidental burns, there was a minor crisis in the home which occurred immediately prior to the child's injury. None of these children have returned re-injured.

Accidental Burns Associated With Extreme Neglect

Case. A 14 month old white female sustained a 13 per cent body surface second degree burn when her six year old sibling, who had been left in charge of the care of four children, placed the patient in a bathtub of hot water. The twice-divorced mother was living with an ex-convict who was known for his violent temper and who had attempted to rape his own daughter by a previous marriage. The living conditions were described as "filthy" and the children were inappropriately clothed for weather conditions. The case had been previously investigated by protective services for neglect. The child was returned home, but because of continued neglect and lack of cooperation, the children were eventually removed and placed in foster care.

Physical evidence. All five children received scald burns. One child had a combination of flame and scald burns. Every child demonstrated significant old injuries consisting of scars, bruises, cigarette burns, old burns, bite marks, strap marks and fractures. The burn did not appear to be the first non-accidental injury. These children were younger in age and all were under twenty months with most under one year of age. The oldest child suffered from the most severe old injuries and the most profound deprivation. Delay in treatment was not significant. Concomitant upper respiratory illness on two occassions appeared to directly precipitate the abuse. Children were described as irritable, cranky, unwilling to mind or be comforted, and consequently were punished. This group had the most severe permanent physical damage: Two children died, and two of the three survivors suffered serious permanent physical impairment. Three children demonstrated moderate to severe withdrawal and had significant developmental delays.

Psychosocial evidence. In all cases of physical abuse there were two adults present and involved in a conflict within the home at the time the abuse occurred. In three cases, a boyfriend's leaving the home, and in one case, the adult male's returning to the home may have precipitated the abuse. Although family dynamics of the crisis which led to abuse appear fairly clear, the identity of the abusive parent could not be determined in every case. In three of five families, there was admitted repeated wife battery. In another family there was suspicion of wife battery. In the fifth family there was verbal abuse but no physical abuse. One half of the families documented chronic unemployment and the second half documented recent unemployment problems. Correlation of suspiciousness with mobility was more pronounced in the above families. Three of the five families moved an average of once a month. Characteristics of abusive mothers include: isolation, suspiciousness, rigidity, dependence, and immaturity. Parents appeared to be responding to their own needs, either through passive withdrawal or through hostility. They reacted with avoidance rather than dealing directly with their children's needs. The hostile mothers presented anger in a very defensive way. They tended to be rigid and saw the question of etiology of the children's injuries as an assault on their individual rights and identities as parents. One mother stated, "You have no right to take my child. Think of how it would make me look." In general, abusive mothers appeared much more difficult to reach emotionally than their neglectful counterparts. Psychosocial evaluation of fathers was not possible due to the inability to require their presence during the hospital stay. It was generally very difficult to contact mothers although their children were hospitalized at the time the interviews were scheduled. Maternal backgrounds of abusive mothers demonstrated three came from emotionally disturbed homes and two from culturally deprived homes.

Disposition. The 40 per cent mortality rate among the abused children and the severity of the subsequent injuries in children who went home suggested the abusive pattern may have been well ingrained at the time of the burn. Inflicted burns appear to require some premeditation, which in itself predicts a poor prognosis. Of the two children who were returned to their homes, one returned to the hospital dead, and the other severely battered. We cannot overly stress the need for intensive intervention with these volatile families.

Predictability. Three out of five children were known to the children's protective unit prior to the burn incident. Two had been previously abused. One child had severe failure to thrive known prior to the burn.

COMMENTS

Our experiences show that non-accidental burns are one of the most serious crimes against children. Physical characteristics such as type of burn and concomitant injuries aid the Child Abuse Team in confirming suspicion of abuse. Specific burn distributions as described by Stone[3] Keene[4] and Lung[5] described as stocking-like distributions on the extermities or radial electric ring burns of the buttocks were not seen. One child had a "donut" distribution burn described by Lenosky[6]. Keene[7] noted that burns and scald appeared to be more calculated and premeditated injuries produced than those produced by sudden outbursts of violence. Scalds, coexisting with other types of injuries of the soft tissues or fractures also present an impressive parallel with Caffey's original example of child abuse[8]. Social characteristics such as excessive mobility, history of unemployment, violence in the home also serve as diagnostic tools.

Keene[9] stated that because injuries such as burns appeared to be more calculated than premeditated that a higher proportion of psychopathic parents might be expected in this group.

Physical evidence. There were a variety of types of burns with two children sustaining flame burns, three scald burns and two from touching a hot object. Only one burn covered more than 15 per cent of the total skin surface. No other physical injuries were found other than the burn. All of the children demonstrated poor physical hygiene. Five of the children had failure to thrive. Ages ranged from four months to six years with most being over one year of age. In two cases, there was a delay in seeking treatment. Although these children had significant burns the mother's explanation for the delays was "I didn't know the burn was that bad." In all children acute respiratory infections was a secondary diagnosis but had not precipitated a family crisis. These mothers seemed almost unaware that their children were ill until it was pointed out to them. Four children demonstrated developmental delays and behavior that included crying, clinging, and extreme passivity. One child died but none of the survivors were permanently physically disabled.
Psychosocial evidence. Mothers tended to live alone and had significant problems with adult relationships and maintaining long-term relationships with individuals of the opposite sex. There was no instance in which an adult male in the home appeared directly involved in the child's injury. In all instances violent activities of the parents occurred within as well as out of the home resulting in jail sentences for the father in two instances. One father attempted suicide. Chronic and acute unemployment was present in all families. Only one family had lived in the same home for more than a five month period. Mobility appeared closely coupled with suspiciousness and financial difficulties. Families frequently indicated that they moved because they were unable to pay the next week's rent. In all cases they lived in sub-standard housing. Mothers were presented as either depressed-overwhelmed, fearful-defensive, or manipulative-sociopathic. Mothers that appeared to have the most empathic responses to their children were those in the depressed-overwhelmed category. These mothers seemed to be reacting to their own low self-esteem and tremendous feelings of lack of control. Mothers in the fearful-defensive group seemed less responsive to their children's needs and more concerned with their feelings of loss of control. They appeared to handle feelings of helplessness with anger and seemed to have a great need to "appear" to be adequate. They were very defensive when it was suggested that they might have played a significant role in their child's injury. This need to maintain appearances was often egocentrically based and at times was an obstacle to these mothers' ability to pick up cues from their children. The manipulative-sociopathic mothers appeared superficial, both in their responses to their children and to other significant adults. They attempted to say and do the socially acceptable things, but appeared to have no depth of commitment to carrying out their responsibilities in regard to their children. This group was designated the most difficult group to treat because of lack of maternal responsiveness to the child's needs. One child in this group was returned home with supervision and never returned for follow-up although the mother repeatedly assured the staff that she would return. She moved within three weeks of the child's discharge and has not been located. A second mother was unable to change her pattern of chronic neglect and eventually her children were placed in foster care. All mothers described chaotic childhoods. Two mothers came from culturally deprived homes, and five came from emotionally disturbed homes fraught with divorce, alcoholism, emotional and possibly physical abuse.
Disposition. Two children were initially placed in foster care. One has returned to his home and the physical conditions within the home have improved. One child remains in foster care and is presently being considered for alternative long-term placement. Four children went home with supervision. Of these four families, one family has been lost to follow-up. None have returned with physical abuse.
Predictability. Five of the seven children were known to the protective unit as members of families previously investigated because of neglectful conditions.

Abuse By Inflicted Burns
Case. A 20 month old negro male received 33 per cent second and third degree burns of the buttocks and legs after being placed in a tub of hot water. He had human bite marks on his arm, black eyes, hematomas of the scalp, cigarette burns of the abdominal and pubic areas, and numerous scars on his neck which appeared to be rope burns. He demonstrated no reaction to pain, maintained a fetal position, and responded only with fearful attentiveness when approached. He had been evaluated extensively in a hospital in another city for failure to thrive several months prior to this admission, and exhibited severe developmental delays at that time. On discharge, this child was placed in foster care.

TABLE I
PHYSICAL AND PSYCHOSOCIAL FINDINGS IN CHILDREN WITH ACCIDENTAL BURNS ASSOCIATED WITH EXTREME NEGLECT

Case	Child's Age	Child's Sex	Child's Race	Maternal Age	Maternal Background	Maternal Characteristics	Marital Status	Mobility	Employment History	Violence	Acute Precipitating Factors
1	12 mos.	F	White	19 years	Educationally deprived	Overwhelmed	Divorced	Yes	Chronic-No	Wife battery	None
2	3 1/2 yrs.	M	White	20 years	Educationally deprived	Manipulative	Separated	Yes	Chronic-No	Wife battery father-prison for violence	None
3	24 mos.	M	White	22 years	Culturally deprived	Defensive	Married	Yes	Chronic-No	Suicide attempts father	None
4	10 mos.	M	Black	19 years	Educationally deprived	Defensive	Single	Yes	Chronic-No	Wife battery child abuse--father	None
5	9 mos.	F	White	23 years	Educationally deprived	Manipulative	Divorced	Yes	Chronic-No	Father in prison for violence	None
6	6 yrs.	F	Black	23 years	Culturally deprived	Overwhelmed	Separated	Yes	Chronic-No	Wife battery	None
7	12 mos.	M	Indian	17 years	Educationally deprived	Manipulative	Single	Yes	Chronic-No	Frequent disturbances at home	None

Case	Type Burn	% of Body Surface Burn	Other Injuries & Conditions	Concomitant Acute Illness	Developmental Delay	Delayed Treatment	Prev. Rep. CPU	Disposition
1	Flame	75	Anemia, poor hygiene	No	No	No	Yes	Died
2	Scald	15	Malnourished, skull fracture (accidental), accidental overdose	No	Yes	Yes	No	Home, lost to follow-up
3	Scald	5	Poor Hygiene	No	No	No	Yes	Home
4	Hot object	1	Anemia, FTT, poor hygiene	Yes	Yes	Yes	Yes	Foster Care, home, removed.
5	Scald	13	Scabies, cellulitis, poor hygiene	No	No	No	Yes	Home
6	Flame	13	FTT, Poor Hygiene	No	Yes	No	Yes	Foster care
7	Hot object	3	Poor Hygiene	No	Yes	No	Yes	Home

TABLE II
PHYSICAL AND PSYCHOSOCIAL FINDINGS IN CHILDREN WITH NONACCIDENTAL BURNS

Case	Child's Age	Child's Sex	Child's Race	Maternal Age	Maternal Background	Maternal Characteristics	Marital Status	Mobility	Employment History	Violence	Acute Precipitating Factors
1	6 mos.	M	Black	20 Yrs.	Educationally deprived	Withdrawn	Single-boyfriend in home	Yes	Acute-No	Physical abuse to mother, source unknown	Acute marital conflict; father left home; child ill.
2	7 mos.	M	White	18 yrs.	Educationally deprived	Withdrawn	Single-boyfriend in home	Yes	Chronic-No	Wife battery	Father left home; acute marital conflict child ill.
3	10 mos.	F	Black	23 yrs.	Educationally deprived	Hostile	Separated (recently)	No	Mother-yes Father-no acute	Verbal abuse	Father left home; marital conflict; child ill.
4.	18 mos.	F	Black	19 yrs.	Culturally deprived	Hostile	Single-boyfriend in home	Yes	Chronic-No	Wife battery	Father returned
5	20 mos.	M	Black	25 yrs.	Culturally deprived	Withdrawn	Married	Yes	Chronic-No	Wife battery	Child chronically ill.

Case	Type Burn	% of Body Surface Burn	Other Injuries & Conditions	Concomitant Acute Illness	Developmental Delay	Delayed Treatment	Prev. Rep. CPU	Disposition
1	Scald	6	Scars, whip marks, rib fracture	Yes	Yes	No	No	Home, re-injured, removed.
2	Scald & flame	15	Skull fracture, old scald burn	Yes	No	No	Yes	Died
3	Scald	10	Scleral homorrhage, scalp contusions	Yes	No	No	No	Foster care, home-died neglect
4	Scald	5	Bruises, strap marks	No	Yes	No	Yes	Foster Care
5	Scald	33	Bruises, cigarette burns bites, rope burns, FTT	No	Yes	No	No	Foster care, removed

The mothers of our patients were isolated, suspicious, rigid, dependent, and immature, some characteristics which could be attributed to the "psychopathic personality." The lack of what Steele[11] called "empathic mothering" is an important factor in the assessment of these parents. The severity of this non-relationship is significant in all of the abusive mothers evaluated.

The high incident of mortality and permanent physical deformity in the burned abused children leads to the conclusion that they should be handled as "top priority" by the agencies involved in their care. Burns in children must not be considered as a purely surgical problem, but must be evaluated in light of the physical, social and emotional components which make up the child's environment.

REFERENCES

1. Keen, J.H., Lendrum, J., and Wolman, B., "Inflicted Burns and Scalds in Children," British Medical Journal, 4, 268 (1975).

2. Stone, N.H., et. al., "Child Abuse by Burning," Surgical Clinics of North America, 50, 420 (1970).

3. Ibid., 422.

4. Keen, J.H., Lendrum, J., and Wolman, B., "Inflicted Burns and Scalds in Children," British Medical Journal, 4, 269 (1975).

5. Lung, R.J., Miller, S., Davis, T., and Graham, W., "Recognizing Burn Injuries as Child Abuse," American Family Physician, 15, 134 (1977).

6. Lenosky, E.F., Hunter, K., "Specific Patterns of Inflicted Burn Injuries," The Journal of Trauma, 17, 842 (1977).

7. Keen, J.H., Lendrum, J., and Wolman, B., "Inflicted Burns and Scalds in Children," British Medical Journal, 4, 269 (1975).

8. Caffey, J., "Multiple Fracture in the Long Bones of Infants Suffering from Subdural Hematoma," Journal of Roentgenology, 56, 163 (1946).

9. Helfer, R. E., and Kempe, C.H., The Battered Child, Chicago, University of Chicago Press, 1968.

10. Elmer, E., "Follow-Up Study of Traumatized Children," Child Abuse and Neglect--The International Journal, 1, 105 (1977).

11. Steele, B.F., and Pollock, C.B., in Battered Child, ed. R. E. Helfer and C. H. Kempe, Chicago, University of Chicago Press, 1968.

Child Abuse and Neglect, Vol. 3, pp. 483 - 490.

0145-2134/79/0601-0483 $02.00/0.

LIFE STYLE PATTERNS IN FAMILIES WITH NEGLECTED CHILDREN

Dagmar Lagerberg, Katarina Nilsson and Claes Sundelin/PRU team

Department of Paediatrics, Academic Hospital, S-750 14 Uppsala, Sweden
Department of Social Services, Box 76, S-751 03 Uppsala, Sweden

The reasoning presented in this paper is based on the findings in an on-going multi-disciplinary study of child abuse and neglect in Uppsala, Sweden.* The study material comprises 26 families with a total of 50 children 0-7 years of age. The families were selected by local social workers and discussed by our research team on two occasions with an interval of at least one year. The selection of cases was based on the criteria of abuse and neglect laid down in the Swedish Child Welfare Act, § 25 a:

The social service agency is directed to take measures...
if anyone below the age of 18 years is being abused in his/her home or is otherwise treated there in a manner that endangers his physical or mental health, or if his development is being jeopardized by incompetence of his parents or other fosterer as a fosterer or their incapability to foster him.

It is the aim of this paper to discuss and analyse characteristic life style patterns encountered in families in which abuse and neglect occur, as well as in families where the children are at risk of having an unfavourable emotional development even though abuse or neglect in the strict sense is perhaps not the predominant feature. In summary, we may call all these children "neglected".

COMMON CHARACTERISTICS

From the legal criteria quoted above, it seems apparent that the families should have characteristics in common. Such common traits have been found in families with abused children or children with failure to thrive, for instance emotional and psychiatric disturbances (Kempe 1971; Smith 1975), alcohol or drug addiction (Barbero and Shaheen 1967), medical problems (Bullard, Glaser, Heagarty and Pivchik 1967), and social maladjustment such as unemployment or poor housing (Barbero and Shaheen 1967; Lynch, Steinberg and Ounsted 1975). What we intend to do here, however, is not to repeat the results of previous studies but to try to find interpretations and explanations and relate such manifest characteristics to some deeper life style patterns. Life style patterns in abusing families have been described previously by Davoren (1974).

Lack of Structure or Continuity

One basic characteristic of the life careers of our families may be called a lack of structure or continuity, perhaps aimlessness. In the typical case, the parents have never kept the same employment for more than a short time. Often the children in one and the same family have different fathers. The mother marries or lives with different men. If the marriage lasts for a long time, it is characterized by quarrels, crises, attempted divorces and new efforts to

*Two other papers relating to this project are: "A Multi-disciplinary Approach to the Child Abuse and Neglect Problem" (Gustafsson, Lagerberg and Larsson) and "Early Signs and Symptoms in Neglected Children" (Jakobsson, Lagerberg and Ohlsson).

go on living together. The family frequently moves into new premises.

Table 1 summarizes some manifestations of a lack of continuity in our families.

TABLE 1 Manifestations of a Lack of Continuity

Characteristic	Number of families n=26
Frequent moves, frequent or unrealistic moving plans	21
Instability or failure in employment or training	18
Marital instability, divorces, crises in interpersonal relationships	21
Children in same family have different fathers, mother has other children placed outside the family	10
None of the above	0

Deviant Health Attitudes

Our families seem to have more health problems than the population at large (Table 2). The picture is dominated by drug and alcohol addiction. To a certain extent the other health problems are secondary to misuse or a general social incapacity.

TABLE 2 Health Problems in the Parents

Health problem	Number of parents n=40
Somatic illness (disease, handicap or functional defect lasting for a long time)	10
Mental illness (inpatient hospital care)	10
Intellectual deficiency	3
Drug and/or alcohol addiction	23
None of the above	10

The manner in which the parents treat their health problems bespeaks a characteristic aimlessness even though on the surface they may behave differently. One pattern is illustrated by the parent who gets fixed in a role of ill health. Different doctors certify his or her inability to work. Financial support is provided, and it seems impossible to rehabilitate the patient and provide a permanent job. Typically, the parent says: "I do really want to work - just wait until I am all right again". A disability pension is discussed. Others ignore their illnesses in an almost self-destructive fashion. First and foremost, this is true for the alcohol and drug abusers, who continue with the abuse in spite of their knowledge of the risks. In some cases this resembles an extended suicide. The general life situation of these parents is so bad, and their freedom of action so restricted that they may not consider it worthwhile to plan for the future. At the same time, their health is a field in which they are still at liberty to decide over themselves.

One thing which seems apparent is that different forms of health information would be completely wasted in the majority of these cases. The parents live here and now and try to make the best of it.

Our psychiatric care resources do not seem to have helped the parents very much. Lack of continuity of care, and variation in attempts at psychiatric treatment may have increased their confusion. Their own lack of assiduity has also contributed to the negative results.

Six of the 50 children suffer from serious physical handicaps or illnesses. These problems augment the burden laid on the parents, who often fail to provide the necessary care.

Social Isolation

The social contacts of the parents of our risk children are, characteristically, so deficient that they may be said to live in social isolation. Those social contacts which do exist are largely with close relatives, while real friendships are very rare. Existing friendships seem to be short, superficial and founded on such common interests as alcohol, drugs and crime. Mutual interests of this kind may also keep brothers and sisters together, as social shortcomings are frequently shared by all members of a family. In many cases, however, the nearest relatives may be important safeguards for the children. They are able to help in acute crises and, formally or informally, function as foster parents.

The relationships between our parents and their relatives are seldom free from complications. Feelings of guilt and inferiority influence the interactional pattern, which may also be characterized by symbiotic, ambivalent dependency. Parents who represent the black sheep in an otherwise well-adjusted family particularly exhibit ambivalence. Contempt and disappointed love go abreast, and caresses easily turn to battering. In some of the parents, particularly single mothers, the degree of isolation is such that an informal web of contacts is almost non-existent. The only contact available in the event of loneliness or sorrow may be the social worker. It is valuable that the social worker is able to function as a provider of organized kindness and contact, but the situation as such reveals human destitution and an immense lack of communication.

How can this isolation be explained? In the general debate, factors such as the segregation in sterile housing areas without communication, unemployment and migration are emphasized as predominant reasons. These factors are generally considered to have a structural cause, which is true in the sense that they are related to the general organization of the community. For our parents, however, the fact is that internal causes are just as frequent as external ones. The parents move repeatedly because they get easily involved in conflicts with their neighbours, or feel pointed out, or inferior, for instance. They are afraid of contacts - but at the same time they feel a need of friendships. Overwhelmed by their own problems, afraid and suspicious, they repel other people. Poor health, periods of alcohol addiction, lack of mental energy and stamina and incapacity to plan and keep appointments render it impossible for them to conform to the requirements of the open labour market - if given a chance. Their poor opportunities in working life seem to be an insurmountable obstacle to deeper social communication, which could otherwise serve as a lever for personal development.

The Feeling of Worthlessness

We shall now describe some characteristic protective mechanisms used by the parents as a form of escapism from an existence which offers little opportunity for joy and satisfaction. These mechanisms permit the parents to maintain some feeling of worth and some idea of life as a good thing.

1. The pattern of marital roles is often asymmetrical. The husband plays an apparent male role. He is the one who talks and who decides. The woman seems oppressed and inferior. In the most pronounced cases sado-masochistic patterns may exist. Repeated wife battering occurs in several cases.

2. A feeling of personal identity is maintained through pronounced role playing (certainly on an unconscious level). The parents exhibit varying pictures of themselves, adapted to the circumstances: the martyr, the person who arranges everything, the good parent, the person who makes new efforts, the person who is in the process of getting to know him- or herself, to mention some of them.

3. It is of great importance to be just like everyone else, to build a pretty façade. External forms are clung to with almost ritual attention. One has to be a real family, to be properly married and to have children. Christmas and birthdays are celebrated with the appropriate attributes. If the children are away from home they must at least come home for Christmas.

4. The power of resistance against commercial pressures is often low. This results in purchases of furniture and costly mechanical equipment on hire-purchase contracts that are almost impossible to pay off.

5. Unrealistic employment and housing plans for the future play an important role, as well as dreams of sudden great positive changes.

6. Particularly in the case of women, the existence of children is decisive for their self-esteem and identity. Pregnancies are often positive experiences, and attitudes towards community child care are not infrequently sceptical or negative. Foster or day care placement of a child engenders a void which may in turn produce a new pregnancy.

Not all parents, of course, display these traits, which may vary in degree. Most of them exhibit some, and a very few show none at all. To us, though, they do seem characteristic to a degree that makes them a pattern.

INTERPRETATION

How can we understand these characteristics? The matter mainly has to be discussed on a basis of conjectures and possible interpretations.

The childhood conditions of almost all parents in our study have been insecure and traumatic. They were deprived of love, appreciation, contact, warmth and opportunities to observe positive behaviour patterns under stable and foreseeable conditions. In the majority of parents there was an early risk of damage to their personality development. During childhood and adolescence their beliefs about their own incompetence and unnecessariness were constantly corroborated (cf. Steele and Pollock 1974). When we meet the parents in our study it is obvious that their self-esteem is substantially undermined. Their low self-esteem and chronic inferiority explain the importance attributed to external appearances, the clinging to objects, and the need to play a role and assume a false identity.

The lack of a position in the labour market and the social isolation make it necessary to base all self-esteem on the intimate family circle. Hence the need for a parental role becomes decisive for their feeling of personal worth.

To see reality as it is arouses anxiety. Our parents phrenetically defend themselves against the patent fact that their life is well on the way to becoming a failure. Lies, or perhaps more accurately self-deception, therefore play an important role in the management of daily life. Feelings of anxiety are suppressed by dreams where one's existence is suddenly transformed in a miraculous and magical way (cf. Lynch and Ounsted (1976) about fantasy as a rescue in similar situations). Uneasiness may also be exorcised by the rejection of a demanding equality in the relationship with one's spouse. Security is achieved through total domination or total subjection. Furthermore, anxiousness may be kept away if one can avoid seeing life as an entirety. Instead, it is transformed into a series of discrete events without any close relationship to one another. Our parents live for a day or an hour at a time. They eat, drink and have fun in many ways. Time passes by. They live half lives, fragments of lives, curtailed lives with a lack of identity and presence. What justifies such a way of living, what makes it a reasonably good life? Very often the parent role is the last resort - what else when there is no communication, no religion, no job, no political anchorage, no friendship? Or perhaps there is no internal dialogue at all - the experience of being incompetent may have led to an inner censorship. The past and present seem to be enclosed by impenetrable barriers - barriers raised by toil, poverty, deceit, humiliations, painfulnesses and shortcomings.

As already mentioned, the reasons for this mode of life lie far back in the past. They seem to form a progressive course which cannot be influenced by one's own efforts.

A typical "life spiral" is shown in Fig. 1.

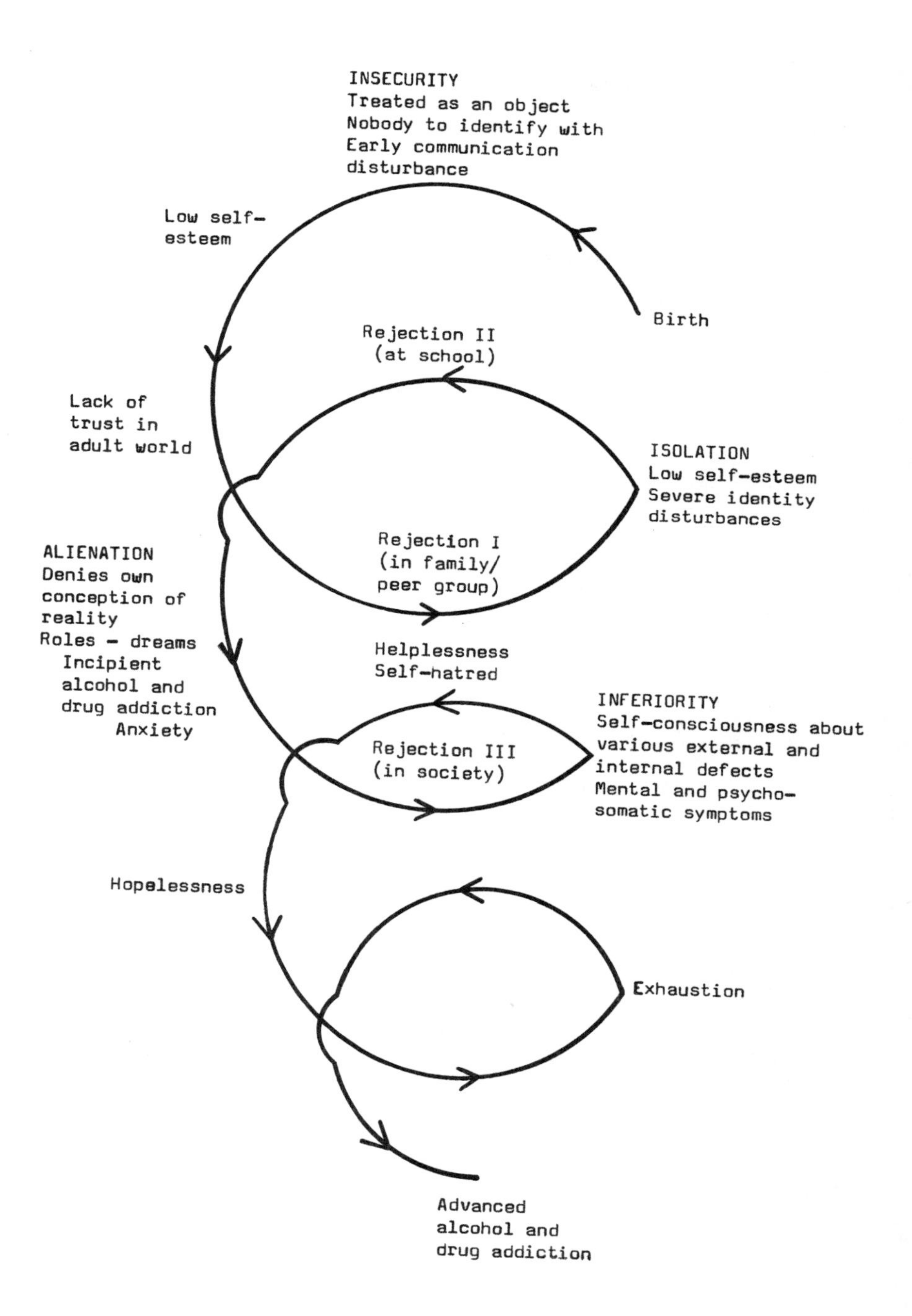

Fig. 1. A typical "life spiral".

THE CHILDREN

What do the parents' conditions mean to the children? How do these conditions influence the parental capacity to foster and socialize a child?

Certainly, it would be unfair to generalize. Each case has its own peculiarities. A home environment may be better than it seems from the outside. All the same, we may draw some inferences without making the picture too coarse or too superficial:

Children need food, clothing and housing. To the same extent, their emotional needs must be met. They require a safe adult environment providing consolation, protection, encouragement, help and security. Furthermore, children need opportunities for quiet occupation with play materials suitable for their age. They need positive examples and models to learn from, and an intelligible system of standards.

We should think our parents have extremely great difficulties in providing these prerequisites, mainly because they themselves have never experienced them. If they are incapable of showing emotions and setting limits in an understandable way, the children's socialization process will fail. Socialization to a large extent consists in bringing about a willingness to collaborate, to abandon the satisfaction of an immediate desire on behalf of another person or a common goal. When demands are made in a rough, harsh and capricious manner by people who are void of self-knowledge, endurance and capacity to make efforts, firm standards will never develop in the children.

From the children's point of view, life is a chaos, a mass of disconnected events. Their conceptions of time, space and continuity become defective. The unreliable attitude of their parents prevents them from finding out what will happen next and deprives them of means to anticipate the consequences of their own actions.

To survive, children living under such threatening conditions may develop a combination of cunning and cowardice. It becomes a question of getting along as well as possible. The child anxiously observes the reactions of the environment. "What is going to happen next? How shall I survive? How shall I master the situation?" Eventually he develops a method for cleverly reading off and anticipating his parents' emotional moods.

All this inevitably fosters insecurity and suspiciousness. Personal integrity becomes almost unachievable if you constantly have to be on guard against what people may do and if there is nobody to be trusted except yourself.

A less adaptive child may create a set of inelastic rules of thumb as a means of survival. Others may just become confused and aggressive. Unfailingly, less adaptive behaviour enhances the risk of recurrent conflicts.

External signs of adaptation in abused children have been discussed, among others, by Kempe (1971) and Leonard, Rhymes and Solnit (1966), who mention the well known phenomena of watchfulness and role reversal. Martin and Beezley (1976) point out the ability of abused children to adapt themselves to different situations, like the "chameleon" (p. 107). Martin (1976), discussing variations in the capacity of abused children to adapt to their environment, emphasizes the internal consequences of an intelligent child's ability to cope (p. 142) - self-respect and internal behaviour controls are damaged, his right to be a child and his own needs are disregarded even by himself.

An important issue stressed by Martin and Beezley (1976) is the fact that one and the same personality trait may be viewed as either good or bad. Politeness, compliance and obedience are good qualities, but the authors stress the price the child has to pay in terms of emotional harm and suffering (p. 108).

In our opinion, it is imperative that all internal consequences for the child's personality development and emotional integrity be considered in the analysis of abuse and neglect, and not only the child's external symptoms and behaviour. It seems to us particularly important to realise the possible obverse side of "good" behaviour like superficial sympathy and compliance - namely cunning, amorality and unreliability.

TREATMENT

How can the professional system help these very unfortunate parents? We do not believe in the possibility of total removal of anxiety, closeness and melancholy, but we do hope the parents may be able to catch a glimpse of an existence beyond their own personal situation, of a way of living different from their present one. In brief, that they may be given hope and trust. If this is utopian then anything else will be even more utopian. Furthermore, we should want to bring the parents back to relying on their own resources and make role playing unnecessary - to let them see that familial communication may involve something of a quiet good will and kindness without strife, toil and surveillance. They must be taught that parenthood can be a joyful experience and to appreciate themselves as they are, without disguise. We wish to make them feel that their life and their duties are important, that their actions matter, and at the same time to make them accept some sense of fun, leisure and play in life. Appreciation of the proportions of life will probably make them less dependent on objects, formalities and conventions.

How shall we bring about such changes? It seems apparent that we have to believe in the possibility of personal growth and maturation in our parents. But how do these occur? At random? In many cases they can be observed following radical religious or political experiences. They may also be elicited through art and love. The pertinent questions are: Can it be assumed that medical and social service agencies are in a position to provide experiences of this kind? And, in such a case, will the parents be able to make use of them?

To answer these questions, the parents' linguistic situation must be analysed. Verbal interaction is a necessary condition for meaningful communication and for mental processes to be influenced in a positive way. We consider this point crucial, as the parents' linguistic patterns seem to reflect their loss of identity, their alienation, inferiority and emotional deprivation.

Language is our major foundation for treatment. We take it for granted that we get to know ourselves, the world and other human beings through language. The linguistic defects of our parents appear as a lack of correspondence between private experiences and feelings, on the one hand, and the common language of society, on the other. In the verbal and conceptual set-up of the parents, significant words are void of meaning or bear meanings different from those generally accepted, for instance the words "care", "trust", "truthfulness", "considerateness", "continuity", "goals", and "identity". Words with emotional undertones fail to arouse emotional reactions and insights. Our parents defend themselves from the verbal means - i.e. the use of words and sentences - to observe their own situation, the painfulnesses of the past and the threats of the future. They are isolated - not only socially, but from their own biographies as well. One consequence of their isolation is the fact that they sometimes play different linguistic roles in different social contexts. In a parrot-like fashion, they repeat words and turns of phrase used by others. Social workers and physicians are well familiar with imitation of professional jargon by patients.

This situation renders meaningful and sincere conversations in a therapeutic setting impracticable. It also distorts the family interactional pattern and prevents straight messages from being given and understood.

The linguistic predicament of our parents affects the possibilities of treatment. If taken seriously, this situation is not favourable. It faces us with the inevitable question: What is meaningful treatment? Maturation and growth will not be achieved in the absence of linguistic means. To provide such means would take time and make heavy demands upon organization and routines. Are we, on the whole, capable of bringing this about?

If we do not sincerely believe in our own capacity to overcome linguistic barriers, we should perhaps not let children suffer while we occupy ourselves with measures which will not give radical changes. Realising this is certainly a distressing procedure to all who wish to give help and support instead of allowing people's lives to be destroyed, but the truth has to be said even when it is painful and disagreeable or seemingly unfavourable to those involved.

Our first treatment goal, then, would be to try to change the parents' pre-linguistic status and bring about meaningful communication. If this proves impossible, maybe we should content ourselves with modest practical goals, for instance seeing that the family's material needs are met and that the children receive emotional compensation outside the family setting.

Such an approach might release us from a bad professional conscience and prevent us from getting crushed by the burden of our own ambitions.

REFERENCES

Barbero, G.J. and Shaheen, E.: Environmental failure to thrive: A clinical view. Journal of Pediatrics 71, 639 (1967).

Bullard, D.M., Jr, Glaser, H.H., Heagarty, M.C. and Pivchik, E.C.: Failure to thrive in the "neglected" child. American Journal of Orthopsychiatry 37, 680 (1967).

Davoren, E. (1974) The Role of the Social Worker. Chapter 6 in: Helfer, R.E. and Kempe, C.H. (eds.): The Battered Child. Chicago and London.

Kempe, C.H.: Paediatric Implications of the Battered Baby Syndrome. Archives of Disease in Childhood 46, 28 (1971).

Leonard, M.F., Rhymes, J.P. and Solnit, A.J.: Failure to Thrive in Infants. A Family Problem. American Journal of Diseases of Children 111, 600 (1966).

Lynch, M.A. and Ounsted, C. (1976) Family oriented therapy. Residential therapy - a place of safety. Human Development Research Unit. University of Oxford. The Park Hospital for Children. Mimeograph.

Lynch, M., Steinberg, D. and Ounsted, C.: Family Unit in a Children's Psychiatric Hospital. British Medical Journal, April 19, 127 (1975).

Martin, H.P. (1976) Factors Influencing the Development of the Abused Child. Chapter 12 in: Martin, H.P. (ed.): The Abused Child. A Multidisciplinary Approach to Developmental Issues and Treatment. Cambridge, Massachusetts.

Martin, H.P. and Beezley, P. (1976) Personality of Abused Children. Chapter 9 in: Martin, H.P. (ed.): The Abused Child. A Multidisciplinary Approach to Developmental Issues and Treatment. Cambridge, Massachusetts.

Smith, S.M. (1975) The Battered Child Syndrome. London-Boston.

Steele, B.F. and Pollock, C.B. (1974) A Psychiatric Study of Parents Who Abuse Infants and Small Children. Chapter 5 in: Helfer, R.E. and Kempe, C.H. (eds.): The Battered Child. Chicago and London.

Child Abuse and Neglect, Vol. 3, pp. 491 - 496.

0145-2134/79/0601-0491 $02.00/0.

ESSENTIAL ELEMENTS OF SUCCESSFUL CHILD ABUSE AND NEGLECT TREATMENT

Anne Harris Cohn, D.P.H.
Berkeley Planning Associates and University of California School of Public Health, Berkeley, California

Not all child abuse is preventable. Society faces an ongoing need to support programs that treat the members of families in which abuse occurs. There is little systemmatically generated knowledge on the most efficient and effective ways to assist parents and children faced with abuse. The purpose of our 40-month study of eleven child abuse and neglect demonstration service programs in the United States was to expand the knowledge base in this area by determining, through evaluative research, the essential elements of successful treatment programs. This paper highlights our findings that pertain to more effective delivery of services to abusive and neglectful parents.

TREATMENT SERVICES FOR PARENTS

A focus of our study was determining the relative effectiveness of different treatment strategies for the parent. In order to study treatment effects, all adults receiving treatment services from the demonstration projects were included in the study population. Data on 1,724 clients, recorded by case managers, included case history information about the nature and severity of the maltreatment, the extent of reincidence during treatment, the services received by the parent and outcome information including the case manager's assessment of the extent to which specific client problems theorized to be related to abusive behavior had been reduced and whether the parents' overall propensity for maltreatment had been reduced.

In discussing what was learned about treatment effectiveness, a number of unavoidable methodological constraints which limit the conclusiveness of findings must be taken into account. Although the study population is similar to the kinds of cases routinely handled by public protective service departments, the projects studied, selected because of the different treatment strategies they proposed to demonstrate, are not necessarily representative of child abuse and neglect treatment programs in general. The study included no control or non-treatment groups. All data were collected from case managers rather than directly from the clients themselves. And, no data were collected on a follow-up basis, after the termination of treatment services.

STUDY POPULATION

The 1,724 parents included in the study population represent a heterogeneous group of families, not substantially unlike those reported to public protective services agencies across the country on key socioeconomic characteristics. In the majority of cases, more than one adult lived in the household (69%), no adult in the household held a high school degree (61%), at least one adult was employed (70%), the reported annual family income was less than $5500 (56%), at least two children were present in the household (72%), and at least one of the children was a preschooler. Most of the 1,724 cases were referred to the projects from social service agencies, schools, hospitals and neighbors or acquaintances; close to 10% were self-referrals. Twenty-eight percent of the cases were labeled as high risk or potential cases; an additional 14% were identified as emotional abusers and neglectors. Four percent of the cases involved sexual abuse. The remaining 54% of the cases had physically maltreated their children -- 31% by physical abuse, 20% by physical neglect and 3% by a combination of both. (The representation of physical abuse cases in this study population is proportionately higher than in caseloads of public protective services cases, due largely to the selective intake criteria of some of the demonstration projects.) Ten percent of the cases required court intervention of some form, although in over 30% of the cases the alleged abuse or neglect was actually established.

Clients, on average, were in treatment six to seven months and had contact with a service provider about once a week. Approximately 30% of the clients received a treatment package which included lay services (lay counseling and Parents Anonymous) along with individual counseling or case management and other services. Only 12% received a group treatment package (including group therapy or parent education classes) along with other services, and over half (54%) received an individual counseling model of service delivery which excluded any lay or group services. Extensive analyses were undertaken to determine if the receipt of any particular service package was related to client characteristics. For the client characteristics measured, no general patterns of service prescription emerged. It may well be that certain factors, such as client motivation, which were not included in this study, would help explain differences in service receipt across clients.

REINCIDENCE DURING TREATMENT

While the absence of reincidence (or incidence) of abuse or neglect during treatment cannot be regarded as a measure of treatment outcome or effect, the presence of reincidence may serve as a good indication of whether a program is, in general, protecting the children in client families. Of the 1,724 parents studied, a full 30% were reported to have severely reabused or neglected their children while they were in treatment. This severe reincidence excluded any reports of emotional abuse, mild physical injuries, emotional neglect or mild physical neglect. While no benchmarks exist in the field by which to assess this experience of the demonstration projects studied, the 30% figure seems high and does raise serious questions about how well these projects, and perhaps child abuse and neglect treatment programs in general, are helping to maintain a safe environment for the abused or neglected child. As shown on Table 1, we found that cases identified as "serious" at intake (multiproblem families with a previous history of maltreatment, in which the current episode was labeled as "severe") were significantly more likely to severely reabuse or neglect their children during treatment than non-serious cases (56% as opposed to 15%). Given that over half of the cases labeled as serious were reported with severe reincidence, it seems apparent that these cases require very special supervision and intervention.

TABLE 1 Relationship between Severe Reincidence During Treatment and Seriousness of the Case*

	Seriousness of Case	
Severe Reincidence	Serious	Not Serious
Yes	56%	15%
No	44%	85%
	(N=622)	(N=1102)

*Chi-square significant at .05.

Further, we found that programs using profesionally trained staff to conduct intakes and treatment planning had lower reincidence rates, suggesting that the protection of the child and the well-being of the family is increased when the most highly qualified workers have initial contact with families, carrying them through the immediate crises they are facing.

The importance of using the most experienced workers for the management of cases was further emphasized through an in-depth study on the case handling practices for a random sample of the 1,724 cases in the study population. Teams of expert clinicians reviewed case handling procedures for 362 cases using an audit technique developed in the medical field of abstracting case records and interviewing case managers. Reviewers then rated the overall quality of case management. Workers with professional training as well as workers with three or more years experience working with child abuse cases were consistently rated as providing higher quality case management than workers without professional training or fewer years of direct clinical experience.

REDUCING PROPENSITY FOR FUTURE ABUSE OR NEGLECT

One indication of treatment effectiveness is a clinician's judgment of whether or not a client's potential for abusive or neglectful behavior has been reduced by virtue of improvement in a number of problem areas. Case managers at the demonstration projects were asked to report, for each client served, whether or not a client's propensity for future maltreatment had been reduced by the end of treatment. As shown on Table 2, of the parents studied, 42% were reported with reduced potential for abuse or neglect. In other words, case managers reported success with less than half of their cases. Given the paucity of comparable studies, it is not known if the experiences of the demonstration projects represent a norm for the field. However, because these projects received special resources and special attention not common in public protective service programs across the country, it may be fair to assume that the projects studied did at least as well in working with clients as most other programs across the country. If this is the case, it suggests that child abuse and neglect programs are not nearly as successful in longer-term protection of children as we might wish.

TABLE 2 Relationships between Reduced Propensity for Future Abuse or Neglect and Service Model Received*

Reduced Propensity	All Cases	Service Model Received		
		Lay	Group	Individual
Yes	42	53	39	38
No	58	47	61	62
		(N=334)	(N=186)	(N=635)

*Chi-square significant at .05.

Those client characteristics measured did not seem to differentiate successful or not successful clients. Additionally, no one service or service package was found to be overwhelmingly related to reduced propensity. The experiences of the demonstration projects did not point to a single best method of service delivery. However, it was the case that clients receiving lay services (lay or parent aide counseling and/or Parents Anonymous) as supplements to their service package were more frequently reported with reduced propensity than clients not receiving these services. Fifty-three percent of those provided with lay services were said to have improved during treatment as opposed to less than 40% of other clients.

ALLEVIATING CLIENT PROBLEMS THAT TRIGGER ABUSE OR NEGLECT

A second way of looking at the outcome of service delivery is to determine whether or not the problems clients exhibited at the time they entered treatment have been ameliorated. Select attitudes, situations and behaviors, theorized to be causally related to abusive and neglectful behavior were measured at intake and again at termination to determine if each was a problem for a particular client and, if so, if this problem was remediated by the end of treatment. As can be seen on Table 3, while projects had more success with some problems (such as reducing the stress in the client's household or improving parent's behavior toward the child) than with others (such as parent's low self-esteem, understanding of self, or sense of independence), for no problem measured did more than 28% of the clients exhibiting the problem improve. Once again, given the lack of comparable studies, we do not know if these findings are reflective of child abuse programs across the country. It is apparent, however, that while projects may have helped clients resolve many problems not measured, of those measured, very few were remediated. If in fact these unremediated problems are related to the propensity to abuse, as theorized in the literature and as generally accepted by the field, then it stands to reason that clinicians reported generally low overall success with cases.

We look to the services provided to clients to determine whether or not different mixes of services are associated with greater success in ameliorating problems. As shown on the table, clients receiving a service package which included lay services (lay counseling and Parents Anonymous) had almost consistently greater success with their problems than those receiving services based on individual counseling; additionally, clients receiving group services (group therapy or parent education classes) did better on most measures than those receiving the individual counseling model. These findings, as those previously reported, suggest that treatment is more effective in helping clients resolve problems theorized to be related to abusive or neglectful behavior when lay and group services are added to the treatment package.

TABLE 3 Relationships between Problem Resolution and Service Model Received*

Problem Resolution	All Cases	Service Model Received		
		Lay	Group	Individual
Reduced stress from living situation	28%	31%	24%	29%
Improved sense of child as person	22	30	32	17
More appropriate behavior toward child	28	35	32	25
Greater awareness of child development	23	29	28	19
Improved ability to talk out problems	25	33	32	21
Improved reactions to crisis situations	23	33	25	20
More appropriate expression of anger	20	28	24	17
Greater sense of independence	18	26	26	14
Better understanding of self	19	28	28	14
Enhanced self-esteem	19	28	19	15

*Chi-square significant at less than or equal to .05 for all relationships.

It was of particular interest to look beyond the mix of services provided to a client and determine if any one discrete service stood out as being more effective than others in problem resolution. We found that parents who participated in Parents Anonymous, irrespective of whatever other services they received, were significantly more likely to have their problems resolved than clients who did not participate in this service. Table 4 highlights this finding. It is reasonable to believe that parents do self-select into this self-help service; however, it is also reasonable to believe that the nature of the service itself goes a long way in enabling parents to better cope with their own problems.

THE LAY SERVICE TREATMENT PACKAGE

This lay service package that was found to be more effective than others generally included case management carried out by a trained, full-time worker. It included services of a lay person (in other words, an individual, usually volunteer, trained on the job and under the ongoing supervision of a professional) who was assigned to the client to serve as a friend, a support, a social contact. This lay counselor or parent aide met with the client once or several times a week and was generally available to help the family in a variety of daily needs. The lay service package may also have included participation in Parents Anonymous, a self-help group of abusive and neglectful parents.

TABLE 4 Relationships between Problem Resolution and Participation in Parents Anonymous

Problem Resolution	Participation in Parents Anonymous	
	Yes (N = 90)	No (N=1523)
Reduced stress from living situation	36%	28%
Improved sense of child as person	37	21*
More appropriate behavior toward child	43	27*
Greater awareness of child development	31	22*
Improved ability to talk out problems	37	25*
Improved reactions to crisis situations	44	22*
More appropriate expression of anger	30	19*
Greater sense of independence	32	18*
Better understanding of self	38	18*
Enhanced self-esteem	38	18*

*Chi-square significant at or less than .05.

There are many reasons why this lay model may have been somewhat more effective than other treatment modalities. The lay counselor or parent aide carries a very small caseload (one to three) and thus has more energy and time to give to each individual client. (Most full-time workers in the Demonstration projects carried 20-25 cases.) The lay counselor's job consists of becoming a client's friend, helping a client break down some of the social isolation he or she is experiencing; workers with large caseloads do not have the time to do this; paid workers generally carry the stigma of authority that does not enable them to do this. A service such as Parents Anonymous encourages parents to help themselves and help others in comparable situations, which appear to foster independence and greater self-esteem among other things; this interaction with others struggling with similar problems (and sometimes seemingly worse problems) helps to put problems and solutions into perspective.

A treatment service model which includes lay services is, as might be expected, less costly than other service models. (The annual expense per case for the lay service model is about $1400 as compared to $1700 for a service model based on individual counseling by paid workers only.) Given the somewhat greater effectiveness of the lay service model, it also appears as a more cost-effective service strategy (approximately $2600 a year per successful case versus $4700 a year for the individual counseling model). More cost-effective than the individual counseling model is a service package which includes professionally provided group services (at a cost of $4000 a year per successful case). Such a group service model was found to be particularly beneficial for physical abusers, as opposed to neglectors or emotional maltreators.

OTHER ASPECTS OF EFFECTIVE TREATMENT

The findings discussed suggest that while treatment programs require highly trained, experienced workers to conduct intakes, treatment planning and general case management, the use of lay, self-help and group services likely improve the effectiveness of treatment. Through a more detailed analysis of data from a subset of cases, the study identified other aspects of case handling that contribute to effective treatment.

First, as shown in Table 5, while not all cases will require lengthy treatment, we found that cases in treatment for at least six months (and generally not longer than 12 to 18 months) were more likely to have reduced propensity for future abuse by the end of treatment (46% versus 22% of those in treatment under six months). In addition, keeping a case in treatment was found to be more cost-effective. Apparently, some amount of contact is necessary before the benefits of treatment are realized.

TABLE 5 Relationships between Reduced Propensity for Future Abuse or Neglect and Select Aspects of Case Handling*

	Length of Time in Treatment		Case Manager Case Load Size	
Reduced Propensity	Less than 6 months	Over 6 months	20 or less	Over 20
Yes	22	46	40	30
No	78	54	60	70

*Chi-square significant at .05 for all relationships.

Second, not only do workers with smaller caseloads (closer to 20 than 40) provide higher quality case management, they also appear to have more success with their cases. Forty percent of those cases managed by workers with smaller caseloads were reported as successes as opposed to 30% of those cases managed by workers with larger caseloads.

Beyond these two factors which are directly related to outcome, we found a number of other case handling variables which are essential aspects of quality case management and which thus have important, although indirect, implications for treatment outcome. The six most notable variables include: immediate (e.g., same day) contacting of client after a report is received for timely crisis intervention; contacting the referral source for background information to avoid unnecessary duplication during investigation and intake; use of a multidisciplinary team review during intake to guarantee a comprehensive treatment plan; the ongoing use of consultants from different disciplines to ensure a continuously responsive treatment plan; maintaining weekly contact between the case manager and the client to ensure timely review of treatment progress; and conducting follow-up four to six weeks after termination to make sure that discontinuation of services was appropriate. Beyond these specific facets of case management, the study suggests that treatment programs, in general, operate more efficiently and effectively if they are housed within or closely linked with the public agency mandated to handle abuse and neglect cases (in the United States this is typically Children's Protective Services) and if the program has established strong, formal working relationships with other agencies in the community working with maltreatment, notably those from the legal, educational, and medical sectors.

CONCLUSIONS

Our evaluation of eleven demonstration projects sought to systemmatically document select aspects of the more effective methods for treating child abuse and neglect. This paper has presented findings about treating the abusive or neglectful parent. The findings affirm the experiences of many small, pioneering programs in the field which have not been subject to national evaluations. Perhaps our findings, coupled with the experiences of others, can begin to form a generally accepted body of knowledge about treating child abuse. And perhaps with this body of knowledge, we can begin to seek ways to improve treatment services for all identified cases of abuse and neglect.

This work, conducted at Berkeley Planning Associates, was supported by the National Center for Health Services Research under contract HRA 106-74-120 and HRA 230-76-0075. Copies of final reports, which detail the study findings, are available through the National Technical Information Service, Washington, D.C., reports numbered PB 278-438 to PB 278-449.

Child Abuse and Neglect, Vol. 3, pp. 497 - 504.
Pergamon Press Ltd., 1979. Printed in Great Britain.

QUELQUES THEMES RELEVES DANS LA PSYCHANALYSE D'UNE EX MERE MALTRAITANTE

Liliane DELTAGLIA
C.M.P.P. 68 Avenue de la République - PARIS 11è - FRANCE -

Madame X est née en 1938 à Paris. Son père, fuyant les massacres dans un pays du Moyen Orient, est arrivé à Paris en 1923, à l'âge de 16 ans. Ouvrier en métallurgie il s'est marié avec une compatriote, exilée comme lui, dont il a eu 4 enfants. La mère est morte de tuberculose en 1941, après avoir été internée pour troubles mentaux graves.

Madame X a vécu une enfance misérable : maladive, elle a été placée pendant plusieurs années après la mort de sa mère. A 7 ans, elle est reprise par son père rentrant d'Allemagne où il avait été envoyé en service du travail obligatoire. Elle est élevée au foyer par la grand-mère paternelle, dure et méchante, et par son père qui s'est mis à boire. Elle fait une scolarité irrégulière et elle est alors qualifiée de débile.

A 13 ans et demi, fuyant le logement taudis et les coups, elle se met à sortir, et à fréquenter des bandes de jeunes. Le père la rejette et c'est alors la série des placements en internat de rééducation où elle est considérée comme une adolescente difficile.

A sa majorité, elle revient à Paris et a diverses aventures, avant de vivre avec son mari actuel, lui-même ancien mineur pré-délinquant.

Elle a un premier enfant qu'elle place et dont elle est séparée pendant près de 3 ans. Elle le reprend et vit seule avec lui et les deux autres enfants qu'elle a eus entre temps, car le mari est absent momentanément du foyer.

Quelques mois plus tard, l'aîné est hospitalisé à la demande de la mère. Mais comme il est dans un état grave et porte des traces suspectes, une action judiciaire est déclenchée qui aboutit à une condamnation de 13 mois de prison avec sursis et 5 ans de mise à l'épreuve. Pendant ce temps, l'aîné est placé et elle a un 4ème enfant.

Cette probation n'est pas tout à fait terminée lorsqu'une enquête de police est de nouveau provoquée par des traces de coups relevées sur la 2è enfant. Pourtant rien n'est prouvé, et il n'y a pas de poursuite pénale; mais cet incident déclenche une mesure d'action éducative (A.E.M.O.). C'est au cours de cette AEMO que les travailleurs sociaux envoient la mère à notre Centre pour être aidée dans ses difficultés éducatives avec ses enfants et en particulier avec l'aîné, revenu au foyer depuis peu. Après une première consultation avec le médecin, elle m'est adressee pour un soutien personnel qu'elle accepte et c'est alors le début du traitement.

MODALITES DU TRAITEMENT

- Madame X a été suivie pendant 5 ans et demi, à raison d'une fois par semaine en face à face pendant 2 ans, puis deux fois par semaine et allongée pendant un peu plus de 3 ans. J'ai donc un "matériel" de 270 séances.

- Une particularité très importante à souligner est que ce traitement a été possible malgré (ou à cause ?) le mandat judiciaire. Mais il faut préciser que je n'ai jamais eu aucun rapport avec le juge chargé de la mesure. Avec l'assistante sociale les rapports ont été limités aux incidents survenus dans la famille, et en particulier lors des fugues de l'aîné.

- D'autre part, je me suis trouvée, sans dommage apparent, dans une situation curieuse puisque pendant près de 2 ans, j'ai fait du psychodrame de groupe avec le fils aîné de Madame X.

- Sur le plan technique, malgré un transfert très positif et immédiat, je suis restée longtemps dans une relation de type aide psycho-sociale : reflet reformulation, renforcement du moi, etc... Lors de la deuxième année, et plus encore après la "mise sur le divan", j'ai adopté la technique psychanalytique et l'interprétation, avec pourtant des retpurs à la première technique, lors d'incidents graves sur le plan du réel (maladies, fugues du fils aîné).

- D'autre part, je suis intervenue plus qu'il n'est habituel de le faire :
  - après des périodes d'absence, j'écrivais à plusieurs reprises pour faciliter le contact
  - il m'est arrivé de donner des "conseils éducatifs" ou encore d'expliquer clairement des aspects théoriques de ce que Madame X découvrait sur elle-même
  - j'ai suggéré des lectures ou encore regardé avec elle ses dessins.

En relisant mes notes, je me suis aperçue que mes interventions avaient eu aussi deux caractéristiques :

- Surtout au début, j'ai "fourni" du matériel fantasmatique à Madame X bloquée dans une répétition du réel, et une attitude de justification. Par la suite elle a repris ce matériel à son compte et l'a élaboré en l'enrichissant de ses propres associations.

- Mes interprétations ont été longtemps centrées sur la défense, et à la relecture m'ont paru assez "traumatisantes". S'agissait-il de mon propre sadisme, ou d'un mécanisme induit par Madame X et son masochisme profond et donc d'une répétition inversée, dans le champ analytique, de ce qui s'était passé dans le réel ?

- Enfin, il faut souligner l'investissement important et réciproque : Madame X est venue aux séances avec une grande régularité; à plusieurs reprises elle m'a fait "oublier l'heure" et j'ai souvent été en admiration devant le travail intérieur qu'elle était capable de faire.

REFLEXIONS SUR QUELQUES THEMES

J'ai pu retrouver dans le traitement de Madame X toutes les phases d'une psychanalyse classique : transfert, régression, dépression, réminiscence, réélaboration, sentiment de renaissance, thèmes oedipiens et pré-oedipiens, etc De multiples pistes auraient donc été utilisables pour l'analyse de cette analyse. J'ai choisi de rapporter quelques thèmes qui sont revenus fréquemment et ont subi une transformation radicale au cours du traitement. Mais ils sont loin d'épuiser toute la richesse de ce matériel.

LA MERE MORTE

"Ma mère est morte à ma naissance, et je me suis toujours sentie coupable de cette mort" a été la première phrase de Madame X. La mort de sa mère a été un point central, un leitmotiv, tout au long de son analyse. Mais ce thème a subi des variations importantes.

- Elle rappelle ses souvenirs d'enfance "pour moi ma mère n'était pas morte, je neposais même jamais de questions, elle était près de moi, ou bien dans les étoiles où je luis parlais... je n'ai jamais vu sa photo, je ne sais pas où est sa tombe... Lors de la fête des mères je me sentais différente des autres enfants... Mes frères et soeurs me rejetaient, disant"tu n'es pas notre soeur".

- Un évènement survient dès la 16è séance :par sa famille elle apprend la vérité : sa mère est morte lorsqu'elle avait près de 3 ans. Ce qui a permis à Madame X d'adhérer pleinement à l'analyse par la découverte des mécanismes inconscients "Mais pourquoi ai-je inventé cette histoire ?"

Puis au fur et à mesure se sont élaborés d'autres points :

- la mort de la mère, réalisation du souhait oedipien de la "petite bonne femme adorant son père"

- la mauvaise mère qui lui a donné un corps dont elle a honte et, bien sûr après un long travail elle reconnait que c'est de son corps de femme qu'il s'agit.

- A la 92ème séance, alors que la mort de la mère est évoquée pour la Xème fois, diverses associations dans un climat émotionnel intense la font évoquer ses propres désirs de mort sur ses enfants.

- Madame X projette sur moi l'inévitable double image : je suis la mauvaise mère qui la déprime, lui fait ressentir son vide, provoque ses malaises. Mais aussi la bonne mère en qui elle a enfin confiance, et avec qui elle peut redevenir petite fille sans craindre la mort.

- Le "roman familial" a également fait de brèves apparitions au cours du traitement : Madame X pense que sa mère a trompé son père qui ne serait donc pas le sien; à un autre moment elle a le fantasme que sa mère n'est pas morte de "mort naturelle".

- Mais ce qui nous semble le plus important, c'est un ensemble d'images fantasmatiques élaborées dès à partir de la 42è séance, et qui s'est poursuivi jusqu'à la fin : Madame X pense que sa mère a voulu sa mort lorsqu'elle la portait. Elle a l'impression d'être née du vide, et non sortie du vantre de sa mère. En outre, elle dit qu'il s'est peut-être passé quelque chose lorsqu'elle était bébé (voir le fantasme de la main sur la bouche). Or rappelons que sa mère était malade mentale.

La séparation les a "tuées toutes les deux" et elle s'est identifiée à une mère morte, se condamnant ainsi à une existence de "morte vivante". Cette idée d'avoir vécu comme si elle était morte a été très très importante, et a fait place à la fin, avec la jubilation que l'on devine, à une véritable renaissance.

A la fin de l'analyse, elle peut dire que cette fois sa mère est bien enterrée (bien qu'elle n'ait jamais recherché sa tombe comme je le lui avais suggéré). Elle apprend que sa mère est morte de tuberculose et non d'une fièvre de lait.

Mais surtout elle peut sans angoisse, admettre les images de bonne et mauvaise mère en elle et autour d'elle. D'autre part, son mari refuse de lui souhaiter la fête des mères en lui disant "tu n'es pas ma mère, mais ma femme".

Enfin les dernières séances de l'analyse ont lieu après le décès de la belle-mère de Madame X. Elle a pu alors revivre un chagrin intense, mais faire un véritable "travail de deuil".

LA CULPABILITE - LA PERSECUTION

Avec la mort de la mère et en relation directe avec elle, au moins au début, la culpabilité et la persécution ont dominé les trois premières années du traitement.

"quand j'étais petite on me traitait de sale race.
"quand on me grondait, je me sauvais, je me serais cachée dans un
"trou de souris, je me faisais du mal pour me punir
"quand je suis passée devant le juge à 14 ans, puis après chez les
"soeurs, je narguais, je me révoltais.
"Encore maintenant quand on me regarde dans le métro, je crois qu'on
"me juge.
"Avec vous, je me sens comme devant un Tribunal, vous cherchez ce
"qu'il y a de mal en moi.

- Madame X me parle aussi longuement de sa révolte devant tout ce qu'elle croit une injustice du sort ou de la société. Quand on fait des reproches à ses enfants c'est comme si c'était à elle, et s'ils font une bêtise elle s'en sent coupable.

- Elle interprête tout en accusation contre elle, et en auto-dépréciation. Mais en même temps, elle rejette violemment toute responsabilité : c'est les soeurs qui ne l'ont pas comprise, c'est les voisins qui lui veulent du mal, c'est la guerre subie par ses grands parents, c'est la mort de sa mère, etc... qui l'ont faite comme elle est.

- Elle est méfiante, ne croit pas en la sincérité, se sent toujours de trop partout, rêve fréquemment qu'elle est encore en pension, pas libre.

- Petit à petit elle reconnaît son propre besoin de détruire la bonne image d'elle-même chez les autres et que c'est son propre comportement qui, dans son adolescence, élevait des barrières entre elle et les autres dont elle attendait tant.

- Après un long travail, elle retrouve une partie de l'origine de cette culpabilité dans les sentiments oedipiens. Mais elle ira plus loin, et parle un jour de la culpabilité d'exister, dans un contexte véritablement Kafkaïen. C'est cette culpabilité pré-existante et omni-présente qui l'a poussée à prendre des attitudes et poser des actes qui lui attirent la punition, pour qu'enfin cette culpabilité soit "nommée". Elle comprend et dit que la prison c'est elle-même.

- Vers la moitié du traitement, elle reconnaît être venue me voir au début par peur qu'on lui retire ses enfants, et avoir craint longtemps que je dise au Juge qu'elle était un danger pour eux.

- L'évolution continue et elle admet que la colère peut la rendre méchante et a failli la rendre criminelle. Elle réalise avec beaucoup d'émotion que "cela a dû être atroce ce que ses enfants ont supporté d'elle".
Sa peur d'être jugée devient à un moment sa peur de découvrir en elle-même qu'elle est un monstre.

- A la fin la culpabilité disparait presque complètement. Elle n'a plus besoin de s'inventer des excuses, se sent à l'aise, et rappelle en souriant son ancienne peur d'être jugée.

LE CORPS

L'évolution de ce thème est inversement proportionnel à celui de la culpabilité. Il n'en n'est pratiquement pas question au début et petit à petit le corps prend une place importante dans son discours et dans son vécu.

Ses souvenirs "corporels" sont tous négatifs : elle dit avoir été mordue par un chien et dans la suite avoir été opérée plusieurs fois, plâtrée, immobilisée etc... Elle s'est toujours sentie mal à l'aise dans sa peau. A 9 ans elle est couverte d'abcès "son corps se décompose".
Dans ses accès de détresse enfantine, elle se griffait, se tapait, se blessait, se privait de manger ou se faisait vomir, buvait son urine.
Les bonnes soeurs lui disaient qu'elle avait le diable au corps, et étouffaient toute expression de féminité.
Ses premières expériences sexuelles ont été traumatisantes et décevantes.
Enfin elle s'identifie aux infirmes et aux clochards. Dans tout cela, elle parle de sa jouissance de souffrir, mais cet élément, amené tardivement, nous a toujours paru un peu artificiel. Enfin elle décrit son obsession de la propreté et diverses phobies.

- Au cours de l'analyse, les rêves les plus importants ont toujours été des images corporelles : tomber, voler, bras coupés, perdre ses dents, manques de toutes sortes.

- Son corps réagit très fort à l'impact émotionnel : lors de certaines séances, elle a chaud, tremble, se sent comme paralysée, a des douleurs à la nuque, à la jambe.

Elle a des hémorragies utérines, et divers autres troubles physiques que chaque fois elle rapporte spontanément aux séances, comme le jour où elle raconte un rêve de bouche pleine et se réveille deux ou trois jours plus tard la muqueuse buccale couverte d'aphtes !

Parallèlement à son sentiment de renaître, elle dit que son corps se réveille et lui fait mal et rappelle que ses opérations d'enfants ne lui ont laissé aucun souvenir de souffrances (annulation psychotique ?).

Très souvent elle parle de son impression de vide, de dégoût d'elle-même, d'étouffements.

A la 79è séance, elle raconte comment elle a appris par sa famille qu'elle avait complètement inventé l'histoire du chien, ce qui la sidère. En fait, elle avait eu une ostéomyélite.

- Une autre fois, elle évoque ses sentiments lors de la naissance de ses enfants. Non seulement elle ressentait le "vide" banal du post-partum, mais en outre elle avait chaque fois le fantasme de se vider complètement avec l'enfant qui emportait ses viscères.

- Ses dessins, : des têtes sans corps, des yeux à l'infini, des têtes - prison, tombes, sont pour elle l'occasion d'élaborer ses fantasmes de scène primitive, de négation de son corps ou d'emprisonnement intérieur.

- Si elle n'est pas frigide, elle préfère de beaucoup la tendresse à l'acte sexuel; pourtant au cours de l'analyse, elle raconte comment ces jours-ci pour la première fois c'est elle qui a demandé un rapport à son mari. Sa masturbation enfantine ou actuelle, ou ses équivalents (elle met un doigt dans sa cicatrice qui aspire comme une ventouse) sont évoqués avec gêne d'abord, avec de plus en plus de liberté ensuite.

- Un des rêves les plus importants de l'analyse est celui où elle s'enlève de la bouche pour me l'apporter bien propre ! un instrument bizarre, mis en elle quand elle était petite, dont elle n'a plus besoin, et que dans la réalité l'une de ses amies (et non moi!) l'aide à reconnaître comme un phallus ! Madame X a pu, autour de ce rêve mieux comprendre sa bi-sexualité et reconnaît que si elle "l'enlève" maintenant c'est qu'elle est bien femme et n'en a plus besoin.

- Par ailleurs, bien que n'ayant utilisé aucune "technique corporelle" je pense avoir participé à plusieurs reprises à une sorte de reconstruction du corps.

- Une fois j'ai exigé qu'elle retire ses mains mises en bouclier derrière sa nuque, pour qu'apparaisse enfin le "danger physique".

- Plusieurs fois, par la verbalisation, le ton de la voix, j'ai pu l'aider à exprimer son vécu corporel.

Comme il est classique au cours d'une analyse, Madame X a changé de coiffure et de toilette, s'est parfumée, etc...
Enfin, lors des dernières séances, elle a exprimé son bonheur d'avoir un corps, sa redécouverte successive de tous ses organes, la disparition des phobies et du vertige.

LE CRI ET LE MOT

- Au début du traitement, Madame X "parle pour ne rien dire" et une seule fois elle évoque un reproche qu'on lui a fait pour des cris qu'elle n'a pas poussés. Ce n'est que la 4ème année qu'elle aborde le thème des cris qu'elle ne peut pas supporter : les cris d'enfants, son mari en colère; puis en remontant dans le temps : les cris de son père ivre.

- Puis c'est très longuement et très fréquemment qu'elle parle de ces cris : "je ne criais pas lorsque j'accouchais, les cris des autres me font mal, les cris de mes enfants me rendaient folle". Elle associe cri et crime et répète à l'infini qu'elle a l'impression que, toute petite, on lui a "mis la main sur la bouche pour l'empêcher de crier". Depuis c'est intérieurement qu'elle crie, ce qui lui donne la nausée, la paralyse, etc...

- Mais elle s'étend aussi longuement sur ses explosions de colère très violentes et fréquentes au début et qui ont pratiquement disparu à la fin. Elle devenait alors "comme une bête sauvage" capable de tuer et chaque fois il s'agissait de circonstances s'organisant autour de la frustration vécue comme un danger vital. Elle associe d'ailleurs longtemps le cri au danger et à la mort, avant de rédécouvrir le cri de la vie.

La dernière année Madame X "perd sa voix" pendant plusieurs mois alors qu'elle ne crie pratiquement plus. Ce n'est que lorsque nous avons élaboré ensemble qu'il s'agissait d'un symptôme "artificiel" destiné à prolonger le traitement que sa voix est redevenue normale.

A la fin Madame X, plagiant Marie Cardinal dit "qu'elle a des mots pour parler" et qu'elle n'a plus besoin de crier. A la maison, le dialogue est devenu plus vivant, elle éteint la télévision, pour qu'on se parle, et elle me rapporte certains échanges familiaux et certaines attitudes éducatives avec ses enfants qui font mon admiration.

CONCLUSION

Voici donc une jeune femme, cataloguée dans son enfance et sa jeunesse comme débile caractérielle, instable, etc... alors qu'elle était probablement pré-psychotique. Pourtant quelques traits la différencient du tableau classique des "jeunes marginales". Lors d'une fugue, elle va elle-même demander de l'aide aux services du Tribunal pour Enfants (comportement que reproduit exactement son fils, 20 ans plus tard).

Elle est capable de bons contacts et enfin elle est restée plusieurs années dans un établissement religieux ou sans doute sa névrose a été renforcée par le climat, mais où en même temps elle a pu se "reconstruire" un peu, en particulier grâce à la phase d'homosexualité positive de l'adolescence. Mais Madame X m'a dit à plusieurs reprises combien elle regrettait maintenant que dans sa jeunesse on ne l'ait pas "forcée à des contacts" ou à une thérapie.

Au cours de son analyse, Madame X s'est révélée d'une intelligence et d'une finesse qui n'ont rien à voir avec le tableau du début de sa vie. Sa transformation, attestée par tout l'entourage, a été spectaculaire et a eu des répercussions, en particulier au niveau des enfants, dont la courbe de développement scolaire a suivi exactement la trajectoire de l'analyse de leur mère.

Et si le fils aîné, traumatisé par les évènements de son enfance, passe une adolescence difficile, nous pouvons espérer que pour les trois autres le "cycle de la reproduction" est enfin brisé.

Child Abuse and Neglect, Vol. 3, pp. 505 - 508.
Pergamon Press Ltd., 1979. Printed in Great Britain.

PSYCHOTHERAPY WITH A CHILD WHO HAS BEEN POISONED

Rolene Szur

Hospital for Sick Children, Great Ormond Street, London W C I, England

Whenever there is a serious physical attack on a child we can see that it is also functioning as a channel for some form or degree of psychological onslaught. In the case of Jason D neither common brutality nor crude neglect were present.

He was an only child, since his brother had died in the hospital following a complicated metabolic disorder, at the age of two and a half years. Jason was born two years later, and surgical repair for hiatus hernia was carried out at three months in the same hospital. He remained a somewhat sickly child and attended the out-patient clinics regularly for some years. He did not sit till twelve months nor walk till three years. In stature he was below the third centile and there were unexplained metabolic disturbances. When tested for intellectual development at age four, and again later because of poor school progress, it was concluded that he probably was within the average range, though performing at a lower level. At this time the social worker wrote that his parents were treating him in an inappropriately infantile way; they explained that disciplining him might endanger his health as frustrations produced an alarming state in which the child raged, rocked and screamed.

By his eighth birthday Jason had been admitted to a medical ward in the Hospital for Sick Children for pain in the eyes, double vision, photophobia and pains in the leg and abdomen. Suspicion that there was a psychogenic element in the symptoms led to a psychiatric interview with the very unwilling mother, who reported that Jason was in constant pain, only able to lie in bed or a push-chair, eyes closed behind dark glasses. Though a lively, friendly boy, she said, when well, he had not been able to attend school for the last two months. Recently he had apparently been having "turns" as she called them, when he would become limp, collapse, scream and wet himself. Throughout the interview Jason lay curled up, whimpering, nodding or shaking his head. Mrs D referred to many stillbirths and infantile defects in her extended family. She complained bitterly about treatment in her childhood when she had been admitted to the Hospital for Sick Children for minor surgery, and then accused the same hospital of responsibility for the older boy's death. In answer to a question she said that her husband left the management of Jason to her. The psychiatrist, noting that the mother appeared to have an investment in the child being ill, hoped to develop some therapeutic relationship with her. However, the latter's hostility became increasingly intense and she refused any further interviews.

Within the following weeks diuretic drugs that had not been prescribed were discovered in the boy's urine, producing a dangerously low level of salt in the blood. Evidence that his mother was administering these was judged to be convincing, although fiercely and persistently denied by her. (Attempting to clear herself, Mrs D offered a sequence of alternative accounts, which were contradicted by factual information.)

It was considered advisable to remove the child from her care and under a 'place of safety order' he was admitted to the In-Patient Unit of the Department of Psychological Medicine, while legal proceedings were taking place. Parental visits were limited and also had to be supervised. This was partly to avoid a recurrence of the poisoning and also because the mother had been overheard whispering to Jason in an attempt to interfere with the ward management of his health care. (Later the court ruled that he be taken into care for an indefinite period.)

At this stage Jason was referred for psychotherapy and I met him for the first time. Because of the unusual way the case had developed I did not meet either of the parents and my information about them and about the early history is based in the first instance on accounts from the psychiatrist who conducted the early interviews and from a social worker who made considerable efforts to help his distressed parents. What stands out in this case is that Jason had been subjected, one may think since early years, to an invasion of his own identity, which was currently being forced into carrying the burden of being little more than a helpless infant, ailing, and bound to the hospital.

One may speculate as to what unconscious needs in his mother were served in this way, and how they were related to her own early experiences in the hospital, in which also her first child had died, and to which she had returned again and again. Our present concern, however, is to attend to the boy and to look at what it has meant to him. The use of debilitating drugs, pain, fear and isolation had combined to reduce him at this stage into a passive instrument of the unfortunate woman's disturbed fantasies, which may indeed be thought of as poisoning his mind or personality, and perhaps eroding the protective barriers which distinguish the self from others, and the inner world from outer reality. His daytime life must have seemed little different from a nightmare.

Following admission to the Unit Jason's physical improvement was rapid and marked, so that soon he was walking about normally and energetically. But at the same time this was in every way a very unsettling time for him. It was reported that he played endless games about poisoning and killing, was rough with other children, extremely provocative to the staff and seemed very disturbed, claiming with apparent conviction to be invulnerable and to have superhuman strength.

A strange little boy, with an odd spiky hair-cut, ill-fitting glasses and clothes, Jason appeared for his first session carrying an assortment of rubbery snakes, monsters and a twisted glass tube. His manner conveyed an unreal air of confidence, with a shallowness of affect and a quick and easy style of relating which suggested that he was very defended against facing the enormous difficulties of his situation. "Have you got a two-way mirror?" he said threateningly. "There were some people watching me, but I worked out a way to watch them, and then smashed it. I'm an escaper," he added. "Don't like the unit. Nearly 'scaped; I was just getting on to a bus when they got me, but I pushed them under the bus and it ran over them." A comment that this was what he probably had wanted to do really, and that children often felt like this when frightened and worried, momentarily seemed to relax his tension, as he answered, a little to my surprise, "Yeah, I just wish I could have." This response suggested he had in fact been able to retain some healthier modes of functioning. It did also seem likely that he was expressing underlying feelings about his mother's intrusiveness, but now transferred to the hospital setting.

In what followed Jason showed something of his state of inner confusion. Using the glass tube, he explained that he was giving the snake a blood transfusion and, concentrating with a serious air, said, "Now this will make him better, and when it gets to the tip of his tail he will die." It was as if the differentiations between good and bad, health and sickness, being alive or dead, had hardly been achieved. The session ended with some scribble writing read out in meaningless scribble words.

At other times he seemed to turn himself into a wild fusion of Superman, Tarzan and Kung Fu killer. Taking a flying leap from the table, he would hurl chairs crashing to the wall and, when I attempted to restrain him, swing round to chop at my arm karate-style. His behaviour gave the impression of requiring me to be the frightened one, and indeed to some extent he did sometimes succeed, especially when his stocky build and heavy shoulders provided quite unexpected strength and force. Sadistic fantasies and morbid preoccupations often filled his sessions. At such times I think he needed a therapist as someone for taking on the fear and panic in a way which could help him towards holding it in, instead of being driven to a choice between overwhelming feelings of persecution or a flight into grandiose illusion. He told me about a recurrent nightmare of a cut off hand and arm coming to thump him. The therapist's function was, in general, mainly to show him that one could survive, not become hostile, but keep thinking as well as one could manage. Sometimes he would respond as if being given a useful piece of information; sometimes sneering, "You're bonkers you are!", sniffling and laughing.

One aim, of course, was to try to help build a more realistic picture of a mother figure as neither idealised and persecuted, nor totally sinister, but perhaps as someone who, while caring for him, might herself be very confused. In explicit terms he maintained a loyalty to his mother and her tales of the cruel doctors, though at times one felt that some of the conviction was wearing thin, and later this was more evident.

There were also more constructive interludes which brought to mind the image of something in the nature of a handyman father as, for example, when he used plasticine to mould a plug for the sink, or made efforts to repair a loose door-hinge. The overall picture of the boy's world which was emerging contained a place for helpful figures as well as destructive, frightening ones, though in a state of continual flux and confusion. Jason had been enmeshed in his mother's paranoid system and it was difficult to know how well he would be able to find an independent individuality of his own. Providing a stable, healthy environment could be very important for his further development. Fortunately a Children's Home was found which was able to provide a very positive place for him, and where he made good progress both socially and academically. His mother continued to visit weekly.

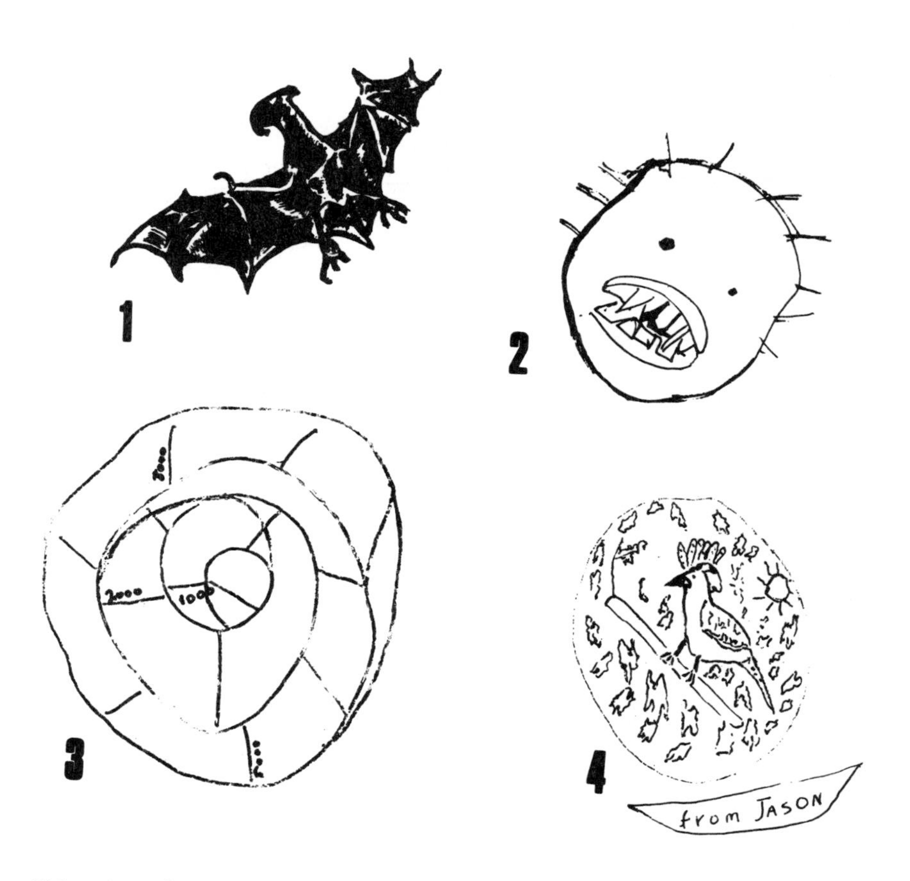

This series reflects something of the gradual changes one saw taking place in the child. The first figure shows the plastic monster which accompanied him to all the early sessions. The second is Jason's drawing of me as a monster which shared my place in the treatment room as a target for wads of wet paper. The third represents his later development of this activity by turning it into a dartboard game we both were meant to play, thus enabling him to express rivalry and aggression towards the therapist in a far more symbolized and mature way. The last one is a drawing made as a gift for me shortly after he had left the Unit; the more positive, creative and integrated qualities here form a marked contrast to the sinister, winged object of the earlier days.

There are, of course, many uncertainties that beset social service placements, and frequent staff changes can make it hard to form personal relationships. It seems to me still somewhat rare for Jason to experience persons as individuals who continue to exist in themselves independently of their attachment to him, and of the parts they play in his real or fantasy world. Occasionally there are some signs of social concern about someone, or a sense of warmth, perhaps in the attachment to his house mother. But it is not easy for him to deal with separateness other than by coldness and "cutting off". This has seemed to apply to his feeling about his mother to some extent.

Since his discharge from the hospital I have continued to keep in contact with Jason and with his social worker. Although the intervals between sessions are often quite long, the thread does not seem to get altogether broken, and perhaps this might be of some use to him.

One may conclude that at the present time Jason appears to have found a place of safety in a psychological and a physical sense. I would think certain personal traits have helped, and attached others who can give him help. Perhaps this has been his 'survival kit', an ability to make the most of anything good and useful which became available, whether it was a piece of plasticine, an attempt to understand or a sound home base.

References

Helfer, R.E. and Kempe, C.H. (1974) The Battered Child: A Psychiatric Study of Parents Who Abuse Infants and Small Children, University of Chicago Press, Chicago and London.

Meltzer, D. (1967) The Psycho-Analytical Process, Heinemann, London.

Rogers, D. et al, Non-accidental poisoning: an extended syndrome of child abuse, British Medical Journal, I, 793-796 (1976).

Child Abuse and Neglect, Vol. 3, pp. 509 - 514.
Pergamon Press Ltd., 1979. Printed in Great Britain.

THE ANALYSIS AND TREATMENT OF CHILD ABUSE BY BEHAVIOURAL PSYCHOTHERAPY

William Reavley - Marie Therese Gilbert

Department of Clinical Psychology,
Graylingwell Hospital, Chichester,
West Sussex.

In this paper we are attempting to describe how we treat child abuse problems by Behavioural Psychotherapy, how our treatment approach evolved and the results we have obtained.

Firstly, some information on our patient population. Between September 1974 and July 1978 we have had 53 cases of child abuse referred to us in the Psychology Department of Graylingwell Hospital. Of these, 26 were referred by social workers, the majority of the remainder (20) were referred by consultant psychiatrists. The others were referred by general practitioners, psychologists and a child guidance clinic. One parent was a self-referral.

TABLE 1

Psychiatric and Related Problems

Agoraphobia	3	5.66%
Anxiety	16	30.18%
Depression	40	75.47%
Dietary	3	5.66%
Interpersonal Difficulties	25	47.16%
Marital Difficulties	25	47.16%
Mental Handicap	1	1.88%
Obsessional Problems	14	26.41%
Personality Disorders	5	9.43%
Sexual Problems	25	47.16%
Social Isolation	21	39.62%
Total number of patients	53	

27 of these patients have completed therapy, 13 are currently being treated, 4 were found to be unsuitable and hence were not taken on for therapy. In our sample there were six patients who were assessed by us as suitable for therapy but who did not take up the offer of treatment. With three patients treatment is pending.

None of our patients presented with child abuse as their only problem. All of our sample presented with psychiatric problems which often needed treatment before the child abuse difficulties could be tackled. The high incidence of "depression" and "anxiety" in our sample is not surprising considering the circumstances in which our patients find themselves. However, the incidence of "obsessional problems" (twenty-six percent), is higher than we expected (Cooper 1970). This warrants further investigation although the high psychiatric morbidity is likely to be partly a function of the setting in which we work.

Behavioural Analysis

Our first patients were referred for treatment of problems other than child abuse. When the behavioural analysis revealed the child abuse difficulties which were described in behavioural language it was a natural progression to apply behaviour therapy treatments. In our behavioural analysis (Kanfer and Saslow 1969), we aim to identify the behavioural excesses (the things the parent does which he should not do) and the behavioural deficits (the things the parent does not do but needs to do to promote the healthy development of the child). A behaviour which often figures as an excess is "shouting" and "cuddling" is frequently a deficit.

Deciding just what is a behavioural excess and a behavioural deficit is an area where value judgements can have a major influence. To minimise the chance of the therapist inflicting his own value system on the patient, as soon as the problem behaviours have been identified by the parent and therapist, the parent is encouraged to define "target" behaviours which fit in with her own values. These target behaviours are definitions of how she would like to behave at the end of therapy.

The behavioural analysis focusses not only on the particular difficulties the parent is experiencing in caring for their child but it also covers many other aspects of the parents' inter - and intra - personal lives. To help us in our assessment we are developing an interview schedule to gather and collate the information we find necessary in order to plan treatment.

Therapy, including the use of measurement

The analysis of the parent's problems into behavioural excesses and deficits, i.e. translation into behavioural language, can often lead to the use of well understood behavioural treatments. But the same deficit or excess in two parents will not necessarily be treated in the same way. Account needs to be taken of the individual's particular resources and how the problem behaviour relates to other behaviours. For example, two parents may complain of severe anxiety in what are apparently very similar situations. As a result of the behavioural analysis, one parent may be taught Anxiety Management, the other may be taught to identify the sequence of events leading up to the anxiety and be encouraged to intervene in this chain to prevent escalation of the anxiety.

It is generally agreed that many parents need to be taught more appropriate behaviours in the handling of their children. We would emphasise the word "taught", because in our experience for the parents to be told how to behave or instructed in a general sense how to tackle particular problems is not enough. The teaching needs to be very concrete. Social Learning theory provides the framework for this teaching, particularly the use of Participant Modelling. For case illustrations see Reavley and Gilbert 1976. This strategy, featuring as it does the prominence of the therapist and then, gradually, the therapist's presence fading from the scene, makes sure that the behaviour being advised actually occurs in the first place and that, over time, the occurrence of the "good" behaviour is not dependent upon the therapist's presence. Parents have reported to us that they often know what it is they ought to do with their child but, because of negative feelings or fear of doing something untoward, they are unable to put it into operation. In these cases Participant Modelling is particularly useful both to alter behaviour and attitudes.

Having identified the behavioural excesses and deficits and the stimuli which seem to provoke the excess behaviours, the next step is to establish baselines of frequency of these behaviours.

The need for baseline measures is explained to the parent and their contributing to the construction of their own record cards increases the likelihood of them keeping accurate records. The measures they keep, initiated at the beginning of our involvement with the parent, help with the analysis of the problems and also give indications as to the success of therapy. Details of some of the measures are reported elsewhere (Reavley, Gilbert and Carver 1978). We have found that these on-going measures are of particular importance in giving feedback to the parent regarding their endeavours to bring about change. Without the detailed records it is sometimes difficult for a parent to recognise the gradual changes which are taking place. Thus the records the parents keep serve to motivate them for, without knowledge of successful change in behaviour, they might well not persist in the efforts necessary.

Attitudes

Certainly in the early stages of therapy, although behaviour may have changed, the parent's attitude may not have altered (Hersen 1973). Marks (1975) high-lighted the importance of measuring both behaviour and attitude. Working with obsessional patients, he showed that those patients whose behaviour changed in the desired direction, but whose attitudes remained unaltered had, at follow up, reverted to their pre-therapy behaviours. Thus, in an attempt to gauge how permament any observed change in behaviour might be, we measure by Semantic Differential the parents' attitudes. The assumption is made that if behaviour change is maintained for a sufficient length of time, then attitudes compatible with the changed behaviour will evolve. However, rather than leave attitude change to occur by itself, we make use of the data the patients have gathered themselves to help bring about attitude change by feeding back to the patients information about those areas in which they have been successful.

At the beginning of therapy, a parent may identify a particular interaction as causing anxiety. As therapy progresses and the parent's rating of anxiety diminishes, she is asked now to discontinue rating anxiety and to rate how much pleasure she is gaining from the situation. The change of "set" may also help to bring about attitude change.

Some of the therapeutic strategies we use, (discussed more fully in Reavley, Gilbert and Carver 1978), such as Positive Self-Talk and Participant Modelling (Bandura et al 1969), have been shown to alter not only behaviour but also attitudes.

Outcome of Therapy

It is very difficult to assess the effectiveness of any therapy but assessing therapy with child abuse cases is particularly difficult. It does not seem appropriate to us to attempt to demonstrate the effectiveness of behaviour therapy with child abuse cases using experimental designs acceptable with other problems. However, we are mindful of the need to examine the claims of any so called "therapy".

We have attempted to assess, in several ways, the outcome of the 27 patients who have completed therapy. In addition to records of how well the patients achieved their individual targets, each patient was rated on the scale illustrated in figure 1, at completion of therapy and at follow up. This is a measure of overall therapeut.c success.

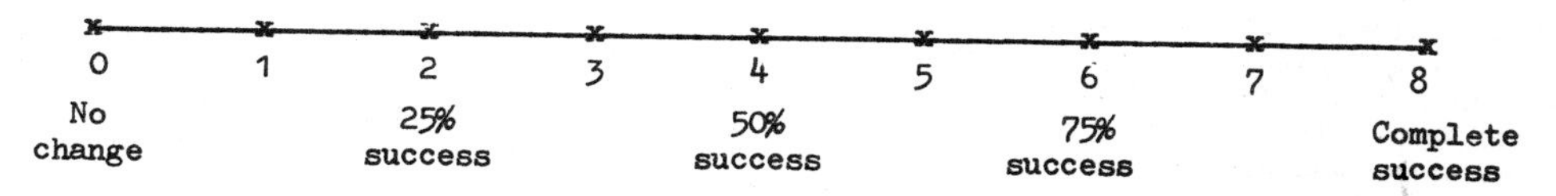

figure 1

The ratings were carried out by therapists and although the therapists agreed criteria for each rating point on the scale, their judgements may not be free from "contamination".

TABLE 2

Therapist Rating of Success

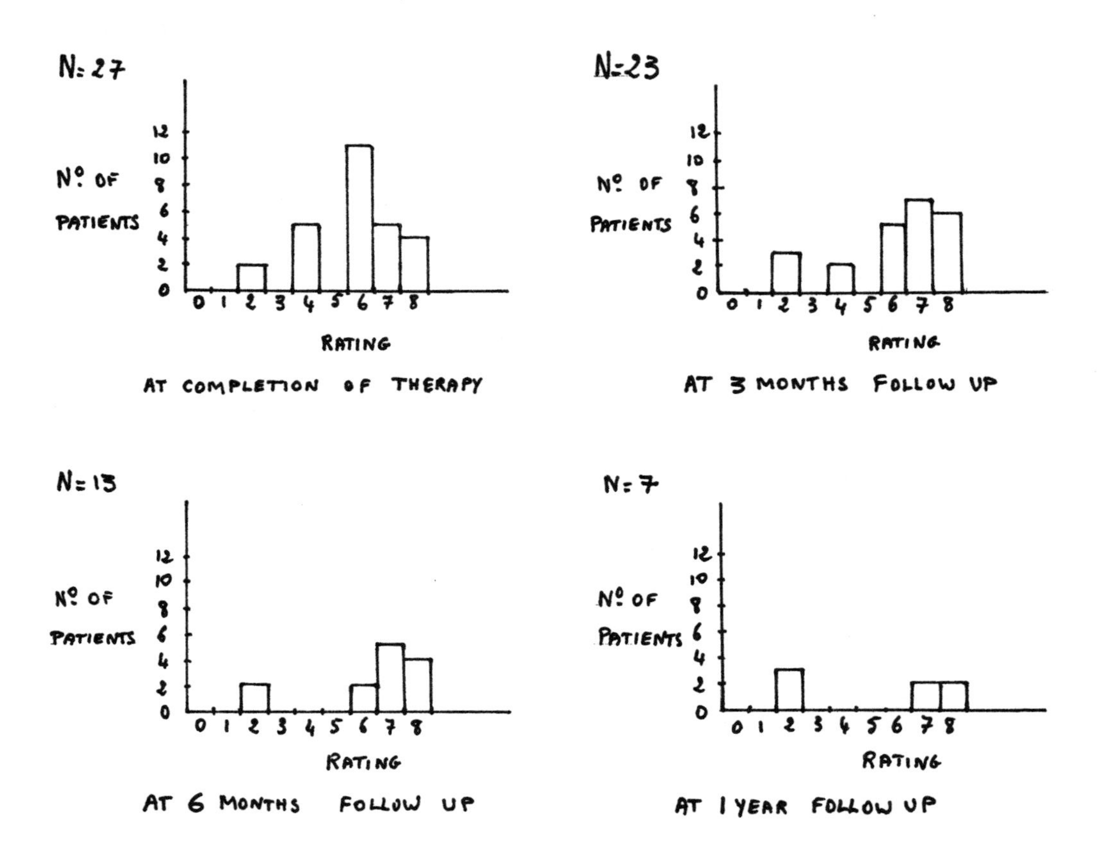

Of the 27 patients who completed therapy ($\bar{x}$ success rating 5.8), two patients (approximately seven percent), who had been rated by the therapist at 2 and 6 at completion of therapy, failed to maintain this level. Their ability to cope with their children deteriorated to such an extent that the children were taken into long-term care. This relapse rate of seven percent compares very favourably with the finding of other studies (Helfer & Pollock 1968, Castle and Kerr 1972). Two parents needed "booster" sessions which they sought themselves. The remainder of our sample had achieved and have maintained target performances and are coping with the care of their children at a satisfactory level. This group consists of 23 patients, who have been followed up by ourselves and social workers. The amount of therapist time needed to achieve these results is contained in Table 3.

TABLE 3

Therapy Time (Completed Cases N = 27)

$\bar{X}$	Number of Sessions	16	(Range 3 to 70)
$\bar{X}$	Number of Hours	24	(Range 3 to 100)

There is a very wide range of time and the number of sessions before completion of therapy. This underlines how, in child abuse, each case is unique and how each situation in each case is also unique. Most cases (16 : 69 percent), were completed within six months.

TABLE 4

Length of Therapy N = 27

Cases	completed	within		3 months		9	33.3%
"	"	between	3 &	6	"	7	25.9%
"	"	"	6 &	9	"	6	22.2%
"	"	"	9 &	12	"	3	11.1%
"	"	"	1 &	2 years		2	7.4%

Our usual practice is to have frequent sessions at the beginning of therapy.

Conclusions

Our conceptualisation and treatment of child abuse have altered and are still altering. We are coming to the conclusion that in many cases although "excess" behaviours like shouting need to lessen in frequency, it is equally, if not more important, to increase the frequency of those behaviours (deficits) that both the parent and the therapist see as desirable. In many cases to promote the showing of affection may be as important as diminishing the frequency of physical abuse. Therapy is often directed towards encouraging the parent to produce more of those behaviours which are lacking and this may have the additional benefit of reducing the frequency of behavioural excesses.

We would like to emphasise that the behavioural psychotherapy approach is not a collection of techniques regularly applied across the board to particular problems. One has to accept that child abuse is probably the final common pathway reflecting a wide variation in causes and problems. Successful therapy is not possible unless a very careful behavioural analysis is made.

It may appear that the practitioner of this approach needs a great deal of training and experience. We are not in a position to make a definite statement on this but we have had a social worker seconded to us for a period of 6 weeks who has gone on to treat a child abuse case independently and successfully by behavioural means. This is very encouraging and an aspect of our work we hope to expand in the future.

Summary

The results from use of behaviour therapy with child abuse cases is very encouraging. Data has been presented to show the approach both economical and rewarding. Our experience suggests that selected social workers may be able to learn to use the approach with a relatively short period of training.

REFERENCES

Bandura A., Blanchard E.B. and Ritter B. (1969). Relative Efficiency of Desensitisation and Modelling Approaches for Inducing Behavioural, Affective and Attitudinal Changes. Journal of Personality and Social Psychology. 5, 16-23.

Castle, Raymond and Kerr, Ann (1972). A Study of Suspected Child Abuse. N.S.P.C.C.

Cooper J. (1970). The Leyton Obsessional Inventory. Psychological Medicine 1, 48-64

Helfer, Ray E. and Pollock, Carl B. (1968). The Battered Child Syndrome. XV Chicago Year Book Publications Inc.

Hersen M. (1973). Self Assessment of Fear. Behaviour Therapy 4, 241-257

Kanfer F.H. and Saslow G. (1970). Behavioural Diagnosis in C.M. Franks (Ed) Behaviour Therapy : Appraisal and Status. New York, McGraw Hill.

Marks I.M. et al (1975). Treatment of Chronic Obsessive Compulsive Neuroses by In Vivo Exposure : A Two Year Follow Up and Issues in Treatment. British Journal of Psychiatry 127, 349-364.

Reavley W. and Gilbert M-T, (1976). The Behavioural Treatment Approach to Potential Child Abuse - Two Illustrative Cases. Social Work Today, 7 6, 166-8. Reprinted in Lee C.M. (Ed) Child Abuse : A Reader and Sourcebook. (1978) Milton Keynes, The Open University Press.

Reavley W., Gilbert M-T and Carver V. (1978). The Behavioural Approach to Child Abuse (2). In Carver, V (Ed), Child Abuse : A Study Text. Milton Keynes, The Open University Press.

Child Abuse and Neglect, Vol. 3, pp. 515 - 519.

0145-2134/79/0601-0515 $02.00/0.

FOSTER CARE ENRICHMENT PROGRAM

Pamela McBogg, Mary McQuiston, and Robert Schrant

The National Center for the Prevention and Treatment of Child Abuse and Neglect of the Department of Pediatrics, University of Colorado Medical Center, Denver, Colorado, 80262, U.S.A.

INTRODUCTION

The Foster Care Enrichment Program of The National Center for the Prevention and Treatment of Child Abuse and Neglect in Denver is an outgrowth of the Center's experience with *Circle House, a short-term residential treatment facility for the entire abusive family. Circle House was staffed by a cadre of therapeutic paraprofessionals and professionals available to the family 24 hours of every day. In essence, what the Center staff learned from the Circle House experience was how to be a foster family to the entire abusive family-- thus, the conception of the Foster Care Enrichment Program which began in August of 1977. The program was carefully planned, after a review of the literature, so that the foster care experience would indeed be a beneficial intervention for the child and family. The preliminary results of the pilot project are encouraging and do suggest that foster care can be an effective family service rather than an often traumatic experience of indeterminate duration.

REVIEW OF THE LITERATURE

A review of the foster care literature was both exciting and depressing: exciting because the literature clearly defined the major problems of foster care[1] and effective solutions to those problems; [2,3,4,5] depressing because the solutions were not sufficiently implemented.

Two major problems exist in most current foster care systems. The first is that children are in temporary foster care much too long without a future on which to plan or build. In some states the average placement for a child is now nearly two years.[6] The second major problem involves the foster parents and their complaints about the system. Foster parents want clarification of their roles with the agency, the child and the child's parents. Further, because roles can and do change, foster parents want ongoing, effective communication with all appropriate parties. Foster parents also want support for the work they do. The support has been suggested in many forms, i.e., money, supervision, training,[7,8] and/or classification of foster parents as to what kinds of children they can best nurture.[9]

Effective solutions to the above problems have been demonstrated. Pike and the Oregon Project[10,11] have shown that making decisions and permanent plans for children can be accomplished and is effective in ending indefinite placement in foster care. Several projects have demonstrated the various roles foster parents can effectively fulfill.[12] All of the literature supports the concept that children in foster care do better both in placement and after placement if the foster parents have a relationship with the natural parents. [13-18] The literature was extremely helpful in determining the goals as well as the methods of the foster care enrichment project.

The Program

The first major goal is to provide safe foster care that facilitates development for the child. In order to accomplish this goal, a number of important factors must be present: the foster

*Described elsewhere in this issue of the Journal.

parents must be nurturing people; visits with the natural parents must be frequent and a positive experience for all parties; and the child, natural family and foster family must receive adequate and appropriate evaluation, treatment and ongoing support.

The second major goal is to determine a feasible,permanent placement plan for the child in the shortest time possible, preferably within three months. After this diagnostic period efforts are directed towards carrying out and supporting that plan until it is a reality for the child. In order to accomplish these goals,the program has three therapeutic components. The component for the natural family consists of thorough psychosocial evaluation followed by appropriate treatment. This treatment includes the foster family services, lay therapist, weekly group therapy at The National Center, and casework by the local agency worker responsible for the case. The component of the program for the child consists of safe, caring foster parents, a thorough developmental evaluation, appropriate therapies and, of course, frequent, productive visits with the natural parents. The component for the foster family consists of much ongoing education. Topics range from those in any good foster care curriculum to understanding the abusive adult, development of abused children, sexual abuse, effective listening techniques, communication, discipline, and dealing with grief, mourning, and separation. This formal education as well as informal sharing of experiences and professional support take place at foster parent group meetings. The foster parents also attend team meetings at which time all treatment persons involved in the case are present. These team meetings facilitate necessary communication as well as clarifying everyone's role and responsibility in regard to any particular family. Professional consultation is also available 24 hours a day. Foster parents are paid $150 a month per child in care in addition to what the local agency pays for foster care. The additional payment is an attempt to adequately compensate foster families, to reward those who do a good job and to pay for services rendered.

Results

Currently, seven foster families participate in the program, and each has had at least one child in placement. The foster families represent both the ethnic variety in the community and the local foster care population. Most are in the middle socioeconomic range, and all but one couple have children of their own. Interestingly, nearly 60% of the families either have adopted children or are awaiting an adoptive placement. Over half of the families had been foster parents previously and wanted to participate in the program because of the relationship with the natural parents and the professional team. The new foster parents were clearly invested in the children. While they were initially a bit scared of interacting with the natural parents, the new foster parents also felt that aspect of the program necessary.

Before discussing the natural families,one other point about the foster parents needs to be made. The professional staff on the project carefully interviewed prospective foster parents and rated them as to their potential of success in the program. The typical criteria of previous childhood history and experience with children were not predictive of adequate performance as foster parents in the program. The atmosphere of acceptance and the ability to care and nurture were not clearly elicited in the initial interviews. The parents in one of the most nurturing foster homes had concerning backgrounds of instability and abuse as children, whereas the foster parents who were initially most impressive because of their ability to intellectualize and converse were, in reality, quite rigid. An appropriate measure, including gut reactions, for predicting nurturing qualities in foster parents is not yet available, and efforts should be directed towards developing such a measure.

The natural families represent the variety of families who utilize foster care. Two newborn infants were admitted to foster care. One was in foster care because mother displayed unusual psychotic behavior during the lying-in period. The other infant was placed at one month of age for failure to thrive and lack of residence and consistent care. Mother was young, immature, unmarried and a prostitute. Children of five families were placed by court order for abuse and neglect. Children in three families were placed voluntarily, but family profiles are similar to those families whose children were placed by court order. Children in six families experienced previous placements. In keeping with the goals of the program, good foster care, including frequent visits with parents and appropriate therapeutic intervention have been established. Permanent plans have been made and are in process. Placement with natural parents using multiple support systems has occurred in four families and termination of parental rights is being sought in three families. In the remaining case, not enough information is yet available to determine and execute a plan, but it is anticipated that the child will be returning home soon after a therapeutic program has been established. There have been no replacements of children in the program nor have any children had to be placed in other foster homes. Table I. summarizes the status of the 10 children from eight families.

TABLE I.

Family and Children	*Age at Entry into F.C.	*# of Months in F.C.E.P.	Placements: V=voluntary C=court ordered	Previous Placements: # of Times and Duration	Permanent Plan	Status in Attaining Permanent Plan
Family A	3 wks	8 mos	C	1 -- 2 wks	Terminate parental rights	In progress
Family B	6 wks	7 mos	C	0 -- 0	Terminate parental rights	In progress
Family C	4 yrs	6 mos	C	2 -- 18 mos	Return home	Accomplished
Family D_1	4 yrs	2 mos	C	3 -- 2 mos	Return home	Accomplished
D_2	2 yrs	2 mos	C	3 -- 2 mos		
Family E	5 yrs	2 mos	V	1 -- 3 mos	Return home	Accomplished
Family F_1	6 yrs	7 mos	C	2 -- 3 yrs	Terminate parental rights	In progress
F_2	9 mos	7 mos	C	1 -- 3 yrs		
Family G	4 yrs	2 mos	V	1 -- 1 mo	Return home	Imminent
Family H	9 yrs	1 mo	V	0 -- 0	None	Evaluation in progress

*F.C. = Regular foster care
**F.C.E.P. = Foster Care Enrichment Program

The majority of natural families, foster families, professionals and paraprofessionals involved with the program are satisfied. Major cudos for the program all involve the combination of relationships which are available: that is, parents and children, foster parents and natural parents, foster parents and program staff, natural parents and therapists, children and therapists. The major criticisms continue to center around systems problems, for example, continuances of court hearings for reasons unrelated to the cases.

Case Illustration

A short case history should serve to highlight pertinent therapeutic aspects of the program. Jason, age four, was voluntarily placed in foster care by his mother who felt Jason might seriously hurt his two-year-old sister and mother might seriously hurt Jason. Jason had been placed originally in a regular foster home but was replaced in the Foster Care Enrichment Program when he became very aggressive, destructive, and uncontrollable. Mother had infrequ-

contact with Jason in the first foster home. Jason was prepared for the transfer as was everyone else involved. He continued to behave inappropriately,but his behavior changed after contacts with mother. Mother had withdrawn from Jason feeling less and less adequate to care for him. After thorough evaluation, it became evident that the natural family had numerous problems, that Jason himself was a disturbed little boy and that the separation from his family and fear of abandonment was a major contributor to his difficult-to-control behavior both at home and in foster care.

Visits though always available to mother had not occurred until insistence by program team members, including the case manager, lay therapist, and foster parents. Foster mother prepared both mother and Jason for visits and was available if needed during visits. Contact of Jason and his mother between visits was maintained by phone. Mother gradually regained confidence in her ability and desire to have Jason return home. She utilized available support systems and was most relieved to know that foster mother also thought Jason was a difficult boy for whom to care. Jason returned home after less than three months in foster care. Mother and Jason both had established and utilized the numerous support systems of the program. The foster family was able to deal with its trauma of separation by maintaining some contact with Jason and mother and by sharing their feelings with other foster parents at the group meeting. Jason continues to need individual psychotherapy. Mother utilizes the foster parents, lay therapist and parents' group to avoid or handle crises. Substantial behavioral changes are slow in coming and crises do occur, but with support the family is able to function.

SUMMARY

In summary then, the preliminary data of the Foster Care Enrichment Program indicates that therapeutic foster care can and does exist and that decisions regarding children in foster care can and should be made in a short period of time. Foster families can be recruited who are able and willing to nurture families as well as children. Easily available professional support is necessary and effective, frequent communication of all parties involved is absolutely essential. Short-term foster care can be effective in alleviating crisis situations, offering a diagnostic safe period and establishing therapeutic relationships.

The Foster Care Enrichment Program has put into effect what has been known for many years to be good foster care. The program has outlined the needs of foster care and its recipients and ways to fulfill and maximize the goals of foster care.

One of the most exacting aspects of our particular program is that the Denver Department of Welfare is actively exploring ways of incorporating program goals and techniques into its larger system.

REFERENCES

1. The Denver Post, New York Times, Nov. 3, 1977, Group to probe problems of foster care children.

2. S. Baslow, Fostering an abusive family: extended-family concept for abusive families, Grant Application (1976).

3. I. W. Fellner and C. Solomon, Achieving permanent solutions for children in foster home care, Child Welfare, March, 178 (1973).

4. M. Garber, The ghetto as a source of foster homes, Child Welfare, May, 246 (1970).

5. E. Glassberg, Are foster homes hard to find? Child Welfare, 44, 453 (1968).

6. C. Hebeler, Children in foster care -- descriptive data. Report to Governor of Colorado, October (1976).

7. Child Welfare League of America, Basic Curriculum for Foster Parenting, Child Welfare League of America (1975).

8. H.D. Stone, Introduction to foster parenting: new curriculum, Children Today, Nov-Dec. (1976).

9. J. L. Simon, The effects of foster care payment levels on the number of foster children given homes, Social Service Review, 9 (4) 405 (1975).

10. A. Emlen, Caseload screening and periodic case review; its value in permanent planning for children in foster care. The Oregon Project, Permanent Planning for Children in Substitute Care Workshop, May 10, 1977.

11. V. Pike, Permanent planning for foster children: the Oregon project, Children Today, Nov-Dec. (1976).

12. J. Mannheimer, A demonstration of foster parents in the co-worker role, Child Welfare, Feb. 104 (1969).

13. E. Jacobson and J. Cockerum, As foster children see it, Children Today, Nov-Dec. (1976).

14. S. Jerkins, Separation experiences of parents whose children are in foster care, Child Welfare, 48, 334 (1969).

15. N. Littner, The importance of the natural parents to the child in placement. Paper presented at the First Conference of Foster Parents in Chicago in 1971. Child Welfare League of America, LIV, March, 175 (1975).

16. D. A. Murphy, A program for parents of children in foster family care, Children Today, Nov-Dec. (1976).

17. H. B. M. Murphy, Long-term foster care and its influence on adjustment to adult life, The Child and His Family, Child at Psychiatric Risk, Anthony and Koupernik(eds.), 3 (1974).

18. E. A. Weinstein, The Self-Image of the Foster Child, Russell Sage Foundation, New York (1960).

Acknowledgments

The authors would like to thank the Denver Department of Welfare and Mary Alice Bramming for their cooperation. We also want to thank the superb foster parents available to children and families.

Child Abuse and Neglect, Vol. 3, pp. 521 - 528.

0145-2134/79/0601-0521 $02.00/0.

THE ALAMEDA PROJECT:A TWO YEAR REPORT & ONE YEAR FOLLOW UP

Theodore J. Stein
School of Social Work
Calif. State Univ.-Sac. CA.

Eileen D. Gambrill
School of Social Work
Univ. of Calif. Berk.-Berk. CA.

INTRODUCTION

Data suggests that more than 50% of the estimated 420,000 children in foster care in the United States will spend their lives in out of home placement. (1) Rather than being the outcome of purposeful decision making, the situation in which these children live is said to result from an absence of case planning. (2) These children are described in the literature as "drifting" in the limbo of long term foster care. (3)

Concern for the plight of such youngsters led to the development and implementation of a two year experimental project which is described in this paper. Providing permanent homes for children in care was the primary objective. Intensive services were offered to natural parents to facilitate their participation in decision making such that permanent plans could be made. One of the following four outcomes could result from such planning: (a) the child could be restored to natural parents; (b) the child could be placed for adoption following parental relinquishment or termination of parental right; (c) an adult could be designated by the court as the child's legal guardian, or (d) the child could remain in long term placement. Comparing the effectiveness of behavioral procedures with those typically used by child welfare workers to resolve identified problems was a second objective. Testing the feasibility of having two workers share the management of each case was a third area for investigation. One of the workers bore responsibility for providing services to natural parents; the other focused attention on the child and foster parents. This article describes the experimental phase of the project and presents data concerning the whereabouts of the children one year after the project terminated. (4)

METHOD

Cases had to meet the following criteria to be included: (a) at least one biological parent had to be present in the county; (b) the child must be under 16 years of age; (c) the child must be in foster home placement. Children in treatment institutions were excluded since other resources were primary treatment agents and because geographic distance made frequent contact between parents and children difficult, and; (d) a decision as to the child's future must not have been made. Such decision making was an objective of the project. The initial caseload was volunteered from the active files of workers in two out of six foster care placement units selected for inclusion in the project. One unit was designated as experimental, the other as control. New intake was randomly assigned to all units. Accepting new cases was contingent on openings in the caseloads of workers. Caseload limits were reached,in the experimental unit, by the end of the first month at which point a second experimental unit was added in order to continue accepting new cases. There were two experimental units and one control for the remainder of the project. Three project workers were hired especially for the study.

A total of 428 children participated in the project over two years, 227 in experimental units and 201 in control. Volunteered cases accounted for 54% in the experimental units and 66% in the control, whereas new intake comprised 46% of the cases in the experimental unit and 34% in the control. Maximum caseload size in the experimental and control units was 35 children in the former and 49 in the latter. In viewing caseload size it is important to remember that all experimental cases were in various stages of decision making and thus were active. Once a case was referred for adoption or guardianship or designated long term care, the case was closed to the project to make room for new intake. In control, all long term cases as well as guardianship on which the court dependency was not dismissed, remained part of the worker's caseload. It is reasonable to conclude that such cases were less active than those in various stages of decision making.

Sample Description

Ninety-nine percent of all children were court dependents, voluntary placements representing only 1 percent in each unit. Eighty-six percent of the children in the experimental unit and 92 percent of the children in the control unit entered care under neglect petitions. Thirteen percent in the former and six percent in the latter entered care under either abuse or combination abuse and neglect petitions. The majority of children in the experimental group were six years old or less (58%) compared to 31% for children in the control units, whereas control cases had a slightly higher percentage of children 7 to 9 years of age (31% compared to 22%).* There were equal percentages of 10 to 12 year olds in both units. More control than experimental children were over 12 years of age (22% compared to 6%). Males and females were almost equally represented across units, as were Caucasian (34% experimental;37% control), Mexican-American (9% and 8%) and Bi-Racial children (9% and 10%). Black children represented a greater percentage of experimental than control cases (48% compared to 37%), while 8% of the control and none of the experimental children were of American-Indian descent. Females headed the majority of families (71% experimental; 74% control). Two-parent families represented 23% of the cases in each unit. Male headed families accounted for only 6% and 4% of the experimental and control cases. The only significant difference between units was in the child's age (X^2= 42.95;5 d of f;p.$\leq$.001).

Reason for placement. For 54 of the 227 experimental unit children (24%) and 47 of the 201 children in the control group (23%) the general definition of the petition under which they entered care (e.g. neglected or abused) was the only information available regarding reason for placement. Additional problem information was obtained from case records for the remaining 173 experimental (76%) and 145 control youngsters (77%). Significant differences between units existed in 3 out of 10 problem areas (X^2=30.6 (9 d of f) p.$\leq$.001):parental drug abuse, cited as the reason for placing 53 experimental cases (21%) compared to 20 in control (10%); alleged physical abuse of the child which was reported for 28 children in the experimental unit (11%) and 9 in the control (5%), and being left unattended with a neighbor or relative reported for 56 children in control (29%) compared to 36 in the experimental units (14%). Other problem areas mentioned included parental use of alcohol, parent in prison, in a psychiatric institution or said to be mentally ill but not hospitalized, children "out of parental control, and the condition of the parent's home." There was a miscellaneous category that included small numbers of youngsters whose parents had been hospitalized for physical illness, children whose medical needs were unmet, and children whose parents had marital difficulties.

Framework for Decision Making

Ninety-five percent of natural parents in the experimental units stated that they wished to have their children restored to their care. There was no attempt at this point to judge the sincerity of their verbal statement. Their motivation and capacity to parent was assessed through the efforts they extended in working toward that goal. Counselor-client contracts were drawn up in all cases and the parents encouraged to sign these. Initial contracts "set-the-stage" for gathering needed assessment information, during prearranged parent-child visits, and they specified outcomes in other areas that could be determined at an early point. If additional problems were identified as cases moved toward restoration, new objectives were added. Minimum standards of parenting were our concern; hence, contingencies for restoration focused only on the relationship between parental behavior and a child's well being. Detailed plans for achieving each objective were described in writing and attached to the contract.

An important part of case planning entails deciding when to "alter course" and pursue new options. Contracts facilitated this process, since they included statements describing alternatives for each case, such as referring a case for adoption, that a worker could pursue if clients did not participate in plans, as well as the time limits within which this would occur. Because of the specificity with which they described objectives and documented progress toward

*Further descriptive information is available from the authors upon request.

their attainment, they could facilitate the transfer of a case to a new worker. (5)

RESULTS

When the project ended in April of 1976, decisions had been made for 145 of the 227 children in the experimental units (64%) and for 148 of the 201 children in the control unit (74%). (see Table 1). Premature closings precluded making decisions, or, if they were made, precluded following them through to completion for the remaining 82 experimental and 53 control unit children. Premature closings included cases where the court jurisdiction changed when a parent moved out of the county, cases where children "ran away" from foster homes and whose status under the law changed from that of a neglected child to a child "in danger of becoming a delinquent."

Cases were closed following restoration to natural parents and dismissal of the court dependency or after adoption or guardianship actions were completed for 41% of the experimental unit children compared to 25% of those in the control unit (see Table 1). Cases were to be closed in the near future for 37% of the children in the former units compared to 15% in the latter. These would be closed once dependencies were dismissed for children who were restored, or when cases were completed for children to be restored, adopted or who were to have court appointed guardians. Overall, 114 experimental unit children (79%) compared to 59 in control (40%) were either out or headed out of care when the project ended. Only 31 children from the former unit (21%) compared to 89 from the latter (60%) were designated long term placement. The difference in outcomes between units was significant ($p. = \leq .001$).

Outcome and Predictor Variables

The question addressed here is what variables might be useful to predict differential outcomes for children in care? Correlations for demographic variables such as family composition, child's age, ethnicity, sex, type of placement, reason for placement or petition under which a child was placed, were low, ranging from zero (age) to .38 (ethnicity).* Since age was the only demographic variable for which there was a significant difference between groups this was further analyzed controlling for length in care. If age had predictive utility, one would expect older children, in care for long periods of time, to comprise the majority of long term cases. The results of this analysis yielded a purely random distribution by age and outcome, controlling for time in care. In general, age had no predictive utility.

Children in the experimental units had a significantly greater chance of leaving foster placement than those in the control unit regardless of the length of time they had been in care (less than 3 years; $p. = \leq .001$; three years or more; $p. = \leq .01$). There was a pronounced change, however at the three year point in time. For experimental cases, the percentage restored or to be restored decreased from 82% to 55% and for control from 44% to 26 percent. There were concommitant increases in the percentage of children designated long term. For experimental the increase was from 18 to 45%; for control from 56 to 74 percent.†

Written contracts were employed by experimental unit workers only. Seventy percent of the children whose parents signed a written agreement were restored. Eighty-five percent of those whose parents would not sign a contract were either referred for adoption, court appointment of a guardian or were designated as long term care. The predictability of restoration compared to alternative outcomes given information as to whether a contract was signed was 57 percent.

ONE YEAR FOLLOW UP

As noted in the introduction, one objective of the project was to test the feasibility of joint case management between a project and county worker. Project workers had been hired expressly for the experiment and their employment terminated when the project ended. These workers received training in behavioral methods of intervention and bore the responsibility for providing intensive services to natural parents. A county worker, who was to provide services to the child in the foster home, did not receive special training. In practice, the division of responsibility was not maintained. As cases moved closer to restoration, project staff worked

* Guttman's lambda was the measure of association used throughout unless otherwise noted.
† Complete data tables are available from the authors on request.

with both the natural parent and child. In all likelihood, collaborating on cases resulted in some informal learning for county personnel. However, several of these workers left the department or were transferred out of foster care units during the follow up year. The result of this change in staffing is that many of the cases in the follow up period were not carried by county workers who had any part in initial decision making. Due to these overall changes in staff composition, follow up data is not presented seperately for experimental and control units. Reporting by units would suggest that we were comparing casework methods used. Such a view would be appropriate only if staff composition in the units was the same as in prior years. Since this was no longer the case, it would be misleading to report data in such a manner. Reference is made to the units children had been in only as appropriate.

Three questions are addressed below: (1) Did the children who left care during the project period remain out of placement? (2) Were plans that were in process when the project ended completed? (3) What was the status of children classified as long term placement at the end of the project?

The Sample

At the end of the project, decisions had been made for 145 experimental and 148 control children. Seventy experimental (48%) and 44 control unit children (30%) had moved out of foster care. A total of 179 children remained in placement. (see Table 1). Of these, 44 in the experimental (30%) and 15 in control (10%) were headed out of placement. Thirty-one in the experimental unit (21%) and 89 in the control (60%) were designated long term care. Cases were closed during the follow up year for 7* of these 179 children for miscellaneous reasons, such as change in court jurisdiction, leaving a total of 172 youngsters for whom follow up data is reported.

RESULTS

Two children who had been restored to their natural parents, one each from experimental and control units, reentered care during the follow up year. New decisions had not been reached for these youngsters at the time of follow up. The remaining 172 children fall into two groups based on decisions made during the project. Fifty-nine children (34%) were headed out of placement and 113 were designated long term care (66%). Case movement during the follow up period for the 59 children is shown in Table 2. Decisions were completed in 64% of the cases, changed in 25% and remained unchanged in 10 percent. Cases that had been referred for adoption accounted for the highest percentage of completed decisions (n=19:79%). Thirteen of the 22 youngsters headed for restoration (59%) were restored and guardianship actions were completed for 6 of thirteen children (46%). Initial decisions were changed for 15 children. Five who were headed for adoption were referred for guardianship, and one child who was a guardianship referral was in the adoption unit. The 6 remaining youngsters for whom guardianship was being pursued, plus two who were to have been restored, were classified as long term placements. The one additional child who was headed for restoration was reported as undecided. The difference between completed, unchanged and changed decisions was not significant. (X^2=4.43 (2 d of f).

Case outcomes for the 113 children classified as long term placements are shown in Table 3.+ For 54% of the children, there was no change in decision status. However, changes did occur for 46%. Sixteen percent of the children from this latter group were restored to their natural parents and 28% are now headed out of placement. No new decisions were reached for two youngsters.

DISCUSSION

As noted in the introduction, more than 50% of the children in foster home care in the United States will grow to maturity in out-of-home placement. The results of the Alameda Project suggest that this figure can be substantially reduced. Although the design of the project precludes partialling out the effects of the various case management procedures, the methods employed were effective for attaining project goals. As such, they provide direction for case

---

*Six of these children had been in experimental, one in control. All had been long term care.

+Twenty-five of the 113 children in the long term category were from experimental units, the remaining 88 were in control.

planning, decision making and problem solving that have heretofore been unavailable to child welfare workers. Only one child from the experimental and one from the control unit reentered care in the follow up year. This suggests that decisions to restore children, whether made by experimental or control unit workers were appropriate. However, as the data in the first part of this report shows, decisions that result in providing children with continuity-in-care were made for a significantly greater number of children in the former units than in the latter.

One factor which is probably highly related to this result is the different use of time by project and county workers. The majority of experimental case contacts were with natural parents while the majority of control case contacts were with foster parents. (6) Based on this data we suggested that caseload size, often cited as a barrier to service delivery, may not be an obstacle to providing services. Workers do provide services, exercising judgement with regard to the client group who will receive the "lion's share." It seems reasonable that only if time is devoted to determining whether natural parents can attain the minimal parenting skills required to regain custody of their children, can decisions be made in a timely manner for children in care. Why foster parents rather than natural parents? First, it has been suggested that workers avoid biological parents because of negative attitudes toward this client group resulting from the stigma associated with the labels assigned to clients, such as neglectful or abusive. (7) The possibility that workers lack problem solving skills has also been suggested (8), and is supported by our data which showed that a significantly greater number of natural parent difficulties were resolved by experimental compared to control workers. (9)

Fifty-four percent of the youngsters classified as long term care at the end of the project remained classified in this manner one year later. If long term care is to provide continuity this decision should remain stable over time. Given that decisions changed for almost 50% of these children, it is reasonable to conclude that this alternative is least likely to result in stability for children. The lack of stability in this outcome category relates to several factors. First, unlike adoption or guardianship, there are no legal safeguards for the foster parent-child relationship. Such cases are subject to yearly court review at which time a child may be returned to natural parents. With few exceptions, when foster parents move out of the county of jurisdiction, the child is replaced in a new home. The absence of a shared definition regarding a minimum period ot time a child is expected to remain in care when designated long term is an additional difficulty. The need for guidelines for use of this category is recognized in the Foster Care and Adoptions Reform Act of 1977 (10) which describes criteria for its use. Because of this difficulty, it has been recommended that long term care be dichotomized to reflect short term placements as well as those expected to last an indefinite period of time. (11) Long term decisions may be made for the purpose of "banking" cases. (12) This occurs when workers designate children as long term shortly after they enter care without exploring alternative outcomes. Our data showed that this approach to case management was used by control staff. (13) Other factors which may account for such categorization of cases include lack of a framework for decision making and deficits in problem solving skills. Once classification occurs, expectations may be established which limit consideration of alternatives. The worker responsible for the initial decision may fully intend to reconsider other options, but the chances of this happening are reduced by the high rate of worker turnover. (14) In view of the relationship between length of time a child is in care and case outcome, decision making of this type is quite problematic.

To date, there have been few controlled investigations directed at identifying methods and procedures to correct the problems of children drifting in foster care. The small number of studies employing experimental designs report either minimal or no success. (15) In view of the magnitude of the problem this study addressed, it is imperative that this work be replicated and the components most relevant to outcome be identified.

SUMMARY

The results of a two year experimental project plus a one year follow up have been reported. Data at the end of the study showed that a significantly greater number of experimental than control unit children were moved out of foster placement when systematic case management procedures were used. Only two children, one each from experimental and control units reentered care in the follow up year. This suggests that decisions to move youngsters out of placement, whether made by experimental or control staff, were appropriate. However, such decisions were made for only a small percentage of control cases relative to those in experimental sections. Reference was made to data previously reported by these authors showing that control workers visited with foster parents with approximately the same frequency as experimental staff saw biological parents. In considering why this occurs, we suggested that perjorative attitudes caseworkers have toward natural parents plus deficits in problem solving skills may function as barriers to service delivery and case planning. In the follow up year almost 50% of the long term care decisions made during the project period were changed. We hypothesized that the instability of this outcome category was due to the absence of legal safeguards protecting the foster parent-child relationship as well as the absence of uniform criteria for designating children in this way. In addition, attention was directed to the use of long term care for case management purposes. Because of the overall success of the project, it was recommended that this work be replicated and that those aspects of the case management process having the greatest bearing on outcome be identified.

REFERENCES

1. Emlen, A.C. (1976) Barriers to Planning for Children in Foster Care:A Summary, Regional Research Institute, Portland; P.6. Gruber, A.R. (1978) Children in Foster Care: Destitute, Neglected,.....Betrayed, Human Services Press, New York; P. 176. Maas,H. & Engler,R. (1959) Children in Need of Parents, Columbia Univ. Press, New York; P. 356. Jeter, H.R. (1963) Children, Problems and Services in Child Welfare Programs, Children's Bureau, Washington, D.C.; P.87.
2. Emlen, ibid. Gruber, ibid. Maas and Engler, ibid. Jeter, ibid.
3. D. Fanshel, The Exit of Children from Foster Care:An Interim Research Report, Child Welfare L, 65-81 (1971). Maas and Engler, ibid.
4. data relative to the second and third objectives can be found in; Stein, T.J., Gambrill, E.D. and Wiltse, K.T. (in-press) Children in Foster Homes:Achieving Continuity in Care, Praeger Publ., New York.
5. additional information describing the use of contracts in the Alameda Project can be found in; Stein, Gambrill and Wiltse, ibid.
6. T.J. Stein and E.D. Gambrill, Early Intervention in Foster Care, Public Welfare 34, 38-44 (1976).
7. M.K. Rosenheim, Notes on Helping Juvenile Nuisances, in Rosenheim, M.K. (ed.) (1976) Pursuing Justice for the Child, Univ. of Chicago Press, Illinois; 43-66. Jenkins, S. and Norman, E. (1975) Beyond Placement:Mothers View Foster Care, Columbia Univ. Press, New York; P.140.
8. E.D. Gambrill and K.T. Wiltse, Foster Care:Plans and Actualities, Public Welfare 34, 12-21 (1974). R.H. Mnookin, Child Custody Adjudication:Judicial Function in the Face of Indeterminancy, Law and Contemporary Problems 39, 226-293 (1975).
9. Stein, Gambrill and Wiltse, op cit.
10. U.S. Congress, House of Representatives. Foster Care Adoption and Reform Act of 1977, 95th Congress, 1st session (1977).
11. Pascoe, D.J. (1974) Review, Synthesis and Recommendations of Seven Foster Care Studies in California, The Children's Research Institute of California, Sacramento;P. 6.
12. Pers, J.S. (1976) Government as Parent:Administering Foster Care in California, Institute of Governmental Studies, Berkeley; P. 87.
13. Stein, Gambrill and Wiltse, op cit.
14. Pisani, J.R. (1976) The Children of the State:Barriers to the Freeing of Children for Adoption, New York State Dept. of Social Services, Albany; P.130. Shapiro, D. (1976) Agencies and Foster Children, Columbia Univ. Press, New York; P.18.
15. Sherman, E.A., Neuman,R. and Shyne, A.W. (1974) Children Adrift in Foster Care:A Study of Alternative Approaches, Child Welfare League of America, New York. Jones, M.A., Neuman,R. and Shyne, A.W. (1976) A Second Chance for Families:Evaluation of a Program to Reduce Foster Care, Child Welfare League of America, New York.

TABLE 1 NUMBER AND PERCENTAGE OF CLOSED CASES AND CHILDREN HEADED OUT OF FOSTER CARE COMPARED TO THOSE DESIGNATED LONG TERM PLACEMENT

	Exp.	Cont.	Experimental (n=145)	Control (n=148)
Closed:				
Dependencies dismissed: children restored to natural parents:	45	31		
Completed:				
Adoptions	12	4		
Guardianship	3	2	60 (41%)	37 (25%)
Children headed Out of placement:				
Restored: Dependency not yet dismissed	10	7		
To be restored	15	7		
Adoption to be completed	17	7		
Guardianship to be completed	12	1	54 (37%)	22 (15%)
Sub-Total: Children out or headed out of care:			114 (79%)	59 (40%)
Long-term placement			31 (21%)	89 (60%)
Total			145	148*

*X^2=58.73 (9 d of f)p.=$\leq$.001. Given the small numbers in some of the cells it was necessary to combine the following categories to do a test of significance: all children restored, whether or not dependencies were dismissed, completed adoption and guardianship cases with those to be completed.

TABLE 2 DECISION STATUS OF CHILDREN HEADED OUT OF PLACEMENT ONE YEAR LATER

Decision Status at End of Project	No. of Children	Status One Year Later		
		Completed	Unchanged	Changed
To be restored	22	13 (59%)*	6 (27%)†	3 (14%)
Incomplete adoptions	24	19 (79%)		5 (21%)
Incomplete guardianship	13	6 (46%)		7 (54%)
Total	59	38 (64%)	6 (10%)	15 (25%)

*Percentages are to horizontal totals

†Categories of unchanged and changed were combined for chi-square test because of the empty cells in the unchanged category.

TABLE 3 DECISION STATUS OF CHILDREN CATEGORIZED AS LONG TERM PLACEMENT ONE YEAR LATER

		Long-Term (n=113)
Status Unchanged		61 (54%)
Decisions Changed:		
were restored	18 (16%)*	
to be restored	12 (11%)	
referred for adoption	6 (5%)	
referred for guardianship	14 (12%)	
undecided	2 (2%)	52 (46%)
	Total	113

*Percentages are to the total number of children

Child Abuse and Neglect, Vol. 3, pp. 529 - 534.
Pergamon Press Ltd., 1979. Printed in Great Britain.

PRISE EN CHARGE D'ENFANTS MALTRAITES ET DE LEUR FAMILLE PAR LE PLACEMENT FAMILIAL THERAPEUTIQUE

Docteur Michelle ROUYER Janine LABOREY
Relais Familial Alésia, 20 bis rue d'Alésia, PARIS I4e - FRANCE

INTRODUCTION

Le placement familial thérapeutique est en France un des moyens d'action qui permet de réaliser une prise en charge simultanée d'enfants maltraités et de leur famille.

Ce type de placement spécialisé accueille un petit nombre d'enfants de 30 à 50, et se caractérise par un encadrement pluridisciplinaire important, 8 à I0 techniciens : médecins, travailleurs sociaux, psychologues, psychiatre, travaillant en étroite collaboration avec des familles d'accueil sélectionnées pour leur capacité d'identification à l'enfant et leur possibilité de coopération au travail d'équipe. En général un seul enfant est confié à chaque famille d'accueil.

FONCTIONNEMENT DU PLACEMENT FAMILIAL

Nous rapporterons ici une expérience de prise en charge de parents maltraitants durant le placement de leur enfant. Elle se déroule depuis 5 ans dans un placement familial non exclusivement réservé à ce type de problème. Actuellement, I3 enfants sur 30 ont subi des sévices graves, tous les enfants admis présentent des troubles de la personnalité. Dans tous les cas c'est l'existence d'une situation familiale pathologique et conflictuelle qui a déterminé ce type de placement.

Les enfants sont âgés de 0 à I2 ans à l'admission, la prise en charge peut se poursuivre jusqu'à I8 ans.

L'indication de placement est une mesure thérapeutique proposée aux parents comme mode de traitement de l'enfant et de leur difficulté relationnelle avec lui. Il s'agit d'un placement temporaire de 2 à 4 ans ou plus durant lequel l'enfant est confié à une famille d'accueil et pourra être soigné en fonction de ses difficultés, il bénéficiera le cas échéant de traitement spécifique : rééducations, psychothérapie, hôpital de jour, impossibles à réaliser avec continuité dans le milieu familial.

Notre désir d'intégration de l'enfant à la vie du quartier où réside sa famille d'accueil nous a conduit à utiliser l'équipement de secteur plutôt que de centraliser les traitements au siège même de notre centre ; de plus, la proximité géographique des familles d'accueil permet aux parents de participer réellement à toutes les décisions prises dans l'intérêt de l'enfant en prenant eux-mêmes contact avec les différentes structures qui ont à s'occuper de l'enfant : école, consultation de Protection Maternelle Infantile, établissement spécialisé, dispensaire d'Hygiène Mentale infantile. Ce choix impose à l'équipe permanente un important travail de coordination mais facilite la prise de responsabilité des parents vis-à-vis de leur enfant.

Notre intervention auprès des parents est systématique dans la perspective d'un maintien de liens réguliers avec l'enfant, au rythme variable d'une fois par semaine à une fois par mois, et d'un retour éventuel dans le milieu familial. Dans le cas où la maladie mentale des parents, leur instabilité professionnelle ne leur permettent pas d'offrir à l'enfant la possibilité d'un retour durable auprès d'eux. Certains placements aboutissent parfois avec l'accord des parents à une admission dans un petit internat de semaine. L'évolution positive de l'enfant, l'existence d'une relation plus harmonieuse avec la famille rend alors possible cette nouvelle orientation.

PREPARATION DU PLACEMENT

Les parents font eux-même la demande d'admission, cependant cette demande est rarement spontanée, ils y sont souvent contraints par la pression des services sociaux alertés par la situation de danger et la menace d'un retrait autoritaire de l'enfant.

Leur accord et leur coopération sont indispensables. Ils gardent tout leur droit sur l'enfant et peuvent légitimement le reprendre s'ils le désirent. Pour qu'un travail soit accompli avec eux, il faut qu'ils acceptent la séparation et le placement comme un traitement qui sera long. L'adhésion des parents est toujours ambivalente, elle sera constamment remise en question au cours de la prise en charge.

Aussi quelque soit l'urgence, la préparation du placement est une étape indispensable : lors des entretiens préliminaires, les indications de séparation, la demande des parents, leur possibilité de mobilisation, la qualité des échanges affectifs avec l'enfant sont des éléments qui doivent être analysés en profondeur et toujours dans une perspective à long terme.

Ces entretiens sont déjà une prise en charge et déterminent la qualité du travail futur, quelle que soit la décision qui sera prise en définitive. Notre rôle ne consiste pas seulement à admettre les enfants qui nous sont adressés mais éventuellement à choisir avec les parents une orientation plus adaptée à leur difficulté.

En effet, dans certains cas le désir d'abandon, le rejet de l'enfant est tel que la mise en oeuvre d'une lourde prise en charge ne saurait restaurer des liens pathologiques et destructeurs et faire évoluer une situation où l'enfant est gravement menacé dans son corps et dans son évolution psychique ; il faut alors privilégier la sauvegarde de l'enfant et tenter d'aider les parents à consentir à un placement stable et définitif, voire à l'adoption.

A l'opposé, malgré une situation familiale très tendue qui semble mettre l'enfant en danger, la relation affective entre parents et enfants apparaît chaleureuse et riche, l'enfant est investi positivement, ses identifications au père et à la mère sont bonnes, les troubles du comportement aussi spectaculaires soient-ils semblent réactionnels à des évènements traumatiques tels que : séparation, hospitalisation, modification de la vie familiale. Le placement dans une famille d'accueil risque d'être mal toléré par les parents et l'enfant, il créera une rivalité insoutenable entre les deux familles qui ne permettra pas à l'enfant de s'adapter. D'autres solutions sont alors préférables comme l'intervention à domicile d'un travailleur social, une prise en charge par un centre médico-psychologique ou même l'internat pour l'enfant.

Les échecs que nous avons rencontrés tels que les ruptures prématurées, l'abandon, les retours impossibles, la persistance d'une situation de danger pour l'enfant sont souvent liés à des erreurs d'appréciation qui s'expliquent par la résistance que nous éprouvons à reconnaître les limites de nos possibilités d'intervention, le désir de donner à l'enfant maltraité des parents idéaux meilleurs que les siens en référence aux fantaisies de chacun concernant le roman familial.

Lorsqu'il s'agit d'enfants maltraités aucune prise en charge valable des parents ne peut être entreprise si l'existence des mauvais traitements n'est pas clairement abordée avec eux dès les premiers entretiens ; en général, les parents se justifient en décrivant le comportement intolérable de l'enfant : anorexie, insomnie, énurésie, encoprésie, instabilité, retard des acquisitions, ces symptômes qui témoignent pour nous de l'existence d'une relation perturbée entre parents et enfant ne sont pas compris comme tels par les parents. L'enfant est rendu responsable des sévices qu'il subit sans que les parents remettent en question : leur exigence excessive, leur rigidité éducative, leur rigidité éducative, leur impossibilité à répondre aux besoins de l'enfant. Seul un long travail pas à pas pourra les amener à accepter différemment l'enfant, tout en sachant que la disparition rapide des mauvais traitements dont nous nous réjouissons n'est pas toujours significative d'une modification fondamentale de la relation parents-enfants. L'agressivité peut s'exprimer alors par des comportements éducatifs rigides ou aberrants, un discours sadique tout aussi dévalorisant pour l'enfant.

La nécessité d'une séparation est longuement analysée avec les parents, avant qu'elle ne soit effective, en fonction des difficultés propres à l'enfant et de la situation de danger dans laquelle il se trouve. La séparation, si elle protège l'enfant, protège aussi les parents contre leurs pulsions destructrices.

Malgré cette préparation et la vigilance accrue de l'équipe thérapeutique, le départ de l'enfant modifie l'équilibre familial et crée une situation critique où surviennent fréquemment des décompensations graves, il peut s'agir d'hospitalisations en milieu psychiatrique, d'accidents somatiques graves, d'incarcération pour un tout autre motif que les mauvais traitements, de grossesses adultérines. Le départ de l'enfant inflige aux parents une blessure narcissique, c'est un constat d'échec qui aggrave le sentiment de dévalorisation de soi, la dépression, souvent masqués par l'impulsivité et la violence. Quand l'enfant est éloigné, s'opère un retournement sur soi de l'aggressivité. L'angoisse qui surgit tout à coup permet d'établir une relation plus authentique avec les parents, sans pouvoir éviter dans certains cas qu'un des deux parents s'éloigne définitivement rompant tous contacts, ou bien que le père et la mère séparés ne se disputent chacun de leur côté la garde de l'enfant placé.

Ces réactions permettent de saisir le rôle joué par l'enfant maltraité dans l'équilibre familial, de comprendre les projections dont il est l'objet, de mettre en évidence comment parents et enfants se sont enfermés dans un type de relation rigide et figée où les mauvais traitements sont devenus le seul mode d'expression des tensions et des conflits au point que l'enfant lui-même arrive à provoquer les sévices par un jeu inconscient et subtil de provocations et de manipulations où les parents s'opposent et se réconcilient à ses dépens.

MODE DE PRISE EN CHARGE DES PARENTS

Après l'admission de l'enfant, les parents seront suivis au centre et en visite à domicile à un rythme fixé d'un commun accord et à leur demande chaque fois qu'un problème se pose à eux, qu'il s'agisse de l'enfant, des conflits avec la famille d'accueil ou par la suite de difficultés personnelles.

La prise en charge des parents est assurée le plus souvent par deux membres de l'équipe auxquels s'adjoint éventuellement le travailleur social du secteur qui les a suivis auparavant, principalement lorsque la situation socio-économique nécessite une prise en charge globale psycho-sociale.

Ces interventions à deux ou trois maximum ont l'avantage de faciliter l'analyse des positions contre-transférentielles que suscitent la provocation et l'ambivalence des parents ; par ailleurs, lorsque surviennent des conflits, le clivage qu'opère les parents entre les divers intervenants permet en général à l'un d'entre eux d'être pour un temps l'interlocuteur privilégié avec lequel les parents peuvent maintenir un lien positif et relativiser les éléments du conflit. Le clivage entre bons et mauvais objets, la méfiance, le sentiment de persécution que les parents vivent dans leur relation avec nous ne font que reproduire ce qu'ils ont vécu dans leur enfance, bien qu'ils expriment avec force qu'ils se veulent différents du père et de la mère qui les ont si mal aimés. Le maintien de liens réguliers avec l'enfant permet d'aborder concrètement les difficultés qu'ils rencontrent avec lui, en référence à leur passé où se retrouvent : mauvais traitements, abandons, carence affective ; nous essayons en jouant le rôle de "moi auxilliaire" de les aider à faire échec à la répétitions de leur propre histoire avec leur enfant.

La survenue d'une nouvelle grossesse est toujours un moment fécond où l'on peut intervenir auprès de la mère avant qu'elle ne soit submergée par l'angoisse et l'ambivalence que suscitent en elle la fragilité du bébé. L'impossibilité pour la jeune mère de faire référence à une bonne image maternelle, le souvenir angoissant des précédentes naissances, très souvent la fragilité de son conjoint ne lui permettent pas d'établir une bonne relation avec le bébé si elle ne sent pas auprès d'elle quelqu'un à qui elle peut faire appel à tous moments, quelqu'un qui ne se contente pas de donner des conseils mais peut, bercer, nourrir, changer devant elle cet enfant qu'elle n'ose pas toucher, où qu'elle secoue lorsque ses cris l'effraie. Tout en restant nous-même très attentifs à son angoisse et à sa tolérance, il est parfois nécessaire d'introduire auprès de la mère une aide ménagère ou de la décharger quelques heures par jour de la présence du bébé.Cette intervention précoce permet d'éviter que ne se reproduise comme auparavant les situations de rejet, de mauvais traitements, de négligences graves dont les premiers enfants ont eu à souffrir.

Nos interventions sont souvent directives, nous incarnons pour les parents une autorité parentale sécurisante qui a été défaillante pour eux. A travers une relation très proche et mouvementée qui nécessite une grande disponibilité, les parents nous éprouvent, nous testent par de nombreux passages à l'acte, ils arrivent peu à peu à exprimer verbalement leurs pulsions agressives. leur sentiment d'échec et de dévalorisation ; les entretiens évoluent alors vers une relation plus psychothérapique, qui aboutit à des demandes individuelles de traitement réalisés à l'extérieur du centre, après une phase que l'on peut qualifier de sevrage pendant laquelle les parents commencent à s'autonomiser par rapport à nous.

L'isolement de certains couples ou de parents célibataires, leur désir de contact ou d'échange lorsqu'ils commencent à ne plus se sentir dévalorisés ou exclus nous ont conduit à élargir notre mode de prise en charge en leur offrant des possibilités d'intégration à des activités de groupe : rencontres de parents, expression corporelle, activités de quartier, sorties cinéma.

Nous avons dans ce texte parlé des parents sans dissocier le père et la mère. Pour 13 enfants maltraités actuellement présents dans notre placement, 5 d'entre eux n'ont de contact qu'avec un seul de leur parent, 3 avec la mère, 2 avec le père. Pour les 8 autres, nous nous efforçons de rencontrer régulièrement le couple, les visites à domicile nous en donnent la possibilité, les parents en nous accueillant chez eux n'ont plus recours à des réactions de prestance, ils sont plus détendus plus authentiques. Ils expriment souvent le désir que nous nous rendions auprès d'eux lorsque l'enfant est au foyer comme si la présence d'un tiers leur permettait d'établir un dialogue différent avec l'enfant.

Après cinq ans de travail, il nous semble important d'intensifier nos interventions auprès des familles, de nous orienter vers une forme de psychothérapie familiale incluant parents et enfants.

PRISE EN CHARGE DES ENFANTS

Le placement dans une famille d'accueil doit permettre à l'enfant de connaître une vie familiale différente, chaleureuse et tolérante. Certains enfants ont connu mauvais traitements et séparations multiples, ils n'ont jamais pu nouer de relations objectales stables et valables. Il s'agira d'abord pour la famille d'accueil d'accomplir un véritable maternage renarcissant permettant à l'enfant d'investir une image maternelle en tant que bon objet. Pour d'autres enfants cette nouvelle expérience de vie leur permettra d'assouplir ou de neutraliser des imagos parentales terrifiantes ou destructrices.

Comme nous l'avons mentionné plus haut, les enfants bénéficient de rééducations ou de psychothérapies à l'extérieur du centre, cependant tous ont une relation privilégiée avec le travailleur social qui les suit au domicile des familles d'accueil, celui-ci représente pour eux une instance protectrice et un modèle d'identification secondaire ; il fait aussi le lien avec la famille d'origine et c'est avec lui, plus qu'avec la famille d'accueil que l'enfant peut parler de ses parents. Il est dangereux de vouloir trop idéaliser la famille de l'enfant, cette idéalisation peut se maintenir tant que les échanges avec la famille sont très courts mais elle risque de s'effondrer au retour définitif de l'enfant; l'acceptation des failles et des manques des parents permet davantage à l'enfant de se situer et de prendre le meilleur de ce qui lui est apporté dans sa famille d'origine comme dans sa famille d'accueil ; il peut ainsi constituer des identifications en mosaïques qui empruntent à l'une et l'autre famille et sans doute au travailleur social qui le suit.

Par ailleurs, l'enfant est reçu par le médecin psychiatre, accompagné par ses parents ou par la famille d'accueil ; il s'agit d'entretiens dynamiques où l'enfant parle de sa place vis-à-vis des parents et des nourriciers. Toute une série de dessins nous sont laissés mettant en scène le roman familial : dessins où l'enfant prince est entouré du roi et de la reine, figurant l'image idéale des parents qu'il cherche à préserver.

Le milieu familial d'accueil permet une observation privilégiée des difficultés de l'enfant. L'enfant maltraité quel que soit son âge tend à reproduire dans sa famille d'accueil les mêmes situations de rejet et d'agressivité qu'il connaît dans sa famille d'origine, son comportement induit des réactions en chaîne qui peuvent opposer violemment non seulement la famille d'accueil et les parents mais encore la famille d'accueil et l'équipe ; il peut s'agir de provocations sous la forme d'opposition passive, refus systématique, mutisme, de comportements auto-destructeurs suicidaires plus subtilement de séductions et de manipulations visant à dissocier et opposer le père et la mère de la famille d'accueil.

Il est impossible de faire une description clinique type de l'enfant maltraité car de nombreux facteurs surajoutés interviennent tels que les placements précoces en institution, les hospitalisations répétées, qui aggravent ou provoquent des carences affectives graves avec carence d'apport et de stimulation entravant le développement physique et mental de l'enfant : hypotrophie, nanisme psychogène sont associés à un retard global des acquisitions ; par ailleurs, il existe des situations familiales déviantes : l'homosexualité du père, la prostitution, la drogue, la présence au foyer d'enfants nés de relations incestueuses qui perturbent gravement l'enfant dans son identité et ses identifications.

Il semble que les enfants très jeunes de moins de deux ans jamais séparés du milieu familial présentent fréquemment un hypercontrôle des affects tels que la capacité d'arrêter brutalement : cris, pleurs, rires, gestes devant l'interdiction maternelle avec une tendance très précoce à la somatisation : eczéma, alopécie, douleurs abdominales, nausées. Ces symptômes sont difficilement mobilisables et réapparaissent pendant longtemps lors de situations traumatisantes. Les enfants plus âgés en dépit d'une intelligence normale ont des blocages intellectuels, l'attention est labile, la vie imaginaire est réduite, langage, jeux, dessins sont pauvres et stéréotypés avec une absence totale de symbolisation.

La famille d'accueil a un rôle difficile car si elle doit aider l'enfant au niveau même de ses difficultés elle doit aussi avec l'équipe valoriser pour l'enfant les aspects positifs de la relation avec sa famille d'origine. L'enfant ne peut évoluer que s'il sent qu'il existe un certain accord entre ses deux familles. Les sentiments agressifs qu'éprouve la famille d'accueil à l'égard des parents maltraitants ne peuvent être dépassés que si elle participe réellement au projet thérapeutique établi par l'équipe et peut avec l'aide constante de celle-ci relativiser et distancier les conflits qui l'oppose aux parents. Le travail de groupe entre l'équipe et les familles d'accueil où la technicité des uns est complémentaire de l'intuition et de la spontanéité des autres permet d'effectuer les réajustements indispensables au traitement de l'enfant et des parents.

Il importe par ailleurs de ne pas minimiser les difficultés de l'enfant, il arrive que seule la vigilance et la tolérance de la famille d'accueil maintienne l'illusion d'une évolution positive alors que la personnalité de l'enfant demeure fragile, que les interdits ne sont pas intériorisés par l'enfant, s'il est privé trop tôt de la protection que lui fournit sa famille d'accueil, l'enfant recourre de nouveau au passage à l'acte, à la provocation.

Par contre, l'apparition de symptômes phobiques ou obsessionnels : peur du noir, des voleurs, rites du coucher, cauchemars témoignent d'une évolution positive de l'enfant, d'une restructuration de la personnalité ; une vie fantasmatique plus riche se manifeste significative d'une accession au stade oedipien. Cette névrotisation inquiète les familles d'accueil lorsqu'elles n'y sont pas préparées ; elles y voient un échec de leur savoir faire et tentent de réduire au plus vite ces symptômes.

CONCLUSION

Il ne peut s'agir que de longues prises en charge, le retour de l'enfant qui a pu se structurer et s'épanouir au cours du placement ne peut être envisagé que lorsque la relation avec les parents s'est modifiée dans le sens d'une plus grande souplesse lorsque la circulation des affects devient plus riche et plus nuancée.

Il est souvent souhaitable que le travail auprès des parents et de l'enfant se poursuive après le retour dans la famille.

Seules l'évolution de l'enfant à l'adolescence, la qualité des investissements à l'âge adulte permettront d'affirmer qu'est enfin rompue la pseudo-hérédité qui fait de l'enfant maltraité un parent maltraitant.

BIBLIOGRAPHIE

KREISLER L. - STRAUS P. : Les auteurs de sévices sur les jeunes enfants - A.F.P.

SOULE M. - NOEL J. : Le placement familial - E.S.F.

STRAUS P. : Recherches sur les enfants victimes de mauvais traitements - Rapport d'enquête 72-75

HADJIISKY F. 1971 : Le parent maltraitant - Thèse.

AUBRY J. 1965 : La carence de soins maternels - Nouvelle Bibliothèque universitaire.

Child Abuse and Neglect, Vol. 3, pp. 535 - 538.
Pergamon Press Ltd., 1979. Printed in Great Britain.

ADOPTING OLDER CHILDREN FROM INSTITUTIONS

BARBARA TIZARD.

THOMAS CORAM RESEARCH UNIT,
41, BRUNSWICK SQUARE,
LONDON WC1N 1AZ.

One possibility for children abused within their own family is to place them in another family for adoption. This possibility is rarely considered; instead, considerable resources are put into keeping the natural family together. Even when the child is removed from his parents to be fostered or institutionalised for a while, the aim of social work policy is usually to keep the child in contact with his natural parents, with a view to eventual restoration. This policy is based on certain implicit values - e.g. parents' rights, the sanctity of the natural family. It is also certainly influenced by a widespread belief that adoption is unlikely to succeed after infancy, and that adoption itself is an unnatural and hazardous mode of childrearing.

The motivation of adopters is often considered suspect. Adopted children are thought to frequent child guidance clinics, and to undergo serious identity crises in adolescence. Most of these anxieties probably derive from the fact that those adopted children whom psychiatrists and social workers see are the tiny minority who are referred to clinics. A very different impression is gained from a study of the great majority of adopted children who are not so referred. Large scale studies of the rate of psychiatric disturbance or behaviour disorder in a whole age group of adopted children make it clear that although a higher proportion of adopted than non-adopted children have problems, especially adopted boys. the great majority of adopted children have no more problems than other children. [1,2]. As to the crisis of adolescence, a large scale Swedish study found that fewer adopted children were considered a problem at fifteen than at eleven.

In the studies referred to so far, the vast majority of children had been adopted in the first year of life. What is the outcome of adopting older children, in particular children who have had damaging experiences in their early years? An American author, Kadushin, has followed-up 91 children placed for adoption between the ages of five and twelve. Many of these children had been removed from their natural parents by a court order, and had been placed in one or more foster homes before being adopted. Six years after adoption, three-quarters of the adoptive parents were satisfied with the adoption; the younger the child had been placed. the greater the parents' satisfaction. [3].

No assessment of the children was made in this study, and its importance lies in the demonstration that the adoption of older children who have had an exceptionally disturbed and unhappy early childhood can bring satisfaction to the adoptive parents and provide the children with a stable and permanent home.

My own study was of thirty children adopted from institutions between the ages of two and seven years. [4]. Unlike Kadushin's children, these children did not have a history of unhappy or disturbed family experiences - all had entered an institution before the age of four months. All were illegitimate, and had been placed in an institution either because their mothers wanted to have them adopted, or because at the time of their birth their mothers felt that they couldn't look after them, but hoped to reclaim them later, or simply because the mothers were uncertain whether to keep the child or not. Why were children who had been offered for adoption soon after birth still in institutions at the age of two? In all cases, it was because the authorities had considered them unsuitable for adoption, either because they were the wrong colour, or because they had a family history of something like epilepsy, or because at birth they had some minor physical imperfection, e.g. a hernia. (These children were born in 1966; today they would almost certainly have been adopted in infancy, despite their colour or family history.)

Of greater contemporary significance were the children who had been taken into care with the hope that their mothers would later reclaim them. I think it's fair to say that often there was little realistic prospect that this would happen - either because the child was extra-marital, and the husband refused to accept him, or because the mother was very young, or was a single parent already struggling to bring up several other children. Eventually, some of them released the children for adoption, but this decision took up to seven years to make. I think, then, it's fair to say that all the initial decisions were made in terms, not of the children's needs, but of the needs of various sets of adults - the needs of prospective adopters, who couldn't be given a less that perfect child, or the needs of the natural mothers, who felt that they "couldn't bear to give up their child" but none the less could not look after them.

However, eventually the 30 children were adopted - mostly between the ages of two and a half and four, although six were adopted between the ages of four and a half and seven and a half. What had been the effect of these years of institutional rearing on the children's development? Before answering this question, it's necessary to give a brief description of the institutions. The 30 children came from over 20 different institutions. In many ways these institutions were of very high quality. They were quite small, generally caring for between 15-25 children, and the staffing was generous. The children lived in small groups of six, each with their own separate accomodation, in the charge of two nurses. Toys and books were plentiful, and considerable efforts were made to provide stimulating experiences.

However, two characteristice of the nursery distinguished them from almost any private family. Large numbers of different adults looked after the children, and close personal relationships between adults and children were discouraged. Both of these characteristics were closely tied up with the function of the institutions as training schools for nursery nurses. On an average 24 different nurses had worked with the children for at least a week in their first two years of life; by the time the children were four and a half the figure had increased to 50. Partly in response to this situation, in all of the nurseries close personal relationships were discouraged. It was argued that if a child became closely attached to a nurse he would suffer when she was at college, or off duty or had left the nursery, and that other staff would find it difficult to handle him, Moreover, the policy of treating all the children in a detached way was seen as the best guide against favouritism.

Thus, although the children were rarely treated unkindly, they were certainly deprived of the close affectionate relationship with a small number of adults which home-reared children in our society generally experience. How did this affect their development? We visited all the children when they were still in institutions at the age of two. 5.6. There was no evidence of the gross retardation or disturbance which used to be described in children in old-style institutions. There were, however differences between these children and a contrast group of working-class London home-reared children. We found that the institutional children talked less than the home-reared children, more of them sucked their thumbs, fewer were toilet trained; in addition tended to cry rather more readily and to be more unwilling to share. At 24 months, their average Cattell Mental Age was 22 months.

However, the major difference between the home-reared and nursery children was in their relationship with adults. The nursery children were much more fearful of strangers. On the other hand, they tended to respond affectionately and to cling to larger numbers of different adults whom they were familiar with. It was not therefore the case that institutional rearing had made the children indifferent to adults, but it was rather as though the limited amount of individual attention and affection which they received awoke in them a craving for more.

We visited the children again when they were four and a half. By this age 26 had been adopted. Those children who remained in the institution were now of average I.Q. They had, however, tended to develop characteristics which the nurses regarded as abnormal. Temper tantrums and aggressiveness with their peers were commoner than amongst home-reared children. Some of the children were described by the staff as cold and fickle - they would follow around after any staff on duty, and demand attention, but they didn't seem to mind which nurse was on duty. This behaviour had been found acceptable in the two-year olds but was recognised by the staff as abnormal by the time the children were four. A smaller group of children were said to be uninterested in adults, whilst a few were believed to have formed a genuine attachment to a particular nurse.[7,8]

What happened to the ex-institutional children after adoption? We visited the children at the age of eight, and found most of them living in comfortable middle-class homes.[9] Apart from two children who had been adopted by their nurses, the adoptive parents were relatively old, that is in their thirties or forties. Rather more than a half were childless; the rest already had children of their own, and they wanted both to enlarge their family and at the same time to give a home to an institutional child. Their motivation to adopt was high - many of them had gone from one adoption society to another, and waited for several years for a child.

The children adopted between the ages of two and four had a mean I.Q. at eight years of 115; their educational attainments were also above average for their age. This finding appeared to be related to the social class of the adoptive home - the minority of children adopted into working-class homes had average I.Qs. According to the adoptive parents, in most respects the children presented no more problems than did the children in the contrast group. Eight per cent had been referred to a child guidance clinic. The only problems described more frequently by the adoptive than the contrast parents were "over-friendliness" and "attention-seeking". Most of the children were also described as unusually affectionate to their parents, but they did not bestow affection indiscriminately to allcomers. Twenty-one of the twenty-five adoptive mothers seen when the child was eight believed that the child was closely attached to them. Only three of the 25 mothers seemed to have little positive feeling for the child, and these were the only mothers who expressed dissatisfaction with the outcome of the adoption.

The children's teachers tended to take a less favourable view of them. Between a half and two thirds of the children were described as very restless, quarrelsome, disobedient, and attention-seeking at school. In our study, age at leaving the institution was not a significant variable in affecting outcome - children who left at two were as likely to be described as attention-seeking and difficult at school as those who left after the age of four. Equally, close parent-child attachments seemed to be formed as often with the children who left the institution relatively late as with those who left relatively early.

Age at leaving the institution did appear to affect the children's I.Q. at eight. Of the children tested at two, and later adopted before the age of four, all had increased in I.Q., most very markedly. But of the children adopted after the age of four and a half only one increased in I.Q. However, since the numbers involved were very small, this finding must be considered highly tentative.

It should be noted that there was considerable variability amongst the adopted children by the age of eight. A few children showed markedly abnormal behaviour - e.g. frequent and violent tantrums both at school and at home and were considered by their parents "not to care much about any one"; however only about a half of the children presented problems to their teachers, and only a third were considered over-friendly and attention-seeking by their parents. We were unable to account for these differences, but there was a tendency for the children who presented the most problems at eight to have been already identified by the nurses as difficult whilst still in the institution.

Judged by a number of criteria, then, most of these adoptions much be considered successful. All 30 placements were stable; only three of the 25 couples we visited when the child was eight expressed reservations so serious as to amount to dissatisfaction; only four considered that the child was not attached to them. The only behaviour problem reputed frequently was attention-seeking behaviour, and this was particularly marked at school. In contrast the children who remained in institutions or who had been restored to their natural families had more frequent and more severe problems.

It may, of course, be argued that the children's difficulties will not become apparent until the identity crisis in adolescence. I would like to make two points here. Firstly,

Bohman's longitudinal study of adopted children showed that their problems diminished as they grew up. Secondly, the identity problems of the adopted child are likely to be less than those of the institutional child, or of the child restored to his natural family. We found that in these natural families a total denial of the child's earlier experiences often occurred. Not only was no explanation offered to the child of why he had been placed in, and then taken out of the institution, but any attempt by the child to refer to his earlier experiences was sometimes cut short and prevented. No explanation was offered to the child, either, of the complex family situation in which he often found himself on restoration - e.g. being reared with a step-family or by grandparents.

The striking characteristic of most of the adoptive parents in our study was their strong desire to rear a child, their willingness to devote much time and energy to him, and their tolerance of difficult and immature behaviour. These are the very characteristics which tend to be missing in parents who abuse their children. From the child's point of view, it seems clear that he would often benefit from adoptive placement. The issues are admittedly complex, but it is important to consider the extent to which we as a society are in collusion with the natural parents, to the extent that we expect and accept that natural parents should bring up children whom they do not really want.

REFERENCES

1. J. Seglow, M. Kellmer Pringle and P. Wedge. (1972) Growing up Adopted, National Foundation for Educational Research in England and Wales.

2. M. Bohman. (1970) Adopted Children and their Families. A Follow-up Study of Adopted Children, their Background, Environment and Adjustment. Stockholm: Proprius.

3. A. Kadushin. (1970) Adopting Older Children, Columbria University Press, New York.

4. B. Tizard. (1977) Adoption: A Second Chance. Open Books, London.

5. Jack and Barbara Tizard. (1971) Social Development of Two-Year old Children in Residential Nurseries, H.R. Schaffer (ed.) The Origins of Human Social Relations. Academic Press, London.

6. B. Tizard and Ann Joseph. The Cognitive Development of Young Children in Residential Care, J. Child Psychol. and Psychiat. 11, 177-186 (1970)

7. B. Tizard and J. Rees. The Effect of Early Institutional Rearing on the Behaviour Problems and Affectional Relationships of Four-year-old children. J. of Child Psychol. and Psychiat. 16, 61-73. (1975).

8. B. Tizard and J. Rees. A Comparison of the Effects of Adoption, Restoration to the Natural Mother, and Continued Institutionalization on the Cognitive Development of Four-year old Children. Child Development 45, 92-99. (1974.)

9. B. Tizard and J. Hodges. The Effect of Early Institutional Rearing on the Development of eight year old children. J. of Child Psychol. and Psychiat. 19. 99-119. (1978).

Child Abuse and Neglect, Vol. 3, pp. 539 - 546.
Pergamon Press Ltd., 1979. Printed in Great Britain.

INTERIM NOTES ON A STUDY OF PSYCHOTHERAPY WITH SEVERELY DEPRIVED CHILDREN

Mrs. Mary Boston

Tavistock Clinic, Dept. for Children and Parents, Belsize Lane, London.

INTRODUCTION

A high rate of behaviour difficulties in children in long stay institutional care has been reported by many writers, e.g. Pringle (1). Wolkind and Rutter (2) report a strong association between behavioural disturbance and even a short period in care although they suggest this may be due to the long term family discord rather than the period in care as such. There is also clinical evidence that a considerable proportion of children who are abused or who suffer deprivation of adequate parental care have parents who have themselves experienced abuse or deprivation. Study needs to be directed towards ways of intervening in this vicious cycle of deprivation.

Where the natural family has broken down, alternative placement becomes necessary but not always successful. It is hard to maintain continuity of adequate substitute care. Difficulties may arise for many reasons, including the children's own responses and disturbance. Repeated breakdown of fostering attempts and the problems of managing children in Homes are sad testimony to the truth of John Bowlby's (3) contention that early deprivation of continuity of emotional care may have serious effects on the child's capacity to establish trusting and secure relationships. Although the controversy continues about the reversibility of the effects of early deprivation and about the importance of different variables, and although recent evidence by Tizard (4) suggests that later adoption may be more successful than fostering because of the greater security it engenders, it will hardly be disputed that many children whose own families have been unable to care for them find it hard to accept and utilise the alternative care that is offered. They may grow up to perpetuate the cycle of deprivation.

These are the children who present considerable problems with regard to therapeutic measures and management. A number of special institutions have attempted to provide a therapeutic group environment and sometimes also individual psychotherapy. Dockar-Drysdale (5) considers the provision of 'primary emotional experience', (as described in her book on the Mulberry Bush School), to be essential for some children before interpretative psychotherapy is possible. Individual psychotherapy on an out-patient basis has usually been unavailable to such children for a variety of reasons. Even where it might be practical, the suitability of severely deprived children for what is often a scarce resource has frequently been questioned. Will such a child be able to make a sustained relationship with the therapist or is the impairment already too great? Or can the necessary support for therapy be provided for children living in Homes or foster care?

THE TAVISTOCK WORKSHOP

Attempts at long term individual psychotherapy with severely deprived children have been reported by Boston (6) and Henry (7). A number of children have been offered intensive psychoanalytic psychotherapy in the Department while living in Children's Homes or in Foster Care and a workshop has been set up to study and co-ordinate the experience gained.

Some features of the psychotherapy of eight boys and seven girls have been discussed so far.

This sample included one family of two girls and a boy, seen together. The rest were seen individually. The age range when starting therapy was $5\frac{3}{4}$ - 14 years. This study is still in its preliminary stages and tentative observations only can be presented.

A major focus has been on the child's own experience of his deprivation; his ways of communicating his thoughts, feelings and phantasies about his situation. An attempt has been made to assess the use the different children make of the relationship with the therapist and their capacity to work usefully. An issue in mind has been whether it is possible to assess which children can make the best use of psychotherapy and if in any cases it may be contraindicated.

A further area of study has been the network of agencies whose active support is necessary if therapy is to take place at all.

In view of the fact that there are so many children in Care (100100 in 1976 in England and Wales) and such a minute proportion of these are likely to receive psychotherapy, consideration has also been given to whether the experience of the psychotherapists can be in any way helpful to the non-therapist helpers in close contact with the children.

THE SUPPORTING NETWORK

Most of the children studied (14 out of 15) have been living in Children's Homes (usually fairly small 'family' groups) while attending for psychotherapy. One was in foster care and one of the 14 went to live with her grandmother during therapy. This inevitably means that many more people are involved in supporting the child in therapy than is the case with the patient from an ordinary family. A minimum number includes the child's social worker and several members of the residential staff. If these change frequently or if Care Practice Officers, Senior Social Workers, escorts and others are involved, the number of different people to whom the child has to relate can be bewilderingly great. The child's own family in some cases may also need to be negotiated with. All this makes the therapist's task in establishing contact with those who care for the child correspondingly difficult and bewildering. A complex tangle of intergroup relations is often encountered and needs to be allowed for.

Experience of this series of cases indicates that unless some attempt is made to establish a good working relationship between clinic staff and residential care staff, regular attendance for therapy may be jeopardised. At review meetings when the child is discussed, plans affecting the continuation of therapy may be made and the therapist or her representative may need to be present. Changes in social workers or residential staff may mean that issues previously discussed and settled may be reversed and negotiations have to start from scratch again.

Some discussion in the workshop has centred on how much contact the therapists themselves need to have with the Homes. The help of a colleague who can consult to the Home, as described by Hutten (8) and Britton (9), offering support to the staff and liason between the Home and Clinic appears in the cases studied to have been a crucial factor in maintaining the children in therapy.

ASSESSMENT FOR PSYCHOTHERAPY

One consideration of the workshop has been the principles on which suitability for psychotherapy can be assessed.

Psychological assessment of such children in general indicates that many of them are intellectually underfunctioning; they appear to be verbally deprived and many of the boys, but few of the girls, have reading difficulties. In school they are very attention-seeking and have difficulties in working on their own; as they get older their behaviour sometimes becomes very aggressive so that transfer to a school for maladjusted children is necessary.

Projective tests indicate a preoccupation with food and with primitive violent feelings in a dangerous world, without any concept of genuine protection. Whether this kind of assessment can contribute to predictions about the use a child would make of psychotherapy is not yet clear and would require further study. Unfortunately not all the children in this sample have been tested.

Historical factors have often been thought to be relevant in predicting response to therapy, a history of severe deprivation being considered to be a contraindication. No detailed conclusions about this can be drawn from this Tavistock sample because the information about the early histories of the children is very sketchy. Possibly this is characteristic of children in Care. Certainly most of the children studied had experienced breakdown of their natural families at an early age and had had at least two or three different placements. In spite of these histories, in all cases except one, psychotherapy was established and attendance maintained over a considerable period of time. A detailed relationship between the severity of deprivation and the use made of the psychotherapy is much more difficult to explore and the data inadequate, though there are some suggestive trends. The quality of the material of those four children who had experienced continuity of care in their early years seems very different from that of the rest of the children who had suffered early deprivation. All the deprived children in this sample have, however, experienced a period of stable care at some time after infancy, either in foster care or with one housemother. It could be speculated that this might be a factor in their responsiveness to therapy. This would be in line with Pringle's (1) finding that a lasting relationship with an adult makes a significant difference to the adjustment of children in long-term institutional care.

More important considerations seem to be the individual ways in which each child has reacted to the deprivation he has experienced and the particular constellation of defences he has built up to protect himself from emotional hurt. It could be that the point at which premature interruption of the separating out process between mother and infant has occurred (Dockar-Drysdale 5), or the kind of parenting experienced in the first six months, might be very relevant, but these facts are seldom known and can only be deduced from the nature of the infantile transference during the course of psychotherapy itself. Britton (10) points out that "the history taken however carefully may not do sufficient justice to some of the details of early infantile care". In the case of one girl where we have early data (a twin born prematurely, kept in an incubator and in hospital in the early months), there does seem to be a link between lack of adequate 'holding' in infancy and the type of personality developed. The only other case known to have had a deprived infancy from birth, a boy who spent his first sixteen months in a residential nursery, was one of those about whose prognosis the workshop felt most concern.

It might be speculated that children whose difficulties stem from environmental deprivation might be expected to make a better response to therapy than those who are disturbed despite ordinary good care. Far more data than we have at present would be required to throw light on this question.

As previously mentioned, the age range of this sample was $5\frac{3}{4}$ - 14 years on starting psychotherapy. A possible trend for the younger children to show a less rigid constellation of defences might be worth exploring further, though this trend is not clear-cut. This would be in accordance with the expectation that younger children would benefit more from psychotherapy. It is noticeable that few really young children have as yet been referred, even though attention was drawn in the workshop to the need for psychotherapeutic assessment at a much earlier stage, before repeated breakdown of fostering has hardened the child's defences (Truckle 11).

The actual reasons why these particular children came into psychotherapy seemed in most cases to be to do with the pain and anxiety invoked in others. They apparently compelled those caring for them to seek help for them, whether it was on account of alarming or appealing behaviour. Very often they were likeable children who were thought to be able to get in touch with their feelings, though this expectation was not necessarily borne out by the course of the therapy (e.g. the one failed case). Seven were referred for being unbearable, or for aggressive behaviour; three at a point of crisis in placement because of breakdown in fostering; four, including one family of three, because of traumatic events.

THE PSYCHOTHERAPY

Few generalisations on such a small sample in a study which has only just commenced can be made. All the patients were different, yet there are a number of common features. Some of the more striking of these will be mentioned.

Attendance

As previously indicated, 14 of the 15 children discussed were established in psychotherapy and were able to make steady progress over the course of time, even though the work in many cases caused considerable difficulties for the therapists concerned. Attendance was maintained over lengthy periods of time. Twelve are still in treatment, having attended for periods varying from eight months to four years. The two who have completed treatment attended for four years and four and a half years respectively. One case was seen five times weekly, one four times weekly, two were seen three times weekly, one twice weekly and the rest were seen once weekly (two increasing to a second session).

Naturally this is a selected sample of children who were presented because psychotherapy was established (apart from the one failed case). Information is available on eleven other cases referred for psychotherapy. Of these eight were successfully established in therapy and three were not.

This material does not confirm the view that severely deprived children are necessarily inaccessible to psychotherapy. Allowance, however, must be made for the fact that there may have been something hopeful about these particular children which led to their being offered this specialised help in the first place.

Improvement outside therapy

In every case where therapy was established an improvement in the child's general behaviour outside the treatment was reported. (This is in contrast to the findings of Brill and Thomas 13). In no case was a deterioration complained of, although reluctance to come to treatment in some cases presented a problem to the staff concerned and sometimes a threat to the continuation of the treatment. In one case a phase of "sexy" behaviour by a hitherto well behaved little girl was attributed in the Home to the therapy. Residential staff, however, more often compared the behaviour of the child in therapy favourably with that of other children not receiving help.

Establishing contact with the patient

An illuminating aspect of this preliminary study has been the nature of the contact made between patients and therapists and the very strong feelings, particularly painful ones, evoked in the therapists.

Naturally, children who have in the past been let down frequently have more difficulty than most patients in establishing a trusting relationship with the therapist. Initial contact has been a problem in most cases, some showing extreme suspiciousness, hostility, withdrawal, or impenetrability. Others make a superficial contact in a conforming way, but there is a feeling of flatness. The therapist may be treated as just another person in a bewildering chain of adults who impinge peripherally on their lives. Many seem to have an intermittent contact, with communication alternating with defensive 'shutting out' behaviour.

In most cases the wish for a continued contact is there, but at the same time the defensive manoeuvres against the emotional pain of a further betrayal of trust are blatantly obvious, and can present considerable technical problems for the maintenance of treatment. The pathetic lack of any expectation of continuity is often shown by remarks such as "Will I be seeing you till the next lady comes?" or "Will I be passed on to someone else?" Whether the defence is to obliterate all notice of differences between people, so that change does not impinge, or to project the anticipated abandonment onto the therapist, problems of frequency and regularity of attendance are highlighted.

Do some children whose early experience has been so depriving need intensive experience of frequent sessions (four or five times a week) in order to feel sufficiently contained and secure to work through some of these conflicting feelings as Boston (6) suggests? Would more frequent sessions from the outset have prevented the breakdown of the case which failed to establish? At present this can only be a matter for speculation. In fact, most of these cases managed with less than three times a week or only once weekly.

Projection of feelings

The most outstanding feature of this study so far has been the extraordinarily painful nature of the therapists' experience, shared by members of the workshop. All the children have managed to convey to their therapists the intensely painful emotional experiences they have suffered, in spite of their individually different ways of communicating.

Many sessions can be described as endless evacuation into the therapists of chaotic, confused and unwanted feelings. This process may be expressed by a stream of talk or abuse or by actually throwing things and attacking the therapist. Silence, too, can be experienced as a 'perpetual silent scream', in the words of one therapist. As one patient described it, 'The session is never ending poo'. These children, as the residential staff well know, take a lot of putting up with. Nevertheless, the ability to search for, and to use, when given the opportunity, an object who can receive these projections may well be a good prognostic sign for these patients. Despair, both for the patient and the therapist, seems to be related to a feeling of there being 'no one and no way for experiences to be caught and held' (another therapist). Many of the children express this feeling in their play by making things fall. An important function of the therapist seems to have been to experience and to bear, and gradually to reflect on, these painful feelings on behalf of the patients. It is only after a considerable period of time that the patients are able, to some extent, to take back some of these feelings and to begin to come to terms with them.

The anxiety about not having enough time comes up frequently in such remarks as 'How long have I got?' and references to thousands of years. This is one of the sources of pain for the therapists. How can a limited amount of therapy ever be enough for children who have been deprived of permanent parents?

Such a deprivation and particularly the awareness of what they have missed is felt by many of the children to be a cruel and torturing experience, which they may enact in reverse in the therapy, inflicting the pain on the therapist. As Bion (13) suggests, the poignancy of the deprivation is rendered more acute when the patient is allowed an opportunity of which he has hitherto been cheated. The feeling of being rejected, of being got rid of as rubbish, may be expressed by behaviour such as soiling or looking uncared for, a reproach to all concerned.

A great sense of grievance that other children are luckier is shown by many of these patients. The loved, privileged babies are attacked in phantasy during sessions, with consequent fears of retaliatory attacks. When infantile parts of the self are confused with these envied babies, self destructuve behaviour may occur. The therapy may be attacked by missing sessions or the therapist abused. Nevertheless, Boston's (6) suggestion that containing physical violence might generally be a problem in the treatment of emotionally deprived children has not so far been entirely borne out by this study. The therapist has only been personally attacked in two cases (both boys) though there has been the menace of violence in some others (also boys). Quite a few, however, including some girls, have shown aggressive and destructive behaviour and there is no doubt that the treatment of these children is an arduous task.

The father figure

The absence of much concept of a firm protective father who can support the mother figure in her containment of all this mess and destruction is striking in many of the patients. This is hardly surprising in view of the fact that only five children (all in one family) in the sample are in current contact with their father. More than half were illegitimate, with unknown fathers. The unknown father tends in phantasy to be a destructive figure with whom the boys are often unconsciously identified. In at least two cases there was the conviction of growing up to become a criminal. Much of the aggressive behaviour seen in therapy can be understood as taking place under the domination of phantasies of being in the shoes of very bad or cruel figures, e.g. a mother who abandons or a sadistic father.

Idealisation

The other side of this picture may be a marked idealisation of parental figures. One girl said angrily, 'Don't call my mother bad or mad'. Many deprived children show terrific family loyalty and touchiness on the subject. Such idealisation may remain very cut off from the child's actual experiences and constitute a very defended area kept apart from the therapist. This idealisation of course matches in intensity the extremely bad parental images inevitably there. The pain of bringing these two aspects of experience together into a more realistic conception of the parents is intense. Sometimes the bad parental image is projected on to the therapist with a consequent threat to the continuation of the therapy. When such a splitting process goes on in the residential setting, it can make the children very hard to manage. It is also hard for foster parents who are attempting to substitute for such idealised parents. A vivid example of a foster child's extreme idealisation of his own mother was given in the workshop. He repeatedly asked, after years, 'Why can't I live with my own Mummy?' Rapid swings from an idealised contact to disillusionment and hostility were noted in some patients.

DISCUSSION

We need to consider what it is that psychotherapists can offer these patients and how it is different from what is offered by other helping people in their lives. Above all these children are deprived of continuity of concerned and caring attention to their emotional needs and no amount of substitute material care can make up for this deprivation. Where there have been frequent changes of substitute parental figures, there may be no-one who knows the child intimately or who remembers events in his life as ordinary parents do. As one of the therapists describes it, care by a succession of different people must be like a series of different mothers who have forgotten. Such fragmenting of relationships and experience in the early months and years makes it difficult for the child to identify with a caring, concerned figure who can help to modify his chaotic and confused feelings - to take inside himself the function of the "ordinary devoted mother " (Winnicott 14), or the mother who can contain and modify the infant's feelings, (Bion 15). In Dockar-Drysdale's words, the baby needs to have enough experience of containment to become himself a container, (5).

It begins to look from the very early stages of this study that children may have many different ways of coping with this early fragmenting of emotional experience. The data is insufficient to sort out which kind of factors, within the child himself or in the events of his life, are likely to lead to particular constellations of defences or personality organisation. Among these 15 children three types of personality appear to be emerging.

There are those children who seem unintegrated, to lack any kind of boundary or containing function, who are experienced by themselves and others as a sort of net, a container full of holes, like the child described by one of the therapists in this study. This leads to an impoverished, two-dimensional type of personality, characterised by an impairment of abstract thinking, a tendency to think, if it can be called thinking, very concretely. Dockar-Drysdale has also pointed out an inability to symbolise shown by some 'unintegrated' children (5). In the Tavistock sample, the children of this type were all girls. If it were true that girls were more likely to react to deprivation in this manner, it might explain Wolkind and Rutter's finding that girls who have been in Care show fewer behaviour disorders than boys (2). Such children may 'get by' unnoticed in a superficially conforming way or even cling to others in a pathetic appealing way. They may elicit more attempts at help and caring from the environment, but their unrewardingness, shown by their inability to hold on to and to develop what they receive, may in the end lead to rejection. It is a matter for speculation whether they will become mothers who in turn will let their babies slip through the net into 'Care'. Some evidence that such girls may well be at risk in later life is given by Wolkind (16).

A second type of child, exemplified by boys in this study, are those who have developed a hard defensive emotional 'armour' to protect themselves against a very vulnerable raw "skin", as it were, underneath. These are the ones who are difficult to reach and tend to be violent and hostile if touched; - the "brick wall" type (Henry 7). It might be speculated that some of these children have kept alive somewhere within, if it can be reached, more capacity to feel than the flat two-dimensional type. They tend to exhibit antisocial behaviour, but Winnicott considers this may in the first place be a manifestation of hope and a plea for help (17). Nevertheless they tend to elicit further environmental rejection by their defensive, hostile behaviour and thus inflict on themselves a "double deprivation" as described by Henry (7). It then becomes progressively more difficult to help them and their defences become hardened. Britton (10) considers the prognosis for deprived children to be better when a strong sense of injustice is retained, rather than a pseudo-compliance and cynical disbelief in any real goodness.

Most of the other children studies so far fall into a more mixed group, where hard, touchy, defensive and sometimes hostile behaviour can alternate with some more hopeful attempts to communicate and understand. It is too early yet to say whether this lack of crystallisation into a more permanent mode of relating is a more prognostically hopeful sign and whether it is related to periods of greater continuity and stability of caring relationships in earlier life.

The sad fact is that the defensive measures which these children have of necessity employed to protect themselves against more than ordinary emotional pain are the very measures which tend to lead to breakdown of foster care or attempts to help them. The role of the child psychotherapist would seem to be the provision of a consistent, reliable framework of concerned attention - a 'space in the therapists' mind', as Hoxter describes (18), for a predictable time in which the child can have a second chance, as it were, for unassimilated infantile feelings and experiences to be understood and integrated within the personality. A space where hostile and negative feelings in particular can be contained and understood should help the child to respond more positively outside the therapy to those who are trying to offer him substitute care and parenting. The child psychotherapist's task is not to attempt to give such parenting nor to attempt to right wrongs of the past, but to help the child to be able to respond to the help of all those other important people who care for him.

The ethical problems involved in the exposure of such hurt children to more pain, by attempting to modify their defences, inevitably touching raw spots, has been a matter for concern in the workshop. The sequestering and limiting of this painful process as far as possible to the consulting room, apart from the child's ordinary life, is probably necessary both for the child and for the residential staff.

Nevertheless all those who care for the child are inevitably recipients of the pain and anxiety projected and need support in being able to recognise and understand such projections. An aspect of the child psychotherapist's function which might be useful for other staff and for children who are unable to have psychotherapy is the concerned attention - the 'space in the mind' which is so difficult to give to the individual child in group care. Winnicott (19) suggests that in providing for children in our care we should "organise ourselves so that in every case there is someone who has time and inclination to know what the child needs".

The idea of a "special time" for each child, where the exclusive attention of a staff member can be given has been suggested. An illustration of such a receptive contact with a child by a field social worker was given in the workshop (Truckle 9). The educational therapy case discussed illustrated a concerned, reliable contact with the educational therapist over a period of time, focussing on shared tasks and play, rather than on interpretative work. This might provide a useful model. It was felt that if such staff members were to be able to be in tune with the painful feelings which might come up they would need the regular support of group discussions with a consultant to the Home. The workshop also considered two small groups of three children (one was a family) where children were seen together over a period of time, after a crisis, and the possibility of this kind of approach being used more widely by staff other than psychotherapists might be well worth considering.

ACKNOWLEDGEMENT

This interim account of psychotherapy with deprived children is based on the work of all who participated at the Tavistock Clinic. I am grateful to the therapists, psychologists and social workers who provided the material, to those who took part in the discussions, to Mrs. E. Holmes for help with the section on testing and to Mr. A. Shuttleworth who, with the help of some others, co-ordinated the recording of the proceedings.

REFERENCES

(1) Pringle, M.K. (1975) The Needs of Children, London Hutchinson.
(2) Wolkind S. and Rutter M., Children who have been "in Care", J. Child Psychol. and Psychiatry 14, 2, 97 (1973).
(3) Bowlby, John, (1951) Maternal Care and Mental Health, World Health Organisation, Geneva.
(4) Tizard, Barbara (1977) Adoption - A Second Chance, Open Books
(5) Dockar-Drysdale, Barbara (1968) Therapy in Child Care, London and Harlow, Longmans.
(6) Boston, M. Psychotherapy with a Boy from a Children's Home, J. of Child Psychotherapy 3,2, 53 (1972).
(7) Henry, Gianna Doubly Deprived, J. of Child Psychotherapy, 3, 4, 15 (1974).

(8) Hutten, Joan (1977) Social Work Consultation to a small Children's Home in Short-term contracts in Social Work, Routledge and Kegan Paul
(9) Britton, R.S. Consultations in Child Care (unpublished).
(10) Britton, R.S. The Deprived Child. To be published in The Practitioner.
(11) Truckle, Brian, First contact with a child in Foster Care: some reflections and their implications for practice, Brit. J. of Social Work, to be published.
(12) Brill K. and Thomas R. (1964) Children in Homes, London, Gollantz.
(13) Bion, W.R. (1959) Attacks on Linking in Second Thoughts, London, Neinemann
(14) Winnicott, D.W. (1965) The Family and Individual Development, London, Tavistock Publications Ltd.
(15) Bion, W.R. (1962) Learning from Experience, London, Heinemann.
(16) Wolkind, S. Women who have been "in care", psychological and social status during pregnancy, J. Child Psychol. and Psychiatry, 18, 2, 179 (1977).
(17) Winnicott, D.W. (1966) Becoming Deprived as a Fact - A Psychotherapeutic Consultation, J. of Child Psychotherapy, 1, 4, 5 (1966).
(18) Hoxter, Shirley (1977) Play and Communication in The Child Psychotherapist and Problems of Young People, ed. by Boston and Daws, London - Wildwood Press.
(19) Winnicott, D.W. (1962) Providing for the Child in Health Crises in The Maturational Processes and the Facilitating Environment (1965) Hogarth, London.

Child Abuse and Neglect, Vol. 3, pp. 547 - 553.

0145-2134/79/0601-0547 $02.00/0.

RISK FACTORS ASSOCIATED WITH CHILD ABUSE

R.K. Oates, A.A. Davis, M.G. Ryan and L.F. Stewart

Community Paediatric Unit, Royal Alexandra Hospital for Children, Camperdown, N.S.W., Australia.

A great deal is now known about the recognition, management and prevention of child abuse (1, 2) and a large literature has accumulated on this subject (3). In recent years there has been a welcome recognition of the developmental and emotional problems of the abused child (4).

One of the difficulties in assessing parents where there is the question of child abuse is that many of the factors found in abusing families can be found in families where a child has not been abused or neglected. It is important to decide in what areas abusing and non-abusing families differ. The aim of this study was to try to clarify some aspects of this question by comparing a group of 56 abused and neglected children and their families with a matched group where child abuse and neglect had not been noticed.

METHOD

Fifty-six children and their families admitted to the Royal Alexandra Hospital for Children over a 3 year period for management of child abuse and neglect (CAN) were traced and reviewed one to three years after the initial presentation.

At review each mother participated in a structured interview which examined her obstetric history, her experiences with the child during the perinatal period, her child-rearing practises and her expectations for the child. The problems of health, housing, finance, domestic friction and social isolation of these families were also explored. The Denver Developmental Screening Test was used to estimate each child's developmental level.

To interpret these results, each family was compared with a control family which was matched for marital status, nationality, education, employment status and socio-economic status of the parents and for age, sex and health of the child. Each control family was selected from the register of the Baby Health Clinic in the same suburb as the family being studied. No regard was paid to regularity of attendance at the Baby Health Clinic when controls were chosen. It was felt that this was a valid selection as each family in the study group was also on the Baby Health Clinic register. The control parents participated in the same structured interview as the study group and their children received the same developmental assessment.

The results were coded and subjected to computer analysis*. The Chi-squared test of significant differences was used to compare the two groups.

---

*Vogelback Computing Center, Northwestern University Version 7.0 June 27, 1977.

RESULTS

Marked differences were found between the two groups in the following areas:

1. General:

The mothers in the two groups perceived their own childhood quite differently. Seventy-nine percent of mothers in the CAN group described their own mothering experiences as lacking in affection compared with two percent of controls ($P < .0001$). Thirty-seven percent of the CAN mothers describe their own mothers' attitude as being one of rejection compared with two percent of controls ($P < .0001$). There was no significant difference between the ages of the mothers in the two groups when the index child was born but the fathers from the CAN group were younger than the control fathers. Twenty-five percent of fathers from the CAN group were between 16 and 21 years of age when the child was born compared with 4% of fathers in the control group ($P = .014$).

The CAN families were larger than the control families. Twenty-nine percent of CAN families had four or more children compared with 14% of controls ($P = .027$).

There were no differences in the nominated religious affiliation of the two groups but those in the control group attended church more frequently. Seventy-five percent of CAN mothers never attended church compared with 38% of controls while 41% of controls attended church at least monthly compared with 20% of CAN mothers ($P = .008$).

2. Pregnancy and Neonatal Period:

The pregnancies in the control group were more likely to have been planned (52% compared with 27%, $P = .0001$). The fathers' reaction to the news of the pregnancy, as described by the mother, was more likely to be unfavourable in the CAN group (See Table 1). Thirty-six percent of these fathers were displeased about the pregnancy compared with the 12% of control fathers.

TABLE 1 Fathers' Reaction to Pregnancy

REACTION TO PREGNANCY	CAN N=56	CONTROL N=56
Delighted	19%	63%
Generally Pleased	43%	25%
Generally Displeased	36%	12%
Father not aware of Pregnancy	2%	0

$x^2 = 22.413$ $P = .0001$

The mothers in the CAN group were less likely to have made preparations, such as purchase of nappies and clothing, for the baby's arrival ($P = .0014$). They were more likely to have chosen a name for only one sex. This is shown in Table 2.

TABLE 2 Name Considered for Baby Before Birth

NAME CHOSEN	CAN N=56	CONTROL N=56
Only male names chosen	43%	27%
Only female names chosen	23%	16%
Name for either sex chosen	34%	57%

$x^2 = 6.118$ $P = .05$

The birth of the baby in the CAN group was often complicated. Fifty-five percent of these births were complicated by prolonged labour, forceps delivery, unusual presentations, caesarian section or a combination of these factors compared with 37% in the control group (P = .0002). The birth was described as a difficult or bad experience by 64% of the CAN mothers compared with 27% of controls ($P < .0001$).

Prematurity or post-maturity occurred more often in the babies from the CAN group (54% compared with 13%, $P < .0001$). Medical problems in the first week of life occurred far more frequently in the CAN group. Fifty-two per-cent of these babies had problems ranging from respiratory distress syndrome, apnoea and infection through to mild jaundice and feeding problems. Medical problems occurred in 9% of controls ($P < .0001$). These factors may have contributed to the lower incidence of attempted breast feeding in the CAN group (20% compared with 66% of controls, $P < .0001$).

3. Mother's Perception of the Child and Child Rearing Methods:
The mothers were asked to describe their babies on a scale from ideal to very poor. The results are shown in Table 3. Mothers from the CAN group were more likely to see their babies as being lower on this scale than mothers from the control group.

TABLE 3 Mothers Perception of Child as a Baby

DESCRIPTION OF BABY	CAN N=56	CONTROL N=56
Ideal	18%	25%
Good/Above Average	25%	45%
Reasonable	12%	27%
Poor/Below Average	25%	3%
Very Poor	20%	0

$x^2 = 7.11$ P = .008

Thirty-four percent of mothers from the CAN group said that they did not enjoy caring for the child. This response was not made by any of the mothers from the control group.

Toilet training was started earlier in the CAN group and punishment was used more often. This is shown in Tables 4 and 5.

TABLE 4 Age Toilet Training Was Started

AGE WHEN TOILET TRAINING STARTED	CAN N=56	CONTROL N=56
Under 6 months	25%	0
6 to 11 months	23%	5%
12 to 17 months	20%	20%
18 to 23 months	11%	46%
24 months and over	21%	29%

$x^2 = 33.32$ $P < .0001$

Physical punishment as a form of discipline was favoured in the CAN group where 54% of mothers used physical punishment frequently compared with 11% of mothers from the control group($P < .0001$). In addition to physical punishment, the children from the CAN group were often told that they were bad or not loved (41%) for misbehaviour compared with 2% of controls ($P < .0001$). Control mothers were more likely to deal with temper tantrums by leaving the child (55% compared with 29%) whereas the CAN mothers were more likely to react to temper tantrums by screaming back at the child or hitting him (55% compared with 12%, $P < .0001$).

TABLE 5 Strictness of Toilet Training

METHOD OF TOILET TRAINING	CAN N=56	CONTROL N=56
Left on pot for long periods, accidents punished	30%	0
Put on pot regularly, moderate disapproval for accidents	50%	50%
Trained when child seems ready, no scolding	20%	50%

$x^2 = 24.41$ $P < .0001$

Mothers from the CAN group were much stricter than the control mothers when the child directed his aggression towards the parents. This is shown in Table 6.

TABLE 6 Punishment for Aggression to Parent

REACTION TO CHILD HITTING PARENT	CAN N=56	CONTROL N=56
Severe Punishment	39%	0
Moderate Punishment	41%	41%
No Punishment	20%	59%

$x^2 = 33$ $P < .0001$

The children from the control group were often given verbal encouragement for good behaviour. This was less common in the abused group as shown in Table 7.

TABLE 7 Verbal Encouragement for Good Behaviour

VERBAL ENCOURAGEMENT	CAN N=56	CONTROL N=56
Rarely	45%	0
Sometimes	37%	27%
Readily	18%	73%

$x^2 = 44.84$ $P < .0001$

Although the parents of the CAN group were more restrictive as regards preventing their children jumping on furniture and making a mess (86% compared with 68%) they were less likely to know what their children were doing at a particular moment and checked on their whereabouts and activities less frequently than the control mothers. This is shown in Table 8.

TABLE 8 Level of Supervision

SUPERVISION	CAN N=56	CONTROL N=56
Checks frequently	21%	62%
Checks fairly often	38%	36%
Practically never checks	41%	2%

x^2 = 31.44 P < .0001

4. Family Relationships:

The mothers in the CAN group thought highly of their partner in only 7% of cases compared with 43% of controls while 54% of the CAN mothers and 11% of the controls held their partner in poor regard (P < .0001).

Important decisions in the CAN families were shared between the partners in 27% of cases compared with 54% of control parents sharing important decisions (P = .015). Frequent disagreement between the CAN partners about child rearing methods occurred in 30% of cases. Forty-six percent of CAN parents did not discuss child rearing practises together at all. This compares with 2% disagreement in the controls and non-participation in 36% (P < .0001). The differences in the mother's perception of how the child's father related to the child are shown in Table 9.

TABLE 9 Father's Relationship with Child

FATHERS RELATIONSHIP WITH CHILD	CAN N=56	CONTROL N=56
Very fond of child	14%	69%
Quite fond of child, interested	38%	20%
Rejects child or not interested	48%	11%

x^2 = 37.07 P < .0001

5. Supports Outside the Family:

The mothers from the CAN group had contact with people less frequently than the mothers from the control group. This is shown in Table 10.

TABLE 10 Degree of Isolation

CONTACT WITH OTHER PEOPLE	CAN N=56	CONTROL N=56
Almost daily	34%	59%
Approximately weekly	16%	32%
Infrequently	29%	7%
Very Rarely	21%	2%

x^2 = 22.73 P < .0001

CAN parents were also less involved in regular social activities (CAN 27%, controls 79%, P < .0001). Opportunities for breaks from the child were less common in the CAN group. Only 48% used baby-sitters compared with 86% of controls (P = .0001).

6. Other Stresses:

The parents in the CAN group also had more problems than the controls in the areas of finance, housing, domestic friction, their own health and the health of other family members. This is shown in Table 11.

TABLE 11 Problem Areas

PROBLEM:	FINANCE	HOUSING	DOMESTIC FRICTION	OWN HEALTH	HEALTH OF FAMILY
CAN	64%	38%	50%	46%	54%
CONTROLS	32%	9%	5%	4%	14%
Significance	$x^2=10.34$ P=.0013	$x^2=11.27$ P=.0008	$x^2=25.69$ $P < .0001$	$x^2=25.19$ $P < .0001$	$x^2=17.56$ $P < .0001$

7. Development of the Child:
The estimate of the child's developmental level with the Denver Developmental Screening Test showed that the children from the CAN group were behind in all areas when compared with the control children. The differences were most marked in language and gross motor skills. Table 12 shows these results.

TABLE 12 Developmental Assessment

	PERCENTAGE FAILING TEST AT CHRONOLOGICAL AGE			
	PERSONAL-SOCIAL	FINE MOTOR-ADAPTIVE	LANGUAGE	GROSS MOTOR
CAN	11%	14%	36%	18%
CONTROLS	5%	2%	8%	2%

DISCUSSION

These two groups of families are superficially similar in terms of marital status, nationality, socio-economic and employment status. However, there are marked differences in the areas of the mother's experiences during the pregnancy and perinatal period, the expectations for the child, child-rearing techniques, family and community support, health of the parents and development of the child. From these results we can make a profile of the family where child abuse is more likely to occur.

The pregnancy is more likely to be unplanned and the father, who may be young, is likely to be unhappy about the pregnancy. The mother, who has often experienced insufficient mothering in her own childhood, may do very little to prepare for the child's arrival and is less likely to have chosen names for a chid of either sex. The birth is often a complicated one and is seen by the mother as being an unpleasant experience. The child is likely to have a medically complicated neonatal period.

As the baby grows into infancy, he is seen by the parent as comparing unfavourably with other children. Child-rearing techniques are likely to be strict with little positive encouragement. This is exemplified by the approach to toilet training, which is commenced early and is likely to be punitive. Decisions about child management are not discussed between the parents and child-rearing responsibilities are often not shared at all. The spouse is likely to be held in low regard by the other partner. Contact with other adults outside the family is infrequent and there are few opportunities to be relieved from the burden of constantly caring for a child who is seen as unrewarding. Domestic friction is common and this is complicated by accommodation difficulties and unsatisfactory budgeting of family finances. Problems of poor health in the parents and other family members are particularly common. The child is likely to be delayed in his developmental milestones, particularly in language development.

The increased risk of child abuse when the pregnancy is complicated by premature delivery and neonatal problems is well recognised (5, 6). This study confirms these findings and also highlights the increased incidence of complicated deliveries, which may have contributed to so many of the mothers in this study describing the birth as a bad experience. Maternal ill-health (7) has only recently been described as contributing to child abuse in families who have other risk factors. This study shows that health problems are much commoner in all family members when compared with controls. This study also points out that CAN mothers are stricter with their children, while at the same time being likely to view the child unfavourably.

It has been shown that families with the potential to abuse their children may be able to be detected in the maternity hospital (8) and in antenatal clinics (9). The factors in this study which distinguish the CAN families from the controls are not difficult to detect and should be looked for in antenatal clinics, maternity hospitals and by nursing and medical staff who come into contact with young children and their families.

As child abuse is known to be likely to occur in successive generations, it seems important that all who deal with parents and children should be aware of the risk factors associated with child abuse, so that appropriate steps can be taken to intervene to break this cycle. Some of the risk factors which are commonly found in CAN families, when compared with controls, have been shown in this study. Factors such as this should be considered when services aimed to reduce the incidence of child abuse and neglect are being planned.

REFERENCES

1.. Kempe C.H. & Helfer, R.E. (1972) Helping the Battered Child and His Family, J.B. Lippincott.

2. Helfer, R.E. & Kempe, CH (1976) Child Abuse & Neglect - The Family & The Community, Ballinger.

3. Jobling, M. (1976) The Abused Child : An Annotated Bibliography, National Children's Bureau, London.

4. Martin, H. (1976) The Abused Child, Ballinger.

5. Klein, M. & Stern, L. Low Birth Weight and the Battered Child Syndrome, Amer. J. Dis. Child. 122, 15 (1971).

6. Baldwin, J.A. & Oliver, J.E. Epidemiology and Family Characteristics of Severely Abused Children, Brit. J. prev. soc. Med. 29, 205 (1975)

7. Lynch, M.A. Ill-Health and Child Abuse. Lancet 2, 317 (1975).

8. Lynch, M.A., Roberts, R. & Gordon, M. Child Abuse : Early Warning in the Maternity Hospital. Develop. Med. Child Neurol. 18, 759 (1976)

9. Gray, J.D., Cutler, C.A., Dean, J.G. & Kempe, C.H. Prediction and Prevention of Child Abuse & Neglect. Child Abuse & Neglect 1, 45 (1977).

Child Abuse and Neglect, Vol. 3, pp. 555 - 563.

0145-2134/79/0601-0555 $02.00/0.

FOLLOW-UP SURVEY OF CASES OF CHILD ABUSE SEEN AT NEWCASTLE GENERAL HOSPITAL 1974-75

A.N.P. Speight, J. M. Bridson and C.E. Cooper

Paediatric Department, Newcastle General Hospital
Newcastle upon Tyne, U.K.

ABSTRACT

Fifty-nine in-patient cases of child abuse were followed up at an interval of 2-4 years. Fifty-six of these were cases of non-accidental injury (NAI), and 3 were of neglect. Of the 59, 41 (69%) had initially been managed under legal sanctions, and 18 (31%) without. Of these 18, 7 (39%) subsequently suffered repeat child abuse. In addition, 3 children suffered repeat NAI while rehabilitation with natural parents was being attempted under legal sanctions. At follow-up there were 44 (75%) children under legal sanctions. Of these, 12 (27%) had been rehabilitated with their natural parents. The remaining 32 (73%) were effectively in long-term care with no active plans for rehabilitation. In the 3-14 year group, NAI was often found to be a marker of severe family pathology; 15 out of the 20 (75%) of these children came into long-term care. There was a marked failure to provide family placements for 32 children in long-term care, only 14 (44%) of them having reached a family placement at the time of follow-up. Reasons for this failure are discussed, as is the probability that neglect/emotional deprivation is being under-diagnosed.

KEYWORDS

Non-accidental injury, child abuse, children in care, fostering, adoption, social work, neglect, deprivation.

INTRODUCTION

Child abuse is a difficult and time-consuming problem for all concerned in its management. Paediatricians can have great influence on both early and late management of cases of child abuse, but may find it difficult to find the time to follow up all their cases. Generalisations from individual cases can be dangerous, and surveys of larger numbers are probably more useful in providing evidence to improve management. This study was undertaken to provide a general picture of the management of all in-patient cases of child abuse seen in one of the two Newcastle teaching hospitals over a two-year period.

METHODS

Cases studied were all the in-patient cases of inflicted injury (non-accidental injury, NAI) and neglect admitted to the Paediatric Department at Newcastle General Hospital over the two calendar years 1974-75. The diagnosis of NAI or neglect had been established at case conference level in each case. In the majority of cases the social work agency involved was a local authority social service department. The details and management of the initial episode were studied by reference to the medical records, together with social reports, case conference minutes and correspondence. An attempt was made to see every child on at least one occasion. However, in 15 cases (25%) this proved impossible because of lack of co-operation by parents, or moves from the area. In all cases, up-to-date reports were obtained from the current social worker. Additional information was sought from health visitors for pre-school children, and from teachers for children of school age. Each child that was seen and assessed clinically with regard to physical health, emotional health and development. In pre-school children a Denver screening test was performed, and in older children reliance was placed on school reports. All this information was used in making the follow-up assessment.

In each case the current social worker was asked for his long-term plan for the child's future. In addition, all the movements of each child were noted during the entire follow-up period, together with episodes of repeat NAI/neglect, changes in legal status and incidents in the natural family. The follow-up period was a minimum of 2 years and a maximum of 4 years, with a deadline for information set at April 1978.

RESULTS

The categories of child abuse are shown in Table I, and the surprisingly small number of neglect cases is dealt with later under 'Discussion'.

TABLE 1 Category of Child Abuse

Non-accidental injury	=	54
Neglect	=	3
Sib. of NAI case	=	2
	TOTAL	59

In addition, there was 1 case in 1975 in which death occured within 24 hours of admission.

Table 2 shows the age incidence at the time of the initial incident.

TABLE 2 Age Incidence

0 - 3 years	39
3 - 6 years	11
6 - 14 years	9

As in most series the younger age group predominates. However, 34% of cases were over 3 years of age at the time of the original diagnosis, and 15% were over 6 years. These figures for the older group are higher than earlier figures from Newcastle (Cooper 1975) perhaps reflecting an increased awareness by professionals of inflicted injury in older children. The fact that there was only one death in this series of 60 cases in 2 years is again vastly different from the earlier study which showed a death rate of 10.4%.

TABEL 3 Legal Action taken at Initial Episode of Abuse

	No legal action	Legal sanctions
0 - 3 years	14	25
3 - 6 years	3	8
6 - 14 years	1	8
	18 (31%)	41 (69%)

This table denotes the legal action taken in relation to the original incident. Legal sanctions consisted of either a Care Order (Children and Young Persons Act, 1969) or a Section 11 resolution (Children's Act, 1948). In the 'No legal action' group, the child was discharged home without sanctions having been taken. In 3 of these cases, Care Proceedings were taken in the Juvenile Court, but Care Orders were not granted.

The families of the 18 children discharged home without legal sanctions were offered various forms of support including social work help, counselling by the health visitor, play group placement, paediatric follow-up and in some cases psychiatric help.

These services were not as well co-ordinated as they might have been, but the most frequent problem was poor parental co-operation, so that in many cases all that remained was a policy of continued surveillance.

Episodes of repeat child abuse

In 39% of the cases sent home without legal sanctions (7 out of 18) a definite repeat episode of child abuse occurred. These episodes consisted of:- 1 subdural haematoma, 2 fractures of long bones, 1 poisoning, and 2 sisters who were initially bruised but subsequently neglected; the final case was a 4 year old girl with psychosocial dwarfism who was sent home for three months where she failed to thrive. (A further account of this case is given under 'Discussion'). Of these 7 cases, 5 became subject to legal sanctions; 1 of these was rehabilitated, the other 4 came into long-term care.

In addition, repeat NAI occurred in 4 cases out of 16 (25%) in which rehabilitation with natural parents was being attempted under legal sanctions. (In one of these cases this episode was in fact the initial episode from the view point of the survey).

In 5 children (from 3 families) the initial episode had been preceded by definite NAI to a sibling (2 of these early episodes having been fatal).

TABLE 4 Management of Children under Legal Sanctions - Status at follow-up

	Rehabilitation	Long Term Care
0 - 3 years	10	16
3 - 6 years	2	8
6 - 14 years	0	8
	12 (27%)	32 (72%)

Table 4 shows the status at follow-up of the 44 children in whom legal sanctions were taken. It will be seen that of the 33 children, 12 (27%) had been rehabilitated with one or both natural parents. The status of these children could be summed up as "reasonably satisfactory". Certainly in none of them did there appear to be a continuing risk of NAI.

The remaining 32 children (72%) were regarded as being in long-term care, because the current social workers had no active plans aimed at rehabilitation with natural parents.

Overall Results

It will be seen that over half the children in this series (32 out of 59, 54%) ended up in long-term care. Nearly three-quarters (32 out of 44, 72%) of the children in whom legal sanctions were taken came into long-term care.

Status of "no legal sanctions" group

As already stated 5 of this group of 18 (28%) subsequently came under legal sanctions. In the remainder, there was a general clinical impression of continuing concern in many of this group, coupled with a lack of co-operation of parents with social workers. The majority could not be seen for the purposes of this survey because of this lack of co-operation. With hindsight there were several cases in which care orders should have been taken at the initial episode with benefit to children and parents alike.

TABLE 5 Placement of Children in Care at Time of follow-up

Age	Fostered	Relative	Institution	TOTAL
0 - 3 years	11	1	* 4	* 16
3 - 6 years	2	2	4	8
6 - 14 years	1	2	5	8
	14 (44%)	5 (15%)	13 (41%)	32

*Includes one child in long-term care in a subnormality hospital, due to brain damage as a result of NAI.

Each group was looked at separately to see what proportion of time had been spent in the various forms of placement.

0 - 3 Year Age Group, Children in Long-Term Care (15 children)

Eleven children appeared to be satisfactorily placed in long-term foster homes, two of them having finally been adopted. However, it was noted that the mean time to reach these "final" placements was greater than 10 months. In addition 3 children in this age group were still in institutions at follow-up, in each case more than 3 years after the original incident. Four children had experienced distressing fostering breakdowns (one having actually suffered NAI at the hands of foster-parents). The mean time to get a Care Order in these children was 3 months, the majority of children spending this period of time in hospital. The following graph shows the total lengths of time accumulated by this group of children in various placements during the follow-up period:

TIME SPENT 0–3 yr GROUP

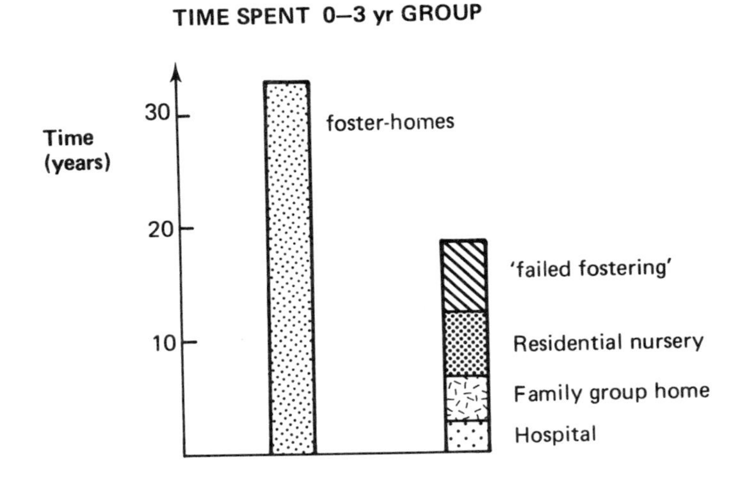

N.B.1 "failed fostering" denotes any foster placement which had to be terminated.

N.B.2 This table excludes the case of the child in the subnormality hospital.

3 - 6 Year Age Group (8 children)

In this group of children there was far more reliance on institutional placements than on family placements compared with the 0 - 3 year group.

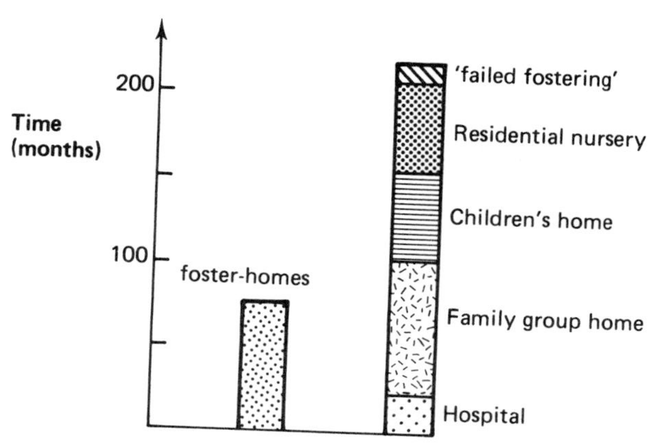

6 - 14 Year Age Group (8 children)

Only one child in this age group had reached a fostered placement, all the rest being placed in a variety of institutions. In the majority of cases fostering did not even appear to have been considered.

General Points 3 - 14 Year Age Group

It will be seen that 15 out of the 20 children in the age range came into long-term care. This reflected the fact that many of these children came from chronically deprived situations, and that relatively minor NAI in this age group turned out to be a marker of serious family pathology. Previous missed opportunities for intervention were noted in several families, often consisting of a dismissal of NAI as "over-chastisement", and recourse to a policy of support rather than intervention. In most families there were several siblings also in need of rescue although action in this direction was often lacking in urgency.

DISCUSSION

Under-Diagnosis of Neglect/Emotional Deprivation

It is striking that only 3 cases in this series were found to be of the neglect/deprivation variety, compared with 54 cases of NAI. This is paralleled by a report (Creighton and Outram 1975) that the N.S.P.C.C. register for 1975 failed to record any cases of this syndrome in either Newcastle or Leeds. The overall incidence of this syndrome for England and Wales was only 3.4% in this report. It seems extremely unlikely that any of these figures reflect the true incidence of serious neglect/deprivation in the community. Certainly failure to thrive in infancy for psycho-social reasons is a common problem in general paediatric practice, and tends not to be treated with as much seriousness as NAI. If neglect/deprivation is being under-diagnosed (and therefore undermanaged), the implications are serious because long-standing emotional deprivation probably causes far greater emotional damage than an isolated incident of NAI. It seems likely that doctors and social workers alike are still preoccupied with the problem of physical injury. Certainly in this series there was evidence that medical staff were under-diagnosing co-existing neglect in the NAI cases. In 10 cases of NAI there was a marked growth spurt in hospital which appeared not to have been appreciated at the time. In addition, developmental and emotional assessments were conspicuous by their absence in many medical records and reports.

It seems likely that at present there are many children suffering neglect and deprivation sufficiently severe to warrant being taken into care, but that at present this will only occur if in addition they are subjected to NAI.

The following case report demonstrates how even gross cases of neglect can be handled with much less urgency than an equivalent case of NAI:-

A 4 year old girl was noticed by the Health Visitor to be coughing and neglected in the house of a family of 8 children. No medical attention had been sought by her parents. In hospital she was found to have severe growth retardation, and a chicken bone in her left main bronchus which had led to severe permanent damage to her left lung. The family situation was found to be disastrous, with father drinking most of the social security money, battering his wife, and all the children having evidence of growth failure. Despite this, the four year old was returned home without even a case conference. Three months later her growth was found to have suffered again and she came into voluntary care. Seventeen months later a Section II resolution was secured, but the remaining 7 siblings were not taken into care until 2 years had passed from the original event. All are now thriving in care with plans for fostering being made.

Initial Decision-Making

In this series 18 cases were discharged home without legal sanctions, although these could probably have been obtained in the majority of cases. In these children, the incidence of repeat abuse was unacceptably high (7 out of 18), which suggests that some of these decisions were based on over-optimistic assessments of families. We would argue that the taking of legal sanctions should be the rule rather than the exception for the majority of cases of significant child abuse. The opposite approach of only taking legal sanctions in the worst cases or as a last resort leaves too many children at risk. Ideally, the Care Order gives control and helps the family to accept their need for help; once this has occurred rehabilitation of the child with his family can proceed both speedily and safely in many cases.

In some of these 18 cases, the decision not to pursue legal sanctions was based on legal advice which took an unduly pessimistic view of the strength of the evidence of NAI. Sometimes this reflectedthe lack of force with which doctors provided the medical evidence at Case Conferences. Many doctors still seem unaware that 100% certainty that an injury has been inflicted is not necessary for the purpose of obtaining a Care Order. In some cases, a significant factor in the Case Conference decision seems to have been the erroneous idea that legal sanctions necessarily imply long-term separation of a child from its natural family.

Rehabilitation with Natural Parents

It will be seen that in 12 cases children were rehabilitated under legal sanctions. In 3 further cases attempted rehabilitation failed because of repeat NAI; it would seem that in these cases the psycho-social evaluation of the family must have been too superficial and over-optimistic. In the remaining cases rehabilitation was always explored but usually failed because of parental lack of motivation or chaotic life-style. In many cases the possibility of rehabilitation was kept open for so long (sometimes for years) that social workers were able to postpone acceptance of the fact that children had effectively come into long-term care, and needed a long-term plan for their upbringing.

In this series over 70% of the children under legal sanctions were in long-term care at the time of follow-up. It is possible that rehabilitation could have been successful in a higher proportion of cases given more resources. At present many cases of NAI in Newcastle are being managed by social workers with heavy case loads and limited experience of working with NAI. It is unrealistic to expect them to be able to provide the time and skilled work necessary for intensive rehabilitation work. This is an argument for more specialization and more resources for the management of child abuse. It is possible that specialist in-patient hospital units such as those at The Park, Oxford (Ounsted 1974) can achieve higher rehabilitation rates, although in Newcastle mothers are always offered admission to the mother and baby units of paediatric wards, or to a Nursery Unit outside the town. Additional services such as groups for mothers, lay befrienders, day foster care, etc. are needed, and more time and special training for all the workers concerned. However, there was a strong impression that the majority of families in this series came from a section of the Newcastle population with a particularly high rate of delinquency and psychopathy, and that many of them would naturally fall into one or other of the categories of untreatable families described by Kempe and Kempe (1978).

Delays in Decision-Making

Ideally, any child subjected to abuse deserves speedy decisions as to his future in keeping with his own "sense of time" (Goldstein, Freud and Solnit 1973). By this criterion, decisions may need to be taken in a matter of days or weeks in the case of younger children. This ideal was virtually never realised in this series except in the cases returned home directly from hospital. In the under 3 year group whose cases were taken to court, delays in the legal process meant that the children spent an average of 11 weeks in hospital awaiting the outcome of legal action. In most of these cases a preferable alternative would have been placement in short-term foster care while awaiting the court case; if early rehabilitation is planned it is better to transfer the child with the mother to a special mother and baby unit. It is of course important to include the father in the treatment plan from the outset.

In this series the worst delays in decision-making occurred after legal sanctions had been obtained. Ideally at this stage there should be intensive work with the natural family to assess the chances of rehabilitation. Rehabilitation should be intensive or not at all. In this series a frequent finding was of a long drawn-out "failed rehabilitation" process often taking several years. As a result, children were denied the chance of alternative family placement. This tendency towards "laissez-faire" decision-making was one of the most important factors in leading to sub-optimal management of children in care. It is essential that a long-term decision is made on a child's future as soon as possible after legal sanctions are obtained. The parent's problems should be fully assessed and they should be given a time limit and intensive help to achieve set objectives; if they fail to meet these objectives a firm decision should be taken not to return the child. This decision should be taken at a special Case Conference and should have a strength and continuity binding on subsequent social workers. Too often this basic decision is not made, and the case becomes an "inactive" one, governed by the statutory 6 monthly review procedure. The final result is that there is avoidance of the fact that a child has effectively "lapsed" into long-term care; as long as this denial persists long-term planning will be inhibited and the child's potential in a family setting never realised. We believe children need families, and substitute families if necessary.

Family Versus Institutional Placement

By any standards the high recourse to institutional care in this series is depressing. Basically this group of children have hardly done any better in this respect than the large mass of children in care for all reasons (Rowe and Lambert 1973).

Apart from the factors discussed above there appeared to be one other factor of prime importance in denying children family placements. This was what can only be described as a basic lack of appreciation of the emotional needs of children on the part of the workers concerned. There seemed to be a lack of awareness of the extreme preferability of family care to institutional care, and a tolerance of the latter even for young children on a long-term basis. Many workers seemed over-pessimistic about fostering children. Reasons for this pessimism may have been past experiences of foster-breakdowns, or more practical difficulties such as the absence of a "waiting-list" of approved couples. For such a worker, keeping a child in an institution is a kind of "safety-first" course, and also a line of least resistance if natural parents are still involved.

Even when foster-placement was decided on in theory there remained difficulties and delays in implementation. For instance, because of the absence of a "bank" of suitable couples, each child had to be advertised separately; all couples responding to these advertisements had then to be assessed from scrath, and this could involve a period of 3 - 6 months. All this work and responsibility devolves on the child's social worker and constitutes quite a disincentive to consider fostering in the first place. A further problem is that assessment and support of foster parents is a skilled occupation and that many junior generic social workers (who managed the majority of these cases) have received no special training in this field. All these factors may have contributed to the findings of this survery concerning delays in finding long-term foster-homes for the children.

Long-Term Fostering Versus Adoption

Apart from the practical difficulties of long-term fostering there are some in-built contradictions in the whole concept. The most obvious is the way in which the foster-parents are handicapped in their natural inclination to commit themselves to the child. The child for his part will sense the inherent lack of permanence in the arrangement. If natural parents are still allowed to have the child home for visits, the child is exposed to a conflict of loyalties. These factors help to explain why many foster placements break down including those in this series.

We would argue that in the majority of cases of younger children coming into long-term care as a result of child abuse, it would be better to regard adoption as the desired method of family placement rather than long-term foster care. Adoption possesses all the advantages and none of the disadvantages of long-term foster care and has been shown to be a successful social manoeuvre (B. Seglow, Pringle and Wedge 1972, Bohman 1973). There is evidence from the work of Kadushin (1970) and Tizard (1977) that even relatively late adoption of children who have been ill-treated or who have spent their early years in institutional care can be very successful.

Role of the Paediatrician

Only paediatricians with a special interest in child abuse have much enthusiasm for following-up all their cases after the initial incident. However there are several cogent reasons why they should. The most obvious is that as this survey shows a child does not cease to be "at risk" just because it had been taken into care! The paediatrician who remains involved can have a vital role in improving subsequent management along the lines already discussed. In addition, he can be an important source of continuity. In this series at follow-up very few cases were still being managed by the original social worker, whereall all four consultants involved were still working in Newcastle. Another reason for remaining involved is that no case is ever closed legally (until adoption or revocation of the Care Order). The paediatrician can also be an important source of support for foster-parents and can give important additional evidence in court e.g. concerning the growth and development of the child, the quality of the parent-child relationship, the value of a foster-placement and the advisability or otherwise of returning a child to his natural parents. A further way in which paediatricians can help abused children is to try to ensure that they receive psychotherapeutic or other special treatment in their own right, which is something that only happens rarely at present.

For all these reasons we feel paediatricians should attempt to follow-up all their cases of child abuse until a satisfactory long-term solution has been achieved.

Prediction and Prevention

In recent years it has been shown that both prediction and prevention of child abuse are feasible (Lynch 1975, Lynch and Roberts 1977, Gray, Cutler, Dean and Kempe 1976). Even where resources are limited it is desirable to set up some form of preventive service, as every case prevented will liberate resources that would have been consumed in managing the case after it had occurred.

Summary

In this series, sub-optimal forms of management were observed at every stage of management. These included:-

(i) Failure to recognise growth failure, neglect and emotional deprivation.

(ii) Failure to treat the above with sufficient seriousness.

(iii) Faulty initial decision-making, leading to repeat child abuse.

(iv) Some examples of ill-advised attempts at rehabilitation, leading to repeat child abuse.

(v) Failure to provide early family placements for children in long-term care.

In addition the fact that all these cases occurred in the first place should remind us that prediction and prevention of child abuse have been shown to be feasible, although little is being done in this direction at the present time.

Acknowledgements

We would like to express our gratitude to all the social workers concerned for their co-operation in providing reports, and help in bringing children for assessment. In addition we thank health visitors and teachers for providing helpful reports, and parents, both natural and foster, for bringing their children to out-patients. Finally we thank Dr. T. C. Noble, Dr. A. P. Kenna and Dr. F. W. Alexander for permission to study their cases.

References

Bohman, M. (1973) Unwanted Children - A Prognostic Study
in Child Adoption No. 72
Journal of the Association of British Adoption Agencies,
4 Southampton Row, London, W.C.1.

Cooper, C. E. (1975) The Doctor's Dilemma - A Paediatrician's View
in Concerning Child Abuse
Franklin, A. F. (Ed.)
Churchill Livingstone, London. pp. 21 - 29

Creighton, S. J. and Outram, P. J. (1975)
in Child Victims of Physical Abuse
National Society for the Prevention of Cruelty to Children
1 - 3 Riding House Street, London. page 5.

Gray, J., Cutler, C., Dean, J. and Kempe, C. H. (1976)
Perinatal Assessment of Mother-Baby Interaction
in Child Abuse and Neglect: The Family and the Community
Helfer, R. E. and Kempe, C. H. (Ed.)
Ballinger Publishing Company, Cambridge, Mass., Ch. 19,pp. 377 - 392.

Goldstein, J., Freud, A. and Solnit, A. J. (1973)
Beyond the Best Interest of the Child
The Free Press, New York, pp. 24 - 26.

Kadushin, A. (1970)
in Adopting Older Children
Columbia University Press (New York and London)

Kempe, R. S. and Kempe, H. (1978)
in Child Abuse
Fontana/Open Books, London. Ch. 8, pp. 128 - 131

Lynch, M. A. (1975)
Ill Health and Child Abuse
Lancet, ii, p. 317

Lynch, M. A. and Roberts, J. (1977)
Predicting Child Abuse: Signs of Bonding Failure in the Maternity Hospital
Brit. Med. J., I, 624.

Ounsted, C., Oppenheimer, R. and Lindsay, J. (1974)
Aspects of Bonding Failure: The Psychopathology and Psychotherapeutic Treatment of Families of Battered Children
in Develop. Med. Child Neurol., 16, 447 - 456.

Rowe, J., and Lambert, L. (1973)
in Children Who Wait
Association of British Adoption Agencies, London, Ch. 111, pp. 34.

Seglow, J., Pringle K. P. and Wedge, P. (1972)
Growing Up Adopted
National Foundation for Educational Research, Slough, England.

Tizard, B. (1977)
in Adoption: a Second Chance
Open Books, London. Ch. 7 pp. 75 - 94 and Ch. 12 pp. 151 - 179.

Child Abuse and Neglect, Vol. 3, pp. 565 - 575.
Pergamon Press Ltd., 1979. Printed in Great Britain.

ABUSE AND RISK TO HANDICAPPED AND CHRONICALLY ILL CHILDREN

Danya Glaser and Arnon Bentovim.

Department of Psychological Medicine.
Hospital for Sick Children, Great Ormond Street, London, W.C.1.

INTRODUCTION

Surveys of populations of abused and neglected children have consistently shown an over representation of handicapped and physically ill children (Lynch 1975 and Friedrich and Boriskin 1976). Handicap and physical illness thus appear to be important factors in the child predisposing to abuse.

The presence of a considerable number of more severely handicapped and chronically ill children in our own hospital population of abused and at risk children led us to examine factors associated with abuse of the handicapped and chronically ill children in their families.

Historical Perspective

Radbill (1974) indicates that for many centuries attitudes to the deformed or handicapped was occasionally to revere but only too often to 'destroy deformed children at birth' and 'expose the weak that the strong only should survive'. These attitudes have obviously changed with gradual development of a compassionate view of the handicapped. There has however been continuing concern about parental attitudes and reaction to chronically handicapped and ill children. Anxiety about possible handicap of the child during pregnancy, the horror and narcissistic blow occasioned by the birth of a sick or handicapped child, and the pain of the loss of the expected normal child are all feelings which have been widely described and recognised. The stigma and burden borne by the families of handicapped children, and their relationship with the helping community which both needs them and yet so rarely satisfies them, has been widely documented (e.g. Bentovim 1972). With this background it is understandable that with growing awareness about abuse in general handicapped children should also be the subject of concern.

Hospital Practice in the Management of Child Abuse

Weekly meetings have been held since 1973 in the Hospital for Sick Children to discuss children thought to be at risk for, or actually abused through, non accidental injury (NAI), neglect, rejection or non-medical failure to thrive. The children discussed and registered at the NAI meetings could be referred by medical, nursing, or social work staff. The only criterion necessary for inclusion was a professional's anxiety about the child and the family, or the presence of actual diagnosed abuse. The children included and discussed here do not constitute the total number of eligible children attending the hospital in the years 1973 to 1977 but only those actually brought up for discussion. Those for instance referred directly to the Department of Psychological Medicine for treatment, or those children already under the care of other agencies were not discussed at NAI conferences.

One of us has previously described the unusual pattern of the sample of children discussed in these meetings (Bentovim 1977):-

(1) Severely injured children referred by other hospitals and requiring resuscitation or special treatment e.g. neurosurgery.
(2) Second referral children who required further investigation or a further opinion about disputed management.
(3) Child abuse presenting as inexplicable medical symptoms e.g. a series of non-accidental poisoning (Rogers et al 1976).
(4) Abuse and risk to our own hospital population of chronically ill or handicapped children.

We present here a review of the children discussed at these meetings with particular emphasis on the last category.

THE STUDY

Aims

In this study we have been particularly interested to seek the answer to a number of questions:
(1) Did the patterns of concern about risk or evidence of abuse take a particular form in the handicapped group.
(2) Were there unusual features e.g. age, differentiating the sick or handicapped children from the previously non handicapped group.
(3) What is the effect of the degree of pre-existing handicap or chronic illness on the severity of risk or abuse.
(4) What was the relationship between the degree of pre-existing social/emotional disturbance in the family and the risk or abuse to the child.
(5) What makes professionals concerned about families of the handicapped and how does the labelling of risk or abuse rise.

The Sample

During the years 1973 - 1977 a total of 189 children were discussed at regular meetings. Fifteen children were excluded because of insufficient information being documented, or because on review there was felt to be little evidence of abuse or the presence of risk factors. For example, where severely handicapped children were appropriately placed in long-term residential care, this was not included as rejection. Cases where abuse had occured in the past and was not of immediate concern during the current attendance were also excluded.

The study deals with 175 children in whom medical, social and where appropriate, psychiatric investigation, documentation and discussion have pointed to a strong likelihood of risk for, or actual abuse.

Characteristics of the Children

TABLE 1. Percentage and Number of Handicapped and Non-Handicapped Abused and At Risk Children

	PRE-EXISTING HANDICAP AND CHRONIC ILLNESS (BEFORE THE ABUSIVE INCIDENT)		NON-HANDICAPPED (BEFORE THE ABUSIVE INCIDENT)		TOTAL
TOTAL	100%	(67)	100%	(107)	174
ABUSED	46%	(31)	75%	(80)	111
AT RISK	54%	(36)	25%	(27)	63

Table 1 shows that in our series of 174 children, 111 (64%) were abused and 63 (36%) were at risk. Sixty seven (38% of the total) were suffering from a pre-existing handicap or chronic illness. It should be noted here that we are primarily dealing with major physical problems (See Table 5). Prematurity and neo-natal separation have not been included in this sick or handicapped group. This large proportion of sick and handicapped children in our series is a reflection of the nature of our hospital and is therefore not comparable with the proportion of handicapped children in other series.

Patterns of Abuse

It could be hypothesised that with a large population of chronically ill and handicapped children attending a specialist children's hospital, the patterns of abuse seen would represent those seen in the general population of handicapped and chronically ill children. It is likely that were there any severe form of injury to any of the children which led to their admission to other hospitals, we would have been informed. Whilst accepting that such assertions require further investigation and follow up, we decided to compare the patterns of abuse in the 67 children who were handicapped or chronically ill before the abusive or at risk incident, with the 107 children who were not. As the source and reason for referral to the Hospital differed, i.e. the non-handicapped children were often referred because of the severity of the injury, this group could not serve as a control group, but as a contrast group to point to suggestive comparisons for future study. As shown in Table 1 we found a marked difference between the handicapped and non-handicapped groups. Whereas 75% of the non-handicapped children had been abused in some way, in the handicapped group abuse occured in 46%.

Examples of Risk and Abuse: Children considered at risk had given rise to concern, without acutal abuse having occured.

> E.g. Case. No. 133. A two year old boy with mild haemophilia had been born in the second marriage of the mother. Father had blamed her for the boy's illness, she could not cope with the boy's behaviour and wanted to 'throw him away'. The mother had great difficulty in working with any helping agencies.

We divided abuse into two groups:- commision of injury and omission of care. The former category includes head injury, poisoning and fractures at the more severe end of the scale and bruising at the other. Under the category of omission of care we have included neglect, rejection, failure of administration of treatment and evidence of non-medical failure to thrive.

> E.g. Case No. 79. A healthy three and a half year old girl who had on several occasions been left alone at home with other young siblings and on one such occasion sustained severe burns in a fire (Neglect).

> E.g. Case No. 101. A two month old baby with congenital diaphragmatic hernia, suffered consequent neo-natal separation from his parents, whose marriage was at that time unstable, and whose mother, who had psychiatric problems did not want him back. (Rejection).

There were several Phenylketonuria children whose diet had been inadequately handled.

Contrasting Patterns of Actual Abuse

On examining patterns of actual abuse, further clear differences between the non-handicapped and handicapped children emerged. This is shown in Table 2. A considerably higher proportion of non handicapped children suffered abuse by commision rather than omission of care (60% of non-handicapped children, 29% of handicapped children) whereas of the handicapped abused group a majority (71%) suffered omission of care. Several of the non-handicapped children were premature and had suffered neo-natal separation from their families, as noted in other series (e.g. Lynch 1975).

Within the category of abuse by omission of care, there is a certain degree of overlap between the non-handicapped and handicapped groups. However, overt signs of rejection appeared more commonly for the handicapped children whereas neglect and failure to thrive were more common in the non-handicapped group.

TABLE 2. PATTERNS OF ABUSE

		HANDICAPPED		NON-HANDICAPPED	
TOTAL ABUSE		(31)	100%	(80)	100%
COMMISSION OF ABUSE	TOTAL	(9)	29%	(48)	60%
	Head injury	(2)		(28)	
	Fractures; Soft Tissue Tears	(2)		(5)	
	Poisoning	(3)		(9)	
	Bruising	(2)		(6)	
OMISSION OF CARE	TOTAL	(22)	71%	(32)	40%
	Failure to thrive; Neglect; Non-administration of medical care	(12)		(17)	
	Rejection	(10)		(5)	

Age Range and Distribution

TABLE 3 AGE DISTRIBUTION OF CHILDREN ABUSED

AGE	0 - 6 months	7 months - 2 years	2 years - 5 years	5 years +	TOTAL
HANDICAPPED	(8) 26%	(7) 22.5%	(7) 22.5%	(9) 29%	(31) 100%
NON HANDICAPPED	(29) 36%	(26) 32%	(18) 23%	(7) 9%	(80) 100%

TABLE 4 AGE DISTRIBUTION OF CHILDREN AT RISK

AGE	0 - 6 months	7 months - 2 years	2 years - 5 years	5 years +	TOTAL
HANDICAPPED	(9) 25%	(15) 42%	(7) 19%	(5) 14%	(36) 100%
NON HANDICAPPED	(11) 41%	(12) 44%	(3) 11%	(1) 4%	(27) 100%

The age range of the children was from birth to 10 years. Tables 3 and 4 show the age distribution of the handicapped i.e. children who had pre-existing handicap or chronic illness before the abusive incident, and non handicapped i.e. children who were not handicapped or chronically ill before the abusive incident, and the distribution of abuse or risk over the age range.

E.g. Case No. 54. A boy of 7 with spina bifida and hydrocephalus whose father was not cooperating with treatment.

E.g. Case No. 3. A mentally handicapped boy of 7 with fits who was poisoned with anticonvulsants.

Several interesting patterns emerged. Over one third (36% of the non-handicapped children were abused by the age of 6 months. Included here were the several children admitted with subdural effusions. This finding of early severe abuse has been documented in other studies (Baldwin and Oliver 1975). The incidence of abuse in these children progressively decreased with age. In contrast to this, in the ill/handicapped group only some 26% suffered abuse in the early months and the rate of abuse remained steady until the age of 5+. The relationship between being at risk and age, does not show a clear pattern.

ANALYSIS OF THE HANDICAPPED AND CHRONICALLY ILL GROUP

Relationships between Degree of Handicap and Illness, Severity of Abuse and Social/Emotional Difficulty in the Families

In order to look for relationships between handicap, abuse and social and emotional disturbance in the families, it has been necessary to quantify the magnitude of these 3 interrelating dimensions. Scores of one to three have allottedto each dimension. It is important to stress that these scores were retrospective and based on clinical impressions. As a result in some individual children it was therefore difficult to arrive at a precise score. In case of doubt scoring was arrived at by consensus. For each child, however, dimensions were scored independently of each other.

Criteria for Scoring Degree of Handicap

I Mild Handicap

Long lasting but minor, and non life threatening quality (cleft lip and palate, epilepsy).

II Moderate handicap

Included chronic conditions amenable to maintenance treatment (e.g. Phenylketonuria), not grossly affecting quality of life, and early problems requiring definitive surgery which successfully reversed the problems, (e.g. intestinal obstruction, mild mental retardation, mild haemophilia).

III Severe handicap

Included chronic irreversible handicap and multiple handicaps (e.g. tracheo-oesophageal fistula, severe mental handicap with epilepsy, severe congenital heart disease).

Scoring for Degree of Risk and Abuse and examples

I At risk

E.g. Case No. 7. A 5 month old boy suffering from a dermal cephalic defect and consequent neonatal separation from mother. Mother had deprived childhood, and the baby was born in her second marriage. Baby had two falls.

II Moderate Abuse - Failure to thrive, neglect, partial rejection, moderate injuries.
E.g. Case No. 34. A baby girl, born with congenital heart disease, to a divorced very young mother. The baby was in care due to the mother's inability to look after her and contact was intermittently maintained.

III Severe Abuse - total rejection, neglect, severe injuries.
E.g. Case No. 111. A one year old girl with congenital heart disease necessitating neonatal surgery and prolonged separation from mother. Mother was an immigrant and culturally isolated. Child suffered fractures of skull and other bones.

Criteria for Scoring Social/Emotional Disturbance in the Family and examples

Here an attempt was made to assess the degree of difficulties existing in the family prior to the emergence of illness or handicap in the child. For this dimension, scoring was impressionistic and examples only can be given.

I Mild social/emotional disturbance e.g. short marriage due to pregnancy; some previous emotional problems in the mother.
E.g. Case No. 105. A working class family with some financial problems, but mother approved as foster mother and daily minder. The child suffered from severe mental handicap and epilepsy and was thought to be at some risk for abuse or rejection.

II Moderate social/emotional disturbance e.g. marital problems , mother was deprived in childhood.
E.g. Case No. 24. A middle class family, mother professional with personality problems, marital problems. The child suffered from bilateral congenital dislocation of the hips, scored as II and was thought to be at risk for abuse.

III Severe social/emotional disturbance e.g. single parent with psychiatric and social or cultural problem; other multiple difficulties.
E.g. Case No. 104. Mother foreign, suffering from psychiatric problems. Father previously married with children. Child suffering from severe congenital rubella, rejected by parents.

(1) Results: Most of the handicapped children were moderately or severely affected (See Table 5 for types of handicap). Ninety per cent were in groups II and III.

There was a considerable magnitude of social/emotional disturbance in this handicapped group, there being only 18% in groups 0 - I, but 34% in group II and 48% in group III.

In contrast, however, the degrees of abuse by emoission of commission were predominantly in the moderate category II (61%).

TABLE 5 TYPES OF HANDICAP

	% of Total Handicapped	Number
Central and Sensory Nervous system Including: Mental handicap, (e.g. rubella), Epilepsy, Spina Bifida, Deafness.	39%	(26)
Gastro Intestinal Including: Tracheo-oesophageal fistula, Intestinal obstruction, Diaphragmatic Hernia, Hare Lip, and Cleft Palate.	28%	(19)
Biochemical and Genetic Including: Phenylketonuria, Adrenogenital syndrome, Blood clotting defects.	15%	(10)
Skeletal Including: Congenital dislocation of the Hip, Arthrogryphosis, Muscular Dystrophy	6%	(4)
Congenital Heart Disease	6%	(4)
Renal	6%	(4)
TOTAL	100%	(67)

(2) The Relationship Between Degree of Handicap and Severity of Abuse

Our first concern was with the possible effects of varying degrees of handicap on patterns of abuse. We controlled for social/emotional disturbance by looking at the relationship of severity of handicap to degree of risk or abuse within two of the social/emotional disturbance categories - mild to moderate (O-II) and severe III.

The division was at the median point of the distribution of numbers in the categories (Tables 6 and 7).

TABLE 6 The Relationship of Degree of Handicap to Risk and Abuse When Mild to Moderate Social/Emotional Disturbance is Present. (Groups O-II) (Total 23).

DEGREE OF HANDICAP	NUMBERS AT RISK	NUMBERS ABUSED BY		TOTAL
		Omission of care (I-III)	Injury and Poisoning (I-III)	
I	2	-	-	2
II	10	1		11
III	5	4	1	10
TOTAL	17	5	1	23

TABLE 7 The Relationship of the Degree of Handicap to Risk and Abuse When Severe Social/Emotional Disturbance is Present (Group III) (Total 32).

DEGREE OF HANDICAP	NUMBERS AT RISK	NUMBERS ABUSED BY		TOTAL
		Omission of Care (I-III)	Injury and Poisoning (I-III)	
I	2	2	-	4
II	3	8	2	13
III	4	10	1	15
TOTAL	9	20	3	32

It was then found that as social/emotional disturbance increased, severity of handicap exerted a decreasingly discriminating influence on severity of risk or abuse. (Fisher's exact probability test significant at $p = < 0.03$ for Table 6 - mild to moderate social/emotional disturbance (0-II): not significant for Table 7 - severe social/emotional disturbance (III). In other words the severity of handicap itself was not a powerful factor associated with severity of abuse when there was severe social/emotional disturbance present.

(3) The Relationship Between Degree of Abuse and Social/Emotional Disturbance

We grouped together the handicapped II and III groups (i.e. the more severely handicapped) and looked at the relationship between degree of abuse and degree of social/emotional disturbance. (Table 8). We found that whereas 20 children in social/emotional group III suffered moderate or severe omissions of care or commission or injury, only 7 in social/emotional group II did so.

TABLE 8 Relationship Between Degree of Prior Social/Emotional Disturbance and Risk or Abuse for More Severely Handicapped Children (Groups II and III) (Total 60)

DEGREE OF SOCIAL/ EMOTIONAL DISTURBANCE	NUMBERS AT RISK	NUMBERS ABUSED BY		TOTALS
		Omission of Care (I-III)	Injury and Poisoning (I-III)	
0	2	-	-	2
I	7	1	1	9
II	15	5	2	22
III	7	17	3	27
TOTAL	31	23	6	60

This difference was significant at $p < 0.001$ on χ^2 test when social/emotional disturbance groups O-II were collapsed and compared with group III. We then examined separately the relationship between degree of social/emotional disturbance and risk or abuse in the moderately handicapped group (I-II), and severely handicapped groups (III) (Tables 9 and 10)

Table 9 Relationship Between Degree of Prior Social/Emotional Disturbance and Risk or Abuse in Moderately Handicapped Children (Groups I and II) (Total 34)

DEGREE OF SOCIAL/ EMOTIONAL DISTURBANCE	NUMBERS AT RISK	NUMBERS ABUSED BY		TOTALS
		Omission of Care (I-III)	Injury and Poisoning (I-III)	
O-II	16	1	1	18
III	5	7	4	16
TOTAL	21	8	5	34

Table 10 Relationship Between Degree of Prior Social/Emotional Disturbance and Risk or Abuse in Severely Handicapped Children (Group III) (Total 32).

DEGREE OF SOCIAL/ EMOTIONAL DISTURBANCE	NUMBERS AT RISK	NUMBERS ABUSED BY		TOTALS
		Omission of Care (I-III)	Injury and Poisoning (I-III)	
O-II	10	4	2	16
III	4	10	2	16

The differences remained significant ($p < 0.001$ and $p < 0.003$ respectively) Tables 9 and 10).

DISCUSSION

In examining patterns of concern we assumed a continuum ranging from presence of risk to actual abuse, either by omission of care or commission of injury.

Relating our findings and our original aims the following can be concluded.
(1) We found that amongst the handicapped/ill group, risk and actual abuse were equally represented. Furthermore, where abuse occured it was far more likely to be by omission of care than commission. Both these findings contrasted markedly with the situation in the previously non-handicapped comparison group. Further investigation with a group controlled for social/emotional factors would be necessary to confirm this finding.
(2) The even age distribution of abuse from birth to age 5 years and over, in the ill/handicapped group, shows a different pattern from that found in the comparison, previously non-handicapped group.

It is possible that the actual physical separation due to hospitalization of the ill/handicapped babies avoids a situation in which abuse might otherwise occur. However, that very separation is considered to be one of the factors contributing to abuse in the non-handicapped children. One mediating factor here could be earlier alerting of professional help and increasing awareness. It is also possible that the handicap exerts a protective influence for the young, potentially abused, handicapped child in an opposite way to that created by minor ill health in actually abused children. We have not assessed the presence of minor illness in our abused non-handicapped children although this was certainly present in many of the cases, and has been documented elsewhere, (e.g. Lynch 1975). However, although possibly protecting initially, the presence of chronic illness or handicap continues to exert pressures which are reflected in the steady rate of abuse with rising age of the children. It should also be noted that regular contact with medical surveillance could lead to moderate degrees of abuse being picked up, rather than being over-looked in the non-handicapped.
(3) Our hypothesis, that actual presence, as well as degree of severity, of illness or handicap would each positively correlate with severity of committed abuse, has been only partially proved. As social/emotional disturbance increases, severity of handicap becomes less important in predicting degree of risk or abuse.

It may be that difference in the degree of handicap are more meaningful to the medical profession than to parents in terms of the impact of the handicap, especially in the presence of severe social/emotional disturbance. There appeared to be a strong positive association between severity of social/emotional disturbance and degree of risk or abuse.
(4) The high rates of considerable social/emotional disturbance in this handicapped group points to a lesser likelihood of ascribing the significantly lower rate of severe physical abuse in the handicapped group to better emotional conditions in the family. It would be interesting to examine social/emotional factors in the non handicapped group in order to substantiate this. It rather appears that the handicap may be exerting a negative influence on occurence of abuse.
(5) A question concerning the relationship between professionals and families of handicapped children arises. Are the professionals' expectations of the parents of handicapped children too great and do we consequently too regularly label reasonable parental feelings as abuse? If this is so, then the amount of actual abuse to handicapped children would appear to be even lower, but it would be necessary to determine the rate in relation to the total population of handicapped children attending the Hospital.

SUMMARY

Our group of children feared to be at risk for, or actually abused could be clearly subdivided into a previously non-handicapped group and a previously handicapped one. Patterns of abuse and age distribution between these two groups have been found to differ considerably.

Within the handicapped group, it appeared that beyond a moderate degree of illness or handicap its increasing severity does not contribute materially to the degree of abuse. The degree of social/emotional stress is the important varying factor.

Acknowledgements

Thanks to Jim Stevenson for data analysis, Edna Waller, Social worker, for making notes available, physicians and surgeons under whose care children were and Pamela Oatey and Deborah Crookes for secretarial assistance.

REFERENCES

Baldwin, J.A. and Oliver, J.E. Epidemiology and Family Characteristics of Severely Abused Children. Brit. J. prev. soc. Med. 29, 205, (1975).

Bentovim, A. Emotional Disturbances of Handicapped Pre-school Children and their Families. Attitudes to the Child. Brit. med. J. 3, 579, (1972).

Bentovim, A. A Psychiatric Family Day Centre Meeting the Needs of Abused or at Risk Pre-school Children and Their Parents. Pergamon Press, Oxford. J. Child Abuse and Neglect. 1, 479 - 485 (1977).

Friedrich, W.N. and Boriskin, J.A. The Role of the Child in Abuse. Amer. J. Orthopsychiat 46 (4) 580, (1976).

Lynch, M.A. Ill Health and Child Abuse. Lancet, 2, 317, (1975).

Radbill J, A History of Child Abuse and Infanticide in Helfer, R.E. and Kempe, C H., (Eds.) (1974) The Battered Child, University of Chicago Press, Chicago, Chicago and London.

Child Abuse and Neglect, Vol. 3, pp. 577 - 582.
Pergamon Press Ltd., 1979. Printed in Great Britain.

INTERPROFESSIONAL COMMUNICATION IN CASE CONFERENCES

Christine Hallett and Olive Stevenson

Department of Social Policy and Social Work, University of Keele, Staffs. England

This paper is based on the findings of a small research study sponsored by the Department of Health and Social Security. The aim of the project was to identify and explore some of the factors affecting interprofessional communication. The method chosen was observation of a sample of case conferences concerning children at risk of abuse or neglect and follow-up interviews with participants from selected conferences. Case conferences on children at risk were selected for study for three main reasons. First, they provide a ready forum in which aspects of interprofessional communication can be examined. Secondly, the published reports of inquiries into cases of child abuse suggest that failures in communication played a major part in several of these tragedies, (ref. 1). Thirdly, since case conferences are widely recognised as vital tools in the management of cases of non-accidental injury (ref. 2), study of their functioning seemed timely and potentially useful. The study was small scale, designed to produce some qualitative insight into interprofessional communication to complement the quantitative material available elsewhere, for example in Castle, 1976 (ref. 3).

Three neighbouring area review committees in England were asked to give notification of all case conferences called in July 1976. The researchers attended 13, as observers, taking no part in the proceedings but noting such matters as: the composition of the conference, the role of the chairperson, the main focus of discussion, the decisions reached, and the communication and interaction among the participants.

Six of the conferences were selected for follow-up interviews with those present. Almost all agreed to participate and 49 were interviewed. Topics discussed included the participants' background and experience of dealing with child abuse and of attending case conferences; the nature of their contact, if any, with members of the family in the case under discussion; their role and area of expertise and their understanding of the role of other participants; their views on the composition of the conference, on communication within it, on its purpose (or purposes), on how it was chaired, and an assessment of its effectiveness.

The interviews explored these issues first in relation to the conferences observed in the study and then drew more widely on the respondents' experience of attending others. From observation and interviews it proved possible to identify a number of factors affecting interprofessional communication in the conferences and some of these are discussed below.

MISSING PEOPLE

At several of the conferences there were 'missing people'. Some had been invited but were unable to attend, others had not been approached. Certain groups of people, in particular general medical practitioners and class teachers, were rarely present in the conferences studied. The importance of the general practitioner's contribution is often stressed, for example, in government circulars (ref. 4), but family doctors were present at only three of the 13 conferences. As one of our respondents said:

> 'The family doctor has never been to the conferences I've been to. They are a law unto themselves.'

Clearly there are practical matters to be taken into account, such as the location, length, and timing of conferences; a clash with surgery hours, for example, would affect doctors' attendance. But these considerations did not seem to provide an answer which satisfied other participants. It was suggested that some general practitioners may feel uncertain about how to share confidential information in fairly large groups of non-medical people. This may be particularly difficult when, as was the case in several of the conferences studied, the identity and role of the participants is unclear to many of those present.

It was also suggested that some family doctors simply 'did not want to know' - not just about case conferences, but about the whole problem of child abuse and the consequences in terms of the doctor's responsibilities under local procedural guidelines and of his relationship with the family concerned. Child abuse is estimated to constitute a very small proportion of the work of most general practitioners (ref. 5) and it is likely that there is an imbalance between the priority accorded these cases by some agencies, notably social services departments, and their importance within a family doctor's total workload.

Whatever the reasons, the absence of general practitioners from many of the conferences studied frequently left a vital information gap about the physical and mental health of those under discussion, particularly the parents. This was not usually filled by health visitors attending on the general practitioner's behalf. It was not clear whether this was because the health visitors were not in possession of the relevant information (and here the brevity of some medical records may be a consideration) or that they felt constrained from disclosing it in the doctor's absence, or whether it was for other reasons.

As well as leaving gaps in information, absenteeism illustrated in some cases the limited usefulness of those who 'come bearing messages' but are not in a position to take the discussion forward. It is of utmost importance that all relevant information should be fed into the conference so that a picture of the child and family can be built up from a variety of perspectives. But information gathering is only one stage of the process. A dynamic interchange of ideas on the basis of shared knowledge is the next step towards decision-making - even though the ultimate responsibility for the case may rest with one agency. Greater flexibility in the location of conferences may help some, for example, class teachers, to exchange views directly with others concerned. Or the key worker might discuss the case with those unable to attend. These and other ways of sharing information and ideas are used but were not always practised in the conferences studied.

CONFIDENTIALITY

One much publicised issue affecting multidisciplinary working is that of confidentiality. Yet most of the respondents said that in practice this posed few, if any, problems for them; they accepted a need to share information responsibly in conferences and several said that they had sought permission from the families involved. One respondent said:

> 'Confidentiality is very little of a problem. The families know and are told that they are being seen by a team of people and therefore they know and expect the information to be shared.'

This is somewhat surprising in view of the 'heat' this often engenders. However, it is probably important that local liaison arrangements with the police were considered to be good and the way in which the police exercised their discretion in this matter generally met with the approval of other workers involved. It is possible that work in other areas would have highlighted more problems in this matter than were encountered in this study.

WHO WAS WHO?

The extent to which those present at the conferences knew the others present and, more important, understood their roles, varied widely. Some participants, usually those most closely involved with the case or responsible for issuing invitations, were clear as to the identity and reasons for attendance of the other members. But many were unclear even when introductions were made, which they were not at all conferences.

Uncertainty arose particularly, although not exclusively, when senior officers accompanied staff from their own agency. It was not uncommon for three members of the social services department to be present - usually a social worker, a senior social worker, and an area officer or equivalent (usually taking the chair) - and health visitors were also often accompanied by a nursing officer. Often senior staff in supervisory roles had no direct contact with the case and contributed infrequently to the discussion.

Those who did not know who these others were or why they were there were unlikely to be enlightened as the conference progressed. Thus there was an air of mystery about the silent fringe and a number of those interviewed commented on feeling inhibited by 'the audience' from contributing to the discussion. One said:

> 'It's not so easy when you don't know people.'

and another:

> 'You don't know what they are there for and you don't know their involvement.'

This is not to suggest that the presence of senior staff, or others there perhaps primarily to learn rather than to contribute, is unnecessary or intrinsically unhelpful. Rather, it is to stress the importance of making introductions which identify participants and make clear their role and reason for attending the conference.

ANXIETY

Clearly some anxiety is inherent in case conferences concerning children at risk. This is engendered in part by realistic concern for the well-being and safety of the children involved, but also, particularly at present, by fear of being found wanting in the event of a tragedy. The conference may, quite properly, increase or decrease anxiety as information is pooled. It is no criticism of the conference if people leave it with an increased level of concern and suspicion about the situation. When anxiety is increased in this sense, there may be relief that a problem has been faced, clarified, and shared - even if it proves to be as bad as or worse than when the worker arrived. There were some conferences at which the problems under discussion were not such as to arouse intense realistic anxiety and yet the atmosphere was, to put it mildly, charged. In contrast, at another conference, although all were very worried about the family, the consensus among members and the controlled, quiet chairing left little doubt that the participants would leave it feeling that the professional communication had been satisfactory.

The important point is - why is this? One must allow for past history concerning the case under discussion or other cases and for the professional interaction which has resulted, for much communication takes place outside formal case conferences. Thus, people enter the room with views about the case and feelings about each other. This is 'given' in the situation and was undoubtedly crucial to the dissatisfaction expressed by most of the participants interviewed in two conferences. At times, 'troubles' in the past were hampering communications as illustrated by the quotations:

> 'It's not worth going over old ground because they all know it.'
>
> 'We have been at five or six conferences and so we all know what we think and this is so awfully difficult.'

The chairperson plays a crucial part in determining to what extent it is appropriate and helpful to bring out underlying conflicts of view and attitude, which in some instances created a tense atmosphere and inhibited genuine sharing of feelings. On the whole, those taking the chair did not do this; whether they should or not is an important matter to discuss further. But it may be necessary for conference participants to recognise that some less experienced members might need help to express their anxiety. It seemed from interviews that some participants found the conference itself an ordeal and failed to convey what they wanted to say, so feeling dissatisfied and uneasy. It is also unfortunate if the fact of having held a case conference is a symbol of 'formal sharing' when, in fact, important matters have not been discussed.

SPECIALISED KNOWLEDGE AND THE USE OF JARGON

Part of the communication in all the conferences involved the use of specialised knowledge and jargon. It was not easy to tell from observation how much of these exchanges was understood by the different occupational groups present. What was striking was that on no occasion did participants seek clarification of points on which they might have been unclear. The interviews yielded vague and perhaps evasive answers on this topic, with several respondents commenting that while they thought *they* had 'broadly understood', they surmised that many others present had not. A few admitted that it was not easy to ask for clarification in such a gathering:

> 'No, I don't find it easy to say, "Would you like to explain in simple language what that means?".'

The main types of 'technical' contribution were: first, those concerned with medical information (at times presented in baffling 'medical shorthand'); secondly, the law relating to children; and, thirdly, the predictors and signs of child abuse. There was a good deal of uncertainty or confusion about the technicalities of the law relating to children and of the broader legal framework within which social services departments have to operate in respect of children at risk. The precise implications of such phrases as 'place of safety order', 'reception into care', 'Section 2 rights', etc. were not always understood by all of those present. Yet these terms were often central to the debate and it was important for them to be clearly understood if all present were to share fully in the decisions or recommendations made by the conference. For example, at a conference called following a place of safety order one of the participants - who disclosed in interview that she was opposed to the conference recommendation to take care proceedings - believed that these had automatically to follow a place of safety order and was unaware that the child could, in fact, have been returned home.

Some of those interviewed spoke openly about their uncertainty regarding the law, saying that they left it to 'the professionals', i.e. the social workers. Others implied that they felt they should know more about it than they did. For example:

> 'I feel guilty about that. One sometimes says something ought to be done, but one doesn't really know what the legal rights are.'

Some of the social services representatives seemed to think that the legal terms were more 'self-explanatory' than proved to be the case, but others, recognising the difficulties, were uncertain as to how best to explain the legal position in the case conferences. They were worried about appearing too didactic or taking up valuable time. A possibility might be for social services departments to list the relevant sections of the law and the requirements to be satisfied, for example, for care proceedings, on a sheet of paper which could be handed out, when appropriate, at case conferences. This would enable those unsure to absorb the information at their own pace. At one conference, for example, a representative of the social services department outlined quite carefully the grounds for care proceedings under Section 1 of the 1969 Act, but it must have been difficult, if not impossible, for those unfamiliar with such phrases as: 'his proper development is being avoidably prevented or neglected or his health is being avoidably impaired or neglected or he is being ill-treated' (ref. 6) to have taken them in and applied them to the case under consideration, especially in a situation where anxiety is running high. One of those interviewed asked about this, said she would understand:

> 'If I sat down and thought about it, yes, but at the time when it's being thrown about, then not at all.'

There was similarly some confusion over the 'warning signs' of child abuse, despite considerable effort made in the areas concerned to inform those likely to come into contact with these problems. There had been short courses, study days, procedural handbooks, and so on. As one respondent said:

> 'We are all under the illusion that everybody knows everything at the moment because there's been so much. We've had mass meetings and things like that.'

Some workers, closely involved in work with child abuse, said they deliberately pointed out the 'danger signs':

> 'I think there's a lot of ignorance about what the warning signs are. So much so that often I tend to over-emphasise these points because I think if I don't other people won't even begin to be aware of them.'

The problem was that such knowledge was 'patchy' and, not surprisingly, it seemed that there was greater clarity about physical signs of abuse than about the more intangible aspects related to the 'feel' of the parent/child interaction, even when these might be relevant to the possibility of physical abuse. When information about the family dynamics was shared it was unclear whether all those present perceived the clues in the same way. For example, at one conference, a social worker voiced her anxieties about the way in which a mother was holding her baby and a health visitor suggested that the mother would be unlikely to hold the baby close to her after a caesarian section. The inference to be drawn from this was not spelled out, and an important task for the chairperson is to elucidate such exchanges so that significant pieces of information are not left 'hanging in the air'.

PROFESSIONAL FRAMES OF REFERENCE

A wider issue than the use of specialised knowledge is the extent to which frames of reference or differences in values and objectives, affected communication among professionals. The evidence from the study is unclear, for, although there were differences of opinion among members, these were not clearly and consistently related to differing professional ideologies. In particular, there was little to support the hypothesis that social workers were 'family focused' while others were 'child focused'. Indeed, it seemed at times, in observing the conferences, that other professionals also found it difficult to manage the balance between their sympathies for the parents and a realistic concern for the child. Nor did it seem that social services departments were being pressed to remove children from the home at the first sign of trouble and without consideration of the longer term implications.

It may be that the absence of doctors from some of the conferences precluded a clear distinction, which might have been expected, between a medical and a social assessment of the case under discussion. Or it may be that within the conference there was a 'blurring' of roles - at times hailed as the hallmark of good interprofessional cooperation. Certainly it seemed that the 'stereotypes' were not much in evidence.

THE LOCATION OF CONFERENCES

Although few respondents initiated this topic, few, if any, dismissed its relevance, either to themselves, or (more often) to others. Generally speaking, it was agreed that those accustomed to being 'on the road' did not mind so much where conferences were held, although one chairperson said that to hold them on social services ground gave greater security and emphasised to others that 'we carry the can'. One doctor thought that holding conferences in their own hospitals forced the doctors into 'taking over'. But it was suggested by one respondent that:

> 'People are happier in their own groove. Consultants have to be dragged outside screaming.'

Similarly, one teacher acknowledged that she felt happier on her own ground.

One suspects that this is not a trivial matter and that location and the physical arrangements generally might profitably be considered, not simply in terms of practical expediency, although that is obviously important, but, on occasions, in relation to the dynamics of a particular set of interprofessional relationships.

CONCLUSION

This paper has focused on some aspects of the process of interprofessional communication in case conferences. The research report contains additional material on the composition and purposes of the conferences, and on the role of the chairperson - vital in ensuring that conference purposes are achieved as effectively and economically as possible (ref. 7).

This small study cannot necessarily be considered as representing problems and trends generally - for there is a good deal of local variation in these matters. Nonetheless, the interviews and observation of these conferences has shed light on the case conference process and indicated some possible areas for improvement.

REFERENCES

1. cf. for example, Report of the committee of inquiry into the care and supervision provided in relation to Maria Colwell, DHSS, HMSO, (1974); Report of the review body appointed to inquire into the case of Steven Meurs, Norfolk County Council, (1975); and Report of the committee of inquiry into the provision and coordination of services to the family of John George Auckland, DHSS, HMSO, (1975).

2. cf. for example, Violence to children - first report from the select committee on violence in the family, HMSO, (1977) and DHSS circular Non-accidental injury to children, LASSL (74) 13 (1974).

3. Castle, R. L. (1976), Case conferences: a cause for concern, NSPCC.

4. DHSS circular Non-accidental injury to children, LASS L (74) 13 (1974) and DHSS circular Non-accidental injury to children: area review committees, LASS (76) 2 (1976).

5. Colwell Report, op. cit. paragraph 137.

6. Children and Young Persons Act 1969, Section 1.

7. Desborough (Hallett), C. and Stevenson, O. (1977) Case conferences: a study of inter-professional communication concerning children at risk, Social Work Research Project, University of Keele.

Child Abuse and Neglect, Vol. 3, pp. 583 - 590.
0145-2134/79/0601-0583 $02.00/0.

CASE CONFERENCES ON CHILD ABUSE: THE NOTTINGHAMSHIRE APPROACH

David N. Jones — Team Member, Nottinghamshire and NSPCC Special Unit; Chairman, British Association of Social Workers Working Party on Child Abuse Registers

Roy McClean — Detective Superintendent, Nottinghamshire Constabulary; Deputy Head Criminal Investigation Department

Roger Vobe — Assistant Director, Nottinghamshire Social Services Department

Most authors on child abuse have stressed the necessity of a multi-disciplinary approach to case management (1, 2, 3, 4). An essential feature of such co-operation, it has been argued, is the case conference. This is convened to share relevant information, share the benefits of differing theoretical and professional skills and perspectives, exchange views and discuss action. UK Government circulars have repeatedly emphasized the value of holding a conference at an early stage in case management (5, 6, 7). It would appear the practice is now universal (7, 8). However there have been criticisms of this view, for example that conferences are time-consuming and therefore expensive, inefficient at eliciting facts and an inappropriate forum for planning action, a breach of confidentiality and an erosion of professional freedom and discretion (eg 9, 10). This paper starts from the assumption that case conferences are essential to the management of child abuse, but that their operation should be considered critically. Our main intention is to present an outline of the system of case conferences which has been operating in Nottinghamshire (Notts) for over a year and which was devised in an attempt to overcome some of the criticisms. Before doing so we present a review of issues relevant to effective case conferences.

We do not intend to repeat the rationale for a case conference system, adequately presented elsewhere (eg 3, 6, 11, 12). A recent report from a working party of the British Paediatric Association and British Association of Social Workers identified eight tasks for the conference: "i) to share knowledge of and concern about the family, including parental biographies and a full family history, ii) to formulate a diagnosis and full family assessment, including degree of risk in relation to the register criteria, iii) to decide whether or not to recommend registration, iv) to formulate immediate treatment plan and long-term aims, v) to allocate responsibility for implementation of plans, vi) to nominate a key worker, vii) to decide whether to inform the parents (and child if appropriate) of the fact and significance of registration, and if so how and when this is to be done, viii) to decide an on-going review procedure" (8, 13). "The conference should consist of the smallest number of people conducive to good case management" (14). "We would expect this to embrace the social worker, health visitor or school nurse, general practitioner, paediatrician, teacher or daycare staff and senior police officer (always where there is suspicion of assault and otherwise as appropriate)" (13).

PREREQUISITES FOR EFFECTIVE CASE CONFERENCES

Case conferences are complex phenomena but little studied. Perhaps this lack of thought and research is a major reason for the widespread concern about their use and the apparent frustration of many expected to attend. The widespread use of case conferences, and the relevant government recommendations followed some well publicised enquiries into tragic deaths of certain children (eg 15, 16, 17). The reports emphasized repeatedly the results of inadequate or no communication between professionals (18). Press criticism sapped the confidence of social workers, in particular, and some seized on case conferences as a means of sharing anxiety and avoiding blame should things go wrong. To some extent this view was supported in government circulars advocating "collective decisions", although there was also recognition of the reality that such decisions could not be binding on agencies with statutory duties nor on professionals with conflicting assessments (7). We suggest that this confusion can be resolved if the conference is seen as advisory rather then executive, each agency and individual being required to assess conference recommendations and retaining the duty to act independently when his conscience and professional judgement so suggest, whilst bearing in mind the value of co-ordinated intervention. The fact that conferences rarely end in disagreement (3) does not detract from the significance of this distinction. We consider this to be fundamental to effective case conference proceedings. The following factors are also important; space prevents a full discussion of each.

1. COMMITMENT Case conferences will be futile unless there is an understanding of and commitment to the principle of inter-agency, multi-disciplinary co-ordination, not only in senior management but also other staff (especially fieldworkers). Lack of commitment results in pointless argument, inappropriate decisions and unilateral action. Commitment derives from training, positive experiences of co-operation and an ability to relate such co-operation to daily practice.

2. CO-OPERATION NOT COERCION Given limited resources, much inter-agency contact consists of one agency trying to persuade, manoeuvre or force another into certain action. This is inevitable in general but inappropriate in the child abuse case conference (12). If participants feel that one person or agency is trying to dominate discussion and dictate action, defensive manoeuvres develop, the conference becomes preoccupied with this conflict and effective communication is blocked. The quality of decisions will be poor.

3. NO WITCH HUNT The case conference should not be an enquiry into what went wrong so as to apportion blame. Mistakes may need to be analyzed, but only to prevent repetition. The task of the conference is to plan future action to help the child and his parents. Should there be a need for an enquiry into questionable practice, this must be conducted elsewhere, preferrably in private (18). If an individual feels his judgement and actions are under attack in the conference, he will become defensive and block effective communication.

4. THEORETICAL/ETHICAL AGREEMENT There must be substantial agreement between those involved about the nature of the problem under consideration and also about ethical issues, especially confidentiality. A recent study of conferences found a surprising absence of clashes of "frames of reference" (19), despite differing attitudes and training. Clearly, if one person sees all child abusers as devils who should be flogged whilst another sees them as mentally ill requiring nothing but sympathy and "tender loving care", effective communication and joint action are impossible.

5. UNDERSTAND FORMAL RELATIONSHIPS Conference members should understand the duties and limitations of those attending, which implies understanding of the functions and systems of accountability of each agency (20). It is also necessary to know what follows if the conference fails to agree, which is rare but can happen (3). In some areas the decision is referred to an ARC sub-committee of senior staff (eg 21). We consider this to be a dangerous practice, especially insofar as decisions are binding on junior staff, required to implement them possibly against their better judgement. In Notts, disagreement is rare, but when present is best handled by routine contact between senior staff and/or reconvening the conference with senior staff present.

6. PROFESSIONAL NOT HIERARCHIC The contribution of each participant, regardless of status, is significant and should be facilitated. Each person must take responsibility for his own observations and assessments. Agencies should ensure that those involved in child abuse cases are not required constantly to "refer up" all matters for decision. This creates delay and can introduce distortions, in particular the needs of the agency, which cannot be totally discounted (eg to protect itself from public criticism), may come to take precedence over the primary concern for needs of the child and his parents. Conference participants must have the assurance that reasonable and well-argued decisions will be endorsed by senior staff (who retain ultimate accountability). In turn senior staff should be prepared to allow justifiable, therapeutic risk-taking. This principle cannot be over-riding but should be pre-eminent (3, 12).

7. UNDERSTAND INFORMAL RELATIONSHIPS This is perhaps the least well documented aspect of case conferences. These can be analyzed at inidividual, group and agency levels. Child abuse conferences can be highly charged, emotional events, particularly for those with little or no previous experience of the problem and for those with contact with the family prior to the incident. Powerful feelings and defences may operate (3, 22, 23), for example denial that anything really serious has happened (a well understood defensive behaviour), anger that the client has "betrayed" a trust and let down the worker, guilt that more should have been done to prevent the incident, fear that one may be subjected to professional and public criticism and that one's future prospects may have been damaged, anxiety about an uncertain outcome perhaps including possible death of the child, jealousy that other professionals are also involved with the family, perhaps jeopardizing a previously intimate relationship, fear of losing control over the work with the family and the outcome of the investigation by being caught up in an inexorable chain of events, despair that nothing is possible to improve things.

The presence of such emotions affect not only the individual but the whole group and can distort communication and decisions. For example the conference may become angry with the individual's apparently irrational response and try to reject him or conversely may become preoccupied with sympathy and attempts to help him to the detriment of consideration of the family under review. Chairmen, in particular, need to be aware of such feelings and attempt to diffuse them. The significance of contributions by those with a heavy emotional involvement must also be carefully assessed (3). It might be appropriate for the conference to consider the implications of such strong feelings for future work with the family. Distorted communication can also follow from rigid adherence of participants to unrealistic stereotypes of other professions.

An appreciation of group dynamics is also essential. Case conferences are nothing but small, task-orientated groups. The insights of social psychology and social groupwork are therefore highly relevant (eg 24, 25 26), indeed they may offer more help in understanding conference process than a grasp of formal systems, such as those recommended by government: the DHSS guidance on co-ordination seems to view this as "the application of static procedures rather than as the negotiation of a dynamic process" (11). The conference may come to mirror the family dynamics, family conflicts being replayed by conference members identifying with particular family members; in this context insights derived from conjoint marital and family therapy are invaluable (eg 27, 28). The chairman should structure proceedings so that these dynamics assist rather than obstruct communication and decision-making. Professionals whose practice requires understanding of these processes should be at an advantage in understanding and using case conference dynamics, although in practice this is not always evident. Social workers should not restrict use of their relationship skills to contact with clients.

Good personal relationships at fieldworker level are essential to team-work and case conferences, yet are sensitive and impossible to impose, although the attitudes of senior staff are relevant. In most cases repeated contact over a long period enhances co-operation and small teams working in settled rural areas or small communities seem to be at an advantage (2). The recent rapid turnover of staff, especially in inner-urban areas and involving social workers, health visitors and junior hospital doctors, inhibits the development of essential informal networks. Senior staff should allow time for staff to make and develop such contacts.

8. FACILITATING STRUCTURES Case conference proceedings should not be formal (3), but must be structured. Work is facilitated when there is a shared understanding of purpose, an agreed agenda and a clearly identified and effective chairman (19, 23). Absence of any one of these elements will tend to lead to unco-ordinated discussion with little sense of purpose and an inability to define clear, agreed decisions. Participants will become increasingly frustrated and may engage in struggles to win over the conference to their understanding of the reason for meeting. Repeated experience of such meetings will result in lack of commitment and increasing absence of essential people. If they have not already done so, Area Review Committees should give urgent attention to these factors. Case conference chairmen should also ensure that hard fact, observation and opinion are clearly differentiated (23).

9. ABILITY TO DELIVER Commitment of individuals and agencies will wane if one or more agencies are repeatedly unable to provide services/resources identified as necessary, and unable to offer any alternative.

10. BE PREPARED It would appear that those attending conferences rarely give much prior, detailed thought to their contribution. Some suggest that key people should provide a written report. In practice, lengthy reports seem to carry less weight than oral statements persuasively argued. The presentation of voluminous written material is a waste of time; it frequently remains unread and is rarely assimilated (19), but a page of relevant factual detail (eg family names, relationships, ages, summary of medical findings and brief chronological account of events) can be valuable. Participants should not come with fixed ideas, unwilling to adapt to new information. Nevertheless some prior thought and assessment is essential and each person should be able to present a summary of their involvement without constant reference to bulky files of ill-ordered notes (23, 29). Supervisory staff should assist fieldworkers by discussion of the case and consideration of worker feelings and assessments.

11. RECORDING A detailed, accurate account of discussions and decisions is essential. Senior staff require to be informed of delicate decisions and the rationale for them; their confidence in the conference process and willingness to support action recommended will be enhanced by reliable recording. The record is also necessary as one factor in the assessment of subsequent action. Should things go wrong, a record would be required by an enquiry. Recording is a skilled task. Conferences by their nature, are discursive and conjectural,

and may involve discussion lasting two hours or more. Some argue this could be done by training clerical staff (19), but in our view recording requires professional skills of assessment and is best done by a social worker with special training and competence.

SOME OTHER RELEVANT ISSUES

The extent of police involvement in child abuse management has been the subject of much debate in this country and elsewhere (eg 2, 4, 14). Early studies of "battering parents" argued that most had such damaged personalities that they were unable to integrate "care" and "control", therapist and punisher (eg 30). This hypothesis implied that the therapist should be unreservedly accepting and not involved in any juvenile or adult court proceedings; if essential, proceedings should be conducted by another person. The former NSPCC Battered Child Research Team attempted to operate this dichotomy and have described the rather disastrous results in a very honest and enlightening section of their recent book (4). The hypothesis, coupled with a stereotype of policemen as rigid, uncaring and authoritarian, only interested in securing conviction at all costs, resulted in many medical and social work personnel refusing to involve the police. In turn the police complained that social workers and others were hiding offenders from justice. More recent experience in the UK suggests that very few parents fit the original description: "some writers have suggested that it is not possible to hold together protective and therapeutic roles but our work does not support that view in most of our cases" (31). The police in many areas have also shown themselves to be "firm yet tactful; thorough yet considerate; and objective yet compassionate" (32). It would appear that the debate has been resolved in most areas, therefore, in favour of police involvement (3, 14, 33), although social workers and doctors in one part of London recently threatened not to attend conferences if the police were invited (34). The government has recommended police involvement (35), a view supported by the British Paediatric Association, British Association of Social Workers (8) and Police Federation.

The value of police attendance is reciprocal. The police frequently possess valuable information about a family, for example calls to domestic incidents. In some cases previous criminal convictions are relevant and the 1976 circular advises disclosure of these to the conference. The police are as concerned about confidentiality as medical and social work professionals, the 1974 Rehabilitation of Offenders Act and certain court cases restricting the disclosure of criminal records. However "it seems clear that there is nothing unlawful in the interchange of confidential information at case conferences. ... the duty to respect confidence is subject to the duty to obey the law" (36). It is also our experience that police involvement rarely damages client/worker relationships, some parents expecting this and understanding and appreciating police intervention more readily than social work (33); in one case a parent sought police help several months after the incident in preference to contacting the social worker already involved. Some parents find the police investigation to be cathartic and guilt relieving whilst others are clearly distressed at the time. In Notts the police are now willing not to investigate particularly sensitive cases, but they are always informed and their views sought.

The role of family doctors in child abuse management is a matter of continuing debate (2, 7, 19). They seem to be the one group conspicuous by their absence from case conferences, with a few notable exceptions. It has been suggested that the doctor's daily routine prevents participation (3), that many prefer to work in isolation and are suspicious of team-work (37) and that many experience an acute conflict of loyalty between parent and child (19). In urban areas many family doctors seem to have little detailed knowledge of their patients and the traditional doctor/patient relationship, based on years of contact, is clearly absent. In such cases their absence from the conference may be less critical, but in general family doctors should have a crucial role. After years of exhortation, perhaps the onus is now on the medical profession to ensure adequate care and treatment for their patients by participation in the multi-disciplinary system accepted by all other groups, including other branches of medicine. One doctor has commented "the G.P. is a notorious butt for despairing neglect by other workers", adding "keep on pestering" (37).

THE NOTTINGHAMSHIRE CASE CONFERENCE SYSTEM

We now present the system adopted in Notts in an attempt to overcome the criticisms of conferences and to facilitate effective discussion and decision-making. Before doing so it is necessary to relate developments culminating in publication of the manual including procedures laid down by all agencies in contact with children in the county for the management of non-accidental injury to children (NAIC) by their staff (38). There was a prompt reaction to public and professional concern about NAIC and a multi-disciplinary Area Review Committee (ARC) was established following government advice (6). Co-terminous boundaries of Area Health Authority and County Council facilitated progress, as did the commitment of senior staff from different disciplines (police, medical, social work etc.) to developing an efficient, multi-disciplinary system.

The ARC decided initially to undertake a review of existing agency practices and attempt to agree standard procedures. Simultaneous consideration was given to different models of inter-agency co-ordination. After several months agreement was reached on the establishment of a Special Unit, administered by the NSPCC and funded by the County Council, central government and the NSPCC. The "Nottinghamshire and NSPCC Special Unit" became operational in May 1976 and is the administrative "hub" of the system. It is staffed by a Unit Leader and three Unit Members (all qualified and experienced social workers), a Unit Administrator and two administrative assistants, with Honorary Consultants in paediatrics, psychiatry and groupwork. This is one of seven NSPCC Units discussed in detail elsewhere (39, 40, 41). The Notts Unit, on behalf of the ARC, is responsible for a) the Area Child Abuse Register (41, 42), b) co-ordinating agency responses to child abuse cases, in particular by convening and recording all initial case conferences, c) offering consultation on all aspects of child abuse management, and d) providing education and training. Unit social workers also carry limited caseloads to ensure essential, continuing experience of practice (43).

The ARC also commissioned a county-wide series of seminars to a) give information about identification and initial management of cases, b) encourage development of a common knowledge base shared between staff of all agencies, and c) undermine prejudices and stereotypes held by any one discipline about others. Unit staff also spoke with all staff, prior to the Unit opening, to discuss the new procedures and Unit operation. This is being reinforced by monthly induction seminars for staff new to the county.

The inauguration of the procedures manual (38) followed 18 months of work by an ARC sub-committee (half-day per fortnight). The case conference was identified as the focus of initial management. It was agreed that each agency was responsible for its own procedures, that no one agency should be dominant and that the ARC could not dictate policy or procedures. The practice of taking votes at case conferences, apparently used in some areas, is dangerous and an abdication of responsibility by the statutory agencies. Progress in Notts was thus by the consent of participating agencies. In practice, each agency submitted its procedures to the sub-committee. These were redrafted into uniform layout for ease of cross-reference and structured around the Unit register and the case conference. The draft was ratified by the agency, following further amendment if required, and the whole manual approved by the ARC. Only minor amendment has been necessary in the first two years.

The procedures advise senior staff of participating agencies to make a register enquiry on initial suspicion of NAIC (41, 42), to establish any history of previous abuse and if present, which agency is supervising. This enquiry is not a registration. If necessary suspicion is investigated by police and social services, or the NSPCC Inspectorate (which is distinct from the Unit). If there is confirmed or suspected abuse the Unit Administrator is requested to convene a conference. The request may come from any agency (occasionally prompted by the Unit), which facilitates good working relationships and respect between agencies, although in practice most come from the social services (community or hospital teams) and the police. The conference should be held within 72 hours of the initial concern, although this is not always possible. In a few very urgent cases it has been possible to meet within 24 hours. A conference after three weeks, as advocated elsewhere (3) is unrealistically delayed. In most cases a single conference has been sufficient.

The ARC agreed that all conferences should be chaired by the SSD Area Director or Principle Hospital Social Worker and attendance should include police, health visitor, family doctor, social worker, and others as appropriate (e.g. probation, hospital staff, legal adviser). A Special Unit Member attends every initial conference as consultant and recorder. The Unit distributes minutes, including a full account of discussion and decisions. The venue is arranged to suit participants, usually the SSD office, but sometimes a hospital, health clinic or probation office, rarely a doctor's surgery, and so far never a police station, although the full ARC does meet at a Divisional Police Headquarters.

Initial reaction to the system was divided between appreciation of clear procedural guidance and fear of excessive bureaucratisation and erosion of individual discretion. However it also became clear that there was widespread frustration with conference proceedings. Criticism focussed on duration (over 1½ hours average) and time-wasting, lack of structure and of shared perception of purpose and decisions. Elimination of these problems was essential to ensure continued co-operation and commitment.

Chairmen were identified as crucial to the system and a working party was established to devise guidance and training. Management Consultants have long recognised the importance of chairmanship training but this is still comparatively new to social welfare agencies. A compulsory, two day training programme was provided for all potential chairmen, the first day being lead by a management consultant discussing group dynamics and chairmanship skills and the second considering child abuse specifically.

A standard case conference format was also devised for the guidance of chairmen, aiming to facilitate presentation of all relevant details and encourage discussion so that rational decisions could be made. The format is based on an aetiological perspective, similar to the approach advocated by the Park Hospital (44); a former member of that team, working in Nottingham, provided the first draft of the format.

The conference opens with identification of participants by name, agency and status, before any confidential matters are discussed. The chairman should then summarise the immediate reason for meeting and explain the format/agenda. Family names, birth dates, addresses are then clarified. The conference next considers the precipitating incident (ie the immediate reason for the conference including referral details, medical evidence of abuse, parental explanations to police, social workers etc., immediate stress factors). Those involved present reports in chronological sequence. Discrepancies are analyzed and discussed. It is essential to discuss these factors at the beginning. They probably generate the greatest anxiety, especially for those with prior contact with the family (see above). To attempt to conclude with the incident, as the culmination of "the critical path", whilst logical, in practice increases anxiety and distorts discussion by blocking consideration of the immediate source of anxiety. We find that there is less danger of participants interpreting all past events as precursors of the abuse if the Notts approach is followed.

Consideration is next given to the life-history and personality of each family member in turn, in order to assess future risk to children and also the need and likely prognosis for medical/social intervention (including police action). Emphasis is placed on distinguishing fact and opinion, and also on the need to consider all children in the household, not merely the abused one. Discussion concludes with consideration of responsibility for future action (ie prosecutio juvenile court proceedings, psychiatric referral, medical and social work intervention, home visiting frequency, key worker and daycare provision). The conference decides whether to recommend registration, given the accepted criteria, and if so who is to discuss this with the parents and who is to complete the Unit quarterly monitor forms. The conference does not decide, but recommends action to constituent agencies and individuals. Subsequent decisions not to follow these recommendations usually lead to a review conference. In practice, conference recommendations have been supported by senior management in all but a handful of cases (probably under 2%).

SUMMARY OF BENEFITS OF THE NOTTINGHAMSHIRE SYSTEM

1. Careful planning resulted in a viable, multi-disciplinary system involving all agencies.
2. Fieldworker commitment followed positive experiences of the benefits of the system.
3. Administration is centralised in a Special Unit but decision-making is decentralised (ie the Unit Administrator, highly skilled in convening conferences, and Unit Members, specialising in child abuse, ensure that procedures are followed and communication occurs, but case management decisions are made by those in contact with the family).
4. The belief that decisions are taken to protect the agency rather than to meet client need is now rarely expressed.
5. The co-ordinating agency (Special Unit) is geographically and administratively independent of all other agencies and is therefore perceived as "neutral". This enhances the professional credibility of Unit Members and of the reports they provide.
6. The system is predictable (ie at a time of stress and uncertainty in case management, administrative procedures are clear, releasing fieldworkers to concentrate energies on client contact, the Unit handling the time-consuming, convening of the conference).
7. Decisions are by agreement and differences recorded (ie no agency is dominant, no individual should feel coerced into agreement, Unit Members provide professional opinion distanced from other agency conflicts).
8. The Unit and system supports professionals in existing health and social agencies (ie knowledge and skills are disseminated throughout the services and not concentrated in a specialist team which in any event could not handle the volume of referrals).
9. Agency and individual accountability is clear. Individuals cannot hide behind a false sense of case conference democracy nor collective decisions.
10. A uniform, predictable but flexible case conference format reduces anticipatory anxiety, facilitates effective communication, reduces time-wasting and encourages good decisions.
11. It would appear that criticism of case conferences has dramatically declined among all professions.

REFERENCES

1. Helfer, R.E. & Kempe, C.H. (eds.) Child abuse and neglect: the family and the community, Ballinger, (1976).

2. Sussman, A. & Cohen, S.J., Reporting child abuse and neglect:guidelines for legislation, Ballinger, (1975), (especially ch 6 Child abuse reporting in four states).

3. Hall, M.H., The team approach, in Carver, V. (ed) Child abuse: a study text, Open University Press, Milton Keynes, (1978).

4. Baher, E. et. al., At risk: an account of the work of the NSPCC Battered Child Research Department, London, RKP, (1976).

5. Department of Health and Social Security, The battered baby, HMSO, London (1970).

6. Department of Health and Social Security, Memorandum on non-accidental injury to children, LASSL(74)13, CMO(74)8, (1974).

7. Department of Health and Social Security, Non-accidental injury to children: reports from Area Review Committees, LASSL (76)2, CMO(76)2, CNO(76)3, (1976).

8. British Association of Social Workers, The central child abuse register, (report of a working party, chairman D.N. Jones), BASW, (1978).

9. Lancet, The, The battered ...., The Lancet, 31.5.75, 1228-9, (1975).

10. Fry, A., NAI: danger of over-reaction, Community Care, 14.7.76, (1976).

11. Carter, J., Co-ordination and child abuse, Social Work Service, 9,22-28, (1976)

12. Tomlinson, T., Inter-agency collaboration:issues and problems, In Borland, M., Violence in the family, Manchester University Press, (1976).

13. British Paediatric Association/British Association of Social Workers, Child abuse registers: a discussion document, unpublished, (1978).

14. First report from the House of Commons Select Committee on Violence in the Family, Violence to children, 329-i, HMSO, London, (1977).

15. Department of Health and Social Security, Report of the committe of inquiry into the care and supervision provided in relation to Maria Colwell, HMSO, London, (1974).

16. Essex Area Health Authority and Essex County Council, Report of the joint committee set up to consider co-ordination of services concerned with non-accidental injury to children (after the death of Max Piazzani), (1974).

17. Lambeth, Southwark and Lewisham Area Health Authority (Teaching), Report of the joint committee of inquiry into non-accidental injury to children with particular reference to the case of Lisa Godfrey, (1975).

18. Lee, C., Official inquiries, ch. 12 in Carver, V. op. cit., (1978).

19. Desborough, C. & Stevenson, O., Case conferences; a study of interprofessional communication concerning children at risk, University of Keele, (1977).

20. Lee, C., & Roberts, B., Roles and functions of the various professions in the recognition and diagnosis of child abuse, ch 7, 8, in Carver, V., op. cit., (1978).

21. Fairburn, A.C., The monitoring system in Bath, in Franklin, A.W. (ed), Child abuse: prediction, prevention and follow-up, Churchill Livingstone, London, 71-78, (1978).

22. Kerr, A., Crisis reaction of parents and professionals to the identification or suspicion of child abuse, ch 14 in Carver, V. op.cit. (1978).

23. Stevenson, O., Obtaining and communicating good information, Ch 16 in Carver, V., op. cit., (1978).

24. Argyle, M., The psychology of interpersonal behaviour, Penguin, Harmondsworth, (1972).

25. Cross C.P., Interviewing and communication in social work, RKP, London (1974).

26. Douglas, T., Groupwork practice, Tavistock, London, (1976).

27. Skynner, A.C.R., A group-analytic approach to conjoint family therapy, Social Work Today, 2, 8, 3-11, 21-25, (1971).

28. Bloch, D. & La Pierre, K., Techniques in family psychotherapy: a primer, Grune and Stratton, New York, (1973).

29. Castle, R.L., Case conferences: a cause for concern?, NSPCC, London, (1976).
30. Court, J., The battered child, Medical Social Work, 22, 1, 11-20, (1969).
31. Pickett, J. & Maton, A., Protective casework and child abuse: practice and problems, Social Work Today, 9, 28, (1978).
32. Wedlake, M., A police view of the present position, in Franklin, A.W., op, cit, (1978).
33. Arthur, L.J.H. et. al., Non-accidental injury in children: what we do in Derby, British Medical Journal, 1, 1363-6, (1976).
34. Morris, P., Police: by invitation only, Community Care, 208, (1978).
35. Department of Health and Social Security/Home Office, Non-accidental injury to children The police and case conferences, LASSL(76)26, HC(76)50, HO 179/76, (1976).
36. British Association of Social Workers, Confidentiality in social work (report of a working party, chairman P. Oakley), BASW, (1977).
37. Stone R., GPs and child abuse, in Franklin, A.W. op. cit., (1978).
38. Nottinghamshire Area Review Committee, Non-accidental injury to children:guidance notes and procedures, Notts County Council, (1976).
39. Owtram, P.J., NSPCC Special Units, Social Work Service, 8, 8-11, (1975).
40. Pickett, J., The management of non-accidental injury to children in the City of Manchester, In Borland, M. op. cit., (1976).
41. Jones, D.N. et. al., Central child abuse registers: the British experience, paper presented to the Second International Congress on Child Abuse and Neglect, (1978).
42. Hill, K.P., Evaluating inquiries to the Notts NAI register, Social Work Today, 9.29, 19-20, (1978).
43. Aims and Structure of the Nottinghamshire and NSPCC Special Unit (1976).
44. Lynch, M.A., Risk factors in the child: a study of abused children and their siblings, ch 4 in Martin, H.P.(ed), The abused child, Ballinger, (1976).

ACKNOWLEDGEMENTS

We acknowledge the help and co-operation of Nottinghamshire Constabulary and Social Services Department, colleagues in both agencies and Members of the Notts and NSPCC Special Unit. We are also indebted to Rhoda Oppenheimer, who provided the first draft of the case conference format.

Roy McClean and Roger Vobe, together with Dr. Peter Barbor (Consultant Paediatrician, Nottingham Children's Hospital), are external lecturers on the management of child abuse cases at the National Police Training College.

Child Abuse and Neglect, Vol. 3, pp. 591 - 600.
Pergamon Press Ltd., 1979. Printed in Great Britain.

THE ISSUE OF REINJURY : AN AGENCY EXPERIENCE

Thomas E. Taw

N.S.P.C.C. Special Unit, Manchester, England.

INTRODUCTION:

Modern society delegates responsibility to record, control and prevent behaviour it defines as a problem. That licence may be questioned if it becomes thought the behaviour is not being prevented.

Thus in child abuse, one review, assessing a 60% 'incidence of rebattering', concluded 'the procedures for handling these cases were ineffective', and moreover related this incidence to the treatment style. In other contexts, e.g. criminal offenders and psychiatric patients, respective rates of recidivism are a conventional index of comparison between different techniques and philosophies. But is this index valid in child abuse?

This paper studies the issue of reinjury, as experienced in a specialist child abuse agency, by both quantitative and qualitative methods.

QUANTITATIVE:

This comprises the record of reinjury during the agency's five years practice. The agency practices social casework with a restricted number of families and also performs management, consultative and educational functions within a major conurbation. (Maton and Pickett, 1978) The services available to families taken on for treatment have several advantages over those more generally available: the potential for intensive contact with families by professionally qualified social workers and health visitor; 24 hour availability; and Therapeutic Day Centre for both children and parents. For this reason accepting a family for treatment is regarded as a significant act. A child of the family must have been notified to the Register for Suspected Non-Accidental Injury to Children (henceforth referred to as 'the Register'). Typically, although not exclusively, this means the child has sustained a non-accidental injury at the hands of an adult caretaker.

Reinjury:

To produce findings, one has to decide first whether the event under inquiry has occurred. In this case 'reinjury' means 'subsequent suspected non-accidental injury'.

As described above, a child's 'registration' is a necessary requirement for the agency's acceptance of the case. The primary condition for 'reinjury', and therefore the base line of this study, is that it is notified to the Register. The Register includes three categories of injury: previous; notified; and subsequent. It is entries to this latter with which we are concerned.

There are several reasons for this choice. The nature of the work is such that references to incidents of varying status abound in case papers. For example, a parent may allege having inflicted, or threaten or express fear of inflicting an injury for which there is no visible evidence. The Register was chosen because:

a) it made the research manageable and comparable. In England there is already a tradition of research based upon the Register into which this would seem to fit.

b) it is explicitly the medium to which actual injuries, rather than alleged or promised attacks, are notified.

c) notwithstanding b) it is assumed that where a significant act of abuse has occurred, even where there is no injury, it is likely to be notified e.g. one entry contained allegations of sexual offences, admitted by the 'father', where medical examination revealed 'no virgo intacta' but no 'other' injuries.

However not all notifications are included. The Register uses the following five point Index of Suspicion:

'1) CERTAIN

2) VERY SUSPICIOUS

3) SUSPICIOUS

i All cases where the injury could conceivably have been caused in the manner described but where the history and/or circumstances of the family indicate a high level of risk e.g. history of serious deprivation, the presence of chronic or acute stress, previous history or suspicious injury, etc.

ii Where there is inadequately explained ingestion of toxic substances.

4) ACCIDENTAL

Injuries medically confirmed as accidental, or witnesses as accidental by a reliable observer.

5) PRODROMAL'

Only those injuries rated 1, 2 or 3 are included in this study. I have quoted in full the guidelines for 3 and 4 because it represents a boundary of my research. Given that one must acknowledge that an injury may not be medically confirmed as accidental, nor witnessed by a reliable observer, and yet could have been caused in the manner described. If so, the potential notifier is thrown back on the 'high level of risk' condition. If he feels that family circumstances do not meet this condition there appears no appropriate category. Two caseworkers, taking the same view of the injury and the family circumstances, could notify the injury, one to category 3 the other to category 4. Of course potential notifiers of subsequent injury may not follow this 'fine print'. Additionally it may be held that by definition, all families with whom the agency works, or even all those where a child has been previously registered, constitute a 'high level of risk'.

A further condition relates to another sense of the term 'subsequent'. Injuries are included in this study only if they occur during the agency's work with the family. Injuries occurring before and after this period are excluded. This is because the study is concerned with 'reinjury' as an index of treatment effectiveness.

Similarly one must not only specify when a relevent 'reinjury' can occur but to whom it can occur. A child may be reinjured, but a family is taken on for treatment. Is each child in the family then subject to the same risk ? A previous study's criterion for the battered child was: 'all those (injuries) for which there was no definite proof of accidental cause'. The criterion for siblings differs significantly 'out of a possible total of 32, 7 siblings were thought to have been injured by their parents'. (Baher and colleagues 1976, p.173)

Children also need to be 'available for possible injury in the home.' (Baher and colleagues 1976). It follows that a fuller study might relate 'reinjury' to the time a child spends at home. Insufficient time, as well as data complications, prevented me doing so, or relating 'reinjury' to a timescale of work with the family, or comparing the 'seriousness' of 'injuries'.

The criteria for children included in the study are therefore;

a) in a family each individual child who is notified to the Register and/or has been subject to a statutory order of a Juvenile Court as a result of abuse to a sibling. My choice of the

Register as base line means there is no medium, nor would there appear to be the same criteria, in notifying 'subsequent injuries' to other siblings.

b) the relevant child must have been at home sometime after the 'notified injury'. In other words children removed from their parents' home who did not return are excluded. This rationale in fact influences the administration of the Register. The fact that a child is in 'permanent care' frequently leads to a premature end to the 'monitoring' which is part of registration. In addition, where monitoring does continue, answers to the question 'is the child still at risk?' typically refer back to the 'natural parents' e.g. 'not as long as she remains in care'.

Change of Management Plan:

A record of 'subsequent injury' is only part of the story. How the professions respond is another. Just as the agency regard initial injury as a necessary precursor to their involvement, preventing 'reinjury' is a significant objective. Conversely failure to prevent 'reinjury' can be reason to question the direction of treatment.

Documentary analysis of case records, the agency having high standards in this regard, allows these responses to be characterised thus:

a) no (distinguishable) change in management plan.

b) gross change i.e. usually the child's separation from his home (e.g. under statutory proceedings, hospitalisation, reception into care) but also the perpetrator's removal from the home (e.g. into custody).

c) qualitative change i.e. some other decided change of plan. Usually this falls into one of three categories: pattern of visiting; talk with the family, often involving expressions of concern; and environmental provision, varying from day care placement to the purchase of a toilet seat.

RESULTS 1973-77

a) Overall

Total cases taken on for treatment	82[1]
Children relevantly involved	99
Children ruled out of study	13
Children subsequently 'injured' i.e. each occasion on which 'subsequent injuries' were notified	33
Children not subsequently injured	53
% of children, relevantly involved and meeting the research conditions, who have been subsequently 'injured'	38%
Total number of subsequent 'injuries'	100
Number of children with one subsequent 'injury'	16
" " " " two " 'injuries'	8
" " " " three " 'injuries'	3
" " " " four " 'injuries'	2
" " " " more than four subsequent 'injuries'	4

b) Responses.

Responses to all subsequent 'injuries'

No change - 57 : Gross change - 22 : Qualitative change - 21

Responses where there has been only one subsequent 'injury' : (16 children)

No change - 3 : Gross change - 10 : Qualitative change - 3

---

[1]There were in fact 81 cases. However, one case taken on in 1974 involved a child who did not return home. The agency continued casework to protect another child, born 1975. To facilitate 'breakdown by year' I have chosen to regard these as two separate cases.

Responses to all first subsequent 'injuries':

No change - 14 : Gross change - 12 : Qualitative change - 7

Responses to 'injuries' to children with 1-3 subsequent injuries: (27 children)

No change - 15 : Gross change - 19 : Qualitative change - 7

Responses to 'injuries' to children with 4 or more subsequent 'injuries' : (6 children)

No change - 42 : Gross change - 3 : Qualitative change - 14

c) Breakdown.

Cases taken on for treatment 1973-1974	28
Children relevantly involved	32
Children ruled out of study	7
Children subsequently 'injured'	14
Children not subsequently injured	11
Percentage subsequently 'injured'	56%
Number of subsequent 'injuries'	31

Responses

No change - 14 : Gross change - 10 : Qualitative change - 7

Cases taken on for treatment 1975	29
Children relevantly involved	35
Children ruled out of study	3
Children subsequently 'injured'	15
Children not subsequently 'injured'	17
Percentage subsequently 'injured'	47%
Number of subsequent 'injuries'	56

Responses

No change - 35 : Gross change - 10 : Qualitative change - 11

Cases taken on for treatment 1976-1977	25
Children relevantly involved	32
Children ruled out of study	3
Children subsequently 'injured'	4
Children not subsequently 'injured'	25
Percentage subsequently 'injured'	14%
Number of subsequent 'injuries'	13

Responses

No change - 8 : Gross change - 2 : Qualitative change - 3

DISCUSSION:

Do these findings accurately record 'reinjury', its significance, and its relationship with work done, either as an indication of effectiveness or as reason for 'change of management plan?' Unfortunately I think it does none of these.

A fundamental weakness of 'recidivist' studies is 'hidden evidance' i.e. equivalent behaviour which is not so defined and recorded. (Creighton and Owtram, 1977; Taylor, Walton and Young, 1973). The effect of differential 'visibility' (Pickett and Maton, 1977) and the difficulties of subjecting 'control' groups to the same criteria are formidable problems in using the data comparatively. At best it is a negative indicator: 'it is quite impossible to demonstrate statistically that reformation, when it does occur, is due to the treatment process'. (Vold, 1958; also Baher and Colleagues, 1976).

Secondly, although my criteria represents the most manageable and comparable instrument of measurement, it has considerable flaws. Variability in interpretation and use of the Register inevitably occur. Entries under 'subsequent injury' vary between one minor injury and 'multiple bruising and abrasions'. The term 'abusing incident' was suggested as more accurate. However 'abusing incident' is a more general concept and the Register does not require their registration. Like 'alleged assaults' they are occasionally noted but typically remain in casework papers. Nevertheless, 'abusing incidents' without visible injury have led to fundamental changes in management plans, including the child's removal from his home.

Moreover the case papers reveal several minor injuries, about whose status doubt is expressed, which were not 'registered'. A major problem is the 'counsel of perfection' involved in the notification criteria: 'all injuries, however minor, and regardless of whether they are thought to be accidental or non-accidental'. It is very doubtful that this criteria is applied literally. For example, a nursery noted 26 occasions when Seymour B had injuries, of which 19 were 'registered' (one as 'accidental'). Incidentally, his sister Hannah had 8 injuries but, not being registered, she was not in this study. Similarly another caseworker found it 'interesting' that Donald, previously 'overprotected', received injuries on 5 separate occasions within 24 days, of which one was 'registered'. The relationship between 'registered' and 'non-registered' injuries is by no means simple.

Sometimes, several incidents or injuries are lumped together. For example, one case involved a period when a Care Order was revoked before it was reinstituted. Entries for this period read:

> 'Sept/Nov. Seen on several occasions with bruising which may be non-accidental.
> May. Twelve further lots of bruising and scratches - no adequate explanation.
> 'various dates: repeated pattern of minor bruising continues.' I would emphasise such entries are exceptional.

Finally, the concept 'reinjury' differs from 'subsequent' in one important respect. It carries the implication there has been previous non-accidental injury. Despite the seriousness with which the agency takes its criterion of actual non-accidental injury, this study includes cases where either there has not been an injured child or, more usually, in retrospect the injury probably was accidental.

One case, deep in the agency's mythology, illustrates the point:

> "we started working on a false basis ... it soon became apparent that the parents' explanations were absolutely right so there was no question of N.A.I., but by this time we had become committed to the family so we continued working with them, a very demanding and needing family in other ways. After a couple of years we began to limit that dependency ... and it was when the caseworker first started saying "well look the time is coming when I'll not be coming to see you any longer". It was then with the threat of losing the social worker that the mother first injured one of her children. It was a moderate injury, a bruise inflicted in the context of chastisement".

This case in fact posed the greatest dilemma for the research categories, although the status of the initial injury was not part of the dilemma. The case was taken on in 1973 with one child injured and 'registered'. It was to be closed when another, older child sustained an admitted non-accidental injury. In other words each child, 3 years apart, received one initial injury. Yet the agency however clearly viewed it as a 'reinjury' in 'the case' and continued casework, a 'qualitative change'.

Although the most difficult, there were several similar 'boundary adjudications' to be made (e.g. a 'subsequent' injury before the 'initial injury' was officially 'registered'). I felt with each succeeding decision I did further violence to the reality of what I was studying.

My innovation also ultimately proved false. Although agency records are of high standard and search was made of all contemporary reports it would be idle to pretend that all changes in 'management plan' are recorded. Rarely too are responses such as 'gross change' due solely to the injury. Typically it is a complex matter and a cumulative process over time, in which the actual injury may play a small part. All one can properly say is the 'gross change' followed the injury.

'Qualitative change' depended upon statements of decided change and as 'actions' often did not carry conviction. Even then the 'changes' sometimes had a tenuous relationship with the injury. There were also inevitable 'boundary adjudications' with 'no change'.

The force of these remarks is not simply directed towards technical aspects of collecting and presenting statistics. These are inevitably the product of the understandings, decisions and interactions between society, deviants and agents of social control (Wiles, 1971). It might serve us better therefore to approach the issue of 'reinjury' more directly.

QUALITATIVE

Whatever 'reinjury' indicates of treatment effectiveness, it remains a sensitive and problematic event for the professional. The following account aims only to sketch some areas of significance, illustrated by a case example, rather than provide a thoroughgoing analysis. However qualitative research could achieve the latter. My methods involved participant observation, documentary analysis and interviews with workers in post.

Such efforts rely on the assumption that when professionals decide a child has been or might have been abused and take action, even if no action, their decisions are ultimately based on a socially accredited body of knowledge which they methodically use. The aim is not to guess which interpretation of events will be made in any given situation, or arrive at criteria for deciding which interpretation is correct. It is rather to discover the inferential procedures and presumptions informing the interpretations that can be made.

First one must review the social distribution of acceptable and/or likely contexts of injury. I have already incorporated such presumptions in the 'quantitative' study. I stipulated that once a child goes into 'care' the issue of likely further non-accidental injury goes into abeyance. Similarly a recurring theme in parental explanations of reinjuries are claims that 'it happened at nursery'. Whatever other judgement is made, caseworkers routinely assume that if it did happen in nursery it loses significance from a 'non-accidental' perspective. In general the physical location of injury, and the numbers and status of those present are significant factors. Further inquiry might explore other issues. For example, when in retrospect the original injury is regarded as accidental; when the actual perpetraor, when known and perhaps legally identified, is no longer within reach of the child; when grandparents have become caretakers; or when only one child is thought likely to be physically abused.

Secondly a central concept in child abuse is 'discrepancy', initially discrepancy between the injury and its explanation. But in any particular situation the nature of the discrepancy will inform the nature of permissible accounts for it. Amongst 'areas of discrepancy' commonly used one can number: the child's development, parent/child interaction; incongruous conduct; parental talk about the child, the attitudes, beliefs and emotions expressed.

On the other hand, explanations delivered with appropriate concern for the child, the conventions of description and the circumstances of the injury, can forestall suspicions of non-accidental injury. That is, if other things stand up e.g. the nature of the child's contribution and the context of the injury; medical opinion; evaluation of biography; the family's acceptance of help; the extent to which a possible act of commission is also understandable as an act of omission.

I need to say something more about 'reinjury's' effect on talk with families. A continuing concern for caseworkers is the extent to which, and the occasions on which, 'injury' is a subject for talk. As described above, parental explanation forms the basis for 'negotiating reality' (Scheff, 1966) about an injury. An important theme for caseworkers is how far talk about 'reinjury' needs to be bounded. That is, the circumstances in which such talk can be left in a general conversational context or needs to be made a special occasion, in which, unilaterally if necessary, the caseworker raises it as a significant issue. Such an occasion can occur at the 'investigative' stage or when the caseworker needs to make explicit his opinion of the injury, or its implications (see Case Example).

Thirdly an important factor is the degree of seriousness and visibility of an injury. Visibility has two dimensions; physical visibility; and visibility as 'non-accidental' material. Each of these varies along a continuum from, respectively, an injury no one sees/everyone accepts as accidental; through, an injury seen by some combination of lay and professional people/its 'accidental' status is subject to various degrees of doubt or dispute; to, an injury to which a parent draws attention and admits inflicting.

The interaction of these dimensions matters a good deal. For example, a neighbour complained about a parent's rough treatment of a child and noticed unusual bruises on his back. The complaint led to the child being examined in nursery the following day. There was a bruise which the nursery had seen previously and had considered too commonplace to make 'visible' to the caseworker. The fact of the bruise's presence the day before took away the force of the original complaint, whilst in turn the complaint caused a re-examination of the injury, including 'talk' with the parents.

The order in which different participants come onto the scene can also matter. For example, on Thursday the nursery reported fresh bruises on a child's cheek and below her eye. They thought it happened outside nursery. The caseworker visited and the parents told him the bruises hadn't been there that morning. On the following Tuesday the health visitor reported seeing bruises to cheek and near the eye. The parents said the caseworker knew about this. Nevertheless, and despite the nursery being unaware of further injury, the caseworker made an abortive home visit; a visit to grandparents; and a further home visit in which he insisted the child was brought down before satisfying himself there was no doubt the bruising was the same. This was a case at a low point where there had been several other injuries.

The seriousness of an injury can outweigh 'non-accidental' considerations. Or, as the 'agency boss' put it, referring to the serious injury discussed below, 'the very fact of the child being hurt is enough'. The following exchange also makes this point:
Agency Boss: '(this injury) came to us with a medical diagnosis as accidental and it seemed consistent enough so it didn't raise the same sort of questions that the other case did'.

Q: 'But no one suggested that wasn't accidental?'

A.B.: 'Right, but these injuries are not so serious as that one'.

This wider concern differs somewhat from other areas of deviancy ascription e.g. 'insanity' (Coulter, 1973, p.138), where professionals seem aware of the necessity to distinguish between <u>this</u> case, as an example of insanity or child abuse, and ordinary behaviour e.g. childhood accidents - however serious their consequences - which are similar in some ways.

Nevertheless, caseworkers are routinely conscious of the extent to which natural justice requirements e.g. thresholds of proof and suspicion, can warrantably be laid aside. In particular, references to injuries frequently take into account how far the weight of evidence would impress a Juvenile Court.

It may already be clear that the meaning attributed 'reinjury' is a complex interplay of things to do with the injury as such, and more general issues concerning the family.

> 'Whenever a caseworker goes into a family ...... in the process of getting to know that family, talking with them, and so on, they come to have a set of perceptions about that family, where their problems are, how they function and how they relate.'

How does 'reinjury' effect this state of affairs? First, at routine times the caseworker, being most directly involved with the family, is largely in control of how the case and family is viewed. 'Reinjury' constitutes a crisis in which this balance is disturbed, at least temporarily:

> 'we need to do a check on our own understanding of that family because it may be the reinjury is saying that we've been missing the way .... the opportunity should be taken, has to be taken where there's reinjury of revising one's whole concept of the case because its easy in the ongoing flow of casework for the caseworker to find himself in a rather comfortable rut, really.'

Secondly, the distinction between 'injury' and 'general' issues can influence where energies are directed:

> 'with the first injury much energy goes into getting a medical diagnosis .... (subsequently) less energy would go into establishing the medical diagnosis .... but the same sort of high degree of energy and emphasis should go on, where there is reinjury, into what's going on in the family, and why that reinjury has occurred'.

Referring to the serious but 'accidental' injury discussed below, and the questions it raised about family dynamics, the same respondent claimed:

> 'we are really dealing with two quite different definitions of suspected abuse in regard to the injuries.'

Thirdly, in constructing the meaning of 'reinjury' in a particular family, workers bear in mind certain practical commonsense ideas about 'injuries' e.g.

> 'there is always the fear that if an injury happens, however it occurs, that if its part of a pattern and happens again it will happen at the same severity or greater.'[2]

Finally one must refer to the concept of 'tolerance'. As the findings illustrate, some cases involve 'frequent' reinjury without apparent change of management plan. Caseworkers sense when they can warrantably tolerate this, balancing the 'worrying aspect' with more positive indicators.

Case Example:

Ray (2½) had suffered 'a high number of logged incidents of possible or suspected abuse', before the agency took over casework. These stopped but the family continued to puzzle. Ray and brother Harold (4) remained slight, pale and hyperactive: 'one of the features of this particular family is that its been very difficult consistently to get to grips and really pinpoint the underlying problems and their overt symptoms.'

The caseworker planned to close the case. Then in Christmas week he was surprised at the incongruity of Mother intending to spend the holiday on her own at her mother's. Over the Christmas, Ray broke his collar bone. After interviewing both parents, largely about their five day delay in seeking medical attention, the caseworker concluded:

> 'the children are very active, Ray in particular and I feel it is likely that the child's injury was the result of an accident but that probably occurred because Father was a bit overwhelmed by the children and left Ray to play unattended in his bedroom'.

The casualty doctor was 'surprised at the delay because he thought there would have been a lot of pain'. There was nothing to suggest non-accidental injury but any associated bruising would probably have cleared up and it was difficult to assess the cause when it was not seen at the time.

After a further home visit, the caseworker commented:

> 'the explanation is consistent, the delay may be due to Christmas and Father's worry over the consequences. Doctors think its accidental which is likely because a fractured clavicle is atypical of N.A.I. and it is the kind of injury often received by little children climbing around.'

In this account one is struck by how much is added to the parental explanation even, on occasions, in the face of their denial e.g. asked whether fear of what people might say caused his delay, Father replied 'no, because it was an accident' and moreover Ray only showed pain when he undressed for bed.

To his supervisor the incident was 'out of the blue'. To the caseworker, recalling his pre-Christmas visit, it was 'almost too much of a coincidence'. Nevertheless, 'I do not think this latest incident is any reason for prolonging my involvement'.

A month later Ray suffered facial and back injuries, having 'fallen from his stool'. The caseworker initially 'phoned the nursery who confirmed Ray was 'always climbing'. Visiting, he heard Mother had again stayed away overnight. Father explained the injuries, denied inflicting them but questioned his ability to cope when Mother was away. They had

---

[2]See Skinner and Castle (1969) and Creighton and Owtram (1977) for opposing research findings concerning this hypothesis.

decided he would not be left again.

The caseworker felt strongly entitled (see discussion on 'talk') to 'make it clear to Mother that she was equally responsible for what had happened because she had left Father alone, and this not long after Ray had a fracture when she left Father to cope over Christmas'.

Father said he didn't want the caseworker to stop coming - he felt safer. The caseworker concluded:

> 'almost a year and now two serious injuries so quickly. I still feel the clavical was an accident although he was left unattended. Notwithstanding this happening, Mother left Father again and I wonder even more about her relationship with the children. I find this second injury less acceptable .... perhaps he hit him causing the fall'.

Thus, although the first remains 'accidental', the two injuries are intrinsically linked:

> 'the fact is you've now got two injuries of the same kind in the same sort of circumstances where the mother has buzzed off ... they forced us to look around at a particular aspect of this family's dynamics which we'd missed up to then ..... that raises questions about causation that we want to test out, think about, the rationale being that having some idea as to cause, then by tackling that root we can prevent those sorts of situations arising again where the child will be hurt whether in this particular case by true accident, inadvertence, neglect or inflicted injury'.

Discussion

We have seen that parental explanation is essential to the process of inquiry. Notwithstanding, judgements upon 'reinjury' routinely occur in settings (either talk between caseworker and supervisor or, in more serious instances, a case conference) to which parents are not party. Criminal charges being rare, it is comparatively unusual to resolve unequivocally the status of a 'reinjury' which a parent denies inflicting. This leaves room for a variety of ad hoc connections between the injury and what is happening in the family.

In this case some embodied commonsense presumptions designed to suggest Ray should be removed from home: when do you say enough's enough: if you don't remove him, nothing will have changed; the severity of the injuries is escalating; why is this child always 'query battered'.

Other links e.g. references to the children being 'very active' and 'always climbing' suggest the ordinariness of the incidents. Thus, to counter arguments that Ray should be removed, 'it seemed to me (caseworker) only fair to the parents to let people know that Ray had received a similar injury to the laceration in the Day Nursery' i.e. an acceptable context.

However, the above account generally makes connections whose message is - 'something wrong'. Even so, these links are only sustained if we overlook alternative, ordinary meanings. For example, the two injuries are linked together in a 'pattern that up to now has been repeated twice'. Subsuming two events in this way invites contortionism: 'the second reinjury and the repeating pattern that that highlighted reinforced the first one and the first the second, right'.

Similarly, 'Mother going away' is the fundamental link, 'raising questions' about family dynamics - 'some problem in the marriage'/'her relationship with the kids' - although she went away on other occasions without mishap.

Finally, the first injury was understood in terms of Ray being left 'unattended' while his father was 'overwhelmed'. Is it abnormal for a 2½ year old to play unattended in his bedroom? Similarly, if 'accident' it was, is it relevant to the injury whether or not his father was 'overwhelmed'?

The caseworker's rebuttal of such queries seems fundamental to the whole process: 'because I think it's quite possible it would'nt have happened in a different household.'

Given the dual concern with 'injury' and 'whole family', and the 'openendedness' of the routine 'reinjury' inquiry such connections seem endemic. They can be understood as linking these two elements of the caseworker's task and providing a sense of control - through-understanding, even if retrospectively. They also provide a guide for future action. The meanings given 'reinjury' are influenced by the caseworker's sense of what room there is for change; in his face-to-face work with the family; in manipulating the environment; and in legal action. Thus, in response to pressure for 'care proceedings', this caseworker argued: 'work has now got something to go on - the question of Mother leaving the child'. In the event, 'as a last resort we brought Mother and child into our nursery to help her and see if it would make any change'.

N.B.

Incidentally, neither injury qualified for my 'quantitative' study; the first being registered 'accidental'; the second falling outside the research period.

REFERENCES.

MATON, A. and PICKETT, J (1978)

'The Multi-Disciplinary Team in an urban setting: The Special Unit Concept'.
A paper presented to the Second International Congress of Child Abuse and Neglect, London, 1978.

BAKER, E., HYMAN, C., JONES, C., JONES, R., KERR, A., MITCHELL, R (1976) "At Risk: An account of the work of the Battered Child Research Dept. NSPCC", Routledge, Kegan Paul, London.

MARRAN, B., MATON, A., OWTRAM, P., PICKETT, J., ROSE, R. (1976) 'Registers of Suspected Non-Accidental Injury: a report on registers maintained in Leeds and Manchester by NSPCC Special Units, ' NSPCC, London.

CREIGHTON, S. and OWTRAM, P. (1977)
'Child Victims of Physical Abuse: A Report on the findings of NSPCC Special Units' registers', NSPCC., London.

MATON, A., and PICKETT, J. (1978)
'Protective casework and child abuse: practice and problems', Social Work Today. Vol. 9 No. 28, 10-18.

VOLD, G.B. (1958) 'Theoretical Criminology' Oxford U.P. London, p.295.

TAYLOR I., WALTON, P AND YOUNG, J. (1973) 'The New Criminology', Routledge, Kegan Paul, London 11-19.

WILES, P.(1971) 'Criminal Statistics and Sociological Explanation of Crime' in 'Crime and Delinquency in Britain' ed. Carson, W. and Wiles, P. London.

SCHEFF, T. (1966) 'Negotiating reality: notes on power in the assessment of responsibility', Social Problems 16 (Summer) 3-17.

COULTER, J. (1973) 'Approaches to Insanity. A Philosophical and Sociological Study', Martin Robertson, London.

SKINNER, A. and CASTLE, R. (1969) '78 Battered Children: A Retrospective Study', NSPCC, London.

Child Abuse and Neglect, Vol. 3, pp 601 - 605.

0145-2134/79/0601-0601 $02.00/0.

AN EPIDEMIOLOGICAL STUDY OF CHILD ABUSE

Susan Jean Creighton

N.S.P.C.C., 1 Riding House Street, London W1P 8AA

ABSTRACT

An analysis is presented of 905 cases notified to N.S.P.C.C. Special Unit Registers of Suspected Non-Accidental Injury during 1976.

INTRODUCTION

In 1976, thirteen per cent of the child population of England and Wales were living in areas covered by Registers of Suspected Non-Accidental Injury. These were maintained by N.S.P.C.C. Special Units sited in Manchester, Leeds, Newcastle upon Tyne, Northampton, Coventry, Nottingham and Goldthorpe. The areas covered by their Registers in 1976 included both Metropolitan Counties and Districts and Non-Metropolitan Counties. Children aged less than 16 years* living in these areas were notified to their Register if they fulfilled the following criteria:-

> "All physically injured children where the nature of the injury is not consistent with the account of how it occurred or where other factors indicate that there is a reasonable suspicion that the injury was inflicted or not prevented by any person having custody, charge or care of the child. In exceptional circumstances, children who have neverrreceived a suspected non-accidental injury but are considered to be at serious risk of injury by the notifier, may be accepted for registration".

905 such children were registered with N.S.P.C.C. Special Units in 1976, mostly by Social Service Departments. Of these, 656 had been injured and 249 were thought to be at serious risk of injury. This represents a registration rate of 0.68 per thousand children and an injury rate of 0.5 per thousand children less than 15 years old. Amongst the injured were 12 children whose injuries were subsequently judged to have been caused accidentally. The data on these has been excluded from the analysis.

The injured children were divided into five categories depending on the type and severity of their injury. These categories were 'Fatal', 'Serious', 'Moderate', 'Failure to Thrive' (F to T) and 'Sexual Abuse'. The 249 uninjured children notified to the Registers as being at serious risk of non-accidental injury were assigned to a separate 'Prodromal' category. All cases which resulted in death, where the cause of death was medically confirmed to be due to non-accidental injury were put in the 'Fatal' category. 'Serious' injuries included all fractures, head injuries, internal injuries, severe burns and ingestion of toxic substances. 'Moderate' injuries included all soft tissue injuries of a superficial nature. Infants and children whose weight fell progressively below that expected for their age, and where there was no medical explanation for the condition, were registered in the 'Failure to Thrive' category. The 'Sexual Abuse' category comprised those children suspected of having been sexually abused but without any accompanying physical injury. Seven children were fatally injured, 91 seriously and 520 moderately, 24 failed to thrive and there were

---

*Four years in Leeds Metropolitan District

two cases of sexual abuse. Three of the dead children came from one family, where the father had killed them, his wife and the cleaning lady, before setting fire to the public house where they lived and committing suicide by throwing himself into the flames.

Table 1 shows the breakdown of cases by severity of injury.

TABLE 1 Number of Registered Children by Severity of Injury

Severity of Injury	Number of Cases	Percentage
Fatal	7	(1.1)
Serious	91	(14.1)
Moderate	520	(80.8)
Failure to Thrive	24	(3.7)
Sexual Abuse	2	(0.3)
Rate per 1,000 under 15's*	0.5	
Accidental injuries	12	
Prodromal	249	
Total registered	905	
Rate per 1,000 under 15's*	0.68	

*Population estimates, 1976 (O.P.C.S., 1977)

The majority of the injured children (81 per cent) received soft tissue injuries only, mostly bruising, with the head and face the commonest site. The percentage of moderately injured children in the sample was larger than that of a previous study (Creighton and Owtram, 1977) on the children registered with the five N.S.P.C.C. Special Units operational in 1975. There was a corresponding decrease in fatal and serious injuries from 22% in 1975 to 15% in 1976. The absolute numbers, as well as the percentages, of fatal and serious injuries fell between the two years in spite ot an increased sample size. The types of injury which have shown the largest decrease have been skull fractures, brain and eye damage i.e. serious head injuries. In view of the concern shown by various authors (Oliver, 1975; Eppler and Brown, 1977) at the proportion of children amongst the mentally retarded population whose symptoms seem to have been initiated by an incident of abuse, this decrease in serious head injuries, since the introduction of registers and their associated management procedures, is an encouraging sign.

THE CHILDREN

The injured children differed significantly from the national distribution of children aged less than 16 in their age, sex and birthweight. They were younger, more likely to be boys and had lower birthweights even when social class was controlled. The younger the child the more likelihood there was of the injury being serious, a finding which has been shown in other epidemiological studies (Friedrich, 1976; Gonzalez-Pardo and Thomas, 1977).

Table 2 shows the distribution of the different categories of severity of injury by the age of the child.

Boys outnumbered girls in the ratio of 5:4 in each group except the 0 - 6 months and the 15 - 16 year olds. Gil (1970) and Friedrich (1976) found that over the age of 12 years girls were more likely to be reported than boys, which Gil ascribed to parental panic at their adolescent daughters' burgeoning heterosexual relationships. The preponderance of girls in the 0 - 6 month age group of the 1976 data is more difficult to explain.

TABLE 2 Severity of Injury by Age of Child

Age of Child	Severity of Injury Fatal	Serious	Moderate	F to T	Sexual Abuse	Total %
0- mths	2 (28.6)	25 (27.4)	36 (6.9)	7 (29.2)		(10.9)
6- mths	1 (14.3)	13 (14.3)	35 (6.7)	4 (16.7)		(8.2)
1- yrs		17 (18.7)	62 (11.9)	4 (16.7)		(12.9)
2- yrs	1 (14.3)	20 (22.0)	121 (23.3)	8 (33.3)		(23.3)
4- yrs		2 (2.2)	43 (8.3)		1 (50)	(7.1)
5- yrs	1 (14.3)	8 (8.8)	145 (27.9)	1 (4.1)		(24.1)
10- yrs	2 (28.6)	5 (5.5)	71 (13.7)		1 (50)	(12.3)
15-16yrs		1 (1.1)	7 (1.3)			(1.2)
Totals	7 (100)	91 (100)	520 (100)	24 (100)	2 (100)	(100)

Information was available on the birth weight of nearly half the sample of injured children. Of these, some 16.1% weighed less than 2,500 grams at birth. This is significantly more (Chi square = 53.2 with 6 df. $p < .001$) than the national distribution of 7.9% for Social Classes IV and V and 'Unsupported Mothers' taken from a recent representative sample (Chamberlain et al., 1975). The birthweights of the 'prodromal' cases showed a similar distribution. There was a high rate of illegitimacy amongst the sample compared to national distributions controlled for age of mother (C.S.O.,6). If only the cases with information on legitimacy are considered the figure rises to 30%. Friedrich (1976) and Smith (1975) found similar rates amongst their samples.

34.5% of the injured children had been injured on a previous occasion, a similar percentage to that of the children registered in 1975. The children who had been injured before registration were, on average, four months younger than those without such a history.

THE PARENTS

Only 52% of the injured children were living with both natural parents at the time of the incident. 22% were living with their mother and a father substitute and 20% were living with one parent alone, usually the mother. These atypical parental situations are associated with a high rate of marital discord in the registered child's family at the time of the incident. Of all the stress factors thought to have had a possible contributory effect, marital discord was cited most frequently.

The mean ages of the male and female caretakers were 30 and 26½ years respectively. The male caretakers were in mainly semi-skilled and unskilled occupations and a third of them were unemployed at the time of the incident. 34% of the male and 12.4% of the female caretakers had a criminal record. Males were just as likely to have committed violent as non-violent offences whereas females were four times as likely to have committed non-violent crimes. Although the ratio of violent to non-violent offences is higher in males than females in the general population (C.S.O.,7) it is not as marked as in this sample.

There was information on the perpetrator in two thirds of the cases. Mothers or mother substitutes were suspected in 44% of these cases and fathers or father substitutes in 46.5%. Siblings, other relatives, other adults or children were implicated in the remainder. In those families where there were two natural parents mothers were suspected in 37% and fathers in 55% of the cases. In families where there were mother or father substitutes, the substitutes were suspected of injuring the child twice as often as the natural parent. When compared to the families with two natural parents the mothers with father substitutes don't differ significantly but the fathers with mother substitutes do (Chi square = 5.1 with 1 df. $p < .025$). There was a slight tendency for mothers to injure younger children and fathers older ones and also for mothers to injure their children more seriously.

Fathers were over twice as liable to prosecution as mothers even though adult court proceedings were brought more often in the case of serious injuries.

THE FAMILIES

Just over half the injured children came from families with three or more children. The equivalent percentage for the national distribution of unskilled and semi-skilled workers is 29.1% (C.S.O.,6). Family sizes ranged from 1 to 12 with an average of 2.9 children. This over representation of large families in the register sample can be partly attributed to earlier parenthood. The injured child was three times as likely to be born to a mother aged less than 20 years as a child from a similar socio-economic background.

Although 50.8% of the children came from families with three or more children 76% of them were either the first or second born in their families. Both the family size and birth order distributions of the injured children differed significantly (Chi square = 196.9 for family size and 17.3 for ordinal position with 3 d.f. $p < .001$) from national samples of similar social class with the register sample having larger families and more fourth and later born children. The differences intween the sample and national distributions in family size were considerably more marked than those of birth order however. This complex interaction between family size and ordinal position was also found in the sample registered in 1975.

THE ENVIRONMENT

The families'type of accommodation, tenure and amenities were found not to differ quantitatively from the national distribution for similar social classes. Nearly half the sample had been living in their present accommodation for less than a year and 30% had been there for less than six months. Only 8% had been resident for over five years compared to 70% for manual workers generally (C.S.O.,6). The mobility of families with abused children remarked on by Gil (1970) is shown clearly in this sample.

The four most frequently quoted stress factors judged to have been present at the time of of the notified injury were marital discord, financial problems, unemployment and a poor self-image on the part of the parents. That this period was a stressful one for the families is indicated by the fact that over 50 per cent of them had four or more stress factors present then.

SUMMARY

There were more school age children registered in 1976 than in previous years, in line with the growing concern of the education authorities over the problem of child abuse. The features which distinguished the 1976 sample from national distributions controlled for social class remained the same. The youngest age groups, boys and low birth weights were all over represented amongst the injured children whilst early parenthood, large families and abnormal family structures, low social class, high unemployment and mobility characterised their parents. In spite of this seeming lack of change workers in the field should be encouraged by the continued decrease in serious injuries, and serious head injuries in particular, shown in successive register samples.

REFERENCES

Central Statistical Office (1975) Social Trends 1975 (no.6), HMSO, London.

Central Statistical Office (1976) Social Trends 1976 (No.7), HMSO, London.

Chamberlain, G.V.P., Chamberlain, R. and Claireaux, A. (1975) British Births 1970, Heinemann, London.

Creighton, S.J. and Owtram, P.J. (1977) Child Victims of Physical Abuse, N.S.P.C.C., London.

M. Eppler and G. Brown, Child abuse and neglect: preventable causes of mental retardation, Child Abuse and Neglect, 1, 309 (1977).

W.N. Friedrich, Epidemiological survey of physical child abuse, Texas Med., 72, 81 (1976).

Gil, D. (1970) Violence against Children: Physical Child Abuse in the United States, Harvard University Press, Cambridge, Mass.

L. Gonzalez-Pardo and M. Thomas, Child abuse and neglect: epidemiology in Kansas, J. Kansas Med. Soc., 78, 65 (1977).

Office of Population Censuses and Surveys (1977) Population estimates 1976 (provisional) 1975 (revised), PP1 no.2, HMSO, London.

J.E. Oliver, Microcephaly following baby battering and shaking, Brit. Med. J., 2, 262 (1975).

Smith, S.M. (1975) The Battered Child Syndrome, Butterworth, London.

Child Abuse and Neglect, Vol. 3, pp. 607 - 614.

0145-2134/79/0601-0607 $02.00/0.

CHILD ABUSE IN INDIA AND NUTRITIONALLY BATTERED CHILD

A. K. Bhattacharyya

Department of Nutritional and Metabolic Diseases
School of Tropical Medicine, Calcutta 700073, India

ABSTRACT

Four available papers on a total of 12 Indian battered baby cases and one unpublished case are reviewed. The clinical and aetiological patterns conform to classical accounts. Although the reported cases are very few, the condition may not be so uncommon under changing social conditions. Impairement in growth and development or death of children resulting from widely prevalent malnutrition and preventable infections in the background of poverty and its concomitants, is considered child abuse in a wider sense and the literature is reviewed. The term, "Nutritionally Battered Child" is suggested for the victim of prolonged and severe protein-energy malnutrition showing extreme failure of growth and development. A brief account of measures that have been adopted in an attempt to protect the huge child population at risk is given.

INTRODUCTION

Cruelty to children has been for ages, a part of human behaviour all over the globe (Ref.1) and India is no exception. Accounts of infanticide are available in Hindu mythology and there are anecdotes on children being sacrificed for achieving devine favour in ancient times. It was only in the earlier part of the ninteenth century that the prejudicial practice of throwing children into the holy river Ganges at its mouth where it enters the Bay of Bengal was abolished by law. Female infanticide was practised by the Rajputs, faced with the difficulty of getting their daughters married (Ref. 2). Infanticide perhaps existed elsewhere in the country for various other reasons. Corporal punishment was very common in schools about three decades back.

These forms of cruelties to children differ considerably from willful but unadmitted and often repetitive physical abuse which is characteristic of the classical 'battered child syndrome' (Ref. 3), now called 'non-accidental injury', in the United Kingdom and 'the abused child' in the United States. With growing concern for healthy child growth and development however, the problem of child abuse should be considered in a much wider sense. While physical assault is commonly reported from the affluent countries, children are subjected to various other forms of inhuman treatment in the socio-cultural and economic milieu of the third world.

With the object of showing the nature and extent of the problem of child abuse in India, this paper (i) reviews briefly the few published Indian reports of classical battered baby cases, (ii) puts forward a wider concept of child abuse and describes the prevailing forms including nutritional deprivation and (iii) characterises two hitherto unrecognised syndromes of prolonged and severe protein-energy malnutrition (PEM) suggesting the term 'nutritionally battered child' for the victim of either syndrome.

CLASSICAL BATTERED BABY CASES IN INDIA

The First Report

A 22-month-old girl and her 10-month-old brother, from a middle income family, were admitted to the hospital attached to the Calcutta School of Tropical Medicine, in April 1966 for having recurrent painful swellings of limbs during the previous 3 months. Radiological pictures were suggestive of multiple fractures of long bones, epiphyseal separations and periosteal reactions. Subsequently, it was revealed that a caretaker subjected the sibs to repeated physical assaults out of jealousy. The sibs could be protected against further abuse. When these two cases were presented in a Clinical Meeting (Ref. 4), the condition seemed to be unknown to the audience. Hence, they were reported subsequently in detail with a review of the literature (Ref. 5).

Subsequent Studies

The author has come across only four papers (Ref. 5,6,7,8) on battered child syndrome in India giving accounts of altogether 12 cases. One case recently seem by the author remains unpublished. Of these 13 cases, 3 were from Calcutta, 2 from Bombay, 3 from Madras and 5 from Poona. Two were newborns and the ages of others were between 1 and 6 months in 3, 6 and 12 months in 2, 18 and 24 months in 4, and 24 and 30 months in 2; 6 were males and 5 females and the sex was not reported in 2. The socio-economic condition (of the 12 families) was high in 2, medium in 2, low in 2, very low in 1 and not stated in 5. The nature of the injuries were : bony fractures with or without epiphyseal separations and periosteal reactions in 7 (involving multiple long bones in 5, multiple long bones and skull bone with ecchymoses and burn scars in 1 and only one humerus in 1), compression fractures of ribs in 1 (newborn), only periosteal reactions in 1 and repeated epistaxis and bruises in 3. One was brought to hospital as having died suddenly. A jealous caretaker was the batter in 2 sibs, a hostile female cousin in 1, the mother in 7 and the father in 1, In 2, the batterer could not be identified but in 1 the father was probably responsible. The battering was caused by the mother in one case as the baby had harelip and cleft palate, she being the sixth successive child born with such defects. Unhappy relations with the husband due to presence of a co-wife was responsible in another. In the third case, the mother was deserted by her husband following the birth of the baby and she felt that the child was responsible for all the misfortune that had befallen her. Three other mothers injured their children (epistaxis and bruises) as "he/she is too bad and gets on to my nerves" (Ref. 8). Yet another had already 6 children and was not keen to have another. The battering father of one 18 month-old child, brought dead to the hospital, without any external injury (autopsy not permitted), developed one year later a psychiatric illness resulting from a guilt complex and confessed of having beaten the child for a minor fault, never thinking of fatal consequences (Ref. 8). Except in this case and in another, the assaults were repetitive in all others and 3 (out of 13) died. Failure to thrive was recorded in only 2.

Comments

The causes of child abuse in the Indian cases reviewed here, do not differ essentially from those reported from the developed countries. In India, remarkable socio-economic changes have taken place during the last three decades. There is increasing urbanization but facilities for housing, transport, good schools and recreation are often very inadequate. Also the age-old large joint families are being replaced by nuclear families and the number of working mothers are increasing. They have fewer children (mostly one or two) now but there is often no creche for the babies and usually they are looked after by maids. In the economically weaker section of the community, poverty may contribute significantly towards child abuse. The environmental factors are therefore unfavourable and there must be many parents psychologically prone to be batterers (Ref. 9). It is very likely that physical assault does occur and many cases go unreported. But despite these, it also appears that the magnitude must be much less in comparison to that in the developed countries. However, socio-anthropological studies must be very extensive to throw any light on the possible magnitude and nature of child battering in a country like India.

CHILD ABUSE IN A WIDER SENSE

The Concept

Human development. A WHO Scientific Group (Ref. 10) has considered that human development embraces every aspect of the maturation process taking place in the human life cycle. It is characterised by phases and transitional events. The development of the child begins in the mother's womb with the fertilisation of the ovum and continues in the subsequent phases - the foetal life, the breast dependence and weaning ages and the pre-school and school years. It is influenced by genetic factors and directly or indirectly, by environmental factors - physical, chemical, biological and social - of which economic condition of the family, education and cultural beliefs and changes in human setting (urbanization for example) are very important ones. Healthy development depends upon the utilization of many areas of scientific knowledge and many components of the health service such as nutrition, communicable diseases, human reproduction and many others. There are critical periods of growth and development (Ref. 11) and clinical and experimental observations show that nutritional failure at younger ages can have permanent consequences.

Child abuse. In accordance with the concept of human development quoted above, one can justifiably suggest that child abuse should be defined in a wider sense, as impaired development of a child for a considerable period or death resulting from any adverse environmental factor that could otherwise be prevented to operate on the basis of scientific knowledge and adequate health services. Further, if this insult is of such a nature in duration and degree that it causes physical disability or mental impairment or both persisting throughout life, this must be considered a very serious form of child abuse. The factors responsible for such child abuse are broadly those involved in healthy child development. The critical period is upto the pre-school age.

The Background

Country size and population. India is a vast subcontinent with an area of about 32.8 million square kilometers and according to 1971 census (Ref. 12), a population of 548 million. About 80% lives in nearly 0.6 million villages with poor transport and communication systems and 20% in about 3000 cities and towns. Children under 14 constitute 41.6% and children under 6, 17% (115 million) of the population. Child mortality (described later) is high but this is over-compensated by high birth rate (35.2% in 1975) and a fall in crude death rate (14.7%) resulting from increase in the average life expectancy (46.4 for males and 45.6 for females) during the last 30 years.

Poverty. A substantial proportion of the population lives below the poverty line or the subsistence level. At 1960-61 prices, this has been considered to be at the level of per capita annual income of 340 Indian rupees or about 43 dollars. In terms of 1973-74 consumers' expenditure, those having a monthly income of 61.80 rupees in rural areas and those having a monthly income of 71.30 rupees in cities are taken to be below the poverty line. According to various sources 40% to 60% of the people live under the poverty line and 25% are very poor. About 40% of the 115 million children live under the poverty line (Ref. 12).

Unemployment. At present, there are about 10 million educated and enlisted unemployed persons. A substantial proportion, particularly from the rural areas is not enlisted and there is a huge illiterate and unemployed or underemployed mass.

Illiteracy. In 1971, the literacy rate, excluding the children under-five, was 21.48% for females and 45.28% for males and 33.84% for the females and males combined. The literacy rate for the urban population was 59.7% compared to only 27.0% for the rural population. 86% of children enter school, those who do not are mostly girls or children from weaker sections of the community. However, of those enrolled in schools, only 40% reach grade V and only 25% reach grade VIII (Ref. 12).

Housing problem. In most cities, accommodation is inadequate and too costly. Many live in congested and filthy slums. In Calcutta, it has been estimated that about 35000 dwell in pavements where babies are also born and reared.

Child feeding. There is a declining trend in breast feeding, depriving the child from the natural, and hygienic food of great economic value (Ref. 13). Otherwise, breast feeding is an usual practice particularly in rural areas. It is often prolonged but hardly adequate after 6 months. However, the proportion of capable mothers varies in different parts of the country (Ref. 12,14,15,16,17). Supplements usually consists of diluted and/or insufficient cow milk or powder and gruels prepared of barley, sago, rice etc. Solids are started after 6 months or even later and complete weaning to cereal-based diets is achieved by 18 months of age in the majority (but not in all) under 'favourable' circumstances. Obviously, this diet is nutritionally inadequate in energy, protein and most other nutrients.

Socio-cultural aspects. The socio-cultural complexities and diversities of the vast Indian subcontinent are intriguing. A huge poor and illiterate or poorly educated mass living in its rural and tribal areas follows largely a traditional life (with old customs and beliefs and methods of child feeding and rearing) which however, is continuously being subjected to modifications under the influence of several rapidly developing industrial zones. The 1971 census recorded that 19.87% of the population was urban. In 1961 census, this figure was 17.98%. However, as the population has increased, actually much more people now live in urban areas. For various reasons, the impact of family planning programmes has fallen mostly on higher income group. Low income families, both in urban and in rural areas, are often larger families (5 or 6 children) with larger number of children of lesser ages; infections and severe nutritional deficiencies are also more frequent in such families (Ref. 12,15). Morbidity depends more on family income rather than on its unitary or joint character (Ref. 12).

Medical education and health services. The western-model of medical education followed in the Medical colleges is not considered suitable for the country's need (Ref. 12,18,19,20,21). The young speciality of paediatrics is developing fast but mostly in teaching institutions. As stated elsewhere, "paediatric nutrition receives almost fragmentary consideration in our undergraduate teaching" (Ref. 19). Health services available mostly in cities and towns are not adequate particularly for the low-income group. However, the real problem is rural health care. The Primary Health Centre, each for a population of about 80,000 to 120,000 and with subcentres, at an average of one for every 10,000 population, functions to provide medical services in all possible forms to in-patients, out-patients and the community. Insufficient medical and paramedical manpower and administrative factors are important reasons for the unsatisfactory working of this vast infra-structure (Ref. 21).

Forms Of Child Abuse

Mortality and morbidity. Perinatal mortality rate (1969 figure) is 63.8 and still birth rate 22.1. Infant mortality rate (1971 figure) is 122 (81 in urban areas and 131 in rural areas) (Ref. 12). Of the total mortality, 37.5% is contributed by mortality in children under 5 years of age (Ref. 22). Only 72% of all those born alive complete 5 years of age. Of the perinatal deaths, 60 to 70% are associated with low birth weight, notably due to maternal malnutrition (Ref. 12) which is directly related to socio-economic status (Ref. 23). By far the most important causes of high childhood morbidity are communicable and preventable infections and malnutrition and very often one favours the other worsening the situation. The morbidity pattern is fairly uniform for rural or urban areas (Ref. 12). Available data based on hospital statistics show that intestinal infections constitute 7 to 15% of all admissions of under-fives. Also of the total admissions in all age groups, 30 to 40% are for all intestinal infections and 55 to 70% for all cases of enteritis and other diarrhoeal diseases in under-fives (Ref. 12). The concept of weanling diarrhoea (Ref. 24) is helpful to understand the effect of inadequate weaning food contaminated with infections. Bacterial invasion of small bowel is a significant cause of diarrhoea in malnourished children (Ref. 15,18). The incidence of common intestinal parasitic infections (ascaris, giardia, hookworm and amoeba) in different parts of the country varies from 13.2 to 78% (Ref. 12,25). Respiratory tract infections (bacterial and viral), boils, measles, diphtheria, whooping cough and tetanus (notably neonatal) are significant contributors to mortality and morbidity (Ref. 12,15). Available epidemiological data indicate the prevalence of tuberculosis in children below the age of 14 years as 2.7%. The annual incidence of new cases is 1.09% and 40% of child population below 14 years and 25% of those below 6 years are positive tuberculin reactors (Ref. 26). Pulmonary, meningeal, visceral and miliary forms are common in hospital practice and 30% of those with meningeal lesions die (Ref. 27). About 20% of severely malnourished children have pulmonary lesions radiologically, this being vary advanced in 8% (Ref. 15).

Malnutrition. By far the commonest form of nutritional failure in children is protein-energy malnutrition (PEM) (Ref. 15). A survey has shown that amongst the under-fives, clinically 2% suffer from severe forms of PEM and 20% from mild-moderate forms (Ref. 28). The prevalence of mild-moderate cases will be much higher (60 to 80%) if anthropometric criteria are used (Ref. 29). In view of the high mortality and morbidity (Ref. 15,22) and significant dwarfism and delayed mental development (Ref. 30), PEM must be regarded as a serious form of child abuse and neglect. Two other nutritional deficiencies, xerophthalmia and rickets, produce permanent and serious disabilities. Xerophthalmia is seen in 2 to 5% of pre-school children (Ref. 16,28). About 20% (Ref. 15) of those with severe PEM develop keratomalacia, a most important cause of preventable blindness. Nutritional rickets occurs with varying regional prevalence, this being 1.8% (Ref. 16) in Calcutta. At times it takes very severe atrophic forms (Ref. 31).

Some classical battered baby cases may fail to thrive. This is well known. Conversely however, as a malnourished child lacks in charm and demands more parental care, thereby decreasing their earning capacity, he may be deprived of affection. It is not known whether this leads to any physical assault or intentional neglect contributing towards recurrent malnutrition commonly observed (Ref. 30).

Exploitation. Born in poverty and squalor, brought up under deprivation of minimum pre-requisites for healthy development, the lives of a large proportion of children are obviously miserable and they have no future. On the contrary, many of these poor human offsprings are exploited in various ways. Under economic compulsions, low income families, use their manual labour in agriculture and in urban areas, they are employed in small trades, in houses, hotels and restaurants (mostly boys) or in hazardous jobs at a very tender age. The worst form of exploitation is however, beggary which ruins the very social and psychological make-up of the growing mind. Beggary is common in children of pavement dwellers in Calcutta and in some other areas (but not in all cities). It is also seen in temples, railway stations and trains. Some are blind or posses grotesque physical deformities. The fact that they are seen to survive for several years in pitiable health, in the same locality raises strong suspicion that the crippling has been done deliberately by their 'care-takers'. Yet another sin is to trap somehow, very young girls to utilise them later as prostitutes. Some reports appear at times in news papers on these types of child abuse but the magnitude has never been assessed and it is impossible to substantiate these reports.

NUTRITIONALLY BATTERED CHILD

Common Types Of PEM

The clinical types of severe PEM, commonly seen in Calcutta (Ref. 15) are : the fatty type including 'classical kwashiorkor' and 'kwashiorkor without dermatosis' and the wasted type including 'nutritional marasmus' and 'marasmic kwashiorkor'. Anthropometrically, both the types show growth failure. Compared to Harvard standard, usually, in the fatty type the weight for age is between 50 and 60%, the height for age between 75 and 85% and the weight for height between 70 and 90% and in the wasted type these are between 35 and 45%, 65 and 85% and 50 and 70% respectively. A common milder form is 'pre-kwashiorkor' which shows no oedema, wasting or skin change but the weight for age, the height for age and the weight for height are usually as low as in the fatty type (Ref. 15,32). The WHO classification on PEM (Ref. 33) is inadequate for many children and particularly for those with pre-kwashiorkor. In a survey, 11% of under-fives were below 60% of weight for age but only 1.83% were clinically marasmic (Ref. 17).

Nutritionally Battered Child

It is generally accepted that a child with kwashiorkor may subsequently develop marasmus if treatment is inadequate and a marasmic child may come later with marasmic kwashiorkor. Less commonly, after a period of recovery, a marasmic child may develop 'fatty' kwashiorkor. Majority of children with severe or mild-moderate PEM survive, get accustomed to a cereal-based family diet and reach population normal and a smaller proportion dies (Ref. 30). However, occasionally weaning is grossly unsatisfactory, intercurrent infections recur too frequently and it may so happen that (i) the pre-kwashiorkor state lingers for years, no history (admittedly, may not be reliable in all) of oedema or emaciation is available and the child remains incredibly small or (2) the child suffers recurrently from kwashiorkor or marasmus with short periods of incomplete recovery from either condition but somehow escapes death. In these two situations, the resulting pictures are extremely severe types of PEM, not described in the available literature. The first type has been called (Ref. 34) 'Prolonged Pre-kwashiorkor' (PPK) and the second (Ref. 35) 'Recurrent Kwashiorkor-Marasmus' (RKM). A detailed study of these syndromes will be published elsewhere but their chief characteristics are described here. Serial photographs of two typical cases are given (Figs.1,2). While PEM should be regarded as a serious form of child abuse, the term, "Nutritionally Battered Child" is suggested particularly for a child with PPK or RKM as both the syndromes result from prolonged and/or repetitive assaults of very severe malnutrition. The prevalence of these syndromes in the community is not known but PPK and RKM were diagnosed in 40 (0.73%) out of 5460 children attending the under-seven Tropical Paediatric Clinic during 1973-1977. During 1967-77, 37 such children, aged 2 to 7 years, could be hospitalised and followed up. The characteristics common to PPK and RKM are : (1) age 2 to 7 years, (2) gross dietary deficiency of energy, protein and other nutrients from early infancy, (3) recurrent diarrhoea and/or respiratory infections, (4) extreme retardation in growth (compared to Harvard standard, weight for age 25 to 40%, height for age 60 to 70% and weight for height 55 to 75%) and development (inability even to stand and to talk), (5) significant hypoalbuminaemia, (6) moderate anaemia, (7) no apparent cause of failure in growth and development except malnutrition and associated infections and (8) clinical and biochemical improvement with adequate diet given for 3 to 6 months in the hospital when they gain in weight, learn to stand, walk and talk but develop a state of dwarfing with still grossly low weight for age and height for age and normal weight for height. The distinguishing features between RKM and PPK are wasting and oedema which are recurrent in RKM but surprisingly not seen in PPK. The long-term effects on physical and mental developments remain to be studied.

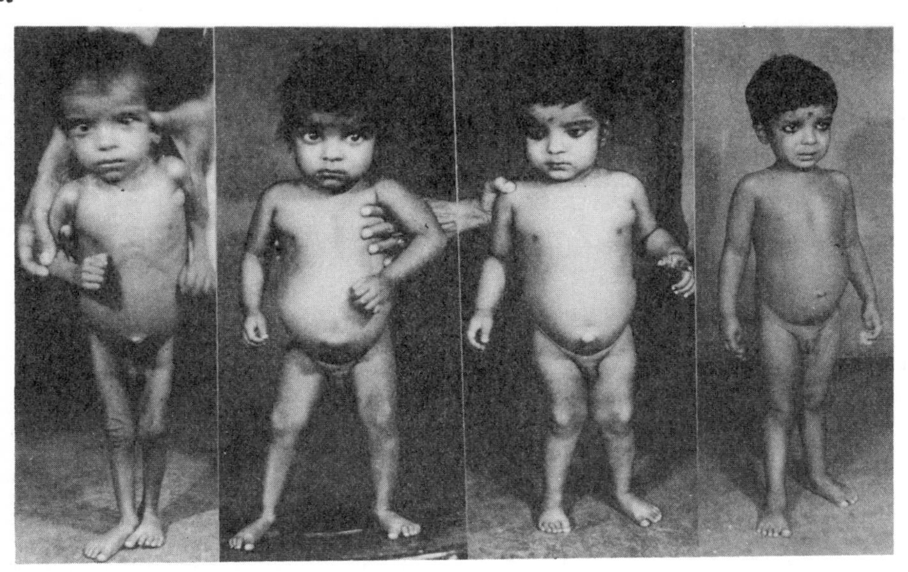

Fig.1. A child with 'Prolonged Pre-Kwashiorkor'. From left to right, first picture on 19.11.74: age 56 months, weight (Wt) 4.7 kg , height (Ht) 64.5 cm, head circumference 44.5 cm, compared to Harvard standard, weight for age (WA) 26%, height for age (HA) 60%, weight for height (WH) 64%, unable to stand and talk. Very thinly built but had no loose skin folds, typical of marasmus. Second picture on 20.1.75 (58 months), third picture on 20.5.75, (62 months), Wt 10.0 Kg (WA 50%), Ht 71.5 cm (HA 63%), WH normal; still unable to stand without support. Discharged on 12.6.75. Fourth picture on 9.4.77 (85 months), Wt 13.1. kg (WA 53%), Ht 96.0 cm (HA 77%), WH 90%, head circumference 49.9 cm (allowance for hairs); able to walk and talk.

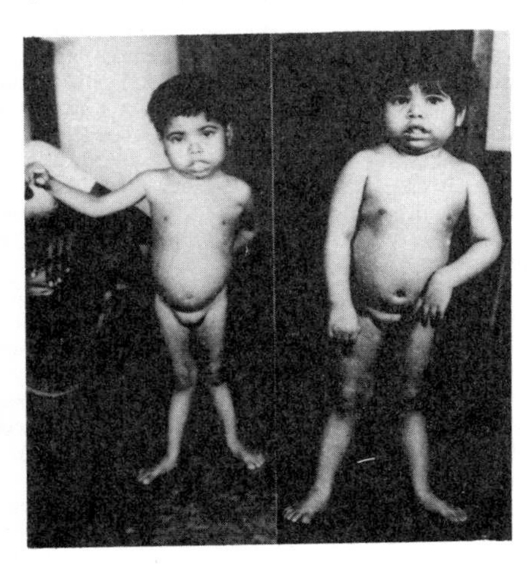

Fig.2. A child with 'Recurrent Kwashiorkor-Marasmus'. Left : on 6.7.77, age 84 months, Wt 7.78 kg, WA 33%, Ht 78.0 cm, HA 64%, head circumsference 44.2 cm, unable to stand without support, talked one or two words; no wasting or oedema; mother said that she had improved a little after her last illness 2 months previously. Right: on 29.9.77, age 87 months, Wt 11.04 kg, WA 45%, Ht 82.0 cm, HA 65%, WH 97%, could walk and talk. This child died of acute diarrhoea and vomiting in home in June, 1978.

PROTECTION

It will be grossly incorrect to assume from the foregoing discussions that nothing has so far been done to protect the huge child population at risk against abuse in the wider sense. The

Constitution of the Republic of India have specified the needs of the children and the duty of the community in meeting them adequately. In fact, there have been many attempts (Ref. 12, 36,37) to improve the situation. Measures adopted by the Indian Council of Child Welfare and the Department of Social Welfare under the five-year plans, through the network of social welfare institutions and community programmes, indicate special concern for the physical, emotional and social care of children. Also there are provisions in the special laws relating to children for their welfare, development and protection. Many States have passed anti-beggary legislation. In others, Municipal and Police Acts provide for measures against begging. Provisions have also been made for rehabilitation and healthy development of children found begging. Factories Act, 1962, statutorily lays down for establishment of creches in every factory where the number of women employees exceeds 50. Employment of young children in factories, shops and establishments is also governed by law. There is definitely increasingly more move to improve health care for rural people, school health and child health services, health and nutrition education and education of children. Reorientation of paediatric medical education has also been under consideration keeping in mind the national needs. More and more emphasis has been laid on the implementation of family planning programmes. The Integrated Child Development Services (ICDS) scheme which is now being implemented in a number of project areas is a step towards human resource development. ICDS provides a package of services : supplementary nutrition, immunisation, health check-up referal services, health and nutrition education and non-formal pre-school education. With encouraging results, the project areas are being gradually extended. However, it would appear that the different measures that have been adopted so far are perhaps too many. Successful implementation of them depends on the co-ordination of several governmental departments and this may be difficult to achieve due to bureaucratic affairs. Failure to involve the community is another important deterrent.

ACKNOWLEDGEMENT

Grateful thanks are due to Prof. A.B. Chowdhury, Director, School of Tropical Medicine, Calcutta, for his kind permission to publish this paper. It is regreted that of the works that have been consulted, many important ones, particularly the individual contributions to the book, "The child in India" (Ref. 12), could not be quoted.

REFERENCES

(1) Radbill, S.X. (1968) A history of child abuse and infanticide. In The Battered Child, Ed by R.E. Helfer and C.H. Kempe, University of Chicago Press, Chicago.

(2) O'malley, L.S.S. (1976) Indian Caste Customs, Rupa & Co, Calcutta.

(3) C.H. Kempe, F.N. Siverman, B.F. Steele, W. Droegemueller and H.K. Silver, The battered child syndrome, J. Amer. Med. Assoc. 181, 17 (1962).

(4) A.K. Bhattacharyya, Multiple fractures. Bull. Calcutta School Trop. Med. 14, 111 (1966).

(5) A.K. Bhattacharyya and J. N. Mandal, Battered child syndrome : a review with a report of two siblings, Indian Pediatr. 4, 186 (1967).

(6) S.M. Merchant, B.D. Patel, J.C.N. Joshipura, S.G. Daftary and J.V. Khatri, The battered child syndrome, Pediatr. Clin. India, 2, 170 (1967).

(7) B.R. Santhanakrishnan, M. Vasantakumar Shetty and V.B. Raju, PITS syndrome, Indian Pediatr. 10, 97 (1973).

(8) M.L. Magotra, Battered baby syndrome, Arch. Child Hlth. 18, 41 (1976).

(9) Court, J. (1974) Characteristics of parents and children. In The Maltreated Child, Ed by J. Carter, Priory Press.

(10) WHO (1972) Human Development and Public Health, Technical Report Series No 485, Geneva.

(11) V. Ramalingaswami, Nutrition, cell biology and human development, WHO Chronicle, 29, 306 (1975).

(12) Gupta, S. Ed (1977) The Child In India, Indian Pediatrics, New Delhi.

(13) Berg. A. (1973) The Nutrition Factor, Brookings Institution, Washington, D.C.

(14) B. Belavady, Nutrition in pregnancy and lactation, Indian J. Med. Res. 57, 8 (1969 August Suppl).

(15) A.K. Bhattacharyya, Studies on kwashiorkor and marasmus in Calcutta (1957-74), I. aetiological and clinical studies, Indian Pediatr. 12, 1103 (1975).

(16) M.K. Chaudhuri, Nutritional profile of Calcutta pre-school children II. clinical observations, Indian J. Med. Res. 63, 189 (1975)

(17) M. Chowdhury, N.Dutta, A.Sarkar and B.Dey, Breast feeding by urban mothers. J. Indian Med.Assoc. 70, 221 (1978).

(18) Morley, D. (1973) Paediatric Priorities In The Developing World, Butterworth & Co (Publishers) Ltd, London.

(19) A.K. Bhattacharyya, The need of pediatric nutrition units, Calcutta Med. J. 68, 233 (1971).

(20) A.B. Chowdhury, Tropical diseases in the tropics, J. Indian Med. Assoc. 69,246 (1977).

(21) B. Roy Chaudhury, Rural health care : problems and priorities, J.Indian Med.Assoc. 70, 230 (1978).

(22) V. Seth and O.P. Ghai, Mortality in protein-calorie malnutrition, Indian Pediatr. 9, 163 (1972).

(23) N.D. Datta Banik, A Study on incidence of different birth weight babies and related factors, Indian Pediatr. 15, 327 (1978).

(24) J.E. Gordon, I.D. Chitkara, and J.B. Wyon, Weanling diarrhoea, Amer. J.Med.Sci. 245, 129 (1963).

(25) S. Madan, S.P. Ghosal and P.C. Sengupta, Intestinal parasitosis: its relation to diarrhoea in Indian children, Indian Pediatr. 14, 899 (1977).

(26) H.B. Dingley, Tuberculosis in India, Indian Pediatr. 13, 879 (1976).

(27) P.M. Udani, U.S.Bhat, S.K.Bhave, S.G. Ezuthachan and V.V. Shetty, Problem of Tuberculosis in children in India - (epidemiology, morbidity, mortality and control programme), Indian Pediatr. 13, 881 (1976).

(28) Indian Council of Medical Research (1974) Studies on Pre-school Children, Technical Report series No 26, New Delhi.

(29) Gopalan, C. and Vijayaraghavan,K. (1971) Nutrition Atlas of India, National Institute of Nutrition, Hyderabad.

(30) A.K. Bhattacharyya, Studies on kwashiorkor and marasmus in Calcutta (1957-74) III. therapeutic and follow-up studies, Indian Pediatr. 12, 1125 (1975).

(31) A.K. Bhattacharyya, and K.N.Dutta, Atrophic rickets (with case reports), Indian J. Radiol. 30, 267 (1976).

(32) A.K. Bhattacharyya, Pre-kwashiorkor, Bull. Calcutta School Trop. Med. 21, 17(1973).

(33) Waterlow, J.C. (1976) Classification and definition of PEM. In Nutrition In Preventive Medicine, Ed by G.H. Beaton and J.M. Bengoa, WHO Monograph No. 62, Geneva.

(34) A.K. Bhattacharyya, Prlonged pre-kwashiorkor, Bull. Calcutta School Trop. Med. 23,22(1975).

(35) A.K. Bhattacharyya, Recurrent kwashiorkor-marasmus, Bull. Calcutta School Trop. Med. 26, in press (1978).

(36) R.P. Devadas and N.K. Murthy, Nutrition of the pre-school child in India, Wld. Rev. Nutr. Diet. 27, 1 (1977).

(37) R. Rajalakshmi and C.V. Ramakrishnan, Formulation and evaluation of meals based on locally available foods for young children, Wld. Rev. Nutr. Diet. 27, 34 (1977).

Child Abuse and Neglect, Vol. 3, pp. 615 - 621.

0145-2134/79/0601-0615 $02.00/0.

"KIDNAPPING" A SOCIAL EVIL

Dr. Meenakshi N. Mehta*, Dr. Shalini S. Bhatt**, and M. G. Gore***

*Prof. of Pediatrics, **Asst. Prof. of Pediatrics, L.T.M.M. College & Hospital, Bombay, India
***Chief Officer & Secretary, Children's Aid Society, Bombay, India

ABSTRACT

Kidnapping has become an important social and judicial problem over the years. Parents usually get worried about a child's sickness and seek advice or help even for minor ailments. However adequate attention is not being paid to his day to day needs. Such a child starts feeling deprived, insecure, unwanted and craves for attention and love outside his home and thus becomes an easy prey for kidnapping. This paper includes study of 100 kidnapped children between the ages of 3 to 16 years, over a period of 3 years in the city of Bombay. Of these children, 96% were girls and majority of them were hindus. Surprisingly 46% of the cases were willing victims. The motives for kidnapping were prostitution (3.4%), selling (4.5%), for the purpose of begging (4.5%), employment and bootlegging (51.6%), vengence (3.5%), sexual gratification (29.1%) and domestic servant (3.4%). Extreme poverty, broken homes, antisocial surrounding, illiteracy and lack of interest on the part of parents were conspiciously observed, which created a background suitable for kidnapping. These 100 kidnapped children were rescued, rehabilitated and restored to their parents.

INTRODUCTION

We are guilty of many errors and many faults but our worst crime is abandoning the children, neglecting the fountain of life. Many of the things we need can wait, the child cannot, right now is the time, his bones are formed, his blood is being made and his senses are being developed. To him we cannot answer "tomorrow" his name is "today" - (Gabrial Mistral).

Amongst the varied problems of child abuse and neglect "kidnapping" has achieved social and judicial importance over the years. The gravity of the problem of "kidnapping" in children is beyond question. In a less priviledged country like India with its vast population and increasing poverty, a child's day to day needs both physical as well as emotional, are not getting fulfilled. Such a child starts feeling deprived, insecure, unwanted and craves for attention and love outside the boundaries of his home and thus becomes an easy prey for kidnapping. Every year more than 4,000 children run away from their homes in Bombay itself.

AIMS AND OBJECTIVES

Here an attempt has been made to study (1) the facts about kidnapped children, namely the personal data of the child, family background, socio-economic conditions and the circumstances leading to being kidnapped. (2) Where ever possible, the rehabilitation i.e. the rescue and restoration of these kidnapped children to their parents or guardians was also studied.

MATERIAL AND METHODS

This paper includes study of 100 kidnapped children of either sex, between the ages of 3 to 16 years, over a period of 3 years in the city of Bombay and its suburbs. These 100 children were selectively chosen amongst the 247 cases of various offences (under section 78 of Bombay Children Act 1948 and section 363 (A) of Indian Penal Code) referred to Probation department, Remand Home, Umerkhadi by the police. 147 cases could not be included as they were either over age i.e. more than 16 years or upcountry cases or the cases which could not be traced for interviews due to vague addresses, constant mobillity or hutments being demolished. 43 cases of these children, had 'run away' by themselves from their homes, and hence were excluded. All above children and their parents were interviewed seperately by probation officers in remand home as well as their houses. The data was recorded and analysed.

OBSERVATIONS

TABLE 1 Distribution of Cases According to Age and Sex

Age in Years	Boys	Girls	Total
3 - 6	-	2	2%
7 - 9	1	11	12%
10 - 12	2	14	16%
13 - 14	1	29	30%
15 - 16	-	40	40%
Total.	4	96	100%

Above table reveals that 96% of the victims are girls and only 4% are boys. The largest no. i.e. 70% of all girls are found in the age group of 13 to 16 years. There is not much difference in lower age groups i.e. 14% between 3 to 9 years and 16% between 10 to 12 years. Average age of the girl who was kidnapped was around 14 years.

TABLE 2 Educational Background

Primary	37%
Secondary	37%
S.S.C.	1%
Not going to School	25%
Total.	100%

From the above table it is seen that 75% of the children had either gone up to primary or secondary school at one time. 25% had not attended school. This shows that, there is high number of dropouts before even reaching the secondary school.

School plays a major role in child's life. Education is not compulsary in India. Few parents can afford to send their children to school and with limited facility of free school, quite a few children remain uneducated and utilise their time either by helping their parents in domestic work or find some employment, the remaining waste their time aimlessly. Thus the educational status of the child gives us some idea about the pattern of the society to which the child belongs. Parental illiteracy and lack of interest towards education also contributes to low educational status of the children.

TABLE 3 Family Background

a) Broken Family

1. Broken homes	20%
2. Unbroken homes	54%
3. Not known	26%
Total.	100%

b) Victims' Parents

1. Both parents	80%
2. Only mother	10%
3. Only father	4%
4. Step father	2%
5. Two fathers (Two husbands)	2%
6. No parents	1%
7. Deserted mother	1%
Total.	100%

The above table shows the pattern of the family amongst the victims. Here it is seen 80% of victims had original parents and hence were complete families. 10% had only mother, 4% had only father and one child had no surviving parents. In two cases the mother was staying with two husbands, two children had step fathers and one mother was deserted. 20% victims belonged to broken homes and in 26% of victims little information regarding their families was available. Surprisingly a sizable number of children were kidnapped even when both the parents were alive. However the children from broken families are more prone for the dangers of being kidnapped and for exploitation. Parental disharmony seems to contribute more significantly for girls being kidnapped than the boys.

A well adjusted child in a closely knit family is not a problem either to himself or to the society. Broken homes, disturbed interfamilial relationship, vices like alcoholism etc. predisposes a child for insecurity and emotional disturbance and lead indirectly either to 'runaway' or being kidnapped.

TABLE 4 Religion of the Victims

1. Hindus	61%
2. Muslims	27%
3. Christians	6%
4. Neobudhist	6%
Total.	100%

From the above table it is found that 61% of victims belonged to Hindu religion, followed by Muslim (27%), Christians (6%) and Neobudhist (6%). This was probably due to high population of Hindus in Bombay city.

Marital Status

99% victims were unmarried before they were kidnapped, of these 40 girls were married after the incidence of kidnapping. This shows that kidnapping did not come in the way of the marriage of the girls.

TABLE 5 Hobbies of the Kidnapped Children

1. Chit chating	3%
2. Wandering	2%
3. Singing	1%
4. Sewing	7%
5. Reading	7%
6. No hobbies	80%
Total.	100%

80% of the children had no hobies at all. Poor and crowded homes do not provide any facilities for indoor occupation and recreational outlet for the children. Thus children tend to spend time in hotels, in wandering and make friendship with vagabonds. Such free children can often fall prey at the hands of kidnappers.

Employment

Out of 100 children only 8 were employed, 4 as domestic servants and 4 in factory as semi and unskilled labourers. 10 years was the youngest age when one of the above victims started working. Their earnings varied from Rs. 2-5/day, Rs. 40 per month being the lowest. Incidently all of them gave their earnings at home, out of necessity.

Parental interest

The parents' interest in the kidnapped children was very poor mainly because of the burden of the heavy work and spending their leisure time in other activities.

TABLE 6 Socio-economic Status of Family

Income/month	Size of the Family Members		Total
	6 or more	4 or less	
Rs. Less than 100	5	7	12%
" 100 - 200	13	11	24%
" 201 - 300	12	6	18%
" 301 - 400	5	4	9%
" 401 - 500	12	4	16%
" 500 Onwards	13	3	16%
No data	2	3	5%
Total.	62	38	100%

The above table shows that about 50% of families in the income level upto Rs. 300/- p.m. are large households. Remaining 50% whose earnings were more than Rs. 300/- p.m. are little better off and definetely not above lower middle class,

TABLE 7 Educational Background of Parents

Illiterate	46%
Literate	6%
Primary Education	36%
Middle School	8%
Graduate	2%
No information	2%
Total.	100%

Regarding educational background 46% were illiterate and 36% were had gone upto primary level only. As regards the occupation 27% were busy in petty business and 47.5% were doing various types of services. 2.5% were retired and 3.5% were unemployed.

TABLE 8 Living Conditions of the Victims

Rented house	82%
Own huts	17%
Footpath dweller	1%
Total.	100%

Poverty striken families have very little choice in the selection of residential locality. They live in slums where professional adult criminals live. Thus children are easily drawn on wrong path way for multipurpose uses. Most of the respondents found that their living accommodation was too small for their large families. It is natural for children to remain outside their house for longer time, out of control or watchful eyes of the parents and therefore exposed to being easily kidnapped.

TABLE 9 Victims in relation to Motives of Offenders

Motives	Male	Female	Total	Percentage
Rape	-	26	26	26
Willing Victims	-	46	46	46
Begging	1	3	4	4
Selling	1	3	4	4
Prostitution	-	3	3	3
Motive not known	2	9	11	11
Any other	-	6	6	6
Total.	4	96	100	100

As seen from above table, 26 victims were being kidnapped for the purpose of rape and as high as 46 i.e. 46% eloped for the purpose of sexual satisfaction. Kidnapping in this category becomes easier because of the offender gets partial or full concurrence of the victim. Majority of these are teenagers with love infatuations.

Accused

Out of 100 cases investigated, data of 89 cases of accused was available. 82 of these were males, 50 of them were in age groups of 16 to 25 years during which human desire in sex indulgence is probably intense. Religion and occupation of the accused had no relation to kidnapping. All the 89 accused were unmarried, 48% were staying alone as paying guests and hence had easy assess for sex. In 46 out of 89 cases the victims were willing to be kidnapped and in such instances, the victims and the accused had acquaintance ranging from less than a month to over 4 years.

DISCUSSION

"Kidnapping" according to Indian Penal Code, takes place when a minor under 16 years of age (if a male) or under 18 years (if a female) is taken or enticed out of the keeping of the lawful guardian of the minor. The question of the consent of the minor does not arise. Kidnapping children is an offence under Indian Penal Code section 78 and 368 (A), these are "victimised" children for various purposes, such as prostitution, selling, begging, bootlegging etc. In the case of victimised child the trial of the accused person was simultaneously conducted in the adult court (if the accused was an adult) or in Juvenile Court if accused was below 18 years of age.

The gravity of the problem of kidnapping in children is beyond question. In under priviledged country like India facilities provided for children, such as schooling, medical check up, child health centres are out of proportion to that of increasing child population. Extreme poverty, broken homes, unsocial surroundings of slums, lack of interest of parents in the child, and illiteracy of parents were consipiciosly observed, which created background conductive to circumstances leading to victimisation of the child. These factors also contribute to Juvenile Deliquency. As "Reckless said that very often to a growing child, his companions mean much more than his family. They influence him very strongly in his use of language, his likes, dislikes and behaviour and attitudes towards others. Due to his close association with his friends at times he acquires anti-social tendencies".

Girls are kidnapped much more frequently than boys. It is obvious that lack of parental control was the main cause of their deviation in falling victims to sex deliquency. As Gibbon says "Girls who face affectional deprivation at homes become heavily involved with boys, so as to acquire substitute affectional gratification from that source". Thus in the present study the percentage of willing victims is 46%. It is conceivable that girls are less heriditorily prone to deliquency and therefore require greater influence from their environment to fall into bad ways.

Amongst the various motives of kidnapping like rape, selling, prostitution, begging, bootlegging etc., though well known, we could not come across kidnapping for the purpose of robbery or stealing i.e. of small jwellery worn by children which is a common practise in Indian households. Quite often public announcements and notices are put up in newspapers, radio and T.V. etc., of these small, tender kidnapped children.

Last year in India there was a big uproar about children being kidnapped for the purpose of some religious ceremony such as offerring of blood of young children by slaughtering them. This is a tribal practise, being considered as a good omen for begining of an important task such as construction of a bridge etc. Similar incidences are not unknown in villages of India due to wrong cultural beliefs.

Management of these kidnapped children depended on the motive behind it. Though rescued, occassionally it took considerable time before they could be finally restored to their parents or guardians. Till then they were kept in various homes of the children's Aid Society - a society dealing with all the aspects of child abuse and neglect. Inspite of restoration and adequate judicial warning the fact remains that once kidnapped chances of repeat kidnapping are quite high in these vulnerable families.

No separation between parent and child, not even death could be as anguishing as the seperation caused by kidnapping. The emotional and the physical needs of the child are often not met within under priviledged countries, societies and families. It is a scene of "Oliver asked for more" i.e. being repeated over and over again.

ACKNOWLEDGEMENT

We take this opportunity to acknowledge Children's Aid Society for giving us facilities and to the Dean, L.T.M.G.Hospital & College, for allowing us to carry out this study. We also wish to express our gratitude to our typist Miss. A.H. Masand for her untiring and excellent typing work.

REFERENCES

1) Cowie, Cowie and Slater. (1968)
Delinquency in Girls, Heinemann, London.

2) Gibbons, Don, C.
Delinquent Behaviour, Portland State University, New Jersey.

3) Kapadia, K.M. and Pillai, S.D. (1971)
Young Runaways, Popular Prakashan, Bombay.

4) Karpman, Benjamin, M.D. (1957)
The Sexual Offender and His Offences, Jullian Press, Inc.

5) Nye F. Ivan. (1958)
Family Relationships and Delinquent Behaviour, New York, Jhon Wiley and Sons, Inc.

6) Punekar, S.D. and Kamala Rao. (1967) Revised Ed.
A Study of Prostitutes in Bombay, Lalvani Publishing House, Bombay.

7) Reckless, Walter C. (1967)
The Crime Problem, Meredith Publishing Company.

Reports

1) Begging by children, How many of them are kidnapped? Central Bureau of Correctional Services, Department of Social Welfare, Government of India, New Delhi, 1971.

2) Gore M.G. (1973). Study of Kidnapped Children in the City of Bombay, Children's Aids Society, Bombay. Central Bureau of Correctional Services, Department of Social Welfare, Government of India, New Delhi.

Child Abuse and Neglect, Vol. 3, pp. 623 - 632.

0145-2134/79/0601-0623 $02.00/0.

CHILD ABUSE: THE LEGISLATIVE RESPONSE IN THE PROVINCE OF ONTARIO

Joseph Paul Chertkow, LL.B., LL.M.

Law Clerk to the Chief Justice of Ontario, (1978)
Toronto, Ontario, Canada

In every cry of every Man,
In every Infant's cry of fear,
In every voice, in every ban,
The mind-forg'd manacles I hear.
- William Blake, "London"

Background

The legal responses to the problem of child abuse and neglect require a rational balancing of important societal values, including the interest of parents and the state in preserving the integrity of the family, the right of children to thrive in a healthy and secure environment, and the interest in achieving administrative efficiency, while maintaining due process and fairness in the treatment of individuals when the state intervenes under statutory power.

The law relating to the protection of children should be evaluated against the fundamental proposition that the power of the state to intervene in the parent-child relationship should only be used when there is reasonable justification for the belief that a child will be harmed permanently by parental conduct.[1]

Professor Monrad G. Paulsen has distinguished four sets of legal provisions relating to child abuse: 1) provisions of the criminal law which may be invoked to punish persons who have inflicted harm upon children; 2) juvenile or family court acts which create procedures resulting in a finding that a child has been neglected; 3) legislation authorizing or establishing protective services for abused and neglected children; and 4) child abuse reporting laws which encourage or require reporting of suspected cases of child abuse.[2]

The legal situation in Canada is complicated by the constitutional division of powers whereby criminal law falls within the exclusive jurisdiction of the federal government, which enacted the Criminal Code,[3] while social welfare legislation for the protection of children (for example the Ontario Child Welfare Act)[4] is regarded as a matter of civil rights within the province.

Criminal Law

Infliction of physical harm against children is not given specific recognition in the Criminal Code. When harm is inflicted on a child, the abuser may be prosecuted under the sections dealing with assault, manslaughter or murder.[5] A recent proposal by the federal Justice Department would amend the Code to allow the courts to punish persons who have inflicted unjustifiable physical pain or mental suffering upon children, thereby giving recognition to the repugnancy of such assaults.[6] It should be noted that one aspect of child abuse which is presently prohibited in the Code concerns various sexual offenses, which recognize the vulnerability of the young.[7]

The Code does aim at certain omissions affecting children. A parent, foster parent, guardian or head of a family is bound under strict conditions to provide necessaries of life for a child under the age of sixteen and commits an offense in failing to perform this duty when the child is in destitute or necessitous circumstances or is at the risk of his life or permanent health.[8] Further, everyone who unlawfully abandons or exposes a child under ten years old so that his life or permanent health is endangered is liable to up to two years imprisonment.[9]

A controversial section of the Code is s. 43 which allows every school teacher, parent or person standing in the place of a parent to use force by way of correction toward a pupil or child, if the force does not exceed what is reasonable in the circumstances. The provision thus preserves the traditional concept of a parental privilege of discipline,[10] since in the absence of such a section the disciplining of a child by corporal punishment would be considered an assault. The federal Justice Department is currently studying the desirability of retaining this section.[11]

A number of commentators have questioned the role of criminal sanctions in the area of child abuse. Criminal proceedings may punish an abusive parent, but may have a highly negative effect on the child's family environment, with little therapeutic benefit to the offender.[12] The deterrent effect of criminal sanctions on abusive parents is doubtful. Moreover, it has been noted that a criminal prosecution may be costly and time consuming, with difficulty in obtaining a conviction because of the requirement that guilt must be proved beyond a reasonable doubt.[13] It appears that in Ontario minimum use has been made of the courts in prosecuting child abusers, save in the most blatant cases, and lack of substantiating evidence is the major reason for the dismissal or withdrawal of charges.[14]

History of Child Welfare Legislation in Ontario

The first comprehensive piece of legislation in Ontario for the protection and care of disadvantaged children was The Children's Protection Act, passed in 1893,[15] and based largely on Scottish legislation of 1854.

The Ontario Act set the pattern for legislation in other provinces, and introduced several important concepts which have been preserved in the modern legislation. The Act recognized the local Children's Aid Society (CAS) as the primary social welfare agency for providing services for children. It is interesting to note that the earliest CAS's actually predated the legislation,[16] having been developed and staffed as charities using the services of volunteers. The approach of the CAS (and indeed, the tone of the legislation) in this period was influenced by the religious and moral notions of the time.[17]

Fundamental to the operation of the Act was the definition of "neglected" child, which in 1893 demonstrated a greater concern for the apprehension of street waifs, beggars, and deserted children than for the problem of child abuse as it is recognized today.[18] The Act required that any child apprehended by CAS officers had to be brought before a judge, and if there was a finding that the child was neglected, he would be delivered to the local CAS pending placement in an approved foster home.[19] The two stage hearing (i.e. a "fact finding" stage and a "dispositional" stage) is still an important aspect of current child welfare legislation. Following an order committing the child to the care of the CAS, there was a suspension of parental rights, and the society became the legal guardian of the child, although there was provision for the parents to make application for the return of the child, in the discretion of the judge.[20]

During the next sixty years, the legislation went through a series of revisions which involved such matters as modification of the definition of neglected child, and expansion of the range of alternatives available to the court and the local C.A.S.'s.[21]

In 1954, The Children's Protection Act[22] was repealed and the relevant provisions were incorporated as Part II of The Child Welfare Act,[23] a statutory scheme which remains intact at present. In 1965, The Child Welfare Act underwent major revisions.[24] The definition of "neglected child" was replaced by a new concept of a "child in need of protection",[25] although the twelve sub-clauses which made up the definition were almost identical.

An important concept introduced by the amendments was that of "Crown wardship",[26] which allowed a judge to order that a child found to be in need of protection was a ward of the Crown in the care of the CAS, signifying that the Crown had all rights and responsibilities of a legal guardian. Thus, rather than committing a child to the care of only one local CAS (a separate corporation in law), the provision allowed the Director of Child Welfare under the Act greater flexibility in the placement of the child.

Another notable provision enacted in 1965 was a reporting requirement[27] to encourage the communication of information of cases of child abuse and neglect.

In 1970,[28] exclusive jurisdiction for hearings under Part II was given to a Judge of the Provincial Court (Family Division). The definition of child in need of protection was expanded to include a child brought before a judge with the consent of the person having charge of him. Further amendments were made in 1975.[29] A new section provided for the temporary placement of a "homemaker" in the home by the CAS in certain cases.[30] Another provision allowed a child to be cared for by a society on this basis of an agreement with the parents (non-ward care agreement) rather than by a court order for wardship.[31]

In December, 1977 the governmental department responsible for the administration of children's services[32] published the "Consultation Paper on Short Term Legislative Amendments" which contained proposals for amendments to The Child Welfare Act. On June 8, 1978, Bill 114[33] was introduced in the provincial legislature, and when passed will effect some major changes in the provisions relating to the protection of children in Ontario.

The Definition of "Child in Need of Protection"

Under the Ontario Act, it is on essential prerequisite to legal intervention that there is a finding of a "child in need of protection". The problem of definition, basic to all statutory enactments, is crucial in considering legal responses to child abuse; as the definition is broadened, identification of child abuse is facilitated.[34]

The Act defines "child" as a boy or girl actually or apparently under sixteen years of age.[35] The definition of "child in need of protection" presently reads as follows.[36]

(b) "child in need of protection" means,

(i) a child who is brought, with the consent of the person in whose charge he is, before a judge to be dealt with under this Part,

(ii) a child who is deserted by the person in whose charge he is,

(iii) a child where the person in whose charge he is cannot for any reason care properly for him, or where that person has died and there is no suitable person to care for the child,

(iv) a child who is living in an unfit or improper place,

(v) a child found associating with an unfit or improper person,

(vi) a child found begging or receiving alms in a public place,

(vii) REPEALED,

(viii) a child whose parent is unable to control him,

(ix) a child who, without sufficient cause, habitually absents himself from his home or school,

(x) a child where the person in whose charge he is neglects or refuses to provide or obtain proper medical, surgical or other recognized remedial care or treatment necessary for his health or well-being, or refuses to permit such care or treatment to be supplied to the child when it is recommended by a legally qualified medical practitioner, or otherwise fails to protect the child adequately,

(xi) a child whose emotional or mental development is endangered because of emotional rejection or deprivation of affection by the person in whose charge he is,

(xii) a child whose life, health or morals may be endangered by the conduct of the person in whose charge he is;

The definition has undergone a series of modifications since first enacted, in a process than can best be called "legislation by addendum". The basic deficiency, as one commentator has noted, is that the definition is too fragmented and legally imprecise to meet the functional needs it is required to fulfill.[37] The eleven sub-clauses direct the attention of the court to different circumstances, without a consistent focus. The definition can be categorized on the basis of parental conduct including consent,[38] conduct of the child[39] and environmental factors.[40] The suggestion can be made that the definition would be more effective if it concentrated upon the observable condition and needs of the child, rather than observable parental conduct.[41] The definition also contains an element of social discrimination in labelling children as in need of protection.[42] Moreover, many of the sub-clauses contain a great degree of subjectivity, and it has been contended that the definition should attempt to utilize scientific assessments, rather than subjective lay evaluations.[43]

Procedure Under Part II of The Child Welfare Act

The Act contains special powers for the apprehension of children suspected of being in need of protection. There is authority for a police officer, the Director of Child Welfare, a local director of a CAS or person authorized by them to take without warrant any child apparently in need of protection to a "place of safety",[44] or such person may apply to a judge for an order requiring the person having charge of the child to produce the child before a judge.[45] In addition, it is provided that a justice of the peace may issue a warrant authorizing a person to search for a child suspected of being in need of protection.[46]

A child detained in a place of safety must be returned to his parent or person in whose charge he was immediately prior to his apprehension or brought before a judge within five days of his detention.[47] During this time the local CAS will obtain and record the information necessary to determine the course of action deemed necessary for the welfare of the child.[48] The CAS may decide to return the child to his own home without taking the case to court, and perhaps continue to work with the child and his family. Alternatively, court proceedings can be avoided where the child is taken into the temporary protective care of the CAS pursuant to an agreement with a parent, for a period not exceeding twelve months.[49] In the case where the CAS determines that an order for supervision in the home is desirable, or that an order for protective care is necessary, there must be a hearing before a Judge of the Provincial Court (Family Division) to determine whether or not the child is in need of protection.[50]

For the purpose of a protection hearing, the judge has the power of summoning any person and requiring him to give evidence on oath.[51] The judge may hear any person on behalf of the child, the CAS, the municipality and a regional welfare administrator of the Ministry or any person authorized by the Minister.[52]

The Act specifically says that the judge shall not proceed to hear or dispose of the matter until he is satisfied that the parent or other person having actual custody of the child had reasonable notice of the hearing or that every reasonable effort has been made to cause them to be notified.[53] There is provision to dispense with such notice if prompt service of notice cannot be effected and any delay might endanger the health or safety of the child, but parental rights[54] are protected by limited the period of protective care by any order to thirty days, unless a further hearing is held.[55]

When a child is shown to be in need of protection, the judge shall make one of three orders:[56]

1) an order that the child be placed with or returned to his parent or other person subject to supervision by the CAS for a period of not less than six months and not more than 12 months.[57]
2) an order that the child be made a ward of and committed to the care and custody of the CAS for such period, not exceeding 12 months, as in the circumstances he considers advisable.[58]
3) an order that the child be made a ward of the Crown until wardship is terminated[59] and that the child be committed to the care of the CAS.

It is essential that the two stages of the hearing not become confused, since a child is not shown to be in need of protection simply because the CAS can demonstrate that it can offer the child preferable circumstances. Before the question of the disposition can arise, a child must be shown to be in need of protection according to objective standards.[60] Unfortunately in practice the distinctive stages and applicable standards are frequently seen to overlap.[61]

An important issue in protection hearings is the degree of formality to be injected into the proceedings. Many commentators have rejected the need for traditional adversarial elements in family court as an unrealistic response to domestic problems.[62] It has been stated that informal proceedings may tend to reduce additional family conflicts.[63] Several provisions of the Act assist in maintaining informality in family court.[64] Indeed, one criticism relates to the lack of systematic recording of reasons for judgment (and case reporting) in family court, with the result that there has been difficulty in developing a body of case law relating to the protection of children.[65]

Despite the deficiencies of the adversary system, the fact remains that the parties to the proceedings are frequently in opposition and their interests may require protection. The difficulty confronting family court is to strike a balance between the function of a social agency and that of a legal institution.[66]

Arguably another functional inconsistency lies in the role of the CAS under the Ontario Act.[67] The CAS is empowered to act as the "accuser of parents", supporter of parents through a casework relationship, planner for children and adviser to the court with respect to the proposed course of action and agent for carrying out the order of the court.[68] It could be contended that the legislative scheme has a dysfunctional effect on the performance of services by the CAS. Moreover, each local society can be regarded as having its own institutional policy objectives, which may be reflected in the proposals made with respect to a child. Thus, it may be more economical to have the child removed from the home and placed in a facility rather than providing home supervision.[69]

Some Recent Legislative Proposals

1. Reporting Requirements

The reporting provision in Bill 114 has been a focus of attention.[70] The Child Welfare Act[71] presently requires "every person" having information of the abandonment, desertion, physical ill-treatment or need for protection of a child to report the information to a CAS or Crown attorney. However, there is currently no penalty for failure to comply with this duty.

A 1977 government paper[72] recommended that mandatory reporting of suspected abuse cases should be required of those obtaining information in a professional or official capacity, which would include physicians, public health nurses, hospital staff, teachers, lawyers and others. The report proposed a maximum fine of $1,000 for failure of a professional to report. These recommendations have been given expression in s. 45 of the new bill.[73] The rationale of limiting mandatory reporting to those acting in the course of professional or official duties is that such individuals have the best opportunity and expertise to detect cases of child abuse.[74]

The nature of reporting legislation has been frequently discussed in legal writing, with prominence given to: 1) the definition of abuse and reportable injuries, 2) the individuals who are subject to the duty to report, 3) the protections granted to those who report, 4) the liabilities and penalties for failure to report, and 5) the value of a central reporting registry.[75]

In dealing with the problem of defining abuse for purposes of reporting, the proposal was for a new definition of abuse[76] as a "condition of physical harm or neglect or sexual molestation". The focus of the definition is thus on the condition of the child rather than the conduct of those responsible for the abuse. It is noteworthy that only the more serious forms of abuse are included, and that emotional and psychological forms of abuse are omitted from the definition.

The approach of the provision in the new bill has been to preserve the duty of "every person" to report, while creating a new professional duty to report, reinforced by a penalty provision.[77] The new provision gives protection from civil liability to both professionals and ordinary citizens who report, unless the giving of information is done maliciously or without reasonable and probable cause.[78]

The decision to require reporting by all professionals conflicts with the view of at least one leading commentator that a reporting requirement should be focused solely upon the medical profession. The contention was that a reporting law should aim to uncover cases of abuse which only medical skill can detect, and that blatant cases of maltreatment are likely to be recognized by others in the community. It can be strongly argued, however, that professionals other than doctors will frequently come into contact with the abused child, that such individuals are capable of recognizing abuse, and that a physician may only see the child when the problem is so serious that medical treatment is required.[79]

The medical profession appears to have been the target of special criticism with respect to the reporting of child abuse.[80] A 1973 government report referred to the relatively low rate of reporting by physicians and public health nurses, as contrasted with other sources.[81] Doctors face special problems of confidentiality arising from the physician-patient relationship, and may regard reporting as a breach of confidence which may result in civil liability. However it is clear that, even under the present legislation, a doctor who has reasonable grounds to suspect abuse is protected from civil action. Moreover, it is possible that failure to report might render a physician liable in negligence to the abused child for breach of his duty of care.[82]

The argument that a compulsory reporting law will deter parents from seeking medical aid for their injured children appears to have little foundation, since many incidents of abusive behaviour result from crisis situations, following which parents will take steps for treatment.[83] However, the suggestion can be made that mandatory reporting may inhibit parents seeking some form of therapy for themselves, since the confidentiality of a psychiatric relationship may be affected.

There is evidence to suggest that an increase in reporting of cases of abuse in parts of Ontario has resulted from greater inter-disciplinary co-operation among professionals in the field.[84] This may indicate that the concerns of advocates of a mandatory reporting law for professionals are being misdirected.

2. Child Abuse Registry

Bill 114 makes provision for registration of suspected cases of child abuse which have been reported to the CAS.[85] A registry presently exists on a purely administrative basis but has been criticized as being arbitrary and inconsistent.[86] The government consultation paper referred to three registry options: a province-wide central registry for identifying information that could be used for "tracking purposes", exchange of information on a local level without use of a registry, or a province-wide registry of non-identifying social information for research and planning purposes only.[87] The scheme adopted in Bill 114 is one for a central registry of identifying information, despite the fact that studies in other jurisdictions have indicated that such registries are costly and not necessarily effective for tracking purposes.[88] The problem results from the fact that the theory of reporting and registration of child abuse cases is based on a model of the abusive parent which has never been empirically confirmed in Ontario.[89]

3. Separate Legal Representation of Children

Child advocacy recognizes that the interests of the child, as an individual directly affecting by protection proceedings, may not coincide with the interests of the child welfare agency making the application in court, nor with the interests of the parents opposing the application.[90]

Under the present Act, it is provided that "the judge may hear any person on behalf of the child".[91] However, a recent case held that there was no authority in a Judge of the Provincial Court (Family Division) to appoint the Official Guardian on behalf of the child, although it was said that a judge could ask the Official Guardian if he wished to make any representations and the judge could hear such representations.[92] The decision is illustrative of the traditional view that the child welfare agency represents the interests of the child and that no other representation is required.

In a 1977 report by a committee to the Attorney-General for Ontario, it was recognized that there are cases in child protection where the child has no real advocate speaking for his or her interests.[93] However the committee was not prepared to recommend that a child be represented in all such proceedings and rather than proposing an amendment which would have established that a child is a "party to the proceedings", it recommended that the judge should have the discretion to appoint counsel to represent the child. However, the committee did not attempt to particularize the method by which legal representation should be achieved.[94]

The committee's recommendation has been implemented by Bill 114,[95] which grants a judge the discretion to appoint legal representation. Several points can be raised in criticism of the provision.[96] Firstly, the decision of legal representation is left entirely to the judge, who may be firmly of the view that the CAS is always best equipped to represent the child. Secondly, although the new provision would allow an order "at any stage in proceedings", it is unlikely that such an order for representation would be made prior to the appearance in court, thereby preventing some important services of a child advocate earlier in the process. Thirdly, the amendment may simply be seen as a solution to the gap in the present legislation, so that judges may routinely refer the question of representation to the Office of the Official Guardian.

An earlier report by the Ontario Law Reform Commission[97] was of the opinion that in view of the traditional connection of the Official Guardian with property interests of children, it would be better to place the new functions of representation in the hands of a new official, the Law Guardian, who would be able to develop new techniques for their discharge. In contrast, the Law Reform Commission of Canada, in a 1974 paper[98] was of the view that counsel for the child should be independent of the court. Obviously, further consideration must be given to the methods and circumstances of legal representation, and thus the proposed amendment is best described as a short term measure.

Among the problems raised by the concept of child advocacy are two possibly conflicting social interests: the right of a child to assert by legal representation his or her own interests as against the rights and responsibilities of adults to make decisions on behalf of the child.[99] Clearly this area of concern requires special expertise, training, and communicative skills, as well as a re-evaluation of the role of the legal practitioner.

NOTES

1. This proposition was adopted by the Ontario Law Reform Commission, Report on Family Law, Part III "Children", p. 64.
2. M.G. Paulsen, "The Legal Framework for Child Protection" (1966), 66 Colum. L. Rev. 679; and "The Law and Abused Children" in R. Helfer & C. Kempe, The Battered Child at p. 153.
3. R.S.C. 1970, c. C-34.
4. R.S.O. 1970, c. 64.
5. The Criminal Code, ss. 244, 245, 212, 214, 215, 218, 219.
6. Toronto Globe & Mail, April 13, 1978, pp. 1-2.
7. Eg. s. 150 (Incest), s. 146 (sexual intercourse with female under fourteen), s. 166 (parent or guardian procuring defilement of a female under fourteen), s. 168 ("corrupting children").
8. Code, s. 197.
9. Code, s. 200.
10. See Paulsen, "The Legal Framework for Child Protection", note 2 at p. 686; Eekelaar "What are Parental Rights?" (1973), 89 Law Q. Rev. 210; Feshbach, "Punishment: Parent Rites versus Children's Rights" in G.P. Koocher (ed.) Children's Rights and the Mental Health Professions (1976).
11. Toronto Globe and Mail, April 13, 1978, p. 1.
12. See B.G. Fraser, "A Pragmatic Alternative to Current Legislative Approaches to Child Abuse" (1974), 12 Amer. Crim. L.R.; B.M. Dickens, "Legal Responses to Child Abuse" (1978), 12 Fam. Law Q. 1: M.G. Paulsen "The Law and Abused Children", note 2, at p. 154.
13. M.G. Paulsen, "The Legal Framework for Child Abuse", note 2, p. 692.
14. C. Greenland, Child Abuse in Ontario (Research Report 3) 1973, p. 26.
15. 56 Vict. c. 45.
16. For example the Children's Aid Society of Metropolitan Toronto was officially established in 1891 to provide a temporary refuge for the care and protection of neglected children.
17. Ontario Law Reform Commission, Study of the Family Law Project (1968), vol. 9, p. 131.
18. S. 13.
19. S. 14.
20. Ss. 15, 17.
21. See S.O. 1908, 3 Edw. 7 c. 59; S.O. 1916, 6 Geo. 5 c. 53; S.O. 1927, 17 Geo. 5 c. 78; S.O. 1928, 18 Geo. 5 c. 46.
22. R.S.O. 1950, c. 53.
23. S.O. 1954, c. 8.
24. S.O. 1965, c. 14.
25. s. 19(1)b.
26. S. 25(c).
27. s. 41, see infra.
28. S.O. 1970, c. 96.
29. S.O. 1975, c. 1.
30. S. 22a.
31. S. 23a.
32. The Children's Services Division of The Ministry of Community and Social Services.
33. "An Act to revise The Child Welfare Act".
34. B.M. Dickens, note 12, p. 9.
35. S. 20(1)(a).
36. S. 20(1)(b).
37. B.M. Dickens, Legal Issues in Child Abuse (1976), p. 5.
38. Eg. ss. 20(1)b(i), (ii), (iii), (x), (xi), (xii).
39. Eg. ss. 20(1)b(vi), (viii), (ix).
40. Eg. ss. 20(1)b(iv), (v).
41. Dickens, note 37, p. 12.
42. See Areen, "Intervention Between Parent and Child: A Reappraisal of the State's Role in Child Neglect and Abuse" (1975), 63 Geo. L.J. 887 at pp. 888-9.
43. Dickens, note 37, p. 12.
44. "place of safety" means a receiving home or foster home or an institution for the care and protection of children: s. 20(1)(f).
45. S. 21(1).

46. S. 22(1).
47. S. 24(1).
48. Current regulations state that a complaint regarding a child in need of protection shall be recorded within 24 hours and investigated within twenty-one days: Reg. 86, R.R.O. 1970, s. 14. However a recent Report of the Task Force on Child Abuse (June 1978) was critical of the laxity of the provision.
49. S. 23a.
50. S. 25(1).
51. S. 25(2).
52. S. 25(3). But apparently no power to appoint a representative for the child: Re Helmes (1976), 13 O.R. (2d) 4.
53. S. 25(4).
54. "Parent" is defined to mean a person who is under a legal duty to provide for a child and includes a person standing in loco parentis: s. 20(1)(e).
55. Ss. 25(7), (8).
56. S. 26(1).
57. By s. 27(7) a parent may apply for termination of a supervision order after 6 months.
58. An order may be renewed but is not to exceed a total of 24 months wardship: s. 31.
59. An order of Crown wardship can be terminated by s. 32 (application by CAS, parent, or ward upon reaching age of 16 years) or by s. 35 (ward attaining 18 years).
60. Dickens, note 12, p. 24.
61. Consultation Paper on Short Term Legislative Amendments (1977), Ministry of Community and Social Services, p. 19; Also note the decision of the Ontario Divisional Court in St. Pierre and Meloche v. Roman Catholic Children's Aid Society for Essex County (1976), 27 R.F.L. 266, where it was held that it is proper for the judge holding a hearing under s. 25 to hear evidence dealing with both the investigative and dispositional issues at the same time.
62. Eg. Law Reform Commission of Canada, Working Paper 1, The Family Court (1974) p. 11 and Dickens, note 12, p. 29.
63. E.C. Duncan, "Recognition and Protection of the Family's Interests in Child Abuse Proceedings" (1974-75) 13 J. of Family Law 803 at p. 813.
64. See s. 46(2) (judge shall exclude public from hearing), s. 28(1) (judge may order presence of child dispensed with), but see Bill 114, s. 31 as to right of child over the age of 10 years to be present in court.
65. Dickens, note 37, p. 7. See now Bill 114, s. 34 which would require that written reasons shall be part of the record. Also see decision in Children's Aid Society of Winnipeg v. Forth et al. (1978), 1 R.F.L. (2d), Man. Prov. Judges Court (Family Division) for an instructive discussion of factors for disposition of child found to be in need of protection.
66. Duncan, note 63, p. 813.
67. S. 6(2) of The Child Welfare Act says that each CAS shall be operated for the purposes of, inter alia (a) investigating allegations or evidence that children may be in need of protection, (b) protecting children where necessary, (c)providing guidance, counselling and other services to families for protecting children or for the prevention of circumstances requiring the protection of children. See also report of The Task Force on Child Abuse (1978), p. 7.
68. B. Chisholm -- The Child as Citizen: Do Children Need Lawyers? at p. 3. See also Report of the Committee on the Representation of Children in the Provincial Court (Family Division), 29 R.F.L. 134 at p. 149.
69. Dickens, note 12, p. 25, and interview with Dr. Dickens on 7/24/78.
70. See Toronto Globe & Mail, June 9, 1978, p. 1.
71. R.S.O. 1970, c. 64, s. 41(1).
72. Consultation Paper, note 61, p. 36.
73. The offense is created by s. 86(1)(f)(ii).
74. See note 72.
75. Eg. Fraser, note 12 supra, Dickens, note 37 supra, Paulsen, note 2 supra, A.M. McCoid "The Battered Child and Other Assaults Upon the Family (Part 1)" (1965) 50 Minn. Law Rev. 1.
76. Consultation Paper, note 61, p. 37 and Bill 114, s. 44(1).
77. Bill 114, ss. 45(1)-(2). Note that the report is to be made exclusively to a CAS.
78. Bill 114, s. 45(3).
79. Fraser, note 12, p. 108.
80. See editorial in Toronto Globe and Mail, July 17, 1978.
81. C. Greenland, note 14 supra at pp. 20-21 and 10 R.F.L. 50.
82. Paulsen, "The Law and Abused Children", note 2 supra at p. 175. Also see Tarasoff v. Regents of the University of California 551 P. 2d 334 (1976).
83. Paulsen, note 82 supra at p. 163; Dickens, note 37 supra at p. 24.

84. Interview with Dr. H. Sohn, Co-ordinator, Child Abuse, Children's Services Division, Ministry of Community and Social Services 7/28/78. Dr. Sohn referred to the increase in reporting in the Ottawa-Carleton region of Ontario in recent years which may be attributable to the "ripple effect" of inter-professional activities.
85. Bill 114, s. 46.
86. C. Greenland, note 14 supra at 10 R.F.L. 51; Task Force on Child Abuse at p. 9.
87. Consultation Paper, note 61, pp. 38-39.
88. Loc. cit.
89. Interviews with Dr. B.M. Dickens, 7/24/78 and Dr. H. Sohn, 7/28/78.
90. See further Dickens, note 37 supra, Chap. VII and B. Chisholm, note 68 supra.
91. S. 25(3).
92. Re Helmes (1976), 13 O.R. (2d) 4 (Div. Ct.).
93. See Report of Committee on the Representation of Children in the Provincial Court (Family Division) at p. 27 ff. and 29 R.F.L. at pp. 146-8.
94. The committee further recommended the establishment of a series of "pilot projects" designed to study, inter alia, the circumstances in which legal representation was required and to assess the relative merits of the existing methods of providing representation.
95. Bill 114, s. 20 (the section also contains a number of factors which the judge should consider in forming the opinion as to representation.
96. These comments were suggested by the submissions made by Justice for Children in response to the Consultation Paper on Short Term Legislative Amendments, and by an interview with Mr. Jeffery Wilson, Counsel for Justice for Children, 7/21/78.
97. Ontario Law Reform Commission, note 1 supra at p. 128.
98. Law Reform Commission of Canada, note 62 supra, p. 40.
99. Report, note 68 supra, 29 R.F.L. 149.

REFERENCES

Areen, J., "Intervention Between Parent and Child: A Reappraisal of the State's Role in Child Neglect and Abuse Cases" (1975), 63 Geo. L.J. 887.

Burke, K.M., "Evidentiary Problems of Proof in Child Abuse Cases: Why Family and Juvenile Courts Fail" (1974-75) 13 J. of Family Law 819.

Child Abuse and Neglect, Report to the House of Commons, (First Session, Thirtieth Parliament, 1974-75-76), Queen's Printer, Ottawa, 1976.

Child Abuse in Ontario, (Research Report 3), Ontario Ministry of Community and Social Services, Research and Planning Branch, Toronto, November, 1973.

The Child Welfare Act, Revised Statutes of Ontario, Ministry of Community and Social Services, Toronto, October, 1977.

The Child Welfare Act, 1978 (Bill 114), Ministry of Community and Social Services, Toronto, June 8, 1978.

Chisholm, B.A., "Do Children Need Lawyers?", The Child as Citizen, Canadian Council on Children and Youth, Ottawa.

Dickens, Bernard M., Legal Issues in Child Abuse, Centre of Criminology, University of Toronto, Toronto, January, 1976.

Dickens, Bernard M., "Legal Responses to Child Abuse" (1978), 12 Family Law Q. 1.

Duncan, E.C., "Recognition and Protection of the Family's Interests in Child Abuse Proceedings" (1974-75) 13 J. of Family Law 803.

Eekelaar, J.M., "What are Parental Rights?" (1973) 89 Law Q. Rev. 210.

Fraser, B.G., "A Pragmatic Alternative to Current Legislative Approaches to Child Abuse" (1974) 12 Amer. Crim. L.R. 103.

Greenland, C., "Reporting Child Abuse in Ontario" 10 Reports of Family Law 44.

Helfer, R.E. and Kempe, C.H. (ed.), The Battered Child (2nd ed. 1974), University of Chicago Press.

Koocher, G.P. (ed.), Children's Rights and the Mental Health Professions (1976) New York, John Wiley & Sons.

Law Reform Commission of Canada, Working Paper 1, The Family Court, Ottawa, 1974.

McCoid, A.H., "The Battered Child and other Assaults Upon the Family (Part 1) (1965) 50 Minn. L. Rev. 1.

Note "Child Neglect: Due Process for the Parent" (1970), 70 Colum. L. Rev. 465.

Ontario Law Reform Commission, Report on Family Law, Part III "Children", Toronto, 1973.

Ontario Law Reform Commission, Study of the Family Law Project, Volume 9, Toronto, 1968.

Paulsen, M.G., "The Legal Framework for Child Protection" (1966), 66 Colum. L. Rev. 679.

Paulsen, M.G., "Child Abuse Reporting Laws: The Shape of the Legislation" (1967), 67 Colum. L. Rev. 1.

Report of the Committee on the Representation of Children in the Provincial Court (Family Division), Ministry of the Attorney General, Toronto, June, 1977.

Report of the Task Force on Child Abuse, Ministry of Community and Social Services, Toronto, June, 1978.

Sussman, A. & Cohen, S.J., Reporting Child Abuse and Neglect: Guidelines for Legislation 1975, Cambridge, Mass. Ballinger Pub. Co.

Van Stolk, M., "The Abused Child and the Law" (1974) 16 Reports of Family Law 1.

Van Stolk, M., The Battered Child in Canada, 1972. Toronto. McClelland and Stewart Ltd.

Child Abuse and Neglect, Vol. 3, pp. 633 - 641.

0145-2134/79/0601-0633 $02.00/0.

CIVIL LIABILITY FOR FAILURE TO REPORT CHILD ABUSE

Orville R. Endicott, Barrister and Solicitor

214 Ava Road, Toronto, Ontario, Canada, M6C 1X1

INTRODUCTION

Research has begun to reveal that the effects of child battering are more far-reaching than the immediate pain and injury endured by its victims. According to Fontana (1973), an abused child grows up "without a sense of self-esteem, a hater and potential killer, a future child abuser learning dreadful lessons in the art of handling his or her own children".[1] While the suffering of child abuse victims as children ought to be enough in itself to prompt a concerted effort to control this phenomenon, the extended effects provide still more incentive to adopt any and all measures which offer a reasonable hope of relieving the problem.

Because the battering of a particular child is usually repeated over a period of some years, or until the child dies, one of the obvious areas of concern is that those who have the authority and the skill to intervene in the homes where child abuse is taking place should be informed by anyone who has a reasonable suspicion that it is happening in a particular family. Over the past decade most Canadian provinces have enacted statutory provisions to encourage such reporting.[2] Besides the mandatory reporting requirement, the statutes also stipulate that the bona fide informer is not subject to any court action by the parent or other person whom he has named in the report as the perpetrator of the abuse. Some of the provinces provide for fines or prison terms for those who are convicted of failing to report information which they possessed about the abuse of a child. All of the American states now have mandatory child abuse reporting laws, although unlike the Canadian provinces, most States name certain occupational groups as those who have a positive duty to report, such as medical and educational personnel. Others are permitted to report and protected from lawsuits when they do, but are not subject to penalties for failing to do so.

There is a growing concern that the reporting laws have not resulted in an appreciable improvement in the level of protection afforded to abused children.[3] Prosecutions for failing to exercise the statutory duty to report are virtually non-existent.[4] It is necessary to ask if anything more can be done to increase the probability of child abuse being reported. Current discussions in Canada are focussing on the possibility of increasing the maximum penalties and of narrowing the field of those classes of persons who are legally obligated to report. Although these contemplated amendments will result in reporting laws similar to those in jurisdictions where there is apparently still serious non-reporting,[5]

---

[1]Fontana, V. (1973). Somewhere a Child is Crying. MacMillan, New York. p. 57.

[2]For example, The Child Welfare Act, Revised Statutes of Ontario 1970, c. 64, s. 41.

[3]Kohlman, Richard J. (1974). Malpractice liability for failing to report child abuse. 49 California State Bar Journal 118. p. 120.

[4]Ibid., p. 121.

[5]Ibid., p. 120.

there may be some value in making the duty more certain and the penalty more severe. As Dickens (1976) puts it, this value may be primarily educational, since actual prosecutions would continue to be rare.[6]

It is the purpose of this paper to explore an additional legal implication of failing to report child abuse when one has a duty to do so. That implication is that certain persons may be civilly liable to a child where compliance with the duty to report would have meant that the child would not have been returned to the environment in which subsequent additional injuries were sustained. Most of the existing statutes provide a public remedy for non-reporting. The question posed here is whether a child who suffers further injuries after a person who had a duty to do so failed to take the necessary action to have him removed from that danger, has a private remedy in negligence against that person for the damages arising out of the subsequent injuries. We will examine this question in the light of the common law and the existing statute law, and then consider the possibility of codifying the civil cause of action in the context of the statute which sets out the reporting obligation.

CIVIL LIABILITY AT COMMON LAW FOR FAILING TO REPORT CHILD ABUSE

Liability Apart from the Reporting Statute

It is possible that an action in negligence without regard to the reporting legislation could be brought on behalf of an injured child against a doctor who had treated previous injuries which were clearly caused by non-accidental means and had failed to report his observations to the appropriate child protection authorities. Such an action would be one of malpractice liability for failing to meet the recognized standard of care in diagnosing or treating the condition. In such a case, "condition" would not refer to the physical injuries which the doctor had treated, but to the dangerous family environment to which the doctor had permitted the child to be returned.

A common law basis for establishing liability in such a case has been recognized by the California Supreme Court in the case of Landeros v. Flood.[7] The standard of care in that case was similar to that applied in Canadian courts in medical malpractice cases, namely that a physician is required to possess and exercise that reasonable degree of knowledge and skill which is ordinarily possessed and exercised by other members of the medical profession in similar circumstances.[8] The question in the Landeros case was whether such a standard can be interpreted to mean that a physician is required to know how to diagnose and treat the battered child syndrome. The California Court of Appeal ruled that it cannot. The reasoning was that "the clinical condition designated as the battered child syndrome is far from being well-defined or clear-cut", and that "physicians in private practice do not encounter a sufficient number of cases to recognize the symptoms of the battered child syndrome".[9] The conclusion was that "in the absence of [a] statute, doctors are under no legal duty to report child abuse cases".[10] On a further appeal, however, the Supreme Court of California ruled that the infant plaintiff was entitled to call expert witnesses to prove that in her case a reasonably prudent physician would have suspected that she was the victim of the battered child syndrome, and would have further investigated that possibility by means of x-rays, and would have notified the child care authorities so that a recurrence of the injuries could have been avoided.[11]

---

[6]Dickens, Bernard M. (1976). Legal Issues in Child Abuse. Centre of Criminology, University of Toronto. p. 21.

[7]Landeros v. Flood (1976), 131 Cal. Rptr. 69, 551 P. 2d 389. (Supreme Court of California).

[8]Ibid., pp. 72-73. Compare the Canadian cases of Crits v. Sylvester, [1956] O.R. 132, aff'd [1956] S.C.R. 991, and Gent and Gent v. Wilson, [1956] O.R. 257.

[9]Landeros v. Flood (1975), 123 Cal. Rptr. 713. (California Court of Appeal). pp. 718 & 719.

[10]Ibid., p. 720.

[11]Landeros v. Flood (1976), 131 Cal. Rptr. 69. (Supreme Court of California). pp. 73-74.

Liability Based on the Statutory Duty to Report

It is an ancient common law doctrine that "wherever a statute enacts anything or prohibits anything for the advantage of any person, that person shall have remedy to recover the advantage given him, or to have satisfaction for the injury done to him contrary to law, by the same statute".[12] While this dictum seems unequivocal, it has been qualified in many decisions over the past two hundred years, to the point where it is now rather uncertain what the law is. With regard to the statutory duty to report child abuse, Dickens (1976) has expressed the opinion that "it is uncertain, but doubtful, whether [the statute] imposes a duty owed to the child under common law, giving him a cause of action if he can show he suffered injury by virtue of its breach".[13] It is obviously necessary to explore in some detail the various aspects of this question in order to determine the bearing which child abuse reporting legislation might have on a civil action on behalf of a child against a person who failed in the duty to report. The uncertainty surrounding this issue arises from the fact that legislatures have declared that a person who becomes aware that a child has been or may be abused must report the situation to the prescribed authorities, but they have been silent as to whether failure to report in such circumstances may result in civil liability to the child who is subsequently injured again by the same custodian. The concluding part of this paper will deal with the question of whether such legislative silence ought to be broken. In this part we will consider civil liability in relation to the existing mandatory reporting laws, whether they are backed by penal sanctions or not.

Possible effects of the breach of a penal statute by the defendant to a civil action. The Supreme Court of California in Landeros v. Flood adopted the view that the defendant physician's responsibility for the harm which the plaintiff child suffered was determinable in the light of what the legislature commanded him to do. That command was issued in a deliberate attempt to preserve persons such as the plaintiff from further injuries of the kind she in fact sustained. The defendant's failure to comply with the statute was taken as compelling evidence that he failed to observe the appropriate standard of care.[14]

In determining the bearing of the Landeros v. Flood decision on the state of the law in other jurisdictions, it should be borne in mind that California enacted in its Evidence Code a presumption of negligence where a defendant has violated a statute.[15] This enactment was a codification of the existing case law in California, which generally reflected judicial opinion in other common law jurisdictions. The Canadian courts have followed the House of Lords in this matter. In Lochgelly Iron and Coal Company v. M'Mullan, Lord MacMillan said,

> Where two persons stand in such relation to each other that the law imposes on one of these persons a duty to take precautions for the safety of the other person, then, if the person on whom that duty is imposed fails to take the proper precautions and the other person is in consequence injured, a clear case of negligence arises.[16]

The question of legislative intention. When the courts attempt to determine the effect of a statute on an issue being tried before them, it is often asked what the intention of the legislature was in enacting the statutory provision. Some take the view that the courts should take statutes at their face value. Others, such as Julius Stone (1936) argue that a statute should be treated not only as a statement of specific rules, but also as a source of judicial reasoning to derive the rules which ought to govern related issues not addressed directly by the statute.[17] The objective, according to those who advocate this position,

---

[12] Anonymous (1703), 87 E.R. 791 (per Holt, C.J.)

[13] Dickens, Bernard M. (1976). Legal Issues in Child Abuse. Centre of Criminology, University of Toronto. p. 18.

[14] Landeros v. Flood (1976), 131 Cal. Rptr. 69. (Supreme Court of California). p. 76.

[15] California Evidence Code, s. 669.

[16] Lochgelly Iron and Coal Company v. M'Mullan, [1934] A.C. 1, cited by Smith, C.J.A. in Ostrash v Sonnenberg (1968), 67 D.L.R. (2d) 311, at p. 323. (Alberta Supreme Court).

[17] Stone, J. (1936). The common law in the United States. 50 Harvard Law Review 4. p. 13.

ought to be to decide cases wherever possible in a manner which is consistent with the aims revealed in the legislation, even if the legislature has not pronounced on the particular question to be decided. There can be no doubt that the objective of a child abuse reporting provision in child welfare legislation is to obtain reports in as many instances as possible where children are in danger, in order that measures can be taken to alleviate that danger. The imposition of civil liability arising out of non-compliance with the statute would create a greater incentive to make such reports, and thus assist in the attainment of the object of the legislation.

Where a statute stipulates a penalty for violating its provisions, the courts have reached various conclusions as to whether the legislature also intended that such a violation should give rise to civil liability for injuries another party suffers as a consequence. The House of Lords has taken the view that if a severe criminal penalty is called for, then that may be regarded as the only remedy intended, but that if there is provision for only a token fine or no penalty at all, then it can be assumed that the remedy of damages would be available.[18] If, as is the case in Ontario's child abuse reporting law,[19] no penalty is prescribed, then it makes sense to assume there is civil liability arising out of non-compliance with the statute. Otherwise the law would have no sanction, and by some standards would therefore not be law.

It has been held that a person who sells ammunition to a child contrary to the Criminal Code of Canada incurs civil liability for the injuries consequently sustained by the child.[20] The decision was based on the fact that there is a common law action for negligence in giving dangerous things to children, and that the Code could be invoked as setting an irrefutable standard of care applicable in such an action.

While it would no doubt clear up a great deal of confusion if legislators would actually say that a civil remedy is available to a child who is injured after a person came under a duty to report his dangerous situation to the responsible authorities and failed to do so, it is at least consistent with the known legislative intention for the courts to grant such a remedy. The purpose of the reporting statutes is to encourage more wide-spread reporting of situations where child abuse is likely to occur. The courts may well regard the recognition of a cause of action by a child against a person who failed to report as a just means of promoting the objectives of the legislation.

Problems of proof of liability. One of the reasons there have been so few convictions for the offence of failing to report child abuse is that the prosecution is faced with the difficult task of proving beyond a reasonable doubt that the report ought to have been made. If the accused who witnessed signs of child abuse had a reasonable doubt as to what these signs meant, then he or she would have a defence against the charge. The fact that the statute often requires reporting even when the person has only a reasonable suspicion, rather than actual knowledge that the child was intentionally injured, does not take away that defence, but rather adds confusion to the question of what mental state of the accused must be proved before guilt can be established under the evidentiary standard of the criminal law. A negligence action on behalf of the injured child against the person who had a duty to report may present less of an evidentiary problem, since the standard of proof required in civil cases is that the plaintiff must show that the balance of probabilities favours him.

Problems of proof can also arise on the basis of whether a subjective or an objective standard ought to be applied. Here we are asking whether a defendant is liable only when it is shown that he had actual knowledge that the child's injuries were non-accidental (the subjective test), or when the injuries were such that a reasonable person in the defendant's position ought to have been able to reach such a conclusion (the objective test). Rowine Hayes Brown (1973), a leading authority on both the medical and the legal aspects of child abuse, said, "When the injuries sustained are out of proportion to the history recited to the physician, he should immediately consider the possibility of abusive treatment".[21] Applying such an objective standard, the courts could find that it is professional malpractice not to pursue

---

[18] Cutler v. Wandsworth Stadium, [1949] A.C. 398. p. 414.

[19] The Child Welfare Act, Revised Statutes of Ontario, 1970, c. 64, s. 41.

[20] Wasney v. Jurazsky, [1933] 1 W.W.R. 155. (Manitoba Court of Appeal).

[21] Hayes Brown, Rowine. (1973). Medical and legal aspects of the battered child syndrome. 50 Chicago-Kent Law Review 45. p. 49.

the medical investigation to the point where the battered child syndrome can at least be considered as a possible underlying factor.

Some jurisdictions have reporting statutes which suggest that a subjective standard would be applied in determining liability for failing to report child abuse. The wording in most of the Canadian provinces, for example is to the effect that "everyone having information" that a child has been abused is obligated to report.[22] Other statutes say that a report must be made whenever a person "has reasonable cause to believe that a child is subject to physical ill-treatment"[23] or words to that effect. The use of the concept of "reasonable grounds" to suspect the existence of abuse would preserve for a civil plaintiff the advantage of having an action in negligence, rather than having to prove that the defendant actually knew he had been abused, but deliberately chose not to make a report.

Causation. Establishing a causal nexus between a failure to report one or more earlier incidents of child abuse and a subsequent battering of the same child by the same adult is a critical element to be considered in a civil action of this nature. The immediate cause of the child's injuries is the infliction of blows, burns, deprivation or other abuse by his adult custodian. The question is whether these acts are to be regarded as the sole legal cause, or whether the failure to take reasonable steps to have the child removed from the dangerous environment or otherwise protected may not be considered as a substantial factor leading to the subsequent injuries. It is a well-established tort law principle that the action of a third party does not necessarily break the chain of causation between the defendant's negligence and the plaintiff's injuries. According to Salmond, "It is a fallacy to suppose that the last cause is the sole cause".[24] This principle becomes particularly relevant where the intervening act is one from which the defendant had a duty to protect the plaintiff. Such a situation is addressed by the American Restatement of Torts:

> If the likelihood that a third person may act in a particular manner is the hazard ... which makes the actor negligent, such an act, whether innocent, negligent, intentionally tortious, or criminal, does not prevent the actor from being liable for harm caused thereby.[25]

In a civil action based on the defendant's duty to report child abuse, the battering of the plaintiff by his parent or guardian is precisely the risk which prompted the legislature to impose such a duty. The failure to report effectively extends in time the risk which the person whose duty it is to report could be instrumental in reducing or ending altogether.

The key to answering the question of causation is to discover whether the intervening act of child abuse was reasonably foreseeable. One of the characteristics of the battered child syndrome which a medical practitioner ought to know is, in the words of Mosk, J. of the Supreme Court of California in Landeros v. Flood:

> ... that the assault on the victim is not an isolated, atypical event but part of an environmental mosaic of repeated beatings and abuse that will not only continue but will become more severe unless there is appropriate medicolegal intervention. If the risk of the resumption of physical abuse is thus a principal reason why a doctor's failure to diagnose and treat the battered child syndrome constitutes negligence, ... the fact that the risk eventuates does not relieve him of responsibility.[26]

It follows that expert testimony is required in order to determine the foreseeability of further injuries which occupied or ought to have occupied the mind of the physician when the child was examined and treated on the earlier occasion.

---

[22] For example, The Child Welfare Act, Revised Statutes of Ontario, 1970, c. 64, s. 41.

[23] The Youth Protection Act, Revised Statutes of Quebec, 1964, c. 220, s. 14j.

[24] Heuston, R.V.F. (1973). Salmond on the Law of Torts, (16th edition), Sweet & Maxwell, London. p. 556.

[25] Restatement (Second) of Torts, (1965), s. 449.

[26] Landeros v. Flood, (1976), 131 Cal. Rptr. 69. (Supreme Court of California). pp. 75-76. Mosk, J. lists several authorities in the fields of medicine and social work to substantiate the repetitive nature of child abuse.

The high probability of repetition of child battering is of course the raison d'etre of the reporting laws. The objective is not to apprehend and punish the abusers so much as to break the pattern of abuse in the home and protect the child from additional torment and from death or life-long physical and emotional scars through continued acts of violence and deprivation. Reporting laws are based on two suppositions as to the possible outcomes: (1) that if the abuse of the child goes unreported, the child is likely to be injured again, and (2) that if the required report is made, adequate measures will be taken to preserve the child from further harm. Both of these suppositions may have to be confirmed in court in order to establish the requisite degree of foreseeability. The action of the child welfare officials is discretionary. If, in a given community, it began to appear unlikely that any effective action would be taken to relieve the plight of an abused child after a report had been made, a non-reporting person may be able to show that he or she could not reasonably be expected to foresee that the making of a report would in fact reduce the risk to the child. Such a plea would not necessarily free a mandated person from an action for violation of the statutory duty as such, but it may be relevant in a civil action by virtue of the fact that foreseeability is an essential factor in determining causation.

Generally speaking, the pleading of a broken chain of causation due to the actions of others is not one which will exculpate a defendant whose failure to report has substantially contributed to the plaintiff's ensuing injuries. A question which may often deserve deeper consideration is that of how great an "affinity of causal likelihood" exists between the defendant's wrong and the plaintiff's injuries.[27] In other words, the court may well ask how significant a factor the breach of the reporting law was in the unfortunate outcome of the child being further injured.

Isaacson (1975) has summed up the essential arguments in favour of finding a casual link between failure to comply with the reporting statute and the continuation of the child's suffering:

> The statute has designated the physician as the conduit to the outside world for the pain of the inarticulate child. Proximate causation is found because a non-reporting doctor allows the battered or otherwise injured child to be returned to parents or guardians who are likely to abuse him again. A non-reporting doctor effectively blocks police and juvenile welfare authorities from aiding the helpless child. A non-reporting doctor should, therefore, bear the civil consequences of his wrong-doing.[28]

Taking into consideration the mandate to report child abuse in the various child welfare statutes and the effect of statutory duties in civil actions, it seems likely that there is a cause of action at common law in favour of infants who suffer abuse after their plight has become known to or ought reasonably to have been suspected by a person who was under a legal duty to report. There are, however, many uncertainties involved in the prosecution of such an action. The next part of this paper will explore the possibility that some of these uncertainties could be resolved by legislation.

CIVIL LIABILITY DEFINED BY STATUTE

We have observed that a great deal of the jurisprudence and scholarly writing on the effects of statutory violations on civil actions arising in connection with the conduct the statute requires or prohibits revolve around the question of whether the legislature intended that there should be a civil remedy. This tendency, coupled with the uncertainty of this area of the law of torts, suggests that it would be valuable to have a statute which expresses as clearly as possible what the civil consequences are of the breach of a penal clause requiring certain groups of people to report actual or suspected child abuse.

In Canada, only a 1973 amendment to Alberta's Child Welfare Act makes any mention of civil liability to the child for failure to report child abuse. The subsection prescribing

---

[27] Malone, E. (1956). Ruminations on cause-in-fact. 9 Stanford Law Review 60. p. 72.

[28] Isaacson, Lon B. (1975). Child abuse reporting statutes: the case for holding physicians civilly liable for failing to report. 12 San Diego Law Review 743. p. 758.

penalties for the violation of the reporting requirement reads as follows:

> (3) Any person who fails to comply with subsection (1) [the reporting requirement], in addition to any civil liability, is guilty of an offence and liable upon summary conviction to a fine of not more than $500 and in default of payment to imprisonment for a term not exceeding six months or to both fine and imprisonment.[29]

Evidently the legislators addressed their minds to the possibility that an action in negligence may be available as a remedy for an injured child. The non-committal reference, however, suggests that they were simply acknowledging the existence or possible existence of an action at common law, rather than declaring that an action exists by legislative fiat. It should be noted that subsection (1) says "any person who has reasonable and probable grounds to believe that a child has been ... ill-treated" is obligated to make a report. The fact that the net is cast so wide is further indication that no statutory cause of action was intended, since only those with certain professional qualifications could be presumed to be subject to an appropriate standard of care.

In the United States, New York and Arkansas have positively enacted civil liability on the part of persons or institutions failing to report when they are under a duty to do so. The New York legislation reads as follows:

> s. 420(2) Any person, official or institution required by this title to report a case of suspected child abuse or maltreatment who knowingly and wilfully fails to do so shall be civilly liable for the damages proximately caused by such failure.[30]

The Arkansas enactment is similar in all material respects.[31] Both States require reports only from members of certain professions, rather than from any person who may have reasonable cause to suspect a child has been abused. The named professions are in the areas of medicine, education, social work and law enforcement.

J. W. Davies (1973) has said, "Much of the difficulty of the action for breach of statutory duty would be avoided if statutes expressly said whether there was a civil action for breach of the duty and, if so, what the limits of the liability were".[32] If this need exists generally, then it would seem also to exist for the particular problem of tying together the violation of the statutory reporting requirement in child abuse cases and the question of the liability of the violator to the victim of further abuse.

Sussman and Cohen (1975) have proposed that the legislation ought to state specifically that a person failing to report "shall be liable for any civil damages proximately caused by his failure to report".[33] To support this proposal, they point to the virtual non-existence of criminal prosecutions under the existing reporting statutes, and suggest that "the threat of civil liability would more efficiently promote reporting".[34] Certainly the inclusion of a provision establishing civil liability in the reporting statute would increase the awareness of the child abuse problem and of the duty to report many times over its present level, and considerably beyond that which a purely penal sanction can generate.

Throughout the foregoing discussion it has been either explicit or implicit that members of the medical profession are the primary ones contemplated as having to face the risk of a civil action for failing to report child abuse. This focus was not by design, but arises necessarily in the light of a presumption that medically trained personnel have special

---

[29] The Child Welfare Act, Revised Statutes of Alberta, 1970, c. 45, s. 41, as amended by the Child Welfare Amendment Act, S.A. 1973, c. 15, s. 8. (This amendment had not been proclaimed when this paper was written).

[30] McKinney's Consolidated Laws of New York, Social Services Law (1973), s. 420(2).

[31] Arkansas Statutes Annotated, 1975 Cummulative Supp., s. 42-816(b).

[32] Davies, J.W. (1974). Torts. In the Annual Survey of Commonwealth Law, 1973. Butterworths, London. p. 443.

[33] Sussman, Alan, and Stephen J. Cohen. (1975). Reporting Child Abuse and Neglect: Guidelines for Legislation. Ballinger, Cambridge, Mass. p. 35.

[34] Ibid.

knowledge and skill in recognizing and analyzing signs of intentionally inflicted wounds. There is no reason to exculpate other persons whose occupations bring them into close, and perhaps much more frequent contact with battered children, such as teachers. It must also be noted, however, that statistics reveal that over three-quarters of the children who are attacked by their parents are of pre-school age.[35] If such attacks are so violent that extensive or permanent injuries are sustained (such as would give rise to a civil action for damages), then the most likely person to be in a position to set in motion the process of rescuing the child is the physician. There are also statistics which reveal serious under-reporting by doctors.[36] It is appropriate that each person mandated to report should, if faced with an action for damages incurred in consequence of his or her failure to report child abuse, be subject at trial to the standard of care normally expected of persons in his or her occupational group.

If legislators are convinced that the problem of child abuse is of serious consequence to large numbers of children, which it is, and a continuing threat to the sound development of future parents and citizens, which it is, then every avenue must be explored to reduce its incidence. This paper has focussed on one of those avenues -- a civil remedy on behalf of injured children against those who could and should have helped to rescue them. While this is not likely in itself to remove the danger of child abuse from children and its blight from society, it can, along with more effective medical, social and legal intervention, contribute to a significant amelioration of the problem.

---

[35] Hayes Brown, Rowine. (1973). Medical and legal aspects of the battered child syndrome. 50 _Chicago-Kent Law Review_ 45. p. 83.

[36] Note. Child abuse and the law: a mandate for change. (1973) 18 _Howard Law Journal_ 200. p. 203. Sussman, Alan. (1974). Reporting child abuse: a review of the literature. 8 _Family Law Quarterly_ 245. p. 270. Greenland. C. (1973). _Reporting Child Abuse in Ontario_. Ministry of Community and Social Services, Toronto.

REFERENCES

Dickens, Bernard M. (1976). _Legal Issues in Child Abuse_. Centre of Criminology, University of Toronto.

Greenland, C. (1973). _Reporting Child Abuse in Ontario_. Ministry of Community and Social Services, Toronto.

Hayes Brown, Rowine. (1973). Medical and legal aspects of the battered child syndrome. 50 _Chicago-Kent Law Review_ 45.

Heuston, R.V.F. (1973). _Salmond on the Law of Torts_, (16th edition). Sweet and Maxwell, London.

Fontana, V. (1973). _Somewhere a Child is Crying_. MacMillan, New York.

Isaacson, Lon B. (1975). Child abuse reporting statutes: the case for holding physicians civilly liable for failing to report. 12 _San Diego Law Review_ 743.

Kohlman, Richard J. (1974). Malpractice liability for failing to report child abuse. 49 _California State Bar Journal_ 118.

Landeros v. Flood (1975), 123 Cal. Rptr. 713. (California Court of Appeal).

Landeros v. Flood (1976), 131 Cal. Rptr. 69, 551 P. 2d 389. (Supreme Court of California).

Malone, E. (1956). Ruminations on cause-in-fact. 9 _Stanford Law Review_ 60.

Note. Child abuse and the law: a mandate for change. (1973) 18 Howard Law Journal 200.

Stone, J. (1936). The common law in the United States. 50 Harvard Law Review 4.

Sussman, Alan. (1974). Reporting child abuse: a review of the literature. 8 Family Law Quarterly 245.

Sussman, Alan, and Stephen J. Cohen. (1975). Reporting Child Abuse and Neglect: Guidelines for Legislation. Ballinger, Cambridge, Mass.

Child Abuse and Neglect, Vol. 3, pp. 643 - 650.
Pergamon Press Ltd., 1979. Printed in Great Britain.

NEGLECT OF THE UNBORN CHILD: AN ANALYSIS BASED ON LAW IN THE UNITED STATES

Donald C. Bross, Instructor in Pediatrics (Family Law), University of Colorado School of Medicine; Staff Attorney, The National Center for the Prevention and Treatment of Child Abuse and Neglect, Denver, Colorado 80220, U.S.A. and Ann Meredyth, J.D., Boulder, Colorado 80303, U.S.A.

"Justice requires recognition that a child has a legal right to begin life with a sound mind and body." [1]

Dangers to the unborn child range from predictable, but rare, genetic disorders to overt, unreasonable abuse. For example, some 200 pregnant and heroin-addicted mothers are seen annually at Hutzel Hospital in Detroit, Michigan alone,[2] approximately 6,000 children were born with fetal alcohol syndrome in the United States in 1977,[3] and at least 22 amphetamine babies were born in Stockholm from 1976 to 1978.[4] Another concern is the child known to be gravely endangered by parental inadequacies even at birth.[5] With increasing attention being directed to preventive medicine on one hand, and child abuse and neglect on the other, it is inevitable that some thought be given to what societies can properly do on behalf of neglected or "abused" unborn.

It is obviously much harder to protect a child still within the mother than when a simple change of custody guarantees physical safety. On the other hand, taking a child from the home is a last resort anytime and assumes that other servies to the family will not suffice. Given that an unborn child cannot be placed in a safer place than the womb, everything else being equal, one may question what else society can do practically, legally, and ethically to protect the neglected or abused unborn.

RIGHTS OF THE MOTHER OF THE UNBORN

Assuming that society might wish to act on behalf of the unborn child _in a limited fashion_, do not the mother's rights prevent _any_ invasion of her privacy? The American abortion decisions of the last ten years have created guidelines for comparing a woman's rights to the rights of her unborn child. The United States Supreme Court has marked the end of the first trimester of pregnancy as the point at which the state may have a "compelling" interest in the _mother's_ life. As its rationale, the court stated:

---

1. _Smith v. Brennan_, 31 N.J. 353, 157 A.2d 497, 503 (1960).

2. "Child Abuse Charged in Neonate Heroin Addiction," _Pediatric News_. September 1977, p. 18.

3. Harrison W. John, "Harming the Innocent," _Listen_, August 1978, Pp.15-16.

4. M. Eriksson, G. Larsson, R. Zetterstrom, "Child Neglect and Abuse in Drug Addicted Families." Second International Congress on Child Abuse and Neglect, London, September 12-15, 1978, _Abstracts_, p. 43.

5. Anthony C. Fairburn, "Removal of the Newborn into Care at Birth," Presentation at the Second International Congress on Child Abuse and Neglect, London, England, Sept. 15,1978.

"This is so because of the now-established medical fact. . . that until the end of the first trimester mortality and abortion may be less than mortality in childbirth. It follows that, from and after this point, a State may regulate the abortion procedure to the extent that regulation reasonably relates to the preservation and protection of maternal health."[6]

The Court further concluded that until the end of the first trimester, the decision to terminate the pregnancy is one for the mother and her doctor "free of interference by the State."[7] Given such absolute discretion over the life of the unborn, there appears to be no basis for regulating any of the mother's conduct with respect to the pregnancy during this first trimester.[8] The manner in which the early pregnancy is conducted, however, may become an evidentiary matter once sufficient time has passed for the life of the unborn to become directly subject to State power.

Under the Roe v. Wade decision the point at which a State's interest in the unborn child is compelling enough to justify intervention on behalf of the child follows after the first trimester:

"With respect to the State's important and legitimate interest in potential life, the 'compelling' point is at viability. This is so because the fetus then presumably has the capability of meaningful life outside the mother's womb. State regulation protective of fetal life after viability, thus has both logical and biological justification. If the state is interested in protecting fetal life after viability, it may go so far as to proscribe abortion during that period, except when it is necessary to preserve the life and health of the mother."[9] (Emphasis added.)

One can be relatively comfortable with the primacy of the pregnant woman's discretion in early pregnancy, and yet be concerned about the quality of the pregnancy carried to term. Pregnancy is, of course, a time-determined process. Whether the woman actively wants a pregnancy or passively submits to it, her control over the growing fetus becomes increasingly limited by nature. The mother's failure to have an abortion early enough results practically in a nearly total abandonment of that option. Legally, under the Roe v. Wade decision,the failure to act becomes a forsaking or waiver of her nearly absolute right to abort. As the unborn child matures, so does the bundle of rights,accruing to all persons in a free society,begin to ripen. In the words of a state court prior to the Roe v. Wade decision, "The essential requirement of due process is that the woman be given the power to determine within an appropriate period after conception whether or not she wishes to bear a child." [10]

Once past the issues of abortion, parental rights in the unborn child must be considered, with great deference to be given to parental discretion.

"At common law, the parents' possessive control over their child was virtually limitless.* * *

"The last 50 years have seen the slow erosion of this doctrine of parental absolutism. Though it is still commonly agreed that the parent may exercise the rights of care, custody and control, these rights are no longer regarded as absolute. Each state, under its police powers and the doctrine of parens patriae, may restrain and regulate parental prerogatives when the parent grossly abuses these rights of care, custody and control.* * *

---

6. Roe v. Wade,410 U.S. 113, 163 (1972).

7. Id.at p. 164.

8. Subsequent decisions make it unlikely that a guardian could, at this point, act on behalf of the child, since even the parents of a pregnant minor or a husband cannot override a woman's decision during the first trimester. For example, see Planned Parenthood v. Danforth, 96 S. Ct. 2831 (1976).

9. Id. at Pp. 163-164.

10. Abele v. Markle, 342 F. Supp 800 (D.Conn., 1972).

"What was formerly referred to as a doctrine of parental absolutes is now more realistically characterized as a presumptive parental right."[11]

Depending on the situation, it is now possible that a court will find that the State has an interest in the health and education of a child that is, in many respects, superior to the interests of the parents or the wishes of children.[12] Even freedom of religion is not a sufficient basis to allow parents to martyr a child.[13] The test remains one of balancing parental rights and the children's rights as they conflict in a specific situation.

LEGAL RECOGNITION OF THE UNBORN

Now permitted clear discretion, under the U.S. Constitution, to take an interest in the viable unborn child, a state must nevertheless provide a common law or statutory basis for including the unborn child within the class of persons or objects over whom courts have jurisdiction. The threshold question of whether unborn children are "persons" for any purpose of the law has been answered differently for different legal matters. For example, the United States Supreme Court has decided that an unborn child is not a "person" under the 14th amendment to the United States Constitution.[14] This ruling does not mean that states cannot define an unborn child as a person,within constitutional guidelines. Also, deciding that the unborn is not a "person," does not totally prevent action on behalf of the unborn. In property, tort and probate law, moreover, there are a considerable number of cases recognizing unborn children as persons.

A range of interests accruing to the unborn child must be examined. Property interests of the unborn have been widely recognized under law. Unborn children have been allowed to inherit, and to benefit from wills, trusts, and ante-nuptial agreements.[15] Courts have evenly split on allowing recovery under Workman's Compensation statutes,[16] with recovery usually depending on the wording of specific laws. Children as yet unborn can also be grantees of real property.[17] The considerable development of property cases relating to the unborn exemplifies the traditional primacy of property issues over issues of individual health and life, especially in the area of children's law. Fortunately, the development of law relative to the life and health of children has accelerated in the United States, especially in the last decade.

There is a great variety of forms of action to protect the person of the unborn child. Crimes against the person of the unborn, torts (claims for compensation for injuries to the unborn), the right to paternal support, eligibility for support of unborn children under the Federal Aid to Families with Dependent Children law, and dependency, abuse and neglect actions are all related to the immediate well-being of the child's person.

Statutes imposing criminal liability have often been found not to apply to the unborn,[18]

---

11. Brian G. Fraser, "Independent Representation for the Abused and Neglected Child: The Guardian Ad Litem," California Western Law Review, Vol. 13, No. 1, 1976-77, Pp.25-26.

12. For example, see Meek v. Pittinger, 374 F. Supp. 639, Aff'd in part, rev'd in part 421 U.S. 1049 (D.C. Pa., 1974).

13. Prince v. Massachusetts,321 U.S. 158 (1944) Matter of Gregory S., 380 N.Y.S.2d 620 (N.Y. Fam. Ct., 1976).

14. Roe v. Wade, supra.

15. Wallis v. Hodson (Ch.1740), 26 Eng.Rep.472; Marsh v. Kirby (Ch.1634), 21 Eng. Rep.512; Hale v. Hale (Ch.1692), 24 Eng. Rep.25; Burdet v. Hopegood (Ch.1718), In Re Holthausen's Will, 175 Misc. 1022,1024, 26 N.Y.S.2d 140,143 (1941). See generally, W.Blackstone, Commentaries 130. See also, 23 Am.Jur.2d,Descent and Distribution, §§88,89; Wills (1st Ed., §1367).

16. Workman's Compensation (1st Ed., §176).

17. Mackie v. Mackie, 230 N.C. 152, 52 S.E.2d 352 (1949).

18. Reyes v. Superior Court 141 Cal. Rptr. 912 (App., 1977).

unless the crime is specifically one against the unborn, as in a criminal abortion.[19] This pattern is not surprising, in that courts are usually unwilling to interpret criminal statutes broadly. Crimes against an unborn, which necessarily must be directed first or primarily against the mother, can be prosecuted on the basis that the mother is the victim. Prosecution for a crime against the mother normally can satisfy society's policies of punishment and deterrence. Since most of the remedies available through the criminal process are of no value, of limited value, or equally available through other legal processes, insofar as protection of the child is the goal, this relative lack of criminal protection does not appear to be of great importance. Finally, in certain cases, criminal prosecution for harm to the unborn may be possible.[20]

As early as 1884,[21] an American court was confronted with the issue of harm to a child _en ventre sa mere_. Deciding that the unborn child was part of the mother, without separate existence, the Massachusetts Supreme Court set a precedent, blocking tort actions for prenatal harm, which lasted until 1946.[22] A total reversal has occurred throughout the United States since 1946, with all states permitting recovery for injuries to the unborn child.[23] The viability question remains but is gradually losing its importance.[24]

Wrongful death caused by prenatal injuries presents a more troubling question for the courts. Wrongful death is a cause of action statutorily created, and it is not a common law action. Most wrongful death statutes are written in language which allows recovery for "death. . .of a person." Fifteen states deny recovery for the wrongful death of a viable, stillborn fetus[25] because the fetus is not "a person" within the meaning of the wrongful death statute, or because the statutory requirement that the decedent would have been able to bring an action would he have lived is not met. Seventeen states have allowed recovery for the wrongful death of a stillborn fetus [26] on the rationale that while the fetus is "a person" is in the statute; that "life" is destroyed when a viable fetus is injured so that it cannot be born alive; and that it is illogical to allow recovery for acts which injure a viable fetus, but not for those which kill.

The _Roe v. Wade_ limitations do not apply to tort actions and it is now possible to recover for injuries to a child caused by conduct prior to a child's conception. This notion may seem so extraordinary, that perhaps specific examples are in order. Transfusing blood type A-RH+ when the mother should have received type A-RH- resulted in recovery for the damages or costs caused by injuries sustained by an infant as a result of the negligent transfusions.[27]

---

19. See discussion and cases cited in _Cheaney v. State_, 285 N.E.2d 265, 268 (Indiana, 1972). This case was limited, as were other criminal abortion decisions, by _Roe v. Wade_, supra.

20. 40 Am.Jur.2d, Homocide §9.

21. _Dietrich v. Northampton_, 138 Mass. 14 (1884) overruled by implication in _Keyes v. Construction Service, Inc._, 165 N.E. 2d 912 (Mass., 1960).

22. _Bonbrest v. Katz_, 65 F. Supp. 138 (D.C. Dist. Cal., 1946).

23. The final state adopting this rule is _Husky v. Smith_, 289 Ala. 52, 265 So.2d 596 (1972).

24. _Smith v. Brennan_, 31 N.J. 353, 157A 2d 497, 504 (1960).

25. R. Kruger, "Wrongful Death and the Unborn: An Examination of Recovery After _Roe v. Wade_," 13 _J. Fam. Law_ 99 at 111,112 (1973-74). Recovery is allowed where the infant is born alive and subsequently dies. By its live birth, the fetus has become a "person" within the meaning of the wrongful death statutes.

26. Id., at p. 113, 114.

27. _Renslow v. Mennonite Hospital_, 351 N.E. 2d 870 (Ill., 1976).

Chromosomal damage in twins related to the taking of birth control pills prescribed prior to pregnancy led to recovery against a pharmaceutical company.[28] Negligent performance of a ceasarian section for one child led over two years later to an occult rupture of the uterus and an emergency caesarian resulting in liability for the defendent physicians because of brain damage to the last-born child.[29]

With tort actions being successfully pursued by parents on behalf of children harmed prenatally or even harmed by events prior to conception, one might assume a right to recover against parents would be easily sustained. In fact, parental immunity doctrines are only gradually being overcome.[30] Willful and wanton conduct on the part of the parent is usually required.[31] Many parents harming their children are "judgment proof" due to poverty. And money damages are normally a very poor way to restore a child prenatally harmed. Restitution is, clearly, less desirable than prevention. Thus, the difficulty of sustaining actions against parents for prenatal injuries need not be greatly concerning if other remedies for protection of the unborn are practical and enforced.

A few further examples of the status of the unborn can be mentioned. Federal payments on behalf of the unborn under the Social Security Act,[32] specifically titled the Aid to Families with Dependent Children program (hereinafter AFDC), have been determined not to be required of States.[33] A regulation of the United States Department of Health, Education and Welfare requiring AFDC payments on behalf of unborn children has been interpreted to provide an option for states to make such payments.[34] In 1974, approximately 60% of the states participating in AFDC disallowed such payments.[35]

A paternity action on behalf of an unborn child may be initiated,[36] although it may have to be continued if the alleged father requests a continuance for blood tests.[37]

Given the numerous ways unborn children have had their property and health protected, the possibility of maintaining an action for dependency, neglect or abuse should not seem unreasonable. In effect, at least two American courts have decided that harm to unborn children can be adjudicated through dependency and neglect proceedings. In _Raleigh Fitkin-Paul Morgan Mem. Hosp. v. Anderson_[38] (hereinafter _Raleigh Fitkin_), the New Jersey Supreme Court ordered that a pregnant woman be given transfusions _if needed to save her life and the life of her unborn child_, despite her religious objections. In the case of _In re Vanessa F._[39] (hereinafter _Vanessa F._), _the mother's prenatal behavior_ led to the birth of an addicted baby, and

---

28. _Jorgensen v. Meade Johnson Laboratories, Inc._, 483 F.2d 237 (10th Cir., 1973).

29. _Bergstresser v. Mitchell_, U.S. Court of Appeals (8th Cir), No.77-1742(Missouri, May 10, 1978); Newsletter of the National Health Lawyers Assoc., Vol. 6, No. 6, June, 1978.

30. Robert H. Mnookin, _Family Law: Child, Family, State_. Unpublished manuscript, 1977, Pp.23, 24.

31. Id., 24.

32. 42 U.S.C. §601 et seq.

33. _Burns v. Alcola_, 420 U.S. 575 (1975).

34. 45 C.F.R. §233.90(c)(2)(ii).

35. Matter of _Rankin v. Lavine_, 41 N.Y.2d 911,394 N.Y.S.2d 618,363 N.E.2d 343(1977).

36. _People v. Estergard_, 169 Colo. 445,457 P.2d 698 (1969).

37. _State v. Morgan_, 31 N.C. App. 128, 228 S.E. 2d 523 (1976).

38. 201 A.2d 537 (N.J., 1964),cert.den.377 U.S. 985, 84 S.Ct. 1894 (1964).

39. (76 Misc.2d 617), 351 N.Y.S.2d 337, 340 (1974) _Id_.at 340.

was implicitly the basis of the court's decision that a child born addicted to heroin is prima facie a dependent or neglected child. These and other cases provide a means of analyzing the various facts or patterns which justify judicial intervention on behalf of the neglected unborn.

FACTUAL PATTERNS SUPPORTING LEGAL INTERVENTION

Three situations involving prenatal harm to children are of sufficient prevalence to justify special attention: medical neglect, harmful drug ingestion, and mental illness.

The issues of medical neglect are sufficiently diverse and complex to merit a wholely separate discussion. The following comments are offered only as an outline of some of the issues. Among the medical conditions threatening the health of a viable fetus would be diabetes in the mother, multiple gestation, toxemia, herpes II infection, premature rupture of membranes and high-risk deliveries generally. The strongest cases for court-ordered treatment are those wherein the very life of the child is in question. Blood transfusion cases are perhaps the most common example of life-threatening refusal to agree to a medical procedure,[40] but any situation in which a mother is unwilling to permit life-saving medical care for a viable fetus is potentially subject to state action. As the condition of concern changes from life-threatening to seriously disabling to disfiguring to merely undesirable, the willingness of American courts to override parental discretion decreases. The risk of severe brain damage,[41] an untreated, herniated umbilical cord,[42] untreated, undescended testicles,[43] and even failure to provide mental health care,[44] have provided a basis for court-ordered treatment in the United States. The failure to consent to surgery for correction of a massive disfigurement of the face and neck,[45] failure to provide proper care for children with primary tuberculosis,[46] and failure to permit vaccinations,[47] have been ruled not to be adequate bases for court-ordered medical intervention. Absent a showing that an illness or condition has been caused by lack of parental care, the illness alone may not be enough to justify intervention.[48] But failure to seek care that is available for children, can lead to sustaining of a dependency and neglect petition[49] or even a criminal conviction[50] for those courts more accepting of the need to give primary consideration to the needs of children. The parents' reasonable objections to a medical procedure must be considered, but a reasonable medical certainty that an operation procedure is required[51] or the presence of a treatable disease[52] may be enough to justify court-ordered intervention.

---

40. For example, see People ex rel Wallace v. Labeny, 411 Ill. 618, 104 N.E.2d 769 (1952); Jehovah's Witnesses in State of Wash. v. King County Hospital Unit No. 1 (Harborview), 278 F. Supp. 488, Aff'd 391 U.S. 961 (D.C. Wash., 1967). Also see Raleigh Fitkin, supra.

41. State v. Perricone, 37 N.J. 463, 181A,2d751 (1962).

42. Matter of Gregory S.,85 Misc. 2d 846, 380 N.Y.S.2d 620 (N.Y. Fam. Ct., 1976).

43. Commission of Social Services v. D., 339 N.Y.S.2d 89, 72 Misc.2d 428 (N.Y. Fam. Ct., 1972).

44. V.A.M.S. In re C________F________B________,497 S.W.2d 831 (Mo.App., 1973).

45. In Re Green, 448 Pa. 338, 292 A.2d 387 (1972).

46. In Re Price's Welfare, 13 Wash. App. 437, 535 P2d 475 (1975).

47. In Re Maria R., 81 Misc.2d 286, 366 N.Y.S.2d 309 (N.Y. Fam. Ct., 1975).

48. Daugaard v. People in Interest of Daugaard, 488 P.2d 1101 (Colo., 1971); In Interest of Gonzales, 323 N.E.2d 42, 25 Ill. App.3d 136 (1974),but cf. footnote 52.

49. Harley v. Oliver, 404 F. Supp. 450 (D.C. Ark., 1975).

50. State v. Clark, 261 A.2d 294, 5 Conn.Cir.689 (Conn.Cir.A.D., 1969).

51. In Re Elwell, 284 N.Y.S.2d 924, 55 Misc.2d 252 (N.Y. Fam.Ct., 1967).

52. In Re Karworth, 799 N.W.2d 147 (Iowa, 1972).

Because medical intervention on behalf of an unborn child would inevitably involve the direct health and safety of the mother as well, there are additional, obvious limitations on such interventions absent in ordinary medical neglect cases. The Roe v. Wade case in dictum indicates that harm to the unborn child may be acceptable when necessary to save the mother's life.[53] The principle of applying the least restrictive alternative state action possible should be applied not only to safeguard the child but to safeguard the mother as well.[54] The process of informed consent should be followed as a means of assuring that all knowledge available to help make an adequate decision will be applied to the conditions of the mother and the unborn child.[55] The clearest case for medical intervention before a child is born would be in situations where the mother's life as well as the child's life would be saved.[56] Another strong example would be a procedure which will save the child's life but be totally benign for the mother. Nearly as compelling should be cases where there are minimal risks for the mother, but the child will be saved from a substantial impairment of function, such as retardation, blindness, paralysis or similar losses.

The second area is drug dependency. The developing fetus of a heroin addict is actively harmed by the mother's drug habits. Any drug taken by a pregnant woman will affect the fetus if the drug is capable of crossing the placenta. Heroin readily passes through the placenta.[57] Note, however, that no law directly prohibits this abuse of the fetus. It is likely babies born of heroin-addicted mothers will be born addicted, will be premature, will have low birth-weights, will have small head circumferences, will have a higher mortality rate and will require a lengthy hospital stay.[58]

Not all babies born to heroin users are addicted. Roughly 50-75% of such babies will manifest symptoms of withdrawal.[59] Three factors determine the severity of an infant's withdrawal: (a) the longer the mother has been on drugs, the more severe will be the baby's withdrawal; (b) the larger the dose the mother takes, the more severe will be the baby's withdrawal; (c) the closer to delivery the mother takes her last dose of heroin, the greater and earlier will be the signs of withdrawal in the baby.[60]

At least two courts have ruled that a child born heroin-addicted is a dependent or neglected child.[61] By implication, earlier monitoring and court-ordered regimens of reduced doses of heroin or methodone might be imposed by courts with juvenile jurisdiction during the last trimester of pregnancy.

Mental illness in an expectant mother presents a third set of factual circumstances wherein a court might order intervention on behalf of the unborn. Where, as a result of mental illness, a person is a danger to themselves or others, involuntary evaluation and treatment is commonly ordered. When a person is mentally ill and pregnant, society's concern reasonably extends to the unborn child as well as its mother. Thus, evaluation and treatment might be considered with a special focus directed at the needs of the unborn child. In situations where there is a history of violence, or harm to previously born children, the factual basis for intervention seems to be especially strong.

---

53. Supra.

54. Shelton v. Tucker, 364 U.S. 479, 488 (1960).

55. For example, see G. Annas, et al. Informed Consent to Human Experimentation: The Subject's Dilemma, Cambridge, Mass: Ballinger (1973) Pp.27-42.

56. This was the situation in Raleigh Fitkin, supra. p.538.

57. Johnson and Johnson, Narcotic Addiction in the Newborn, 1 (1972).

58. L. P. Finnegan; J.F. Connaugton; J.P. Emich; and W.F. Willand, "Comprehensive Care of Maternal Addicts," 1 Contemp - Drug 795, 804-806.

59. Id., p. 802.

60. S. Burman, The Heroin Babies: Going Cold Turkey at Birth, N.Y. Times, Jan. 9, 1972, Magazine 18.

61. See In re Vanessa F., supra., and In re Baby X, Oakland County, Michigan, Probate Court No. N-33772, July 22, 1977.

LEGAL AND PRACTICAL ALTERNATIVES FOR THE PROTECTION OF THE UNBORN

The alternatives which should be examined in prenatal neglect cases include the following. The alternatives represent increasingly intrusive steps and therefore require an increasingly strong medical, social, or psychiatric basis. All of these steps assume that adequate attempts at voluntary compliance have been undertaken.

1. Document prenatal behavior harmful to the child as a method of establishing a syndrome or pattern of conduct justifying immediate court action as soon as the child is born.

2. Ask the court to take jurisdiction over the unborn child, and to appoint a guardian ad litem for the unborn child.

3. Ask the court to order a social investigation of the family.

4. Ask the court to order a medical or psychiatric examination of the mother (or father).

5. Ask the court to order a medical regimen, following the application of informed consent principles and considering primarily procedures benign or beneficial to the mother.

6. As the court to order fetal monitoring or other intervention, if and only if, relatively benign to the mother.

7. The most restrictive alternative possible is an order of confinement. Involuntary confinement or restriction of physical activities creates special problems of right to travel, and special concerns of due process under law. While such a step could occur only under the most extraordinary of circumstances, involuntary evaluation and treatments do occur rather frequently in mental health cases and cannot be ruled out in some prenatal abuse cases.

PROTECTING THE NEONATE BASED ON PRENATAL EVENTS

Whether or not a situation demands extensive prenatal intervention, extending consideration of the behavior of parents towards children to the prenatal period can be legally useful. By beginning documentation of situations where unborn children are clearly at risk for death or serious injury after birth based on the prenatal behavior of parents, those situations which justify immediate intervention after birth but are sometimes difficult to prove can more readily be managed.

This article should not end without pointing out one of the many limitations of law. Perhaps the most generally significant type of prenatal neglect is the failure to obtain even one prenatal visit to a doctor.[62] One prenatal visit can "equalize" neonatal morbidity and mortality among the various social and economic classes in the United States. One must look more to general cultural values and institutional structures if prenatal visits are to become a more universal practice.

---

62. Dr. C. Henry Kempe, personal communication, August 1978.

AUTHOR INDEX

SUBJECT INDEX